Web Technologies:
Concepts, Methodologies, Tools, and Applications

Arthur Tatnall
Victoria University, Australia

Volume II

INFORMATION SCIENCE REFERENCE

Hershey · New York

Director of Editorial Content: Kristin Klinger
Development Editor   Julia Mosemann
Senior Managing Editor: Jamie Snavely
Managing Editor: Michael Brehm
Assistant Managing Editor: Carole Coulson
Typesetters: Michael Brehm, Carole Coulson, Elizabeth Duke, Christopher Hrobak, Jamie Snavely, Sean Woznicki
Cover Design: Lisa Tosheff
Printed at: Yurchak Printing Inc.

Published in the United States of America by
        Information Science Reference (an imprint of IGI Global)
        701 E. Chocolate Avenue
        Hershey PA 17033
        Tel: 717-533-8845
        Fax: 717-533-8661
        E-mail: cust@igi-global.com
        Web site: http://www.igi-global.com/reference

and in the United Kingdom by
        Information Science Reference (an imprint of IGI Global)
        3 Henrietta Street
        Covent Garden
        London WC2E 8LU
        Tel: 44 20 7240 0856
        Fax: 44 20 7379 0609
        Web site: http://www.eurospanbookstore.com

Library of Congress Cataloging-in-Publication Data

Web technologies : concepts, methodologies, tools and applications / Arthur
Tatnall, editor.
        p. cm.
  Includes bibliographical references and index.
  ISBN 978-1-60566-982-3 (hbk.) -- ISBN 978-1-60566-983-0 (ebook) 1. World
Wide Web. 2. Internet. 3. Information technology. I. Tatnall, Arthur.
  TK5105.888.W377 2010
  004.6'7--dc22
                                2009037778

British Cataloguing in Publication Data
A Cataloguing in Publication record for this book is available from the British Library.

All work contributed to this book set is original material. The views expressed in this book are those of the authors, but not necessarily of the publisher.

Additional Research Collections found in the
"Contemporary Research in Information Science and Technology"
Book Series

Data Mining and Warehousing: Concepts, Methodologies, Tools, and Applications
John Wang, Montclair University, USA • 6-volume set • ISBN 978-1-60566-056-1

Electronic Business: Concepts, Methodologies, Tools, and Applications
In Lee, Western Illinois University • 4-volume set • ISBN 978-1-59904-943-4

Electronic Commerce: Concepts, Methodologies, Tools, and Applications
S. Ann Becker, Florida Institute of Technology, USA • 4-volume set • ISBN 978-1-59904-943-4

Electronic Government: Concepts, Methodologies, Tools, and Applications
Ari-Veikko Anttiroiko, University of Tampere, Finland • 6-volume set • ISBN 978-1-59904-947-2

Knowledge Management: Concepts, Methodologies, Tools, and Applications
Murray E. Jennex, San Diego State University, USA • 6-volume set • ISBN 978-1-59904-933-5

Information Communication Technologies: Concepts, Methodologies, Tools, and Applications
Craig Van Slyke, University of Central Florida, USA • 6-volume set • ISBN 978-1-59904-949-6

Intelligent Information Technologies: Concepts, Methodologies, Tools, and Applications
Vijayan Sugumaran, Oakland University, USA • 4-volume set • ISBN 978-1-59904-941-0

Information Security and Ethics: Concepts, Methodologies, Tools, and Applications
Hamid Nemati, The University of North Carolina at Greensboro, USA • 6-volume set • ISBN 978-1-59904-937-3

Medical Informatics: Concepts, Methodologies, Tools, and Applications
Joseph Tan, Wayne State University, USA • 4-volume set • ISBN 978-1-60566-050-9

Mobile Computing: Concepts, Methodologies, Tools, and Applications
David Taniar, Monash University, Australia • 6-volume set • ISBN 978-1-60566-054-7

Multimedia Technologies: Concepts, Methodologies, Tools, and Applications
Syed Mahbubur Rahman, Minnesota State University, Mankato, USA • 3-volume set • ISBN 978-1-60566-054-7

Virtual Technologies: Concepts, Methodologies, Tools, and Applications
Jerzy Kisielnicki, Warsaw University, Poland • 3-volume set • ISBN 978-1-59904-955-7

Free institution-wide online access with the purchase of a print collection!

INFORMATION SCIENCE REFERENCE
Hershey · New York

Order online at www.igi-global.com or call 717-533-8845 ext.100
Mon–Fri 8:30am–5:00 pm (est) or fax 24 hours a day 717-533-7115

List of Contributors

Contents

Volume I

Section I. Fundamental Concepts and Theories

This section serves as the foundation for this exhaustive reference tool by addressing crucial theories essential to the understanding of Web technologies. Chapters found within these pages provide an excellent framework in which to position Web technologies within the field of information science and technology. Individual contributions provide overviews of the mobile Web, semantic Web, and Web 2.0, while also exploring critical stumbling blocks of this field. Within this introductory section, the reader can learn and choose from a compendium of expert research on the elemental theories underscoring the research and application of Web technologies.

Section II. Development and Design Methodologies

This section provides in-depth coverage of conceptual architectures, frameworks and methodologies related to the design and implementation of Web technologies. Throughout these contributions, research fundamentals in the discipline are presented and discussed. From broad examinations to specific discussions on particular frameworks and infrastructures, the research found within this section spans the discipline while also offering detailed, specific discussions. Basic designs, as well as abstract developments, are explained within these chapters, and frameworks for designing successful Web sites, Web-based applications, and Web portals are provided.

Volume II

Section III. Tools and Technologies

This section presents extensive coverage of the technology that informs and impacts Web technologies. These chapters provide an in-depth analysis of the use and development of innumerable devices and tools, while also providing insight into new and upcoming technologies, theories, and instruments that will soon be commonplace. Within these rigorously researched chapters, readers are presented with examples of the tools that facilitate and support the emergence and advancement of Web technologies. In addition, the successful implementation and resulting impact of these various tools and technologies are discussed within this collection of chapters.

Section IV. Utilization and Application

This section introduces and discusses the utilization and application of Web technologies. These particular selections highlight, among other topics, the application of semantic Web technologies to e-tourism, e-banking, and in car repairs as well as the adoption of Web services in digital libraries. Contributions included in this section provide excellent coverage of today's online environment and insight into how Web technologies impact the fabric of our present-day global village.

Section V. Organizational and Social Implications

This section includes a wide range of research pertaining to the social and organizational impact of Web technologies around the world. Chapters included in this section analyze social marketing, e-government, Web vendors, and Web tourism. The inquiries and methods presented in this section offer insight into the implications of Web technologies at both a personal and organizational level, while also emphasizing potential areas of study within the discipline.

Volume III

Section VI. Managerial Impact

This section presents contemporary coverage of the managerial implications of Web technologies. Particular contributions address Web software engineering and Web-enabled employee life-cycle process management. The managerial research provided in this section allows executives, practitioners, and researchers to gain a better sense of how Web technologies can inform their practices and behavior.

   Tobias Kollmann, University of Duisburg-Essen, Campus Essen, Germany
   Christoph Stöckmann, University of Duisburg-Essen, Campus Essen, Germany
   Carsten Schröer, University of Duisburg-Essen, Campus Essen, Germany

Section VII. Critical Issues

This section addresses conceptual and theoretical issues related to the field of Web technologies, which include issues related to usage, as well as failures and successes in Web implementation. Within these chapters, the reader is presented with analysis of the most current and relevant conceptual inquires within this growing field of study. Particular chapters address privacy concerns in Web logging, Web information extraction, and Web rules. Overall, contributions within this section ask unique, often theoretical questions related to the study of Web technologies and, more often than not, conclude that solutions are both numerous and contradictory.

   Joseph Wood, LTC, US Army, USA
   James Grayson, Augusta State University, USA
   Hui-Lien Tung, Paine College, USA
   Margo Bergman, Northwest Health Services Research & Development (HSR&D), USA
   Tina Marshall-Bradley, Paine College, USA
   W.F. Lawless, Paine College, USA
   Donald A. Sofge, Naval Research Laboratory, USA

   Stefan Dietze, Open University, UK
   Alessio Gugliotta, Open University, UK
   John Domingue, Open University, UK

   Paulo Cesar G. Costa, George Mason University, USA
   Kathryn Blackmond Laskey, George Mason University, USA
   Thomas Lukasiewicz, Oxford University Computing Laboratory, UK

   Oscar Corcho, Universidad Politécnica de Madrid, Spain
   Silvestre Losada, Intelligent Software Components, S.A., Spain
   Richard Benjamins, Intelligent Software Components, S.A., Spain

   Livia Predoiu, University of Mannheim, Germany
   Heiner Stuckenschmidt, University of Mannheim, Germany

Volume IV

Section VIII. Emerging Trends

This section highlights research potential within the field of Web technologies while exploring uncharted areas of study for the advancement of the discipline. Chapters within this section highlight emerging semantic Web applications, Web personalization, and learning on the Web. These contributions, which conclude this exhaustive, multi-volume set, provide emerging trends and suggestions for future research within this rapidly expanding discipline.

Preface

Since its development just two decades ago, the World Wide Web has grown to become the infrastructure that supports innumerable applications essential to everyday life. It's not an exaggeration to claim that if you can think it, you can create a Web page about it. We use Web sites and the information they contain to create and connect with a seemingly unlimited amount of information. As such, it is important to understand the tools and technologies that support the continued growth of the Web and contribute to its role as an increasingly-pervasive aspect of our lives.

With the constant changes in the landscape of Web technologies, it is a challenge for researchers and experts to take in the volume of innovative advances and up-to-the-moment research in this diverse field. Information Science Reference is pleased to offer a four-volume reference collection on this rapidly growing discipline, in order to empower students, researchers, academicians, and practitioners with a wide-ranging understanding of the most critical areas within this field of study. This collection provides the most comprehensive, in-depth, and recent coverage of all issues related to the development of cutting-edge Web technologies, as well as a single reference source on all conceptual, methodological, technical and managerial issues, and the opportunities, future challenges and emerging trends related to the development, application, and implications of Web technologies.

This collection entitled, **"Web Technologies: Concepts, Methodologies, Tools, and Applications"** is organized in eight (8) distinct sections, providing the most wide-ranging coverage of topics such as: 1) Fundamental Concepts and Theories; 2) Development and Design Methodologies; 3) Tools and Technologies; 4) Utilization and Application; 5) Organizational and Social Implications; 6) Managerial Impact; 7) Critical Issues; and 8) Emerging Trends. The following provides a summary of what is covered in each section of this multi-volume reference collection:

Section 1, *Fundamental Concepts and Theories*, serves as a foundation for this extensive reference tool by addressing crucial theories essential to the understanding of Web technologies. Chapters such as "Tips for Tracking Web Information Seeking Behavior" by Brian Detlor, Maureen Hupfer, and Umar Ruhi and "A Proposed Template for the Evaluation of Web Design Strategies" by Dimitrios Xanthidis, David Nicholas, and Paris Argyrides provide analyses of user behavior and Web design. "Mobile Social Web; Opportunities and Drawbacks," by Thorsten Caus, Stefan Christmann, and Svenja Hagenhoff presents an overview of recent trends in mobile Web usage, which is becoming an increasingly important area of study as more and more people obtain Internet access for their wireless devices. Later selections, such as "Web 2.0 and E-Discovery" by Bryan Kimes and "The Power and Promise of Web 2.0 Tools" by G. Andrew Page and Radwan Ali explore the application of Web 2.0 as well as the issues companies must address as a result. These and several other foundational chapters provide a wealth of expert research on the elemental concepts and ideas which surround Web design and access.

Section 2, *Development and Design Methodologies*, presents in-depth coverage of the conceptual design and architecture of Web sites, services, and systems. "Paralingual Web Design and Trust in E-

Government," by Roy H. Segovia, Murray E. Jennex, and James Beatty and "Designing Medical Research Web Sites" by Jonathan Grady, Michael B. Spring, and Armando J. Rotondi discuss context-specific Web design projects, highlighting the importance of recognizing the specific needs and requirements of different development initiatives. The latter half of this section introduces concepts that relate to the development of Semantic Web services. Chapters such as "A Semantic Web-Based Approach for Building Personalized News Services" by Flavius Frasincar, Jethro Borsje, and Leonard Levering and "Building Semantic Web Portals with a Model-Driven Design Approach" by Marco Brambilla and Federico M. Facca offer specific considerations for the creation of Semantic Web services, while later selections such as "Rule Markup Languages and Semantic Web Rule Languages" by Adrian Paschke and Harold Boley and "Semantic Web Rule Languages for Geospatial Ontologies" by Philip D. Smart, Alia I. Abdelmoty, Baher A. El-Geresy, and Christopher B. Jones present more technical considerations relating to the use and communication of rule languages in the Semantic Web. With 20 contributions from leading international researchers, this section offers copious developmental approaches and methodologies for Web services and technologies.

Section 3, *Tools and Technologies*, presents extensive coverage of the various tools and technologies used in the development and implementation of Web services and applications. This comprehensive section opens with the chapters "New Paradigms: A Collaborative Web Based Research Tool," by Hamish Holewa, and "Adaptability and Adaptivity in The Generation of Web Applications," by Raoudha Ben Djemaa, Ikram Amous, and Abdelmajid Ben Hamadou, which describe new tools that support the development of Web applications and the challenges faced in the management and creation of new technology. "Migrating Web Services in Mobile and Wireless Environments," by Myung-Woo Park, Yeon-Seok Kim, and Kyong-Ho Lee revisits Web use on wireless devices, specifically exploring the mitigation and replication of Web services among mobile devices. Later selections such as "Web 2.0 Technologies: Social Software Applied to Higher Education and Adult Learning" by Teresa Torres-Coronas, M. Arántzazu Vidal-Blasco, Ricard Monclús-Guitart, M. José Simón-Olmos, and Araceli Rodríguez-Merayo and "Interactive Whiteboards in the Web 2.0 Classroom" by David Miller and Derek Glover provide insight into the use of specific Web tools (namely social software and interactive whiteboards) in educational settings. In all, this section provides coverage of a variety of Web tools and technologies under development and in use.

Section 4, *Utilization and Application*, describes the implementation and use of an assortment of Web technologies. Including chapters such as "Semantic Web Take-Off in a European Industry Perspective" by Alain Léger, Jean Charlet, Johannes Heinecke, Paola Hobson, Lyndon J.B. Nixon, François Goasdoué, and Pavel Shvaiko and "Semantic Web for Media Convergence: A Newspaper Case" by Ferran Perdrix, Juan Manuel Gimeno, Rosa Gil, Marta Oliva, and Roberto García provide specific insight into the application of Web tools and technologies in both the professional and private sector. "Mailing Lists and Social Semantic Web" by Sergio Fernández, Jose E. Labra, Diego Berrueta, Patricia Ordóñez de Pablos, and Lian Shi describes the use of mailing lists and presents a method for extracting data from these lists. Later selections, such as "A Context-Based Approach to Web 2.0 and Language Education" by Gary Motteram and Susan Brown and "Exploring the Effects of Web-Enabled Self-Regulated Learning and Online Class Frequency on Students' Computing Skills in Blended Learning Courses" by Pei-Di Shen and Chia-Wen Tsai suggest approaches and consider the impact of Web-based learning on student performance. Contributions found in this section provide comprehensive coverage of the practicality and current use of Web technologies.

Section 5, *Organizational and Social Implications*, includes chapters discussing the impact of Web technology on social and organizational practices. Chapters such as "Building Trust in E-Commerce through Web Interface," by Muneesh Kumar and Mamta Sareen and and "Swift Trust in Web Vendors:

The Role of Appearance and Functionality," by Xin Li, Guang Rong, and Jason B. Thatcher discuss the growth and influence of e-commerce and the important role trust plays in impacting e-marketplaces. Specific Web implementation and resulting implications of such initiatives are explored in selections such as "Assessing the Performance of Airline Web Sites: The ARTFLY Case" by Elad Harison and Albert Boonstra and "Aviation-Related Expertise and Usability: Implications for the Design of an FAA E-Government Web Site" by Ferne Friedman-Berg, Kenneth Allendoerfer, and Shantanu Pai. This section continues with discussions of Web accessibility and customization, concluding with a discussion of educational implications of Web technology. Overall, these chapters present a detailed investigation of how Web technology is implemented and how this implementation impacts the individual and society as a whole.

Section 6, *Managerial Impact*, presents focused coverage of Web services and technology as it relates to improvements and considerations in the workplace. "Employee Life-Cycle Process Management Improvement with Web-Enabled Workflow Systems" by Leon Welicki, Javier Piqueres Juan, Fernando Llorente Martin, and Victor de Vega Hernandez presents a real-world case of constructing a Web-enabled worklflow for managing employee-life cycle processes, which include hiring and dismissing of employees. "Web Engineering in Small Jordanian Web Development Firms: An XP Based Process Model" by Haroon Altarawneh and Asim El-Shiekh describes a model for small Web project development and explains, from a managerial perspective, how this differs from the more large-scale implementation projects adopted by larger firms. In all, the chapters in this section offer specific perspectives on how work and Web technologies interact and inform each other to create more meaningful user experiences.

Section 7, *Critical Issues*, addresses vital issues related to Web technology, which include privacy and quality, among other topics. Chapters such as "Privacy Concerns for Web Logging Data" by Kirstie Hawkey explore the issues that must be considered when collecting user data and offer recommendations for enhancing privacy. Later selections, such as "Search Engine-Based Web Information Extraction" by Gijs Geleijnse and Jan Korst, continue the discussion of information gathering and extraction which, in this chapter, is discussed in terms of approaches to expressing and sharing structured information in Semantic Web languages. This section continues by asking unique questions about information literacy, as well as presenting new solutions to questions about the social Web and Web services profiling.

The concluding section of this authoritative reference tool, *Emerging Trends*, highlights areas for future research within the field of Web technology, while exploring new avenues for the advancement of the discipline. Beginning this section is "The Social Semantic Desktop: A New Paradigm Towards Deploying the Semantic Web on the Desktop" by Ansgar Bernardi, Mehdi Jazayeri, Stefan Decker, Cédric Mesnage, Ludger van Elst, Knud Möller, Gunnar Aastrand Grimnes, Michael Sintek, Tudor Groza, Leo Sauermann, and Siegfried Handschuh. This selection presents the Social Semantic Desktop project, addressing design considerations of a project whose aim is to blur the lines between individual applications and users' physical workspace. Trends in marketing are explored in "Social Media Marketing; Web X.0 of Opportunities" by Lemi Baruh with the aim of introducing new techniques for advertisers whose aim is to reach consumers through social media. These and several other emerging trends and suggestions for future research can be found within the final section of this exhaustive multi-volume set.

Although the primary organization of the contents in this multi-volume work is based on its eight sections, offering a progression of coverage of the important concepts, methodologies, technologies, applications, social issues, and emerging trends, the reader can also identify specific contents by utilizing the extensive indexing system listed at the end of each volume. Furthermore to ensure that the scholar, researcher and educator have access to the entire contents of this multi volume set as well as additional coverage that could not be included in the print version of this publication, the publisher will provide unlimited multi-user electronic access to the online aggregated database of this collection for the life of the edition, free of charge when a library purchases a print copy. This aggregated database provides far more contents than what can be included in the print version in addition to continual updates. This unlimited access, coupled with the continuous updates to the database ensures that the most current research is accessible to knowledge seekers.

The diverse and comprehensive coverage of Web technologies presented in this four-volume authoritative publication will contribute to a better understanding of all topics, research, and discoveries in this developing, significant field of study. Furthermore, the contributions included in this multi-volume collection series will be instrumental in the expansion of the body of knowledge in this enormous field, resulting in a greater understanding of the fundamental concepts and technologies while fueling the research initiatives in emerging fields. We at Information Science Reference, along with the editor of this collection, hope that this multi-volume collection will become instrumental in the expansion of the discipline and will promote the continued growth of all aspects of Web technology.

Chapter 2.19
Rule Markup Languages and Semantic Web Rule Languages

Adrian Paschke
Freie Universität Berlin, Germany

Harold Boley
National Research Council, Canada

ABSTRACT

Rule markup languages will be the vehicle for using rules on the Web and in other distributed systems. They allow publishing, deploying, executing and communicating rules in a network. They may also play the role of a lingua franca for exchanging rules between different systems and tools. In a narrow sense, a rule markup language is a concrete (XML-based) rule syntax for the Web. In a broader sense, it should have an abstract syntax as a common basis for defining various concrete languages addressing different consumers. The main purposes of a rule markup language are to permit the publication, interchange and reuse of rules. This chapter introduces important requirements and design issues for general Web rule languages to fulfill these tasks. Characteristics of several important general standardization or standards-proposing efforts for (XML-based) rule markup languages including W3C RIF, RuleML, R2ML, SWRL as well as (human-readable) Semantic Web rule languages such as TRIPLE, N3, Jena, and Prova are discussed with respect to these identified issues.

INTRODUCTION AND MOTIVATION

Web rule languages provide the required expressiveness enabling machine-interpretation, automated processing and translation into other such Web languages, some of which also being the execution syntaxes of rule engines. One of these languages may act as a "lingua franca" to interchange rules and in-

DOI: 10.4018/978-1-60566-402-6.ch001

tegrate with other markup languages, in particular with Web languages based on XML and with Semantic Web languages (e.g. W3C's RDF Schema, OWL and its new OWL 2 version) for ontologies serialized in RDF/XML or directly in XML. Web rule languages may also be used for publication purposes on the Web and for the serialization of external data sources, e.g. of native online XML databases or RDF stores. Recently, there have been several efforts aiming at rule interchange and building a general, practical, and deployable rule markup standard for the (Semantic) Web. These encompass several important general standardization or standards-proposing efforts including RuleML (www.ruleml.org), SWRL (www.w3.org/Submission/SWRL/), SWSL (http://www.w3.org/Submission/SWSF-SWSL/), R2ML (oxygen.informatik.tu-cottbus.de/rewerse-i1/?q=R2ML), RIF (www.w3.org/2005/rules/), and others such as XCL (http://www.altheim.com/specs/xcl/1.0/), designed as a concrete (serialization) syntax for ISO's Common Logic (CL) standard.

In this chapter, a system of general requirements and design choices for Web rule languages will be introduced and instantiations discussed in the context of the current prominent general Rule Markup Languages and Semantic Web rule languages. This chapter is intended to be of help to a wide audience. In particular, it is targeted to rule practitioners who want to serialize the declarative rules of their applications in a general rule markup language, and publish and interchange them on the Web. Rule practitioners will find here a discussion of general design criteria with examples from the current rule markup languages. These examples, together with a discussion of advantages and drawbacks, will offer guidance to readers when declaratively representing their own rule-based applications in a Web rule language. The structure of the rest of this chapter is as follows: Section 2 introduces current rule markup languages and rule interchange formats as well as Semantic Web rule languages. Section 3 comprises the main part of this chapter, discussing important

design issues and characteristics of the introduced rule languages. Section 4 presents future research issues in Web rule language design. Section 5 concludes this chapter with a summary.

WEB RULE LANGUAGES

Rule markup (serialization) languages have been developed for the Web-based interchange of, e.g., privacy policies, business rules, and - as focused here - Semantic Web rules. Rules are central to knowledge representation for the Semantic Web (Boley, 2007), hence are increasingly considered as being side by side with ontologies, e.g. in W3C's layered Semantic Web architecture (2007 version shown in Figure 1).

Rule interchange in an open format is important for all higher Semantic Web layers, including a Web of Trust and, generally, a Pragmatic Web (Paschke et al, 2007), and is crucial for applications in eBusiness, eGovernment, eHealth, etc. This section introduces major *rule markup languages* including RuleML, R2ML, and RIF, as well as human-readable *Semantic Web rule languages* such as TRIPLE and N3, and platform-specific rule engine languages such as Jena and Prova.

Rule Markup Languages

We characterize rule languages as rule markup languages if they are serialized in XML, employ URIs/IRIs for constants etc., and can interface with Web ontology languages.

RuleML

The Rule Markup Language (RuleML, www.ruleml.org) is a markup language developed to express a family of Web rules in XML for deduction, rewriting, and reaction, as well as further inferential, transformational, and behavioral tasks. It is defined by the Rule Markup Initiative (www.ruleml.org), an open network of individuals and

Figure 1. Semantic Web Layer Cake [adapted from (W3C, 2007)]

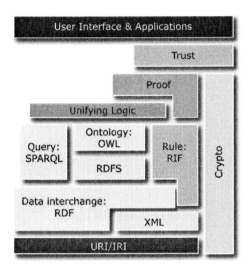

groups from both industry and academia that was formed to develop a canonical Web language for rules using XML markup and transformations from and to other rule standards/systems. It develops a modular, hierarchical specification for different types of rules comprising facts, queries, derivation rules, integrity constraints (consistency-maintenance rules), production rules, and reaction rules (Reaction RuleML, http://ibis. in.tum.de/research/ReactionRuleML), as well as tools and transformations from and to other rule standards/systems.

Datalog RuleML is defined over both data constants and individual constants with an optional attribute for IRI (URI) webizing. Atomic formulas have n arguments, which can be positional terms or, in Object-Oriented Datalog, slots (F-logic-like key->term pairs); OO Datalog also adds optional types and RDF-like oids/anchors, via IRIs (Boley, 2003). Inheriting all of these Datalog features, Hornlog RuleML adds positional or slotted functional expressions as terms. In Hornlog with equality, such uninterpreted (constructor-like) functions are complemented by interpreted (equation-defined) functions. This derivation rule branch is extended upward towards First Order

Logic, has subbranches with Negation-As-Failure, strong-Negation, or combined languages, and is parameterized by 'pluggable' built-ins.

SWRL

The Semantic Web Rule Language (SWRL, www.w3.org/Submission/SWRL/) is defined as a language combining sublanguages of the OWL Web Ontology Language (OWL DL and Lite) with those of the Rule Markup Language (Unary/Binary Datalog).

The specification was submitted to W3C in May 2004 by the National Research Council of Canada, Network Inference (since acquired by webMethods), and Stanford University in association with the Joint US/EU ad hoc Agent Markup Language Committee.

Compared to Description Logic Programs (DLP), a slightly earlier proposal for integrating description logic and Horn rule formalisms by an overlapping authoring team, SWRL takes the opposite integration approach: DLP can be seen as the 'intersection' of description logic and Horn logic; SWRL, as roughly their 'union'. For DLP, the resulting rather inexpressive language corresponds to a peculiar looking description logic imitating special rules. It is hard to see the DLP restrictions, which stem from Lloyd-Topor transformations, being either natural or satisfying. On the other hand, SWRL retains the full power of OWL DL, but adds rules at the price of undecidability and a lack of complete implementations, although the SWRL Tab of Protégé has become quite popular (http://protege.cim3.net/cgi-bin/wiki.pl?SWRLTab).

Rules in SWRL are of the form of an implication between an antecedent (body) conjunction and a consequent (head) conjunction, where description logic expressions can occur on both sides. The intended interpretation is as in classical first-order logic: whenever the conditions specified in the antecedent hold, then the conditions specified in the consequent must also hold.

R2ML

R2ML (http://oxygen.informatik.tu-cottbus.de/rewerse-i1/?q=R2ML) was developed as a subproject in the EU Network of Excellence REWERSE (http://oxygen.informatik.tu-cottbus.de/rewerse-i1/). The R2ML project is about the design of integrity and derivation rules on the basis of the Rule Markup Language (RuleML) and the Semantic Web Rule Language (SWRL). R2ML defines a general markup framework for integrity rules, derivation rules, production rules and reaction rules. Rule concepts are defined with the help of MOF/UML, a subset of the UML class modeling language proposed by the Object Management Group (OMG) for the purpose of 'meta-modeling', i.e. for defining languages conceptually on the level of an abstract (semi-visual) syntax. From these MOF/UML language models concrete markup syntax is obtained by applying a mapping procedure for generating corresponding languages from parameterized schemas.

W3C RIF

The W3C Rule Interchange Format (RIF) Working Group (http://www.w3.org/2005/rules/wiki/RIF_Working_Group) is an effort, influenced by RuleML, to define a standard *Rule Interchange Format* for facilitating the exchange of rule sets among different systems and to facilitate the development of intelligent rule-based application for the Semantic Web. For these purposes, *RIF Use Cases and Requirements* (RIF-UCR) have been developed. The RIF architecture is conceived as a family of languages, called *dialects*. A *RIF dialect* is a rule-based language with an XML syntax and a well-defined semantics.

So far, the RIF working group has defined the *Basic Logic Dialect* (RIF-BLD), which semantically corresponds to a Horn rule language with equality. RIF-BLD has a number of syntactic extensions with respect to 'regular' Horn rules, including F-logic-like frames, and a standard

system of built-ins drawn from *Datatypes and Built-Ins* (RIF-DTB). The connection to other W3C Semantic Web languages is established via *RDF* and *OWL Compatibility* (RIF-SWC). Moreover, RIF-BLD is a general Web language in that it supports the use of IRIs (Internationalized Resource Identifiers) and XML Schema data types. The RIF Working Group has also defined the *Framework for Logic Dialects* (RIF-FLD), of which RIF-BLD was shown to be the first instantiation. RIF-FLD uses a uniform notion of terms for both expressions and atoms in a Hilog-like manner.

Current efforts of the RIF Working Group are expected to introduce a *Core* (RIF-Core) in the intersection of RIF-BLD and a new *Production Rule Dialect* (RIF-PRD) influenced by OMG's PRR, which can then be further extended or supplemented by reaction rules.

Semantic Web Rule Languages

In contrast to the XML-based rule markup languages in the previous section, the Semantic Web rule languages described in this section are human-readable rule languages, using an ASCII syntax based, e.g., on the ISO Prolog syntax standard. Typically, they are designed as compact presentation languages for human consumption. While they may be serialized in an XML-based rule markup language such as RuleML or RIF, e.g. for interchange purposes, they can also be employed directly: dynamically interpreted by platform-specific rule engines (at runtime) or statically translated into executable code (at compile time).

TRIPLE

TRIPLE (http://triple.semanticweb.org/) was designed as a practical rule language for linked-data applications. It is an RDF query, inference, and transformation language for the Semantic Web extending F-logic with modules. TRIPLE rules have been used to implement RDFS and other schema languages.

N3 / Turtle

Notation3 (w3.org/TeamSubmission/n3/), more commonly known as N3, is a shorthand non-XML serialization of Resource Description Framework (RDF) models, designed with human readability in mind: N3 is much more compact and readable than RDF/XML serializations. N3 has several features that go beyond the serialization of RDF models, such as support for RDF-based rules. Supporting the triple pattern syntax of SPARQL, Turtle (w3.org/TeamSubmission/turtle/) is a simplified, RDF-only subset of N3.

Jena Rules

The default representation format in Jena (jena. sourceforge.net/) for a rule in the rule-based reasoner is a Java Rule object with a list of body terms (premises), a list of head terms (conclusions) and an optional name and an optional direction. However, in Jena2 a rather simple parser is included which allows rules to be specified in reasonably compact form in text source files.

Prova

Prova (http://www.prova.ws/) is both a (Semantic) Web rule language and a highly expressive distributed (Semantic) Web rule engine which supports complex reaction rule-based workflows, rule-based complex event processing, distributed inference services, rule interchange, rule-based decision logic, dynamic access to external data sources, Web Services, and Java APIs. Prova follows the spirit and design principles of the W3C Semantic Web initiative and combines declarative rules, ontologies and inference with dynamic object-oriented programming and access to external data sources via query languages such as SQL, SPARQL, and XQuery. One of the key advantages of Prova is its separation of logic, data access, and computation as well as its tight integration of Java, Semantic Web technologies and enterprise service-oriented computing and complex event processing technologies.

DESIGN AND CHARACTERISTICS OF WEB RULE LANGUAGES

General requirements that need to be addressed by a rule markup language include semantic expressiveness and clarity, computational efficiency and Web scalability, machine-readable and machine-interpretable syntaxes, usability by both human users and automated agents, compact representation, interchangeability with other formats, means for serialization and persistence, as well as tool support in authoring, parsing/generating, and verifying rules. An important property that refers to development-time software engineering quality is the extensibility of the language and its interoperability with other representation formats. In this section, general language design principles, together with a selection of four important issues and criteria for rule markup language design, are identified and characteristics of the current rule markup languages RIF, RuleML, R2ML, SWRL (DAML Rules) as well as specific Semantic Web rule languages are exemplified with respect to them. Further design issues and requirements for Web rule languages have been elaborated in, e.g., (Wagner et al, 2005), (Bry and Marchiori, 2005), (Boley, 2007), and (Paschke, 2007).

Language Design Principles

Given the large design space of rule languages and rule concepts, the specification of a rule markup language is a difficult integration and conceptualization challenge that calls for balancing many (interrelated) design choices with respect to semantics, syntax, and pragmatics. In this subsection, we will raise four (markup) language design principles and will illustrate the actual design choices of the current rule markup languages with examples.

1. Criteria of Good Language Design

Rule markup language should be clear, compact, precise and easily adaptable. They should strive to fulfill typical criteria for good language design (Codd, 1971) - as known from logic, databases and programming - such as minimality, referential transparency and orthogonality:

- *Minimality* requires that the language provides only a small set of needed language constructs, i.e., the same meaning cannot be expressed by different language constructs
- *Referential transparency* is fulfilled if the same language construct always expresses the same semantics regardless of the context in which it is used
- *Orthogonality* asks for pairwise independent language constructs, thus permitting their meaningful systematic combination

The RuleML family follows these design principles as far as possible and provides only a set of needed language constructs which can be applied in every meaningful combination. This leads to a compact homogeneous syntax which is easier to maintain, learn, read and understand by end users, as well as easy to process automatically by machines (e.g. translators).

SWRL and RIF, which build on RuleML, basically follow this compact minimalistic design approach. However, SWRL introduces a more fine-grained distinction of constructs than RuleML, e.g. of Atoms into various types of specialized atoms such as *classAtom*, *datarangeAtom*, and *invidiualPropertyAtom*, which can be formed from unary predicates (classes), binary predicates (properties), and equalities or inequalities.

R2ML introduces further differentiated types of terms and atoms. This leads to a rich structure-

preserving syntax with many highly specialized constructs. For instance, variables in R2ML are provided in the form of *ObjectVariable* (i.e. variables that stand for objects), *DataVariable* (i.e. variables that stand for data literals), and *GenericVariable* (i.e. variables that do not have a type), whereas RuleML (as well as SWRL and RIF) only provide a generic Var construct. Like RuleML, R2ML defines the notion of an individual (constant) and distinguishes between objects and data with the notions of an *object name* and *data value*.

The main design goal of the specific Semantic Web rule languages such as TRIPLE, Jena, and (following ISO Prolog syntax) Prova is to provide a terse scripting syntax with a minimal set of needed constructs. RuleML's POSL syntax combines and extends the terse ISO Prolog and F-logic syntaxes.

2. Different Syntactic and Semantic Layers

A complete specification of Web rule languages consists of a formalization of their syntax, semantics and, often left implicit, pragmatics. As implied by their name, the syntax of markup languages always includes the concrete syntax of (XML) markup, perhaps indirectly through other languages such as via RDF/XML. Often, there is another more or less concrete syntax such as a compact shorthand or presentation syntax, which may be parsed into the XML markup. While a presentation syntax can already disregard certain details, an abstract syntax systematically replaces character sequences with abstract constructors, often in a (UML) diagram form or as an abstract syntax tree (AST). Together with different token dictionaries, it can be used to generate corresponding concrete syntaxes. The semantics is formalized in a model-theoretic, proof-theoretic, or procedural manner, sometimes in more than one. When rules and speech-act-like performatives, such as queries and answers, are transmitted between different systems, their pragmatic interpretation, including their pragmatic context, becomes relevant, e.g. in order to explain the effects of performatives - such as the assertion or retraction of facts - on the internal knowledge base (Paschke et al, 2007).

A general distinction of three modeling layers can be adopted from OMG's model driven architecture (MDA) engineering approach (http://www.omg.org/mda/):

- A platform specific model (PSM) which encodes the rule statements in the language of a specific execution environment
- A platform independent model (PIM) which represents the rules in a common (standardized) interchange format, a rule markup language
- A computational independent model (CIM) with rules represented in a natural or visual language

The *CIM level* comprises visual and verbal rendering and rule modeling, e.g. via graphical representation or a controlled natural language syntax for rules, mainly intended for human consumption. Graphical representations such as UML diagrams or template-driven/controlled languages can also be used as presentation languages.

In order to facilitate rule modeling, R2ML provides a UML-based Rule Modeling Language (URML) (Lukichev and Wagner, 2006) which allows visual rule modeling based on UML class models and OCL constraints. RuleML on the CIM level provides several tools that use a controlled natural rule language approach. Among them are TRANSLATOR (Hirtle, 2006), which is based on Attempto Controlled English (ACE) (Fuchs et al, 2006), the open source Reaction RuleML editor (http://ibis.in.tum.de/research/ReactionRuleML/index.htm#editor), which uses a template driven approach, and the commercial RuleManager (Ensig, 2007). The Protégé tool (http://protege.stanford.edu/) provides facilities for modeling SWRL rules, but only on the PIM level, i.e. rules

are directly written in the concrete SWRL XML syntax. RIF, being a rather new standard under development, currently does not provide any such tool support.

The *PIM level* should enable platform-independent machine interpretation, processing, interchange and translation into multiple PSM execution syntaxes of concrete rule engines. Hence, the concrete XML (or RDF/XML-based) syntax of a Web rule language such as RuleML, SWRL or R2ML resides on this level, whereas the abstract syntax is on the borderline between the PIM and CIM levels. The abstract syntax can be defined, e.g., with the help of a suitably general grammar definition language such as the EBNF formalism, used, e.g., in the definition of the abstract syntax of OWL, RuleML, RIF, and SWRL, or with the help of a MOF/UML model, as, e.g., in PRR, R2ML, and RuleML. (Wagner et al, 2004) (Giurca and Wagner, 2005).

The *PSM level* is the result of translating/mapping PIM rule (interchange) languages into execution syntaxes which can be directly used in a specific execution environment such as a rule engine. A general distinction can be made between a compiled language approach, where the rules are statically translated into byte code (at compile time), as e.g. done in the rule engines Take (http://code.google.com/p/take/) and Drools (www.jboss.org/drools/) versus interpreted scripting languages, which are dynamically interpreted (at run-time), as e.g. in the rule engines Prova (Paschke, 2006b) and OO jDREW (Ball et al., 2005). While the compiled approach has obvious efficiency benefits, the interpreted approach is more dynamic and facilitates, e.g., updates at run-time. Often, Semantic Web Rule Languages are directly executable by their respective rule engines; hence reside on the PSM level. As an intermediate step between the concrete PSM level and the PIM level an abstract representation is often introduced, such as N3, which provides an abstract rule syntax based on the RDF syntax, or POSL and Prova, which both provide ANTLR grammars (http://www.jdrew.org/oojdrew/demo/ translator, http://www.prova.ws/gram.html) which are transformed into ASTs as the basis for further translation into interchange markup languages such as RuleML or other, specific execution formats.

The correct execution of an interchanged PIM-level rule set serialized in a rule markup language depends on the semantics of both the rule program and the platform-specific rule inference engine (IE). To address this issue, the IE and the interchanged rule set must reveal their intended/ implemented semantics. This may be solved via explicit annotations based on a common vocabulary, e.g. an (Semantic Web) ontology which classifies the semantics. Annotations describing the semantics of an interchanged rule set could even be used to find appropriate IEs on the Web to correctly and efficiently interpret and execute the rule program; for example, (1) by configuring the rule engine for a particular semantics in case it supports different ones, (2) by executing an applicable variant of several interchanged semantic alternatives of the rule program, or (3) by automatic transformation approaches which transform the interchanged rule program into a rule program with an applicable semantics; cf. XTAN (http:// www.w3.org/2008/02/xtan/). Another approach is to specify additional meta test cases for testing typical properties of well-known semantics, where by the combination of succeeded and failed meta tests the unknown semantics of an IE can often be uniquely determined (Paschke, 2006).

We remark that, traditionally, rule-based systems have been supported by two types of inferencing algorithms: forward-chaining and backward-chaining. A general rule markup language, as a lingua franca, should support translation and interpretation of both reasoning directions, perhaps again using pragmatic annotations (where by default chaining should be bidirectional, as with the direction attribute in RuleML).

Independently from the semantics of an interchanged rule program, the pragmatic context in which the interchange takes place is important for the target environment, in order to know how the received information should be used and which actions should be taken with respect to the pragmatic aspects. A standard nomenclature of pragmatic performatives is defined by the Knowledge Query and Manipulation Language (KQML) (www.cs.umbc.edu/kqml/) and the FIPA Agent Communication Language (ACL) (FIPA, 2000), which define several speech-act-theory-based communicative acts.

3. Modular Specialized Schema Layers vs. Flat General Schema

There are two basic design principles for the concrete rule markup syntax. The language (or language family) may be implemented in one flat (monolithic) general XML schema or in a layered structure, where semantically related constructs are defined within separate modules that are added to the different language layers of the Web rule language (cf. http://www.ruleml. org/modularization/) . This leads to a hierarchical structure where higher language layers build on sublayers and add more expressiveness by extending them. The layers are not necessarily organized around expressiveness/efficiency to the language core.

R2ML follows the first approach and provides one quite large, flat XML schema for all different rule types and language constructs. In contrast, RuleML (also SWRL and RIF) follow the layered design principle and define new constructs within separate modules which are added to the respective layers in the RuleML language family. The layered and uniform design makes it easier to learn the language and to understand the relationship between the different features, and it provides a certain guidance to users who might be interested only in a particular subset of the features and who do not need support for the full expressiveness of the language. The modularization allows for easy extension of the language's representation capabilities, using the extensibility of XML Schema (e.g. a redefine of an XML Schema group definition), without breaking the core language standard. This development path provides a stable, useful, and implementable language design for rule developers to manage the rapid pace of change on the Semantic Web and modern rule systems. Apart from that, modules facilitate the practical and extensible development of a rule language family by bundling language constructs into layers which can be developed, compiled, tested and managed separately. The modularization also enforces the principle of information hiding and can provide a basis for data abstraction. However, a monolithic schema is easier to read by humans than an unevenly modularized one and, by now, some of the extant XML processing tools and editors do not fully support modular XML Schema definitions. This calls for flattening a layered schema on demand via automatic modular-to-monolithic translators, thus combining the advantages of modular development and maintenance with the advantages of monolithic delivery (for some validators and (object model) transformers, e.g. based on JAXB https://jaxb.dev.java.net/).

4. XML Elements vs. Attributes

A general question regarding the implementation of a concrete rule markup language is where to use XML elements and where attributes to define the rule constructs and the rule information content. A general discussion on this element-vs.-attribute issue can be found in the OASIS Cover pages (http://xml.coverpages.org/elementsAndAttrs.html):

- If the information in question could be itself marked up with elements, put it in an element.
- If the information is suitable for attribute form, but could end up as multiple attributes of the same name on the same element, use child elements instead.

- If the information is required to be in a standard DTD-like attribute type such as ID, IDREF, or ENTITY, use an attribute.
- If the information should not be normalized for white space, use elements. (XML processors normalize attributes in ways that can change the raw text of the attribute value.) (cf. http://www.ibm.com/developerworks/xml/library/x-eleatt.html)

Accordingly, RuleML's general markup conventions provide common principles for its language hierarchy. XML elements are used for representing language constructs as trees while XML attributes are used for distinguishing variations of a given element and, as in RDF, for webizing. Variation can thus be achieved by different attribute values rather than requiring different elements. Since the same attribute can occur in different elements, an orthogonal, two-dimensional classification ensues, which has the potential of quadratic tag reduction.

For example, recent work in RuleML led to orthogonal dimensions extending the RuleML 0.9 role tags for argument, <arg...>, and slots, <slot>. So far, the *unkeyed* <arg index="..."> was always *ordered*, as indicated by the index attribute, and the *keyed* <slot> was always *unordered*, as indicated by the lack of an index attribute. This was generalized by allowing an optional index attribute for both role tags, as shown by the independent distinctions in the following key-order matrix:

```
ordered unordered
keyed <slot index="..."> <slot>
unkeyed <arg index="..."> <arg>
```

Two extra orthogonal combinations are obtained from this system. First, *keyed, ordered* children permit positionalized slots, as in this cost fact (see Figure 2).

Here, slot names item, price, and taxes are provided, e.g. for readability, as well as index

Figure 2.

```
<Atom>
  <Rel>cost</Rel>
  <slot index="1"><Ind>item</Ind><Ind>jewel</Ind></slot>
  <slot index="2"><Ind>price</Ind><Data>6000</Data></slot>
  <slot index="3"><Ind>taxes</Ind><Data>2000</Data></slot>
</Atom>
```

positions 1-3, e.g. for efficiency.

Second, *unkeyed, unordered* children permit elements acting like those in a bag (finite multiset), as in this transport fact:

```
<Atom>
<Rel>transport</Rel>
<arg><Ind>chair</Ind></arg>
<arg><Ind>chair</Ind></arg>
<arg><Ind>table</Ind></arg>
</Atom>
```

Here, the arguments are specified to be commutative and 'non-idempotent' (duplicates are kept).

For a general discussion of positional vs. unordered representations see (Boley, 2006).

R2ML differs from RuleML, SWRL and RIF as it implements an attribute solution and defines user information content in attributes. For instance a typed object variable "?driver" is represented as follows:

```
<r2ml:ObjectVariable
r2ml:name="driver"
r2ml:classID="userv:Driver" />
```

A distinction of positional vs. slotted (named-argument) predicates and functions, as in RuleML and RIF, does not exist in R2ML.

Expressive Layering

From the perspective of knowledge representation, the main adequacy criterion for a rule markup language is its *epistemological adequacy*, which addresses the ability of the language to represent all relevant knowledge under consideration. Among other representation issues, a general rule interchange format should allow to coherently represent derivation rules, reaction rules, integrity rules, and deontic rules in a homogeneous syntax (Wagner et al, 2005). We use the following general rule classification:

- Facts may comprise various kinds of information such as asserted atoms (formulas), individual-class memberships (of ontology classes), (object-oriented) instances, stored data (e.g., relational, XML), states and event occurrences which might be qualified, e.g., by priorities, temporally, etc.
- Derivation rules infer conclusions from conditions (as in Datalog and Horn logic), where facts (see above) are a special case with constantly true conditions
- Transformation rules specify term rewriting, which can be considered as derivation rules of logics with (oriented) equality
- Integrity rules (or integrity constraints) are assertions which express conditions (or queries) that must always be satisfied. Besides enforcing data integrity, they can constrain, e.g., the rule system structure, its information content, or its behavior:

Figure 3. RuleML rule language family

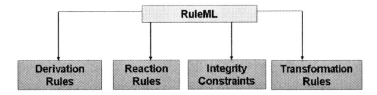

- ◦ *Structural constraints* (deontic assignments)
- ◦ *State constraints*
- ◦ *Process constraints*
- Deontic rules describe rights and obligations, e.g., of institutions and agents in the context of evolving states (situations triggered by events/actions) and state transitions, where integrity rules (see above) are a special case ('introspectively') affecting the rule set itself
- Reaction rules are (behavioral / action) rules that react on occurred events (external events or changed conditions) by executing actions, where production rules are a special case with events restricted to changed conditions

Because of this broad variety of rules relevant to the Semantic Web, a general rule markup language such as RuleML should have a hierarchical structure that reflects the relevant rule dialects or sublanguages, covering the knowledge representation needs of various subcommunities (cf. Figures 3 and 4).

The main branches contain subbranches, e.g. derivation rules monotonically disallowing or non-monotonically allowing negation as failure (NAF). Branches also exhibit a layering structure with sublanguages of different expressive power, e.g. for monotonic derivation rules proceeding from function-free Horn logic (Datalog) through either full Horn logic or disjunctive Datalog up to first-order logic (FOL). This hierarchy does not form a strict tree (but a directed acyclic graph), i.e. some sublanguages are shared by several more expressive languages; e.g., a sublanguage of conditions is shared by derivation rules and reaction rules. A basic classification of rule languages is introduced by the RuleML family with Derivation Rule Markup Languages (that is, Derivation RuleML), Production Rule Markup Languages (that is, Production RuleML which is a subfamily of Reaction RuleML), Reaction RuleML Markup Languages (that is, Reaction RuleML, http://ibis. in.tum.de/research/ReactionRuleML/), and Transformation Markup Languages (that is, Functional RuleML, http://www.ruleml.org/fun/), as well as other specializations, e.g. dialects for deontic rules (e.g. covered by the RBSLA language (Paschke, 2005)), defeasible rules (Defeasible RuleML, http://defeasible.org/RuleML/) and uncertainty / fuzziness (Fuzzy RuleML, http://www.image. ntua.gr/FuzzyRuleML/).

The coverage of rule markup languages can be roughly divided into logic-based rule formalisms, usually variants of first-order predicate logic, and not logic-based rule formalisms such as (early) production rule systems. In this chapter, we mainly focus on logic-based derivation rule markup languages, but most of the general rule markup languages such as RuleML and R2ML also support the serialization of production rules and reaction rules (e.g., Reaction RuleML covers different types of reaction rule languages). In fact, RuleML and R2ML provide a roughly similar coverage, whereas, e.g., SWRL acts as a more specialized language for homogeneously combining Datalog rules with OWL, hence does not cover, e.g., reaction rules.

Figure 4. RuleML 0.91 derivation RuleML subfamily

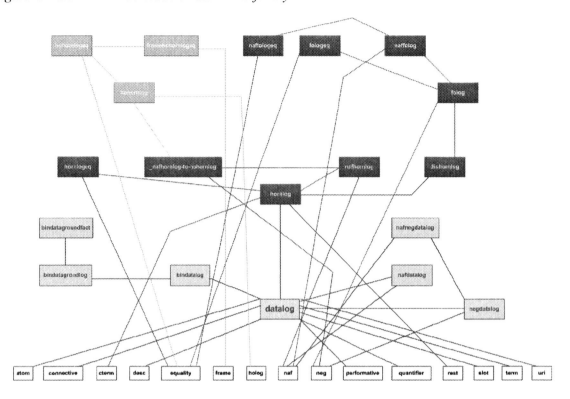

Rules and Object Descriptions

With its URIs (http://www.w3.org/Addressing/), the Web provides a global addressing (URL) and naming (URN) mechanism for objects. A URI consists of a URI scheme name (http:, file:, etc.) followed by other information that is interpreted relative to the URI scheme. The method for assigning meanings to names varies from one URI scheme to the next, and within each scheme for different sets of names. Each scheme's specification describes how its URIs are intended to be used in certain contexts. As a result, any naming framework must provide mechanisms to enable the creation of new names while avoiding conflicts with existing ones. URIs are also central to the Semantic Web, where RDF metadata are used to describe those objects or resources with classes and properties, which are themselves defined by ontologies (in RDF Schema or OWL). Since SHOE (Heflin et al, 1999), Semantic Web rule languages have as-

sociated URIs with constant symbols, predicate names, and other language constructs for reference and disambiguation. For example, the constant symbol Georgia could be associated with the unique 'homepage' URI http://www.georgia.gov to refer to and disambiguate the state in the Southeastern U.S. in contrast to other entities having the same English name such as the country at the east coast of the Black Sea.

There have been attempts to differentiate the Web notion of URIs into two subnotions, as discussed in (Halpin, 2006): URLs (Uniform Resource Locators), for access, and URNs (Uniform Resource Names), for naming. This distinction is independent from the recent IRI (Internationalized) versions of URIs. In the context of Web knowledge representation, especially for Web rules as explored in POSL, RuleML, and RIF, three central URI uses are emerging (Boley, 2007), given here in the order of further needed research (orthogonal to research in URI normalization (Boley, 2003)).

First, a URI can be used, URL/access-style, for module import (transitive import for nested modules), where it is an error if dereferencing the URI does not yield a knowledge base valid with respect to the expected representation language.

Second, a URI can be used, URN/naming-style, as the identifier of an individual constant in the representation language, where URI dereferencing is not intended as part of the formal knowledge representation. If dereferencing is attempted as part of the metadata about the informal knowledge representation, it should retrieve a descriptive 'homepage' about the individual.

Third, a URI can be used, naming-style, as the identifier of a class, property, relation, or function, and at the same time, access-style, where dereferencing yields (a "#"-anchor into) a knowledge base formally defining that identifier (albeit perhaps partially only, as for an RDF Schema knowledge base just giving the superclasses of a class).

Here are examples for the three URI uses in connection with rules.

First, a module of U.S. states could be imported into the current rulebase using the URL/access-style URI http://modeg.org#us-state.

Second, the URI http://en.wikipedia.org/wiki/Pluto can be used URN/naming-style to refer to a celestial body originally considered a planet, as in this rule specifying its years of planethood (a URI is enclosed in a pair of angular brackets, <... >):

```
planet(<http://en.wikipedia.org/
wiki/Pluto>,AD[?year]):-
lessThanOrEqual(1930,?year),
lessThanOrEqual(?year,2006).
```

As part of the formal rule knowledge, the Pluto URI is employed only for naming. The rule can also be employed as metadata about informal knowledge through ('semantic search engine') queries like planet(?which,2005), because one of its solutions will bind ?which to the URI, whose dereferencing ('clicking') will then retrieve Pluto's Wikipedia entry.

Third, for certain formal purposes a URI like http://termeg.org#MiniVan is needed just to provide a name; for other formal purposes, also to provide a total or partial definition found by using that same URI access-style (say, the partial definition of being rdfs:subClassOf both http://termeg.org#Van and http://termeg.org#PassengerVehicle).

In most rule markup languages as well as the specific Semantic Web rule languages, the (user-defined) vocabulary names are globally unique standard identifiers in the form of URI references. Morover, they often define specific builtins for handling URIs such as the SWRL builtins *swrlb:resolveURI (from XQuery op:resolve-uri)*, which is satisfied iff the URI reference in the first argument is equal to the value of the URI reference in the second argument resolved relative to the base URI in the third argument, or *swrlb:anyURI*, which is satisfied iff the first argument is a URI reference consisting of the scheme in the second argument, host in the third argument, port in the fourth argument, path in the fifth argument, query in the sixth argument, and fragment in the seventh argument.

All classes in R2ML are URI references. A class is a type entity for R2ML objects and object variables. Similarly, a *reference property* as well as a *datatype predicate* in R2ML is a URI reference.

RIF uses *internationalized resource identifiers* or *IRIs* (symbol space rif:iri) as constants similar to RDF resources.

Rule-Ontology Combination

A rule markup language should be reasonably integrated with the Semantic Web and should be able to refer to external Semantic Web vocabularies by means of URIs or IRIs, e.g. to use their taxonomic vocabularies as type systems and their individuals as external constants/objects. Domain-independent rules can then be interpreted (relative to each vocabulary) in a domain-dependent manner (with a precise semantics). Accordingly, the original rule set can be much easier interchanged and managed/maintained in a distributed environment. Also, the core Web rule language stays compact and can be easily extended for different vocabulary languages (RDFS, OWL, OWL 2, etc.) on a "per-need-basis".

In recent years, quite an effort has been made to develop a dual expressiveness layering of assertional and terminological knowledge as well as their blends (Antoniou et al., 2005, Kifer et al, 2005). To retain decidability of querying, the *assertional bottom layer* usually consists of Datalog (function-free) assertions, perhaps restricted to unary/binary predicates. For the *terminological bottom layer*, an irreflexive version of RDF Schema's subClassOf can be employed, which could later be extended towards the rhoDF (Munoz et al., 2007) fragment of RDF. The two layers can be blended through a hybrid combination (rhoDF classes used as types for Datalog constants and variables, and subClassOf defined with order-sorted semantics) or a homogeneous integration (rhoDF classes used as unary predicates in the body of Datalog rules, and subClassOf defined as special rules with Herbrand-model semantics).

The higher layers can develop Datalog into Horn (as in Prova's or OO jDREW's hybrid implementation) and FOL (First-Order Logic) assertions, rhoDF into ALC and SHIQ terminologies with classes and properties, and appropriate blends (Rosati, 2006) (Rosati, 2006a), e.g. as advancements of our hybrid DatalogDL (Mei et al, 2007b) or homogeneous ALCuP (Mei et al, 2007). For certain purposes, especially in the early modeling phases, the assertional layers can move even beyond FOL, including towards higher-order and modal logics, as started as part of the RuleML family (Boley, 2006).

To permit the specification of terminologies independent of assertions, a hybrid approach is proposed here adopting the CARIN (Levy and Rousset, 1998) principle as a working hypothesis:

A terminological predicate is not permitted in the head of a rule. Intuitively, terminological classes cannot be (re)defined by assertional clauses, because a terminology establishes more stable 'background' knowledge extended by assertions that constitute more volatile 'foreground' knowledge.

Such a hybrid lower layer can use sort restrictions as simple terminological queries in Datalog rule bodies, which in higher layers are extended to terminological queries involving properties, ALC expressions, etc. In the spirit of (Kifer et al, 2005), this should lead to a more realistic Semantic Web architecture with simplified foundations and better computational properties. Our fine-grained bottom-up approach also complements the recent differentiation of OWL-Lite into OWL 1.1 (later: OWL 2) Tractable Fragments (Grau et al., 2006).

The following example uses classes of a sub-ClassOf terminology as variable sorts (types) of slightly extended Datalog rules, namely of Horn logic rules employing (unary) functions only for measurement units.

The terminology forms a DAG (cf. Figure 5) that introduces Vehicle-rooted classes and exemplifies multiple inheritance of MiniVan from Van and PassengerVehicle (the ">" infix is used between a superclass and a subclass):

```
Vehicle > Van
Vehicle > PassengerVehicle
Van > MiniVan
PassengerVehicle > MiniVan
PassengerVehicle > Car
```

The following RuleML/POSL rules specify registration fees for vehicles. The first rule specifies a vehicle variable typed by the Van class, while the second refers to the Car class (the ":" infix is used between a variable and its type):

Figure 5. A vehicle terminology (cf. (W3C, 2000))

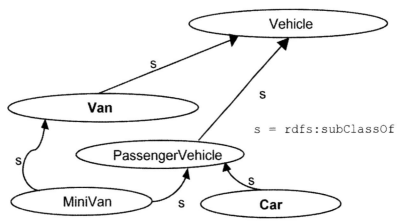

A registration query for a given vehicle class will thus unify only with correspondingly sorted rule conclusions, hence directly branch into the appropriate rule premises (the emiweight and emispeed premises compute the fees from the emissions as well as the weights and speeds for Vans and Cars, respectively). The previous section has shown URI-'webized' versions of these terminological classes.

R2ML rules may refer to a vocabulary which can be R2ML's own vocabulary or an imported one (such as RDF(S) and OWL). R2ML's internal default vocabulary is a serialization of a UML fragment of class diagrams. R2ML uses XML Schema datatypes as its standard datatype

```
registration(?V:Van,CAD[?R:Deci
mal]):-
emission(?V,CO2[?E]),
weight(?V,kg[?W]),
emiweight(CAD[?R],CO2[?E],kg[?W
]).
registration(?V:Car,CAD[?R:Deci
mal]):-
emission(?V,CO2[?E]),
speed(?V,kmh[?S]),
emispeed(CAD[?R],CO2[?E],kmh[?S
]).
```

set. R2ML distinguishes between plain and typed literals and typed and untyped variables. A *DataTerm* is a *DataVariable*, a *DataLiteral*, or a *DataFunctionTerm*. An *ObjectVariable* is a variable that stand for objects of a particular class type, a *DataVariable* is a variable that stand for data literals, and a *GenericVariable* is a variable that does not have a type. For instance, an *ObjectVariable* contains an optional reference to a class which is used as its type:

```
<r2ml:ObjectVariable
r2ml:name="driver"
r2ml:classID="userv:Driver" />
```

R2ML allows both typed and untyped individuals. For instance, a *TypedLiteral* consist in a lexical value and a type that is an RDF datatype or a user defined datatype (subclass of rdfs:Literal):

```
<r2ml:TypedLiteral r2ml:type
Literal="xs:positiveInteger"
r2ml:lexicalValue="90"/>
```

RuleML supports order-sorted terms permitting typed individuals, variables (exemplified above) and data literals (Boley, 2003). Therefore,

RuleML/XML defines an optional type attribute for specifying a term's (user-defined) type. Besides referring to the default XML Schema datatypes, typed terms may also link into external object class hierarchies via their fully qualified class names (e.g. Java classes) or taxonomies such as RDF Schema class hierarchies, thus reusing the OO class models and Semantic Web's light-weight ontologies as pluggable external order-sorted type systems. For example:

```
<Var type="rdf://
owl:Vehicle">V</Var>
<Ind type="xml://
xsd:string">abc</Ind>
<Var type="java://java.lang.
Number">X</Var>
```

A *Data* term in RuleML contains a fixed value, like an RDF literal. It may be optionally associated with an XML Schema built-in datatype using the xsi:type attribute. For example:

```
<Data
xsi:type="xs:dateTime">2002-10-
10T17:00:00Z</Data>
```

This open order-sorted typing approach of RuleML provides higher levels of abstractions and allows ad-hoc polymorphism with respect to coercion, i.e., automatic type conversion between subtypes, and overloading, i.e., defining multiple cases (rules with the same head except for types) taking different argument types. The ability to integrate external Semantic Web vocabularies, data types and object oriented class hierarchies as type systems provides syntactic expressiveness for easy extension of the language with domain-specific terminologies, and it facilities rule interchange across domain boundaries due to the explicit semantic definition of the used vocabulary, e.g., a Semantic Web ontology.

As in RuleML, RIF provides an optional type attribute for typed constants / individuals and a set of default XML Schema primitive data types such as xsd:long, xsd:integer, xsd:decimal, xsd:string, rdf:XMLLiteral and rif:text. For example:

```
<Const
type="rif:iri">dc:creator</
Const>
<Const type="xsd:string">abc</
Const>
```

However, variables are not typed directly in a prescriptive form using, e.g., the type attribute in the variable construct to denote that a variable X is of type T, i.e. $X{:}T$. Instead, RIF defines classification terms for class memberships, and also for subclass relationships (cf. F-logic's ":" and "::"):

- t#s is a *membership term* if t and s are terms.
- t##s is a *subclass term* if t and s are terms.

These classification terms are used to describe subclass hierarchies and membership constraints, e.g. expressing that a variable is of a certain class (type).

In SWRL, a homogeneous combination of OWL (OWL DL and OWL Lite) and RuleML (Unary/Binary Datalog), atoms can be of the form $C(x)$, $P(x,y)$, *sameAs(x,y)* *differentFrom(x,y)*, or *builtIn(r,x,...)* where C is an OWL description or data range, P is an OWL property, r is a built-in relation, x and y are either variables, OWL individuals or OWL data values, as appropriate. In the context of OWL Lite, descriptions in atoms of the form $C(x)$ may be restricted to class names. That is, SWRL defines a rule language on top of OWL ontologies and hence directly supports the definition of class ontologies and their properties which can be used to type variables. For an example, see Figure 6.

Figure 6.

```
<!-- Each person that is a qualified driver can be added to a car rental as
additional driver-->
<ruleml:Implies
   xmlns:ruleml="http://www.ruleml.org/0.91/xsd"
   xmlns:owlx="http://www.w3.org/2003/05/owl-xml"
   xmlns:swrlx="http://www.w3.org/2003/11/swrlx"
   xmlns:srv="http://www.eurobizrules.org/ebrc2005/eurentcs">

   <ruleml:body>
     <swrlx:classAtom>
       <owlx:Class owlx:name="srv:Rental"/>
       <ruleml:Var>rental</ruleml:Var>
     </swrlx:classAtom>
     <swrlx:classAtom>
       <owlx:Class owlx:name="srv:Person"/>
       <ruleml:Var>person</ruleml:Var>
     </swrlx:classAtom>
     <swrlx:classAtom>
       <owlx:Class owlx:name="srv:QualifiedDriver"/>
       <ruleml:Var>person</ruleml:Var>
     </swrlx:classAtom>
   </ruleml:body>
   <ruleml:head>
     <swrlx:individualPropertyAtom swrlx:property="srv:additionalDriver">
       <ruleml:Var>rental</ruleml:Var>
       <ruleml:Var>person</ruleml:Var>
     </swrlx:individualPropertyAtom>
   </ruleml:head>
</ruleml:Implies>
```

This homogeneous integration approach is adopted by R2ML from SWRL, while in RuleML without OWL one would refer to the external ontology which defines the vocabulary classes and their properties.

EXTERNAL DATA INTEGRATION AND DATA PROCESSING

Often Web rules refer to or describe functions and queries over data stored in an external database which can be anything from log files to Web sources or relational databases, data warehouses, or XML or RDF databases such as native XML databases or RDF triple stores. The rule language must allow for the direct dynamic integration of these secondary data storages as facts or object values into the rules in order to reduce redundancy and high memory consumption. It should also support outsourcing of expensive (pre-)processing of data to external systems, e.g., of mathematical functions to procedural implementations such as Java, or of SQL/SPARQL aggregation queries (constructive views) to database management systems or RDF triple stores. A tight combination of declarative and object-oriented programming with rich procedural attachments and language built-ins, e.g. for querying, will facilitate the integration of existing functionalities, tools, and external data sources into rule executions at run time.

Procedural attachments are procedure calls to external user-defined computational models of a standard programming language, e.g., directly to

Figure 7.

```
<swrlx:builtinAtom swrlx:builtin="&swrlb;#multiply">
    <ruleml:var>inches</ruleml:var>
    <ruleml:var>feet</ruleml:var>
    <owlx:DataValue owlx:datatype="&xsd;#int">12</owlx:DataValue>
</swrlx:builtinAtom>
```

Java or C# methods. Therefore, procedural attachments are a crucial extension of a modern Web rule language. They permit the combination of the benefits of declarative (rule-based) as well as procedural and object-oriented languages, e.g., to delegate computation-intensive tasks to optimized object code or to invoke procedure calls on object methods which cannot be easily expressed in a declarative rule-based way. Procedural attachments should be supplemented with a typed logic approach with external type systems such as Java or Semantic Web ontologies, e.g. to assign external objects to typed variables, and with mode declarations in order to safeguard the usage of built-ins and calls to external functionalities.

(Procedural Attachments). A procedural attachment is a function or predicate whose implementation is given by an external procedure. Two types of procedural attachments are distinguished:

- *Boolean-valued attachments (or predicate attachments)* which call methods that return a Boolean value, i.e., that are of Boolean sort (type).
- *Object-valued attachments (or functional attachments)* which are treated as functions that take arguments and return one or more objects, i.e., that are of a function sort. This also includes access to public object fields.

(Built-Ins). Built-in predicates or functions are special restricted predicate or function symbols in the rule language for concrete domains, e.g., built-ins for strings, numerics, Boolean values,

date, time, intervals, lists, etc.

All Web rule languages discussed in this chapter provide support for built-ins and some of them also for general procedural attachments.

SWRL provides an extensible library of built-in functions (http://www.daml.org/2004/04/swrl/builtins.html) co-developed with RuleML. SWRL's built-ins approach is based on the reuse of existing built-ins in XQuery and XPath, which are themselves based on XML Schema Part 2: Datatypes. SWRL built-ins are called via a built-in atom, swrlx:builtinAtom, which identifies a built-in using the swrlx:builtin attribute and lists its arguments as subelements. SWRL built-ins are identified using the http://www.w3.org/2003/11/swrlb namespace, currently also used by RuleML. This is an example of calling the multiply built-in (see Figure 7).

SWRL does not provide direct support for procedural attachments, but it could easily adopt this feature from Reaction RuleML.

R2ML by default supports SWRL and XPath2 built-ins as predicate names of atoms *r2ml:DatatypePredicateAtom* and symbols of functions *r2ml:DatatypeFunctionTerm*. Functions and operators like addition, subtraction, etc. are translated into corresponding R2ML function terms. The operands of the functions implied by the built-ins are enclosed by *r2ml:dataArguments* and might be class attributes, class operations, data variables, typed variables, or further nested built-in functions. However, mode declarations are missing (see Figure 8).

R2ML supports procedural attachments in order to access public data fields of objects which might be bound to object variables (see

Figure 8.

```
<r2ml:DatatypePredicateAtom
  r2ml:datatypePredicate="swrlb:lessThan">
    <r2ml:dataArguments>
       <r2ml:DataVariable r2ml:name="y"/>
       <r2ml:TypedLiteral r2ml:lexicalValue="4"
                          r2ml:datatype="xs:positiveInteger"/>
    </r2ml:dataArguments>
</r2ml:DatatypePredicateAtom>
```

Figure 9.

```
<r2ml:AttributeFunctionTerm r2ml:attributeID="userv:Car.price">
    <r2ml:contextArgument>
       <r2ml:ObjectVariable r2ml:name="car"
                          r2ml:classID="userv:Car"/>
    </r2ml:contextArgument>
</r2ml:AttributeFunctionTerm>
```

Figure 9).

For reactive rules such as production rules, R2ML supports assignments of action expressions in order to call object methods as actions in the action part (see Figure 10).

The RIF built-ins (http://www.w3.org/2005/rules/wiki/DTB) overlap with the functions and predicates defined in XQuery 1.0 and XPath 2.0 Functions and Operators.

Syntactically, built-in predicates and functions in RIF are enclosed by external terms of the form:

'External' '(' Expr ')'

where Expr is a UNITERM, i.e. either a Boolean-valued function expression / predicate or an object-valued functional expression. Since RIF does not support a general typed rule language, it requires special guard predicates for all of its supported datatypes to ensure the correct usage of the arguments of built-ins:

Figure 10.

```
<r2ml:AssignActionExpression r2ml:propertyID="status">
    <r2ml:contextArgument>
       <r2ml:ObjectVariable r2ml:name="ticket"/>
    </r2ml:contextArgument>
    <r2ml:TypedLiteral r2ml:lexicalValue="Escalate"
                r2ml:datatypeID="xs:string"/>
</r2ml:AssignActionExpression>
```

Figure 11.

```
<!- a call to a builtin function -->
<Expr>
    <Fun per="builtin" uri="swrlb:stringConcat"/>
        <Var type="java://java.lang.String" mode="+">String1</Var>
        <Var type="java://java.lang.String" mode="+">String2</Var>
</Expr>

<!-- a call to a builtin predicate -->
<Atom>
    <Rel per="builtin" uri="rif:dateTime-equal"/>
        <Var type="xml://xs:dateTime" mode="+">Time1</Var>
        <Var type="xml://xs:dateTime" mode="+">Time2</Var>
</Atom>
```

```
External("op:numeric-greater-
than"^^rif:iri(
?diffdays
"10"^^xsd:integer))
External(
"www.w3.org/2007/rif-builtin-
predicates#isInteger"^^rif:iri(
?diffdays))
```

Note that the above example shows the RIF presentation syntax, not the concrete RIF XML syntax.

RIF-FLD foresees procedurally attached user-defined function terms or predicates to be wrapped as external terms but does not define a concrete approach for calling procedural actions yet. However, it supports frame terms *t[p1->v1 ... pn->vn]* which can be used to describe properties of objects.

The RuleML family (through its Reaction RuleML branch) provides an open flexible approach for pluggable external built-in libraries safeguarded by type and mode declarations. It explicitly denotes the usage by the attribute per= *"plain|value|effect|modal|builtin"* on functional expressions and atomic relations. A *<Rel>* or *<Fun>* using "plain" is left uninterpreted, using *"value"* is interpreted purely for its value, using *"effect"* is interpreted impurely both for its value and its (side-)effect action, e.g. by a procedural attachment, using *"modal"* is interpreted as pure modality, and using *"builtin"* as a built-in (Figure 11).

The mode ("+": input; "-": output; "?": input or output) and type declarations ensure the correct usage of arguments in built-ins, i.e. that built-ins are called with ground values (not free variables) of the expected types.

RuleML provides a concise integration of procedural attachments. Methods of external object classes can be called, including calls to object constructors and calls to object instance and static object methods as well as access to public object fields. Constructed objects and returned result objects can be assigned to variables. Nested selection patterns can be defined over the result object collections such as "forall ?X where ?X=Person(age > 30 and age < 40)" (see Figure 12).

Most of the specific Semantic Web rule languages such as Jena and Prova support all "standard" built-ins of Web Rule languages as well as many additional built-ins e.g. for meta interpretations of literals, exception handling, console printouts, collections, iterations/enumerations, object property constraints, or access to system environment properties. For instance, Prova supports several query built-ins to access

Figure 12.

```
<!-- Assign the constructed Java object to the variable
     Date = java.io.Calendar.getInstance() -->
<Equal>
  <Var>Date</Var>
  <Expr>
     <!-- class -->
     <oid><Ind uri="java://java.util.Calendar"/></oid>
     <!-- constructor -->
     <Fun per="effect">getInstance</Fun>
  </Expr>
</Equal>

<!-- Use the bound object of the variable and call a function
     "isSet" of the object -->
<Atom>
    <!-- object previously assigned to Date -->
    <oid><Var>Date</Var></oid>
    <Rel per="effect">isSet</Rel>
    <Data>1</Data>
</Atom>

<!-- Call a static C# method -->
<Atom>
    <oid><Ind uri="c-sharp://System.Console"/></oid>
    <Rel uri="WriteLine"/>
    <Data>Hello World</Data>
</Atom>
```

files, XML data sources via DOM, XPath, and XQuery, RDF data sources via RDF triples and SPARQL and RDFS/OWL ontologies, as well as various homogeneous or heterogeneous inference queries using external DL reasoners such as, e.g., Pellet. Prova also provides a tight and natural Java integration. Methods of classes in arbitrary Java packages can be dynamically invoked from Prova rules. The method invocations include calls to Java constructors creating Java variables and calls to instance and static methods for Java classes as well as public object data fields.

FUTURE TRENDS

A general rule markup language such as RuleML or RIF covers many different rule types and rule families. Some of the language families such as classical production rules historically only define an operational semantics, while other rule families such as logical rules (see RuleML family in the section about expressive layering) are based on a model-theoretic and/or proof-theoretic semantics. A general research question is whether there exists a unifying semantic framework for all different rule types. Work in this direction is pursued, e.g. in RIF (http://www.w3.org/2005/rules/wiki/FLD) and Reaction RuleML (transactional transition semantics for reaction rules subsuming all other RuleML rules). However, since there is no general consensus on one particular semantics for all expressive rule languages, an exclusive commitment to one particular semantics for a Web rule language should be avoided (even in well-researched fields such as logic programming several semantics such as well-founded semantics and answer set semantics are competing). Nevertheless, for certain subfamilies a preferred semantics can still be given and semantic mappings between rule families be defined.

General rule markup languages need to include practical language constructs which might not (yet) have a standard formal semantics based on classical model-theoretic logic. For instance, procedural calls to external (object) functions, operational systems, data sources and terminological descriptions, are often vital to deal with practical real-world settings of distributed Web applications. Recent research, e.g. in RuleML and RIF-PRD, is done on adopting such practical language constructs without a standard formal semantics but with a non-standard one. While there is a risk that these concessions to non-standard semantics might endanger the benefits of formal semantics for the overall rule language, they turn out to be a crucial means to avoid limitations of standard rule representations in the exploration of rule markup languages. The rule component will rarely run in isolation, but interact with various external components, hence call for functionalities such as efficient object-oriented or relational/SQL-style retrieval and aggregation methods that are common in modern information systems.

Further examples of useful practical constructs are the annotation of rules and rule sets with additional metadata such as rule qualifications, rule names, module names, Dublin Core annotations, etc., which eases, e.g., the modularization of rules into rule sets (bundling of rules), the creation of constructive views over internal and external knowledge (scoped reasoning), as well as the publication and interchange of rules / rule sets on the Web. Advanced rule qualifications such as validity periods or rule priorities might for example safeguard dynamic updates (e.g. the incorporation of interchanged rules into the existing rule base), where conflicts are resolved by rule prioritizations.

Another domain of research is the engineering and maintenance of large rule-based applications, where the rules are serialized and managed in a distributed manner, and are interchanged across domain boundaries. This calls for support of verification, validation and integrity testing (V&V&I), e.g. by test cases that are written in the same rule markup language and are stored and interchanged together with the rule program. A proposal for self-validating rule bases adapting a test-driven development approach from extreme programming in Software Engineering has been made for RuleML (Paschke et al, 2006) and for RIF (Paschke et al, 2005).

CONCLUSION

In this chapter several important requirements and design choices for a rule markup language have been described. It was shown how the current Web rule language proposals address these issues and what characteristics derive from those solutions. Commonalities as well as differences between the languages were presented and illustrated with concrete examples. Discussions of the advantages and disadvantages of the language design approaches reveal that all approaches legitimately coexist at this stage, as all have their strengths and weaknesses.

REFERENCES

W3C (2000). W3C Resource Description Framework. Candidate Recommendation. Retrieved from, http://www.w3.org/TR/2000/CR-rdf-schema-20000327/

W3C (2007). Semantic Web Layer Cake. Retrieved from, http://www.w3.org/2007/03/layerCake.png

Antoniou, G., Damasio, C. V., Grosof, B., Horrocks, I., Kifer, M., Maluszynski, J., et al. (2005). *Combining rules and ontologies — A survey.* Deliverables I3-D3, REWERSE. Retrieved from, http://rewerse.net/deliverables/m12/i3-d3.pdf

Ball, M. Boley, Hirtle, H.D., Mei, J., & Spencer, B. (2005). The OO jDREW reference implementation of RuleML. In *Proceedings of Rules and Rule Markup Languages for the Semantic Web* (RuleML-2005) (pp. 218-223). (LNCS 3791).

Boley, H. (2003). *Object-oriented RuleML: User-level roles, URI-grounded clauses and order-sorted terms* (. LNCS, 2876*, 1–16.

Boley, H. (2006). The RuleML family of Web rule languages. In *Proceedings of the Fourth Workshop on Principles and Practice of Semantic Web Reasoning*, Budva, Montenegro (LNCS 4187, pp. 1-15).

Boley, H. (2007). *Are your rules online? Four Web rule essentials.* RuleML (pp. 7-24).

Bry, F., & Marchiori, M. (2005). *Ten theses on logic languages for the Semantic Web.* PPSWR (pp. 42-49).

Codd, E. (1971). Alpha: A data base sublanguage founded on the relational calculus of the database relational model. In *Proceedings of ACM SIG-FIDET Workshop on Data Description, Access and Control,* San Diego, CA.

Ensing, M. (2007). *The rule manager: A graphical business rules environment.* Demo at RuleML-2007. Retrieved from, http://2007.ruleml.org/docs/Acumen%20Business%20-%20RuleML.pdf

FIPA. (2000). *FIPA agent communication language.* Retrieved December 2001, from http://www.fipa.org/

Fuchs, N.E., Kaljurand, K., & Schneider, G. (2006). *Attempto controlled English meets the challenges of knowledge representation, reasoning, interoperability and user interfaces.* FLAIRS 2006.

Giurca, A., & Wagner, G. (2005). Towards an abstract syntax and direct-model theoretic semantics for RuleML. *RuleML, 2005,* 45–55.

Grau, B. C., Calvanese, D., De Giacomo, G., Horrocks, I., Lutz, C., Motik, B., et al. (2006). *OWL 1.1 Web ontology language tractable fragments.* W3C Member Submission. Retrieved from, http://www.w3.org/Submission/owl11-tractable/

Halpin, H. (2006, May). *Identity, reference, and meaning on the Web.* WWW 2006 Workshop on Identity, Reference, and the Web. Retrieved from, http://www.ibiblio.org/hhalpin/irw2006

Heflin, J., Hendler, J., & Luke, S. (1999). *SHOE: A knowledge representation language for Internet applications* (Technical Report CS-TR-4078) (UMIACS TR-99-71).

Hirtle, D. (2006). *TRANSLATOR: A TRANSlator from LAnguage TO rules.* Canadian Symposium on Text Analysis (CaSTA), Fredericton, October 2006.

Kifer, M., de Bruijn, J., Boley, H., & Fensel, D. (2005). A realistic architecture for the Semantic Web. In A. Adi, S. Stoutenburg, & S. Tabet (Eds.), *RuleML* (LNCS 3791, pp. 17-29).

Levy, A. A., & Rousset, M.-C. (1998). CARIN: A representation language combining horn rules and description logics. *Artificial Intelligence, 104*(1-2), 165–209. doi:10.1016/S0004-3702(98)00048-4

Lukichev, S., & Wagner, G. (2006). Visual rules modeling. In I. Virbitskaite & A. Voronkov (Eds.), *Proceedings of the 6th International Conference Perspectives of Systems Informatics* (LNCS 4378, pp. 467-673).

Mei, J., Lin, Z., & Boley, H. (2007). *ALCuP: An integration of description logic and general rules, Web reasoning and rule systems.* In First International Conference, RR 2007 (LNCS 4524, pp. 163-177).

Mei, J., Lin, Z., Boley, H., Li, J., & Bhavsar, V. C. (2007b). The DatalogDL combination of deduction rules and description logics. *Computational Intelligence, 23*(3), 356–372. doi:10.1111/j.1467-8640.2007.00311.x

Munoz, S., Perez, J., & Gutierrez, C. (2007). Minimal deductive systems for RDF. In E. Franconi, M. Kifer, & W. May (Eds.), *ESWC* (LNCS 4519, pp. 53-67).

Paschke, A. (2005). *RBSLA: A declarative rule-based service level agreement language based on RuleML.* CIMCA/IAWTIC 2005 (pp. 308-314).

Paschke, A. (2006). *Verification, validation and integrity of distributed and interchanged rule based policies and contracts in the Semantic Web.* Int. Semantic Web and Policy Workshop (SWPW'06), Athens, Georgia.

Paschke, A. (2006b). *A typed hybrid description logic programming language with polymorphic order-sorted DL-typed unification for Semantic Web type systems.* OWL-2006 (OWLED'06), Athens, Georgia.

Paschke, A. (2007). *Rule-based service level agreements - Knowledge representation for automated e-contract, SLA and policy management.* IDEA Verlag GmbH, München.

Paschke, A., Boley, H., & Dietrich, J. (2005). *RIF use case. Rule interchange through test-driven verification and validation.* Retrieved from, http://www.w3.org/2005/rules/wg/wiki/Rule_Interchange_Through_Test-Driven_Verification_and_Validation, 2005.

Paschke, A., Boley, H., Kozlenkov, A., & Craig, B. L. (2007). Rule responder: RuleML-based agents for distributed collaboration on the pragmatic Web. *ICPW, 2007,* 17–28. doi:10.1145/1324237.1324240

Paschke, A., Dietrich, J., Giurca, A., Wagner, G., & Lukichev, S. (2006). *On self-validating rule bases.* Int. Semantic Web Enabled Software Engineering Workshop (SWESE'06), Athens, Georgia.

Rosati, R. (2006). The limits and possibilities of combining description logics and datalog. In T. Eiter, E. Franconi, R. Hodgson, and S. Stephens (Eds.), *RuleML* (pp. 3-4). IEEE Computer Society.

Rosati, R. (2006a). *Integration ontologies and rules: Semantic and computational issues.* Reasoning Web.

Wagner, G., Antoniou, G., Tabet, S., & Boley, H. (2004). The abstract syntax of RuleML - towards a general Web rule language framework. *Web Intelligence, 2004,* 628–631.

Wagner, G., Damásio, C. V., & Antoniou, G. (2005). Towards a general Web rule language. *Int. J. Web Eng. Technol, 2*(2/3), 181–206. doi:10.1504/IJWET.2005.008483

KEY TERMS AND DEFINITIONS

Built-in Predicates or Functions: Special restricted predicate or function symbols in the rule language for concrete domains, e.g., built-ins for strings, numerics, Boolean values, date, time, intervals, lists, etc.

Deontic Rules: Describe rights and obligations, e.g., of institutions and agents in the context of evolving states (situations triggered by events/actions) and state transitions, where integrity rules (see above) are a special case ('introspectively') affecting the rule set itself.

Derivation Rules: Infer conclusions from conditions (as in Datalog and Horn logic), where facts are a special case with constantly true conditions.

Facts: Various kinds of information such as asserted atoms (formulas), individual-class memberships (of ontology classes), (object-oriented) instances, stored data (e.g., relational, XML), states and event occurrences which might be qualified, e.g., by priorities, temporally, etc.

Integrity Rules (or integrity constraints): Assertions which express conditions (or queries) that must always be satisfied.

Procedural Attachment: A function or predicate whose implementation is given by an external procedure.

Reaction Rules are (Behavioral / Action) Rules: (Re)act on occurred events (external events or changed conditions) by executing actions, where production rules are a special case with events restricted to changed conditions.

Rule Interchange Format: A common interchange format, such as e.g. W3C RIF or RuleML, for different rule types and rule families.

Rule Markup Language: A concrete markup-based rule syntax using e.g. XML for the Web.

Semantic Web Rule Language: A rule language specifically tailored for the semantic web with a human-friendly syntax, e.g., a scripting syntax (as opposed to a Rule Markup Language for the Semantic Web).

Transformation Rules: Specify term rewriting, which can be considered as derivation rules of logics with (oriented) equality.

Chapter 2.20
Semantic Web Rule Languages for Geospatial Ontologies

Philip D. Smart
Cardiff University, UK & University of Glamorgan, UK

Alia I. Abdelmoty
Cardiff University, UK & University of Glamorgan, UK

Baher A. El-Geresy
Cardiff University, UK & University of Glamorgan, UK

Christopher B. Jones
Cardiff University, UK & University of Glamorgan, UK

ABSTRACT

Geospatial ontologies have a key role to play in the development of the geospatial-Semantic Web, with regard to facilitating the search for geographical information and resources. They normally hold large volumes of geographic information and undergo a continuous process of revision and update. Limitations of the OWL ontology representation language for supporting geospatial domains are discussed and an integrated rule and ontology language is recognized as needed to support the representation and reasoning requirements in this domain. A survey of the current approaches to integrating ontologies and rules is presented and a new framework is proposed that is based on and extends Description Logic Programs. A hybrid representational approach is adopted where the logical component of the framework is used to represent geographical concepts and spatial rules and an external computational geometry processor is used for storing and manipulating the associated geometric data. A sample application is used to demonstrate the proposed language and engine and how they address the identified challenges.

INTRODUCTION AND BACKGROUND

The Internet is the single largest information resource in the world that is however still not being used to its full potential. To fully unlock the potential of such a large knowledge resource and to enable its effective utilisation by both human and

DOI: 10.4018/978-1-60566-402-6.ch007

machine agents, information on the Web needs to be machine-understandable using semantic as opposed to syntactic (e.g. HTML) markup languages and tools. At the heart of this vision are ontologies which, in the context of the web, are logical theories that act to constrain and derive information (Guarino,1995). They provide the necessary semantics and machine understanding to the sheer volumes of information contained on the Web.

A significant proportion of information resources on the web are geographically referenced. Nearly 17% of all web queries contain place names (Sanderson & Kohler, 2004) and the web, powered by the simplicity of recent applications such as Google Maps, is increasingly being seen as a medium for the storage and exchange of geographic data in the form of maps. A geographic or geospatial ontology is a model of terminology and structure of geographic space as well as records of entities in this space (Egenhofer, 2002). This chapter considers the development and management of geospatial ontologies on the Semantic web. By analyzing the nature and complexity of the geographical concepts and data to be handled by these ontologies, we evaluate the suitability of the current semantic web tools and suggest an appropriate platform to represent and develop these ontologies.

In particular, geographical concepts are complex, normally associated with geometric representations of their boundaries and location and exhibit implicit spatial relationships that need to be computed and derived. Qualitative spatial reasoning as well as computational geometry procedures are both established complementary techniques for the representation and manipulation in this domain. In addition, maintaining the spatial integrity of large geospatial ontology bases is crucial for their realization. Ontology representation languages such as OWL are limited in their ability to handle the challenges in this domain. In this chapter, a survey of current approaches to integrating rules and ontologies is

presented. Two approaches are identified, namely a hybrid approach where both systems of ontologies and rules are kept distinct and communicate only through an interface, and a homogeneous approach where one system is mapped to and becomes accessible from the other.

In the second section, we first discuss the representational and manipulation challenges facing ontology management systems that aim to support geospatial domains. OWL as an ontology representation language is evaluated against those challenges and the need for a integrated rule layer is highlighted. In the third section, current approaches to integrating rules and ontologies (logic programming and Description Logic) are identified and classified. Based on a comparative evaluation of both approaches, a homogenous approach to integration, namely, Description Logic Programs is chosen as a suitable platform for the development of geospatial ontology management systems. In the fourth section, the potential and further extensions of this new approach are described. In the fifth section, the implementation of the approach is briefly sketched and demonstrated using a sample geospatial ontology described in the chapter, followed by conclusions and future outlook in the final sections.

MANAGING GEOSPATIAL ONTOLOGIES

In this section we consider a typical geospatial ontology model, as shown in Figure 1. The model is based on OGC guidelines for simple geographic features, see (OGC Technical Committee, 1999; Vretanos, 2005), and other models commonly used in existing geospatial ontology development (Fu et al., 2005, Smith & Frew, 1995). The terminology of the geo-ontology is relatively plain with regards to the number and type of constructs used. This reflects typical geographic ontology developments which, beyond the complex representation of geometry, are relatively sparse (parsimonious (Jones

Figure 1. An example geospatial ontology

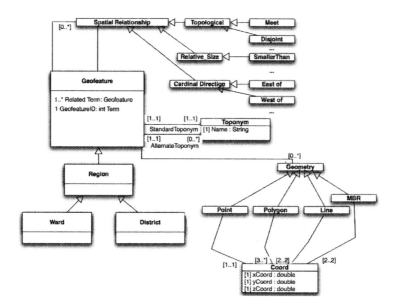

et al., 2001)) and fit to purpose. In this section, issues related to the representation and management of such geospatial ontologies are discussed and OWL's ability to handle them is evaluated.

In Figure 1, a geofeature is a representation of any geographic phenomena that exist in space, e.g. a forest, a building or a road. As such, its location and boundary can be specified using a geometric entity of point, line or polygon. Also, as it is located in space, the relationships it exhibits with other geographical features are of interest, e.g. it may be inside (topological), north of (directional) or near to (proximity) another feature. Some of these relationships may be stored explicitly or need to be computed from the features geometric entities.

Representational Requirements

Consider the map scene in Figure 2. The map shows sample administration regions in Wales. Two Unitary Authorities are shown; Cardiff and Newport along with some of their contained Wards.

The ontology in Figure 1 can be used to represent this map of Places. In particular, it can be represented using OWL as shown below. Examples from the axioms in the TBox (terminology or model) and the ABox (asserted knowledge) are shown. The logic-based syntax used here is that of OWL-DL.

TBox
$Geofeature \subseteq =1.GeofeatureID \cap \geq 1.RelatedTerm \cap \forall RelatedTerm.Geofeature$
...
$Region \subseteq Geofeature$
$Country \subseteq Region$
$Ward \subseteq Region$
$UnitaryAuthority \subseteq Region$
ABox
Cardiff: UnitaryAuthority
Newport: UnitaryAuthority
Roath: Ward
Wales: Country
Cathays: Ward
Cardiff Meets Newport
Roath Inside Cardiff
Cardiff Inside Wales
Roath Meets Cathays

Figure 2. A sample geographic scene showing administrative regions in Wales

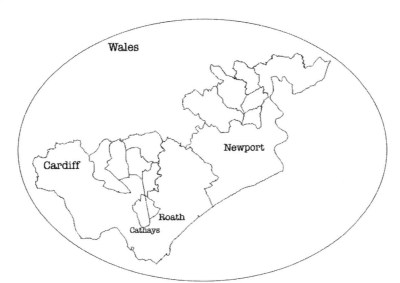

The geometry of geographic regions is normally complex and can consist of a large number of points. For example, the Unitary Authority of Cardiff in Figure 2 is represented by over 1,000 points, presenting a large storage and management overhead on the ontology language. An experiment with a small geospatial ontology of geographic regions was constructed in OWL, using the Jena2 library. The base OWL ontology, without the associated geometry, contained 1,000 individual places with two data attributes (ID and name). The ontology occupied approximately 2.2mb of persistent storage space and 16mb of system memory to reason with. Adding the associated geometry for each place, represented as general classes and data properties, the ontology grew to around 100mb on persistent storage and the memory overhead increased to over 1gb. Even then, spatial queries e.g. all Wards in Wales, are not supported within OWL as currently its associated reasoning engines e.g. Racer (Haarslev et al., 2001) or Fact (Horrocks, 1998), do not contain the necessary algorithms to perform polygon in polygon geometry operations etc.

To support the geospatial domain, an ontology management system needs to consider the following requirements.

- Support the representation of basic spatial data models, spatial data types and relationships.
- Provide a scalable capacity for handling and searching over large geometric data stores.

Manipulation Requirements

Manipulating geospatial ontologies involves the search, computation and retrieval of spatial properties and relationships. Two paradigms are possible: quantitative, using computational geometric procedures for structuring and search along with qualitative, using qualitative spatial reasoning techniques. Indeed, both paradigms are complementary and can be used together.

In this section, both paradigms are explored to understand the issues they pose to geospatial ontology management systems.

Table 1. Part of a spatial composition table for topological relations between simple regions. 1 denotes the universal relation.

	DISJOINT	**MEET**	**OVERLAP**	**INSIDE**	**CONTAINS**
DISJOINT	1	DISJOINT, MEET, OVERLAP, COVEREDBY, IN-SIDE	DISJOINT, MEET, OVERLAP, INSIDE, COV-EREDBY	DISJOINT, MEET, OVERLAP COVEREDBY, IN-SIDE	DISJOINT
MEET	DISJOINT, MEET, OVERLAP COVERS, CONTAINS	DISJOINT, MEET, OVERLAP COVEREDBY, COV-ERS, EQUAL	DISJOINT, MEET, OVERLAP, INSIDE, COV-EREDBY	OVERLAP, COVEREDBY, INSIDE	DISJOINT
OVERLAP	DISJOINT, MEET, OVERLAP CONTAINS COVERS	DISJOINT, MEET, OVERLAP, COVERS, CONTAINS	1	OVERLAP, COVEREDBY, INSIDE	DISJOINT, MEET, OVERLAP COVERS, CON-TAINS
INSIDE	DISJOINT	DISJOINT	DISJOINT, MEET, OVERLAP INSIDE, COV-EREDBY	INSIDE	1
CONTAINS	DISJOINT,MEET, OVERLAP CONTAINS COVERS	OVERLAP,COVERS CONTAINS	OVERLAP, COVERS CONTAINS	OVERLAP,COVERS COVERED-BY, INSIDE, CONTAINS EQUAL	CONTAINS

Geometric Manipulation

As noted in the previous section, geospatial ontologies will normally be associated with large geometric ontology bases representing the ground location associated with geographic phenomena. Simple manipulation of these phenomena will involve the computation of their spatial properties, such as length or area and relationships such as near or inside. Traditional computational geometry algorithms need to be implemented to compute these properties. Also, spatial databases and information systems normally employ different forms of spatial data structures and indexing techniques to facilitate searching over large geometric stores.

Hence, a geospatial ontology management system needs to consider the following requirement.

- Support basic geometric computational and spatial search functions to manipulate the geometric data stores.

Qualitative Spatial Representation and Reasoning

Over the past two decades much work has been conducted on the development of qualitative spatial approaches to represent and reason over space and spatial relations (Frank, 1992; Freska, 1992; Gahegan, 1995; Egenhofer et al., 1999; El-Geresy, 2004). Qualitative spatial manipulation is import and complements quantitative geometric processing in space, especially so when precise geometric information is missing or simply not needed for the context of operation. Qualitative approaches are based on the exploitation of the nature of the structure of space and the qualities of the spatial relationships themselves for deriving implicit information. Results of these approaches are documented in what is known as composition table of spatial relations such as the one shown in Table 1.

Entries in the table are possible relationships between two regions (A and C) resulting from the composition of relationships with another region B, i.e. $R_1(A,B) \otimes R_2(B,C) \rightarrow R_3(A,C)$.

As an example, consider the spatial relations defined in the ontology in the previous section. A new relationship can be derived as follows, where $\otimes$ denotes the composition of two relations:

Inside $\otimes$ Inside $\rightarrow$ Inside

*(Roath**Inside**Cardiff) $\otimes$ (Cardiff**Inside**Wales) $\rightarrow$ (Roath**Inside**Wales)*

Entries in spatial composition tables can be seen as a set of first order compositional inferences, and can be represented as a set of deduction or inference rules of the form:

$\forall x,y,z: R_1(x,y) \wedge R_2(y,z) \rightarrow R_3(x,z)$

where R_1, R_2 and R_3 are spatial relations, for example,

$\forall x,y,z$ $\text{Inside}(x,y)$ $\wedge$ $\text{Meet}(y,z)$ $\rightarrow$ $\text{Disjoint}(x,z)$

where x, y and z are region variables, substituted for geofeature instances in the geospatial ontology. The rule entails that the region bound to the variable x is disjoint from the region bound to the variable z, if x is inside another region y, and y meets (touches) z.

Hence, another requirement for the geospatial ontology management system is as follows.

- Support the representation of spatial composition rules for qualitative spatial reasoning.

Maintaining the Consistency of Geospatial Ontologies

'Consistency describes the absence of any logical contradictions within a model of reality' (Nectaria & Egenhofer, 1996). Errors in the description of the location and shape of geographical entities are common, especially on the web, when data provided and manipulated by users may not be complete or accurate. Such errors can propagate to inconsistencies in the spatial relationships and consequently to wrong information being stored in the ontology bases. Erroneous updates to the data may go undetected unless appropriate spatial integrity rules are declared and applied.

Cockcroft (1997) catagorised spatial integrity rules as 1) topological, maintaining the accuracy of topological information (which applies to all spatial relations) 2) Semantic, concerning the meaning of geographical features and how they should legally be allowed to interact 3) user defined, analogues to user defined business rules. Topological constraints can be further subdivided to structural errors, geometric errors, and topo-semantic constraints (Servigne et al., 2000).

Consider again our example ontology and a new fact to be inserted as follows.

Roath Disjoint Wales

Although this fact is valid from the point of view of the ontological model, i.e. it asserts the existence of a spatial relationship between two regions, its spatial consequence implies an inconsistency as the explicit relationships already stored implies that Roath must in fact be inside Wales.

*(Roath**Inside**Cardiff) $\otimes$ (Cardiff**Inside**Wales) $\rightarrow$ (Roath**Inside**Wales)*

To detect this inconsistency, we need not only to encode the appropriate qualitative spatial rule but also the following integrity constraint

$\forall x,y,z$ $\text{Inside}(x,y) \wedge \text{Inside}(y,z) \wedge \text{Disjoint}(x,z) \rightarrow \text{error}$

Different types of spatial integrity constraints can be encoded to maintain the consistent spatial structure and properties of the geospatial ontology bases. For example the following constraint indicates that if an object is inside another it must also be smaller in size.

$\forall x,y$ $\text{Inside}(x,y) \wedge \text{SmallerThan}(y,x) \rightarrow \text{error}$

A final consideration for the geospatial ontology management system can therefore be as follows.

- Support the expression and implementation of spatial integrity constraints over geospatial ontology bases.

Summary

Description logics (DL) are a powerful representational tool for describing real world concepts, their attributes and relationships. Key reasoning mechanisms of any DL are checking concept satisfiability and inferring subsumption hierarchies. On the terminological level a DL reasoner will infer concept hierarchies based on concept subsumption. On the level of asserted knowledge (instance level) each individual's type is inferred if not already explicit.

The description logic underpinning OWL-DL (*SHOIN*(D)) has purposefully been restricted to preserve decidability and in large tractability of the language. Such restrictions lead to representation and reasoning limitations. In addition to these, several limitations can be recognized with OWL as a platform to support the management of geospatial ontologies (Abdelmoty et al., 2005). These limitations, some as highlighted in previous sections, are now summarized below.

- OWL's first order, open world semantics in combination with the non unique name assumption is not suitable for constraint checking (Bruijn et al., 2005). Extensions to OWL have been proposed to overcome this limitation, for example by translating subsets of OWL to a logic program that assumes both unique name and closed world assumptions (Bruijn et al., 2005; Grosof et al., 2003), as well as by locally closing certain domain concepts using autoepistemic constructs.
- "Triangular knowledge" can not be represented directly in OWL (Horrocks, 2005). In particular, inference patterns of the form, $\forall$ x,y,c: rel_1 (x,y) $\wedge$ rel_2(y,c) $\rightarrow$ rel_3(x,c) can not be represented. This is the typical form of a spatial compositional inference rule.
- The description logic underpinning OWL-DL does not support spatial data types. Representation of geometric objects using generic class and property constructs is not ideal and will have potentially high implications on storage overheads (Haarslev et al. 1998).
- OWL does not support geometric computation, analysis or spatial indexing. Simple computational geometry calculations such as area and distance calculations are not possible to represent and consequently more complex spatial search queries are also not possible.
- Tableaux based reasoners (as used in most DL reasoners) are poor for query answering over individuals (Bruijn et al., 2005). Instance bases of geospatial ontologies are likely to be very large. Logic programming reasoning engines are more suitable platforms for reasoning in this case.

Realising the limitation of OWL, a rule layer has recently been proposed in the semantic web stack. Adding a rule layer to the existing ontology layer (typically a DL variant) will help to overcome some of the representational and reasoning limitations of OWL. In the next section a survey is given of existing approaches to the integration of logic programs and description logics, or less formally rules and ontologies.

INTEGRATION OF RULES AND ONTOLOGIES

Work on adding a rule layer to the semantic web technology stack was initiated by the W3C at the turn of the century. A fundamental challenge in facilitating the addition of this rule layer is finding means of integrating rules (Logic Programs - LPs) and ontologies (a descriptions logic- DL),

Figure 3. *Different paradigms; a) ontologies in DLs and b) Logic programming systems*

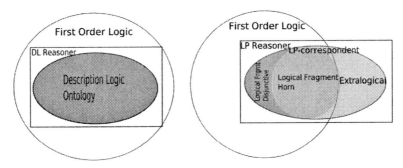

and in doing so handling the following semantic differences between logic programs and the DL subset of classical first order logic.

- First order languages have open world semantics, while LPs adhere to closed world semantics.
- DLs do not assume the unique name assumption, whereas all individuals in a logic program are assumed unique.

In addition, an integrated framework for rules and ontologies will face the following issues.

- Computational complexity of the resulting system. The decidability and tractability of the resulting reasoning system. The realisation and practical utilisation of the combined frameworks need to provide pragmatic reasoning procedures (with at most a polynomial time complexity).
- The modularity of the reasoning process. The choice is between combining both systems into a single logical language with a uniform reasoner or retaining different reasoners.

Figure 3 illustrates the differences between ontologies, as DL fragments of first order logic and rule systems as logic programming fragments of the same logic. The integration of the DL structural component with the LP relational

component is the subject of much work and debate. Current approaches can broadly be classified into two categories based on the degree of overlap between the two models in the resulting system; the *hybrid approach* and the *homogeneous approach* as described below.

Rule + Ontology: A Hybrid Approach

A hybrid approach is essentially a modular approach to the integration of rules and ontologies. It is sometimes referred to as loose integration or the integration of rules and ontologies through strict semantic separation (Eiter et al., 2006). Reasoning distinction between the ontology (DL) component and the relational (rule) component is maintained (Rosati, 2005). The ontology component is a description logic variant i.e. ALC and upwards, and the rule component is typically some identified flavor of Datalog (for example Datalog or $Datalog^{\vee}$).

A complete hybrid knowledge base K is represented by a pair $K = <\Sigma,\Pi>$, where Σ represents the ontological (DL) component and Π represents the relational (rule) component. Π contains rule and ontology predicates maintaining a strict separation between both. Typically a rule r in the relational component Π has the form:

$H \leftarrow B_1 \wedge ... \wedge B_n : O_1 \wedge O_m$ $m \geq 1, n \geq 1$

where H and B are both rule predicates (head and body predicates respectively) and O

Figure 4. Hyrbid Rule + Ontology Integration

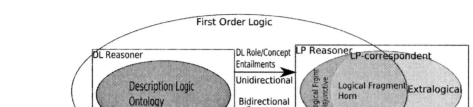

represents an ontology predicate. The ontology or structural predicates act as constraints on the interpretation of the relational component. Interaction between the rule and ontology reasoners take place through a safe interface (Eiter et al., 2006). The flow of information through the interface is either unidirectional or bidirectional.

In the unidirectional approach, reasoning is performed over the ontology using an ontological reasoning engine (DL reasoner). Entailments from the DL reasoner ($\Sigma \models \omega$) are fed, as a starting point, into the rule reasoner. Rules are interpreted such that they must satisfy the ontology predicates p in ω. Early unidirectional approaches combined unexpressive structural variants with unexpressive relational variants. For example AL-Log (Donini et al., 1998) uses the foundational DL namely *ALC* with Horn Datalog while introducing the, now common, rule safety condition to maintain decidability. That is, rule safety constraints the use of each variable that appears in the head of the rule to also appear in the body of the rule. Moreover, only concepts are allowed as constraints in the relational component. CARIN (Levy & Rousset, 1995) overcame this limitation with a more expressive DL (*ALCNR*), and allowed both concept and role constraints whilst maintaining decidability using a form of role safety.

To further enhance reasoning, a complete synergy of structural and relational reasoning can be catered for by introducing a bidirectional flow of information. Iterative reasoning is then performed on both components until no more inferences can be drawn. This approach was adopted by Eiter at al. (2004), namely Description Logic Programs, and DL+log (Rosati, 2006).

Homogenous Rule + Ontology Integration

Homogenous approaches present a complete or tight integration of both the ontology Σ and rule Π components resulting in a single logical language *L*. No syntactic or semantic distinctions are made in *L* between the ontology and rule predicates and both can be interpreted under the same reasoning umbrella.

All works based in this approach employ a mapping (typically a recursive mapping) from one language to the other. Approaches that involve mapping the rule language to the ontology language exist. However, more common are approaches mapping from the ontology language to the rule language, thus opening the possibility of using existing rule engines for reasoning tasks (query answering etc). The mapping process involves either completely combining both languages (expressive union), or embedding one language into the other (intersection).

Expressive union of the structural and relational component is depicted in Figure 5 as the union of the entire LP and DL fragments within FOL. The union brings about substantial computational

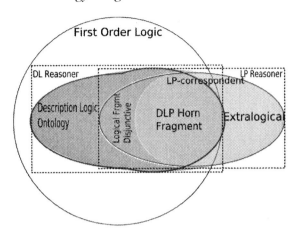

Figure 5. Homogenous Rule + Ontology Integration

complexities that often leads to undecidability, even if the languages of each are simplistic, see (Schmidt-Schauß, 1989) for the proof. W3C's candidate rule language SWRL (Patel-Schneider et al., 2004) is an example of unifying OWL-DL with a Horn based rule language which does lead to undecidability.

Intersecting the structural and relational components into their common fragment can help to retain decidability and tractability if for example, their common fragment corresponds to the horn subset of FOL. Description Logic Programs (Grosof et al., 2003) represent a complete ontology paradigm that is formed by the intersection of the description logic underpinning OWL-DL with Horn Datalog. The result is a sound, highly tractable and practical paradigm from which further extensions can be be layered (Hitzler, 2005). Over the past few years a number of extensions have been considered to DLP. For example, by considering disjunctive logic programs a larger fragment of DL can be mapped into the combined language *L* (Motik & Volz, 2003), and in (Krötzsch et al., 2008) which extended the reasoning potential of DLPs, while not adversely effecting the decidability and tractability of the language.

DLPs are also at the heart of the W3C's alternative (to SWRL) candidate rule language WRL (Angele et al., 2005). WRL-core is the base representation paradigm of WRL and represents an ontology language in its own right.

Comparison of the Two Approaches

Augmenting ontologies with rules is of benefit in general and offer potential solutions to the representational limitations of ontology languages such as OWL, or indeed to most description logics.

Of the hybrid approaches, early techniques either used unexpressive DL variants (e.g. AL-Log *ALC*), or only permitted class constraints in the relational component. Unidirectional approaches produce only a subset of all inferences possible from the combination of both components. On the other hand, bidirectional approaches suffer from higher, often intractable, and therefore unacceptable worst case complexities (EXPTIME or NEXPTIME see (Eiter et al., 2004)). The use of two separate reasoning engines to obtain a unified output could be an inconvenient obstacle to reasoning and may add an additional cost to run-time performance.

Of the homogenous approaches, SWRL is undecidable and as such is not mature enough for full scale implementation. WRL-Flight is promising and supports integrity constraints thanks to both a closed word and unique name assumption. However, its perfect model semantics is not as compatible with most existing ordinary logic programming engines. Disjunctive logic programs exhibit high computational complexities (typically higher than polynomial time i.e. NEXPTIME or NEXPTIME^{NP} (Eiter et al., 1997)), due to the possibility of multiple minimal models (each minimal model increases the size of the search space exponentially).

The most tractable of all approaches is, unsurprisingly, the least expressive logic, namely, Description Logic Programs (DLPs). A DLP can be trivially mapped to existing logic programming or production system engines e.g. XSB (Sagona et al., 1993) or Rete (Forgy, 1982) respectively. Logic programs or productions systems do not assume classical first order semantics. Making intuitive closed world and unique name assumptions make them more suitable models for integrity checking tasks. Finally, logic programs will scale well to reasoning over individuals (Krotzsch et al., 2006); a very desirable property, in particular for the geospatial domains.

Approaches to Integrating Spatial Logics and Ontologies

Current approaches to utilizing spatial logic and reasoning in ontologies are based on the homogeneous approach to integration and propose extending existing description logics with spatial concrete domains and qualitative spatial reasoning algorithms. The method provides a means to employ spatial reasoning for deduction and satisfiability checking of spatial information asserted into the description logic.

Haarslev et al. proposed an extension to ALCRRP(D) DLs to include a concrete spatial domain and hence support spatio-terminological reasoning (at the concept level) (Haarslev et al., 1998). However, the proposal was limited to support only one specific spatial data type; a polygon.

Wessels (2001) proposed the ALCI$_{rcc}$ DL that includes role axioms derived from the spatial com-

position tables, based on the Region Connection Calculus (RCC) (Cohn et al., 1997), a theoretical variant of the 9-intersection model shown in the previous section, again for topological reasoning. The RCC spatial role axioms can be used to check the topological satisfiability of spatial individuals. However, as noted in their work, the proposal is only decidable if RCC-5 or a more general family of the spatial logic is used – for example by replacing the distinction between within and coveredby with the more general part-of relation.

To be of practical use, Wessels (2003) also argues for layerd hybrid deductive geographic information system that employs the DL ALCI$_{rcc}$, and recognizes the limitations of adding geometry to a description logic, previously mentioned.

The full potential of using an integrated logical and geometric framework to support a general spatial ontology is yet to be realized. The potential of such a framework to serve geospatial domains has been recognized in some recent proposals (Chen et al., 2005; O'Dea et al., 2005; Smart et al.). Exiting approaches to combine spatial logics with description logics to form new geospatial ontology language, highlight some important issues. Both proposals above are limited in their application both from a representational and reasoning perspective. In particular, the following issues still need to be addressed.

- Existing DLs need to include complex role composition constructs in order to effectively store spatial compositional inference rules such as those described in table 1, as well as role compositions that allow head disjunctions. A separate rule representation layer is needed.
- A spatial ontology will need to support a general set of spatial data types, such as regions, points, and lines. Restricting geospatial ontologies to spatial logics that work over simple polygonal shapes limits their general applicability.

Figure 6. Proposed DLP approach to representing geospatial ontologies and rules

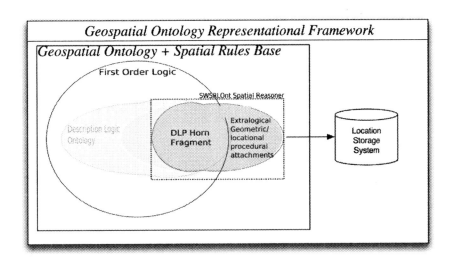

- Geometric processing of spatial data is better suited to dedicated external geometric reasoning engines. Hence, 'outsourcing' the geometric component of the ontologies to external components outside the DLs and logic programming seems a reasonable choice.

A SEMANTIC WEB RULE AND ONTOLOGY LANGUAGE FOR GEOSPATIAL DOMAINS

From the above survey of approaches to integrating rules and ontologies and the analysis of the requirements of the geospatial domains, we propose the use of Description Logic Programs DLP (a homogeneous approach to integration of rules and ontologies) as a basis for representing and reasoning in geospatial domains. To further support the particular requirements of these domains, an integrated framework combining both the logical and the computational approaches to geospatial data processing is also proposed. Figure 6 depicts the new proposed language framework for representing geospatial onotlogies. In this section,

we examine how this framework can support the requirements identified in the second section and also outline any necessary further extensions.

DLP for Representing Geospatial Ontologies

The geospatial ontology in section 2 can be captured, without loss in a DLP. It is of interest to note that a large percentage of currently developed ontologies are also within the representational abilities of the DLP fragment (Volz, 2004). A transformation function, named DLP-Fusion (Grosof et al., 2003), is needed to translate OWL-DL to DLP. The representation of the geometric component of geo-features is decoupled from the ontology component and delegated to an external specialized system as described below.

DLP-Fusion, OWL-DL to DLP

DLP-Fusion is a syntactical, semantic preserving, bidirectional mapping between OWL-DL and the Horn fragment of FOL, resulting in a new ontology paradigm namely a Description Horn Logic

Table 2. Example DLP-Fusion mapping

DL Axiom	First Order Rule Syntax
Region $\subseteq$ Geofeature	Region(x) $\rightarrow$ Geofeature(x)
Ward $\subseteq$ Region	Ward(x) $\rightarrow$ Region(x)
Topological $\subseteq$ Spatial_Relationship	Topological(x,y) $\rightarrow$ Spatial_Relationship(x,y)
Meet $\subseteq$ Topological	Meet(x,y) $\rightarrow$ Topological(x,y)
Roath: Ward	Ward(Roath)
Wales: Country	Country(Wales)
Roath Inside Cardiff	Inside(Roath,Cardiff)

(DHL) ontology.

The mapping function, denoted T, takes DL axioms of the form $(C \subseteq D)$, $(S \equiv B)$, $(T \subseteq \forall P.D)$, $(T \subseteq \forall P^-.D)$, $(a: D)$, $(<a,b>: P)$, $(P \subseteq Q)$, $(P \equiv Q)$, $(P \equiv Q^-))$, $(P^+ \subseteq P)$ and converts them into a rule of the form $A \rightarrow B$. The geospatial ontology in figure 3 can be directly mapped using this transformation. Examples are shown in Table 2.

Where x and y are spatial variables from the domain of individuals in the geospatial ontology.

DLP for Qualitative Spatial Reasoning

Unlike OWL, the Horn fragment of first order logic is sufficient to represent triangular knowledge or role composition of the form (where R_1, R_2 and R_3 are spatial relations, and x,y and z are spatial variables):

$$\forall x,y,z \; R_1(x,y) \wedge R_2(y,z) \rightarrow R_3(x,z)$$

For example from the composition Table 1, we can now represent the compositional inference:

$$\forall x,y,z \; Disjoint(x,y) \wedge Contains(y,z) \rightarrow Disjoint(x,y)$$

Of note, OWL-DL can represent transitive roles, for example: $R_1(x,y) \wedge R_1(y,z) \rightarrow R_1(x,z)$, but not those involving three different relations as shown in the example above.

As DLPs are the logic programming equivalent of a Horn rule, they too can capture such spatial compositional inferences. However, Horn rules

are limited to compositional inferences with a definite head (one head predicate). To employ more general qualitative spatial reasoning calculi disjunctive rules are required; rules that allow head disjunctive of the form:

$$R_1(x,y) \wedge R_2(y,z) \rightarrow R_3(x,z) \vee \ldots \vee R_n(x,z)$$
for example:

Contains(x,y) $\wedge$ Meet(y,z) $\rightarrow$ Overlap(x,z) $\vee$ Contains(x,z)

To work around this problem, spatial calculi have been proposed that can be directly mapped to Horn rules (Schockaert& Cock, 2007). Such spatial calculi are currently being tested with the proposed DLP approach, but the results are not included in this chapter.

In addition to representing qualitative rules, a DLP can be extended to include procedural attachments that implements, through calls to external geometric processing systems, spatial operators for the computation of spatial properties and relationships. A reasoning synergy is then possible to compute required properties which could not be derived automatically using the spatial logic.

DLP for Integrity Maintenance

Classical Horn Logic assumes a first order semantics, including the open world and non unique name assumptions. However, the logic programming equivalent of Horn logic, that used by DLPs, assumes a more intuitive closed world and unique name assumption and is consequently

Figure 7. DLP based geo-ontology software framework

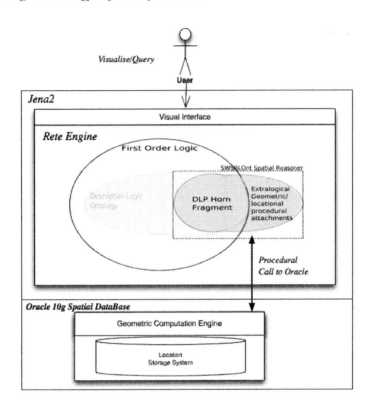

a suitable language for expressing and implementing integrity constraints.

Integrity rules are headless rules, where satisfaction of all body predicates leads to a conflicting knowledge base. In addition to this general form of integrity rules, representation of 'default' rules and rule exceptions is also desirable. Consider for example, a rule that states that rivers and roads do not intersect. It may be desirable to express exceptions to this rule in the case where the entities in fact do intersect in a "ford". Enumerating rule exceptions is therefore a desirable quality. Extension to DLP to support a form of default logic, e.g. Courteous Logic (Grosof et al., 1997) is needed.

A backward chaining mode of inference is used in the implementation of logic programs, where querying the system results in exhaustive rule evaluation. On the other hand, integrity rules must continually monitor the ontology to find inconsistencies as and when they arise and as such need to work in a forward chaining mode. However, forward and backward reasoning modes can be made to work together, an interleaved mode (Eisenstadt & Brayshaw, 1990). Then, predicates in the forward system can be determined on the fly from the backward system, and no longer have to be contained explicitly in the geo-ontology as facts. This is advantageous in reducing storage and memory overheads, but has an adverse effect on reasoning speed. That is, not all facts need to be stored in the geo-ontology, but querying the backward system requires evaluation of, in the worst case, the entire rule set for each query.

PROTOTYPE APPLICATION

A system has been developed that implements the DLP proposed framework above within the Jena2

Figure 8. Geo-ontology visualisation tool

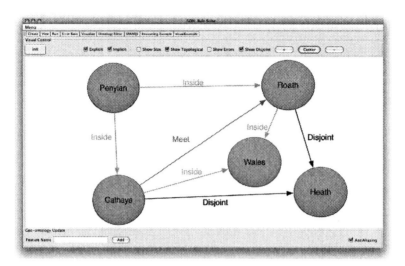

Semantic Web toolkit (Carroll et al., 2003). The rule engine is based on the Rete pattern matching production system (Forgy, 1982). A complete spatial rule base of topological spatial compositions has been developed. The geometric processing component is developed using the Oracle 10g Spatial database management system. Figure 7 shows a concrete instantiation of the framework in Figure 6.

Evaluation of the system is currently ongoing on synthetic as well as real data sets. A small example based on the ontology in section 2 is demonstrated below. The following are examples of both an integrity and deduction rule in the system.

Topological deduction rule:

[<label>ContainsEqualContains</label><ruleGroup>Topological</ruleGroup>: Equal(?x ?c) AND Contains(?c ?y) --> Contains(?x ?y)]

Topological integrity rule:

[[<label>InsideDisjointIntegrity</label><ruleGroup>Topological</ruleGroup>: Region(?x) AND Region(?y) AND Region(?z) AND inside(?x ?y) AND Disjoint(?y ?z) AND Inside(?x ?z) --> error(?x ?z)

Figure 8 shows a screenshot of the ontology depicted as a graph of regions (as red circles) and relations (different colored edges).

A new region (Penylan) as well as two new relationships are introduced to the ontology as found using the web mining technique in (Schockaert et al., 2008), these are:

Penylan: Ward

Penylan inside Roath

Penylan inside Cathays

The reasoning engine detects the inconsistencies as a result of this update as shown in Figure 9, where edges resulting in the error are highlighted (in red).

Figure 9. Topological inconsistencies

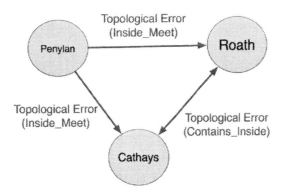

The three relationships between Cathays, Roath and Penylan are all highlighted indicating an inconsistent spatial scene. In reality, *Penylan* and *Roath* are neighbours, as shown in the Google maps view in Figure 10. To find this inconsistency, the following integrity rules were triggered.

[[<label>Inside_Meet</label><ruleGroup>Topological</ruleGroup>: Region(?x) AND Region(?y) AND Region(?z) AND Inside(?x ?y) AND Meet(?y ?z) AND inside(?x ?z) --> error(?x ?z)]

Where, Penylan is inside Cathays and Roath meets Cathays means that Penylan can not be inside Cathays, but it is hence the rule implies an error.

[[<label>Contains_Inside</label><ruleGroup>Topological</ruleGroup>: Region(?x) AND Region(?y) AND Region(?z) AND Contains(?x ?y) AND Inside(?y ?z) AND Meet(?x ?z) --> error(?x ?z)]

Where, Roath contains Penylan and Roath meets Cathays means that Cathays can not contain Cathays, but it is hence the rule implies an error.

Figure 10. Google Maps View ©2008 Google Map Data ©2008 Tele Atlas

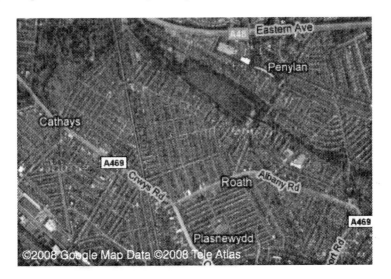

FUTURE TRENDS

Further to the current development of the proposed framework, the following are ongoing research tasks:

- Evaluating the scalability using large ontology bases. In particular, large place ontologies are developed using some real data sets obtained from national mapping agencies and multiple resources on the web.
- Evaluating the value of encoding hybrid spatial reasoning rules using multiple types of spatial relations.
- Explore more expressive DLP fragments for an enriched geo-ontology representation paradigm with increased reasoning and integrity potential.
- Deployment or testing of the proposed framework for realistic application scenarios, for example, representing and maintaining Wikipedia articles.

CONCLUSION

This chapter proposes a new framework for the development and management of geospatial ontologies on the Semantic web. Challenges in representing and manipulating geospatial knowledge in large onotology bases are identified and used to specify requirements for the new framework. OWL as the Semantic Web ontology language was evaluated and its limitations identified to handle those requirements.

To overcome the limitations of OWL, the current approaches to the integration of ontologies and rules are reviewed and classified. A rule layer will allow for the complex semantics of geospatial ontologies to be represented, including the expression of qualitative spatial logic rules for the specification and derivation of spatial properties and relationships.

Description Logic Programs is a homogeneous approach to integrating both OWL-DL ontologies with classical Logic Programs. DLPs was proposed as the most suitable approach as it provides a tractable, and hence scalable, base for the expression of spatial rules and integrity constraints.

The DLP approach was then examined to analyse its benefits and a new framework was proposed in which it can be implemented to serve this domain. The implementation of the framework is briefly sketched and demonstrated using a sample ontology used for demonstration purposes throughout the chapter. Initial testing of the approach demonstrates its efficiency and effectiveness. Evaluation experiments are currently being done to test the scalability of the approach to realistic geospatial ontology development on the Web.

REFERENCES

Abdelmoty, A. I., Smart, P. D., Jones, C. B., Fu, G., & Finch, D. A. (2005). Critical evaluation of ontology languages for geographic information retrieval on the Internet. *In Journal of Visual Languages & Computing* (pp., 331–358).

Angele, J., Boley, H., Bruijn, J., & Fensel, D. (2005). *Web Rule rule Language language (WRL).* Retrieved 2008, from http://www.w3.org/Submission/WRL

Bruijn, J., Lara, R., Polleres, A., & Fensel, D. (2005). OWL DL vs. OWL flight: Conceptual modeling and reasoning for the semantic Semantic Web. In *Proceedings of the 14th international conference on World Wide Web* (pp. 623-632). New York: ACM Press. New York, NY, USA.

Carroll, J. J., Dickinson, I., Dollins, C., & Reynolds, D. (2003). *Jena: Implementing the Semantic Web recommendations.* (Internet Report). Retrieved 2007 from http://dsonline.computer.org/0211/f/wp6jena.htm.

Chen, H., & Fellah, S. & Bishr., Y. A. (2005). Rules for geospatial Semantic Web applications. In *W3C Workshop on Rule Languages for Interoperability.*

Cockcroft, S. A. (1997). Taxonomy of spatial data integrity constraints. *GeoInformatica, 4*(1), 327–343. doi:10.1023/A:1009754327059

Cohn, A. G., Bennett, B., Gooday, J., & Gotts, N. M. (1997). Qualitative spatial representation and reasoning with the region connection calculus. *GeoInformatica, 1,* 275–316. doi:10.1023/A:1009712514511

Donini, F. M., Lenzerini, M., Nardi, D., & Schaerf, A. (1998). AL-log: Integrating datalog and description logics. *Journal of Intelligent Information Systems, 10*(3), 227–252. doi:10.1023/A:1008687430626

Egenhofer, M. J. (2002). Toward the semantic geospatial web. In *Proceedings of the tenth ACM international symposium on Advances in geographic information systems* (pp. 1-4). ACM Press.

Egenhofer, M. J., Mark, D. M., & Herring, J. (1999). *The 9-Intersection: Formalism and its use for natural-language spatial predicates.* Report, National Center for Geographic Information and Analysis.

Eisenstadt, M., & Brayshaw, M. A. (1990). Knowledge engineering toolkit: The first of a two-part series presenting a knowledge-engineering toolkit for building expert systems. *Byte Magazine, 15*(10), 268–282.

Eiter, T., Gottlob, G., & Mannila, H. (1997). Disjunctive Datalog. *ACM Transactions on Database Systems, 22* (pp., 364-418) Vol 22.

Eiter, T., Ianni, G., Polleres, A., Schindlauer, R., & Tompits, H. (2006). Reasoning with rules and ontologies. In *Reasoning Web, Second International Summer School 2006, Lisbon, Portugal* (LNCS 4126, pp. 93-127).

Eiter, T., Lukasiewicz, T., Schindlauer, R., & Tompits, H. (2004). Combining answer set programming with description logics for the semantic Semantic Web. In *KR2004: Principles of Knowledge Representation and Reasoning* (pp. 141–151). Menlo Park, CA: AAAI Press, Menlo Park, California.

El-Geresy, B. A., & Abdelmoty, A. I. (2004). SPARQS: A qualitative spatial reasoning engine. *In Journal of Knowledge-Based Systems, 17,* (pp. 89-102): Vol 17.

Forgy, C. (1982). Rete: A fast algorithm for the many patterns/many objects match problem. *Journal of Artificial Intelligence, 19,* 17037. doi:10.1016/0004-3702(82)90020-0

Frank, A. (1992). Qualitative spatial reasoning about distances and directions in geographic space. *Journal of Visual Languages and Computing* (LNCS 639, pp. 343–371).

Freksa, C. (1992). Using orientation information for qualitative spatial reasoning. In *Theories and methods of spatio-temporal reasoning in geographic space* (pp. 162–178).

Fu, F., Jones, C. B., & Abdelmoty, A. (2005). Building a geographical ontology for intelligent spatial search on the Web. In *IASTED - International Conference on Databases and Applications part of the 23rd Multi-Conference on Applied Informatics, Innsbruck, Austria* (pp. 167-172).

Gahegan, M. (1995). Proximity operators for qualitative spatial reasoning. In *Spatial information theory: A theoretical basis for GIS* (LNCS 988, pp. 31-44).

Gerevini, A., & Renz, J. (2002). Combining topological and size information for spatial reasoning. *Artificial Intelligence, 137*, 1–42. doi:10.1016/S0004-3702(02)00193-5

Grosof, B. N. (1997). Prioritized conflict handling for logic programs, In *Proceedings of the International Symposium on Logic Programming* (pp. 197-211). Cambridge: MIT Press.

Grosof, B. N., Horrocks, I., Volz, R., & Decker, S. (2003). Description logic programs: combining logic programs with description logic. In *Proceedings of the 14th international conference on World Wide Web 03* (pp. 48-57).

Guarino, N. (1995). Formal ontology, conceptual analysis and knowledge representation. *International Journal of Human-Computer Studies, 43*, 625–640. doi:10.1006/ijhc.1995.1066

Haarslev, V., Lutz, C., & Moller, R. (1998). Foundations of spatioterminological reasoning with description logics. In *Principles of knowledge representation and reasoning* (pp. 112–123).

Haarslev, V., & Muller, R. (2001). RACER system description. In *Proceedings of the First International Joint Conference on Automated Reasoning* (pp. 701-706).

Hitzler, P., Haase, P., Krtzsch, M., Sure, Y., & Studer, R. (2005). DLP isn't so bad after all. In *Proceedings of the 1st Workshop on OWL: Experiences and Directions (OWLED-05). CEUR Workshop Proceedings* (Vol. 188).

Horrocks, I. (2005). OWL rules, ok? In *W3C Workshop on Rule Languages for Interoperability*.

Horrocks, I. R. (1998). Using an expressive description logic: FaCT or fiction? In *KR'98: Principles of Knowledge Representation and Reasoning* (pp. 636-645).

Jones, C. B., Alani, H., & Tudhope, D. (2001). Geographical information retrieval with ontologies of place. In *Spatial Information Theory: Foundations of Geographic Information Science, International Conference: COSIT* (LNCS 2205, pp. 322-335).

Krotzsch, M., Hitzler, P., Vrandecic, D., & Sintek, M. (2006). How to reason with OWL in a logic programming system. In *Rules and Rule Markup Languages for the Semantic Web, Second International Conference* (pp. 17–28). IEEE Computer Society.

Krötzsch, M., Rudolph, S., & Hitzler, P. (2008). Description logic rules. In *Proceedings of the 18th European Conference on Artificial Intelligence (ECAI-08)* (pp. 80–84). IOS Press.

Levy, A. Y., & Rousset, M. C. (1995). Combining rules and description logics: An overview of CARIN. In *Proceedings of the International Symposium on Logic Programming* (pp. 635). Cambridge: MIT Press.

Motik, B., & Volz, R. (2003). Optimizing query answering in description logics using disjunctive deductive databases. In *Proceedings of the 10th International Workshop on Knowledge Representation meets Databases, Hamburg, Germany* (Vol. 79).

Nectaria, T., & Egenhofer, M. J. (1996). Multiresolution spatial databases: Consistency among networks. In *Integrity in Databases-Sixth International Workshop on Foundations of Models and Langauges for Data and Objects* (pp. 119–132).

O'Dea, D., Geoghegan, S., & Ekins, C. (2005). Dealing with geospatial information in the Semantic Web. In *Proceedings of the 2005 Australasian Ontology Workshop: AOW '05* (pp. 69-73). Australian Computer Society, Inc.

OGC Technical Committee. (1999). *OGC, abstract feature specification* (Tech. Rep.) Retrieved 2008, from: http://www.opengis.org/techno/specs.htm.

Patel-Schneider, P. F., Horrocks, I., Tabet, H. B. S., Grosof, B., & Dean, M. (2004). *SWRL: A Semantic Web rule language combining OWL and RuleML* (Internet Report). Retrieved 2008, from http://www.w3.org/Submission/2004/SUBM-SWRL-20040521/.

Rosati, R. (2005). Semantic and computational advantages of the safe integration of ontologies and rules. In *Principles and Practice of Semantic Web Reasoning, Third International Workshop, PPSWR 2005, Dagstuhl Castle, Germany* (LNCS 3703, pp. 50-64).

Rosati, R. (2006). DL+log: Tight integration of description logics and disjunctive datalog. In *Proceedings of the Tenth International Conference on Principles of Knowledge Representation and Reasoning* (pp. 68-78). AAAI Press.

Sagonas, K., Swift, T., & Warren, D. (1993). *XSB: An overview of its use and implementation* (Tech. Rep). Retrieved 2006, from http://citeseer.ist.psu.edu/195039.html

Sanderson, M., & Kohler, J. (2004). Analyzing geographic queries. In *Workshop in Geographic Information Retrieval.*

Schmidt-Schauß, M. (1989). Subsumption in KL-ONE is undecidable. In *Proceedings of the 1st International Conference on Principles of Knowledge Representation and Reasoning* (pp. 421-431). Toronto, Canada.

Schockaert, S., & Cock, M. (2007). Reasoning about vague topological information. In *Proceedings of the Sixteenth ACM Conference on Information and Knowledge Management* (pp. 593-602).

Schockaert, S., Smart, P. D., Abdelmoty, A. I., & Jones, C. B. (2008). Mining topological relations from the Web. In *DEXA Workshops* (pp. 652-656). IEEE Computer Society.

Servigne, S., Ubeda, T., Puricelli, A., & Laurini, R. (2000). Methodology for spatial consistency improvement of geographic databases. *GeoInformatica*, 7–34. doi:10.1023/A:1009824308542

Smart, P. D., Abdelmoty, A. I., Jones, C. B., & El-Geresy, B. A. (2007). A framework for combining rules and geo-ontologies. In *Web Reasoning and Rule Systems: First International Conference, RR 2007, Innsbruck, Austria* (LNCS 4524, pp. 133-147).

Smith, T. R., & Frew, J. (1995). Alexandria digital library. *Communications of the ACM, 38*(4), 61–62. doi:10.1145/205323.205340

Volz, R. (2004). *Web Ontology reasoning with logic databases*. PhD thesis, AIFB, University of Karlsruhe.

Vretanos, P. (2005). *Open geospatial consortium filter encoding implementation specification* (Tech. Rep.). Retrieved 2008, from http://www.opengis.org/techno/specs.htm.

Wessel, M. (2001). Obstacles on the way to spatial reasoning with description logics – Some undecidability results. *Working Notes of the 2001 International Description Logics Workshop (DL-2001) Vol. 49*, Stanford, CA, USA.

Wessel, M. (2003). Some practical issues in building a hybrid deductive geographic information system with a DL component. In *Proceedings of the 10th International Workshop on Knowledge Representation meets Databases (KRDB 2003)* (Vol. 79). Hamburg, Germany.

KEY TERMS AND DEFINITIONS

Description Logics: Successors to Semantic Networks and Frame Based Languages which can represent both asserted and structural knowledge. Modern description logics stem from KL-ONE which formalized the ideas of Semantic Networks and Frames. A description logic can describe the world in terms of properties or constraints that specific individuals have to satisfy.

Geospatial Ontologies: A specilisation of ontology that represent only knowledge from the geographic and spatial domain.

Geospatial Rules: Rules or logical rules of inference represent dynamic, relational knowledge as opposed to static structural knowledge. A rule is an inference of the form PREMISE implies CONCLUSION, mimicking human cognitive reasoning processes. If the PREMISE condition holds, then the CONCLUSION condition is deducible. Geospatial rules are those that represent and reason with geographical and or spatial knowledge.

Integration of Rules and Ontologies: How to integrate description logic ontologies with classical rule based logic programs, while preserving semantics and maintaining decidability and tractability. Approaches are either based on the union or the intersection of the two languages.

Interleaved Mixed Mode Reasoning: Allowing knowledge querying using backward rule sets during the course of forward inferencing. Facts in the premise of forward rules can be found directly from explicit facts or implicitly through additional inferences.

Ontology: Those things that *exist* are those things that have a formal representation within the context of a machine. Knowledge commits to an ontology if it adheres to the structure, vocabulary and semantics intrinsic to a particular ontology i.e. it conforms to the ontology definition. A formal ontology in computer science is a logical theory that represents a conceptualization of real world concepts.

Qualitative Spatial Reasoning: Representation of continuous properties of the world by discrete symbols, and then reasoning over such symbols without recourse to more expensive (computationall) quantitative knowledge. Qualitative knowledge and reasoning better mimics human spatial reasoning processes.

Section III
Tools and Technologies

This section presents extensive coverage of the technology that informs and impacts Web technologies. These chapters provide an in-depth analysis of the use and development of innumerable devices and tools, while also providing insight into new and upcoming technologies, theories, and instruments that will soon be commonplace. Within these rigorously researched chapters, readers are presented with examples of the tools that facilitate and support the emergence and advancement of Web technologies. In addition, the successful implementation and resulting impact of these various tools and technologies are discussed within this collection of chapters.

Chapter 3.1
New Paradigms:
A Collaborative Web-Based Research Tool

Hamish Holewa

International Program of Psycho-Social Health Research, Central Queensland University, Australia

ABSTRACT

The chapter aims to document the challenges associated with the management of an international research program and to look at innovative, information technology (IT) based ways of tackling these. Through the medium of a case study, insights gained from practical experience developing and implementing an original Web based collaborative research management tool are discussed. This tool is based on a centralised model of information distribution and access. It was designed following a reductionist analysis of existing research processes and procedures. The ways in which the integration of responsive IT processes into the management of a large international research program have removed redundancies and increased automation and research efficiency are also discussed.

INTRODUCTION

This chapter presents, through the medium of a case study, insights gained from practical experience developing and implementing an original web based collaborative research tool to assist and enhance the management of an existing, qualitative research program. The case example used is that of the International Program of Psycho- Social Health Research (IPP-SHR). This case study provides the reader with insights into the ways in which information technology (IT) processes can be used to overcome problems associated with the post-modern research environment. Within this context the major challenges are to address the fragmented nature of research locations, staff and project administration within a global setting.

Technological advances have paved the way for global research, enabling it to transcend physical, geographical and cultural boundaries. However, there are still great challenges to be overcome in conducting a truly international research program. The chapter aims to document the challenges associated with the process and management of a large international research program and to look at innovative, IT based ways of tackling these.

DOI: 10.4018/978-1-59904-970-0.ch005

The International Program of Psycho-Social Health Research (IPP-SHR) provides international leadership through research, publication, education, media, newsletters and podcasting activities in the area of psycho-social health research. This program, explores a broad range of psycho-social health issues including: the lived experience of serious and terminal illness; haematology and oncology; palliative care; indigenous health; rural and remote health; mental health; obstetrics; bio-ethics; and the interface between patients and the health care system. The core aim of IPP-SHR is to 'make a difference' by informing policy and service delivery in the real world of health care.

This program utilises qualitative, or natu-ralistic, research methodology, which seeks to document the voice of the research participant from their own world view (Streubert & Carpenter 1995). Such methodologies are underpinned by a philosophical perspective that listens to, rather than imposes on the experience of others and has a sensitivity to the disempowered and marginal-ized (Latimer et al. 2003) The large and diverse amount of the data gained from using such meth-odologies, coupled with diverse and geographical isolated data collection sites of an International program, necessitated the design and construction of a central based management system.

After extensive literature searches in ma-jor databases, consultation with software and project management vendors, collaboration and discussion with international leaders in qualita-tive methodologies, it was evident that no such program existed to meet the specific requirements of IPP-SHR or collaborative multi-site qualitative research projects. As such, to meet the challenges and technical difficulties associated with IPP-SHR's methodology and operation, an internet based research tool was designed. Server side technologies were utilized to achieve a central research portal for IPP-SHR practitioners to use and collaborate through, independent of their physical location. The maturing of server side and Internet connectivity and speed are major contributors to the success of such a system. The system uses a central website, where users with appropriate security credentials like correct user name, password and encryption key can deposit files related to the research processes, implement automatic work flow processes for dictation, tran-scription and coding processes, view work and project flows and progress, schedule appointments and stipulate task for other users or team members. The system improves research efficiency and lowers research costs. This is achieved through a streamlined website portal offering best practice security, enhanced ethics compliance, limiting or reducing redundancy between processes and team members, and providing accurate information on the process and state of each particular research project. The software also provides team building and mentoring activities through the use of project reporting, a bulletin board, discussion forums and team feedback.

BACKGROUND AND CHALLENGES

The research paradigm and context within which IPP-SHR operates presents unique challenges. Although the program has developed gradually over the last decade, it has only recently evolved to the level of national and international research data collection and collaboration. As a qualitative research program with a focus on the human in-terface of health care, the challenge is collecting and managing the magnitude and complexity of data gained from naturalistic methodologies over extensive geographical areas. This section details the challenges and problems associated with running a decentralized, location unspecific international research program. It also introduces the equity and ethical considerations associated with research.

IPP-SHR operates in an environment, charac-terised by the fragmentation of location, staff skills and expertise, participant groups, disciplinary focus and broad topic interests. Translated to the practicalities of research activities, this means, data collection and analysis occurs in many geographical locations and time zones and focuses on a multiplicity of research topics. Additionally staff management needs to address a multiplicity of duties and responsibilities, and access and control of project information, some of which is confidential. Also posing challenges are the practical necessities of enabling simultaneous access by multiple team members to a broad range of specific documents, and creating processes for multi-site data entry and analysis.

As a core component of IPP-SHR's philosophy is to 'make a difference,' and to, 'document the human experience of human illness,' IPP-SHR's qualitative methodology focuses on a phenomenological perspective using exploratory, iterative and open–ended interviews. A phenomenological perspective is used with data analysis and process as its inherent aim is to document and record the particular phenomena or appearance of things as a lived experience (Streubert & Carpenter 1995). Data gathered during the interviewing process is then transcribed verbatim and analysed from the view point of the participiant (McGrath & Holewa 2006). Such analyses and exploration is undertaken without imposing specific theoretical or conceptual frameworks on the interview or data analyses to ensure that the individual experience is recorded (Polit & Hungler, 1995). As such, it is methodologically important for the data management system to not only store data correctly and without corruption but to ensure that research staff can engage in a rigorous data analysis process. IPP-SHR has a particular pride and a documented history of ensuring a rigorous data analysis process by which the findings are driven by a meticulous coding of all statement by participants.

Due to the rigour of IPP-SHR's application of qualitative methodologies, even relatively small research projects produce large amounts of data. For example, a small project in which ten participants are interviewed will on average produce over two hundred pages of language texts, excluding supplementary data such as descriptive statistics. The sheer quantity of data produced by IPP-SHR's qualitative methodologies necessitates that the discrete processes of qualitative research (i.e. verbatim recording and transcription of interviews, managing coding processes) be streamlined.

Although, the data gained in IPP-SHR projects is usually qualitative, occasionally descriptive data is also included. Thus, any system that is to facilitate and streamline IPP-SHR's research processes also needs to be scalable and flexible so as not to disadvantage collaboration and research efficiency if projects required support for different methodologies. Additionally, each project has differing qualitative methodological requirements, which vary according to project size, participant numbers, interviews per participant, and timeframes. As such, any software implementation needs to support IPP-SHR's diverse projects which requires flexibility, scalability and durability, plus continuity of access over extended periods of time.

Additional requirements and challenges posed to the development of a software system are stipulated by the regulatory and policy frameworks within which IPP-SHR operates. Human Research Ethic Councils (HREC) stipulate privacy, informed consent, confidentiality, and audit requirements for research approval involving humans (Australian Federal Government 1988; NHMRC 2003; AIATS 2004). Additionally, audit requirements necessitate data be stored in a confidential and secure location for a period of time from five to seven years. The challenges imposed by such policy and regulatory frameworks require IPP-SHR to store and be legally liable for any information which is gathered throughout the research process. This is particularly important within IPP-SHR's operating paradigm due to the decentralized composition of IPP-SHR research projects and staff. Document control, ethical requirements and privacy issues represent a major concern and challenge for the research process and for any software system designed to support such research.

IPP-SHR research practitioners have not previously been exposed to a high level of IT involvement and had a reticence based on lack of familiarity. Consequently, an additional challenge for incorporation and implementation of the system was the development of comprehensive and supported training packages. The case study highlights the need for mutual understanding from both academic and IT disciplines in developing the system and the positive outcomes that can be gained from incorporating such diverse professional viewpoints. This case study profiles the importance of IT leadership and innovation in meeting the outlined challenges.

DESIGN AND IMPLEMENTATION

Design and implementation of the technological interface created for the research program required a detailed understanding and high level analysis of the challenges, backgrounds, procedures, needs and desires of proposed users of the system. This required both research practitioners and IT consultants to have a high level of cooperation and effective discourse focussed on the needs and wishes of the research practitioners. Although research practitioners bring to their work an understanding of the role and function of IT, this was insufficient for translating their work into an innovative and original incorporated system. What became evident in this experience was the need to provide IT leadership, collaboration and experience in translating the research work components and wishes into a sustainable and useable system.

Design and implementation of the system needed to be in a bottom up fashion. Effective translation, education and implementation assisted in establishing a self perpetuating and learning experience for users. Users are able to

see advances that technology can make and can suggest, modify and drive new innovations and uses. Understanding this user determined innovation variable allows users and IT designers to implement user friendly software with practical outcomes which correctly and efficiently operationalises research processes. That is, by a process of continual feedback and discussion between research practitioners and IT consultants, both parties were able to understand and learn the constraints, practicalities and possibilities of automating the research process. Development and specification of the software requirements was partly informed by the Institute of Electrical and Electronics Engineers (IEEE) document (1998) referring to recommended practice for software requirement specifications.

Such in-depth discourse between the two professional groups and the development of a thorough understanding of the research processes allowed for extra innovative features to be created and other unnecessary ones to be omitted. This assisted in producing an effective program with an efficient design. For example, features such as user control and public and private files where not proposed in the original design, however after extensive consultation this feature was warranted as crucial. This was in particular reference to identifiable participant data which, in line with HREC agreements, only authorised persons should be able to view. Without consultation and ongoing discussion between both professional groups, this feature would have been omitted from the final product. Additionally, features proposed by the IT professionals were omitted as they did not add value and could potentially complicate use of the final software interface.

All parties agreed on final software specifications before commencement of programming and software construction. The use of specification allowed for accurate budgeting and timeframe projections. It also allowed for a medium in which users from both professional groups could suggest and implement changes before programming.

This is particularly important in relation to the ethical imperative of efficient and effective use of resources, as changes made to the system once programmed are costly and expensive compared to alterations made in the pre–programming stage. (Diaz & King, 2002)

This considered, laborious and collaborative consultative period before manufacture of the software began is an essential step for any project which bridges two disparate disciplines. Continual communication between research practitioners and IT consultants, coupled with a referable specification documents, allowed for greater flexibility, increased innovation and design features, producing a software package that is of direct use and benefit to its intended users.

WORKFLOW ANALYSIS, PROGRAM SPECIFICATIONS AND IMPLEMENTATION

Extensive research and market searches indicated that no suitable, scalable and location-independent software was available to serve the unique demands and constraints faced by the research group. Although there are numerous research software packages specifically designed for qualitative methodologies (e.g. NUD*IST or Atlas/ti) (Barry 1998) there was an absence of project management software which incorporated qualitative methodologies and associated workloads. In order to fill this gap, a software program was designed to handle such programmatic demands and incorporate data analysed within the major qualitative data analyses programs. A full working commercial version of this program can be found at www.quadrant-pm.com

A reductionist analysis of the workflow and procedures that IPP-SHR uses to operationalise its research was critical for successful design and implementation of the software program. This process involved detailing and referencing every activity conducted by researchers. All components produced by the research process were discretely assigned a unique identifier. Components were then tracked in order to ascertain a step by step understanding of the research process. For example, the interviewing of a participant produced a component, "audio voice file," this file was then forwarded to the transcriber, who by transcribing the audio voice file produced another component, "text document of interview verbatim". The flow and process of information creation (arrangement of participant interview) to research output (publishing and dissemination of information) was tracked and compiled into a flow diagram. (See Figure 1)

After construction of the flow diagram each process was analysed to identify redundant processes and avenues through which automation and efficiency could be increased. For example a redundant process found was the duplication of communication occurring between team members in the activity of scheduling an interview. Although, in its simplest form, scheduling can be achieved through one person (enrols the participant, schedules and conducts the interview, compiles and stores documents relating to the interview and transcribes the interview) this is a rarity due to the aforementioned operating challenges of the research program. It is IPP-SHR's experience that there can be up to four people involved in the process of arranging, conducting and transcribing an interview. Similar issues of redundancy and repetition of tasks were found within the interface between transcription, coding and recording keeping.

Analysis of data flow and information creation in Figure 1 suggested that many tasks undertaken within a project only need be completed once if every member involved had access to such information. As such, a centralised distribution model of information storage, provision and access was developed to enable this streamlining to occur. Using the centralised model, users of the system, with appropriate rights and security credentials, have access to each component of information that is relevant to the specific needs of their task. This enables users to maintain up-to-date information and accurate data repositories, which assists in smooth and efficient running of research processes. Furthermore, duplication, redundancy and errors are reduced as only one record exists per each research instance per project. Instead, for example, of four team members keeping individual records of each particular research instance and co-ordinating changes between each other, only one record is kept and only one change is made. Using the model in relation to interviewing, scheduling would be provided to the centralised data source (such as a web based calendar) and information given to other members associated with such interview will be provided from such source.

Figure 1. Procedural, sequential information creation and flow (©2007, Hamish Holewa. Used with permission)

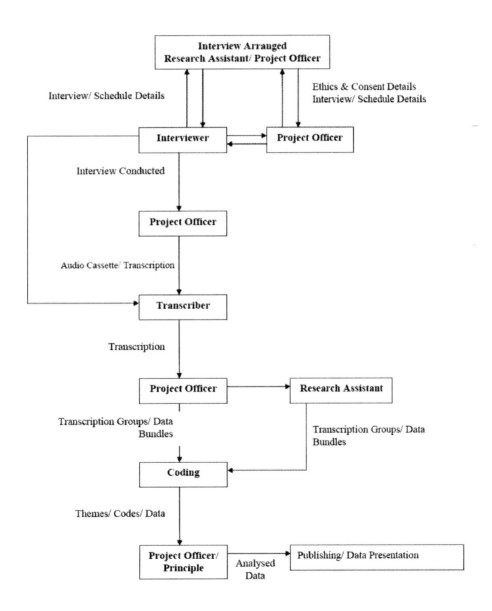

Figure 2. Centralised and distributed information flow (©2007, Leena Hiltunen. Used with permission)

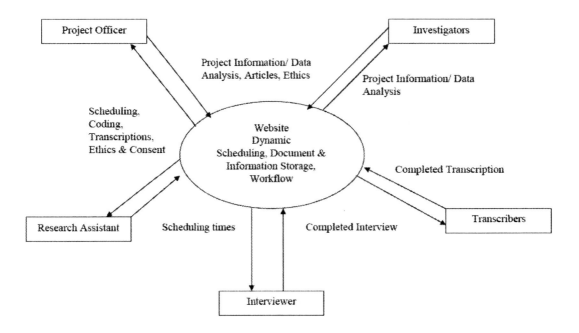

As shown in Figure 2, research staff interacts individually with the central dynamic website and information flow occurs via a centralised, distributed model. This distinctly contrasts with the processes formerly used, whereby information flow was procedural, sequential and task oriented. Once information has been created, research team members with appropriate security credentials can access the most up-to-date source of information through a website portal without needing to ask other team members for the status and latest version of such information.

The depicted system in Figure 2 also removes unnecessary and redundant tasks with the motivation of increasing automation and realising efficiencies through the process. Once, implemented and configured, simple procedural and reporting tasks are completed automatically. In previous work flow the researchers were involved in a six step processes which included: (1) research assistant (RA) enrols participant; (2) schedules an interview time; (3) organises HREC compliance such as informed consent and project description procedures; (4) the interviewer (INT) completes the interview and produces a digital recording; (5) the recording is sent to the transcriber (TRS) who completes transcription processes; and, (6) send completed transcription to RA or project officer (PO), who initiates coding and qualitative analysis. At any point in the process, each member is reliant on another member to complete their scheduled task, record appropriate details and ensure HREC and other policy guidelines are complied with. Furthermore, the PO or investigator may have to contact up to four people to receive an accurate report on the progress of the research project.

A major advance has been achieved on the automation and reduction of the described processes. This is done through the automatic storage and referencing of documents and information (participant details, consent forms, digital interview files, transcriptions) which is completed at each stage and by each individual person responsible for such tasks. Once each task is completed by the assigned research team member, the team member interfaces with the website portal and flags its completion and uploads the accompanied file or information. The website will then contact the next research team member within the process. For example, once an interviewer has completed the interview, this is flagged within the system and the corresponding sound file is uploaded to the website portal. Once uploaded, the website sends an alert to the transcriber of the need for an interview to be transcribed. This process reduces record keeping times and ensures an up-to-date report on progress.

The distributed, centralised model of project work flow implementation has been realised through the use of four discrete online modules operating within the project management portal. These four modules are as follows: calendar and scheduling; project workflow and progress; document and version control; and administration. Included are different levels of user access and control and differing levels of information categories, ranging from public to private. Access to the website portal occurs through a computer with internet connectivity and browser support. The website server runs on a combination of client and server side code attached to a centralised database. Most computation and processing is completed on the remote server and, apart from internet connectivity, there is little computational demand on client computers.

SELF DIRECTED LEARNING COMMUNITIES

The development of a community, centred upon online collaborative applications, is a well regarded method for increasing the use and accessibility of a system and for encouraging users to engage in self directed interaction and learning (Neus, 2007). The implementation and use of community

based initiatives has been successful within this case study. The provision of a message board, collaborative document sharing applications, version control and work processes has encouraged community building and increased collaboration and use of the service. It has also facilitated self directed learning and enquiry and has supported a forum for public discussion.

Evidence associated with the development of an online community and self directed learning stemmed from online dialogue evident within the bulletin board feature and the minimum formal training needed for new users. Through anecdotal records and conversions with users of the system, it was noted that software training and learning was largely conducted within the system. Although, software training was required for initial users of the system, the historical dialogue between such users provided a self directed learning environment for new users, and assisted in development of an environment conducive to posting public comments and asking questions to the group of users. However, it should be noted, that the development of such a community of self- directed learning may be further successful due to the separate and disparate physical location of the users. It is unclear whether such development of a bulletin board and self- directed learning would have developed if user where located in the same physical space, e.g. in the same office.

The central place assumed by the software within the research program creates a responsive medium through which staff concerns, ideas and issues can be raised. This enables research staff to pose research-related questions and comments, and provide direct feedback on the program's usability. The facilitation of such open communication allowed for quick development of ideas and creative problem solving. It also helped to foster team culture and shared identity, whilst acting as an effective training tool.

The software program's ability to dynamically provide users with up-to-date project information has encouraged individual and team ownership of the research projects. As the program allows for instant viewing of research project status and progress, research members are also able to identify any aspects of the research process hindering overall progress. Additionally, staff training and supervision, early identification of potential problems, and feedback were facilitated by the availability and ease of gauging project progress.

FUTURE ADVANCES AND ETHICAL IMPLICATIONS

It is anticipated the further development of the system will occur through a user driven, evolutionary response. Increased and synchronised communication avenues are predicted with a decreasing need of physical presence. This is particularly evident with the advent of increased access and data throughput, as a result of increasing bandwidths and the emergence of new and maturing technologies (Choudrie & Dwivedi, 2007). It is envisaged that access to the research collaboration tool will occur through more diverse means, and not be limited to a computer with Internet connectivity. This has strong positive implications for the processes of qualitative research, as many research activities are conducted in the setting of the participant and away from traditional computing equipment. There is potential to limit the redundant activities presently associated with scheduling, interviewing and recording by allowing handheld or portable devices access to the software.

Additionally, the immediacy of information access between research staff and the potential for real-time communication is an important avenue for future advances. Instant Messaging and Voice-Over-Internet-Protocol advances have the potential to contribute to stronger group collaboration, communication and a sense of community. The use of such technologies also has the potential to lower communication costs and providing greater access to research opportunities for marginalised or disadvantaged groups. The adoption and inclusion of such technologies, has the opportunity to lower research costs, providing greater potential outputs from fewer resources.

Increased security represents another domain in which future advancements may occur. This aligns with the ethical imperative of maintaining rigorous privacy and confidentiality protocols within the research process, particularly when using centralised models of information storage collaboration and project management work. The transfer, storage and processing of information within the aforementioned system is governed by strict HREC and other policy requirements. Effective system security, regulating access and use, is paramount to fulfilling the ethical and policy requirements of privacy, confidentiality and cost effective use of research resources. Although the system currently uses best practice security practices, such as encryption, user access and password, security certificates and user training, the advent of increased processor and computational capabilities and increased internet users and connectivity means that security issues are a priority area for ongoing future advancement.

The software program has the potential to increase user engagement between researchers, health professionals and stakeholders in qualitative research processes, especially for groups whose lack of access to traditional research institutions may have formerly acted as a barrier to participation. This use of IT solutions within qualitative research has the potential to bridge geographical and social communication gaps, opening up the potential for increased collaboration and information sharing between researchers worldwide. From IPP-SHR's experience implementing and using such a program, it is evident that the integration of IT management structures into a qualitative research program can be instrumental in bridging geographical constraints and fostering global research collaboration. The potential of this new technology is clearly evidenced by the way in which it has enabled IPP-SHR to effectively engage in research collaboration that spans national boundaries and multiple time zones.

CONCLUSION

This chapter has presented, through the medium of a case study, insights gained from the practical experience of developing and implementing an original web based collaborative research tool to assist and enhance the management of an existing qualitative research program. This tool is based on a centralised model of information distribution and access and was designed following a reductionist analysis of existing research processes and procedures. The ways in which the integration of responsive IT processes into the management of a large international research program have removed redundancies and increased automation and research efficiency has also been discussed. The program opens up avenues for increased research participation and collaboration and makes an important contribution to overcoming the challenges that a fragmented, globalised environment poses.

REFERENCES

AIATS. (2000). Ethical guidelines for research. Australian Institute of Aboriginal and Torres Strait Islander Research. Retrieved March 18,2007, from http://aiatsis.gov.au/research_program/gratns/gratns_assests/ ethics_guidelines.pdf

Australian Federal Government. (1988). *Privacy Act 1988* Australia Privacy Policy. Australian Federal Government. Retrieved March 18,2007, from http://www.comlaw.gov.au/com-law/management.nsf/lookupindexpagesbyid/I P200401860?OpenDocument

Barry, C. A. (1998). Choosing Qualitative Data Analysis Software: Atlas/ti and Nudist Compared *Sociological Research Online,* 3(3). Retrieved March 17, 2007, from http://www.socresonline.org.uk/socresonline/3/3/4.html

Choudrie, J., & Dwivedi, Y.,K. (2007). Broadband impact on households consumers: online habits and time allocation patterns on daily life activities. *International Journal of Mobile Communications,* 5(2), 225–241. doi:10.1504/IJMC.2007.011817

Diaz, M., & King, J. (2002). How CMM impacts quality, productivity, rework and the bottom line. *CrossTalk,* 15(3), 9–16.

IEEE – Software Engineering Standards Committee of the IEEE Computer Society. (1998). *IEEE recommended practice for software requirements specifications.* USA

Latimer, J., et al. (Eds.). (2003). Advanced Qualitative Research for Nursing. Oxford, Malden, MA: Blackwell Publishing.

McGrath, P., & Holewa, H. (2006). Missed Opportunities: Nursing insights on end-of-life care for haematology patients. *International Journal of Nursing Practice,* 12(5), 295–301. doi:10.1111/j.1440-172X.2006.00585.x

Neus, A. (2007). Managing Information Quality in Virtual Communities of Practice. Lessons learned for a decade's experience with exploding Internet communication. *The 6th International Conference on Information Quality at MIT.* Retrieved March 18, 2007, at http://opensource.mit.edu/papers/neus.pdf

NHMRC. (2003). Values & ethics: guidelines for ethical conduct in Aboriginal and Torres Strait Islander health research. National Health and Medical Research Council. Retrieved March 18, 2007, http://www.nhmrc.gov.au/publications/synopses/e52syn.htm

Polit, D., & Hungler, B. (1995). Nursing research: principles and methods. 5th Ed. Philadelphia: Lippincott.

Streubert, K., & Carpenter, D. (1995). Qualitative research in nursing: Advancing the humanistic imperative. Philadelphia: Lippincott.

KEY TERMS

Information Technology (IT): As defined by the Information Technology Association of America, IT is "the study, design, development, implementation, support or management of computer-based information systems, particularly software applications and computer hardware."

Phenomenology: A method of inquiry based around the exploration, description and analysis of a particular phenomenon, untainted by presupposed theories, beliefs and assumptions.

Psycho-Social Research: Research processes which aim to explore and document social and psychological aspects of the human experience.

Qualitative Research: A non-numerical research methodology which aims to describe and understand, rather than explain, human behaviours and experiences.

Redundant Processes: Unnecessary process or tasks that through analyses of such process can be removed without affect the output of such tasks.

Server Side Technology: A form of web server technology in which users' requests are fulfilled by running a script directly on the web server to generate dynamic HTML pages. It is used to provide interactive web sites capable of interfacing with databases and other data stores.

Chapter 3.2
Adaptability and Adaptivity in The Generation of Web Applications

Raoudha Ben Djemaa
MIRACL, Tunisie

Ikram Amous
MIRACL, Tunisie

Abdelmajid Ben Hamadou
MIRACL, Tunisie

ABSTRACT

This article proposes a generator for adaptive Web applications called GIWA. GIWA's objective is to facilitate the automatic execution of the design and the generation of Adaptable Web Applications (AWA). Characteristically, the effort in this work has to be pursued with special attention to both issues applied to AWA: adaptability and adaptivity. The architecture of GIWA is based on three levels: the semantic level, the conceptual level and the generation one. Using GIWA, designers specifies, at the semantic level the features of Web application. The conceptual level focuses on the creation of diagrams in WA-UML language; the extended UML by our new concepts and new design elements for adaptation. At the generation level, GIWA acquires all information about users' preferences and their access condition. Consequently, the generated pages are adaptable to all these information. An evaluation and a validation of GIWA are given in this article to prove our adaptation.

INTRODUCTION

The growing demand for data-driven Web applications has led to the need for a structured and controlled approach to the engineering of such applications. Both designers and developers need a framework that in all stages of the engineering process allows them to specify the relevant aspects of the application. The engineering becomes even more complicated when we include notions of adaptation. Here, we address both adaptations during the presentation generation, for example to reflect user preferences or platform used, as well as adaptation inside the generated presentation.

The need for adaptation arises from different aspects of the interaction between users and Web applications. Users' categories which deal with these systems are increasingly heterogeneous due to their different interests, preferences, and the use of number of devices (PC, WebTV, PDA, WAP phone, etc...). User's preferences and interests can be deduced from his and browsing history.

Adaptive Web engineering is meant to provide a systematic and disciplined approach for designing, generating and maintaining adaptive Web applications (Cingil, 2000). For this reason, recently several models and methodologies have been proposed for supporting the development of adaptive Web applications. The main goal of such models is to help designers to reason in a structured way about aspects that are specific to hypermedia, such as links, structure and navigation, and to express adaptation in the design process. Moreover, such models and methodologies should help engineers to manage the overall complexity of Web development which requires a variety of activities, such as organizing the structure, choosing the contents and the presentation modality, some of them involving automated generation of Web page (Brusilovsky, 1998). So, methodologies usually provide guidelines for performing such activities and suitable models for expressing the results of such operations.

In our previous works (Ben Djemaa, 2006a; 2006b, 2006c; Ben Djemaa, 2007; Ben Djemaa, 2008) we have presented a methodology for AWA which guides the designer through different steps of the design process, each of them yielding a specific model that is being interpreted by the GIWA tools. The GIWA methodology is based on several following steps: requirement analysis, conceptual design, adaptation design and generation.

The requirement analysis step (Ben Djemaa, 2005) represents the application domain. This step expresses the purpose and the subjects of the Web application through the functionality model and defines the target audience through the audience model. The result of these two models is a set of audience classes together with an informal description of their functional space. In GIWA,

the functional space is determined by a semi automatic algorithm called AGCA.

In the Conceptual Design step (Ben Djemaa, 2008), the functional space for each audience class is represented using traditional conceptual modeling: use case diagram, sequence diagram, class diagram, etc. In GIWA, conceptual model is represented in a specific notation called Web Adaptive Unified Modelling Language (WA-UML) (Ben Djemaa, 2008). This new notation increases the expressivity of UML while adding labels and graphic annotations to UML diagrams. This extension of UML defines a set of stereotypes and constraints, which make possible the design of conceptual model. These models are translated and exported in XML files in a data repository.

The adaptation design level (Ben Djemaa, 2007) is based on the profile model, which takes into account the user's devices capabilities (hardware and software), Users' preferences presentation (desired layout, navigation patterns, etc.) and personal information (eg. Age, sex, language, etc...).

In this article we concentrate on the generation level. At this level the designer is invited to instantiate previous models using the specific interfaces offered by GIWA. Only the aspects related to the two first levels (requirement analysis and conceptual design) are instantiated by the designer. Information related to the devices' capabilities are dynamically captured by the system (using Logs files) and then stored in the profile model. At the end of the step of instantiation, the GIWA deployment can be launched.

Characteristically, the effort in this work has to be pursued with special attention to both issues applied to AWA: adaptability and adaptivity. Adaptability can be defined as the facility of an application to be configurable according to a set of decisions taken by the user, which usually define his preferences and/or background. Whereas adaptivity denotes the capacity of the application to alter the profile model according to the user's behaviour during the application run and adapt dynamically to the current state of the user model to any user.

The article is structured as follows. In Section 2 we provide an overview of related works. In section 3 we present an overview of the different models of GIWA. Section 4 presents the architecture of GIWA and some examples of interfaces which illustrated the prototype. In section 5 we present our experimental design and the carrying out of the experiment using the design. Finally, section 6 concludes the article and suggests future research directions.

RELATED WORKS

For a long time, Web application engineering has been synonymous with ad hoc development and not supports a systematic process. Aspects like adaptation and generation process complicate the design process of Web application engineering and bring its complexity beyond the level that is easily handled by a single human developer. Therefore, to support a systematic development process, a strong methodology (supported by a suite of tools) can help to keep the design process at a practical level. Recently, different approaches for modeling and engineering adaptive hypermedia system have emerged. Approved hypermedia design principles, such as those defined in OOHDM (Schwabe, 1998) or in RMM (Isakowitz, 1995; Isakowitz, 1998) have been enhanced with the notions of adaptation and personalization in a further extension of OOHDM (Rossi, 2001) or the RMM-based Hera methodology (Frasincar, 2001; Frasincar, Houben, 2002). UWE (Koch, 2000, 2001) included a design methodology for adaptive hypermedia applications (AHDM) and a development process for such applications (AHDP). In the AMACONT project authors have introduced a component-based XML document format (Fiala, 2003). This project enables to compose adaptive Web applications by the aggregation of reusable document components.

All these methodologies were originally designed for Adaptive Hypermedia Application (AHA) and do not deal comfortably with Adaptive Web Application (AWA). These methodologies are very much data-driven or implementation oriented and do not covers the lifecycle of adaptive Web applications. Still, most solutions have been originally developed for a manual hypermedia design process and are not particularly well-suited in the context of automated hypermedia design.

Methodologies like RMM, UWE or AMA-CONT are not specifically targeted to support dynamic adaptation. For these methodologies, personalization means that the application acknowledges the user's situation and its information delivery are adapted. They may be able to solve adaptability problems to some extent but they do not address the real problem of adaptivity relating to the devices' capability (hardware and/ or software). On the other hand, most of the currently existing methodologies lack a profile model that would allow for the design of truly adaptive Web applications. In fact, this model can play a significant role in such applications: our aim is to include this aspect in the personalization of the hypermedia presentations that get generated. Generating adaptive presentations requires a clean separation of concerns, as is advocated in (Frasincar, 2002).

OVERVIEW OF GIWA MODELS

In GIWA, Web applications data are defined by different models such functionalities model, audience model and profile model.

The Functionalities Model

Met with the increasing needs of Web applications users, we propose a functionalities model, gathering users' informational and functional needs. In this model, functionalities are classified into three functional classes: Static Informational (SI),

Dynamic Informational (DI) and Professional (P) ones. The Static Informational functional class gathers all functionalities enabling the users to have access to the system to acquire static information being in a specific URL Web page. This class translates the set of the static informational users' needs. Using hypertext and hypermedia links, the user is capable to exploit a functionality of information's consultation.

The Dynamic Informational functional class regroups all functionalities enabling the users to have access to the system to acquire dynamic information. This class translates the set of the dynamic informational users' needs. Using techniques of research by a search engine, the user is capable to exploit a research functionality of information.

The Professional functional class is devoted to the representation of the users' functional needs. Indeed, Web applications are based on technologies which make their contents dynamic, enabling, thus, the user to modify the applicative state of the server by carrying out a set of functionalities.

Each of these functional classes, represented above, will be decomposed by the designer into a set of elementary functionalities representing both informational and functional needs. These functionalities, describing every functional class, are three:

- Static Informational Functionality (SIF) displaying a static Web page being in a specific URL.
- Dynamic Informational Functionality (DIF) displaying a dynamic Web page constructed from one (or several) "SELECT" server query (s). It is about a selection from the database without affecting the applicative server's state.
- Profession Functionality (PF) displaying a dynamic Web page constructed from one (or several) server query: UPDATE, ADD or DELETE. The execution of this functionality affects the applicative server's state.

At the lowest level of the Functionalities Model, the concept "Functional Space" provides each actor with a list of authorized functionalities.

In Figure 1 we present the Functionalities' meta-model (using the UML notation). This figure illustrates the inheritance and composition links existing between the concepts constituting the Functionalities Model (Functional Class, Functionality and Functional Space). We notice that the Informational Functionality class executes link (hypertext and hypermedia link classes) and the Informational Functionality class uses a query of consultation (Query research class) which makes it possible to select and to organize the presented information. In this case, the Query class is composed of several classes representing various clauses of a simple query like in SQL. In this meta-model we present:

- The SQL Select clause by a Projection class which defines the expected structure of the query result;
- The SQL From clause by the Source class which introduces the collections from which the result is built;
- The Where clause by the Selection class which specifies a predicate allowing to filter the collections;

A query produces a result modelled by a Result class. A relation of dependence exists between the classes Query and Result: any modification made to a query has a direct influence on the result. In addition, the Profession functional class uses another type of query which updates the database system (Query Updating class). It also implements the composition of the classes representing the following clauses: The Insert clause represented by the class Insertion; the Delete clause represented by the class Delete and the Update clause represented by the class Modification.

In our approach, the Functionalities Model implementation is carried out in two stages. During the first stage, the designer is invited to define

Figure 1. Representation of the meta-model of the model of the functionalities

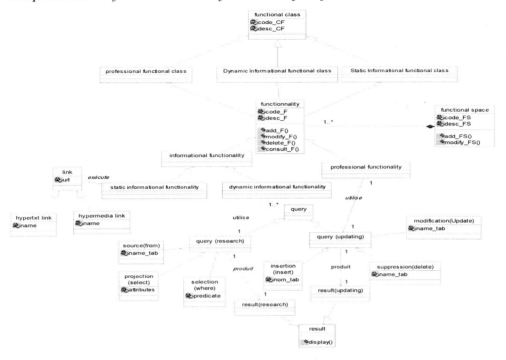

the first three levels of the model. The fourth level, relating to the functional space of the actors, is approached only after having defined the list of the actors involved in the application. However, this list is defined in the following section.

The Audience Model

The goal of this model is to define the actors' list of a Web application. Indeed, for this type of application, besides the human users (defines as of the physical actor) that exploits the Web system, we can distinguish services (representing roles played by the human users) or systems (devices, data processing system, Web service,...). In this context, to take account these distinctions, we propose three categories of actors classified as follows: physical actor, logical actor and system actor.

Physical actor represents a human user (or human user group) who visits the application Web. This actor interacts with the system to search or consult information (to execute an informational functionality) and possibly to modify the state of the system (to execute a professional functionality). For example, in the case of an application of library in line; Subscribers and Visitors are some physical actors.

Logical actor represents a role played by a human user (or a human user group) to assure the maintenance of the Web application. This actor assures all actions and functionalities that participate in the configuration and the administration of the system (to execute a professional functionality). For example, in the case of a Web application of a library the Webmaster and the Bookseller are some logical actors.

System Actor represents a computer system, an access device or a Web service, etc. These systems are connected generally to the application to provide news to the system or to update data. It is the external sources that will be charged automatically in the system.

In our approach, we have proposed an algorithm which generates the list of these different actors of the Web application starting from the concept of Functionality. We have presented in (Ben Djemaa, 2007), the process of operations of this algorithm.

The hierarchy of actors generated by this algorithm cannot describe a model for users because the definite actors are not all human actors. Therefore, in the goal to define an audience model (that leans logically on the human users), we propose to differentiate the human users by the concept "audience class" to inhuman one (systems) and, therefore to distinguish between "logical audience class" and "physical audience class".

By definition, an audience class is a potential user group which belongs to the application target audience and which has the same informational and functional needs. These classes are not necessarily disjoined (a user can belong to several classes of audience).

In Figure 2 we present the meta-model of our audience model. This figure illustrates the inheritance and composition links existing between the concepts constituting the Functionalities Model (Functional Class, Functionality and Functional Space).

To evaluate the audience model, we have proposed in (Ben Djemaa, 2005) an EPMA (Evaluation Process of the Audience Model) which evaluates the result generated by the algorithm of actor generation. This process is based on several mathematical symbols and formulas follow to check the distribution of the informational and functional needs between the actors for the application.

Profile Model

In our approach we proposed a new model specific for adaptive Web application called Profile Model (Ben Abdallah, 2008). In Figure 3 we show the different dimensions treated in this model to generate adaptive Web applications.

This model represents an abstract specification of the presentation in terms of users' profiles. In

Figure 2. Meta-model of the audience model

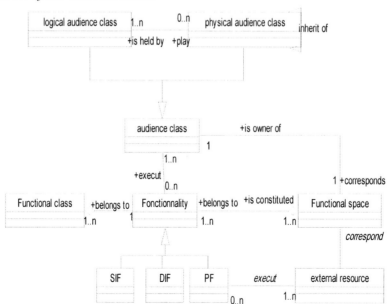

Figure 3. Profile model

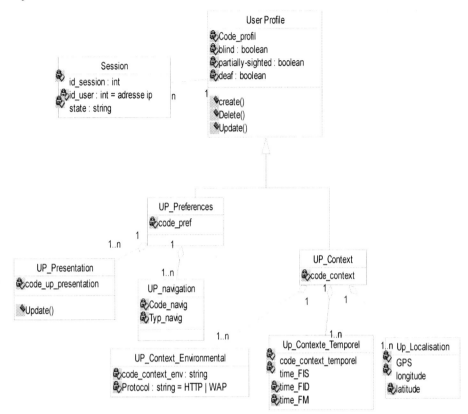

fact, this model needs to take into account the users' preferences (Up_preferences) and the user's context (UP_context). The first aspect is composed of preferences of presentation and preferences of navigation. The second aspect dealt with the environmental context (hardware and software), the temporal context (the preferred time to execute a FIS, FID or FM functionality) and the localisation (GPS information's) context.

Users' preferences presentation will be defined through specific techniques of data presentation and different media in the Web page. In fact, to take into account the adaptation of the different media in a Web application we have defined a model of media adaptation which presents preferred choices for users for each type of media: visual, video and audio one. (cf. Figure 5).

UP_context_Environmental has a number of components, each component grouping a number of attributes. In Figure 4 we defined three profiles components (UP_Network, UP_Hardware and UP_software). UP_Hardware component has a number of attributes (eg. Support_image specifies if the device is able to display images and ScreenSize defines the dimensions of the device display).

Both adaptability and adaptivity are considered in our approach. These concepts are treated differently in the profile model. Users' preferences presentation will be defined through specific charters (composition and graphical charters). Each of these charters can be choice by the user after the generation of his Web application (adaptability) and he can also modify some information at his system use (adaptivity). This dimension of the profile model will be detailed in the following section. Users' preferences navigation and information about the context of user is a

Figure 4. Environnemental context / user profile

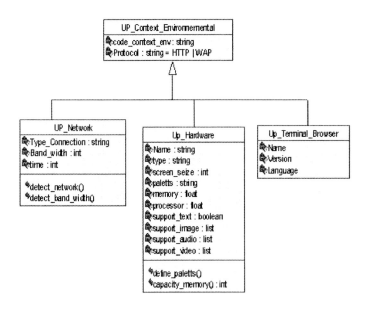

Figure 5. Model of media adaptation in GIWA

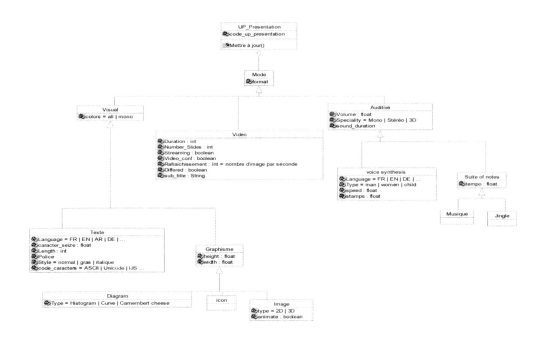

dimension which is automatically captured by GIWA (adaptivity).

To generate Web interfaces, the user does not need all dimensions or sub-dimensions or all information characterizing a dimension. A profile is thus an instantiation partial of this model according to the user's needs, to the type of application and to the execution environment.

Different engines and processes are defined in GIWA to instantiate these models and to generate adaptable interfaces Web. The architecture of GIWA is detailed in the following section.

ARCHITECTURE OF GIWA

GIWA's target is to facilitate the automatic execution of the design and the automatic generation of adaptive Web interfaces. It should be possible to program the Web applications in such a way that it can automatically execute the process specified by the design. Figure 6 depicts three different activities of the proposed generator GIWA: Semantic level, Conceptual level and Generation level.

The semantic level instantiates specific data contents of the Web application defined by different semantic model us functionality model, audience model and profile model.

The conceptual level focuses on the creation of diagrams in WA-UML. In fact, in this level we propose an AGL which supports the new design elements that we proposed. This AGL is based on Argo_UML. Thus, in this extension of Argo_UML, we introduce new types of diagrams to represent the different diagrams of our extension, namely, WA-UML.

The generation level focuses on the process of Web page generation and describes how the generator GIWA dynamically adjusts to varying user preferences into chosen implementation platform (HTML, WML, SMIL, etc.).

Semantic Level of GIWA

Figure 7 depicts different steps of GIWA in the semantic level. For a designer modelling an adaptive Web application using GIWA consists firstly, in instantiating the functionalities' model.

Once instantiated, this model is translated into XML files to be stored in the data repository ❶ and the system execute the algorithm of generation of audience classes ❷ which built the audience model. Then this model is validating by a specific process called PVMA❸. The last is also translated into XML file ❹ which contains the functional space for each audience class. At this stage, the content is adapted to each audience class. But to adapt the user's presentation preferences, the designer is invited to instantiate the profile model using specific interfaces offered by GIWA that treat respectively by following axes:

Figure 6. Architecture of GIWA

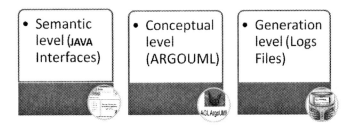

Figure 7. The semantic level of GIWA

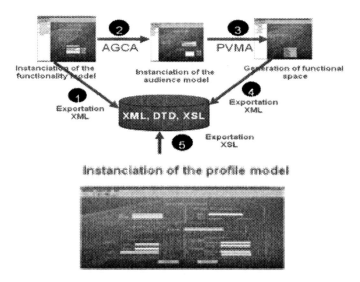

- Personal information about the user like name, age, sex, language.
- Users' presentation preferences defined in by two charters called composition and graphical charters (defined in the model of media adaptation (cf. Figure 4)).

After instantiation, the profile model is exported in XSL files in the data repository❺. At this stage GIWA treat the aspect of adaptability which appears through the choice of a graphical charter and through the composition of page after generated users' application. Figure 8 presents some interfaces of GIWA to instantiated the functionality model, the audience model and the profile model.

Conceptual Level

In the Conceptual level, the functional space for each audience class is represented using different conceptual modeling (use case diagram, sequence diagram, class diagram, etc) which are represented in WA-UML (Ben Djemaa 2006c; Djemaa, 2008). While this article is not solely devoted to the conceptual issue, we do want to

shortly demonstrate how the functional space for each user, is modeling. In fact, diagram and meta-model of WA-UML are detailed in our work in (Ben Djemaa, 2008).

In this article we propose an AGL which supports the new design elements that we proposed in WA-UML. The last is based on Argo_UML because it permits to guide the user in the use of the UML notation through a mechanism of critiques and help messages. In addition, the source code of Argo_UML is available on the Web making it possible to analyze its inner workings. Thus, in this extension of Argo_UML, we introduce new types of diagrams to represent the different diagrams of our extension. In Figure 9 we present the different steps of the conceptual level in GIWA.

The XML files generated by the semantic level are extracted from the data repository ❻ to be imported into the AGL supporting the new design elements that we proposed.

This AGL is based on Argo_UML. So, in our use of Argo_UML, we introduce new types of diagrams to represent the new diagrams of our extension WA-UML (Ben Djemaa, 2008). In these diagrams, the user can add, displace and copy the different design elements as well as replace faces

Figure 8. Interfaces of the semantic level in GIWA

The instantiation of the functionality model

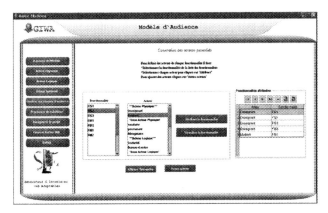

The application of the PVMA

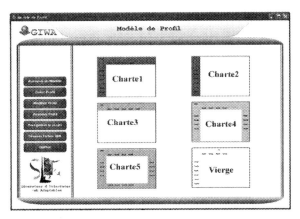

Composition charter of GIWA

continued on following page

Figure 8. continued

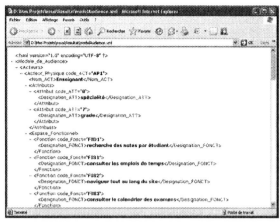

XML file of the audience model

Figure 9. Conceptual level of GIWA

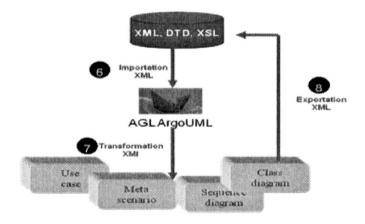

and publish their properties as used in Argo_UML. Figure 10 shows some examples of new icons of WA-UML presented by Argo_UML.

All conceptual diagram of WA-UML can be described with the new AGL based on Argo_UML❼. The last diagram is translated in XML files ❽.

In Figure 11 we present some diagrams of GIWA at the conceptual level. Us an example we present conceptual diagrams related to E-commerce application.

Generation Level

The previous sections dealt with the engineering process of GIWA. This section focuses on the process of generation of adaptive Web applications and describes how the system is dynamically adjusted to varying audience classes.

The generation level focuses on the process of Web page generation and describes how the generator GIWA dynamically adjusts to varying user

Figure 10. New icons in WA-UML

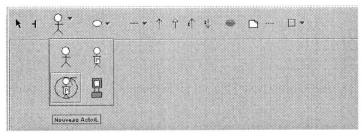

(a) New actors in WA-UML

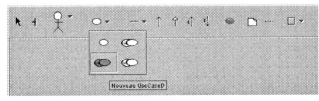

(b) New use cases in WA-UML

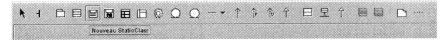

(c) New classes in WA-UML

preferences into chosen implementation platform (HTML, WML, SMIL, etc.). The target of this step is to facilitate the automatic generation of adaptive Web interfaces. It should be possible to program the Web applications in such a way that it can automatically execute the process specified by the design. The tool is based on a collection of engines, which interpret the models provided by the designer during the generation process. (cf. Figure 12).

According to the user/devices profile (refers aspect of adaptivity) is captured by the GIWA using data from logs files to be stored on the server according to a RDF vocabulary (W3C, 2002) ❾ and then to instantiate the profile model (user/devices profile) by specific capabilities (e.g. bandwidth, display resolution,…). Finally, XML, RDF and XSL files are extracted from the data repository ❿ and they are sent to the PARSER in order to apply some adaptation rules for each media (text, image, sound and video) and finally to publish the HTML page corresponding to the

devices user (PC, PDA, cell phone or desktop browse) ❿.

In adaptation media rules (Abdallah, 2008), we use the media properties defined in profile model, e.g. we can test if the dimensions of a particular image fit the size of the screen. Note that the adaptation based on user preferences can be treated in the same way as the adaptation based on device capabilities.

We proposed several adaptation rules for different Medias (text, image, sound and video).

R1 is an example of an adaptation rule for text media. This rule dimensions the size of the screen to adapt the size of the text to the hardware device or to user who is partially-sighted person or blind person. In appendix 1 we present the rest of adaptation rules for text media.

R1: ClientPage.Media.Texte.size_caracter >

$$\sqrt{\frac{height\_screen * width\_screen}{length\_text}})$$

∧ (¬ UserProfile. partially-sighted person

Figure 11. Examples of WA-UML diagrams

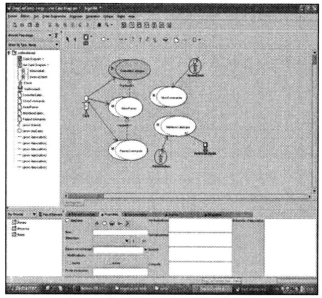

An example of WA-UML use case diagram

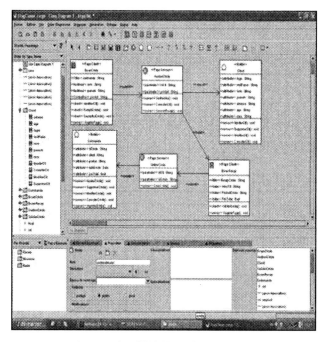

An example of WA-UML class diagram

continued on following page

Figure 11. continued

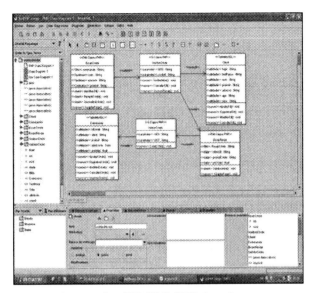

An example of WA-UML PHP class diagram

Figure 12. Generation level of GIWA

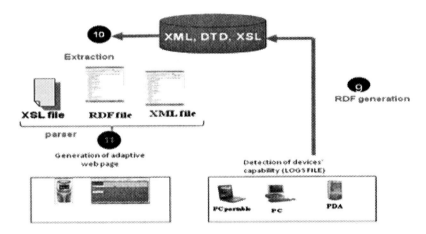

∨ ¬ UserProfile. blind person)

∧(UserProfile.Up_Context.Up_Context_En-vironmental.DeviceCaracteristic.Up_Hardware.support_text))

→t₁ Resize_text(ClientPage.Media.Text.size_caracter, E(

$$\sqrt{\frac{height\_screen * width\_screen}{length\_text}}))$$

R 2 presents an example of adaptation rules for an image media. This rule adapts the size of the image to be displayed by the device. In appendix 2 we present the rest of adaptation rules for image media.

R2: ClientPage.Media.image.Hauteur > User-Profile.Up_Context.Up_Hardware.hauteur ∨ Cli-

entPage.Media.image.largeur > UserProfile.Up_
Context.DeviceCharacteristic.Up_Hardware.
Largeur →t2 Resize_image(ClientPage.Media.
image,UserProfile.Up_Context.Up_Context_En-
vironmental.Up_Hardware.hauteur,UserProfile.
Up_Context.Up_Context_Environmental.De-
viceCharacteristic .Up_Hardware.largeur)

R 3 presents an example of adaptation rules
for sound media. This rule deletes the sound in
the Web page where the device doesn't support it
or where the user is a deaf person. In appendix 3
we present the rest of adaptation rules for sound
media.

R3: UserProfile.deaf ∨ ¬ UserProfile.
Up_Context.Up_Context_Environmental.De-
viceCharacteristic .Up_Hardware.support_sound
∨ ClientPage.Media.audio.sound.jingle →t3 de-
lete_sound(ClientPage.Media.audio).

R 4 presents an example of adaptation rules
for video media. This rule is applied to substitute
a video by an image if the device is enabling to
display this video. In appendix 4 we present the
rest of adaptation rules for video media.

r18:¬UserProfile.Up_Context.Up_Con-
text_Environmental.DeviceCharacteristic
.Up_Hardware.support_Video ∧UserProfile.
Up_Context.Up_Context_Environmental.Up_
Hardware.support_image →t18Convert_video_
to_image(ClientPage.Media.video,UserProfile.
Up_preference.Up_presentation.Charte.Mo-
dalite.Visual.graphic.format,number_image:1
default)

In Figure 13 we present the simulation of GIWA
for a user who connected with a PC.

In Figure 14 we present other interfaces of
GIWA related to user who connected to the system
using cell phone (Nokia SDK 5100).

EXPERIMENTATION AND EVALUATION

Evaluating systems is a difficult task, and it

Figure 13. Simulation of GIWA using PC

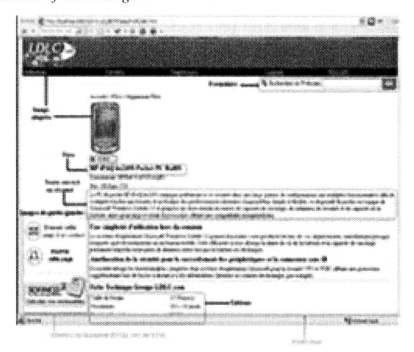

becomes even more difficult when the system is adaptive. It is of crucial importance to be able to distinguish the adaptive features of the system from the general usability of the designed tool.

The evaluation of our GIWA system was designed to address the goals of the system, namely to help users to design and generate adaptive web applications. So firstly, we wanted to measure the usability of GIWA and testing the ability of the process, during its three levels (i.e. semantic, conceptual and generation), to design and generate adaptive interfaces. Secondly, we were also interested in subjects' own evaluation of how well the adaptive system worked compared to the non-adaptive one, and whether they felt in control of the adaptive parts of the system. A last difficulty in making studies of adaptive systems is in the procedure of the study.

Design of the Experiment

The study was done in the laboratory of MIRACL.

Subjects were videotaped, and the computer screen was recorded on the same videotape. The subjects' actions were tracked using DRUM (Diagnostic Recorder for Usability Measurement) and descriptive statistics of task completion time, actions performed inefficient use of the system, and others could be easily computed using this tool. There were 8 subjects in the study, 3 female and 5 male, all employed at the laboratory that had developed and used the target domain SDP. All had experience with World Wide Web (WWW) and hypermedia development. Subjects spent in total, approximately three hours in carrying out the steps of the experiment, out of which two hour was spent testing the three level of GIWA. The rest of the time was used for questions on the subject's background, a small diagnostic test of their understanding of certain concepts in the on-line manual before using our system and after using our system, and finally answering some questions about their preferences regarding GIWA and the adaptive versus the non-adaptive

Figure 14. Simulation of GIWA using cell phone (Nokia SDK 5100)

system. Details of the steps of the experiment are presented below.

Each of the subjects followed three steps in this experiment, related to each level of GIWA. We proposed for them an example of web application related to the "teaching gate" of our institute. The two first steps related to the semantic and the conceptual level that were designed to test the explanations provided by the system rather than test the usefulness of the system as such. These two steps also served as a means to introduce subjects to the development of Web applications. The third step concerned the generation level that was realized for both of the two devices: the PC and the cell phone.

In the first step, a subject was given a set of functionalities related to the "teaching gate" with different types (FIS, FID, and FM), and was asked to use the generator to complete the following three tasks:

- **Task 1:** Instantiate the functionality model by adding, for each functionality, the code and the description, and generate the XML file for this model.
- **Task 2:** Apply the AGAC (Algorithm of Generation of Audience Classes).
- **Task 3:** Apply the PVMA and generate the XML file of the audience model.

In the second step the subject was given the XML file generated by the first step and asked to use the ArgoWA-UML to complete the following three tasks:

- **Task 4:** Import the XMI File related to the semantic level and created the use cases of the application.
- **Task 5:** create the sequence and classes diagrams with the new icons of WA-UML.
- **Task 6:** choose a Web language (PHP, JSP, ASP) and generated the technical class diagram.

In the third of the three above mentioned steps the subject was given the XML file generated by the second step and asked to use firstly a Pc and secondly, a cell phone, to complete the following three tasks:

- **Task 7:** connected to GIWA by taping: http://localhost:8080/GIWA/index.html (for PC) http://localhost:8080/GIWA/index.wml (for cell phone).
- **Task 8:** create an account and then choose a profile or create a new profile.
- **Task 9:** choose the XML file related to the conceptual model of the application "teaching gate" and generated the results by PC and cell phone.

The design goal of these nine tasks (1 to 9) was to oblige the users to actively use all the commands provided, while at the same time expose their own patterns of command sequences when performing the various tasks.

Results of Carrying out the Experiment

Usability of the System

Our results are divided into those concerning:

- Some remarks concerning the task completion time, where we can see a weak tendency that users spend some time to achieve the first task.
- The actions in ArgoWA-UML that the subjects have to do (clicking on icons, making menu-choices, clicking on association, etc) to build WA-UML conceptual diagrams are less than the action of building UML diagrams. Thus, this confirms the result that conceptual level of GIWA is a semi automatic one.
- Adaptive Web pages generated by cell

telephone are more interesting than those generated by a PC for most of users.

- The subjects' satisfaction with the system, where they compare the result (page generated) and their preferences described at the semantic level.
- The passage between the three levels of GIWA was not too clear by some of users.
- Combination of design and generation in GIWA is approved by users.

User Satisfaction

After the subjects had used the two variants of GIWA, we asked them to provide their viewpoints on various aspects of the generator. We did this through ten questions, and they were also asked to freely comment on various aspects of the system. For the ten questions the subjects put a cross on a scale grading from 1 to 7 - the interpretation of the scales can be seen from the statements left and right of the Table 1.

In the evaluation column of the Table 1 we present the interpretation of the scales which can be seen from the statements left and right. The x-axes represents the number of user for each scale, the y-axes represents the different interpretation of user for each question.

In Table 1 we see the result of the queries on how the subjects perceived the adaptive system in using GIWA. As we can see, the subjects preferred the adaptive system (mean 5.25); they also like the combination of design and generation in GIWA (mean 5.25); and they felt that the system made good adaptations to their needs (mean 4.75). Also, they claimed that they saw when the system changed the inferred task (mean 4.75).

Evaluating adaptive systems is often done through comparing a non-adaptive version of the system to an adaptive system. Our study is no exception from this approach. Still, an adaptive system should preferably be designed in such a way that the adaptivity is only one instrument in the repertoire of design techniques that together will form the tool that in its whole meets the users' needs and individual differences.

There are few studies of adaptive systems in general and even fewer of adaptive hypermedia. In the studies of adaptive hypermedia by (Boyle 1994; Kaplan 1993) the main evaluation criterion is task completion time. This should obviously be one important criterion by which some systems should be evaluated. In our case, though, the goal of the adaptive hypermedia system is to generate the right needs according to the user's preferences. The time spent in retrieving information is not as relevant as is the quality of the search and the result. Apart from task completion time, Boyle and al. also measured reading comprehension through a diagnostic test put to the subjects after having used their system. Kaplan and al. measured how many nodes the users visited - in their case the more nodes the users visited the better.

CONCLUSION

The research described in this article targets the support of automated generation Web interfaces in the context of adaptive Web application. Specifically, for Web applications involving various functionalities (informational or professional one), the implementation requires a structured approach.

This article develops a generator called GIWA supporting both design aspect and generation one. The architecture of GIWA is based on three levels: the semantic level, the conceptual level and the generation level.

The primary focus of the GIWA is to provide engineering support for adaptive Web applications that automatically generate hypermedia presentations in response for each ad hoc user's requirements. GIWA guides the designer through the different steps of the generation process, each of them yielding a specific model that is being interpreted by the GIWA tools to achieve the objective of automatic presentation generation.

Table 1.

NUM	Questions	Means	Evaluation		
1	How efficiently would you be able to Work with GIWA?	4,87	Badly, the generator gets in the way		Good, the work would be very efficient
2	Did you like using GIWA?	5,37	No, it is very demanding and unpleasant to use.		Yes, I really liked using it.
3	Do you feel in control while using GIWA?	4,25	No, it feels as if the generator controls me.		Yes, I can make the generator do what I want.
4	Did you easily get lost in the information space?	4,75	I got lost several times and did not know where I was.		I knew all along exactly where I was.
5	Did you find it easy to get started?	5,12	No, in the beginning it was very difficult.		Yes, it is possible to get started right away.

continued on following page

Table 1. Continued

6	Are the different Steps of GIWA easy to under-stand and use?	4,62	No, it is difficult to find the right icon and use it.		Yes, they are eas-ily understood.
7	Did you like the combination of de-sign and genera-tion in GIWA?	5,25	No, there are too many details and it is confusing.		Yes, the interface of GIWA is very appealing.
8	Did you see when the adaptations hap-pened in GIWA?	4,75	No, I never saw that the system changed.		Yes, it was ob-vious when the generator changed task and opened new operation.
9	Did the adaptive system make good adapta-tions to your needs?	4,75	No, I repeatedly had to change the answers I got in order to find the right information.		Yes, it managed to get relevant information.
10	Did you prefer the adaptive or the nodaptive system?	5,25	The noadaptive Was definitely bet-ter.		The adaptive Was definitely better.

In GIWA, we have distinguished two kinds of adaptation: adaptability (implemented at the semantic level) and adaptivity (implemented at the generation level). Adaptability is based on information about user preferences presentation (a.g. font color, page layout etc.) and user preferences navigation stored in the profile model before browsing starts. Adaptivity is considered in GIWA to provide a system which is able to automatically adapt a given presentation to the user device capabilities (hardware and software configuration). Information about device capabilities are captured from Logs Files and stored then in the profile model. The prototype of GIWA has been built by different engines and equipments. The prototype uses java interfaces to instantiated models at the semantic level. At the second level GIWA uses Argo_UML to create conceptual diagrams which are translate in XML files to be generated in Web pages at the generation level. In the last, XML and RDF files are used to store the data and XSL files to specify transformations between consequent steps.

We have presented an experiment to evaluate our generator GIWA. Results showed significant performance gains, both in design and in generation step. While our experiment provided several revealing results, there are many issues regarding adaptive web generation worthy of further study. It would be interesting to experiment and evaluate GIWA with blind and sighted users. Also interesting is how the framework generalizes between various users.

The work presented in this article provides different opportunities for future research. The future work includes further developments to facilitate adaptation at all levels of the generation process. Firstly we plan the extension of the ArgoWA-UML tool that is currently built to support the semi automatic transition from design models to a running implementation of adaptive Web applications. Secondly we plan to extend adaptivity in GIWA in order to dynamically elaborate and modify both the functional space and the navigation patterns, learning from the user's behaviour.

ACKNOWLEDGMENT

The authors would like to thank Ben Abdallah Fatma, who helped in the design and the development of a part of media adaptation.

REFERENCES

Abdallah, F., Amous, I., Ben Djemaa, R., & Ben Hamadou, A. (2008). Génération d'Interfaces Web Adaptable au Contexte et aux Préférences des Utilisateurs. Les huitième journées scientifiques des jeunes chercheurs en Génie Electrique et Informatique (GEI'2008) (pp. 103-112), Sousse, Tunisie.

Ben Djemaa, R., Amous I., & Ben Hamadou, A. (2005, September). Towards an approach for adaptive Web applications' requirements engineering. The 7th International conference on Information integration and Web-based Application and Services (IIWAS05) (pp. 19-21). Kuala Lumpur.

Ben Djemaa, R., Amous I., & Ben Hamadou A. (2006a, May). Design and implementation of adaptive Web application. *In 8th International Conference on Enterprise Information Systems ICEIS'06 (pp. 23- 27), Paphos Cyprus.*

Ben Djemaa, R., Amous I., & Ben Hamadou A. (2006b, February). GIWA: A generator for adaptive Web applications. In *Proceedings of the Advanced International Conference on Telecommunications and International Conference on Internet and Web Applications and Services (AICT/ICIW 2006) IEEE (pp. 23-25), Guadeloupe, French Carabeen.*

Ben Djemaa, R., Amous I., & Ben Hamadou A. (2006c). Use case and meta-scenarios for modelling Adaptive Web Applications. In *proceeding of IEEE 1st International Conference on Digital Information Management (ICDIM)*. 06-08 December, 2006. Christ College, Bangalore, India, pp. 283-288.

Ben Djemaa, R., Amous I., & Ben Hamadou A. (2007, May). Adaptable and adaptive Web applications: From design to generation. *International Review on Computers and Software (IRECOS), 2(3), 198-207.*

Ben Djemaa, R., Amous I., & Ben Hamadou, A. (2008, April/June). Extending a conceptual modeling language for adaptive Web applications. *International Journal of Intelligent Information Technologies (IJIIT), 4*(2), 37-56.

Boyle, C., & Antonio, O. (1994). MetaDoc: *An Adaptive Hypertext Reading System. User Models and User Adapted Interaction*, (UMUAI), 4, 1-19.

Brusilovsky, P. (1998). Methods and Techniques of Adaptive Hypermedia. In P. Brusilovsky, A. Kobsa, & J. Vassileva (Eds.), *Adaptive Hypertext and Hypermedia* (pp. 1-43). Kluwer Academic Publishers.

Cingil, I., Dogac, A., & Azgin, A. (2000). A broader approach to personalization. Communication of the ACM, 43(8), 136-141.

Fiala, Z., Hinz,, M., Meissner K., & Wehneer, F. (2003). A component-based component architecture for adaptive dynamic Web documents. *Journal of Web engineering, 2(*1), 58-73.

Fons, J., Pelechano, V., Pastor, O., Albert, M., & Valderas, P. (2003). *Extending an OO Method to Develop Web Applications.* The Twelfth International World Wide Web Conference (pp. 20-24), Budapest, Hungary.

Frasincar, F., & Houben, G.-J. (2002). Hypermedia presentation adaptation on the semantic Web. In P. de Bra, P. Brusilovsky, & R. Conejo (Eds.), *Proceedings of the 2nd International Confer-*

ence on Adaptive Hypermedia and Adaptive Web-Based Systems (AH 2002)* (pp. 133-142), Malaga, Spain.

Frasincar, F., Houben, G.-J., & Vdovjak, R. *(2001).* An RMM-Based Methodology for Hypermedia Presentation Design. *In Proceedings of the 5th East European Conference on Advances in Databases and Information Systems (ADBIS 2001), LNCS 2151 (pp.* 323-337), Vilnius, Lithuania.

Isakowitz, T., Stohr, A., & Balasubramanian, E. (1995). RMM: A methodology for structured hypermedia design. *Communications of the ACM, 38*(8), 34-44.

Isakowitz, T., Kamis, A., & Koufaris, M. (1998). *The Extended RMM Methodology for Web Publishing.* Center for Research on Information Systems.

Kapla, C., Justine, F., & James, C. (1993). Adaptive Hypertext Navigation Based On User Goals and Context. *User Modeling and User-Adapted Interaction, 3,* 193-220.

Koch, N. (2000). Software Engineering for Adaptative Hypermedia Systems-Reference Model, Modelling Techniques and Development Process. Ph.D Thesis, Fakultät der Mathematik und Informatik, Ludwig-Maximilians Universität München.

Koch, N. (2001). The Authoring Process of the UMLbased Web Engineering Approach. 1*st International Workshop on Web-Oriented Software Technology. The Tenth International Conference on the World Wide Web,* Hong Kong.

Rossi, G., Schwabe, D., & Guimaraes, R. (2001) Designing Personalized Web applications. *The Tenth International Conference on the World Wide Web, Hong Kong.*

Schwabe, D., & Rossi, G. (1998*).* Developing hypermedia applications using OOHDM. *In Proceedings of Workshop on Hypermedia development Process, Methods and Models* (pp. 85-94).

Villanova-Oliver, M., Gensel, J., Martin, H., & Erb, C. (2002). *Design and generation of adaptable Web information systems with KIWIS.* In Proceedings of the 3rd IEEE Conference on Information Technology TCC-2002, Las Vegas, USA World Wide Web Consortium.

Argo UML. http://www.tigris.org. eXtensible Stylesheet Language, XSL Specification – version 1.0, W3C Recommendation. Retrieved October 15, 2001 from http://www.w3.org/TR/xsl/ World Wide Web Consortium, 2002.

RDF Vocabulary Description Language 1.0: RDF Schema, W3C Working Draft. Retrieved April 30, 2002 from http://www.w3.org/TR/rdf-schemadix.

APPENDIX

Appendix A: Adaptation rules for Text Media

R5: (ClientPage.Media.Text.color $\not\subset$ UserProfile.Up_preference.Up_presentation.Charte.Modalite. Visual.colors) $\vee$ (ClientPage.Media.Text.color$\notin$UserProfile.Up_Context.Up_Context_Environmental. DeviceCharacteristic.Up_Hardware.palette) $\rightarrow$ t5: Modify_color(ClientPage.Media.Text.color, color)

R6 :ClientPage.Media.Text.police$\neq$UserProfile.Up_preference.Up_presentation.Charte.Modalite. Visual.Text.police $\wedge$ (UserProfile.partially-sighted person $\vee$ UserProfile.blind_man $\vee$ UserProfile. Up_Context.Up_Context_Environmental.DeviceCharacteristic.Up_Hardware.support_Text$\wedge$UserProfile. Up_Context.Up_Context_Environmental.DeviceCharacteristic.Up_Hardware.support_image)$\rightarrow$t6 Convert_text_to_image(ClientPage.Media.Text)

Appendix B: Adaptation rules for Image Media

R7: (ClientPage.Media.image.color$\not\subset$UserProfile.Up_preference.Up_presentation.Charte.Modalite. Visual.colors)$\vee$(ClientPage.Media.image.color $\notin$ UserProfile.Up_Context.Up_Context_Environmental. DeviceCharacteristic . Up_Hardware.palette)$\rightarrow$t7 color_image(ClientPage.Media.image.color, color)

R8: UserProfile.Up_Context.Up_Context_Environmental.Protocole_de_transfert="HTTP"$\wedge$ClientPage.Media.image.size_File > UserProfile.Up_Context.Up_Context_Environmental.DeviceCharacteristic.Up_Hardware.memory $\rightarrow$ t8 $\wedge/\vee$ t_{10} $\vee/\wedge$ t_{13} convert_gif (ClientPage.Media.image)

R9: $\neg$ UserProfile.Up_Context.Up_Context_Environmental.DeviceCharacteristic .Up_Hardware. support_image $\wedge$ $\neg$ UserProfile.Up_Context.Up_Context_Environmental.DeviceCharacteristic .Up_ Hardware.support_Text $\wedge$ UserProfile.blind_man $\rightarrow$t9 Delete (ClientPage.Media.image

Appendix C: Adaptation rules of Sound Media

R10: UserProfile.mal_entendant $\vee$ $\neg$ UserProfile.Up_Context.Up_Context_Environmental.DeviceCharacteristic .Up_Hardware.support_sound $\vee$ $\exists$ClientPage.Media.audio.sound.jingle $\rightarrow$t10 Delete_sound(ClientPage.Media.audio).

R11: ClientPage.Media.audio.size_File > UserProfile.Up_Context.Up_Context_Environmental. DeviceCharacteristic .Up_Hardware.memory $\rightarrow$t11 Stereo_to_mono(ClientPage.Media..audio) $\wedge / \vee$ Reduct_sampling(ClientPage.Media..audio)$\wedge/\vee$Convert_sound(ClientPage.Media..audio, UserProfile. Up_preference. Up_presentation. Charte .Modalite.auditive.format)

Appendix D: Adaptation rules of Video Media

R12: $\neg$ UserProfile.Up_Context.Up_Context_Environmental.DeviceCharacteristic .Up_Hardware. support_Video$\wedge$$\neg$UserProfile.Up_Context.Up_Context_Environmental.DeviceCharacteristic .Up_Hardware.support_image $\wedge$ $\neg$ UserProfile.Up_Context.Up_Context_Environmental.DeviceCharacteristic. Up_Hardware.support_sound $\rightarrow$t12 Delete_video(ClientPage.Media.video)

This work was previously published in International Journal of Information Technology and Web Engineering, Vol. 4, Issue 2, edited byG. I. Alkhatib and D. C. Rine, pp. 20-44, copyright 2009 by IGI Publishing (an imprint of IGI Global).

Chapter 3.3
Migrating Web Services in Mobile and Wireless Environments

Myung-Woo Park
Yonsei University, South Korea

Yeon-Seok Kim
Yonsei University, South Korea

Kyong-Ho Lee
Yonsei University, South Korea

ABSTRACT

Mobile devices enabled with Web services are being considered as equal participants of the Web services environment. The frequent mobility of devices and the intermittent disconnection of wireless network require migrating or replicating Web services onto adjacent devices appropriately. This article proposes an efficient method for migrating and replicating Web services among mobile devices through code splitting. Specifically, the proposed method splits the source code of a Web service into subcodes based on users' preferences for its constituent operations. The subcode with a higher preference is migrated earlier than others. The proposed method also replicates a Web service to other devices to enhance its performance by considering context information such as network traffic or the parameter size of its operations. To evaluate the performance of the proposed method, the effect of the code splitting on migration was analyzed. Furthermore, to show the feasibility of the proposed migration method, three application scenarios were devised and implemented.

INTRODUCTION

Web services (Huhns & Singh 2005; Stal, 2006), which are independent from operating systems and programming languages, have gained momentum as an enabling technology to realize business processes on distributed network environments such as the Web. Additionally, the technology of mobile devices is continually developing and thus allows for a new form of Web services, that is, mobile Web services (Schall, Aiello, & Dustdar, 2006; Sirirama, Jarke, & Prinz, 2006). However, it is difficult to provide Web services on mobile devices seamlessly, since wireless and mobile environments still involve unstable connectivity, unlike the typical client-server environment.

If Web services autonomously migrate among mobile devices in this unstable wireless environment, seamless provisioning of services would be possible. When a service cannot be provided during movement of a device, it can be migrated to an adjacent mobile device and provide its functionality continuously. Additionally, requests can be distributed by replicating the service to other devices when the requests are concentrated on one device. Moreover, in the case of a client's request for a service that takes large parameters such as bitmap image files as input, the service itself can be replicated and executed on the client side, resulting in saving resources.

Recently, research on Web service migration has been performed. However, most of the research targets desktop and wired environments or does not consider constraints such as low bandwidth of wireless and mobile environments. Therefore, the research approaches might take much longer time to migrate.

To resolve this issue, this article proposes a method for migrating Web services through code splitting. Specifically, an original code, which implements the functionality of a service, is split into subcodes based on users' preferences to its constituent operations. The subcodes of higher preference are migrated earlier to minimize the latency of the operations of high priority and raise the efficiency of Web services migration and replication in wireless and mobile environments. To evaluate the performance of the proposed method, the effect of the code splitting on migration was analyzed. Furthermore, to show the feasibility of the proposed migration method, three application scenarios were devised and implemented.

Meanwhile, how to determine when and where to migrate services is an important issue. The migration of a service may be carried out by the request of a service provider or the change of context information, such as the shortage of battery level and the location change of a device.

It involves developing the context model and strategies or policies relevant to the migration of Web services. If a migration of a service is requested, the proposed framework collects the context information of neighboring devices based on the migration policy of the service. It computes the suitability values of candidate devices and determines a target host. To establish a migration policy, the proposed method is based on our previous approach (Kim & Lee, 2007), which is based on WS-Policy (2006). In this article, we do not discuss the context model and migration strategies, but focus on describing the migration method itself.

Meanwhile, the process of identifying when and where to migrate services is also an important issue. The migration of a service may be caused by context changes such as the battery shortage and location change of a device. For the seamless provisioning of a service, we have to determine which device is the most suitable target host. This process involves a mechanism to describe context models and migration strategies, which are relevant to the migration of Web services in mobile environments. For example, a service provider should be able to specify that if the CPU usage-ratio of an origin host is over 80%, a service should be migrated to a new device, which has enough processing power and supports J2ME. For this purpose, we propose a method to establish the context model and migration policy to determine when and where to migrate services in mobile environments (Kim & Lee, 2007). The method determines a target host based on the migration policy of a service as well as the information collected from devices in the neighborhood of the origin host that is hosting the service. In this article, we do not discuss the process of determining when to migrate a service to a specific target host, but focus on how to migrate a service to a target host efficiently.

The organization of this article is as follows. First, a brief survey of previous works is presented. Next, the methods of splitting Web services codes and migrating and replicating them are described. Next, the effect of splitting codes on migration is analyzed through experiments, and three application scenarios are implemented to show the feasibility of the proposed migration method. Finally, we summarize the conclusions and further studies.

RELATED WORK

We summarize the conventional methods about Web service migration and also discuss previous works concerning code mobility, which do not target Web services but are related with migration. Pratitha and Zaslavsky (2004) propose a framework and strategies for migrating Web services. Based on context information such as network bandwidth, their method selects a target server, to which a service should be migrated. Moreover, their method defines service modules in advance according to context information and selects a proper module to the corresponding context.

Hammerschmidt and Linnemann (2005) propose a migration framework, which supports Web services based on Tomcat-Axis. Particularly, since instances are supported, connections do not need to be restarted after migration. Ishikawa, Yoshioka, Tahara, and Honiden (2004) propose the migration of mobile Web services, which are defined as composite Web services. Particularly, agents that execute several services in a composite Web service can migrate to an appropriate host. An endpoint of each service in a composite Web service can be changed; however, the endpoint of a composite Web service does not change. The method of Mifsud and Stanski (2002) monitors context information of available target hosts and migrates Web services to a specific target host.

Meanwhile, Kern, Braun, Fensch, and Rossak (2004) propose a more rapid execution of mobile agents through splitting and arranging codes which implement the functionality of agents. A

shortcoming of this method is that the execution order of agent functions in each host must be fixed. The middleware for an ad-hoc network proposed by Bellavista, Corradi, and Magistretti (2004) can receive and execute a list of binary files from neighboring devices. Montanari, Lupu, and Stefanelli (2004) propose a middleware framework which can implement migration policies application independently.

Previous works are mostly based on desktop and wired environments, and therefore the latency of Web services are too long to apply to wireless and mobile environments. Therefore, it is difficult to deal with a service migration efficiently in mobile and wireless environments. In this article, we aim at presenting how to migrate services quickly and to reduce the latency of service requests during migration.

SPLITTING WEB SERVICE CODES

We describe a splitting method of Web service codes. For the splitting and migration method, the framework of Figure 1 is proposed.

The code splitter splits a Web service code and saves them in a code repository in a component form. The migration manager encapsulates components and instances in a transportable form, and unpacks the encapsulated form and saves it at the resource space. The service execution manager manages the execution of a service, which stops and restarts the service execution. The context manager collects context information from the current and adjacent mobile devices and decides when and where to migrate services. The channel manager takes charge of the establishment of network connections. The logger records the execution history of the modules of the framework.

How to split a Web service code by the code splitter in the proposed framework is shown in Figure 2. In our method, it is assumed that the original source codes of Web services are proportionate to their compiled codes.

Figure 1. The proposed framework

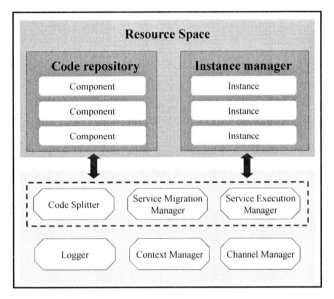

Figure 2. The process of splitting codes

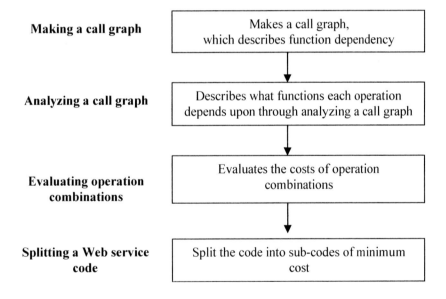

Making and Analyzing a Call Graph

A code that implements a Web service is analyzed and represented with a call graph, and the dependency among functions (or methods) is derived from the call graph. The proposed method for computing the dependency among functions is based on the method of Grove and Chambers (2001). The functions exposed as operations in a WSDL interface are recorded particularly and are used in the next analyzing step. After making the call graph, it is analyzed in order to determine functions, upon which each operation depends.

The analysis progresses following nodes, to which each operation node is connected. Figure 3 illustrates the making and analyzing of a call graph.

Evaluating Operation Combinations and Splitting a Web Service Code

A condition required in code splitting is that each split code should contain at least one operation and exists in a class form so that it can be compiled. The code split must have all the functions upon which its operations depend. However, if operations depend on functions in common, code splitting is impossible or inefficient. Copying appropriate codes of functions can solve this problem. In the call graph of Figure 3, Operations 1, 2, and 3 commonly depend on Function E, and therefore disjoint code splitting is impossible. However, if Function E is copied, it is possible to split the code, as shown in Figure 4.

It is possible but somewhat inefficient to copy all the function codes that are used in common. In Figure 4, Functions B, C, D, and E need to be copied in order to split Operations 2 and 3, and those four functions are almost a half of all the function code, including operations. Therefore, whether functions would be copied should be de-

termined for efficient code splitting. Alternately, an original code is split based on which operations will exist in a class, and then the combination of operations can decide which functions need to be copied.

The selection of the optimal code split is related to both the total size of the codes split and users' preferences to operations. If a code segment has not arrived in a target server, it is impossible to invoke its operation. In this case, users' dissatisfaction with the service would be raised. The proposed method transmits a code segment of higher priority earlier to minimize its service discontinuance. So, the dissatisfaction rate of a code segment at a certain time is proportionate to the time to migrate the total codes that include it and the code segments with a higher priority. The dissatisfaction would be also proportionate to user preferences. User preferences can be statistically calculated from users' previous requests by the logger. In this article, the dissatisfaction with a service migration is formulated and computed by a cost function as follows:

$$Cost = \sum_{i=1}^{n} (p_i \times \sum_{j=1}^{i} S_j) \qquad (1)$$

Figure 3. An example of making and analyzing a call graph

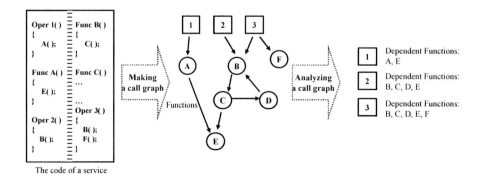

Figure 4. An example of copying functions

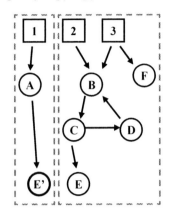

Dependent Functions:
A, E

Dependent Functions:
B, C, D, E

Dependent Functions:
B, C, D, E, F

where $i < j \rightarrow p_i \geq p_j$, $p_i = p_j \rightarrow S_i \leq S_j$, n is the number of partitions, p_i ($0 \leq p_i \leq 1$) is the sum of user preferences to operations in the ith partition, and S_j ($0 \leq S_j \leq 1$) is the total code size of jth partition.

The proposed method computes the costs of every possible combination of code split. It finds the combination of minimum cost that corresponds to the optimal split of operations. The original service code is split according to the optimal combination. Each partition of operations and their functions is compiled and saved as a component in the code repository.

MIGRATING AND REPLICATING WEB SERVICES

The proposed method handles both migration and replication. The former occurs when an origin server cannot provide a service any more because of some reasons (e.g., battery shortage and a nonservice area). The replication of a service is done when the service needs to be copied to a different server temporarily to maintain its quality. Example cases are as follows: 1) when network bandwidth becomes more crowded and traffic slows down; 2) when the number of requests from a particular location grows rapidly; and 3) when a client wants to use a service with large parameters.

When the migration of a service occurs, its endpoint should be changed as the corresponding endpoint of the target host. In the case of replication, a new endpoint is added to the existing list of endpoints of an origin server. The context manager selects between migration and replication depending on context information.

Migrating Web Services

When the battery level of an origin server becomes very low or a service cannot be provided any more due to the location change of its device into a nonservice area, the service should be migrated to an appropriate target device. If a target server accepts the migration request, the components and instances in a transportable form are transmitted, as shown in Figure 5. Specifically, existing requests on the execution queue of the service execution manager are processed on the server, selected between the origin server and the target server for faster execution. This is basically the same with the case of a service request during migration. At the same time, instances and their associated components on the resource space are transmitted in order of the user preference.

Whenever a component and/or its instance arrive, the service execution manager of the target server deploys the operations of the component.

Figure 5. An example procedure of Web services migration

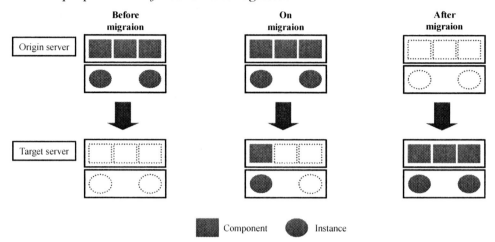

As soon as all the components and instances have arrived at the target server, they are deleted on the origin server. If the components and instances of a service have not arrived at the target server due to any reason, the process of migration halts. Additionally, the origin server searches again for a new target server. The former target server maintains the components and instances already arrived for a certain period of time. After the time period, the target server deletes them.

If a service is requested during its migration, the proposed method determines which server between the origin and target servers executes the request faster. Figure 6 describes the control flow of the process. In the case where the component of the operation called has already transmitted to the target server, t_o is the time to receive the instance from the target server, execute it on the origin server, respond its result to a client, and transmit the instance updated to the target server, that is, synchronize two instances between the two servers. t'_n includes the time to notify a client that the request should be made to the target server and the time for the client to request the operation to the target server and receive its response. Figure 7(a) describes the case of Figure 6.

In the case where the code has not been transmitted yet, t'_o corresponds to the time required to respond to the client request and transmit the instance and component of the operation to the target server. t''_n includes the time to forward the component and client request to the target server and execute the operation on the target server. It also contains the time for the origin server to notify a client that the result should be received from the target server and for a client to receive the result from the target server. Figure 7(b) illustrates the case of Figure 6.

Replicating Web Services

The replication of a Web service is classified into two cases: the replications of a service to another server, and to the client requesting it.

Replication to Another Server

The method of replication is similar to that of migration. If a target server accepts a replication request, the corresponding components and instances are transmitted. However, all the instances

Figure 6. The flow of processing in case of a service call on migration

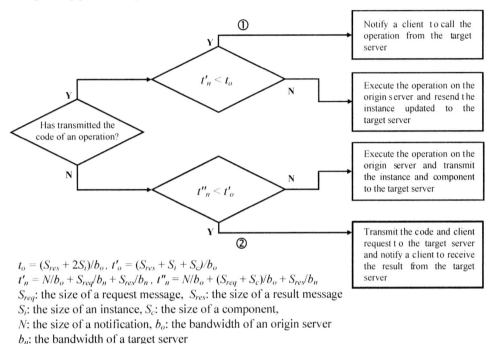

$$t_o = (S_{res} + 2S_i)/b_o, \quad t'_o = (S_{res} + S_i + S_c)/b_o$$
$$t'_n = N/b_o + S_{req}/b_n + S_{res}/b_n, \quad t''_n = N/b_o + (S_{req} + S_c)/b_o + S_{res}/b_n$$

S_{req}: the size of a request message, S_{res}: the size of a result message
S_i: the size of an instance, S_c: the size of a component,
N: the size of a notification, b_o: the bandwidth of an origin server
b_n: the bandwidth of a target server

Figure 7. Service requests during the migration process

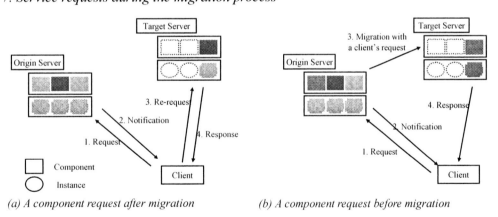

(a) A component request after migration   *(b) A component request before migration*

do not need to be transmitted, and after finishing the replication process the components are not deleted from its origin server. The instances that have been transmitted to the target server are deleted on the origin server. When a replication occurs, the origin server records the target servers on the list of replications. Additionally, the origin server may request the target server to delete the replicated service. If a service is requested during replication, the same processes with the case of migration are applied.

Figure 8 is an example of a service replication, where an origin server with three components and five instances communicates with five clients. The context manager decides which server should be selected as the target server and which instances

Figure 8. An example of Web services replication

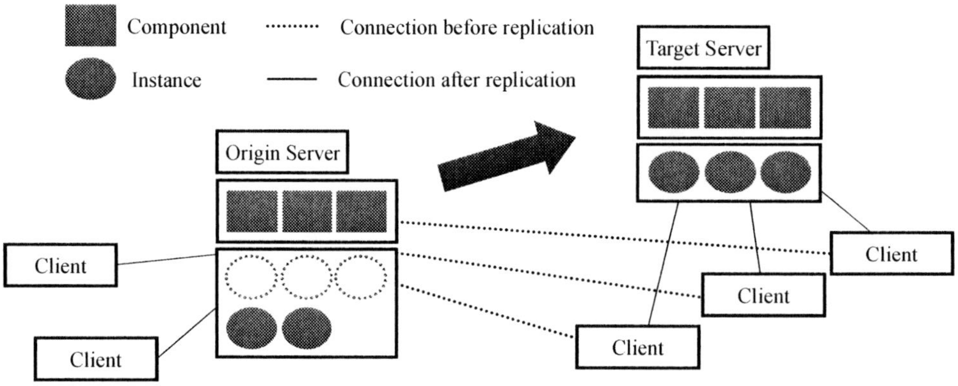

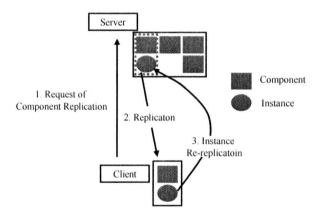

Figure 9. Component replication

should be migrated. For example, after copying three components and three instances, the target server and three clients would reconfigure their connections. The three instances would be removed from the origin server, resulting in reducing traffic on the origin server.

Replication to a Client

If a service requires a large message as an input parameter, a client may want to download the service code of a smaller size and execute it on his or her device, as illustrated in Figure 9.

To do this, a client should examine the component information about an operation and compare the sizes of the parameter and component. If a component were downloaded, an origin server would record the client on the replication list. Likewise, the origin server may request the client to delete the component.

If a replication is requested during migration or replication, a server, from which the component would be downloaded more quickly, should be determined, as shown in Figure 10. While t''_o indicates the download time of the component and instance from the origin server, t'''_n corresponds

Figure 10. The flowchart for a replication request during migration or replication

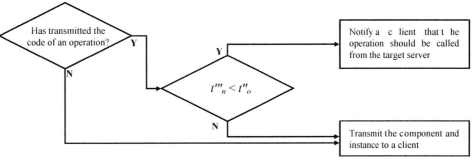

$t''_o = (S_c + S_i)/b_o$
$t'''_n = N/b_o + S_{req}/b_n + (S_c + S_i)/b_n$
S_c: the size of a component, S_i: the size of an instance
N: the size of a notification, S_{req}: the size of a request message
b_o: the bandwidth of an original server, b_n: the bandwidth of a target server

to the time to notify the client that the component and instance would be downloaded from a new server and when the client would receive them from the new server.

EXPERIMENTAL RESULTS

We have experimented evaluating the effect of the proposed code splitting approach on migration. Additionally, to show the feasibility of the proposed migration and replication, three application scenarios were implemented and tested. The tests were conducted on devices, which have an Intel(R) PXA270 processor, a memory of 62.28M, and the Windows Mobile 2003 operating system.

Code Splitting

To evaluate the performance of the proposed code splitting method, we measured the time to split codes from three different experiments. First, to investigate how much the method is affected by the dependency among operations, we experimented with test data, where Web services consist of 10 operations and each operation calls 3 functions.

Second, concerning the number of functions called by an operation, the test was done with services, which contain 10 operations and 20 functions. Here we varied the number of functions, which are called by an operation, from 2 to 20. The third test is about the number of operations in a service. Web services contain operations that call 10 functions. Here the number of operations was varied from 1 to 10. In our experiments, the dependencies between operations and functions were randomly selected. In each experiment, the size of the functions also varied from 1 KB (kilobyte) to 100 KB.

Evaluation in Terms of the Dependency between Operations

If operations in a service share functions in common, we can say that they depend on each other. We define the dependency of operation a in a service as:

operation_dependency(a) = the number of operations sharing functions in common with a
/ the total number of operations in a service

(2)

715

Figure 11(a) shows the experimental results of the relation between the average value of operation dependencies and the time taken to split codes. The figure shows that operation dependency and splitting time are scarcely related. If a Web service has many functions shared by its operations, the possibility of splitting would be low. Otherwise, the possibility of splitting would be high. Since only the functions shared by operations are copied, the number of copied functions is limited, resulting in increasing a limited amount of time. Consequently, the operation dependency is shown to be unrelated to the splitting time. Moreover, Figure 11(b) shows that the dependency is unrelated to the total size of the codes split. The test was done with services, whose operations and functions have the size of about 10 KB.

Evaluation in Terms of the Number of Functions Called by Operations

The experimental result of Figure 12(a) shows that as the number of functions called by operations grows, splitting time increases. Nodes in a call graph represent functions or operations. The number of functions called by operations determines the number of edges among function nodes. As the number of connections among nodes, we need more time to analyze and split the graph.

Figure 12(b) shows the relationship between the number of functions called by an operation

Figure 11. An experimental result on operation dependency

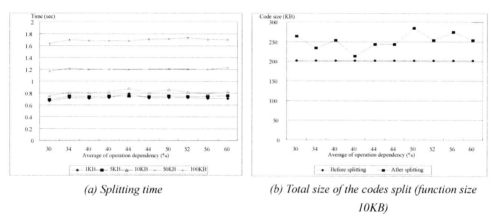

(a) Splitting time   (b) Total size of the codes split (function size 10KB)

Figure 12. An experimental result on the number of function calls

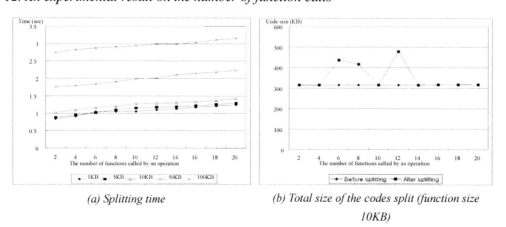

(a) Splitting time   (b) Total size of the codes split (function size 10KB)

and the size of the codes split. The test was done with services, whose operations and functions have the size of about 10 KB. In the cases where the numbers of the function called are 2 or 4—since the numbers are relatively small and each operation did not share functions—there was no difference in the size of the codes split before and after splitting. No regularities were found while increasing the number of functions called by an operation until it reached 12. In the case of 14 or more functions, operations called more than 70% of functions in this test. Splitting did not happen since too many functions needed to be copied otherwise.

Evaluation in Terms of the Number of Operations

As shown in Figure 13, there is a close correlation between the number of operations and the splitting time. An increase in the number of operations results in an exponential growth of the splitting time since all possible combinations of operations need to be considered to determine the code splitting of minimum cost.

As a result, we find that the splitting time of a service is related with its code size, the number of functions called by operations, and the number of operations, while the dependency among operations seldom affects the splitting time. In particular, the splitting time grows exponentially

as the number of operations increases. We have a plan to consider this matter to enhance the processing time of the proposed method.

Migration and Replication

To show the feasibility of the proposed migration method, we implemented three application scenarios.

Migrating Web Services to a Mobile Device

The first scenario is about the migration of a Web service, which provides traffic information about a particular bridge. As described briefly in Figure 14, we assume that a service offers information about the traffic and weather situation of bridge continuously by migrating from a car leaving the bridge to a car arriving at the bridge. The service should be migrated to a new server because its origin server is leaving the bridge and so it cannot be provided any more. Additionally, the connections from clients should be reconfigured to the new car.

Figure 15(a) shows the log information of an origin server, which hosts the service. When the car is about to leave the bridge, a client calls the service to get information on traffic speed (getAveVel) and temperature (getTemperature). The service is being migrated to a new server

Figure 13. An experimental result on the number of operations

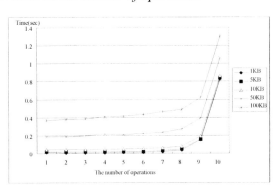

Figure 14. A scenario of service migration

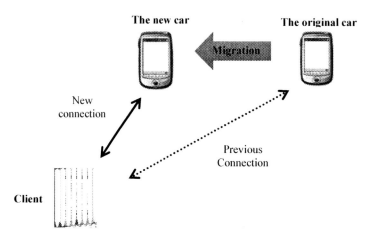

Figure 15. Log information of servers

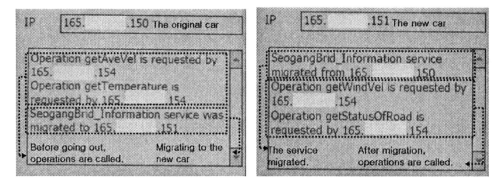

arriving at the bridge. Figure 15(b) shows the log information of a car, to which the service has arrived and its two operations, that is, getWindVel and getStatusOfRoad, have been requested by the client

Replicating Web Services to a Mobile Device

This scenario is about a service replication for providing art information seamlessly in a museum. The museum in the scenario provides a Web service, which offers information about artists and their artworks, and if necessary, replicates the service to guiding devices, resulting in reduced network traffic.

Figure 16 provides a brief description of this scenario. Visitors or clients are served from the museum server, which collects the information and adjacent guiding devices and maintains their list. If the requests to the origin server increase suddenly, the origin server will an appropriate device, to which its service should be replicated. If a target device accepts the replication request from the origin server, the service code is replicated to the target device and the connections between the origin server and clients are reestablished in order to provide the service seamlessly.

While Figures 17(a) and 17(c) illustrate the interaction between the museum and its visitor before replication, Figures 17(b) and 17(d) show the interaction between the device of a guide and

Figure 16. A scenario of service replication

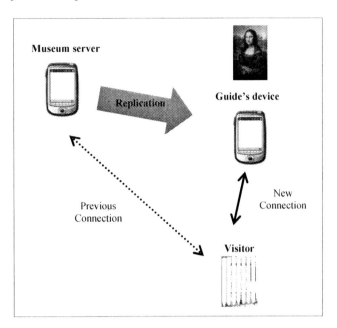

Figure 17. Screenshots of the server and client

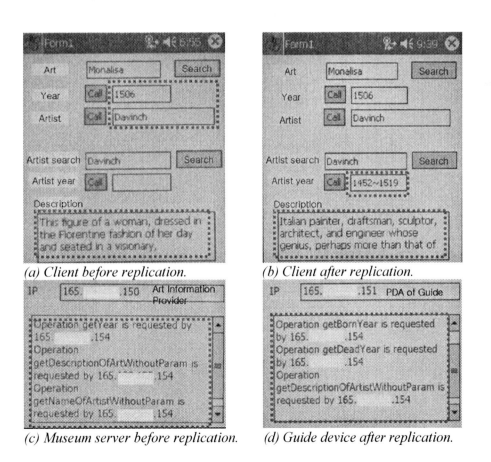

(a) Client before replication.

(b) Client after replication.

(c) Museum server before replication.

(d) Guide device after replication.

the visitor after replication. Once a client calls an operation, the service provider maintains the instance and thus enables the client to call other operations of the same service without parameters. After the client calls operation getYear with parameter Monalisa, he or she could call two operations, such as getDescriptionOfArtWithoutParam and getArtistWithoutParam, without parameters. As shown in Figures 17(b) and 17(d), we find that the client could call three operations with no parameters (e.g., getBornYear, getDeadYear, and getDescriptionOfArtistWithoutParam). This

is due to the fact that the instance of the service was replicated to the target server.

As described before, an origin server maintains a list of replicated services and may request a target server to delete the service replicated. Figure 18(a) shows that an origin server replicates a Web service to a target server and records the service and its target server. As shown in Figure 18(b), after replication, the origin server can request to the target server to delete the service replicated. Figure 18(c) indicates that the service was deleted from the target server according to the request of the origin server.

Figure 18. Deletion of the service replicated

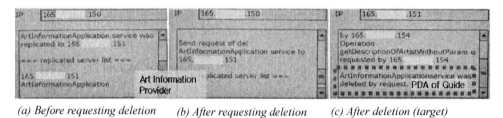

(a) Before requesting deletion   (b) After requesting deletion   (c) After deletion (target)

Figure 19. Replicating a component to a client

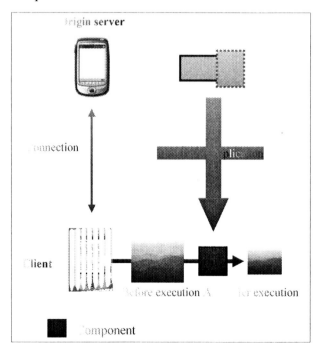

Figure 20. An example of component replication

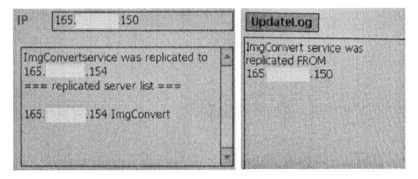

(a) Log information of a server   (b) Log information of a client

Replicating Components to a Client

There may be a case where if a service requires a large amount of input and output messages, it is more efficient to download and execute the service at a client side. In the scenario of Figure 19, an origin server provides a service of converting images and a client wants to resize an image. The client does not transmit a large image file as a parameter; instead, the client resizes the image by executing the service component replicated from the origin server.

Figure 20(a) shows the log information of the origin server, which provides the image conversion service. Figure 20(b) is the log information of the client that uses the service replicated. Likewise, the origin server records the service replicated and the client. It may also request the client to delete the service replicated.

Comparison with Previous Works

Table 1 shows the comparison result of the proposed method with previous works. The method of Pratitha and Zaslavsky (2004) migrates services to a target server, which is selected based on context information. Services are composed of service modules, which have been defined in advance depending on context. However, as the size of a service increases, it takes a lot of resources to migrate the service. They do not handle the migration of service instances and the replication of services. Hammerschmidt and Linnemann (2005) support the migration of instances to reduce network traffic and resource consumption on an origin server. Among the methods concerning code mobility, Bellavista et al. (2004) and Montanari et al. (2004) support the migration of binary codes, but do not offer the instance migration.

In this article, we present a method for migrating and replicating Web services on mobile and wireless environments. Based on the context information of mobile devices, the proposed method selects between migration and replication. Additionally, service instances are preserved during migration and replication. The proposed framework does not consider the reconfiguration of services after migration. The reconfiguration involves increases in code size since it requires codes—which are relevant to each context—to be implemented. Therefore, it may be not suitable for wireless and mobile environments.

Table 1. Comparison with previous works

Methods \ Features	Web services	Instance preservation	Reconfiguration	Supporting mobile and wireless environments	Context –awareness
Pratitha and Zaslavsky (2004)	O*	X	O	X	O
Hammerschmidt and Linnemann (2005)	O	O	X	X	X
Ishikawa, Yoshioka Tahara, and Honiden (2004)	O	X	X	X	X
Mifsud and Stanski (2002)	O	X	X	X	X
Kern and Braun (2005)	X	O	X	X	X
Bellavista, Corradi, and Magistretti (2004)	X	X	X	O	O
Montanari, Lupu, and Stefanelli (2004)	X	X	X	X	O
The proposed method	O	O	X	O	O

* O: supported, X: not supported

CONCLUSION AND FUTURE STUDY

This article presents an efficient method for migrating and replicating Web services through code splitting. Specifically, a service is split into subcodes based on users' preferences to its constituent operations. The subcodes of higher preference are migrated earlier to minimize the discontinuance of the operations of high priority and raise the efficiency of Web services migration and replication in wireless and mobile environments. From experimental results, we found that the proposed splitting method depended on the size of a Web service and the number of functions called by its operations. In particular, as the number of operations increased, the splitting time grew at an exponential rate. Moreover, the proposed migration method was experimented under three application scenarios. Experimental results show that the proposed migration method helps services to be provided continuously.

The proposed method selects an optimal combination of code split, on which the source code is split and compiled into components. However, it may be necessary to merge and split the codes split repeatedly since user preferences may change rapidly and frequently. Therefore, to reflect the changing desires and preferences of users dynamically at runtime, we have a plan to enhance the proposed migration method to make it possible to accommodate user feedback at runtime.

ACKNOWLEDGMENT

This work was supported by the Korea Research Foundation Grant funded by the Korean Government (MOEHRD) (KRF-2005-041-D00690).

REFERENCES

Bellavista, P., Corradi, A., & Magistretti, E. (2004, September 20-22). Lightweight code mobility for proxy-based service rebinding in MANET. In Proceedings of the 1st International Symposium on Wireless Communication Systems, Port Louis,

Mauritius (pp. 208-214).

Grove, D., & Chambers, C. (2001). A framework for call graph construction algorithms. ACM Transactions on Programming Languages and Systems, 23(6), 685-746.

Grove, D., DeFouw, G., Dean, J., & Chambers, C. (1997, October 5-9). Call graph construction in object-oriented languages. In Proceedings of the ACM SIGPLAN Conference on Object-Oriented Programming Systems Languages and Applications, Atlanta (pp. 108-124).

Hammerschmidt, B. C., & Linnemann, V. (2005, February 22-25). Migrating stateful Web services using Apache AXIS and P2P. In Proceedings of the IADIS International Conference on Applied Computing, Algarve, Portugal (pp. 433-441).

Huhns, M. N., & Singh, M. P. (2005). Service-oriented computing: Key concepts and principles. IEEE Internet Computing, 9(1), 75-81.

Ishikawa, F., Yoshioka, N., Tahara, Y., & Honiden, S. (2004, July 19-20). Toward synthesis of Web services and mobile agents. In Proceedings of AAMAS Workshop on Web Services and Agent-based Engineering (WSABE), New York (pp. 227-245).

Kern, S., & Braun, P. (2005, September 20-22). Towards adaptive migration strategies for mobile agents. In Proceedings of the Second GSFC/IEEE Workshop on Radical Agent Concepts (WRAC) (pp. 334-345). NASA Goddard Space Flight Center Visitor's Center Greenbelt, MD.

Kern, S., Braun, P., Fensch, C., & Rossak, W. (2004, October 25-29). Class splitting as a method to reduce migration overhead of mobile agents. In Proceedings of the International Conference on Ontologies, Databases and Application of Semantics (ODBASE'04), Agia Napa, Cyprus (pp. 1358-1375).

Kim, Y.-S., & Lee, K.-H. (2007). An efficient policy establishment scheme for Web services migration. In Proceedings of the International Conference on Convergence Information Technology (ICCIT'07) (pp. 595-600).

Mifsud, T., & Stanski, P. (2002, October 8-11). Measuring performance of dynamic Web service migration using LAMS. In Proceedings of the 10th International Conference on Software, Telecommunications and Computer Networks (SoftCOM), Venice, Italy (pp. 214-218).

Montanari, R., Lupu, E., & Stefanelli, C. (2004). Policy-based dynamic reconfiguration of mobile-code applications. Computer, 37(7), 73-80.

Pratistha, I. M., & Zaslavsky, A. B. (2004, March 14-17). Fluid: Supporting a transportable and adaptive Web service. In Proceedings of the 2004 ACM Symposium on Applied Computing, Nicosia, Cyprus (pp. 1600-1606).

Schall, D., Aiello, M., & Dustdar, S. (2006). Web services on embedded devices. Web Information System, 1(1), 1-6.

Sirirama, S. N., Jarke, M., & Prinz, W. (2006, February 19-22). Mobile Web services provisioning. In Proceedings of the Advanced International Conference on Telecommunicatons and International Conference on Internet and Web Application and Services, Guadeloupe, France (pp. 120-126).

Stal, M. (2006). Using architectural patterns and blueprints for service-oriented architecture. IEEE Software, 23(2), 54-61.

This work was previously published in International Journal of Web Services Research, Vol. 6, Issue 2, edited by L. Zhang, pp. 1-19, copyright 2009 by IGI Publishing (an imprint of IGI Global).

Chapter 3.4
Applying Web–Based Collaborative Decision–Making in Reverse Logistics:
The Case of Mobile Phones

Giannis T. Tsoulfas
University of Piraeus, Greece

Costas P. Pappis
University of Piraeus, Greece

Nikos I. Karacapilidis
University of Patras, Greece

ABSTRACT

The increasing environmental concerns and the technological advances have boosted the post-use treatment of nearly all kinds of products and a new area for research and application has emerged described by the term "reverse logistics." In this chapter, parameters that may affect reverse logistics operation are discussed from a decision-making perspective, so that alternative design options may be proposed and evaluated. In particular, these parameters are used for the qualitative evaluation of the reverse supply chain of mobile phones in Greece. For this purpose, we present an illustrative application of a Web-based decision support tool that may assist collaborative decision-making in conflicting environments, where diverse views, perspectives, and priorities shared among stakeholders have to be considered.

DOI: 10.4018/978-1-60566-114-8.ch018

INTRODUCTION

The increasing environmental concerns and the technological advances have boosted the post-use treatment of nearly all kinds of products, regardless of their size, composition, and initial value. Relevant legislative frameworks have been enforced in developed countries aiming at apportioning the responsibilities related to the recovery of end-of-life products. In addition, specific targets regarding product design and recovery rates are set, networks' requirements are suggested and, last but not least, voluntary schemes are applauded. As a result, further extensions in research and applications of supply chain management have emerged described by the term "reverse logistics." De Brito and Dekker (2004) defined reverse logistics as "the process of planning, implementing and controlling backward flows of raw materials, in process inventory packaging and finished goods, from a manufacturing, distribution or use point, to a point of recovery or point of proper disposal." In this definition both economic and environmental dimensions of reverse logistics are implied, indicating the potential benefits that companies would have by adopting such practices.

Reverse logistics is a multidisciplinary area of research. For example, operations research, environmental analysis, marketing, and informatics have all a significant role to play in order to assist decision-making regarding the design and operation of reverse supply chains. Moreover, reverse logistics is often regarded in conjunction with forward logistics, since they are interrelated. However, the distinguishing characteristics of reverse supply chains introduce new dimensions in decision-making aspects. In particular, the main differences between forward and reverse supply chains, as stated by Fleischmann, Krikke, Dekker, and Flapper (1999) and Krikke, Pappis, Tsoulfas, and Bloemhof-Ruwaard (2002), are the following:

- In contrast to forward supply chains, in reverse supply chains there are a lot of sources of "raw materials" (used products), which may enter the reverse flow at low or no cost at all, and significantly fewer "customers" (recyclers, remanufacturers, etc.).
- The economic value of inputs in reverse supply chains is lower than the one in the case of forward supply chains.
- In the case of reverse supply chains, offer does not follow demand.
- The economic efficiency of reverse supply chains is precarious, since it is not sure that there will be markets to exploit their outputs.
- Reverse supply chains are characterized by higher uncertainty regarding issues like quality, volumes, and composition of reverse flows.

From this perspective, it is important to identify the parameters that may affect reverse logistics operation so that alternative design options are proposed and evaluated. In Tsoulfas, Dasaklis, and Pappis (2007), a first attempt to define and categorize them is presented. Given these parameters, in this chapter we discuss a qualitative evaluation of the reverse supply chain of mobile phones in Greece, as presented by Pappis, Tsoulfas, and Dasaklis (2006). For this purpose, we make use of a Web-based decision support tool that may assist collaborative decision-making (CDM) in conflicting environments, where diverse views, perspectives, and priorities shared among stakeholders have to be considered.

The remainder of the chapter is structured as follows: First, the parameters affecting reverse logistics operation are discussed. Then, the reverse supply chain of mobile phones in Greece is briefly presented. Next, the CDM tool is presented, followed by its illustrative application regarding the reverse supply chain of mobile phones in Greece. Finally, some concluding remarks are outlined.

PARAMETERS AFFECTING REVERSE LOGISTICS OPERATION

Three major categories of parameters that may affect reverse logistics operation are identified: product-dependant, organizational, and social. These parameters, which cannot be addressed independently since they may interact with each other, may form a nonexhaustive basis for analysis in the following decision-making situations:

a. When assessing the current situation regarding the operation of reverse supply chains;

b. When exploring alternative options for the reverse supply chain activities, as well as their interaction with the external environment.

Figure 1. The various flows between the two major sessions of reverse supply activities

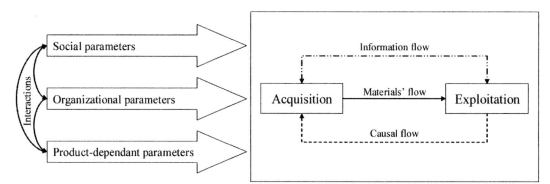

Generally speaking, reverse supply chains may be considered as the conjunction of two major sessions of activities: acquisition and exploitation. The first one refers to the activities that aim at the physical transportation of used products and the second one includes the activities targeting final value extraction or environmentally sound management. Although exploitation follows acquisition when the materials' flows are regarded, it may be considered as a necessary condition for the acquisition in the causal chain. To be more specific, the ability to exploit used products may trigger their acquisition. Otherwise, it would be purposeless to acquire used products without having in mind how to treat them. In addition, information exchange between these sessions is bidirectional and repeated. The relationships between the two major sessions of reverse supply activities are illustrated in Figure 1, where the parameters affecting these operations are regarded as influential factors.

Product-Dependent Parameters

Product-dependant parameters refer to the particular characteristics of products that determine their post-use treatment from a technical and an economic point of view. In particular:

- *The weight or the volume of used products and the infrastructure needed* is a decisive

criterion for the development of reverse logistics activities, since several operations, such as collection, storage, and transportation, may be affected. Generally speaking, large products may require special machinery and equipment for handling, transportation, and so forth, whereas small products may call for big quantities to be collected before being transported.

- *The composition and the technical characteristics of used products* may be another decisive issue, since they determine the ways used products should be treated in order to preserve their value and to prevent them from harming the environment.

- *The way used products are replaced by new ones* is another important parameter for the implementation of reverse logistics. It is obvious that replacements, which occur in the same place or using the same distribution means for the return of used products, have positive effects on the reverse supply chain operation, both from an economic and an environmental perspective.

- *The remaining value of used products* is considered to be a very significant issue for consumers and manufacturers, since they can both benefit from the post-use treatment of used products. Consumers may achieve reduced prices for new products replacing used ones, while manufacturers can extract value from used products by re-furbishing, reusing, or recycling them.

- *Direct reuse or reuse after minor treatment* is a situation commonly perceived in the case of packaging materials and may offer significant benefits to companies and the environment, as the useful life cycle of used products is extended and the production of new ones is avoided.

- *The capability to change the usage of used products or to provide them to different markets (e.g., second hand)* may be another important criterion. Generally, in such situations no special treatments are necessary and the life cycle of products is extended.

Organizational Parameters

Organizational parameters refer to issues regarding the stakeholders involved in the recovery of used products. In particular:

- *The recovery networks structure* is a decisive element for reverse logistics activities. Generally speaking, companies have two options: either they will handle the recovery processes themselves (even by using outsourcing practices), or they will participate in wider networks, usually by financially supporting them. The first option is commonly adopted when companies can achieve significant return rates, whereas the second scheme is preferred, especially when used products are widely dispersed.

- *Asset control policies* that are adopted by some companies can contribute to the effective operation of reverse logistics. Such cases are often met, for example, in the automotive sector and in the electronics industry. By using such practices, companies actually sell services rather than the product itself. As a result, they can have improved control of their products and, at the same time, fulfill their customers' needs,

with whom they can easier communicate.

- *Marketing* is a very important criterion for the implementation of reverse logistics. Companies may participate in campaigns for promoting collection of used products and they can indicate recovery options in the products themselves or in their packages.

- *Economic motivation* is a means used in many industrial sectors in order to involve consumers in the recovery activities. Usually, consumers prepay a certain amount of money as a deposit and they get it back when they return the product or the package to collection facilities.

Social Parameters

Social parameters involve attitudes and values prevailing in societies that may determine practices regarding recovery of used products. In particular:

- *Social habits* may significantly affect the results of reverse logistics activities, since individual attitudes are often affected by mainstreams. Recovery of used products seems to find a more fertile ground in big cities rather than in small communities.

- *Legislation* is a decisive parameter affecting the recovery of used products. In particular, the principle of shared responsibility and the "cradle to grave" perspective have been elevated in legislative frameworks around the world. Furthermore, explicit targets are posed and certain benefits are offered in some cases (e.g., tax relieves, improved financial eligibility, etc.).

- *Social awareness* is a critical issue regarding reverse logistics practices, especially with respect to consumers' attitudes. In developed countries, the environmental standards stemming from social demand are higher. Education is of particular importance regarding this parameter, not solely in schools, but also in corporate environments.

THE REVERSE SUPPLY CHAIN OF MOBILE PHONES IN GREECE

Facts

In 2002, the total number of mobile phones in use worldwide exceeded the number of land-lines (Donner, 2005). According to the International Telecommunication Union the mobile subscribers in 2006 were more than 2.5 billions (International Telecommunication Union, 2007). According to the same source, the subscribers in Greece were around 11 million.

Typically, mobile phones are used for only 1½ years before being replaced (Fishbein, 2002). These obsolete mobile phones are mainly replaced due to fashion trends and the rapid technological improvements, as new features are added in mobile phones. Other reasons for replacement are the incompatibility with a new provider, or the fact that they no longer function. Less than 1% of mobile phones retired and discarded annually are recycled and the majority is accumulated in consumers' desk drawers, store rooms, or other storage, awaiting disposal (Most, 2003). Of this small percentage recovered, some are refurbished and put into use or used for replacement parts. If these options are not possible, some metals are recycled. The refurbishment process can significantly aid to the prolongation of a mobile phone's life cycle and therefore prevent it from early entry into the waste stream. The recycling process keeps discarded phones out of disposal facilities and reduces the need for raw materials used to make new products.

In the case of Greece, Appliances Recycling S.A. is the authorized collective take-back and recycling organisation for all electrical and electronic waste in Greece (Pappis et al., 2006). Actually, all service providers and importers are obliged by law to cooperate with Appliances Recycling

S.A., since they are the only authorized take-back organisation in Greece right now. The program relies on in-store collection and special bins have been installed in retail stores. In addition, several bins have been put on central city spots, as the result of cooperation with local municipalities. Recycling Appliances S.A. aimed at covering 67% of Greek mobile phones population by the end of 2006, while their corresponding target for 2008 is 90% (http://www.electrocycle.gr). The used mobile phones collected have been destined only abroad for further treatment, since no appropriate facilities exist in Greece. In the recycling process, the plastic parts of mobile phones are incinerated and utilised as a fuel to melt the metal mixture. Then metals are separated using electrolytic refining and mechanical (e.g., magnetic segregation) procedures.

The possible routes of used mobile phones and the affected activities in the forward supply chain (grey color) are illustrated in Figure 2.

Major Concerns

Mobile phones contain a great number of metals such as copper, aluminium, iron, nickel, silicon, lead, antimony, beryllium, arsenic, silver, tantalum, and zinc. Some of these metals are toxic and hazardous for mankind and the environment. This variety of valuable metals raises very significant issues regarding the gradual exhaustion of natural resources. In addition, the side effects of this exhaustion are also important. For example, the mining of tantalum has been identified as a serious threat to gorillas clinging to survival in the Democratic Republic of Congo (Macey, 2005). Apart from metals, mobile phones contain also brominated flame retardants, which are used in the plastic parts and cables in order to reduce the risk of fire. When burned in incinerators, these substances have the potential to pollute the air and to pose threats for the workers in recycling facilities, since dioxins and furans can be formed. When buried in landfills, they may leach into soil

Figure 2. The possible routes of used mobile phones and the affected activities in the forward supply chain (grey color)

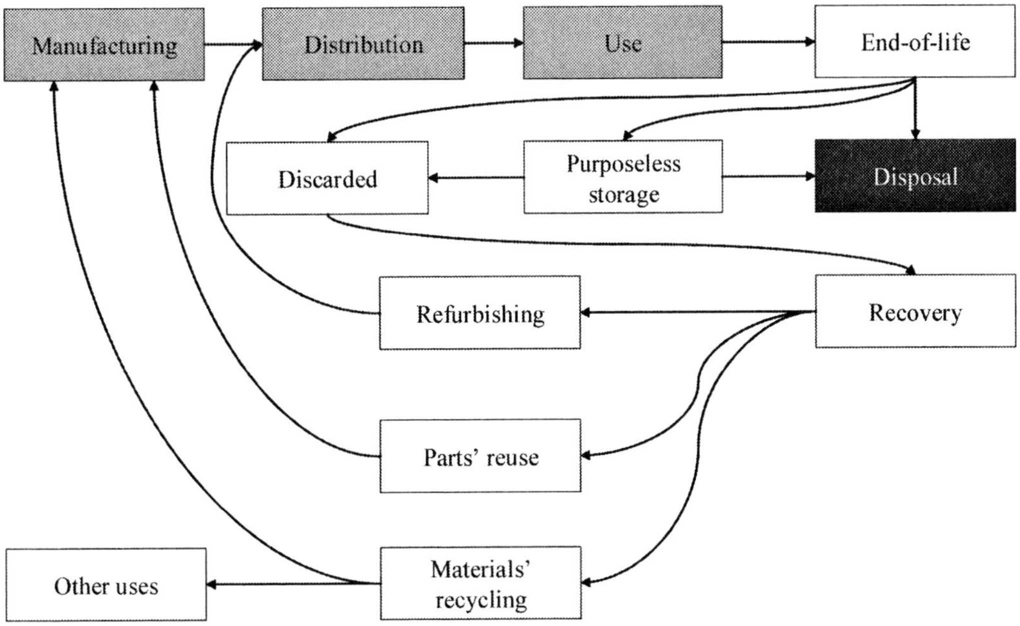

and drinking water.

The environmental impact of the substances mentioned above is of great concern because some of them, like flame retardants and lead, are considered to be persistent, bioaccumulative, and suspected carcinogens. Relative legislation enforcement in the European Union aims at the restriction of the use of certain hazardous substances in electrical and electronic equipment, such as mobile phones (RoHS Directive) (European Union, 2003a). In addition, the WEEE Directive draws the frame regarding the post-use treatment of electrical and electronic equipment (European Union, 2003b).

Apart from the environmental concerns related to the treatment of used mobile phones, there are some important economic issues as well. Indeed, many substances contained in mobile phones are valuable as it is relatively more expensive to acquire them as primary raw materials (e.g., lead, zinc).

It is obvious that decision-making procedures regarding the operation of reverse supply chains get more complicated, due to the involvement of diverse parties. For example, in the case of mobile phones, manufacturers, distributors, service providers, recovery operators, and recyclers would be the participants of such a decision-making situation. Moreover, even different departments of these stakeholders might have diverse views of the situation.

The Decision-Making Situation

From an OEMs' perspective, reverse logistics implementation in the case of mobile phones is determined by their interaction with several stakeholders, as shown in Figure 3.

Thus, reverse logistics managers are responsible for taking into account and coordinating all stakeholders' requirements. Correspondingly, similar actions are necessary among the different departments within a company. Consequently, a conflicting decision-making environment is formed, where the factors "place" and "time" may pose restrictions. Such decision-making

Figure 3. OEMs and their interactions with stakeholders in reverse logistics activities

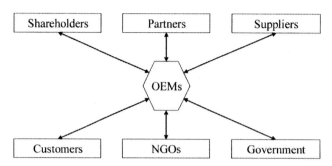

situations may be dealt with Web-based CDM tools and a corresponding approach is presented in the sequel.

A WEB-BASED TOOL FOR COLLABORATIVE DECISION-MAKING

Approaching Conflicting Decision-Making Situations

Choices in decision-making cannot generally be addressed by individuals working alone or even by several people working separately and then merging their pieces of work. Instead, they have to be addressed through collaborative work among stakeholders with diverse views, perspectives, and priorities.

Information and Communication Technology (ICT) infrastructure to support people working in teams has been the subject of interest for quite a long time (Fjermestad & Hiltz, 2000). Such systems aim at facilitating group decision-making processes by providing forums for expression of opinions, as well as qualitative and quantitative tools for aggregating proposals and evaluating their impact on the issue in hand. They may exploit intranet or Internet technologies to connect decision-makers in a way that encourages dialogue and, at the same time, stimulates the exchange of knowledge. Accordingly, recent

computer-based knowledge management systems (KMS) focus on providing a corporate memory, that is, an explicit, disembodied, and persistent representation of the knowledge and information in an organization, as well as mechanisms that improve the sharing and dissemination of knowledge by facilitating interaction and collaboration among the parties involved (Bolloju, Khalifa, & Turban, 2002).

CDM may provide a means for a well-structured decision-making process. Usually, CDM is performed through debates and negotiations among the parties involved. Conflicts of interest are inevitable and support for achieving consensus and compromise is required. Decision-makers may adopt and suggest their own strategy that fulfils some goals at a specific level and may have arguments supporting or against alternative solutions. In addition, they have to confront the existence of insufficient information. Generally speaking, efficient and effective use of information technology in the collection and dissemination of information and knowledge produced by diverse sources, the evaluation of alternative schemes, the construction of shared meanings, and the associated feedback learning process are critical factors for the decision-making process (Clases & Wehner, 2002).

The Web-Based Tool

Given the above issues, a Web-based tool has been implemented that supports the collaboration conducted in decision-making situations, by facilitating the creation, leveraging, and utilization of the relevant knowledge. This tool is based on an argumentative reasoning approach, where discourses about complex problems are considered as social processes and they may result in the formation of groups whose knowledge is clustered around specific views of the problem (Karacapilidis, Adamides, & Pappis, 2004). In addition to providing a platform for group reflection and capturing of organizational memory, this approach augments teamwork in terms of knowledge elicitation, sharing, and construction, thus enhancing the quality of the overall process. This is due to its structured language for conversation and its mechanism for evaluation of alternatives. Taking into account the input provided by the individual experts, the proposed tool constructs an illustrative discourse-based knowledge graph that is composed of the ideas expressed so far, as well as their supporting documents. Moreover, through the integrated decision support mechanisms, experts are continuously informed about the status of each discourse item asserted so far and reflect further on them according to their beliefs and interests on the outcome of the discussion. In addition, the overall approach aids group sense-making and mutual understanding through the collaborative identification and evaluation of diverse opinions.

The proposed tool builds on a server-client network architecture. It is composed of two basic components, namely the *collaboration visualization module* and the *collaborative decision making module*. The former provides a shared Web-based workspace for storing and retrieving the messages and documents deployed by the discussion participants, using the widely accepted XML document format (http://www.w3.org/XML). This module actually provides the interfaces through which participants get connected with the system via Internet (by using a standard Web browser; there is no need of installation of any specific software in order to use the tool). Exploitation of the Web platform renders, among others, low operational cost and easy access to the system. The knowledge base of the system maintains all the above items (messages and documents), which may be considered, appropriately processed and transformed, or even re-used in future discussions. Storage of documents and messages being asserted in an ongoing discussion takes place in an automatic way, upon their insertion in the discussion. On the other hand, retrieval of knowledge is performed through appropriate interfaces, which aid participants in exploring the contents of the knowledge base and exploit previously stored or generated knowledge for their current needs. In such a way, our approach builds a "collective memory" of a particular community. On the other hand, the collaborative decision-making module is responsible for the reasoning and evaluation purposes of the system. Alternative mechanisms for these purposes can be invoked each time, upon the participants' wish and context under consideration. These mechanisms follow well-defined and broadly accepted algorithms (based on diverse decision making approaches, such as multi-criteria decision-making, argumentation-based reasoning, utility theory, risk assessment, etc.), which are stored in the tool's model base.

The basic discourse elements in the proposed tool are *issues, alternatives, positions,* and *preferences.* In particular, issues correspond to problems to be solved, decisions to be made, or goals to be achieved. They are brought up by users and are open to dispute (the root entity of a discourse-based knowledge graph has to be an issue). For each issue, the users may propose alternatives (i.e., solutions to the problem under consideration) that correspond to potential choices. Nested issues, in cases where some alternatives need to be grouped together, are also allowed. Positions are asserted in order to support the selection of a specific course of action (alternative), or avert the users' interest from it by expressing some objection. A position may also refer to another (previously asserted) position, thus arguing in favor or against it. Finally, preferences provide individuals with a qualitative way to weigh reasons for and against the selection of a certain course of action. A preference is a tuple of the form (position, relation, position), where the relation can be "more important than" or "of equal importance to" or "less important than." The use of preferences results in the assignment of various levels of importance to the alternatives in hand. Like the other discourse elements, they are subject to further argumentative discussion.

These four types of elements enable users to contribute their knowledge on the particular problem (by entering issues, alternatives, and positions) and also to express their relevant values, interests and expectations (by entering positions and preferences). In such a way, the tool supports both the rationality-related dimension and the social dimension of the underlying collaborative decision-making process. Moreover, the tool continuously processes the elements entered by the users (by triggering its reasoning mechanisms each time a new element is entered in the graph), thus enabling users to become aware of the elements for which there is (or there is not) sufficient (positive or negative) evidence, and accordingly conduct the discussion in order to reach consensus.

ASSESSING THE OPERATION OF THE REVERSE SUPPLY CHAIN OF MOBILE PHONES IN THE CASE OF GREECE

An illustrative application of the Web-based tool presented earlier is conducted regarding the qualitative assessment of the operation of the reverse supply chain of mobile phones in the case of Greece. In this application, decision-makers A, B, and C explore interventions in the operation of the chain as well as their possible interaction with the external environment. The parameters that affect reverse logistics operations are used as a basis for the discourse. The decision-making process may reveal flaws of current practices as well as improvement potentials and areas to focus on.

Figures 4 and 5 correspond to instances of collaboration concerning the *"Recovery network structure,"* and *"Marketing,"* respectively. In these instances, the stakeholders participate in an argumentation-based decision-making process. More specifically, in the instance shown in Figure 4, the issue under consideration is *"Priorities in improving the recovery network's structure,"* while three alternatives, namely *"Extended cooperation with local municipalities," "Collection bins in super markets,"* and *"Collection programs in schools,"* have been proposed so far (by C, A, and B, respectively). The three stakeholders have argued about them by expressing positions speaking in favor or against them.

For instance, *"People visit super markets at least once a week"* is a position (asserted by A) that argues in favor of the second alternative, while *"It is time-consuming"* is a position (asserted by B) that argues against the first alternative. As also shown in Figures 4 and 5, argumentation can be conducted in multiple levels. Furthermore, users may also assert preferences about positions already expressed. As shown in Figure 5, user C has expressed a preference concerning the relative importance between the positions *"It is very expensive to initiate a nationwide campaign"* and *"The timing is excellent,"* arguing that the first position is of bigger importance for him. Users may also express their arguments in favor or against a preference.

When clicking on a discourse item, detailed information about it is provided in a dedicated window of the basic interface of the tool. More specifically, this part contains information about the user who submitted the selected discussion element, its submission date, any comments that the user may have inserted, as well as links to related Web pages and multimedia documents that

Figure 4. Instances of collaboration concerning "Priorities in improving the recovery network's structure"

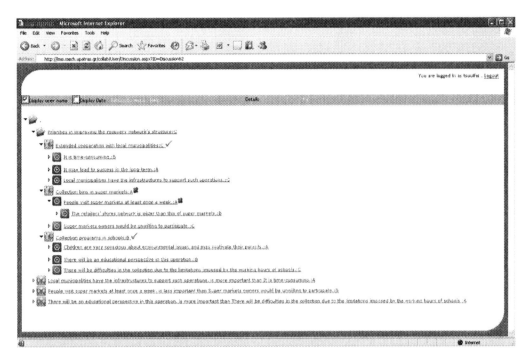

Figure 5. Instances of collaboration concerning "Marketing interventions"

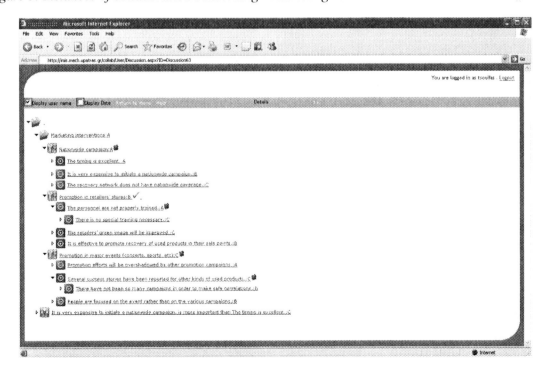

the user may have uploaded to the tool in order to justify this element and aid his/her peers in their contemplation.

Further to the argumentation-based structuring of a discourse, the tool integrates a reasoning mechanism that determines the status of each discourse item in order to keep users aware of the discourse outcome. More specifically, alternatives, positions, and preferences of a graph have an *activation label* (it can be *"active"* or *"inactive"*) indicating their current status (inactive entries are indicated with a red "x"). This label is calculated according to the argumentation underneath and the type of evidence specified for them. In the instance of Figure 4, the position *"People visit super markets at least once a week"* is inactive because, according to the argumentation rule holding for this specific discussion, it has been defeated by the position *"The retailers' stores network is wider than this of super markets."* Activation in the tool is a recursive procedure; a change of the activation label of an element is propagated upwards in the discourse graph. Depending on the status of positions and preferences, the mechanism goes through a scoring procedure for the alternatives of the issue. A detailed presentation of more technical details concerning the argumentation-based reasoning and scoring mechanisms of the tool can be found in Karacapilidis and Papadias (2001).

At each discourse instance, the tool informs users about what is the most prominent (according to the underlying argumentation) alternative solution (this is shown by a green "tick" sign). In the instance shown in Figure 4, *"Extended cooperation with local municipalities"* and *"Collection programs in schools"* are equally justified as best solutions, while in the instance shown in Figure 5 *"Promotion in retailers' stores"* is the better justified solution so far. However, this may change upon the type of the future argumentation; each time an alternative is affected during the discussion, the issue it belongs to is updated, since another alternative solution may be indicated by the tool.

CONCLUSION

The introduction of reverse logistics in supply chain management has created new decision-making dimensions. Consequently, parameters that may affect the operation of reverse supply chains should be evaluated. In this chapter, a qualitative approach has been discussed with respect to such parameters, aiming at facilitating and augmenting decision-making in reverse supply chains. In such cases, several stakeholders get involved, including governments, producers, distributors, and customers. As a result, decision-making procedures get more complicated due to increased levels of conflicts of interests but also due to practical reasons. For example, it is not always easy to get all stakeholders together in a round table. As it has been illustrated in this chapter, ICT may support decision-making procedures in conflicting environments by providing the means to structure dialogue, disseminate information, and last but not least, facilitate the associated reasoning process.

FUTURE RESEARCH DIRECTIONS

The parameters affecting reverse logistics operation may guide decision-makers towards identifying possible modifications in supply chain activities as well as in other corporate issues, such as marketing and supplier selection. Further research should be devoted to explore the interactions among these parameters and the ways they affect the reverse supply chains' operation and success. In addition, research efforts should also focus on how reverse supply chains may interact with forward supply chains and on relevant expedient strategies that aim at making the extended supply chains more efficient. Moreover, the qualitative evaluation of the reverse supply chains of different products may reveal the determinant parameters for each case, helping to create a body of knowledge based on thorough observations. In particular, it is important to identify the circumstances under which reverse supply chains are impeded and the options to improve their operation. Such knowledge may be exploited in developing organizational memory, a process which, beyond storing individual and collective knowledge, is related to organizational learning, decision-making, and competitive capability issues.

Apart from economic criteria, additional criteria (environmental, social, etc.) get increasingly involved in decision-making problems, leading to more complex decision-making situations. Moreover, such problems may not be usually addressed by formal models or methodologies. Instead, an argumentative practical reasoning approach seems to offer a more convenient solution. Thus, decision-making tools should focus on facilitating the cooperation of the different parties involved towards well-structured decision-making processes. The corresponding technologies should further exploit the advances in ICT in order to deliver applications of enhanced performance to decision-makers, while efficiently and effectively addressing communication and collaboration requirements. In particular, it is important to develop a more human-centric view of the problem, which appropriately structures and manages the underlying human interaction. The CDM tool discussed previously in this chapter may be exploited in order to retrieve useful information and knowledge, as well as to reason according to previous cases or predefined rules. The proposed tool may be enhanced with intelligent agent technologies, which are able to facilitate a variety of decision-makers' tasks and actions by acting on their behalf, as well as to automate system's processes.

ACKNOWLEDGMENT

The project is co-funded by the European Social Fund and national resources - EPEAEK II.

REFERENCES

Bolloju, N., Khalifa, M., & Turban, E. (2002). Integrating knowledge management into enterprise environments for the next generation decision support. *Decision Support Systems, 33*(2), 163–176. doi:10.1016/S0167-9236(01)00142-7

Clases, C., & Wehner, T. (2002). Steps across the border: Cooperation, knowledge production and systems design. *Computer Supported Cooperative Work, 11*(1/2), 39–54. doi:10.1023/A:1015207530896

de Brito, M. P., & Dekker, R. (2004). A framework for reverse logistics. In R. Dekker, K. Inderfurth, L. N. van Wassenhove, & M. Fleischmann (Eds.), *Quantitative approaches to reverse logistics* (pp. 3-27). Berlin, Germany: Springer-Verlag.

Donner, J. (2005, June 7-8). *Research approaches to mobile use in the developing world: A review of the literature.* Paper presented at the International Conference on Mobile Communication and Asian Modernities, Hong Kong.

European Union. (2003a). Directive 2002/95/EC of the European Parliament and of the Council of 27 January 2003 on the restriction of the use of certain hazardous substances in electrical and electronic equipment. *Official Journal of the European Union.*

European Union. (2003b). Directive 2002/96/EC of the European Parliament and of the Council of 27 January 2003 on waste electrical and electronic equipment (WEEE). *Official Journal of the European Union.*

Fishbein, B. K. (2002). *Waste in the wireless world: The challenge of cell phones.* INFORM Inc., New York, USA.

Fjermestad, J., & Hiltz, S. R. (2000). Group support systems: A descriptive evaluation of case and field studies. *Journal of Management Information Systems, 17*(3), 115–159.

Fleischmann, M., Krikke, H. R., Dekker, R., & Flapper, S. D. P. (1999). *Logistics network (re)-design for product recovery and reuse* (Management Report 17). Rotterdam, The Netherlands: Erasmus University of Rotterdam.

International Telecommunication Union. (2007). *Basic indicators: Population, GDP, total telephone subscribers and total telephone subscribers per 100 people.*

Karacapilidis, N., Adamides, E., & Pappis, C. P. (2004, September 20-25). An IS framework to support the collaborative design of supply chains. In M. Negoita, R. J. Howlett, & L. C. Jain (Eds.), *Knowledge-based intelligent information and engineering systems: Proceedings of the 8th International Conference, KES 2004,* Wellington, New Zealand, Part II (pp. 62-70). Berlin/Heidelberg, Germany: Springer-Verlag.

Karacapilidis, N., & Papadias, D. (2001). Computer supported argumentation and collaborative decision making: The HERMES system. *Information Systems, 26*(4), 259–277. doi:10.1016/S0306-4379(01)00020-5

Krikke, H. R., Pappis, C. P., Tsoulfas, G. T., & Bloemhof-Ruwaard, J. (2002). Extended design principles for closed loop supply chains: Optimising economic, logistic and environmental performance. In A. Klose, M. G. Speranza, & L. N. Van Wassenhove (Eds.), *Quantitative approaches to distribution logistics and supply chain management* (pp. 61-74). Berlin/Heidelberg, Germany: Springer-Verlag.

Macey, R. (2005, March 10). Mobile phones kill great apes. *Sydney Morning Herald.*

Most, E. (2003). *Calling all cell phones: Collection, reuse, and recycling programs in the U.S.* INFORM Inc., New York, USA.

Pappis, C. P., Tsoulfas, G. T., & Dasaklis, T. (2006, July 2-5). *Assessing alternative reverse logistics policies for the recovery of used mobile phones.* Paper presented at the EURO XXI Conference, Reykjavik, Iceland.

Tsoulfas, G. T., Dasaklis, T., & Pappis, C. P. (2007, May 9-11). Identifying success factors for reverse logistics activities. In *Proceedings of the 2nd International Conference ECO-X 2007,* Vienna, Austria (pp. 39-46).

ADDITIONAL READING

Adamides, E., & Karacapilidis, N. (2006). A knowledge centred framework for collaborative business process modelling. *Business Process Management Journal, 12*(5), 557–575. doi:10.1108/14637150610690993

Ahn, H. J., Lee, H. J., Chob, K., & Park, S. J. (2005). Utilizing knowledge context in virtual collaborative work. *Decision Support Systems, 39*(4), 563–582. doi:10.1016/j.dss.2004.03.005

Álvarez-Gil, M. J., Berrone, P., Husillos, F. J., & Lado, N. (2007). Reverse logistics, stakeholders' influence, organizational slack, and managers' posture. *Journal of Business Research, 60*(5), 463–473. doi:10.1016/j.jbusres.2006.12.004

Angell, L. C., & Klassen, R. D. (1999). Integrating environmental issues into the mainstream: An agenda for research in operations management. *Journal of Operations Management, 17*(5), 575–598. doi:10.1016/S0272-6963(99)00006-6

Boons, F. (2002). Greening products: A framework for product chain management. *Journal of Cleaner Production, 10*(5), 495–505. doi:10.1016/S0959-6526(02)00017-3

Bowen, F. E., Cousins, P. D., Lamming, R. C., & Faruk, A. C. (2001). The role of supply management capabilities in green supply. *Production and Operations Management, 10*(2), 174–189.

Chouinard, M., D'Amours, S., & Aït-Kadi, D. (2005). Integration of reverse logistics activities within a supply chain information system. *Computers in Industry, 56*(1), 105–124. doi:10.1016/j.compind.2004.07.005

Courtney, J. (2001). Decision making and knowledge management in inquiring organizations: Toward a new decision-making paradigm for DSS. *Decision Support Systems, 31*(1), 17–38. doi:10.1016/S0167-9236(00)00117-2

Dowlatshahi, S. (2000). Developing a theory of reverse logistics. *Interfaces, 30*(3), 143–155. doi:10.1287/inte.30.3.143.11670

Eichner, T., & Pethig, R. (2001). Product design and efficient management of recycling and waste treatment. *Journal of Environmental Economics and Management, 41*(1), 109–134. doi:10.1006/jeem.2000.1126

Evangelou, C., Karacapilidis, N., & Tzagarakis, M. (2006). On the development of knowledge management services for collaborative decision making. *Journal of Computers, 1*(6), 19–28.

Fleischmann, M., Krikke, H. R., Dekker, R., & Flapper, S. D. P. (2000). A characterization of logistics networks for product recovery. *Omega, 28*(6), 653–666. doi:10.1016/S0305-0483(00)00022-0

Forgionne, G., Gupta, J., & Mora, M. (2002). Decision making support systems: Achievements, challenges and opportunities. In M. Mora, G. Forgionne, & J. Gupta (Eds.), *Decision making support systems: Achievements and challenges for the new decade* (pp. 392-403). Hershey, PA: Idea Group.

Georgiadis, P., & Vlachos, D. (2004). The effect of environmental parameters on product recovery. *European Journal of Operational Research, 157*(2), 449–464. doi:10.1016/S0377-2217(03)00203-0

Gungor, A., & Gupta, S. M. (1999). Issues in environmentally conscious manufacturing and product recovery: A survey. *Computers & Industrial Engineering, 36*(4), 811–853. doi:10.1016/S0360-8352(99)00167-9

Handfield, R., Sroufe, R., & Walton, S. (2005). Integrating environmental management and supply chain strategies. *Business Strategy and the Environment, 14*(1), 1–19. doi:10.1002/bse.422

Karacapilidis, N. (2006). An overview of future challenges of decision support technologies. In J. Gupta, G. Forgionne, & M. Mora (Eds.), *Intelligent decision-making support systems: Foundations, applications and challenges* (pp. 385-399). London: Springer-Verlag.

Khanna, M., & Anton, W. Q. (2002). Corporate environmental management: Regulatory and market-based pressures. *Land Economics, 78*(4), 539–558. doi:10.2307/3146852

Liebowitz, J., & Megbolugbe, I. (2003). A set of frameworks to aid the project manager in conceptualizing and implementing knowledge management initiatives. *International Journal of Project Management, 21*(3), 189–198. doi:10.1016/S0263-7863(02)00093-5

Malhotra, Y. (2005). Integrating knowledge management technologies in organizational business processes: Getting real time enterprises to deliver real business performance. *Journal of Knowledge Management, 9*(1), 7–28. doi:10.1108/13673270510582938

Mora, M., Forgionne, G., Gupta, J., Cervantes, F., & Gelman, O. (2003, September 3-5). A framework to assess intelligent decision-making support systems. In V. Palade, R. J. Howlett, & L. C. Jain (Eds.), *Knowledge-based intelligent information and engineering systems: Proceedings of the 7th International Conference, KES 2003, Oxford, UK, Part II* (pp. 59-65). Berlin/Heidelberg: Springer-Verlag.

Muckstadt, J., Murray, D., Rappold, J., & Collins, D. (2001). Guidelines for collaborative supply chain system design and operation. *Information Systems Frontiers*, 3(4), 427–453. doi:10.1023/A:1012824820895

Nonaka, I. (1994). A dynamic theory of organizational knowledge creation. *Organization Science*, 5(1), 14–37. doi:10.1287/orsc.5.1.14

Provis, C. (2004). Negotiation, persuasion and argument. *Argumentation*, 18(1), 95–112. doi:10.1023/B:ARGU.0000014868.08915.2a

Ravi, V., & Shankar, R. (2005). Analysis of interactions among the barriers of reverse logistics. *Technological Forecasting and Social Change*, 72(8), 1011–1029. doi:10.1016/j.techfore.2004.07.002

Richey, R. G., Chen, H., Genchev, S. E., & Daugherty, P. J. (2005). Developing effective reverse logistics programs. *Industrial Marketing Management*, 34(8), 830–840. doi:10.1016/j.indmarman.2005.01.003

Rogers, D. S., & Tibben-Lembke, R. S. (1999). *Going backwards: Reverse logistics trends and practices*. Pittsburgh: Reverse Logistics Executive Council.

Shapiro, J. (2001). Modeling and IT perspectives on supply chain integration. *Information Systems Frontiers*, 3(4), 455–464. doi:10.1023/A:1012876804965

Shim, J. P., Warkentin, M., Courtney, J. F., Power, D. J., Sharda, R., & Carlsson, C. (2002). Past, present and future of decision support technology. *Decision Support Systems*, 33(2), 111–126. doi:10.1016/S0167-9236(01)00139-7

Tibben-Lembke, R. S., & Rogers, D. S. (2002). Differences between forward and reverse logistics in a retail environment. *Supply Chain Management*, 7(5), 271–282. doi:10.1108/13598540210447719

Tsoulfas, G. T., & Pappis, C. P. (2006). Environmental principles applicable to supply chains design and operation. *Journal of Cleaner Production*, 14(18), 1593–1602. doi:10.1016/j.jclepro.2005.05.021

This work was previously published in Web-Based Green Products Life Cycle Management Systems: Reverse Supply Chain Utilization, edited by H. Wang, pp. 401-415, copyright 2005 by Information Science Reference (an imprint of IGI Global).

Chapter 3.5
WSBen:
A Web Services Discovery and Composition Benchmark Toolkit[1]

Seog-Chan Oh
General Motors R&D Center, USA

Dongwon Lee
The Pennsylvania State University, USA

ABSTRACT

In this article, a novel benchmark toolkit, WSBen, for testing web services discovery and composition algorithms is presented. The WSBen includes: (1) a collection of synthetically generated web services files in WSDL format with diverse data and model characteristics; (2) queries for testing discovery and composition algorithms; (3) auxiliary files to do statistical analysis on the WSDL test sets; (4) converted WSDL test sets that conventional AI planners can read; and (5) a graphical interface to control all these behaviors. Users can fine-tune the generated WSDL test files by varying underlying network models. To illustrate the application of the WSBen, in addition, we present case studies from three domains: (1) web service composition; (2) AI planning; and (3) the laws of networks in Physics community. It is our hope that WSBen will provide useful insights in evaluating the performance of web services discovery and composition algorithms. The WSBen toolkit is available at: http://pike.psu.edu/sw/wsben/.

INTRODUCTION

A *Web Service* is a set of related functionalities that can be loosely coupled with other services programmatically through the Web. Examples of web applications using Web services include weather forecasting, credit check, and travel agency programs. As a growing number of Web services are available on the Web and in organizations, finding and composing the right set of Web services become ever more important. As a result, in recent years, a plethora of research work and products on Web-service discovery and composition problems have appeared[2]. In addition, the Web service research community has hosted open competition programs (e.g., ICEBE05[3], EEE06[4]) to solicit algorithms and software to discover pertinent Web services and compose them to make value-added functionality. Despite all this attention, however, there have been very few test environments available for evaluating such algorithms and software. The lack of such a testing environment with flexible features hinders the development of new composition algorithms and validation of the proposed ones. Therefore, the need for a benchmark arises naturally to evaluate and compare algorithms and software for the Web-service discovery and composition problems. As desiderata for such a benchmark, it must have (a large number of) web services in the standard-based WSDL files and test queries that can represent diverse scenarios and situations that emphasize different aspects of various Web-service application domains. Often, however, test environments used in research and evaluation have skewed test cases that do not necessarily capture real scenarios. Consider the following example.

Example 1 (Motivating) *Let us use the following notations: A Web service w ∈ W, specified in a WSDL file, can be viewed as a collection of operations, each of which in turn consists of input and output parameters. When an operation op has input parameters $op^i = \{p_1,...,p_n\}$ and output parameters $op^o = \{q_1,...,q_n\}$, we denote the operation by $op(op^i, op^o)$. Furthermore, each parameter is viewed as a pair of (name, type). We denote the name and type of a parameter p by p.name and p.type, respectively. For the motivating observation, we first downloaded 1,544 raw WSDL files that Fan and Kambhampati (2005) gathered from real-world Web services registries such as XMethods or BindingPoint. We refer to the data set as PUB06. For the purpose of preprocessing PUB06, first, we conducted WSDL validation according to WSDL standard, where 874 invalid WSDL files are removed and 670 files are left out. Second, we removed 101 duplicated*

WSDL files at operation level, yielding 569 valid WSDL files. Finally, we conducted type flattening and data cleaning processes subsequently. The type flattening process is to extract atomic types from user-defined complex types using type hierarchy of XML schema. This process helps find more compatible parameter faster. Details are found in (Kil, Oh, & Lee, 2006). The final step is the data cleansing to improve the quality of parameters. For instance, substantial number of output parameters (16%) was named "return", "result", or "response" which is too ambiguous for clients. However, often, their more precise underline meaning can be derived from contexts. For instance, if the output parameter named "result" belongs to the operation named "getAddress'", then the "result" is in fact "Address". In addition, often, naming follows apparent pattern such as getFooFromBar or searchFooByBar. Therefore, to replace names of parameters or operations by more meaningful ones, we removed spam tokens like "get" or "by" as much as we could.

We measured how many distinct parameters each WSDL file contained. Suppose that given a parameter p ∈ P, we denote the number of occurrences of p.name as #(p.name). That is, #("pwd") indicates the number of occurrences of the parameter with name of "pwd". Figure 1 illustrates #(p.name) distributions of PUB06 and the ICEBE05 test set, where the x-axis is #(p. name) and the y-axis is the number of parameters with the same #(p.name) value. The distribution of PUB06 has no humps. We also plotted a power-function, over the #(p.name) distribution, and found that the exponent is 1.1394. Although 1.1394 does not suffice the requirement to be the power law (Denning, 2004), the distribution is skewed enough to be seen as the Zipf-like distribution. Indeed, the parameters such as "license key", "start date", "end date," or "password" have a large #(p.name) value, while most parameters appear just once. This observation also implies the existence of hub parameters, which appear in Web services frequently, and serve important roles on the inter-connections between Web services. On the contrary, the distribution of ICEBE05 test set has four humps equally at around 1, 100, 200, and 800 with the highest value at third hump. This distribution shape differs considerably from PUB06, the real public Web services. This implies that the test environments of ICEBE05 do not necessarily capture characteristics of real Web services.

In conclusion, as demonstrated in the example, our claim is that *any Web-services discovery and composition solutions must be evaluated under diverse configurations of Web services networks* including two cases of Figure 1. However, to

our best knowledge, there have been no publicly available benchmark tools. To address these needs and shortcomings, therefore, we developed the *WSBen* - a <u>W</u>eb-<u>S</u>ervice discovery and composition <u>Ben</u>chmark tool. The main contributions of WSBen is to provide diverse Web service test sets based on three network models such as "random", "small-world", and "scale-free" types. These three network models have been shown to model many real-world networks sufficiently (Albert & Barabasi, 2002). We also present three use cases in different communities to demonstrate the application of WSBen. In addition, we propose a flexible framework, by which we can study real Web service networks, and establish the design

Figure 1. #(p.name) distributions. (left) PUB05. (right) ICEBE05.

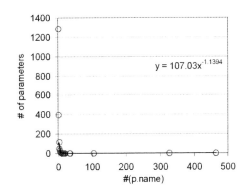
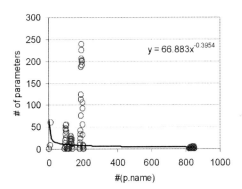

Table 1. Summary of notation

Notation	Meaning
w, W	Web service, set of Web services
p, P	Parameter, set of parameters
r, r^i, r^o	Request, initial and goal parameter sets of r
$G_p(V_p, E_p)$	Parameter node network
$G_{op}(V_{op}, E_{op})$	Operation node network
$G_{sw}(V_{sw}, E_{sw})$	Web service node network
$G_{op}^f(V_{op}^f, E_{op}^f)$	Full-matching operation node network
$G_{cl}(V_{cl}, E_{cl})$	Parameter cluster network
$g_{r^i}(p)$	Minimum cost of achieving $p \in P$ from r^i in G_p
xTS	WSBen's 5-tuple input framework (e.g., *baTS*, *erTS* and *nwsTS* are instances)

foundation of WSBen. As a whole, this article is based on two of our earlier works (Kil et al., 2006; Oh, Kil, Lee, & Kumara, 2006). Extended from the previous works, this article describes how WSBen is designed and works to generate test sets from the software architecture perspective, and furthermore introduces three use cases to highlight the practical benefits of WSBen. Table 1 summarizes important notations used in this article.

This article is organized as follows. First, in the background section, we review concepts and techniques required for the WSBen development, especially focusing on the complex network theory. Second, in the related works section, we discuss related studies in the literature as well as surveying existing world-wide challenges with regard to Web services and Semantic Web. Third, in the overview of WSBen section, we present WSBen with its design concept, test set generation mechanism, key functions and characteristics. Fourth, in the use cases of WSBen section, we illustrate how WSBen can be exploited to obtain research benefits, especially by demonstrating three use cases. We expect three use cases enough to provide vigorous experiments and evaluation of our WSBen. Finally, conclusions are provided.

BACKGROUND

In this section, we review prerequisite techniques and concepts required to build WSBen. First, we revisit the definition and complexity of Web-service discovery and composition problems. Second, we introduce three complex network topologies based on which WSBen is designed to populate WSDL test files. Finally, we explain our conceptual methodology to project a bipartite Web-service network consisting of three distinct nodes (parameter, operation, and Web service) and heterogeneous arc types into three distinct Web-service networks, each of which consists of single node and uniform arc. The main benefit

of projecting Web-service networks is that it can allow for straightforward analysis on referred network's characteristics. Throughout this article, we will use our conceptual Web-service network concept in order to analyze real public Web-service networks as well as WSDL test file sets generated by WSBen.

Web-Service Discovery and Composition

Suppose that a Web service w has one operation so that a Web service can be considered as an operation, and input and output parameter sets of w are denoted by w^i and w^o, respectively. When one has a request r that has initial input parameters r^i and desired output parameters r^o, one needs to find a Web service w that can fulfill such that (1) $r^i \supseteq w^i$ and (2) $r^o \subseteq w^o$. Finding a Web service that can fulfill r alone is referred to as *Web-service discovery* (WSD) problem. When it is impossible for one Web service to fully satisfy r, on the other hand, one has to compose multiple Web services $\{w_1, w_2,...,w_n\}$, such that (1) for all $w_k \in \{w_1, w_2,...,w_n\}$, w_k^i can be applicable when w_k^i is required at a particular stage in composition, and (2) $(r^i \cup w_1^o \cup w_2^o...\cup w_n^o) \supseteq r^o$. This problem is often called as *Web-service composition* (WSC) problem. In addition, one can also consider different matching schemes from the operation perspective – "partial" and "full" matching. In general, given w_1 and w_2, if w_1 can be invoked at the current information state and $w_1^o \supseteq w_2^i$, then w_1 can "fully" match w_2. On the other hand, if w_1 cannot fully match w_2, but w_1 can match a subset of w_2, then w_1 can "partially" match w_2. When only full matching is considered in the WSC problem, it can be seen as a single-source shortest path problem whose computational complexity is known as polynomial (Bertsekas, 2000). On the other hand, when both full and partial matching must be considered concurrently, the problem becomes a decision problem to determine the existence of a solution of k operators or less for propositional STRIPS planning, with restrictions on negation in pre- and post-conditions (Nilsson, 2001). Its computational complexity is proved to be NP-complete (Bylander, 1994). Therefore, when the number of Web services to search is not small, finding an optimal solution to the WSC problem (i.e., a chain of Web services to invoke) is prohibitively expensive, leading to approximate algorithms instead.

Complex Network Models

There are many empirical systems to form complex networks such as the scale-free network and the small-world network, in which nodes signify the elements of the system and edges represent the interactions between them.

Definition 1 (Random network) *A network is defined as the random network on N nodes, if each pair of nodes is connected with probability p. As a result, edges are randomly placed among a fixed set of nodes. The random network can be constructed by means of the Erdos-Renyi's random-graph model (Erdos, Graham, & Nesetril, 1996).*

Definition 2 (Regular network) $Rg_{(N,k)}$ *is defined as the regular network on N nodes, if node i is adjacent to nodes $[(i+j)\bmod N]$ and $[(i-j)\bmod N]$ for $1 \leq j \leq k$, where k is the number of valid edge of each node. If $k = N - 1$, $Rg_{(N,k)}$ becomes the complete N-nodes graph, where every node is adjacent to all the other $N - 1$ nodes.*

We can define some metrics to quantify the characteristic properties of the complex networks as follows:

- L: The average shortest distance between reachable pairs of nodes, where the distance between nodes refers to the number of hops between the nodes. $L(p)$ is defined as L of the randomly rewired Watts-Strogatz graph (Watts & Strogatz, 1998) with probability p. L_{random} is identical to $L(1)$.

- C: The average clustering coefficient. Suppose that for a node i with v_i neighbor,

$$C_i = \frac{2E_i}{v_i(v_i - 1)},$$

where E_i is the number of edges between v_i neighbors of i. C is the average clustering coefficient C_i for a network. $C(p)$ is defined as C of the randomly rewired Watts-Strogatz graph with probability p. C_{random} is identical to $C(1)$.

Definition 3 (Small-world network) *Small-world networks are characterized by a highly clustered topology like regular lattices and the small network diameter, where the network diameter suggests the longest shortest distance between nodes. Specifically, small-world networks are $C \succ C_{random}$ and $L \approx L_{random}$ (Delgado, 2002).*

By using the Watts-Strogatz model (Watts, 1999; Watts & Strogatz, 1998), we can construct networks that have the small-world properties. The model depends on two parameters, connectivity (k) and randomness (p), given the desired size of the graph (N). The Watts-Strogatz model starts with a $Rg_{(N,k)}$ and then every edge is rewired at random with probability p; for every edge (i, j), we decide whether we change j node (the destination node of (i, j)) with probability p. The Watts-Strogatz model leads to different graphs according to the different p as follows:

- When $p = 0$, an $Rg_{(N,k)}$ is built.
- When $p = 1$, a completely random network is built.

Otherwise, with $0 < p < 1$, each edge (i, j) is reconnected with probability p to a new node k that is chosen at random (no self-links allowed). If the new edge (i, k) is added, the (i, j) is removed from the graph. The long-range connections (short-cuts) generated by this process decrease the distance between the nodes. For intermediate values of *p*, there is the "small-world" region, where the graph is highly clustered yet has a small average path length.

Definition 4 (Scale-free network) *Networks are called scale-free networks if the number of nodes that have v number of neighbor nodes is proportional to* $P_w(v) \propto v^{(-\gamma)}$, *where γ is typically greater than two with no humps.*

Barabasi and Albert provided several extended models (Albert, Jeong, & Barabasi, 1999; Delgado, 2002) to provide the scale-free properties. The extended model uses an algorithm to build graphs that depend on four parameters: m_0 (initial number of nodes), *m* (number of links added and/or rewired at every step of the algorithm), *p* (probability of adding links), *q* (probability of edge rewiring). The procedure starts with m_0 isolated nodes and performs one of the following three actions at every step:

- With the probability of *p*, $m (\leq m_0)$ new links are added. The two nodes are picked randomly. The starting point of the link is chosen uniformly, and the end point of the new link is chosen according to the following probability distribution:

$$\Pi_i = \frac{v_i + 1}{\sum_j (v_j + 1)} \quad (1)$$

where Π_i is the probability of selecting the *i* node, and v_i is the number of edges of node *i*.
The process is repeated *m* times.
- With the probability of *q*, *m* edges are rewired. For this purpose, *i* node and its link l_{ij} are chosen at random. The link is deleted. Instead, another node *z* is selected according

to the probabilities of Equation (1), and the new link l_{iz} is added.
- With the probability of $1 - p - q$, a new node with *m* links is added. These new links connect the new node to *m* other nodes chosen according to the probabilities of Equation (1).
- Once the desired number *N* nodes are obtained, the algorithm stops. The graphs generated by this algorithm are scale-free graphs, and the edges of the graphs are constructed such that the correlations among edges do not form. When *p* = *q*, the algorithm results in a graph, whose connectivity distribution can be approximated by

$$P(v) \propto (v+1)^{-\frac{2m(1-p)+1-2p}{m}+1} \quad (2)$$

where *v* is the number of edges.

Diverse Web Service Network Models

A set of Web services form a network (or graph). Depending on the policy to determine nodes and edges of the network, there are varieties: Web service level (i.e., coarse granularity), operation level, and parameter level (i.e., fine granularity) models. The graph at the middle of Figure 2 has a bipartite graph structure and consists of three distinct kinds of vertices (i.e., parameter, operation, and web-service node) and directed arcs between bipartite nodes (i.e., operation nodes and parameter nodes). An edge incident from a parameter node to an operation node means that the parameter is one of the inputs of the corresponding operation. Reversely, an edge incident from an operation node to a parameter means that the parameter is one of the outputs of the corresponding operation. The graph has two Web services, labeled `WS1` and `WS2`. `WS1` has two operations `Op11` and `Op12`, and `WS2` has one operation, `Op21`, respectively. There are seven parameters, labeled `P1` to `P7`. According to the node granularity, we can project the upper graph into three different Web service networks.

- Parameter-Node Network: A graph $G_p(V_p, E_p)$, where V_p is a set of all parameter nodes and E_p is a set of edges. An edge (p_i, p_j) is directly incident from input parameters $p_i \in V_p$ to output parameters $p_j \in V_p$, where there is an operation that has an input parameter matching p_i and an output parameter matching p_j. For example, `P1→Op11→P3` in the upper graph is projected into `P1→P3` in the parameter node network. Figure 3 shows the parameter node network for PUB06 and the ICEBE05 test set.

- Operation-Node Network: A graph $G_{op}(V_{op}, E_{op})$, where V_{op} is a set of all operation nodes, and E_{op} is a set of edges. An edge (op_i, op_j) is incident from operation $op_i \in V_p$ to operation $op_j \in V_p$, here op_i can fully or partially match op_j. For example, `Op11` partially matches `Op12` which, in turn, fully matches `Op21` in the upper graph. Therefore, `Op11→Op12→Op21` can be shown in the operation node network. In particular, the fully matching operation node network, G_{op}^f has only `Op12→Op21`.

- Web-service Node Network: A graph $G_{ws}(V_{ws}, E_{ws})$, where V_{ws} is a set of all web-service nodes, and E_{ws} is a set of edges. An edge (ws_i, ws_j) is incident from web-service node $ws_i \in V_{ws}$, to $ws_j \in V_{ws}$, where there is at least one edge between any operation in ws_i and any operation in ws_j. For example, since `WS1` possesses `Op12` and `WS2` possesses `Op21` in the upper graph, `WS1→WS2` appears in the Web service node network.

RELATED WORKS

Constantinescu, Faltings, and Binder (2004)

Figure 2. Web services networks: (a) WSDLs, (b) Conceptual Web service network, (c) Web service networks from diverse models, (d) Parameter node network, G_p, (e) Operation node network, G_{op}, (f) Fully invocable operation node network, G_{op}^f, and (g) Web service node network, G_{ws}

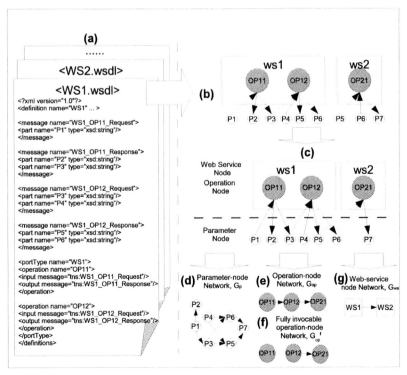

Figure 3. Diverse parameter networks. (left) PUB05. (right) ICEBE05

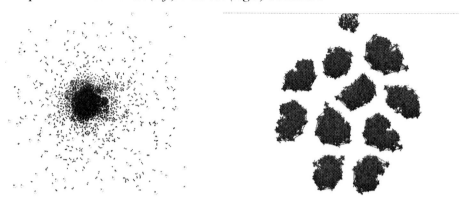

proposed a scalable syntactic test bed where Web services are generated as transformation between sets of terms in two application domains. For doing that, they first defined parameter sets corresponding to application domains and then, connected those parameter sets randomly and constructed a service graph which structure (i.e., nodes and arcs) is similar to the parameter cluster network of WSBen. However, WSBen takes a significant different approach to construct its parameter cluster networks in that WSBen does not simply connect parameter sets at random but simulates topologies of real Web service networks. WSBen is inspired by extensive studies on real Web services, and therefore is designed to support various Web service network topologies and distributions. As a result, WSBen can present more realistic testing situation for researchers who want to test their Web service discovery or composition algorithms than that of Constantinescu et al. (2004).

XMark (XMark, 2006) is an XML benchmark suite that can help identify the list of functions which an ideal benchmark should support. WSBen uses XMark as a reference model to identify necessary functions to simplify the testing process. One feature that is offered by XMark but not by WSBen is the provision of solutions to queries. In other words, XMark provides queries and their corresponding solutions but WSBen gives requests only because the optimal solution to a Web service composition problem may not be obtained in the reasonable time window due to the problem's inherently high complexity.

There are three unique challenges that have been established to investigate research issues with regard to Web services and Semantic Web. First is the Semantic Web Services Challenge[5]. This venue invites application submissions for demonstrating practical progress towards achieving the vision of the Semantic Web. According to the event, it has the overall goal to advance our understanding of how semantic technologies can be exploited to produce useful applications for the Web. Second is the Web Services Challenge[6]. This venue solicits approaches, methods, and algorithms in the domain of Web-service discovery and composition. This event evaluates participants' approaches based on their quantitative and qualitative performance results on discovery and composition problems. The Web Services Challenge is more driven by common problems, but the Semantic Web Challenge concentrates more on the environment. As such, the Semantic Web Challenge places more focus on semantics while the Web Services Challenges favors applied and short-term solutions (Brian, William, Michael, & Andreas, 2007). Third is the Service Oriented Architecture Contest[7] which asks participants to openly choose particular domain-specific problems and show their best approaches for them. There are unique characteristics for each venue so that they have undoubtedly contributed to advance the state-of-art technologies in Web services and Semantic Web. Among these challenges, WSBen can be exploited especially for the Web Services Challenge to provide various benchmark environments, discovery and composition problems by varying Web-service network topologies.

As for WSC, there are two main approaches, depending on the use of domain knowledge. First, the template-workflow based approach is to use software programs and domain experts to bind manually-generated workflows to the corresponding concrete Web services. METEOR-S (Sivashanmugam, Verma, Sheth, & Miller, 2003) is an example of this approach. Second, various AI planning techniques have been applied to the WSC problem, ranging from simple classical STRIPS-style planning to an extended estimated regression planning (McDermott, 2002). We believe that our WSBen is complementary for AI Planning based tools for the WSC problem. In fact, we demonstrate how WSBen can be used to compare the performance of AI planners for the WSC problems in the illustrative use-cases section. In this article, meanwhile, we do not propose how METEOR-S can make use of WSBen for a test case generation

tool. It is because METEOR-S consists of three modules such as process designer, configuration module, and execution environment, where the execution environment requires executable Web services but WSBen can generate only WSDL files without real implementation.

Overview of WSBen

In this section, we present a novel benchmark tool titled WSBen, which provides a set of functions to simplify the generation of test environments for WSD and WSC problems.

Overview of WSBen

At a higher level, a Web service can be assumed as a transformation between two different application domains, and each can be represented by a cluster. This assumption was the basis in developing WSBen. From the perspective of graph theory, WSBen builds *Parameter Cluster Network*, which consists of clusters and directed edges connecting two different clusters. These directed edges become Web service templates from which WSBen generates Web services as users specify. Formally, the parameter cluster

Figure 4. Overview of WSBen

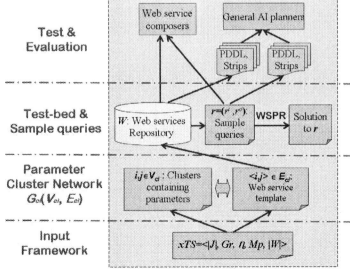

network is defined as follows:

Definition 5 (Parameter Cluster Network) *A directed graph $G_{cl}(V_{cl}, E_{cl})$, where V_{cl} is a set of clusters and E_{cl} is a set of directed edges that are incident from input clusters $i \in V_{cl}$ to output clusters $j \in V_{cl}$. Here, cluster i and j contain a set of non-overlapping parameters denoted by Pa_i and Pa_j, respectively, where $Pa_i \cap Pa_j = \phi$. Each directed edge is also called a Web service template, from which WSDL files are generated.*

Figure 4 shows the overview of WSBen. In detail, WSBen consists of the following functionalities:

- Input framework: Users can specify and control the generated synthetic WSDL files and their characteristics. For this purpose, WSBen provides an input framework *xTS* = <$|J|$, G_r, η, G_p,$|W|$>. *xTS* applies existing complex and random network models to specify G_r. Each element of *xTS* will be discussed in more detail below.
- Parameter cluster network, $G_{cl}(V_{cl}, E_{cl})$: If *xTS* is given by users, based on the first four elements, WSBen generates G_{cl}. Each cluster of G_{cl} is filled with some number of atomic parameters. In this network, Web services are defined as transformations between two different clusters. That is, <i, j> $\in E_{cl}$ becomes Web service templates. The role of Web service templates in the test set generation will be illustrated.
- Test set and sample requests: By randomly selecting the Web service templates (arcs of the parameter cluster network), WSDL files are generated. Once a test set is generated, users can generate sample test requests r = <r^i, r^o>. The generation process of test sets and test requests will be illustrated.
- Test and evaluation: WSBen can export both the Web service WSDL files and test requests into files in PDDL (McDermott, 1996) and

STRIPS format, enabling concurrent comparison with state-of-the-art AI planners.

WSBen input framework: *xTS*

WSBen input framework, *xTS* consists of five tuples, <$|J|$, G_r, η, G_p,$|W|$>. In detail:

1. $|J|$ is the total number of parameter clusters.
2. G_r denotes a graph model to specify the underlying topology of a parameter cluster network. G_r can be on of the following three models discussed in the Background section:

   - *Erdos-Renyi*($|J|$, p): This model has such a simple generation approach that it chooses each of the possible

   $$\frac{|J|(|J|-1)}{2}$$

   edges in the graph with $|J|$ nodes with probability p. The resulting graph becomes the same as the binomial graph.

   - *Newman-Watts-Strogatz*($|J|$, k, p): The initialization is a regular ring graph with k neighbors. During the generation process, new edges (shortcuts) are added randomly with probability p for each edge. Note that no edges are removed, differing from Watts-Strogatz model.

   - *Barabasi-Albert*($|J|$, m): This graph model is generated by adding new nodes with m edges that are preferentially attached to existing nodes with a high degree. The initialization is a graph with m nodes and no edges. Note that the current implementation of WSBen is limited because it can only generate the simplified version of the extended Barabai-Albert model, by setting $p = q = 0$ and $m_0 = m$, resulting in graphs with γ = 2.0 ± 0.1, where γ is the exponent of a power function $P_w(v)$ defined over connectivity v range in the form of $P_w(v) \propto v^{-\gamma}$.

3. η denotes the parameter condense rate. With η, users can control the density of partial-matching cases in produced Web services.

4. M_p denotes the minimum number of parameters a cluster can contain. In other words, clusters may have a different number of parameters but all clusters must have at least M_p number of parameters.

5. $|W|$ denotes the total number of Web services of a test set.

With $|J|$ and G_r, the first two input elements of *xTS*, we can build G_{cl} with each empty cluster. Thus, we need a procedure to fill each empty cluster with parameters. For this purpose, WSBen uses the following procedure:

1. A parameter cluster network G_{cl} with empty clusters is built by specifying $|J|$ and G_r.

2. Co-occurrence probability of each cluster is measured by the following probability:

$$\Delta_j = \frac{k_j}{\max_{j \in V_{cl}} k_j} \eta \qquad (3)$$

where Δ_j is the co-occurrence probability of cluster j, and k_j is the edge degree of cluster j.

η is the parameter condense rate which is given by users.

3. $|Pa_j|$ is measured based on the following equation.

$$|Pa_j| = \frac{M_p}{\Delta_j} \qquad (4)$$

where Pa_j is the set of parameters contained in cluster j.

4. For each j cluster, atomic parameters are generated up to $|Pa_j|$, with duplicated parameters forbidden (i.e., $\forall i, j \in V_{cl}, Pa_i \cap Pa_j = \phi$).

Once a complete parameter cluster network, $G_{cl}(V_{cl}, E_{cl})$ is built, WSBen repeats the following procedure until $|W|$ number of Web services are generated:

1. A Web service template $<i, j>$ is chosen at random from E_{cl}.

2. WSBen generates a WSDL file, in which each input parameter is selected from i cluster with probability Δ_i, and each output parameter is selected from j cluster with probability Δ_j.

Figure 5 illustrates how WSBen builds G_{cl} and generates WSDL files based on the G_{cl}. Suppose that *xTS* = $<8, Barabasi - Albert$ (8, 2), 0.8, 1.5, 100> is given. Then, the generation steps are as follows:

1. WSBen generates a graph of *Barabasi-Albert*(8,2). The direction of each edge is determined at random.

2. Δ_j and $|Pa_j|$ are specified. For example, Cluster 5 has nine parameters as shown in Figure 5. That is, $|Pa_5| = 9$, as

$$\Delta_5 = \frac{k_j}{\max_{j \in V_{cl}} k_j} \eta = \frac{1}{5} \times 0.8 = 0.16,$$

resulting in

$$|Pa_5| = \frac{M_p}{\Delta_5} \approx 9.$$

3. Pa_j is specified. For example $Pa_5 = \{17,18,19,20,21,22,23,24,25\}$ as shown in Figure 5 because $|Pa_5| = 9$ and for $\forall i, j \in V_{cl}, Pa_i \cap Pa_j = \phi$. Note that the parameter names are automatically generated, and thus do not contain any semantics.

4. Finally, G_{cl} is built and WSBen generates $|W|$ Web services. For example, in Figure 5, WS1 is instanced from a Web service template $<3, 1> \in E_{cl}$. Note that $\Delta_1 = 0.16$ and $\Delta_3 = 0.8$. $\Delta_1 = 0.16$ suggests that the occurrence probability of each parameter in Cluster 1 has 0.16. Due to the low probability, only "1" and "9" are selected from Cluster 1. Similarly, $\Delta_3 = 0.8$ means that the occurrence probability of each parameter in Cluster 3 has 0.8. Due to the high probabil-

Figure 5. Test set generation with <8, Barabasi – Albert (8, 2), 0.8, 1.5, 100>

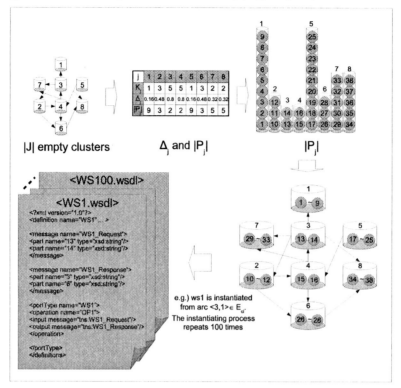

ity, all parameters in Cluster 3 that are "13" and "14" are selected. In the case where no parameter is generated, dummy parameters "S" and "T" are filled in the input and output parameters, respectively.

The state, $s \in S$ is a collection of parameters in $|P|$. Therefore, r^i and r^o are states. The test request r is constructed such that r^o is farthest away from r^i in a parameter space in terms of $g_{r^i}(p)$ - the cost of achieving $p \in P$ from a state r^i. To obtain $g_{r^i}(p)$, we propose following *Forward Searching* algorithm.

Forward Searching: $g_{r^i}(p)$ can be characterized by the solution of a recursive equation as follows:

$$g_{r^i}(p) = \min_{w \in Ow(p)} [c(w) + \max_{p' \in w^i} g_{r^i}(p')] \qquad (5)$$

where $c(w)$ is an invocation cost of a Web service,

Algorithm 1. Forward searching algorithm of WSBen

Test Request Generation

```
Input   : r^i
Output: g_{r^i}(p) for all p reachable from r^i
1: s = r^i; C = φ; d = 1;
2: while (δ ≠ φ) do
3:      δ = {w | w ∈ Ω(s), w ∉ C};
4:      for p in w^o(w ∈ δ) do
5:              if g_{r^i}(p) = ∞ then
6:                      g_{r^i}(p) = d; s = s ∪ {p};
7:      C = C ∪ δ; d++;
```

$w \in W$ and is assumed to be 1. $Ow(p)$ is a set of Web services: $Ow(p) = \{w \in W \mid p \in w^o\}$. At first, $g_{r^i}(p)$ is initialized to 0 if $p \in r^i$, and to ∞ otherwise. Then, the current information state s is set to r^i (Line 1 in Algorithm 1). We denote $\Omega(s)$ by a set of Web services $w \in W$ such that $w^i \subseteq s$. That is, w can be invoked or applicable in the state s.

Every time for $\forall w \in \Omega(s)$, each parameter $p \in w^o$ is added to s, and $g_{r^i}(p)$ is updated until $\Omega(s)$

stops to increase, meaning that this process ends with finding $g_{r^i}(p)$ for all parameters reachable from r^i (Lines 2-6 in Algorithm 1).

We can use Equation (5) to drive the lower bound of the optimal cost of WSC solutions. Note that the invocation cost of a Web service is assumed to be 1. Thus, the optimal cost of a WSC problem coincides with the minimum number of Web services required to solve the WSC problem. For a set of parameters A, we can regard the following cost function:

$$g_{r^i}^{max}(A) = \max_{p \in A} g_{r^i}(p) \qquad (6)$$

The cost of achieving a set of parameters cannot be lower than the cost of achieving each of the parameters in the set. Thus, $g_{r^i}^{max}(A)$ is the lower bound of the optimal cost of achieving r^o from r^i.

Based on the forward searching algorithm, WSBen create a test request r, as follows:

1. WSBen selects a Cluster $j \in G_{cl}$ at random.
2. WSBen copies all parameters in the Cluster j (i.e., Pa_j) into r^i, and then r^o is constructed so that it consists of the first five largest parameters in terms of $g_{r^i}(p)$. Consequently, parameters in r^o are farthest away from parameters in r^i in a parameter space.

As a default, WSBen repeats the above procedure five times, generating five request sets for each test set.

Implementation

As shown in Figure 6, WSBen provides user interfaces to specify *xTS* and several parameters, which are required to form a parameter cluster network and generate WSDL files. WSBen is implemented in Python, and run on Python 2.3 or later. It runs on Unix and Windows. For the creation, manipulation, and functions of complex networks, we used a Python package called NetworkX[8].

Figure 6. WSBen user interface

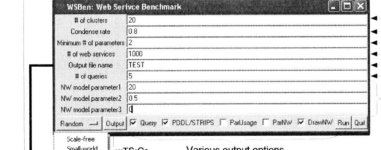

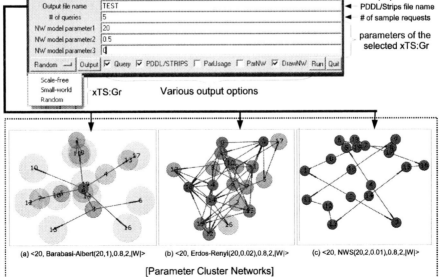

Current implementation of WSBen is limited as follows: (1) it supports only the exact matching without type compatibility check, and (2) each Web service contains only one operation so that a Web service can be viewed as equivalent to an operation. Therefore, w^i and w^o indicate the input and output parameter set of a Web service, w.

Figure 6 also shows three sample parameter cluster networks, where each circular node represents a cluster and edges with heads denote the Web service template, from which Web services are instanced. The size of node is proportional to the number of parameters in the node, while the transparency level of a node's color is inversely proportional to the degree of the node. For example, in the left cluster network, Cluster 18 can be considered a hub cluster in that it has the high degree. Therefore, it is presented by a small circle with denser color.

Following the mechanism of WSBen explained so far, we can build three illustrative test set frameworks by specifying *xTS* as follows:

1. *baTS* = <100, *Barabasi – Albert* (100, 6), 0.8, 5, |*W*|>
2. *nwsTS* = <100, *Newman – Watts – Strogatz*(100, 6, 0.1), 0.8, 5, |*W*|>
3. *erTS* = <100, *Erdos – Renyi*(100, 0.006), 0.8, 5, |*W*|>

Figures 7 and 8 show that there are distinctive differences between *baTS*, *nwsTS*, and *erTS* in

terms of G_p and outgoing edge degree distribution.

ILLUSTRATIVE USE CASES OF WSBEN

In this section, we present three use cases to demonstrate the application of WSBen: (1) evaluating Web-service composition algorithms; (2) comparing performance of AI planners; and (3) estimating the size of giant component. These use cases are prepared to provide vigorous experiments and evaluation for assessing the usage of WSBen. For each use case, we will provide three Web-service test sets by varying *xTS* with three parameter cluster networks such as "random", "small-world", and "scale-free" types. Note that these three network models have the expression power enough to model many real-world networks sufficiently (Albert & Barabasi, 2002). This implies that our generated test cases can be appropriate for representing diverse real-world Web-service networks. Furthermore, these three Web-service test sets are significantly distinctive from each other in terms of their Web-service network topologies and degree distributions as we have shown in the previous section. This indicates that we have sufficient reason to analyze

Figure 7. G_p of baTS, erTS, and nwsTS when |W| = 1,000

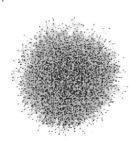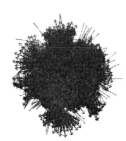

Figure 8. Outgoing edge degree of baTS, erTS, and nwsTS when |W| = 1,000

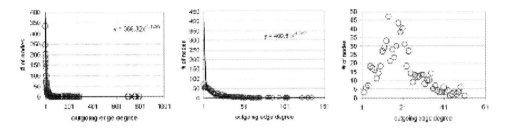

Figure 9. Composed services using WSPR for three test sets. (left) baTS with |W| = 5,000. (center) erTS with |W| = 5,000. (right) nwsTS with |W| = 5,000

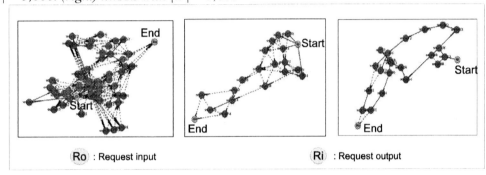

how different network topologies can affect the performance of Web-service applications or environments.

Evaluating Web-Service Composition Algorithms

Recently, many WSC researches have been reported in the Web service community. As such, the EEE06 Web-service composition contest holds as many participants as 11. Among the 11 WSC algorithms, we choose a WSC algorithm named WSPR (Oh, Lee, & Kumara, 2007), which was proved effective and efficient in the contest, in order to demonstrate the application of WSBen.

In this case, we use three test sets generated by WSBen: (1) *baTS* with |W| = 5,000; (2) *erTS* with |W| = 5,000; and (3) *nwsTS* with |W| = 5,000. The resultant composed services generated by WSPR

are shown in Figure 9, where WSPR addressed a request for each of the three test sets. Note that WSBen can automatically create sample requests for a given test set. In the graph, each composed solution has nodes such as "*Ri*" and "*Ro*", which represent the initial condition and goal state, respectively. Other nodes represent Web services. The directed arcs indicate the invocation flow, where a solid edge means full-matching invocation and a dotted edge represents partial-matching invocation. From the experiments based on diverse test sets such as *baTS*, *erTS*, and *nwsTS*, we can understand how different network models of G_{cl} influences the performance of WSC algorithms. In general, given the same number of clusters, the *Barabasi-Albert* model generates G_{cl} with a greater number of parameters, and a larger variance of the number of parameters between clusters than the *Newman-Watts-Strogatz* and *Erdos-Renyi* models do. Due to the greater number of parameters and larger variance, *baTS* needs more partial-matching Web services to fulfill the given requests than others. The increasing need for partial-matching Web services leads to increasing number of Web services in the composed service. This is the reason that the *baTS* case has more Web services to create a resultant composed service as shown in Figure 9 (left).

Comparing Performance of AI Planners

We demonstrate how WSBen can be used to compare the performance of AI planners. For this purpose, we choose three prominent AI planners – Graphplan (Blum & Furst, 1997), Blackbox (Kautz & Selman,1996), and IPP[9]. Blackbox and IPP are extended planning systems that originated from Graphplan. In particular, Blackbox is extended to be able to map a plan graph into a set of clauses for checking the satisfiability problem. Consequently,

it can run even in large number of operators. For comparing the performance of three planners, we use two evaluation metrics as follows:

1. τ(Time): It measures how long an algorithm takes to find a right solution, in seconds. This is a measure of computational efficiency.
2. #W: The number of Web services in a right solution. This is a measure of effectiveness.

All AI planners run with their default options, except that the maximum number of nodes for Blackbox and Graphplan was set to 32,768 and 10,000, respectively. Commonly, the time to read operator and fact files is not included in τ. Blackbox and IPP accept only the PDDL format, while Graphplan accepts only the STRIPS format for their operator and fact files. Note that an operator file corresponds to a test set, and a fact file corresponds to a test request file. Also note that WSBen provides a function to convert test

Table 2. Results over baTS with $|W| = 3,000$

Requests	BlackBox		GraphPlan		IPP	
	#W	τ	#W	τ	#W	τ
r_1	61	478.69	-	-	-	-
r_2	-	-	-	-	-	-
r_3	5	5	5	0.09	5	26.22
r_4	9	27.78	9	0.11	9	28.56
r_5	4	1.4	4	0.04	4	23.97

Table 3. Results over erTS with $|W| = 3,000$

Requests	BlackBox		GraphPlan		IPP	
	#W	τ	#W	τ	#W	τ
r_1	75	38.09	-	-	-	-
r_2	50	16.02	-	-	-	-
r_3	22	18.68	-	-	22	24.78
r_4	23	4.38	-	-	23	21.06
r_5	38	4.01	-	-	38	21

sets and requests into PDDL and STRIPS files automatically. The experiments were performed on Linux with three Intel® Xeon™ CPU, running at 2.4GHz with 8GB RAM.

Tables 2, 3, and 4 shows the results of the five test requests for each of *baTS*, *erTS*, and *nwsTS* with $|W|$ = 3,000. Graphplan ran out of memory in many cases. IPP also failed to solve the some requests. As a whole, Blackbox showed better performance than others, meaning that it can solve more requests than others. It is because Blackbox uses the local-search SAT solver, Walksat, for the satisfiability problem, so that Blackbox can run relatively well even with a large number of operators.

We can estimate the size of giant component in a service network using random graph theory. Often it is believed to be important to have a large and dense giant component in a service network. Otherwise, the isolated services will never have a chance to provide any services to clients. Newman, Strogatz, and Watts (2001)

suggested the theoretical framework in order to estimate the giant component size in networks by using random graph theory. In order to see if their theoretical framework works, we generated the g_{op}^f with different network size for each of following cases:

1. *Random model*: <50, *Erdos − Renyi*(100, 0.6), 0.8, 5, $|W|$>
2. *Scale-free model*: <50, *Barabasi − Albert*(100, 6), 0.8, 5, $|W|$>
3. *NWS model*: <50, *Newman − Watts − Strogatz*(100, 6, 0.1), 0.8, 5, $|W|$>

For each of these networks, we measured the real size of giant components. Then, we calculated the theoretical size of giant components according to the estimation model of Newman et al. (2001). The comparisons between real and theoretical sizes are summarized in Figure 10. For g_{op}^f based on the random parameter cluster network in Figure 10(A), the theoretical value of the giant component

Table 4. Results over nwsTS with $|W|$ = 3,000

Requests	BlackBox		GraphPlan		IPP	
	#W	τ	#W	τ	#W	τ
r_1	48	571.63	-	-	48	29.52
r_2	35	114.67	-	-	35	28.57
r_3	24	192.99	-	-	24	30.19
r_4	26	11.88	-	-	26	28.39
r_5	31	111.21	-	-	-	-

Figure 10. Comparison of real and theoretical size of giant components: (A) random, (B) scale-free, and (C) NWS models.

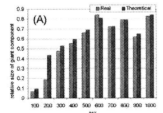 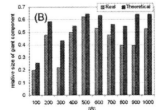 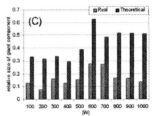

Estimating the size of giant component

size is very close to the measured one for each synthetic network. This implies that even a simple random model may be very helpful to estimate the inter-operable portion of such networks with random topology without even analyzing the available network beyond its degree distribution. However, Figure 10(B) shows that the estimation model is not a good model for Scale-free type. There is a considerable gap between theory and real value for many of the synthetic networks in this type. The deviation between theory and actual networks becomes more dramatic for the *NWS* (small world phenomenon and highly clustered property) type shown in Figure 10(C). The results show that the random network model might be good generative model for such Web services networks if these networks are entirely random, which is also in accordance with the basic assumption by Newman et al. (2001).

CONCLUSION

A novel Web-service benchmark toolkit, WSBen, is presented with three use cases in different application domains. The WSBen development is inspired by the study on real-world Web services, and is designed to provide diverse scenarios and configurations which users can fine-tune easily. As a result, using WSBen, users can conduct extensive experimental validation on their Web-service discovery and composition algorithms. It is our hope that WSBen will provide useful insights to the design and development of Web-services discovery and composition solutions and software. The latest version of WSBen is available at: http://pike.psu.edu/sw/wsben/. Further research is needed to extend WSBen to support approximate and semantic matching among Web services. Also, we plan to discover additional applications where the WSBen can be used.

ACKNOWLEDGMENT

Authors would like to thank Hyunyoung Kil and Ergin Elmacioglu for their help on the design and implementation of WSBen, and Professor Soundar R. T. Kumara at Penn State for his helpful comments on the earlier draft of this article.

REFERENCES

Albert, R. & Barabasi, A. (2002). Statistical mechanics of complex networks. *Reviews of Modern Physics, 74*(1), pp. 47-95.

Albert, R. & Barabasi, A. (2000). Topology of evolving networks. *Phys. Rev. Lett., 85*, pp. 5234-5237.

Albert, R., Jeong, H. & Barabasi, A. (1999). The diameter of the world wide web. *Nature, 401*, pp. 130-131.

Bertsekas, D. (2000). *Dynamic programming and optimal control*, volume 1, 2nd ed. Athena Scientific, Boston.

Blum, A. & Furst, M. (1997). Fast planning through planning graph analysis. *Artificial Intelligence, 90*, pp. 281-300.

Brian, B., William, C., Michael, J., & Andreas, W. (2007). WSC-07: Evolving the web services challenge. *In Proc. of 9th IEEE International Conference on E-Commerce Technology and 4th IEEE International Conference on Enterprise Computing, E-Commerce, and E-Services (CEC-EEE 2007)*, pp. 505-508, Tokyo, Japan.

Bylander, T. (1994). The computational complexity of propositional STRIPS planning. *Artificial Intelligence, 69*(1-2), pp. 165-204.

Constantinescu, I., Faltings, B. & Binder, W. (2004). Large scale testbed for type compatible service composition. In *Proc. of 14th International Conference on Automated Planning and Scheduling (ICAPS)*, pp. 23-28, Whistler, British Columbia, Canada.

Delgado, J. (2002). Emergence of social conventions in complex networks. *Artificial Intelligence*, *141*, pp. 171-185.

Denning, J. P. (2004). Network laws. Communications of the ACM, 47(11), pp. 15-20.

Erdos, P, Graham, R., & Nesetril, J. (1996). *The mathematics of Paul Erdos*. Springer-Verlag, Berlin, Germany.

Fan, J., & Kambhampati, S. (2005). A snapshot of public Web services. *SIGMOD Record, 34*(1), pp. 24-32.

Kautz, H. & Selman, B. (1996). Unifying SAT-based and graph-based planning. In *Proc. of the 16th International Joint Conference on Artificial Intelligence (IJCAI)*, pp. 318-325, Stockholm, Sweden.

Kil, H., Oh, S., & Lee, D. (2006). On the Topological Landscape of Semantic Web services Matchmaking. In *Proc. of 1st International Workshop on Semantic Matchmaking and Resource Retreival (SMR2006)*, pp. 19-34, Seoul, Korea.

McDermott, D. (1996). A heuristic estimator for means-ends analysis in planning. In *Proc. of the third International Conference on Artificial Intelligence Planning Systems (AIPS)*, pp. 142-149, Edinburgh, Scotland.

McDermott, D. (2002). Estimated-regression planning for interactions with Web services. In *Proc. of the sixth International Conference on Artificial Intelligence Planning and Scheduling Systems (AIPS)*, pp. 67-73, Toulouse, France.

Newman, M. E. J., Strogatz, S. H., & Watts, D. J. (2001). Random graphs with arbitrary degree distributions and their applications. *Phys. Rev. E, 64*(026118).

Nilsson, J. (2001). *Artificial Intelligence: a new synthesis*. Morgan Kaufmann, San Francisco, CA.

Oh, S., Kil, H., Lee, D., & Kumara, S. (2006). WS-Ben: a Web-services discovery and composition benchmark. In *Proc. of the fourth International IEEE Conference on Web service (ICWS)*, pp. 239-246, Chicago.

Oh, S., Lee, D., & Kumara, S. (2007). WSPR: a heuristic algorithm for Web-service composition. *Int'l J. of Web services Research (IJWSR), 4*(1), pp. 1-22.

Sivashanmugam, K., Verma, K., Sheth, A., & Miller, J. (2003). Adding semantics to Web services standards. In *Proc. of the first IEEE International Conference on Web services (ICWS)*, pp. 395-401, Las Vegas, NV.

Watts, D. J. (1999). *The dynamics of networks between order and randomness*. Princeton Univ. Press, Princeton, NJ.

Watts, D. J., & Strogatz, S. H. (1998). Collective dynamics of small-world networks. *Nature, 393*(4), pp. 440-442.

XMark. An XML Benchmark Project. Retrieve on September 17, 2006 from, http://monetdb.cwi.nl/xml/.

ENDNOTES

[1] This article is a substantial extension from the short version that appeared in the proceedings of the 4th International IEEE Conference on Web Services (ICWS), held in Chicago, USA, 2006. The work of Seog-Chan Oh was done while the author was with the Pennsylvania State University.

[2] As of August 2007, according to the estimation of Google Scholar, there are about 2,360 scholarly articles mentioning "Web Services Composition".

[3] http://www.comp.hkbu.edu.hk/~ctr/wschallenge/

[4] http://insel.flp.cs.tu-berlin.de/wsc06/

5   The Semantic Web Services Challenge (2007): http://sws-challenge.org/wiki/index.php/Main_Page

6   The Web Services Challenge (2007): http://www.wschallenge.org/wsc07/

Chapter 3.6
Architecture of the Organic.Edunet Web Portal

Nikos Manouselis
Greek Research & Technology Network (GRNET S.A.), Greece

Kostas Kastrantas
Greek Research & Technology Network (GRNET S.A.), Greece

Salvador Sanchez-Alonso
University of Alcalá, Spain

Jesús Cáceres
University of Alcalá, Spain

Hannes Ebner
Royal Institute of Technology (KTH), Sweden

Matthias Palmer
Royal Institute of Technology (KTH), Sweden

Ambjorn Naeve
Royal Institute of Technology (KTH), Sweden

ABSTRACT

The use of Semantic Web technologies in educational Web portals has been reported to facilitate users' search, access, and retrieval of learning resources. To achieve this, a number of different architectural components and services need to be harmonically combined and implemented. This article presents how this issue is dealt with in the context of a large-scale case study. More specifically, it describes the architecture behind the Organic.Edunet Web portal that aims to provide access to a federation of repositories with learning resources on agricultural topics. The various components of the architecture are presented and the supporting technologies are explained. In addition, the article focuses on how Semantic Web technologies are being adopted, specialized, and put in practice in order to facilitate ontology-aided sharing and reusing of learning resources.

INTRODUCTION

Following their introduction and commercial growth after 2000, Web portals have lately attracted increased research interest that focuses on a variety of aspects such as their business models, interface design, technical development, or their quality (Mahadevan, 2000; Tatnall, 2005a; Moraga et al., 2006; Tatnall, 2007). The term Web portal has been initially used to refer to well-known Internet search and navigation sites that provided a starting point for web visitors to explore and access information on the World Wide Web (Warner, 1999; Winkler, 2001). A Web portal can be generally viewed as a single, distilled view of information from various sources that integrates information, content, and other software services or applications (Averweg, 2007). Therefore, today Web portals can be simply defined as *gateways to information and services from multiple sources*, and their continuous development has been highlighted by relevant publications (Tatnall, 2005b).

A type of Web portals with particular interest are educational ones (Conceicao et al., 2003; Boff et al., 2006). Educational Web portals generally serve as gateways to information and services of some learning or teaching relevance and may cover a variety of types. They range from institutional Web portals that provide access to course listings and institutional information (such as Ethridge et al, 2000), to community portals that serve the needs of particular communities of learning and practice (such as DeSanctis et al., 2001; Luke et al., 2004). One category of educational portals that have recently received considerable interest (Neven & Duval, 2002; Richards et al., 2002; Hatala et al., 2004) is that of Web portals that provide access to some organized collection of learning resources. These portals usually facilitate users' access to the content in one or more learning repositories – that is, to database systems that facilitate the storage, location and retrieval of learning resources (Holden, 2003). Popular examples include both independent learning resources' portals such as MERLOT (http://www.merlot.org) and Teachers' Domain (http://www.teachersdomain.org/), as well as portals that list or aggregate learning resources from various other sources (e.g. other portals or repositories) such as OERCommons (http://www.oercommons.org).

Richards et al. (2002) stress that Web portals with learning resources may offer a wide variety of services based on what they seek to give to the user community behind them, although the more common are those aimed at facilitating users' search, access, and retrieval of the resources. For this purpose, they include services that will facilitate these processes, utilizing different types of user-related information (such as personal preferences) or resource-related information (such as the learning resource characteristics). One of the most recent trends in portal development is the use of Semantic Web technologies (Maedche et al., 2001). Semantic Web is an evolving extension of the World Wide Web (WWW) in which web content can be expressed not only in natural language, but also in a format that can be read and processed by software systems, thus permitting them to find, share and integrate information more easily (Berners-Lee, 1998). Numerous applications and case studies of Semantic Web technologies (e.g. ontologies for annotating information and expressing its semantics in a machine-processable manner) have been reported during the past few years. For instance, the World Wide Web Consortium (W3C) reports on several systems that have been put in production in existing organizations, as well as a number of commercial products (http://esw.w3.org/topic/CommercialProducts). Yet, the Semantic Web technologies have not so far reached the wide public. Some of the experts in the field claim that the reason is that large-scale applications, serving the needs of large user communities, have not been delivered yet (Shadbolt et al., 2006). To further illustrate their potential (and especially for Web portals), there is a need for implementing state-of-the-art Semantic Web technologies in large-scale applications. In the context of educational Web portals, this involves the semantic annotation of big collections of learning resources and their access and use from existing communities of users.

This article aims to contribute to this development by presenting such a large-scale implementation effort. More specifically, it discusses how semantic annotation and Semantic Web technologies are being adopted, specialized, and put in practice in order to set up a technical infrastructure that will facilitate sharing and reusing of learning resources for an educational Web portal. The case study is the Organic.Edunet Web portal, a portal that serves the needs of learning and teaching communities of the agricultural sector, by facilitating their access to a network (also called a federation) of learning repositories with learning resources on Organic Agriculture (OA) and Agroecology (AE) topics.

The article is structured as it follows. First, a short review of the way Semantic Web approaches are being implemented in similar applications is carried out. A description of the Organic.Edunet initiative is given, and the rationale for developing the Organic.Edunet Web portal is outlined. The main part of the article focuses on the description of the technical architecture of the Web portal, and on the way Semantic Web technologies are implemented in it. A discussion of perceived benefits and potential challenges is later carried out, to finally provide the main conclusions of this work.

BACKGROUND

Educational Semantic Web

From its initial conception around 1989 (Berners-Lee, 1998), the WWW (or simply, the Web) has been designed as an information space, with the goal that it should be useful not only for human-to-human communication, but also for machines

that would be able to mediate and help. As Berners-Lee reports, one of the major obstacles to this has been the fact that most information on the Web is designed for human consumption, and even if it was derived from a very well specified database, the structure of the data is not evident to an automated software system browsing the Web. On the contrary, in his vision of the Semantic Web, data recovery for a particular context of use should be a routine, automated process. This is the reason why the empowering role of Semantic Web technologies has already been acknowledged in various contexts, such as education and training (Aroyo & Dimitrova, 2006). In this new paradigm, data would be specifically oriented to machine consumption by means of formal descriptions based on the existence and wide availability of ontologies, knowledge models of a given domain. Ontologies, which can be defined as collections of concepts representing domain-specific entities, the relationships between those concepts, and the range of admissible values for each concept (Daraselia et al., 2004) are in fact the key element of the Semantic Web. Ontologies serve as knowledge models for each particular domain of science, thus allowing to unambiguously represent, refer, and describe entities in that domain, and serving as the basis for interoperability and common understanding under formal and strict semantics.

Since the Web is becoming a popular educational medium at schools, universities and professional training institutions, a prominent new stream of research on the Educational Semantic Web has been established. Research studies already report semantic-based annotation and sharing of learning resources. For example, Forte et al. (1999) report on the principles underlying the semantic and pedagogic interoperability mechanisms built in the European Knowledge Pool System, a distributed repository of learning objects developed by the European research project ARIADNE (http://www.ariadne-eu.org).

In addition, Soto et al. (2007) designed an ontology schema capable to bring more flexibility to the description of the entities stored in semantic learning object repositories and, at the same time, to facilitate automated functions and task delegation to agents. Furthermore, Sicilia et al. (2005) describe the design of a learning object repository approach to what they called "semantic lifecycle" and illustrate thus through the concrete architecture of a semantic learning object repository prototype.

Moreover, semantic web applications are becoming more and more usual in education & training contexts. Sancho et al. (2005) for instance, applied these technologies to e-learning personalization by combining the information provided by ontologies, and the user profile, to create personalized units of learning. Santos et al. (2006) described an approach to promote interoperability among heterogeneous agents that are part of an educational portal. Their main contribution was to provide a means for social agents to communicate with agents outside its original scope through the use of semantic web technologies. Other implementations of Semantic Web technologies in educational portals also exist in the literature (Woukeu et al., 2003; Tane et al., 2004; Moreale & Vargas-Vera, 2004; Verdejo et al., 2004; Kotzinos et al., 2005).

To further illustrate the potential of the Educational Semantic Web, there is a need for implementing state-of-the-art Semantic Web technologies in large-scale applications that involve the semantic annotation of big collections of learning resources and their access and use from existing communities of users.

Organic.Edunet

To further promote the familiarization of consumers with the benefits of OA and AE - for their own health as well as for the benefits of the environment - the most dynamic consumer groups have to be properly educated. Young people at all stages of formal education have to be carefully approached through relevant educational programs in the curricula of all kinds of educational institutions, from elementary schools to relevant university departments. But apart from raising the awareness and education level of consumers, agricultural professionals must also be properly educated. By "agricultural professionals" we refer to the different types of future agricultural experts (e.g. natural production experts, veterinary experts, agricultural economists, extension officers, etc.), who study in agricultural universities around Europe, and who should be provided with a wide range of information related to OA and AE theories, methods, practices, and economic/environmental impacts.

Both groups (pupils and young agricultural students) constitute user groups of high importance. Children constitute tomorrow's consumers, and they have to be properly approached and educated so that their nutritional, as well as their ecological and environmental awareness are developed. Students of agricultural universities constitute tomorrow's agricultural professionals. They are expected to guide farmers through the adoption of OA and AE principles, or to serve themselves as the next generation of farmers/producers. Therefore, these two user groups have to be carefully approached through publicly available, quality, and multilingual educational content.

In this direction, the Organic.Edunet initiative (http://www.organic-edunet.eu), a European project that is funded by the *eContentplus* Programme and which involves 15 partners from 10 countries, aims to facilitate access, usage and exploitation of digital educational content related to OA and AE. Organic.Edunet will deploy a multilingual online federation of learning repositories, populated with quality content from various content producers. In addition, it will deploy a multilingual online environment (the Organic.Edunet Web portal) that will facilitate end-users' search, retrieval, access and use of the content in the learning repositories. In this way, digital content resources that can be used to educate European youth about the benefits of OA and AE, will become easily accessible, usable and exploitable.

To achieve its aims, Organic.Edunet adopts state-of-art technologies that have been developed and tested in several research initiatives, but have yet to be proven in a real-life context. A characteristic example involves the implementation of Semantic Web technologies that have been previously developed in the context of the "LUISA: Learning Content Management System Using Innovative Semantic Web Services Architecture" EU project (http://www.luisa-project.eu/). The main characteristics of the LUISA architecture are its service-orientation and the built-in capabilities for semantic querying. For this purpose, semantic Web Services are involved, reusing the EU framework WSMO (http://www.wsmo.org/) for the brokering of multiple repositories. WSMO (which stands for Web Service Modeling Ontology) provides ontological specifications for the core elements of Semantic Web services. Taking the Web Service Modeling Framework (WSMF) as reference, WSMO defines four different ele-

ments for describing semantic Web Services: ontologies that provide the terminology used by other elements, goals that define the problems that should be solved by Web Services, Web Services descriptions that define various aspects of a Web Service, and finally mediators which bypass interpretability problems. In the following section, we describe the overall architecture of the Organic. Edunet infrastructure, and how technologies such as the ones adopted from LUISA are engaged.

ORGANIC.EDUNET INFRASTRUCTURE

Overall Architecture

The overall architecture of Organic.Edunet is illustrated in Figure 1. The main elements of this architecture are the following:

Figure 1. Overall architecture of Organic.Edunet

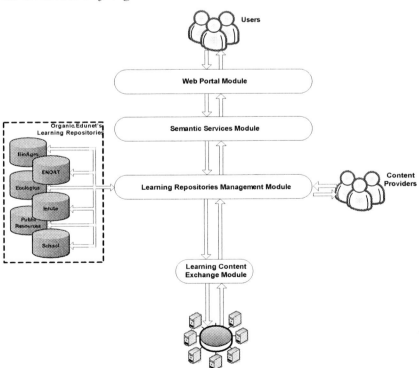

- *Learning Repository Management Module*: includes the suite of tools that the Organic.Edunet content providers will use to create a digital collection of learning resources, to describe resources with appropriate metadata, and to publish resources in their own learning repository. Overall, six learning repositories are expected to be set up by the Organic.Edunet content providers (namely the Bio@gro, ENOAT, ECOLOGICA/COMPASS, Intute, School, and Public Resources ones).
- *Learning Resource Exchange Module*: concerns the connection of the Organic. Edunet federation with other federations of learning repositories, using open standards and specifications for the exchange of search queries and the harvesting of metadata. Organic.Edunet is expected to be connected with two external federations; the Learning Resource Exchange (LRE) of the European Schoolnet (http://lre.eun.org) and the ARIADNE Foundation (http://www.ariadne-eu. org/).
- *Semantic Services Module*: it is the core of the Semantic Web technologies' application in the architecture, and supports the semantically-enabled services that the Organic. Edunet Web portal will offer, by reasoning upon a number of integrated ontologies.
- *Web Portal Module*: refers to the end-user visible parts of the whole infrastructure, allowing users (including school teachers and pupils, university teachers and students,

Figure 2. Overview of the learning repository management module components

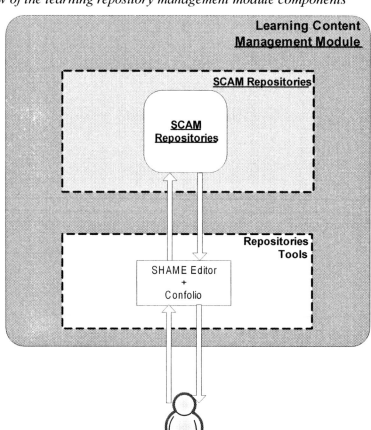

researchers etc.) to search, locate, retrieve and access learning resources on OA and AE throughout the whole Organic.Edunet federation.

Each module is further detailed in the paragraphs that follow.

Learning Repository Management Module

This module deals with the way content producers organize, annotate and publish learning resources and metadata in an Organic.Edunet repository. As illustrated in Figure 2, each of the Organic.Edunet content providers is expected to collect and annotate its learning resources, according to a multilingual application profile of the IEEE Learning Object Metadata (LOM) standard (LTSC, 2002). Two existing software tools are being adapted and integrated for this purpose:

- A configurable metadata editor built upon the code-library SHAME (available as Open Source at http://shame.sourceforge.net). With this code-library application programmers can develop flexible and easily extensible annotation tools for Semantic Web-based metadata. SHAME implements the Annotation Profile Model (Palmér et al., 2007a; Palmér et al., 2007b). This model is a configuration mechanism for the annotation of metadata and leaves the question of metadata standard compliance up to a metadata expert and not to the application developer.
- The electronic portfolio system Confolio (http://www.confolio.org) that allows the flexible management of folder-based repository interfaces.

The content providers will use the integration of the SHAME editor and the Confolio tool in order to upload (if desired) their resources and the associated metadata into a learning repository that is called SCAM (Standardized Contextualized Access to Metadata), an Open Source Semantic Web repository solution for learning resources (Palmér et al., 2004). Figure 3 presents how a SCAM repository is accessed, using a combination of technologies.

The repository backend is resource-oriented and will store its metadata according to a Resource Description Framework (RDF, www.w3.org/RDF/) representation of the Organic.Edunet IEEE LOM application profile. The repository provides a range of connection interfaces, allowing the most appropriate to be chosen for each situation. An interface which exposes the repository closest to the internal representation is the REST (Representational State Transfer), a resource-based software architecture building fully on top of well established standards such as the HTTP protocol (Fielding, 2000). This makes it very easy to build interactive web applications on top of this interface.

The Confolio repository front-end builds on top of the REST-based web services exposed by the repository and an AJAX (Asynchronous JavaScript and XML) toolkit, which enables cross-browser compatibility and operating system independent application. The basic operations of Confolio can be separated in two groups: administrative (e.g. creation of new portfolios of learning resources) and end-user (e.g. creation of folders and description of resources using the SHAME metadata editor).

Using the Learning Repository Management Module, Organic.Edunet content providers may collect resources, annotate them using metadata conforming to the developed application profile, reviewing and approving resources, and then releasing resources for publication. Then, the metadata of the resources stored in a particular Organic.Edunet repository are (a) made available for harvesting from the Semantic Services Module and (b) made available for harvesting and/or search federation to external federations.

Figure 3. Overview of technology layers in a SCAM repository

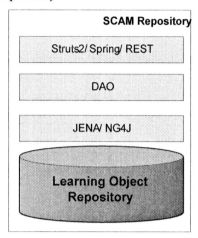

Learning Resources Exchange Module

The Learning Resources Exchange Module allows for the communication of the Organic.Edunet repositories with external federations. Organic. Edunet will aim at the connection with the LRE and ARIADNE federations by adopting two widely used protocols and specifications:

- For communicating with ARIADNE: the Open Archives Initiative Protocol for Metadata Harvesting (OAI-PHM, http://www. openarchives.org/OAI/openarchivesprotocol.html) for making metadata available for harvesting from the ARIADNE services.
- For communicating with LRE: the Simple Query Interface (SQI, http://www.prolearn-project.org/lori) for serving/exchanging queries with the LRE services.

Metadata is transformed from its RDF representation into an XML representation, in order to be available for the external federations. Additional possibilities also exist for further interconnecting the Organic.Edunet repositories, due to their SCAM basis, e.g. the SPARQL Protocol

and RDF Query Language - a W3C standardized query language and protocol for accessing RDF data (http://www.w3.org/TR/rdf-sparql-query/).

Semantic Services Module

The Semantic Services Module is the core engine behind the Organic.Edunet Web portal that allows offering users with semantic search capabilities. To support this, it is based on a semantic representation of the learning resources' metadata, as well as a number of ontologies that are engaged during search queries to provide reasoning capabilities. More specifically, metadata is transformed into an ontological representation inside a sub-module called LOMR.

The LOMR (standing for Learning Object Metadata Repository) is not itself a metadata repository but rather a framework which provides Web Service interfaces to any given, "real" learning object repository. LOMR instances allow developers to select the best repository implementation for a given application need, enabling specialized components, such as custom query resolvers and result composers, to benefit from the availability of different, heterogeneous LOMR instances. LOMR main features include the storage of learning object metadata in semantic format, the provision of a service-oriented interface and the import of metadata in non-semantic formats, among others.

In addition, LOMR offers semantic services to the Web Portal Module, following WSMO. It uses the Web Services Modeling Language (WSML, http://www.wsmo.org/wsml/) in order to provide formal syntax and semantics for WSMO, since it is richer in reasoning capabilities than the OWL Web ontology language (http://www.w3.org/TR/owl-features/) recommended by the W3C. Interoperability can be easily achieved through translating WSML to OWL through open source tools that are publicly available, such as the Web Service Modeling Toolkit (WSMT, http://wsmt.

Figure 4. Illustration of the way the Learning Resources Exchange Module operates

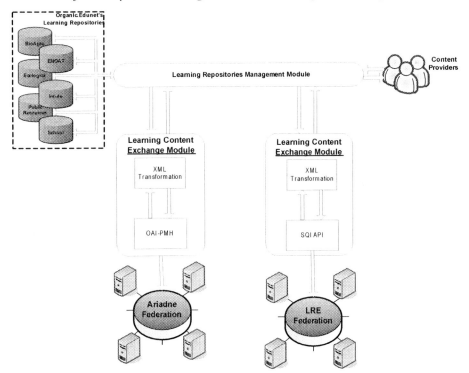

sourceforge.net) and WSMO Studio (WSMO4J, http://wsmo4j.sourceforge.net).

As a starting point, three ontologies are expected to be used by the Semantic Services Module. The first ontology will represent the domain area (OA and AE). It will serve all subject classification purposes, as well as allow for reasoning related to the semantics of the OA and AE concepts themselves. For example, searching for resources that have been classified using some concepts or terms related to the ones that the user has initially indicated. The popular AGROVOC (http://www.fao.org/aims/ag_intro.htm) ontology of FAO will be used as a basis for the construction of this ontology. The second ontology will be a geographical one. It will help reasoning related to the geographical origin and/or coverage of resources and their associated languages. For instance, it may allow users from a particular geographical region to search for resources in

languages that have been indicated as related to the particular region, even if this has not been indicated in the initial search query. The third ontology will be representing IEEE LOM. It is expected to allow reasoning related to semantics of the LOM structure itself, such as searching for information in other elements than the ones that a user has initially indicated.

In LOMR, metadata will be harvested from the individual Organic.Edunet repositories using an appropriate harvesting mechanism. As Figure 5 shows, the RDF representations stored in the SCAM repositories will be converted to the WSML representation that LOMR requires. Once all the metadata information is stored in the LOMR repository in the formal, ontology-based format, LOMR will be able to expose various functionalities through semantic Web Services (described according to WSMO), allowing a wide variety of interactions with the Organic.Edunet Web portal.

Figure 5. Overview of the Semantic services module

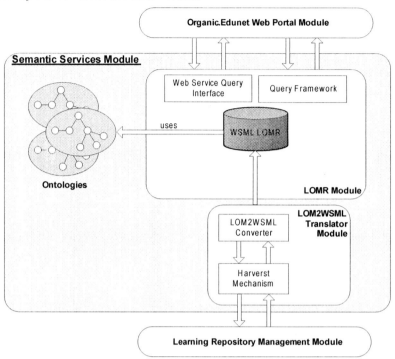

Web Portal Module

The final module of the Organic.Edunet architecture is the Web Portal one. It actually comprises the online environment that will interact with the various user roles (school teachers & pupils, university teachers and students). For this purpose, it entails a role-filtering mechanism that will allow each user category to be presented with a user interface tailored to its specific needs. Apart from allowing users to semantically search and retrieve learning resources using the Semantic Services Module, the Web Portal Module will also provide the users with the option of evaluating/ rating learning resources. Multi-dimensional numerical evaluations will be stored in appropriately defined evaluative metadata (Vuorikari et al., 2008). Then, they will give input to a collaborative filtering mechanism that will recommend users to look at resources that other users with similar preferences liked in the past (Manouselis & Costopoulou, 2007).

DISCUSSION

Benefits

As it has been described in the presentation of the Organic.Edunet portal architecture, there is a number of benefits expected from the adoption of Semantic Web technologies. The following paragraphs will go into more detail on these benefits.

The use of ontologies for the classification of learning resources will allow the refinement and expansion of queries. Users currently have to rely on keyword-based searches: for instance, a teacher looking for learning resources on the advantages of the use of organic fertilizers might try something like "advantages organic fertilizers" in Google (or in any other keyword-based search engine). A search on these keywords would return results containing either the terms "organic" or "fertilizer" or "advantage" or a combination of them, but many of those would be seen as non ap-

Figure 6. Elements of the Web portal module

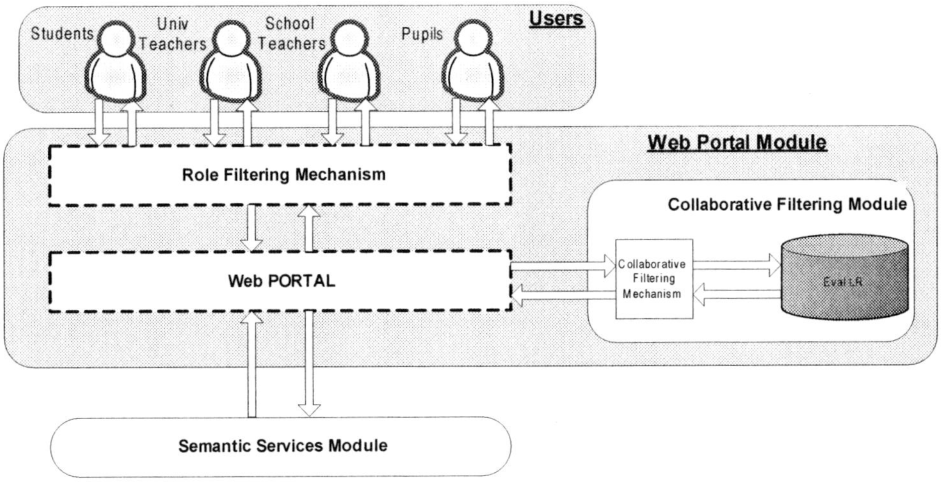

propriate for most users. An example on the kind of (inadequate) resources that might be retrieved with this method –traditional keyword-based searches– would be the following:

- Commercial information on products by companies selling *organic fertilizers.*
- Resources on the *advantages* of non-*organic fertilizers* (matching the three keywords used for the search).
- Resources criticizing the use of *organic fertilizers* and discouraging users on its application due to their low efficiency and high prices.
- Resources on the elaboration of *organic* yoghurt (as they would match to at least one of the keywords provided).

Contrary to these examples, the use of ontologies for the description of materials would force the search engine to stick to strict-matching criteria to unambiguous definitions. It would also allow to search only educational-oriented materials explicitly annotated with the predicates such as "IsAbout" or "Provides BackgroundOn", which are related to e.g. organic fertilizers. This would even allow users to find just those learning

resources explaining the advantages of the use of organic fertilizers and not criticizing them, and would allow users avoid suggestions for learning resources on other topics.

In addition, the use of ontologies will further enhance the search and browsing services offered to the users. More specifically, users will be able to browse through learning resources by selecting concepts of the ontologies used, together with an expression of their relationships. In a learning objects portal on organic farming, these technologies would help to easily access similar materials to a given one, as the relationships in the ontology would provide the ability to navigate from one instance to another. An example would be a search on learning objects about organic pest control, which would return e.g. a case study on the use of several types of insecticide-fungicide dust for use on fruit trees. Thus, portal users could navigate from the relationship from this object to fruit trees, and find e.g. learning objects on the commercialization of organic apples, or even lectures on organic fungicides applicable only to specific geographical regions.

Learning resources in current public repositories often have a high variability in their characterizations: from anything in digital format to well-defined educational oriented learning materials including metadata conformant to the IEEE LOM standard (McGreal, 2004). The description of all the knowledge about the domain of learning objects in the form of an ontology, and the use of this ontology as the basis for a learning object portal on organic farming, would provide the portal with the flexibility necessary to seamlessly accommodate different conceptualizations. It would also provide the ability to interact with external systems, even if each of these systems have a different understanding of what a learning object is, how their metadata should look like, etc. This model would eventually provide the users with a number of different functionalities, adapted to each particular concept of learning object, and not necessarily restricted by only one of these conceptualizations, applying technologies already in practice (Soto et al., 2007).

Challenges

Apart from the benefits, a number of challenges have also to be dealt with during the implementation of the Organic.Edunet architecture:

- The process of selecting, developing, and specifying the ontologies to be used (especially as far as domain-dependent ones such as the OA & AE ontology are concerned) is demanding and time-consuming, and needs the help of a number of experts from different disciplines. To make all the experts reach agreements is not always straight-forward (Sánchez-Alonso et al., 2008.).
- The process of engineering a new ontology often implies checking the new knowledge against the commonsense knowledge and general terms in an upper ontology. This process, which has to be carefully carried out, can be summarized in four iterative phases as described by Sánchez-Alonso & García (2006): (1) find one or several terms that subsume the category under consideration,

(2) check if the mapping is consistent with the rest of the subsumers inside the upper ontology, (3) provide appropriate predicates to characterize the new category, and (4) edit it in an ontology editor to come up with the final formal version.

- Even though semantic web technologies are attractive and promise many benefits, they are not, unfortunately, ready for production use yet. Ontology-management systems hardly support the large ontologies needed for most production environments, and thus should be preferably used for research and experimentation purposes. A good example of the lack of maturity of these technologies are the APIs for ontology persistence in Java available today: Jena, Sesame and Protégé's persistence APIs find many difficulties in managing medium to large sized ontologies.
- Although the Organic.Edunet portal is based on a distributed architecture, the semantic module calls for a centralized repository that harvests the data from all repositories in the federation. Even though the harvesting tests carried out so far have shown good results, scalability, size and performance issues might arise as the project progresses and have an impact in the development.

CONCLUSION

To further illustrate the potential of Semantic Web technologies in Web portal applications, experiences from large-scale implementations are required. Especially in the case of Web portals that provide access to learning resources, the implementation of Web portals with services that are based on Semantic Web technologies that will be tested semantically annotating large collections of learning resources, and by being accessed and used from communities of users with numerous members. In this direction, this article presented a large-scale implementation effort that engages Semantic Web in order to set up a technical infrastructure that will facilitate sharing and reusing of learning resources for the agricultural domain. The next steps of this work concern reporting the results from the actual implementation, deployment, and initial testing of the technologies that are integrated in the Organic. Edunet Web portal.

ACKNOWLEDGMENT

The work presented in this article has been funded with support by the European Commission, and more specifically the project No ECP-2006-EDU-410012 "Organic.Edunet: A Multilingual Federation of Learning Repositories with Quality Content for the Awareness and Education of European Youth about Organic Agriculture and Agroecology" of the *e*Content*plus* Programme.

REFERENCES

Aroyo, L., Denaux, R., Dimitrova, V., & Pye, M. (2006). Interactive Ontology-Based User Knowledge Acquisition: A Case Study. *Lecture notes in computer science, 4011*, 560.

Averweg U. (2007), Portal Technologies and Executive Information Systems Implementation, in A. Tatnall (Ed.), *The Encyclopedia of Portal Technology and Applications*, Hershey, PA: Idea Group Publishing.

Berners-Lee, T. (1998). Semantic Web Road Map. *W3C Design Issues. URL http://www. w3. org/ DesignIssues/Semantic. html, Oct.*

Boff E., Rizzon Santos E., Vicari R.M., "Social Agents to Improve Collaboration on an Educational Portal," Sixth IEEE International Conference on Advanced Learning Technologies (ICALT'06), IEEE Computer Press, 896-900, 2006.

Conceicao S., Sherry L., Gibson D., Amenta-Shin, G.,"Managing Digital Resources for an Urban Education Portal". in Proc. of World Conference on Educational Multimedia, Hypermedia and Telecommunications (ED-MEDIA 2003), Honolulu, Hawaii, June 23-28, 2003.

Daraselia, N., Yuryev, A., Egorov, S., Novichkova, S., Nikitin, A., & Mazo, I. (2004). *Extracting human protein interactions from MEDLINE using a full-sentence parser*, 20, 604-611. Oxford Univ Press.

DeSanctis G., Wright M., Jiang L., "Building A Global Learning Community", Communications of the ACM, 44 (12), 80 – 82, December 2001.

EC (2004), European Action Plan for Organic Food and Farming, COM 415, Brussels 10 June 2004.

Ethridge R.R., Hadden C.M., Smith M.P., "Building a Personalized Education Portal: Get a Behind-the-Scenes Look at LSU's Award-Winning System", Educause Quarterly, 23(3), 12-19, 2000.

Fielding, R. T. (2000). Chapter 5: Representational State Transfer (REST), Architectural Styles and the Design of Network-based Software Architectures, Dissertation.

Forte, E., Haenni, F., Warkentyne, K., Duval, E., Cardinaels, K., Vervaet, E., et al. (1999). Semantic and pedagogic interoperability mechanisms in the ARIADNE educational repository. *SIGMOD Rec., 28*(1), 20-25.

Hatala M., Richards G., Eap T., Willms J., "The interoperability of learning object repositories and services: standards, implementations and lessons learned", in Proc. of the 13th International World Wide Web Conference, New York, NY, USA, 19-27, 2004.

Holden, C. (2003). From Local Challenges to a Global Community: Learning Repositories and the Global Learning Repositories Summit. Version 1.0, Academic ADL Co-Lab, November 11.

Kotzinos D., Pediaditaki S., Apostolidis A., Athanasis N., Christophides V., "Online curriculum on the semantic Web: the CSD-UoC portal for peer-to-peer e-learning", in Proc. of the 14th International Conference on World Wide Web, Chiba, Japan, 307 – 314, 2005.

LTSC (2002). IEEE Standard for Learning Object Metadata, 1484.12.1-2002. IEEE Learning Technology Standards Committee, 2002.

Luke R., Clement A., Terada R., Bortolussi D., Booth C., Brooks D., Christ D., "The promise and perils of a participatory approach to developing an open source community learning network", in Proc. of the 8th Conference on Participatory Design on "Artful integration: interweaving media, materials and practices", 11 – 19, Toronto, Ontario, Canada, 2004.

Maedche, A., Staab, S., Stojanovic, N., Studer, R., & Sure, Y. (2001). SEAL - A framework for developing SEmantic Web PortALs. *Lecture Notes in Computer Science*, 2097(1-22), 46.

Mahadevan B., "Business Models for Internet based E-Commerce: An Anatomy", California Management Review, 42(4), 55-69, 2000.

Manouselis N., Costopoulou C. (2007). Experimental Analysis of Design Choices in Multi-Attribute Utility Collaborative Filtering, International Journal of Pattern Recognition and Artificial Intelligence (IJPRAI), Special Issue on Personalization Techniques for Recommender Systems and Intelligent User Interfaces, 21(2), 311-331.

McGreal, R. (2004). Learning Objects: A Practical Definition. *International Journal of Instructional Technology and Distance Learning, 1*(9), 21-32.

Moraga A., Calero C., Piattini M., "Comparing different quality models for portals", Online Information Review, 30 (5), 555-568, 2006.

Moreale E., Vargas-Vera M., "Semantic Services in e-Learning: an Argumentation Case Study", Educational Technology & Society, 7 (4), 112-128, 2004.

Neven F., Duval E., "Reusable learning objects: a survey of LOM-based repositories", in Proc. of the 10th ACM International Conference on Multimedia, Juan-les-Pins, France, 291 – 294, 2002.

Palmér M, Enoksson F, Nilsson M, Naeve A (2007a). Annotation Profiles: Configuring forms to edit RDF. In: Proceedings of the Dublin Core Metadata Conference. DCMI Conference Papers, United States.

Palmér, M., Enoksson, F., Naeve, A (2007b). LUISA deliverable 3.2: Annotation Profile Specification,.

Palmér, M., Naeve, A., Paulsson, F., (2004), The SCAM-framework – helping applications to store and access metadata on the semantic web, Proceedings of the First European Semantic Web Symposium (ESWS 2004), Heraklion, Greece, May, 2004, Springer, ISBN 3-540-21999-4.

Richards, G., McGreal, R., Hatala, M., & Friesen, N. (2002). The Evolution of Learning Object Repository Technologies: Portals for On-line Objects for Learning. *Journal of Distance Education*, 17(3), 67-79.

Sánchez-Alonso S., Cáceres J., Holm A.S., Lieblein G., Breland T.A., Mills R.A., Manouselis N., "Engineering an ontology on organic agriculture and agroecology: the case of the Organic.Edunet project", in Proc. of the World Conference on Agricultural Information and IT (IAALD AFITA WCCA 2008), Tokyo, Japan, 24 - 27 August, 2008.

Sánchez-Alonso, S. and García, E. (2006) Making use of upper ontologies to foster interoperability between SKOS concept schemes. Online Information Review, 30(3), pp. 263-277.

Sancho, P., Martínez, I., & Fernández-Manjón, B. (2005). Semantic Web Technologies Applied to e-learning Personalization in< e-aula>. *Journal of Universal Computer Science, 11*(9), 1470-1481.

Santos, E. R., Boff, E., & Vicari, R. M. (2006). Semantic web technologies applied to interoperability on an educational portal. In *Proc. of Intelligent Tutoring Systems, 8th International Conference*, 4053, 308-317.

Shadbolt N., Berners-Lee T., Hall W. (2006). The Semantic Web Revisited, *IEEE Intelligent Systems*, 21(3), 96-101, May/June.

Sicilia M. A, García E. Sánchez-Alonso S, and Soto J. (2005). A semantic lifecycle approach to learning object repositories. In *Proceedings of ELETE 2005 - eLearning on Telecommunications*, Lisbon, Portugal.

Soto, J., García, E. and Sánchez-Alonso, S. (2007). Semantic learning object repositories. *International Journal of Continuing Engineering Education and Life-Long Learning*, 17(6), pp. 432-446.

Stokes E., Edge A., West A. (2001). Environmental education in the educational systems of the European Union, Environment Directorate-General, European Commission, April.

Tane J., Schmitz C., Stumme G., "Semantic resource management for the web: an e-learning application", in Proc. of the 13th International World Wide Web Conference, New York, NY, USA, 1-10, 2004.

Tatnall, A. (2005b), "Portals, Portals Everywhere...", in Tatnall, A. (Ed.), Web Portals: the New Gateways to Internet Information and Services, Hershey, PA, Idea Group Publishing, 1-14.

Tatnall, A., Ed. (2005a). Web Portals: the New Gateways to Internet Information and Services. Hershey, PA, Idea Group Publishing.

Tatnall, A., Ed. (2007). Encyclopaedia of Portal Technology and Applications. Hershey, PA, Information Science Reference.

Verdejo M.F., Barros B., Mayorga J.I., Read T., "Designing a Semantic Portal for Collaborative Learning Communities", in Selected Papers from the 10th Conference of the Spanish Association for Artificial Intelligence (CAEPIA03), Current Topics in Artificial Intelligence, LNCS 3040, Springer Berlin/Heidelberg, 251-259, 2004.

Vuorikari R., Manouselis N., Duval E. (2008). Using Metadata for Storing, Sharing, and Reusing Evaluations in Social Recommendation: the Case of Learning Resources, in Go D.H. & Foo S. (Eds.) *Social Information Retrieval Systems: Emerging Technologies and Applications for Searching the Web Effectively*, Hershey, PA: Idea Group Publishing.

Warner, S. (1999). Internet portals, what are they and how to build a niche Internet portal to enhance the delivery of information services. In *Proceedings of 8th Asian-Pasific SHLL Conference*.

Winkler, R. (2001). Portals – The All-In-One Web Supersites: Features, Functions, Definition, Taxonomy. SAP Design Guild, Edition 3. Retrieved May 2, 2008, http://www.sapdesignguild.org/editions/edition3/portal_definition.asp.

Woukeu A., Wills G., Conole G., Carr L., Kampa S., Hall W., "Ontological Hypermedia in Education: A framework for building web-based educational portals", in Proc. of World Conference on Educational Multimedia, Hypermedia and Telecommunications (ED-MEDIA 2003), H Honolulu, Hawaii, June 23-28, 2003.

This work was previously published in International Journal of Web Portals, Vol. 1, Issue 1, edited by J. Polgar, pp. 71-91, copyright 2009 by IGI Publishing (an imprint of IGI Global).

Chapter 3.7
Interactive Whiteboards in the Web 2.0 Classroom

David Miller
Keele University, UK

Derek Glover
Keele University, UK

ABSTRACT

This chapter summarizes the work underway to chart, critically evaluate, and systematize the introduction of interactive whiteboards (IWB) into modern foreign language classrooms in England. It is suggested that there is a developmental cycle whereby teachers take some time to understand the technology and become competent in its use. They then look to its advantages in presentation and the motivation of students before becoming aware of its pedagogical value and develop a changed classroom practice. This cycle is based upon enhanced teacher understanding of the nature of interactivity and the potential offered by the IWB in meeting a variety of learning needs. The relationship between IWB use and Web 2.0 arises from the potential of both to add impetus for teachers to structure lesson development and enhance activity. It is supported by teacher understanding of questioning techniques, and increasingly, by consideration of the use of gestures at the IWB. While IWBs are not a solution to all learning problems, it is suggested that they offers scope for greater student involvement and understanding in the learning process.

INTRODUCTION

The interactive whiteboard (IWB) is part of the growing variety of equipment used in conjunction with a computer and data projector to incorporate software, Internet links and data equipment for whole class use. Increasingly schools are equipping each subject area, and in many cases every classroom, with an interactive whiteboard to supplement or replace traditional white or blackboards. This is happening in many parts of the world, for example in Mexico there has been a focus on IWB installation and use, wherever possible, to ensure that the full potential of the equipment and associated software can underpin quality lessons to be taught on the widest possible scale. This shows a fundamental belief that IWB technology and pedagogy can make

DOI: 10.4018/978-1-60566-190-2.ch027

a difference across a range of subjects (Hennessey, Wishart & Whitelock, 2007; Belli, 2005; McFarlane, 2005). Research shows that this may be true for certain young people and for a period of time but that fundamental changes promoting continued educational achievement are only possible where teachers recognize the significance of the word "interactive" and develop their approaches to teaching to promote this. Such approaches are concerned with driving student involvement and increasing understanding. They are based on the recognition of students' differing learning needs in order to ensure conceptual understanding and cognitive development (Armstrong et al., 2005; Hall & Higgins, 2005; Kent, 2006; Smith et al., 2005; Sturcke, 2004; Jones, 2004).

Glover and Miller (2003) have traced the pattern of increasing use in terms of the influence of "missioners, tentatives and luddites" within schools. More importantly they have demonstrated that teachers need to be helped through a three-stage development process so that they can move from traditional to increasingly more interactive approaches, specified as:

a. *Supported didactic*, where the teacher makes some use of the IWB but only as a visual support to the lesson and not as integral to conceptual development.

b. *Interactive*, where the teacher makes some use of the potential of the IWB to stimulate student responses from time to time in the lesson and to demonstrate some concepts.

c. *Enhanced interactivity*, where the teacher develops the materials so that the students focus upon the IWB as a means of prompting, explaining, developing and testing concepts for most of the lesson.

It is only at the third stage that the potential of the board as the focus of learning based upon a new understanding of the learning process, is recognized and realized by the teacher (Miller & Glover, 2004; Ziolkowski, 2004; Watson, 2006).

The capacity to use the equipment in this way is dependent upon both technical fluency in the use of the equipment and associated software, and pedagogic understanding and flexibility to exploit the possibility of interactivity between teacher and student, and student and student. To achieve this has much in common with the educational development of all ICT and reflects a move, whether recognized or not, to the use of the Web 2.0 platform (Belshaw, 2007). Web 2.0 is here understood to be related to a focus on learning through concentration on multimedia use, age and ability linked group and individualized learning, and an awareness of variations in personal learning styles (Xhakli, 2008). This brings with it a change of emphasis from the teacher centered transmissive approach to learning to one characterized by interactivity, collaboration, user-generated content and immediacy of feedback. This is based on short attention switches from the teacher to the IWB as a mediating agency allowing access to other ICT technology within the classroom.

In a sense the IWB presents a new meta-language for classroom use. It certainly has developed its own vocabulary, which offers new technical terms. These become part of the basic language from initial training sessions with phrases such as "calibration," "drag and drop," and "hide and reveal" being early concepts for the user to understand. With the use of the interactive potential, phrases such as "virtual manipulatives" (Weiss, 2005) signify understanding of both process and pedagogic possibility, and as the integration of technology and pedagogy becomes better understood teachers and learners become aware of associated words from subject specific areas such as "the use of artifacts," which in both mathematics and modern languages has its own significance within the IWB focused classroom.

Language, however, is more than vocabulary, and IWB users become aware of the use of intonation, whereby the same word or phrase used in a different way signifies another meaning. This can be illustrated by considering the word "interactive" which is seen to operate at three levels — as indicating that there is a relationship between the technology and the user whereby a physical action leads to changes in the visual content on the boards; as an instruction to a user when using the board; or to one planning the sequence of conceptual developments and seeking a process by which movement on the board can lead to action in the brain of the recipient and subsequent action in the classroom.

This argument suggests that teaching and learning is limited by what occurs on the desk or the board but there is an intermediary in the process. This is the teacher, however defined; who acts as a mediator in the process of learning and who, we have noticed, develops a set of gestures as the non-verbal aspect of language. While not all users have the same hand and face gestures for similar aspects of mediation, research shows that users make consistent use of the same non-verbal expressions as lessons proceed (Miller & Glover, 2006).

This chapter concentrates on the outcomes of research that has been centered on the way in which IWB users, both teachers and learners, have developed their use of hardware and software to enhance teaching and learning in modern foreign language teaching. Our work was based on recent research and practice publications that highlighted the way in which IWBs could be a support in target language teaching. Research has also highlighted the role of ICT in language teaching and directed teachers to the use of the Internet, streaming videos and downloaded resources as a stimulant to interest in the classroom. Interactivity, however, is a feature of the Web 2.0 philosophy and this may extend beyond the classroom to include e-mail correspondence, blogging, and the use of *realia*. These are shown in the developing shareware from the Teacher Resource Exchange in England (tre.ngfl.gov.uk/server.php). As yet, though, there is very little modern language and IWB specific research. Glover et al., (2007) deal with the research outlined below in more detail and Gray et

al., (2007) examine the integration of the IWB with teaching in the lower secondary school. Both are however, reporting on the need to move from didactic to more interactive approaches.

Our illustrations are taken from research into the learning of modern foreign languages within ten schools in England in 2004. These schools were all at an early stage of technology use and the experience of teachers in these schools accords with that of all new learners in that they have had to gain both competence and confidence in working with technology in enhancing pedagogy.

IWB AND MODERN LANGUAGE TEACHING

The selected schools were known to have previously good OfSTED (national inspection service) reports and were therefore likely to be showing good practice. Overall 13 lessons were video-recorded for subsequent analysis according to the following framework:

- The timeline and activity sequence in each lesson. This usually included a revision starter, and then moved through vocabulary use to sentence construction and grammatical understanding.
- Classroom management issues. These included the way in which the room was set out for the lesson, the nature of the environment to favor or inhibit IWB use for all students in the room, the integration of the IWB with traditional textbooks and other resources and the use of student groupings for learning activities.
- Enhancement from IWB use was sought within a framework of revision of past work, establishing new principles and data, sequencing of information and learning, as well as the demonstration of processes and reinforcement of learning through recall and the use of examples.

- The contribution of IWB use to cognitive development was assessed through the establishment of aims, the use of varied learning styles, stepped learning sequences with revision as needed, problem solving, and recall and discussion as a bridge to further learning.
- The contribution of IWB use to the conceptual development of discrete elements in the lesson through the identification of processes, manipulation of data, and review to ensure understanding and application as part of cognitive development.
- The nature of IWB techniques used within the lesson and the way in which these are perceived by students.
- An assessment of the teaching style used in the lesson.
- Identification of practical and pedagogical issues arising from the use of IWB technology in its contribution to effective learning.
- Measurement of the percentage of the lesson when the IWB was the focus of teaching and learning.

Structured interviews were also undertaken with ten teachers to probe aspects of their understanding of presentational, motivational and pedagogical issues inherent in technology use. The interviewers attempted to identify the reasons why, and how, teachers felt that the IWB made a difference to learning. Two groups of ten students each were interviewed in two schools to gain some triangulation with teacher opinion. There appears to be a run-in period of between eighteen months and two years while teachers develop competence in handling the technology, in developing fluency in its use and in establishing a battery of basic screens to support their teaching. Whilst teachers may have developed these skills their practice could still be grounded in older styles of teaching — or these styles may emerge in some lessons but not in others according to the needs of the topic and the class context.

PRESENTATION

During the lesson observation notes were made of the techniques used in the presentation of materials. In some lessons teachers used several techniques, in others they used just two or three but exploited them to the full as a further spur to learning. Overall, the frequency of use was as shown in Table 1.

Observation and interview evidence was also used to explore the processes by which IWB use promoted interactivity as understood by teachers in the lessons. In using techniques the four most common methods of securing interactivity were:

- Drag and drop, matching a response to a stimulant.
- Hide and reveal, opening a hidden response when the stimulant was understood.
- Matching equivalent terms, e.g. vocabulary in different languages.
- Movement, to demonstrate principles, e.g. sentence construction.

Students were also observed writing (and replacing) words, e.g. as they explained a story in a village mapped from the IWB, and shading e.g. to show rooms in a house where one would watch TV. In all of these the aim of the teachers was to: "have a number of children working at the board so that they could gain competence and confidence and to get others involved especially where we were using competitive approaches to keep them all involved" (Male teacher, Spanish lesson).

Teachers made use of superimposition by moving phrases or words and putting them alongside vocabulary or in sentences, and considerable use of matched verbal and visual representation of vocabulary. They made use of the coloring potential for parts of speech, and shading, to mark parts of a sentence as construction developed.

Nine of the teachers made some comment about higher standards of presentation as a result of the

Table 1. Use of techniques in IWB focused teaching

Techniques	Example	No of lessons (n=13)
Movement and animation	Cycle route on map	11
Drag and drop	Vocabulary	10
Overwriting of screen	Verb endings	10
Verbal and visual linkage	Sounds and objects	10
Superimposition	Labeling	10
Hide and reveal	Sentence construction	10
Shading	Comprehension	5
Imported sound	Clip	4
Gap infilling	Sentence construction	4
Internet access	Life in village	4
Highlighting	Parts of speech	4
Automatic responses	Vocabulary	4
Applet development	Describing actions	3
Tools	Connecting lines	2

use of IWB software and in each of the student groups there were three references to the way in which writing on the board had improved. According to teachers, it was "sort of professional looking" and "much easier to read than the writing we used to have."

At the same time both teachers and students spoke of the problems of "over-writing" where teachers made notes on diagrams on the board, and where "the writing looks odd, sort of angular." This is partly due to the level of fluency developed in the use of the pen on the IWB, but also related to the precision generated by the software.

Although increasing, at the time there were few commercial or professional programs specifically designed for teaching modern languages using the IWB. As a result practitioners speak of the need to develop their own materials often through electronically scanning textbooks, or from downloaded Internet material. In three of the lessons characterized as "supported didactic" a page of sketches had been scanned from a textbook and this lacked the movement, color and vitality of comparable material built up by the teacher from clipart collections, but given interest through at-

taching sounds. This incorporation of sound was a feature of half the lessons observed in modern languages. Four of the 13 lessons also made use of passages from the Internet as the basis of a comprehension activity and in two lessons students working with laptops were asked to pursue this at a higher level while the others in the class worked at the IWB.

Observation suggests that the use of the presentational aspects of the IWB varies as students get older. Year seven students (aged 11-12) showed enthusiasm and interest when filling in missing words in a competitive situation—the capacity for the IWB to have associated sounds for success and failure added to this. By year nine (aged 13-14), however, it appears that students are less willing to participate in either volunteering to write on the board unless all students are involved, or as a member of a small group at the board; completing "hide and reveal" type statements or hazarded answers, and demonstrating verbal relationships to the rest of the class. Indeed, there is some evidence that by this stage students will attempt to subvert some of the presentational advantages through spotting wrong results so that they incur the "noise of failure," or give the wrong answer to "appear to be one of the gang."

One skilled teacher pointed out, however, that this does not mean that students have outgrown the board. Rather they expect the teacher to be fluent in its use and to lead their learning in such a way that their consolidation takes place individually in their exercise books following teacher use of IWB materials. Discussion showed that even to age 16 students appreciate its value when the IWB is a source of further material for comprehension, or when it is used to demonstrate grammatical rules in action.

Consideration of the content and approach of the observed lessons indicates that the more didactic teaching was in lessons where there were fewer activities in the lesson period, where the pace was more limited and where there were longer periods of textbook or exercise work. In these lessons there were also fewer techniques used and teachers tended to make use of "drag and drop" or "hide and reveal" more than in lessons that used movement, automation (manipulatives) and color changes. In the lessons characterized by enhanced interactivity there was a tendency to use more activities with several techniques and a combination of commercially or professionally produced materials with those developed by the teacher. These lessons had greater pace and tended to use the IWB as the focus of all activity including board-based exercises and extension work. A year nine group learning German followed a three minute revision starter with three activities building vocabulary through highlighting, drag and drop and hide and reveal; building phrases through pair work drawing upon matching of vocabulary, gender and translation, to sentence construction based on an Internet activity. The lesson concluded with revisiting screens and the use of color highlighting to identify rules for case and gender agreement.

Teachers commented on, and used, color highlighting and arrows to indicate movement and positioning for parts of speech and to indicate verb endings. Over half the lessons observed made some use of associated sound, imported pictorial material and "real" newspaper or magazine extracts as a basis for comprehension work and the application of vocabulary. It was agreed that this was the greatest presentational advantage in that pre-prepared materials could be highlighted, expanded, developed and analyzed by over-written comment. In discussion respondents also considered the issues of "savability." All except two participants had a battery of screens that they used as they prepared their lessons. The general view was that although it took time to prepare lessons for IWB use they could then be stored and used in three ways:

1. Catalogued by topic and then drawn out as each lesson was prepared.
2. Catalogued by lesson and then copied if the same screen was to be used in another lesson.
3. Catalogued by intended year group and then developed with further material if being used in a different context.

Teachers were less ready to regularly link their presentation to the printer so that materials could be made available for students. In 9 of the 13 observed lessons there was an element of copying from the IWB at some stage in the lesson. Table 2 shows the results of an analysis of the copying used in observed lessons:

Some copied activity characterizes all the teaching described as "modified didacticism," but also occurs in the other styles of IWB use. It seems that teachers are less willing to explore or use the copying facility than is claimed by the promoters of IWB technology. The more positive view emerges from a linguist who commented on the time saved by being able to print off materials for those needing extra help.

Table 2. Analysis of copying activity during observed lessons (multiple activities possible)

Nature of copying activity	Number of language lessons (n=9)
Examples for exercises	6
Rules of grammar or process	4
Copied screen as a record	2
Aims of the lesson	1
Homework material	3

MOTIVATION

In all the discussions with teachers it has been difficult to sort out the motivational factors from the presentational or pedagogic in the successful use of the IWB. Seven of the teachers made reference to the intuitive use of the technology as a feature in the everyday lives of students and felt that the schools should be offering a high level of presentation and attractiveness so that "what happens in school should not be seen as a poor relation to what they see on TV and computer screens."

Our evidence suggests that the major features that encourage student motivation are as follows:

- The intrinsic stimulation provided by the combination of the visual, kinesthetic and auditory paths to learning.
- Those aspects of classroom management that lead to a focus on the IWB with linked desk activities throughout the lesson.
- The stepped learning that characterizes much IWB teaching offering constant challenges with frequent assessment of achievement as a stimulant to further involvement.
- The particular advantages for slower learning students or those who need reinforcement through the presentation of data or processes with more than one learning style (i.e. the ability of the board to allow material to be presented or represented in a variety of ways.

The observed lessons show, however, that older and more able students gain from the IWB because they appreciate the visualization of structures more readily than through verbally dominated approaches. A German lesson for 15-16 year olds exploited the IWB to build up and then analyze sentences in terms of constituent vocabulary, constructional frameworks and comprehension alongside continuous and enthusiastic encouragement from the member of staff who constantly referred them back to earlier screens. It was not simply the IWB, but also the way in which it had become integrated into the teaching method in a highly personal way combining visualization and encouragement of all students, that enhanced learning.

Another factor in the motivation of students stemmed from the way in which teachers exploited a "different type of contact with the lesson in the student's hands." Good practice obviously builds upon knowledge of particular groups and of individuals within the groups and a realistic assessment was that "the IWB still doesn't mean that we shall have a lesson where all the students are paying attention all the time." Boys, for example, are generally more ready to demonstrate or complete work at the IWB than girls of the same age. Older boys were more ready to demonstrate in part because it provides an opportunity for them to show their superiority in technological fields when teachers comment upon inadequacies of programs or available tools, while girls were more concerned about "being right" before they would commit themselves to the board. Evidence from the two student groups showed that they thought that "lessons had less wasted time" and that "they moved with more pace so that they didn't want them to come to an end." If there is one single motivational factor during lessons it appears to be that the immediacy of response ensures maintained interest. Seven of the teachers refer to the enhanced engagement in lessons and four referred to the ways in which the use of the IWB encouraged participation.

Although there was general agreement that teachers needed to consider aspects of lighting, student seating arrangements, sight lines, and the area of the board in use by students considering their physical characteristics, the observed lessons highlighted continuing issues. In four of the 13 lessons tables were organized in such a way that students were in rows at right angles to the board, or at grouped tables where half of the students naturally had their backs to the board. This problem is not subject specific but is related to the size of the room, access problems and the need for teachers to move around while desk work is in progress. In three classrooms light infiltration rendered vision difficult for those seated at the near front of the sides of the rooms. Amelioration was achieved in one school by using laptops with the same screen program so that vision was achieved and in another by breaking the lesson up in such a way that board activity was distinct from grouped activity. The latter was dependent upon group work using laptops and linked audio material while one group worked with the IWB and then groups moved to different activities in a subsequent lesson.

When the student groups were asked to identify why lessons were of greater interest than in traditional teaching they identified:

- The inherent interest of color, shading, dynamics, hide and reveal and demonstration.
- The sequential development of ideas and exemplars resulting from pre-prepared and commercial software.

- The availability of games that support learning, require responses that can be immediately assessed and then linked to a scoring system with team races or noughts and crosses.
- The "fun" arising from the use of pictorial matter and the immediacy of any processing built into the programs.
- The opportunity to revisit earlier concepts and examples in underpinning understanding.

Where lessons have such a dynamism and attraction it is likely that they will offer interest and challenge. This supports both revision of earlier work and enhanced understanding of new work. Above all as one teacher commented this offers "credible media for a new age." Teachers were conscious, however, of the time demands for preparation even when using commercial materials, and four referred to the problems of technology that could inhibit slick use of the IWB.

These data show that those lessons characterized by enhanced interactivity focused on the board for a greater proportion of the lesson, while those where the board was a support for more didactic approaches used the board for a significantly more limited period. For linguists more of the lesson may have to take place away from the board, e.g. in practicing vocabulary use, constructing sentences, and repeating words and phrases. The most interactive lessons were those where these activities were linked to the board. In four of the 13 lessons this led to a combination of choral reading, repetition of phrases and word completion using sentences from the board. Overall time on task is greater when the IWB is the focus of teaching and learning.

There was considerable concern that there could be a novelty value in the use of the new technology, "but we have to remember that students are used to this at home" and "that they think advanced technology now." One teacher commented "there is now danger that if we don't use the technology we will be seen as lacking in some way." All the respondents accept this but it is clear that teachers have developed strategies to ensure that there should be a continuing upward progression in learning and attainment. In a year seven French lesson the teacher used an introductory activity based upon naming colors, then moved to five vocabulary development exercises and finished with a learning check linked to boys versus girls scoring to ensure that momentum was maintained, that all the students were taking part and that visual stimulation was used to the full with a total of ten screens during the 35 minute lesson. That said, the dynamism of the teacher was important in supporting continuing learning — even broken with a two minute march to the French alphabet to stimulate renewed activity.

While it would be easy to claim great advantages for the IWB in motivating students at all ages it is evident that it is the quality of the teaching that ensures progress. Comparison was made of two lessons of vocabulary development with year seven groups. In one there were seven screens used in the course of the lesson but these were interspersed with pair work, a brief exercise and a discussion about rooms in the house. The students were animated throughout. In a comparable lesson, again with seven screens used, the teaching approach was much more didactic, there was little variation in activity from stage to stage in the lesson and the inter-relationship between teacher and learners was authoritarian and defensive. In such circumstances the lesson could not have the vigor, and "fun" element shown with a different teacher.

But there is another subtle influence noted by four of the respondents. This is because the constant progression in an interactive situation absorbs those who might otherwise become fidgety in a traditional classroom situation. They, in turn are less "nagged" during the lesson, enjoyment increases and motivation is supported: "It enhances collaborative work. This may just take the form of kids shouting out, correcting each other, say in a multiple-choice selection. This is very noticeable. As the teacher you too are working in a community, where you are visible. It does give a sense of competition, of expectation, the idea of can you beat it?" (male teacher, Spanish lesson).

PEDAGOGY

It was clear that teachers were using the learning of concepts as a basis for cognitive understanding. As a result in all but two of the 13 lessons there were discernible cognitive aims and a series of activities to explore, develop, explain and reinforce subsequent understanding. This was summed up one teacher as follows: "Sustained learner interest works in a number of different levels. It is not just a gimmick ... the interaction is important, like kids coming out to the board, having choices, e.g. they can decide on the verb ending, find the stem and match up the right pronoun. It makes concrete in their minds how the language works" (male teacher, German lesson).

There was a high level of understanding that students learn in different ways. This was seen where a pattern of viewing pictures, learning associated vocabulary, repeating its use in sentence construction, and then undertaking written or spoken group work ensured that: "we both enjoy teaching and learning more ... you can give clearer examples which are more interesting because of access to color and clip art. It's more aesthetically pleasing and is good for visual and kinesthetic learners and it's useful in that you can jumble up sentences and get them involved in reconstruction" (male teacher, French lesson).

Although there was some use of commercially developed activities, such as a short color recognition program — "we have developed our own materials from a number of sources, including download from the net, magazine and picture scanning and my own extensive library of clip art images" — this was seen to have advantages in that what was developed was meeting specific needs. Two teachers, however, expressed reservations — one about the time taken to produce good professional looking materials, and the other about "the danger of getting too structured and then unable to work flexibly if a problem occurs in the learning process for a particular topic" (female teacher, French lesson).

Teachers were all conscious of the need to maximize interactivity between themselves, the students and the learning materials. This is achieved through developing the opportunity to use "visual manipulation" so that concepts can be illustrated and worked upon by the students; the growth of shared evaluation of resources and the use of shared materials developed within subject areas, and exploitation of immediacy of feedback either through programmed software or through the use of presentational tools as with the colors program in French, or with right and wrong answer symbols. These programs are most effective as starters or for work with the least able when rapid responses and moving on enhance word manipulation.

There was also much debate about the place of traditional textbooks, exercise books, homework and other data sources in teaching. Over-writing was seen to offer scope for assisting cognitive development by "showing the same thing in different ways." Much of the Internet use was to download games and activities that did just this by underpinning learning of vocabulary and phrase development, or even with some audio links to check pronunciation. Most importantly, however, were the ways in which the IWB was being used to underpin lesson structure and to enhance cognitive development. Teachers variously appear to use a structure of:

- Setting objectives with or without revisiting earlier IWB slides.
- Using a bright and lively starter including "drag and drop," "hide and reveal" and multiple answers to stimulate interest, to offer a chance for brainstorming

as a bridge to the main part of the lesson, and to revise necessary associated learning.

- Proceeding to the main part of the lesson where the IWB is the focus of much activity being used for illustration, explanation, sequenced ideas and the development of main principles. The progression was through the use of vocabulary and its application in sentences reinforced by practice and comprehension. During this section of the work the approach was distinguished by challenged responses with the emphasis on understanding and then using language correctly — with practice in the completion of sentences on the IWB reinforced by group activities. In this way, as one teacher commented, "you move the students with you." Interview respondents identified a tension between those who thought that time taken in managing the students' use of the IWB while others were watching could be seen as a loss to active learning but in eight language lessons students were given tasks alongside the work being illustrated on the board so that all the students were active.
- Concluding with a plenary session involving the use of recall, examples and previously worked material to ensure understanding and to act as the basis for extension work. This section of the lesson was more usually concerned with revisiting vocabulary and structures and then looking at an associated screen requiring comprehension or conversation as a consolidation for the lesson.

Awareness of the need for cognitive development and the place of concepts within this was shown in the frequent reference to sequencing of ideas, the availability of a range of pre-prepared examples appropriate "to age and ability," adaptability of materials to allow for "alternative approaches and the use of different ways of learning." This was through vocabulary understanding and pronunciation, and through phrase and sentence construction to use in verbal and aural comprehension. Three linguists outlined the use of supportive materials from the net or other sources, and three referred to the need to help students understand the technology e.g. in the use of pens and programs, so that they could become fluent in the interactivity required if whole class participation was to be assured.

There were comments that dependence on sequenced slides in some pre-prepared materials in PowerPoint and Excel, as well as in some of the commercial materials, could inhibit flexibility in revisiting ideas and in offering alternative explanations appropriate to "whether they can learn verbally or not." This was not seen to be a problem in the observed lessons because of the technological fluency shown in accessing screens. There was a general view amongst those interviewed that when the staff have the time to develop their materials and access to appropriate technological support it was possible to use the IWB to generate faster and more effective learning, with tighter planning and the implementation of lesson plans according to the need to cover the prepared material.

There was frequent reference in the interviews to the need to match materials to the needs of the students and that some differentiation of task, activity or outcome required teachers to be flexible, adaptable, and "aware of the ways in which consolidation can occur without going back to old fashioned practices such as copying." This was illustrated in a comparison between two groups learning and applying clothing vocabulary showing that the more able group moved on to determine the difference between summer and winter clothing while using similar screens of information.

In pedagogic review the teachers also drew attention to the clear match of objectives to activities and the understanding of these by students so that they could use the board to help in their evaluation of progress. They showed an awareness of what the IWB could offer and in the two most stimulating lessons Web 2.0 approaches were integrated into the teaching. In one lesson there were five groups working at their own level in differing learning situations. These included the use of an interactive software program at the IWB, access to the net by a group using a laptop, randomized questioning in pairs with an interactive program on a desktop, and the preparation of a presentation by a group working with PowerPoint. It is possible that all these approaches can exist individually without being specifically labeled as Web 2.0 but they are now being used to shift the emphasis from teacher to student, from lecture to learning.

THE DEVELOPING AGENDA

Arising from the agenda it appears that there are two pedagogic areas for further investigation. The first is the relationship between the teacher, the student and the materials involved. For enhanced interactivity to occur this has to be understood as a chain reaction where the IWB is a means of mediation between learners and learning. There are four elements in this process:

a. *Teaching approach.* Ernest (1994) suggests a simple scale for the approach used by teachers. At the lowest level the teacher is an "instructor" concerned with the presentation of concepts as rules followed by practice. At the higher level the teacher is "facilitator" offering approaches that enhance understanding, and at the highest level the teacher is a "mediator" bridging between student understanding and development. In their use of the interactive whiteboards the instructor is concerned with elements of presentation. Conversely the mediator deals with issues arising from questions and thereby regards the interactive whiteboard as a vehicle for interaction with students.

b. *The use of the interactive whiteboard.* In both the approaches discussed above, it is evident that the interactive whiteboard enhances the role of the teacher regardless of where s/he is on the spectrum. The teacher-as-instructor will be working with prepared material, to be presented in a logical sequence, and often with a PowerPoint sequence as the basis of the teaching. The material is likely to be focused on statements of facts and definitions, headings etc. but there will also be examples to be copied and exercises to be completed. Such material is likely to be organized, clear and monotone. On the other hand, the teacher-as-mediator will be concerned with how the IWB can support the features of mediation such as modeling and coaching in relation to the topic under consideration. In collaborative classrooms, modeling serves to share with students not only what one is thinking about the content to be learned, but also the process of communication and collaborative learning. Modelling may involve thinking aloud (sharing thoughts about something) or demonstrating (showing students how to do something in a step-by-step fashion). Coaching involves giving hints or cues, providing feedback, redirecting students' efforts, and helping them use a strategy. A major principle of coaching is to provide the right amount of help when students need it — neither too much nor too little so that students retain as much responsibility as possible for their own learning (Tinzmann et al., 1990). This can be seen in the selection of appropriate adjectives or in the search for word meanings. Miller, Glover and Averis (2005) have suggested that as competence improves teachers become more ready to develop and use manipulatives as the basis of interaction. This is seen to particularly good

effect in consideration of the accommodation available at differing costs within a French holiday town where the input of so many Euros into a slot machine then produced a range of menus for description and selection. It is our contention that the use of particular manipulations might be used effectively to support the role of teacher-as-mediator (Miller, Glover, Averis & Door, 2005).

c. *Questioning.* Experienced and effective teachers use questioning intuitively. They probably think little about the nature or level of the question but proceed as they think fit. Inexperienced and poor teachers appear not to have such skills. Much has been written about the nature of questions and the art of questioning. Mason (2000), in his commentary on the work of many in this field, clearly demonstrates the complexities of the process and relates questioning to both conceptual and cognitive development. Analysis of the video recorded lessons suggests that open and closed questions and those focusing on product or process are frequently used but are only partially helpful in developing higher order learning.

d. *Learning Models.* The fourth element in developing interactivity stems from the learning model espoused by the teacher. Observations have been made on the way in which teachers use the constructivist and social-constructivist views of learning as defined by Piaget (Piaget & Inhelder, 1974) and Vygotsky (1978). Students construct concepts and meaning, as a solo activity, based on their own experience. Associated with this model is the notion of "cognitive conflict" whereby children are exposed to something that is different from (conflicts with) their currently perceived models. From Vygotsky, the focus is on the social-constructivist view of language and the extent to which it is linked with the formation of knowledge. Furthermore, all knowledge is a social construction and based on shared views and images. In language teaching the social context of much learning offers scope for constructivist learning to be enhanced. The opportunity to call on a vast range of Internet resources helps when technological fluency allows access.

GESTURE

In the introduction to this chapter we spoke of the impact of intonation on language understanding and we return to this in considering the way in which teachers, and indeed board-using students, gesture while mediating between board and class.

There is an increasing awareness that teaching is a multi-modal activity drawing upon a range of communicatory activity including verbal, visual and interpersonal communication, as well as associated technology. Jewett (2004) has shown that knowledge of multi-modal perception and pedagogy can support both teachers and taught. Abrahamson (2003) outlines the role of artifacts or bridging tools, including gesture in that learning process. Watson and De Geest (2005) outline the need for consideration of all aspects of communication in teaching and learning, and Rasmussen et al (2004) explore the use of consistent gesture as part of these multi-modal approaches. Goldin-Meadow and Wagner (2005) take these patterns of gesture further and consider the impact of these on both learners and their learning environment through reflection of the state of knowledge and subsequent change through cognitive understanding.

There is considerable evidence of the way in which the teachers using enhanced interactive approaches were constantly using recognizable gesture patterns. One female teacher used all-embracing movements to secure attention at the start of most lessons almost sweeping the students along with her as she summed up her aims and then moved towards the IWB. During starter periods her hands were used in a quick to and fro movement linking students to the IWB but ensuring that the pace of the lesson was maintained. In the main section of the lesson her movements were slower, often indicating building or process stages, and then opened in an invitational way as explanation was returned to the students for consolidation. There was then a return to quicker, pointing and sequencing gestures as stages were revisited in the plenary section of the lesson. When asked about the pattern of interaction the teacher referred to "the need to keep them on their toes, but to feel that we were learning together."

Ferscha et al., (2005) attempt to extend the gesture typology with three families of gestures — hand gestures, gestures of an artifact held permanently (e.g. an IWB pen) and gestures that are detached from the hand and manipulated occasionally (e.g. change of software). All of these convey messages by the way in which they are used. While such a system is of potential value for user interface computer technology development it does not offer the sort of vocabulary of gestures that match the instinctive activity by teacher and student in the classroom. However, it is the basis of gesture sensing devices and could well offer an insight into a typology because it may be that students read more into body language, as shown when recall of an IWB screen fails and frustration is indicated, or when invitations are issued for students to work at the IWB and they respond with acceptance gestures.

In our analysis of video-recorded lessons it was possible to ascertain the reliance on gesture by both teacher and students and the combination of gesture as explanation, indication and invitation. The IWB both encourages and reinforces learning through the use of visual as well as more transitory gestures that offer shapes in the air. During this lesson gestures were used and emulated in an often involuntary manner, in all three areas of gesture; hand, software and artifact. The hand movements that mediated technology and learning through movements were:

- *Invitational*, with the use of movement linking students to the IWB, offering the pen for use, showing a step and offering an opportunity for participation – often encouraged with IWB software.
- *Displaying*, with hand gestures pointing to material on the IWB and then using movement, highlighting or overwriting to indicate content or process.
- *Blocking*, with hand gestures putting a barrier between the students and the IWB as a result of mistakes or the need to re-think a process and then followed by an invitational reinforcement of process and use of drag and drop and over-writing to support this.
- *Sequencing*, with the gestures to indicate progression and using gestures to pose a question and then to work through sequences of example questions.

It would seem that students learn not only because of the difference in presentation but also because the IWB offers additional modes of gesturing that support verbal and visual explanation. It may be that this kinaesthetic quality will meet the needs of those who cannot readily learn with didactic approaches. Our observations suggest that where teachers are using enhanced interactivity with the IWB they are employing considerable gesturing to great advantage

ACHIEVING INTERACTIVITY

The starting point for the effective use of IWB technology has to be in teacher training. Nevertheless, the move from traditional didactic approaches to changed pedagogy is complex. It has been recognized that although UK student teachers are required to have a basic knowledge of computer use as a requirement for certification many already have a high degree of computer literacy and technological understanding. Whether

this can be harnessed to enhance teaching appears to be related to other factors including the nature of curriculum development programs, school technology resource levels, and individual teachers' planning and reflection. Kennewell (2001) suggests that effective evaluation of ICT use will prompt more awareness of, and adaptation to, the complexity of influences in the classroom. More pessimistically, Robertson (2003) argues that despite the potential impact of ICT on teaching and learning it remains a marginal influence on student attainment. He argues that other significant changes have been more willingly achieved in education and that the slow pace of change in ICT may be related to social, anthropological and cultural aspects of the human and computer interaction. Kirschner and Selinger (2003) point to the disparate technological competence of teachers and the children they teach and argue that if ICT is to be a core technology then teachers need to recognize not only how to use the different technologies but also follow through a five stage development from pre-novice through novice, apprentice, and practitioner to expert user. The elements of this stage are the ability to reflect, evaluate and adapt both content and approach to address student needs. If this is to be achieved, then the work of teacher educators takes on a major role extending beyond the "how to" to the "why" of ICT and the use of interactive whiteboards (Sturkle, 2004).

This requires understanding of the potential of Web 2.0 tools in association with IWB use to change the way in which teachers encourage learning. Interactivity may be a matter of question and answer but Web 2.0 approaches in modern language teaching may open the way for the use of interactive software, as for example in vocabulary extension work; for the use of the net in developing comprehension; for the use of search engines in preparing presentations, and for enhanced understanding of the cultural context. In this way presentation spurs motivation and this, in turn, promotes higher attainment. This is especially so where collaborative group work has been developed to meet differing learning styles. Web 2.0 tools provide the means of both conceptual and cognitive development.

However at the time of the investigation it was not possible to podcast and share videos. These technologies offer considerable opportunities (and threats) for teachers and pupils. The possibilities will undoubtedly be constrained by the technical, pedagogical and attitudinal backgrounds of the teachers. Further limiting factors will be the way in which uses of some Web 2.0 technologies are "censored" and restricted by school firewalls.

In language teaching students may find considerable benefits in using (and creating) products that may help them with their study. Generally the technological skills will be within the grasp of learners — but the option to demonstrate and use these skills may be overlooked.

Even at the most basic technological level this may require fundamental changes in aspects of initial teacher education. In simple terms, the assertion that mentoring teachers should be at least competent in ICT use was found wanting by Cuckle and Clarke (2003) who comment on the considerable variation in student support between schools. When that competence occurs for Knezek and Christensen (2002) the focus of subsequent change is determined by evidence that:

as teachers progress from lower level, simple applications toward full integration of technology in the classroom in support of higher cognitive functions, attitudes progress in predictable patterns along with changes in their needs. (p. 375)

Once established as teachers and in continuing professional development there is some evidence that successful one-to-one coaching can be achieved where the technologically adept students are paired with teachers having a much wider pedagogic experience to mutual

benefit (Matthew et al., 2002). Mooij (2004) argues that teachers have to be aware not only of the technical aspects of newer technologies but also of the curricular and instructional gains that can be made, and more importantly of the way in which technology and pedagogy can be integrated to achieve flexible and individually sensitive learning situations. Triggs and John (2004) have demonstrated the need for working groups at departmental, whole-school and educational service levels, interconnecting for professional growth through the sharing of technical and pedagogic experience.

The recurrent theme is one of a discrete way of teaching and learning using ICT and Taylor (2004) suggests that this requires a three stage development from personalization to achieve fluency in using the technology, through pedagogic sensitivity to its potential, to the development of contingent thinking to allow responsive and reflective use of materials. In the context of continuing professional development, this requires strong support within teacher training institutions and the schools with whom they work in partnership. This will then help teachers who have been inappropriately, or inadequately, trained in the pedagogy and do not realize the need to develop interactivity through the use of a variety of teaching and learning styles, artefacts and gesture — in short, coping with the affordances of the technology (Conole & Dyke, 2004). Failure to make a significant pedagogic change will, we suggest, lead to wasted opportunities and the danger that equipment with the potential to change understanding, application and the conceptual development of learning will be at worst, unused, and at best a presentational aid.

For this to occur there has to be further consideration of the professional development provided for users. Glazer and Hannafin (2006) building on Vygotsky's social constructivist approaches suggest that this exploration of what happens in the classroom is best undertaken as a social enterprise where peers rely on the expertise and support of one another to adopt innovative practices: "Reciprocal interactions in a community of practice, where teachers take responsibility for each other's learning and development, may provide an effective means of supporting situated professional learning" (p. 179). Contextual work by Schrum et al. (2005) points to the need for departments to continually refine, reassess and redevelop their teaching approaches. Eekelen et al. (2005) have shown that this process needs to be regulated rather than self-regulated and unstructured — with implications for those responsible for professional development, and Tearle (2003) shows that this is particularly true of learning in technology based contexts where the learning culture is fundamental to teacher involvement and shared experience

CONCLUSION

There appears to be a learning curve for both teachers and students. The former need time to develop their technological fluency, apply pedagogic principles to the available materials or to the development of materials, and then to incorporate the IWB seamlessly into their teaching. Few teachers base all their lesson on the IWB all the time, and over half those interviewed stressed that the IWB has to be seen as part of the equipment available but that there was still a need for the use of texts, exercises and other media. Teachers then appear to become more aware of the nature of interactivity and its stimulation as the basis for conceptual development and cognitive understanding. Students also need to have a range of manipulative skills if they are to take part in lessons without loss of self-esteem as technologically incompetent. Even so good practitioners ensure that all students have access to the board, and are given help if there are signs of unhappiness with the medium.

It is only when basic technological fluency and pedagogical understanding has been achieved that teachers can then overcome the novelty factor. Our evidence suggests that there is an initial period where interest is stimulated by the cleverness of the technology, but after a period students are more aware of three great gains:

1. Brighter and clearer presentation of material
2. Stepped learning and the ability to recall earlier material
3. Rapid responses to interactive examples so that learning is reinforced or revisited

Where students have reached this stage, they accept the IWB as part of the battery of learning resources offered to them and progress beyond novelty to enhanced learning. At this stage any possible behavioral problems are usually overcome because students are caught up in the sequence and pace of learning and appear to "take off" in their understanding, achievement and consequent self-esteem.

There is evidence that language teaching is being transformed by competent and confident teachers but this is not to suggest that the IWB is a panacea for all ills. As yet, there is only a limited shift in classroom practice and student learning and transformation will require markedly changed teacher understanding. Our evidence suggests that there is a teacher progression from supported didactic to enhanced interactivity in their classroom and pedagogical management. Where there is still reliance on the copying of material, textbook exercises and minimal conceptualization of learning so that it can be interactive, the gains are minimized. Effective learning is inhibited where the IWB is given a novelty value by the teacher so that it becomes something different, where the physical surroundings are not conducive to IWB use and where the lesson lacks pace. It is not sufficient to argue that the use of the IWB will, of itself, bring the classroom into the Twenty First Century and the visually stimulated environment. Effective teaching requires that the technology and the pedagogy are directed towards enhanced and structured understanding. "I love my board because it gives so much to the kids," as one teacher said, may be the clue that enthusiasm can be regenerated not just in the students but in the staff also.

REFERENCES

Abrahamson, D. (2003). Embodied spatial articulation: a gesture perspective on student negotiation between kinaesthetic schemas and epistemic forms in learning mathematics. In McDougall, D. E., & Ross, J. A. (Eds.). *Proceedings of the 26ᵗʰ Annual Meeting of the International Group for the Psychology of Mathematics Education 2*, 791-797.

Armstrong, V., Barnes, S., Sutherland, R., Curran, S., Mills, S., & Thompson, I. (2005). Collaborative research methodology for investigating teaching and learning: The use of interactive whiteboard technology. *Educational Review, 57*(4), 457–469. doi:10.1080/00131910500279551

Belli, M. (2005). Technology is not white and black. *Times Educational Supplement*. Retrieved May 1, 2008, from: http://www.tes.co.uk/search/story/?story_id=2063467

Belshaw, D. (2007). Flattening the world: How to harness Web 2.0 tools to engage learners inside and outside the classroom. *In-service development day Kings Heath Leading Edge Partnership*. Retrieved November 27, 2007, from: http://www.slideshare.net/edte.ch

Conole, G., & Dyke, M. (2004). What are the affordances of information and communication technologies? *ALT-J, 12*(2), 113–124. doi:10.1080/0968776042000216183

Cuckle, P., & Clarke, S. (2003). Secondary school teachers, mentors and student teachers' views in the value of ICT in teaching. *Technology, Pedagogy and Education, 12*(3), 377–391. doi:10.1080/14759390300200168

Eekelen, I., Boshuizen, H., & Vermunt, J. (2005). Self-regulation in higher education teacher learning. *Higher Education, 50*(3), 447–447. doi:10.1007/s10734-004-6362-0

Ernest, P. (1994). The impact of beliefs on the teaching of mathematics. In Bloomfield, A. & Harries, T. (Eds.). *Teaching and Learning Mathematics*. Derby: Association of Teachers of Mathematics.

Fersha, A., Resmerita, S., Holzmann, C., & Reichor, M. (2005). Orientation sensing for gesture-based interaction with smart artefacts. *Computer Communications, 28*(13), 1552–1563. doi:10.1016/j.comcom.2004.12.046

Glazer, E. M., & Hannafin, M. J. (2006). The collaborative apprenticeship model: Situated professional development within school settings. *Teaching and Teacher Education, 22*(2), 179–193. doi:10.1016/j.tate.2005.09.004

Glover, D., Miller, D., Averis, D., & Door, V. (2007). The evolution of an effective pedagogy for teachers using the interactive whiteboard in mathematics and modern languages: An empirical analysis from the secondary sector. *Learning, Media and Technology, 32*(1), 5–20. doi:10.1080/17439880601141146

Glover, D., & Miller, D. J. (2003). Players in the Management of Change: introducing interactive whiteboards into schools. *Management in Education, 17*(1), 20–23. doi:10.1177/08920206030170010701

Goldin-Meadow, S., & Wagner, S. M. (2005). How our hands help us learn. *Trends in Cognitive Sciences, 9*, 234–241. doi:10.1016/j.tics.2005.03.006

Gray, C., Pilkington, R., Hagger-Vaughan, L., & Tomkins, S. A. (2007). Integrating ICT into classroom practice in modern foreign language teaching in England: Making room for teachers' voices. *European Journal of Teacher Education, 30*(4), 407–429. doi:10.1080/02619760701664193

Hall, I., & Higgins, S. (2005). Primary school students' perceptions of interactive whiteboards. *Journal of Computer Assisted Learning, 21*(2), 102–117. doi:10.1111/j.1365-2729.2005.00118.x

Hennessy, S., Wishart, J., & Whitelock, D. (2007). Pedagogical approaches for technology-integrated science teaching. *Computers & Education, 48*(1), 137–152. doi:10.1016/j.compedu.2006.02.004

Jewitt, C. (2004). *Knowledge, Literacy and Learning: Multimodality and New Technologies.* London: Routledge Falmer.

Jones, K. (2004). Using Interactive Whiteboards in the Teaching and Learning of Mathematics: a research bibliography. *Micro Math, 20*(2), 5–6.

Kennewell, S. (2001). Interactive whiteboards — Yet another solution looking for a problem. *Information Technology in Teacher Education, 39,* 3–6.

Kent, M. (2006). Our journey into whiteboard hell. *Times Educational Supplement.* Retrieved May 1, 2008, from: http://www.tes.co.uk/search/story/?story_id=2287557

Kirschner, P., & Selinger, M. (2003). The state of affairs of teacher education with respect to information and communications technology . *Technology, Pedagogy and Education, 12*(1), 5–17. doi:10.1080/14759390300200143

Knezek, G., & Christensen, R. (2002). Impact of new information technologies on teachers and students. *Education and Information Technologies, 7*(4), 369–376. doi:10.1023/A:1020921807131

Mason, J. (2000). Asking mathematics questions mathematically. *International Journal of Mathematical Education in Science and Technology, 31*(1), 97–111. doi:10.1080/002073900287426

Matthew, K., Callaway, R., Letendre, C., Kimbell-Lopez, K., & Stephens, E. (2002). Adoption of ICT by teacher educators: one-on-one coaching. *Technology, Pedagogy and Education, 11*(1), 45–62. doi:10.1080/14759390200200122

McFarlane, A. (2005). The taming of the whiteboard. *Times Educational Supplement.* Retrieved May 1, 2008, from: http://www.tes.co.uk/search/story/?story_id=2153815

Miller, D., & Glover, D. (2004). *Enhancing mathematics teaching through new technology: The use of the interactive whiteboard.* Retrieved May 1, 2008, from: http://www.keele.ac.uk/depts/ed/iaw/nuffield.htm.

Miller, D. J., Glover, D., & Averis, D. (2005). Developing Pedagogic Skills for the Use of the Interactive Whiteboard in Mathematics. *British Educational Research Association, Glamorgan.* Retrieved September 25, 2007, from: http://www.keele.ac.uk/depts/ed/iaw/docs/BERA%20Paper%20Sep%202005.pdf.

Miller, D. J., & Glover, D. C. (2006) *Enhanced secondary mathematics teaching: gesture and the interactive whiteboard.* Paper presented at the British Educational Research Association Annual Conference, University of Warwick, September 6-9.

Miller, D. J., Glover, D. C., Averis, D., & Door, V. (2005). The Interactive Whiteboard — A literature survey. *Technology, Pedagogy and Education, 14*(2), 155–170. doi:10.1080/14759390500200199

Mooij, T. (2004). Optimising ICT effectiveness in instruction and learning. *Computers & Education, 42*(1), 25–44. doi:10.1016/S0360-1315-(03)00063-0

Piaget, J., & Inhelder, B. (1974). *The child's construction of quantities*. London: Routledge & Keegan Paul.

Rasmussen, C., Stephan, M., & Allen, K. (2004). Classroom mathematical practices and gesturing. *The Journal of Mathematical Behavior, 23*, 301–323. doi:10.1016/j.jmathb.2004.06.003

Robertson, J. W. (2003). Stepping out of the box: rethinking the failure of ICT to transform schools. *Journal of Educational Change, 4*(94), 323–344. doi:10.1023/B:JEDU.0000006047.67433.c5

Schrum, L., Burbank, M. D., Engle, J., Chambers, J. A., & Glassett, K. F. (2005). Post-secondary educators' professional development: Investigation of an online approach to enhancing teaching and learning. *The Internet and Higher Education, 8*(4), 279–289. doi:10.1016/j.iheduc.2005.08.001

Smith, J., Higgins, S., Wall, K., & Miller, J. (2005). Interactive whiteboards: boon or bandwagon? A critical review of the literature. *Journal of Computer Assisted Learning, 21*(2), 91–101. doi:10.1111/j.1365-2729.2005.00117.x

Sturcke, J. (2004). ICT strategy? 'Just keep taking the tablets'. *Times Educational Supplement*. Retrieved May 1, 2008, from: http://www.tes.co.uk/search/story/?story_id=2055679

Taylor, L. (2004). How student teachers develop their understanding of teaching using ICT. *Journal of Education for Teaching, 30*(1), 43–56. doi:10.1080/0260747032000162307

Tearle, P. (2003). Enabling teachers to use information and communications technology for teaching and learning through professional development: influential factors. *Teacher Development, 7*(3), 457–472. doi:10.1080/13664530300200222

Tinzmann, M. B., Jones, B. F., Fennimore, T. F., Bakker, J., Fine, C., & Pierce, J. (1990). *What Is the Collaborative Classroom?* NCREL: Oak Brook.

Triggs, P., & John, P. (2004). From transaction to transformation: information and communication technology, professional development and the formation of communities of practice. *Journal of Computer Assisted Learning, 20*(6), 426–439. doi:10.1111/j.1365-2729.2004.00101.x

Vygotsky, L. S. (1978). *Mind in society*. Cambridge, MA: Harvard University Press.

Watson, A., & De Geest, E. (2005). Principled teaching for deep progress: improving mathematical learning beyond methods and materials. *Educational Studies in Mathematics, 58*, 209–234. doi:10.1007/s10649-005-2756-x

Watson, D. (2006). Understanding the relationship between ICT and education means exploring innovation and change. *Education and Information Technologies, 11*(3/4), 199. doi:10.1007/s10639-006-9016-2

Weiss, D. F. (2005). Keeping it real: The rationale for using manipulatives in the middle grades. *Mathematics Teaching in the Middle School, 11*(5), 238–242.

Xhakli, K. (2008). *Going online: How innovative projects can transform education and ICT opportunities*. Kosovo: IPKO Institute.

Ziolkowski, R. (2004). Interactive Whiteboards: Impacting Teaching and Learning. *Media & Methods, 40*(4), 44.

KEY TERMS

Artifact (BE Artefact): Artifact is an object or item. However it can also be the on screen representation of an object or an item.

Gesture: This is a term encompassing human actions here associated with the use of the interactive whiteboard e.g. hand and body movements and facial expressions. There is evidence that users develop consistent hand and facial gestures e.g. in seeking responses, rejecting wrong responses and that learners assimilate these as part of the teaching package offered by individual teachers.

Interactive Whiteboard (IWB): An interactive whiteboard consists of a computer linked to a data projector and to a touch sensitive large electronic screen usually fixed to a wall. Images from the computer are then displayed onto the whiteboard by means of the data projector. These images can be manipulated at the electronic screen usually by means of a special pen or a finger (this depends on the properties of the electronic screen). The term interactive whiteboard often refers only to the electronic screen.

Interactivity: Interactivity is an approach to learning in which teacher and learner interact to ensure understanding, enhance conceptual development and stimulate debate. Learning is stimulated through participation rather than through rote or passive learning which characterises didactic approaches.

Motivation: In this context, is an outcome of presentation because of the greater interest offered to learners and the reinforcing of concepts through learner engagement.

Presentation: Presentation is the use of the software potential of the interactive whiteboard to enhance the way in which words, concepts, ideas and relationships are displayed. Design, color, movement and more complex virtual manipulatives offer a superior way of showing data on an interactive whiteboard with the intention of prompting learner participation. The use of a variety of means of display may meet the needs of learners with differing learning styles.

Social Constructivist Approaches: These are based upon the complex interaction between teacher and learner, or between learners, and relate to the way in which we learn from each other with greater facility once the social network of the context is known and when the culture of the learning group has been developed.

Virtual Manipulatives: A virtual manipulative is a computer program that represents a piece of equipment on a computer screen. Examples include a cannon that can fire cannon balls, a protractor for measuring angles and a geoboard where you can place and manoeuvre "elastic bands" on a grid on "nails." Virtual manipulatives are most commonly written in Flash and JavaScript.

This work was previously published in Handbook of Research on Web 2.0 and Second Language Learning, edited by M. Thomas, pp. 506-525, copyright 2009 by Information Science Reference (an imprint of IGI Global).

Chapter 3.8
Web 2.0 Technologies:
Social Software Applied to Higher Education and Adult Learning

Teresa Torres-Coronas
Universitat Rovira i Virgili, Spain

Ricard Monclús-Guitart
Universitat Rovira i Virgili, Spain

Araceli Rodríguez-Merayo
Universitat Rovira i Virgili, Spain

M. Arántzazu Vidal-Blasco
Universitat Rovira i Virgili, Spain

M. José Simón-Olmos
Universitat Rovira i Virgili, Spain

ABSTRACT

Web 2.0 technologies are playing an important role in building social capital through increasing flows of information, and building on knowledge and human capacity of learning. The purpose of this chapter is to show the role that social software, a component of Web 2.0 technologies, can play in higher education and adult learning. This chapter focuses on the role of Web 2.0 technologies in promoting learning. New learning paradigms and pedagogical applications are also discussed.

DOI: 10.4018/978-1-60566-739-3.ch059

INTRODUCTION

Education has traditionally been conducted face-to-face, with professors performing outstanding magisterial classes in front of the learners. During the centuries, students and professors have shared the same time and same space frame. Nowadays, things are quite different. Information technology (IT) is a reality affecting the whole education system from primary school to higher education and adult learning. IT is having a considerable impact on the learning providers, on the learning process itself and, of course, on any agent involved in the process.

History has demonstrated that technology affects education profoundly. Considering the definition of technology broadly, one may say that prehistoric people used primitive technologies to teach skills to their young (Frick, 1991). Whenever a new medium entered the picture, a new wave of educational delivery arrived. Radio, television, and now computers have all impacted the field of distance education. Though some studies (see Russell, 1999) report no significant differences in performance between face-to-face instruction and technology supported environments.

Nowadays, campuses are networked, faculty post their notes on Web pages, students access the library from their rooms, and entire classes can have discussions via chat software (Rice-Lively, 2000). This development has recently come to be labeled under the by now commonly accepted term e-learning (Hudson, 2003).

The European e-Learning Action Plan 2001 (European Commission, 2001) defines e-learning as the use of new multimedia technologies and the Internet to improve the quality of learning by facilitating access to resources and services as well as remote exchanges and collaboration. This requires new e-interaction and e-communication competencies and a reorganization of e-learning structures. Components can include content delivery in multiple formats, management of the learning, and a networked community of learners (Gunasekaran, McNeil, & Shaul, 2002). Internet/World Wide Web have meant that opportunities have been identified for developing distance learning activity into a more advanced online environment. It is known as Virtual Learning Environment (VLE), which eliminate geographical barriers while providing increased convenience, flexibility, individualized learning, and feedback over traditional classroom (Kiser, 1999). Higher education institutions devote substantial resources to providing students with access to internet-based information, VLEs

and other forms of e-learning. These efforts are predicated upon an assumption that "university students are inherently inclined towards using the internet as a source of information within their day-to-day lives and, it follows, disposed towards academic use of the internet" (Selwyn, 2008, p. 12).

But, today, the traditional approach to e-learning is currently changing from the use of Virtual Learning Environment (VLE) to e-learning 2.0, an approach that combines the use of complementary tools and Web services -such as blogs, wikis, trackback, podcasting, videoblogs, and other social networking tools- to support the creation of ad-hoc learning communities. In this context, most of the current research tends to be concerned with the potential of the worldwide Web and other internet applications to accelerate university students' learning and knowledge-building, and support interactivity, interaction and collaboration (Selwyn, 2008).

This proposal aims to provide an introductory perspective on the learning impacts of new media and Web 2.0 information and communication technologies on the e-learning environment. Web 2.0 technologies are playing a crucial role in building of social capital through increasing flows of information, and building on knowledge and human capacity for learning. Social software has emerged as a major component of the Web 2.0 technology movement. But, how can social software play a role in higher education and adult learning? To answer this question, this proposal will focus on the role of Web 2.0 technologies in promoting learning. Pedagogical applications, which stem from their affordance of collaborative knowledge discovery, will be discussed. At the same time the chapter will also explore the pedagogical methodology involved considering that e-learning Web 2.0 leads us from constructivism to navigationism. Finally, some suggestions are made for future research in this field.

BACKGROUND

Social Software and Web 2.0 Technologies as a Must for a Digital Life

The term social software is generally attributed to Tim O'Reilly. Social software includes a large number of tools used for online communication, e.g. instant messaging, text chat, internet fora, Weblogs (or blogs for short), wikis, social network services, social guides, social bookmarking, social citations, social libraries and virtual worlds.

O'Reilly (2005) presented Web 2.0 as a second stage in the development of the Web. He describes Web 2.0 as an "architecture of participation" where collective intelligence generates a "network effect" leading to Websites that become more valuable as more people participate (O'Reilly, 2003). For McGee and Begg (2008) "Web 2.0 represents a group of Web technologies with a user-centric focus that actively change and evolve with user participation" (p. 164). Web 2.0 is referred to as a technology (Franklin & Van Harmelen, 2007) and at the same time as a community-driven online platform or an attitude rather than technology (Downes, 2005).

Web 2.0 technologies are already having a significant impact on the way in which we communicate in both our personal and professional lives. Mejias (2005) wrote down a list of non-definitive kinds of social software applications, arranging technologies according to their social function (learning, selling, classifying, defining communities, and so on). Mejias (2005) stated that most social software products incorporate functions from more than one category and, also, most of them pose challenges to pedagogical approaches. And, these challenges are today instructors' challenges.

Organizational structures in the 21st century are also increasingly networked and with virtual teams becoming the norm. Virtual team working requires tools that enable the exchange of documents and information and collaborative creation. Wikis and blogs have taken relatively little time to become part of the suite of tools used for collaborative virtual projects. In this new organizational landscape, enterprise social or "collaborative software is probably the most visible current

Table 1. Different types of social software and its applications

Social software	Applications
Multiplayer gaming environments	Multi-User Dungeons (MUDs), Massively-Multiplayer Online Games (MMOGs).
Discourse facilitation systems	Synchronous: instant messaging (IM) and chat (e.g. Windows® Live Messenger, AOL Instant Messenger, Yahoo® Instant Messenger, Google™ Chat, Skype™); chat. Asynchronous: e-mail, bulletin boards, discussion boards, moderated commenting systems (e.g. Slashdot)
Content management systems	Blogs, wikis, document management (e.g. Plone™) and, Web annotation utilities.
Product development systems	Especially for Open Source software (e.g. Sourceforge.net®, Libresource)
Peer-to-peer (P2P) file sharing systems	Napster®, Gnutella, BitTorrent™, eMule, iMesh
Selling/purchasing management systems	eBay™
Learning management systems (LMSs):	Blackboard, WebCT, Moodle
Relationship management systems	Friendster®, Orkut
Syndication systems	list-servs, RSS aggregators
Distributed classification systems	Flickr®, del.icio.us.

challenge. Interpersonal communication has become an integral part of the process of content creation, hence the value placed on communities and networks" (Abell, Chapman, Phillips, Stewart & Ward, 2006, pp. 244-245).

Enterprise Social Software is a term describing social software in "enterprise" (business) contexts -definition provided by Wikipedia- [http://en.wikipedia.org/wiki/enterprise_social_software/]. It includes social and networked modifications to company intranets and other classic software platforms used by large companies to organize their communication'. Enterprise 2.0 is a paradigm shift. Organizations are increasingly focusing on leveraging internal information and on connecting people to people and people to content. Web 2.0 tools and techniques focus on collaboration and information/knowledge sharing. Business Information Survey explores the penetration of Web 2.0 tools. Results show that there is great strategic interest in social technology and Web 2.0 tools and techniques, but not much serious deployment yet (Foster, 2008). But, in our digital world, *digital natives* (Prensky, 2001) eagerly embrace social software developing the skills necessary to engage with social and technical change, and to continue learning throughout the rest of their lives..

As workers live Web 2.0 digital lives, organizations also will need to update their e-learning corporate practices. In that sense, Trondsen (2006) predicts strong uptake of virtual worlds in corporate learning and notes a number of pilot projects underway in company learning contexts. As students live Web 2.0 digital lives, instructors need to begin to deeply explore and develop new learning paradigms with these technologies and practices. And, finally, as the students of today grow into the leaders of tomorrow, they will bring these technologies into their organizations, making their use an essential part of the future of world of work and life-long learning.

Learning Paradigm Shifts

Since many years ago, different theories have been developed to explain how we learn. Behaviorism, cognitivism, and constructivism are the three broad learning theories most often utilized in the creation of learning environments. Neither of these views can be regarded as exclusively right or wrong. It is, however, necessary to know that constructivism is presently accepted as the most relevant of the three. In the pedagogical arena it is a must to analyze how these models allow instructors to create the circumstances best suited to facilitate student learning.

The first one, behaviorism, is a worldview that assumes a learner is essentially passive, responding to environmental stimuli. It stems from the work of Pavlov –the father of classical conditioning- and Skinner –the father of operant conditioning. Behavior theorists define learning as nothing more than the acquisition of new behavior. Learning is "any more o less permanent change in behaviour which is result of experience" (Borger & Seaborne, 1966, p.16). The behaviourist definition of learning focuses on the behavioural outcomes of learning, rather than on knowledge, attitudes and values.

After the behavioural theories came cognitive ones. The most influential theorists were Piaget and Vygotsky. Cognitivism theories seek to explain how the brain processes and stores new information. People are rational beings that require active participation in order to learn, and whose actions are a consequence of thinking. The learner is viewed as an information processor.

Constructivism as a paradigm posits that learning is an active, constructive process. According to a constructivist view, learning is seen as the individualized construction of meanings by the learner. The learner is an information constructor. Constructivist learning theories posit that knowledge is built by the learner, not supplied by the teacher (Piaget, 1967). People, by reflecting on their experiences, actively construct their own subjective representations of objective reality. Each of us generates our own mental models, which we use to make sense of our experiences. Learning, therefore, is simply the process of adjusting our mental models to accommodate new experiences.

In the present landscape of technological change, important transformations are underway in terms of how we teach and learn. There is a growing shift on the need to support the acquisition of knowledge and competencies to continue learning throughout life. "With respect to ICT, we are witnessing the rapid expansion and proliferation of technologies that are less about "narrowcasting", and more focussed on creating communities in which people come together to collaborate, learn and build knowledge" (McLoughlin & Lee, 2007, p. 664). So, constructivist approaches have grown to include social constructivism, which refers "to learning as the result of active participation in a community" where new meanings are co-constructed" (Brown, 2006, p. 111). Different learning strategies have been designed based on a community supported constructionist approach in which constructionism strategy –a strategy connected with experiential learning and based upon constructivist theories of learning- is situated in a supportive community context (Bruckman, 1998). This approach emphasizes the importance of social aspect of learning environment. The construction of new knowledge is the aim of these learning theories.

But beyond constructivism and social constructivism new paradigms are emerging. Brown (2006) focus on navigationism as the last learning paradigm shift. In this new learning paradigm the emphasis will be on knowledge navigation. Learning activities will be focused on exploring, connecting, evaluating, manipulating, integrating and navigating. Learning will take place when learners solve contextual real life problems through active engagement in problem-solving activities, and networking and collaboration. Siemens' principles of connectivism (Siemens, 2004) provides a summary of the connectivist learning skills required within a navigationist learning paradigm:

- Learning is a process of connecting specialized nodes or information sources.
- Capacity to know more is more critical than what is currently known.
- Nurturing and maintaining connections is needed to facilitate continual learning.
- Ability to see connections between fields, ideas, and concepts is a core skill.
- Currency (accurate, up-to-date knowledge) is the intent of all connectivist learning activities.
- Decision making is itself a learning process.

Connectivist learning skills are required to learn within a navigationist learning paradigm. And this is why Brown (2006) states that "connectivism is part and parcel of navigationism," (p. 117) a learning paradigm that needs further development. The main practical implication of Brown's work is that teachers and trainers should become coaches and mentors within the knowledge and digital era and learners should acquire navigating skills for a navigationist learning paradigm. To enhance e-learning Web 2.0 over time, it is vital for instructors to ground their designs on established learning theories and report how related learning experiences are integrated with Web 2.0 tools so instructors can determine what Web 2.0 tools have the greatest effect on learner motivation and performance. E-learning Web 2.0 is the key solution to equipping people with the evolving knowledge and skills that will be needed to adapt to the continuously changing nature of the information society. At the same time, the major aim in education is to produce autonomous learners. For Franklin and van Harmelen (2007, p. 21) "the growing Personal Learning Environment (PLE) movement has a significant Web 2.0 following which claims that PLEs are social software

Table 2. Comparison of characteristics of Web 1.0 versus Web 2.0 educational Websites. Source: McGee and Begg (2008, p. 167)

Web 1.0	Web 2.0
Course Websites using content management systems. An expert (course director) produces a syllabus which resides on a curriculum Website. Single Website, which displays the same content and design for all users. Posting problem based learning cases to a curriculum Website.	Faculty blogs, student discussion groups. Podcasts. Students in a course contribute to syllabus content with questions and answers to supplement expert materials. Personal Websites, with customized data sources and layout for individual users Small groups have their own Website to which they add learning objectives and educational content related to their coursework

tools that help or enable learners to take control of their own education" and learning processes throughout their lives.

POSSIBILITIES AND APPLICATIONS OF WEB 2.0 TOOLS

As Owen, Grant, Sayers, and Facer (2006) state "Web 2.0 will lead to e-Learning 2.0, to a rethinking of the relationship between technology and learning, to the development of educational practices that place the learner at their heart through the creation of collaborative, community-based learning experiences. To explore this further we touch now on the key theme of the potential shift in thinking from 'e-learning' to 'c-learning' (p. 10). Virtual communities of learning also offer the promise of bridging the worlds of work and education.

Some of the key attributes of social software in relation to education are that it (Owen et al., 2006): "Delivers communication between groups, enables communication between many people, provides gathering and sharing resources, delivers collaborative collecting and indexing of information, allows syndication and assists personalization of priorities, has new tools for knowledge aggregation and creation of new knowledge and, delivers to many platforms as is appropriate to the creator, recipient and context".

To help apply Web 2.0 to education McGee and Begg (2008, p. 167) summarize briefly the key differences between Web 1.0 and Web 2.0 (see Table 2). The new user-centered paradigm in which users are both producers and consumers of content and services has evolved from previous Web developments. The Web before the dot.com crash is usually referred to as Web 1.0. O'Reilly (2005) cites a number of examples of how Web 2.0 can be distinguished from Web 1.0, such as Web 1.0 was mainly a platform for information, but Web 2.0 is also a platform for participation. Web 1.0 tools can be used for the delivery of the course materials and for communication but Web 2.0 tools (such as blogs) can be integrated in a e-learning environment to a shift from a "knowledge transfer model" to a "knowledge construction model" as presented by Virkus (2008).

If one were to apply Web 2.0 concepts, "the lecture notes could become wikis (Wikipedia), the slides would become an image sharing collection (akin to Flick®), and students would subscribe to audio and video recordings (on a site like iTunes™), ideally all within an integrated "virtual learning environment." This online environment would allow students to create their own views of their learning material and combine, with their own notes and external information resources. In Web 2.0 parlance this is a "mash up," where content from different sources is combined by a user to create something new" (McGee & Begg, 2008, p. 167). Web 2.0 is suitable for educational and lifelong learning, because our knowledge society is built on digital environments of work and social communication, and educational practices must

Table 3. Educational applications of Web 2.0. Source: Franklin & Van Harmelen (2007, pp. 5-7)

Web 2.0 tool	Description	Educational application
Blogs	A system that allows an author to publicly display time-ordered articles.	A blogger can build up a corpus of interrelated knowledge. Teachers can use a blog for course announcements, news and feedback. Blogs can be used with syndication technologies to enable groups of learners and teachers to easily keep track of new posts.
Wikis	A system that allows one or more people to build up a corpus of knowledge in a set of interlinked Web pages.	Wikis can be used for the creation of annotated reading lists by one or more teachers. Wikis are suited to the incremental accretion of knowledge by a group, or production of collaboratively edited material.
Social bookmarking	It provides users the ability to record (bookmark) Web pages, and tag those records with significant words (tags) that describe the pages being recorded.	To build up collections of resources. Groups of users with a common interest can team together to use the same bookmarking service to bookmark items of common interest.
Media-sharing services	Sstore user-contributed media that allows users to search for and display content. Compelling examples include YouTube™ (movies), iTunes® (podcasts and vidcasts), Flickr® (photos), Slideshare (presentations), DeviantArt (art work) and Scribd (documents).	Podcasts can be used to record lectures. Podcasts can be used to supply audio tutorial material. Instructional videos and seminar records can be hosted on video sharing systems.
Social networking and social presence systems	Systems that allow people to network together for various purposes, such as Facebook© and MySpace® (for social networking / socialising), LinkedIn® (for professional networking), Second Life™ (virtual world) and Elgg (for knowledge accretion and learning).	LinkedIn® acts, at a professional level, as a model of educational use in the way in which it can be used to disseminate questions across the community for users seeking particular information. There are a wide variety of educational experiments being carried out in Second Life.
Collaborative editing tools	These allow users in different locations to collaboratively edit the same document at the same time, such as Google™ Docs & Spreadsheets.	For collaborative work over the Web.
Syndication and notification technologies	A world of newly added and updated shared content. A feed reader (or aggregator) is used to centralize all the recent changes in the sources of interest, and a user can easily use the reader/aggregator to view recent additions and changes. This relies on protocols called RSS (Really Simple Syndication) and Atom to list changes (these lists of changes are called feeds, giving rise to the name feed reader).	Feed Readers enable students and teachers to become aware of new blog posts in educational blogging scenarios, to track the use of tags in social bookmarking systems, to keep track of new shared media, and to be aware of current news

foster a creative and collaborative engagement of learners with this digital environment in the learning process (Guntram, 2007, p. 17).

Table 3 summarizes some educational applications of Web 2.0 tools included in Franklin and Van Harmelen's (2007) work.

To embed Web 2.0 tools and processes within mainstream higher education practice the following need to be in place (Collis & Moonen, 2008, p. 100):

- Both instructors and students must value an educational approach where learner participation and contribution are balanced with acquisition.
- A pedagogical approach must be used that reflects contribution-oriented activities where students create some of their own learning resources.
- The approach must be scaffolded in practice by interlinked support resources for

both instructors and students. Uncertainty must be reduced as much as possible for the students in terms of what is expected of them, and to what standard.

- The processes as well as the products produced by the students must be assessed as part of overall course assessment practices.

In higher education and adult learning educational applications of Web 2.0 tools add extra value to the learning experience and have an unlimited potential. So far, we have briefly summarized the increasingly varied ways in which these new tools can be used to construct the navigationist learning paradigm. This new learning paradigm 2.0 represents an opportunity to revolutionize the way human beings learn, interact, innovate and develop.

FUTURE TRENDS

Different subjects need to be explored in detail to step up research —educational, socio-economic and technological— in the field of e-learning 2.0 and in the use of Web 2.0 tools in higher education and adult learning.

- Special attention need to be devoted to using emerging technologies (GRID, Web 3.0) for the development of innovative applications for education and training. In this new technological environment, the question of how to motivate and socialize the student as an active learner needs also to be raised. As Hvid and Godsk (2006) state "e-learning platforms needs an aesthetic perspective instead of mainly addressing usability and function". (p. 210)
- In the near future, portable and personal technologies will offer new opportunities to connect people and to create new e-learning 2.0 environments. We are only

beginning to understand the opportunities that mobiles technologies provide for learning. As Wilson (2006) points out "Web platforms that allow moblogging (blogging from mobile phones), vlogging (video blogging) and other forms of 3G-enabled participation are increasingly popular and show clearly the potential for user-generated 3G content to be integrated in an architecture of participation" (p. 239). Mobile technology will play a key role in the new e-learning 2.0 paradigm.

- e-Learning 2.0 indicators need to be further developed in order to monitor progress in the use of Web 2.0 in formal and informal education.
- Education methods, learning communities organization are essential aspects in this context.
- Research also needs to provide a holistic view of students' actual use of the social software in higher education and adult learning.
- Another key issue for any future research is to explore what forms of knowledge students obtain from social software and, most importantly, how students use such knowledge. In-depth qualitative research should be carried out to understand how is built through Web 2.0 technologies.
- The concept of virtual campus and virtual networks for cooperation and collaboration needs to be revisited.
- In the virtual world, social networking functions can enable learners to aggregate into communities of interest and evolve into communities of learning or practice. We need to understand the formation of these communities and ways to facilitate the contribution of cybersocial networking to the learning and engagement of students and teachers (Computing Research Association, 2005).

- E-learning Web 2.0 may be able to reach learners who are disadvantaged by the digital divide. If it also important to define a research agenda which takes into account individual differences in learning, and special needs education to exploit the potential of Web 2.0 technology to provide remedial measures in the case of disability, exclusion, difficulty in gaining access to learning, or where conventional education does not work.

- Finally, special attention needs to be given to the promotion of gender equality in building e-learning 2.0 communities and social capital.

Bearing in mind all these agendas, e-learning 2.0 are likely to be a fertile research field.

CONCLUSION

Each new wave of technological innovation promises to revolutionize education, as we know it. The emergence of e-learning Web 2.0 is currently affecting most colleges, universities, and corporations. Now it is time to step back and question the pedagogical principles that inform our learning paradigms because Web 2.0 technologies have to be implemented taking into account pedagogical perspectives. The use of Web 2.0 technologies in higher education and adult learning is still a new technological phenomenon which will only "become valuable in education if learners and teachers can do something useful with it" (OECD, 2001, pp. 24-25).

REFERENCES

Abell, A., Chapman, D., Phillips, P., Stewart, H., & Ward, S. (2006). Roles in the e-landscape: Who is managing information? *Business Information Review, 23*(4), 241–251. doi:10.1177/0266382106072249

Borger, R., & Seaborne, A. (1966). *The psychology of learning.* Harmondsworth: Penguin Books.

Brown, T. H. (2006). Beyond constructivism: Navigationism in the knowledge era. *Horizon, 14*(3), 108–120. doi:10.1108/10748120610690681

Bruckman, A. (1998). Community support for constructionist learning. *Computer Supported Cooperative Work: The Journal of Collaborative Computing, 7,* 47–86. doi:10.1023/A:1008684120893

Collis, B., & Moonen, J. (2008). Web 2.0 tools and processes in higher education: Quality perspectives. *Educational Media International, 45*(2), 93–106. doi:10.1080/09523980802107179

Computing Research Association. (2005). *Cyber infrastructure for education and learning for the future: A vision and research agenda.* Retrieved September 15, 2008, from http://www.cra.org/reports/cyberinfrastructure.pdf

Downes, S. (2005). e-Learning 2.0. *eLearn Magazine: Education and Technology in Perspective.* Retrieved September 15, 2008, from http://www.elearnmag.org/subpage.cfm?section=articles&article=29-1

European Commission. (2001). *The elearning action plan. Designing tomorrow's education.* Retrieved September 15, 2008, from http://eurlex.europa.eu/LexUriServ/LexUriServ.do?uri=COM:2001:0172:FIN:EN:PDF

Foster, A. (2008). Business information survey. *Business Information Review, 25*(1), 13–31. doi:10.1177/0266382107088221

Franklin, T., & Van Harmelen, M. (2007). *Web 2.0 for content for learning and teaching in higher education,* JISC, Bristol. Retrieved September 15, 2008, from http://www.jisc.ac.uk/media/documents/programmes/digitalrepositories/Web2-content-learning-and-teaching.pdf

Frick, T. (1991). *Restructuring education through technology.* Bloomington, IN: Phi Delta Kappa Educational Foundation.

Gunasekaran, A., McNeil, R. D., & Shaul, D. (2002). E-learning: Research and applications. *Industrial and Commercial Training, 34*(2), 44–53. doi:10.1108/00197850210417528

Guntram, G. (Ed.). (2007). *Open educational practices and resources. OLCOS Roadmap 2012.* Salzburg Research EduMedia Group, Salzburg. Retrieved September 15, 2008, from, available at: http://www.olcos.org/cms/upload/docs/olcos_roadmap.pdf

Hudson, B. (2003). Promoting collaboration in and international online learning community. *Industrial and Commercial Training, 35*(3), 88–93. doi:10.1108/00197850310470294

Hvid, M., & Godsk, M. (2006, June). *The pleasure of e-learning - Towards aesthetic e-learning platforms.* In Proceedings of the 12th International Conference of European University Information Systems, University of Tartu & EUNIS, Tartu, Estonia, (pp. 210-212).

Kiser, K. (1999). 10 things we know so far about online training. *Training (New York, N.Y.), 36*(11), 66–74.

McGee, J. B., & Begg, M. (2008). What medical educators need to know about "Web 2.0". *Medical Teacher, 30*(2), 164–169. doi:10.1080/01421590701881673

McLoughlin, C., & Lee, M. J. W. (2007, December). S*ocial software and participatory learning: Pedagogical choices with technology affordances in the Web 2.0 era.* In ICT: Providing choices for learners and learning. Proceedings ASCILITE (pp. 664-675), Singapore. Retrieved September 15, 2008, from http://www.ascilite.org.au/conferences/singapore07/procs/mcloughlin.pdf

Mejias, U. (2005). *A nomad's guide to learning and social software.* Retrieved September 15, 2008, from http://knowledgetree.flexiblelearning.net.au/edition07/download/la_mejias.pdf

O'Reilly, T. (2003). *Architecture of participation.* Retrieved September 15, 2008, from http://www.oreillynet.com/pub/wlg/3017

O'Reilly, T. (2005). *What is Web 2.0?* Retrieved September 15, 2008, from http://www.oreillynet.com/pub/a/oreilly/tim/news/2005/09/30/what-is-Web-20.html?page=1

OECD. (2001). *OECD E-learning: The partnership challenge.* Paris: OECD.

Owen, M., Grant, L., Sayers, S., & Facer, K. (2006). *Social software and learning.* FutureLabs. Retrieved September 15, 2008, from http://www.futurelab.org.uk/research/opening_education.htm

Piaget, J. (1967). *Six psychological studies.* New York, NY: Vintage Books.

Prensky, M. (2001). Digital natives, digital immigrants. *On the Horizon, 9*(5). Retrieved September 15, 2008, from http://www.marcprensky.com/writing/Prensky%20-%20Digital%20Natives,%20Digital%20Immigrants%20-%20Part1.pdf

Rice-Lively, M. L. (2000). Bordeless education at UT-Austin GSLIS. *Texas Library Journal, 76*(2), 58–60.

Russell, T. L. (1999). *The no significance difference phenomenon.* Raleigh, NC: North Carolina State University Press.

Selwyn, N. (2008). An investigation of differences in undergraduates' academic use of Internet. *Active Learning in Higher Education, 9*(1), 11–22. doi:10.1177/1469787407086744

Siemens, G. (2004). *Connectivism: A learning theory for the digital age.* Retrieved September 15, 2008, from http://www.elearnspace.org/Articles/connectivism.htm

Trondsen, E. (2006). *Virtual worlds for learning and training.* Menlo Park, CA: SRI Consulting Business Intelligence.

Virkus (2008). Use of Web 2.0 technologies in LIS education: experiences at Tallinn University, Estonia. *Program: Electronic Library and Information Systems, 42*(3), 262-274.

Wilson, J. (2006). 3G to Web 2.0? Can mobile telephony become an architecture of participation? *Convergence: The International Journal of Research into New Media Technologies, 12*(2), 229–242. doi:10.1177/1354856506066122

KEY TERMS

Collaborative Learning: An educational approach based the idea that learning is a naturally social act. The learner actively constructs knowledge by formulating ideas into words, and these ideas are built upon through reactions and responses of others. In other words, collaborative learning is not only active but also interactive. It is a student-centered approach in which social software tools are currently used for building and sharing knowledge.

Connectivism: A learning theory for the digital era. It is based upon the idea that knowledge is networked and so the act of learning takes place inside virtual networks and communities through social interaction. It is a networked model of learning.

E-Learning (electronic learning): Technology-supported learning and delivery of content via all electronic media. These may include Internet, intranets, computer-based technology, or interactive television. They may also include the use of e-technology to support traditional methods of learning, for example using electronic whiteboards or video conferencing. This terms covers a wide set of applications and processes, such as Web-based learning, computer-based learning, virtual classrooms, and digital collaboration.

Personal Learning Environments (PLE): A learning environment in which learners manage their own learning by selecting, integrating and using various software tools and services. It takes advantages of Web 2.0 affordances such as collaborative information and knowledge sharing.

Social Capital: A cross-disciplinary concept referring to the benefits of social networks and connections. Social capital is constructed and maintained in the interaction between individuals or groups. Social networks promote different types of social capital: bonding –referring to horizontal ties between individuals-, bridging – referring to ties that cut across different communities- or linking –referring to vertical ties.

Social Software: Software that allows the creation of communities and resources in which individuals come together to learn, collaborate and build knowledge. It is also known as Web 2.0 and it supports social interaction and collaborative learning. Current typical examples include Flickr® and YouTube™ –as audiovisual social software.

Virtual Learning Environments (VLE): A set of teaching and learning tools designed to enhance a student's learning experience by including computers and the Internet in the learning process. The principal components of a VLE package include curriculum mapping, student tracking, online support for both teacher and student, electronic communication, and Internet links to outside curriculum resources. There are a number of commercial VLE software packages available, including Blackboard, WebCT, Lotus® LearningSpace, and COSE.

This work was previously published in Handbook of Research on E-Learning Applications for Career and Technical Education: Technologies for Vocational Training, edited by V. C.X. Wang, pp. 779-790, copyright 2009 by Information Science Reference (an imprint of IGI Global).

Chapter 3.9
SWELS:
A Semantic Web System Supporting E-Learning

Gianluca Elia
University of Salento, Italy

Giustina Secundo
University of Salento, Italy

Cesare Taurino
University of Salento, Italy

ABSTRACT

This chapter presents a prototypal e-learning system based on the Semantic Web paradigm, called SWELS (Semantic Web E-Learning System). The chapter starts by introducing e-learning as an efficient and just-in-time tool supporting the learning processes. Then a brief description of the evolution of distance learning technologies will be provided, starting from first generation e-learning systems through the current Virtual Learning Environments and Managed Learning Environments, by underling the main differences between them and the need to introduce standards for e-learning with which to manage and overcome problems related to learning content personalization and updating. Furthermore, some limits of the traditional approaches and technologies for e-learning will be provided, by proposing the Semantic Web as an efficient and effective tool for implementing new generation e-Learning systems. In the last section of the chapter, the SWELS system is proposed by describing the methodology adopted for organizing and modeling its knowledge base, by illustrating its main functionalities, and by providing the design of the tool followed by the implementation choices. Finally, future developments of SWELS will be presented, together with some remarks regarding the benefits for the final user in using such system.

INTRODUCTION

In a context of rapid environmental and technological change, characterized by an increasing obsolescence of knowledge, organizations need to accelerate the renewal and to increase the effectiveness of their managerial competences. Such continuous change is a determinant of continuous learning processes that calls for the capacity to organize at all levels of the organization new working processes that have to be more knowledge intensive, multidisciplinary, and collaborative.

DOI: 10.4018/978-1-60566-034-9.ch006

This requires a profound rethinking of the processes supporting the design, development, and delivery of learning (McCrea et al., 2000) in a way that the learning process becomes more effective, just-in-time, and customized.

As a consequence, learning should not be a passive activity which is only done when people are in the educational institutions without knowing how the knowledge is used in the real world. It should be a continuous and active process performed under a specified goal and situation where the knowledge is really needed. Moreover, as huge amount of knowledge becomes available through Internet in the information society, it becomes possible for people to access the knowledge they need when necessary. In such a circumstance, the most important thing about having a lot of knowledge is to know how to find the knowledge, to be ready to understand and master the new knowledge, and to create knowledge for future use to close the loop of knowledge production and consumption. For these reasons, the goal of education and learning should be augmented to include training of learning capability and creativity of the learners (Mizoguchi, 2000).

Such considerations are some prominent drivers of the e-learning. Since e-learning applications are accessible from anywhere at any time, ICT-based learning environment has been gaining increasing attention from the research community.

In this context, the recently emerged (VLE) Virtual Learning Environments revealed themselves very effective from the pedagogical point of view, especially if they are compared with the previous (CBT) Computer Based Training and (WBT) Web Based Training systems.

However, VLE did not completely solve the problems related to the organization and navigation of the learning materials. Indeed, most of the current Web-based learning solutions show some limits in accessing the right knowledge, as well as in the learning pattern navigation process (given that they do not allow a complete and multi-

dimensional vision of the knowledge available, therefore users are obliged to follow the learning modules according to a linear path designed for a generic learner). In addition, there is the need to optimize the processes related to learning resource organization and aggregation, and the subsequent access and reuse of such resources with respect to a not scheduled learner profile.

Our focus here is on the creation of a Web-based learning environment that enables fast, just-in-time and relevant learning. Indeed, current Web-based solutions do not meet the above mentioned requirements, and some pitfalls are for example information overload, lack of accurate information, and content that is not machine-understandable.

These limits suggest the application of Semantic Web technologies (Barnes-Lee, 2000) to e-learning as means for implementing new generation e-learning systems. The Semantic Web technologies support the innovation process in a learning environment, exploiting the opportunity to create and manage data that are *machine understandable* and not *only machine readable* (Secundo et al., 2004).

An effective way to apply the Semantic Web approach to e-learning could be the use of the ontology backbone, which allows the *ontology-based* description of the learning materials (knowledge base), adding small semantic annotations to each learning object created (Nejdl, 2001). By using an ontology-based approach, learning resources can be easily organized into customized learning patterns and delivered on demand to the learner, according to her/his profile and knowledge needs.

Moreover, such an approach allows to virtuously combine the content description process with the content navigation one: content description to easily identify the learning resources required to achieve the desired learning goals; content navigation to minimize the required time for accessing the learning resources by adopting the right approach of exploring the learning space.

Therefore, according to this approach and to the alignment between e-learning and Knowledge Management we present an application of the KIWI approach called SWELS (Semantic Web E-Learning System). This tool is a prototypal e-learning system based on the Semantic Web paradigm which main functionalities are:

- The creation of an ontology-based view;
- The semantic representation and visualization of learning modules (knowledge base);
- Learning modules (knowledge base) accessing;
- The visualization of the structure of the ontology.

Moreover, SWELS provides an innovative functionality to learners--the opportunity to navigate a domain ontology explicitly. By explicitly navigating the domain ontology, learners not only have the direct access to the knowledge they need inside the knowledge base, but also they are empowered in reaching the following goals (Secundo et al., 2004):

1. The complete exploration of the knowledge base, keeping the awareness and the visibility of the learning path performed to reach the extracted knowledge;
2. The gradual, but deep, understanding of the semantic structure of the knowledge domain they are exploring, through the comprehension of the meanings of concepts and relations of the ontology.

The chapter starts by introducing e-learning as an efficient and just-in-time tool supporting the learning processes, arisen from the learning requirements of the new, dynamically changing knowledge society. Then a brief description of the evolution of distance learning technologies will be provided, starting from first generation of e-learning systems (CBT) through the current Virtual Learning Environments and MLEs (Managed Learning Environments), by underling the main differences between them and the need to introduce standards for e-learning with which to manage and overcome problems related to learning content personalization and updating. Furthermore, some limits of the traditional approaches and technologies for e-learning will be provided, especially referring to the knowledge organization and access as well as to the learning content navigation. At this point, the Semantic Web will be proposed as an efficient and effective tool for implementing new generation e-learning systems, since that the application of such technology to e-learning provides an ontology-based description and organization of learning materials around small pieces of semantically annotated learning objects. In the last section of the chapter the SWELS e-learning system is proposed. The description of such an innovative solution starts with some insights on the methodology adopted for organizing and modeling the Knowledge Base of SWELS, then the main functionalities of the e-learning system will be illustrated; following, the design of the tool together with the implementation choices will be provided; finally, future developments and some remarks will be presented regarding the benefits for the final user (the learner) in using such system.

E-LEARNING: A TECHNOLOGY FACILITATING THE LEARNING PROCESSES

Learning is a critical support mechanism for organizations to compete, not only from the point of view of education, but also from the point of view of the New Economy (Drucker, 2000). The incredible velocity and volatility of today's markets require just-in-time methods for supporting the need-to-know of employees, partners, and

Table 1. Summary of problems and needs in education (Adapted from: Koper, 2004)

Dimension	Problems/Needs
I. Changes in Societal Demands	1. Current higher education infrastructure cannot accommodate the growing college-aged population and life-long learning enrolments, making more distance education programs necessary. 2. Knowledge and information are growing exponentially and Lifelong learning is becoming a competitive necessity. 3. Education is becoming more seamless between high school, college, and further studies.
II. Changes in Learning Teaching process	4. Instruction is becoming more learner-centred, non-linear, and self-directed. 5. There is an increasing need for new learning and teaching strategies that a) is grounded in new instructional design research and b) exploit the capabilities of technology. 6. Learning is most effective when learners are engaged in solving real-world problems; learning environments need to be designed to support this problem-centred approach. 7. Students demand more flexibility; they are shopping for courses that meet their schedules and circumstances. 8. Higher-education learner profiles, including online, information-age, and adult learners, are changing. 9. Academic emphasis is shifting from course-completion to competency. 10. The need for faculty development, support, and training is growing. 11. Instructors of distance courses can feel isolated.
III. Changes in Organization of Educational Institutions	12. There is a shift in organizational structure toward decentralization. 13. Higher education outsourcing and partnerships are increasing. 14. Retention rates and length of time taken to completion concern administrators, faculty members, students and tax payers. 15. The distinction between distance and local education is disappearing. 16. Faculty members demand reduced workload and increased compensation for distance courses. 17. Traditional faculty roles are shifting or unbundling.

distribution paths.

Time, or the lack of it, is the reason given by most businesses for failing to invest in learning. Therefore, learning processes need to be fast and just-in-time. Speed requires not only a suitable content of the learning material (highly specified, not too general), but also a powerful mechanism for organizing such material. Also, learning must be a customized on-line service, initiated by user profiles and business demands. In addition, it must be integrated into day-to-day work patterns and needs to represent a clear competitive edge for the business. In a few words, learning needs to be relevant to the (semantic) context of the business of people and organizations (Adelsberger et al., 2001).

In this scenario, Web-based learning environments have been gaining increasing attention from the research community, since e-learning applications can represent real facilitator of the learning processes both in business and in academic contexts. The following table (Table 1) underlines some problems and needs that can be effectively overcome with e-learning; such problems and needs are summarized and grouped on several e-learning domain dimensions (Koper, 2004):

But, what does e-learning mean? E-learning is the use of Internet technologies to create and deliver a rich learning environment that includes a broad array of instruction and information resources and solutions, the goal of which is to enhance individual and organizational performance (Rosenberg, 2006). E-learning is not just concerned with providing easy access to learning resources, anytime, anywhere, via a repository of learning resources, but is also concerned with supporting such features as the personal definition of learning goals, and the synchronous and asynchronous communication, and collaboration, between learners and between learners and instructors (Kolovski et al., 2003). It aims at replacing old-fashioned time/place/content predetermined learning with a just-in-time/at work-place/customized/on-demand process of learning (Stojanovic et al., 2001).

Traditional learning process could be characterised by centralised authority (content is selected by the educator), strong push delivery (instructors push knowledge to students), lack of a personalisation (content must satisfy the needs of many), and the linear/static learning process (unchanged content). The consequences of such organisation on the learning are expensive, slow and too unfocused (problem-independent) learning process.

But dynamically changed business environment puts completely different challenges on learning process--fast, just-in-time (cheap) and relevant (problem-dependent) learning, as mentioned above. This can be solved with the distributed, student-oriented, personalised, nonlinear/dynamic learning process--e-learning. The principle behind e-learning is that the tools and knowledge needed to perform work are moved to the knowledge workers--wherever and whoever they are.

In the recent years, new breeds of IS (Information System) known as LMS (Learning Management Systems) and LCMS (Learning Content Management Systems) are evolving to enable learning in organisations (Brennan et al., 2001). In essence, LMS replace isolated and fragmented learning programmes with a systematic means of assessing and raising competency and performance levels throughout the organisation, by offering a strategic IS solution for planning, delivering, and managing all learning events, including both online and classroom-based learning (Greenberg, 2002). LMS are often coupled with LCMS which facilitate the management and administration of the learning content for the online learning prgrammes in the form of learning objects (Brennan et al., 2001).

E-LEARNING SYSTEMS: FROM VIRTUAL LEARNING ENVIRONMENTS TO MANAGED LEARNING ENVIRONMENTS

In the 90s the primary impact of the Internet technologies on distance learning was mainly on the possibility of having different ways for aggregating and delivering learning content. Indeed, the application of such technologies to the learning processes has introduced a set of opportunities and advantages: the possibility to generate and transport on the Web multimedia audio/video flows at low costs (therefore promoting the diffusion of synchronous learning environments on asynchronous ones); the use of standard technologies for information exchange that allow to dynamically and effectively structure and navigate learning content; the possibility for learners to acquire knowledge and to continuously revise and update it by adapting the learning environment to their needs. In other words, Web-based learning environments shifted from stand-alone technologies towards highly integrated e-learning and knowledge management infrastructures and tools enabling the creation of learning communities and supporting the collaboration between members and organizations. However, in the last years Internet technologies failed in the process of creating and managing learning contents in a way that they could be easily and dynamically reused and updated. This because of the inability of trainers and learning managers to create learning materials that could be fast and easily adapted to the learning needs of learners as well as to the new ways of content delivery. Such considerations have been driven the shift from first generation e-learning systems, based on the delivery of Web-based learning content and on the basic Internet standards, towards second generation ones, based on "ad-hoc" e-learning standards (Damiani et al., 2002).

Second generation e-learning systems are based on the creation of VLEs that have risen from the integration between e-learning and knowledge management solutions. The primary aim of VLEs is to allow people to share knowledge, interests and experiences, thereby encouraging the creation of Virtual Learning Communities based on blended learning solutions in which face-to-face and virtual classroom meetings are combined with Web-based learning patterns to provide to learners a complete, interactive and effective learning experience. Nevertheless, if from one side VLEs revealed themselves very effective from the pedagogical point of view (especially if considered in relation to the e-learning platform of first generation), from the other side they showed some limits as regards to the problem of learning content aggregation and organization, and the subsequent access and reuse by learners with a non scheduled user profile. The classification and management of contents are the strength points of the so-called MLE. MLEs privilege the content design, creation, and management in respect to the content delivery infrastructure, considered as an element with which the content has to interoperate. The main goal of MLEs is to manage in an integrated way a complete system for analyzing, developing, and evaluating competences, for scheduling and organizing learning patterns, for managing roles and virtual classrooms, for tracking the learners and for final evaluation of the competences reached (Secundo et al., 2004). The complete separation proposed by MLEs between the management infrastructure and the final output of the learning material is enabling the development and the diffusion of standards for e-learning in several applicative contexts (Lockwood et al., 2001):

- DRM (Digital Right Management) and privacy management;

- Low level formats for learning content;
- Metadata for content description
- Personalization of content according to the learner profile and to the linguistic/social/cultural environment;
- XML-based models and languages for structuring and describing dynamic learning patterns (i.e., Educational Modeling Language);
- Technologies and methodologies for interoperability with Internet/Intranet delivery infrastructures.

Nowadays there are several key international players (including IEEE, IMS, ARIADNE, ADL and AICC) that are focusing their efforts on the issues of interoperability and reuse, resulting in a multitude of standards that can be used for building interoperable learning systems. These attempts at building learning platforms for interoperability are mainly targeted to ease the need of LMSs for adaptation to standards, but as a consequence, learners can be expected to gain more freedom. For example, the goal of SCORM (Sharable Content Object Reference Model) is to provide a reference model for content that is durable (survives system changes), interoperable (between systems), accessible (indexed and searchable) and reusable (able to be modified in different contexts and by different tools). This will hopefully allow students to move more freely between LMSs and even to combine several services from different LMSs.

SOME LIMITS OF TRADITIONAL APPROACHES AND TECHNOLOGIES FOR E-LEARNING

Current approaches, models and technologies for e-learning introduce, on the other hand, several problems. First, most content providers have large monolithic systems where adaptation to standards will not significantly change the underlying teacher-learner model. Students will be presented with material in a context often leading up to some form of (standardized) test. New and more interesting methods for learning--such as techniques for collaboration, annotation, conceptual modeling, and so forth.--will not profit from such adaptation. Second, even though monolithic, closed or proprietary systems will be able to exchange learning resources, course-like structures and keep track of students with the help of those standards, they will need to go through yet another process of adaptation to the next big batch of agreements on learning technologies, such as e.g. profiling and tracking of student performance. Third, the current perspective on metadata is too limited. Anyone who has something to say about a learning resource should be able to do so. This includes learners, teachers and content contributors such as authors and providers. Communicating this metadata is equally important as it can help, direct or encourage others to actively participate and learn. Proposed solutions, such as the adoption of SCORM, will result in learning resources (and their metadata) that will reappear in different versions and formats rather than dynamically evolve and improve (Naeve et al., 2001).

In a few words, today many of the e-learning systems available on market lack in specific functionalities for the creation and delivery of dynamic, modular learning paths that match the knowledge needs in a contextualized (according to learner's current activities) and individualized (according to learner's experiences, competences profiles, learning history and personal preferences) way.

This suggests a strong integration among e-learning and knowledge management functionalities to define a rich learning environment with wealth and variety of resources available just-in-time to learners, both through structured and unstructured knowledge objects through interaction with other people (Elia et al., 2006). The key to success is therefore the ability to reduce the cycle time for learning and to adapt "content, size and style" of learning to the learner and to the business. Therefore, to overcome such problems,

a new learning framework is required, based on the key points mentioned above and opened to a multitude of new services. In order to be effective, it needs a powerful language for expressing facts about resources and schemas that will allow machines as well as humans to understand how these facts are related without relying on heuristics. Moreover, there is a need for expressing facts about remote (identifiable) objects without accessing remote data stores.

EMERGING PERSPECTIVES OF E-LEARNING IN THE SEMANTIC AGE

In an e-learning environment, the learning content should be oriented around small modules (the so called learning objects) coupled with associated semantics (the metadata) so that learners are able to find what they need in a specific moment and context. Furthermore, these modules should be related by a "dependency network" or "conceptual Web" to allow individualised learning. Such a dependency network permits, for example, the learning objects to be presented to the learner in an orderly manner, with prerequisite material being presented first. Additionally, in an e-learning environment, the learner should be able to add extra material and links (i.e., annotate) to the learning objects for their own benefit or for that of later students. This framework lends itself to an implementation based on the Semantic Web, incorporating cooperating software agents, which additionally make use of appropriate Web services to provide the functionality. The facilities the applications based on these technologies can provide, include allowing e-learning content to be created, annotated, shared, and discussed, together with supplying resources such lecture notes, student portfolios, group projects, information pages, discussion forums, and question-and-answer bulletin boards. Moreover, such applications allow students to benefit from more interaction with their peers (for example, sharing resources found on the Web), as well as with the instructors and tutors, by also providing an easy way for sharing and archiving information, whether of general interest or specific to a group project they are involved in (Kolovski et al., 2003).

T first generation WWW was a powerful tool for research and education, but its utility is hampered by the inability of the users to navigate easily the huge amount of sources for the information they require. The Semantic Web is a vision to solve this problem. It is proposed that a new WWW architecture will support not only Web content, but also associated formal semantics (Barnes-Lee, 1998). The idea is that the Web content and the related semantics (or metadata) will be accessed by Web agents, allowing these agents to reason about the content and produce intelligent answers to user queries. The Semantic Web, in practice, comprises a layered framework: an XML layer for expressing the Web content (the structure of data); a RDF (Resource Description Framework) layer for representing the semantics of the content (the meaning of data); an ontology layer for describing the vocabulary of the domain; and a logic layer to enable intelligent reasoning with meaningful data (Stojanovic et al., 2001).

Within an e-learning framework, the Semantic Web provides the technology that allows a learning object to be (Naeve et al., 2001):

- **Described with metadata.** Since a resource can have uses outside the domains foreseen by the provider, any given description (metadata instance) is bound to be incomplete. Because of the distributed structure of RDF, a description can be expanded or new descriptions following new formats (schemas) can be added. This allows for creative uses of content in new and unforeseen ways. Hence, one of the most important features of the current Web - the fact that anyone can link anything to anything--has been carried over into RDF.

- **Annotated.** Every resource identifiable by an URI can be annotated, with personal notes and links by anyone.
- **Extended.** In terms of content (structured, by means of XML descriptors), permitting multiple versions to exist. Indeed, successive editing of the content can be done via special RDF-schemas allowing private, group consensus or author-specific versions of a common base document. The versioning history will be a tree with known and unknown branches, which can be traversed with the help of appropriate versioning tools.
- **Shared by, and communicated to, anyone** who has expressed an interest in such content. RDF is application independent. Since the metadata is expressed in a standard format, which is independent of the underlying schemas, even simplistic applications can understand parts of complex RDF graphs. If the learner's favourite tool does not support the corresponding schemas, it can at least present them in a rough graph, table or whatever standard form it has for describing resources and their properties. If more advanced processing software is available (such as logic engines), more advanced treatment of the RDF descriptions is possible.
- **Certified.** There is no reason why only big organizations should certify learning resources. Individuals, such as teachers, may want to certify certain content as a quality learning resource that is well suited for specific learning tasks.

Apart from these uses, it is possible to invent new schemas describing structures, personalization, results from monitoring and tracking, processes and interactions that can enrich the learning environment in various ways.

The key property of the Semantic Web architecture (common-shared-meaning, machine-processable metadata), enabled by a set of suitable agents, establishes a powerful approach to satisfy the e-learning requirements: efficient, just-in-time, and task relevant learning. Learning material is semantically annotated and for a new learning demand it may be easily combined in a new learning course. According to his/her preferences, a learner can find useful learning material very easily. The process is based on semantic querying and navigation through learning materials, enabled by the ontological background. So, the Semantic Web can be exploited as a very suitable platform for implementing an e-learning system, because it provides all means for the ontology development, the ontology-based annotation of learning materials, as well as their composition in learning modules and proactive delivery of the learning materials through e-Learning portals.

In the following table (Table 2), the most important characteristics (or pitfalls) of the traditional learning and improvements achieved using the e-learning environment are showed; furthermore, a summary view of the possibility to use the Semantic Web for realizing the e-learning requirements is presented (Drucker, 2000; Stojanovic et al., 2001).

An important aspect related to the use of Semantic Web in educational contexts is how to represent a course in a formal, semantic way so that it can be interpreted and manipulated by computers as well as humans (i.e., the creation and management of data that are machine understandable and not only machine readable). This process is known in the literature as "educational modeling." A semantic model is developed using a variety of methods: literature research, expert group discussions, validation sessions, and so forth, and the result is described with a formal modeling language, like UML. The UML class diagrams can be translated to RDF-Schema and/ or OWL Web Ontology Language, depending on the richness of the model. XML-Schema's (XSD) and other semantic bindings like Topic Maps can also be generated from the UML models (Koper, 2004). A semantic representation of

learning content provides efficient solutions to the following problems (Koper, 2004):

- The development of Web-based courses that are flexible, problem-based, non-linear, incorporate multimedia and are adaptive to learner characteristics, is expensive and extremely time-consuming. A semantic framework can help the course developers in the structuring and integration of the development work. In addition, authoring and design support agents and tools could be created to help the developers to do their jobs more effectively and efficiently.

- An explicit notation of learning content can preserve and share knowledge about effective learning designs. It gives the possibility to build and share catalogues of effective learning patterns that can be communicated very precisely and can be adapted to other contexts, problems, and content.

- Instantiation of an e-learning course in current LMSs (Learning Management Systems) can be a time-consuming job that has to be repeated for every new run of the course. One has to assign users, create groups, but also has to set-up the communication and collaboration services (e.g., discussion forums, workspaces, etc.) mostly by hand. A representation of a course that includes a specification of the set-up of the services enables the automation of this instantiation process.

- When the representation of the learning material includes a semantic, higher level description of the interactive processes that occur during the learning process, software agents can interpret these to support learners and staff in managing the workflow of activities in learning. These agents can also support the filtering of the

Table 2. Differences between training and e-learning and main benefits of applying Semantic Web technologies to e-learning (Adapted from Drucker, 2000; Stojanovic et al., 2001)

Dimension	Training	e-Learning	Semantic Web
Delivery	Push--Instructor determines agenda	Pull--Learner determines agenda	Knowledge items (learning materials) are distributed on the Web, but they are linked to commonly agreed ontologies. This enables the creation of user-specific learning patterns, by semantic querying for topics of interest.
Responsiveness	Anticipatory--Assumes to know the problem	Reactionary--Responds to problem at hand	Software agents on the Semantic Web may use commonly agreed service language, which enables co-ordination between agents and proactive delivery of learning materials in the context of actual problems. The vision is that each user has his/her own personalised agent that communicates with other agents.
Access	Linear--Pre-defined progression of knowledge	Non-linear --Allows direct access to knowledge in whatever sequence makes sense to the situation at hand	User can describe situation at hand (goal of learning, previous knowledge) and perform semantic querying for the suitable learning material. The user profile is also accounted for. Access to knowledge can be expanded by semantically defined navigation.
Symmetry	Asymmetric --Training occurs as a separate activity	Symmetric --Learning occurs as an integrated activity	The Semantic Web offers the potential to become an integration platform for all business processes in an organisation, including learning activities.
Modality	Discrete-- Training takes place in dedicated chunks with defined starts and stop	Continuous --Learning runs in the parallel loops and never stops	Active delivery of information (based on personalised agents) creates a dynamic virtual learning environment.
Authority	Centralized --Content is selected from a library of materials developed by the educator	Distributed --Content comes from the interaction of the participants and the educators	The Semantic Web will be as decentralised as possible. This enables an effective co-operative content management.
Personalization	Mass produced-- Content must satisfy the needs of many	Personalized- -Content is determined by the individual user's needs and aims to satisfy the needs of every user	A user (using personalised agent) searches for learning material customised for her/his needs. The ontology is the link between user profile and needs, and characteristics of the learning material.
Adaptiveness	Static-- Content and organization/taxonomy remains in their original authored form without regard to environmental changes	Dynamic-- Content changes constantly through user input, experiences, new practices, business rules and heuristics	The Semantic Web enables the use of knowledge provided in various forms, by semantic annotation of content. Distributed nature of the Semantic Web enables continuous improvement of learning materials.

appropriate resources to be used during the performance of an activity.

- Adaptation to individual learner characteristics (i.e., his/her learner profile) is highly desirable, since learners have not the same learning pre-requisites, skills, aptitudes or motivations. However, such adaptation can only be done realistically when the adaptation is wholly or at least partially automated (therefore, including descriptions of the conditions for adaptation). Otherwise, it becomes a very demanding work for the learner and/or his/her learning manager.

- A semantic annotation of learning content enables and facilitates sharing and re-use of learning objects (that is one of the major objectives in the field of e-learning). This sharing and re-use is needed to make the content development process more efficient. On the contrary, if learning objects are not semantically represented, it might be hard to find them on local or remote repositories, hard to integrate them into new contexts and--relating to the problem of interoperability and learning object exchange among different LMSs--hard to interpret and structure them in the correct way.

- An explicit semantic representation can serve as a means to create more advanced and complex, but consistent learning designs than is possible without such a representation. This is a characteristic of any language with semantic that enables one to write, read, rewrite and share meaning (e.g., natural language).

SWELS: AN E-LEARNING SYSTEM BASED ON SEMANTIC WEB TECHNOLOGIES

According to the alignment between e-learning and knowledge management approaches, a prototypal e-learning system based on the Semantic Web paradigm has been implemented called SWELS. Such system has been designed and developed at the eBMS (e-Business Management Section) () of the Scuola Superiore ISUFI, University of Lecce (Italy) and it is the result of a research activity under the KIWI project.

This paper represents an extended version of a previous publication that the authors G. Secundo, A. Corallo, G. Elia G. Passiante (2004) published in the proceedings of the International Conference on Information Technology Based Higher Education and Training, May 29th--June 2th, 2004 Istanbul, Turkey.

The SWELS system is intended to be an innovative tool for knowledge acquisition and competence development of learners and knowledge workers that exploits Semantic Web technologies in order to provide an effective and useful support to online learning processes. The system, indeed, is conceived as a tool with which to potentially overcome the limits of the current e-learning applications in terms of learning content creation and delivery, that is, the inability of existing tools to create dynamics and adaptive learning paths that match the learning profile of learners as well as their knowledge needs. SWELS points out a proactive behaviour based on a matching process among the profile of the user, his/her interests as well as his/her just-in-time choices during the learning activities, and the learning content available in the knowledge base; as a consequence learning resources can be easily organized into customized learning patterns and delivered on demand to the user.

Learning materials which SWELS refers to are focused on "Change Management and Leadership" knowledge domain, that has been modeled through a domain ontology. Such an ontology contains the list of concepts and semantic relations with which to provide a semantic description of the learning objects (text files, images, graphs, as well as multimedia audio-video files) of the domain.

KNOWLEDGE BASE ORGANIZATION AND MODELING

Learning materials (i.e., the knowledge base) are described by means of a domain ontology that provides a semantic representation of con-

Figure 1. A representation of knowledge base flexibility

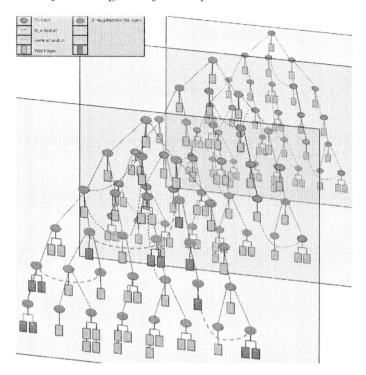

tent, adding small semantic annotations to each learning resource. In particular, the knowledge base modeling process can be organized in two main steps:

1. Definition of the knowledge base ontology. The ontology definition consists in identifying the learning module structure and defines the abstract notions and vocabulary that will be available for the learner to conceptualize the learning modules.
2. Description of the knowledge resources. Knowledge items are tagged with one concept belonging to the ontology. In this way, learner can identify each resource and, using the ontological relationships, he/she can explore new resources tagged by different domain concepts.

Such a description of learning content allows an effective organization of them in the knowl-

edge base, therefore providing to learners the possibility to have an explicit navigation of the domain ontology.

The two main advantages for the final users are, from one hand a complete exploration of the modeled knowledge base, which allows them to have a total awareness of the available content, as well as the visibility of the performed learning path to reach the required knowledge. So, learners are conscious both of the total amount of knowledge present in the knowledge base, and of the knowledge extracted till then and of knowledge heritage to explore in the future. From the other hand, learners can understand, step by step, the semantic structure of the knowledge domain they're exploring by surfing the ontology, by gradually being aware of the meanings of ontology's concepts and relations.

This approach to the knowledge base organization and modeling provides more flexibility for learners as regard to the learning content

Figure 2. Use case diagram

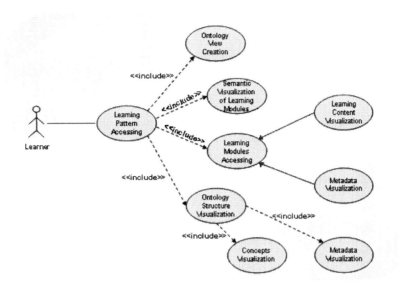

access, since that they can explicitly browse the knowledge base and dynamically configure their learning patterns (Figure 1).

FUNCTIONAL DESCRIPTION OF SWELS

The interaction between the learner and the system can be represented through a use case diagram that shows the main functionalities of the tool (Figure 2).

As the use cases show, in order to have access to the dynamically created learning patterns, learners have to perform a set of different steps.

The following state chart diagram describes the overall behaviour of the system by underling the logic sequence of the states and the list of the state transitions related to the user events according to interaction between learner and system described before (see Figure 3).

CREATION OF THE ONTOLOGY-BASED VIEW

When a learner accesses the SWELS, he/she has to select the domain ontology and the relation by which creating the ontology view. When predicate is chosen, the tool generates the taxonomic representation of the ontology, through a tree-structure (Figure 4).

SEMANTIC REPRESENTATION AND VISUALIZATION OF LEARNING MODULES

After the ontology view creation, the learner can generate his/her own personalized learning pattern by browsing the concepts of the ontology. By clicking on each concept, a list of elements will be shown:

Figure 3. State chart diagram

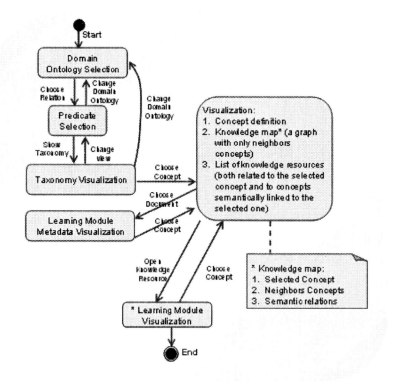

- Concept definition (top of the page);
- List of knowledge resources indexed on the selected concept (body of the page-- with blank relation);
- List of knowledge resources indexed on concepts linked to the selected concept through one of the ontology relationships (body of the page – with specified relation).

Such information is organized in the tab "Documenti" (Knowledge Resources) as follows (Figure 5).

Ontology Structure Visualization

When a learner selects the specific concept which he/she is interested to, together with the semantic visualization of the learning modules, SWELS generates also a knowledge map containing both the selected concept and the neighbour concepts. Such a graph is organized in the tab "Grafico" (Graph) of the application, and represents the semantic boundary of the concept (specifying the neighbour concepts, the semantic connections and the direction of these connections). The semantic boundary is illustrated through a radial layout (neighbourhood view) --as TGViz one (a Plug-in of Protégé) and Visualizer one (a Plug-in of OntoEdit)--to give to the learner an explicit and immediate representation of the ontology structure (Figure 6). It is important to note that, referring to each triple (subject, predicate, object), the direction of the arrows connecting two concepts goes from the subject to the object of the triple; this allows the learner to have a unique interpretation of the semantic map.

In this way, two different and complementary representations of the domain ontology are available: the tree-structure (on the left of the page)

Figure 4. Ontology view creation

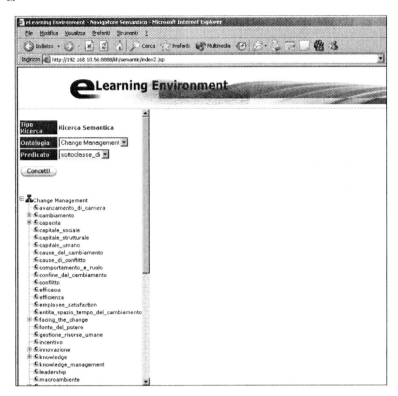

Figure 5. Semantic representation and visualization of learning modules

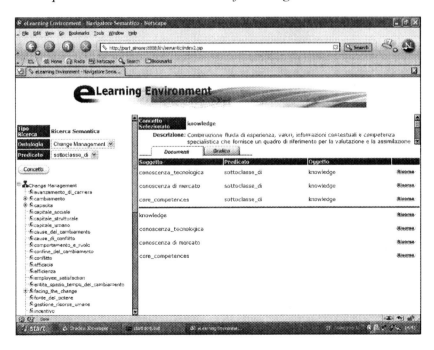

Figure 6. Ontology structure visualization

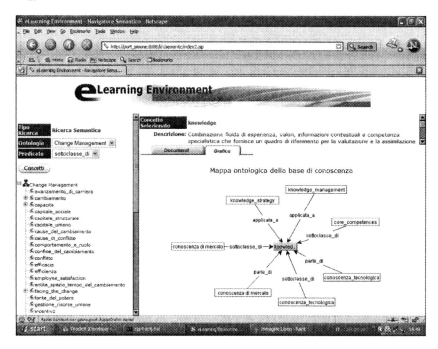

and the graph-structure (on the right). This choice allows a better understanding of the knowledge domain (since that it provides two different ways for representing the knowledge available in the domain) and gives the learner the opportunity to select and extract the right learning resources according to his/her "learning profile."

Learning Module Accessing

By clicking on the button "Risorsa" (Resource), in the list of the knowledge resources indexed in the tab "Documenti" (Figure 5), the learner has the direct access to the chosen learning module; in this way, the selected learning module will be launched in a new browser window and he/she can attend it autonomously (Figure 7).

Moreover, the learner can also access metadata describing knowledge resources, by clicking on resource name. In this way, Dublin Core metadata (Dublin Core Metadata Initiative, 2006) will be shown (Figure 8).

Design of The Tool

Concerning the design of SWELS, we decided to adopt the MVC (Model-View-Controller) design pattern (Figure 9) since that it allows enterprise applications to support multiple types of users with multiple types of interfaces. By representing the logic architecture of the system with such a "Three Tier" model, it is possible to keep separated core business model functionalities from the presentation and the control logic that uses those functionalities. Such separation permits multiple views to share the same enterprise data model, which makes supporting multiple clients easier to implement, test, and maintain (Sun Microsystems, Inc., 2002).

According to the Three Tier model adopted for the SWELS design, the first diagram proposed is the package diagram that shows developed class packages and the dependencies among them (Fowler et al., 1999) (Figure 10).

Figure 7. Learning module accessing

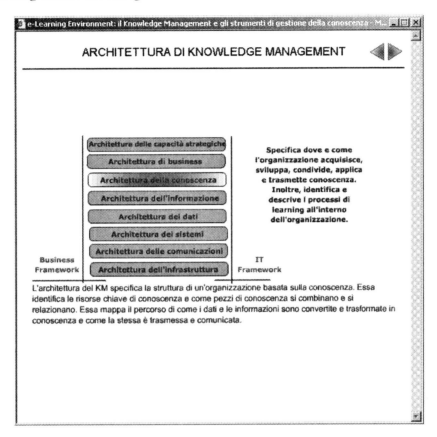

Going on in the description of the SWELS design, following are shown the class diagrams describing the types of the objects in the system and the various kinds of static relationships that exist among them. In particular, we propose the class diagram related to the ontology view creation (Figure 11), the class diagram related to the semantic visualization of the learning modules (Figure 12), and the class diagram related to the ontology structure visualization (Figure 13).

Technological Issues

With regard to implementation choices, SWELS is a J2EE Web-based application, developed according to the MVC (Model-View-Control) pattern (which implies together the use of Servlets as well as JSPs technologies), by using two suitable frameworks:

- *Jakarta Struts*, an open source framework for creating Java Web applications that utilize a MVC architecture. The framework gives three key components: a "request" handler provided by the application developer that is mapped to a standard URI, a "response" handler that transfers control to another resource which completes the response, a tag library that helps developers create interactive form-based applications with server pages (The Apache Software Foundation, 2006).
- *Oracle9iAS Toplink*, an ORM (Object Relational Mapping) framework for implementing the 'Model' layer that is free only for non-commercial applications.

Furthermore, the ontology is codified in RDFS and is stored in a relational database. The DBMS

Figure 8. E-learning metadata

is Oracle 9i; the relational database schema for the application is the following (Figure 15):

Finally, the standard for e-learning metadata is Dublin Core; the implementation of SCORM 1.2 is a work-in-progress.

These implementation choices give the tool a high level of flexibility and scalability; indeed, it can be used on several knowledge bases by developing a specified domain ontology and by exploiting the potentialities of ORM framework.

Empirical Evidence

During the exciting experience of conceptualization, design and implementation phases of SWELS, some attempts to validate the effectiveness of the whole approach were made. Specifically, we refer to a process realized on empirical evidence basis to acquire some insights for improving the overall system. This process is articulated in two test phases--the 'alpha test' phase and the 'beta test' phase.

The "Alpha test" phase was performed by the team involved in the implementation of the system itself. From one side, software developers tested

Figure 9. The MVC (Model-View-Controller) design pattern

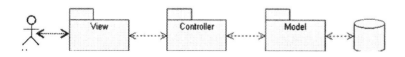

Figure 10. Package diagram

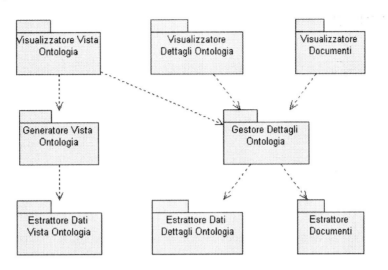

Figure 11. Class diagram for the ontology view creation

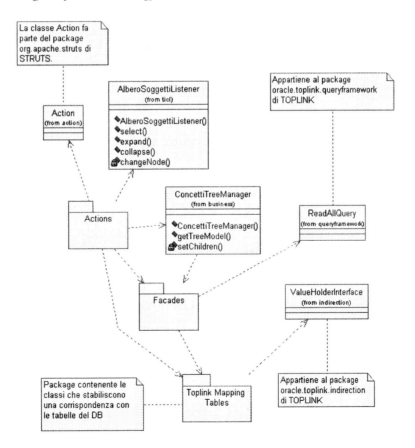

Figure 12. Class diagram for the semantic visualization of the learning modules

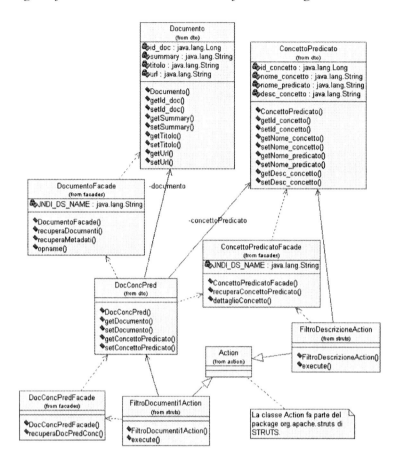

many times and under different conditions each functionality of the system. They also executed a general test for the overall system to evaluate its robustness and the coherence of data management and tracking systems. From the other side, the subject matter experts, after the design phase and the coordination of teams involved into the content creation process, executed a double-layer control: one for the exactness of how each topic was expressed, and one for the semantic link about different topics. Both tests revealed a set of enhancements that have been implemented in the new version of SWELS.

The "Beta test phase" was performed by involving a group of 20 students attending an International master program at the eBMS of Scuola Superiore ISUFI,. They used SWELS

(platform and contents) as an additional learning tool during the attendance of the module on "Change Management and Leadership." After one week, at the end of this module, a face-to-face discussion meeting was organized with the participation of an outstanding professor in this field. Final impressions of master participants about SWELS were extremely positive, because they represented a sort of personal assistant to deepen and clarify some difficult concepts of the module and, above all, to have a systemic vision of the general topic.

Future Developments of Swels

The next steps that we aim to develop in the future are:

Figure 13. Class diagram for the ontology structure visualization

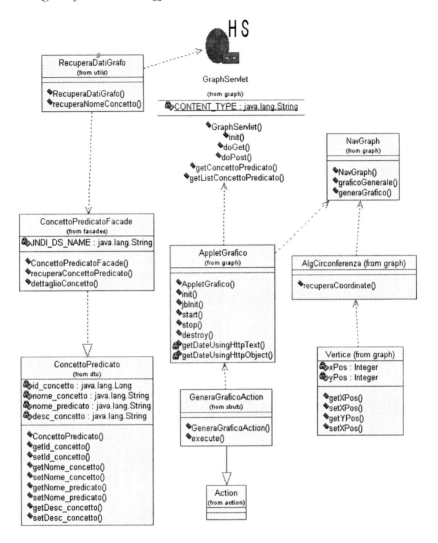

- The implementation of an interactive radial layout layer (i.e., an interactive graphical interface to activate the "conceptual semantic boundary"). In our opinion, this improvement could make SWELS more effective, since that learners can immediately access learning modules, by directly clicking on the concepts shown in the radial graph.
- The ontological representation of two further learning dimensions: the typology and characteristics of the learning resource (i.e., assessment, difficulty level, etc.) and the learner profile expressed in terms of interests and knowledge gaps (by tracking the learning pattern dynamically created by learners).
- The integration of SWELS into a LMS, that means the development of a personal learning agent integrated into a LMS that proactively configures and recommends personalized learning paths to the learners according to their learning profile.

Figure 14. Integrating struts framework in MVC architectures

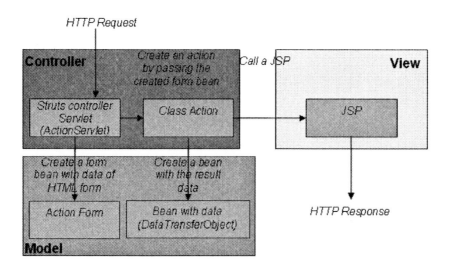

Finally, a large scale experimentation of the system should be organized in order to evaluate the effectiveness of SWELS and, more in general, of the learning approach embedded in SWELS.

CONCLUSION

SWELS platform is the result of applying Semantic Web technologies to e-learning. Such a strategic choice allows learners and knowledge workers to increase the effectiveness of their learning process since it enables a personalized access to learning materials as well as a complete and deep understanding of the knowledge domain. Indeed, from the point of view of the final users, the main benefits of using SWELS are:

- The explicitation of tacit knowledge contained in the knowledge base conceptualization process and held in the minds of subject matter experts as well as domain designers;
- The systematization of knowledge through an explicit indexing of knowledge resources

through simple and complex semantic assertions;
- A more direct access to the knowledge domain by explicitly navigating and browsing the ontology map;
- A more flexible structure of the learning materials that can be easily recombined and described for other purposes and learning goals in other knowledge domains.

In our beliefs, this approach could provide a new way in which students learn, since it is based on a learner-centric strategy characterized by:

- The role of personal tacit knowledge and learning experiences as the starting point and the knowledge background of future learning patterns;
- A solution-oriented approach for creating just-in-time new learning patterns;
- The possibility to fulfill the personal skill gap by actively participating and self-exploring the knowledge base;

Figure 15. Relational schema of the database implemented

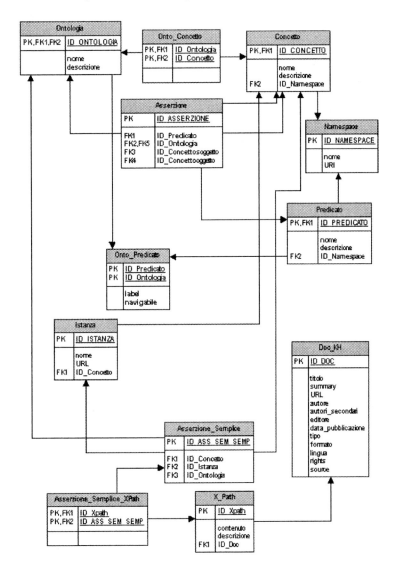

- A stimulus to the "knowledge curiosity" of learners in deepening specific knowledge domains;
- The development of knowledge, skills and attitudes conceived as capacity for effective actions and problem solving;
- A set of customized training curricula consistent to learners' needs, their own time and place, without compromising its effectiveness (Keegan, 2000);

- A dynamic creation of learning paths, starting from different knowledge resources semantically annotated, according to the learner interests and knowledge needs, expressed by them in real time.

REFERENCES

Adelsberger, H., Bick, M., Körner, F., & Pawlowski, J. M. (2001). Virtual education in business information systems (VAWI)--Facilitating collaborative development processes using the Essen learning model. In H. Hoyer (Ed.), *20th ICDE World Conference on Open Learning and Distance Education. The Future of Learning – Learning for the Future: Shaping the Transition.*

Barnes-Lee, T. (1998), Semantic Web Roadmap. *W3C Design Issues.*

Barnes-Lee, T. (2000). What the Semantic Web can represent.

Brennan, M., Funke, S., & Andersen, C. (2001). The learning content management system--a new e-Learning market segment emerges. *IDC White Paper.,*

Damiani, E., Corallo, A., Elia, G., & Ceravolo, P. (2002, November). *Standard per i learning objects: Interoperabilità ed integrazione nella didattica a distanza.* Paper presented at the International Workshop eLearning: una sfida per l'Università - Strategie Metodi Prospettive, Milan, Italy.

Drucker, P. (2000). Need to know: Integrating e-learning with high velocity value chains. *Delphi Group White Paper.*

Dublin Core Metadata Initiative. (2006). Dublin Core Metadata Terms., Retrieved on May 26, 2003, from http://dublincore.org

Elia, G., Secundo, G., & Taurino, C. (2006), Towards unstructured and just-in-time learning: The "Virtual eBMS" e-Learning system. In A Méndez-Vilas, A. Solano-Martin, J. Mesa González, & J.A. Mesa González (Eds.), *m-ICTE2006: Vol. 2. Current Developments in Technology-Assisted Education* (pp. 1067-1072). FORMATEX, Badajoz, Spain.

Fowler, M., & Scott, K. (Eds.). (1999). *UML Distilled Second Edition--A Brief Guide to the Standard Object Modelling Language.* A. Wesley.

Greenberg, L. (2002). LMS and LCMS: What's the Difference? *Learning Circuits, ASTD.*

Keegan, M. (Ed.). (2000). *e-Learning, The engine of the knowledge economy.* Morgan Keegan & Co.

Kolovski, V., & Galletly, J. (2003). Towards e-learning via the Semantic Web. In B. Rachev, & A. Smrikarov (Eds.), In *Proceedings of the 4th International Conference on Computer Systems and Technologies--CompSysTech'2003* (pp. 591 - 596). ACM New York, NY, USA.

Koper, R. (2004). Use of the Semantic Web to solve some basic problems in education. *Journal of Interactive Media in Education*, (6): 1–23.

Lockwood, F., & Gooley, A. (Eds.). (2001). *Innovation in open and distance learning - successful development of online and Web-based learning.* London, Kogan Page.

McCrea, F., Gay, R. K., & Bacon, R. (2000). *Riding the big waves: a white paper on the B2B e-Learning Industry.* San Francisco/Boston/New York/London: Thomas Weisel Partners LLC.

Mizoguchi, R. (2000). IT revolution in learning technology, In *Proceedings of SchoolNet 2000*, Pusan, Korea (pp. 46-55).

Naeve, A., Nilsson, M., & Palmer, M. (2001), E-learning in the semantic age. CID, Centre For User Oriented It Design. Stockhom, Sweden. Retrieved on September 30, 2006

Nejdl, W. (2001). Learning repositories--Technology and context. In A. Risk (Ed.), *ED-Media 2001 World Conference on education multimedia, Hypermedia and Telecommunications: Vol. 2001, N. 1.*

Rosenberg, M. J. (Ed.). (2006). *Beyond E-Learning: Approaches and technologies to enhance knowledge, learning and performance.* Pfeiffer.

Secundo, G., Corallo, A., Elia, G., & Passiante, G. (2004). An e-Learning system based on semantic Web supporting a Learning in Doing Environment. In *Proceedings of International Conference on Information Technology Based Higher Education and Training--ITHET 2004.* IEEE XPlore,

Stojanovic, L., Staab, S., & Studer, R. (2001, October 23-27). eLearning based on the Semantic Web. In W. A. Lawrence-Fowler & J. Hasebrook (Eds.), In *Proceedings of WebNet 2001--World Conference on the WWW and Internet,* Orlando, Florida. (pp.1174-1183). AACE.

Sun Microsystems, Inc. (2002). Java Blueprints--Model-view-controller.

The Apache Software Foundation. (2006). Apache Struts.

Chapter 3.10
Web Services Discovery with Rough Sets

Maozhen Li
Brunel University, UK

Bin Yu
Level E Limited, UK

Vijay Sahota
Brunel University, UK

Man Qi
Canterbury Christ Church University, UK

ABSTRACT

Web services are emerging as a major technology for building service-oriented distributed systems. Potentially, various resources on the Internet can be virtualized as Web services for a wider use by their communities. Service discovery becomes an issue of vital importance for Web services applications. This article presents ROSSE, a Rough Sets based Search Engine for Web service discovery. One salient feature of ROSSE lies in its capability to deal with uncertainty of service properties when matching services. A use case is presented to demonstrate the use of ROSSE for discovery of car services. ROSSE is evaluated in terms of its accuracy and efficiency in service discovery.

INTRODUCTION

Web services are emerging as a major technology for developing service-oriented distributed systems. Potentially, many resources on the Internet or the World Wide Web can be virtualized as services for a wider use by their communities. Service discovery becomes an issue of vital importance for Web service applications. As shown in Figure 1, discovered services can either be used by Web service applications or they can be composed into composite services using workflow languages such as BPEL4WS (Andrews Curbera, Dholakia, Goland, Klein, Leymann et al., 2003). UDDI (Universal Description, Discovery and Integration, http://www.uddi.org) has been proposed and used for Web service publication and discovery. However, the search mechanism supported by UDDI is limited to keyword matches. With the development of the Semantic Web (Berners-Lee, Hendlet, & Lassila, 2001), services can be annotated with metadata for enhancement of service discovery. The complexity of this metadata can range from simple annotations, to the representation of more complex relationships between services based on first order logic.

One key technology to facilitate this semantic annotation of services is OWL-S (Martin, Paolucci, McIlraith, Burstein, McDermott, McGuinness et al., 2004), an OWL (Web Ontology Language, http://www.w3.org/TR/owl-features/ Reference) based ontology for encoding properties of Web services. OWL-S ontology defines a service profile for encoding a service description, a service model for specifying the behavior of a service, and a service grounding for invoking the service. Typically, a service discovery process involves a matching between the profile of a service advertisement and the profile of a service request using domain ontologies described in OWL. The service profile not only describes the functional properties of a service such as its inputs, outputs, pre-conditions, and effects (IOPEs), but also non-functional features including service name, service category, and aspects related to the quality of a service. In addition to OWL-S, another prominent effort on Semantic Web services is WSMO (Roman, Keller, Lausen, Bruijn, Lara, Stollberg et al., 2005), which is built on four key concepts—ontologies, standard WSDL based Web services, goals, and mediators. WSMO stresses the role of a mediator in order to support interoperation between Web services.

However, one challenging work in service discovery is that service matchmaking should be able to deal with uncertainty in service properties when matching service advertisements with service requests. This is because in a large-scale heterogeneous system, service publishers and requestors may use their pre-defined properties to describe services, for example, in the form of OWL-S or WSMO. For a property explicitly used in one service advertisement, it may not be explicitly used by another service advertisement within the same service category. As can be seen from Table 1, the property P_1 used by the service advertisement S_1 does not appear in the service advertisement S_2. When services S_1 and S_2 are matched with a query using properties P_1, P_2 and P_3, the property P_1 becomes an uncertain property when matching S_2. Similarly, the property P_3 becomes an uncertain property when matching

Figure 1. A layered structure for service-oriented systems

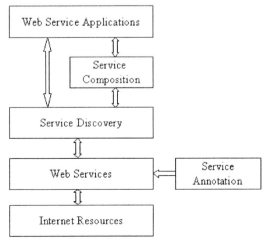

S_1. Consequently, both S_1 and S_2 may not be discovered because of the existence of uncertainty of properties even though the two services are relevant to the query.

It is worth noting that properties used in service advertisements may have dependencies, for example, both P_1 and P_3 may be dependent properties of P_2 when describing services S_1 and S_2 respectively. Both S_1 and S_2 can be discovered if P_1 and P_3 (which are uncertain properties in terms of the user query) can be dynamically identified and reduced in the matching process. To increase the accuracy of service discovery, a search engine should be able to deal with uncertainty of properties when matching services.

In this article, we present ROSSE, a Rough Sets (Pawlak, 1982) based Search Engine for Web service discovery. One salient feature of ROSSE lies in its capability to deal with uncertainty in service properties (attributes) when matching service advertisements with service requests. Experiment results show that ROSSE is more effective in service discovery than existing mechanisms such as UDDI keyword matching and OWL-S matchmaking.

The remainder of this article is organized as follows. The ROSSE Design section presents the design details of ROSSE. The ROSSE Case Study section gives a case study to demonstrate the use of ROSSE for discovery of car services. The ROSSE Implementation and Evaluation section evaluates ROSSE from the aspects of accuracy and efficiency in service discovery. The Related Word section discusses some related work, and the Conclusion and Future Work section concludes the article.

ROSSE DESIGN

ROSSE considers input and output properties individually when matching services. For the simplicity of expression, input and output properties used in a service request are generally referred to as service request properties. The same goes to service advertisements.

Figure 2 shows ROSSE components. The Irrelevant Property Reduction component takes a service request as an input (step 1), and then it accesses a set of advertised domain services (step 2) to remove irrelevant service properties using the domain ontology (step 3). Reduced properties will be marked in the set of advertised domain services (step 4). Once invoked (step 5), the Dependent Property Reduction component accesses the advertised domain services (step 6) to discover and reduce indecisive properties which will be marked in advertised domain services (step 7). Invoked by the Dependent Property Reduction component (step 8), the Service Matching and Ranking component accesses the advertised domain services for service matching and ranking (step 9), and finally it produces a list of matched services (step 10).

In the following sections, we describe in depth the design of ROSSE components for service matchmaking and discovery. Firstly, we introduce Rough sets for service discovery.

Rough Sets for Service Discovery

Rough sets method is a mathematic tool that can deal with uncertainty in knowledge discovery. It is based on the concept of an upper and a lower

Table 1. Two service advertisements with uncertain service properties

service advertisements	property	property	property
S_1	P_1	P_2	
S_2		P_2	P_3

approximation of a set as shown in Figure 3. For a given set X, the yellow grids (lighter shading) represent its upper approximation, and the green grids (darker shading) represent its lower approximation. We introduce Rough sets for service discovery in the following way.

Let

- Ω be a domain ontology.
- U be a set of N service advertisements, $U = \{s_1, s_2, ..., s_N\}$, $N \geq 1$.
- P be a set of K properties used in the N service advertisements, $P = \{p_1, p_2, ..., p_K\}$, $K \geq 2$.
- P_A be a set of M properties used in service advertisements which are relevant to a service request R within the domain ontology Ω,
- $P_A = \{p_{A1}, p_{A2}, ..., p_{AM}\}$, $P_A \subseteq P$, $M \geq 1$.
- X be a set of service advertisements relevant to the service request R, $X \subseteq U$.
- $\underline{X}$ be the lower approximation of the set X.
- $\overline{X}$ be the upper approximation of the set X.

According to the Rough sets theory, we have

$$\underline{X} = \{x \in U : [x]_{P_A} \subseteq X\} \qquad (1)$$

$$\overline{X} = \{x \in U : [x]_{P_A} \bigcap X \neq \varnothing\} \qquad (2)$$

For a property used by a service request $p \in P_A$, we have

- $\forall x \in \underline{X}$, x definitely has property p.
- $\forall x \in \overline{X}$, x possibly has property p.
- $\forall x \in U - \overline{X}$, x absolutely does not have property p.

The use of "definitely," "possibly" and "absolutely" are used to encode properties that cannot be specified in a more exact way. This is a significant addition to existing work, where discovery of services needs to be encoded in a precise way, making it difficult to find services which have an approximate match to a query.

Advertised domain service properties may be irrelevant (having no effect on service matching) or relevant (having an impact on service matching). Certain properties used by advertised services may be redundant which can be reduced without losing essential classificatory information. The concept of the reduct is fundamental for Rough sets theory (Winiarski, 2001). Service property reduction can be considered as a process of finding a smaller (than the original one) set of properties with the same or close classificatory power as

Figure 2. ROSSE components

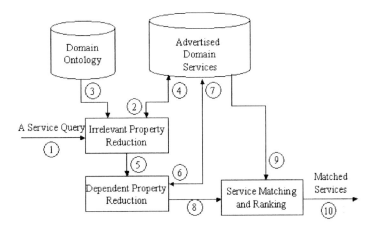

Figure 3. Approximation in Rough sets

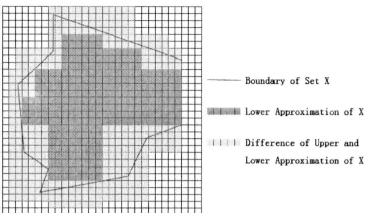

the original set. For a service query, the most relevant properties of advertised services can be determined after property reduction.

Reducing Irrelevant Properties

When searching for a service, a service request may employ some properties which are irrelevant to the properties used in a service advertisement within one domain ontology. These irrelevant properties used in service advertisements should be removed before the service matchmaking process is performed.

Let
- p_R be a property used in a service request.
- p_A be a property used in a service advertisement.

Following the work proposed in (Paolucci, Kawamura, Payne, & Sycara, 2002), we define the following relationships between p_R and p_A:

- **exact** match, p_R and p_A are equivalent or p_R is a subclass of p_A.
- **plug-in** match, p_A subsumes p_R.
- **subsume** match, p_R subsumes p_A.
- **nomatch**, no subsumption between p_R and p_A.

For each property used in a service request, the Irrelevant Property Reduction component uses Algorithm 1 to remove irrelevant properties from advertised services. For those properties used in service advertisements that have a nomatch result, they will be treated as irrelevant properties. Service advertisements are organised as service records in a database. Properties are organised in such a way that each property uses one column to ensure the correctness in the following reduction of dependent properties. As a property used in one service advertisement might not be used in another one, some properties may have empty values. For a service request, a property with an empty value in a service record becomes an uncertain property. If a property in an advertised service record is marked as nomatch, the column associated with the property will be marked as nomatch. As a result, all properties within the column including uncertain properties (i.e., properties with empty values) will not be considered in service matchmaking.

Reducing Dependent Properties

Properties used by service advertisements may have dependencies. Dependent properties are indecisive properties which have no effect on

Algorithm 1. Reducing irrelevant properties from service advertisements

```
1: for each property p_A used in service advertisements
2:   for all properties used in a service request
3:     if p_A is nomatch with any p_R
4:       then p_A is marked with nomatch;
5:     end if
6:   end for
7: end for
```

service matching. Building on the work proposed in (Jensen, Shen, & Tuson, 2005), we designed Algorithm 2 to reduce dependent properties from advertised services.

Let

- Ω, U, P, P_A be defined as in the Rough Sets for Service Discovery section.
- P_A^D be a set of L_D decisive properties for identifying service advertisements relevant to the service request R in terms of Ω,
- $P_A^D = \{p_{A1}^D, p_{A2}^D, ..., p_{AL_D}^D\}$, $P_A^D \subseteq P_A$, $L_D \geq 1$.
- P_A^{IND} be a set of L_{IND} indecisive properties for identifying service advertisements relevant to the service request R in terms of Ω,
- $P_A^{IND} = \{p_{A1}^{IND}, p_{A2}^{IND}, ..., p_{AL_{IND}}^{IND}\}$, $P_A^{IND} \subseteq P_A$, $L_{IND} \geq 1$.
- $IND()$ be an indiscernibility relation.
- f be a mapping function from a property to a service advertisement.

Then

$$IND(P_A^{IND}) =$$
$$\{(x,y) \in U : \forall p_{Ai}^{IND} \in P_A^{IND}, f(x, p_{Ai}^{IND}) = f(y, p_{Ai}^{IND})\}$$

$$\text{(3)}$$

$$P_A^D = P_A^{IND} - P_A \qquad \text{(4)}$$

For a service request, the Dependent Property Reduction component uses Algorithm 2 to find the decisive properties in service advertisements.

Specifically, service advertisements with the maximum number of nonempty property values are used in the algorithm as targets to find indecisive properties. The targeted services can still be uniquely identified without using these indecisive properties. All possible combinations of individual indecisive properties are checked with an aim to maximally remove indecisive properties which may include uncertain properties whose values are empty. In the mean time, the following service discovery process is speeded up due to the reduction of dependent properties.

Computing Match Degrees

The Service Matching and Ranking component uses the decisive properties to compute the match degrees of advertised services related to a service request.

Let

- Ω, U, P, P_A be defined as in the Rough Sets for Service Discovery section.
- P_R be a set of M properties used in a service request R. $P_R = \{P_{R1}, P_{R2}, ..., P_{R3}\}$, $M \geq 1$.
- P_A^D be a set of L_D decisive properties for identifying service advertisements relevant to the service request R in terms of Ω,
- $P_A^D = \{p_{A1}^D, p_{A2}^D, ..., p_{AL_D}^D\}$, $L_D \geq 1$.
- $m(p_{Ri}, p_{Aj})$ be a match degree between a property P_{Ri} and a property P_{Aj} in terms of Ω, $P_{Ri} \in P_R, 1 \leq i \leq M$, $P_{Aj} \in P_A^D$, $1 \leq j \leq L_D$.
- $v(P_{Aj})$ be a value of the property P_{Aj}, $P_{Aj} \in P_A^D$, $1 \leq j \leq L_D$.

Algorithm 2. Reducing dependent properties from advertised services

```
S is a set of service advertisements with the maximum number of nonempty
        property values relevant to a service request;
    PA is a set of properties used by the S set of service advertisements;
    PAD is a set of decisive properties, PAD ⊆ PA;
    PAIND is a set of individual indecisive properties, PAIND ⊆ PA ;
    PAIND_Core is a set of combined indecisive properties,
        PAIND_Core ⊆ PAIND;
    PAD = Ø; PAIND = Ø; PAIND_Core = Ø;
1:  for each property p∈ PA
2:     if p is an indecisive property for identifying the S set of services
3:        then
4:        add p into PAIND;
5:        PAIND_Core = Ø;
6:        add p into PAIND_Core;
7:     end if
8:  end for
9:  for i=2 to sizeof(PAIND)-1
10:     calculate all possible i combinations of the properties in PAIND;
11:     if any combined i properties are indecisive properties for identifying
             the S set of services
12:        then
13:        PAIND_Core = Ø;
14:        add the i properties into PAIND_Core;
15:        continue;
16:     else if any combined i properties are decisive properties
17:        then break;
18:     end if
19:  end for
20:  PAD = PA-PAIND_Core;
21:  return PAD;
```

- $S(R, s)$ be a similarity degree between a service advertisement s and the service request $R, s \in U$.

Algorithm 3 shows the rules for calculating a match degree between a property used in a service request and a property used in a service advertisement. A decisive property with an empty value has a match degree of 50% when matching each property used in a service request. A property used in a service advertisement will be given a match degree of 100% if it has an exact match relationship with a property used in a service request. A match degree of 50% will be given if it has a plug-in relationship with a service request property and the relationship is out of five generations. Similarly, a property used in a service advertisement will be given a match degree of 50% if it has a subsume relationship with a service request property and the relationship is out of three generations.

Algorithm 3. The rules for calculating match degrees between properties used in service requests and service advertisements respectively

```
1:   for each property p_{Aj} ∈ P_A^D, v(p_{Aj}) ≠ NULL
2:     for each property p_{Ri} ∈ P_R
3:       if  p_{Aj} is an exact match with p_{Ri}
4:         then  m(p_{Ri}, p_{Aj}) = 1;
5:       else if p_{Aj} is a plug-in match with p_{Ri}
6:           then if p_{Ri} is the kth subclass of p_{Aj} and 2≤k≤5
7:           then m(p_{Ri}, p_{Aj}) = 1-(k-1)×10%;
8:             else if p_{Ri} is the kth subclass of p_{Aj} and k>5
9:               then m(p_{Ri}, p_{Aj}) = 0.5;
10:          end if
11:      else if p_{Aj} is a subsume match with p_{Ri}
12:          then   if p_{Aj} is the kth subclass of p_{Ri} and 1≤k≤3
13:              then m(p_{Ri}, p_{Aj}) = 0.8-(k-1)×10%;
14:              else if p_{Aj} is the kth subclass of p_{Ri} and k>3
15:      then m(p_{Ri}, p_{Aj}) = 0.5;
16:          end if
17:      end if
18:    end for
19:  end for
20:  for each property p_{Aj} ∈ P_A^D, v(p_{Aj}) = NULL
21:    for each property p_{Ri} ∈ P_R
22:      m(p_{Ri}, p_{Aj}) = 0.5;
23:    end for
24:  end for
```

Each decisive property used for identifying service advertisements has a maximum match degree when matching all the properties used in a service request. $S(R, s)$ can be calculated using formula (5).

$$S(R,s) = \sum_{j=1}^{L_D} \sum_{i=1}^{M} \max(m(p_{Ri}, p_{Aj})) \bigg/ L_D$$

(5)

Using the formula (5), ROSSE calculates a matching degree for each service advertisement related to a service request. The similarity degrees are used to produce a lower and an upper approximation set of discovered services.

ROSSE CASE STUDY

In this section, we present a use case of ROSSE to discover vehicle services. Figure 4 shows the

Figure 4. Ontolgogies used in the search scenario

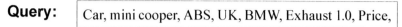

Query: Car, mini cooper, ABS, UK, BMW, Exhaust 1.0, Price,

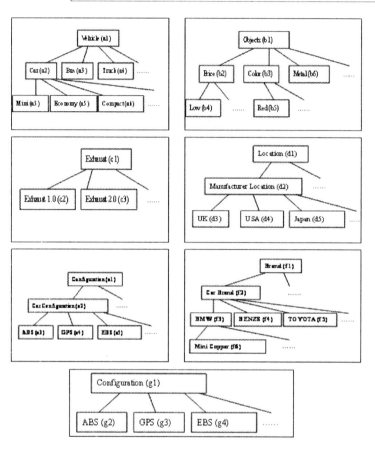

ontologies used in this scenario defining the classifications of *vehicles, objects, exhausts, locations, configurations, brands* respectively. Two ontologies are used to classify configurations of vehicles represented respectively by *e1-e5* and *g1-g4*. Relevant vehicle services are registered with ROSSE. In the following sections, we describe how services are matched in terms of the following query to search for car services that sell red BMW mini coopers that have an exhaust of 1.0, and are configured with ABS, manufactured in the UK. Price information is also provided by the car services.

Building a Decision Table

A service decision table is used to compute dependent properties among services. As the number of services registered with ROSSE can be tremendous, the decision table is constructed by sampling registered services. For a specific query, ROSSE randomly selects a certain number of services records. A service record is selected as long as one of its properties has a valid relationship with a property used in a service query. The relationship can be *exact, plug-in* or *subsume* as defined in algorithm 1 which is described in the Reducing Irrelevant Properties section.

Table 2. A segment of the decision table used for discovery of car services

properties \ services	f6	g2	d3	f3	c2	b2	b3	d2	c1	e1/g1	d1	b6
S_1	1	1	1	1	1	0	0	0	0	0	1	1
S_2	0	1	0	1	0	0	0	0	0	0	1	1
S_3	0	1	0	1	0	0	1	1	1	1	0	0
S_4	0	1	0	0	0	1	1	1	0	1	0	0
S_5	0	1	1	0	1	0	0	0	0	1	0	0
S_6	1	1	1	1	1	1	0	0	0	0	0	0
S_7	0	1	0	0	0	0	1	1	1	0	0	0
S_8	1	1	1	1	1	0	0	0	0	1	0	0
S_9	0	1	0	1	0	0	0	0	0	0	1	1
S_{10}	0	1	0	0	0	0	0	0	1	0	1	0
S_{11}	0	1	0	0	1	0	0	1	0	0	0	0
S_{12}	0	1	0	1	0	0	0	0	1	0	1	1
S_{13}	1	1	1	1	1	1	1	0	0	1	0	0

Table 3. Computed dependent properties

properties \ services	f6	g2	d3	f3	c2	b2	b3	d2	c1	e1/g1	d1	b6
S_1	1	1	1	1	1	0	0	0	0	0	1	1
S_2	0	1	0	1	0	0	0	0	0	0	1	1
S_3	0	1	0	1	0	0	1	1	1	1	0	0
S_4	0	1	0	0	0	1	1	1	0	1	0	0
S_6	1	1	1	1	1	1	0	0	0	0	0	0
S_6	1	1	1	1	1	1	0	0	0	0	0	0
S_7	0	1	0	0	0	0	1	1	1	0	0	0
S_8	1	1	1	1	1	0	0	0	0	1	0	0
S_9	0	1	0	1	0	0	0	0	0	0	1	1
S_{10}	0	1	0	0	0	0	0	0	1	0	1	0
S_{11}	0	1	0	0	1	0	0	1	0	0	0	0
S_{12}	0	1	0	1	0	0	0	0	1	0	1	1
S_{13}	1	1	1	1	1	1	1	0	0	1	0	0

Table 2 shows a segment of the decision table with 13 service records for discovery of car services. As can be seen from Table 2, properties of advertised services that are relevant to the car service query are *f6, g2, d3, f3, c2, b2, b3, d2, c1, e1/g1, d1, b6*. If a property in a service record is marked with *1*, this means that the property is used by the service in its advertisement. For example, the service S_1 has properties of *f6, g2, d3, f3, c2, d1,* and *b6* in its advertisement. A property marked with *0* in a service record means that the service does not have the corresponding property in its advertisement, for example, properties such as *b2, b2, d2, c1,* and *e1/g1* are not used by the service S_1 for advertisement. However, it should be noted that a property marked with 0 in a service record does not necessarily mean this property is not

relevant to the service. Such a property might be an inherent property of the service. ROSSE deals with properties marked with 0 as uncertain properties when matching services.

Computing Dependent Properties

Once a service decision table is constructed, the next step is to compute dependent properties. Using the algorithm 2 presented in the Reducing Dependent Properties section, properties *g2, d3, f3,* and *c2* are indecisive properties which are reduced from the decision table in matching services as shown in Table 3. Table 4 shows the segment of the decision table without dependent properties.

Table 4. The segment of the decision table without dependent properties

properties \ services	f6	b2	b3	d2	c1	e1/g1	d1	b6
S_1	1	0	0	0	0	0	1	1
S_2	0	0	0	0	0	0	1	1
S_3	0	0	1	1	1	1	0	0
S_4	0	1	1	1	0	1	0	0
S_5	0	0	0	0	0	1	0	0
S_6	1	1	0	0	0	0	0	0
S_7	0	0	1	1	1	0	0	0
S_8	1	0	0	0	0	1	0	0
S_9	0	0	0	0	0	0	1	1
S_{10}	0	0	0	0	1	0	1	0
S_{11}	0	0	0	1	0	0	0	0
S_{12}	0	0	0	0	1	0	1	1
S_{13}	1	1	1	0	0	1	0	0

Table 5. Computation of matching degrees

Match Degrees properties \ services	100%					95%	90%	
	f6	b2	b3	d2	c1	e1/g1	d1	b6
S_1	1	0	0	0	0	0	1	1
S_2	0	0	0	0	0	0	1	1
S_3	0	0	1	1	1	1	0	0
S_4	0	1	1	1	0	1	0	0
S_5	0	0	0	0	0	1	0	0
S_6	1	1	0	0	0	0	0	0
S_7	0	0	1	1	1	0	0	0
S_8	1	0	0	0	0	1	0	0
S_9	0	0	0	0	0	0	1	1
S_{10}	0	0	0	0	1	0	1	0
S_{11}	0	0	0	1	0	0	0	0
S_{12}	0	0	0	0	1	0	1	1
S_{13}	1	1	1	0	0	1	0	0

Computing Match Degrees

Decisive properties are used for computing the similarities between an advertised service and a service request. For each decisive property used in a service advertisement and a property used in the service query, a maximum matching degree can be computed using ontologies defined in Figure 4. Table 5 shows the matching degrees of the decisive properties used in the exemplified 13 service records. It should be noted that both *e1* and *g1* refers to the same property *Configuration*, but they use different ontology definitions as shown in Figure 4. The matching degree of *Configuration* to the *ABS* property used in the query is computed in such way that a mean of two matching degrees using the two ontology definitions (i.e., 100% and 90%) is computed which is 95%.

It is worth noting that for an uncertain property which is marked with the number of 0 in a box of Table, a matching degree of 50% is given. Based on the formula (5) presented in the Comupting Match Degrees section, the similarity degree between an advertised service and a service query can be computed. In the car service query case, for example, service S_1 has a similarity degree of 66.25% and service S_{13} has a similarity degree of 74.375%.

ROSSE IMPLEMENTATION AND EVALUATION

ROSSE is implemented with Java on a Pentium IIII 2.6G with 512M RAM running Red Hat Fedora Linux 3. Figure 5 shows the homepage of ROSSE. It has two registries for service registration, a UDDI registry and an OWL registry. The UDDI registry is used to register services with WSDL interfaces, and the OWL-S registry is used to register services with OWL-S interfaces. The UUID of a WSDL service registered with the UDDI registry is used to uniquely identify semantic annotation records of the registered service. In this way, WSDL services registered with ROSSE can be matched with semantic inferences instead of using keywords only. jUDDI (http://ws.apache.org/juddi) and mySQL (http://www.mysql.com) are used to build the UDDI registry and UDDI4J (http://uddi4j.sourceforge.net/) is used to query the registry. OWL-S API (http://www.mindswap.org/2004/owl-s/api) is used to parse OWL-S documents to register services with OWL-S interfaces with the OWL-S registry in ROSSE.

ROSSE provides graphical user interfaces to register services. Figure 6 shows a page to register a *vehicle* service that has a WSDL Interface, and Figure 7 shows the four steps used to semantically

Figure 5. ROSSE user interface

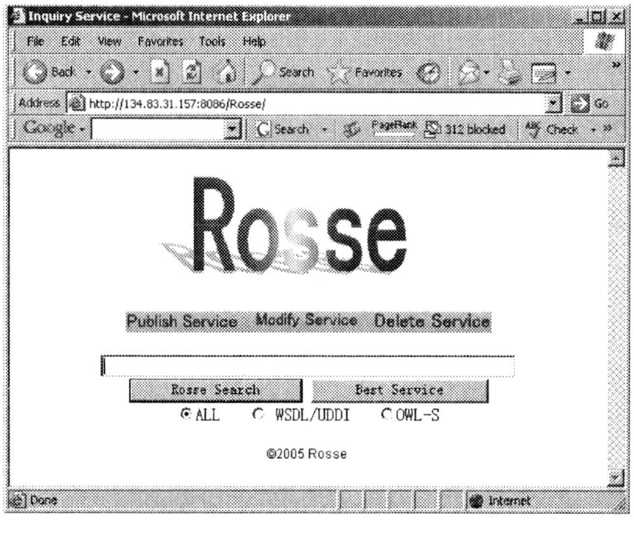

Figure 6. Registering a service that has a WSDL interface

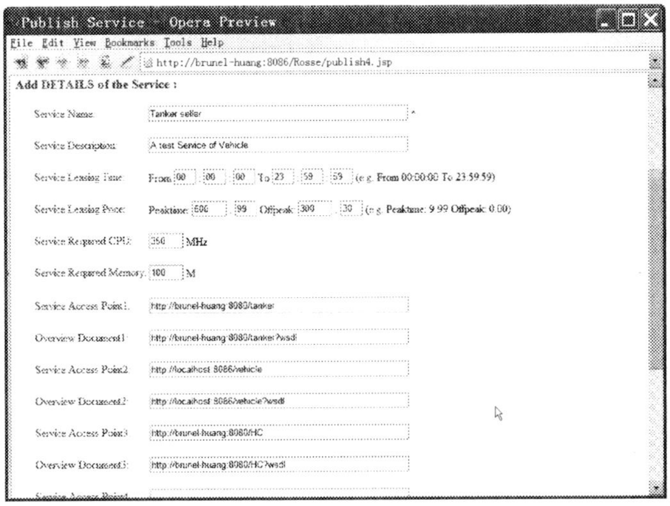

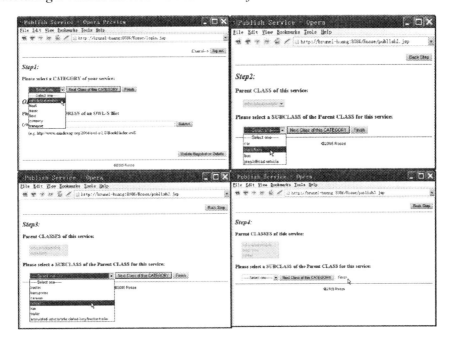

Figure 7. Annotating a vehicle service with semantic information

annotate the *vehicle* service. Figure 8 shows the registration of a zip code finding service with an OWL-S interface in ROSSE.

For a service request, ROSSE computes a matching degree for each service advertisement in terms of its functional input and output properties using formula (5). As shown in Figure 5, ROSSE can discover services with WSDL interfaces or OWL-S interfaces. It can also discover the best service from service advertisements which has

Figure 8. Registering OWL-S services with ROSSE

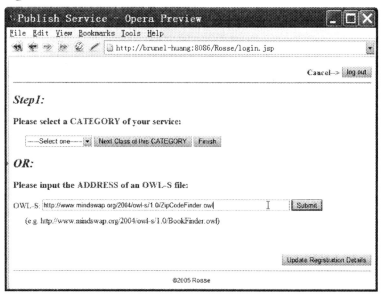

Figure 9. Pizza ontology structure

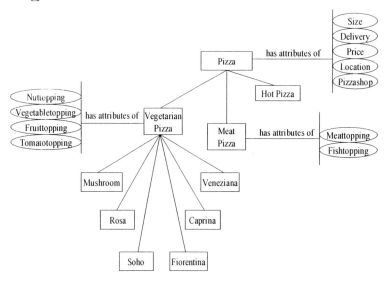

the highest matching degree related to a service request.

In this section, we evaluate the accuracy and efficiency of ROSSE in service discovery. We compare ROSSE with UDDI and OWL-S respectively. RACER (Haarslev & Möller, 2001) was used by OWL-S to infer the relationships between properties used in service queries and service advertisements. We implemented a light weighted reasoning component in ROSSE to overcome a high overhead incurred by RACER. The component uses the Protégé OWL API (http://protege.stanford.edu/plugins/owl/api/) to parse OWL documents.

We designed Pizza services for the tests using the Pizza ontology defined by http://www.co-ode.org/ontologies/pizza/pizza_20041007.owl. Figure 9 shows the Pizza ontology structure. The approach adopted here can be applied to other domains—where a specific ontology can be specified. The use of service properties needs to be related to a particular application-specific ontology.

ROSSE Accuracy in Service Discovery

Precision and recall are standard measures that have been used in information retrieval for measuring the accuracy of a search method or a search engine (Rijsbergen, 1979). We performed 4 groups of tests to evaluate the precision and recall of ROSSE in service discovery using 10 service records in each group. Each service had 5 properties of which 2 properties were dependent properties. For a service query, each group had 3 relevant services. The 10 services in group 1 did not have uncertain properties, but group 2 had 3 services with uncertain properties, group 3 had 5 services with uncertain properties and group 4 had 7 services with uncertain properties. Properties such as *Size, Price, Nuttoping, Vegetariantopping,* and *Fruittopping* were used by the advertised services. Table 6 shows the evaluation results.

In the tests conducted for group 1, both OWL-S and ROSSE have a precision of 100%. This is because all service advertisements in this group do not have uncertain properties (i.e., properties with empty values). UDDI discovered 4 services, but only 2 services were relevant to the service query with a precision of 50%, and a recall of 66.7%. In the tests of the last 3 groups where advertised services have uncertain properties, OWL-S cannot discover any services producing a precision of 0 and a recall of 0. Although UDDI can still discover some services in these tests, the precision of each group is low. For example, in the tests of group 3 and group 4 where the service property certainty rates are 50% and 30% respectively, UDDI cannot discover any relevant services. ROSSE is more effective than both UDDI and OWL-S in dealing with uncertain properties when matching services. For example, ROSSE is still able to produce a precision of 100% in the tests of the last 3 groups albeit with a low recall which is 33.3%.

ROSSE Efficiency in Service Discovery

We have registered 10,000 Pizza service records with ROSSE for testing its efficiency in service discovery. Service discovery involves two processes, one is service matchmaking and the other is service accessing (i.e., accessing matched services). We compared the efficiency of ROSSE in matching services with that of UDDI and OWL-S

Table 6. ROSSE accuracy in service discovery

Service Property Certainty Rate	UDDI		OWL-S		ROSSE	
	Precision	Recall	Precision	Recall	Precision	Recall
100%	50%	66.7%	100%	100%	100%	100%
70%	33.3%	33.3%	0	0	100%	33.3%
50%	0	0	0	0	100%	33.3%
30%	0	0	0	0	100%	33.3%

Figure 10. ROSSE efficiency in service matchmaking

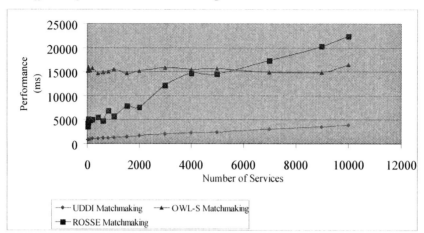

respectively, and the evaluation results are plotted in Figure 10. We also compared their efficiency in accessing matched services, and the results are plotted in Figure 11.

From Figure 10 we can see that UDDI has the least overhead in matching services. This is because UDDI only supports keyword based exact matching. UDDI does not support the inference of the relationships between requested service properties and advertised service properties which is a time consuming process. We also observe that ROSSE has a better performance in service matchmaking than OWL-S when the number of advertised services is less than 5500. This is because ROSSE used a simpler reasoning component than RACER which was used by OWL-S for matching services. However, the overhead of ROSSE in service matchmaking increases when the number of services gets larger. This is due to the overhead caused by a reduction of dependent properties. The major overhead of OWL-S in matching services is caused by RACER which is sensitive to the number of service properties instead of the number of services.

From Figure 11 we can see that the ROSSE matchmaking algorithm is most efficient in accessing matched services due to its reduction of dependent properties. The OWL-S has a similar performance to UDDI in this process.

RELATED WORK

Service matchmaking is becoming an issue of vital importance in service-oriented systems. UDDI has been proposed to support service publication and discovery. However, the search mechanism supported by UDDI is limited to keyword matches and does not support any inference based on the taxonomies referred to by the tModels. Various extensions (Miles, Papay, Dialani, Luck, Decker, Payne et al., 2003; Powles & Krishnaswamy, 2005; Shaikh Ali, Rana, Al-Ali, & Walker, 2003) have been proposed to complement UDDI with rich descriptions and powerful match mechanisms in support of service discovery.

Among the extensions, the UDDI-M approach (Miles et al., 2003) is flexible in attaching metadata to various entities associated with a service, but this approach assumes the properties used in service advertisements and in service requests are consistent. Semantic Web service technologies such as OWL-S and WSMO have been proposed to enhance service discovery with semantic annotations. However, the classical OWL-S matching algorithm (Paolucci et al., 2002) cannot deal with uncertainty in service properties when matching service advertisements with service requests. This work has been extended in various ways in applying Semantic Web services for

Figure 11. ROSSE efficiency in accessing matched services

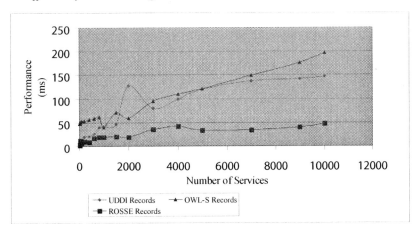

service discovery. For example, Jaeger, Rojec-Goldmann, Mühl, Liebetruth, and Geihs (2005) introduce "contravariance" in matching inputs and outputs between service advertisements and service requests using OWL-S. Li & Horrocks (2004) introduce a "intersection" relationship between a service advertisement and a service request. Majithia, Ali, Rana, and Walker (2004) introduce reputation metrics in matching services. However, these OWL-S based methods still cannot deal with missing (uncertain) properties.

WSMO introduces mediators trying to support distinct ontologies employed by service requests and service advertisements. However, the discovery mechanism (Keller, Lara, Polleres, Toma, Kifer, & Fensel, 2004) proposed in WSMO requires that properties used by both the goals and services should be consistent.

Compared with the work mentioned above, ROSSE matchmaking can deal with uncertain properties in matching services. It takes all service advertisements belonging to one service category into one search space to dynamically identify and reduce irrelevant and dependent properties which may be uncertain properties related to a service request.

CONCLUSION AND FUTURE WORK

In this article we have presented ROSSE for service discovery. ROSSE is novel in its capability to deal with uncertainty of service properties for high accuracy in service discovery. The preliminary experimental results achieved so far are encouraging. However, the following issues need to be considered for ROSSE enhancement:

- It has been shown that finding a minimal reduct in Rough set is a problem of NP-hard when the number of attributes gets large (Skowron & Rauszer, 1992). Heuristic methods need to be investigated to speed up the process in service property reduction.
- Services registered with ROSSE could be tremendous. Scalability is one the issues that need to be tackled. UDDI Version 3 (http://uddi.org/pubs/uddi_v3.htm) provides larger support for multiple registries, but the specification does not specify how these registries should be structured for enhanced scalability in service registration. Distributed Hash Table (DHT) based Peer-to-Peer (P2P) systems such as Chord (Stoica, Morris, Liben-Nowell, Karger, Kaashoek, Dabek et al., 2003) and Pastry (Rowstron &

Druschel, 2001) have shown their efficiency and scalability in content lookup. Scalability in ROSSE can be improved with DHT structured P2P systems.

- Advertised services may be further described in terms of their non-functional properties related to QoS such as reliability and cost. One challenge is how to model such QoS data so that functionally matched services can be evaluated in terms of their QoS properties.

- Currently ROSSE only supports keyword-based queries. It is expected that complex queries to be supported in ROSSE, for example, queries with a range or fuzzy queries.

REFERENCES

Andrews, T., Curbera, F., Dholakia, H., Goland, Y., Klein, J., Leymann, F. et al. (2003). Business Process Execution Language for Web Services version 1.1.

Berners-Lee, T., Hendler, J. & Lassila, O. (2001). The Semantic Web, *Scientific American*, Vol. 284 (4), pp. 34-43.

Haarslev, V. & Möller, R. (2001). Description of the RACER System and its Applications, *Proc. of 2001 International Workshop on Description Logics (DL-2001)*, Stanford, USA.

Jaeger, M., Rojec-Goldmann, G., Mühl, G., Liebetruth, C. & Geihs, K. (2005). Ranked Matching for Service Descriptions using OWL-S, *Proc. of Communication in Distributed Systems (KiVS) 2005*, Kaiserslautern, Germany.

Keller, U., Lara, R., Polleres, A., Toma, I., Kifer, M. and Fensel, D. (2004). WSMO Web Service Discovery. Retrieved on XXX from, http://www.wsmo.org/2004/d5/d5.1/v0.1/20041112/d5.1v0.1_20041112.pdf

Li, L. & Horrocks, I. (2004). A software framework for matchmaking based on semantic web technology. *Int. J. of Electronic Commerce, 8*(4), pp. 39-60.

Majithia, S., Ali, A., Rana, O., & Walker, D. (2004). Reputation-Based Semantic Service Discovery, *Proceedings of WETICE 2004*, Italy.

Martin, D., Paolucci, M., McIlraith, S., Burstein, M., McDermott, D., McGuinness, D. et al. (2004). Bringing Semantics to Web Services: The OWL-S Approach, *Proceedings of the First International Workshop on Semantic Web Services and Web Process Composition (SWSWPC 2004)*, San Diego, California, USA.

Miles, S., Papay, J., Dialani, D., Luck, M., Decker, K., Payne, T. et al., (2003). Personalised Grid Service Discovery, *IEE Proceedings Software: Special Issue on Performance Engineering, 150*(4), pp. 252-256.

Paolucci, M., Kawamura, T., Payne, T. & Sycara, K. (2002). Semantic Matching of Web Service Capabilities, *Proceedings of the 1st International Semantic Web Conference (ISWC)*, Berlin.

Pawlak, Z. (1982). Rough sets. *International Journal of Computer and Information Science, 11*(5), pp. 341-356.

Powles, A. & Krishnaswamy, S. (2005). Extending UDDI with Recommendations: An Association Analysis Approach, *Proceedings of WSMDEIS 2005*, Miami, USA.

Roman, D., Keller, U., Lausen, H., Bruijn, J., Lara, R., Stollberg, M. et al., (2005), Web Service Modeling Ontology, *Applied Ontology, 1*(1), pp. 77 - 106.

Rowstron A. & Druschel, P. (2001). Pastry: Scalable, distributed object location and routing for large-scale peer-to-peer systems, *Proceedings of Middleware 2001*, pp. 329-350, Lecture Notes in Computer Science, Springer.

ShaikhAli, A., Rana, O., Al-Ali, R., & Walker, D. (2003). UDDIe: An Extended Registry for Web Service, Proceedings of SAINT Workshops, Orlando, Florida, USA, 2003.

Skowron, A. & Rauszer, C. (1992). The discernibility matrices and functions in information systems, *Decision Support by Experience - Application of the Rough Sets Theory*, R. Slowinski (ed.), Kluwer Academic Publishers, pp. 331-362.

Stoica, I., Morris, R., Liben-Nowell, D., Karger, D., Kaashoek, M., Dabek et al. (2003). Chord: A Scalable Peer-to-Peer Lookup Protocol for Internet Applications, *IEEE/ACM Transactions on. Networks, 11*(1), pp. 17-32.

Winiarski, R. (2001). Rough sets methods in Feature Reduction and Classification, *Int. J. Appl. Math. Comput. Sci., 11*(3), pp. 565-582.

Jensen, R., Shen, Q., & Tuson, A. (2005). Finding Rough Set Reducts with SAT, *Proceedings of the 10th International Conference on Rough Sets, Fuzzy Sets, Data Mining, and Granular Computing (RSFDGrC)*, pp. 194-203, Lecture Notes in Computer Science, Springer, Regina, Canada.

Rijsbergen, C. (1979). *Information Retrieval*, 1979, Butterworths: London.

This work was previously published in International Journal of Web Services Research, Vol. 6, Issue 1, edited by L.-J. Zhang, pp. 69-86, copyright 2009 by IGI Publishing (an imprint of IGI Global).

Chapter 3.11
Generating Join Queries for Large Databases and Web Services

Sikha Bagui
The University of West Florida, USA

Adam Loggins
Zilliant Inc., USA

ABSTRACT

In this data-centric world, as Web services and service oriented architectures gain momentum and become a standard for data usage, there will be a need for tools to automate data retrieval. In this article the authors propose a tool that automates the generation of joins in a transparent and integrated fashion in heterogeneous large databases as well as Web services. This tool reads metadata information and automatically displays a join path and a SQL join query. This tool will be extremely useful for performing joins to help in the retrieval of information in large databases as well as Web services. [Article copies are available for purchase from InfoSci-on-Demand.com

INTRODUCTION AND RELATED WORKS

As we are working with more and more data, the sizes of databases are getting larger and larger. As businesses are going global, Web services are becoming a standard for sharing data (Srivastava et al., 2006; Resende and Feng, 2007). Enterprises are moving towards service oriented architectures where several large databases may be layered behind Web services, hence databases are having to become adaptable with loosely-coupled, heterogenous systems (Srivastava et al., 2006) too. In such scenarios of Web services and service oriented architectures, which may be dealing with several loosely coupled heterogeneous large databases, it is no longer humanly possible to have handy all the information on all the tables and primary keys in all the large databases. Although considerable work is being done on the challenges associated with Web services addressing the problem of multiple Web services to carry out particular tasks (Florescu et. al., 2003; Ouzzani and Bouguettaya, 2004), most of this work is targeted towards work-flow of applications, rather than coordinating how data can be retrieved from multiple large databases in Web services via SQL (Srivastava et al., 2006). In this article we try to address one aspect of this problem of retrieving data from multiple heterogeneous large databases using SQL. Specifically, we present a tool that automatically formulates joins by reading the metadata of databases in the context of very large databases or in the context of Web services which may employ the use of several large heteregenous databases.

Let us look at an example of a query presented to a Web service: *Suppose a health insurance company needs to verify the salary, health, and travel patterns of a person before determining the amount of health insurance he/she needs to pay. In a Web service, this will require joining of several tables. And, of course, no one person will have knowledge of all the primary key/foreign key relationships between the tables to join in the Web services.*

When databases were smaller, it was possible to have knowledge of most of the tables and primary key/foreign key relationships in databases, and SQL join queries could easily be built by joining tables in databases. But, in large databases layered behind Web services, it will not be possible to have knowledge of all the database schemas.

The join operation, originally defined in the relational data model (Codd 1970, 1972), is a fundamental relational database operation, facilitating the retrieval of information from two relations (tables). Writing efficient joins is simple for small databases since few relations are involved and one has knowledge of the complete database schema. But, writing efficient joins is a challenge in large database scenarios and Web services where it may not be possible to have a complete picture of the database schema and it's relations.

Since joins are one of the most time-consuming and data-intensive operations in relational query processing, joins have been studied discussed extensively in the literature. Mishra and Eich (1992) present a very comprehensive study of works that have been done on joins. Query optimization issues in joins, and devising strategies for distributed join processing have also been discussed by many, for example, Kim et al. (1985), Perrizo et al. (1989), Segev (1986), Swami and Gupta (1988), Yoo and Lafortune(1989), and Yu et al (1985, 1987). These works have to be extended in the context of databases for Web services and service oriented architectures. Srivastava, et. al (2006) addresses the problem of query optimization over Web services on a much broader scale.

In this article we present a tool that we have developed that will: (i) read the meta data of databases, that is, search the database model or schema and discover the relationships between the tables using table indexes defined in the database catalogs; (ii) find efficient join paths between the tables to be joined; and, (iii) generate a SQL join query (in ANSI SQL standard).

This rest of the article is organized as follows: Section two briefly describes relational databases with respect to the join operation; section three presents an architectural overview of our tool; section four presents the configuration details of our tool; section five describes how we tested our tool and presents some results; and section six presents the conclusion. Some relevant code portions are presented in the appendices.

RELATIONAL DATABASES AND THE JOIN OPERATION

In relational databases, data is stored in the form of tables or relations. Each table has information on a particular subject or concept and is composed of a group of "related" attributes. The attributes in a table are all "related" in the sense that they describe the subject or concept of the table. For example, there could be a table called Employee, with attributes emp_lastName, emp_midName, emp_firstName, emp_ssn, emp_birthdate, city, state, homePhone, cellPhone, deptnum, etc. All these attributes describe an Employee. Likewise, there could be another table called Department, with attributes, dept_Name, dept_Number, dept_manager, dept_location, etc. Here again, all these attributes describe a Department. Now, if we want information that is partly in the Employee table and partly in the Department table, for example, if we want to know which employee is working for a department located in LA, we have to perform a "join" of the Employee table and the Department table on some common attribute (usually the primary key field of one table and the foreign key field of the other table). In this case we would perform this join with a simple SQL query where Employee.deptnum = Department.dept_Number.

Usually, when a join query is composed, one has to determine which tables contain the information needed to answer the query, and has to join those tables by the key fields. This is possible if there are few tables and one has a conceptual idea of the databases. But how do we compose joins when there are hundred of tables, with an unknown (large number) of attributes per table in a database – the scenario for Web services. Moreover, the conceptual schema of the databases could be constantly evolving or changing.

So, the join operation is used to combine related tuples from two relations into single tuples that are stored in a resulting new relation. The desired relationship between the tuples or some attributes in the tuples is specified in terms of the join condition. In its simplest form, the join of two tables or relations, R and S is written as:

$$R \bowtie_{r(a) \, \Theta \, s(b)} S$$

where $r(a) \, \Theta \, s(b)$ defines the join condition; a and b are the attributes, usually the key fields of the respective tables R and S (usually indexed); and Θ defines the join condition that must hold true between the attributes a and b of R and S, respectively. The Θ operation can be any one of the following: $=, \neq, >, <, \geq$ or $\leq$. The join condition also includes multiple simple conditions of the form shown above connected with the logical connective AND (Earp and Bagui (2000), Elmasri and Navathe (2007)):

condition AND condition AND condition

AN ARCHITECTURAL OVERVIEW OF OUR TOOL

We developed a tool that extracts configuration information from system tables in databases in Web services. The primary keys of the tables in the databases are extracted. Primary key/foreign key relationships are determined. A list of table indexes is also constructed – this information is also obtained from the metadata of the databases. This information is then stored in an XML configuration document. A Java interface is then used to activate a GUI that takes, as input parameters, the names of tables that need to be joined. Then, a search routine is called that generates the table's neighbor nodes (tables) – that is, information on which table is linked to which table. From here, join paths are generated, from where a valid join path is then selected, and the final product is a SQL join query generated from the valid join path.

Below we present the algorithm of our tool.

Algorithm of our Tool

Input: *Activate GUI, input parameters, that is, the names of the tables that have the final information that is required (tables to be joined).*

Figure 1. Architectural overview of our tool

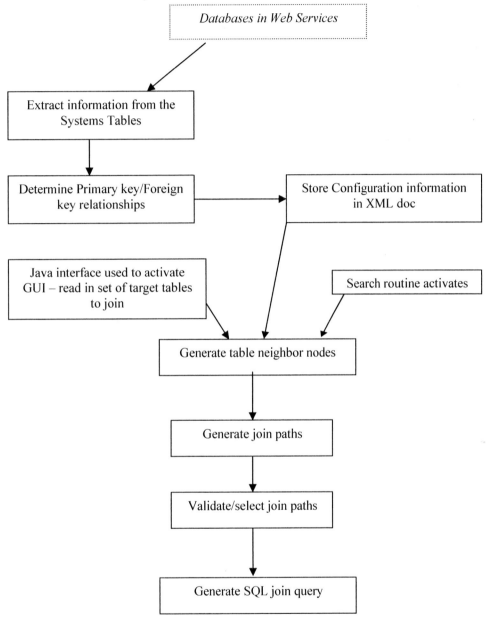

Output: *SQL Query.*

Method:

1. *For all the metadata in the required database catalogs in Web services*

    a.   *Read the primary keys of the tables*

    b.   *Check for primary key/foreign key relationships and generate primary key/ foreign key relationship table*

2.   *Call Search Routine*

3.   *Generate join paths*

4.   *Generate SQL query*

Figure 2. UML for tool

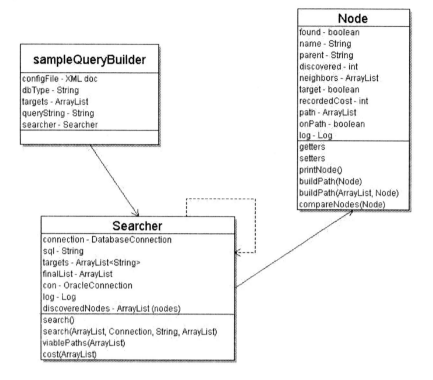

Figure 1 presents the architectural overview of our tool.

TOOL CONFIGURATION DETAILS

The UML class diagram of the tool is presented in Figure 2.

The first step is to extract the list of tables in the database from the information available in the Systems Table of the databases. This is done using the following SQL query:

```
SELECT table_name
FROM System_tables
WHERE table_type = 'TABLE'
```

The next step is to determine the primary key/foreign key relationships between the tables and indexes used for the relationships. This is done using the following SQL queries:

```
SELECT DISTINCT scr.PKTABLE_NAME AS lo-
calTable,
scr.PKCOLUMN_NAME AS localCol,
scr.FKTABLE_NAME AS foriegnTable,
scr.FKCOLUMN_NAME AS foriegnCol,
scr.FK_NAME AS key
FROM System_CROSSREFERENCE scr
WHERE scr.PKTABLE_NAME = '-tablename-'
```

And,

```
SELECT DISTINCT scr.PKCOLUMN_NAME AS local-
Col,
scr.FKCOLUMN_NAME AS foriegnCol
FROM System_CROSSREFERENCE scr
WHERE scr.PKTABLE_NAME = '-tablename-'
AND scr.FKTABLE_NAME = '-tablename2-'
```

This configuration information is stored using an XML document, presented in appendix 1. The XML document creates a table of the form:

Table(localTable, localColumn, foreignTable, foreignColumn)

Then, a search routine, as can be seen from UML diagram (Figure 2), reads, as input parameters, a list of table names to find relationships between, and searches for the relationships between the tables by looking up the primary key/foreign key relationships between the tables. The code of the Searcher class is presented in appendix 2. The sampleQueryBuilder class develops the GUI. This class takes in the database type (in this case, hypersonic) as the input parameter, the XML configuration file (presented in appendix 1), the table names, and calls the Searcher class, which then creates the nodes.

The Search Routine

The search routine reads, as input parameters, a list of table names to find relationship between, and searches for relationships between the tables. Below we present the algorithm of our search routine.

Algorithm of Search Routine

Until all targets are found
a.   *Read in the tables to be joined*
b.   *Determine the relationships between the tables*
c.   *For all tables*
    i.   *Find all neighbors*
    ii.   *If targets are found stop else find neighbors of new tables*

For example, let us assume that we have the following tables in a database schema:

{A, B, C, D, E, F, G, H, I, J, K, L}

And assume that you do not know the primary key/foreign key relationships between the tables.

Now, we need information that is partly in table A, partly in table D and partly in table I. That is, we want to see if tables A and D can be joined and if tables A and I can be joined. We need to determine if the following links, as shown in Figure 3, exist.

The algorithm takes the first table: A, and finds all its neighbors. A's neighbors are all the tables that A links to. Now suppose for example, it was found that A's neighbors are B, C, and D, that is, A links to B, C, and D, as in Figure 4.

That is, A's primary key is in tables B, C and D as the foreign key, as shown in Figure 5.

So, one of the targeted links have been found, A-D. But, all the targeted links have not been found, so the algorithm keeps running until all the targeted links have been found. So now, the algorithm stores the links A-B, A-C, A-D, as shown in Figure 4.

Next the routine finds the neighbors of tables B, C, and D. Now suppose for example, B's neighbor is E, C's neighbor is F and D's neighbor is G and H. So now we have found the following links A-B, A-C, A-D, A-B-E, A-C-F, A-D-G, A-D-H, as shown in Figure 6.

Next search routine finds the neighbors of E, F, G and H. Now suppose that E links to I and J, and F links to K and L, as shown in Figure 7.

The algorithm now stops since the targeted tables have been found: A links to D directly: A-D. And, A links to B which links to E which links to I: A-B-E-I. The algorithm now keeps only these two paths as the valid join paths. Using these join paths, the next step was to generate a SQL join query.

Generating the SQL Query

Our algorithm to create the SQL join query goes down the shortest join path first. The shortest path is A-B-E-I. So, the joins will be in the form (see Box 1).

As shown in Figure 8.

TESTING THE TOOL

We tested our tool using the hypersonic database and the Java Business Process Management (JBPM) in the context of Web services. The hypersonic database (HSQLDB), freely available on the Web at http://www.hsqldb.org/, is a leading SQL relational database engine written in

Figure 3. Are these tables linked?

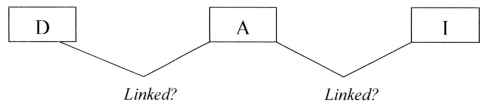

Figure 4. Neighbors of Table A

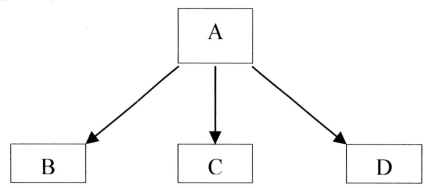

Figure 5. Primary key/Foreign key relationships

TableA(<u>PrimaryKeyOfA</u>, AttributeA1, AttributeA2)
TableB(<u>PrimaryKeyOfB</u>, AttributeB1, PrimaryKeyOfA)
TableC(<u>PrimaryKeyOfC</u>, AttributeC1, PrimaryKeyOfA)
TableD(<u>PrimaryKeyOfD</u>, AttributeD1, PrimaryKeyOfA)

Figure 6. Neighbors of Tables B, C, and D

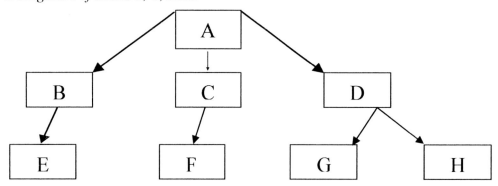

Figure 7. Neighbors of Tables E, F, G, and H

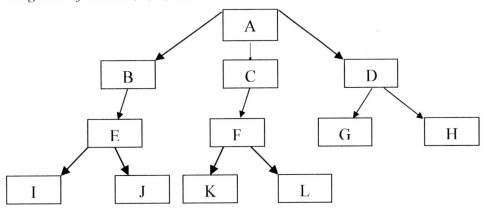

Box 1.

Table A	INNER JOIN	Table B	ON	A.X = B.X
Table B	INNER JOIN	Table E	ON	B.X = E.X
Table E	INNER JOIN	Table I	ON	E.X = I.X
Table A	INNER JOIN	Table D	ON	A.X = D.X

Figure 8. Join paths

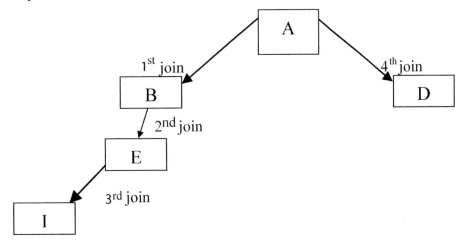

Java. The HSQLDB database engine offers both in-memory and disk-based tables and supports embedded and server nodes.

The JBPM data model, available at http://www.jboss.com/products/jbpm, is a business friendly open source piece of software with an architecture that will run standalone or can be embedded with

any Java application. JBPM (or JBOSS JBPM) presently has a fully-formed table schema of 38 tables with multi-table relationships. Figure 9 shows a snapshot of a portion of the complicated multi-table schema of the JBPM data model. These tables house data that record the state of a process as it progresses through its life cycle. The

Figure 9. Schema of the JBPM data model

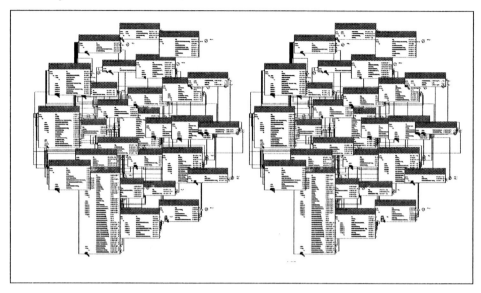

JBPM_ProcessInstance table, for, example, stores the process instance id along with start and end dates; the JBPM_ProcessDefinition table stores the various definitions that are present for use by the application along with their versions.

Running the Application

Step 1: *From the GUI interface (shown in Figure 10), the user selects a data source (of the database). We selected JBOSS, as shown in Figure 10.*

Step 2: *The next step will be to select the tables that you want to join from that data source (the*

schema of the JBOSS data source is given in Figure 9). We selected the JBPM_ACTION and JBPM_BYTEBLOCK tables. This was an arbitrary selection, and the user can select any table or any number of tables by selecting the **select another** *tab (shown in Figure 11). We will illustrate this software by using two tables. After the user selects the tables, as shown in Figure 11, the user clicks the* **find relations** *tab.*

Step 3: *Once you click* **find relations**, *you will get join path displayed in Figure 12.*

Figure 10. The GUI interface

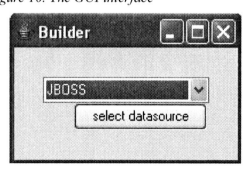

Figure 11. Selecting tables using the GUI

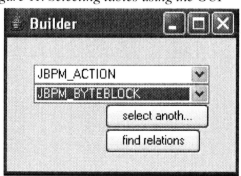

Figure 12. The join path

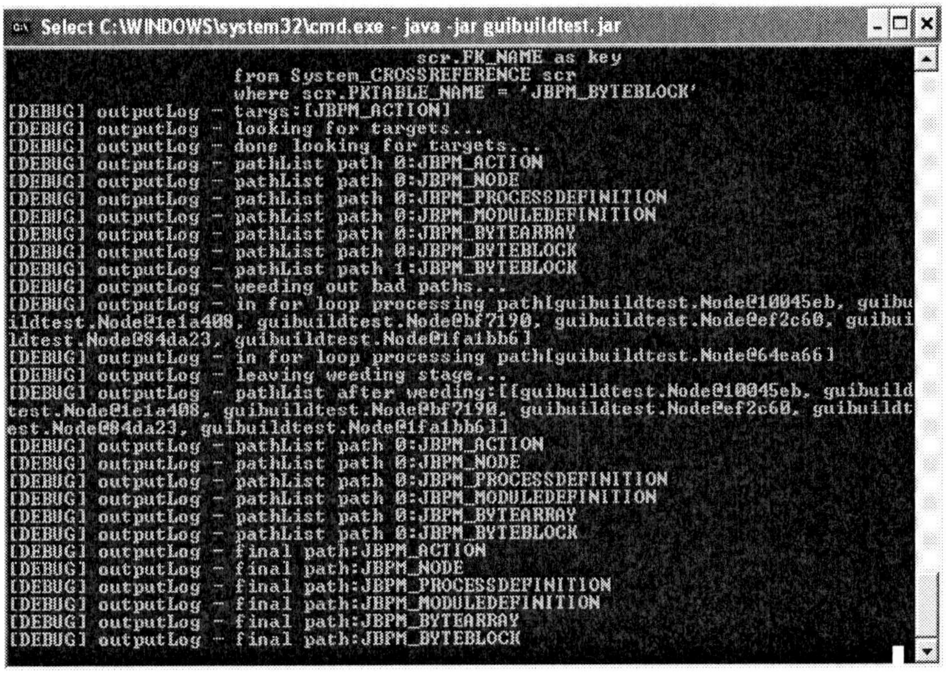

From Figure 12's output screen we can see that there is join path from the JBPM_ACTION table to the JBPM_NODE table to the JBPM_PROCESS-DEFINITION table to the JBPM_MODULEDEF-INITION table to the JBPM_BYTEARRAY table to the JBPM_BYTEBLOCK table.

This join path generates the ANSI SQL join query shown in Figure 13.

Results

Using the large database, JBPM, we ran several tests to test our software. Below we present the results of some of the test runs. The first column shows the tables that needed to be joined. The second column shows the number of tables that the algorithm needed for the output. The third column shows the resulting number of 2-table joins that the algorithm required for the output. And the last column shows the number of milliseconds it took to produce the output for this particular join.

On the average, six tables needed to be joined to obtain the results of 2 table joins, and the time averaged 53.2 mil seconds; 4 tables needed to be joined to obtain the results of 3 table joins, and

Figure 13. ANSI SQL join query generated

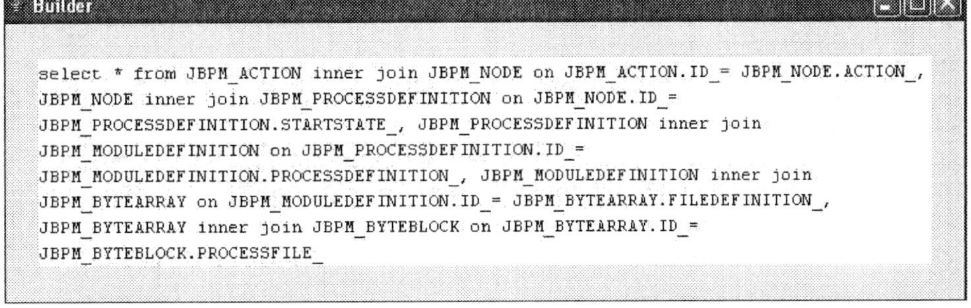

```
select * from JBPM_ACTION inner join JBPM_NODE on JBPM_ACTION.ID_ = JBPM_NODE.ACTION_,
JBPM_NODE inner join JBPM_PROCESSDEFINITION on JBPM_NODE.ID_ =
JBPM_PROCESSDEFINITION.STARTSTATE_, JBPM_PROCESSDEFINITION inner join
JBPM_MODULEDEFINITION on JBPM_PROCESSDEFINITION.ID_ =
JBPM_MODULEDEFINITION.PROCESSDEFINITION_, JBPM_MODULEDEFINITION inner join
JBPM_BYTEARRAY on JBPM_MODULEDEFINITION.ID_ = JBPM_BYTEARRAY.FILEDEFINITION_,
JBPM_BYTEARRAY inner join JBPM_BYTEBLOCK on JBPM_BYTEARRAY.ID_ =
JBPM_BYTEBLOCK.PROCESSFILE_
```

Table 1.

Tables to be joined	Number of tables to be joined	Number of 2-table joins required	Total Number of different tables joined to get result	Number of mil seconds it took to build the query
JBPM_ACTION, JBPM_BYTEARRAY	2	4	8	94
JBPM_ACTION, JBPM_RUNTIMEACTION	2	2	4	32
JBPM_NODE, JBPM_ACTION, JBPM_EVENT	3	2	4	47
JBPM_TASKINSTANCE, JBPM_SWIMLA-NEINSTANCE, JBPM_SWIMLANE	3	4	8	47
JBPM_LOG, JBPM_COMMENT, JBPM_PRO-CESSINSTANCE	3	4	8	31
JBPM_VARIABLEINSTANCE, JBPM_LOG, JBPM_TOKEN, JBPM_TOKENVARI-ABLEMAP	4	3	6	31
JBPM_ACTION, JBPM_PROCESSDEFINI-TION, JBPM_TRANSITION	3	2	4	47
JBPM_PROCESSDEFINITION, JBPM_VARI-ABLEINSTANCE, JBPM_PROCESSIN-STANCE	3	2	4	94
JBPM_PROCESSINSTANCE, JBPM_NODE	2	2	4	78
JBPM_LOG, JBPM_VARIABLEINSTANCE	2	1	2	31
JBPM_VARIABLEINSTANCE, JBPM_PRO-CESSDEFINITION	2	2	4	47
JBPM_ID_PERMISSIONS, JBPM_ID_GROUP	2	-	-	16
JBPM_POOLEDACTOR, JBPM_PROCESSIN-STANCE	2	3	6	62
JBPM_TIMER, JBPM_TASK	2	2	4	31
JBPM_ACTION, JBPM_PROCESSIN-STANCE	2	3	6	125
JBPM_PROCESSDEFINITION, JBPM_RUN-TIMEACTION	2	2	4	47
JBPM_PROCESSINSTANCE, JBPM_COM-MENT	2	2	4	47
JBPM_SWIMLANE, JBPM_DELEGATION	2	1	2	140
JBPM_ACTION, JBPM_EVENT, JBPM_LOG, JBPM_SWIMLANE, JBPM_SWIMLANEIN-STANCE	5	5	6	204
JBPM_PROCESSDEFINITION, JBPM_PRO-CESSINSTANCE, JBPM_NODE, JBPM_TO-KEN, JBPM_TASKINSTANCE	5	5	6	266

Figure 14. Number of mil seconds to build a SQL join query for 2 tables

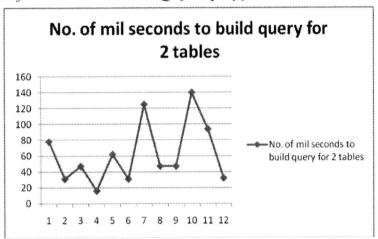

Figure 15. Number of mil seconds to build a SQL join query for 3 tables

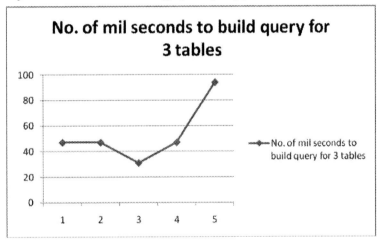

the time averaged 62.5 seconds; six tables needed to be joined to obtain the results of 4 table joins, and the time averaged 46.5 mil seconds; six tables needed to be joined to obtain the results of 5 table joins, and the time averaged 235mil seconds.

Figure 14 presents a graphical representation of the number of milliseconds it took to build a query for two table joins, and Figure 15 presents a graphical representation of the number of milliseconds it took to build a query for three table joins.

CONCLUSION

This tool will generate join paths and a SQL join query from large databases as well as large databases in Web services. The user only needs to know which tables he/she wants to join, but does not have to know the join path needed to join them (the primary key/foreign key relationships between the tables). The software finds the join path between the tables selected, and displays a SQL join query. This software is a very important step forward in the process of retrieving information efficiently from large databases as well as large databases used in Web Services and Service Oriented Architectures.

ACKNOWLEDGMENT

The authors would like to thank the Editor, Dr. Ghazi Alkhatib, and the referees of this article for their constructive suggestions, which led to the present improved version of this article.

REFERENCES

Codd, E. (1970). A Relational Model for Large Shared Data Banks, *CACM, 13*(6).

Codd, E. (1972). Further Normalization of the Data Base Relational Model. *Data Base Systems.* Prentice Hall.

Earp, R., & Bagui, S. (2000). Oracle's Joins, *Oracle Internals, 2*(3), 6-14.

Elmasri, R., & Navathe, S.B. (2007). *Fundamentals of Database Systems*, (5th ed.). Boston, MA: Pearson Education.

Florescu, D., Grunhagen, A., & Kossmann, D. (2003). XL: A platform for Web services. *Proceedings of First Biennial Conference on Innovative Data Systems Research (CIDR).*

Kim, W., Reiner, D. S., & Batory, D. S. (1985). *Query Processing in Database System.* New York: Springer-Verlag.

Mishra, P., & Eich, M.H. (1992). Join Processing in Relational Databases. *ACM Computing Surveys, 24*(1), 63-113.

Ouzzani, M., & Bouguettaya (2004). A. Efficient access to Web services. *IEEE Internet Computing, 8*(2), 34-44.

Perrizo, W., Lin, J.Y.Y., & Hoffman, W. (1989, June). Algorithms for distributed query processing in broadcast local area networks. *IEEE Trans. Know. Data Eng., 1*(2), 215-225.

Resende, L., & Feng, R. (2007, June 12-14). Handling Heterogeneous Data Sources in a SOA Environment with Service Data Objects (SDO). *SIGMOD'07*, Beijing, China.

Segev, A. (1986, March). Optimization of join operations in horizontally partitioned database systems. *ACM Trans. Database Systems, 11*(1), 48-80.

Srivastava, U., Munagala, K., Widom, J., & Motwani, R. (2006, September 12-15). Query Optimization over Web Services. *VLDB '06*, Seoul Korea.

Swami, A., & Gupta, A. (1988). Optimizing large join query. *Proceedings of SIGMOD*, 8-17.

Yoo, H., & Lafortune, S. (1989, June). An intelligent search method for query optimization by semi-joins. *IEEE Trans. Knowl. Data Eng., 1*(2), 226-237.

Yu, C. T., Chang, C. C., Templeton, M., Brill, D., & Lund, E. (1985). Query Processing in a fragmented relational database system: Mermaid. *IEEE Trans. Software Eng. SE-11*, 8, 795-810.

Yu, C. T., Guh, K. C., Zhang, W. Templeton, M., Brill, D., & Chen, A. L. P. (1987). Algorithms to process distributed queries in fast local networks. *IEEE Trans. Comput. C-36, 10*, 1153-1164.

APPENDIX A

Storing the configuration information using an XML document

```xml
<?xml version="1.0" encoding="UTF-8"?>
<!--
   Document    : configDoc.xml
   Author      : Owner
-->
<config>
   <datasource id="TEST1">
       <driver>org.postgresql.Driver</driver>
       <url>jdbc:postgresql://localhost:5432/TEST1</url>
       <username>postgres</username>
       <password>****</password>
             <type>postgres</type>
   </datasource>
   <datasource id="school">
       <driver>oracle.jdbc.driver.OracleDriver</driver>
             <url>jdbc:oracle:thin:@unix.cslab.uwf.edu:1521:STUDENT_COURSE</url>
             <username></username>
             <password></password>
   </datasource>
       <datasource id="JBOSS">
       <driver>org.hsqldb.jdbcDriver</driver>
             <url>jdbc:hsqldb:E:\Graduate_Project\guibuildTest\hypersonic\localDB</url>
             <username>sa</username>
             <password></password>
                   <type>hypersonic</type>
       </datasource>
   <DBType id="oracle">
           <query id="tables">
                 select table_name
                 from ALL_IND_COLUMNS
             </query>
       <query id="table_relation">
             select con.table_name as localtable,
                   concol.column_name as localColumn,
                   icol.TABLE_NAME as foreignTable,
                   icol.Column_name as foreignColumn,
                   con.Constraint_name as key
                 from all_constraints con,
                     all_ind_columns icol,
                     all_cons_columns concol
```

```
              where con.constraint _ type = 'R'
              and con.R _ constrant _ name = icol.Index _ Name
              and con.constraint _ name = concol.Constraint _ Name
         </query>
</DBType>
<DBType id="hypersonic">
    <query id="tables">
              select table _ name
              from System _ tables
              where table _ type = 'TABLE'
     </query>
     <query id="table _ relation">
              select distinct scr.PKTABLE _ NAME as localTable,
                              scr.PKCOLUMN _ NAME as localCol,
                              scr.FKTABLE _ NAME as foriegnTable,
                              scr.FKCOLUMN _ NAME as foriegnCol,
                              scr.FK _ NAME as key
              from System _ CROSSREFERENCE scr
              where scr.PKTABLE _ NAME = '-tablename-'
     </query>
</DBType>
<DBType id="postgres">
    <query id="tables">
    select distinct tabs.tablename as table _ name
    from pg _ catalog.pg _ tables tabs
    where tabs.schemaname = 'public'
    </query>
    <query id="table _ relation">
    select localTab.tablename as localTable,
         locCol.column _ name as localColumn,
         refTab.tablename as foriegnTable,
         refCol.column _ name as foriegnColumn,
         keys.FK as key
    from pg _ catalog.pg _ indexes localTab,
         constraint _ column locCol,cvs
         constraint _ column refCol,
         pg _ catalog.pg _ indexes refTab,
         (select locTab.conname as localTabIndex,
                 refTab.conname as foriegnTabIndex,
                 con.conname as FK
         from pg _ catalog.pg _ constraint con,
             pg _ catalog.pg _ constraint locTab,
             pg _ catalog.pg _ constraint refTab
         where con.contype = 'f'
```

```
                and con.conrelid = locTab.conrelid
                and con.confrelid = refTab.conrelid ) keys
        where localTab.indexname = keys.localTabIndex
        and refTab.indexname = keys.foriegnTabIndex
        and locCol.constraint _ name = keys.localTabIndex
        and refCol.constraint _ name = keys.foriegnTabIndex
        and localTab.tablename = locCol.table _ name
        and refTab.tablename = refCol.table _ name
        </query>
    </config>
```

This work was previously published in International Journal of Information Technology and Web Engineering, Vol. 4, Issue 2, edited by G. I. Alkhatib; D. C. Rine, pp. 45-60, copyright 2004 by IGI Publishing (an imprint of IGI Global).

Section IV
Utilization and Application

This section introduces and discusses the utilization and application of Web technologies. These particular selections highlight, among other topics, the application of semantic Web technologies to e-tourism, e-banking, and in car repairs as well as the adoption of Web services in digital libraries. Contributions included in this section provide excellent coverage of today's online environment and insight into how Web technologies impact the fabric of our present-day global village.

Chapter 4.1
The Role of Web Services:
A Balance Scorecard Perspective

Pauline Ratnasingam
University of Central Missouri, USA

ABSTRACT

This chapter aims to examine the extent of Web services usage and quality, applying the balanced scorecard methodology in a small business firm as an exploratory case study. This chapter contributes to guidelines and lessons learned that will inform, educate, and promote small businesses on the importance of maintaining the quality of Web services.

INTRODUCTION

The Internet, a rapidly expanding global computer and communication infrastructure, has facilitated the emergence of digitization and globalization that in turn has permitted businesses to extensively engage in foreign investments. Forrester Research suggests that e-commerce in the U.S. will grow 19%, reaching $230 billion by 2008. Today, firms are attempting to attain their value chain goals by offering to sell products and services. Web services have become a significant part of small business,

as they are used to facilitate the seamless flow of business transactions and are known to offer many benefits.

However, studies also show that the lack of effective use, quality, and security in Web service applications is one of the main reasons why firms fail to realize the full potential of their IT investments (Benko & McFarlan, 2003). It is imperative that small businesses focus on the quality of Web services and their operations given the extent to which Web service applications are used in business processes in this fast changing market conditions. Enforcing and maintaining the quality of Web services does not only involve a set of security analyses and audit procedures that most firms conduct periodically, but rather it is a continual process that needs to align a rigorous methodology. Such methodology is the balanced scorecard, which is a set of quantifiable measures that aim to monitor and manage a firm's strategic performance. This chapter aims to examine the extent of Web services usage and quality by applying the balance scorecard methodology in a small business firm.

The balanced scorecard is needed to align, monitor, and adjust the factors that impact the quality

DOI: 10.4018/978-1-60566-042-4.ch016

of Web services. Previous studies applying the balanced scorecard in the context of Web services and quality is limited. Only 10% of the organizations executed their implementation strategy to apply the balanced scorecard methodology because they experienced barriers in formulating a vision, allocating resources (i.e., human resources), and managing change (Niven, 2003). This chapter aims to examine the extent of Web services usage and quality, applying the balanced scorecard methodology in a small business firm as an exploratory case study. The next section discusses the theory of balanced scorecard and Web services followed by the development of a framework which integrates the critical success factors. Then we discuss the research method and provide a description of the background information of the firm. We then test the framework via an exploratory case study and report the findings. The findings contribute to guidelines and lessons learned that will inform, educate, and promote small businesses on the importance of maintaining the quality of Web services. Finally, we conclude the chapter with contributions and directions for future research.

BACKGROUND INFORMATION: THE BALANCED SCOREBOARD

The balanced scorecard deployed to measure the effective use and quality of Web services among small businesses focuses on a system that enforces measurement and feedback, thereby imposing quality, continuous improvement, employee empowerment, and strategic performance that aim to sustain the competitive and strategic objectives. The balanced scorecard measures the performance of Web services in a small business firm from four perspectives, namely, learning and growth, internal business processes, customer, and financial perspectives, which are discussed below. Each of these four perspectives is further categorized by their objectives (as in what are

their outcomes?) measures (as in how to achieve their outcomes?) targets, that is, accountability (as in how do we know that we have achieved it?), and initiatives (as in what actions to take?). Further, the balanced scorecard is based on three time dimensional timelines, namely, yesterday, today, and tomorrow. The next section presents a discussion of the four perspectives.

1. The *learning and growth perspective* aims to measure the human, information, and organizational capital. Human capital includes the skills, knowledge, expertise, the extent of training given to employees, and the business cultural attitudes. Do small business employees have the skills/competencies to operate the Web service application and align it with their internal business processes effectively in order to meet their customers' objectives of using Web services? Information capital aims to measure effective communication and information sharing. Do small business employees possess the information required to achieve objectives? Organizational capital aims to monitor the soft areas of the employees, such as, learning and growth, culture, leadership, knowledge sharing, and teamwork. Do small businesses have the ability to sustain growth and change that in turn enhances the quality of Web services?

2. The *internal business process perspective* aims to measure performance that permits small businesses to be aware of the quality of their products and services. Web services, considered as system quality, are defined as "the conformance to explicitly stated functional and performance requirements, explicitly stated development standards, and implicit characteristics that are expected of all professionally developed software" (Solano, De Ovalles, Rojas, Padua, & Morales, 2003, p. 67). Similarly, Ortega, Perez, and Rojas (2000) suggest that product effectiveness should include characteristics

such as timeliness, functionality, reliability, usability, efficiency, maintainability, and probability. Small businesses need to be aware of the following questions when assessing the quality of their Web services performance. Does our internal business processes applying Web services conform to the mission of small businesses? Does the internal business processes meet our customer requirements? There are two types of processes under strategic management. First, the mission oriented-process focuses on the strategic goals of small businesses, and second, the support processes are more repetitive and are used in the daily operations that in turn enforce benchmarking. The balanced scorecard provides a diagnostic feedback into the various internal processes, thereby guiding and improving the business processes involved in the use of Web services on a continuous basis. What must small businesses do well internally in order to achieve the objectives they set forth to achieve quality in Web services? Where does the Web services "process" start, and where does it end?

3. The *customer perspective* focuses on meeting the needs of the customers, retaining existing customers, and gaining customer satisfaction. What do customers expect or demand from the use of Web services? Dimensions of customers experience include time, quality, price or cost, accessibility, reputation, and relationship. Who do we define as our customers? How do our customers see us? How do Web services create value for our customers?

4. The *financial perspective* aims to provide timely and accurate financial information. By implementing a centralized database, it is hoped that processing can be standardized and automated. Further, both risk assessment and cost benefit analysis can be easily conducted in order to ensure that the bottom line of small businesses is achieved. What accountability do small businesses that use Web services have to financial stakeholders? In many respects, the financial perspective represents "end in mind" of the small business strategic vision. Small business managers are able to examine the outcomes of their business performance that provide strategic financial feedback and show the trends of their business performance using Web services overtime. Figure 1 presents the perspectives of the balanced scorecard.

WEB SERVICES

Web services are creating a service-oriented architecture that provides technical solutions and e-collaborations among value chain partners (Chan, Kellen, & Nair, 2004; Yen, 2004). Web services refer to a new breed of Web applications as self-contained, self-describing modular applications that can be published, located, and invoked across the Web. Businesses use existing software components specified as services to perform business operations in a "service-oriented architecture." Similarly, Web services refer to a set of software applications or components developed using a specific set of application programming interface (API) standards and Internet-based communication protocols. The objective is to enable these applications or components to invoke function calls and exchange data among themselves over the standard Internet infrastructure. We define Web services as "modular Internet-based business functions that perform specific business tasks to facilitate business interactions within and beyond the organization." Further, Web services generate sustainable competitive advantage for firms supporting their core competencies and adding value to the execution of the corporate strategy. The technology's fullest potential will not be realized if it is used only for improving the operational efficiency of existing business processes. Therefore,

Figure 1. The balanced scorecard perspectives

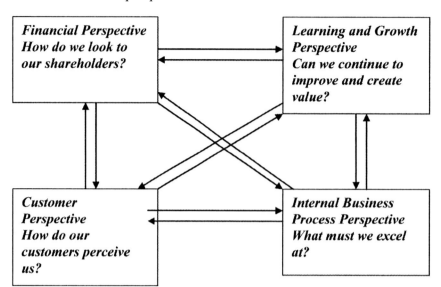

we focus on the quality of Web services usage by applying a rigorous methodology called the balanced scorecard methodology as it measures the effective use and quality of Web services from four perspectives, namely, learning and growth, internal business processes, customer, and financial perspectives, thereby providing a holistic view.

The Web Services Architecture

The Web services architecture is made up of three layers of technology. At the foundation (the bottom layer) is the software standards and communication protocols that provide a common language for Web services and enable applications to be connected. Standards and protocols are often cited as the strategic value that Web services bring (Hagel, 2002; Hagel & Brown, 2001). The service grid (the middle layer) provides a set of shared utilities from security to third-party auditing, to billing and payment so that critical business functions and transactions over the Internet can be conducted. This layer publishes the services that serve as entry points for queries to find service descriptions. In short, the service grid plays two

roles. First, it helps the Web service requestors and providers to find and connect with one another; secondly, it creates a trusted environment essential for carrying out mission-critical business activities, thereby contributing to technology trust. Finally, the top layer consists of a diverse array of application services. It is in this top layer where the day-to-day operations will be most visible to employees, customers, and trading partners. The top layer performs the service binding and invocation. Similarly, three are layers of Web services, namely, basic services, composite services, and managed services. While basic services manage the publication, discovery, selection, and binding, composite services facilitate the coordination, conformance, monitoring, and quality of service. Finally, managed services provide the market certification rating and operations support.

Table 1 presents the three layers of the Web services architecture adapted from Hagel and Brown (2001).

Table 1. The Web services architecture

Top Layer – Application Service   Web services runs on any application platform as long as it has a Web server connected to the Internet.

Middle Layer – Service Grid
 The service grid layer provides four types of utilities:
     (1) Service management utilities (i.e., provisioning, monitoring, ensuring quality of service, synchronization, conflict resolution)
     (2) Resource knowledge management utilities (i.e., directories, brokers, registries, repositories, data transformation)
     (3) Transport management utilities (i.e., message queuing, filtering, metering, monitoring, routing, resource orchestration)
     (4) Shared utilities (i.e., security, auditing, and assessment of third party performance, billing and payment)

Bottom Layer – Software Standards and Communication Protocols
 Software standards include:
     (1) Web service description language (WSDL) to describe the Web service
     (2) Universal, description, discovery and integration (UDDI) to advertise, syndicate as a central organization for registering, finding, and using Web services)
     (3) Web services flow language (WSFL) to define work flows
     (4) XML (format for data exchange and description)
     (5) Communication protocols including simple object access protocol (SOAP) to communicate that are for calling Web services, HTTP, and TCP/IP)

FRAMEWORK OF THE BALANCED SCORECARD FOR WEB SERVICES

The framework of balanced scorecard for Web services was developed by integrating the theory of balanced scorecard and Web services. The framework consists of critical success factors or indicators that make up the objectives, measures, targets, and initiatives. The goal of these critical success factors is to evaluate the effective use and quality of Web service applications. Table 2 below illustrates the framework of the balanced scorecard in Web services, which serves as a measurement tool, thereby ensuring the quality of Web services.

RESEARCH METHOD

Case studies were chosen as an appropriate method to evaluate the effective use and quality of Web services among small businesses as it elicited subtle and rich data needed, thereby increasing our understanding in the use and quality of Web services applying the balanced scorecard methodology (Yin, 1994).

We attempted to identify the critical success factors in the effective use and quality of Web services by deploying the balanced scorecard framework for small businesses based on the objectives (what are the outcomes?) measures (how to achieve the outcomes?), targets, that is, accountability and initiatives (how do we know that we have achieved it?), and initiatives (what actions to take?) for all the four perspectives (i.e., learning and growth, internal business processes, customer, and financial perspectives).

In this study we interviewed the managers of the firm in the agricultural industry. Initial entry into the case site was obtained by making telephone calls to key representatives in the organization. A brief description and purpose of the study was discussed before requesting them to participate. The telephone conversation was followed by an e-mail to the respondents with an attachment of the file describing the purpose of the study. Once confirmation of their willingness to participate in the study was received, appointment dates for interview sessions were arranged with the managers in the firm. Evidence for the exploratory case study data came from the hand written notes taken during the two (90 minutes) face-to-face interviews and the tape recorded data. In addition, analysis of existing documents relating to Web service applications, day-to-day

Table 2. Framework of the balanced scorecard in Web services

Balanced Scorecard Perspectives	Relationship to Effective use and Quality of Web Services via the Critical Success Factors (or Indicators)
(1) *(1) Learning and growth perspective* *How can we continue to improve and create value in the use of Web services?*	*Objectives:* employees must be well trained and are expected to perform their day-to-day business operations applying Web services *Measures:* provide online training, user manuals, standard operating procedures, help desk, and reward employees with high productivity *Targets:* fewer customers and stakeholder complaints *Initiatives:* ongoing monitoring of employees performance, focus on the culture, climate, and commitment of the organization.
(2) *Internal business process perspective* *What processes do we need to excel further when using Web services?*	*Objectives:* to achieve high quality and productivity of the services provided via Web services *Measures:* apply best business practices, reliable, accurate, and timely information. Focus on the usability, interoperability of the system *Targets:* increased profit and fewer customers and stakeholders complaints *Initiatives:* ongoing audit and applying the quality assurance plan on a regular basis
(3) *Customer perspective* *How can we enhance our business reputation with our customers via Web services?*	*Objectives:* satisfaction of customers and stakeholders, reputation of the firm and the quality of their products and services *Measures:* open, frequent communications, providing excellent quality services, provide value for money and reliable operations *Targets:* increase in profit and sales *Initiatives:* training employees, ongoing weekly meetings with employees; regular review and reflection of the goals and mission of the company
(4) *Financial perspective* *How are we perceived by our shareholders and other stakeholders invested in our firm?*	*Objectives:* increase in profits, rate of return *Measures:* increased productivity, increase quality of services provided, apply the return on capital employed, economic value added and free cash flow *Targets:* profit figures, increased shareholders value *Initiatives:* advertising their company products, attending trade shows, business conferences and seminars, word of mouth, control operating costs, maximize potential use of Web services

interactions, operating procedures, Web sites, and internal security policies were analyzed. The tape recorded data was transcribed to identify concepts via pattern matching to the balanced scorecard framework.

FINDINGS: BACKGROUND INFORMATION OF FIRM A

Firm A is a small business seed manufacturer and seller of wild flower and bird seeds located in Kingsville. It is a family owned business with 10 employees and the owner has been in this business for 23 years. They sell a variety of wild flowers seeds including the annual mix, shade, and suns. They also supply bird seeds to regular stores, residential customers, and fulfill large bids from the government for beautifying the land, such as for the city of Blue Springs and the Tiffany Springs highway. Their main form of Web service application is their business-to-consumer (B2C) Web site implemented in 2003, which has embedded IT solutions, e-mail, and fax. Table 3 presents the background information of Firm A.

In this section we report the findings of the exploratory case study from the hand written notes taken during the face-to-face interview with the manager of Firm A.

Web Services Quality in the Learning and Growth Perspective

Firm A found that the learning capability in applying best business practices was important for their business performance. Although only six

Table 3. Background information of firm A

Background Characteristics	Firm A
Type of industry	Agricultural industry
Size of Firm	Small business
Type of ownership	Family owned
Number of employees	10
Type of Web service application	B2C Web site & embedded IT solutions
Type and number of customers/business partners	Regular store customers, government bid contracts, Web customers
Annual revenue in US$	$1.5 million
How long have they being in business?	23 years
Mode of attracting customers	Advertise in the local newspaper, Web page

employees were assigned to operate their computer systems, they had to abide to best business practices that included changing their passwords every 10 days and not disclosing pricing information to any other employees other than the manager and two other employees in the accounts department. Each employee was given limited access rights and was unable to see the detail information of the transaction.

The manager noted, *"We continually improve our employee skills by providing training to our employees in order to increase the potential use of Web services."*

Web services were deployed to facilitate information sharing and collaboration among employees and business units.

Web Services Quality in Improving Internal Business Processes

The internal business process perspective focused on the quality and use of Web services in activities such as supply chain management, customer relationship management, and research and development. The balanced scorecard provided a systemic quality approach to assess Web services as it allowed the software processes to be efficiently and effectively balanced. The manager noted, *"We applied the quality assurance plan which included the following critical success factors: timeliness of obtaining information or processing the transaction, accuracy as in achieving integrity in the content of the message, confidentiality, access rights, non-repudiation, reusability, portability, reliability, security and efficiency of the Web service applications were considered in this perspective."*

The manager indicated that, *"Further, with industry-accepted standards and protocols, Web services provided a standard interface allowing integration among heterogeneous platforms, thus facilitating efficient and effective collaboration between departments that use different IT systems. Finally, Web services' service-oriented architecture allows firms to build a flexible IT infrastructure that enables faster decision-making and response to market changes."*

Hence, through the orchestration of modular, loosely coupled software components, Web services enable an "assemble line approach" to software development, resulting in a responsive IT infrastructure for designing and building faster application development and enterprise applications.

We argue that Web services technology, with its industry-accepted standards and protocols, can enhance internal business operations by enabling process automation, increasing interoperability and reducing integration complexity, and improving process design.

Web Services Quality in Improving Customer Retention and Relationships

The customer perspective is the core of the business strategy. The manger noted, *"Our Web services and IT solutions offered us with unique business processes and customer value propositions that determined the correct business processes thereby creating better customer relationships."*

The manager also noted, *"We have key attributes of Web services that create customer value propositions such as; enhanced customer intimacy via open communications, improved customer retention, and better customer value. Beyond the quality and specifications of its products and services we try to satisfy our customers by meeting their needs and offering quality goods and services."*

These attributes that serve as critical success factors were derived from the balanced scorecard methodology which comprises of objectives, measures, targets, and initiatives.

The manager indicated, *"Web services made our firm's IT infrastructure more flexible and adaptable, affording the organizational agility to meet the ongoing customers' changing requirements."*

Web Services Quality in Improving Financial Position

The use of the balanced scorecard methodology allowed for improved capability of learning and innovation, better internal business processes, and the enhanced customer value that in turn served as performance drivers for increased financial returns.

The manager noted, *"Web services has directly influenced our shareholder value as it influenced our firm's financial strategy, productivity and revenue growth."*

Further, he added, *"For example, in the financial perspective we aimed to create value for*

the shareholders and there is a balance between growth and productivity. Further, return on capital employed and economic value indicators are added."

LESSONS LEARNED

The findings suggests a cyclic process that was created with the use of the balanced scorecard approach to evaluate the quality of Web services applications and in order to integrate quality, provide a strategic map, and indicate how information will be disseminated so that the potential use of Web services can be attained. The processes adapted from Kaplan and Norton (2000) included:

- **Analysis of the sector, its development and role of company:** Refers to the identifications of the key goals in the use of Web services and establishing the characteristics and requirements for the industry.
- **Establishing or confirming the company's strategic plan:** Refers to the establishment or confirmation of a strategic plan, intensifying the internal and external analysis of the earlier processes, and ensuring that agreements are arrived towards the quality of Web services.
- **Translating the strategy into operational terms:** Refers to the actual actions taken to ensure that best business practices, standards, and quality procedures that were followed in the use of Web services. For example, in the financial perspective they aim to create value for the shareholders and there is a balance between growth and productivity. Return on capital employed and economic value indicators are added. Likewise, in the customer's perspective, the growth in terms of volume generated from customers was examined. Further, segments that value quality and innovation were emphasized. In the internal business

process perspective they try to differentiate between basic operating processes and operating excellence in the support services via the use of Web services. The product and service quality were measured through the product quality index indicator using the market share in order to gain profit from the investment in the financial perspective. Finally, in the learning and growth perspective, three strategic objectives were identified, namely, basic competencies and skills (referring to the skills expected of the employees), technology (referring to the Web services applications used in the value chain), and climate for action (referring to organization commitments that must be implemented by the human resources department).

- **Aligning the organization with the strategy:** Refers to the alignment of business unit goals with the organization's goal in the use of Web services.
- **Making the strategy everyone's daily job:** Refers to the linking of the employees with the business unit and the organization's strategy.
- **Making the strategy an ongoing process:** Refers to proposing a process for managing the strategy by integrating the tactical management and the strategic management in the use of Web services.
- **Promoting change through management leadership:** Refers to the involvement of the management team in the change process.

CONCLUSION

In this chapter we discussed the role of Web services usage and quality, applying the balanced scorecard methodology. We developed a framework that presented the balanced scorecard's four business perspectives (i.e., learning and growth, internal business processes, customer, and financial perspectives) and tested it via an exploratory case study of a small business firm within the agricultural industry. Then we reported the findings based on the impact of Web services quality on the four perspectives. The findings suggest that the lessons learned evolve over a set of processes that are aimed at integrating quality into the potential use of Web services.

The contribution of this study was attributed to the framework, which provided guidelines for measuring Web services usage and quality, applying the key Web services features that gave rise to business values that were matched with strategic initiatives that small businesses can have in each of the business perspectives. Web services further drive the quality of IT strategy as it is fully aligned with overall business strategy, thereby focusing on the key organizational capabilities and sustainable competitive advantage.

This study contributes to the theory as it extends the current literature of Web services to include the balanced scorecard framework of measure to its usage and quality. Further, the study contributes to practice as small businesses using Web services will benefit from the balanced scorecard as they will have a system which provides them with timely, cost-effective, scalable, manageable and reliable feedback on their strategic performance. The business issues including effective organizational performance and successful strategy implementation will be greatly enhanced. Further, the balanced scorecard gives a holistic view of the small business by simultaneously examining its performance from four perspectives. It is able to translate an organization's vision and strategy into specific objectives, monitored through a coherent set of performance indicators. Future research should aim to apply the balanced scorecard framework for Web services via a survey or multiple case studies with firms across different sections in the industry so that the findings can contribute to a generic framework.

REFERENCES

Benko, C., & McFarlan, F. W. (2003). *Connecting the dots: Aligning projects with objectives in unpredictable times.* Boston: Harvard Business School Press.

Chan, S. S., Kellen, V., & Nair, C. (2004). *Adopting Web services for B2B e-collaboration: Research directions.* Paper presented at the International Resources Management Association Conference, Innovations through Information Technology (pp. 1191-1193).

Hagel, J. (2002). Edging into Web services. *The McKinsey Quarterly, 4.*

Hagel, J. III, & Brown, J. S. (2001). Your next IT strategy. *Harvard Business Review, 79*(9), 105–115.

Kaplan, R., & Norton, D. (2000). *The strategy focused organization.* Harvard Business School Press.

Niven, P. R. (2003). *Balanced scorecard. Step-by-step for government and non-profit agencies.* John Wiley & Sons.

Ortega, M., Perez, M., & Rojas, T. (2000). *A model for software product quality with a system focus.* Paper presented at the 4th World Multi Conference on Systematic Cybernatics.

Solano, J., De Ovalles, M. P., Rojas, T., Padua, A. G., & Morales, L. M. (2003, Winter). Integration of systemic quality and the balanced scorecard, privacy and security in e-business. *Information Systems Management,* 66–81. doi:10.1201/1078/43203.20.1.20031201/40086.9

Yen, V. C. (2004). *Applications development with Web services.* Paper presented at the International Resources Management Association Conference, Innovations through Information Technology (pp. 875-876).

Yin, R. K. (1994). *Case study research: Design and methods* (2nd ed.). Thousand Oaks, CA: Sage Publications.

APPENDIX: CASE STUDY QUESTIONNAIRE

A) Demographic Section

1.   Name of your organization?
2.   Your job title?
3.   How long have you worked in your present organization?
    A.   Less than a year
    B.   Between 1-5 years
    C.   Between 6-10 years
    D.   Between 11-20 years
    E.   Over 20 years
4.   How long have you had your present position?
    A.   Less than a year
    B.   Between 1-2 years
    C.   Between 3-5 years
    D.   Between over 5 years
5.   What is your organization's reach?
    A.   Local
    B.   Regional
    C.   National
    D.   Global
6.   What is your organization's size?
    A.   Large > 500 employees
    B.   Small-Medium-Enterprise 1-499 employees
7.   Please name the type of industry your organization is or provide the NAICS code?
8.   Please indicate which of the following terms best describes your organization's main business activity
    A.   Retail/wholesale trade
    B.   Manufacturing/distribution
    C.   Computers/communications
    D.   Financial services
    E.   Education
    F.   Health
    G.   Government services
    H.   Other services
    I.   Other ---
9.   What is the main role of your organization?
    A.   Buyer
    B.   Seller
    C.   Manufacturer
    D.   Supplier
10. Please indicate which of the following types of business transactions are actively supported by the IT systems in your organization?

    A.   Purchase orders

    B.   Invoices

    C.   Advance shipping notices

    D.   Product information

    E.   Payment transactions

11.   Please indicate the type of business applications and tools your organization implemented, or will be implementing?

    A.   EDI – Value-Added-Network

    B.   Internet-based EDI

    C.   Extranets

    D.   Intranets

    E.   E-mail

    F.   B2C or B2B shopping cart

    G.   Other types of Web service applications

    H.   Other --

12.   Please indicate the number of business partners your organization has? (business partners refer to those who are contracted legally to do business with the firm)

    A.   1-20

    B.   21-50

    C.   51-100

    D.   101-499

    E.   Over 500

13.   Approximately what is your annual revenue, in millions? (please estimate)

    A.   0-1m

    B.   1-10m

    C.   10-100m

    D.   100-500,

    E.   500-1,000m

    F.   Over 1,000m

14.   Approximately how much does your organization spend annually on information technology? (please estimate)

    A.   0-100,000

    B.   100,000-500,000

    C.   500,000-1m

    D.   1-5m

    E.   Over 5m

15.   Please indicate how your organization chose your business partners?

    A.   Advertising on your Web page

    B.   Screening of business partners

    C.   Based on past reputations

    D.   Other --

16.   When did your organization start implementing a balanced scorecard system? Please indicate the year.

17. Please indicate the importance of implementing a balanced scorecard system in your organization's current business strategy
    A. No importance/not considered
    B. Small consideration
    C. Nominally part of strategy
    D. Substantially part of strategy
    E. Crucial to strategy
18. On average how often does your organization meet face-to-face with your business partners?
    A. At least once per week
    B. At least once per month
    C. More than once a month
    D. Other ---
19. Please indicate how your organization maintains your business partners
    A. Verbal agreements
    B. Legal business partner agreements (written)
    C. Screening of business partners (based on a performance assessment)
    D. Other --

Questions on your Firm's Application of the Balanced Scorecard on Web Services

How did your firm implement a balanced scorecard methodology? What is the vision of your organization towards the use of Web services? Do your employees have a solid understanding of your firm's use of Web services? Why was the balanced scorecard important in measuring your business performance? What benefits did your firm experienced from the quality of Web service applications? What risks/challenges did your firm experienced from using Web services?

Learning and Growth Perspective

Do small business employees have the skills/competencies to operate the Web service application and align it with their internal business processes effectively in order to meet their customers' objectives of using Web services?

Do small business employees possess the information required to achieve objectives?

Do small businesses have the ability to sustain growth and change that in turn enhances the quality of Web services?

How does the balanced scorecard impact the quality of Web services in the learning and growth perspective?

How was the data gathered, analyzed, evaluated for feedback so that appropriate actions can be taken to improve the learning and growth perspective?

What skills do your employees possess regarding performance management and more specifically, developing performance measures in the balanced scorecard framework?

(This question relates to what qualification requirements do the senior employees who undertake the role of a balanced scorecard auditor or quality control manager has? The purpose is to ensure that they have the adequate skills to completely measure the firm's performance).

Do your employees have the right skills/competencies to operate the Web service applications?

Do your employees have the tools and information they require to make effective decisions that impact customer outcomes?

Do your employees possess the information required to achieve objectives?

Does your organization have the ability to sustain growth and change?

Do your employees face difficulties when accessing critical information needed to serve customers?

Internal Business Process Perspective

Does the internal business processes applying Web services conform to the mission of small businesses?

Does the internal business processes meet their customer requirements?

What must small businesses do well internally in order to achieve the objectives they set forth to achieve quality in Web services?

Where does the Web services "process" start, and where does it end?

How does the balanced scorecard impact the quality of Web services in the internal business processes? How were the data gathered, analyzed, evaluated for feedback so that appropriate actions can be taken to improve the internal business process perspective?

Do your employees know how their day to day actions contribute to the organization's success? (how and why)

What must your firm do well internally in order to achieve the objectives set forth in the customer perspective?

Customer Perspective

What do customers expect or demand from the use of Web services? Dimensions of customers experience include; time, quality, price or cost, accessibility, reputation, and relationship.

Who do we define as our customers?

How do our customers see us? How does Web services create value for our customers?

How does the balanced scorecard impact the quality of Web services and its relationship with customers' perspectives? What factors are evaluated in the customers' perspective?

How the data was gathered, analyzed, evaluated for feedback so that appropriate actions can be taken to improve the customer perspective?

Who does your firm define as your customers?

What do your customers expect or demand from your firm? (factors pertaining to time, quality, price or cost, accessibility, reputation, relationship and image).

Do you require anything from your customers? (in order to meet your customers demands – is there anything you need from them?)

You have a unique value proposition for customers (for example cost, technical superiority, customer intimacy).

What factors does your firm excel in as in evidence of past successes thereby providing accountability to your stakeholders that you are satisfying customer expectations?

(This question relates to what factors do the firm excel in as in evidence of past successes thereby providing accountability)

Financial Perspective

What accountability do small businesses that use Web services have to financial stakeholders?

How does the balanced scorecard impact the quality of Web services performance from a financial perspective? What factors are evaluated in the financial perspective?

How are the data gathered, analyzed, evaluated for feedback so that appropriate actions can be taken to improve the financial perspective?

What reporting mechanisms are deployed in your firm in order to enforce accountability?

Does your firm create significant value from intangible assets such as employee knowledge and innovation, customer relationships, and a strong culture. (how and why)

Does your senior management team spend time together discussing variances from plan and other financial issues? (How often?)

Does your organization clearly define the performance targets for both financial and non-financial indicators? (how and why)

Chapter 4.2
Semantic Web Take–Off in a European Industry Perspective

Alain Léger
France Telecom R&D, France

Johannes Heinecke
France Telecom R&D, France

Lyndon J.B. Nixon
Freie Universität Berlin, Germany

Pavel Shvaiko
University of Trento, Italy

Jean Charlet
STIM, DPA/AP-Hopitaux Paris & Université Paris 6, France

Paola Hobson
Motorola Labs, UK

François Goasdoué
LRI, CNRS et Université Paris Sud XI, France

ABSTRACT

Semantic Web technology is being increasingly applied in a large spectrum of applications in which domain knowledge is conceptualized and formalized (e.g., by means of an ontology) in order to support diversified and automated knowledge processing (e.g., reasoning) performed by a machine. Moreover, through an optimal combination of (cognitive) human reasoning and (automated) machine processing (mimicking reasoning); it becomes possible for humans and machines to share more and more complementary tasks. The spectrum of applications is extremely large and to name a few: corporate portals and knowledge management, e-commerce, e-work, e-business, healthcare, e-government, natural language understanding and automated translation, information search, data and services integration, social networks and collaborative filtering, knowledge mining, business intelligence and so on. From a social and economic perspective, this emerging technology should contribute to growth in economic wealth, but it must also show clear cut value for everyday activities through technological transparency and efficiency. The penetration of Semantic Web technology in industry and in services

DOI: 10.4018/978-1-60566-066-0.ch001

is progressing slowly but accelerating as new success stories are reported. In this chapter we present ongoing work in the cross-fertilization between industry and academia. In particular, we present a collection of application fields and use cases from enterprises which are interested in the promises of Semantic Web technology. The use cases are focused on the key knowledge processing components that will unlock the deployment of the technology in industry. The chapter ends with the presentation of the current state of the technology and future trends as seen by prominent actors in the field.

CURRENT SITUATION

As a result of the pervasive and user-friendly digital technologies emerging within our information society, Web content availability is increasing at an incredible rate but at the cost of being extremely multiform, inconsistent and very dynamic. Such content is totally unsuitable for machine processing, and so necessitates too much human interpretation and its respective costs in time and effort for both individuals and companies. To remedy this, approaches aim at abstracting from this complexity (i.e., by using ontologies) and offering new and enriched services able to process those abstractions (i.e., by mechanized reasoning) in a fully – and trusted - automated way. This abstraction layer is the subject of a very dynamic activity in research, industry and standardization which is usually called "Semantic Web" (see for example, DARPA, European IST Research Framework Program, W3C initiative, OASIS). The initial application of Semantic Web technology has focused on Information Retrieval (IR) where access through semantically annotated content, instead of classical (even sophisticated) statistical analysis, aimed to give far better results (in terms of precision and recall indicators). The next natural extension was to apply IR in the integration of enterprise legacy databases in order to leverage existing company information in new ways. Present research has turned to focusing on the seamless integration of heterogeneous and distributed applications and services (both intra- and inter-enterprise) through Semantic Web Services, and respectful of the legacy systems already in place, with the expectation of a fast return on investment (ROI) and improved efficiency in e-work and e-business.

This new technology takes its roots in the cognitive sciences, machine learning, natural language processing, multi-agents systems, knowledge acquisition, automated reasoning, logics and decision theory. It can be separated into two distinct – but cooperating fields - one adopting a formal and algorithmic approach for common sense automated reasoning (automated Web), and the other one "keeping the human being in the loop" for a socio-cognitive Semantic Web (automated social Web) which is gaining momentum today with the Web 2.0 paradigm[1].

On a large scale, industry awareness of Semantic Web technology has started at the EC level with the IST-FP5 thematic network Ontoweb[2] [2001-2004] which brought together around 50 motivated companies worldwide. Based on this experience, within IST-FP6, the Network of Excellence Knowledge Web[3] [2004-2008] made an in-depth analysis of the concrete industry needs in key economic sectors, and in a complementary way the IST-FP6 Network of Excellence REW-ERSE[4] was tasked with providing Europe with leadership in reasoning languages, also in view of a successful technology transfer and awareness activities targeted at the European industry for advanced Web systems and applications. This impetus will continue and grow up in the EU IST-FP7 [2007-2013][5].

The rest of the chapter is organized as follows. Four prototypical application fields are presented in Section 2, namely (1) healthcare and biotechnologies, (2) knowledge management (KM), (3) e-commerce and e-business, and finally, (4) multimedia and audiovisual services. Finally, Section

3 reports on a current vision of the achievements and some perspectives are given.

Overall Business Needs and Key Knowledge Processing Requirements

Use Case Collection

In order to support a large spectrum of application fields, two EU FP6 Networks of Excellence NoE-Knowledge Web and NoE-REWERSE are tasked with promoting transfer of best-of-the-art knowledge-based technology from academia to industry. The networks are made up of leading European Semantic Web research institutions that co-ordinate their research efforts while parallel efforts are made in Semantic Web education to increase the availability of skilled young researchers and practitioners and last but not the least, in pushing the take-up in Business and Industry.

In order to accelerate the transfer from research to industry, the objective of an Industry-Research co-operation is to establish a working relationship between Semantic Web researchers and an industry partner, in which research results being produced in an area of Semantic Web research will be prototypically applied to the industry partner's selected business case. The co-operation not only seeks to achieve an individual success story in terms of some specific research and a given business case, but also to establish the value of Semantic Web technologies to industrial application in a more general sense. It achieves this by demonstrating the use of Semantic Web technology in a business setting, exploring their usefulness in solving business problems and ensuring future applicability by directing researchers towards meeting industrial requirements in their work.

In NoE-Knowledge Web, an Industry Board was formed at the beginning of the network to bring together potential early adopters of Semantic Web technologies from across a wide spread of industry sectors. Industry Board members have been involved in many initiatives of the Knowledge Web Industry Area, including the collection of business use cases and their evaluation. In order to more directly achieve close co-operation between researchers and industry, each research activity in the network was invited to select a use case whose requirements closely correlated to what would be achieved in their research work. Results have been collected and reported in July 2007[6].

Currently in 2007, this Industry Board consisted of about 50 members (e.g., France Telecom, British Telecom, Institut Français du Pétrole, Illy Caffè, Trenitalia, Daimler AG, Thalès, EADS, ...) from across 14 nations and 13 economic sectors (e.g., telecoms, energy, food, logistics, automotive,...).

The companies were requested to provide illustrative examples of actual or hypothetical deployment of Semantic Web technology in their business settings. This was followed up with face-to-face meetings between researchers and industry experts from the companies to gain additional information about the provided use cases. Thus, in 2004, a total of 16 use cases were collected from 12 companies. In 2007, through many workshops and Industry forum sessions at major Semantic Web conferences, more than a hundred use cases were available or illustrative of the current trend to introduce Semantic Web technology in the main stream.

As shown in Figure 1, where the use cases are broken down according to the industry sector, collected cases are from 9 industry sectors, with the highest number of the use cases coming from the service industry (19%) and media & communications (18%) respectively. This initial collection of use cases can be found in (Nixon L. et al., 2004), and an updated selection is available on the Knowledge Web Industry portal[7].

The co-operations have been a very challenging activity, given the early state of much cutting edge Semantic Web research and the differences in perspective between academia and business. However, successes have been reported, not only

Figure 1. Breakdown of use cases by industry sector

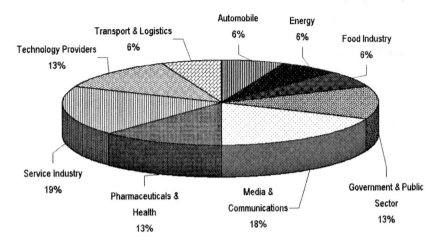

Use Case Analysis

in the production of some prototypical solutions and demos which can be shown to industry and business top managers, but also in making researchers more aware of the importance of their work to solving business problems and the earlier recognition by academics of industry needs and expectations and so integrating them to their research agenda.

Hence, the Industry-Research co-operations in NoE-Knowledge Web and NoE-REWERSE must be seen as a significant first attempt to align the ambitious cutting edge work on Semantic Web technologies done by leading researchers in Europe and the real world business problems encountered by the European industry which may find a potential solution in those same Semantic Web technologies. Given a continued rise in awareness among Semantic Web researchers of the applicability of their work to industry and the continued rise in awareness among industry of the potential of the work of Semantic Web researchers, which has been begun in IST-NoEs, in IST-R&D projects, but also clearly in industry (SMEs and large companies), the technology transfer is gradually evolving.

A preliminary analysis of the use cases has been carried out in order to obtain a first vision (end of 2004) of the current industrial needs and to estimate the expectations from knowledge-based technology with respect to those needs. The industry experts were asked to indicate the existing legacy solutions in their use cases, the service functionalities they would be offered and the technological locks they encountered, and eventually how they expected that Semantic Web technology could resolve those locks. As a result, this analysis has provided an overview of:

- Types of business or service problems where the knowledge-based technology is considered to bring a plausible solution.
- Types of technological issues (and the corresponding research challenges) which knowledge based technology is expected to overcome.

Figure 2 shows a breakdown of the areas in which the industry experts thought Semantic Web technology could provide a solution. For example, for nearly half of the collected use cases, data integration and semantic search were areas

Figure 2. Breakdown of use cases by industry sector

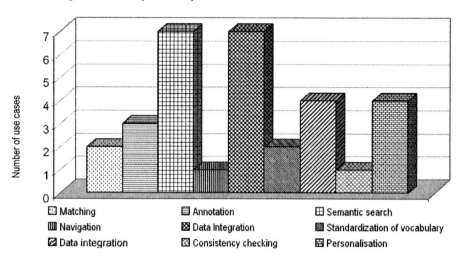

where industry was looking for knowledge-based solutions. Other areas mentioned, in a quarter of use cases, were solutions to data management and personalization.

Figure 3 shows a breakdown of the technology locks identified in the use cases. There are three technology locks which occur the most often in the collected use cases. These are: (1) ontology development, i.e., modeling of a business domain, authoring, reusing existing ontologies; (2)

knowledge extraction, i.e., populating ontologies by extracting data from legacy systems; and (3) ontology mapping, i.e., resolving semantic heterogeneity among multiple ontologies.

Below, an illustration is given, with the help of a use case from the collection, how a concrete business problem can be used to indicate the technology locks for which knowledge-based solutions potentially might be useful. This use case addresses the problem of intelligent search of

Figure 3. Preliminary vision of technology locks in use case

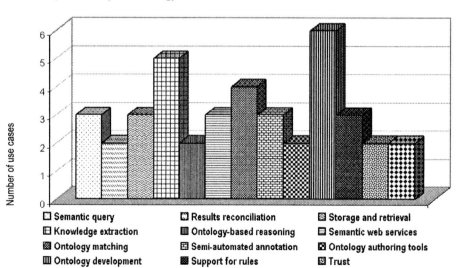

documents in the corporate data of an international coffee company.

The company generates a large amount of internal data and its employees encounter difficulties in finding the data they need for the research and development of new solutions. The aim is to improve the quality of the document retrieval and to enable personalization services for individual users when searching or viewing the corporate data. As technology locks, the expert mentioned here the corporate domain ontology development and maintenance, and semantic querying.

Eventually, this analysis (by experts estimations) has provided with a preliminary understanding of scope of the current industrial needs and the current concrete technology locks where knowledge-based technology is expected to provide a plausible solution. However, to be able to answer specific industrial requirements, there is the need to conduct further a detailed technical analysis of the use cases, thereby associating to each technology lock a concrete knowledge processing task and a component realizing its functionalities.

Knowledge Processing Tasks and Components

Based on the information processing needs identified during the technical use cases analysis (Shvaiko P. et al., 2004), a typology of common knowledge processing tasks and a library of high level components for realizing those tasks, was built, see Table 1. The first tentative typology includes twelve processing tasks. Let us discuss knowledge processing tasks and components of Table 1 in more detail:

- *Ontology management, ontology merging and ontology manager.* These tasks and component are in charge of ontology maintenance (e.g., reorganizing taxonomies, resolving name conflicts, browsing ontologies, editing concepts) and merging

multiple ontologies (e.g., by taking the union of the axioms) with respect to evolving business case requirements, see (Dou D. et al., 2005) (McGuiness D. et al., 2000) (Protégé[8]), OAEI-2007 Ontology Alignment Evaluation Initiative[9], NeOn[10] (Networked Evolving Ontologies) and Ontology Matching survey site[11].

- *Ontology matching, matching results analysis, producing explanations and match manager.* These tasks and component are in charge of (on-the-fly and semi-automatic) determination of semantic mappings between the entities of multiple schemas and ontologies, see (Rahm E. et al., 2001) (Shvaiko P. and Euzenat, 2005), (Euzenat J. and Shvaiko P., 2007). Mappings are typically specified with the help of a similarity relation which can be either in the form of a coefficient rating match quality in the (0,1] range (i.e., the higher the coefficient, the higher the similarity between the entities, see (Billig A. et al., 2002) (Ehrig M. et al., 2004) (Euzenat J. et al., 2004) (Do H. H. et al., 2002) (Zhong J. et al., 2002) or in the form of a logical relation (e.g., equivalence, subsumption), see (Giunchiglia F. et al., 2003) (Giunchiglia F. et al., 2004). The mappings might need to be ordered according to some criteria, see (Di Noia T. et al., 2003) (Do H. H. et al., 2002).

Finally, explanations of the mappings might be also required, see (Dhamankar R. et al., 2004) (Shvaiko P. et al., 2005). Matching systems may produce mappings that may not be intuitively obvious to human users. In order for users to trust the mappings (and thus use them), they need information about them. They need access to the sources that were used to determine semantic correspondences between terms and potentially they need to understand how deductions and manipulations are performed. The issue here is to present explanations in a simple and clear way to the user.

- *Data translation and wrapper.* This task and component is in charge of automatic manipulation (e.g., translation, exchange) of instances between heterogeneous information sources storing their data in different formats (e.g., RDF, SQL DDL, XML ...), see (Hull R. 1997) (Petrini J. et al., 2004) (Velegrakis Y. et al., 2005) (Halevy A. et al., 2006). Here, mappings are taken as input (for example, from the match manager component) and are the support for generating query expressions that perform the required semantic and syntactical manipulations with data instances coming from heterogeneous environment.

- *Results reconciliation and results reconciler.* This task and component is in charge of determining an optimal solution, in terms of contents (no information duplication, etc.) and routing performance, for returning results from the queried information sources, see (Preguica N. et al., 2003).

- *Composition of Web services and planner.* This task and component is in charge of automated composition of Web services into executable processes (Orchestration). Composed Web services perform new functionalities by specific on demand interaction with pre-existing services that are published on the Web, see surveys from (Chan et al., 2007) (Berardi et al., 2005) (Hull et al., 2005) (Pistore et al., 2005) (Roman et al., 2005) (Traverso P. et al., 2004) (Cardoso et al., 2003) (McIlraith et al., 2001). From a business viewpoint, it remains a key challenge to be overcome, as the businesses react very positively to the need for a very effective integration technology and for more agility in a very competitive worldwide economy. In the meantime, reducing interoperability problems will open opportunities for easier innovative solutions and for the increase in cooperation between enterprises. This

should result in re-combinations of businesses the technology provides and so will have a profound impact on business and economic workflows.

- *Content annotation and annotation manager.* This task and component is in charge of automatic production of metadata for the contents, see aceMedia[12] for multimedia annotation. Annotation manager takes as input the (pre-processed) contents and domain knowledge and produces as output a database of content annotations. In addition to the automatic production of content metadata, prompt mechanisms offer the user the possibility to enrich the content annotation by adding extra information (e.g., title, name of a location, title of an event, names of people) that could not be automatically detected.

- *Automated reasoning.* This task and component is in charge of providing logical reasoning services (e.g., subsumption, concept satisfiability, instance checking tests), see (Haarslev V. et al., 1999-2007). For example, when dealing with multimedia annotations, logical reasoning can be exploited in order to check consistency of the annotations against the set of spatial (e.g., left, right, above, adjacent, overlaps) and temporal (e.g., before, after, during, co-start, co-end) constraints. This can certify that the objects detected in the multimedia content correspond semantically to the concepts defined in the domain ontology. For example, in the racing domain, the automated reasoner should check whether a car is located on a road or whether the grass and sand are adjacent to the road.

- *Semantic query processing and query processor.* This task and component is in charge of rewriting a query posed by a human being or a machine, by using terms which are explicitly specified in the model of domain knowledge in order to provide

Table 1. Typology of knowledge processing tasks & components

N	Knowledge processing tasks	Components
1	Ontology Management	Ontology Manager
2	Ontology Matching	Match Manager
3	Ontology Matching results Analysis	Match Manager
4	Data Translation	Wrapper
5	Results Reconciliation	Results Reconciler
6	Composition of Web Services	Planner
7	Content Annotation	Annotation manager
8	Reasoning	Reasoner
9	Semantic Query Processing	Query Processor
10	Ontology Merging	Ontology Manager
11	Producing explanations	Match Manager
12	Personalization	Profiler

semantics preserving query answering, see (Mena E. et al., 1996) (Halevy et al., 2001) (Calvanese et al., 2002) (IST-IP aceMedia 2004). Examples of queries are "Give me all the games played on grass" or "Give me all the games of double players", in the tennis domain. Finally, users should be able to query by sample content e.g. an image. In this case, the system should perform an intelligent search of images and videos (e.g., by using semantic annotations) where, for example, the same event or type of activity takes place.

- *Personalization and profiler.* This task and component is in charge of tailoring services available from the system to the specificity of each user, see (Antoniou G. et al., 2004). For example, generation and updating of user profiles, recommendation generation, inferring user preferences, and so on. For example users might want to share annotations within trusted user networks, thus having services of personal metadata management and contacts recommendation. Also, a particular form of personalization, which is media adaptation, may require knowledge-based technology and

consistent delivery of the contents to a broad range user terminals (e.g., PDA, mobile phone, portable PC).

KEY APPLICATION SECTORS AND TYPICAL TECHNOLOGY PROBLEMS

Healthcare and Biotechnologies

The medical domain is a favourite target for Semantic Web applications just as the expert system was for artificial intelligence applications 20 years ago. The medical domain is very complex: medical knowledge is difficult to represent in a computer format, making the sharing of information even more difficult. Semantic Web solutions become very promising in this context.

One of the main mechanisms of the Semantic Web - resource description using annotation principles - is of major importance in the medical informatics (or sometimes called bioinformatics) domain, especially as regards the sharing of these resources (e.g. medical knowledge on the Web or genomic database). Through the years, the IR area has been developed by medicine: medical thesauri are enormous (e.g., more than 1,600,000 terms in Unified Medical Language

System, UMLS[13]) and are principally used for bibliographic indexation. Nevertheless, the MeSh thesaurus (Medical Subject Heading) or UMLS have been used to provide data semantics with varying degrees of difficulty. Finally, the Web services technology allows us to imagine some solutions to the interoperability problem, which is substantial in medical informatics. Below, we will describe current research, results and expected perspectives in these biomedical informatics topics in the context of Semantic Web.

Biosciences Resources Sharing

In the functional genomics domain, it is necessary to have access to several databases and knowledge bases which are accessible separately on the Web but are heterogeneous in their structure as well as in their terminology. Among such resources, we can mention SWISSPROT[14] where the gene products are annotated by the Gene Ontology[15], Gen-Bank[16], etc. When comparing these resources it is easy to see that they propose the same information in different formats. The XML language, which acts as a common data structure for the different knowledge bases, provides at most a syntactic Document Type Definition (DTD) which does not resolve the semantic interoperability problem.

One of the solutions comes from the Semantic Web with a mediator approach (Wiederhold G., 1992) which allows for the accessing of different resources with an ontology used as the Interlingua pivot. For example and in another domain than that of genomics, the NEUROBASE project (Barillot C. et al., 2003) attempts to federate different neuro-imagery information bases situated in different clinical or research areas. The proposal consists of defining an architecture that allows the access to and the sharing of experimental results or data treatment methodologies. It would be possible to search in the various data bases for similar results or for images with peculiarities or to perform data mining analysis between

several databases. The mediator of NEUROBASE has been tested on decision support systems in epilepsy surgery.

Ontologies for Coding Systems

The main usage of ontologies in medical domain is as index of coding system: after using thesauri for indexing medical bibliography (PubMed with the Mesh[17]), the goal is to index Electronic Health records with medical concept in order to enhance information retrieval or to allow epidemiological studies. For that purpose, several countries intend to use the SNOMED, an international classification of concepts organized in eight axes (Spackman et al., 2002). Except the problem of languages, this classification exists in two versions: a classification of 160,000 concepts (SNOMED-I V3.5) and an ontology, which is the evolution of the preceding one, of 330,000 concepts, SNOMED CT. The use of ontologies of such a size is difficult. Some authors describe them as *Reference Ontology* which cannot be accessed without an *interface ontology* (Rosenbloom et al., 2006). Notwithstanding, UK national health system (NHS) is integrating SNOMED CT and it will be interesting to examine the results of this industrial deployment[18].

Web Services for Interoperability

The Web services technology can propose some solutions to the interoperability problematic. We describe now a new approach based on a "patient envelope" and we conclude with the implementation of this envelope based on the Web services technology.

The patient envelope is a proposition of the Electronic Data Interchange for Healthcare group (EDI-Santé[19]) with an active contribution from the ETIAM[20] society. The objective of the work is on filling the gap between "free" communication, using standard and generic Internet tools, and "totally structured" communication as promoted by CEN (in the Working Group IV "Technology for Interoperability"[21]) or HL7[22]. After the worldwide analysis of existing standards, the proposal consists of an "intermediate" structure of information, related to one patient, and storing the minimum amount of data (i.e. exclusively useful data) to facilitate the interoperability between communicating peers. The "free" or the "structured" information is grouped into a folder and transmitted in a secure way over the existing communication networks (Cordonnier E. et al., 2003). This proposal has reached widespread adoption with the distribution by Cegetel.rss of a new medical messaging service, called "Sentinelle", fully supporting the patient envelope protocol and adapted tools.

After this milestone, EDI-Santé is promoting further developments based on ebXML and SOAP (Simple Object Access Protocol) in specifying exchange (see items 1 and 2 below) and medical (see items 3 and 4 below) properties:

1. *Separate what is mandatory* to the transport and management of the message (e.g., patient identification from what constitutes the "job" part of the message.
2. *Provide a "container" for the message*, collecting the different elements, texts, pictures, videos, etc.
3. *Consider the patient as the unique object of the transaction.* Such an exchange cannot be anonymous. It concerns a sender and an addressee who are involved in the exchange and who are responsible. A patient can demand to know the content of the exchange in which (s)he is the object, which implies a data structure which is unique in the form of a triple {sender, addressee, patient}.
4. *The conservation of the exchange semantics.* The information about a patient is multiple in the sense that it comes from multiple sources and has multiple forms and supporting data (e.g., database, free textual document, semi-structured textual document, pictures). It can

be fundamental to maintain the existing links between elements, to transmit them together, e.g., a scanner and the associated report, and to be able to prove it.

The interest of such an approach is that it prepares the evolution of the transmitted document from a free form document (from proprietary ones to normalized ones as XML) to elements respecting HL7v3 or EHRCOM data types. In France, the GIP-DMP[23] retains such an approach (in conjunction with the Clinical Document Architecture of HL7[24]) for the implementation of the exchanges of the *Dossier Médical Personnel* (a future national electronic health record).

What is Next in the Healthcare Domain?

These different projects and applications highlight the main consequence of the Semantic Web being expected by the medical communities: the sharing and integration of heterogeneous information or knowledge. The answers to the different issues are the use of mediators, a knowledge-based system, and ontologies, which should be based in the mid term on normalized languages such as RDF, OWL but also in addition to come OWL-S, SAWSDL, WSML, SWRL, or RuleML. The work of the Semantic Web community must take into account these expectations, see for example the FP6 projects[25,26,27]. Finally, it is interesting to note that the Semantic Web is an integrated vision of the medical community's problems (thesauri, ontologies, indexation, and inference) and provides a real opportunity to synthesize and reactivate some research directions (Charlet J. et al., 2002).

Knowledge Management

Leveraging Knowledge Assets in Companies

Knowledge is one of the key success factors for enterprises, both today and in the future. Therefore, company knowledge management (KM) has been identified as a strategic tool. However, if for KM, information technology is one of the foundational elements, KM in turn, is also interdisciplinary by its nature. In particular, it includes human resource management as well as enterprise organization and culture[28]. KM is viewed as the management of the knowledge arising from business activities, aiming at leveraging both the use and the creation of that knowledge for two main objectives: capitalization of corporate knowledge and durable innovation fully aligned with the strategic objectives of the organization.

Conscious of this key factor of productivity in an ever faster changing ecosystem, the European KM Framework (CEN/ISSS[29], KnowledgeBoard[30]) has been designed to support a common European understanding of KM, to show the value of this emerging approach and to help organizations towards its successful implementation. The Framework is based on empirical research and practical experiences in this field from all over Europe and the rest of the world. The European KM Framework addresses all of the relevant elements of a KM solution and serves as a reference basis for all types of organizations, which aim to improve their performance by handling knowledge in a better way.

Benefits of Knowledge-Based KM

The knowledge backbone is made up of ontologies that define a shared conceptualization of an application domain and provide the basis for defining metadata that have precisely defined se-

mantics, and are therefore machine-interpretable. Although the first KM approaches and solutions have shown the benefits of ontologies and related methods, a large number of open research issues still exist that have to be addressed in order to make Semantic Web technology a complete success for KM solutions:

- Industrial KM applications *have to avoid any kind of overhead as far as possible. A seamless integration of knowledge creation* (i.e., content and metadata specification) and knowledge access (i.e., querying or browsing) into the working environment is required. Strategies and methods are needed to support the creation of knowledge, as side effects of activities that are carried out anyway. These requirements mean emergent semantics that can be supported through ontology learning, which should reduce the current time consuming task of building-up and maintaining ontologies.

- *Access to as well as presentation of knowledge has to be context-dependent.* Since the context is setup by the current business task, and thus by the business process being handled, a tight integration of business process management and knowledge management is required. KM approaches can provide a promising starting point for smart push services that will proactively deliver relevant knowledge for carrying out the task at hand more effectively.

- *Conceptualization has to be supplemented by personalization.* On the one hand, taking into account the experience of the user and his/her personal needs is a prerequisite in order to avoid information overload, and on the other hand, to deliver knowledge at the right level of granularity and from the right perspective at the right time.

The development of knowledge portals serving the needs of companies or communities is still a manual process. Ontologies and related metadata provide a promising conceptual basis for generating parts of such knowledge portals. Obviously, among others, conceptual models of the domain, of the users and of the tasks are needed. The *generation of knowledge portals* has to be supplemented with the (semi-) automated evolution of portals. As business environments and strategies change rather rapidly, *KM portals have to be kept up-to-date in this fast changing environment.* Evolution of portals should also include some mechanisms to *'forget' outdated knowledge.*

KM solutions will be based on a combination of intranet-based functionalities and mobile functionalities in the very near future. Semantic technologies are a promising approach to meet the needs of mobile environments, like location-aware personalization and adaptation of the presentation to the specific needs of mobile devices, i.e., the presentation of the required information at an appropriate level of granularity. In essence, employees should have access to the KM application *anywhere* and *anytime.*

Peer-to-peer computing (P2P), social networking (W2.0), combined with Semantic Web technology, will be a strong move towards getting rid of the more centralized KM approaches that are currently used in ontology-based solutions. W2.0 scenarios open up the way to derive consensual conceptualizations among employees within an enterprise in a bottom-up manner.

Virtual organizations are becoming more and more important in business scenarios, mainly due to decentralization and globalization. Obviously, semantic interoperability between different knowledge sources, as well as trust, is necessary in inter-organizational KM applications.

The integration of KM applications with *e-learning* (e.g., skill management in companies) is an important field that enables a lot of synergy between these two areas. KM solutions and e-learning must be integrated from both an organizational and an IT point of view. Clearly, interoperability and integration of (metadata)

standards are needed to realize such integration.

Knowledge management is obviously a very promising area for exploiting Semantic Web technology. Document-based portals KM solutions have already reached their limits, whereas semantic technology opens the way to meet KM requirements in the future.

Knowledge-Based KM Applications

In the context of geographical team dispersion, multilingualism and business unit autonomy, usually a company wants a solution allowing for the identification of strategic information, the secured distribution of this information and the creation of transverse working groups. Some applicative solutions allowed for the deployment of an Intranet intended for all the marketing departments of the company worldwide, allowing for a better division of and a greater accessibility to information, but also capitalisation on the total knowledge. There are four crucial points that aim at easing the work of the various marketing teams in a company: (1) Business intelligence, (2) Skill and team management[31], (3) Process management[32] and (4) Rich document access and management[33].

Thus, a system connects the "strategic ontologies" of the company group (brands, competitors, geographical areas, etc.) with the users, via the automation of related processes (research, classification, distribution, knowledge representation). The result is a dynamic semantic system of navigation (research, classification) and collaborative features.

At the end from a functional point of view, a KM system organises skill and knowledge management within a company in order to improve interactivity, collaboration and information sharing. This constitutes a virtual workspace which facilitates work between employees that speak different languages, automates the creation of work groups, organises and capitalises structured and unstructured, explicit or tacit data of the company, and offers advanced features of capitalisation

(Bonifacio M. et al., 2005) (Brunschweig B. et al., 2005) (Nordheim D. et al., 2005).

Eventually, the semantic backbone makes possible to cross a qualitative gap by providing cross-lingual data.

E-Commerce and E-Business

Electronic commerce is mainly based on the exchange of information between involved stakeholders using a telecommunication infrastructure. There are two main scenarios: business-to-customer (B2C) and business-to-business (B2B).

B2C applications enable service providers to promote their offers, and for customers to find offers which match their demands. By providing unified access to a large collection of frequently updated offers and customers, an electronic marketplace can match the demand and supply processes within a commercial mediation environment.

B2B applications have a long history of using electronic messaging to exchange information related to services previously agreed among two or more businesses. Early plain-text telex communication systems were followed by electronic data interchange (EDI) systems based on terse, highly codified, well structured, messages. A new generation of B2B systems is being developed under the ebXML (electronic business in XML) heading. These will use classification schemes to identify the context in which messages have been, or should be, exchanged. They will also introduce new techniques for the formal recording of business processes, and for the linking of business processes through the exchange of well-structured business messages. ebXML will also develop techniques that will allow businesses to identify new suppliers through the use of registries that allow users to identify which services a supplier can offer. ebXML needs to include well managed multilingual ontologies that can be used to help users to match needs expressed in their own language with those expressed in the service

providers language(s) see (Guarino N. 1999) (Zyl J. et al., 200) (Lehtola A. et al., 2003) (Heinecke J. et al., 2003) (Benatallah B et al., 2005).

Knowledge-Based E-Commerce and E-Business Value

At present, ontology and more generally knowledge-based systems appear as a central issue for the development of efficient and profitable e-commerce and e-business solutions. However, because of the actual situation i.e. the partial standardization of business models, processes, and knowledge architectures, it is currently difficult for companies to achieve the promised ROI from knowledge-based e-commerce and e-business.

Moreover, a technical barrier exists that is delaying the emergence of e-commerce, lying in the need for applications to *meaningfully share information*, taking into account the lack of reliability, security and eventually trust in the Internet. This fact may be explained by the variety of e-commerce and e-business systems employed by businesses and the various ways these systems are configured and used. As an important remark, such *interoperability problems* become particularly severe when a large number of trading partners attempt to agree and define the standards for interoperation, which is precisely a main condition for maximizing the ROI indicator.

Although it is useful to strive for the adoption of a single common domain-specific standard for content and transactions, such a task is often difficult to achieve, particularly in cross-industry initiatives, where companies co-operate and compete with one another. Some examples of the difficulties are:

- *Commercial practices* may vary widely, and consequently, cannot always be aligned for a variety of technical, practical, organizational and political reasons.

- *The complexity of a global description* of the organizations themselves: their products and services (independently or in combination), and the interactions between them remain a formidable task.
- It is not always possible to establish *a priori rules* (technical or procedural) governing participation in an electronic marketplace.

Adoption of a single common standard may limit business models which could be adopted by trading partners, and therefore, potentially reduce their ability to fully participate in e-commerce.

A knowledge-based approach has the potential to significantly accelerate the penetration of electronic commerce within vertical industry sectors, by *enabling interoperability at the business level*. This will enable services to adapt to the rapidly changing business ecosystem.

Knowledge-Based E-Commerce and E-Business Applications

The Semantic Web brings opportunities to industry to create new services[34], extend markets, and even develop new businesses since it enables the inherent meaning of the data available in the Internet to be accessible to systems and devices able to interpret and reason at the knowledge level. This in turn leads to new revenue opportunities, since information becomes more readily accessible and usable. For example, a catering company whose Web site simply lists the menus available is less likely to achieve orders compared to one whose menus are associated with related metadata about the contents of the dishes, their origin (e.g., organic, non-genetically modified, made with local produce), links to alternative dishes for special diets, personalised ordering where a user profile can be established which automatically proposes certain menu combinations depending on the occasion (e.g., wedding banquet, business lunch). The latter case assumes that both provider-side knowledge generation and

knowledge management tools are available, such that the asset owner can readily enhance their data with semantic meaning, and client-side tools are available to enable machine interpretation of the semantic descriptions related to the products being offered, such that the end user can benefit from the available and mined knowledge. Examples of some possible application areas were studied by the Agent Cities project[35].

In the e-business area Semantic Web technology can improve standard business process management tools. One prototypical case is in the area of logistics. The application of knowledge technology on top of today's business management tools enables the automation of major tasks of business process management[36] see (Semantic Web Case Studies for eBusiness 2005).

In one of the Knowledge Web Industry-Research co-operations, a number of scenarios within the **B2B integration scenario** were identified, involving data mediation, discovery, and composition of services. All of these use cases have been evaluated according to a community-agreed methodology defined by the SWS challenge methodology with satisfying success levels defined by the methodology. This is an important step when proving the added value of the Semantic Web service technology applied to B2B integration domain. In addition, the standardization process has been partially finalized within the OASIS Semantic Execution Environment Technical Committee (OASIS SEE TC) and W3C Semantic Annotations for WSDL and XML Schema (W3C SAWSDL WG). However, the standardization process in both groups is still ongoing, but under business pressure has concluded respectively on SAWSDL in 2007 and SESA framework early 2008.

The Industry-Research co-operation has *demonstrably solved a business case from the B2B domain*. We have shown how the technology deals with requirements from B2B domain and how this technology reacts to changes in back-end systems which might occur over the system's lifetime.

Figure 4. Semantic Web services integration in B2B

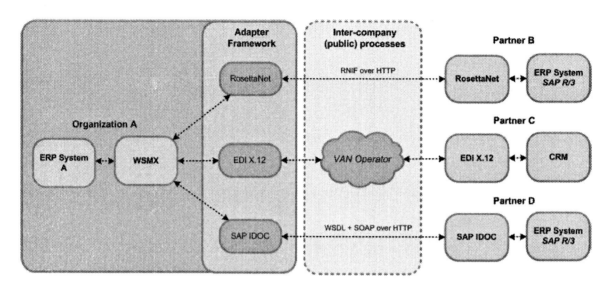

The research is not yet ready for industry. It must be shown how the technology is layered on the existing infrastructure and how it interacts with existing systems. For this purpose some parts of the technology need to be standardized (such as grounding mechanisms built on SAWSDL or the architecture). In particular, the grounding mechanism built on SAWSDL provides a "common interface" between semantic descriptions and non-semantic descriptions (in our case WSDL). The standardization is still ongoing while at the same time, the alignment of service semantics with this grounding mechanism must be further finalised. While it has been demonstrated how this is possible to be done and what the added value of this approach is, *the complexity of business standards still needs to be addressed.*

In addition, a prototype is available[37] and has been provided to NoE-Knowledge Web industry partners see Figure 4. The following scenarios have been realised as part of the Semantic Web Services Challenge:

- **Mediation Scenario** (http://sws-challenge. org/wiki/index.php/Workshop_Budva). Addressing the mediation scenario for

B2B integration when proprietary back-end systems of one company needed to be integrated with a partner using RosettaNet standard. Whole scenario has been successfully addressed.

- **Discovery Scenario** (http://sws-challenge. org/wiki/index.php/Workshop_Athens). Addressing discovery scenario when a supplier needed to be discovered and selected from suitable ones. Whole scenario has been successfully addressed.

- **Composition Scenario** (http://sws-challenge.org/wiki/index.php/Workshop_ Innsbruck). Addressing composition scenario when more services can satisfy the user need. Whole scenario has been successfully addressed.

Work will continue and the co-operation plans to address additional scenarios of the SWS challenge, namely scenarios when services can be filtered based on non-functional properties (QoS, financial, etc.). In addition, a tutorial was given on SWS in the context of business process management at ICWS'07 conference, and the authors co-organize the workshop on service composition and SWS challenge held at the Web Intelligence conference[38] (Vitvar T. et al., 2007a) (Vitvar T. et al., 2007b) (Hasselwanter T. et al., 2007).

Multimedia and Audiovisual Services

Practical realisation of the Semantic Web vision is actively being researched by a number of experts, some of them within European collaborative projects, and others within company specific initiatives. Earlier projects such as SEKT[39] and DIP, mainly focused on enhancing text based applications from a knowledge engineering perspective. Although significant benefits in unlocking access to valuable knowledge assets are realised via these projects, in various domains such as digital libraries, enterprise applications, and financial services, it was soon recognised that there was a challenging and potentially highly profitable area of research into the integration of multimedia and Semantic Web technologies for multimedia content based applications. Projects such as aceMedia, BOEMIE, and MESH are examples of initiatives aiming to advance the use of semantics and reasoning for improved multimedia applications such as automated annotation, content summarisation, and personalised content syndication.

The drive for application of semantic technologies in the multimedia and content domains comes from a proliferation of audiovisual devices and services which have led to an exponential growth in available content. Users express dissatisfaction at not being able to find what they want, and content owners are unable to make full use of their assets. Service providers seek means to differentiate their offerings by making them more targeted toward the individual needs of their customers. Semantic Web technology can address these issues. It has the potential to reduce complexity, enhance choice, and put the user at the center of the application or service, and with today's fast mobile data services and availability of wifi, such benefits can be enjoyed by consumers and professional users in all environments using all their personal devices, in the home, at work, in the car and on the go.

Semantic Web technologies can enhance multimedia based products to increase the value of multimedia assets such as content items which are themselves the articles for sale (songs, music videos, sports clips, news summaries, etc) or where they are used as supporting sales of other goods (e.g. promotional images, movie trailers etc). Value is added in search applications, such that returned items more closely match the user's context, interests, tasks, preference history etc, as well as in proactive push applications such as personalised content delivery and recommendation systems, and even personalised advertising. However, applications such as content personalisation, where a system matches available content to the user's stated and learned preferences, thereby enabling content offerings to be closely targeted to the user's wishes, rely on the availability of semantic metadata describing the content in order to make the match. Currently, metadata generation is mostly manual, which is costly and time consuming. Multimedia analysis techniques which go beyond the signal level approach to a semantic analysis have the potential to create automatic annotation of content, thereby opening up new applications which can unlock the commercial value of content archives (Stamou et al., 2006) (Stamou et al., 2005).

Automated multimedia analysis tools are important enablers in making a wider range of information more accessible to intelligent search engines, real-time personalisation tools, and user-friendly content delivery systems. Such automated multimedia analysis tools, which add the semantic information to the content, are critical in realising the value of commercial assets e.g. sports, music and film clip services, where manual annotation of multimedia content would not be economically viable, and are also applicable to users' personal content (e.g. acquired from video camera or mobile phone) where the user does not have time, or a suitable user interface, to annotate all their content.

Figure 5. Automated semantic annotation in aceMedia

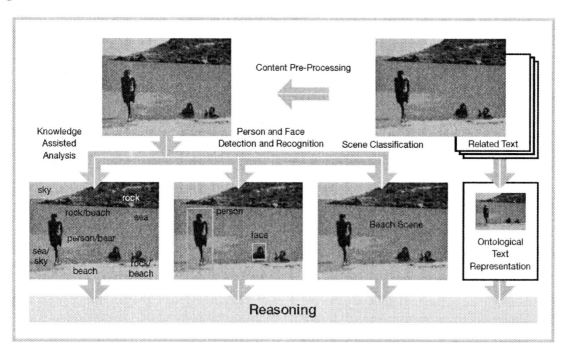

Multimedia ontologies are needed to structure and make accessible the knowledge inherent in the multimedia content, and reasoning tools are needed to assist with identification of relevant content in an automated fashion. Although textual analysis and reasoning tools have been well researched, and despite the projects funded by the European Commission in the 6th framework, fewer tools are available for semantic multimedia analysis, since the problem domain is very challenging. However, automated multimedia content analysis tools such as those being studied within aceMedia[40] are a first step in making a wider range of information more accessible to intelligent search engines, real-time personalisation tools, and user-friendly content delivery systems.

Furthermore, interoperability of multimedia tools is important in enabling a wide variety of applications and services on multiple platforms for diverse domains. The W3C Multimedia Semantics Incubator Group reported on interoperability issues[41] and it is clear that a common framework using Semantic Web languages tools is essential for full exploitation of the potential of multimedia assets. Interoperability is essential in achieving commercial success with semantic multimedia applications, since it enables multiple manufacturers, content providers and service providers to participate in the market. This in turn enables consumer confidence to be achieved, and a viable ecosystem to be developed.

Knowledge Enhanced Multimedia Services

In aceMedia the main technological objectives are to discover and exploit knowledge inherent in multimedia content in order to make content more relevant to the user; to automate annotation at all levels (see Figure 5) ; and to add functionality to ease content creation, transmission, search, access, consumption and re-use.

Users access multimedia content using a variety of devices, such as mobile phones and set-top-boxes, as well as via broadband cable or wireless to their PC. Through exploitation of Semantic Web tools, aceMedia has created a system which provides new and intuitive ways for users to enjoy multimedia content, such as intelligent search and retrieval, self-organising content, and self-adapting content. For example, using aceMedia's automatic metadata generation, a user can annotate content taken with her mobile phone, then seamlessly upload it to her PC where further automatic metadata generation takes place. aceMedia tools enables the content to be automatically organised into thematic categories, according to the user's preferences, and using extensions to DLNA/UPnP (networked digital home) standards, the content can be automatically pushed to other users (as specified by the content owner) according to chosen rules. For example, our user might automatically receive new pictures of herself on her mobile phone or PC which were acquired and annotated on the device of one of her friends or family.

The aceMedia use case highlighted a number of future direction, issues and new challenges with respect to semantic multimedia content analysis and manipulation within a Semantic Web framework. Apart from the requirements with respect to formal uncertainty representations and more effective reasoning and management tools support, two dimensions of significant importance include:

- *Cross-media analysis*, where additional requirements are posed due to the multimodality of knowledge considered, and their semantic modelling and integration, and
- *Non-standard approaches to reasoning*, as purely deductive reasoning alone proves not sufficient

Other projects which can use the results of this co-operation: particularly K-Space[42], X-Media[43], BOEMIE[44] and MESH[45] constitute research consortiums working on the same topic. As, in the case of aceMedia, the main research directions focus on the exploitation of formal explicit knowledge and (possibly extended) inference services for the extraction of semantic descriptions from multimedia content. Additional aspects include among other scalability, logic programming and DL-based reasoning integration for non-standard inference support, and ontology evolution (Stoilos G. et al, 2005) (Petridis K. et al., 2006) (Dasiopoulou S. et al., 2007).

Leveraging Social Network Knowledge for Movie Recommendations

Another interesting reported multimedia experiment is MediaCaddy (Garg S. et al., 2005) aiming at providing *movie or music recommendations* based on published online *critics, user experience and social networks*. Indeed, for the entertainment industry, traditional approaches to delivering meta-content about movies, music, TV shows, etc. were through reviews and articles that were done and published in traditional media such as newspapers, magazines and TV shows. With the introduction of the Internet, non-traditional forms of delivering entertainment started surfacing. The third quarter of 2003 in the U.S was the best ever for broadband penetration bringing such services as content on-demand and mobile multimedia. As of today more than 5000 movies and 2,500,000 songs are available on line. In the next couple of years this figure is expected to grow in leaps and bounds. With such a phenomenal rise in content over IP, a new need for secondary metacontent related to the movies/music emerged. Initially this was through movie reviews or music reviews published on Web portals such as Yahoo, MSN and online magazine portals as well as entertainment sales sites such as Netflix.com and Amazon.com.

Most consumers today get information about media content primarily from reviews/articles in entertainment/news magazines, their social network of friends (one user recommends a song or movie to a friend), acquaintances and advertisements. In most of the cases, one or all

Figure 6. Conceptual model of content navigation system from the MediaCaddy project

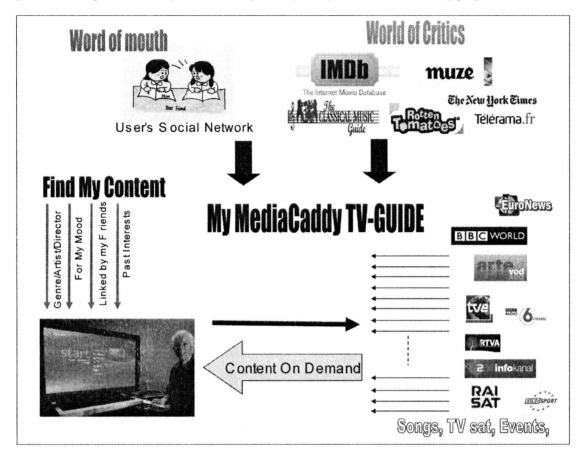

of the above influence user's opinion about any content (s)he chooses to consume. In addition, a new breed of customizable meta-content portal has emerged, which specifically targets the entertainment industry. Examples of such portals include Rotten Tomatoes[46] and IMDB[47]. However, these services today are typically accessed via Web portals thereby limiting the interactions and access to the information for a user in a non-PC environment.

MediaCaddy is a recommendation and aggregation service built around a self-learning engine, which analyzes a click stream generated by user's interaction and actions with meta-content displayed through a UI. This meta-content (Music /Movies/ TV reviews/ article/ synopsis/ production notes) is accessed from multiple Internet sources

and structured as an ontology using a semantic inferencing platform. Figure 6 illustrates the conceptual model of MediaCaddy

This provides multiple benefits, both allowing for a uniform mechanism for aggregating disparate sources of content, and on the other hand, also allowing for complex queries to be executed in a timely and accurate manner. The platform allows this information to be accessed via Web Services APIs, making integration simpler with multiple devices and UI formats. Another feature that sets MediaCaddy apart is its ability to achieve a high level of personalization by analyzing content consumption behaviour in the user's personal Movie/Music Domain and his or her social network and using this information to generate music and movie recommendations.

Prominent Applications

Finally we list some excellent illustrations of the applications of Semantic Web technology, as selected from a worldwide competition[48] which offers participants the opportunity to show the best of the art.

- Multimedia e-culture demonstrator, is to demonstrate how novel semantic-Web and presentation technologies can be deployed to provide better indexing and search support within large virtual collections of cultural heritage resources, 1st Prize 2006, http://e-culture.multimedian.nl/demo/search
- CONFOTO, Essen, Germany. CONFOTO is an online service which facilitates browsing, annotating and re-purposing of photo, conference, and people descriptions. 1st Prize 2005: http://www.confoto.org/
- FungalWeb, Concordia University, Canada. "Ontology, the Semantic Web, Intelligent Systems for Fungal Genomics".2nd Prize 2005: http://www.cs.concordia.ca/FungalWeb/
- Bibster – A semantics-based Bibliographic P2P system. http://bibster.semanticweb.org
- CS AKTive space – Semantic data integration. http://cs.aktivespace.org (Winner 2003 Semantic Web challenge)
- Flink: SemWeb for analysis of Social Networks. http://www.cs.vu.nl/~pmika (Winner 2004 Semantic Web challenge)
- Museum Finland: Sem. Web for cultural portal. http://museosuomi.cs.helsinki.fi (2nd prize 2004 Semantic Web challenge)
- Also see Applications and Demos at W3C SWG BPD. http://esw.w3.org/mt/esw/archives/cat_applications_and_demos.html

CONCLUSION AND FUTURE TRENDS

In 2000, three prominent authors in the Semantic Web activity expounded in a seminal Scientific American paper (Berners-Lee T. et al., 2001) the Semantic Web vision. In the time since then, the Semantic Web has become real. Currently, there are hundreds of millions of RDF triples, on tens of thousands of Web pages, and thousands of ontology pages have been published using RDF schema and OWL, with a growing level of industrial support. This very active support from industry is witnessed at worldwide key conference[49] very focused on the applications of the Semantic Web Technology. Indeed, about 100 talks on industry experience in testing and deploying the technology and about 30 technology showcases and 10 workshops or tutorials were actively followed by hundreds of attendees (300 at STC 05, 700 at STC 06, 730 at STC 07 and 210 at the 1st ESTC 2007) mostly from the industry.

However, the Semantic Web is still in its early days and there are many exciting innovations on the horizon.

A keynote speech[50] foresaw (Hendler J. & Lassila O., 2006) a "re-birth of AI" (or the end of the AI-winter) thanks to big-AI applications (Deep Blue, Mars Rover, Deep Space 1, Sachem-Usinor) and Web AI (IR, NLP, Machine Learning, Services, Grid, Agents, social nets) needed due to the tremendous amount of data continuously available on the Web and the emergence of new ways of doing things (loose coupling of distributed applications or services, new business models, etc.).

From 2000 to 2007, three major endeavours have paved the way for the future: DARPA, W3C and EU IST where DARPA and EU IST funded projects particularly were clearly forces towards production of recommendations to W3C (RDF-S, OWL, Rules, …), for fast adoption in industry. In the meantime, 2003 saw early government adoption and emerging corporate interest, in 2005 the emergence of commercial tools, lots of open source software and even good progress in the problem of scalability (tractable reasoning over 10 million triples has already been claimed by Oracle[51]). So, *significant corporate activity is clearly noticeable today compared to 7 years ago*:

- Semantic (Web) technology companies are starting and growing: Cerebra, Siderean, SandPiper, SiberLogic, Ontology Works, Intellidimension, Intellisophic, TopQuadrant, Data Grid, Software AG, OntoText, Autonomy, FAST, Exalead, iSoco, Jouve, Mondeca, Sirma, Pertim, Biovista, etc.
- Semantic Web technology appears in the strategic plans of large corporations: Nokia, SAP AG, IBM, HP, Adobe, Cisco, Oracle, Sun, Vodaphone, Renault, AGFA, Cable and Wireless, Novartis, JP Morgan Chase Bank, Wells Fargo, Swiss Life, Boeing, Audi, Elsevier etc.
- Outreach to industry is also demonstrated through a newly launched W3C initiative (2007): "Semantic Web Education and Outreach Interest Group - Case Studies and Use Cases". Case studies include descriptions of systems that have been deployed within an organization, and are now being used within a production environment[52].
- Government projects in and across agencies: US, EU, Japan, Korea, China, FAO, etc.
- Life sciences/pharma is an increasingly important market, e.g. the Health Care and Life Sciences Interest Group at W3C[53]
- Many open source tools are available: Kowari, RDFLib, Jena, Sesame, Protégé, SWOOP, Wilbur etc. see the W3C SWAD initiative[54]
- Related technologies are taking off: Google Base (taxonomies for resource descriptions), Web 2.0 initiatives for mash-up applications, etc.

- Enterprise Web 2.0 can be the catalyst for a more collaborative business environment[55]. The BBC World Service had done a lot of work to try to create a more collaborative work environment. As it turned out, the BBC's internal forums, which only cost the company about 200 pounds, got the company to be more collaborative than the more formal initiatives did.

Then, it is also witnessed that adding a few semantics to current Web applications - meaning "not harnessing the full picture at once but step by step" – gives a significant push in applications: richer metadata, data harvesting and visualization, Web-based social network, digital asset management, scientific portals, tools for developers, and so gradually closing the semantic gap.

What has been Learned from AI?

- Cross-breeding with AI succeeded, stand-alone AI did not!
- Tools are hard to sell (needed too much skill and education)
- Reasoners are a means, not an end (a key component but not the end)
- Knowledge engineering bottleneck (Ontology development and management)

What has been Learned from the Web?

- The magic word: Distribute, interconnect and Share Roadmap!
- PC era [1980-1990] – autonomous computing and Ethernet
- Internet 1st generation [1990-2000] - Web 1.0), "read-only Web", Web sites and Companies' portals
- Social Networks [2000-2010] - Web 2.0, corporate Knowledge Management and social nets

- Semantic Web [2007 – 2020] - Web 3.0 – merging social net with automated Semantic Web
- Web OS [2020-2030] - Web 4.0

However, it must be clear that there are still **key technology locks** identified today that needs academic research and R&D investments for a full uptake of the technology (Cuel et al., 2007):

- **Ontology and reasoning:**
  - **The development of medium size to large ontologies is a challenging task:** e.g. modelling of business domains, unified and industry-grade methodology, best practices and guidelines, re-use of existing ontologies and simple tools to use.
  - **Automated update of ontologies and knowledge bases:** e.g. ontology maintenance by extraction of new knowledge facts and concept reasoning (abduction, learning), knowledge base population from legacy databases, data warehouse and data on the Web, consistency checking.
  - **Ontologies interoperability:** Overcome inevitable heterogeneity in spite of KR standards via e.g. automated mapping (concepts, properties, rules, graphs, …) in particular in the open context of the Web and the social Web (Web 2.0).
  - **Scalability:** Be capable to process business and real applications needs e.g. approximate reasoning, reasoning on inconsistent ontologies, ontology and reasoning modularization, distribution and cooperation.
  - **KR expressivity and tractability trade-off:** Maintaining the just needed KR expressivity to avoid tractability and decidability issues, there are many open problems in this area. Look for reasoning algorithm optimizations (!), measure experimental complexity and lastly may be relax the completeness property.
  - **Rules - Logic Programming and KR:** Moving towards a deeper and broader automation of business process intra- and inter-enterprise require the addition of semantic rules technology.

e.g. Rules in communicating applications, Rules to describe / represent service process models, Rules for policies and contracting, etc. (see e.g. RuleML W3C[56])

- **Semantic Web Services and sevices oriented computing** (Papazoglou et al., 2006):
  - **Discovery:** Automated service discovery, reasoning on non functional parameters like QoS and cost.
  - **Composition:** Business and industrial processes automated. I/O signature and behavioural composition (Inputs, Outputs, pre-conditions, effects and message protocols). Robustness in a versatile and inconsistent context. Composition driven by high level business needs (Business Rules).
  - **Management:** Web services supervision, self-healing service, self-optimizing service, self-configuring service, self-protecting service.
  - **Design tools:** Unified design principles for engineering service applications, associating a service design methodology with standard software development and business process modelling techniques, service governance, test and proof checks.
  - **Pilots and standard platforms.** The most prominent (2007):

  WSMX[57] (Fensel et al., 2005) probably the most complete architecture to date, experimented on business cases and in transfer to OASIS

  SAWSDL[58]: some running prototypes, industrial pilots and transfer to W3C (Sivashanmugam, 2003) (METEOR-S[59])

  OWL-S[60] (Ankolenkar, 2004) (OWL-S MX[61])

  SWSF[62]

  In summary, the Semantic Web is "an interoperability technology", "a architecture for interconnected communities and vocabularies" and "a set of interoperable standards for knowledge exchange"[63]. Firstly, layman users facing the unmanageable growth of data and information, and secondly companies facing the huge amounts and volatility of data, applications and services, all require urgently automated means that master this growing complexity. In such de-facto context, no individual is able to identify knowledge patterns in their heads, no company (and employees!) is able to always shorter its products and service lifecycle and self adapt rapidly enough to survive.

The performance of semantic technologies clearly shows efficiency gain, effectiveness gain and strategic edge. Those facts are based on a survey[64] of about 200 business entities engaged in semantic technology R&D for development of products and services to deliver solutions and also recently witnesses at the ESTC 2007 industry oriented major event. From an academic and technological viewpoint, most things that have been predicted have happened - the semantic chasm is closing. Some things happened faster than anticipated like – triple store scaling, cooperation tools, enhanced SOA middleware, meta-data tagging tools, semantically-aware development environments and last but not the least, the unpredicted huge rise of Web 2.0 user-oriented technology[65] – and others still need to be realized: ontologies are there (but very little interlinking and the need is huge especially in the healthcare domain), public information sources and public re-usable ontologies (as RDF, OWL, etc.), standard Rules (SWRL, WSML, etc.) and Logic Programming integration to Ontology languages, scalable and robust reasoners, technology transparency for the final user and the practitioners, and these technologies must mature into enterprise-class products, etc.

Pervasive computing is just emerging.

ACKNOWLEDGMENT

This work has been possible thanks to the three large European consortia REWERSE, Knowledge Web and aceMedia. Acknowledgements are also for the large gathering of international conferences mixing research results and prospects from academia and industry: ESWC, ISWC, ASWC, ICWS, WWW, STC etc. Lastly, credits go also directly to the numerous people, in research labs in academia and in industry who are contributing so strongly to make semantic technology a real momentum in industry.

IST-REWERSE is a NoE supported by the European Commission under contract FP6-506779 http://rewerse.net

IST-Knowledge Web is a NoE supported by the European Commission under contract FP6-507482 http://knowledgeweb.semanticweb.org

IST-aceMedia is an Integrated Project supported by the European Commission under contract FP6-001765. http://www.acemedia.org

REFERENCES

Ankolenkar A., Paolucci M., Srinivasan N., and Sycara K., (2004). *The owl services coalition, owl-s 1.1 beta release*. Technical report, July 2004.

Antoniou, G., Baldoni, M., Baroglio, C., Baumgartner, R., Bry, F., & Eiter, T. (2004). Reasoning Methods for Personalization on the Semantic Web. *Annals of Mathematics . Computing & Telefinformatics, 2*(1), 1–24.

Barillot, C., Amsaleg, L., Aubry, F., Bazin, J.-P., Benali, H., & Cointepas, Y. (2003). Neurobase: Management of distributed knowledge and data bases in neuroimaging. [New-York, NY.]. *Human Brain Mapping, 19*, 726–726.

Benatallah, B., Hacid, M. S., Léger, A., Rey, C., & Toumani, F. (2005). On automating Web services discovery. *The VLDB Journal, 14*(1), 84–96. doi:10.1007/s00778-003-0117-x

Berardi, D., Calvanese, D., De Giacomo, G., Lenzerini, M., & Mecella, M. (2005). Automatic Service Composition based on Behavioral Descriptions. *International Journal of Cooperative Information Systems, 14*(4), 333–376. doi:10.1142/S0218843005001201

Berners-Lee, T., Hendler, J., Lassila, O. (2001). The Semantic Web. *Scientific American Journal* (May 2001).

Billig A. and Sandkuhl K. (2002). Match-making based on semantic nets: The xml-based approach of baseweb. *1st workshop on XML-Technologien fur das Semantic Web*, 39–51.

Bonifacio, M., & Molani, A. (2005). Managing Knowledge needs at Trenitalia. *Proceedings of the Second European Semantic Web Conference* ESWC 2005, Industry Forum proceedings.

Brunschweig, B., & Rainaud, J. F. (2005). Semantic Web applications for the Petroleum industry. *Proceedings of the 2nd European Semantic Web Conference,* ESWC 2005 Industry Forum

Cardoso, J., & Sheth, A. (2003). Semantic e-workflow composition. [Technical description of the composition of a workflow.]. *Journal of Intelligent Information Systems, 21*(3), 191–225. doi:10.1023/A:1025542915514

Chan, M. K. S., Judith, B., & Luciano, B. (2006). *Survey and Comparison of Planning Techniques for Web Services Composition.* Technical Report.

Charlet J., Cordonnier E., Gibaud B. (2002). Interopérabilité en médecine: quand le contenu interroge le contenant et l'organisation. *Revue Information, interaction, intelligence, 2*(2), 37-62.

Cordonnier, E., Croci, S., Laurent, J.-F., & Gibaud, B. (2003). Interoperability and Medical Communication Using "Patient Envelope"-Based Secure Messaging. *Medical Informatics Europe Congress, 95,* 230–235.

Cuel R., Deleteil A., Louis V., Rizzi C. (2008). *Knowledge Web Technology Roadmap: The Technology Roadmap of the Semantic Web.* To appear early 2008.

Dasiopoulou, S., Saathoof, C., Mylonas, Ph., Avrithis, Y., Kompatsiaris, Y., & Staab, S. (2007). Introducing Context and Reasoning in Visual Content Analysis: An Ontology-based Framework. In Paola Hobson, Ioannis Kompatsiaris (Editors), *Semantic Multimedia and Ontologies: Theories and Applications.* Springer-Verlag.

Description Logics for Information Integration. (2002). *Computational Logic: Logic Programming and Beyond.* LNCS; Vol. 2408, pp 41 – 60. London, UK: Springer-Verlag.

Dhamankar, R., Lee, Y., Doan, A., Halevy, A., & Domingos, P. (2004). iMAP: Discovering complex semantic matches between database schemas. *Proceedings of the 2004 ACM SIGMOD international conference on Management of data,* pages 383 – 394.

Di Noia, T., Di Sciascio, E., Donini, F. M., & Mongiello, M. (2003). A system for principled matchmaking in an electronic marketplace. *Proceedings of the 12th international conference on World Wide Web,* WWW 2003, 321–330.

Do, H. H., & Rahm, E. (2002). COMA - a system for flexible combination of schema matching approaches. In *Proceedings of Very Large Databases* VLDB 2002, 610–621.

Dou, D., McDermott, D., & Qi, P. (2005). Ontology translation on the Semantic Web. *Journal on Data Semantics, 3360,* 35–57.

Ehrig, M., & Staab, S. (2004). QOM: Quick ontology mapping. *Third International Semantic Web Conference,* ISWC 2004, LNCS 3298, 683–697.

Euzenat, J., & Shvaiko, P. (2007). *Ontology Matching.* Springer-Verlag.

Euzenat, J., & Valtchev, P. (2004). Similarity-based ontology alignment in OWL-lite. *Proceedings of European Conference on Artificial Intelligence* ECAI 2004, 333–337.

Fensel, D., Kifer, M., de Bruijn, J., Domingue, J. (2005). *Web service modeling ontology (wsmo) submission*. w3c member submission.

Garg, S., Goswami, A., Huylebroeck, J., Jaganathan, S., & Mullan, P. (2005). MediaCaddy - Semantic Web Based On-Demand Content Navigation System for Entertainment. *Proceedings of the 4th International Semantic Web Conference*, ISWC 2005. LNCS 3729, 858 – 871.

Giunchiglia, F., & Shvaiko, P. (2003). Semantic matching. *Knowledge Engineering Review Journal*, *18*(3), 265–280. doi:10.1017/S0269888904000074

Giunchiglia, F., Shvaiko, P., & Yatskevich, M. (2004). S-Match: an algorithm and an implementation of semantic matching. In *Proceedings of the First European Semantic Web Symposium*, ESWS2004, LNCS 3053, 61–75.

Guarino, N., Masolo, C., & Vetere, G. (1999, May). OntoSeek: Content-Based Access to the Web. *IEEE Intelligent Systems*, *14*(3), 70–80. doi:10.1109/5254.769887

Haarslev, V., Moller, R., & Wessel, M. (1999-2007). *RACER: Semantic middleware for industrial projects based on RDF/OWL, a W3C Standard*.

Halevy, A. (2001). Answering Queries Using Views: A Survey. *The VLDB Journal*, *10*(Issue 4). doi:10.1007/s007780100054

Halevy, A., Rajaraman, A., & Ordille, J. (2006). Data Integration: The Teenage Years. 10-year best paper award. *VLDB*.

Hasselwanter, T., Kotinurmi, P., Moran, M., Vitvar, T., & Zaremba, M. (2006). WSMX: a Semantic Service Oriented Middleware for B2B Integration. In *Proceedings of the 4th International Conference on Service Oriented Computing*, Springer-Verlag LNCS series, Chicago, USA.

Heinecke, J., & Cozannet, A. (2003). Ontology-Driven Information Retrieval. a proposal for multilingual user requests. *Workshop on Ontological Knowledge and Linguistic Coding at the 25th annual meeting of the German Linguistics*, Feb. 26-28, 2003.

Hibbard, J. (1997). Knowledge management-knowing what we know. *Information Week* (October 20).

Hull R., (1997), Managing Semantic Heterogeneity in Databases: A Theoretical Perspective, Tutorial at *PODS 1997*.

Hull, R., & Su, J. (2005). Tools for composite Web services: A short Overview. *SIGMOD Record*, *34*, 2. doi:10.1145/1083784.1083807

Lehtola, A., Heinecke, J., & Bounsaythip, C. (2003). Intelligent Human Language Query Processing in mkbeem. Workshop on Ontologies and Multilinguality in User Interface, in the *Proceedings of Human Computer Interface International*, HCII 2003, 4, 750-754.

McGuinness, D. L., Fikes, R., Rice, J., & Wilder, S. (2000). An environment for merging and testing large ontologies. Proceedings of the *Seventh International Conference on Principles of Knowledge Representation and Reasoning* (KR2000), Breckenridge, Colorado, 483–493.

McIlraith, S. A., Son, T. C., & Zeng, H. (2001). Semantic Web services. *IEEE Intelligent Systems . Special Issue on the Semantic Web*, *16*, 46–53.

Mena, E., Kashyap, V., Sheth, A., & Illarramendi, A. (1996). Observer: An approach for query processing in global information systems based on interoperability between pre-existing ontologies. *Proceedings of the First International Conference on Cooperative Information Systems* CoopIS'96, 14–25.

Nixon, L., Mochol, M., Léger, A., Paulus, F., Rocuet, L., Bonifacio, M., et al. (2004). *Prototypical Business Use Cases*. (Technical report Deliverable 1.1.2), Knowledge Web IST-NoE.

Norheim, D., & Fjellheim, R. (2006). Knowledge management in the petroleum industry. *Proceedings of the 3rd European Semantic Web Conference*, ESWC 2006 Industry Forum.

Papazoglou M., Traverso P., Dustdar S. and Leymann F. (2006). *Service-oriented computing research roadmap*. Technical report.

Petrash, G. (1996). Managing knowledge assets for value. *Proceedings of the Knowledge-Based Leadership Conference*, Linkage Inc., Boston, MA, October 1996.

Petridis, K., Bloehdorn, S., Saathoff, C., Simou, N., Dasiopoulou, S., Tzouvaras, V., et al. (2006). Knowledge Representation and Semantic Annotation of Multimedia Content. *IEEE Proceedings on Vision Image and Signal Processing, Special issue on Knowledge-Based Digital Media Processing*, Vol. 153, No. 3, pp. 255-262, June 2006.

Petrini, J., & Risch, T. (2004). Processing queries over RDF views of wrapped relational databases. In *Proceedings of the 1st International workshop on Wrapper Techniques for Legacy Systems*, WRAP 2004, Delft, Holland, 2004.

Pistore, M., Roberti, P., & Traverso, P. (2005). Process-Level Composition of Executable Web Services: "On-thefly" Versus "Once-for-all" Composition. The Semantic Web: Research and Applications. *Proceedings of ESWC 2005*, Heraklion, Crete, Greece. LNCS 3532, Springer Verlag.

Preguica, N., Shapiro, M., & Matheson, C. 2003). Semantics-based reconciliation for collaborative and mobile environments. In *Proccedings of the Eleventh International Conference on Cooperative Information Systems,* CoopIS 2003, LNCS 2888, 38-55.

Rahm, E., & Bernstein, P. (2001, Dec.). A survey of approaches to automatic schema matching. *Very Large Databases Journal, 10*(4), 334–350. doi:10.1007/s007780100057

Roman, D., Keller, U., Lausen, H., de Bruijn, J., Lara, R., & Stollberg, M. (2005). Web Service Modeling Ontology . *Applied Ontology Journal, 1*(1), 77–106.

Rosenbloom ST, Miller RA, Johnson KB. (2006). Interface terminologies: facilitating direct entry of clinical data into electronic health record systems. *Journal of the American Medical Informatics Association.*

Semantic Web Case Studies and Best Practices for eBusiness (SWCASE). At *ISWC2005*, online version

Shvaiko, P., & Euzenat, J. (2005). A survey of schema-based matching approaches. [JoDS]. *Journal on Data Semantics, 4*, 146–171. doi:10.1007/11603412_5

Shvaiko, P., Giunchiglia, F., Pinheiro da Silva, P., & McGuinness, D. L. (2005). Web explanations for semantic heterogeneity discovery. In *Proceedings of the Second European Semantic Web Conference*, ESWC 2005, 303-317.

Shvaiko, P., Léger, A., Paulus, F., Rocuet, L., Nixon, L., Mochol, M., et al. (2004). *Knowledge Processing Requirements Analysis*. Technical report Deliverable D 1.1.3, Knowledge Web IST-NoE.

Spackman, K. A., Dionne, R., Mays, E., & Weis, J. Role grouping as an Extension to the Description Logic of Ontylog Motivated by Concept Modeling in SNOMED. *Proceedings of the AMIA Annual Symposium 2002*, San Antonio, Texas, p. 712-6, November, 9-13, 2002.

Stamou, G., & Kollias, S. (2005), *Multimedia Content and the Semantic Web: Standards, Methods and Tools*. Wiley.

Stamou, G., van Ossenbruggen, J., Pan, J., & Schreiber, G. (2006). Multimedia annotations on the Semantic Web. *IEEE MultiMedia, 13*(1), 86–90. doi:10.1109/MMUL.2006.15

Stoilos, G., Stamou, G., Tzouvaras, V., Pan, J. Z., & Horrocks, I. (2005). A Fuzzy Description Logic for Multimedia Knowledge Representation. In *Proc. of the International Workshop on Multimedia and the Semantic Web*, pp 12-19, ESWC 2005, Heraklion, Grece, June 2005.

Traverso, P., & Pistore, M. (2004). Automated composition of Semantic Web services into executable processes. In *Proceedings of the Third International Semantic Web Conference,* ISWC 2004, 380–394, 2004.

Velegrakis, Y., Miller, R. J., & Mylopoulos, J. (2005). Representing and querying data transformations. *Proceedings of the 21st International Conference on Data Engineering* ICDE 2005, 81-92.

Vitvar, T. Zaremba M., Moran M., Haller A., Kotinurmi P. (2007b). Semantic SOA to Promote Integration of Heterogeneous B2B Services. *The 4th IEEE Conference on Enterprise Computing, E-Commerce and E-Services* (EEE07), IEEE Computer Society, July, 2007, Tokyo, Japan.

Vitvar, T., Zaremba, M., & Moran, M. (2007a). Dynamic Service Discovery through Meta-Interactions with Service Providers. In *Proceedings of the 4th European Semantic Web Conference* (ESWC2007), Springer-Verlag LNCS series, Innsbruck, Austria.

Wiederhold, G. (1992). Mediators in the architecture of future information systems. *IEEE Computer, 25*(3), 38–49.

Wiig, K. (1997). Knowledge management: where did it come from and where will it go? *Journal of Expert Systems with Applications, 13*(1), 1–14. doi:10.1016/S0957-4174(97)00018-3

Zhong, J., Zhu, H., Li, J., & Yu, Y. (2002). Conceptual graph matching for semantic search. In *Proceedings of the 10th International Conference on Computational Science,* 2393 (2002), 92-106

Zyl, J., & Corbett, D. (2000). A framework for Comparing the use of a Linguistic Ontology in an Application. *Workshop Applications of Ontologies and Problem-solving Methods,* ECAI'2000, Berlin Germany, August, 2000.

ADDITIONAL READINGS

W3C http://www.w3.org/2001/sw/

Annual Semantic Web applications challenge: http://challenge.semanticweb.org

Journal of Web semantics (Elsevier)

The Semantic Web: research and Applications LNCS series: LNCS 2342 (ISWC 2002), LNCS 2870 (ISWC 2003), LNCS 3053 (ESWS 2004), LNCS 3298 (ISWC 2004), LNCS 3532 (ESWS 2005), LNCS 4011 (ESWC 2006), LNCS4273 (ISWC 2006), LNCS 4519 (ESWC 2007), LNCS 4825 (ISWC 2007).

ENDNOTES

[1] http://www.web2con.com
[2] http://www.ontoweb.org
[3] http://Knowledge Web.semanticweb.org
[4] http://rewerse.net
[5] http://cordis.europa.eu/fp7/home_en.html
[6] Knowledge Web Deliverable D 1.1.4v3 http://knowledgeweb.semanticweb.org/ semanticportal/deliverables/D1.1.4v3.pdf
[7] http://knowledgeweb.semanticweb.org/ o2i/
[8] http://protege.stanford.edu/index.html
[9] http://oaei.ontologymatching.org/2007/
[10] http://www.neon-project.org

[11] http://www.ontologymatching.org/

[12] http://www.acemedia.org

[13] http://www.nlm.nih.gov/research/umls/umlsmain.html

[14] http://us.expasy.org/sprot/

[15] http://obo.sourceforge.net/main.html

[16] http://www.ncbi.nlm.nih.gov/Genbank/index.html

[17] http://www.ncbi.nlm.nih.gov/sites/entrez

[18] http://www.connectingforhealth.nhs.uk/

[19] http://www.edisante.org/

[20] http://www.etiam.com/

[21] http://cen.iso.org/ and http://www.tc251w-giv.nhs.uk/

[22] http://www.hl7.org/

[23] http://www.d-m-p.org/docs/EnglishVersion-DMP.pdf

[24] http://www.hl7.org/Special/Committees/structure/index.cfm#Mission

[25] http://www.cocoon-health.com

[26] http://www.srdc.metu.edu.tr/webpage/projects/artemis/index.html

[27] http://www.simdat.org

[28] Some of the well-known definitions of KM include: (Wiig 1997) " Knowledge management is the systematic, explicit, and deliberate building, renewal and application of knowledge to maximize an enterprise's knowledge related effectiveness and returns from its knowledge assets"; (Hibbard 1997) "Knowledge management is the process of capturing a company's collective expertise wherever it resides in databases, on paper, or in people's heads and distributing it to wherever it can help produce the biggest payoff"; (Pettrash 1996) "KM is getting the right knowledge to the right people at the right time so they can make the best decision".

[29] http://www.cenorm.be/cenorm/index.htm

[30] http://www.knowledgeboard.com

[31] Semantic Web, Use Cases and Challenges at EADS, http://www.eswc2006.org Industry Forum.

[32] See for example in the Petroleum industry (Nordheim D. et al., 2005)

[33] See for example Use of Ontology for production of access systems on Legislation, Jurisprudence and Comments (Delahousse J. et al., 2006) http://www.eswc2006.org/industry.html

[34] E.g. see the EU Integrated project "DIP Data, Information, and Process Integration with Semantic Web Services", http://dip.semanticweb.org/

[35] agentcities RTD project http://www.agentcities.org/EURTD/

[36] Semantic Business Automation, SAP, Germany http://www.eswc2006.org Industry Forum

[37] http://sws-challenge.org/2006/submission/deri-submission-discovery-phase3/ http://sws-challenge.org/2006/submission/deri-submisson-mediation v.1/ http://sws-challenge.org/2006/submission/deri-submisson-mediation v.2/

[38] http://events.deri.at/sercomp2007/

[39] Semantically Enabled Knowledge Technologies http://www.sekt-project.com/

[40] http://www.acemedia.org

[41] http://www.w3.org/2005/Incubator/mmsem/

[42] http://www.kpace-noe.net

[43] http://www.x-media-project.org

[44] http://www.boemie.org

[45] http://www.mesh-ip.eu

[46] http://www.rottentomatoes.com

[47] http://www.imdb.com/

[48] Annual Semantic Web applications challenge: http://challenge.semanticweb.org

[49] Semantic Technology Conference http://www.semantic-conference.com/; European Semantic Technology Conference http://www.estc2007.com/

[50] SemWeb@5: Current status and Future Promise of the Semantic Web, James Hendler, Ora Lassila, STC 2006, 7 March 2006, San José, USA

[51]   Oracle Database 10g using RDF natively supported by the 10g Enterprise Edition

[52]   http://www.w3.org/2001/sw/sweo/public/UseCases/

[53]   http://www.w3.org/2001/sw/hcls/

[54]   Semantic Web Advanced Development for Europe http://www.w3.org/2001/sw/Europe/

[55]   Forester, Erica Driver, October 2007

[56]   http://www.w3.org/2005/rules/wg/wiki/RuleML

[57]   http://www.oasis-open.org/committees/semantic-ex/faq.php, http://www.wsmx.org http://sourceforge.net/projects/wsmx

[58]   http://www.w3.org/TR/sawsdl/

[59]   http://lsdis.cs.uga.edu/projects/meteor-s/

[60]   http://www.w3.org/Submission/OWL-S/

[61]   http://www-ags.dfki.uni-sb.de/~klusch/owls-mx/index.html

[62]   http://www.w3.org/Submission/SWSF/

[63]   ESTC 2007 Keynote speech from Susie Stephens (Oracle)

[64]   Semantic Wave 2006, Part-1 Mills Davis

[65]   Web 2.0 and its related phenomena becomes increasingly interesting for businesses.

In January 2007 a research programme conducted by the Economist Intelligence Unit and sponsored by FAST gauged the relevance of Web 2.0 to large corporations throughout the world and across a wide range of industries. The research, which consisted of an online survey plus follow-up interviews with senior executives at large public corporations, found that Web 2.0 now has significant implications for big business across a wide range industry sectors. By 2006, and even earlier at some companies, the world's multinationals began to see many Web 2.0 technologies as corporate tools. In fact, according to the survey, 31% of companies think that use of the Web as a platform for sharing and collaboration will affect all parts of their business (Economist Intelligence Unit (2007): Serious business. Web 2.0. goes corporate. A report from the EIU sponsored by FAST. Also to mention two majors initiatives: MySpace with 300 million users (Dec 2007) http://www.myspace.com and Facebook with 60 millions users (Nov 2007) http://www.facebook.com

This work was previously published in Semantic Web for Business: Cases and Applications, edited by R. García, pp. 1-29, copyright 2009 by Information Science Reference (an imprint of IGI Global).

Chapter 4.3

A Strategic Framework for Integrating Web 2.0 into the Marketing Mix

Samantha C. Bryant
Philip Morris, USA

ABSTRACT

Marketing strategy set by the marketing mix has remained fundamentally the same through years of other business disciplines being significantly disrupted by emerging technologies. Emerging Web 2.0 technologies such as wikis, blogs, YouTube, and virtual worlds are not only affecting how companies tactically approach marketing, but also their marketing strategies. This chapter will explore the impact of Web 2.0 technologies on marketing and brand management and how companies can leverage these technologies to strengthen relationships between their brands and consumers through a Web 2.0 marketing mix. This new Web 2.0 marketing mix supplements the traditional four-p marketing mix (price, product, promotion, and placement) with a new "p" lens: participation. The focus of this analysis is on B2C marketing of products and services only.

INTRODUCTION

Marketing has gone through a number of evolutions and technology has revolutionized a number of disciplines. New generations of consumers are consuming media in a different fashion than before. Gone are the days of the 30-second Super Bowl advertisements and here are the days of Facebook, Flickr, and MySpace. Collaborating and participating on the Internet is the preferred entertainment.

Web 2.0 technologies such as wikis, blogs, YouTube, and *Second Life* are changing the behavior of consumers like never before.

- Empowering them with knowledge from a myriad of sources
- Enabling them to self-organize around brands and share their passion (or dissatisfaction) for a brand
- Enabling them to act as marketers of brands

Marketing strategy set by the marketing mix has remained fundamentally the same through years of other business disciplines being significantly disrupted by emerging technologies. However, Web

DOI: 10.4018/978-1-60566-122-3.ch003

2.0 is not only affecting how companies tactically approach marketing, but also their marketing strategies.

This chapter will explore the impact of Web 2.0 technologies on marketing and brand management and how companies can leverage these technologies to strengthen relationships between their brands and consumers through a Web 2.0 marketing mix. The focus of this analysis is on business-to-consumer (B2C) marketing of products and services only.

BACKGROUND: WEB 2.0 TECHNOLOGIES AND MARKETING

Web 2.0 technologies, also known as social software technologies, are a second generation of Web-based communities and services that facilitate collaboration and sharing between users. Web 2.0 does not refer to an update to any technical specifications of the Web but to changes in the way it is being used. These technologies are built on an architecture of participation ("Web 2.0," 2007).

Little has been published about Web 2.0 technologies, particularly about their effect on marketing. In 2004, *High Intensity Marketing* explored the effects of a new emerging stream of networked technologies on marketing. However, these technologies were the mere beginning of what was to explode a few years later as Web 2.0. (Mootee, 2004). *Wikinomics: How Mass Collaboration Changes Everything* discussed Web 2.0 technologies, with examples of companies' use to interact with their consumers and improve their product offerings (Tapscott & Williams, 2006). The American Marketing Association (AMA) is one of the largest professional organizations for marketers and is trusted to provide relevant marketing information to experienced marketers. One channel through which it educates its members is conferences. The AMA has just begun to acknowledge how Web 2.0 is disrupting traditional

marketing theory. In 2008, the AMA hosted its first conferences on Web 2.0 (social media) and marketing. The conferences focused on how companies need to recognize the impact social media has on their brands and how they can benefit from using social media as new marketing tools (American Marketing Association, 2007a).

Not surprisingly, the most written about this relationship between Web 2.0 technologies and marketing has been via Web 2.0 technologies themselves, particularly blogs. Blogs, also known as weblogs, are shared online journals or diaries where people can post entries via the Web. Live-Journal, Blogger, and WordPress are examples of online blog services where users can post their thoughts with an emphasis on user interaction within the community. LiveJournal is one of the most popular, with currently over 14 million journals and communities. Numerous individuals blog daily about what they are witnessing and hearing about in the marketing world. These same individuals then harness the power of Web 2.0 by linking to each other's blogs and commenting on the author's thoughts. What results is insightful speculation about trends emerging as a result of Web 2.0's impact on marketing and brand management.

THE TRADITIONAL MARKETING MIX (FOUR *P*S)

With such revolutionary technologies disrupting consumers' lives, many businesses wonder what the implication is to the marketing of their products and brands.

The marketing mix, invented in the 1950s, is the mix of controllable marketing variables that a company uses to pursue the desired level of sales in the target market. The most common model of these factors is the four-factor classification called the four *P*s. Optimization of the marketing mix is achieved by assigning the amount of the marketing budget to be spent on each element of the marketing mix so as to maximize the total contribution to the firm (American Marketing Association, 2007b).

The four *P*s of the traditional marketing mix are product, pricing, promotion, and placement.

- **Product:** The product aspects of marketing deal with the specifications of the actual goods or services, and how it relates to the user's needs and wants. Generally, this also includes supporting elements such as warranties, guarantees, and support.
- **Pricing:** Pricing refers to the process of setting a price for a product, including discounts. The price need not be monetary; it can simply be what is exchanged for the product or services, such as time, energy, psychology, or attention.
- **Promotion:** Promotion includes advertising, sales promotion, public relations, and personal selling, and refers to the various methods of promoting the product, brand, or company.
- **Placement:** Placement or distribution refers to how the product gets to the customer, for example, point-of-sale placement or retailing. This *p* is also the place, referring to the channel by which a product or service is sold (e.g., online vs. retail), to which geographic region or industry, and to which segment (young adults, families, professionals; American Marketing Association, 2007b).

While effective for setting marketing strategy since its creation, the traditional marketing mix lacks relevancy when it comes to Web 2.0. A new term coined Marketing 2.0 is being used to describe the impact Web 2.0 has had on the discipline of marketing. Companies are finding many uses of Web 2.0 technologies to successfully connect with their consumers. These are discussed in the next section.

ISSUES AND EXAMPLES: THE EFFECT OF WEB 2.0 TECHNOLOGIES ON MARKETING AND BRAND MANAGEMENT

Numerous companies are integrating Web 2.0 technologies into their portfolio of marketing channels. Let us explore some Web 2.0 technologies and how they are affecting marketing strategy.

Second Life (Virtual World)

A virtual world is a computer-based simulated environment intended for its users to inhabit and interact, usually represented in the form of graphical representations of avatars. *Second Life* is an Internet-based virtual world developed by Linden Research, Inc. that is a massive multiplayer online game. *Second Life* enables its users to interact with each other through motional avatars, providing an advanced level of a social network service. Residents can explore, meet other residents, socialize, participate in individual and group activities, and create and trade property and services with one another.

Second Life has received much media attention regarding its benefits to the business world, most significantly from a cover story in *Business Week* in April 2006 that brought the virtual world to the attention of the masses, including a number of business leaders. The unique avatar population in the virtual world *Second Life* topped 7 million in 2007, with about 4 million distinct individuals participating in the online world (Rose, 2007).

Second Life has been recognized to have so much marketing potential that new companies have been established to assist companies with establishing their presence. For example, Millions of Us, an agency specializing in virtual worlds, designs and measures marketing programs for clients across a wide spectrum of platforms, especially *Second Life* (*Millions of Us*, 2007). Another company, The Electric Sheep Company, is the largest company in the world dedicated to designing experiences and add-on software for 3-D virtual worlds and has implemented major projects in both *Second Life* and There (another virtual world) technologies (Carter, 2007).

In addition to Millions of Us and The Electric Sheep, REPERES has formed as the first market research institute in *Second Life*. REPERES performs quantitative research by surveying avatars and qualitative research via private interviews with avatars. REPERES assists companies in the development of their products and offers in *Second Life* using the following:

- A panel of avatars that are representative of the overall population of *Second Life* in terms of nationality, gender, and age; this panel is called upon to address issues faced by brands seeking to establish themselves or develop an offer on *Second Life*
- An understanding of behaviors, innovations, and trends in *Second Life*
- A space for tests and cocreation projects to be tried and evaluated (*REPERES Second Life*, 2007)

In mid-2006, Scion sensed an opportunity to engage the technology and design-oriented communities of *Second Life*. Millions of Us and Scion collaborated to create Scion City, a *Second Life* island that housed the first virtual-world car dealership, representing the first time a major auto manufacturer created a presence in a virtual world. *Second Life* residents had the opportunity to not only purchase all three Scion models in the dealership, but also customize them to make them their own. This is consistent with Scion's approach to allow buyers to customize numerous aspects on real-world cars as well. This launch was such a success that Scion and Millions of Us have continued to work together to extend Scion's presence in *Second Life* through the following:

- The expansion of Scion City into a full-fledged urban environment where residents

are able to develop their own homes and businesses around the Scion dealership
- A simultaneous real and virtual launch of Scion's 2008 line at the Chicago Auto Show, meaning the new vehicle was launched in both *Second Life* and the real world at the same time
- Free expert-led customization classes in *Second Life* for consumers to learn how to personalize their virtual Scions; consumers can then showcase their designs in a Scion gallery in *Second Life*

The Scion xB launch received substantial media attention, and the buzz only grew with each subsequent release and event. Scion City has organically developed its own culture and loyal base of residents; one even created a MySpace page chronicling the evolution of this community, which shows the convergence and power of Web 2.0 technologies working together (*Millions of Us*, 2007).

While Scion was the first major automobile manufacturer with a significant presence in *Second Life*, numerous car companies have followed suit, including Pontiac, Mercedes, BMW, Nissan, and Toyota. Mercedes-Benz operates a car dealership that sells virtual cars and gives away branded racing suits to avatars. BMW even allows avatars the opportunity to test drive their vehicles.

At the 2007 Food Marketing Institute Supermarket Convention and Educational Exposition, Kraft Foods, Inc. unveiled more than 70 new products. Kraft chose to showcase these new offerings at a virtual supermarket in *Second Life*. Online, consumers and convention attendees could interact with Kraft's latest products and take part in online forums with Kraft experts. By having new products introduced online, consumers could see, "touch," and learn about the product before it was able to hit physical supermarket shelves (Kraft Foods, 2007).

In addition to Scion and Kraft, numerous other brands have built a presence in *Second Life*, including Adidas, Dell, Reebok, Sony BMG, Vodaphone, Sun, Sears, AOL, and Circuit City.

Reebok opened a virtual store that is an extension of its real-world RBK custom campaign. The store sells plain white sneakers by size and then features coloring machines for avatars to customize their shoes. Reebok grounds also contain a basketball court for avatars to play on.

Adidas owns an island that features branded video clips and billboards. Avatars who purchase Adidas shoes at the store may then bounce on a trampoline next to the store, demonstrating Adidas' shoes' bounciness.

Wired magazine reports that at least 50 major companies have a *Second Life* presence (Rose, 2007). YouTube is a video-sharing Web site where users can upload, view, and share video clips. So many brands and products have moved in that a YouTube video of brands in *Second Life* has been developed (Hayes, 2007).

Widgets

A widget is a small application that can be embedded on different Web pages. Widgets represent a new indirect marketing channel that enters consumers' lives via other Web 2.0 technologies and effectively promotes a brand, product, or service and generates awareness. A widget can be placed by users onto their personalized home pages, blogs, or other social networking pages. The widget is not intrusive advertising as a consumer must actively choose to add the widget.

The content on widgets can include blogs, live discussions, bookmarks to other Web sites, webcasts, video, games, and more. Companies are already capitalizing on widgets to market their brands, products, and services. On its traditional Web site, CBS lets consumers select widgets to embed in their social networking profiles or blogs to allow them (and everyone else who views their pages) to see advertising about the shows. For example, CBS launched a constantly updating rich-media widget to promote a new series.

Consumers can watch full episodes directly on the widget, get short mini clips of some of the stars, send the widget to a friend, link out to download ring tones, and more. The widget is designed to stand out on any site it is placed on ("CBS Mobile Launches Widget to Promote New Animated Series," 2007).

Sony promoted the film *Zathura* via widgets vs. a traditional online option like banner ads. Widgets enabled Sony to provide an application related to the movie and more importantly allowed users to interact with it. The widget was offered via Freewebs, a Web site that enables consumers to easily create their own Web sites at no cost. The 11 million Web site owners of Freewebs were able to embed the widget within their Web sites, and 11,000 Web sites took this up within 6 weeks. The widgets were viewed 600,000 times, and long after the original movie was out of theaters, thousands of widgets were still delivering content (Jaokar, 2006).

To enable PC users to experience a game offered on a different gaming system (Xbox), interactive agency AKQA created a weather widget to promote the *Microsoft Flight Simulator X* game for the Xbox. The widget allows users to virtually fly and find out the weather at any airport through a live feed from the National Weather Service. In the first 2 months, users downloaded the widget more than 150,000 times, spending an average of 23 minutes with the flight simulator, the agency says (Steel, 2006).

Numerous other companies are using widgets to market their products and services. Reebok created a widget that allows users to display customized pairs of RBK shoes for others to critique. Radio stations are offering widgets that stream a station's broadcast live. Airlines including American Airlines and Air France offer a ticket purchasing widget that allows a consumer to purchase a ticket through the widget without having to visit the airlines' Web sites. (Guiragossion, 2007).

Having a user add a widget to a personalized site that is visited by individuals who share similar interests is an effective way to share your marketing message with those who would find it most relevant. By adding the widget to his or her page, the user is showing endorsement for the brand, making others trust the brand.

Flickr (Tagging)

Tagging is the assignment of descriptive contextual tags to data, such as Web links stored with memorable words for easy future access. An example is Flickr, an online photo-management and -sharing application that allows users to collaboratively organize their photos by tagging them with descriptors that are searchable.

On Flickr, users can post pictures and tag them with words that describe the photo so others can search and view the photos. One quick search on Flickr reveals 88,923 pictures tagged with Coke, 4,650 with Crayola, 3,472 for Vitamin Water, and 32,367 for Heineken. One user posted a picture entitled "Just been to the Heineken Experience," described as a photo taken of the photographer's friend after an exciting trip to the Heineken Experience tourist attraction housed in the former Heineken brewery on the Stadhouderskade in Amsterdam. The administrator for a group entitled Got Heineken? contacted the user and invited them to join the Heine group. The Heine group invites members to post pictures of themselves holding a nice ice-cold Heineken or simply a photograph of anything related to Heineken. There is no official indication that Heineken is sponsoring it. Currently, the group has 363 photos posted by 212 members.

Eurostar, the United Kingdom's high-speed train, recognized that moving from Waterloo to St. Pancras International Station was a significant event in the brand's life. Eurostar set up an account with Flickr, EurostarForTomorrow, to promote the move to a new station. Eurostar posted a number of photos of the new station, and collected a number of photos other users have taken and saved them as favorites. This was an effective way to generate interest about the Eurostar brand and promote a significant event in the brand's history. It also recognized Eurostar consumers who had taken photos of Eurostar and shared them with others on Flickr (Terret, 2007).

Social Networks

Social networks are another Web 2.0 technology disrupting traditional marketing strategy. Social networks are Web sites designed to allow multiple users to publish content. Users are able to connect with those sharing similar interests and to exchange public or private messages. Facebook and MySpace are popular examples. Facebook is a social utility that connects users with other people by enabling them to publish profiles with text, photos, and videos; to review friends' profiles; and to join a network. MySpace allows users to create a community and share photos, journals, and interests with a growing network of mutual friends. Some marketers are making their own social networking sites such as Coke's mycokerewards.com and USA Network's Characters Welcome Web site.

For those brands that have not created their own social networking site, existing social networks enable consumers to create brands for themselves and assist others with creating their brands. At MySpace, brands have member profiles and make friends with other MySpace members. At Facebook, members join Facebook brand groups, just like they join Facebook fraternity or hobby groups, and can even display brand logos on their personal profiles.

Social branding may prove to be the ultimate product placement strategy. Companies can create a page for their brand or product. For example, Big Sky Brands, maker of Jones Soda, created its own page. In addition to company information and a list of retailers carrying the Big Sky Brand's products, its MySpace page contains a blog with discussions about the new Jones Activated Energy Boosters, the latest extension to the brand family.

The blog also talks about promotions, such as the Hot Topic and Jones Soda Carbonated Candy Summer Promo. Currently, Big Sky Brands has 495 friends who, in the comments section of the page, engage in discussions about how much they love the brand and which products are their favorites. The site also links to Big Sky Brands Music MySpace page, another site dedicated to empowering their consumers with Big Sky Brands' enthusiasm through the medium of music (Big Sky Brands, 2007).

In addition to this official Big Sky Brands Web site, a number of unofficial MySpace pages have been developed to support Jones Soda. The majority of these page owners have become MySpace friends of Big Sky Brands. In contrast, Swiffer WetJet also has a number of MySpace pages, but none are sponsored by Procter & Gamble.

Virtual worlds, widgets, tagging, and social networks are Web 2.0 technologies offering opportunities for companies to integrate them into their marketing mix. The next section provides a simple framework to help leverage Web 2.0 to supplement and enhance their marketing efforts.

SOLUTIONS AND RECOMMENDATIONS: A REVISED MARKETING MIX TO MAXIMIZE THE BENEFITS OF WEB 2.0 TECHNOLOGIES

A characteristic of Web 2.0 is an architecture of participation that encourages users to add value to the application as they use it. Tapscott and Williams (2006) argue in their book *Wikinomics: How Mass Collaboration Changes Everything* that the economy of Web 2.0 is based on mass collaboration that makes use of the Internet. Companies can leverage the collective power of their consumers by leveraging Web 2.0 technologies to enable the consumers to participate in the marketing of the brand.

Idris Mootee (2004) in his book *High Intensity Marketing* examines the role of strategic marketing in the network economy, which is relationship driven, network centered, technology enabled, and information intensive. Mootee developed an analytical model supplement to the traditional marketing ps called "The New 4P's." Mootee's new four ps are participation, peer-to-peer communities, predictive modeling, and personalization. Participation focuses on allowing consumers to choose their products, providing valuable insights to companies about consumers' needs and wants. Mootee cites Dell, Procter & Gamble, and Levi's as examples. Mootee also briefly touches on consumers playing a role in defining and owning brands, such as Burton snowboards.

Participation is more relevant than ever with the Web 2.0 revolution, but it is more than a supplemental p to the marketing mix. Participation should now encompass all of the four ps as a lens through which the ps should be approached. The previous section explored a number of examples of B2C companies successfully leveraging Web 2.0 technologies to market their products. Applying a participation lens to the marketing mix can lead similar companies to similar success.

To be more successful at marketing using Web 2.0 technologies, the traditional four-p marketing mix discussed earlier (price, product, promotion, and placement) should be approached with a new p lens: participation. This is the Web 2.0 marketing mix.

In this new marketing mix, each of the four elements is approached by enabling consumers to participate in it. Let us explore how consumers are currently participating in each p of the marketing mix and the steps a company can take to capitalize on that interaction and encourage more.

Web 2.0 technologies provide a medium for consumers to directly participate with companies and their brands. Consumers can write blogs about their favorite brands, define themselves and create communities in social networks like Facebook and MySpace by associating themselves with brands, develop their own commercial advertisement for brands and post them on YouTube, and tag pictures they have uploaded of their brands on Flickr.

In addition, Web 2.0 technologies enable companies to more readily identify brand evangelists: those consumers that are devoted to a brand or product and preach their devotion to the world.

Companies can make it even easier for consumers to participate in their marketing by evaluating each *p* in their marketing mix and fostering involvement by their consumers via Web 2.0 technologies. Let us specifically examine each marketing mix element.

Product

The product aspects of the marketing mix are the specifications of the actual goods or services, and how they relate to the user's needs and wants. The scope of a product generally includes supporting elements such as warranties, guarantees, and support.

In *Wikinomics: How Mass Collaboration Changes Everything*, Tapscott and Williams (2006) explore a new generation of "prosumers" who treat the world as a place for creation, not consumption. These prosumers can be engaged to participate in all aspects of a product, from identifying consumers' unmet needs to the development of a new product to supporting the product once in a consumer's hands. Companies need to encourage consumers to participate in their products and recognize the contributions that are made. There is an allure of prestige and sense of social belonging that develops within prosumer communities (Tapscott & Williams).

Web 2.0 provides immediate feedback about products. Companies do not need a Web site to harness the power of the numerous discussions of products on Web sites beyond the control of the company. Blogs are a great tool to identify latent consumer needs and wants. Communities are free focus groups of very raw, unscripted feelings not tainted by groupthink, or the act of

reasoning or decision making by a group that often occurs in traditional focus groups. Companies can also learn more about the total product life cycle beyond just the physical product, and identify additional uses for it. Companies can gain valuable customer insight and interaction via Web 2.0 in a quicker and cheaper fashion than traditional market research.

Flickr can be an avenue for trend spotting. Trend spotting is a relatively new consumer research methodology that seeks to anticipate what consumers will desire in the future and to keep existing products relevant. For example, on Flickr, a company can search for what consumers are carrying in their purses. Companies can ask consumers to participate in identifying product trends by sending out a call to action to post photos of what is in their purses. Maybe Capital One with their "What's in your wallet?" campaign could ask consumers to post Flickr photos of what is in their wallets, including a Capital One credit card. While a company may not know a lot about the consumer, Web 2.0 enables it to reach into consumers' lives and learn more about their behaviors (Brighton, 2005).

Lego fostered an early prosumer community. Lego's Mindstorms enables users to build working robots out of programmable bricks. Users reverse-engineered the products and shared feedback with Lego. Lego developed a Web site for users to share their discoveries and inventions with other enthusiasts and the company. Users can even virtually develop their own models and then order the bricks to physically build it. This enables Lego's consumers to become a decentralized virtual design team, far larger than the number of the in-house designers (Tapscott & Williams, 2006).

Procter & Gamble is also successfully leveraging the powers of Web 2.0 to enhance its research and development efforts for new products. The research and development team had a success rate of less than 20%, below industry standards of 30%. Via the Web, Procter & Gamble turned to the outside world for new and better ideas, and now more than 35% of the ideas come through the Web, resulting in success for 80% of Procter & Gamble's new product launches.

One example was the discovery of a way to put edible ink pictures on potato chips. The solution came from an Italian professor at the University of Bologna who had invented an ink-jet method for printing edible images. This technology helped the company get the new Pringles Prints potato chips out in a single year, about half the normal time for such a process (Stephens, 2007).

Cadbury brought back the discontinued Wispa chocolate bar after a campaign on Web sites like Facebook, MySpace, and YouTube demanded its return. The chocolate company says that it is frequently contacted by consumers asking for old favorites to be reintroduced, but said the numbers that had joined the Internet campaign to relaunch Wispa were unprecedented (Wallop, 2007).

In the support stage of the product life cycle, brands have an opportunity to engage with consumers during a crisis using Web 2.0. Consumers are pretty responsive to companies and brands who engage, especially when there is a problem. Speaking at Nielsen Business Media's Next Big Idea Conference, EVP of strategic services at Nielsen Online Pete Blackshaw focused his remarks on brand intelligence as he explained how companies can "defensively" market their products by turning negative trends in the marketplace to their advantage. Blackshaw noted the surge in the blog traffic surrounding consumer crises, such as the Mattel toy lead paint and poisonous pet food recalls from brands including Alpo and Mighty Dog, are opportunities for brands to have a touch point with consumers. Companies, said Blackshaw, should learn to "manage around the spikes, listen, react," and move money out of mass media and into online channels, asking consumers to participate in the support of a product, even during a recall (Kiley, 2007).

Pricing

The pricing *p* of the marketing mix refers to the process of setting a price for a product, including discounts. The price need not be monetary; it can simply be anything exchanged for the product or services, including time, energy, psychology, or attention.

Companies can leverage Web 2.0 to learn more about value that consumers perceive about brands and what consumers perceive they are paying for a product beyond just the monetary value. For example, online Web services such as eBay and craigslist let the consumer (or market) determine the price for products.

Consumers are able to discuss prices online via blogs or social networking sites for plane tickets, HDTVs, furniture, cars, and so forth. They can even let other consumers know where to find the best discounts.

A mashup is a Web page or application that integrates complementary elements from two or more sources. The most popular mashups include Google Maps as a source to identify certain things on a map. For example, one mashup shows secret fishing holes in the United States via a Google map. Mashups help locate the best price, such as CheapGas.

Beyond monetary value, companies can also get see what consumers are forfeiting other than money by choosing their brands or products. For example, a number of loyal Starbucks consumers are concerned about the impact they are making to the environment by enjoying Starbucks coffee in a new cardboard cup everyday with a cardboard sleeve. These consumers found a Web site that sold inexpensive reusable cloth holders to protect hands from the hot coffee cup and were elated to share it with one another. Starbucks could learn about this concern of its consumers and address it, possibly by offering this reusable cloth sleeve product in stores or developing one of their own.

Promotion

Promotion is the element of the marketing mix where consumers can most readily participate and add value to the marketing of a brand. This includes advertising, sales promotion, public relations, and personal selling, and refers to the various methods of promoting the product, brand, or company.

Consumers can develop an advertisement for a product or brand and then publish that ad for free on YouTube, tagged with keywords to inform others of the ad.

Companies may also use Web 2.0 to promote their brands with an advertisement. Smirnoff developed a viral marketing video for the launch of their new Raw Tea product. The video was placed on YouTube and at this time had over 4 million views (Iamigor, 2006). The Web 2.0 technology enabled consumers to access the video on YouTube and then participate in disseminating the information by informing their friends about the video. The launch of Raw Tea also included a Web site with the videos and a sharing capability. By placing the advertisement on a Web 2.0 site, Smirnoff made it easier for their consumers to participate by rating and sharing the video on a site they already frequent.

A wiki is any collaborative Web site that users can easily modify via the Web, typically without restriction. A wiki allows anyone using a Web browser to edit, delete, or modify content that has been placed on the site, including the work of other authors. One popular wiki is Wikipedia, a free encyclopedia that anyone can edit. Wikipedia is updated every second by thousands of active contributors, making it an up-to-date reference source vs. a printed encyclopedia that is updated monthly or yearly.

Wikis capture the knowledge of the collective whole. Consumers can define your product or brand on Wikipedia. Consumers define what a brand stands for or describe a product, including its intangible intrinsic value. Companies should check for accuracy but not stifle the participation by their consumers to define the brand.

A key to enabling consumers to participate in promotion is to make it easy to search and find areas where other consumers talk about your brand, product, or service, or create your own site where consumers can talk about what you are interested in learning more about. Procter & Gamble developed a social networking site for women called Contessa. The intention of the social network is not about selling products, but for P&G to learn more about its women consumers and learning about their needs and habits (Ives, 2007).

Placement

Placement or distribution refers to how the product gets to the customer, for example, point-of-sale placement or retailing. This fourth *p* of the marketing mix has also sometimes been called *place*, referring to the channel by which a product or service is sold (e.g., online vs. retail), to which geographic region or industry, and to which segment.

Companies can distribute their products via Web 2.0. American Apparel operates a clothing store in *Second Life* that sells virtual clothing for avatars. American Apparel has run promotions in *Second Life* where after purchasing a clothing item in *Second Life*, a consumer receives a coupon for a discount on the same or similar item at an American Apparel store in the real world (Jana, 2006).

Coke established the Virtual Thirst Pavilion in *Second Life*. It sponsored a contest to develop a Virtual Thirst vending machine. The winning vending machine will be rolled out throughout *Second Life*, making this real-world distribution channel as ubiquitous in *Second Life* as it is in the real world. Coke did not intend for consumers to merely replicate an existing real-world vending machine but to create a portable device for Second Life's in-world digital society that unleashes a refreshing and attention-grabbing experience, on demand. Our goal is to enable individual creativity in pursuit of a "vending" machine that can exist only in your wildest imagination. Virtual worlds make it possible for such innovations to occur, and we selected Second Life as the most conducive to this experiment,

says Michael Donnelly, director of global interactive marketing (Coca-Cola, 2007). This *Second Life* contest establishes a new distribution channel for the brand in a virtual world, but also taps into consumers' creativity for ideas for real-world distribution mechanisms.

On Flickr, in addition to tagging photos, a user may add notes that are visible when someone viewing the photo scrolls over a particular aspect of it. For new product introductions, such as a new pair of Nike shoes, a photo of the shoe may be uploaded to Flickr with associated tags (Nike, new, shoe, blue, limited edition, New York store) and notes that can link to a Web site where the shoe may be purchased.

Companies can even create a mashup using Google Earth to locate products that are not widely distributed such as specific shoe sizes. Online retailers such as Amazon.com and Travelocity are building widgets that can drive traffic to their sites for consumers to make purchases.

CHALLENGES

The consumer defines the brand; a brand is not what a company defines it as, but what a consumer says it is. Via Web 2.0, consumers have numerous avenues to add their interpretation of brands, for better or worse. Brands need to relinquish control to get influence. Two barriers to adoption are regulation of content and security.

One of the reasons Web 2.0 technologies like YouTube and Flickr are successful is because they are authentic: "The lack of corporate polish adds to the feeling that there are real people behind the idea" (Moore, 2006).

What does it say about a brand to have a presence or be communicated via these technologies? Before embracing participation in Web 2.0, a company must determine if a brand is compatible with the spirit of Web 2.0. Web 2.0 is more about spirit, concepts, and principles than definition. It is imperative that a brand be in accordance with that spirit before launching an initiative. If a brand is incompatible with this experience of openness and exchange, it is advised to create or use another brand or subbrand as a workaround for Web 2.0 initiatives to protect the integrity of the core brand (Smagg, 2007).

The best action for a company to take may be no action at all as long as it is recognized that Web 2.0 technologies are having an effect on marketing. In summer 2007, *Wired* magazine exposed *Second Life* for not achieving the commercial potential that was initially expected. A trip to Starwood Hotels' Aloft Hotel in *Second Life* was described as creepy due to the entire place being deserted, compared to the movie *The Shining*, where a tenant at a deserted hotel goes psycho due to the isolation—not exactly the reputation Starwood wanted for its new hotel chain brand. The NBA sought to capitalize on Web 2.0 for its marketing efforts by developing both an island in *Second Life* and a channel on YouTube. The YouTube channel saw over 14,000 subscribers with 23 million views, while the *Second Life* island had a mere 1,200 visitors. Those numbers are not as surprising when it is revealed that the traffic in *Second Life* is slightly more than 100,000 Americans per week (Rose, 2007).

In late 2007, IBM broadcast a television advertisement featuring two employees of an unknown company talking about avatars from a virtual world. The dialogue is as follows:

"This is my avatar. It's all the latest rage. I can do business, I even own my own island! It's innovation!" "But...can you make money?" "Um... virtual or real money?" "Real money. The point of innovation is to make real money." "Oh. My avatar doesn't know how to do that." (Vielle, 2007)

While the advertisement is mocking the value of Web 2.0 technologies, in a roundabout way, IBM is capitalizing on Web 2.0 to market its "Stop Talking. Start Doing." campaign. Yet, in mid-2007, IBM established a presence in *Second Life*, the virtual IBM Business Center staffed by real IBM sales representatives from around the world. In the press release for the launch of this virtual center, IBM boasts it has over 4,000 employees active in *Second Life*. The question remains: Is IBM not seeing the value from this investment in a Web 2.0 technology, or did it create the advertisement mocking avatars merely to generate interest for the IBM brand because avatars are popular at the moment? It also could have been buzz for its own presence in *Second Life* (IBM, 2007).

IMMEDIATE ACTION FOR COMPANIES

Companies should use Web 2.0 to assist with keeping a pulse on their brands' and products' involvement in Web 2.0 technologies. Most brands already have a Web 2.0 presence, and most likely, it is not officially endorsed by the brand.

Web 2.0 technologies make it very simple for a marketer to quickly and easily learn about what consumers are saying about a brand or product. RSS or real simple syndication is any of various XML (extensible markup language) file formats suitable for disseminating real-time information via subscription on the Internet. RSS has become a popular technology for bloggers and podcasters to distribute their content. NewsGator is a free Web-based RSS news reader that consolidates news and updates from the Web, blogs, premium content providers, and internal applications and systems and automatically delivers them to users.

RSS feeds can be set up to find and aggregate information about a brand or product from blogs, podcasts, and so forth, and be sent out via e-mail every morning to keep a marketer updated. Technorati is an RSS service that searches and organizes blogs and other forms of user-generated content (photos, videos, voting, etc.). Technorati is currently tracking over 110 million blogs and over 250 million pieces of tagged social media. The home page will immediately update you on "what's percolating in blogs now," but a quick search of your brand's name will share what is hot about your brand at the moment. It is an easy way to monitor the brand's image (*Technorati*, 2007).

Quick monthly visits to Web 2.0 Web sites can also keep marketers up to do date about their brands (and the competition). Visit Flickr and type in your brand name. Cheerios returns over 8,000 images, many showing how Cheerios plays a role in the everyday life of a child. Marketers will be happy to find this is consistent with the brand's image, values, and positioning.

Visit YouTube and type in your brand name. A McDonald's marketer may be interested to find that some commercials are tagged as creepy and racist and are not positively portraying the megabrand. However, a video containing the McDonald's menu song has had over 1.5 million views. The McDonald's menu song was a song listing all of McDonald's menu items from a promotion in 1989. Reviewing the thousands of comments about the video reveals that consumers are excited to view this video on YouTube and remember memorizing the song in 1989 when it was advertised during television commercials. This is definitely some valuable insight available for McDonald's.

Visit MySpace and type in your brand name or visit http://www.myspace.com/brandname. Mountain Dew does not have an official page, but a 21-year-old from Southern California owns http://www.myspace.com/mountaindew. JC from Newport Beach, California, owns Nike. In addition to learning about consumers' thoughts on your brand, this exploring can also result in insights about your loyal consumers who add your brand to their MySpace pages.

Visit Wikipedia and type in your brand name. Wikipedia's American Express entry has a wealth of historical information, including advertising. The entry is up to date with AmEx's most recent promotions, including its Member's Project. Anyone can contribute to a wiki, so periodically verifying information is correct and adding updates can benefit a brand ("Web 2.0," 2007).

With Web 2.0 technology, companies can quickly and inexpensively make things happen. You can have your advertising messages spread on the Web like a wildfire with social bookmarking sites, RSS, and other Web 2.0 methods, and without having to pay anything for it, have thousands of people coming to your Web site in a matter of days. What would have cost you millions of dollars in investment and a dedicated team of developers may now be accomplished with these Web 2.0 tools by a couple of guys in a garage in just a few days (Beaudoin, 2007).

Web 2.0 technologies intermingle with each other as well, so a presence in one Web 2.0 technology can give you a presence in others. For example, MySpace allows its members to blog on their pages and add YouTube videos.

FUTURE TRENDS

The Web is not going anywhere and will only continue to evolve. More Web applications will be developed and compete for consumers' time and attention. As consumers become accustomed to communicating and collaborating on the Web, they may choose to take marketing your brands into their own hands. Companies should be delighted at this occurrence. It is best to identify and monitor these actions as they transpire, but not take actions to impede them. If a consumer is passionate enough to devote energy toward positively marketing your brand, you can be sure that once disgruntled they will also take action, only this time it could be detrimental.

CONCLUSION

Web 2.0 technologies will not replace traditional marketing such as direct mail or TV advertisements, but instead are new complementing marketing channels that many consumers will expect their brands to communicate through.

Companies that feel Web 2.0 technologies are a right fit for their brands should take action to market their brands using the Web 2.0 marketing mix as a guide. Enabling consumers to participate in each aspect of the marketing mix will help brands remain relevant in today's changing world.

REFERENCES

American Marketing Association. (2007a). *Beyond Marketing 2.0: Harnessing the power of social media for marketing campaign results.* Retrieved December 28, 2007, from http://www.marketing-power.com/aevent_event1221988.php

American Marketing Association. (2007b). *Dictionary of marketing terms.* Retrieved October 15, 2007, from http://www.marketingpower.com/mg-dictionary-view1876.php

Beaudoin, J. (2007). *Web 2.0 for marketers ebook review on Web 2.0 portals.* Retrieved November 26, 2007, from http://www.web20portals.com/web-20-marketing/web-20-for-marketers

Big Sky Brands. (2007). *MySpace.* Retrieved November 26, 2007, from http://www.myspace.com/bigskybrands

Brighton, G. (2005). Flickr kills trendspotting. *PSFK.* Retrieved September 27, 2007, from http://psfk.com/2005/03/flickr_kills_co.html

Carter, B. (2007, October 4). Fictional characters get virtual lives, too. *The New York Times.* Retrieved November 12, 2007, from http://www. nytimes.com/2007/10/04/arts/television/04CSI. html?_r=1&ex=1192161600&en=6994ec8ad 88ab2d8&ei=5070&oref=slogin CBS mobile launches widget to promote new animated series. (2007). *MuseStorm.* RetrievedDecember 28, 2007, from http://www.musestorm.com/site/jsp/ spotlight/1042.jsp

Coca-Cola. (2007, April 16). *Coca-Cola launches competition to design online "virtual thirst" coke machine.* Retrieved October 14, 2007, from http://www.virtualthirst.com/virtualthirst-socialmediarelease.html

Guiragossion, L. (2007, October 29). A thousand ways to widget in the age of Web 2.0 marketing. *Web 2.0 Marketing.* Retrieved December 28, 2007, from http://web2pointzeromarketing. blogspot.com

Hayes, G. (2007). *A video comp of major brands in Second Life.* Retrieved December 28,2007, from http://www.youtube.com/ watch?v=tEGHJuCbGdo

Iamigor. (2006, August 2). *Tea partay.* Retrieved October 15, 2007, from http://www.youtube.com/ watch?v=PTU2He2BIc0

IBM. (2007, May 15). *Live IBM sales people to staff new virtual IBM business center.* Retrieved October 15, 2007, from http://www-03.ibm.com/ press/us/en/pressrelease/21551.wss

Ives, B. (2007, December 1). More Web 2.0 stories, part two: Procter and Gamble embraces the wisdom of the Web for new product ideas. *The FASTForward Blog.* Retrieved December 28, 2007, from http://www.fastforwardblog. com/2007/12/01/more-web-20-stories-part-two-proctor-gamble-embraces-the-wisdom-of-the-web-for-new-product-ideas

Jana, R. (2006, June 27). American Apparel's virtual clothes. *Business Week.* Retrieved September 26, 2007, from http://www.businessweek.com/ innovate/content/jun2006/id20060627_217800. htm

Jaokar, A. (2006, October 25). *Ajit Jaokar's mobile Web 2.0 blog: The widget widget Web.* Retrieved October 12, 2007, from http://www.web2journal. com/read/289798.htm

Kiley, D. (2007). Using bad news to a brand's advantage. *Business Week.* Retrieved November 14, 2007, from http://www.businessweek.com/ the_thread/brandnewday

Kraft Foods. (2007). *Kraft foods goes digital to unveil more than 70 new products in first-ever virtual supermarket in Second Life.* Retrieved October 12, 2007, from http://www.kraft.com/ mediacenter/country-press-releases/us/2007/ us_pr_04192007.htm

Millions of Us. (2007). Retrieved October 12, 2007, from http://www.millionsofus.com

Moore, J. (2006). *Five reasons why...* Retrieved October 16, 2007, from http://brandautopsy. typepad.com/brandautopsy/2006/08/five_reasons_wh.html

Mootee, I. (2004). *High intensity marketing.* Canada: SA Press.

Rose, F. (2007). How Madison Avenue is wasting millions on a deserted Second Life. *Wired Magazine.* Retrieved November 12, 2007, from http:// www.wired.com/techbiz/media/magazine/15-08/ ff_sheep?currentpage=all

Second Life, R. E. P. E. R. E. S. (2007). Retrieved October 12, 2007, from http://www.reperes-secondlife.com

Smagg, C. (2007). *15 golden rules for Web 2.0.* Retrieved October 12, 2007, from http://visionary-marketing.wordpress.com/2007/07/03/web20

Steel, E. (2006). Web-page clocks and other "widgets" anchor new Internet strategy. *Wall Street Journal*. Retrieved November 12, 2007 from http://marcomm201.blogspot.com/2006/11/marketing-widgets-you-saw-it-here-first.html

Stephens, R. (2007). *P&G Web 2.0 success story*. Retrieved December 27, 2007, from http://www.rtodd.com/collaborage/2007/11/pg_web_20_success_story.html

Tapscott, D., & Williams, A. (2006). *Wikinomics: How mass collaboration changes everything*. New York: Portfolio.

Technorati. (2007). Retrieved December 28, 2007, from http://technorati.com

Terret, B. (2007). Brand in good Web 2.0 project shock. *Noisy Decent Graphics*. Retrieved December 28, 2007, from http://noisydecentgraphics.typepad.com/design/2007/11/brand-in-good-w.html

Vielle, T. (2007). IBM avatar commercial. *SL Universe*. Retrieved December 31, 2007, from http://sluniverse.com/php/vb/showthread.php?t=2797

Wallop, H. (2007). Cadbury plans Wispa revival. *Telegraph*. Retrieved November 28, 2007, from http://www.telegraph.co.uk/news/main.jhtml?xml=/news/2007/08/18/nwispa118.xml

Web 2.0. (2007). *Wikipedia*. Retrieved September 15, 2007, from http://en.wikipedia.org/wiki/Web_2.0, http://en.wikipedia.org/wiki/American_Express

Chapter 4.4
Applying Semantic Web Technologies to Car Repairs

Martin Bryan
CSW Group Ltd., UK

Jay Cousins
CSW Group Ltd., UK

ABSTRACT

Vehicle repair organizations, especially those involved in providing roadside assistance, have to be able to handle a wide range of vehicles produced by different manufacturers. Each manufacturer has its own vocabulary for describing components, faults, symptoms, etc, which is maintained in multiple languages. To search online resources to find repair information on vehicles anywhere within the European Single Market, the vocabularies used to describe different makes and models of vehicles need to be integrated. The European Commission MYCAREVENT research project brought together European vehicle manufacturers, vehicle repair organisations, diagnostic tool manufacturers and IT specialists, including Semantic Web technologists, to study how to link together the wide range of information sets they use to identify faults and repair vehicles. MYCAREVENT has shown that information sets can be integrated and accessed through a service portal by using an integrated vocabulary. The integrated vocabulary provides a 'shared language' for the project, a reference terminology to which the disparate terminologies of organisations participating in the project can be mapped. This lingua franca facilitates a single point of access to disparate sets of information.

CURRENT SITUATION

Repair scenarios for resolving a vehicle breakdown are varied, and can take place in a garage (repair by a qualified mechanic in a franchised or independent workshop) or by the roadside (repair by a qualified mechanic working for a Road Side Assistance (RSA) organisation, or a repair by a vehicle driver). For legal liability reasons, 'driver-assisted' repair scenarios only cover minor or temporary repairs of the type covered in owner's manuals, such as changing a vehicle wheel or a fuse.

In workshop scenarios, access to repair information may be provided through online access to repair information systems. Information may be provided publicly by a manufacturer for all users, or specifically to franchised dealers who are provided with

DOI: 10.4018/978-1-60566-066-0.ch002

access to information systems that are specific to the makes and models they retail.

Access to repair information in roadside scenarios is more complicated. A vehicle driver may not have access to the vehicle's owner's manual. In the context of a roadside repair by a mechanic working for an RSA, the mechanic might have access to repair information through a computer located in their van. RSA organisations, however, rely heavily on the detailed knowledge of their highly trained staff to diagnose faults without the aid of documentation. RSA mechanics aim to repair as many vehicles as possible at the roadside, but need to identify as early as possible if a car will need to be taken to a garage for repair. If the repair requires specialist equipment the RSA must be able to identify the nearest garage with suitable equipment that the car may be taken to for repair.

Fault diagnosis precedes vehicle repair in both repair scenarios. Details of the type of fault are ascertained at the point of contact with the customer, be this through direct conversation with the vehicle owner at a service centre, or by conversation through a call centre operator when a motorist initially reports a problem. When contact is made through a phone call it is important that call centre operators analyze the customer's situation in as much detail as possible. They have to be able to identify whether the problem is one that might be repairable at the roadside or whether a recovery vehicle is likely to be needed from the responses received to an ordered set of questions.

Customer contacts rarely lead to a detailed fault diagnosis because vehicle owners typically have insufficient knowledge of their vehicles to identify the cause of a problem. At best they can describe the symptoms produced by the fault and the conditions in which the symptoms manifest themselves (e.g. won't start when it is too cold). In many cases these descriptions can be used to identify the type of diagnostic tests that may have to be carried out before the cause of the problem can be identified.

PROBLEM STATEMENT

With the ever increasing use of electronics in vehicle components, identifying and correcting faults at the roadside or in an independent workshop is becoming a challenge. While the use of on-board diagnostic tools to report faults electronically via dashboard messages can assist mechanics, identifying the cause of a fault from such messages is not always a simple process. When faults are reported over the phone from remote locations sufficient diagnostic information may only be obtainable if the vehicle can be connected directly to the call centre information centre using tools such as personal digital assistants (PDAs) or mobile phones that can be connected to the vehicle's diagnostic ports.

A roadside assistance vehicle cannot contain the wiring schematics for all models of vehicles. Although, under European Union Block Exemption Regulation (European Commission, 2002), manufacturers provide access to all their repair information, repairers at the roadside are not always easily able to find the repair information that they need, particularly if this is related to a previously unreported fault, while physical and business constraints impose restrictions on the set of spare parts, tools, etc, that can be available in the workshop or repair van at any one time. Consequently, the following problem areas can be identified:

- Practical limitations exist on the level of information that can be provided in any repair context. There is variability in the amount and quality of information that is available to describe a fault and its associated symptoms and conditions in order to support fault diagnosis.

- Environmental variables such as geographical location, repair equipment, and spare part availability may combine to constrain the speed with which a repair can be affected, and determine the location at which the repair takes place.
- Logistics and supply chain management and facilitation can provide advance warning of required spare parts or repair equipment at the point of initial fault diagnosis, supporting decision processes such as the direction of a vehicle to an appropriate repair location or the triggering of inventory supply processes to pre-order required parts and arrange their delivery to the repair location.
- Maintenance of acceptable response times that meet customer expectations.

The MYCAREVENT project addresses these issues by facilitating the diagnosis of faults and the provision of repair information at the location where the fault is first described, be this in a workshop or at the roadside.

The MYCAREVENT project provides a single point of entry – a portal – through which a user can access services to support the description and diagnosis of a fault, and to search for and retrieve repair information from a variety of content providers. For this to be achievable, however, it must be possible to associate the terms used by the vehicle owner to describe the problem that has occurred with the terms used by the content provider to describe content or how to detect and solve the fault causing the problem. It should be noted that content can be of variable quality and scope – for example, repair information from a vehicle's manufacturer will typically apply to specific makes of vehicle, whereas information from third parties like technical specialists working for RSAs, or technical data for an automotive part or content from a third party information provider, may be more generic in application.

SOLUTION DESCRIPTION

The Mobility and Collaborative Work in European Vehicle Emergency Networks (MYCAREVENT) research project was sponsored by the IST (Information Society Technology) program of the European Commission. The 3-year project brought together leading manufacturers from the automotive sector, academic researchers and commercial IT suppliers to develop facilities for the provision of repair information to remote users in the automotive aftermarket. Remote access, for example a roadside repair, is enabled by the use of mobile services. Research focused on service development, process and organization management, e-business, communication networks and human-computer interaction. Work in MYCAREVENT has been organized in nine work packages:

WP 1: Project Management
WP 2: Use Case and Business Model
WP 3: Ontologies
WP 4: Mobile Communication
WP 5: Remote Services
WP 6: Service Portal
WP 7: Mobile Applications
WP 8: Training
WP 9: Demonstration and Dissemination

The relationships between these packages are illustrated in Figure 1.

WP1 supported project management, establishing and monitoring the administration and leadership of the MYCAREVENT project. It needs no further discussion here.

WP2 developed the fundamental business model and use cases that scope the project requirements and identify the customers, actors, processes, and the constraints on the legal and organisational environment within which the project solution operates.

The project scope can best be understood by looking at the project's three pilot scenarios, which demonstrate the functionality provided by the solutions and identify their targets:

Figure 1. MYCAREVENT work package relationships

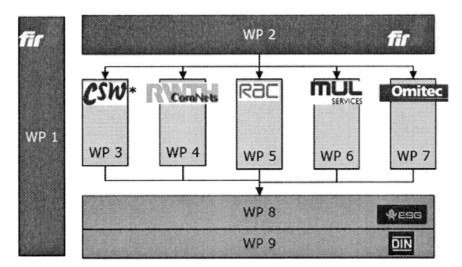

- **Pilot I** was designed to demonstrate possible solutions for original equipment manufacturer (OEM) workshops and OEM roadside technicians who require remote access to the MYCAREVENT service portal to obtain instructions for specific repairs.
- **Pilot II** was designed to demonstrate how the concept of access to car repair information via the MYCAREVENT service portal could be extended to help mechanics working in independent workshops and roadside assistance services to identify faults.
- **Pilot III** was designed to demonstrate the concept of "Driver Self Help" in those scenarios where the driver can carry out simple repairs using advice provided by the MYCAREVENT service portal.

The ontology work package (WP3) defines the information structures that enable cross-system interoperability and the integration of content from disparate sources and heterogeneous databases.

The mobile communications and devices work package (WP4) provides a secure and reliable communication service between users (roadside assistants, drivers, and mechanics) and the service portal. These services are intended to enable the exchange of fault codes and repair information from remote locations, such as those required to carry out roadside repairs.

The remote services work package (WP5) allows a driver to search for self- help information, such as that provided in the owner's handbook, using standard Web browser software that resides on their smart-phone or PDA.

The service portal work package (WP6) defines the core project portal, the gateway for accessing repair information.

The mobile applications work package (WP7) allows the MYCAREVENT Service Portal to be used to deliver automated diagnostic tests to trained mechanics. This requires the application of additional access security and other middleware services within the portal interface.

The role of WP3 Ontology and WP6 Service Portal work packages is explained further in the following sub-sections.

OBJECTIVES

The MYCAREVENT Service Portal acts as a *gateway* to technical information on automotive diagnosis, repair and maintenance that is available from automotive manufacturers and independent organisations supporting the aftermarket.

To ensure high user acceptance, the MYCAREVENT work packages use innovative *state-of-the-art technologies* to find the 'right' information for user needs. To make this possible the service portal includes the following subsystems:

- *Core e-business infrastructure* for the flexible implementation of workflow and business processes.
- *Service data backbone* providing secure links to services as well as manufacturer and third party information repositories.
- An ontology-based *advanced query service (AQS)* for guided navigation through different data resources and terminologies.
- *Expert system hub* combining the capabilities of distributed (specialised) expert system nodes.
- *Authoring tools* for specific types of technical information, such as the interactive circuit diagrams (IACD) used to identify faults in electronic systems.

The remainder of this section explains how the ontology-based advance query service applies Semantic Web technologies to identify solutions to repair problems.

OVERVIEW

The MYCAREVENT Ontology work package was responsible for the development of the models, data structures and terminology sets used to support the work carried out by the service portal. The work package drew on the expertise of data modelling specialists, implementers and content providers (including OEM and RSA organisations) to build an agreed set of 'information artefacts' to be used across all MYCAREVENT services. The Ontology work package developed:

- A *Generic and integrated information reference model (GIIRM)* (MYCAREVENT, 2005), providing a high-level conceptual model of the MYCAREVENT mobile service world.
- A set of W3C XML Schemas derived from the GIIRM, which are used for the representation of data in messages, metadata and interfaces.
- Terminology for populating the GIIRM, enabling repair information, symptoms and faults to be described in a generalized way.
- A W3C Web ontology language (OWL) (McGuinness, 2004) ontology, derived from the GIIRM and the terminology, in which data sources can be registered for access by MYCAREVENT applications.

Details

Since the publication of Tim Berners-Lee's futuristic paper on The Semantic Web in *Scientific American* in May 2001 (Berners-Lee, 2001) the concepts that form the backbone of a system that can add semantics to Web resources has begun to form. As was pointed out in that paper:

For the Semantic Web to function, computers must have access to structured collections of information and sets of inference rules that they can use to conduct automated reasoning.

The goal of the MYCAREVENT ontology work was to link together collections of information created by different vehicle manufacturers, component suppliers and repair organizations in such a way that we can use the collected information to conduct automated reasoning wherever possible.

The start point for the work package was the development of a formal model that could record the relationships between the information components used to identify and repair faults. This top-level model was designed to be generalized enough to apply to any type of repairable product.

Figure 2 shows a diagrammatic representation of the *MYCAREVENT Generic and Integrated Information Reference Model (GIIRM)* which was developed to manage the inter-relationship between information message components exchanged between information suppliers and the service portal. The diagram is expressed in the Object Management Group's Unified Modeling Language (UML) (Object Management Group, 2007).

The information required to populate the classes defined in this model are supplied by information providers in the form of Information Bundles that conform to the ISO/IEC 14662 Open-EDI Reference Model (ISO/IEC 14662, 2004). In this standard Information Bundles are defined as:

The formal description of the semantics of the recorded information to be exchanged by parties in the scenario of a business transaction. The Information Bundle models the semantic aspects of the business information. Information bundles are constructed using Semantic Components.

A unit of information unambiguously defined in the context of the business goal of the business transaction. A Semantic Component may be atomic or composed of other Semantic Components.

The model allows, therefore, for simple (i.e. 'atomic') and composite (i.e. 'non-atomic') attribute values, represented in the model using the concept of the 'representation class' which can be either an atomic datatype or a non-atomic composite data type as defined by the 'Naming and design principles' established in Part 5 of the ISO Metadata Registries (MDR) standard (ISO/IEC 11179-5, 2005). The GIIRM has foundations in abstract concepts and existing standardisation work. This design philosophy and layer of abstrac-

tion provides a generic model independent of any detail specific to implementation. It is, therefore, a platform-independent model.

To simplify the process of identifying relevant information sources, the model includes the concept of a Term. Terms can be used to describe a vehicle instance, its build specification, a system or subsystem used in the build specification, a condition under which a problem was detected, a symptom of the problem or a detected fault. Terms can be grouped into Terminologies that can be applied by different manufacturers within their documentation and information delivery systems.

Users of the MYCAREVENT Service Portal may or may not be aware of the terms used by manufacturers within their documentation. Users need to be able to enter terms that they are familiar with for describing problems, etc. The MYCAREVENT Advanced Query Service (AQS) needs to be aware of the relationships between the terms applied by a particular user community and the terms applied by a particular manufacturer. Terminology, and the mapping of terms in one terminology to terms in another terminology, is central to the AQS as it enables the querying of disparate information sources. The parameters of a search query can be established by a user using their preferred terminology, which may be manufacturer-specific or generalized using a MYCAREVENT specific term set. This search context is then passed to the AQS, which translates the MYCAREVENT terminology into the terminology used to describe the content that will be searched to retrieve information. This level of indirection allows disparate corpora of information to be searched using their own terminology. From an integration perspective, the AQS enables content integration using metadata describing repair information content created by OEMs or third parties, or through direct interface to a vehicle information source system.

The AQS has been developed using open-source technology to enable the latest develop-

Figure 2. MYCAREVENT generic and integrated information reference model

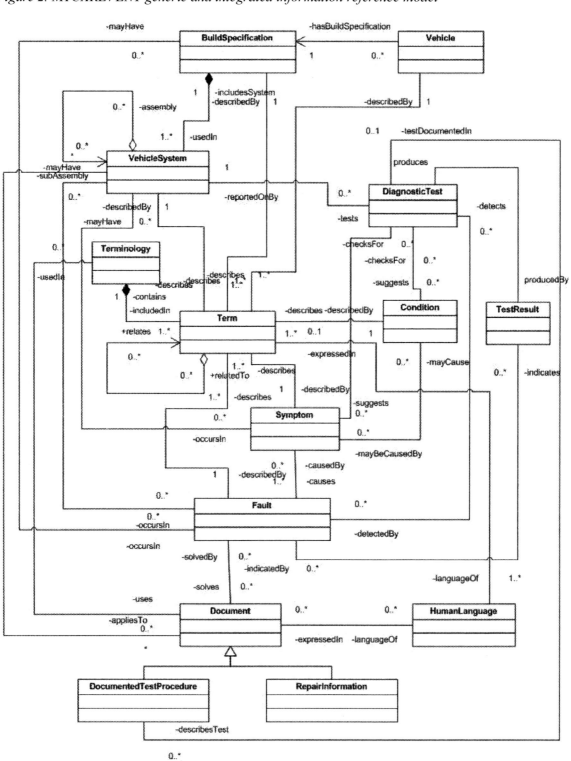

ments in Semantic Web technology to be adopted. It uses the Jena RDF triple store ("Jena", n.d.) to record OWL classes and individual occurrences of these classes. The Jena 2 Database Interface allows W3C Resource Description Framework (RDF) (Klyne, 2004) triples to be stored in MySQL, Oracle, PostgreSQL or Microsoft SQL databases, on both Linux and WindowsXP platforms.

An important feature of Jena 2 is support for different kinds of inference over RDF-based models (for RDFS, OWL, etc). Inference models are constructed by applying *reasoners* to models (Dickinson I, 2005). The statements deduced by the reasoner from the model can appear in the inferred model alongside the statements from the model itself. RDF Schema (RDFS) (Brickley, 2004) reasoning is directly available within Jena: for OWL an external reasoner needs to be linked to the Jena engine through a Reasoner Registry. The Pellet reasoner (Clark & Parsia, 2007) is used within MYCAREVENT to ensure that all inferred relationships are identified prior to searching. Jena includes an OWL Syntax Checker that can be used to check that OWL files are correctly formed.

Jena includes an implementation of the SPARQL query language (Prud'hommeaux, 2007) called ARQ. SPARQL has been developed as part of the World Wide Web Consortium (W3C) Semantic Web activity to provide a transportable technique for RDF data access that serves a similar purpose to the structured query language (SQL) used to access information held in a range of relational databases. The MYCAREVENT AQS generates SPARQL queries, based on the objects in the GIIRM, which are used to identify the concepts being referred to by terms entered by users. Because the query service is based on RDF it can query the contents of any OWL data property used to record information about an individual class member within the MYCAREVENT ontology, or any language-specific RDF label associated with a class or individual, irrespective of whether or not it is a term that has been specifically declared within a terminology.

SEARCHING AND RETRIEVING REPAIR INFORMATION

The key to the success of the MYCAREVENT portal is to allow users to ask questions using terms that they are familiar with and to use these questions to generate alternative versions of the question that OEM and other information provision systems associated with the portal can answer. The workflow steps used to establish a search query are described in the following sections.

MYCAREVENT queries are implemented in a controlled, context sensitive, manner to provide guidance to users as they enter information into the service portal. Figure 3 shows the information components used to identify the type of vehicle to be repaired within the portal.

Users complete each field in turn. As they do so the options available to them in the next field are restricted using the ontology. So, for example, as soon as the user identifies the make of vehicle to be repaired, the set of options that can be used to complete the model field is reduced to the set of models appropriate for the entered make. Completing the model field restricts the range of years that can be entered in the Year field, selecting a year restricts the set of Series that can be selected, and so on.

For countries such as the UK where a vehicle registration number decoder is accessible it is possible to enter the vehicle registration number (VRN) into a field displayed under the Decoder tab and have the entered number return information that has been recorded about the year of manufacture, engine type, fuel type, etc, by the vehicle registration authority. Alternatively the manufacturer's vehicle identification number (VIN) can be used to automatically identify system components. Where a decoding service is not available each field in the vehicle description has to be completed in turn.

When as much information on the vehicle as is available has been recorded the user can be shown a list of available services, which can range

Figure 3. MYCAREVENT Repair Information Form

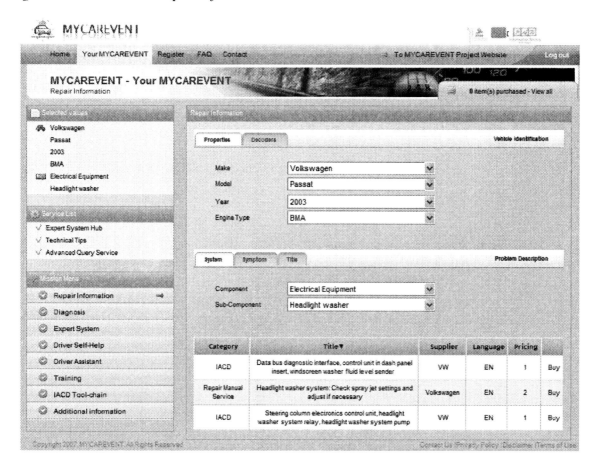

in complexity from a set of online technical tips through the use of the advanced querying system to identify relevant information resources to the use of an expert system to diagnose problems.

By reducing the set of selectable options at each stage to that recorded in the ontology we not only refine the search criteria but also reduce the likelihood that subsequent queries will be rejected. Only those services that are relevant to the type of vehicle to be repaired and the service that is being employed to repair it are offered to users so that, for example, users are not prompted to carry out tests using diagnostic equipment that is not fitted to the vehicle or accessible to the repairer, and are prompted to carry out all tests that must be performed to identify a specific fault.

THE ROLE OF THE MYCAREVENT ONTOLOGY

The ontology used by the AQS consists of a series of specializations of the concepts in the GIIRM. These concepts reflect the core classes and properties of the information required to describe and assert associations between faults, symptoms, conditions, vehicles, vehicle systems, diagnostic tests, terminology, repair information documents and human language. These classes are further sub-classed or specialised to refine concepts from the abstract and generic model level to a lower and more 'concrete' or 'real world' level that aligns with the business requirements. To illustrate, if business analysis shows that a particular information provider has circuit diagram, repair procedure,

Figure 4. Specialization of generic model classes

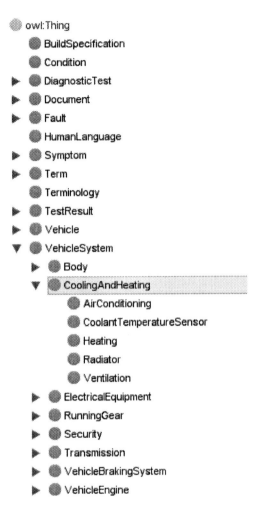

and owner manual types of repair information document, then the terminology used to describe document types is enhanced to include these new kinds of document, and within the ontology new document sub-classes are created to reflect these document types. The development process keeps the terminology and ontology in alignment with each other, and with the GIIRM which defines the base model and so ensures interoperability across the portal and database(s) accessed by it.

Figure 4 shows how the Vehicle System class is specialized into two levels of sub-class. Each class has associated with it multilingual labels, and a set of properties. Figure 5 shows the proper-

ties associated with the Vehicle class as they are displayed using the Protégé ontology editor used to maintain the MYCAREVENT ontology.

As a value is assigned to each of these properties within the MYCAREVENT System Identification form, the set of related properties that can be found by querying the triple store is reduced. Only those entries that are used in matched terms need to be displayed to users when they are required to select options for a currently empty field. The order in which responses are requested can be optimized to ensure that the minimum set of options is provided at each response point.

Figure 5. Properties of a vehicle

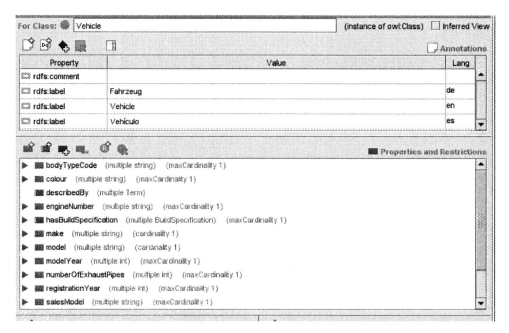

In MYCAREVENT users never see the underlying ontology while completing the basic Repair Information form shown in Figure 3. They do not need to browse the class tree, or know which properties they are dealing with. The ontology is simply used as a Web service by applications that need to request data from users, so that they can restrict the set of choices offered to users to that appropriate for the currently identified processing context, which is shown in the top right-hand window on the display. The role of the ontology is, therefore, to reduce information overload for users.

In later stages of the process, when accessing data using the Symptoms and Title tabs, users are prompted to enter keywords that are searched against lists of symptoms or the titles of documents. In these scenarios matches can only be made in those situations where the title contains relevant wording, or where the symptoms entered match symptoms recorded in one of the terminologies.

ALTERNATIVES

On-line access to information for vehicles is available from a variety of sources, including individual OEMs and third party automotive data suppliers. Subscription models vary, but typically documents are only available to paying subscribers and may require the installation of specialist software or training in the use of a specialized information retrieval system. For an individual user requiring access to information for a variety of vehicles, the availability of a single portal through which multiple sources of information can be accessed and queried is an attractive option. Rather than paying multiple subscriptions and having the burden of maintaining integration with multiple information access points, the portal provides a central point of access from which a user can search for and retrieve information.

Each manufacturer and third party information provider maintains their own vocabulary of terms for describing components, faults, symptoms, etc, in multiple human languages. If a trained mechanic knows which terms a manufacturer has applied to the fault they have identified then it is possible to search the manufacturer's database using a free text search. But if a mechanic is not familiar with the terms used by a specific manufacturer, there are unlikely to be any synonyms for them provided by information suppliers.

The issue of understanding the meaning of a particular terminology is not confined to metadata describing different types of vehicle systems, but applies to data recorded as codified values as well. On-board and plug-in diagnostic devices report faults using a set of codes. Some codes are internationally agreed, and will identify the same fault in a number of vehicles. Other codes are manufacturer specific. As with terminology, descriptions and names for fault codes may be maintained in a variety of human languages. For manufacturer specific codes the same code may be used to identify different problems in different makes of cars. Without access to a decoder that turns the codes into meaningful descriptions of faults for a specific vehicle build specification, knowing the code does not necessarily help the repairer.

Manufacturers of diagnostic tools need to ensure that their decoders are always up-to-date, providing the correct interpretation of codes for the latest models. Users of such tools need to be able to update their tools regularly to ensure the correct analysis of faults. While many OEMs already provide an up-to-date tool set for their vehicles through their BER portals, the extent of this is not consistent across manufacturers, and so a central point for updating information online provides one approach to addressing any gap which may arise between the release of new vehicle types and the availability of tools to diagnose their problems, other than those provided by the vehicle manufacturer.

By providing a central point for searching for repair information, issues such as the need to ensure this content is up-to-date, and legal liability for any claim arising from errors, need to be taken into account. For access across the single European market, irrespective of language and affiliation, however, centralized diagnostic services of the type that can be supplied using the MYCAREVENT service portal provide a viable alternative once agreement can be obtained from OEM and other content providers for making the information available online through the service portal.

COST AND BENEFITS

In 2004 the European Commission reported, in their European Competitiveness Report (European Commission, 2004a) that the automotive industry, as one of Europe's major industries, contributes about 6% to total European manufacturing employment and 7% to total manufacturing output. Total value added produced in the motor vehicles industry in the EU-15 in 2002 was roughly the same as in the US, some €114 billion.

With 209 million passenger cars in use in 2002 the European Union (EU-25) is by far the largest single market for cars in the world. It accounts for roughly 38% of all cars on major international markets. On average, four out of ten EU inhabitants own a car. According to the ACEA, the European Automobile Manufacturers Association, 15 million new passenger cars were registered in the EU and EFTA in 2006.

According to the EU report, it is expected that 90% of all future innovation in vehicle manufacturing will be driven by IT. This affects both the electronics dominated spheres of multimedia entertainment and navigation systems and the traditional mechanical components such as the chassis, body, engine or brakes. For instance, the percentage of electronics in the chassis is expected to increase from 12% to 40% in the next decade. Similar developments are expected for safety features, e.g. pedestrian protection, traction control, backward driving cameras, night-view display on the windscreen, sensor controlled brakes or fuel economy regulation. Product differentiation will be increasingly driven by electronics: for example, performance tuned variants of the same engine will differentiate suppliers. The value of electronic components in vehicles could rise from its current 20% today to 40% by 2015.

Since October 2002 motor vehicle distribution and servicing agreements within the EU have come under the new Block Exemption Regulation (BER). Under the new regulations repairers cannot be required to use original spare parts. Only if repair costs arise which are covered by the vehicle manufacturer, for example warranty work, free servicing and vehicle recall work, can the vehicle manufacturer insist on the use of original spare parts. Other than that, matching quality spare parts of other manufacturers or of independent suppliers can be used.

The automotive aftercare market had a turnover of around €84 billion per annum at the end of the 20th century; automotive replacement parts account for around half of this figure, some 45% of which is supplied by independent aftermarket (IAM) suppliers (European Commission, 2004b). The 210 million motorists in the EU spend on average €400 each per year and approximately €5,000 during the average vehicle lifetime on repair and maintenance.

Major service providers in the automotive industry are franchised dealers (120,000 dealers employing 1.5 million people in 1999) and independent repair shops (160,000 garages employing about 600,000 people). In addition, 18,000 roadside service vehicles fulfil 14 million missions a year.

By providing a single access point through which details of electronically available information can be searched, using generic Semantic Web technologies rather than manufacturer-specific solutions, the MYCAREVENT Service Portal simplifies and speeds up the task of finding information on how to repair vehicles with specific problems. With over a million potential customers it provides a cost-effective solution to information distribution.

By using ontologies to establish relationships between the terms used by vehicle owners and repairers to describe faults and the terms used by manufacturers to classify and describe faults, the MYCAREVENT Advanced Query Service can provide a more flexible solution to finding information, resulting in a higher likelihood of mechanics being able to find the information they need in a timely manner.

RISK ASSESSMENT

Each manufacturer produces thousands of models, each of which can have many build specifications. Model details and build specifications have to be defined prior to manufacture, but cannot be used within the service portal until the product is released. Unless the release date is known in advance, data relating to vehicle models, build specifications, system components, etc, cannot be added to the ontology at the time they are captured by the manufacturer, but need to be made available at the point when relevant documentation is released.

Manufacturers are naturally reluctant to maintain two sets of information, which could get out of step with one another. It must be possible to automatically convert information in local systems into the form that can be used by the AQS. As an alternative it should be possible to turn a query to the AQS into a query to the manufacturer's product database.

Another area of risk is in the level at which data is described, and the equivalence of terminology at different levels. A constraint on the MYCAREVENT ontology is that it currently only recognizes two levels in the system component hierarchy, system and sub-system. If a manufacturer uses a multi-level system hierarchy this needs to be flattened into a two level hierarchy for reference within the service portal. This means that entries at lower levels in the hierarchy have to become members of the appropriate higher level sub-system, thus restricting the level of refinement that can be applied to queries. This restriction is necessary because otherwise it would not be easy to convert AQS queries to queries that could be applied to manufacturer-developed services that can only handle two levels of querying.

Where diagnostic information is a requirement for identifying build specifications and associated repair information, obtaining the necessary information without access to OEM-provided diagnostic equipment can be a problem, especially in roadside breakdown scenarios. Unless the repairer can send appropriate information to the portal it will not be possible to retrieve relevant repair instructions. For this reason, other MYCAREVENT work packages have concentrated on how to get information from on-board diagnostic devices to a portal, diagnostic tool or expert system capable of identifying the cause of the problem.

Not all concepts are applicable to all makes, or to all models made by a specific manufacturer. Where a feature is specific to a particular manufacturer it is not to be expected that other content providers to the portal (be they manufacturers or third party information providers) will have equivalent terms in their terminology. If a user requests information on this subject for another make of vehicle the system will not be able to match the term. In such cases a number of strategies can be adopted to find appropriate terms, including:

- Identifying the term in the terminology of another manufacturer and informing the user that this term is manufacturer-specific
- Identifying the sub-system with which the term is associated by the originating manufacturer and offering a set of terms associated with the same sub-system that are used by the manufacturer of the vehicle being repaired
- Identifying other terms that include one or more of the words in the entered term, which may or may not identify higher-level concepts

- Identify other terms that include the largest identifiable substring of the entered term in compound nouns such as those used in German.

Expanding terminologies to cover all European languages, particularly agglutinative languages such as Finnish and Hungarian, where there are many compound words that could be derived from a term, will make identifying potential matches much harder. For such languages it will be vital to be able to define relationships between alternative references to a term within terminologies.

Identifying which terms have significance in which documents is another problem area. Unless the sub-systems that documents refer to are unambiguously recorded in either the data or metadata associated with a document, and the faults that can be solved using a document are recorded in the ontology or manufacturer's information base, refining queries down to the level of identifying documents that are specific to a particular problem with a given sub-system will not be possible. The best that can be achieved is to identify the set of documents that refer to a particular sub-system and allow users to determine from metadata describing the type of document, etc, whether it may be suitable for solving the problem.

Relying on user selection of suitable documents introduces another risk. Manufacturers want to be paid for preparing and supplying data. Users only want to pay for information that they know will solve their problem more efficiently than alternative solutions. If the cost of information is too high users will not risk purchasing something that may not solve the problem. If the cost of information is too low manufacturers, or third party documenters, supplying the information will not be able to recover the cost of preparing the information for distribution. Because of legal liability concerns, and the requirements by the BER, manufacturers are reluctant to supply information units which do not contain all the legally required warnings, safety notices, etc, that can apply to the repair scenario.

OEMs want to supply units of information that are known to contain all relevant details for the sub-system(s) that are connected with the fault.

The rate at which documents change is also a concern to information suppliers. It is not possible to maintain an up-to-date repository that includes all repair information generated by all vehicle manufacturers, even if an efficient enough content management system was available to store and access them. The best a service portal can expect is to receive metadata about which documents are available for which sub-systems, and the roles those documents serve. If the metadata supplied with each document fails to identify the type of faults that the document can help to correct, it will not be possible to associate faults with the documents that can be used to repair them. These risks were identified and confirmed by the OEMs involved in the project, and in some cases would prevent them from being able to integrate their content with MYCAREVENT.

The key strength of using an ontology-based approach to service portal management is that it reduces information overload on users, who otherwise would find it difficult to find their way through the maze of specifications and information types supplied by different manufacturers. By minimizing the set of options provided at each stage in the process, the MYCAREVENT advanced query service makes it possible to identify information resources provided by a range of manufacturers through a single reference point.

Until manufacturers are able to provide information as to which faults can be solved using which documents a weakness of the service portal is that it will necessarily rely on users making the final choice between a range of information resources that cover a particular component. Where diagnostic tests are available their results can be used to narrow down the range of possibilities. When diagnostics are implemented an associated problem is that of identifying the relationships between symptoms, the conditions they can occur under and the diagnostic test results that can

be used to identify specific faults. At present this information is generally not available from manufacturers. Until it is systematically recorded the efficient identification of faults within the portal will be difficult.

The recording of the symptoms reported when a particular fault has occurred is, however, also an opportunity for the service portal. By recording the symptoms reported by users, the conditions under which they occur and the fault that was eventually identified as the cause of the problem within the service portal it should become possible, over time, to generate statistics that can be used to predict the likelihood of a particular fault being the cause of an exhibited symptom.

The size of the European automotive industry is another major risk. If all vehicle suppliers adopted the system, and it covered all cars in current production, the potential user community could be as many as 2,000,000 people. Several portals would be required to cope with such a load. To keep the systems synchronised it would be necessary to adopt a time-controlled update system, with updates being scheduled for early in the morning when system use is low. A separate system would have to be assigned the task of receiving information from manufacturers and accumulating them ready to carry out a single daily update of online portals. The downside of these process integration issues would be that any changes made to documentation, build specifications, etc, would not be available on the day they were recorded by the manufacturer. This risk can be managed using Trading Partner Agreements and Service Level Agreements between the portal and the information providers, following standard practices for managing business relationships.

Expanding the proposed system to cover all vehicles would also require significant expansion of system functionality, because commercial vehicles have a much wider range of build specifications. One vehicle manufacturer reported to have 93,000 build specifications for trucks. Part of the reason for this is that there are more distinguishing features, such as type of steering, number of axles, body type, couplings, etc, used to define the build of a commercial vehicle. For such vehicles it becomes important to use the unique vehicle identification number (VIN) rather than its vehicle registration number (VRN) to obtain accurate details of the build specification.

FUTURE RESEARCH DIRECTIONS

As Tim Berners-Lee pointed out in his seminal paper on the Semantic Web (Berners-Lee, 2001):

Traditional knowledge-representation systems typically have been centralized, requiring everyone to share exactly the same definition of common concepts such as "parent" or "vehicle". But central control is stifling, and increasing the size and scope of such a system rapidly becomes unmanageable.

Two important technologies for developing the Semantic Web are already in place: eXtensible Markup Language (XML) and the Resource Description Framework (RDF). XML lets everyone create their own tags—hidden labels such as <author> or <title> that annotate Web pages or sections of text on a page. ... Meaning is expressed by RDF, which encodes it in sets of triples, each triple being rather like the subject, verb and object of an elementary sentence. These triples can be written using XML tags.

An ontology is a document or file that formally defines the relations among terms. ... We can express a large number of relations among entities by assigning properties to classes and allowing sub-classes to inherit such properties. ... Ontologies can enhance the functioning of the Web in many ways. They can be used in a simple fashion to improve the accuracy of Web searches—the search

program can look for only those pages that refer to a precise concept instead of all the ones using ambiguous keywords. More advanced applications will use ontologies to relate the information on a page to the associated knowledge structures and inference rules.

The real power of the Semantic Web will be realized when people create many programs that collect Web content from diverse sources, process the information and exchange the results with other programs. ... The Semantic Web, in naming every concept simply by a URI, lets anyone express new concepts that they invent with minimal effort. Its unifying logical language will enable these concepts to be progressively linked into a universal Web.

The need has increased for shared semantics and a Web of data and information derived from it. One major driver has been e-science. For example, life sciences research demands the integration of diverse and heterogeneous data sets that originate from distinct communities of scientists in separate subfields. ... The need to understand systems across ranges of scale and distribution is evident everywhere in science and presents a pressing requirement for data and information integration.

The need to integrate data across a range of distributed systems is by no means restricted to the scientific community. It is a fundamental characteristic of any e-business scenario that needs to be linked to back-office systems or to systems, such as those used for payment management, run by other companies. OWL allows the UML-based modelling techniques that are fundamental to the design and maintenance of back-office systems to be swiftly integrated with the XML-based messaging approach that has been widely adopted for inter-system communication.

The trend towards globalisation that characterises today's business environment is established and set to continue. Increasingly, demands are placed upon organisations to integrate information from diverse sources and to deliver new products and value propositions in narrower timescales. To meet these demands IT organisations need to evolve towards loosely coupled systems where services can be assembled to support the execution of business processes in a flexible way. A service oriented architecture (SOA) is not the only answer, though – for an SOA to be effective, a common view on to the data of the organisation needs to be available, so that data can be provided when and where needed to the processes consuming that data.

RDF-based data integration has a lot to offer because it provides a way to access information held in disparate systems without imposing a new structure on source data. If metadata is available, or can be generated, a metadata-based approach provides a framework structuring, processing and querying information sources.

The use of OWL and Semantic Web technologies moves us beyond simple metadata to structures where additional rules that determine the logical meaning of the data can be layered on top of existing data by the application of an ontology. Ontologies allows rules to be specified which can be reasoned over using methodologies such as description logics, allowing inferred models of data to be constructed. Not only is the explicit meaning of the data recorded, but the implicit meaning of the data can also be inferred and exposed by applying such rules to data.

The use of ontology-based approaches is another step along the path from the computer to the conceptual world used by humans. Now programming has progressed from binary assembler languages to 4th generation object-oriented paradigms, ontologies allow knowledge to be encoded as data structures in a way that reflects the understanding and semantics of the domain and of human users. Data can be modelled in a manner that is more intuitive and conceptually closer to the way humans think. Ontologies allow humans to use their own terminology to model the domain in a way that reflects how they understand it and speak about it. Furthermore, they can now encode knowledge and logic about the data structure, moving it out of application logic.

In this chapter we have said nothing about how OWL's limited set of description logic (DL) rules can be used to constrain the values assigned to ontology properties or to infer membership of a class from the presence or absence of property values. MYCAREVENT has not identified any points at which rules more complex than those needed to constrain cardinality or to ensure that all object properties are members of a given class or set of classes need to be applied to repair scenarios. But in many business scenarios more complex rules, including access control rules and permissions management, will be needed to ensure that business constraints can be met. The presence of an alternative, expert-system based approach to rule definition and application within MYCAREVENT has meant that the service portal team has not fully investigated the role that inferencing rules might play in the development of e-business applications, though a number of possibilities have been identified, including ones related to digital rights management and skill-based access control to information resources.

Work began in 2006 on a W3C Rule Interchange Format (RIF), an attempt to support and interoperate across a variety of rule-based formats. RIF (see www.w3.org/2005/rules for details) will eventually address the plethora of rule-based formalisms: Horn-clause logics, higher-order logics, production systems, and so on. Initially, however, the Phase 1 rule semantics will be essentially Horn Logic, a well-studied sublanguage of first-order logic which is the basis of logic programming. Among the deliverables scheduled from the RIF Working Group for the end of 2007 is:

A W3C Recommendation on using this rule interchange format in combination with OWL. This document is needed to help show implementers and advanced users how these technologies overlap and the advantages and limitations around using them together. This document must clearly state which features of OWL can be mapped to (or otherwise interoperate with) Phase 1 rules and which cannot, and software using this mapping must be demonstrated during interoperability testing. The document may also discuss rule language extensions to cover the excluded OWL features.

A second phase, scheduled to be completed in 2009, will extend rule processing to provide full first-order logic, negation, scoped negation-as-failure and locally closed worlds.

Until RIF tools are readily available, OWL users will have to make use of proposals such as that for a Semantic Web Rule Language (SWRL) (Horrocks, 2004) that extends OWL's built-in set of simple rule axioms to include Horn-like rules. While MYCAREVENT has not currently identified any rules it needs to deploy within the AQS which cannot be implemented using predefined SPARQL queries, it is anticipated that there will be other applications based on the GIIRM for which more complex queries of the type provided by SWRL may be needed. It will be interesting to see, as RIF develops, whether the additional functionality offered by adopting Horn-clause or higher-order logics provides a simpler solution to the type of reasoning currently being performed by the expert system currently used to identify the causes of problems within MYCAREVENT.

CONCLUSION

The automotive market has become one of the most important and complex industries in the EU, due to the rapid development and change in electronics, electrics, software and hardware. Economically, it is a major contributor to the EC economy, accounting for circa 6% of total European manufacturing employment and 7% of total manufacturing output.

Due to the EU Block Exemption Regulation, service providers have the right to access different kinds of repair information, training material and tools.

The MYCAREVENT project gathered partners from across Europe to establish a model of excellence leveraging innovative applications and state-of-the-art technologies, to offer a way for making the market more transparent, competitive and lucrative. It developed and implemented new applications and services which could be seamlessly and securely accessed by mobile devices deploying Semantic Web technologies. These tools allow us to provide manufacturer-specific car repair information that matches problems identified by Off/On-Board-Diagnostic systems.

Breakdown information is presented in different languages. Mobile workers in different countries can interact with service portals of independent service suppliers as well as those of car manufacturers. Using the MYCAREVENT Service Portal it becomes possible to provide a single point of access to information for any make of car, so ensuring that any car manufactured in Europe can be repaired in any European workshop or by any European roadside assistance organisation, irrespective of the preferred language of the owner or the mechanic.

REFERENCES

Berners-Lee, T. (2001). The Semantic Web. *Scientific American*, (May): 2001.

Brickley, D., & Guha, R. (2004). *RDF Vocabulary Description Language 1.0: RDF Schema*, W3C.

Clark & Parsia LLC. (2007). *Pellet: The Open Source OWL DL Reasoner*.

Deliverable, M. Y. C. A. R. E. V. E. N. T. D3.2 (2005) *Generic and Integrated Information Reference Model*. L.3.2_Generic_and_Integrated_Information_Reference_Model_DT_v01.00.pdf

Dickinson, I. (2005). *HOWTO use Jena with an external DIG reasoner.*

European Commission. (2002). *EC Regulation 1400/2002; Application of Article 81(3) of the Treaty to categories of vertical agreements and concerted practices in the motor vehicle sector.*

European Commission. (2004). The European Automotive Industry: Competitiveness, Challenges, and Future Strategies, *European Competitiveness Report 2004,*

European Commission. (2004). *Proposal for a Directive of the European Parliament and of the Council amending Directive 98/71/EC on the Legal Protection of Designs.* Extended Impact Assessment.

Horrocks, I., et al. (2004). *SWRL: A Semantic Web Rule Language Combining OWL and RuleML.*

ISO/IEC 11179-5:2005. *Information technology -- Metadata registries (MDR) -- Part 5: Naming and identification principles.*

ISO/IEC 14662:2004. *Information technology -- Open-edi reference model.*

Jena – A Semantic Web Framework for Java.

Klyne, G., & Carroll, J. (2004). *Resource Description Framework (RDF): Concepts and Abstract Syntax,* W3C.

McGuinness, D., & van Harmelen, F. (2004). *OWL Web Ontology Language Overview,* W3C.

Object Management Group. (2007) *Unified Modeling Language (UML).*

Prud'hommeaux, E., & Seaborne, A. (2007) *SPARQL Query Language for RDF,* W3C.

Shadbolt, N., Berners-Lee, T., & Hall, W. (2006). The Semantic Web Revisited. *IEEE Intelligent Systems, 21,* 96–101. doi:10.1109/MIS.2006.62

Chapter 4.5

The Web Strategy Development in the Automotive Sector[1]

Massimo Memmola
Catholic University, Italy

Alessandra Tzannis
Catholic University, Italy

ABSTRACT

Especially in recent years, a transformation is ongoing: the Web, besides being a means of information sharing (internal-external), becomes a powerful tool for saving costs, reducing the distribution structure, initiating distance transactions, and ever more, becomes a mechanism of integration with the external environment and a catalyst of experiences for all stakeholder. Starting from the identification of the key elements, potentialities, and of the impact of the Internet on firms' performance, competitiveness, effectiveness, and efficiency, this chapter is focused on the changes in the automotive sector due to the integration between business strategy and Web strategy. Therefore, starting from the consideration of a clear identification and subsequent sharing need of strategic goals, a research work will be presented exploring, on the basis of an interpretative model, the Internet potential in the automotive sector in order to achieve the identification of an optimal path definition and development of Web strategy. This objective will be developed through a desk analysis focused on the strategic positioning of the current businesses in the automotive sector (i.e., complexity evaluation of the presence on the Internet, strategic architecture, quality, and effectiveness of this presence).

INTRODUCTION

I need a new car!

Centy, as I affectionately call my old car, is gasping its last breaths. The "poor thing" has really had it, but then, it is really old; 10 years have passed from that happy day it made its entry in our family.

However, I am not so sure I like the idea of searching for a worthy successor. I am not an automobile fan, and my knowledge of them is rather limited. I am, however, sensitive to environmental problems, and I try my best to reduce the impact of my own person on the ecosystem as much as I can, considering its balance has already been seriously damaged.

What bothers me most is the idea of the long search ahead of me. I do not have any particularly difficult requests, but I want to consider such an

DOI: 10.4018/978-1-60566-024-0.ch009

important purchase very carefully, avoiding hurried decisions. I need a sensible family vehicle, with a good balance between performance, consumption, and above all cost. I need to acquire information, but just the idea of going from one dealer to another puts me in a bad mood. I can not stand having to waste time on this, and above all, having to pollute for a car I do not even own yet!

Also, interaction with the dealers is more often than not rather uncomfortable. At times—especially the more prestigious brand dealers—they treat you with a presumptuousness as if you were a nuisance, a matter that needs to be settled as quickly as possible. Other times, for the more sporty brands, they give you so many figures and acronyms, that they make you feel like "you did not do your homework" as in your school days. Lastly, with some there is feeling of a lack of transparency, something like "tell 'm everything but not really the truth."

Of course I do not want to demonize all car dealers. These are only impressions, and on top of that, only personal ones. But I do believe that, at least once, we have all felt the uneasiness I described above, either completely or in part.

I am holding the yellow pages in my hands, ready to copy my city's car dealers addresses on a piece of paper, but then a question just comes to mind, popping up almost unconsciously: "Why not use the Internet?"

I do most of my work nowadays through the Web: I keep in touch with my friends scattered around the world, I keep my bank account, book my holidays, buy music, and lately I have also taken care of my physical well-being using the telemedicine services offered by my city's health department. But then I say to myself: "But for a car it is different!" But is it really? Why would the Internet not have brought about the same changes in life style, in the way of thinking, of buying, in the automotive sector as it did in other areas?

I start my Web search by typing the word "car" into the search engine. Promptly a long list appears with sites specialized in online car sales.

I am starting to question my beliefs. Some sites only offer general information, deferring the sale to a moment of real interaction. There are some sites though that are true virtual car dealerships, and allow you to get through the whole buying procedure on their site, with even a home delivery service of the newly purchased car. So after all I would not spend too much time, as I did with Centy.

However, I do not feel ready for an online purchase. I have identified the model that seems right for me, but I need some extra information. Through the faithful search engine, I reach the Web site of the car manufacturer. I am welcomed into a very sophisticated ambient. I click on "Product Range" and I find myself in a virtual car dealer showroom.

The models are well-presented, with clear 3D images. The technical features provided are exhaustive for each model. I discover the "car configurator," a very interesting tool that allows you to configure your car by choosing the color, the interior, the optional features, and, once the final price has been determined, to have access to another service that allows one to request personalized financial options.

It is also possible to print out a customized brochure showing the specific car model with the chosen color, interior, and optional extras. I find out that the site offers me the possibility to not only get to know my local dealer, but also book a test-drive at my pleasure.

And there is more! The site offers a whole series of services that I would never have imagined that go well beyond the usual general information about the manufacturer. I realize that the contents vary according to the phase of the purchasing process: when the customer is in the process of choosing a car, the customer can benefit from tools that compare the models and optional extras, and that allow people to create the car that is closest to their expectations. Afterwards, some gadgets that make the car look closer and more real, can be downloaded (pictures and videos). Once the purchase has been completed, the customer can monitor the delivery process to see when it will arrive at the customer's door and after that, book the assistance and maintenance services, activating an SMS reminder service.

Often the Web becomes an occasion to create a community of customers of the same brand. Various services have been created to this end, from the normal forum to the more sophisticated blog, that allow an almost one-to-one interaction with the manufacturer, offering the possibility to interact in various ways and degrees with the managers, and to know the reasons behind some project choices, or to be informed about new models before they are launched on the market.

I also find an online magazine that I can virtually read and that, very coincidentally, not only contains car related articles, but "talks" about environment, style, and sports. I realize I am understanding, really entering the brand's life style. Once I own the car, through the Web site, I can request a loyalty card that, apart from working as a credit card on the main international circuits, allows me to obtain discounts not only for the car's assistance (i.e., maintenance, repairs etc.), but also in many shops in line with the brand's style and features.

At this point I am ready to leave the virtual world to get back to the real one. I can calmly think about my visit to the dealer where I booked my test drive. I have got all the information I need and I have made my choice. I could even make the purchase online. I have seen that some sites offer this possibility, but entering the dealer's showroom will allow me to satisfy the emotional value of the purchase, that is, to hold tight the steering wheel of the long-desired vehicle, breathe in the "smell of new," touch the dashboard. The Internet is not able to satisfy these senses, at least not yet!

The lines above are obviously fantasy, but they are not science fiction, as they describe a situation that is very likely in the light of the information and service contents that we have found on the Web analyzing the companies' Web sites of the automotive sector during our research work. We had to use our creativity simply because we imagined an ideal Web site that should hold all the solutions, information, and services that in reality the car manufacturing companies activate only partially in their portals.

It has rightly been observed that the Web represents "a new space, a new territory, made of computers, connections, software and above all, information…inhabited by individuals, companies, and by organizations; a place made of games, commerce and exchange" (Porter, 2001).

Comparing the results of our research with similar ones in other branches, such as banking (Frigerio, in this book), tourism (Yaobin, Zhaohua & Bin, 2007), retail business (Duke, Chul, Sang-II & Soung, 2006), and the health sector (Baraldi & Memmola, 2007), it seems that the automotive sector is, generally speaking, running far behind the others. The feeling that we get is that the companies belonging to this branch, even though they have been developing a "public presence" on the Web for quite a time, have hardly exploited its potential, limiting themselves in various cases to a low profile Web strategy, structured as a source of information rather than as a service. The Internet has therefore played a role up to now that is not dissimilar from any other media that allows a company to develop a one-way communication with the customers, and more generally, with the company's stakeholders.

This delay and lack of sensitivity toward "evoluted usage forms" of the Internet's potentialities can be partly justified by the strong emotional value linked to the purchase of a car, leading the customer to the dealer's showroom to touch the product that the customer is going to buy, to verify its qualities, thereby trusting tactile senses to guide and reassure. And it must be said that past attempts to develop forms of e-commerce in the automotive field, although they requested the purchase to be finalized at the dealer's, did not have much success.

Over the past years however, this trend has been changing dramatically. According to a research carried out by McKinsey (2003), during the next 10 years we will see the third revolution in the automotive sector, after the creation of the Ford mass production factory and the lean production of the Toyota Production System. Customers of the automotive branch, according to the research, will be expecting "hightest performance" for the same price, generating strong pressure on cost reduction and innovation capacity in the automotive companies. These factors will, without a doubt, lead to a whole new set-up of these companies' supply chain.

In fact, various companies are starting to grasp the idea that the Web can become an essential component in the so-called "low cost car strategy" to which many companies (e.g., Renault, Tata, General Motors, Fiat, Volkswagen, and Toyota) are decidedly heading. Through the Web the distribution network, which currently represents an important part of a car's final price, can be removed or reduced to a minimum.

Not only! The Web becomes the privileged instrument of interaction with the so-called "iPod generation," who through the company's portal or a specific product site, can contribute to the various steps of the product's project or image definition (e.g., accessories, internal and external graphic features, etc.). In this sense Fiat's experience with its Web site www.500wantsyou.com is surely significant.

Finally the Web can play a vital role in supporting customer relationship management (CRM) policies, or in the broadening of the product system with a series of complementary services linked to the automotive world (e.g., assistance, insurance, loans, etc.).

This chapter presents the results of a complex research aiming to define in what measure and with which modes the companies of the automotive sector are using the potentialities of the Internet to create value for their main stakeholders.

POTENTIALS OF THE INTERNET FOR THE AUTOMOTIVE SECTOR

Why does the Internet continue to receive so much attention? Why are the Internet and its potentialities always being discussed? What makes the Internet a better technology than so many others that preceded it? Does the Internet really change the way "to do business"? Does the Internet create new business models or does it change the existing ones?

Quite a few years after the boom of the New Economy and the subsequent enlivenment of the managerial literature at the turn of the century, perhaps the question will receive more sensible answers and above all, be sustained by a longer experience. The Internet surely is a surprising technology through which it is possible to communicate, interact, sell or distribute products and services, and above all, create a powerful tool to bind customers through communities in the form of forums, chat groups, blogs, user groups, and so forth.

What mainly distinguishes the Internet from previous technologies is that it sums up all their features and all their potentials in one low-cost standard, that is, through the Web people can watch TV, listen to the radio, and talk over the telephone. Therefore it may make more sense to talk about Media strategy rather than Web strategy: to underline the necessity, from a company's viewpoint, to govern the various interactive channels, on and off the Web, in a harmonious and coordinated way.

The Internet, therefore, changes or can change the way to do business. It has rightly been observed that the brick and mortar companies, that is, which existed before or which were not founded in function of the Internet, have to develop their own business model in order to seize opportunities, taking into account the limits (but also the strong points) of the current situation.

The most important thing is not to succumb to the charms of the Internet, which is only a tool after all, a dependent variable of the model of analysis of the company's governance. It is therefore necessary to align the choices that have been made within this scope with those which have determined the business strategy, selecting the Internet's best potentialities that better fit the purpose, thereby carefully studying realization time and modes.

The Internet as a Media and a Geographical Distance Reduction Tool

The Web facilitates exchange based relations, overcoming the obstacles of time and space. More than 10 years since the diffusion of the Internet, this may seem very obvious. According to the authors, this is the main reason behind its success though. The Internet is certainly not the only media available: the alternatives are the press, television, and radio. As said above, the Internet is extraordinary because it summarizes them all; at the same time developing interaction and the possibility to realize a communication process that is not just one way.

As in other areas, also in the automotive sector this potential allows re-examination of the development logic of the supply chain (e-procurement), the distribution processes (relations with the dealers), and of the relationship with and assistance to the customer. Therefore, it does not matter if the dealer is located far from the manufacturer; through the company's Intranet[2] the dealer will be able to see if a particular model is available or, alternatively, how long the production will take. A small size, niche manufacturer will be able to offer cars for sale to potential customers all over the world, even if the manufacturer has no dealerships at all.

The Internet as a Means to Rationalize Time

The Internet enables efficient time use, as a result of its power to reduce or dilate it. The first distinctive feature appears when looking for information about a particular car, the Web offers the possibility to find it quite quickly. In the same way the Internet allows a time dilation realization if services, streamlining the transaction, are implemented (e.g., booking of test-drive, of assistance services, etc.).

Web Externalities at the Base of the Internet

Technologies or products present Web externalities if their value is proportional to the amount of users, that is, the more the users, the higher the value (Katz & Shapiro, 1986). In order to grasp the meaning of these words, think of the usefulness of a telephone that can be used to talk to only one person. The value of such a phone would most certainly be lower than that of a phone which has a potential for worldwide communication. Clearly, the more people connected to the telephone system, the higher its value will be for its users. The Internet represents, in this sense, clear proof of this: the higher the number of people connected, the higher is the value of the Net.

The authors have had a clear demonstration of this potential, participating at a discussion forum about a new small Italian car manufacturing company. The continuously increasing number of participants and their interactions is progressively creating a pressure group aimed at demanding the satisfaction of the customers' wishes on the manufacturer's part.

The Internet as a Distribution Channel

The Internet, in general, operates as a distribution channel for all products with high information content that can be digitized (e.g., software, music, videos, images, plane tickets, various services related to banking, insurances, and even healthcare).

In the automotive sector, the Internet could be an interesting substitute for the existing distribution channels. Through the Web, low-cost cars could be sold, making it necessary to reduce the cost of the value creation channel as much as possible. And there is more! The Web could act as the main distribution channel for all those companies that have difficulties with traditional approaches, for example, small size or niche manufacturers or companies of a collateral sector such as car tuning.

The Internet as a Tool to Reduce Asymmetrical Information

Information is asymmetrical when, in a transaction, one party holds information that is relevant to the same transaction that the counterparty does not have. A classic example, printed in all economics books, is that of the transaction of a used car: here the asymmetry lies in the fact that the buyer does not only ignore the real condition of the car, but often does not even have the means to know if the asking price is congruous with the market value, or to evaluate the technical features. The Web offers such information, for example, the prices asked by different dealers for similar models, or consumers' associations that certify the quality of the product one intends to buy.

The reduction of these asymmetries can work both ways. Through the Web a car manufacturer can get to know about the expectations, tastes, and opinions of its customers. A very good example is Fiat's blog *quellichebravo* and it's Web site www.500wantsyou.com, gathering information essential for the development of new products.

The Internet as a Transaction Cost Reduction Tool

In the automotive sector too, the Internet could reduce the costs of the transaction process, as a direct consequence of the above-analyzed elements. Often in fact, companies have to do research work to find suppliers that offer the raw materials needed for the requested quality standards; the customers have to acquire information on the products' features, on the prices, and, in general, on the alternatives offered by the market; the dealers have to acquire information on the customer's financial situation, or interact with the headquarters to evaluate availability and delivery terms of each model. In the above activities, surely the majority of the information necessary to the transaction's completion can be easily obtained on the Web.

The Internet as a Tool to Support Corporate Governance and Personnel Training Courses

Finally, the Internet's technology is revealed as an irreplaceable tool sustaining the following activities:

- The company's analysis, control, and governance (business intelligence systems, ERP systems that are ever more oriented towards Web-based applications).
- Distance training of operators, with huge cost savings and significant benefits regarding the service level.
- Management of the company's information service and integration (through Intranet and management networks) of the company's divisions, organizational units, production sites, and dealerships.

OBJECTIVES AND METHODOLOGY OF THE RESEARCH

Objectives of the Research

This research work, carried out through a general survey of the Web sites of the main companies of the automotive sector, aimed at verifying how and to what extent these companies are currently exulting the potentials offered by the Internet to create value for the major stakeholders. In particular, the aim was to collect data that would allow us to evaluate:

- The strategic positioning—obviously on the Internet—of the companies of the automotive sector.
- What results have been achieved, or rather how much of the potential offered by the technology, is being used by the companies to define their own public presence on the Web.
- If and to what degree the strategic initiatives are successful in terms of visibility and registered traffic.

The Methodology of the Research

R. M. Grant (1998) defines the main objective of a company's strategy as the aim of "guiding the management's decisions to excellent results through the search of a competitive advantage; it is simultaneously a means of communication as of co-ordination inside companies."

In a correlated way, the Web strategy could be defined as that systemic set of decisions and actions aimed at determining in what measure and through which modes the company's positioning on the Internet can constitute an advantage in the pursuit of the company's strategy.

It is evident that business and Web strategies need to undergo an integrated process of definition, development, and implementation. On the other hand, if through the business strategy the company's management can understand what to use the web for, through the Web strategy it should be able to understand how to use it. The colonization of the virtual space offered by the Web should then be realized through a progressive alignment and a systematical evaluation (Memmola, 2007) of:

- The company's main strategic orientations.
- The degree of acceptance and awareness of the Internet's potentials on the part of the company's internal and external stakeholders (i.e., customers, personnel, suppliers, dealers, etc.).
- The possible impact on the organizational structure and internal processing.
- The company's general usage logic of other information and communication technologies sustaining its processing.
- The costs and benefits linked to the service or information contents activated one by one on the Web.
- The performance measurement mechanisms enabling the evaluation of the project's success.

However, the creation of a strategy (business strategy or Web strategy) consistent with the internal and external environment in which the company operates is not sufficient. Porter (2001) observes that it is essential to also "act upon" the strategic positioning, that is, on the ability to do business in a different way than the competitors, in order to create value for the customers, that is, not imitable. Which means using the Internet and ICT solutions in order to apply an univocal characterization of the product system to the image, the quality, and to complementary services rather than to the distribution logistics in such a way that it will be impossible, or at least very difficult, for the competitors to copy.

It is subsequently necessary to define the strategic profile of the Internet presence, in order to be able to continue with the positioning of the single company compared to the direct competitors, and to do the necessary categorizations and possible benchmarking actions.

According to Vittori (2004) and Buttignon (2001), the evaluation of a company's approach to the Web is normally based on the technological dimension (i.e., show-case or static site, interactive site), the recipients of the communication process (i.e., B2B, B2C, suppliers, customers, etc.), or on the goal(s) of the site (i.e., e-commerce, customer service, branding, database creation, etc.).

Such orientations are not consistent with the objectives and the set-up that we have put into practice in our research work. In order to proceed with the evaluation of the strategic positioning of the companies of the automotive sector, we have used the model created by Angehrn (1997) that goes under the acronym of ICDT, which stands for *information, communication, distribution, transaction*. This approach explains in a simple, but effective way, the sort of strategic approach used by companies for the definition of their own Web site, evaluating how and to what degree they are using the potentials offered by the Internet.

The model's name (Figure 1) derives from the segmentation of the Internet's virtual space into four main spaces: the v*irtual information space* (VIS), the *virtual communication space* (VCS), the *virtual distribution space* (VDS), and the *virtual transaction space* (VTS). This segmentation highlights the fact that "the Internet has extended the traditional market space by providing new spaces in which economic agents can interact by exchanging information, communicating, distributing different types of products and services and initiating formal business transaction" (Angehrn, 1997). In particular:

- VIS: The space that companies use to introduce themselves to customers or other stakeholders; in essence, it is a "one way," low-cost communication channel that the companies of the automotive sector use to present their organizational structure, mission, commitment to the environment, and linked services (e.g., assistance, maintenance) or complementary products (e.g., secure driving courses etc.).

- VCS: Offers the possibility to create a space on the Web to build relationships and exchange ideas and opinions; in this case, the aim of automotive companies is that of customer retention through the creation of virtual communities such as a forum, a chat, or a blog where customers and fans may exchange information or express their views on products, brand, services, and so forth.

- VDS: The Internet offers a new, efficient, and inexpensive distribution channel, suitable for a variety of services and products. All companies offering goods or services that can be digitized (e.g., e-books, videos, music, etc.), but also companies wanting to offer services to support their traditional products (e.g., online assistance, training, etc.) can benefit. Obviously, the automotive companies belong to the latter category and they can, for instance, offer the customer the possibility to download their car instructions manual, to receive reminder services for car maintenance, and so forth.

- VTS: The space allows one to realize remote transactions with different interlocutors (e.g., customers, suppliers, personnel, etc.); this Internet scope has traditionally been identified as e-commerce, related to the online sale of goods or a series of contents which in any case "assists" the transaction process (e.g., booking of test-drives, maintenance and repair services, job offers, etc.).

With Angehrn's model, a "map" of the Internet presence can be drawn up, aiming at offering a synthetic and prompt view of the Web strategy pursued by the company (Figure 2).

Figure 1. The ICDT model (Angehrn, 1997). © 1997. Albert A. Angehrn. Used with permission

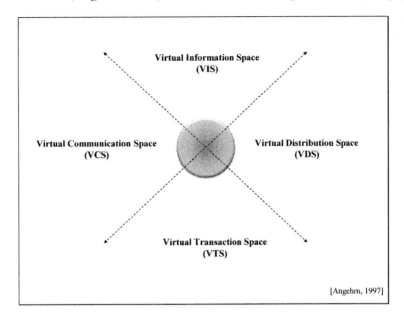

To this end the Web site is ideally divided into a series of minimum units of analysis (MUAs). A MUA represents an area inside the site characterized by the homogeneousness of the contents (informative or service) representing a precise "occupation" area of the Net's virtual space. As such, it does not necessarily coincide with the single Web page, but can be spread over more pages and can share the same page with other MUAs. In the VIS area the MUAs which can

Figure 2. Creation of the map of the Internet presence

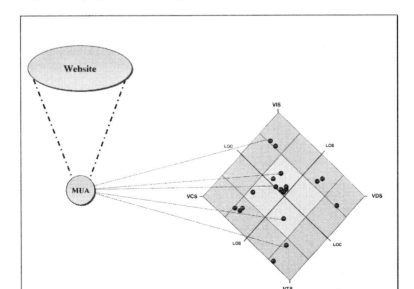

be activated are mainly informative ones, for example, those informing about the company's history, mission, product range and, so forth. In the VDS area instead, a MUA does normally have the task to give a content service, such as a reminder service for the car maintenance. Each single MUA will then be placed within its virtual correspondent area (i.e., VIS, VDS, VCS, VTS). The more external the MUA, the higher the degree of technological sophistication (LOS) and the level of content customization (LOC) measured along the orthogonal axes in the figure.

The Internet presence map allows us to evaluate and compare how and to what degree the automotive companies are using the Web to pursue their business strategy. It is therefore possible to work out a taxonomy of the strategic approaches to the Internet that we have divided into four main scenarios (Figure 3):

- The *low profile strategy*: In this scenario (represented by typology X in Figure 3) the company, although present on the Net, is (almost) unable to exploit its opportunities. Probably, the company's top management does not consider the Internet's technology as a means through which the company can pursue its business strategies, or the company has not clearly defined what the Web should be used for, or even, it may simply represent the company's answer to their stakeholders' low degree of acceptance and awareness of the Internet.

- The *medium profile strategy*: The scenario (typology Y in Figure 3) defines an operative context in which the company seems only interested in exploiting a few opportunities that the Web is able to offer. Very likely, in this situation the company's top management is still not fully aware of the opportunities that the Web can offer, or in any case it does not want to make substantial investments in this technology, due to

the fact that the stakeholders do not value the Internet very highly.

- The *high profile strategy*: In this case (typology Z in Figure 3) the Web strategy starts to actively support the pursuit of the institutional strategy. The company, although it started exploiting the Web as a mere low-cost communication tool, is now starting to significantly broaden and qualify its presence on the Web, "aggregating" other types of virtual space (e.g., VTS, VDS, VCS).

- The *very high profile strategy*: In a context as the one represented by Company K in Figure 3, the top management considers the Web strategy an essential part of the business strategy and the stakeholders accept and are aware of the opportunities offered by the Internet. The occupation of the virtual space offered by the Internet is homogeneous and characterized by high levels of technological sophistication and of content customization; the company also "lives" through, and on the Web. An essential part of the relationship with the customers (or the other stakeholders) is lived through this means of interaction.

The "colonization" of these virtual spaces can obviously be developed according to different approaches and modes. Subsequently, the evaluation of the strategic positioning on the Internet of the automotive companies has been carried out through the consideration of four analytical viewpoints:

- The **complexity of the Internet presence**, or the intensity with which a company uses the Internet to sustain its institutional activities. An intensive and extensive usage of this technology will very likely be realized through a Web site that has got "plenty of" content able to give information about the company (VIS), furnish goods/services

Figure 3. The taxonomy of the strategical approaches to the Internet

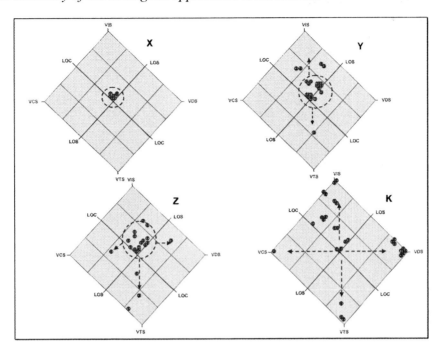

(VDS), create virtual places of communication (VCS) and carry out transactions (VTS).

- The **strategic architecture of the Internet presence**, or the more or less balanced modes through which the company has continued with the colonization of the different virtual spaces made available by the Internet, privileging some stakeholder typologies (e.g., private customers, suppliers, dealers, rental companies, business customers, etc.) and, perhaps, neglecting other typologies.
- The **quality of the Internet presence**, measured by the LOS and by the LOC of the contents proposed by the Web site.
- The **effectiveness of the Internet presence**, in terms of visibility (based on the main search engines) and success (visitors' count) of the company's Web site.

The Complexity of the Internet Presence

The aim of this analytical perspective is to measure the consistency of the Internet presence in the automotive sector, not so much in terms of the Web site's number of pages, but content richness serving the purposes of:

- Providing information about the VIS area.
- Distributing services in the VDS area.
- Creating spaces for virtual communication in the VCS area.
- Realizing transactions in the VTS area.

The higher the number of contents offered in the various areas, the higher the degree of complexity that can be attributed to the site, which is measured through two indicators:

- The amount of MUAs counted in the site.
- The content usability index (CUI).

Table 1. Methodology for analysing the Internet presence

Step 1: Internet presence complexity	• examine Web site contents and classify them in MUAs • assess the existence of other structural features (e.g., foreign language version, native language search engine, Web site map, Extranet)
Step 2: Internet presence strategic architecture	• position retrieved MUAs in corresponding virtual space areas (VIS, VDS, VCS, VTS) • verify Web site use of Internet potential
Step 3: Internet presence quality	• assign the LOS of each MUA • assign the LOC of each MUA
Step 4: Internet presence effectiveness	• verify Web site visibility by means of the most common search engines • measure average Web site traffic

The concept of MUA has been explained above, whereas the CUI allows one to measure, in complex terms, the existence of a series of "structural characteristics" that have been activated within the site to improve content usability. It is in fact logical to suppose that when the amount of content increases, for a Web site user looking for information, the degree of complexity increases accordingly; the presence of an internal search engine or a site map can be very helpful to this end. We also wanted to consider the site's usability by a particular category of stakeholders, that is, people with poor eyesight, verifying the possibility of easy modification of character size, background color, or the existence of a voice describing the contents. The CUI is thus the outcome of the ratio between the number of structural characteristics deemed noteworthy according to the methodology of the research, that is:

• Site map.
• Search engine.
• Site accessibility by poor sighted people (character size and background modification, etc.).
• Reserved area/Extranet.

An Extranet area can be defined as a company's nonpublic presence on the Internet. Whereas the use of an Intranet is totally private, within the company and by personnel only, an Extranet may give information and contents outside the company's scope in a reserved way. In fact, customers can use it to share information or services (the so-called customer clubs). Therefore, although the Extranet is not a tool aimed at improving the legibility of the site's contents, it actually increases the degree of complexity of the Internet presence.

The Strategic Architecture of the Internet Presence

Building a Web presence allows a company to use virtual space, which areas (i.e., VIS, VDS, VCS, VTS) can be used in various ways and to various extents, depending on the company's Web strategy.

This analytical perspective allows one to highlight the Web strategy followed by the company in the "colonization" of such space in terms of:

• Number of occupied virtual spaces, in order to evaluate the size of the presence built on the Internet.
• Exploitation degree of the Net's potential in global terms and of each typology of virtual space (VIS, VDS, VTS, VCS).
• Stakeholder typologies that the company is privileging (or, possibly, neglecting).

The indicators used to evaluate these aspects are respectively:

• The degree of "colonization," resulting from the simple enumeration of the Internet's virtual space areas occupied by the company (VIS, VCS, VDS, VTS).

- The *coverage index*, or the degree of coverage of the virtual space considered as a whole and of each single area.
- The *coverage index* in respect to the different stakeholder categories, that is, the degree of coverage of the demand for information and services expressed by the site's users (i.e., customers, dealers, suppliers, etc.), who for whatever reason are interested in the company.

Defining the degree of colonization of the Internet's virtual space is a simple but effective way to measure the evolutionary phase of a company's Web strategy. However, since an area can also be "colonized" through only one MUA, it is clear that this indicator furnishes a very approximate indication that needs to be integrated by the study of the mean coverage and the single area coverage index. If the degree of colonization indicates the company's presence in one of the Internet's virtual areas, through the coverage index it is possible to assess how much the company is benefitting, through its site, from the opportunities offered by the Net in that specific area.

In particular, the coverage index for each area (VIS, VDS, VCS, VTS) is fixed according to the ratio between:

- The number of MUAs found in the company's site for each area.
- The total number of MUAs found in the same area during the research.

The average coverage index is subsequently calculated through the mean average of the values calculated in each single area and supplies a synthetic, though approximate measure, of how much the company is exploiting the advantages offered by the Internet in general terms.

Finally, the coverage index regarding the different stakeholder categories is the outcome of the relation between:

- The number of MUAs found in the site that relate to a particular stakeholder category.
- The total number of MUAs that relate to the same stakeholder category found during the research.

The Quality of the Internet Presence

With regard to the qualitative dimension of the Web contents, the objective of the research work aims at using a measurement process that would be able to take into account the technical aspects as well as the traceability of the contents within the site, and that would respond as much as possible to people's informative or service needs.

Among the many alternatives, the drivers that have been adopted by the research methodology to evaluate the Internet presence are the LOS and the LOC, presented with their mean value through the MUAs found in the sites of the analyzed companies.

The evaluation of the level of sophistication (in the broadest sense of the word) is linked to the technology used. A progressive variable scale from 1 to 15 has been used to represent the various intermediate situations that can occur through:

- A MUA based on static pages realized with programs that were not specifically ideated for the Internet (e.g., MS Word, Powerpoint, etc.).
- A MUA based on real pages with the most modern tools of multimedial presentation (e.g., Flash View animations, audios, videos, images) and with a high degree of interactivity.

The level of customization is also based on the possibility to "cut" the offered site contents, according to the user's specific customization or service needs. In this case too, a progressive evaluation scale from 1 to 5 has been used. These values represent the extremes of a continuum of intermediate solutions that can turn up between:

- A MUA based on static pages, without any possibility of customizing the content, and without any additional services.
- A MUA based on pages that allow the creation of dynamic, customized contents with accessory services, for example, to build your own customized home page.

The Effectiveness of the Internet Presence

We wanted to complete the evaluation process of the Internet presence of the companies of the automotive sector through an analysis that would express the degree of "success" obtained by the Web sites. This intention implies, nevertheless, the solution of two methodological matters:

- The first concerns the need to translate in actual terms the very concept of "a Web site's success."
- The second is closely linked to the first and concerns the finding of variables able to give a measurement as objectively as possible.

There are basically two sorts of goals a company can have when setting up a Web site:

- Maximizing its visibility on the Web and therefore be reached by the highest number of potential users.
- Maximizing the use of the Web site by all the stakeholders.

The higher the degree of the above goal accomplishment, the more effective (and successful) the Internet presence will be, thereby also solving the second critical point, that is, the effectiveness level measurement of a company's Internet presence. The measurement has been obtained through the combined consideration of:

- A traceability index resulting from the major Italian and international search engines.
- A ranking of the Web site's registered traffic supplied by "Alexa.com," which draws up an international "hit parade" based on the registered traffic.

The first indicator tells how easy it is to "reach" the Web site through the major search engines (e.g., Yahoo.com, Google.com, Msn.com, Altavista. com, Virgilio.com, Arianna.com). As keywords, we have used, with an incremental approach, the company's name, the name of a product of the company, and lastly, a series of other information (i.e., the dealers and the promotions related to the company, a product's accessories line). The index is equal to the sum of the mean of the positive results (search engines with positive outcome compared to the total number of search engines) obtained for each level of measurement (i.e., company, product, and other information). A result is positive when the search engine has included the searched information in the first seven proposals (normally visualized on the first page of the search results).

Alexa.com is a site that makes a classification of all Web sites worldwide, giving them points according to the number of registered visitors. Alexa.com uses an evaluation model that takes into account both the number of accesses to the site, and the number of pages visited within the site. The number of accesses quantifies the number of visitors that have accessed the site on a particular day. The number of pages visited is calculated by the amount of internal URLs requested by the same visitor. Obviously the repeated request of the same URL, on the same day, is counted as a single page. The site with the highest combination of accesses and visited pages will be given a value equal to 1.

The evaluations furnished by Alexa.com relate to all the active sites on the Web. Therefore, a data normalization process had to be carried out in order to obtain a classification specifically related to the analyzed companies.

MAIN FINDINGS

The Research Reference

This project was developed to focus on the Italian customer point of view. We took into account all the car-maker operating in Italy at the time of the research[3] from the databases of the National Association of Italian Automobile Manufacturers (ANFIA) and National Union Foreign Car Dealers (UNRAE). The study took into consideration the Italian version of the Web site, or when this was not available, original language Web sites. This choice was made following two criteria:

- Automotive companies, except for a few cases, are global in nature. They develop a different approach in terms of products and services offered, reflecting the specific characteristics and the importance of the market, depending on each geographical area (state or continent). We decided, therefore, to evaluate their strategic positioning in a specific market area: Italy, in our case.
- The international sites of larger sized companies (singled out by domain name_company.com) are simply "entry systems" through which they are readdressed to the site of the country or language (singled out, for example, by domain name_company.it or name_company.uk).

Obviously, this decision may have an impact on the results of the research, which are in fact influenced by the strategic choice which the company decides to follow in that specific market. Nevertheless, research does not imply any change or adjustment to the framework which remains the same, regardless of the geographic area considered.

The research sample examines 56 automotive companies that roughly fall into two macro categories: generalist companies and niche companies. The first category includes those automotive companies with differentiated offer (in terms of price level and type/model of car and service features), multiple targets, and different strategic areas of market covered; while the second category includes automotive companies that have a strong brand and image, often part of a group, offer a limited range of luxury cars and focus on a segment, target type, or special use. These tend to present a higher level price range with many customized options (even if the variable is not discriminatory) (see Table 2).

For each dimension of analysis (e.g., complexity, strategic architecture, quality, effectiveness) a positive and negative benchmark was created, defining the average value of 5% of companies with the best and worst performances, respectively.

Analysis of the Internet Presence Complexity

The complexity of the Internet presence was evaluated through the combined consideration of the following indicators:

- Number of MUA activated within the Web site.
- CUI, calculated on presence or absence, within the site, of fixed structural characteristics such as: a) site map, b) internal search engine, c) accessibility to site for poor sighted people, and d) reserved area (Extranet).

The research identifies a total of 56 MUAs variously distributed in the different areas where it is possible to articulate the virtual space of Internet (VIS, VDS, VCS, VTS). Three distinct clusters (see Table 3) stand out from the Web sites of the Analyzed companies:

Table 2. Macro categories of reference of the analyzed companies sample

Generalist Manufacurers	Niche Manufacturers
• Alfa Romeo • Audi • BMW • Cadillac • Chevrolet • Chrysler • Citroen • Dacia • Daihatsu • Dodge • Fiat • Ford • Honda • Hyundai • Jaguar • Jeep • Kia • Lancia • Land Rover • Lexus • Mazda • Mercedes • Mitsubishi • Nissan • Opel • Peugeot • Renault • Saab • Seat • Skoda • Ssangyong • Subaru • Suzuki • Tata • Toyota • Volkswagen • Volvo	• Abarth • Aston Martin • Bentley • Corvette • Daimler • Dr • Ferrari • Hummer • Lada • Lamborghini • Lotus • Maserati • Mayback • Mini • Pagani • Porsche • Rolls-Royce • Santana • Smart

- **Cluster A**: Companies, using the Web, with a high number of informative or service contents, with over 30 activated MUAs.
- **Cluster B**: Companies with an average profile approach and between 25 and 30 activated MUAs
- **Cluster C**: Companies with a low profile approach and less than 25 MUAs.

The simple enumeration of MUAs must not be misleading. We are not looking at performance criteria and stating that a company that activates a higher number of MUAs inside its site is better than one that activates just a few. A company's Internet strategy is nothing more than a "translation" of its business strategy on the Web. This explains how the activation of some MUAs, for example, those supplying informative content or provide a booking service for their company museum, is typical of companies that focus on tradition and historical authenticity of their brands as an added value element (e.g., Alfa Romeo, Ferrari, Lamborghini, Maserati, etc.)

From the above considerations, it results that the number of activated MUAs is not a satisfactory indicator of the complexity of the Internet

Table 3. Cluster of 56 analyzed companies

Companies with less than 25 MUA	Companies with between 25 and 30 MUA	Companies with over 30 MUA
Daimler	Honda	Citroen
Lada	Suzuki	Ford
Dr	Bmw	Jaguar
Abarth	Hyundai	Mazda
Pagani	Kia	Saab
Rolls-Royce	Seat	Volkswagen
Mayback	Chevrolet	Volvo
Santana	Ferrari	Lotus
Jeep	Smart	Porsche
Chrysler	Subaru	Fiat
Dodge	Audi	Skoda
Lamborghini	Cadillac	Lancia
Tata	Nissan	Alfa Romeo
Dacia	Land Rover	Mercedes
Hummer	Mini	Renault
Daihatsu	Mitsubishi	Maserati
Toyota	Opel	
Bentley	Peugeot	
Ssangyong		
Lexus		
Aston Martin		
Corvette		

presence, which gives way to the introduction of the second indicator, the CUI as previously defined.

Overlapping the two parameters used to evaluate the complexity of the Internet presence, certain inconsistencies come to light: one would expect a high number of CUIs to result from a high number of MUAs, due to greater usability of the numerous contents offered. In fact, in several situations this hypothesis is denied by sites which, faced with a rather large number of activated MUAs, present a quite low CUI index (Alfa Romeo, Volkswagen, Volvo, Saab).

The good positioning of Maserati, Renault, Mercedes, and Lancia stands out. Alfa Romeo's situation is worth mentioning since it presents the greatest number of activated MUAs with a poor usability level due to the absence of basic navigational instruments (i.e., site map, search engine, accessibility for poor sighted people) on which the CUI index was developed. It is usually the general manufacturers who offer the greatest number of contents, compared with the niche manufacturers. Lotus is an exception, which even if it belongs to the second category, shows up in the higher part of the second quadrant.

Analysis of the Strategic Architecture and Internet Presence

This perspective of analysis recognizes the strategic profile of the Internet presence of companies

Figure 4. The complexity of the Internet presence

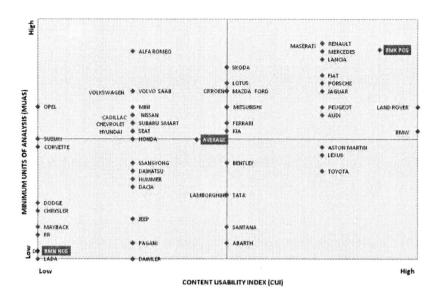

more in the automotive sector than in other areas of research. A company pursues a high profile Web strategy the moment it achieves a presence that is:

- "Widespread" in each of the areas in which the use of the Internet virtual space has been developed (degree of colonization).
- Quantitatively important in terms of number of MUAs activated compared to those potentially activeable (coverage index).

The results of the research demonstrate a generally elevated degree of colonization (average value 3.57) as a consequence of the fact that the automotive companies have predisposed Web sites with at least one MUA in each virtual space. Nevertheless, the potential of the Internet is still only used to a limited degree, that is, less than half of its potential. The average value of the coverage index is just 37%. The fact that many companies still only have a weak presence in the areas of greater value content such as VDS, VCS, and VTS (the coverage indices specific to these areas are generally very low) contributes to this result.

Nearly all of the analyzed companies, however, adopt an Internet strategy which concentrates on the information space (VIS), in which the contents are expressed in information regarding the company structure, the products and services offered by the company, the prices of the products or services, contacts, and so forth.

There are five distinct clusters of indexing (Figure 5):

- **Cluster A:** Companies with a Web strategy of medium/high profile that develop a widespread presence in all the areas and with an over average coverage index. Companies nearest to the positive benchmark like Alfa Romeo, Maserati, Fiat, Volkswagen, Renault, Lotus, but also Cadillac, Jaguar, Smart, Land Rover, and Audi, who show lower degrees of exploitation of the Internet opportunities, appear in this cluster.
- **Cluster B:** Companies with a medium profile Web strategy which develop a widespread presence in all the areas and with a coverage index value in line with or lower

Figure 5. The strategic architecture of Internet presence

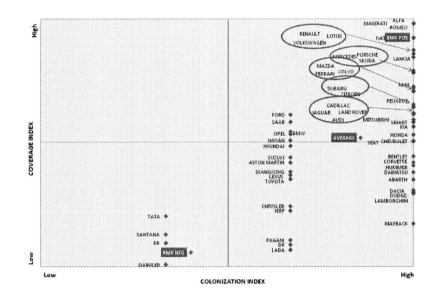

than average, for example, Honda, Seat, Chevrolet, Corvette, Hummer, Abarth, and so forth.

- **Cluster C:** Companies with a Web strategy of average profile which develop a presence limited to three areas, but with an average coverage index value (e.g., Ford, Saab, Opel, Nissan, Aston Martin, and Toyota).
- **Cluster D:** Companies with an average/low Web strategy profile which develop a presence limited to three areas, but with a consistently lower than average coverage index value (e.g., Chrysler, Jeep, Pagani, DR, and Lada).
- **Cluster E:** Companies with a low profile Web strategy which develop a presence limited to only two areas and with a lower than average coverage index value (e.g., Tata, Santana, Rolls Royce, and Daimler Jaguar).

Another evaluation parameter of strategic architecture of the Internet presence concerns the

evaluation of informative or service contents activated for each individual stakeholder category.

Figure 6 shows the performance of the average coverage index of the automotive sector with regard to the Italian market compared with the informative or service contents activated for each stakeholder; it is possible to develop the following considerations:

- It is confirmed the trend highlighted in the previous lines underlining that the companies in this sector are not yet able to fully exploit the potential of the Internet. On average, the index of coverage for each category of stakeholder varies its range from a low of 41% to a maximum of 54%.
- Certain categories of stakeholders (i.e., suppliers, business customers, rental companies, public companies, new employees) are more privileged than others (e.g., partners, employees, protected categories).
- The relatively low coverage for private customers shows how the potential of the Internet, compared with those who may be classified as the institutional recipients

Table 4. Stakeholder considered in the research

Stakeholder	Description
Providers	Companies providing semifinished goods (e.g.m alloy wheels, plastic wheel cover, piston, connecting-rod, etc) or providing services (financial companies, consulting, etc.) for the analyzed company.
Partner	Companies that, participating in the design or development of the product, may be considered a strategic partner of the analyzed company (e.g., Microsoft developing in collaboration with Fiat the Blue & Me service or Brembo, a world leader in braking, involved with a decisive role in the design of a new model).
New Employee	Those who are interested in starting a working relationship with the company analyzed (e.g., work with us...).
Employee	Those who have an employment relationship with the company analyzed.
Dealers	Companies that are holders of a concession of sales of the company analyzed (includes the car dealers and the so called "authorized" and "retailers").
Car Rental Companies	The car rental societies.
Private Customers	Actual customers or prospects of the analyzed company.
Business Customers	This category is different from the previous one because it does not refers to private customers in a B2C logic, but to companies in a B2B logic. Expectations at a content or service level are obviously different from the previous stakeholder identified.
Persons With Disability	Those who are actual or prospect customers of the analyzed company, carrying a form of disability.
Public Administration	The public corporations (e.g., state, region, province, municipality) which may be interested in the territorial development policy implemented by the analyzed company.

of the Web site remains high and largely unexplored; this result is the consequence of a large number of MUAs related to this type of stakeholders (see Figure 7) a still relatively modest coverage especially in more "advanced" areas such as the VDS, the VCS, and the VTS.

Analysis of the Quality of the Internet Presence

The quality of the Internet presence is intended as the level of technological sophistication of the distributed contents and the possibility to enter in a personalized or assisted way. The following parameters of evaluation have been used to develop such a perspective analysis:

Figure 6. The stakeholder coverage index

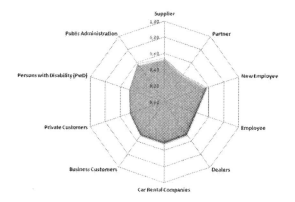

Figure 7. MUAs per stakeholder

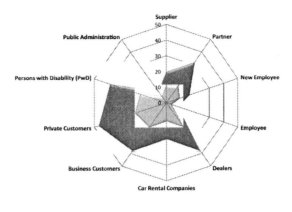

- Level of technological sophistication (LOS)
- Level of customization (LOC)
- Measured on a scale from 1 to 5.

As a first approximation, Figure 7 shows the indexing of automotive companies regarding the qualitative dimension of their presence on the Internet. Although in this case the significant differences noted in other analysis perspectives were not evident. Three distinct clusters however arise:

- **Cluster A:** The first group basically shows the presence of companies like Mini, Ferrari, Maserati, and Alfa Romeo and assumes a "pioneering" position regarding the qualitative characterization of their presence on the Net. The more sophisticated the technology, the higher the possibility to allow customization of the Web site content; this is far superior compared to the average value of the two parameters.
- **Cluster B:** The second group in the position of "chasers" is particularly noteworthy considering it combines the majority of the companies present on the market with performances that are not far or around the average measured value.
- **Cluster C:** A final group of "latecomers" who present a considerable weakness in respect to this dimension of analysis, consisting of those companies that have values close to the negative benchmark, such as Aston Martin, Santana, Tata, Lada, and so forth.

A further evaluation takes into consideration the balance between LOS and speed of access to the contents in each individual Web site. Most of the sites (41%) present a "strong preference" for LOC rather than LOS (with higher values of the first index than the second one). So the companies tend to favor highly customized contents over technology, which ends up being a little sacrificed. Only 11 of the 56 analyzed companies, in fact, consider the level of sophistication more important than the level of content customization.

A final consideration concerns the alignment between business strategy and Internet strategy. Companies with greater evocative power, with a middle to high position in terms of market level or which target the young or a niche, tend to present sites that focus on aspects of emotional involvement, full of images or interactive contents. The aim, in this case, is to create a bond with the brand rather than the mere gratification of informative demands.

In this sense, it can be noted: how Mini stands out thanks to a technologically advanced site and to highly customized contents; how Fiat has a good position, thanks, above all, to new ideas introduced for the launching of the new Fiat 500; how Ferrari has one of the richest sites regarding service contents and high path diversification; and how Abarth presents an extremely distinguished image from a technological point of view, offering the possibility to customize the site structure, its aspect, colors, and music, almost achieving the type of tuning which is at the basis of this brand's philosophy.

Analysis of the Effectiveness of the Internet Presence

The measure of success of the strategic choices by companies in the automotive sector regarding Web positioning was achieved through the combined consideration of the following parameters:

- A tracing index of the site through a panel of search engines.
- A ranking, created by Alexa.com, which supplies an indication of the traffic registered by the Web site.

Generally speaking, the Web sites of automotive companies enjoy good visibility: 63% of them presents a high traceability index (more than 2), 23% presents average visibility (with an index between 1.60 and 2), and only 8 out of the 56 companies presented a decidedly low visibility.

Concerning registered average traffic, the results of the research offer two considerations:

- A substantial aggregation of performance values corresponding to the positive benchmark; with the exception of a few companies (e.g., Fiat, Nissan, Volvo) great

differences in terms of traffic registered do not exist in the surveyed Web sites.
- The consistent distance which exists between the average reference values and the companies which present a performance close to the negative benchmark (Figure 7). The companies in question (i.e., DR, Hummer, Ssangyong) are relatively new on the Italian market, or have an extremely focused offer. In our view, these could be the main reasons for such different results.

Focusing the attention on the companies present in the quadrant II, it is possible to note the existence of four clusters:

- **Cluster A:** Companies that have an effective presence on the Web with a high level of visibility and traffic registered. Companies like Fiat, Nissan, Volvo, Alfa Romeo, Ford, Citroen, Mercedes, and so forth, which are closest to the positive benchmark, are included in this first area.
- **Cluster B:** Companies that record high levels of traffic, but show a lower visibility compared with the search engines we used (e.g., BMW, Mazda, Audi, Suzuki, Subaru, Mini, etc.).
- **Cluster C:** Companies which present high visibility levels, but at the same time achieve a relatively worse performance in terms of recorded traffic (e.g., Volkswagen or Jaguar) who therefore present atypical behavior.
- **Cluster D:** "Follower" companies with visibility levels and recorded traffic lower than the average (e.g., Jeep, Tata, and Chrysler).

The previous arguments refer to the dynamics of competitive interaction among companies in the automotive sector specific to the Italian market. As in every other research area, also with regard to this perspective of analysis, the reference was

Figure 8. The quality of the Internet presence

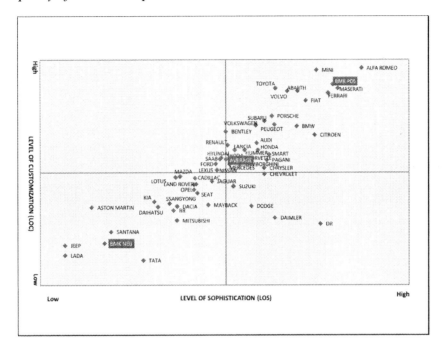

the Italian language Web sites of Italian automotive companies, whose contents, in certain cases, are not managed directly, but by a branch or the Italian importer. It is evident that the results obtained in terms of visibility, but above all recorded traffic inside the Web site, are influenced by the competitive positioning that the company achieves in the real world. In other words, the particularly high performance rate of Fiat, Alfa Romeo, and Lancia is also a consequence of the fact that the study deals with well-known national brands with high values of brand awareness. On the contrary, the results of Chrysler or Jeep can be fit into the logic of a minor diffusion of these brands, having almost a niche presence on the Italian market.

We have therefore tried to repeat the evaluation of this perspective of analysis using original language sites of the different companies (singled out by the extension .com or from the extension of the country of origin as, for example, Lotus [www.lotuscars.co.uk]). The results shown in Figure 8 are, evidently, more consistent compared to the impact that different automotive companies, or rather their brand names, have on the international scene; Toyota, Mercedes, Chevrolet, Ford, and Volkswagen are the players who achieve the highest performance levels. Italian brands undergo a decisive reduction, with the exception of Ferrari which, although it is a niche producer, has an international standing. Lancia's case is noteworthy; the brand name is present on the Italian market, but not particularly diffused on the international scene, which in this new evaluation presents performance levels that are a lot lower than the average.

LIMITATIONS AND FURTHER RESEARCH AREAS

In order to present a complete view of the phenomenon, the methodology used to analyze the presence of automotive companies on the Web inevitably experiences a few structural limits which may be clarified as follows:

Figure 9. The effectiveness of the Internet presence

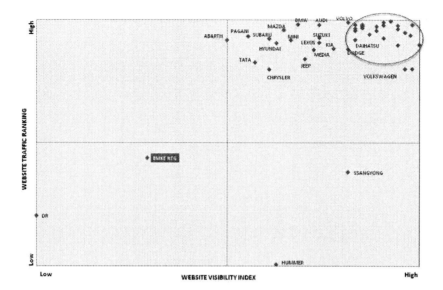

- The Internet is an ongoing reality. The research project photographs the situation as it was at the time of the analysis of the Web sites, which took place in the months of March and April 2007.
- The aim of this research is to provide an objective evaluation of the presence on the Internet. Even though a precise scale of evaluation of the LOS and of the possibility to proceed to a customization of the contents offered by the Web site (LOC) had been defined, there are inevitable elements of subjectivity present in this phase which cannot be eliminated.
- The research examines the Italian user's point of view. We have already discussed the reasons for this choice which, however, do not prejudice the possibility of applying this methodology to any other geographical context. It was in our interest, furthermore, to evaluate the dynamics of the competitive positioning of the companies in the automotive sector in a specific geographical area.

The research presented in this chapter is the first phase of a complex project, still being carried out, which also includes the development of an in-depth analysis through a series of case histories which help to fully explain the possible definition paths of the Web strategy of an automotive company.

The intent is to move from an analysis which takes place "outside" of the company, which is resolved in the evaluation of the "finished product" of the Web strategy, through the site to an analysis "within" the company. The aim is to have a complete vision of the phenomenon object of the survey, studying the path of preparation, definition, and successive implementation of the Internet strategy, the critical aspects and the duration of development, the impact on the organization, and the expectations and requirements of the persons either directly or indirectly involved.

CONCLUSION

This research would not have had much sense 15 years ago. More to the point, it would have been

Figure 10. The effectiveness of the Internet presence (focus on 2nd quadrant)

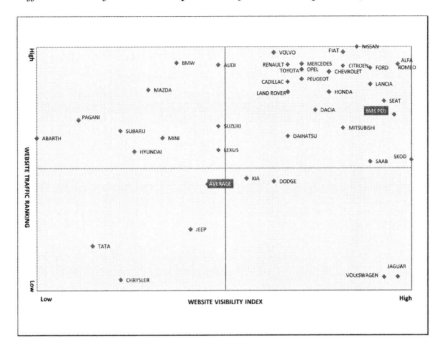

Figure 11. The effectiveness of the Internet presence (international positioning)

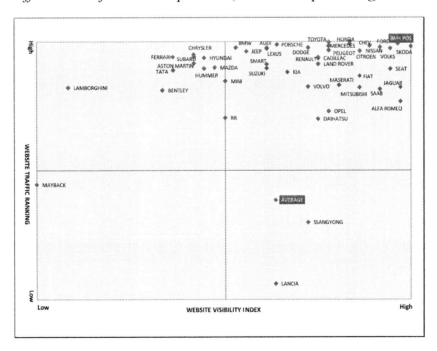

impossible to carry out. The raw materials on which our study is based would have been missing, or, anyway, the object phenomenon of the survey would have had totally different levels and dimensions.

It is in this simple and obvious reflection, but absolutely corresponding to the truth, that the extraordinariness of Internet must be found. It is almost banal to say that Internet has overturned the logics and paradigms of our daily life. This same book has been written through the Internet! Its authors have interacted virtually over the Net, without ever having met physically.

Inevitably, Internet also changes the company logics and paradigms. Thanks to (or because of) this technology, the way to run a company has changed. The Web "opens" new opportunities. And again, not even these are new concepts. Very concisely it is possible to affirm that through a redesigning of the company proceedings, the Net paves the way for improved performance in terms of lower costs, higher quality, and greater capacity of innovation. The Internet is a remarkable instrument for interaction with the company stakeholders, while other media provide only one-way channels of communication. Through the Net it is possible to improve logistics and interaction. Parallel considerations can be made for other phases of the company's value chain, such as the distribution and the relationships with the car dealers in the case of automotive companies. Finally, the Web could become the preferred instrument for interaction with customers (not just the private ones, but also business-to-business), in order to fully understand their expectations and requirements, gain their loyalty, and even involve them in the design and launching of new products (as Fiat did with the site 500wantsyou. com concerning the new Fiat 500).

The feeling which emerges from the results of this research is that companies in the automotive sector are not fully exploiting the opportunities.

Frequently, a limited use of the Web is witnessed, focused on the less complex areas, such as the allocation of contents usually of the informative sort and low technological level. Although it cannot be said that automotive company sites are merely digital transpositions of the brochures or product catalogues, wider areas of improvement could be made, both in terms of services offered and greater personalization of the proposed navigation routes. In general terms, it can be stated that the focus is still basically on the product and on the image associated with the product.

A further consideration examines the approach to the Net, which does not always seem to occur strategically, but often with a logic tied to the improvisation or an image of the Internet as a mere communication tool. In several cases, the impression is that the Web site "frees" itself from the logics of strategic positioning that the company follows in the real world in order to follow merely commercial or promotional logics, on one hand, or to present the product and the company sometimes too quickly and superficially. Companies rarely demonstrate awareness that the investment in this technology must come through an appropriate alignment with the institutional strategy of the company (Minard, 2001), with a correct review of the main operative mechanisms and company governance.

If we were to retrace the results of our analysis to different steps of the purchasing process, it can be stated that the initial stages of seeking basic information and presentation of product alternatives are definitely well covered, with often complete contents and of a multimedia sort. The phase of the actual transaction, and above all, the one linked to the management practices of post sales services (e.g., assistance, maintenance, etc.) tends to be poorly managed, with a few exceptions. The "pioneeristic" practices allow the online management of accessory services such as financing, purchase or ordering, and possible payment for maintenance/repairs, or the activation of a reminder service which advises the client when to proceed with maintenance.

The contents allowing companies to gain customer loyalty both through playful components (e.g., screen savers, images, logos, wallpaper but also real videogames) and through mechanisms of online community (e.g., forums, chats, blogs and also personalized credit cards) are beginning to catch on. At times contents are increased without adequate attention to their usability, causing confusion and a frequent absence of a profiling logic of the user, of the user's interests and needs.

The road towards a mature use of the Web by the automobile companies is still a long one, at least judging from the results we have gleaned from our research. The question, or rather, the questions that must be asked at this point are: What is it worth? Is it worth investing in the Web? How can the Web, through either its more traditional ways or from its more evolved declinations (like the various blogs, Wikipedia, YouTube, and Facebook) help to accomplish the corporate strategy of a company?

These are important questions, we realize, that could generate a specific trend of research. As far as we are concerned, having studied the Internet phenomenon for several years, we have become more aware of the fact that it is not a question of how much to invest, but rather how to invest. The success and choice effectiveness of the strategic positioning on the Web are influenced by the company's brand, but they also depend heavily on the grade of originality of the informative contents or proposed services.

We would like to conclude with a sentence from one of our many "specialists" we met during the planning phases of our research work: "The point is that on the Internet we are all guests... and as guests, we have to bring something!" What is required, therefore, is to gain the attention, "bringing something which is not normally present in the home of our host, or rather, on the Net," that is, contents that are new and original. But, in order to avoid that, this becomes an exercise for its own sake, it is necessary "to understand what type of invitation we have received and how we intend to behave accordingly." We must know what the expectations of our stakeholders are and how we can achieve them on the Web. By doing this, the corporate strategy of our company will be realized.

REFERENCES

AA. VV. (2002). *Stanford-Makovsky Web credibility study 2002: Investigating what makes Web sites credible today.* Retrieved June 23, 2008, from www.webcredibility.org

Alemi, F. (2000, Fall). Management matters: Technology succeeds when management innovates. *Frontiers of Health Services Management, 17*(1), 17–30.

Angehrn, A. (1997, August). Designing mature Internet business Strategies: The ICDT model. *European Management Journal, 15*(4), 361–369. doi:10.1016/S0263-2373(97)00016-9

Angehrn, A., & Meyer, J. F. (1997, Summer). Developing mature internet strategies (cover story). *Information Systems Management, 14*(3), 37–43. doi:10.1080/10580539708907058

Baraldi, S., & Memmola, M. (2006). How healthcare organisations actually use the internet's virtual space: A field study. *International Journal of Healthcare Technology and Management, 7*(3/4), 187–207.

Buttignon, F. (2001). *Strategia e valore nella net-economy.* Milan, Italy: Il Sole 24 Ore.

Duke, H. C., & Chul, M. K., Sang-II, K., & Soung, H. K. (2006, December). Customer loyalty and disloyalty in Internet retail stores: Its antecedents and its effect on customer price sensitivity. *International Journal of Management, 23*(4), 925–942.

Elango, B. (2000). Do you have an Internet strategy? *Information Strategy: The Executive's Journal, 16*(3), 32–38.

Glaser, J. P. (2002). *The strategic application of information technology in health care* organizations (2nd ed.). San Francisco: Jossey-Bass.

Grant, R. M. (2005). *Contemporary strategy analysis 5/e*. Oxford, UK: Blackwell.

Kaplan, R. S., & Norton, D. P. (2004). *Strategy maps*. Boston: Harvard Business School Press.

Katz, M. L., & Shapiro, C. (1986). Technology adoption in the presence of network externalities. *The Journal of Political Economy, 94,* 822–841. doi:10.1086/261409

Malcolm, C. (2001, February). Making a healthcare Web site a sound investment. *Healthcare Financial Management, 2*(74), 74–79.

Malec, B., & Friday, A. (2001). *The Internet and the physician productivity: UK & USA perspectives.* Paper presented at the EHMA Congress, Granada.

Memmola, M. (2007). The development of a Web strategy in a healthcare organization: A case history. In L. Al-Hakim (Ed.), *Web mobile-based applications for healthcare management* (pp. 1-35). Hershey PA: Information Science Publishing.

Minard, B. (2002). CIO longevity and IT project leadership. *IT Health Care Strategist, 4*(1), 3–7.

Porter, M. E. (2001, March). Strategy and the Internet. *Harvard Business Review, 79*(3), 62–79.

Robert, M., & Racine, B. (2001). *E-strategy.* Milan, Italia: McGraw-Hill.

Shapiro, C., & Varian, H. R. (1999). *Information rules*. Boston: Harvard Business School Press.

Vittori, R. (2004). *Web strategy*. Milano, Italia: Franco Angeli editore.

Yaobin, L., Zhaohua, D., & Bin, W. (2007, June). Tourism and travel electronic commerce in China. *Electronic Markets, 17*(2), 101–112. doi:10.1080/10196780701295974

ENDNOTES

[1] This chapter is the result of joint research work done by all authors. Nevertheless, Massimo Memmola is the author of section I, II and III; all other authors have equally contributed to section IV, V and VI, the discussion and the conclusion.

[2] The research was drawn up in February, 2007; The analysis of the Web site took place in March and April, 2007.

[3] A net that can be accessed only by users of a particular company/organization.

Chapter 4.6
Using Semantic Web Services in E-Banking Solutions

Laurent Cicurel
iSOCO, Spain

José Luis Bas Uribe
Bankinter, Spain

Sergio Bellido Gonzalez
Bankinter, Spain

Jesús Contreras
iSOCO, Spain

José-Manuel López-Cobo
iSOCO, Spain

Silvestre Losada
iSOCO, Spain

ABSTRACT

Offering public access to efficient transactional stock market functionalities is of interest to all banks and bank users. Traditional service oriented architecture (SOA) technology succeeds at providing reasonable, good Web-based brokerage solutions, but may lack extensibility possibilities. By introducing Semantic Web Services (SWS) as a way to integrate third party services from distributed service providers, we propose in this chapter an innovative way to offer online real-time solutions that are easy-to-use for customers. The combined use of ontologies and SWS allows different users to define their own portfolio management strategies regardless of the information provider. In deed the semantic layer is a powerful way to integrate the information of many providers in an easy way. With due regard for more development of security technological issues, research on SWS has shown that the deployment of the technology in commercial solutions is within sight.

INTRODUCTION

When operating on the stock market, investors make their decisions on the basis of huge amount of information about the stock evolution, economic and politic news, third parties recommendation and other

DOI: 10.4018/978-1-60566-066-0.ch016

kind of sources. Thanks to the proliferation of the Internet banks the profile of an average investor is changing from a financial expert to common people making small investments on the online stock market. In addition to the business generated around the stock market operations, banks use their online stock market application to attract new and to reinforce the customer commitment.

Banks, as any other commercial organization, needs to optimize the deployment of new products and services to the market. The deployment time of new services or applications is an important issue in a highly competitive market, since it defines the future market share and revenues. Online banks are looking for technologies and architectural paradigms that would allow them to design, implement and deploy new services on a low cost basis and in a short time period. New services often imply integration of many already existing applications, some of them internal and others external to the organization.

This is the case of online stock brokerage solutions adopted by online banks. An online stock brokerage application proposes to the user to buy and sell its stock options via a computerized network. Banks are willing to offer an easy to use application including as much information and as many options as possible without incurring large development costs. We will show that the use of the Semantic Web technology, combined with a service-oriented architecture (SOA), greatly reduces the cost and effort of developing and maintaining an online stock brokerage solution.

A broker based on a semantic service oriented architecture has all the advantages of a service oriented architecture (e.g. modularity, reusability) combined with the advantages of Semantic Web technologies. Semantic Web technology main advantage is to give a clear semantic inside (and eventually outside) the enterprise which reduces the communication confusions (technical or human). This also leads to higher maintainability of the products and to a better automatisation of the system mechanisms. These advantages applied to

SOA will be extended in the proposed solution of this chapter. Next section will first exposes the current situation of brokerage applications based on classical SOA.

CURRENT SITUATION: BROKERAGE APPLICATION BASED ON WEB SERVICES

Banking companies have invested heavily in the last few years to develop brokerage solutions based on a new dominant paradigm in the IT World: service oriented architecture (SOA). The concept of this paradigm is not new: propose a loosely coupled distributed system architecture where independent services provide functionality, so that the difficulty is divided which leads to reduce the development cost and improve the reusability. But the technologies to implement this paradigm are relative new. Web Services are one of the solutions that appeared a couple of years ago and that made the success of this paradigm. For this reason Web Services are often confused with the SOA paradigm.

In this section we first present in more detail the business case for the brokerage application that we propose. We will then explain why a service oriented architecture implemented using Web Services technologies is a suitable solution. The solution properties will be detailed and it will be shown that this kind of architecture is suitable for brokerage application. We then present what the benefits of such an architecture are from both, a technical and a business point of view.

Web-Based Brokerage Applications

Introduction

As a major interface between the financial world and the non-financial world, banks always try to improve their services related to the stock market. As the Internet represents one of the most interesting communication channels of recent years, banks are interested in using this channel to improve the quality of their service and thus increase their image and revenue. Such banks or bank departments have been called eBanks or online banks. We have identified three different strategies for online Banking:

- **Technological leader profile:** Banks that focus their strategy on technology and consider the Internet an opportunity to improve their markets. Also, the Internet specialized banks, usually recently founded banks (not subsidiaries) that have earn a significant market share, even though they do not offer their clients a wide range of products.
- **Follower banks profile:** Banks that first considered the Internet as a threat. When the market has matured, they changed their strategy from a defensive position to a competitive attitude towards those who were the first leaders in Internet banking. In some cases, subsidiary entities were created so as not to cannibalize their own market share.
- **Non "internetized" banks:** Banks that did not invest in the Internet because of their small size, their strategy or other reasons. However, they are a minority in terms of market share.

In these days, banks that already have Web-based brokerage application in place choose the technological leader strategy, while those banks that are only now considering developing their own applications follow the second strategy. Other mediums are also possible:

- **Branches:** Too expensive for Banks. Only for high end clients.
- **Phone banking service:** Expensive for banks. Only for selected clients
- **Mobile services (SMS, mobile phone applications):** Cheap for banks, usually free or at a small fee per service usage.

However, the Internet medium, as a cheap and universal way to perform banking operations is the highlighted solution of this business case.

In current brokerage solutions banks usually only offer the service of making the operations (buy, sell) but rarely integrate the search of relevant information to make the transaction decision. The delivery of this 'hard to integrate' functionality search, is, however, a useful to provide to the end user, who wants to buy and sell stock knowing the most relevant and current information. The user usually searches this information on external pages independently of the bank services. Some of these are free services which propose information of the stock market in real-time or with a minimum delay. Web pages such as Yahoo Finance (http://finance.yahoo.com/), Google Finance (http://finance.google.com), Reuters UK (http://uk.reuters.com/home), Xignite (http://preview.xignite.com/), Invertia (http://www.invertia.com) are good examples of financial information from different providers with different degrees of quality.

However, the need to search the information on several Web pages and then navigate to the brokerage application to execute the transaction is a waste of time and adds unwanted complexity to the end user. The idea is to build an online broker that merges and provides a unified or single point of access to information and operational services. In that way, the user will have an unified environment which integrates most of the tools required to fulfil his/her wishes of buying and selling stocks. A comparison of a traditional brokerage application interaction and the new interaction we proposed is showed in Figure 1. In the traditional interaction, the user must retrieve the information from each Data Provider (Yahoo Finance, etc.) independently and only then do the brokerage action (i.e. buy or sell). In the unified environment we propose, all the interactions are performed through the brokerage application and the brokerage application take care of showing the best data information regarding the user context (user profile, portfolio of the user, etc.).

In the next section we define the functional and non-functional requirements of our business

Figure 1. Brokerage application interaction comparison

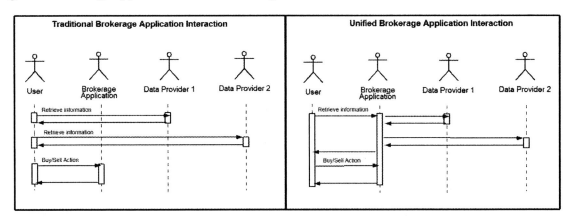

case. The following sections present one relatively new but already commonly used way of using a service oriented architecture (SOA) to implement these requirements. This solution, however, has some problems exposed later on that we resolve exposing a new and innovative way using SOA combined with Semantic Web Technologies.

Functional Requirements

The functional requirements the brokerage application must support in order to fulfil the business case are summarised below:

- **Stock market consultation functionalities:** The application should be able to retrieve information about the stock market such as the price of a share, volume of a share, historical information, etc. Several sources can be used to obtain the information necessary to the supply the user with the information they require to make the trade.
- **Customer information consultation functionalities:** The application should be able to obtain easily the customer information such as his portfolio, buy and sell history and recent searches by the user.
- **Operational functionalities:** Invocation of operations on the stock market using the

bank services: buy, sell.
- **Complex conditional queries:** Possibility to write a complex order in terms of conditions such as "if the stock value of Cisco is higher than X and its volume is lower than Y, ..." that may use different source of information. Logical combinations of the conditions should be possible.
- **Simple entry point of all services:** Complete integration of the conditional queries and operational functionalities within one simple entry point.

Non Functional Requirements

The non-functional requirements that the brokerage application must fulfil are:

- **Highly maintainable:** As the stock market is an entity subject to rapid change, it must be possible to maintain the application in an optimal way.
- **Usability:** The application is aimed at non-expert end users. The application should as usable as possible in order to present to the end user a friendly and easy-to-use interface.
- **Extensibility of the information source:** Possibility to easily add and change the providers of the banking information services.

And to extend and choose the categories of information that the user wants to see. For example, if the user is executing a buy or sell transaction the user may want to see different sets of information.

Solution Based on SOA/ Web Services

Introduction

During the last four decades, software design has been prone to many changes. After abstracting software code from the hardware infrastructure, computer scientists thought to write code in so called black-boxes and invented function oriented software design. The next big revolution was object oriented software design, in which data was intended to be packaged in objects where objects are metaphors of real world entities. Objects were then abstracted in components in order to manage the problem of the increasing number of objects. A component can be defined as a set of objects that has a coherent meaning as a standalone entity. What is the next level of abstraction? A composition of components will always be a component if we only focus on the data that these components contain. The composition must then be thought of a set of components that fulfil a given task. By doing so the packaging is no longer data-oriented but service-oriented, the set of components does no more contain information and methods to access to this information but is a black-box that offers one specific service. The services can then be composed in more abstract services and be part of the entire system, a service-oriented system.

Choosing service-oriented applications allows the clear separation of the users (commonly called 'consumers') from the service implementation (commonly called 'producers'). By having this distinction, the application can then be distributed on several platforms and possibly across networks. Each platform can have its own technology and can be located in any physical place.

The software design has fundamentally changed in system design.

The Organization for the Advancement of Structured Information Standards (OASIS) defines the service oriented architecture as follows (MacKenzie et al, 2006):

A paradigm for organizing and utilizing distributed capabilities that may be under the control of different ownership domains. It provides a uniform means to offer, discover, interact with and use capabilities to produce desired effects consistent with measurable preconditions and expectations.

In this definition a service is designed as an entity with on one hand measurable preconditions and on the other hand measurable expectations. It can be reformulated as the input and output of a function in a typical programming paradigm, but in a service the input (precondition) and the output (expectation) are no data but state of the world or effect on the world.

We must clearly separate the architecture from the underlying technology that can be implemented. The Web Services made the fame of the SOA, but there exists other technologies which are totally suitable to be used in a Service-oriented Architecture such as: RPC, DCOM, CORBA, or WCF (Donani, 2006).

In the following subsection we present a standard SOA for a brokerage application using Web Services as the underlying technology.

Architecture

An overview of the architecture of a brokerage application based on a SOA/Web Service architecture (Booth et al., 2004) is described in Figure 2.

The Web Services are physically located in either the service provider such as Bankinter or Xignite that provides their own Web Services, or in a specific Web Service container in the case that the Web Service provider does not provide a Web

Figure 2. SOA Architecture of a brokerage application

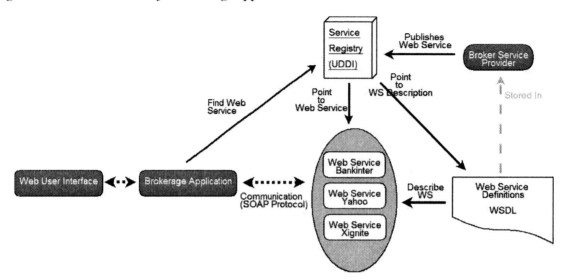

Service Interface and some wrapping mechanisms are needed. This is the case with the above yahoo based Web Service in which analysis (wrapping) of the Web page is needed to extract the right information.

The Web Service Descriptions are stored inside a Broker Service Provider which publishes all the descriptions and is in charge in managing the publication inside a Service Registry.

Through this registry, Web Services can be found and communication between the application and the Web Service is done using the SOAP.

This quite simple and elegant architecture has a lot of advantages that are explained in the following subsections on a technical and business perspective.

Benefits of SOA on a Technical Perspective

SOA is finding increased adoption across more and more business domains. This evolution can be explained by a set of technical benefits. The two most important ones are the following:

- **Reuse:** By decentralizing the systems in self contained atomic Web Services, a

SOA allows the redundancy inside the system to be reduced since the Web-services can be used more than once for different purposes. This allows also delivering new functionalities in shorter time.

- **Loosely-coupled:** In a loosely-coupled system, each entity (Web Services) makes its requirements explicit and makes few assumptions about other entities. This permits not being aware where we locate the Web Services and thus increases the IT efficiency (critical Web Services can have an adapted hardware framework), improve the Quality of Service and reduce the costs. Another advantage of a loosely-coupled system is to have standard interfaces. This way there is no need for technical people to know about the whole details of the system and allows a strategically organisational separation of skills inside the project team.

Benefits of SOA on a Business Perspective

As many times the decision of choosing an architecture is done on a business level, it is important for an architecture type to have good benefits on a business perspective. The main SOA advantages are:

- **Business effectiveness:** If one word could be chosen to describe a SOA, it would be the word "agility". By using loosely-coupled services, the responsiveness to market is highly increased. Each process of the system is better controlled and allowed a deployment of resources based on the business needs.
- **Cost efficiency:** Service-oriented architectures Enables reduction of the development costs by separating the skills and efforts in specific development areas. The separation in services allows putting the resources in the technical areas that correspond best to their skills and thus reduce the costs of training or hiring new resources. The maintenance costs of such systems are also highly reduced because of well separated services and technology and location independence. Last cost reduction is the price/performance optimization based on the freedom to select the adequate platform.
- **Risk reduction:** Dividing problems in smaller parts always has the advantage to reduce the risk of a project, thus SOA is based on this division, we can say that the risk of projects based on SOA are inherently reduced. Another point is the risk reduction of the system deployment which can be done incrementally.

Problem Statement

We have presented the benefits of using a SOA based on Web Services to develop brokerage applications. However, there are a number of points in which the standard SOA is unable to respond:

- **Web services heterogeneity:** In the Web Service technologies, the information is described at a syntactical level. For example, in WSDL XML Schema technology is used to describe what the interchanged objects are. However, this kind of technology only allows describing the type of the objects: string, date, integer etc. The semantic of what the objects are is missing. This adds inside the project development a lot of potential problems:

Misunderstanding of what is interchanged (if the documentation is badly done, errors can be quickly done)

Integration problems due to different type definition (for example, one service could describe an address with different fields while the service consumer use an unique string)

- **Poor visibility:** As defined by the standardization group OASIS inside the OASIS SOA Reference Model, the visibility *refers to the capacity for those with needs and those with capabilities to be able to see each other* (MacKenzie, 2006. In standard SOA, the visibility is mainly provided by means of a registry which lists the available services. By having only a syntactic description of the Web Service, the visibility is highly reduced and more efforts in terms of search and analysis are needed by any entity that wants to consume a Web Service.
- **Manual work:** In standard SOA system, an important effort of Web Services integration is needed in order to develop the entire system. The orchestration (composition) of the necessary Web Services corresponds to one the highest effort time spent inside the project due to the mostly manual work that these efforts imply. Middleware is often used in order to solve the orchestration. Mediation (data conversion) is on this topic the major problem. The previously cited visibility problem also implies

a lot of effort time because of the manual effort spent during the localization of each Web Service.

All these points constitute the problems of actual brokerage application based on pure SOA. However, as discussed earlier SOA has a lot of advantages. This encourages us to re-use this solution and improve it. The proposed solution of the next section aims at solving these problems of the actual solution by adding semantic technologies to this SOA paradigm.

SOLUTION: BROKER BASED ON SEMANTIC WEB SERVICES

As seen in the previous section, SOA technology provides a number of powerful concepts that when applied to brokerage applications allow us to construct flexible and easily extensible systems. However, problems have been identified with this kind of technical approach; those problems are responsible for an important part of the cost of such applications. The identified problems were *vocabulary heterogeneity, poor visibility* of the services and *manual work* needed in the development and maintenance phases. If we succeed developing a homogeneous vocabulary for Web Services, then we would increase the visibility and reduce the manual work. Three solutions were proposed in (Verma et al., 2007):

- **Pre-agree on all terms (operation name, parameters):** This implies a high oral communication between the development team and a lot of documentation writing. Pre-agreeing on the terms with no formally technical structure implies a high risk for any company due to the risk of losing common knowledge or getting integration problems.
- **Comment all aspects of a service:** In this solution, the comments are added inside the IT components. Each service contains the description of what the service proposes to do. Operation names and the semantic of the parameters are described in natural language.
- **Semantic descriptions:** This solution envisages a formal description of the services, called annotation. The services are not described using natural language but with the proper mechanism of the chosen technology.

This last solution, called Semantic Web Service (SWS), is the one that we propose in this section because it represents the most advanced and thus suitable of these three solutions. The annotation is done by using so called semantic technologies, in which the components of the system (here Web services) are formally described by using semantic resources (usually ontologies). This technology is the base of the vision of Tim Berners-Lee who put the base of a Web where the computer will be able to optimally understand and compute the information (Berners-Lee, 2001). We will explain how the use of ontologies, which is the base of most semantic system, adds visibility to the components by homogenizing the vocabulary used. We will also point out how this enhancement leads to a reduction of manual work and thus a reduction of cost.

Powerful Functionalities

The aim of annotating Web Services is not only to add clarity in the Web Service definitions but also to allow the Web Service to be read by machines. This machine-readability makes the power of the SWS by adding to the system the following functionalities:

- **Power to reason:** The machine is able to "understand" what the Web Service is doing. It is able to interpret the messages that are interchanged. The messages are no more only pure data structure but are structured in such a way that the data can be analyzed and transformed (mediated). For example, if a SWS receives information of a "client" but expected a "person", he is able to infer that a client is a person and is able to extract the right information. The whole information space is structured and coherent. Axioms are responsible of maintaining this space coherent and reasoners are the medium to do this. As described in the functional requirements, the brokerage system needs a system that is able to handle a unique point entry. The reasoning capabilities given by SWS fit perfectly to these requirements, the queries can be interpreted by the system and the system can identify what the user's wishes are. Additionally, as the machine is able to interpret what the input of the user is, it is able to help the user at the moment of maintaining the system. For example, a company has a brokerage application that allows the user to buy stocks. However, for marketing purposes the number of times that the customer can buy depends on the profile of the customer. In this case, the maintainer of the brokerage system could want to add a new type of client. With a SWS-based system, this is highly simple, as the only action to do is to add the concept of this new type in the ontology and add the information on how many operations he can do. No additional development efforts are needed and no risk of adding errors in the application is run. If the maintainer makes an error in adding the information inside the ontology, the reasoner will warn him before he put it in production.

- **Automatic discovery:** Formally describing what each Web Service does adds the functionality of automatically discovering them. This means that a query written in a formal language can be interpreted so that

the correct Web Services with the appropriate functionalities and Quality of Service parameters are found. This allows a better decoupling between: what the user wants and what the system proposes. By separating these two parts, the system gets more flexible. This SWS functionality responds to the functional requirements about the processing of complex queries. The user expresses a complex query in Natural Language or through a Web Interface, this query is translated into the corresponding formal language and this formal query can then be used to retrieve the best Web Services. More than one Web Service can be accessible for the same functionality; the system takes care at choosing the more adapted one. In terms of maintainability, the separation of the SWS is also important in the sense that adding new duplicated SWS of other providers does not require modifying the application. If new types of SWS are added, some extents must be added to the query generation functionality of the brokerage application. But this task remains relatively easy because of the use of ontologies which takes care of the coherence of the system. The automatic discovery responds to the non functional property of the "extensibility of the information source".

- **Automatic orchestration:** SWS support the automatic orchestration or composition of Web services (Medjahed, 2003). By orchestration, we mean the composition of the Web Services in order to provide a more complex service. As Semantic Web Services are semantically annotated, the system has enough information to handle a user query and respond to it by assembling the Web Services. Automatic orchestration provides an easy way to combine a usable interface to the user, with one entry point that provides the three main requirements:

979

stock market consultation, costumer information consultation and operational invocation.

SWS Technologies

The Semantic Web Service technologies have been in the last few years under intensive research world-wide. In the actual states, two approaches have been developed. Each one of these approach were part of research projects and their validity was proven by the deployment of concrete use-cases. The two approaches are:

- **Pure Semantic Web Services:** These technologies represent a way to write pure Semantic Web Services. By pure, we mean that they are written directly in a formal language and are independent from any non-Semantic Web Services. Of course, all SWS technologies need to be able to be connected with non-Semantic Web Services (called grounding) in order to support any already developed Web service system. But the idea is to be able to build new Semantic Web Services that will not carry on the "old" non semantic technologies. There are two main technologies based on this approach: OWL-S (Martin et al, 2003) based on the OWL ontology language and WSMO (Fensel et al., 2007) (de Brujin, Bussler et al., 2005)based on the WSML (de Brujin, Fensel et al., 2005) ontology language. The first is mainly a North American development effort, while the second one has been developed within EU-funded projects (Sekt, DIP, Knowledge Web, ASG and SUPER projects). They both are submitted to the W3C and have the necessary specification, development tools and execution engines.
- **Semantic Annotation of Web Services:** The second approach consists in directly annotating the WSDL with semantic information. Two main specification efforts are

actually done: WSDL-S (Akkiraju et al., 2005) that is at the Member Submission stage in W3C and SAWSDL(Farell et al., 2007) that is a W3C proposed recommendation. Main advantage of these approaches is that the annotation is done directly in the WSDL / XML Schema. Thus, the evolution of existing systems is facilitated. Other advantage is that these specifications are ontology language independent, thus execution engine can be developed for any chosen ontology language. Both languages have the necessary development tools.

Tools already exist and are operational to model and run Semantic Web Services. Most of them were part of a research project and are freely available on the Internet. For modelling SWS, the following tools are available:

- **WSMO Studio[1]:** A SWS and semantic Business Process Modelling Environment. Also support SAWSDL. As described by the name, this tool supports the WSMO Framework. It is Eclipse-based and the last version is 0.7.2 released on 29/11/2007 (in the moment that this chapter is written: end of 2007)
- **Web Service Modelling Toolkit (WSMT)[2]:** A lightweighted framework for the rapid creation and deployment of the tools for SWS. It supports WSMO Framework. It is Eclipse-based and the last version is 1.4.1 released on 13/09/2007 (in the moment that this chapter is written: end of 2007)
- **Radiant (Gomadam, 2005)[3]:** A WSDL-S / SAWSDL Annotation Tool developed by the University of Georgia. The annotation is made using OWL ontologies. It is Eclipse-based and the last version is 0.9.4beta released on 29/05/2007 (in the moment that this chapter is written: end of 2007).
- **ODE SWS (Corcho, 2003)[4]:** A toolset for design and composition of SWS. It is based

on UMPL and some work has been done to integrate OWL-S.

- **OWL-S IDE (Srinivasan, 2006)[5]:** A development environment supporting a SWS developer through the whole process from the Java generation, to the compilation of OWL-S descriptions, to the deployment and registration with UDDI. The last version is 1.1 released on 26/07/2005 (in the moment that this chapter is written: end of 2007).

- **OWL-S Editor (Elenius, 2005)[6]:** A Protégé Ontology Editor plugin for a easy creation of SWS. The last version was released on 04/11/2004 (in the moment that this chapter is written: end of 2007).

The following SWS Engines are available:

- **WSMX[7]:** The reference implementation of WSMO

- **Internet Reasoning Service III (IRS-III)[8]** (Domingue et al, 2004): A SWS framework, which allows applications to semantically describe and execute Web services.

- **OWL-S tools:** A series of tools WSDL2OWL-S, Java2OWL-S, OWL-S2UDDI, etc. are available at: http://www. daml.ri.cmu.edu/tools/details.html

Through these tools represent good proofs of the viability of the technology. That said, further development would be required to adapt them to the needs of real world system. Professional benchmarks would be needed to identify efficiency and security lacks and allow the development of professional SWS frameworks.

We gave a short overview of the existing SWS technologies and we explain now how these technologies can be applied to brokerage applications.

Approach and Architecture

The approach taken for creating a brokerage application with SWS is to use the SWS engine as a central component of the architecture. By taking advantage of the reasoning capacities of the SWS engine, it is possible to build a simple and extendible Brokerage Application. New Semantic Web Services are added directly in the engine and we minimize the development costs of managing new services. The SWS engine "understands" the semantic of the new added SWS and only few modifications are needed inside the Brokerage Application itself. This approach has been proven during the DIP project on a use-case (see the two screenshots Figure 3 And 4) that simulated a brokerage application with Bankinter and external Web Services. The user can enter a complex query composed of several conditions and one action to be taken. The conditions are connected with logical operators (AND/OR). The conditions can be of the types:

- *If the price of a specific stock is higher than a given price.*
- *If the value of an index is lower than a given value.*
- *If the expert recommendation is equal to a specified one.*
- *If the variation of the value of a given stock is higher.*

For each information that needs to be retrieved, the SWS Engine is responsible for discovering the best suitable Semantic Web Service, eventually by composing multiple Semantic Web Services (orchestration) and invoke the one (/ones) that correspond to the given Quality of Services parameters (time to respond, localization, etc.). If a Semantic Web Services is grounded on some other service systems (like normal Web Services), it is in charge of getting the information and converting it into the semantic language. The Brokerage

Figure 3. First screenshot of the SWS based brokerage prototype

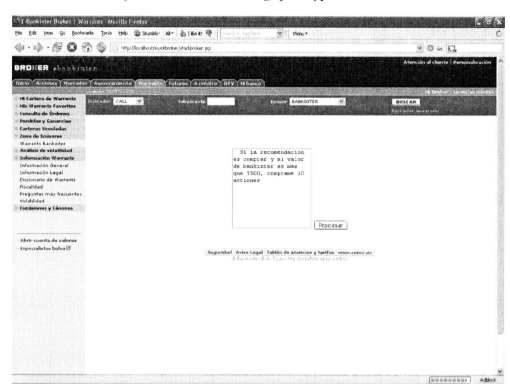

Figure 4. Second screenshot of the SWS based brokerage prototype

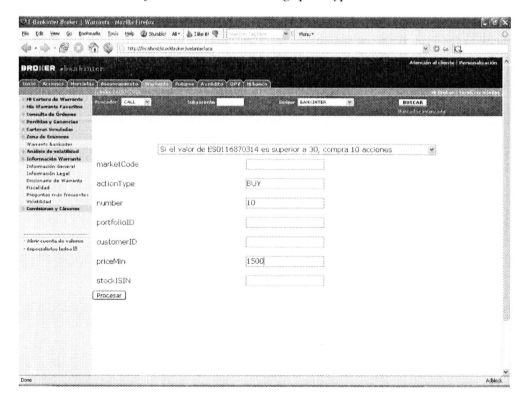

application then returns the result of the execution to the Web Interface.

Figure 5 shows the architecture that implements this approach. The three main components are:

- The Web User Interface that should respond to the Usability non-functional requirement.
- The Brokerage Application that should support all the functional requirements and that is in charge of the communication with the SWS Engine.
- The SWS Engine that is in charge of managing the semantic resources: discovering, invoke and orchestrate the SWS.

The brokerage application prototype developed in DIP has been developed using J2EE technologies. The application makes use of Natural Language Processing technologies to offer a simplified interface to the user. Receiving one sentence as input, the brokerage application is able to identify what is the user intention and automatically retrieve the information that it needs to invoke the SWS. These parameters are used to generate a WSMO goal (de Brujin, 2005) formally describing

the user intention. This goal is the entry point to the SWS Engine.

As SWS Engine, WSMX (Bussler et al., 2005)[9] was chosen over IRIS-III (Domingue et al., 2004) (Cabral et al., 2006)[10] in order to prove the correct implementation of this SWS Engine inside the research project. From the input goal provided by the brokerage application and some optional Quality of Service parameters, the SWS engine discovers the necessary SWS and invokes the retrieved SWS in the right order (orchestration). The brokerage application can then have access to all the information it needs to check the condition provided by the user and if the conditions are validated execute the buy/sell order through another call to the SWS engine.

The Financial ontology, exhaustively described in (López-Cobo, 2008) plays a major role in all the tasks of the SWS engine and is the pillar of the whole brokerage application. It describes the vocabulary of the application and is used to annotate the SWS on both levels: the functionality description (capability) and the interface (message exchange).

By using an architecture based on the Financial ontology and the SWS engine, we provide a flex-

Figure 5. Brokerage application architecture

ible and maintainable application and provide to the brokerage system the whole benefits of using SWS technologies.

In the next section, we describe in a higher level the cost and benefits of adopting such architecture.

COST AND BENEFITS

From a business point of view, the profits of the proposed solution must not be focused on new incomes neither on costs, although they both exist. The resulting application is intended to create a new product, by giving new options to manage their portfolio. These options could have been developed using a more traditional approach but, due to the complex and usually mature architectures used by the financial institutions, the costs would have been significantly higher, both the development and the future sub-applications costs.

Also, a more traditional approach (i.e. without semantic technologies) would have implied agreements with the information providers (data formats, relevant data, how to provide the information, how to access to the data, etc), which will usually implied a one-by-one Trading Partner Agreement (TPA). The semantic layer gives us the ability to smartly read the provided data and therefore to manage it easily. It is also easy to add new providers with this approach. Finally, data is accessed when required and if required, making use of the Web Service advantages.

The costs and benefits, from the technical point of view, must be also considered. The Cost/Benefits ratio in terms of adapting actual systems, although not trivial, is not as dramatic change as the one that was performed in the transition to the Internet era.

Banks were usually based on main frame architectures. The scenario in these last 10-20 years has changed from a exclusive main-frame scenario, where only the bank employees had access to the IT transactional systems, to a Web Based scenario where virtually any customer, anywhere at anytime could be using the bank transactional. This transition meant high investments on scaling the main frame architecture to a 24*7 architecture adding several layers: Web servers, application servers, database servers, security layers...

Fortunately a Web Service scenario is more natural in the actual client-servers environment, therefore, in terms of cost/benefits the investment is lower. The same reasoning can be applied to a SWS scenario, where besides the new Web Service layer to be added, semantic pieces appear to complete the puzzle.

Therefore, taking the chance of adding semantic layers to an existing bank architecture implies low economical risk since no major implications are needed to expand the current architecture.

As a result, and taking into account the business opportunity, the small amount of effort required to create and maintain the service, and the technical prerequisites, the SWS approach emerges as a smart solution to create the new service at a reasonable level of cost, both for the developer and, which is more important, for the final user.

RISK ASSESSMENT

From a business point of view, alternatives are almost always more expensive but it could depend on how each Financial Institution manage its own Stock Market Services. What is more, in several cases the solution could be so complex that it could be considered as 'nearly impossible' to develop without studying in depth what is going to be modified, (Stock Market applications are critical tasks for Financial Institutions due to the volatility of the market and the quality assurance that is required in this specific market).

At the same time, the new proposed service is intended to give better utilities to the clients. These kinds of services are actually free, although the final user must manage with them. So the price of the service for the final clients could not be high and thus, it has to be developed at a reasonable cost. There are some risks when the use of SWS is considered:

- **Security issues:** No doubt this is the major functional risk to be considered when deploying SWS technologies. On banking environments security is the mayor column on which all the architecture must be built. All the security issues must be clarified and solved before any transactional application using real customer banking data is deployed to the real world. If this milestone is not achieved all the SWS-based applications will be forced to handle only with public data and the real value of semantic applications will remain as a proof-of-concept not as a real-world-application.

- **Evolution issues:** SWS techniques are in their first steps of use in business environments. As these techniques become more familiar they will evolve and this evolution could mean scalability issues that should be treated as any other scalability issues inside any corporation environment. Although the semantic techniques are mature their wide use could imply changes that would mean changes on the semantic platform. However these two evolution issues are natural to any IT development or to the deploy of any new technology. The IT business, no matter if it is the banking business or any other, has got enough experience to handle these potential risks.

FUTURE TRENDS

The evolution of the Stock Market and its associated services must be forecasted as part of the global social tendencies: people (and investors) are requiring more and more sophisticated products and services allowing them to make their own decisions. If we consider that information

aggregators are the Internet 'killer applications' (i.e.: Google, Yahoo, You Tube, etc) investors are expected to make use of Stock Market data aggregators (in fact, the actually use them: Yahoo! Finances, Invertia, etc), making their own buying/ selling decisions and finally performing them in their favourite Stock Market site.

None of these services are designed to perform automatic operations that completely fulfil the investor requirements, nor of them are prepared to perform a personalised strategy when data aggregation is required. There are several solutions for professional investors but they are available at a high cost, thus they are only interesting when high volumes are regularly performed (high volume both in terms of number of transactions and in terms of money invested). But there they are not an option for individuals.

Our tests[11] reveal that people usually make use of at least two Stock Market services just to fulfil their information requirements. The SWS is intended to aggregate them and, in the near future, to automatically perform the actions according to the investor strategy, combining sources and retrieving specific data form them.

CONCLUSION

Responding to the need of maintainable and efficient brokerage applications, we have presented in this chapter a novel approach that combines the SOA architecture and the semantic technologies. By using the proposed solution, we resolve the three identified problems of a non-semantic SOA solution: heterogeneity of the vocabulary used in the services which reduces the maintainability and possibilities of evolution of the application, the poor visibility which reduces the possibility for automatic discovery and the lot of manual work that is generated by this poor visibility and the lack of automatic composition possibilities.

We exposed the advantages of a solution based on Semantic Web services: reasoning functionalities, automatic discovery and automatic orchestration. Such functionalities allow us to build an architecture centralized on the SWS engine and have a really flexible system.

The feasibility to build such brokerage application has been demonstrated during the European project called DIP. The output of these projects is a framework called WSMO associated with an ontology language (WSML) and execution engines (WSMX and IRS-III). The European Commission continues to invest money in the research in Semantic Web Services for example in the SUPER project which aims to take advantage of the Semantic Web Services in order to improve Business Process Management Systems. A lot of research is also done in other technologies such as OWL-S. The high activity of these research projects reflects the important interest that should have industrial investor in such technology. The Semantic Web services are ready and continue to be improved.

Companies should consider the benefits of SWS on two levels: the strategic level and the tactical one. On the strategic level, the SWS give the possibility to build highly maintainable applications and profits from a loosely coupled architecture. On a tactical level, a company should see the benefits on other projects where the ontologies that have been created for the SWS are reused and form a common base for the applications. Using such Semantic technologies is interesting for companies because it promotes the homogeneity of the systems inside the company. The intra-company and inter-company applications are then much easier integrable.

REFERENCES

Akkiraju, R., Farrell, J., Miller, J., Nagarajan, M., Schmidt, M., Sheth, A., & Verma, K. (2005) *Web Service Semantics - WSDL-S,*

Berners-Lee, T., Hendler, J., & Lassila, O. (2001). The Semantic Web. *Scientific American, 284,* 34–43.

Booth, D., Haas, H., McCabe, F., Newcomer, E., Champion, M., Ferris, C., & Orchard, D. (2004) *Web Services architecture.*

Bussler, C., Cimpian, E., Fensel, D., Gomez, J. M., Haller, A., Haselwanter, T., et al. Zaremba Maciej, Zaremba Michal (2005). *Web Service Execution Environment (WSMX).*

Cabral, L., Domingue, J., Galizia, S., Gugliotta, A., Norton, B., Tanasescu, V., & Pedrinaci, C. (2006) *IRS-III: A Broker for Semantic Web Services based Applications,* The 5th International Semantic Web Conference (ISWC 2006), Athens, GA, USA, Corcho, O., Fernández-López, M., Gómez-Pérez, A., and Lama, M. (2003). *ODE SWS: A Semantic Web Service Development Environment.* VLDB-Workshop on Semantic Web and Databases, 203-216. Berlin, Germany.

de Brujin, J., Bussler, C., Domingue, J., Fensel, D., Hepp, M., Keller, U., et al. (2005). *Web Service Modeling Ontology (WSMO).*

de Brujin, J., Fensel, D., Keller, U., Kifer, M., Lausen, H., Krummenacher, R., et al. (2005). *Web Service Modeling Language (WSML).*

Domingue, J., Cabral, L., Hakimpour, F., Sell, D., & Motta, E. (2004). IRS-III: A platform, and infrastructure for creating WSMO-based Semantic Web services. In *Proc. Of the Workshop on WSMO Implementations.* CEUR Workshop Proceedings

Donani M.H. (2006). SOA 2006: State Of The Art. *Journal of Object Technology,* 5.

Elenius, D., Denker, G., Martin, D., Gilham, F., Khouri, J., Sadaati, S., & Senanayake, R. The OWL-S editor-A Development Tool for Semantic Web Services. In *The Semantic Web: Research and Applications.* Series: Lecture Notes in Computer Science, Vol. 3532, 78-92. Springer Berlin / Heidelberg 2005. ISBN: 978-3-540-26124-7

Farell, J., & Lausen, H. (2007) *Semantic Annotations for WSDL and XML Schema.*

Fensel, D., Lausen, H., Polleres, A., Brujin, J. d., & Stollberg, M. Romand D., Domingue J. (2007). *Enabling Semantic Web Services – The Web Service Modelin Ontology.* Springer.

Gomadam K., Verma K., Brewer D., Sheth A. P., Miller J. A. (2005) Radiant: A tool for semantic annotation of Web Services, *ISWC 2005.*

López-Cobo, J. M., Cicurel, L., & Losada, S. *Ontology Management in eBanking applications.* In *Ontology Management. Semantic Web, Semantic Web Services, and Business Applications.* Series: Semantic Web and Beyond, Vol. 7. Hepp, M.; De Leenheer, P.; de Moor, A.; Sure, Y. (Eds.) 2008, Approx. ISBN: 978-0-387-69899-1

MacKenzie, M., Laskey, K., McCabe, F., Brown, P. F., & Metz, R. (2006) *Reference Model for Service Oriented Architecture 1.0.*

Martin, D., Burstein, M., Hobbs, J., Lassila, O., McDermott, D., McIraith, S., et al. (2003). *OWL-S: Semantic Markup for Web Services.*

Medjahed, B., Bouguettaya, A., & Elmagarmid, A. K. (2003). Composing Web services on the Semantic Web. *The VLDB Journal, 12*(4), 333–351. doi:10.1007/s00778-003-0101-5

Srinivasan, N., Paolucci, M., & Sycara, K. (2006). Semantic Web Service Discovery in the OWL-S IDE. In *Proceedings of the 39th Annual Hawaii international Conference on System Sciences - Volume 06* (January 04 - 07, 2006). HICSS. IEEE Computer Society, Washington, DC, 109.2.

Verma K., Sheth A. (2007). Semantically Annotating a Web Service. *IEEE Computer Society,* March/April 2007, 11, 83-85.

ENDNOTES

[1] http://www.wsmostudio.org/download. html

[2] https://sourceforge.net/projects/wsmt/

[3] http://lsdis.cs.uga.edu/projects/meteor-s/ downloads/index.php?page=1

[4] http://kw.dia.fi.upm.es/odesws/

[5] http://projects.semwebcentral.org/projects/ owl-s-ide/

[6] http://owlseditor.semwebcentral.org/

[7] http://www.wsmx.org/

[8] http://kmi.open.ac.uk/projects/irs/

[9] http://www.wsmx.org

[10] http://kmi.open.ac.uk/projects/irs/

[11] Done inside the DIP (http://dip.semanticweb. org/) project, Deliverable 10.10.

This work was previously published in Semantic Web for Business: Cases and Applications, edited by R. García, pp. 336-352, copyright 2009 by Information Science Reference (an imprint of IGI Global).

Chapter 4.7
Innovating through the Web:
The Banking Industry Case

Chiara Frigerio
Università Cattolica del Sacro Cuore, Italy

ABSTRACT

In recent years, the financial services industry has been witness to considerable consolidation (Berger & Udell, 2006; De Nicolò, Bartholomew, Zaman, & Zephirin, 2004; Figueira, Neills, & Schoenberg, 2007) and organizational progress in order to sustain two main objectives: efficiency and commercial effectiveness (Epsten, 2005; Sherman & Rupert, 2005). In order to sustain customer-oriented and efficiency strategies, banks have started to explore new ways of conducting their business, introducing areas of innovation in their services, practices, and structures to offer the most complete array of services possible (Quinn et al., 2000). On the other hand, new services and products drive retail banks to explore new ways of producing or delivering these novelties. This is true especially for Internet banking services that offer services to customers 24/7, and it becomes clear that adding new services, that is, trading online or bill payments, is easily and quickly geared towards improving commercial effectiveness. The following chapter aims at describing to what extent the Internet has developed new services and businesses, and what are the main figures of the phenomenon in Europe. Moreover, the Internet has introduced new coordination processes within each financial institution. Let us think about Intranet portal, content management tools, and business process management suites, which are now quite spread in banks due mainly to their technological ease-of-use. Thus, Internet is representing an innovation wave extremely relevant for the financial industry as a whole, and the effects on banks' performance is emerging. What do we expect in the near future? In all probability, the usage of Web-based application will be bigger and bigger also in other contexts of the bank processes, even if some risks could occur when clear strategies and change management practices do not direct the innovation.

INTRODUCTION: INNOVATION AND WEB BANKING

The banking system is undergoing remarkable strategic and organizational change processes, which will consolidate and spread even in the future. Such changes are not to be considered as a contingent change in the design and development criteria of the business, but they point out an innovation character which extends far beyond those boundaries. The application fields of innovation criteria are numerous (e.g., technological, organizational, commercial) even though two main critical issues often hinder

DOI: 10.4018/978-1-60566-024-0.ch012

the creation and spread of innovation: a) the origin of innovation, that is, the characteristics of the innovation source; and b) the possibility to know beforehand the effects of innovation and to keep its sustainability in the long run.

With reference to the subject of the origin of innovation, the most traditional theoretic version counters the organizational process innovation with the innovation of product and service. "Product innovation is given by the introduction of a new product or service to meet the market request or a particular external customer, while process innovation is defined as a new element which is introduced into the organizational processes in order to produce a product or to distribute a service" (Damanpour & Gpalakrishanan, 2001, pp. 47-48). Organizations develop product or service innovation in order to increase their market shares or to improve their strategic positioning, while they innovate in the process in order to achieve economies of scale and increase profitability (Utterback & Abernathy, 1975). The innovation of the first type allows the development of the first phases of the life cycle of a product/service, therefore it involves relevant investments and high risks. On the contrary, organizations that operate process innovations generally develop themselves at the time in which the product/service is in a maturity phase, therefore in the long term. For this reason, process innovation generally requires less investment (Anderson a& Tushman, 1991; Barras, 1990).

Moreover, by overcoming the dichotomy between product/service innovation and process innovation it is possible to consolidate an approach which takes into consideration the combination of both drives within an innovation policy (See Figure 1). Therefore, both product/service and process innovation may be combined and may generate added value within a short period and with minor costs (board 3). Therefore, in some cases, the ability to innovate is measured both in the product/service part as well as in the process one. The convergence of the innovation strategic approaches is ensured by organizational mechanisms which have the role of coordinating and managing skills, relations, and innovation processes as a whole.

With reference to the second critical issue source, managerial literature associates to innovation the characteristics of "radicality." An innovation is radical when its adoption process over time develops in nonlinear maturity phases, characterized by times of performance growth on discontinuous effects. The main obstacle in the innovation management is given by the difficulty of previously predicting moments in which a performance leap and the relevant extent of the performance growth will take place. The effects of innovation may be even more uncertain if the innovation recipient is a little controllable, being it external (e.g., the customer). As a matter of fact, the lack of control over the external party prevents knowing the cause-effect relationship of the leverages affecting the innovation adoption process. Such leverages may also be generated or limited by solicitations which are outside the bank-to-client relationship, difficult to foresee and to manage.

All the above mentioned introductory considerations may be useful in evaluating one of the main innovation areas developed by the banking industry over the last 20 years, that is, the Web.

As a matter of fact, the introduction of this technology immediately generated a great application interest from financial institutions and was directed mostly towards:

a. Development and management of both relationships with the outside (i.e., stakeholder and clients) and the inside (i.e., cooperators and employees), through the use of the Internet and the Web as innovations in the publication and circulation of contents or services.

b. The development of "core banking" applications and information systems in Web-based environments characterized by integrability and pace of important achievements.

Figure 1. Product/service/process innovation

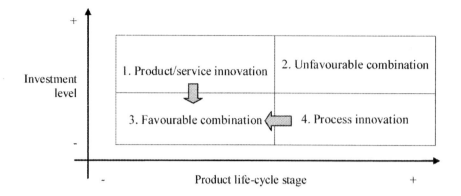

This chapter aims at exploring the first applicability area, by describing how and in which way the Web development in such a context has been innovative. Specifically, it analyzes first the characteristics of *Internet banking* and then those of *Intranet banking*. By the first term, we refer to the development of distribution channels of product/services alternative to the physical presence, based on Web technology and distributed through Internet. In this area, product innovations went and go hand-in-hand with process/channel innovations. As a matter of fact, certain products specifically created for the Internet channel, like c/a, loans, and financial services, are supported by new management processes, aimed at providing procedure efficiency and standardization. The joint product and process innovation enables to support further innovation strategies aimed, on the one side, at creating increasingly customer behaviour-oriented products and, on the other, at improving processes even in nonefficient areas. To support the theory concerning the mutual relationship of product and service innovation, one may consider the evidence substantiated by the "multichannel service strategies," characterized by the presence of cross-channel and cross-customer product/services and processes.

Therefore, though the evolution of the Internet, the banking phenomenon is continuous and steady; another application area of the Web use, less visible but equally active, is the one of Intranet banking. Intranet is an information support available for members of an organization aimed at providing easy and immediate access to organizational and training information, thus reducing distribution costs and the level of information dispersion which potentially increases the job complexity and employee dissatisfaction.

The development of information technology-based innovations, like Web banking, raises the issue of the importance of an assessment of the threats of technology innovation. It is enough, for instance, to look at the problem of trade (products and channels), organization (production processes and innovation delivery), and information (data and information flows) integration, deriving from the implementation of an Internet strategy. The lack of integration represents one of the main defeating threats of the innovation implementation process (Ciborra, 1996). As a matter of fact, the latter is effective only when it is a part of a whole and is not out of context. Another technology innovation challenge is represented by the speed and the direction of the standard implementation process. Specifically in the Web banking industry, the interoperability requirements are essential. Technology innovations which may vary the widespread standards are particularly critical and difficult to implement.

INTERNET BANKING: A HISTORICAL SUMMARY

Internet banking started growing at the beginning of the 90s and saw its maximum development at the end of that same decade.

Its importance in the definition of bank commercial and marketing strategies was immediately clear. The development of applications which would allow customers to remotely operate by means of their home PC was minimally complex and fairly cheap. But the decisional factor of the main business plans on Internet banking was the evaluation of the transaction marginal efficiency. As a matter of fact, since the first analysis it was clear that the cost of the process of a transaction opened on a virtual channel was considerably lower than the physical one (e.g., that of a promoter branch agency). This scenario initially led some banks and then most of them to adopt an Internet strategy.

Especially in the leading banking groups in Europe, the potentials made available by Internet led to the creation of units fully dedicated to the management of virtual customers (both retail and corporate). Such units were often legally autonomous companies, that is, subsidiaries of the parent bank. However, the strategy of direct banks (i.e., those which were exclusively present on the virtual channel) does not have a long life. As a matter of fact, on the one hand, besides the totally dedicated channel, banking groups keep the possibility of operating their accounts via alternative channels (often by using the same virtual bank technology). On the other hand, certain companies born to represent the mere virtual channel of their parent bank start creating, little by little, within a multichannel

perspective "light" branches with employees able to support customers. This was, for example, the Italian case of Banca 121. The current situation is characterized by a higher number of universal banks integrating Internet service into their offer. Only a few operators are solely virtual and they are generally specialized in online trading. This last service has long been considered by most operators as the killer-application of Internet banking. At a time when investments in negotiable securities had high returns, online trading developed considerably and, in certain cases, it replaced the figure of the financial promoter or of the financial manager. Subsequently, the development of further services, not only linked to brokerage, allowed also the development of more complete Internet strategies for retail banking (e.g., c/a transactions, circulars, requests for consulting support) and also for private banking, characterized by sophisticated and demanding clients.

The e-commerce phenomenon for banks has not yet given the expected results. Some banks have activated e-commerce initiatives both in the business-to-business (B2B) as well as in the business-to-consumer (B2C) areas. English and Spanish banks proved to be the most active in this situation. Besides payment management, often accompanied by the creation of special credit cards in the case of B2C, banks also offer partnership formal guarantee services (especially in the case of B2B portals) and of special financing. We have progressively witnessed the passage from an activity of incubator and partnership, still present in the less developed areas, to the activity of facilitating or aggregating, though the few existing cases do not allow us to consider e-commerce for banks as a consolidated phenomenon.

THE PRESENCE ONLINE: AN ANALYSIS OF WEB SITES

A recent survey carried out in 2003 allowed the comparison of the Web world experience of the

European banking key-players, with particular reference to strategies and behaviours (Carignani & Frigerio, 2003).

The survey targeted seven European countries (i.e., France, Germany, Italy, Scandinavian Countries, Spain, Switzerland, UK), selected among those having a higher level of Internet usage penetration and characterized by important investments through alternative channels. To this purpose, the survey analyzed: first the German market, considered as the widest and most developed market of the European scenario; the British one, whose financial and banking tradition is, in many aspects, similar to the US banking system; the Scandinavian system, important for the extremely widespread Internet use among the population; and the Swiss one, characterized by a peculiar banking tradition in retail and private banking. Other significant experiences closer to the Italian context are the one of France, characterized by a good spread of alternative channels, and the one of Spain which, regardless of the disadvantage compared to its European competitors, is now coming up strongly into the direct banking sector with interesting offers.

With regards to the individual banks selected within each chosen country, in Germany, whose banking system still represents today the reference model of all operators of the Old Continent, and in the UK, the survey investigated traditional banks which chose to invest hugely in new channels by implementing rather aggressive strategies, and the most significant examples of direct banks born as spin-offs of the major banking groups of their respective countries. This way it is possible to monitor and compare the direct banking initiatives of both leading banks and followers. With reference to the French market, the survey focused merely on the main traditional banks in terms of customers, as well as on volumes and on the three most successful initiatives in the e-banking field. In the Scandinavian banking industry, which, as previously mentioned, is strongly geared towards the use of innovative channels, the attention was

focused on those banking institutions which have adopted the most interesting and innovative initiatives from a technological point of view and which, for this reason, may represent a reference model for banks of other countries like ours, where Internet penetration is still low, though growing, and the population is still little accustomed to use technological channels. Considering the central role given to the Italian situation within our research, a wide sample of banking institutions was selected. In particular, attention was given to those banks which form part of the major groups of the country, as well as to single institutions having a considerable volume of customers.

From the analysis of data provided in the field of the strategic choice made, both Italian and European banks show the trend of looking at electronic channels as a way of diversifying their offer. The search for new services which may be offered online, thus contributing to increasing the added value given by the bank, is pursued by 68% of Italian banks and 38% of European banks. Price leadership is a primary value just for 10% of Italian banks (typically those which are merely remote) and of 19% of foreign banks. This value makes even more sense if it is compared to the result given by the same survey carried out in 2000. As a matter of fact, in that occasion, it appeared that price reduction represented the main objective of Italian banks, followed by the advertising channel. Moreover, 24% of European banks are aiming at product differentiation, by introducing new products and services which have a different configuration for the Web.

Going more into details with regards to the implemented strategies, the types of services offered have been analyzed, also comparing the offer of other transfer services by remote banking.

All European and Italian banks which took part in the survey declared they offer online transfer services, information, and value-added services. Call centers basically provide the same offer variety. Actually, the range of operations which may be carried out through the use of the most recent

Figure 2. Internet banking strategies

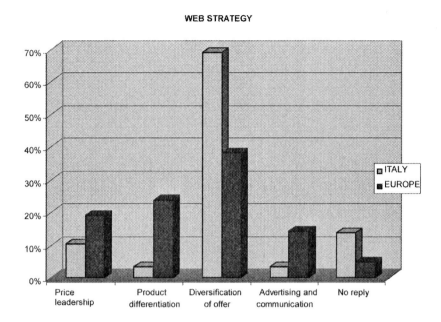

Banks also offer many value-added services; simulation tools and communication services (e.g., forum, newsletter, mailing) are among the most

e-banking technologies is not so wide. Among banks which are equipped with Wap technology, only 70% are able to offer transfer services but only 30% more innovative services, which bring a value added to the overall offer of the bank. SMS messages are used mainly as an information tool. Moreover, the few banking institutions which have extended to the Web TV/digital television their interaction means with customers are trying to develop transfer services which are mostly of transactional type.

The online trading expansion has pushed banks to disclose market information. This information area is mostly explored by foreign banking institutions; to this effect, 94% of European sites, compared to 84% of Italian sites, dispose of a dedicated area. The majority of banks offer services for customers while visitors may consult only stock exchange quotations. The service is almost exclusively supplied by a specialized information provider.

Banks also offer many value-added services; simulation tools and communication services (e.g., forum, newsletter, mailing) are among the most

available services. Seventy-four percent of Italian Web sites and 53% of foreign Web sites taking part in the sample offer financial simulators which support customers in the most efficient portfolio choices. Here again, one can notice the will of our virtual banks to aim at clients information. In Europe, the percentage is higher in Switzerland and Great Britain where banking institutions have a long tradition in managing savings. Discussion forums are present in some banks, especially in Central Europe, but they are also rapidly developing in southern banking institutions.

Financial information is the most widely value-added service (100%) offered by Italian banks, followed by product information (93%), market trend graphics (90%), and online help like FAQ, e-mail, and demos, which represent 86%, 86%, and 79% of the surveyed population, respectively. On the other end of the rating scale are multilingual supports (10%), trading simulators, and online financial consultancy (24% each). The latter, in particular, shows a certain growth compared to the previous survey, but is still too weak to be considered representative.

The European sample, on the other hand, shows a somehow different trend. The multilingual support is present in all European countries, with the exception of Great Britain, and the same goes for financial stimulators. To the possibility of asking for advice by mail or to finding an answer to frequent doubts, thanks to the FAQs, European financial institutions prefer to offer financial calculators and asset allocation instruments (though still in embryo).

From the institutional analysis of the Web site, it shows that 94% of banks of the sample deem it indispensable to offer visitors and customers information about the bank. A good 92% of Italian sites describe the structure of the banking institution and its history, while just 79% of foreign banks provide this kind of content. Moreover, listed banks offer the possibility to consult and download the latest balances and relating reports, as well as the most significant press articles. Italian banking institutions seem to give this information area a higher value rather than their foreign counterpart, as well as with regards to the array of news available on the site. All the analyzed Web sites contain their product catalogue. In this regard, there is a difference in price listing: while 83% of Italian Web sites make reference to prices, only 21% of European Web sites make this information available to visitors. Generally speaking, however, the information available concerning this issue is poor and incomplete with regards to contents and presentation clarity.

Access speed for the display of the Internet banking service and of online trading has considerably increased (8.75 seconds on average). Italian sites have a higher uploading speed compared to European ones, thanks to the reduced presence of simulators and other value-added services and to the improvement of pages design. In order to optimize the page opening time, HP got equipped with direct service links and improvements were made in the site design. Italian banks got higher scores in the design of Web pages (on average 4.1 against a mean European score of 3.73). The number of images per page has reduced in order to increase browsing speed; legible characters are used, as well as dark tones for the background and light tones for writing. Well aware that the browsing difficulty constitutes a discouraging factor for the average net surfer, banks are paying particular attention to this aspect of their site.

INTRANET BANKING AS AN ORGANIZATIONAL INTEGRATION TOOL

As we were saying, the study on the effects of the use of the Web technologies in the financial and banking industry cannot overlook the intercompany application scope. Banks are traditionally considered as complex, large-size organizations, characterized by geographical widespread location and organizational and product differentiation. Due to the frequent merge and acquisitions transactions (M&As), the organizational complexity has lately grown. As a matter of fact, the search for economies of scale in a minimally differentiated market characterized by end customers being highly sensitive as far as the "price" variable is concerned, pushed the bank top management to increase the volume of products and services offered and to be present in a wide range of markets. The trend is therefore to look for economies through merge and integration projects whose main objective is to increase the company size and to extend the bank geographical boundaries even in international contexts. The search for these situations of strong boost towards volumes has an immediate effect on the competition of the industry, which becomes, on the one hand, increasingly global and, on the other, increasingly based on efficiency and innovation parameters.

Against a rather widespread strategic choice of dimensional growth within the banking industry, the distinguishing factor, on the one hand, and challenging factor, on the other, is represented by the integration pace issue, that is, the time needed

Figure 3. Value-added services offered by online banks

VALUE ADDED SERVICES

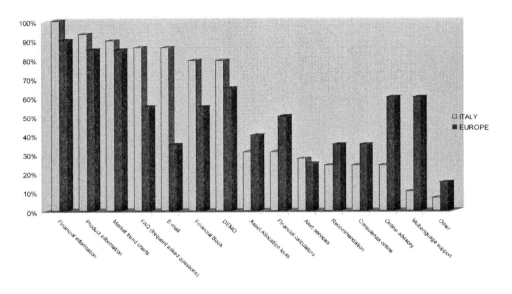

to carry out strategic plans. Therefore, the success factor consists of the ability to create the conditions so that organizational systems and mechanisms change and reach a sound configuration in the shortest time possible.

Within this scenario, a role of paramount importance is played by technologies and information systems in triggering changes through the specification of common practices and procedures in the operations and information management. Lorence and Lorsch (1967) had already pointed out that the need for integration originates from organizational differentiation.

Increasing abilities aimed at managing organizational interdependencies are considered one of the most evident effects of the spread of information technology (Agliati, 1996). In this context the importance of an extensive application of different ICT solutions is stressed, aimed at facing both operational interdependence (i.e., linked to intermediate and final input and output flows which are created as an effect of division of labour) and information interdependence (i.e.,

referring to the need to exchange information in order to face and solve problems encountered during task performance) (Ferraro, 2000).

A common aspect refers to the progressive increase of internal communication flows channeled through *groupware* applications and, in case of larger organizations, the presence of dedicated Intranet and company portals. The networks (namely *Intranet*) increase the capability of collecting, processing, and redistributing "codified" knowledge. The same infrastructures allow users to exchange messages and different texts, forward requests, consult specialized document files, benefit from remote training and coaching courses, and so forth. The use of such instruments for communication purposes is led by the growing use of solutions and services coming from third parties (i.e., external suppliers or companies referring to the same banking group).

The introduction of the Internet paradigm for the communication and exchange management is not so strong; as an example, the use of *Extranet* in the relationships with external partners is still marginal. Sometimes the relationship with certain *outsourcers* (with the exclusion only of persons in charge of the management information system) uses the support offered by similar tools.

Entrusting the operational phases to outside bodies, with the consequent need to carry out systematic controls on the work performed by the supplier and on the creation of working *teams* of specialists coming from the extra-banking world, may be the reason behind the development, in the future, of computerized applications addressed to external counterparts both at the top and at the bottom of the company organizational limits. Should this trend gain ground, we may witness a further expansion of the limits of information systems, with clear repercussions on the bodies in charge of the operation and management of the said systems.

Numerous banks have realized how *Intranets* may increase the visibility of the organization, since they make clear the existence of knowledge, *routine,* and interconnections between all parties contributing to the same process. In certain fields the analysis perspective is widened and this ends up by making the same organization function *transparently* towards the different players.

INTRANET APPLICATIONS: THE CASE OF CONTENT MANAGEMENT AND OF BUSINESS PROCESS MANAGEMENT

Information systems, in their totality, are essential tools aimed at achieving coordination. Proof of this are the investments that financial institutions make in order to adopt innovative technologies alongside the most traditional corporate information systems.

A survey carried out by CeTIF[1] on a sample of 9 banking groups and 2 service centers, ended in March 2005, showed the existence of significant innovative projects in the fields of content management (CM) and business process management

(BPM). By the first term we refer to a set of solutions that automate, partially or fully, the process of creation and publication of contents (*CMt*) and of documents (*document management*) for users inside the bank (Intranet, internal portals) and outside the bank (Extranet, Web etc.). By the second term we refer to the set of *workflow* technologies which manage and monitor the business process, by integrating it with traditional applications.

Both such technologies may be considered innovative business integration tools, though their role may be considered of coordination support and of automation (or, to a certain extent, of decision support), respectively.

However, their choice must be explained in the light of the organizational change that major credit institutions have started in the past few years. Many of the cases considered show that the implementation of CM or BPM solutions was followed up by information system integrations or migrations (48%), merge or acquisitions (23%), and, in the case of BPM, after process revision projects (25%). Though the implementation of both projects derived from common organizational needs, the data clearly show a different trend of the first ones compared to the second ones (Figure 4).

Sixty-fiver percent of interviewed banks declared that they are presently carrying out, or they will soon carry out, CM projects, while only 54% of the sample declared that they are presently carrying out or they are planning to carry out in the short term BPM projects. About 10% of banks have planned investments in BPM in the long term. Therefore it becomes evident that CM projects are more widespread than BPMs among financial institutions, which means that CM support technology is more widespread than BPM support technology.

When considering the volume of the projects, we realize that if, on the one hand, CM may have reached a good circulation because it is applied quite frequently to performance information and product/market information processes (pic. 3), on

Figure 4. CM and BPM projects in financial institutions

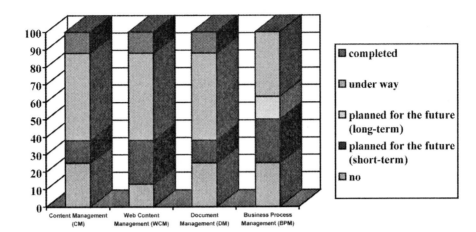

the other hand, BPM is spread only in the field of credits and information processes (38%), finance and treasury (25%), and auditing and risks (23%). In certain cases (i.e., purchase invoice cycle, information processes, collectionsm and payments), the BPM extends also outside the boundaries of the credit institution, involving also customers or, often, suppliers.

This Difference May be Due to Different Factors

First of all, the factors may be the causes and the relating expected results which boosted the innovation introduction in both technological applications. The survey shows that both CM and BPM projects are mostly induced by exogenous market forces and by the consequent need to reduce the so called *"time to market"* (71%). If, on the one side, the market pressure and the introduction of the customer-oriented culture get, in theory, banks to look for ways to improve internal processes and communication integration, on the other side, reality shows that the equipment with tools bringing immediate and recognizable advantages, mostly outside the bank itself, was made easier at first. Therefore, CM projects, aiming at facilitating information publication

and maintenance to the outside public and, only in a second phase, inside the financial institution, have anticipated the BPM projects. The latter are seen as management excellence solutions within processes (68% of interviewed institutions) and as tools implemented to overcome difficulties due to the need for technical modernization of the traditional information systems (44%). The results expected from the two solutions seem to be very different, with consequent differences in the implementation technical difficulties, in costs, and in the identification of organizational effects. If, on the one hand, CM solutions are applied by the bank alongside the existing ones, without the need of organizational changes and important technological integrations, on the other hand, BPM solutions are based on rather more complex technologies, characterized by organizational uncertainty.

Even the analysis of the obstacles faced by CM and BPM projects may be useful to understand the origin of the different spread of such projects. Aggregated data show a common sensitivity towards the cost factor (about 24% of the sample indicated costs as the main obstacle to such initiatives) and the relating difficulty in defining the return on investment (ROI). Another strong obstacle is due to the cultural and organizational reluctance (78%) to the change brought about by these technological innovations. On the other hand, difficulties relating to technologies (18%) do not seem to be a fundamental inhibitor factor. The empiric evidence show, however, a difference between the obstacles to the CM and BPM projects, with particular reference to the cultural and organizational aspects. The reasons are to be found, first of all, in the characteristics of managers and users of these technological innovations and, secondly, in their implementation modalities.

In the case of CM, 44% of respondents state that the people in charge of these projects are active in the lines of business (LOB), while 32% are active in the human resource management (HR) or in the organization. At present, only 18% of financial institutions have "created" a new professional position (i.e., *knowledge officer*) which centralizes content management in one organizational area; the new trend seems to confirm the growth of this organization solution. BPM projects, instead, are managed by the LOB in 24% of the cases, and by the IT area in 32% of the cases. When looking at the characteristics of users of the above mentioned technologies, important differences arise. CM solutions are more and more spread among customers rather than being centrally used. This entail the support of the training structure whose task is to create professional people able to manage the content publication process, as well as, in certain cases (about 50% of the sample), the relevant monitoring process. Even BPM are spread amongst users that manage the processes which make the object of this study. In particular, with regards to processes, a need of coordination and rationalization of business procedures in the most interdependent areas arose. Bank information systems are made up by parallel and integrated applications, often based on different and complex information structures. However, there is no need to create *ad hoc* professional figures which manage the BPM process and project. As a matter of fact, BPM tools often go hand in hand with or replace transactional information systems which

play the main role by completing their integration and automation capacity.

Moreover, CM and BPM projects differentiate for their application modality. While CM is characterized by a *big-bang* implementation logic, which introduces technologies in a sole phase, BPM is often characterized by a modular implementation system.

AN INNOVATION EVOLUTION PERSPECTIVE

It is estimated that the difference in the present status of CM and BPM will fade more and more due to the growing awareness that internal processes are the very same business apparatus; this is due even in the light of the recent regulations on operational risks and also because the two technologies may eventually complement each other.

In particular, the survey shows that the differences between the two technologies may be due, on the one hand, to a lesser knowledge of the BPM technological tool compared to the CM one, and on the other, to the lack, limitedly to the BPM projects, of the domino (or *isomorphism*) effect which is common during the technological innovation application phases and which leads to a resemblance of technological choices by financial institutions.

We hereby would like to hypothesize a hidden link between the two technologies and the presence of an "incremental" effect between them. In order to verify this hypothesis, one must look first of all at the technological and organizational innovation which CM on the one side and BPM on the other bring about.

CM technological innovation may be summarized with the introduction of documental integration tools for archive management and in distributed environments. From a functional point of view, CM allows the automated management of the lifecycle of a document, as well as the need to trace the documents and information contained therein. For this reason, such tools are considered as tools enabling the spread of the internal knowledge of the credit institution.

From a technological point of view, BPM introduces innovation integration between the information systems. Moreover, from a functional point of view, they lead to the identification of process interdependencies and to their management harmonization. Moreover, it is a preparatory tool aimed at the process mapping, which can be used for a range of activities (e.g., risk management, auditing system, definition of internal regulations, etc.).

According to this short synthesis, an evolution perspective for the two technologies seems to take form. The common characteristics may be outlined as follows:

- **Process concept:** Both technologies imply a strong idea of organization through processes. In the case of CM, this merely refers to the document creation and publication processes, while in the case of BPM, this concept is also extended to other business processes.
- **Culture of change:** It shows that the organizational change following the introduction of such technologies is difficult to manage, though it is characterized by different factors. The bank should be able to change and, for this purpose, the management *sponsorship* is important.
- **Organizational and technological monitoring:** The technology innovation seems to be linked to the need of monitoring its implementation from both the technological and organizational point of view.
- **Technological flexibility:** Technological innovation goes hand in hand with the flexibility concept, seen as a capability to "adapt" to the company structures and systems.

We therefore believe that BPM is an evolution and extension of the CM concept (Figure 5).

CM projects are therefore destined to evolve towards BPM projects extended to other processes, whenever the financial institution is able to recognize the CM as a technological innovation tool.

SOME USEFUL INSIGHTS

The considerations made on Web-based technologies, both Internet and Intranet, enable one to draw interesting conclusions already outlined at the beginning of this chapter and concerning the innovation characteristics.

Empirical evidence leads us to focus on how the theory may explain the following:

1. Which are the technological innovation signs? Can they always be measured? Does technological innovation progresses through stages or is it an on-going process?
2. Is technological innovation unique? Does it make sense to speak about innovation of each technology sector (automation, decision-making support, coordination)?
3. What is the relationship between technological innovation and organizational efficiency/effectiveness?

Innovation is a synonym of "change or improving evolution of a situation" and surely not a novelty. Some writers consider technological innovation as technology flexibility or as an improvement of performance. Here we would rather exclude such definitions, since the definitions of flexibility and performance may be ambiguous and "contaminated" by other concurrent factors (Maggi, 2003). For this reason, it is therefore believed that technological innovation is not measurable per se. However, the innovation process may be seen as an *on-going process*, more or less fast, characterized by a constant change in technology, players, and structures. This concept

Figure 5. The technological innovation stages

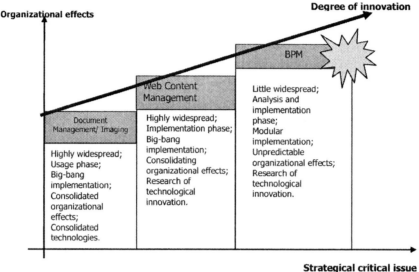

leads us to consider technological innovation as a natural process, only little conscious of the fact that it is stimulated by the implementation of certain technologies which may affect the pace (by increasing it or stopping it) and the process awareness.

Hence, we conclude that the answer to the second question is negative. The division in classes, given at the beginning of this chapter and recognized as valid by the organizational literature, seems not to be relevant in the case of innovation. We could at least "defend" such classification by construing it as typology, that is, as a set of types (rather than classes) which do not have precise demarcation limits and which constitute some archetypes. The concept of technological innovation, however, remains an extensive concept, not referable to any typology.

The third questions leads to wider considerations. Though the concept of organizational efficiency and technological innovation has been highlighted by many interlocutors, the gathered data, however, do not provide empirical evidence. The reason shall be found in the lack of a lon-

gitudinal analysis over a longer temporal span, for the determination of effects produced by information technology. However, a qualitative consideration can be drawn: The two technologies showed different efficiency values against the same technology use. This proves, as a first estimate, that information technology does not have a certain and determining role for reaching organizational efficiency, though it may influence both the information need, as well as the information processing capability. Therefore, its effects seem mediated by organizational and contextual variables, leading to different values with regards to effectiveness.

Therefore, the objective of this chapter is to define to what extent information technology may affect the organizational efficiency, that is, the capability to reduce the operating costs of the organizational structure. On this point, the interviewed persons stressed the high importance given to the role of information technology. IT enables the processing of great volumes of data, a deeper control, the cost cutting in terms of communication and transactions. Hence a new question arises: Does any information technology have an impact on transaction costs and on operating costs? The answer seems to be yes, though the impact magnitude on efficiency is different. While automation and communication technologies highly influence the economic management of the institution, decision-making support technologies have an indirect impact, more difficult to asses beforehand.

CONCLUSION

This study dealt with technology innovation, with particular reference to Web technologies. The different empirical evidence shows that technology may be a tool to improve the service/product offered, as well as an efficiency tool. As a matter of fact, the implementation of Internet technologies brought about, on the one hand, the development of a considerable number of Internet strategies for products and services of Italian banks. On the other hand, Internet technologies supported the coordination as well as the organizational integration phases of the same banks.

Process and content innovation mainly implies a change in the cultural attitude and, for the time being, it is still determined mostly by endogenous variables.

The analysis of the collected data leads us to draw some last conclusions:
- Information systems are affected by information technology; in order to determine the information system, one cannot do without knowing the development and implementation status of the technology.
- Information systems are affected by the task uncertainty, by coordination and control mechanisms, and by communication tools; the organizational (micro-) variables affect the definition of the information system.
- The information system is an organizational planning factor; it is able to affect the organizational efficiency and therefore the organizational structure.
- Besides information systems, the organizational structure is affected by other variables; this observation leads us to consider the absence of technologic determinism.
- Information technology has a mediated role in defining the organizational effectiveness and a direct role in the organizational efficiency management.

However, the role played by the said technologies affects the organizational structures in a different way.

REFERENCES

Agliati, M. (Ed.). (1996). *Tecnologia dell'informazione e sistema amministrativo*. Milan: Egea.

Anderson, P., & Tushman, M. L. (1991). Managing through cycles of technological change. *Research Technology Management, 34*(3), 26–31.

Barras, R. (1990). Interactive innovation in financial and business services: The vanguard of the service revolution. *Research Policy, 19*, 215–237. doi:10.1016/0048-7333(90)90037-7

Berger, A. N., & Udell, G. F. (2006). A more complete conceptual framework for SME finance. *Journal of Banking & Finance, 30*(11), 2945–2966. doi:10.1016/j.jbankfin.2006.05.008

Buckingham, R., Hirschheim, R. A., Land, F. F., & Tully, C. J. (1987). Information systems curriculum. A basis for course design. In Buckingham et al. (Ed.), *Information systems education: Recommendations and implementation* (pp. 72-113). Cambridge: CUP.

Carignani, A., & Frigerio, C. (2003). *European Web banking strategies*. Università Cattolica, Milan, CeTIF Research Centre.

Ciborra, C. U. (1996). Improvisation and information technology in organizations. In *Proceedings of the 17th International Conference on Information Systems*, Cleveland, OH (pp. 369-380).

Damanpour, F., & Gopalakrishnan, S. (2001). The dynamics of the adoption of product and process innovation in organizations. *Journal of Management Studies, 38*(1), 45–65. doi:10.1111/1467-6486.00227

De Nicolò, G., Bartholomew, P., Zaman, J., & Zephirin, M. (2004). Bank consolidation, internationalization, and conglomeration: Trends and implications for financial risk. *Financial Markets, Institutions, & . Instruments, 13*(4), 173–217.

Epstein, M. J. (2005). The determinants and evaluation of merger success. *Business Horizons, Elsevier, 48*, 37–46. doi:10.1016/j.bushor.2004.10.001

Ferraro, F. (2000). L'analisi organizzativa: l'individuo. In R. Mercurio & F. Testa (Eds.), *Organizzazione, assetto e relazioni nel sistema di business* (pp. 52-76). Torino: Giappichelli.

Figueira, C., Neills, J., & Schoenberg, R. (2007). Travel abroad or stay at home? Investigating the patterns of bank industry M&As in the EU. *European Business Review, 19*(1), 23–39. doi:10.1108/09555340710714135

Frigerio, C. (2005). *Process IT Innovation in banking*. Università Cattolica, Milan, CeTIF Research Centre.

Lawrence, P. R., & Lorsch, J. W. (1967). *Organization and environment, graduate school of business administration*. Boston: Harvard University.

Maggi, B. (2003). *De l'Agir Organisationnel*. Toulose: Editions Octares.

Quinn, J. B., Anderson, P., & Finkelstein, S. (2005). Leveraging intellect. *The Academy of Management Executive, 19*(4), 78–94.

Sherman, H. D., & Rupert, T. J. (2006). Do bank mergers have hidden or foregone value? Realized and unrealized operating synergies in one bank merger. *European Journal of Operational Research, 168*(1), 253–268. doi:10.1016/j.ejor.2004.05.002

Utterback, J., & Abernathy, W. (1975). A dynamic model of product and process innovation. *Omega, 3*(6), 639–656. doi:10.1016/0305-0483(75)90068-7

ENDNOTE

[1] The research mentioned was carried out by the author between March 2004 and October 2004 through a quali-quantitative analysis, in the form of semi-structured questionnaires and interviews (Frigerio, 2005).

This work was previously published in Business Web Strategy: Design, Alignment, and Application, edited by L. Al-Hakim; M. Memmola, pp. 219-234, copyright 2009 by Information Science Reference (an imprint of IGI Global).

Chapter 4.8
Semantic Web for Media Convergence:
A Newspaper Case

Ferran Perdrix
Universitat de Lleida, Spain & Diari Segre Media Group, Spain

Juan Manuel Gimeno
Universitat de Lleida, Spain

Rosa Gil
Universitat de Lleida, Spain

Marta Oliva
Universitat de Lleida, Spain

Roberto García
Universitat de Lleida, Spain

ABSTRACT

Newspapers in the digitalisation and Internet era are evolving from mono-channel and static communication mediums to highly dynamic and multi-channel ones, where the different channels converge into a unified news editorial office. Advanced computerised support is needed in order to cope with the requirements arising from convergent multimedia news management, production and delivery. Such advanced services require machines to be aware of a greater part of the underlying semantics. Ontologies are a clear candidate to put this semantics into play, and Semantic Web technologies the best choice for Web-wide information integration. However, newspapers have made great investments in their current news management systems so a smooth transition is required in order to reduce implementation costs. Our proposal is to build an ontological framework based on existing journalism and multimedia standards and to translate existing metadata to the Semantic Web. Once in a semantic space, data integration and news management and retrieval are facilitated enormously. For instance, Semantic Web tools are being developed in the context of a media house that are capable of dealing with the different kinds of media managed in the media house in an integrated and transparent way.

DOI: 10.4018/978-1-60566-066-0.ch009

Figure 1. *Traditional news information flux (left) and the new trend of convergent news flux (right)*

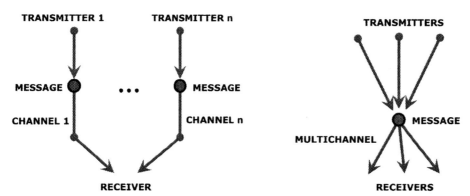

CURRENT SITUATION

Web news publishing is evolving fast, as the majority of Internet services, and nowadays this service is trying to adapt information to a way that best fits users' interests in order to increase its use. With that, newspapers are expecting to profit more from their news sites. In parallel, many of the newspaper companies are changing into news media houses. They own radio stations and video production companies that produce content unsupported by traditional newspapers, but that is delivered by Web newspapers or new mobile services. Initially, Web news was a mere reproduction of those in the printed edition. Nowadays, they are constantly updated and provide new services for those users interested on reaching this information as soon as possible and enjoying new ways of interaction with them (Eriksen & Ihlström, 2000; Lundberg, 2002; Ihlström, Lundberg, & Perdrix, 2003).

Consequently, news industry communication model is changing from the traditional one shown on the left of Figure 1 to the one shown in the right. In the former, each channel is considered separately (press, TV, radio, Internet, mobile phones…) and implies his way creating his own message, transmitting over this channel and using his own interface in order to show the message to the receivers. On the other hand, the latter is based on an information convergence flux. In this model,

transmitters make information in collaboration with other transmitters and produce messages that include as media as it is necessary (video, text, audio, images…). Finally, receivers choose the channel that best fits their needs in order to get access to messages.

The previous situation is the one faced in the context of the Diari Segre Media Group[1], which is a journalism holding that in the last years has been facing this convergence trend. This holding started 25 years ago with a newspaper edition. Today produces three press editions in two languages, three radio stations, six television regional channels and several Internet Websites. Nowadays, all the editorial staff is applying the convergence of information flux approach during news generation and management. Therefore, they are required to be versatile journalists because they cannot be specialized in any concrete media. They must deal with video, image and text edition. Moreover, they must write in different ways, for instance for press news or for radio or TV voiceover.

On the other hand, the Diari Segre archive system is changing to a new repository build from the combination of text, images, video and audio files. In this sense, archive management is becoming a big issue and it requires deep improvements in terms of content search, relations among news (e.g. historical relations among news items) or information retrieval interfaces. The archive system must be a very productive and comprehensive tool in order to assist journalists while they create new content. This business case details how Semantic Web technologies are being explored in the context of the Diari Segre Media Group in order to face this new challenges.

In general, it has been observed that media houses must adapt to the requirements imposed by this new model. First of all, there are changes in how they reach consumers. News are build up from a combination of different content types (video, audio, the traditional text plus images, etc.) and are delivered to users through different channels and adapted to many kinds of devices (PC, PDA, smart phones, etc.). Therefore, formats must be selected and adapted according to the device and connection the user is using. These operations include transcoding of formats, resizing of images or recoding for higher levels of compression. Moreover, multi-channel distribution must take into account that for each channel one must define its own content, aesthetic and interaction model. These characteristics define what an interactive channel is (McDonald, 2004).

However, changes are not just restricted to the relation with consumers. Digital media eliminates many time and space restrictions and changes editorial team routines. Moreover, all different media converge into a unified news object that is produced by interdisciplinary teams. Consequently, more efficient and effective means for news management are needed in order to facilitate coordination and production of these multimedia assets.

The news industry is currently using content management solutions for these means, but the additional requirements of a convergent editorial office stress the need for advanced knowledge management and information retrieval. Currently, there are specific standardisation efforts in the journalism domain, together with more generic ones in the multimedia domain, which carry some uniformity to the newspaper content management systems. However, as it is introduced in the following subsections, they just provide data structures and schemas that facilitate systems interoperability. They do not facilitate knowledge management and information retrieval tasks. These tasks are currently carried out mainly by the documentation department, who is in charge of the news archival process using legacy tools.

Journalism Metadata

One of the main standardization frameworks in the journalism domain is the International Press Telecommunications Council[2], an international consortium of news agencies, editors and newspapers distributors. IPTC has developed standards like the Information Interchange Model[3], News-Codes[4] (formerly the Subject Reference System), the News Industry Text Format[5] or NewsML[6].

Currently, almost all of them have evolved towards XML-based standards to represent and manage news along their whole lifecycle, including their creation, exchange and consumption. For instance, NewsML is used to represent news as multimedia packages and NITF deals with document structure, i.e. paragraphs, headlines, etc. On the other hand, the Subject Reference System (SRS), now part of IPTC NewsCodes, is a subject classification hierarchy with three levels and seventeen categories in its first level.

Moreover, a new family of these journalism standards has been just proposed, expanding the range of available metadata. The new suite, known as the IPTC G2, is actually a series of specifications and XML components that can be shared among all IPTC G2 components for maximum efficiency.

IPTC G2 Standards make possible the integration of any news item with text, photos, graphics, video or other media. The News Architecture model (NAR) is used in order to package any combination of these items. Moreover, it makes stronger use of IPTC's robust metadata taxonomy suite, which is based on NewsCodes, and better interacts with other IPTC-G2 standards.

This standard contains hooks for managing news items, and its flexibility allows news providers to choose whether to support all of the IPTC G2-standards XML tags or a compact subset. It's the cost-effective way of managing news, whether for a Web site, news aggregator, newspaper, radio or television station.

Multimedia Metadata

All the previous initiatives are centred on the journalism specific aspects of a semantic newspaper. However, as has been pointed out, newspapers are evolving towards the digital multimedia domain. Therefore, they stress more and more their multimedia management requirements.

In the multimedia metadata domain, as it is extensively shown in the literature (Hunter, 2003; Einhoff, Casademont, Perdrix, & Noll, 2005), the MPEG-7 (Salembier, & Smith, 2002) standard constitutes the greatest effort for multimedia description. It is divided into four main components: the Description Definition Language (DDL, the basic building blocks for the MPEG-7 metadata language), Audio (the descriptive elements for audio), Visual (those for video) and the Multimedia Description Schemes (MDS, the descriptors for capturing the semantic aspects of multimedia contents, e.g. places, actors, objects, events, etc.).

In addition to MPEG-7, which concentrates on content description, MPEG-21 defines an open framework for multimedia delivery and consumption. This standard must be also considered because it focuses on the content management issues for full delivery and consumption chain, from content creators' applications to end-users' players. The different MPEG-21 parts deal with diverse aspects like Digital Rights Management or Digital Items, the definition of a fundamental content unit for distribution and transaction very useful for convergent media management.

Problem Statement

As has been pointed out in the description of the current situation in many media houses, archivists classify news using a proprietary hierarchical thesaurus while journalists search this information when they need to inform themselves on subjects, histories or events. This search can be performed in extreme situations, e.g., lack of time, or lack of knowledge in relation to the archive system. This is reflected in the way journalists formulate their queries. The gap between archivists' and journalists' mental models implies that more flexible content categorization and search systems are needed. This trend is even bigger when we consider cross-media content production and coordination in order to get multimedia and multichannel news. Therefore, in order to take advantage of the possibilities offered by the digital medium to exploit a newspaper archive, the aspects that can be improved include:

- Keyword search falling short in expressive power
- Weak interrelation between archive items: users may need to combine several indirect queries manually before they can get answers to complex queries
- Lack of a commonly adopted standard representation for sharing archive news across newspapers
- Lack of internal consensus for content description terminology among reporters and archivists
- Lack of involvement of journalist in the archiving process

These shortcomings are difficult to deal with if the existing standards are used as provided. The main standards that have been presented, both in the journalism and multimedia domains, are based on XML and specified by XML Schemas. The more significant case is the MPEG-7 one. It is based on a set of XML Schemas that define 1182 elements, 417 attributes and 377 complex types. NewsML and NITF are also very big standards, they define more than 100 elements, and the NewsCodes hierarchy of subjects defines more than one thousand different subjects.

The complexity of these standards makes it very difficult to manage them. Moreover, the use of XML technologies implies that a great part of the semantics remains implicit. Therefore, each time an application is developed, semantics must be extracted from the standard and re-implemented.

For instance, if we use XQuery in order to retrieve MPEG-7 SegmentType descriptions from an XML database, we must be aware of the hierarchy of segment types and implement an XQuery that has to cover any kind of multimedia segment, i.e. VideoSegmentType, AnalyticClipType, AudiSegmentType, etc.

If the intended interpretation of the segments structure was available for computerised means, semantic queries would benefit from the corresponding formal semantics. Consequently, a semantic query for SegmentType will retrieve all subclasses without requiring additional developing efforts. This is not possible with XML tools because, although XML Schemas capture some semantics of the domain they model, XML tools are based on syntax. The captured semantics remain implicit from the XML processing tools point of view. Therefore, when an XQuery searches for a SegmentType, the XQuery processor has no way to know that there are many other kinds of segment types that can appear in its place, i.e. they are more concrete kinds of segments.

The previous example only illustrates one kind of difficulty derived from the use of just syntax-aware tools. Another example is that the lack of explicit semantics makes MPEG-7 very difficult to extend in an independent way, i.e. third party extensions. The same applies for MPEG-21 or the journalism standards. Moreover, standards from both worlds share many concepts so it would be possible, and easier, to integrate them once their implicit semantics are available from a computer processing point of view.

Proposed Solution

In this chapter, we explore Semantic Web technologies (Berners-Lee, Hendler & Lassila, 2001) as a way to overcome many of the challenges of digital and convergent media houses. The size and complexity of the stored information, and the time limitations for cataloguing, describing and ordering the incoming information, make newspaper archives a relatively disorganised and difficult to manage corpus. In this sense, they share many of the characteristics and problems of the World Wide Web, and therefore the solutions proposed in the Semantic Web vision are pertinent here.

In order to implement more advanced newspaper content management applications, they should be more informed about the content they are managing. They are not just files with some weak interrelations. There is a lot of knowledge embedded in these pieces of content and in their interrelationships. In order to make computers aware of it, their implicit semantics must be formalised, for instance using ontologies. Semantic Web technologies facilitate the building blocks for Web ontologies, which add the facilities for Web-wide ontology sharing and integration. The latter is a key feature for convergent and globalised media houses.

In order to build an ontological infrastructure for the Semantic Newspaper, it is important to consider the state of the art of the metadata initiatives in the journalism domain, which have been introduced in the current situation description section. Additionally, digital newspapers have stressed the requirements of multimedia management. Digital news is managed as multimedia packages that integrate text, images, video, audio, etc. Therefore, it is also important to consider the current situation in the more general multimedia metadata domain.

We have undertaken the application of the Semantic Web proposals to the newspapers world by following a smooth transition strategy (Haustein, & Pleumann, 2002). This strategy advises about keeping compatibility, at least initially, with current newspaper content management systems and journalism and multimedia standards. Consequently, we have rooted our proposed approach on existing journalism and multimedia standards and provide a methodology to move them, together with existing data, to the Semantic Web domain.

Objectives

The objective is then to design a Semantic Web-based platform that is an extension of previously working systems in mass media companies, particularly in the context of the Diari Segre Media Group. The manual creation of semantic instances for news items, at a regular daily pace, is indeed a feasible goal as long as this process is integrated into existing systems and it just causes a slightly greater work load while producing observable benefits. Consequently, the introduction of new semantic documentation tools requires a careful work of analysis, design, testing and balancing of the additional burden that such tools may impose on archivists, journalists or readers.

In order to produce a semantic platform that seamlessly integrates into newspapers content management systems, the first objective is to develop an ontological framework based on existing standards. Once this ontological infrastructure based on existing journalism and multimedia standards is developed, the objective is then to put it into practice in the context of an architecture based on Semantic Web tools for semantic integration, querying and reasoning. However, all this effort must end up reaching users through applications that offer to them the extra benefits of semantic metadata while avoiding them the burden of dealing with the underlying extra complexity.

Overview

The proposed solution is detailed in Section 3. First of all, Section 3.1 presents the methodology that produces an ontological framework based on existing standards. This methodology is based on two mappings. The first one from XML Schema, the language used in most of the considered standards, to ontologies based on the Semantic Web language Web Ontology Language (OWL) (McGuinness & Harmelen, 2004). The second one is based on the previous one and makes it possible to map from XML metadata, based on XML Schemas previously mapped to OWL, to Semantic Web metadata, based on the Resource Description Framework (RDF) (Becket, 2004).

The ontologies produced using this methodology constitute the foundation on top of which an architecture based on Semantic Web technologies is built. This architecture, described in Section 3.2, takes profit from the semantics formalised by these ontologies and loads Semantic Web metadata based on them in order to offer services like semantic integration, semantics queries or logic reasoning. These services are used in order to build applications that facilitate managing heterogeneous media repositories and the underlying knowledge. One example of such an application is given in Section 3.3.

The described application builds on top of a text-to-speech and a semantic annotation tool. The generated annotations are based on existing standards ontologies and loaded into the proposed semantic architecture, which makes it possible to manage audio, audiovisual and text content in an integrated way. However, the key point here is to offer all the semantic services to users in a usable and accessible way. To this end, the application is based on a user interface that provides an object-action interaction paradigm best suited for heterogeneous information spaces. The interface does not solely facilitate content management, it also allows browsing the underlying domain knowledge, formalised using specialised ontologies, and constitutes a useful tool in media houses in order to facilitate news tracking and producing new content.

SOLUTION DETAILS

This section provides a detailed description of the proposed solution. The different modules are described in the following subsections starting from the methodology used in order to benefit from existing standards and produce ontologies that formalise them. These ontologies make possible to develop an architecture that takes profit from their semantics in order to offer advanced services like semantic integration, querying and reasoning. Finally, these services are used in order to build an application that makes the benefits emerging from semantic metadata and ontologies available for end users.

XML SEMANTICS REUSE METHODOLOGY

In order to put into practice the smooth transition strategy, the first step has been to reuse existing standards in the journalism and multimedia fields, which have been for long very active in standardization.

However, as has been highlighted in current situation analysis, all the more recent standards are based on XML and lack formal semantics that facilitate applying a Semantic Web approach. Therefore, in order to facilitate the transition from current standards and applications to the semantic world, we have applied the XML Semantics Reuse methodology (García, 2006).

The main caveat of semantic multimedia metadata is that it is sparse and expensive to produce. If we want to increase the availability of semantic multimedia metadata and, in general, of semantic metadata, the more direct solution is to benefit from the great amount of metadata that

has been already produced using XML, which is extensively used by many newspaper content management systems.

There are many attempts to move metadata from the XML domain to the Semantic Web. Some of them just model the XML tree using the RDF primitives (Klein, 2002). Others concentrate on modelling the knowledge implicit in XML languages definitions, i.e. DTDs or the XML Schemas, using Web ontology languages (Amann, Beer, Fundulak, & Scholl, 2002; Cruz, Xiao, & Hsu, 2004). Finally, there are attempts to encode XML semantics integrating RDF into XML documents (Lakshmanan, & Sadri, 2003; Patel-Schneider, & Simeon, 2002).

However, none of them facilitates an extensive transfer of XML metadata to the Semantic Web in a general and transparent way. Their main problem is that the XML Schema implicit semantics are not made explicit when XML metadata instantiating this schemas is mapped. Therefore, they do not benefit from the XML semantics and produce RDF metadata almost as semantics-blind as the original XML. Or, on the other hand, they capture these semantics but they use additional ad-hoc semantic constructs that produce less transparent metadata.

Therefore, we propose the XML Semantics Reuse methodology, which is implemented by the ReDeFer project[7] as an XML Schema to OWL plus and XML to RDF mapping tool. This methodology combines an XML Schema to Web ontology mapping, called XSD2OWL, with a transparent mapping from XML to RDF, XML2RDF. The ontologies generated by XSD2OWL are used during the XML to RDF step in order to generate semantic metadata that makes XML Schema semantics explicit. Both steps are detailed next.

XSD2OWL Mapping

The XML Schema to OWL mapping is responsible for capturing the schema implicit semantics. This semantics are determined by the combination of

Table 1. XSD2OWL mappings from XML Schema building blocks to OWL ones plus an explanation of why they are interpreted as equivalent modelling constructs

XML Schema	OWL	Explanation
element | attribute	rdf:Property owl:DatatypeProperty owl:ObjectProperty	Named relation between nodes or nodes and values
element@substitutionGroup	rdfs:subPropertyOf	Relation can appear in place of a more general one
element@type	rdfs:range	The relation range kind
complexType|group |attributeGroup	owl:Class	Relations and contextual restrictions package
complexType//element	owl:Restriction	Contextualised restriction of a relation
extension@base restriction@base	rdfs:subClassOf	Package concretises the base package
@maxOccurs @minOccurs	owl:maxCardinality owl:minCardinality	Restrict the number of occurrences of a relation
Sequence choice	owl:intersectionOf owl:unionOf	Combination of relations in a context

XML Schema constructs. The mapping is based on translating these constructs to the OWL ones that best capture their semantics. These translations are detailed in Table 1.

The XSD2OWL mapping is quite transparent and captures a great part XML Schema semantics. The same names used for XML constructs are used for OWL ones, although in the new namespace defined for the ontology. Therefore, XSD2OWL produces OWL ontologies that make explicit the semantics of the corresponding XML Schemas. The only caveats are the implicit order conveyed by xsd:sequence and the exclusivity of *xsd:choice*.

For the first problem, *owl:intersectionOf* does not retain its operands order, there is no clear solution that retains the great level of transparency that has been achieved. The use of RDF Lists might impose order but introduces ad-hoc constructs not present in the original metadata. Moreover, as has been demonstrated in practise, the element ordering does not contribute much from a semantic point of view. For the second problem, owl:unionOf is an inclusive union, the solution is to use the disjointness OWL construct, *owl:disjointWith*, between all union operands in order to make it exclusive.

To conclude, one important aspect is that the resulting OWL ontology may be OWL-Full depending on the input XML Schema. This is due to the fact that, in some cases, the XSD2OWL translator must employ *rdf:Property* for those xsd:elements that have both data type and object type ranges.

XML2RDF Mapping

Once all the metadata XML Schemas are available as mapped OWL ontologies, it is time to map the XML metadata that instantiates them. The intention is to produce RDF metadata as transparently as possible. Therefore, a structure-mapping approach has been selected (Klein, 2002). It is also possible to take a model-mapping approach (Tous, García, Rodríguez, & Delgado, 2005).

XML model-mapping is based on representing the XML information set using semantic tools. This approach is better when XML metadata is semantically exploited for concrete purposes. However, when the objective is semantic metadata that can be easily integrated, it is better to take a more transparent approach.

Transparency is achieved in structure-mapping models because they only try to represent the XML metadata structure, i.e. a tree, using RDF. The RDF model is based on the graph so it is easy to model a tree using it. Moreover, we do not need to worry about the semantics loose produced by structure-mapping. We have formalised the underlying semantics into the corresponding ontologies and we will attach them to RDF metadata using the instantiation relation *rdf:type*.

The structure-mapping is based on translating XML metadata instances to RDF ones that instantiate the corresponding constructs in OWL. The more basic translation is between relation instances, from *xsd:elements* and *xsd:attributes* to *rdf:Properties*. Concretely, *owl:ObjectProperties* for node to node relations and *owl:DatatypeProperties* for node to values relations.

However, in some cases, it would be necessary to use *rdf:Properties* for *xsd:elements* that have both data type and object type values. Values are kept during the translation as simple types and RDF blank nodes are introduced in the RDF model in order to serve as source and destination for properties. They will remain blank for the moment until they are enriched with semantic information.

The resulting RDF graph model contains all that we can obtain from the XML tree. It is already semantically enriched due to the *rdf:type* relation that connects each RDF properties to the *owl:ObjectProperty* or *owl:DatatypeProperty* it instantiates. It can be enriched further if the blank nodes are related to the *owl:Class* that defines the package of properties and associated restrictions they contain, i.e. the corresponding *xsd:complexType*. This semantic decoration of the graph is formalised using *rdf:type* relations from blank nodes to the corresponding OWL classes.

At this point we have obtained a semantics-enabled representation of the input metadata. The instantiation relations can now be used to apply OWL semantics to metadata. Therefore, the semantics derived from further enrichments of the ontologies, e.g. integration links between

different ontologies or semantic rules, are automatically propagated to instance metadata due to inference.

However, before continuing to the next section, it is important to point out that these mappings have been validated in different ways. First, we have used OWL validators in order to check the resulting ontologies, not just the MPEG-7 Ontology but also many others (García, Gil, & Delgado, 2007; García, Gil, Gallego, & Delgado, 2005). Second, our MPEG-7 ontology has been compared to Hunter's (2001) and Tsinaraki's ones (2004).

Both ontologies, Hunter's and Tsinaraki's, provide a partial mapping of MPEG-7 to Web ontologies. The former concentrates on the kinds of content defined by MPEG-7 and the latter on two parts of MPEG-7, the Multimedia Description Schemes (MDS) and the Visual metadata structures. It has been tested that they constitute subsets of the ontology that we propose.

Finally, the XSD2OWL and XML2RDF mappings have been tested in conjunction. Testing XML instances have been mapped to RDF, guided by the corresponding OWL ontologies from the used XML Schemas, and then back to XML. Then, the original and derived XML instances have been compared using their canonical version in order to correct mapping problems.

Ontological Infrastructure

As a result of applying the XML Semantics Reuse methodology, we have obtained a set of ontologies that reuse the semantics of the underlying standards, as they are formalised through the corresponding XML Schemas. All the ontologies related to journalism standards, i.e. NewsCodes NITF and NewsML, are available from the Semantic Newspaper site[8]. This site also contains some of the ontologies for the MPEG-21 useful for news modelling as convergent multimedia units. The MPEG-7 Ontology is available from the MPEG-7 Ontology site[9]. These are the ontologies that are going to be used as the basis for the semantic newspaper info-structure:

- **NewsCodes subjects ontology:** An OWL ontology for the subjects' part of the IPTC NewsCodes. It is a simple taxonomy of subjects but it is implemented with OWL in order to facilitate the integration of the subjects' taxonomy in the global ontological framework.
- **NITF 3.3 ontology:** An OWL ontology that captures the semantics of the XML Schema specification of the NITF standard. It contains some classes and many properties dealing with document structure, i.e. paragraphs, subheadlines, etc., but also some metadata properties about copyright, authorship, issue dates, etc.
- **NewsML 1.2 ontology:** The OWL ontology resulting from mapping the NewsML 1.2 XML Schema. Basically, it includes a set of properties useful to define the news structure as a multimedia package, i.e. news envelope, components, items, etc.
- **MPEG-7 ontology:** The XSD2OWL mapping has been applied to the MPEG-7 XML Schemas producing an ontology that has 2372 classes and 975 properties, which are targeted towards describing multimedia at all detail levels, from content based descriptors to semantic ones.
- **MPEG-21 digital item ontologies:** A digital item (DI) is defined as the fundamental unit for distribution and transaction in MPEG-21.

System Architecture

Based on the previous XML world to Semantic Web domain mappings, we have built up a system architecture that facilitates journalism and multimedia metadata integration and retrieval. The architecture is sketched in Figure 2. The MPEG-7

OWL ontology, generated by XSD2OWL, constitutes the basic ontological framework for semantic multimedia metadata integration and appears at the centre of the architecture. In parallel, there are the journalism ontologies. The multimedia related concepts from the journalism ontologies are connected to the MPEG-7 ontology, which acts as an upper ontology for multimedia. Other ontologies and XML Schemas can also be easily incorporated using the XSD2OWL module.

Semantic metadata can be directly fed into the system together with XML metadata, which is made semantic using the XML2RDF module. For instance, XML MPEG-7 metadata has a great importance because it is commonly used for low-level visual and audio content descriptors automatically extracted from its underlying signals. This kind of metadata can be used as the basis for audio and video description and retrieval.

In addition to content-based metadata, there is context-based metadata. This kind of metadata higher level and it usually, in this context, related to journalism metadata. It is generated by the system users (journalist, photographers, cameramen, etc.). For instance, there are issue dates, news subjects, titles, authors, etc.

This kind of metadata can come directly from semantic sources but, usually, it is going to come from legacy XML sources based on the standards' XML Schemas. Therefore, in order to integrate them, they will pass through the XML2RDF component. This component, in conjunction with the ontologies previously mapped from the corresponding XML Schemas, generates the RDF metadata that can be then integrated in the common RDF framework.

This framework has the persistence support of a RDF store, where metadata and ontologies reside. Once all metadata has been put together, the semantic integration can take place, as shown in the next section.

Figure 2. News metadata integration and retrieval architecture

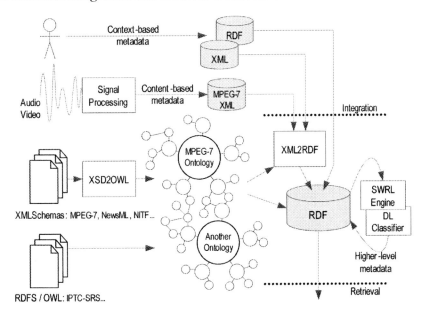

Semantic Integration Outline

As mentioned in the introduction, one of the main problems in nowadays media houses is that of heterogeneous data integration. Even within a single organization, data from disparate sources must be integrated. Our approach to solve this problem is based on Web ontologies and, as the focus is on multimedia and journalism metadata integration, our integration base are the MPEG-7, MPEG-21 and the journalism ontologies.

In order to benefit from the system architecture presented before, when semantic metadata based on different schemes has to be integrated, the XML Schemas are first mapped to OWL. Once this first step has been done, these schemas can be integrated into the ontological framework using OWL semantic relations for equivalence and inclusion: *subClassOf, subPropertyOf, equivalentClass, equivalentProperty, sameIndividualAs*, etc. These relations allows simple integration relations, for more complex integration steps that require changes in data structures it is possible to use Semantic Web rules (Horrocks, Patel-Schneider, Boley, Tabet, Grosof, & Dean, 2004).

These relationships capture the semantics of the data integration. Then, once metadata is incorporated into the system and semantically-decorated, the integration is automatically performed by applying inference. Table 2 shows some of these mappings, performed once all metadata has been moved to the semantic space.

First, there are four examples of semantic mappings among the NITF Ontology, the NewsML Ontology and the IPTC Subjects Ontology. The first mapping tells that all values for the *nitf:tobject. subject* property are from class *subj:Subject*. The second one that the property *nitf:tobject. subject.detail* is equivalent to *subj:explanation*. The third one that all *nitf:body* instances are also *newsml:DataContent* instances and the fourth one that all *newsml:Subject* are *subj:Subject*. Finally, there is also a mapping that is performed during the XML to RDF translation. It is necessary in order to recognise an implicit identifier, *nitf:tobject.subject.refnum* is mapped to rdf:ID in order to make this recognise this identifier in the context of NITF and make it explicit in the context of RDF.

Table 2. Journalism and multimedia metadata integration mapping examples

Semantic Mappings
∀ nitf:tobject.subject . subj:Subject
nitf:tobject.subject.detail ≡ subj:explanation
nitf:body ⊆ newsml:DataContent
newsml:Subject ≡ subj:Subject
XML2RDF Mappings
nitf:tobject.subject.refnum → rdf:ID

SEMANTIC MEDIA INTEGRATION FROM HUMAN SPEECH

This section introduces a tool, build on top of the ontological infrastructure described in the previous sections, geared towards a convergent and integrated news management in the context of a media house. As has been previously introduced, the diversification of content in media houses, who must deal in an integrated way with different modalities (text, image, graphics, video, audio, etc.), carries new management challenges. Semantic metadata and ontologies are a key facilitator in order to enable convergent and integrated media management.

In the news domain, news companies like the Diari Segre Media Group are turning into news media houses, owning radio stations and video production companies that produce content not supported by the print medium, but which can be delivered through Internet newspapers. Such new perspectives in the area of digital content call for a revision of mainstream search and retrieval technologies currently oriented to text and based on keywords. The main limitation of mainstream text IR systems is that their ability to represent meanings is based on counting word occurrences, regardless of the relation between words (Salton, & McGill, 1983). Most research beyond this limitation has remained in the scope of linguistic (Salton, & McGill, 1983) or statistic (Vorhees, 1994) information.

On the other end, IR is addressed in the Semantic Web field from a much more formal perspective (Castells, Fernández, & Vallet, 2007). In the Semantic Web vision, the search space consists of a totally formalized corpus, where all the information units are unambiguously typed, interrelated, and described by logic axioms in domain ontologies. Such tools enabled the development of semantic-based retrieval technologies that support search by meanings rather than keywords, providing users with more powerful retrieval capabilities to find their way through in increasingly massive search spaces.

Semantic Web based news annotation and retrieval has already been applied in the Diari Segre Media Group in the context of the Neptuno research project (Castells, Perdrix, Pulido, Rico, Benjamins, Contreras, & Lorés, 2004). However, this is a partial solution as it just deals with textual content. The objective of the tool described in this section is to show how these techniques can also be applied to content with embedded human-speech tracks. The final result is a tool based on Semantic Web technologies and methodologies that allows managing text and audiovisual content in an integrated and efficient way. Consequently, the integration of human speech processing technologies in the semantic-based approach extends the semantic retrieval capabilities to audio content. The research is being undertaken in the context of the S5T research project[10].

As shown in Figure 3, this tool is based on a human speech recognition process inspired

Figure 3. Architecture for the Semantic Media Integration from Human Speech Tool

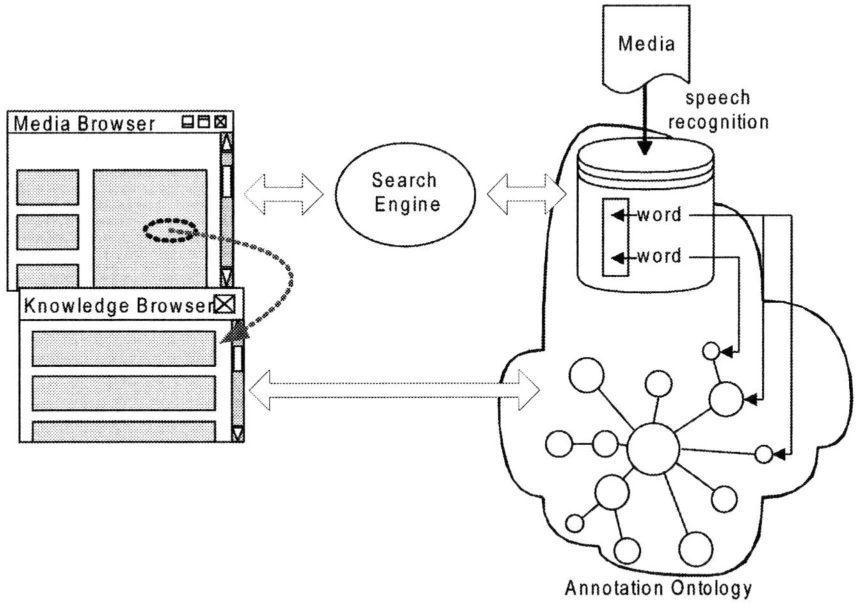

Annotation Ontology

by (Kim, Jung, & Chung, 2004) that generates the corresponding transcripts for the radio and television contents. From this preliminary process, it is possible benefit from the same semi-automatic annotation process in order to generate the semantic annotations for audio, audiovisual and textual content. Keywords detected during speech recognition are mapped to concepts in the ontologies describing the domain covered by audiovisual and textual content, for instance the politics domain for news talking about this subject. Specifically, when the keyword forms of a concept are uttered in a piece of speech, the content is annotated with that concept. Polysemic words and other ambiguities are treated by a set of heuristics. More details about the annotation and semantic query resolution processes are available from (Cuayahuitl, & Serridge, 2002).

Once audio and textual contents have been semantically annotated (Tejedor, García, Fernández, López, Perdrix, Macías, et al., 2007), it is possible to provide a unified set of interfaces, rooted on the semantic capabilities provided by the annotations. These interfaces, intended for journalists and archivist, are shown on the left of Figure 3. They exploit the semantic richness of the underlying ontologies upon which the search system is built. Semantic queries are resolved, using semantic annotations as has been previously described, and retrieve content items and pieces of these contents. News contents are packaged together using annotations based on the MPEG-21 and MPEG-7 ontologies, as it is described in Section 3.3.1. Content items are presented to the user through the Media Browser, detailed in Section 3.3.2, and the underlying semantic annotations and the ontologies used to generate these annotations can be browsed using the Knowledge Browser, described in Section 3.3.3.

Semantic News Packaging Using MPEG Ontologies

Actually, in an editorial office there are a lot of applications producing media in several formats. This is an issue that requires a common structure to facilitate management. The first step is to treat each unit of information, in this case each new,

Figure 4. Content DI structure

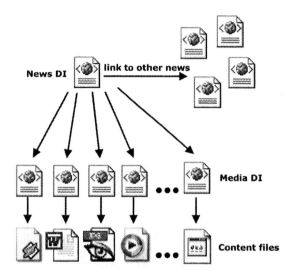

as a single object. Consequently, when searching something upon this structure, all related content is retrieved together.

Another interesting issue is that news can be linked to other news. This link between news allows the creation of information threads. A news composition metadata system has been developed using concepts from the MPEG-21 and MPEG-7 ontologies. It comprises three hierarchical levels as shown in Figure 4.

The lower level comprises content files, in whatever format they are. The mid level is formed by metadata descriptors (what, when, where, how, who is involved, author, etc.) for each file, mainly based on concepts from the MPEG-7 ontology generated using the methodology described in Section 3.1. They are called the Media Digital Items (Media DI).

These semantic descriptors are based on the MPEG-7 Ontology and facilitate automated management of the different kinds of content that build up a news item in a convergent media house. For instance, it is possible to generate semantic queries that benefit from the content hierarchy defined in MPEG-7 and formalised in the ontology. This way, it is possible to pose generic queries for any kind of segment (e.g. *AudioSegmentType,*

VideoSegmentType...) because all of them are formalised as subclasses of *SegmentType* and the implicit semantics can be directly used by a semantic query engine.

Table 3 shows a piece of metadata that describes an audio segment of a Diari Segre Media Group news item used in the S5T project. This semantic metadata is generated from the corresponding XML MPEG-7 metadata using the XML to RDF mapping and takes profit from the MPEG-7 OWL ontology in order to make the MPEG-7 semantics explicit. Therefore, this kind of metadata can be processed using semantic queries independently from the concrete type of segment. Consequently, it is possible to develop applications that process in an integrated and convergent way the different kinds of contents that build up a new.

The top level in the hierarchy is based on descriptors that model news and put together all the different pieces of content that conform them. These objects are called News Digital Items (News DI). There is one News DI for each news item and all of them are based on MPEG-21 metadata. The part of the standard that defines digital items (DI) is used for that. DI is the fundamental unit defined in MPEG-21 for content distribution and transaction, very useful for convergent

Table 3. MPEG-7 Ontology description for a audio segment generated from XML MPEG-7 metadata fragment

```
<?xml version="1.0"?>
<rdf:RDF
xmlns:mpeg7="http://rhizomik.net/ontologies/2006/03/Mpeg7-2001.owl#">
<mpeg7:AudioType rdf:about="http://rhizomik.net/audio/2007-01-13.mp3">
<mpeg7:Audio>
<mpeg7:AudioSegmentType>
<mpeg7:MediaTime>
<mpeg7:MediaTimeType>
<mpeg7:MediaTimePoint
rdf:datatype="&xsd;time">01:27.0</mpeg7:MediaTimePoint>
<mpeg7:MediaDuration
rdf:datatype="&xsd;time">P5S</mpeg7:MediaDuration>
</mpeg7:MediaTimeType>
</mpeg7:MediaTime>
</mpeg7:AudioSegmentType>
</mpeg7:Audio>
</mpeg7:AudioType>
</rdf:RDF>
```

media management. As in the case of MPEG-7 metadata, RDF semantic metadata is generated from XML using the semantics made explicit by the MPEG-21 ontologies. This way, it is possible to implement generic processes also at the news level using semantic queries.

On top of the previous semantic descriptors at the media and news level, it is possible to develop an application for integrated and convergent news management in the media house. The application is based on two specialised interfaces described in the next subsections. They benefit from the ontological infrastructure detailed in this chapter, which is complemented with ontologies for the concrete news domain. However, the application remains independent from the concrete domain.

Media Browser

The Media Browser, shown in Figure 5, takes profit from the MPEG-21 metadata for news and MPEG-7 metadata for media in order to implement a generic browser for the different kinds of media that constitute a news item in a convergent newspaper. This interface allows navigating them and presents the retrieved pieces of content and the available RDF metadata describing them. These descriptions are based on a generic rendering of RDF data as interactive HTML for increased usability (García, & Gil, 2006).

The multimedia metadata is based on the Dublin Core schema for editorial metadata and IPTC News Codes for subjects. For content-based metadata, especially the content decomposition depending on the audio transcript, MPEG-7 metadata is used for media segmentation, as it was shown in Table 3. In addition to the editorial metadata and the segments decomposition, a specialized audiovisual view is presented. This view allows rendering the content, i.e. audio and video, and interacting with audiovisual content through a click-able version of the audio transcript.

Two kinds of interactions are possible from the transcript. First, it is possible to click any word in the transcript that has been indexed in order to perform a keyword-based query for all content in the database where that keyword appears. Second, the transcript is enriched with links to the ontology used for semantic annotation. Each word in the transcript whose meaning is represented by an ontology concept is linked to a description of that concept, which is shown by the Knowledge Browser detailed in the next section. The whole interaction is performed through the user Web

Figure 5. Media Browser interface presenting content metadata (left) and the annotated transcript (right)

browser using AJAX in order to improve the interactive capabilities of the interface.

For instance, the transcript includes the name of a politician that has been indexed and modelled in the ontology. Consequently, it can be clicked in order to get all the multimedia content where the name appears or, alternatively, to browse all the knowledge about that politician encoded in the corresponding domain ontology.

Knowledge Browser

This interface is used to allow the user browsing the knowledge structures employed to annotate content, i.e. the underlying ontologies. The same RDF data to interactive HTML rendering used in the Media Browser is used here. Consequently, following the politician example in the previous section, when the user looks for the available knowledge about that person and interactive view of the RDF data modelling him is shown. This way, the user can benefit from the modelling effort and, for instance, be aware of the politician party, that he is a member of the parliament, etc.

This interface constitutes a knowledge browser so the link to the politician party or the parliament can be followed and additional knowledge can be retrieved, for instance a list of all the members of the parliament. In addition to this recursive navigation of all the domain knowledge, at any browsing step, it is also possible to get all the multimedia content annotated using the concept currently being browsed. This step would carry the user back to the Media Browser.

Thanks to this dual browsing experience, the user can navigate through audiovisual content using the Media Browser and through the underlying semantic models using the Knowledge Browser in a complementary an inter-weaved way. Finally, as for the Media Browser, the Knowledge Browser is also implemented using AJAX so the whole interactive experience can be enjoyed using a Web browser.

ALTERNATIVES

There are other existing initiatives that try to move journalism and multimedia metadata to the Semantic Web world. In the journalism field, the Neptuno (Castells, Perdrix, Pulido, Rico, Benjamins, Contreras, et al., 2004) and NEWS (Fernández, Blázquez, Fisteus, Sánchez, Sintek, Bernardi, et al., 2006) projects can be highlighted.

Both projects have developed ontologies based on existing standards (IPTC SRS, NITF or NewsML) but from an ad-hoc and limited point of view. Therefore, in order to smooth the transition from the previous legacy systems, more complex and complete mappings should be developed and maintained.

The same can be said for the existing attempts to produce semantic multimedia metadata. Chronologically, the first attempts to make MPEG-7 metadata semantics explicit where carried out, during the MPEG-7 standardisation process, by Jane Hunter (2001). The proposal used RDF to formalise a small part of MPEG-7, and later incorporated some DAML+OIL construct to further detail their semantics (Hunter, 2001). More recent approaches (Hausenblas, 2007) are based on the Web Ontology Language (McGuinness & Harmelen, 2004), but are also constrained to a part of the whole MPEG-7 standard, the Multimedia Description Scheme (MDS) for the ontology proposed at (Tsinaraki, Polydoros, & Christodoulakis, 2004).

An alternative to standards-based metadata are folksonomies (Vanderwal, 2007). Mainly used in social bookmarking software (e.g. del.icio.us, Flickr, YouTube), they allow the easy creation of user driven vocabularies in order to annotate resources. The main advantage of folksonomies is the low entry barrier: all terms are acceptable as metada, so no knowledge of the established standards is needed. Its main drawback is the lack of control over the vocabulary used to annotate resources, so resource combination and reasoning becomes almost impossible. Some systems combine social and semantic metadata and try to infer a formal ontology from the tags used in the folksonomy (Herzog, Luger & Herzog, 2007). In our case we believe that it is better to use standard ontologies both from multimedia and journalism fields than open and uncontrolled vocabularies.

Moreover, none of the proposed ontologies, for journalism of multimedia metadata, is accompanied by a methodology that allows mapping existing XML metadata based on the corresponding standards to semantic metadata. Consequently, it is difficult to put them into practice as there is a lack of metadata to play with. On the other hand, there is a great amount of existing XML metadata and a lot of tools based on XML technologies. For example, the new Milenium Quay[11] cross-media archive system from PROTEC, the worldwide leadership in cross-media software platforms, is XML-based. This software is focused on flexibility using several XML tags and mappings, increasing interoperability with other archiving systems. The XML-based products are clearly a trend in this scope. Every day, new products from the main software companies are appearing, which deal with different steps in all the news life-cycle, from production to consumption.

Nowadays, commercial tools based on XML technologies constitute the clear option in newspaper media houses. Current initiatives based on Semantic Web tools are constrained due to the lack of "real" data to work with; they constitute a too abrupt breaking from legacy systems. Moreover, they are prototypes with little functionality. Consequently, we do not see the semantic tools as an alternative to legacy systems, at least in the short term. On the contrary, we think that they constitute additional modules that can help dealing with the extra requirements derived from media heterogeneity, multichannel distribution and knowledge management issues.

The proposed methodology facilitates the production of semantic metadata from existing legacy systems, although it is simple metadata as the source is XML metadata that is not intended for carrying complex semantics. In any case, it constitutes a first and smooth step toward adding semantic-enabled tools to existing newspaper content management systems. From this point, more complex semantics and processing can be added without breaking continuity with the investments that media houses have done in their current systems.

COST AND BENEFITS

One of the biggest challenges in media houses is to attach metadata to all the generated content in order to facilitate management. However, this is easier in this context as in many media houses there is a department specialized in this work, which is carried out by archivists. Consequently, the additional costs arising from the application of Semantic Web technologies are mitigated due to the existence of this department. It is already in charge of indexation, categorization and content semantic enrichment.

Consequently, though there are many organizational and philosophy changes that modify how this task is currently carried out, it is not necessary to add new resources to perform this effort. The volume of information is another important aspect to consider. All Semantic Web approaches in this field propose an automatic or semi-automatic annotation processes.

The degree of automation attained using Semantic Web tools allows archivists spending less time in the more time consuming and mechanical tasks, e.g. the annotation of audio contents which can be performed with the help of speech-to-text tools as in the S5T project example presented in Section 3.3. Consequently, archivists can spend their time refining more concrete and specific metadata details and leave other aspects like categorization or annotation to partially or totally automatic tools. The overall outcome is that, with this computer and human complementary work, it is possible to archive big amounts of content without introducing extra costs.

Semantic metadata also provides improvements in content navigability and searching, maybe in all information retrieval tasks. This fact implies a better level of productivity in the media house, e.g. while performing event tracking through a set of news in order to produce a new content. However, it is also important to take into account the gap between journalists' and archivists' mental models, which is reflected in the way archivists categorise content and journalist perform queries.

This gap is a clear threat to productivity, although the flexibility of semantic structures makes it possible to relate concepts from different mental models in order to attain a more integrated and shared view (Abelló, García, Gil, Oliva, & Perdrix, 2006), which improves the content retrieval results and consequently improves productivity.

Moreover, the combination of semantic metadata and ontologies, together with tools like the ones presented for project S5T, make it possible for journalists to navigate between content metadata and ontology concepts and benefit from an integrated and shared knowledge management effort. This feature mitigates current gaps among editorial staff that seriously reduce the possibilities of media production.

Another point of interest is the possibility that journalists produce some metadata during the content generation process. Nowadays, journalists do not consider this activity part of their job. Consequently, this task might introduce additional costs that have not been faced at the current stage of development. This remains a future issue that requires deep organisational changes, which are not present yet in most editorial staffs, even if they are trying to follow the media convergence philosophy.

To conclude, there are also the development costs necessary in order to integrate the Semantic Web tools into current media houses. As has been already noted, the choice of a smooth transition approach reduces the development costs. This approach is based on the XSD2OWL and XML2RDF mappings detailed in Section 3.1.

Consequently, it is not necessary to develop a full newspaper content management system based on Semantic Web tools. On the contrary, existing systems based on XML technologies, as it is the common case, are used as the development platform on top of which semantic tools are deployed. This approach also improves interoperability with other media houses that also use XML technologies, though the interoperation is performed at the semantic level once source metadata has been mapped to semantic metadata.

RISK ASSESSMENT

In one hand we can consider some relevant positive aspects from the proposed solution. In fact, we are introducing knowledge management into the newspaper content archive system. The proposal implies a more flexible archive system with significant improvements in search and navigation. Compatibility with current standards is kept while the archive system allows searching across media and the underlying terms and domain knowledge. Finally, the integrated view on content provides seamless access to any kind of archived resources, which could be text, audio, video streaming, photographs, etc. Consequently, separate search engines for each kind of media are no longer necessary and global queries make it possible to retrieve any kind of resources.

This feature represents an important improvement in the retrieval process but also in the archiving one. The introduction of a semi-automatic annotation process produces changes in the archivist work. They could expend more time refining semantic annotation and including new metadata. Existing human resources in the archive department should spend the same amount of time than they currently do. However, they should obtain better quality results while they populate the archive with all the semantically annotated content. The overall result is that the archive becomes a knowledge management system.

On other hand, we need to take into account some weaknesses in this approach. Nowadays, Semantic Web technologies are mainly prototypes under development. This implies problems when you try to build a complete industrial platform based on them. Scalability appears as the main problem as it was experienced during the Neptuno

research project (Castells et al., 2004) also in the journalism domain.

There is a lack of implementations supporting massive content storage and management. In other words, experimental solutions cannot be applied to real system considering, as our experience has shown, more than 1 million of items, i.e. news, photos or videos. This amount can be generated in 2 or 3 months in a small news media company. A part from the lack of implementations, there is also the lack of technical staff with Semantic Web development skills.

Despite all these inconveniences, there is the opportunity to create a platform for media convergence and editorial staff tasks integration. It can become an open platform that can manage future challenges in media houses and that is adaptable to different models based on specific organizational structures. Moreover, this platform may make it possible to offer new content interaction paradigms, especially through the World Wide Web channel.

One of these potential paradigms has already started to be explored in the S5T project. Currently, it offers integrated and complementary browsing among content and the terms of the underlying domain of knowledge, e.g. politics. However, this tool is currently intended just for the editorial staff. We anticipate a future tool that makes this kind of interaction available from the Diari Segre Web site to all of its Web users. This tool would provide an integrated access point to different kinds of contents, like text or news podcasts, but also to the underlying knowledge that models events, histories, personalities, etc.

There are some threats too. First of all, any organizational change, like changing the way the archive department works or giving unprecedented annotation responsibilities to journalists, constitutes an important risk. Changes inside an organization never be easy and must be well done and follow very closely if you want to make them successful. Sometimes, the effort-satisfaction ratio may be perceived as not justified by for some journalist or archivists. Consequently, they may react against the organisational changes required in order to implement rich semantic metadata.

FUTURE TRENDS

The more relevant future trend is that the Semantic Web is starting to be recognised as a consolidated discipline and a set of technologies and methodologies that are going to have a great impact in the future of enterprise information systems (King, 2007). The more important consequence of this consolidation is that many commercial tools are appearing. They are solid tools that can be used in order to build enterprise semantic information systems with a high degree of scalability.

As has been shown, the benefits of semantic metadata are being put into practice in the Diari Segre Media Group, a newspaper that is becoming a convergent media house with press, radio, television and a World Wide Web portal. As has been detailed, a set of semantics-aware tools have been developed. They are intended for journalist and archivists in the media house, but they can be also adapted to the general public at the portal.

Making the Diari Segre semantic tools publicly available is one of the greatest opportunities and in the future, with the help of solid enterprise semantic platforms, is the issue where the greatest effort is going to be placed. In general, a bigger users base puts extra requirements about the particular needs that each user might have. This is due to the fact that each user may have a different vision about the domain of knowledge or about searching and browsing strategies. In this sense, we need some degree of personalisation beyond the much more closed approach that has been taken in order to deploy these tools for the editorial staff.

Personalisation ranges from interfaces, to processes or query construction approaches applying static or dynamic profiles. Static profiles could be completed by users in when they first register. Dynamic profiles must be collected by the system based on the user system usage (Castells et al., 2007). Per user profiles introduce a great amount of complexity, which can be mitigated building groups of similar profiles, for instance groups based on the user role.

Moreover, to collect system usage information while users navigate through the underlying conceptual structures makes it possible to discover new implicit relations among concepts with some semantic significance, at least from the user, or group to which the user belongs, point of view. If there are a lot of users following the same navigation path between items, maybe it would be better to add a new conceptual link between the initial and final items. Currently, this kind of relations can only be added manually. In the near future, we could use the power of Semantic Web technologies in order to do this automatically. This would improve user experience while they search or navigate as the underlying conceptual framework would accommodate the particular user view on the domain.

To conclude this section, it is also important to take into account the evolution of the standards upon which the ontological framework has been build. On the short range, the most import novelty is the imminent release of the NewsML G2 standard (Le Meur, 2007). This standard is also based on XML Schemas for language formalisation. Therefore, it should be trivial to generate the corresponding OWL ontologies and to start mapping metadata based on this standard to semantic metadata. More effort will be needed in order to produce the integration rules that will allow integrating this standard into existing legacy systems augmented by Semantic Web tools.

CONCLUSION

This research work has been guided by the need for a semantic journalism and multimedia metadata framework that facilitates semantic newspaper applications development in the context of a convergent media house. It has been detected, as it is widely documented in the bibliography and professional activity, that IPTC and MPEG standards are the best sources for an ontological framework that facilitates a smooth transition from legacy to semantic information systems. MPEG-7, MPEG-21 and most of the IPTC standards are based on XML Schemas and thus they do not have formal semantics.

Our approach contributes a complete and automatic mapping of the whole MPEG-7 standard to OWL, of the media packaging part of MPEG-21 and of the main IPTC standard schemas (NITF, NewsML and NewsCodes) to the corresponding OWL ontologies. Instance metadata is automatically imported from legacy systems through a XML-2RDF mapping, based on the ontologies previously mapped from the standards XML schemas. Once in a semantic space, data integration, which is a crucial factor when several sources of information are available, is facilitated enormously.

Moreover, semantic metadata facilitates the development of applications in the context of media houses that traditional newspapers are becoming. The convergence of different kinds of media, that now constitute multimedia news, poses new management requirements that are easier to cope with if applications are more informed, i.e. aware of the semantics that are implicit in news and the media that constitute them. This is the case for the tools we propose for archivists and journalists, the Media Browser and the Knowledge Browser. These tools reduce the misunderstandings among them and facilitate keeping track of existing news stories and the generation of new content.

REFERENCES

Abelló, A., García, R., Gil, R., Oliva, M., & Perdrix, F. (2006). Semantic Data Integration in a Newspaper Content Management System. In R. Meersman, Z. Tari, & P. Herrero (Eds.), *OTM Workshops 2006*. LNCS Vol. 4277 (pp. 40-41). Berlin/Heidelberg, DE: Springer.

Amann, B., Beer, C., Fundulak, I., & Scholl, M. (2002). Ontology-Based Integration of XML Web Resources. *Proceedings of the 1st International Semantic Web Conference*, ISWC 2002. LNCS Vol. 2342 (pp. 117-131). Berlin/Heidelberg, DE: Springer.

Becket, D. (2004). RDF/XML Syntax Specification. World Wide Web Consortium Recommendation.

Berners-Lee, T., Hendler, J., & Lassila, O. (2001). The Semantic Web. *Scientific American, 284*(5), 34–43.

Castells, P., Fernández, M., & Vallet, D. (2007). An Adaptation of the Vector-Space Model for Ontology-Based Information Retrieval. *IEEE Transactions on Knowledge and Data Engineering, 19*(2), 261–272. doi:10.1109/TKDE.2007.22

Castells, P., Perdrix, F., Pulido, E., Rico, M., Benjamins, R., Contreras, J., et al. (2004). Neptuno: Semantic Web Technologies for a Digital Newspaper Archive. In C. Bussler, J. Davies, D. Fensel, & R. Studer, (Eds.), *The Semantic Web: Research and Applications: First European Semantic Web Symposium*, ESWS 2004, LNCS Vol. 3053 (pp. 445-458). Berlin/Heidelberg, DE: Springer.

Castells, P., Perdrix, F., Pulido, E., Rico, M., Benjamins, R., Contreras, J., & Lorés, J. (2004). *Neptuno: Semantic Web Technologies for a Digital Newspaper Archive*. LNCS Vol. 3053 (pp. 445-458).Berlin/Heidelberg, DE: Springer.

Cruz, I., Xiao, H., & Hsu, F. (2004). An Ontology-based Framework for XML Semantic Integration. *Proceedings of the Eighth International Database Engineering and Applications Symposium*, IDEAS'04, (pp. 217-226). Washington, DC: IEEE Computer Society.

Cuayahuitl, H., & Serridge, B. (2002). Out-of-vocabulary Word Modelling and Rejection for Spanish Keyword Spotting Systems. *Proceedings of the 2nd Mexican International Conference on Artificial Intelligence.*

Einhoff, M., Casademont, J., Perdrix, F., & Noll, S. (2005) ELIN: A MPEG Related News Framework. In M. Grgic (Ed.), *47th International Symposium ELMAR: Focused on Multimedia Systems and Applications* (pp.139-142). Zadar, Croatia: ELMAR.

Eriksen, L. B., & Ihlström, C. (2000). Evolution of the Web News Genre - The Slow Move Beyond the Print Metaphor. In *Proceedings of the 33rd Hawaii international Conference on System Sciences*. IEEE Computer Society Press.

Fernández, N., Blázquez, J. M., Fisteus, J. A., Sánchez, L., Sintek, M., Bernardi, A., et al. (2006). NEWS: Bringing Semantic Web Technologies into News Agencies. *The Semantic Web - ISWC 2006*, LNCS Vol. 4273 (pp. 778-791). Berlin/Heidelberg, DE: Springer.

García, R. (2006). XML Semantics Reuse. In *A Semantic Web Approach to Digital Rights Management*, PhD Thesis (pp. 116-120). TDX.

García, R., & Gil, R. (2006). Improving Human-Semantic Web Interaction: The Rhizomer Experience. *Proceedings of the 3rd Italian Semantic Web Workshop*, SWAP'06, Vol. 201 (pp. 57-64). CEUR Workshop Proceedings.

García, R., Gil, R., & Delgado, J. (2007). A Web ontologies framework for digital rights management. *Artificial Intelligence and Law, 15*(2), 137–154. doi:10.1007/s10506-007-9032-6

García, R., Gil, R., Gallego, I., & Delgado, J. (2005). Formalising ODRL Semantics using Web Ontologies. In R. Iannella, S. Guth, & C. Serrao, Eds., *Open Digital Rights Language Workshop*, ODRL'2005 (pp. 33-42). Lisbon, Portugal: AD-ETTI.

Hausenblas, M., Troncy, R., Halaschek-Wiener, C., Bürger, T., & Celma, O. Boll, et al. (2007). *Multimedia Vocabularies on the Semantic Web*. W3C Incubator Group Report, World Wide Web Consortium.

Haustein, S., & Pleumann, J. (2002). Is Participation in the Semantic Web Too Difficult? In *Proceedings of the First International Semantic Web Conference on The Semantic Web*, LNCS Vol. 2342 (pp. 448-453). Berlin/Heidelberg: Springer.

Herzog, C., Luger, M., & Herzog, M. (2007). Combining Social and Semantic Metadata for Search in Document Repository. Bridging the Gap Between Semantic Web and Web 2.0. *International Workshop at the 4th European Semantic Web Conference* in Insbruck, Austria, June 7, 2007.

Horrocks, I., Patel-Schneider, P. F., Boley, H., Tabet, S., Grosof, B., & Dean, M. (2004). *SWRL: A Semantic Web Rule Language Combining OWL and RuleML*. W3C Member Submission, World Wide Web Consortium.

Hunter, J. (2001). Adding Multimedia to the Semantic Web - Building an MPEG-7 Ontology. *Proceedings of the International Semantic Web Working Symposium* (pp. 260-272). Standford, CA.

Hunter, J. (2003). Enhacing the Semantic Interoperability of Multimedia through a Core Ontology. *IEEE Transactions on Circuits and Systems for Video Technology, 13*(1), 49–58. doi:10.1109/TCSVT.2002.808088

Ihlström, C., Lundberg, J., & Perdrix, F. (2003) Audience of Local Online Newspapers in Sweden, Slovakia and Spain - A Comparative Study. In *Proceedings of HCI International* Vol. 3 (pp. 749-753). Florence, Kentucky: Lawrence Erlbaum Associates.

Kim, J., Jung, H., & Chung, H. (2004). A Keyword Spotting Approach based on Pseudo N-gram Language Model. *Proceedings of the 9th Conf. on Speech and Computer*, SPECOM 2004 (pp. 256-259). Patras, Greece.

King, R. (2007, April 29). Taming the World Wide Web. *Special Report, Business Week.*

Klein, M. C. A. (2002). Interpreting XML Documents via an RDF Schema Ontology. In *Proceedings of the 13th International Workshop on Database and Expert Systems Applications*, DEXA 2002 (pp. 889-894). Washington, DC: IEEE Computer Society.

Lakshmanan, L., & Sadri, F. (2003). Interoperability on XML Data. *Proceedings of the 2nd International Semantic Web Conference*, ICSW'03, LNCS Vol. 2870 (pp. 146-163). Berlin/Heidelberg: Springer.

Le Meur, L. (2007). How NewsML-G2 simplifies and fuels news management. Presented at *XTech 2007: The Ubiquitous Web*, Paris, France.

Lundberg, J. (2002). *The online news genre: Visions and state of the art.* Paper presented at the 34th Annual Congress of the Nordic Ergonomics Society, Sweden.

McDonald, N. (2004). Can HCI shape the future of mass communications. *Interaction, 11*(2), 44–47. doi:10.1145/971258.971272

McGuinness, D. L., & Harmelen, F. V. (2004). *OWL Web Ontology Language Overview*. World Wide Web Consortium Recommendation.

Patel-Schneider, P., & Simeon, J. (2002). The Yin/Yang Web: XML syntax and RDF semantics. *Proceedings of the 11th International World Wide Web Conference*, WWW'02 (pp. 443-453). ACM Press.

Salembier, P., & Smith, J. (2002). Overview of MPEG-7 multimedia description schemes and schema tools. In B.S. Manjunath, P. Salembier, & T. Sikora (Ed.), *Introduction to MPEG-7: Multimedia Content Description Interface*. John Wiley & Sons.

Salton, G., & McGill, M. (1983). *Introduction to Modern Information Retrieval*. New York: McGraw-Hill.

Sawyer, S., & Tapia, A. (2005). The sociotechnical nature of mobile computing work: Evidence from a study of policing in the United States. *International Journal of Technology and Human Interaction, 1*(3), 1–14.

Tejedor, J., García, R., Fernández, M., López, F., Perdrix, F., Macías, J. A., et al. (2007). Ontology-Based Retrieval of Human Speech. *Proceedings of the 6th International Workshop on Web Semantics*, WebS'07 (in press). IEEE Computer Society Press.

Tous, R., García, R., Rodríguez, E., & Delgado, J. (2005). Arquitecture of a Semantic XPath Processor. In K. Bauknecht, B. Pröll, & H. Werthner, Eds., *E-Commerce and Web Technologies: 6th International Conference*, EC-Web'05, LNCS Vol. 3590 (pp. 1-10). Berlin/Heidelberg, DE: Springer.

Tsinaraki, C., Polydoros, P., & Christodoulakis, S. (2004). Integration of OWL ontologies in MPEG-7 and TVAnytime compliant Semantic Indexing. In A. Persson, & J. Stirna, Eds., *16th International Conference on Advanced Information Systems Engineering*, LNCS Vol. 3084 (pp. 398-413). Berlin/Heidelberg, DE: Springer.

Tsinaraki, C., Polydoros, P., & Christodoulakis, S. (2004). Interoperability support for Ontology-based Video Retrieval Applications. *Proceedings of 3rd International Conference on Image and Video Retrieval, CIVR 2004*. Dublin, Ireland.

Vanderwal, T. (2007) *Folksonomy Coinage and Definition*.

Vorhees, E. (1994). Query expansion using lexical semantic relations. *Proceedings of the 17th ACM Conf. on Research and Development in Information Retrieval*, ACM Press.

ADDITIONAL READING

Kompatsiaris, Y., & Hobson, P. (Eds.). (2008). *Semantic Multimedia and Ontologies: Theory and Applications*. Berlin/Heidelberg, DE: Springer.

ENDNOTES

1. http://www.diarisegre.com
2. IPTC, http://www.iptc.org
3. IIM, http://www.iptc.org/IIM
4. http://www.iptc.org/NewsCodes
5. NITF, http://www.nitf.org
6. http://www.newsml.org
7. http://rhizomik.net/redefer
8. http://rhizomik.net/semanticnewspaper
9. http://rhizomik.net/ontologies/mpeg7ontos
10. http://nets.ii.uam.es/s5t
11. Milenium Quay, http://www.mileniumcross-media.com

This work was previously published in Semantic Web for Business: Cases and Applications, edited by R. García, pp. 170-193, copyright 2009 by Information Science Reference (an imprint of IGI Global).

Chapter 4.9
Applying Semantic Web to E-Tourism

Danica Damljanović
University of Sheffield, UK

Vladan Devedžić
University of Belgrade, Serbia

ABSTRACT

Traditional E-Tourism applications store data internally in a form that is not interoperable with similar systems. Hence, tourist agents spend plenty of time updating data about vacation packages in order to provide good service to their clients. On the other hand, their clients spend plenty of time searching for the 'perfect' vacation package as the data about tourist offers are not integrated and are available from different spots on the Web. We developed Travel Guides - a prototype system for tourism management to illustrate how semantic web technologies combined with traditional E-Tourism applications: a.) help integration of tourism sources dispersed on the Web b) enable creating sophisticated user profiles. Maintaining quality user profiles enables system personalization and adaptivity of the content shown to the user. The core of this system is in ontologies – they enable machine readable and machine understandable representation of the data and more importantly reasoning.

INTRODUCTION

A mandatory step on the way to the desired vacation destination is usually contacting tourist agencies. Presentations of tourist destinations on the Web make a huge amount of data. These data are accessible to individuals through the official presentations of the tourist agencies, cities, municipalities, sport alliances, etc. These sites are available to everyone, but still, the problem is to find useful information without wasting time. On the other hand, plenty of systems on the Web are maintained regularly to provide tourists with up-to-date information. These systems require a lot of efforts from humans - especially in travel agencies where they want to offer tourists a good service.

We present Travel Guides – a prototype system that is combining Semantic Web technologies with those used in mainstream applications (cp. Djuric, Devedzic & Gasevic, 2007) in order to enable data exchange between different E-Tourism systems and thus:

- Ease the process of maintaining the systems for tourist agencies
- Ease the process of searching for perfect vacation packages for tourists

The core of Travel Guides system is in ontologies. We have developed domain ontology for tourism and described the most important design principles in this chapter.

As ontologies enable presenting data in a machine-readable form thus offering easy exchange of data between different applications, this would lead to increased interoperability and decreased efforts tourist agents make to update the data in their systems. To illustrate increased interoperability we initialized our knowledge base using data imported from some other system. We built an environment to enable transferring segments of any knowledge base to the other by selecting some criteria - this transfer is possible even if the knowledge bases rely on different ontologies.

Ontology-aware systems provide the possibility to perform semantic search – the user can search the destinations covered by Travel Guides using several criteria related to travelling (e.g., accommodation rating, budget, activities and interests: concerts, clubbing, art, sports, shopping, etc.). For even more sophisticated search results we introduce user profiles created based on data that system possesses about the user. These data are analysed by a reasoner, and the heuristics is residing inside the ontology.

The chapter is organized as follows: in next section we describe different systems that are developed in the area of tourism which use semantic web technologies. In the central section we first discuss problems that are present in existing E-Tourism systems, and then describe how we solve some of these problems with Travel Guides: we give details of the design of the domain ontology, the creation of the knowledge base and finally system architecture. To illustrate Travel Guides environment we give an example of using this system by providing some screenshots. Finally, we conclude and give the ideas of future work and also future research directions in the field.

BACKGROUND

E-Tourism comprises electronic services which include (Aichholzer, Spitzenberger & Winkler, 2003):

- Information Services (IS), e.g. destination, hotel information.
- Communication Services (CS), e.g. discussion forums, blogs.
- Transaction Services (TS), e.g. booking, payment.

Among these three services *Information Services* are the most present on the Web. Hotels usually have their Web sites with details about the type of accommodation, location, and contact information. Some of these Web sites even offer *Transaction Services* so that it is possible to access the prices and availability of the accommodation for the requested period and perform booking and payment.

Transaction Services are usually concentrated on sites of Web tourist agencies such as Expedia, Travelocity, Lastminute, etc. These Websites sometimes include *Communication Services* in the form of forums where people who visited hotels give their opinion and reviews. With emerging popularity of social web applications many sites specialize in CS only (e.g., www.43places.com).

However, for complete details about a certain destination (e.g., activities, climate, monuments, and events) one often must search for several sources. Apparently all of these sources are dispersed on different places on the Internet and there is an "information gap" between them. The best way to bridge this gap would be to enable communication between different tourist applications.

For *Transaction Services* this is already partly achieved by using Web portals that serve as mediators between tourists and tourist agencies. These portals (e.g., Bookings.com) gather vacation packages from different vendors and use Web services to perform booking and sometimes payment. *Communication Services* are tightly coupled with *Information Services*, in a way that the integration of the first implies the integration of the latter. Henriksson (2005) discusses that the one of the main reasons for lack of interoperability in the area of tourism is the tourism product itself: immaterial, heterogeneous and non-persistent. Travel Guides demonstrates how Semantic Web technologies can be used to enable communication between *Information Services* dispersed on the Web. This would lead to easier exchange of communication services, thus resulting in better quality of E-Tourism and increased interoperability.

Hepp, Siorpaes and Bachlechner (2006) claim that "Everything is there, but we only have insufficient methods of finding and processing what's already on the Web" (p. 2). This statement reveals some of the reasons why Semantic Web is not frequently applied in real-time applications: Web today contains content understandable to humans hence only humans can analyse it. To retrieve information from applications using computer programs (e.g., intelligent agents) two conditions must be satisfied: 1) data must be in a machine-readable form 2) applications must use technologies that provide information retrieval from this kind of data.

Many academic institutions are making efforts to find methods for computer processing of human language. GATE (General Architecture for Text Engineering) is an infrastructure for developing and deploying software components that process human language (Cunningham, 2002). It can annotate documents by recognizing concepts such as: locations, persons, organizations and dates. It can be extended to annotate some domain-related concepts, such as hotels and beaches.

The most common approaches for applying Semantic Web in E-Tourism are:

1. Making applications from scratch using recommended standards
2. Using ontologies as mediators to merge already existing systems
3. Performing annotations in respect to the ontology of already existing Web content

One of the first developed E-Tourism systems was onTour (http://ontour.deri.org/) developed by DERI (Siorpaes & Bachlechner, 2006; Prantner, 2004) where they built a prototype system from scratch and stored their data in the knowledge base created based on the ontology. They developed domain ontology following the World Tourism Organization standards, although they considered a very limited amount of concepts and relations. Later on, they took over the ontology developed as a part of Harmonize project and now planning to develop an advanced E-Tourism Semantic Web portal to connect the customers and virtual travel agents (Jentzsch, 2005).

The idea of Harmonize project was to integrate Semantic Web technologies and merge tourist electronic markets yet avoiding forcing tourist agencies to change their already existing information systems, but to merge them using ontology as a mediator (Dell'erba, Fodor, Hopken, & Werthner, 2005).

The third approach is very challenging for researchers as with the current state of the Web it is not easy to add semantics to the data without changing the technologies used to develop the Web applications. Cardoso (2006) presents a system that creates vacation packages dynamically using previously annotated data in respect to the ontology. This is performed with a service that constructs itinerary by combining user preferences with flights, car rentals, hotel, and activities on-fly. In 2005, Cardoso founded a lab for research in the area of Semantic Web appliance in E-Tourism. The main project called SEED (Semantic E-Tourism Dynamic packaging) aims to illustrate the appliance of Web services and Semantic Web in the area of tourism. One of the main objectives of this project is the development of OTIS ontology (Ontology for Tourism Information Systems). Although they discuss the comprised concepts of this ontology, its development is not yet finished, and could not be further discussed in this chapter.

On the other side, Hepp et al. (2006) claim that there are not enough data in the domain of tourism available on the Web - at least for Tyrol, Austria. Their experiment revealed that existing data on the Web are incomplete: the availability of the accommodation and the prices are very often inaccessible.

Additionally, most of E-Tourism portals store their data internally, which means that they are not accessible by search engines on the Web. Using Semantic Web services, e.g. Web Service Modelling Ontology - WSMO (Roman et al., 2005) or OWL-based Web service ontology - OWL-S (Smith & Alesso, 2005) it would be possible to access data from data-intensive applications. SATINE project is about deploying semantic travel Web services. In (Dogac et al., 2004) they present how to exploit semantics through Web service registries.

Semantic Web services might be a good solution for performing E-Tourism *Transaction Services*, and also for performing E-Tourism *Information Services*, as they enable integrating homogenous data and applications. However, using Semantic Web services, as they are applied nowadays, will not reduce every-day efforts made by tourist agents who are responsible for providing current data about vacation packages and destinations. Data about different destinations are not static – they change over time and thus require E-Tourism systems to be updated. With the current state of the development of E-Tourism applications, each travel agency performs data update individually.

In Travel Guides we employ Semantic Web technologies by combining the first and the third approach. We use the first approach to build the core of the system, and to initialize the repository, whereas in later phase we propose using annotation tools such as GATE to perform semi-automatic annotation of documents and update of knowledge base accordingly. Some of the existing Knowledge Management platforms such as KIM (Popov, Kiryakov, Ognyanoff, Manov & Kirilov, 2004) use GATE for performing automatic annotation of documents and knowledge base enrichment. Due to the very old and well-known problem of syntactic ambiguity (Church & Patil, 1982) of human language widely present inside the Web content that is used in the process of annotation, we argue that the role of human is irreplaceable.

The core of the Travel Guides system is in ontologies. Many ontologies have been already developed in the area of tourism. Bachlechner (2004) has made a long list of the areas that need to be covered by E-Tourism relevant ontologies and made a brief analysis of the developed domain and upper level ontologies. Another good summary of E-Tourism related ontologies is given in (Jentzsch, 2005).

However, no ontology includes all concepts and relations between them in such a way that it can be used without any modifications, although some of them such as Mondeca's (http://www.mondeca.com) or OnTour's ontology (Prantner, 2004) are developed following World Tourism Organization standards. While developing Travel Guides ontology we tried to comprise all possible concepts that are related to the area of tourism and also - tourists. Concepts and relations that describe user's activities and interests coupled with built-in reasoner enable identifying the user as a particular type: some tourists enjoy comfort during vacation, whereas others don't care about the type of the accommodation but more about the outdoor activities or the scenery that is nearby.

Most of the developed ontology-aware systems nowadays propose using a RDF repository instead of using conventional databases (Stollberg, Zhdanova & Fensel, 2004). RDF repositories are not built to replace conventional databases, but to add a refinement which is not supported by conventional databases, specifically – to enable representing machine-readable data and reasoning. In Travel Guides system we distinguish between data that are stored in RDF repositories and those that are stored in conventional databases. In RDF repositories we store machine-understandable data used in the process of reasoning, and relational databases are used to store and retrieve all other data – those that are not important in this process and also being specific for each travel agency which means they are not *sharable*. We propose *sharable* data to be those that could be easily exchangeable between applications. This way, applications can share a unique repository

which means that if, for instance, a new hotel is built on a certain destination and one tourist agency updates the repository, all others can use it immediately.

We suggest this approach as Semantic Web technologies nowadays are still weak to handle a huge amount of data, and could not be compared by performance with relational databases in the terms of transaction handling, security, optimization and scalability (cf. Guo, Pan & Heflin, 2004).

APPLYING SEMANTIC WEB TO E-TOURISM

E-Tourism Today

Searching for information on a desired spot for vacation is usually a very time-consuming. Figure 1 depicts the most frequent scenario which starts with the vague ideas of the user interested in travelling, and ends with the list of tourist destinations. In most of cases the user is aware of a few criteria that should be fulfilled (the distance from the shopping centre, sandy beach, a

Figure 1. The usual scenario of searching the Internet for a 'perfect' vacation package

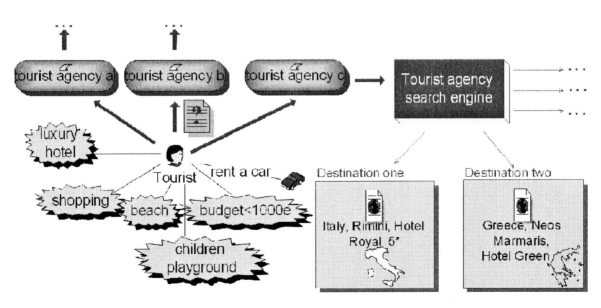

possibility to rent a car, etc.), as well as of some individual constraints (prices, departure times, etc.). After processing the user's query (using these criteria as input data), the search engine of a tourist agency will most likely return a list of vacation packages. It is up to the user to choose the most appropriate one. If the user is not satisfied with the result, the procedure is repeated, with another tourist agency. This scenario is restarted in N iterations until the user gets the desired result. The essential disadvantage of this system is a lack of the integrated and ordered collection of the tourist deals. Tourist deals are dispersed on the Web and being offered from different tourist agencies each of which maintain their system independently.

Additional problem with existing E-Tourism applications is the lack of interactivity. It is always the user who provides the criteria for the search/ query and who analyzes the results returned.

The problem of dispersed information about tourist deals would be reduced totally if all vacation packages would be gathered at one place - the Web portal. This assumption could not be taken as realistic, but apparently the distribution of the tourist offers would be decreased by adding the tourist offers of each tourist agency into the portal. Although the portals are more sophisticated than simple Web applications, they usually do not compensate for the lack of interactivity.

Some of the popular Web tourist agencies, such as Expedia, expand their communication with the user by offering various services based on user selection during visiting their site. Namely, they track user actions (mouse clicks) so that when user browse throughout the site the list of user recently visited places is always available. In case the user provides his personal e-mail they send some special offers or advertisements occasionally. Although their intentions are to improve communication with their clients, this kind of service can be irritating sometimes. Developing more sophisticated user profiles would help developing more personalized systems thus avoiding spamming the user with an unattractive content.

Creating user profiles is widely used in many applications nowadays, not only in the area of tourism. In order to create his/her profile, the user is usually prompted to register and fill in few forms with some personal info such as location, year of birth, interests, etc. Filling these forms sometimes can take a lot of time and thus carries the risk of 'refusing' the user. The best way is to request a minimum data from the user on his first log in, and then update his data later step by step.

Travel Guides

Disadvantages of traditional E-Tourism systems imply requirements for a new system that is focusing on the integration of *Information Services* present on the Web and also on introducing sophisticated *user profiles*. Travel Guides prototype system has been developed to satisfy these requirements by combining semantic web technologies with those used in traditional E-Tourism systems.

Using semantic web technologies enables representing the data in machine-readable form. Such a representation enable easier integration of tourist resources as data exchange between applications is feasible. Integration of tourist resources would decrease efforts tourist agents make in tourist agencies to maintain these data. The final result would affect the tourist who will be able to search for details about destinations from the single point on the Web.

In Travel Guides we introduce more sophisticated user profiles – these are to enable personalization of the Web content and to act as agents who work for users, while not spamming them with commercial content and advertisements. For example, if during registration the user enters that he is interested in extreme sports, and later moves on to the search form where he does not specify any sport requirement, the return results could be filtered in a manner that the first listed are those that are flagged as "adventurer destinations".

Developing sophisticated user profiles requires analyse of the user behaviour while visiting the portal. This behaviour is determined by the data the system collects about the user: his personal data, interests, activities, and also the data that system tracks while 'observing' the user: user selection, mouse clicks, and the like. To be able to constantly analyze the user's profile the portal requires intelligent reasoning. To make a tourism portal capable of intelligent reasoning, it is necessary to build some initial and appropriate knowledge in the system, as well as to maintain the knowledge automatically from time to time and during the user's interaction with the system. Simply saving every single click of the user could not be enough to make a good-quality user profile. It is much more suitable to use a built-in reasoner to infer the user's preferences and intentions from the observations.

Any practical implementation of the aforementioned requirements leads to representing essential knowledge about the domain (tourism) and the portal users (user profiles) in a machine-readable and machine-understandable form. In other words, it is necessary to develop and use a set of ontologies to represent all important concepts and their relations.

When ontologies are developed, it is necessary to populate the knowledge base with instances of concepts from the ontology and with relevant relations. After some knowledge is created, it needs to be coupled with a built-in inference engine to support reasoning. Finally, it is essential to enable input in the system from the user as reasoning requires some input data to be processed.

In the next sections we describe the ontology we developed to satisfy the requirements, followed by the knowledge base creation and the architecture of the system that enables processing the input from end users.

Travel Guides Ontologies

The Travel Guides Ontologies are written in OWL (Antoniou & Harmelen, 2004) and developed using Protégé (Horridge, Knublauch, Rector, Stevens & Wroe, 2004). To develop a well-designed ontology, it was important to:

1. *Include all important terms in the area of tourism* to represent destinations in general, excluding data specific for any tourist agency. For instance, information about a city name, its latitude and longitude, and the country it belongs to is to be included here.
2. *Classify user interests and activities* so that they can be expressed in the manner of a collection of user profiles, and identify the concepts to represent them.
3. *Identify concepts to represent the facts about destinations* that are specific for each tourist agency. This information is extracted from expert knowledge, where an expert is a tourist agent who would be able to classify destinations according to the different criteria; for instance, if the destination is a family destination, a romantic destination, etc. After identifying these concepts they need to be connected with other relevant concepts, e.g. create relations between destination types and relevant user profile types.

Representing aforementioned three steps in a manner of a formal representation of concepts and relations results in the creation of the following:

1. *The World ontology*, with concepts and relations from the real world: geographical terms, locations with coordinates, land types, time and date, time zone, currency, languages, and all other terms that are expressing concepts that are in a way related to tourism or tourists, but not to vacation

packages that could be offered by some tourist agencies. This ontology should also contain the general concepts necessary for expression of semantic annotation, indexing, and retrieval (Kiryakov et al., 2003).

2. *The User ontology* containing concepts related to the users – the travellers who visit the Travel Guides portal. This ontology describes user interests and activities, age groups, favourite travel companies, and other data about different user profiles.

3. *The Travel (Tourism) ontology* contains concepts related to vacation packages, types of vacations, and traveller types w.r.t. various tourist destinations. It includes all terms being specific to vacation packages offered in tourist agencies and being important for travellers, like the type of accommodation, food service type, transport service, room types in a hotel, and the like. It is this ontology that makes a connection between users and destinations. This is accomplished by creating user profiles for the users, and determining the type of destination for each vacation package. Finally, user profiles are linked to relevant destination types (and vice versa).

After the evaluation of existing domain and upper-level ontologies, we have found that the one that suits the Travel Guides the best is the PRO-TON ontology (Terziev, Kiryakov and Manov, 2005). PROTON upper-level ontology includes four modules, each of which is a separate ontology. For the purpose of Travel Guides development, the Upper module of PROTON (Terziev et al., 2005) was used as *the World ontology*. This module was extended to fit *the Tourism (Travel) ontology*. The PROTON Knowledge management module (Terziev et al., 2005) was extended to serve as *the User ontology*.

The World Ontology

The PROTON upper level ontology contains all concepts required by Travel Guides World ontology. In addition, it contains concepts and relations necessary for information extraction, retrieval and semantic annotation. PROTON class we used the most frequently in our World ontology is the class **Location**. Figure 2 depicts the hierarchy of the class **Location** and its subclasses in the PROTON Upper Level ontology.

The classes and properties from PROTON used in Travel Guides are shown in Figure 3. Following aliases have been used instead of full namespaces: pkm for PROTON Knowledge Management, psys for PROTON System Module, ptou for PROTON Upper Module, and ptop for Proton Top module.

For more information about PROTON ontology we refer reader to (Terziev et al., 2005).

The User Ontology

PROTON Knowledge Management (KM) ontology has been extended to suit *the User ontology* needs. The most frequently used classes are: **User, UserProfile**, and **Topic**. According to the PROTON documentation, **Protont:Topic** (the PROTON top module class) is "any sort of a topic or a theme, explicitly defined for classification purposes". For the needs of Travel Guides, **protont:Topic** class has been extended to represent user interests and activities. Its important relations and concepts are depicted in Figure 4.

For determining user profile types, the age and the user preferred travel company is of a great importance hence relevant concepts have been created inside the ontology: **AgeGroup** is a representation of the first and the **TravelCompany** is a representation of the latter (Figure 5). For example, if the user selects that he/she travels with family very often, he/she could be considered as a **FamilyType**.

Figure 2. The Location class and its subclasses in the PROTON Upper Level ontology

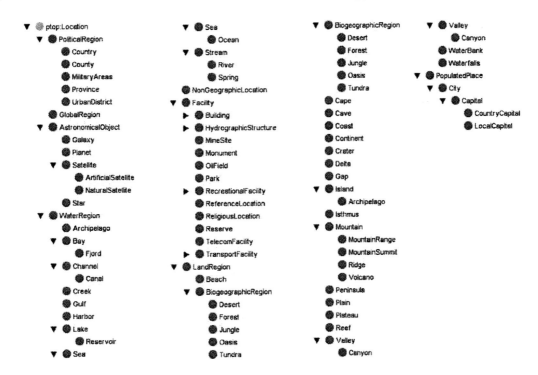

Figure 3. The classes and properties from the PROTON ontology frequently used in Travel Guides

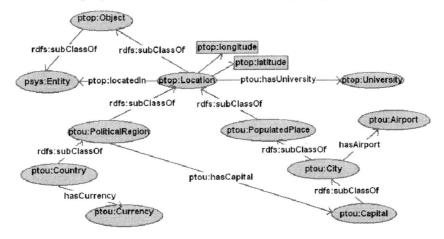

The **UserProfile** class is extended to represent various types of tourists. These profiles are made based on user interests and activities. Figure 6 depicts various types of user profiles.

In practice, many tourists would be determined to belong to more than one type of user profiles. For this purpose, there is a property *weight* that could be assigned for each type of user profile. It is this property that reflects the importance of certain profiles. For example:

User *hasUserProfile* **Adventurer** (*weight* = 2),
User *hasUserProfile* **ClubbingType** (*weight* = 1).

Figure 4. The most important concepts and their relation in the User ontology

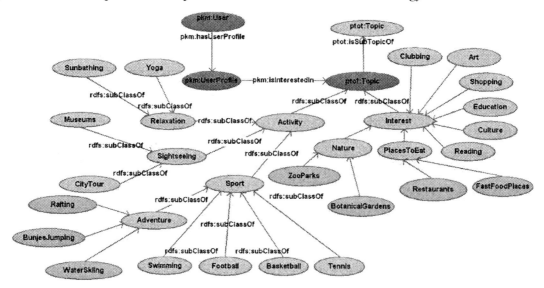

Figure 5. Extension of PROTON Group class

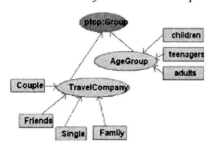

In this case the user profile is a mixture of the **Adventurer** and the **Clubbing** type, but due to the *weight* values adventure destinations have a priority over those that are "flagged" as great-night-life destinations.

Travel Guides User Ontology is available on-line at http:// goodoldai.org.yu/ns/upproton.owl.

Tourism (Travel) Ontology

In order to design the domain ontology for the area of tourism as well as to "link" tourist destination types to the user profile types, we extended the PROTON Upper module ontology. The class **Of-fer** is extended with the subclass of **TouristOffer** representing a synonym term for vacation package

offered in a tourist agency. Figure 7 depicts the **TouristOffer** class and types of destinations assigned to tourist offers. These types are used as indicators of types of tourist offers which are later being assigned to relevant user profile types.

Figure 8 depicts classes and relations between them in *the Travel ontology*. Since the Travel ontology is an extension of the PROTON Upper module ontology, there are some concepts and relations from PROTON that are frequently used. They all have appropriate prefixes.

As shown on Figure 8, a vacation package being an instance of **TouristOffer** class *isAttractiveFor* certain type of **UserProfile**, where this type is determined by user's interests and activities.

Travel Guides Travel Ontology is available on-line at http://goodoldai.org.yu/ns/tgproton.owl.

Travel Guides Knowledge Base
Due to a huge amount of data that is stored inside the knowledge base (KB), it is essential that its structure allows easy maintenance. To meet this requirement, we represent the KB as a collection of *.owl* files (Figure 9). The circle on the top represents the core and contains concepts such as continents and countries used by all other parts of the KB.

Figure 6. Subclasses of PROTON UserProfile class

Figure 7. The extended ptou:Offer class in Travel Guides Tourism ontology

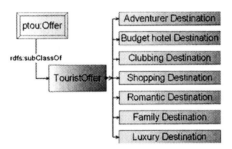

The other parts are independent *.owl* files that are country specific and contain all destinations inside the country, all hotels on the destinations and finally all vacation packages related to the hotels. For the clarity of the presentation Figure 9 depicts only 3 elements of the KB apart from the core. Ideally, the number of these elements is equal to the number of existing countries.

To alleviate the creation, extensions, and maintenance of the KB, and also to address the interoperability issue, we explored some other ontology-based systems that include instances of concepts that are of interest to Travel Guides system. We have built an environment that enables exploiting instances of classes (concepts) and relations of the arbitrary KB in accordance to the predefined criteria. We considered using KIM KB and also WordNet (Fellbaum, 1998). As

KIM KB contains more data that are of interest to Travel Guides system and also is built based on the ontology whose core is PROTON ontology (Popov et al, 2004), we successfully exploited it to build our core (continents and countries). This core is available online at http:// goodoldai.org.yu/ ns/travel_wkb.owl, and is used to initialize other elements of the KB.

This way we avoided entering permanent data about various destinations manually, and also showed that it is possible to share the knowledge between different platforms when it is represented using RDF structure and achieve interoperability - the content of one application can be of use inside the other application, even if they are based on different ontologies. Our environment for knowledge base exploitation is applicable for any knowledge base and ontology; the only precondition is selection of criteria that will define the statements to be extracted.

Apart from many concepts (e.g., organizations and persons), KIM Platform KB includes data about continents, countries and many cities. The environment created inside Travel Guides enables extracting of concepts by selecting some of the criteria, e.g., name of the property. We selected *hasCapital*, as this property has class **Country** as a domain and class **City** as a range. Our environment extracts not only the concepts that are directly related to the predefined property, but also

Figure 8. Concepts and relations in the Travel Guides Travel ontology

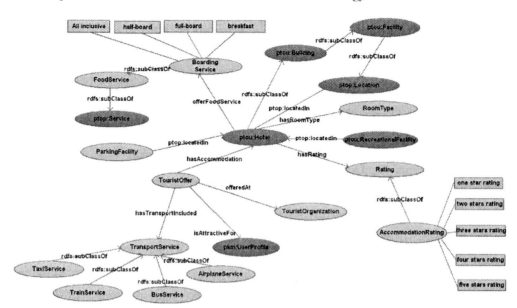

Figure 9. Organization of the knowledge base inside the Travel Guides system

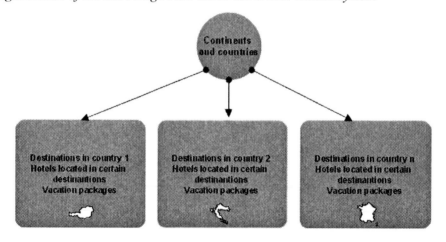

all other statements that are the result of transitive relations of this property. For example, if defined relation **Country** *isLocatedIn* **Continent** exists, statements that represent this relation will also be extracted.

Figure 10 depicts some of the classes and relations whose instances are imported during the KB extraction.

Ideally, the knowledge base should contain descriptions of all destinations that could (but need not necessarily) be included in the offers of the tourist agencies connected to the portal.

The Portal Architecture

This section gives details about the architecture of Travel Guides system (Figure 11) and its design. The system comprises following four modules:

Figure 10. Classes and relations whose concepts are imported during KB extraction

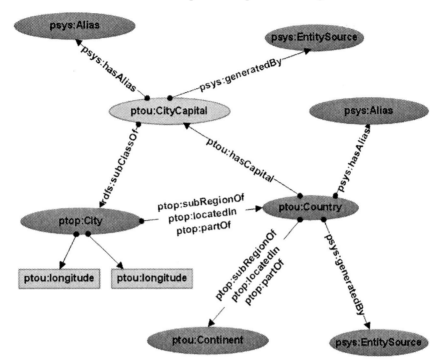

Figure 11. Travel Guides Architecture

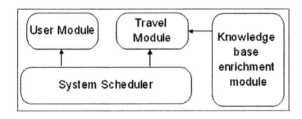

1. **User Module:** For generating user profiles and maintaining user data.
2. **Travel Module:** For generating and maintaining vacation packages and all other data related to vacation packages and destinations.
3. **System Scheduler Module:** For update of the knowledge base. It communicates with:
   o User Module when updating user profiles
   o Travel Module when updating data about vacation packages and destinations.
4. **Knowledge base enrichment module:** For knowledge base enrichment based on annotations in respect to the ontology. It communicates with Travel Module to update knowledge base with new instances and relations between them.

Following are details about key modules.

User Module

User Controller (Figure 12) accepts requests from the user (via *User registration form*) and fires appropriate actions. Actions (at the presentation layer) are directly connected to the business layer of the system represented by *User Manager* (UM). The UM has the following roles:

- Store and retrieve data about the user.
- Observe and track the activities of the user during his visit to the portal.

For manipulation with data stored in the database UM uses the *User DAO* (User Data Access Object). These data are user details that are not subject to frequent changes and are not important for determining the user profile: the username, password, first name, last name, address, birth date, phone and email.

For logging user activities during visiting the portal UM uses *User Log DAO*.

When reasoning over the available data about the user and determining user profile types UM use the User Profile Expert. The *User Profile Expert* is aware of the *User ontology* and also of the User profile knowledge base (*User kb*) that contains instances of classes and relations from the User ontology.

The data about users are collected in two ways:

Figure 12. User module components

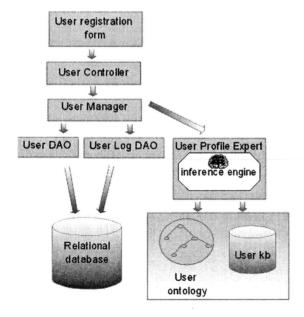

1. Using User interface: the user is prompted to fill the forms to input data about him/herself. These data are: gender, birth date, social data (single, couple, family with kids, friends), the user's location, profession, education, languages, interests and activities (art, museums, sightseeing, sports, exploring new places during vacation, animals, eating out, nightlife, shopping, trying local food/experiencing local customs/habits, natural beauties, books), budget, visited destinations.
2. The system collects data about the user's interests and preferences while the user is reading about or searching for vacation packages using the portal. Each time the user clicks on some of the vacation package details, the system stores his/her action in the database, and analyse it later on.

Travel Module

Travel Module generates and maintains data about vacation packages, destinations and related concepts. The User interface of Travel Module component comprises following forms (Figure 13):

1. *Recommended Vacation Packages* form: This form shows the list of vacation packages that the user has not explicitly searched for - system generates this list automatically based on the user profile.
2. *Vacation Packages Form*: This form is important for travel agents when updating vacation packages data.
3. *Vacation Package Semantic Search Form*: This form enables semantic search of vacation packages.

Each of the available forms communicates with the *Controller* who dispatches the requested actions to the *Travel Manager (TM)*. The Travel Manager is responsible for fetching, storing and updating the data related to vacation packages. It includes a mechanism for storing and retrieving data from the database using *Vacation Package DAO* (Data Access Object). The data stored in the database are those that are subject to frequent changes and are not important in the process of reasoning: start date, end date, prices (accommodation price, food service price, and transport price), benefits, discounts and documents that contain textual descriptions with details about the vacation packages. Some of these data are used in the second phase of retrieving a 'perfect' vacation package, when the role of the inference engine is not important. Retrieving a 'perfect' vacation package is performed in two steps:

1. Matching the user's wishes with certain destinations – the user profile is matched with certain types of destinations. To perform

this TM uses the *Travel Offer Expert* (TOE) and the *World Expert* (WE) components.

2. The list of destinations retrieved in the first step is filtered using the constraints the user provided (for example, the start/end dates of the vacation). TM filters retrieved result using the *Vacation Package DAO*.

TOE and *WE* components include inference engines. These inference engines are aware of the ontologies and knowledge bases: TOE works with *Travel ontology* and a knowledge base (*Travel kb*) created based on this ontology. WE uses the *World ontology* and the knowledge base (*World kb*) created based on it.

After the initial knowledge base is deployed into Travel Guides application, its further update could be performed semi-automatically by *Knowledge base enrichment module (KBEM)* deployed inside Travel Guides. For example, when a new hotel is built, the knowledge base should be enriched with this information. This can be performed either by:

- Using the Travel Guides environment, where a tourist agent or administrator manually enters the name and other data about the new hotel (Figure 13).
- Performing annotation of the relevant content with regards to the Travel Guides ontology, semi-automatically (Figure 14).

Knowledge Base Enrichment Module (KBEM)

Semi-automatic annotation process starts with *Crawler* actions. Crawler searches the Internet and finds potentially interesting sites with details about destinations, hotels, beaches, new activities in a hotel, news about some destinations, popular events, etc. The result (HTML pages) is transformed into .*txt* format and redirected to JMS (Java Message Service) to wait in a queue for annotation process (*aQueue*). JMS API is a messaging

Figure 13. Travel Module Components

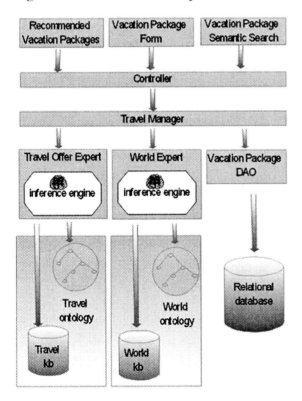

standard that allows application components based on the Java 2 Platform, Enterprise Edition (J2EE) to create, send, receive, and read messages. It enables distributed communication that is loosely coupled, reliable, and asynchronous.

Annotation Manager consumes these plain documents and connects to the *Annotation Server* to perform process of annotation with regards to Travel Guides ontologies. After the annotation process is completed, the annotated documents are sent to JMS to wait in a queue for verification (*vQueue*). The *Notification Manager* consumes these massages and sends an e-mail to the administrator with the details about annotated documents (e.g., location of the annotated documents). The administrator starts *Annotation Interface* and performs the process of verification. The output of the annotation process is correctly annotated documents.

Retrieved annotations that refer to the new concepts/instances could be further used to enrich the KB and also for semantic search over the knowledge store that includes processed documents. Similar approach uses KIM Platform: they provide querying of the knowledge store that includes not only the knowledge base created w.r.t. ontologies, but also annotated documents (Popov et al., 2004).

Annotation of documents performed by KBEM would be simplified in case that verification step is skipped. The implementation of the system would also be simpler. In addition, there would not be a human influence, but the machine would do everything by itself. This would lead to many missed annotations, though. A machine cannot always notice some "minor" refinements as humans can. For example, if in the title "Maria's sand" the machine notices "Maria" and finds it in the list of female first names, it will annotate it as an instance of a class **Woman**. "Maria" can be an instance of a woman, but in this context it is a part of the name of a beach. These kinds of mistakes would happen frequently, and the machine

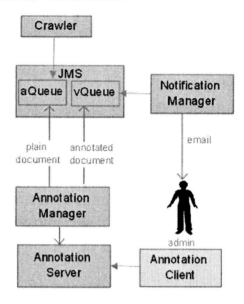

Figure 14. Knowledge base enrichment module inside the Travel Guides

would annotate them in wrong ways, if it does it automatically without any verification.

An Example of Using Travel Guides

Travel Guides users are divided in 3 groups, each of which contributing to the knowledge base in its own way.

End users (i.e., tourists) visit this portal to search for useful information. They can feed the system with their personal data, locations, and interests, which then get analyzed by the system in order to create/update user profiles. Note that the system also uses logged data about each user's activities (mouse clicks) when updating the user's profile. User profile form for feeding the system with user personal information, activities and interests is depicted on Figure 15.

On the left hand side there is a section with results of system personalization. This section provides a list of potentially interested destinations for the tourist. The section is created based on the user profile analyse, which means that offered

Figure 15. The User profile form in Travel Guides

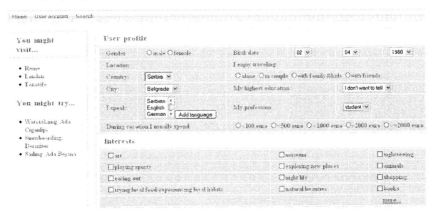

Figure 16. The Search form in Travel Guides

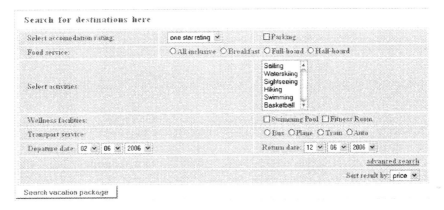

destinations should be matching user wishes, interests and activities. To explicitly search for a 'perfect' vacation package the user uses form shown on Figure 16.

Tourist agents create vacation packages and similar offers in tourist agencies. They feed and update the database with new vacation packages and also knowledge base with new information about destinations. To do this, they fill appropriate forms and save the filled-in information (Figure 17).

To successfully fill in this form and save the vacation package, the hotel has to be selected. If the hotel does not exist in the system, it has to be entered before creating the new vacation package.

Figure 18 depicts a form for entering a new hotel into the KB.

Portal administrators mediate the knowledge base updates with destinations not covered by the tourist agencies connected to the portal. This process is very similar to the process conducted by tourist agents. The major difference is that this part of the knowledge base contains mostly static and permanent information about some geographical locations, such as countries, their capitals, mountains, rivers, seas, etc. all over the world. The idea is that tourist agents can use this part of the knowledge base as the basis for creating new vacation packages and other tourist offers.

Figure 17. The Vacation package form in Travel Guides

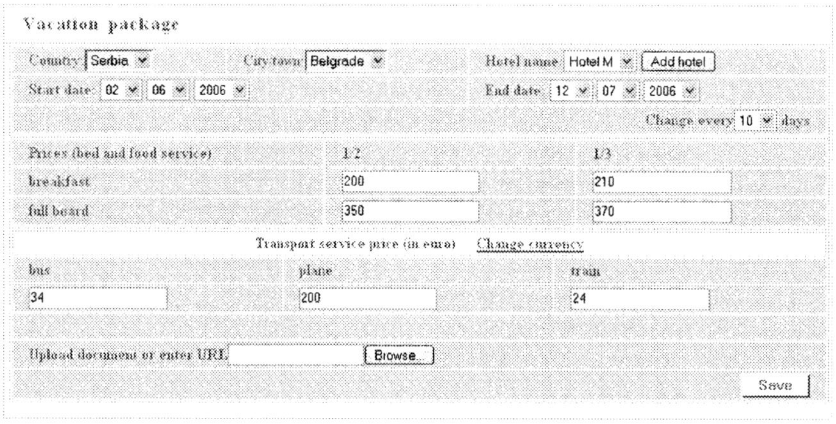

Figure 18. Entering a new hotel using the Travel Guides environment

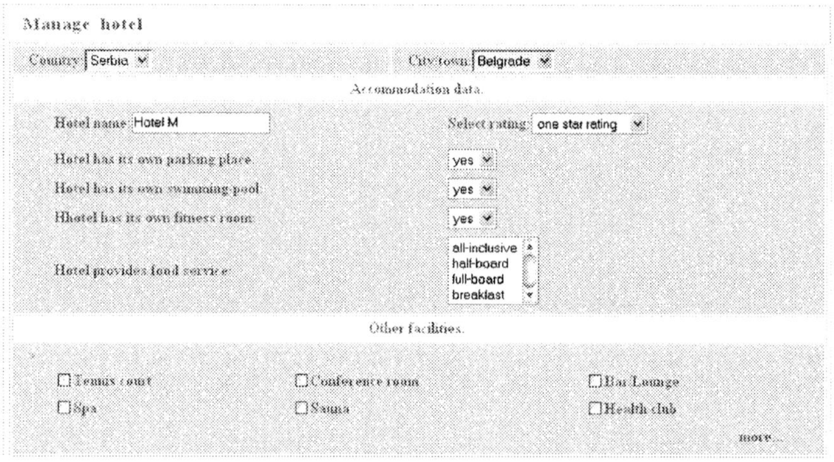

CONCLUSION

Representing tourism-related data in a machine-readable form can help the integration of E-Tourism Information Services. If tourism sources would be centralized in a unique repository, the maintenance efforts would be significantly decreased. Integration of all E-Tourism sources would result in the possibility to search for tourist deals from one place – this would drastically reduce the time tourists spend while searching various tourism-related Web sites.

Built-in heuristics inside ontologies and use of a reasoner enable implying the user profile types for different tourists w.r.t. their activities and interests. Coupled with the destination types which are derived from the specific vacation package descriptions, user profiles can improve the process of searching for the perfect vacation package. Additionally, building a good quality user profiles provides personalization of dynamically created content.

The system's prototype described here includes a limited collection of vacation packages. The main precondition for its evaluation and usability would be feeding it with vacation packages from real tourist agencies.

As Travel Guides focus on integration of Information Services, such as information about destinations, hotels and the like, it would be worth exploring the possibility to integrate such a system with existing applications that offer Transactional Services, so that it can be possible to book and pay for recommended vacation packages after searching repository with available tourist offers covered by Travel Guides. In addition, there are opportunities to extend Travel Guides or to develop an independent module for integration of Communication Services, so that tourists can contribute to the system knowledge about the destinations and express their experience as well.

Finally, as the current version of Travel Guides ontology supports only representing hotel accommodation, there is a space for future improvements that include extending types of accommodations with hostels, private apartments for rent, and campgrounds.

FUTURE RESEARCH DIRECTIONS

Integrating semantic web technologies in traditional existing Web applications has a lot of space for improvement. The most popular way to perform this integration is by employing ontologies as they enable presenting data in machine readable form, reasoning and running intelligent agents, semantic Web services and semantic search. Each of these is partly applied in E-Tourism applications nowadays. However, current state of the art in this field is not mature enough to be used in industry, meaning that there is lots of space for different research topics, some of which could be implied from reading this chapter.

Reasoning over ontologies is very expensive due to the state of development of current inference engines. Development of better and faster reasoner is a precondition for using ontologies in large scale applications. At the moment, only few ontology-based systems exist in the area of tourism, among which Mondeca (www.mondeca.com) is applying the most of them to tourism in different regions in France. Their ontologies define the structure of data they are working with but the use of a reasoner is on the minimum level.

Emerging popularity of social web applications raises another interesting field of research, specifically information retrieval from user created content. Existing Natural Language Processing Tools are still weak to extract and retrieve meaningful answers based on the understanding of the query given in a form of natural language. For example, searching a social web application (e.g., a forum with reviews of different hotels), it would be hard to find 'the hotel in the posh area' using mainstream search engines as some of the posts might talk about luxury hotels, but not using 'posh' to describe them. Developing Natural Language Processing tools that could analyse text so that machines can understand it is a field with lots of research opportunities that would contribute not only to the E-Tourism applications, but to all applications on the Web.

Improving the process of automatic annotation and developing algorithms for training such a process would be another important contribution. Up to date, only Named Entities (e.g., organisations, persons, locations) are known to be automatically retrieved to the reasonable level of accuracy. Additionally, as current systems for performing annotation process usually require the knowledge and understanding of the underlying software such as GATE, research in this field can lead to developing more user-friendly interfaces to allow handling annotations and verifications without any special knowledge of the underlying software. The most natural way would be that similar to using tags in Web 2.0 applications, or any other simple way that requires no training for the user.

REFERENCES

Aichholzer, G., Spitzenberger, M., Winkler, R. (2003, April). Prisma Strategic Guideline 6: eTourism. Retrieved January 13, 2007, from: http://www.prisma-eu.net/deliverables/sg6tourism.pdf

Antoniou, G., Harmelen, F. V. (2004). Web Ontology Language: OWL. In Staab, S., Studer, R. (Eds.): Handbook on Ontologies. International Handbooks on Information Systems, Springer, pp. 67-92.

Bachlechner, D. (October, 2004), D10 v0.2 Ontology Collection in view of an E-Tourism Portal, E-Tourism Working Draft. Retrieved January 15, 2007 from: http://138.232.65.141/deri_at/research/projects/E-Tourism/2004/d10/v0.2/20041005/#Domain

Cardoso, J. (2006). Developing Dynamic Packaging Systems using Semantic Web Technologies. Transactions on Information Science and Applications. Vol. 3(4). 729-736.

Cunningham, H. (2002). GATE, a General Architecture for Text Engineering. Computers and the Humanities. 36 (2). 223–254.

Church, K., Patil, R. (1982). Coping with Syntactic Ambiguity or How to Put the Block in the Box. American Journal of Computational Linguistics, 8(3-4).

Dell'erba, M., Fodor, O. Hopken, W., Werthner, H. (2005). Exploiting Semantic Web technologies for harmonizing E-Markets. Information Technology & Tourism. 7(3-4). 201-219(19).

Djuric, D., Devedzic, V. & Gasevic, D. (2007). Adopting Software Engineering Trends in AI. *IEEE Intelligent Systems*. 22(1). 59-66.

Dogac, A., Kabak ,Y., Laleci, G., Sinir, S., Yildiz, A. Tumer, A. (2004). SATINE Project: Exploiting Web Services in the Travel Industry. eChallenges 2004 (e-2004), 27 - 29 October 2004, Vienna, Austria.

Fellbaum, C. (1998). WordNet - An Electronic Lexical Database. The MIT Press.

Guo, Y; Pan, Z; and Heflin, J. (2004). An Evaluation of Knowledge Base Systems for Large OWL Datasets. The Semantic Web – ISWC 2004: The Proceedings of the Third International Semantic Web Conference, Hiroshima, Japan, November 7-11, 2004. Springer Berlin/Heidelberg. 274-288.

Henriksson, R., (November, 2005), Semantic Web and E-Tourism, Helsinki University, Department of Computer Science. [Online]. Available: http://www.cs.helsinki.fi/u/glinskih/semanticweb/Semantic_Web_and_E-Tourism.pdf

Hepp, M., Siorpaes, K., Bachlechner, D. (2006). Towards the Semantic Web in E-Tourism: Can Annotation Do the Trick? In Proc. of 14th European Conf. on Information System (ECIS 2006), June 12–14, 2006, Gothenburg, Sweden.

Horridge, M., Knublauch, H., Rector, A., Stevens, R., Wroe, C. (2004). A Practical Guide To Building OWL Ontologies Using The Protege-OWL Plugin and CO-ODE Tools Edition 1.0. The University of Manchester, August 2004. [Online]. Available: http://protege.stanford.edu/publications/ontology_development/ontology101.html

Jentzsch, A. (April, 2005) XML Clearing House Report 12: Tourism Standards. Retrieved September 6, 2007, from http://www.xml-clearinghouse.de/reports/Tourism%20Standards.pdf

Kiryakov, A., Popov, B., Ognyanoff, D., Manov, D., Kirilov, A., Goranov, M., (2003), Semantic Annotation, Indexing, and Retrieval, Lecture Notes in Computer Science, Springer-Verlag. Pages 484-499.

Popov, B., Kiryakov,A., Ognyanoff, D.,Manov, D., Kirilov, A. (2004). KIM - A Semantic Platform For Information Extraction and Retrieval. Journal of Natural Language Engineering, Cambridge University Press. 10 (3-4). 375-392.

Prantner, K. (2004). OnTour: The Ontology [Online]. Retrieved June 2, 2005, from http://E-Tourism.deri.at/ont/docu2004/OnTour%20-%20 The%20Ontology.pdf/

Roman D., Keller, U., Lausen, H., Bruijn J. D., Lara, R., Stollberg, M., Polleres, A., Feier, C.,Bussler, C., Fensel, D. (2005). Web Service Modeling Ontology. Applied Ontology. 1(1): 77 - 106.

Siorpaes, K., Bachlechner, D. (2006). OnTour: Tourism Information Retrieval based on YARS. Demos and Posters of the 3rd European Semantic Web Conference (ESWC 2006), Budva, Montenegro, 11th – 14th June, 2006.

Smith, C. F., Alesso, H. P. (2005). Developing Semantic Web Services. A K Peters, Ltd.

Stollberg, M., Zhdanova, A.V., Fensel, D. (2004). "h-TechSight - A Next Generation Knowledge Management Platform", Journal of Information and Knowledge Management, 3 (1), World Scientific Publishing, 45-66.

Terziev, I., Kiryakov, A., Manov, D. (2005). D1.8.1 Base upper-level ontology (BULO) Guidance, SEKT. Retrieved January, 15th, 2007 from: http://www.deri.at/fileadmin/documents/deliverables/Sekt/sekt-d-1-8-1-Base_upper-level_ontology__BULO__Guidance.pdf

ADDITIONAL READING

Bennett, J. (2006, May 25). The Semantic Web is upon us, says Berners-Lee. Silicon.com research panel: WebWatch. Retrieved January 3, 2007, from: http://networks.silicon.com/Webwatch/0,39024667,39159122,00.htm

Bussler, C. (2003). The Role of Semantic Web Technology in Enterprise Application Integration. IEEE Data Engineering Bulletin. Vol. 26, No. 4, pp. 62-68.

Cardoso, J. (2004). Semantic Web Processes and Ontologies for the Travel Industry. AIS SIGSEMIS Bulletin. Vol. 1, No. 3, pp. 25-28.

Cardoso, J. (2006). Developing An Owl Ontology For e-Tourism. In Cardoso, J. & Sheth, P. A. (Eds.). Semantic Web Services, Processes and Applications (pp. 247-282), Springer.

Davidson, C., Voss, P. (2002). Knowledge Management. Auckland: Tandem.

Davies, J., Weeks, R., Krohn. U. (2003a). Quiz-RDF: Search Technology for the Semantic Web. Towards the Semantic Web: Ontology-Driven Knowledge Management, pp. 133-43.

Davies, J., Duke, A., Stonkus, A. (2003b). OntoShare: Evolving Ontologies in a Knowledge Sharing System. Towards the Semantic Web: Ontology-Driven Knowledge Management, pp. 161-177.

Djuric, D., Devedžić, V.,Gašević, D. (2007). Adopting Software Engineering Trends in AI. IEEE Intelligent Systems. 22(1). 59-66.

Dzbor, M., Domingue, J., Motta, E. (2003). Magpie - Towards a Semantic Web Browser, In Proc. of the 2nd International Conference (ISWC 2003), pp. 690-705. Florida, USA.

Edwards, S. J., Blythe, P. T., Scott, S., Weihong-Guo, A. (2006). Tourist Information Delivered Through Mobile Devices: Findings from the Image. Information Technology & Tourism. 8 (1). 31-46(16).

Engels R., Lech, T. (2003). Generating Ontologies for the Semantic Web: OntoBuilder. Towards the Semantic Web: Ontology-Driven Knowledge Management, pp. 91-115.

E-Tourism Working Group (2004). Ontology Collection in view of an E-Tourism Portal. October, 2004. Retrieved January 13, 2007, from: http://138.232.65.141/deri_at/research/projects/e-tourism/2004/d10/v0.2/20041005/

Fensel, D., Angele, J., Erdmann, M., Schnurr, H., Staab, S., Studer, R., Witt, A. (1999). On2broker: Semantic-based access to information sources at the WWW. In Proc. of WebNet, pp. 366-371.

Fluit, C., Horst, H., van der Meer, J., Sabou, M., Mika, P. (2003). Spectacle. Towards the Semantic Web: Ontology-Driven Knowledge Management, pp. 145-159.

Hepp, M. (2006). Semantic Web and semantic Web services: father and son or indivisible twins? Internet Computing, IEEE. 10 (2). 85- 88.

Heung, V.C.S. (2003). Internet usage by international travellers: reasons and barriers. International Journal of Contemporary Hospitality Management, 15 (7), 370-378.

Hi-Touch Working Group (2003). Semantic Web methodologies and tools for intraEuropean sustainable tourism [Online]. Retrieved April 6, 2004, from http://www.mondeca.com/articleJITT-hitouch-legrand.pdf/

Kanellopoulos, D., Panagopoulos, A., Psillakis, Z. (2004). Multimedia applications in Tourism: The case of travel plans. Tourism Today. No. 4, pp. 146-156.

Kanellopoulos, D., Panagopoulos, A. (2005). Exploiting tourism destinations' knowledge in a RDF-based P2P network, Hypertext 2005, 1st International Workshop WS4 – Peer to Peer and Service Oriented Hypermedia: Techniques and Systems, ACM Press.

Kanellopoulos, D. (2006). The advent of Semantic web in Tourism Information Systems. *Tourismos: an international multidisciplinary journal of tourism.* 1(2), pp. 75-91.

Kanellopoulos, D. & Kotsiantis, S. (2006). Towards Intelligent Wireless Web Services for Tourism. IJCSNS International Journal of Computer Science and Network Security. 6 (7). 83-90.

Kanellopoulos, D.,Kotsiantis, S., Pintelas, P. (2006), Intelligent Knowledge Management for the Travel Domain ,GESTS International Transactions on Computer Science and Engineering. 30(1). 95-106.

Kiryakov, A. (2006). *OWLIM: balancing between scalable repository and light-weight reasoner.* Presented at the Developer's Track of WWW2006, Edinburgh, Scotland, UK, 23-26 May, 2006.

Maedche, A., Staab S., Stojanovic, N., Studer, R., Sure, Y. (2001). SEmantic PortAL -

The SEAL approach. In D. Fensel, J. Hendler, H. Lieberman, W. Wahlster (Eds.) In Creating the Semantic Web. Boston: MIT Press, MA, Cambridge.

McIlraith, S.A., Son, T.C., & Zeng, H. (2001). Semantic Web Services. IEEE Intelligent Systems 16(2), 46-53.

Missikoff, M., Werthner, H. Höpken, W., Dell'Ebra, M., Fodor, O. Formica, A., Francesco, T.(2003) HARMONISE: Towards Interoperability in the Tourism Domain. In Proc. ENTER 2003, pp. 58-66, Helsinki: Springer.

Passin, B., T.(2004). *Explorer's Guide to the Semantic Web*. Manning Publications Co., Greenwich.

Sakkopoulos, E., Kanellopoulos, D., Tsakalidis, A. (2006). Semantic mining and web service discovery techniques for media resources management. International Journal of Metadata, Semantics and Ontologies. Vol. 1, No. 1, pp. 66-75.

Singh, I., Stearns, B., Johnson, M. and the Enterprise Team (2002): Designing Enterprise Applications with the J2EE Platform, Second Edition. Prentice Hall. pp. 348. Online: http://java. sun.com/blueprints/guidelines/designing_enter-prise_applications_2e/app-arch/app-arch2.html

Shadbolt, N., Berners-Lee T., Hall, W. (2006). The Semantic Web Revisited. IEEE Intelligent Systems. 21(3). 96-101.

Stamboulis, Y. Skayannis P. (2003). Innovation Strategies and Technology for Experience-Based Tourism. Tourism Management. Vol. 24, pp. 35-43.

Stojanovic, LJ., Stojanovic N.,Volz, R. (2002). Migrating data-intensive Web sites into the Semantic Web. Proceedings of the 2002 ACM symposium on Applied computing, Madrid, Spain, ACM Press. 1100-1107.

Sycara, K., Klusch, M., Widoff, S., Lu, J. (1999) Dynamic service matchmaking among agents in open information environments. ACM SIGMOD Record. Vol. 28(1), pp. 47-53.

World Tourism Organization, 2001, Thesaurus on Tourism & Leisure Activities: http://pub.world-tourism.org:81/epages/Store. sf/?ObjectPath=/Shops/Infoshop/Products/1218/SubProducts/1218-1

WTO (2002). Thesaurus on Tourism & Leisure Activities of the World Tourism Organization [Online]. Retrieved May 12, 2004, from http://www.world-tourism.org/aciduis ciduisi bla facillum nulla feuguer adignit amet

This work was previously published in The Semantic Web for Knowledge and Data Management: Technologies and Practices, edited by Z. Ma and H. Wang, pp. 243-265, copyright 2009 by Information Science Reference (an imprint of IGI Global).

Chapter 4.10

E–Tourism Image:
The Relevance of Networking for Web Sites Destination Marketing

Lluís Prats-Planagumà
Universitat de Girona, Spain

Raquel Camprubí
Universitat de Girona, Spain

ABSTRACT

The competitiveness of tourism destinations is a relevant issue for tourism studies, moreso, is a key element on the daily basis of tourism destinations. In this sense, the management of tourism destinations is essential to maintain competitive advantages. In this chapter tourism destination is considered as a relational network, where interaction and cooperation is needed among tourism agents, to achieve major levels of competitive advantage and a more effective destination management system. In addition, the perceptions of tourists are obtained from two main sources. The first one is the social construction of a tourism destination previous to the visit and the second one is obtained from the interaction between tourists and tourism destination agents during the visit. In this sense, the management of tourism destination to emit a homogenous and collective image is a factor that can reduce the gap if dissatisfaction from the previous and real tourist perception. The authors specifically discuss the importance of a common agreement of tourism agents on virtual tourism images projected through official Web sites, considering that the literature focused mainly in how to promote and sell destinations trough Internet but not in terms of exploiting a destination joint image. Finally, in order to analyze the integration of a tourism product and determine their consequences in tourism promotion an empirical research has been done, using the case of Girona's province. The main findings determine that, although interactions among tourism agents can improve destination competitiveness, little cooperation in tourism promotion on Web sites is achieved, as well as a few uses of technological resources in the Web sites to facilitate to tourists a better understanding of tourism resources in the area.

INTRODUCTION

Each tourism destination can be considered a market in itself. At these destinations tourism suppliers (i.e., accommodations, restaurants, museums, and tour-

DOI: 10.4018/978-1-60566-134-6.ch009

ism offices, among others) interact simultaneously with the tourists who consume these products or services. For that reason a market approach is more appropriate than a supply or a demand one.

A tourism destination is the geographical area where a set of tourism agents interact and intervene in tourism activities. These interactions, from a supply point of view, help develop a relational network at the destination. A relational network is the set of economic and personal relationships established among a number of agents who share goals, cooperation systems, knowledge, reputation, and image, among other elements, in common. These elements help the destination network generate collective learning and knowledge, and consequently, achieve greater levels of competitiveness than individual agents would obtain.

In addition, from the demand point of view, these interactions within the destination help minimize the existing gap between perceived and real images. All tourists have a socially constructed image of a destination (Urry, 1990; Galí & Donaire, 2005; Larsen & George, 2006), which conditions their decision-making, and it is important for the tourism agents involved in the network to control the image of a destination.

This control has two simultaneous benefits. The first one, related to the tourism demand, is the potential to influence tourist decision-making. The second one is related to the tourism supply chain: the competitive advantage brought to tourism destinations by projecting a real image.

Internet is a very important channel that helps tourism agents to achieve these two benefits derived from this control in three aspects. First, a number of authors assume the relevance of Internet as a tourism destination image generator (Baloglu & Pekan, 2006; Choi, Lehto & Morrison, 2007; Hashim, Murphy & Muhammad Hashim, 2007); although "research on the Internet as an image formation agent is still at an infancy stage" (Choi, Lehto & Morrison, 2007, p. 118). Second, Internet brings a great number of opportunities to tourism image formation, contributing to destination im-

agery formation to consumers (Hashim, Murphy & Muhamd Hashim, 2007) and giving to tourism destination an opportunity to improve destination marketing through the use of "Internet's unique features, such as geographical interactivity with audience, low-cost accessibility, world-wide, hyperlinks with other travel suppliers and design flexibility, to attract more tourists and better position their state in the intense competition for visitors" (Lee, Cai & O'Leary, 2006, p. 816). Third, Internet and destination websites, in particular, act as an information tool for tourists, being an influencing element in their decision-making. This article will discuss the attainment of these two benefits and the relevance of Internet in them using the tourism image and social network theories to clarify how supply and demand interact in a tourism destination. A conceptual model will be proposed as part of a theoretical market approach to tourism destinations, which integrates supply and demand, explains interactions between them and highlights the relevance of this scope of analysis to better understand the dynamics of a tourism destination and the possibility of improving its competitive advantage. In addition, the article demonstrates the necessity of using this integrated approach for planning and managing a tourism destination to improve its competitiveness and highlight this theoretical view.

One of the elements that can be planned with an integrated approach, mainly because it helps to establish scale economies in terms of promotion, it is the promotional website content of a destination. Usually different agents take part in this promotion, Destination Marketing Organization's (DMO) local governments, private companies or associations creating different sources of information. Apart from these possible scale economies this will also help in terms of unification of the destination image. If this image is homogeneous gives also an extra value of competitive advantage preventing incoordination.

Finally, a case study is conducted in order to analyze network configuration trough promotional websites in Internet and determine if the tourism product of a destination is integrated and promoted globally or, on the contrary, each tourism agent acts independently. Results show the existence of a reduced network, that means a little integration of the tourism products in the province of Girona.

This article is organized in five main sections. The first explains the process of tourism image formation and how the tourism agents that intervene in this process affect the image that tourists have of tourism destinations, from the perspective of the social construction of tourism images. The second focuses on the network configuration of the destination, taking into account the tourism agents who take part in the tourism system and how networking can generate competitive advantages. The third part presents a theoretical model of an integrated market approach to tourism destinations. The forth section presents a case study, which analyze the network configuration of tourism products in the province of Girona. Finally, the conclusions based on the theoretical model and the case study is drawn, the model's limitations are considered and proposals for future research are made.

HOW TOURISTS PERCEIVE DESTINATIONS

Social Construction of Tourism Destination Images

Images have been used in a number of contexts and disciplines: psychology perceives the image as a visual representation; thought behavior geography emphasizes the association of impressions, knowledge, emotions, values and beliefs; and marketing focus on the relationship between image and behavior of consumers (Jenkins, 1999). The majority of academics from the 1970s to the present day agree that tourism image is "the sum of beliefs, ideas, and impressions that a person

has of a destination" (Crompton, 1979).

Gunn (1988), in her main academic study mentions "all of us have images of destinations, whether or not we have traveled to them. These images may be sharp or vague, factual or whimsical, but in all cases they are indicative of likes and dislikes." (p. 23) This means that all places have an image, which has not appeared out of nowhere, but they have consciously or unconsciously been created by "somebody". In this sense, one needs to think about how a tourism destination image is constructed.

From the realization of a task and its reiterated repetition by people in a society, this task ends up being institutionalized by this society. The acceptance of this task as habitual makes it "settle" in this society and form part of its traditions, so in that sense, the reality of this society has been constructed collectively (Berger & Luckmann, 1968). Using this approach to tourism image, it could be contemplated that a tourism image is constructed socially in the same way as a task is accepted as a normal way to do something in a society.

Tourism images are full of visual elements and signs that evoke socially constructed images (Urry, 1990), for example a couple of lovers in Paris suggest romantic Paris. In this sense, the image construct implies some overriding impression or stereotype (Mazanec & Schweiger, 1981). However, this tourism image does not always reflect the reality, because "the tourism image is, at the same time, a subjective construction (that varies from person to person) and a social construction, based on the idea of collective imagination" (Galí & Donaire, 2005, p. 778).

Variations in tourism image are complex if one considers how these images are formed, a little bit at a time. As Gallarza, Gil and Calderón (2002) have exposed "image is not static, but changes depending essentially in two variables: time and space". (p. 72) The influence of time on image is demonstrated in a number of studies on tourism image (Gartner, 1986; Gartner & Hunt, 1987;

Figure 1. Seven-stage model of a tourism experience (Source: Gunn, 1972)

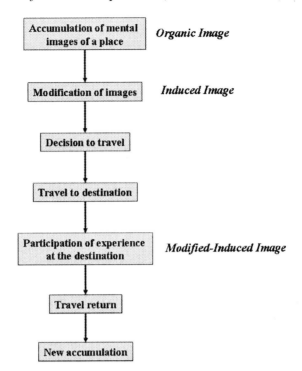

Chon, 1991; Selby & Morgan, 1996), especially if one considers its formation as a process (Gunn, 1972). At the same time, the space variable also influences the image of a tourism destination. Some studies in this field show that the distance between potential tourists and the tourism destination affects the perceived image of the place (Miossec, 1977; Talisman-Kosuta, 1989; Gallarza, Gil & Calderón, 2002). Considering the dynamic nature of tourism, image is useful if the effect of marketing actions on time and space variables (Gallarza Gil & Calderón, 2002; Talisman-Kosuta, 1989) is taken into account. In this manner the periodic evaluation of tourism image is relevant (Talisman-Kosuta, 1989).

How is the Image of a Tourism Destination Formed?

Accepting as valid the fact that tourism image is socially constructed (Urry, 1990; Larsen & George, 2004; Galí & Donaire, 2005), some studies point

to the existence of factors or components that form part of every tourism image and influence its formation process (Baloglu & McCleary, 1999; Gallarza, Gil & Calderón, 2002; Beerli & Martín, 2004). In this sense, Gartner (1993) mentions that some authors have systematized the elements that influence the process of tourism image formation in different conceptual models. At the same time, it is possible to find a number of authors who focus on the existence of a formation process of the tourism image, which is made up of different stages that contribute to how a tourism image is formed (i.e., Gunn, 1972; Govers & Go, 2004).

One of the most important models that show how a tourism image is formed is the seven-stage process of tourism experience, which has been developed by Gunn (1972). This model shows that images held by potential visitors, nonvisitors, and returned visitors differ (Gunn, 1972). (Figure 1)

At the first stage, potential tourists assimilate general information, such as, newspapers, television documentaries, books, and school lessons. This process generates an organic image of the destination; this is because the mere mention of these places evokes images, which are not necessarily tourism images.

The second stage implies a modification of perceived images based on consulting tourism information (i.e., tourism posters, guides, articles in specialized reviews, etc.). These changes in perceived images are influenced by induced images, which are the result of a conscious effort to develop, promote, and advertise a destination.

When the potential visitor has a perceived image based on the organic and induced images of the place, then they are prepared to make a decision. Other factors such as previous experience or the money available are also taken into consideration.

Travel to the destination may condition the image that a visitor has, but the key factor of a new change in a visitor's perceived image is their personal experience at the destination, as well as their participation in different activities, such as, visiting museums or the use of tourism services such as accommodation. At this stage, visitors have a modified-induced image, which is the result of the balance between the perceived image before visiting the destination and the perceived image after the visit.

Returning home after traveling, visitors evaluate and make reflections about their experience and discuss it with other travelers. At the final stage, tourists accumulate new information if one considers that this is a circular process. In this sense, it is widely recognized in academic literature that experienced tourists will become a "source of information" for other potential visitors, which will be based on their experience at the destination (Balogru & McCleary, 1999; Beerli & Martin, 2004).

As is noted in this model, the creation and modification of tourism images are constant and demonstrate the dynamism of the tourism image. The space variable shows these phenom-

ena through the contact of visitors with tourism destinations.

Image Management as a Competitive Advantage

Academic literature recognizes the need to manage tourism image, as it is one of the most important factors that influences the decision-making process of tourists that choose a destination to spend their holidays (Gartner, 1993; Govers & Go, 2004). Gunn (1972), in her model explains that tourism images are conditioned by the actions of a number of agents that influence the creation of tourism images. Although it is agreed that the tourism image is socially constructed, agents intervene in this process emitting images, which end up being consolidated and accepted as valid in a specific society.

According to Gartner's (1993) agents' classification, there are four types of agents. The first, Overt Induced is a kind of agent who promotes the creation of a specific tourism image of the tourism destination in a conscientious way, to influence a tourist's process of decision-making. Gartner (1993), makes a distinction between these agents, who are of two types. On one hand, Overt Induced I are "the promoters of the destination [that] construct an image of the salient attributes of the destination in the minds of the targeted audience" (Gartner, 1993, p. 197) with the traditional forms of advertising (i.e., television, radio, brochures, etc.). In this case, one could also include tourism businesses of the destinations, such as, accommodation, restaurants, activities, and so on. On the other hand, Overt Induced II are usually "tour-operators, wholesalers or organizations who have a vested interest in the travel decision process, but which are not directly associated with a particular destination area" (Gartner, 1993, p. 199). As Gartner (1993), mentions "destination area promoters do have some control over the images projected through tour operator" (p. 199) because if the tourism image does not conform to the reality of the destination it could create dissatisfactions to both locals and visitors (Govers & Go, 2004).

The second, Covert Induced are agents that apparently emit a tourism image that is not induced. In this case the author also defines two types of Covert Induced agents. The first is called Covert Induced I, who is related to a recognizable spokesperson who recommends a destination to support a higher level of credibility of tourism destination advertising. The second is Covert Induced II, this category corresponds to people or organizations who write articles, reports or stories about a particular place. Often this published information is a result of a familiarization tour for travel writers or special interest media groups. These actions increase credibility and allow destination promoters to project a specific image.

The third kind of agents is called Autonomous. These agents are people or organizations who produce reports, documentaries, movies, and news articles independently without the specific aim of creating a tourism image of a place.

The last group of agents that Gartner (1993), identifies is called Organic, and is related to information and opinions about a place that a person receives from other people, from their previous experience in this place, Unsolicited Organic corresponds to people who give information about a destination where they have been, without having been specifically asked by the other interlocutor, for example, when this is a topic of conversation with friends in colleges. The existence of Solicited Organic agents implies that individuals actively search for information about a destination and somebody informs them using their own experience. Friends or relatives usually constitute these kind of agents, who have a high level of credibility and are an extremely important part of the destination selection process.

When people visit a destination they become an Organic (pure) agent, having the capability to give information in a solicited or unsolicited way.

This model shows that the task of Overt Induced

agents, in this context, is undeniable, especially if one considers the sustainable competitive advantage of the destination. Sustainable competitive advantage is generally based on either core competences or unique resources that are superior to those possessed by competitors and are difficult to imitate (Johnson & Scholes, 1999; Aaker, 2001). Govers and Go (2004, p. 169), established that superior resources for a tourism destination "are generally to be found in either its unique and natural environment (climate, wildlife or landscape) or its cultural heritage" and also mention that "competitive advantage might be created through core competences, such as, the host community's existing unique capabilities in attracting visitors from outside." (i.e., destination's ability to stage world class events, festivals or exploit its folklore and prevailing traditions).

Following these considerations, the management of tourism image is viewed as a management tool (Ritchie, 1993). Govers and Go (2004), propose that it is necessary "to formulate a plan for projecting the 'right' image" (p. 170) as one of the essential parts of tourism development strategy. Gartner (1993), mentions the importance of considering the "image mix", as a continuum of factors that have to be taken into account to decide which agents will intervene in the formation of tourism image, as well as, the amount of money budgeted for image development, characteristics of target market, and demographic characteristics or timing. This task is obviously attributed to promoters of the destination who can select the right mix of image formation agents to maximize their scarce resources (Gartner, 1993).

THE NETWORK CONFIGURATION AND A TOURISM DESTINATION

Tourism Destination Agents

Tourism agents are an essential part of the system and of any destination, therefore they have been

Figure 2. Tourism destination agents

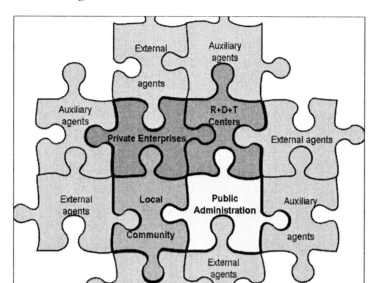

identified. Some definitions that are more applicable to industrial destinations, like innovation systems, clusters, milieux innovateurs, or industrial districts, always consider three main types of agents. Moreover, it is considered that tourism specificity needs another main agent who helps to define the situation of the system and therefore needs to complete it.

Two other types of agents support these main agents at all times and are also necessary to maintain the main set of agents stable. Figure 2 illustrates these agents in detail.

Following this scheme, those organizations that take part directly in generating the tourism experience are private companies. These include basic tourism companies, and also others whose main activity is related to tourism.

Public administrations are those organisms of governmental function that take part in the tourism processes and whose intervention can generate new legislations, give incentives for research, planning, and others.

Research, development, and training centers (R+D+T) are the essential elements capable of

generating specialized training and/or research in the scope of tourism, such as, universities, research institutes, or consultants.

These three main agents appear in the academic literature on innovation systems (Lundvall, 1992; Nelson, 1993), as well as, in clusters and industrial districts. In addition, the tourism scheme proposed by Gunn (1997), and later adapted by the OMT (1999) is taken, and the tourism industry as a functional tourism system (Prats & Balagué, 2005) is conceptualized. They demonstrate that the local community also has an essential role in the development of tourism activity, and consequently of the system. The local community is defined as the inhabitants of a territory. These people are individuals or organizations without economic aims, such as, NGO's, civic organizations, or others. The relevance of local community in tourism is emphasized, seeing that civic movements have been able to modify important decisions in city-planning, ecological subjects, or others, restraining or impelling tourism.

After describing the basic elements, the tourism auxiliary agents can be defined as those agents who do not have activities directly related to the tourism industry, but who support the main agents. Looking at the economic theories, the auxiliary agents are some of the receivers of the multiplying effect (McIntosh, Goeldner & Ritchie, 2000). And the external agents are those tourism agents who are part of other destinations, but who interact with one or more internal agents.

The set of agents in a tourism destination is basically located in the same geographical territory. However, a territory by itself does not have enough conditions for their collective coordination, and also the proximity does not generate synergies by itself, but it can contribute to their effectiveness with other dimensions shared between the agents (Zimmermann, 2001). A good example of an agent who belongs to a distant destination could be a specialized tour operator who commercializes destinations, which are geographically distant but relationally close.

Relational Networks

The use of relational networks in the analysis of a company's competitive advantage can be related to several approaches in the fields of economics or sociology, among others (Sorensen, 2004). Therefore, in the most static frame, this analysis has appeared within the network of individual companies who have useful and important connections with other companies, becoming more than just a unit inside an atomized market (Håkansson & Snehota, 1995). In this sense, these companies must be analyzed considering their relationships with other companies outside the network and also the existing relationships among other companies within the network (Holmen, Pedersen & Torvatn, 2005).

In relation to the most dynamic frame, it is observed that it was contemplated not to see the innovation process as a linear and consecutive process, meaning that the result of the initial stage brings up the following one and so on. Innovation is considered an intensive activity in both knowledge (Sundbo, 1998; Roberts, 2001) and learning. It is also totally accepted as a key element in the innovation process. Thus, innovation also arises and takes place through the interactions between companies (Sorensen, 2004), and between these companies and other relevant actors who are important for their activity (Prats & Guia, 2005). These ties must be understood as intense flows of knowledge and, therefore, essential for innovation, and also for competitiveness.

However, Sorensen (2004) presents a definition that considers networks as the set of conscious and accepted business relationships, whether formal or informal, with transmission of resources, immaterial or material, within the company's scope. In any case, it is useful to adopt the perspective of social network analysis, which studies specific relationships between a defined series of elements, like people, groups, organizations, countries or events, among others (Molina, 2001). It is necessary to consider that social network analysis is based on relationships and not on the attributes of elements. Then, a social network can be defined as the group of people, organizations or other social entities connected by a set of significant relations (Wellman, 1997).

Granovetter (1985) and Hite (2003), affirm that the existing relationships within social networks influence economic actions, and Hite (2003), distinguishes seven different types of ties that can take place inside a social network: the main three are business ties, personal ties, and hollow ties, and the other four types are formed as a result of the relationship between the main types.

Porter (1990), with his five forces model and his later approach to clusters, universalized the necessity to maintain the business or commercial ties that had been previously valued by Becattini (1979), and other authors. Other theories such as the industrial districts theory show that personal relationships have to be considered as a value that contributes to empower the agents' ties making them more efficient and trustworthy (Becattini, 1979). Hollow ties appeared only recently in network theories and have become very common, because they represent all those ties that you accept with the mediation of a third person, so your trust in the relationship is not with the agent to whom you are related, but with the agent who did the mediation (Prats, Camprubí & Comas, 2005).

It seems evident then, that a tourism destination can be defined as a relational network. In every single destination exist relationships among its agents (Prats, Guia & Molina, 2007), considering the specificities of the tourism product, and the existence of the different types of ties able to generate an active and beneficial set of agents and relationships. As an example, a tourism package is integrated by different items that are provided by various companies, which are linked though some kind of relationship. However, tourists do not distinguish that these items belong to different companies, although they need a perfect integration of them, in order for the tourism products to be successful. Another example can be the usual sectorial associations, where hotels, travel agencies or other tourism agents are associated in order to gain power in front of the suppliers or in front of the administration.

Networking as a Generator of Competitive Advantage

If different agents interact among themselves, it can be argued that these interactions often allow the agents to have joint benefits from infrastructures, common engineering, and transfer of tacit knowledge. It also makes productive combinations and interactions more difficult to carry out in atomization or individual isolation.

Even with the continuous growth of the on-line travel expenditure, the academic literature focused mainly in how to effectively build and evaluate hospitality and tourism websites (Han & Mills, 2006). Moreover the analysis is focused on individual perspectives comparing different websites as example, but there are not published results related to collective image construction trough

websites. "Because destination images influence tourist behavior, a destination must be favorably differentiated from its competition and positively positioned in the minds of consumers" (Hudson & Ritchie, 2006, p. 388), and this can be achieved also by the common internet promotion.

Belonging to a destination or relational network involves interacting with other members, which is usually transformed into routines of the organization. This is what Rallet and Torre (2004) call the belonging logic. This logic and interaction will be easier a priori if there is a common knowledge; this is called logic of similarity.

The interaction of these agents generates a number of factors that determine if a destination or local innovation system is successful or not in all scopes. A first and fundamental factor is the internal and external relationships that take place in the system. These relationships can be very different and they have been summarized into two characteristic groups.

On the one hand, depending on the relational structure that is adopted in a system, the degree of success will vary. In this factor the key element is the degree of connectivity that is obtained, understanding that the better the connectivity between the agents is, the closer it will be to "the ideal" system. It is understood that good internal connectivity will contribute to a more fluid circulation of knowledge between the agents, and this will increase the trust among them. But at the same time, an excess of internal connectivity can make the trust on external agents decrease to such an extent that they are considered intruders (Zimmerman, 2001). The lack of trust between external agents could have serious consequences in the new knowledge generation, because the closure of relational networks in itself could limit information flows that come from outside, blocking the possibility of generating new knowledge and collective learning (Lazerson & Lorenzoni, 1999).

On the other hand, however, it must also be observed that the quality of relationships within

Figure 3. Tourism local innovation system model (Source: Prats & Guia, 2005; Prats, Guia and Molina, 2007)

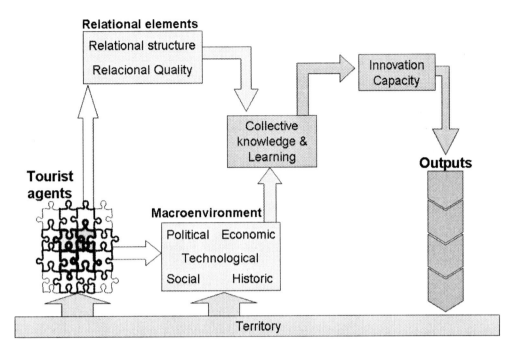

a system such as this, affects its success. The key element in this factor is trust, as a greater trust between the elements of a system will transmit more relevant information, and greater benefits for the whole destination will increase.

Another determining factor is the macro-environment, which is divided into five elements: (1) political, such as, decisions or political elements that affect the system; (2) economic, for instance economic situations that affect the system; (3) technological, which has two levels: (a) the hard level such as the automation level, and (b) the soft level such as the training level of the population; (4) social, this contributes to the system culture, for example the degree of associationism or the cultural level; and finally, (5) historical macro-environment, which gives perspective and historical experience, such as, political periods or natural disasters.

Using the agents' interactions and macro-environment variables, tourism destinations should

be able to generate essential collective knowledge and learning for the evolution of the system. The main purpose of this collective knowledge and learning is being able to generate a constant innovation capacity that will bring dynamism to the system as shown in Figure 3.

This innovation capacity allows the system to obtain four successive outputs, which can be observed in Figure 4. Each stage must be achieved to obtain the desired results. If an "ideal" configuration of the system is obtained, the four outputs will also be obtained, and this will revert again to the tourism destination.

The first unquestionable output of the innovation capacity is innovations in any of their modalities. In the opinions of Prats and Guia (2005) the innovation must allow the system to generate a competitive advantage, allowing the destination to satisfy the needs of the tourists better than the competitor's destinations.

The competitive advantage, consequently,

Figure 4. Tourism local innovation system outputs (Source: Prats and Guia, 2005)

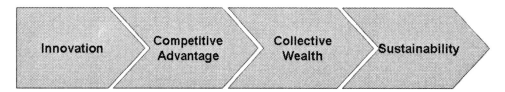

must contribute to the system's collective wealth, which in turn increases the wellbeing of all the agents who join it. Wellbeing is understood to be an improvement of the quality of life of all the elements, which is not based solely on the economic, environmental, or social benefits at an individual level, but is a perfect balance between all of them at a collective level.

This balance allows the system to become sustainable and generates a new and better situation that is a territory improvement, and which also feeds the agents and the macro-environment, varying the behavior of the system constantly, forcing it to reframe itself, and be constantly dynamic.

DESTINATION TOURIST PERCEPTION & NETWORK CONFIGURATION: A THEORETICAL PROPOSAL

The tourism image perceived by tourists and represented in Gunn's model (1972) has a close connection with tourism destinations, and in particular, with agents that interact in the promotion of the destination.

The seven-stages of tourism experience (Gunn, 1972), show interactions between tourists and tourism agents. This materializes, initially, in the process of searching for information, which is done voluntarily by tourists; and later, if tourists travel to the destination the tourism image is again modified by direct contact with tourism agents.

In this context, direct contact and coordination

among internal and external agents of the tourism destination are also necessary, so that tourists can perceive a real tourism image of the destination both before and after traveling to the destination. If this situation occurs, it will be easier for tourism destinations to maintain their competitive advantage in a sustainable way.

Therefore, tourism destinations, which are established as a network and based on trust among its members, can better guarantee a unique tourism image, which is more coherent with the reality of the tourism destination. This configuration has a close relationship with the structure of network, the quality of ties, and its macro-environment. Moreover, the innovation capacity generated has to be useful to adapt the induced image to the tourism product.

Figure 5 shows a market approach model, which focuses on demand and supply simultaneously and explains the relationship between them, taking into account the multiple factors that affect the behavior of tourism agents. As a consequence the competitive advantage of tourism destinations is explained.

In this model the interaction between tourism agents and tourists is highlighted, giving an overall picture of what happens in a destination. In this context, those tourism agents who interact frequently with tourists tend to be public administrations, private companies, and the local community.

First, public administrations have a direct relationship with tourists through the promotional actions of tourism destinations. These agents act as induced agents of tourism images by acting as

Figure 5. Market approach of tourism destination: Conceptual model

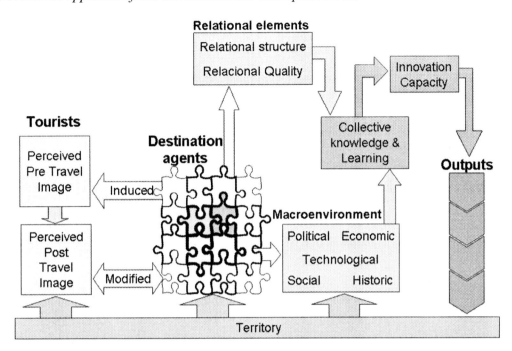

promoters and developers of destinations. In this case, following Gartner's classification (1993), public administrations act as Overt induced agents I, who emit an induced tourism image, which influences both the tourists' perceived image of a destination and the decision-making process at the moment of choosing a destination (Gartner, 1993).

Second, tour operators, as they form part of the private companies of a destination, also act as Overt induced agents II, because they have a clear interest in influencing the decision-making process of tourists at the time of selecting a destination. Public administrations, as well as tour operators, influence the "perceived pre-travel image" of tourists.

When the potential tourist travels to a destination and becomes a real tourist a direct interaction between tourists and tourism companies takes place, and this influences the perceived image of the place that tourists had before going there, creating a new image of the place (Gunn, 1972).

Finally, the local community has a strong

relationship with the tourist and usually the tourist's real image is strongly modified by this kind of contact. In the author's opinion a key factor at this level is the perception the local community has of the tourism activity and the benefits that the inhabitants receive from it, because if a local community thinks that the benefits and damages that tourism causes are in perfect balance or in a more beneficial situation for the local community, these inhabitants will contribute to the tourists well-being, otherwise they will behave to the contrary.

Tourism research and training centers play a secondary, but fundamental role, especially as they might condition the induced tourism image through research projects, and simultaneously, they could also influence perceived tourism images indirectly by training the tourism workers who help tourists during their stay.

Therefore, the influence on "perceived post-travel image" comes from tourism companies, as well as the local community and research and training centers.

This model shows that, the relationships between tourists and tourism agents are systematic and necessary throughout the whole process. This means that this interaction is essential both before a tourist travels to a destination as well as during his/her stay.

If tourists do not go to a destination, this might mean that tourism agents cannot control the factors that generate the appropriate knowledge and transmit the right image to convince tourists. However, other uncontrollable factors exist, such as, the travel time needed, the distance to the destination, the money available or to what extent a tourism product fulfils tourist needs.

When tourists are dissatisfied with their visit because the "perceived post-travel image" is extremely different from the "perceived pre-travel image", there is another scenario where the agents have not transmitted the reality of the destination. In this situation tourism agents had the innovation capacity, but they had not used it in the correct way to obtain the desired image outputs. This context shows the importance of communication and coordination among all the tourism agents of a destination, to induce a real and homogenous image.

CASE STUDY

As we mentioned before, tourism products and even more evident tourists doesn't understand political boundaries, but regional and local governments use it to divide the territory. This situation causes management and commercialization problems that don't help to emit a coherent image of the whole destination to the possible tourists. These scenarios can be avoided developing networks for product commercialization that includes all the Overt induced I agents. Is one of the easiest way to start a network, because in that sense they can share marketing costs entering to scale economies.

We analyzed the public institutions' websites of a tourism destination in a local and regional level in order to know if tourism product is configured globally through collaboration between destination's tourism agents; or in a contrary way the tourism product is fragmented. This can help us to understand the level of tourism image coherence that is transmitted to tourist through Internet.

Methodology

In order to analyze how a tourism product is promoted in a local and regional level a website analysis of public institutions from the Girona's province, which has been conducted during the first trimester of the year.

The Girona's province is situated in the northeastern of Catalonia and their capital is the city of Girona. It is a very rich region in terms of natural resources and heritage; and it has a very privileged placement between the sea and the oriental Pyrenees. Tourism activity is mainly developed in the coastal area, although in Pyrenees tourism is also a relevant activity for their economy. In general terms, Girona's province is integrated by two tourism brands: (a) Costa Brava for the coastal area, and (b) Girona's Pyrenees for the mountain area. These two brands divide their territory and facilitate their promotion.

Websites of 41 public institutions have been analyzed, taking into consideration three labels of public institutions: (a) DMO of the province, (b) regional institutions, and (c) local institutions.

The existence of a section in their website related to tourism activities has been the criteria to select websites. In this context, we have analyzed the role of public agents that act as Overt induced I, following the Gartner's nomenclature (1993) as we mentioned above.

Data collection has been done taken into consideration the level of public institution searching the existing relationship among them. Three kinds of data have been collected. Firstly, it has been detected direct and indirect links that are placed into de website and which is the linked agent. Secondly,

Figure 6. Relational map of direct web links

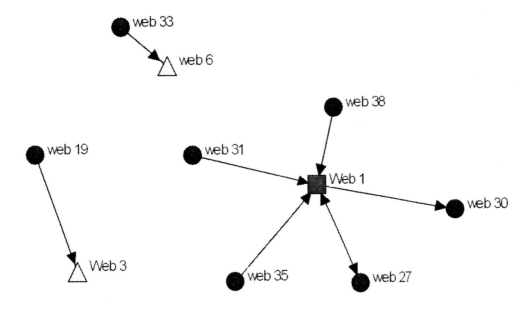

it has been observed the quality of detected links and it has determined their typology (advertising links, friends' links or partners' links). Finally, it has been also analyzed the e-marketing resources that have been used in the websites.

In order to analyze data, it has been used UCI-NET 6.0 software (Borgatti, Everett & Freeman, 2002), which is a software specialized in social network analysis in a qualitative and quantitative way. In our case it has been used the application to represent graphically the social network.

Data Analysis

Observing the network that can be drowned after the analysis, is possible to assure that don't exist a common commercialization network in the Costa Brava destination. From the 41 analyzed webs only 10 have direct links with other promotion agent. The main problem is that only one of these links is bidirectional. This means that the rest maybe are not well developed links.

Another element to extract from this relational map is the fact that only 2 of 8 regional institutions appeared on it, and always as link receiver and not

as a link creator, which means that they promote the tourism elements independently from the municipalities that they represent. (Figure 6)

Jumping to the technological elements included into the webs that can help to emit a better image five different types of them were analyzed, the type of compelling web system, the multimedia systems divided into sound, video and photography galleries, and finally the interaction with the tourists represented by interactive maps (Table 1).

What is really shocking is that the main Catalan destination, only have little technological and interactive elements to attract tourists. This is done by the historical tourism tradition of the destination

Table 1. Use of technological and interactive web resources

Type	N
Advanced Compelling	18
Video	2
Sound	1
Photographic galleries	11
Interactive maps	4
Total	36

Figure 7. Percentage of technological and interactive web resources

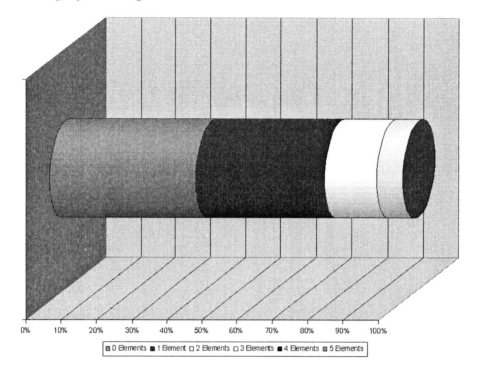

when an intensive promotion to attract tourists never was needed. Most of the mature tourism destinations have a similar problem.

One third of the tourism Web sites of the destination don't have any of the mentioned elements and nearly half of them only have one. This situation sorts out that the emitted image trough websites and technological elements are really poor. At least one of the webs that have three of these elements is the one of the main DMO maybe the most visited site. The problem is that in this site there is not all the information related with destination as we can imagine for the link system showed before. (Figure 7)

CONCLUSION

Discussion

Initially, it has to be mentioned that it is important to observe demand and supply in an integrated way.

This integrated vision gives a greater innovation capacity, in particular, regarding the destinations' tourism agents; who have a broader view of the possibilities of maintaining and improving the sustainable competitive advantage of the destination; allowing to consider the tourists' key role and how the tourism agents' interact with them, as well as when this interaction takes place, and what the basic tools that maintain this relationship are.

In this context it is assumed, as justified earlier, that a tourism destination's image is constructed socially during a complex process in a seven-stage tourism experience. Moreover, the necessity to manage this image is accepted as a method that influences the tourists' process of decision-making and for that reason it is necessary to pay special attention to the agents who take part in this.

Nowadays, Internet is positioned as a relevant tool to contribute to destination imagery formation as well as and information source for tourists that can influence their decision-making. At the same time, it is commonly accepted that city marketing differs in many ways of destination marketing, but if it is analyzed the common projected image trough websites the division line disappears. So we can assume that a big city like Barcelona can have the same number of official emitting image websites than a regional destination like Costa Brava.

In the authors' opinion, social network analysis is a perfect approach for studying tourism destinations. In this sense, they have highlighted the interaction among tourism agents to create a tourism product or service adequate to tourists' needs, as one of the most important factors. One of these interactions can be done in terms of public agents' promotion for the whole destination; this can be materialized though official websites and links those appear in it.

As can be seen, in the case study, the promotion through websites in Girona's province does not help to create a coherent and jointly destination image. This situation can be avoided with a better and wide interaction among the public agents, materializing it through their websites. In addition, probably, the low use of technological and interactive resources in websites is done by the hard sedimentation of tourism industry in this region, and in our opinion these elements will need to be improved if tourism destination goes into a declining process of their life cycle.

Limitations and Future Research

The work that has been presented in this article opens a wide field of future research that takes into consideration all the agents mentioned in the presented model. This empirical analysis will contemplate if having a whole picture of the market will contribute to really improving the planning and management of tourism destinations, as discussed.

In this first conceptualization the autonomous and organic agents from Gartner's model (1993), who generate an uncontrolled tourism image by induced agents, have not been considered. In future research, it would be necessary to revise the conceptual model and include autonomous and organic agents, to have a better proxy, taking into account that tourists also interact with autonomous and organic agents before traveling to the destination.

In the authors' opinion, it could also be interesting to consider the difference between real and potential tourists in future revisions of the model. This reflection could have relevant implications, especially for observing the induced tourism image and searching for explanations for a tourist's reasons to travel to a specific destination and not to others.

REFERENCES

Aaker, D. (2001). *Strategic market management.* (6th ed.). New York, NY: John Wiley and Sons.

Baloglu, S., & McCleary, K. W. (1999). A model of destination image formation. *Annals of Tourism Research, 26*(4), 808–889. doi:10.1016/S0160-7383(99)00030-4

Baloglu, S., & Pekan, Y. A. (2006). The website design and Internet site marketing practices of upscale and luxury hotels in Turkey. *Tourism Management, 27,* 171–176. doi:10.1016/j.tourman.2004.07.003

Becattini, G. (1979). Dal sttore industriale al distretto industrialle. Alcune considerazione sull'unità dell'economia industriale. *Revista di Economia e Politica Industriale, 1.*

Beerli, A., & Martín, J. D. (2004). Factors influencing destination image. *Annals of Tourism Research, 31*(3), 657–681. doi:10.1016/j.annals.2004.01.010

Berger, P. L., & Luckmann, T. (1968). *Social construction of reality.* Amorrortu: Buenos Aires.

Borgatti, S. P., Everett, M. G., & Freeman, L. C. (2002). *Ucinet 6 for Windows: Software for social network analysis*. Harvard: Analytic Technologies.

Choi, S., Lehto, X. Y., & Morrison, A. M. (2007). Destination image representation on the web: Content analysis of Macau travel related Web sites. *Tourism Management, 28*, 118–129. doi:10.1016/j.tourman.2006.03.002

Chon, K. S. (1991). Tourism destination image modification process: Marketing implications. *Tourism Management, 12*(1), 68–72. doi:10.1016/0261-5177(91)90030-W

Crompton, J. L. (1979). An assessment of the image of Mexico as a vacation destination and the influence of geographical location upon the image. *Journal of Travel Research, 18*(4), 18–23.

Galí, N., & Donaire, J. A. (2005). The social construction of the image of Girona: A methodological approach. *Tourism Management, 26*, 777–785. doi:10.1016/j.tourman.2004.04.004

Gallarza, M. G., Gil, I., & Calderón, H. (2002). Destination Image – Towards a conceptual framework. *Annals of Tourism Research, 29*(1), 56–78. doi:10.1016/S0160-7383(01)00031-7

Gartner, W., & Hunt, J. (1987). An analysis of state image change over a twelve year period (1971-1983). *Journal of Travel Research, 16*(2), 15–19. doi:10.1177/004728758702600204

Gartner, W. C. (1986). Temporal influence on image change. *Annals of Tourism Research, 13*, 635–644. doi:10.1016/0160-7383(86)90006-X

Gartner, W. C. (1993). Image formation process. *Journal of Travel & Tourism Marketing, 2*(2), 191–215. doi:10.1300/J073v02n02_12

Govers, R., & Go, F. M. (2004). Cultural identities constructed, imagined and experienced: A 3-gap tourism destination image model. *Tourism, 52*(2), 165–182.

Granovetter, M. S. (1985). Economic action and social structure: The problem of embeddedness. *American Journal of Sociology, 91*, 481–510. doi:10.1086/228311

Guia, J., Prats, L., & Comas, J. (2006). The destination as a local system of innovation: The role of relational networks. In L. Lazzeretti, & C. Petrillo (Eds.), *Tourism local system and networking*. Elseivier: Amsterdam.

Gunn, C. A. (1972). *Vacationscape: Designing tourist regions*. Washington DC: Taylor and Francis/University of Texas.

Gunn, C. A. (1988). *Vacationscape: Designing tourist regions*. New York: Van Nostraud Reinhold.

Gunn, C. A. (1997). *Vacationscape: Developing tourist areas*. Washington DC: Taylor and Francis.

Håkansson, H., & Snehota, I. J. (Eds.). (1995). *Developing relationships in business networks*. London: Routledge.

Han, J. H., & Mills, J. E. (2006). Zero acquaintance benchmarking at travel destination Web sites: What is the first impression that national tourism organizations try to make? *International Journal of Tourism Research, 8*, 405–430. doi:10.1002/jtr.581

Hashim, H. H., Murphy, J., & Muhamad Hashim, N. (2007). Islam and online imagery on Malaysian tourist destination Web sites. *Journal of Computer-Mediated Communication, 12*(3), 16. doi:10.1111/j.1083-6101.2007.00364.x

Hite, J. M. (2003). Patterns of multidimensionality among embedded network ties: A typology of relational embeddedness in emerging entrepreneurial firms. *Strategic Organization, 1*(1), 9–49.

Hjalager, A. M. (2000). Tourism destinations and the concept of industrial districts. *Tourism and Hospitality Research, 2*(3), 199–213.

Holmen, E., Pedersen, A. C., & Torvatn, T. (2005). Building relationship for technological innovation. *Journal of Business Research, 58*(9), 1240–1250. doi:10.1016/j.jbusres.2003.10.010

Hudson, S., & Ritchie, J. R. B. (2006). Promoting destinations via film tourism: An empirical identification of supporting marketing initiatives . *Journal of Travel Research, 44*, 387–396. doi:10.1177/0047287506286720

Jackson, J., & Murphy, P. (2002). Tourism destinations as clusters: Analytical experiences from the World. *Tourism and Hospitality, 4*(1), 36–52.

Jenkins, O. H. (1999). Understanding and measuring tourist destination images. *International Journal of Tourism Research, 1*, 1–15. doi:10.1002/(SICI)1522-1970(199901/02)1:1<1::AID-JTR143>3.0.CO;2-L

Johnson, G., & Scholes, K. (1999). *Exploring corporate strategy*. Harlow, UK: Prentice Hall.

Larsen, G., & George, V. (2004, February). The social construction of destination image – A New Zeland firm example. *Working Papers, 4/01*.

Lazerson, M., & Lorenzoni, G. (1999). The firms that feed industrial districts: A return to the Italian source. *Industrial and Corporate Change, 8*(2), 235–266. doi:10.1093/icc/8.2.235

Lee, G. M., Cai, L. A., & O'Leary, J. T. (2006). An analysis of brand-building elements in the U. S. state tourism Web sites. *Tourism Management, 27*, 815–828. WWW.Branding.States.US. doi:10.1016/j.tourman.2005.05.016

Lundvall, B. A. (Ed.). (1992). *National systems of innovation. Towards a theory of innovation and interactive learning*. London: Pinter Publishers.

Mazanec, J., & Schweiger, G. (1981). Improved marketing efficiency through multi-product brand names? An empirical investigation of image transfer. *European Research, 9*(1), 32–44.

McIntosh, R. W., Goeldner, C. R., & Ritchie, J. R. B. (2000). *Turismo: Planeación, administración y perspectivas*. Mexico D.F.: Limusa Willey

Miossec, J. M. (1977). L'image touristique comme introduccion à la géographie du tourisme. *Annales de Geographie*, 55–70. doi:10.3406/geo.1977.17568

Molina, F. X. (2001). European industrial districts: Influence of geographic concentration on performance of the firm. *Journal of International Management, 7*(4), 277–294. doi:10.1016/S1075-4253(01)00048-5

Nelson, R. (1993). *National innovation systems*. New York, NY: Oxford University Press.

OMT. (1999). *Desarrollo turístico sostenible: Guia para administradores locales*. Madrid: OMT.

Porter, M. E. (1990). *The competitive advantage of nations*. London: The McMillan Press.

Prats, L., & Balagué, J. (2005). Cohesión y sostenibilidad, elementos clave en la competitividad del territorio turístico: El caso de la Costa Brava. *Retos Turísticos, 3*(3), 8–15.

Prats, L., Camprubí, R., & Comas, J. (2005). Network ties relevance on the destination business relationships. In Universidade do Algarve (Eds.), *Recent developments in tourism research*. Faro: University of Algarve.

Prats, L., & Guia, J. (2005). The destination as a local system of innovation. In C. Petrillo & J. Swarbrooke (Eds.), *Networking and partnership in destinations and development management* (pp. 121-136). Arnhem: ATLAS.

Prats, L., Guia, J., & Molina, F. X. (2007). Tourism local innovation systems or how tourism destinations evolve. In M. Smith & L. Onderwater (Eds.), *Destinations revisited. Perspectives on developing and managing tourist areas* (pp. 35-53). *Arnhem: ATLAS*

Rallet, A., & Torre, A. (2004). Proximité et localisation. *Economie Rurale, 280.*

Ritchie, J. R. (1993). Crafting a destination vision: Putting de concept of residence responsive tourism into practice. *Tourism Management, 14,* 279–289. doi:10.1016/0261-5177(93)90006-7

Roberts, J. (2001). Challenges facing service enterprises in a global knowledge-based economy: Lessons from the business services sector. *International Journal of Services Technology and Management, 2*(3), 402–433. doi:10.1504/IJSTM.2001.001612

Selby, M., & Morgan, N. G. (1996). Reconstructing place image: A case study of its role in destination market research. *Tourism Management, 17,* 287–294. doi:10.1016/0261-5177(96)00020-9

Sorensen, F. (2004). *Tourism experience innovation networks.* Doctoral dissertation. Roskilde University, Denmark.

Sundbo, J. (1998). *The theory of innovation: Entrepreneurs, technology and strategy.* Cheltenham, UK: Edward Elgar.

Telisman-Kosuta, N. (1989). Tourism destination image. In S. F. Witt & L. Moutinho (Eds.), *Tourism marketing and management handbook* (pp. 557-561). Cambridge: Prentice Hall.

Urry, J. (1990). *The tourist gaze.* London: Sage: Wellman, B. (1997). An electronic group of virtually a social network. In S. Kiesler (Ed.), *Culture of the internet.* Mahwah: Lawrence Erlbaum.

Chapter 4.11
Successful Web–Based IT Support Services:
Service Provider Perceptions of Stakeholder–Oriented Challenges

Vanessa Cooper
RMIT University, Australia

Sharman Lichtenstein
Deakin University, Australia

Ross Smith
RMIT University, Australia

ABSTRACT

Web-based self-service systems (WSSs) are increasingly leveraged for the delivery of after-sales information technology (IT) support services. Such services are offered by IT service providers to customer firms and increasingly involve business partners. However little is known of the challenges faced by IT service providers as a result of the involvement of the other firms and their employees (end-users). This paper reports related findings from an interpretive study of IT service provider perceptions in six multinational IT service provider firms (Cooper, 2007). The findings highlight that, for IT service providers, (1) it is important to consider and resolve the needs and concerns of other key stakeholders, and (2) significant challenges exist in doing so. The main contribution of the paper is the identification of the key challenges involved. Important implications for theory and practice are discussed.

INTRODUCTION

The continued maturation of the Internet has been accompanied by a corporate shift from the provision of goods to the provision of services, with parallel development of relevant new business models and marketing paradigms (Rust, 2001). Many businesses have developed *E-services*, defined as the provision of services by electronic networks such as the internet (Rust, 2001). Despite the increasing importance of E-services to business success, electronic commerce researchers have been slow to investigate associated issues. As the E-services value chain requires different types of processes and offers greater flexibility in comparison with offline services, there are new research challenges to be explored (Hofacker et al., 2007).

An important new source of value presented by E-services is *supplementary E-services* such as electronic provision of pre- and post-sales customer support for purchased services and products (Hofacker et al., 2007). Experts further suggest that the successful provision of supplementary E-services may be more important strategically to service providers and vendors than the quality of originally-purchased services and products (Otim & Grover, 2006; Piccoli et al., 2004). Marketing of supplementary services (offline and online) can provide differentiation, improve customer service, increase customer retention and lower service costs (Levenburg & Klein, 2006; Reichheld & Schefter, 2000).

This article focuses on the provision by service providers of supplementary E-services to customer firms ("enterprise customers") using the World Wide Web ("Web"). To leverage this market successfully, vendors and service providers aim to improve the implementation and delivery of E-services by employing a systematic approach. One such approach is a Net-based Customer Service System (NCSS) which has been described as "a network-based computerised information system that delivers service to a customer either directly (e.g. via a browser, PDA, or cell phone) or indirectly (via a service representative or agent accessing the system)" (Piccoli et al., 2004 p.424).

This article focuses on the use of a key type of NCSS based on a Web interface – a *Web-based Self-Service System (WSS)*. Self-service is gaining importance in contemporary organisations primarily for cost reduction reasons (Doyle, 2007).

This article explores the context of *managed information technology (IT) support services*. In this setting IT service providers employ WSSs to provide after-sales IT support to enterprise customers.

Key stakeholders comprise the service provider firm and its employees, business partners and their employees, and enterprise customers and their employees. As this article will show, the involvement of the key stakeholders results in significant challenges for IT service providers aiming to provide successful after-sales support by means of a WSS. These challenges will be explored in the article by examining the IT service provider perspective.

A knowledge transfer lens is used to explore this topic as the transfer of after-sales IT support knowledge (such as IT solutions) from an IT service provider firm to a customer firm is central to the concept of successful after-sales Web-based support services (CSI 2002; Koh et al., 2004).

This article draws on a large study investigating the successful provision of managed after-sales IT support when facilitated by WSSs (Cooper, 2007). The perspectives of six large multinational IT service providers were obtained and analysed. The views of IT service providers are important to understand for improved service provision (Pitt, 1998). Our study focuses on the use of operational IT support services, relating to (1) assembling and operating the core IT environment, and (2) providing key value-adding services such as the Service (Help) Desk (Peppard, 2001).

Five further sections complete this article. Section 2 provides a theoretical background by reviewing representative literature. Section 3 outlines the research design. Section 4 describes the key challenges relating to stakeholders, identified when an IT service provider transfers after-sales IT support-oriented knowledge to enterprise customers when WSSs are used to facilitate service provision. Section 5 discusses the key challenges. Section 6 summarises the main points, draws conclusions, reflects on the limitations of the findings and offers suggestions for future research.

THEORETICAL BACKGROUND

We first situate WSSs within a Customer Relationship Management (CRM) context as the strategic goals of supplementary services - such as after-sales support provision using WSSs - include improving customer service and increasing customer retention (Levenburg & Klein, 2006). We then review the use of WSSs for after-sales IT support provision to enterprise customers. Next a stakeholder-oriented framework of successful Web-based enterprise customer service drawn from earlier findings highlights the importance of stakeholder relationships and related knowledge flows. Finally, the section reviews the knowledge transfer process and the transfer of after-sales support knowledge from an IT support organisation to an enterprise customer.

Customer Relationship Management

In recent years CRM has emerged as a potentially powerful organisational strategy to enable a vendor or service provider to better identify and satisfy customer needs and retain customer loyalty. Enhanced customer relationships may also lead to improved customer-related operational effectiveness and a higher return on investment for the organisation (Barua et al., 2004).

To improve the customer service experience and meet other CRM objectives, the aggregation of data, information and knowledge about the customer is important. Specialised software applications that perform electronic CRM (eCRM) have been developed for this purpose. A common example of an eCRM application is a Web interface, supported by database and data mining tools which record past customer transactions and analyse data to identify customer segments, match products to customer profiles, and better understand target demographics and psychographic characteristics (Brohman et al., 2003). Customer service agents can utilise this "customer intelligence" to potentially up-sell or cross-sell products and services (Brohman et al. 2003). A WSS is an important type of operational eCRM application (Geib et al., 2005; Khalifa & Shen, 2005) and is discussed below in the context of managed IT support services.

WSS and After-Sales IT Support for Enterprise Customers

A WSS is a Web-based information system that enables organisations to move from labour-intensive manual processes towards low-cost automated Web-based self-service (Pujari 2004). WSSs can facilitate the offering of customer support services for pre-sales, sales, and after-sales activities. They are underpinned by complex information systems, complemented by a customer contact centre, and integrated with a multi-channel service strategy (Negash *et al.* 2003).

WSSs offer important advantages to service providers and customers (Geib et al., 2006; Pujari 2004). Such advantages include electronically leveraging the Web interface, customer/service-provider (and customer/customer) interactions, knowledge management (KM) principles and self-service principles in order to capture and provide information and knowledge useful for pre-sales, sales and after-sales support.

In managed IT service environments, WSSs offer informational, transactional, and proactive support services. Informational support includes "break-fix" support which provides customers experiencing technical problems with resolutions to their problems. This type of support includes (1) unassisted support such as answers to Frequently Asked Questions (FAQs) and the download of software patches and (2) assisted support such as peer-to-peer online fora, e-mail and online chat. Other informational support includes the provision of information and knowledge to assist with enquiries and enable customers to access best-practice – for example, by the publication of White Papers. Transactional support includes case tracking, whereby the customer initially documents their IT problem scenario, requests assistance from the support organisation, and is subsequently able to monitor the support organisation's progress in resolving this problem. Proactive support includes the embedding of problem detection support software on customer end-user computers, and personalised messages directing the customer to potential product or service purchases. In the study reported in this article we consider primarily informational and transactional supplementary support services.

WSSs can reduce customer support expenses by empowering employees (Support Agents). These employees provide support in the form of knowledge such as solutions to customers' IT problems. WSSs boost Support Agent productivity by providing access to a comprehensive knowledge base that includes many solutions, delivering convenient and higher quality support, and increasing customer loyalty and retention.

Non-IT businesses outsource IT support services to service providers because IT is not their core competency, service levels are likely to improve, and Total Cost of Ownership should be reduced (CRMInd, 2006; SSPA, 2004). Furthermore, client firms are often receptive to Web-based support delivery (SSPA, 2004). Thus the Web is considered by customer firms as an important channel for IT support delivery.

Despite the potential benefits of a WSS to service providers and enterprise customers, there has been a long-reported dissatisfaction with Web-based self-service (Barnes et al., 2000; Meuter et al., 2003; Ragsdale, 2007). Clearly success from the use of a WSS cannot be assumed and the criti-

cal success factors (CSFs) and challenges involved should be identified and addressed.

The study that is reported in this article identified a set of CSFs (Cooper et al, 2005, 2006a, 2006b; Cooper, 2007) and also identified important challenges, as perceived by IT service providers, many of which relate to other key stakeholders. In the next section we develop a stakeholder-oriented framework which situates WSSs in a broader enterprise customer service context and highlights the interactions with stakeholders.

STAKEHOLDER-ORIENTED RELATIONAL WEB-BASED ENTERPRISE CUSTOMER SERVICE

A broad definition of stakeholders is "all those parties who either affect or who are affected by an organisation's actions, behaviours and policies" (Mitroff, 1983). Management concerns about stakeholders arise because stakeholders have varying perspectives of the underlying problems and their ideal solutions may differ. It is important to business success that a firm resolve conflicting stakeholder needs (Hatch, 1997).

Experts report that the needs, roles, responsibilities, relationships and other interactions of stakeholders are especially important to the success of business-to-business (B2B) commerce (Chua et al., 2005; Kandampully, 2003; Pan, 2005; Ritter & Gemunden, 2003; Schultze & Orlikowski, 2004; Singh & Byrne, 2005). In B2B, businesses are increasingly interdependent and the stakeholder issues must be carefully managed (Kumar & van Dissel, 1996). However stakeholder roles and responsibilities along the value chain are complex (Chi & Holsapple, 2005; Ritter & Gemunden, 2003). Chi and Holsapple propose a model of stakeholder collaboration in B2B highlighting three behavioural processes: knowledge sharing, participative decision-making and conflict governance. Other reasons for understanding stakeholder issues in B2B commerce include the need to manage stakeholder expectations (Singh & Byrne, 2005).

Stakeholder relationships in services are different to mere service encounters and are associated with emotions and expectations (Gutek et al., 1999). Such relationships and associated knowledge flows are important in managed IT services environments (Dahlberg & Nyrhinen, 2006; Xu, 2007) as the quality of knowledge exchange influences the quality of outsourcing relationships (Gong et al., 2007). Of interest to this article, the adoption of WSSs can potentially strengthen stakeholder relationships (Bhappu & Schultze, 2006).

From the evidence above and a review of the literature (Cooper, 2007) we have developed a framework (Cooper et al., 2006a) that conceptualises key stakeholders and relationships in a B2B service context. Such a framework can be helpful in understanding complex knowledge transfer from service providers to customer firms. As mentioned earlier, such knowledge transfer is central to the provision of IT support. The framework in Figure 1 depicts key relationships between the main stakeholder types and a WSS. It shows three key types of stakeholder organisations which may be involved in support provision – a support organisation (previously termed "service provider"), business partner, and customer organisation – and their interaction with one another directly and indirectly via a WSS. At each organisation there are corporate entity representatives (for example, managers) interacting with end-users. The framework clearly highlights the interdependencies found in the multi-stakeholder managed IT support environment.

Knowledge Transfer for IT Support of Enterprise Customers Using WSS

The key knowledge process explored in this article is inter-organisational knowledge transfer. We focus on reviewing staged processual and network models of knowledge transfer for reasons of relevance.

Researchers advocating a staged processual approach to knowledge transfer argue that this can unlock the inner workings of the process and enable a more nuanced identification of barriers and enablers (Szulanski 1996). Staged inter-organisational knowledge transfer models include

Figure 1. A stakeholder-oriented relational framework for web-based enterprise customer service (Cooper et al, 2006a)

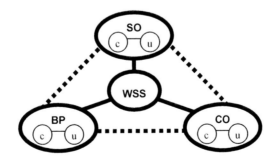

LEGEND
SO = Support Organisation   c = Corporate Entity   WSS = Web-based Self-service System
BP = Business Partner Organisation u = End-User Entity   ___ = Relationship via WSS
CO = Customer Organisation   - - - = Direct Relationship

Figure 2. Knowledge transfer in managed after-sales Web-based IT support (Cooper et al, 2006a)

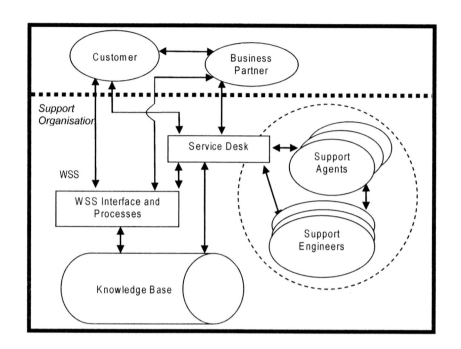

those developed by Cranefield and Yoong (2005) and Nieminen (2005). Cranefield and Yoong's (2005) model comprises six stages: engaging; defining; seeking; articulating; integrating; and disseminating. Among the benefits of this model is its identification of key organisational influences on knowledge transfer during each stage. However the factors identified as most relevant to knowledge transfer in an inter-organisational context are the need for fit between the transferred knowledge and the receiving organisation's current organisational objectives and traditional discipline area, and the need to avoid use of "non-transferable examples" which cannot be readily transferred to other organisational contexts. Nieminen's (2005) model of inter-organisational knowledge transfer focuses on the role of a receiving organisation in enabling knowledge transfer. He writes of the need for a receiving organisation to have a range of competencies among its employees in order to reduce any significant absorptive gap (Lane &

Lubatkin, 1998) between the two firms involved in the transfer. Researchers proposing a networking approach to knowledge transfer also adopt a relational approach based on understanding how patterns of connections between individuals and groups facilitate knowledge sharing and knowledge transfer (Kakabadse et al., 2003).

We next describe the knowledge transfer process in the managed IT support context (Figure 2) drawing on literature and empirical data from a case study (Cooper, 2007). IT service providers respond to enterprise customers' after-sales enquiries, incidents and problems regarding core IT products and services by providing and transferring support-oriented knowledge. The knowledge is complex and based on solutions to the enquiries, incidents and problems reported.

Both tacit and explicit knowledge may be transferred. Tacit knowledge is knowledge that resides in the mind and is difficult to articulate. Explicit knowledge is a representation of knowledge. An example of explicit knowledge in the managed after-sales IT support context is an IT solution stored in a knowledge base.

As shown in Figure 2, when a customer firm experiences IT incidents or problems, IT professionals at the firm may use the telephone channel or Web interface to obtain a solution. When the telephone is chosen, first tier Support Agents identify potential solutions by accessing tacit knowledge or by using the WSS to search the solutions knowledge base. More complex problems are escalated to more experienced Support Agents. Tiers of Support Engineers resolve the most difficult problems by drawing on valuable tacit knowledge. New and evolving solutions are captured in the knowledge base as explicit knowledge and organised for reuse. Successive efforts are made by Support Agents to address related customer questions. Such efforts aim to assist the customer firm in institutionalising support-oriented knowledge. Business partners may assist in the knowledge transfer process by providing partial solutions or other support and may have access to the service provider's WSS knowledge base.

RESEARCH DESIGN

Initially a comprehensive literature review was undertaken. Next, in 2005 an in-depth case study was conducted at the Australian headquarters of a large best-in-class multinational IT services organisation, "ServIT" (a pseudonym). ServIT had previously secured prestigious global awards for its WSS. It defined a successful WSS as one that delivers increased customer satisfaction while reducing service provision costs and this definition of success was used throughout the project. Case data was collected from semi-structured interviews with twelve senior customer service managers, IT support managers and support staff, observations of WSS use, document collection,

and a focusing workshop (Rockart, 1979) with participation by five senior customer service managers and IT support managers. Case study data were analysed using qualitative content analysis techniques (Mayring 2000) by two researchers working independently to identify the key challenges relating to stakeholders. A set of CSFs for the transfer of after-sales IT solution-oriented knowledge to enterprise customers when a WSS is used, and a set of key challenges, have been identified.

In 2006 a focus group of Australian senior customer service and IT support managers from an additional five large multinational IT service provider organisations, all with successful WSSs, was conducted, seeking to confirm and extend the findings from the ServIT case study. In the focus group discussion it became clear that, while the WSS of each company was successful, various challenges remained. Two researchers working independently confirmed and extended the set of CSFs and key challenges working inductively from the transcript. *Many of the challenges were found to be related to other stakeholders and it is these challenges which are the focus of this article.*

The quality of the findings was assured by appropriate techniques. Achieving validity in qualitative research requires a fair, honest and balanced account from the viewpoint of someone who lives in the social situation (Neuman, 2006). Construct validity was assured in the study by use of multiple sources of evidence. Participants were also given copies of interview summaries and the outcomes from each phase of the research were provided to participants for confirmation. Reliability was increased via a case study protocol (Yin 2003) to document all procedures and problems. Triangulation was achieved by collecting and analysing data from a variety of sources at ServIT and establishing consistency of results. The results of the cross-organisational focus group added another level of triangulation.

FINDINGS

The six participating IT service providers utilised WSS strategies to increase customer satisfaction while reducing the cost of IT support provision. Each firm offered a suite of informational, trans-actional and proactive support services using WSSs. Twenty-seven CSFs were identified. While the CSFs are not the focus of this article they are summarised for reference in the Appendix. The CSFs were also classified non-orthogonally into six categories:

- Organisational Commitment and Readiness: The organisation must manage the policies, processes and cultural issues which will affect its ability and willingness to embrace Web-based Self-service.
- Manage for Strategic and Operational Benefits: The WSS strategy must assist the organisation in attaining its strategic and operational objectives.
- KM Capabilities and Processes: The organisation must practice the principles of knowledge management and implement associated knowledge management processes, to maximise the benefits received from the WSS strategy.
- IT Infrastructure Capability: The organisation must have an adequate IT infrastructure in place, to enable it to participate in Web-based Self-service.
- Experience Management: The WSS should manage the stakeholder's experience, both at the corporate and end-user level. The stakeholder experience will directly affect satisfaction levels and therefore ongoing use of the WSS.
- Content: The WSS must contain useful, accurate and up-to-date content in order to resolve the end-user's support issue or knowledge requirement.

These six categories were believed by the IT service provider participants in the study to apply to *all* three stakeholder organisations (that is, those shown in Figure 1). This finding is discussed further in the next section, as it presented one of the main challenges for IT service providers. Further details of the CSFs may be found in earlier publications (Cooper et al, 2005, 2006a, 2006b).

SERVICE PROVIDER PERCEPTIONS OF STAKEHOLDER-ORIENTED CHALLENGES

This section summarises the eight major challenges faced by IT service provider firms, pertaining to key stakeholders. Representative quotes from the ServIT case study and cross-organisational focus group illuminate the challenges. Company names are pseudonyms for reasons of anonymity. The reader is reminded that the findings have been derived from the perspective of the IT support firm only. A further comment on this limitation is made at the end of the article.

First, participants strongly believed that <u>all</u> stakeholder viewpoints should be considered by an IT support organisation when planning, implementing and managing a WSS for after-sales IT support provision. Similar findings were made for electronic business settings more generally by Kandampully (2003) and Singh and Byrne (2005). However our study highlighted the potential for different stakeholder types to hold unique perceptions. For example, while a support organisation may find the transfer of IT solutions to a customer firm highly desirable, it was questioned by IT service provider participants whether end-users at a customer enterprise would feel the same way:

I think the provider [support organisation] is interested in transferring knowledge so [that] they don't have a problem any more and they can manage their costs and help the customers. [However, the customer firm's end-user is thinking] I am interested, not in receiving knowledge ... [but] I am interested in my problem being fixed. Don't give me all this stuff [the details of the problem and solution]. Tell me what the problem is so I can fix it. I don't want the transferring of any knowledge. (Senior IT Architect, I-Systems)

This is an important finding deserving of further research. If an end-user at a customer firm does not wish to learn from a provided IT solution, how can a support organisation ensure such learning? Proposed cost and efficiency benefits to a support organisation stemming from knowledge transfer may have negative implications for customer satisfaction. It should be noted however that end-users at a customer firm have specialised job roles with role-based knowledge needs. Thus, for example, while some end-users may only desire a resumption of IT operations using a supplied solution, other personnel such as Database Administrators are likely to be highly interested in learning about a solution and gaining more general support knowledge which could be useful at a future time. On the other hand if a professional at an enterprise customer has full knowledge of a solution the customer organisation may become increasingly independent of the support organisation. Ultimately the success of the support organisation can be affected. Thus there may be a level of knowledge which a support organisation may wish to retain and not transfer to customer firms.

Second, participants questioned whether the different stakeholder types might interpret the requirements for CSFs (Appendix) differently. For example, for *CSF-9 Ease of use* participants mentioned that regular end-users of the WSS interface would prefer an efficient interface, whereas novice users would prefer easy-to-use interfaces. As a second example, for *CSF-1 Cost-effectiveness* some participants mentioned that cost-effectiveness

to a support organisation, when a WSS is used, is not the same as cost-effectiveness from the perspective of an end-user at the customer firm. End-users are concerned with efficiency gains and usefulness of the knowledge gained from the WSS to perform their jobs (Cenfetelli et al., 2005), rather than the financial costs involved.

Cost effectiveness, from both the end-user of the service and for ServIT, are equally important, but I think you will find some subtleties in [how they are] both explained as cost-effectiveness. For an end-user it's 'Can I actually get the results quickly from my perspective?' From ServIT's perspective, it is 'Can we actually reduce the cost of this service for our customers so that we are actually making a profit? (Consulting Services Division Manager, ServIT)

Third, as described earlier, the six CSF categories were found to apply to *all three* stakeholder organisations. This finding supports prior research by Schultze and Bhappu (2005) who note that customers are often partly responsible for a service provider's success. Clearly, a support organisation will have very little control over whether a customer organisation and business partner organisation do, in fact, address the six CSF categories. As a result, performance measurement and management of WSS strategies in a B2B context will be challenging.

Kurnia and Johnston (2002) note the importance of industry capability in internet trading for corporate adoption of an inter-organisational system. Thus if corporate customers and business partners in a managed IT support situation do not manage the CSFs, the support organisation's WSS may not be successful. As electronic commerce environments are increasingly interdependent (Kumar & van Dissel, 1996; Kurnia & Johnston 2002), a support organisation may benefit from providing further assistance to business partners and customer organisations to better manage the key factors.

One promising strategy may be for a support organisation to conduct education and training programs with partner and customer organisations to increase their awareness and understanding of CSFs. Such education and training could be provided by online support, training, newsletters and so on. Indeed participants also identified the importance of education and training in terms of developing relationships with the customer and ultimately meeting key objectives for CRM. Thus education and training programs will not only provide partner and customer firms with the required knowledge to increase their awareness of WSSs but will provide an opportunity for the support organisation to better understand the needs of the customer and business partners in a WSS context. This finding supports current literature highlighting the importance of developing relationships with enterprise customers when providing support services (Peppers & Rogers, 2001; Pujari, 2004).

A second strategy that is more challenging would be to ensure, when developing external service contracts, that customer and business partner organisations are obliged to meet minimum standards relating to CSFs. Any failure to address CSFs at customer firms and business partners would affect the ability of a support organisation to service them effectively. However such a strategy may be incompatible with the development of improved relationships with business partners and customer firms. It is also important to recall that this study only investigated the IT support organisation perspective. While IT support organisations identified the CSFs as important also for partner and customer firms to address, studies of partner and customer perspectives of CSFs may provide quite different results. This question should be explored in future research.

Fourth, the interesting issue was raised of whether relationships are possible—or even enabled—by a WSS. A two-way relationship was posited by several participants, whereby if an end-user trusts the Web-site and the organisation behind it, this trust forms part of the relationship, with the WSS simply providing the connection:

Although it is a piece of software, it is the front end of a company. For instance, if I feel I have a positive relationship with my Netbank Web-site because I trust it, then that is part of the relationship. (IT Customer Consultant, DistSystems)

Others, however, saw Web-based relationships as perhaps one-way only, whereby it was questioned whether there is a relationship between the end-user and the providing organisation, when the end-user uses the WSS anonymously.

Fifth, it was also suggested that stakeholder relationships can be more complex than Figure 1 allows. Participants observed that relationships with stakeholder types may vary.

We can have the relationship with either both the customer and the business partner or we can have it directly with the customer or we could just have it with the business partner...I mean there are just so many different combinations that that relationship can actually take. (IT Customer Consultant, DistSystems)

Consequently in some instances Figure 1 should be modified. For example, for supporting some customer firms a business partner is involved, while for supporting other customers there are no business partners involved.

The complexity of relationships would also increase as stakeholder organisations increase in size. Multiple relationships would be developed at the individual, departmental and corporate levels. This finding is significant as while it has been acknowledged in a growing body of literature that developing relationships with partners is important (e.g. Vlachopoulou & Manthou, 2003), there is very little literature concerning partner-unit-based relationships.

Sixth, intellectual property (IP), security and privacy issues were found problematic for stakeholder-oriented reasons. Inter-organisational firms in collaborative relationships must protect certain knowledge which may be strategic (Solitander 2006). In the present study, service provider firms were concerned about the loss of IP in the leverage of user fora for customer support. In such fora, end-users may provide solutions to reported problems however it can be unclear who owns the IP that is the solution. Scholars have noted that in customer co-production of service, as illustrated by this situation, new models of digital governance and customer-based innovation are needed (Rai & Sambamurthy, 2006).

IT support organisations, business partners and customers frequently operate across international borders. Support organisations must consider issues of security, privacy and IP within the context of off-shore environments (Rai & Sambamurthy, 2006; Tafti, 2005). The IT service providers in this study expressed uncertainty about the ability of national legal systems to deal with such complex issues. For example, customer end-users may be unaware of the location where their personal information is stored and retrieved. Further, while customer organisations may be aware that, in some instances, third parties such as a support organisation's business partners have access to their stored personal information, they may not be aware of the eventual *use* of this information or its accessibility. A perceived potential privacy violation may lead to unforeseen competitor problems – for example, where business partners compete with a customer enterprise. Sensitive information, knowledge and IP may indeed be compromised (Rai & Sambamurthy, 2006).

A really interesting one that is going through the legal battles now and it comes back to privacy. As a main [support] organisation, you have information that could be of a private nature. If you then make the information available to another

organisation that does not have the same privacy policy as you, and then [if they] were to use that information in such a way that it violates somebody's privacy, who is ultimately responsible? That is a huge legal question that is being tested now. Does it come back to the original person or the person who let the information go? (Emerging Technology Consultant, OpSys)

Seventh, understanding the complexities of the business partner alliance was an issue. Not all service providers participating in the study agreed with the distinction between a business partner relationship and a customer/supplier relationship. For example, a participant from one organisation claimed that his organisation did not have business partners, while others claimed that their organisations were, in fact, partners of his organisation. It was advocated that the distinction between a business partner and customer/supplier relationship, surrounds whether the relationship is a one-off transaction, or whether it is an ongoing relationship. In an enterprise IT services context, however, there is an apparent blurring of relationships. In some projects, organisations may be considered business partners, while in others they would be considered competitors:

DistSystems, DataCorp, OpSys and I-Systems can say, we have been working together as business partners and as competitors and sometimes even on the same bid…on the one hand you compete, in the next 30 seconds, I might be talking to OpSys about something we are competitors about, and in another thing we are working together on, you switch hats, you switch alliances, it is just the way things are these days…. (Senior Systems Consultant, I-Systems)

Some of the complexities of business partner alliances surround intellectual property and security and privacy, discussed earlier. Lei (1997) argues that, with respect to strategic alliances, regardless of the various types of legal structures which may be put in place, over time companies will absorb and internalise skills, regardless of the amount of formal, legal ownership that is demarcated by the alliance structure. Further, Ferdinand and Simm (2007) suggest a need for increased research on illegal inter-organisational knowledge transfer. Participants in our research study also expressed a need for greater understanding of this complex area. They believed it likely that associated concerns would continue in the foreseeable future.

Eighth, managing customer contributions to service was considered an important challenge. The growing literature on co-production highlights the productivity benefits as well as the managerial challenges that arise when customers become "partial employees" (Benapudi & Leone, 2003). The advantages of co-production include decreased cost of service provision and greater control and autonomy for the customer, while disadvantages include the difficulty of controlling service quality when customers are actively involved in the production process (Schultze & Bhappu, 2005).

In the study IT service providers raised concerns relating to the contribution of knowledge by customers to their own service fulfillment, optimisation and improvement. At ServIT when customers interacted and shared resolution-knowledge in online for a the knowledge was not captured permanently. Further, the online fora were open to a variety of end-users causing new issues of accuracy and liability:

ServIT has ventured into the hosting of forums. Solutions can be provided by non-ServIT people and that's a potential conflict between the reliability of our knowledge and the fact that we are opening up [knowledge] to end-users, which could have a good result, but there is a danger that we are facilitating the [incorrect] solution. (IT Manager, ServIT)

ServIT invests significant resources in its legal team and explicitly states in the terms and conditions of using the WSS and in support contracts that ServIT will not be responsible for any degradation of a customer's systems, if an enterprise customer decides to act upon information derived from the WSS. Another challenge is that while ServIT monitors fora content, it relies more on a "merit" based system whereby forum users are allocated merit points by original posters (of questions) when they provide valuable responses. A system of points aggregation motivates users to share valuable knowledge and thus contribute to E-service provision. However, the researchers found from forum observations that this scheme occasionally led to highly successful users moving on to create their own sites independently of the service provider, such was their fame and following.

Other potentially negative impacts of customer co-contribution include potential defamation in the fora. While the terms and conditions of posting to online fora state that users should not post defamatory statements, such defamation sometimes eventuates.

DISCUSSION

The findings above suggest a need for industry sector improvement. For the IT support industry to learn to do things better, learning at the industry level is needed. Prior studies suggest the importance of business learning in a network context (c.f. Knight, 2002). This would entail new collaborative electronic business projects focused on IT support provision involving IT service providers, business partners and customer organisations. According to Cameron's (2005) review of prior relevant studies, there are four important influences to consider for successful electronic business collaboration: motivation, capability, communication and coordination.

First, organisations must be motivated to participate in collaborative projects. Second, the desire to increase organisational capability (skills and knowledge) can be a powerful motivator. Third, it is important to communicate about the value of such collaborative projects within organisations. Fourth, industry groups can assist in coordinating such projects for successful conclusions.

As many of the key challenges identified in the previous section centre on the potential for stakeholder conflict, the development of individual IT service contracts (including service requirements) with customer firms and business partners requires attention. This process should entail greater clarification and negotiation of stakeholder needs. The objectives of each organisation should be articulated during joint planning, which is an important aspect of business collaboration in supply chains (Holsapple & Jin, 2007). Holsapple and Jin note several other important collaborative decisions typically made in a supply chain. The findings from our study suggest a need for focused studies seeking to identify key problem points in decision-making where stakeholder conflicts are influential so that the overall process can be improved to avoid or manage such conflicts. Chi and Holsapple (2005) propose a model of stakeholder collaboration in B2B highlighting three behavioural processes: knowledge sharing, participative decision-making and conflict governance. Our study provides support for the importance of such processes.

The findings and discussion above also suggest a need for supporting infrastructure. Electronic marketplaces offer a recognised structure which may be useful to support both collaborative IT support projects and specific supply chains (Markus & Christiaanse, 2003). However there are also challenges in using electronic marketplaces successfully. In a recent case study of an electronic marketplace, the key influences affecting its success were the loss of social capital, nature of communication channels used, time taken to

reach critical mass, and power imbalances among participants (Driedonks et al., 2005).

The risk of reduced service quality was identified in the practice of customer co-contribution to service. This concern was noted more generally for online service provision by Schultze and Bhappu (2005). There may be ways for IT service firms to better monitor customer contributions via user fora and capture the high quality solutions (which currently are not captured). Related questions of knowledge ownership must be resolved. However regulatory issues at different geographic locations cloud the resolution of such questions.

Indeed there were several areas identified where IT service providers suffer from inadequate regulatory support. The security, privacy and IP issues experienced in the often-offshore managed IT support environment highlight the need for clarification and awareness of relevant regulations and laws at industry, national and international levels. IT support companies also seek to understand how to share knowledge with business competitors within strategic alliances while maintaining a competitive advantage. New theories are sought to underpin such knowledge sharing in an increasingly collaborative global business environment.

The six IT service provider companies in our study uniformly noted that the key objective for use of a WSS for after-sales IT support was to increase customer satisfaction while reducing support costs. This objective was expected to be achieved by relational as well as transactional methods. However as the study showed, the successful accomplishment of both goals can be problematic (also found by Bunduchi, 2005). Research is beginning to appear on the enabling of relationships in service provision when the internet is used to facilitate service provision. In a business to consumer (B2C) context, Sigala (2007) explored online travel service provision and found that the communication aspect of the online service played a key role in relationship development. Where provider-consumer communication was enhanced by use of relevant communication tools, relationships and client satisfaction were improved. Thus IT support organisations may find that the path to satisfying the relational aspect of WSS success is by better leveraging the internet's communication tools and customising communication-oriented content.

Some of the challenges identified in our study relate to the process of knowledge transfer. For example, it was noted that a customer firm end-user may not be interested in institutionalizing transferred IT solutions. Cranefield and Yoong (2005), in identifying key challenges in inter-organisational knowledge transfer, highlighted the need for a fit between the knowledge received and the receiving organisation's objectives. If a customer firm does not prioritise the institution-alization of IT solutions throughout the firm, its employees will not make the effort to learn the solutions transferred from the service provider and will simply apply them to resolve the initial problem. This suggests a need for IT service providers to educate their customers about the importance of institutionalizing IT solutions to their organisation. Nieminen (2005) noted that for knowledge transfer to take place, a receiving organisation must be capable of absorbing shared knowledge. Such capability may be missing from the customer firms which are receiving IT solutions.

CONCLUSION

This article has identified and discussed eight major stakeholder-oriented challenges in the provision of managed after-sales IT support services via WSSs to enterprise customers, from the perspective of multinational IT service providers. Specifically:

- All stakeholder viewpoints should be considered by an IT support organisation when planning, implementing and managing a WSS for after-sales IT support provision;
- Different stakeholder types might interpret the requirements for CSFs differently;
- The six CSF categories identified apply to *all* three stakeholder organisations, however a support organisation will have very little control over whether a customer organisation and business partner organisation do, in fact, address these categories. Thus performance measurement and management of WSS strategies in a B2B context will be difficult;
- It is problematic whether relationships are possible, or even enabled by a WSS;
- Stakeholder relationships can be more complex than Figure 1 allows;
- Intellectual property, security and privacy issues can be problematic for stakeholder-oriented reasons;
- Understanding the complexities of the business partner alliance can be an issue; and
- Managing customer contributions to service is an important challenge.

The findings demonstrate that best-in-class IT service providers face diverse challenges to better understand and resolve potential conflicting stakeholder needs in this context.

Theoretically this article provides numerous insights into the key challenges faced by IT service providers, relating to the different stakeholders, in the provision of B2B after-sales IT support services via WSSs. The article also highlights a need for new theories which integrate WSS strategies across the multiple stakeholders involved. Our findings further suggest that relationship development by WSSs is poorly understood by the companies involved and that further research is needed to develop new understandings.

This article also assists IT service providers by recommending that all stakeholder viewpoints and issues should be considered when planning, implementing and managing WSSs in the managed after-sales IT support context. Addressing diverse stakeholder needs may be particularly challenging in some areas such as security, privacy and IP. Such emerging challenges highlight the complexities of working with business partners which are also considered competitors. Greater collaboration is needed with better supporting infrastructure and regulation.

While the findings from this article are limited by the context (managed after-sales IT support) and scope (the IT support organisation perspective only was studied), they are indicative of possible concerns that other types of service providers may have in offering supplementary E-services using WSSs. Thus the findings provide a foundation for exploration in other settings. Investigating the customer and business partner perspectives would also provide valuable balance to the views expressed and analysed in this article.

ACKNOWLEDGMENT

This article is a significantly extended and updated version of a article published in the *Proceedings of the 20th Bled eConference (Bled07)*, Bled, Slovenia, 4-6 June 2007. The authors are grateful to the anonymous reviewers whose valuable advice helped improve the quality of this article.

REFERENCES

Barnes, J.G., Dunne, P.A. and Glynn, W.J. (2000). Self-service and Technology: Unanticipated and Unintended Effects on Customer Relationships. Handbook of Services Marketing and Management, Swartz, T.A. and Iabocobucci, D. (eds.), Sage Publications, Thousand Oaks, California, 89-102.

Barua, A., Konana, P., Whinston, A.B. and Yin, F. (2004). An Empirical Investigation of Net-enabled Business Value. *MIS Quarterly.* 28(4), December, 585-620.

Benapudi, N. and Leone, R.P. (2003). "Psychological Implications of Customer Participation in Co-production", *Journal of Marketing.* 67(1), January, 14-28.

Bhappu, A.D. and Schultze, U. (2006). The Role of Relational and Operational Performance in Business-to-Business Customers' Adoption of Self-Service Technology. *Journal of Service Research.* 8(4), 372 – 385.

Brohman, M.K., Watson, R.T., Piccoli, G. and Parasuraman, A. (2003). Data Completeness: A Key to Effective Net-based Customer Service Systems, *Communications from the Association for Computing Machinery.* 46(6), 47-51.

Bunduchi, R. (2005). Business Relationships in Internet-based Electronic Markets: The Role of Goodwill Trust and Transaction Costs. *Information Systems Journal.* 15 (4), 321–341.

Cameron, J. (2005). Ten Concepts for an eBusiness Collaborative Project Management Framework. In *Proceedings of eIntegration in Action: 18ᵗʰ Bled eConference*, June 6-8 2005, Bled, Slovenia.

Cenfetelli, R., Benbasat, I. and Al-Natour, S. (2005). Information technology mediated customer service: A functional perspective. In *Proceedings of ICIS 2005*, Las Vegas, USA.

Chi, L. and Holsapple, C. (2005). Understanding Computer-mediated Interorganisational Collaboration: A Model and Framework. *Journal of Knowledge Management.* 9(1), 53-75.

Chua, C.E.H., Khoo, H.M., Straub, D.W., Kadiyala, S. and Kuechler, D. (2005). The Evolution of E-commerce Research: A Stakeholder Perspective. *Journal of Electronic Commerce Research.* 6(4), 262-280.

Cooper, V.A. (2007). Knowledge Transfer in Enterprise IT Support Provision using Web-based Self-Service, unpublished PhD Thesis, Deakin University, Melbourne, Australia.

Cooper, V.A., Lichtenstein, S. and Smith, R. (2006a). Enabling the Transfer of Information Technology Support Knowledge to Enterprise Customers Using Web-based Self-service systems: Critical Success Factors from the Support Organisation Perspective, in *Proceedings of Seventeenth Australasian Conference on Information Systems (ACIS 2006)*, Adelaide, Australia.

Cooper, V., Lichtenstein, S. & Smith, R. (2006b) Knowledge transfer in enterprise information technology support using web-based self-service systems, *International Journal of Technology Marketing*, 1(2), 145-170.

Cooper, V.A., Lichtenstein, S. & Smith, R. (2005) Emerging Issues in After-sales Enterprise Information Technology Support Using Web-based Self-service Systems, in *Proceedings of Sixteenth Australasian Conference on Information Systems (ACIS 2005)*, University of Technology Sydney, 30 November – 2 December, 2005, Sydney.

Cranefield, J. and Yoong, P. (2005). Organisational Factors Affecting Inter-organisational Knowledge Transfer in the New Zealand State Sector: A Case Study. *The Electronic Journal for Virtual Organisations and Networks*. 7, December.

[CRMInd] CRMIndustry.com (2006). 2006 State of IT Outsourcing. Summary report, <http://www.crmindustry.com/industry_research/outsourcing.htm> (Accessed 03 June 2008).

[CSI] Consortium Service Innovation (2002). Getting Started with KCS. Official Consortium Service Innovation Site, <http://www.thinkhdi.com/files/pdfs/GettingStartedKCS.pdf> (Accessed 03 June 2008).

Dahlberg, T. and Nyrhinen, M. (2006). A New Instrument to Measure the Success of IT Outsourcing. In *Proceedings of the 39th Hawaii International Conference on System Sciences (HICSS'2006)*, IEEE Society Press.

Doyle, S. (2007). Self-service Delivery and the Growing Roles of Channels. *The Journal of Database Marketing & Customer Strategy Management*. 14(2), January , 150-159.

Driedonks, C., Gregor, S. and Wassenaar, A. (2005). Economic and Social analysis of the Adoption of B2B Electronic Marketplaces: A Case Study in the Australian Beef Industry. *International Journal of Electronic Commerce*. 9(3), Spring, 49-72.

Ferdinand, J. and Simm, D. (2007). Re-theorizing External Learning: Insights from Economic and Industrial Espionage. *Management Learning*. 38(3), 297-317.

Geib, M., Kolb, L. and Brenner, W. (2006). Collaborative Customer Management. Financial Services Alliances. In (Fjermestad, J. and Romano, N.C. (eds)), *Electronic Customer Relationship Management*, Armonk, New York.

Gong, H., Tate, M. and Alborz, S. (2007). Managing the Outsourcing Marriage to Achieve Success. In *Proceedings of Hawaii International Conference on the System Sciences (HICSS'07)*, IEEE Society Press.

Gutek, B., Bhappu, A.D., Liao-Troth, M.A. and Cherry, B. (1999). Distinguishing between Service Relationships and Encounters. *Journal of Applied Psychology*. 84(2), 218-233.

Hatch, M.J. (1997). *Organisation Theory: Modern, Symbolic and Postmodern Perspectives*. Oxford:UK, Oxford University Press.

Hofacker, C. F., Goldsmith, R.G., Bridges, E. and Swilley, E. (2007). E-Services: A Synthesis and Research Agenda. *Journal of Value Chain Management*. 1(1/2), 13-44.

Holsapple, C.W. and Jin, H. (2007). Connecting Some Dots: E-commerce, Supply Chains and Collaborative Decision Making. *Decision Line.* 38(5), October, 14-21.

Kakabadse, N.K., Kakabadse, A. and Kouzmin, A. (2003). Reviewing the Knowledge Management Literature: Towards a Taxonomy. *Journal of Knowledge Management Practice.* 7(4), 75-91.

Kandampully, J. (2003). B2B Relationships and Networks in the Internet Age. *Management Decision.* 41(5), 443-451.

Khalifa, M. and Shen, N. (2005). Effects of Electronic Customer Relationship Management on Customer Satisfaction: A Temporal Model. In *Proceedings of the 38th Annual Hawaii International Conference on System Sciences (HICSS'05),* IEEE Society Press.

Knight, L. (2002). Network Learning: Exploring Learning by Interorganizational Networks. *Human Relations.* 55(4), 427-454.

Koh, C., Ang, S. and Straub, D.W. (2004). IT Outsourcing Success: A Psychological Contract Perspective. *Information Systems Research.* 15(4), 356-373.

Kumar, K. and van Dissel, H.G. (1996). Sustainable Collaboration: Managing Conflict and Cooperation in Interorganisational Systems. *MIS Quarterly,* 20(3), 279-300.

Kurnia, S. and Johnston, R. (2002). A Review of Approaches to EC-enabled IOS Adoption Studies. In *Proceedings of the 35th Annual Hawaii Conference on System Sciences (HICSS'02),* IEEE Society Press.

Lane, P.J. and Lubatkin, M. (1998). Relative Absorptive Capacity and Inter-organisational Learning, *Strategic Management Journal.* 19(5), 461-477.

Lei, D.T. (1997). Competence-building, Technology Fusion and Competitive Advantage: The Key Roles of Organisational Learning and Strategic Alliances. *International Journal of Technology Management.* 14(2/3/4), 208-37.

Levenburg, N.M. and Klein, H.A. (2006). Delivering customer services online: identifying best practices of medium-sized enterprises. *Information Systems Journal.* 16(2), 135-155.

Markus, M.L. and Christiaanse, E. (2003). Adoption and Impact of Electronic Marketplaces. *Information Systems and E-Business Management.* 1(2), January, 139-155.

Mayring, P. (2000). Qualitative Content Analysis, Forum Quality Social Research, (1)2. <http://www.qualitative-research.net/fqs-texte/2-00/2-00mayring-e.htm> (Accessed 3 June 2008).

Mitroff, I.I. (1983). *Stakeholders of the Organisational Mind.* Jossey-Bass. San Francisco, CA.

Meuter, M.L., Ostrom, A., Bitner, M.J. and Roundtree, R. (2003). The Influence of Technology Anxiety on Consumer Use and Experiences with Self-service Technologies. *Journal of Business Research.* 56(11), 899-906.

Negash, S., Ryan, T. and Igbaria, M. (2003). Quality and Effectiveness in Web-based Customer Support Systems. *Information and Management.* 40(8), September, 757-768.

Neuman, W.L. (2006). *Social Research Methods: Qualitative and Quantitative Approaches,* Sixth Edition. Allwyn & Bacon, Boston, Massachusetts.

Nieminen, H. (2005). Organisational Receptivity – Understanding the Inter-organisational Learning Ability, *Electronic Journal of Knowledge Management.* 3(2), 107-118.

Otim, S. and Grover, V. (2006). An Empirical Study on Web-based Services and Customer Loyalty. *European Journal of Information Systems.* 15(6), 527-541.

Pan, G.S.C. (2005). Information Systems Project Abandonment: A Stakeholder Analysis. *International Journal of Information Management.* 25(2), 173-184.

Peppard, J. (2001). Bridging the Gap Between the IS Organisation and the Rest of the Business: Plotting a Route. *Information Systems Journal.* 11(3), 249-260.

Peppers, D. and Rogers, M. (2001). *One to One B2B: Customer Development Strategies for the Business-to-Business World*, Currency Doubleday, New York.

Piccoli, G., Brohman, M.K., Watson, R.T. and Parasuraman, A. (2004). Net-based Customer Service Systems: Evolution and Revolution in Web-site Functionalities. *Decision Sciences.* 35(3), 423-455.

Pitt, L.F., Berthon, P. and Lane, N. (1998). Gaps Within the IS Department: Barriers to Service Quality. *Journal of Information Technology.* 13(3), 191-200.

Pujari, D. (2004). Self-service with a Smile? Self-service Technology (SST) Encounters Among Canadian Business-to-Business. *International Journal of Service Industry Management.* 15(2), 200-219.

Ragsdale, J. (2007). Self-Service Success Continues to Decline; How Web 2.0 Can Help, Service and Support Professional Association, US.

Rai, A. and Sambamurthy, V. (2006). Editorial Notes – The Growth of Interest in Services Management: Opportunities for Information Systems Scholars. *Information Systems Research.* 17(4), 327 – 331,

Reichheld, F.F. and Schefter, P. (2000). E-Loyalty: Your Secret Weapon on the Web. *Harvard Business Review.* 78(4), July-August, 105-112.

Ritter, T. and Gemunden, H.D. (2003). Inter-organisational Relationships and Networks: an Overview. *Journal of Business Research.* 56, 691-697.

Rockart, J.F. (1979). Chief Executives Define their own Data Needs. *Harvard Business Review.* 57(2), March-April, 81-93.

Rust, R.T. (2001). The Rise of E-Service, *Journal of Service Research*, 3(4), May, 283-284.

Schultze, U. and Bhappu, A.D.P. (2005). Incorporating Self-Serve Technology into Co-production Designs. *International Journal of E-Collaboration.* 1(4), 1-23.

Schultze, U. and Orlikowski, W.J. (2004). Practice Perspective on Technology-mediated Network Relations: The Use of Internet-based Self-serve Technologies. *Information Systems Research.* 15(1), 87-106.

Sigala, M. (2007). Investigating the Internet's Impact on Interfirm Relations: Evidence from the Business Travel Management Distribution Chain. *Journal of Enterprise Information Management.* 20(3), 335-355.

Singh, M. and Byrne, J. (2005). Performance Evaluation of e-Business in Australia. *Electronic Journal of Information Systems Evaluation.* 8(2).

Solitander, M. (2006). Balancing the Flows: Managing the Intellectual Capital Flows in Inter-organisational Projects. *Electronic Journal of Knowledge Management.* 4(2), 197-206.

SSPA (2004). *2005 Support Demand Research Series.* Tech Strategy Partners and Service & Support Professionals Association.

Szulanski, G. (1996). Exploring Internal Stickiness: Impediments to the Transfer of Best Practice Within the Firm. *Strategic Management Journal.* 17, Special Issue, 27-43.

Tafti, M.H.A. (2005). Risk Factors Associated with Offshore IT Outsourcing. *Industrial Management & Data Systems.* 105(5), 549-560.

Vlachopoulou, M. and Manthou, V. (2003). Partnership Alliances in Virtual Markets. *International Journal of Physical Distribution and Logistics Management.* 33(3), 254-267.

Xu, L. (2007). Outsourcing and Multi-party Business Collaborations Modelling. *Journal of Electronic Commerce in Organisations.* 5(2), 77-96.

Yin, R.K. (2003). *Case Study Research, Design and Methods*, Fourth Edition. Sage Publications, Newbury Park.

APPENDIX.

CSFs for Knowledge Transfer from a Support Organisation to a Customer Organisation using WSSs (A)

Critical Success Factor	Description
CSF-1 Cost Effectiveness	The cost equation for providing/using web-based self-service must be better, or at least not worse, than providing/using non-web-based self-service.
CSF-2: Provision of Additional Services and Cross-Selling Opportunities	Current WSS transactions are used proactively as an opportunity to offer the customer organisation additional advice and services
CSF-3: Critical Mass: Knowledge Content and Knowledge Contributors	A sufficient number of end-users must proactively contribute sufficient knowledge content to the WSS knowledge base, to encourage all parties to initially use, and to continue to use, the WSS as a means of resolving their support issues or information requirements
CSF-4: Usefulness: Provision of Knowledge Which Meets User Requirements	The WSS must provide the functionality and knowledge required to meet the objectives of all stakeholders. For example, for the end-user customer, it should resolve a specific technical or business problem, or provide other required knowledge resources.
CSF-5: Ability to Provide Efficiency	Use of the WSS to resolve a support issue or provide other knowledge resources must be perceived as efficient by all parties. This is inclusive of not only the performance of the WSS tool but the surrounding processes for using the WSS.
CSF-6: Access, Connectivity, Availability and Performance	The providing organisation, relevant business partners and the customer organisation must have sufficient technology infrastructure in place, to enable all parties to participate in web-based self-service.
CSF-7: Effective Information Architecture and Search Engine	The WSS must have an effective Information Architecture and Search Engine such that the information system that organises and retrieves knowledge in the knowledge base is perceived as effective by end-users.
CSF-8: Security, Privacy and Assurance	All stakeholders using WSS must feel secure, private and confident in all aspects of WSS transactions including the stored data components of transactions. Issues surrounding information security and information privacy, and the need to keep confidential related company secrets (intellectual property) must be addressed.
CSF-9: Ease of Use/Usability	An end-user must perceive that use of the WSS does not demand excessive cognitive or ergonomic effort.
CSF-10: Early Positive Experience	The first few end-user experiences with the WSS must result in a positive outcome, where end-user needs are met and they feel valued, in order for the end-user to adopt WSS long term.
CSF-11: Positive Experience	Using the WSS on an ongoing basis must result in a positive outcome, where corporate customer needs and all types of end-users' needs are met and they also feel valued. A positive experience is closely related to customer organisation/end-user satisfaction
CSF-12 Confidence in Solution	The customer organisation/end-user must feel confident that the solution provided by the WSS will resolve their issue and will not result in further issues. They must also have self-confidence in their own ability to apply the offered solution.
CSF-13: Customer Focus: Understand Customer and their Requirements	The support organisation (and relevant business partners) must understand the individual business and technical needs of individual customer organisations and their end-users. With this understanding, WSS must be tailored to meet those individual needs.

APPENDIX.

CSFs for Knowledge Transfer from a Support Organisation to a Customer Organisation using WSSs (B)

Critical Success Factor	Description
CSF-14: Positive Relationship	The relationship between the support organisation, business partners and the customer organisation must be one which supports open communication and trust. This positive relationship should exist at both the corporate and end-user levels.
CSF-15: Provision of Additional Support: Education & Training	Additional assistance, or education and training in respect to how to use the WSS must be provided by the support organisation as requested by end-users.
CSF-16: Employee Focus	Management within the support organisation, business partner and customer organisations must have an understanding of the work processes and conditions which will affect the ability and willingness of employees to adopt the WSS and associated strategies. With this understanding, management must focus on meeting the needs of their employees where possible, in order to maximise employee productivity and the benefits received from the WSS strategy.
CSF-17: Culture	The support organisation should foster an environment that recognises that WSS is part of the way it wants to conduct business. In addition, an open, sharing culture is needed. The culture should extend to customer organisations and business partners.
CSF-18: Marketing and Awareness of Web-based Service	Marketing programs which raise awareness of and support for, the adoption of WSS, must be in place.
CSF-19: Knowledge Creation, Capture and Re-Use	Knowledge capture processes to ensure that valuable knowledge is created and captured into the WSS knowledge base by end-users must be in place. Knowledge reuse processes to ensure that this knowledge is subsequently accessed and re-used by end-users, must also be in place.
CSF-20: Knowledge Validation	Processes must be in place to ensure the accuracy of the knowledge which is captured into the WSS knowledge base and to ensure that once it is captured, it is frequently reviewed and updated for currency.
CSF-21: Knowledge Storage/Retrieval	Processes must be in place to ensure that the structure and format of captured knowledge facilitate findability.
CSF-22 : Presentation of Knowledge	The knowledge must be presented in a form which maximizes the understanding acquired by end-users.
CSF-23: Measurement & Feedback of WSS	Sufficient measurement and feedback methods for assessing the effectiveness of the WSS strategy must be in place.
CSF-24: Alignment and Integration	There must be alignment and integration between the WSS and other channels' support processes, as well as with related business processes, in the context of the business/industry environment.
CSF-25: WSS Override and Recovery	The capability for the end-user or WSS to over-ride transactions initially made via the WSS, must be in place, whereby if an end-user is not finding a satisfactory resolution via the WSS, the transaction is directed to an alternative mode of service delivery (e.g. a chat session or telephone call).
CSF-26: Ease of Re-initiation	A process must be in place whereby an end-user can easily re-initiate a support transaction to re-locate a previously retrieved resolution or other knowledge resource.
CSF-27 Top Management Support	Top management must provide ongoing support and commitment to the WSS and associated strategies.

This work was previously published in International Journal of E-Services and Mobile Applications, Vol. 1, Issue 1, edited by A. Scupola, pp. 1-20, copyright 2009 by IGI Publishing (an imprint of IGI Global).

Chapter 4.12
Mailing Lists and Social Semantic Web

Sergio Fernández
Fundación CTIC, Spain

Diego Berrueta
Fundación CTIC, Spain

Lian Shi
Fundación CTIC, Spain

Jose E. Labra
University of Oviedo, Spain

Patricia Ordóñez de Pablos
University of Oviedo, Spain

ABSTRACT

Electronic Mailing lists are a key part of the Internet. They have enabled the development of social communities who share and exchange knowledge in specialized and general domains. In this chapter the auhtors describe methods to capture some of that knowledge which will enable the development of new datasets using Semantic Web technologies. In particular, the authors present the SWAML project, which collects data from mailing lists. They also describe smushing techniques that normalize RDF datasets capturing different resources that identify the same one. They have applied those techniques to identify persons through the mailing lists of open source communities. These techniques have been tested using a dataset automatically extracted from several online open source communities.

INTRODUCTION

Early forms of electronic mailing lists were invented almost as soon as electronic Mail (e-Mail) and are a cornerstone of Internet, allowing a lot of people to keep up to date on news related with their interests. Besides direct messaging between individuals, mailing lists exist as private or public forums for information exchange in communities with shared interests. Mailing list archives are compilations

DOI: 10.4018/978-1-60566-272-5.ch004

of the previously posted messages that are often converted into static HTML pages for their publication on the web. They represent a noteworthy portion of the contents that are indexed by web search engines, and they capture an impressive body of knowledge that, however, is difficult to locate and browse.

The reason for this difficulty can be traced back to the translation procedure that run to transform the e-mail messages into static HTML pages. This task is fulfilled by scripts that create static HTML pages for each message in the archive. In addition, some indexes (by date, by author, by thread) are generated and usually split by date ranges to avoid excessive growth.

On the one hand, this fixed structure reduces the flexibility when users explore the mailing list archives using their web browsers. On the other hand, most of the meta-data that were associated to each e-mail message are lost when the message is rendered as HTML for presentational purposes.

We propose to use an ontology and RDF (Resource Description Framework, Klyne 2004) to publish the mailing list archives into the (Semantic) Web, retaining the meta-data that were present in the messages. Additionally, by doing so, the information can be merged and linked to other vocabularies, such as FOAF (Brickley and Miller, 2005).

The rest of the chapter is organized as follows: in section 2 we describe the main developments of Social Semantic Web related with mailing lists. In section 3, we explain several techniques to collect RDF datasets from mailing lists and other social sources. Section 4 contains a description of the SWAML project that collects those RDF datasets from mailing lists. In section 5, we describe several applications that consume that data. In section 6, we discuss some experiments that we have done over those datasets. Finally, in section 7 we present some conclusions and future work.

SOCIAL SEMANTIC WEB

The Semantic Web vision tries to develop new ways to integrate and reuse the information published on the web. To that end, the W3C has developed several technologies, like RDF, which enable to add metadata descriptions that contain meaningful values and global properties to resources. The resulting metadata forms a graph model which can be easily linked with other graphs (Berners-Lee, 2006) incrementing the knowledge represented by the original graph. Those values and properties formalize the knowledge of a particular. In 2004, the W3C consortium developed OWL (Patel-Schneider et al, 2004), a web ontology language which facilitates the definition of those formalizations, called ontologies. Based on description logics, OWL has been adopted as the standard ontology language with several available editors, reasoners and tools. There have been also a number of ontologies developed in OWL for different purposes and with different level of detail, from generic to domain-specific ones.

On the other hand, in the last years, the concept of Web 2.0 has attracted a lot of interest. One of the key aspects of Web 2.0 applications is the social part of the web. Users are not considered as mere consumers of information, but also as producers. People want to share knowledge, establish relationships, and even work together using web environments. It is necessary to develop people-oriented web technologies which can represent people interests and that enable the integration and reuse of people related information in the same way that the semantic web vision advocates. These technologies can be seen as social semantic web and we expect that there will be more and more applications making use of them.

One of the first developments is the FOAF vocabulary, which represents basic properties of people, like their name, homepage, etc. as well as the people they know. FOAF descriptions are very flexible and can be extended to other domains. There are already web portals which export their user profiles in FOAF format and the number of FOAF applications is increasing.

Apart from FOAF, there are other ontologies related to the social semantic web. In particular, SIOC (Semantically-Interlinked Online Communities), provides a vocabulary to interconnect different discussion methods such as blogs, web-based forums and mailing lists (Breslin 2005, Breslin 2006). Although we will apply mainly SIOC to mailing-lists, it has a wider scope than just mailing lists, and generalizes all kinds of online discussion primitives in the more abstract sioc:Forum concept. Each forum represents an online community of people that communicate and share a common interest. The goal of SIOC is to interconnect these online communities.

Other relevant concepts of the ontology are sioc:User and sioc:Post, which model respectively the members of the communities and the content they produce. Instances of these three classes (forums, users and posts) can be linked together using several properties.

The SIOC ontology was designed to express the information contained both explicitly and implicitly in Internet discussion methods. Several software applications, usually deployed as plug-ins, are already available to export SIOC data from some popular blogging platforms and content management systems. The effort, however, is focused on web-based communities (blogs, discussion forums), while little has been done so far to extend the coverage to legacy non-web communities, such as mailing lists and Usenet groups.

SIOC classes and properties are defined in OWL, and their instances can be expressed in RDF. Therefore, they can be easily linked to other ontologies. The obvious choice here is FOAF, which provides powerful means to describe the personal data of the members of a community.

Mailing lists can be easily described by instantiation of the SIOC classes and properties. Each mailing list can be represented by an instance of sioc:Forum (a subclass of Forum might be used instead, although it is not required). Messages sent to the list and their replies become instances of sioc:Post.

Finally, people involved into the list are instances of sioc:User. The SIOC ontology provides a property to link forums and users, namely sioc:has_subscriber. We argue that being subscribed to a mailing list is just one of the roles a user can play with respect to a forum. Moreover, the list of subscribers is often available only to the system administrator for privacy reasons. On the other hand, it is easy to collect the set of people who post to the list, i.e., the people actively involved in the forum. Depending on the settings, the latter may be a subset of the former, in particular in those mailing lists that forbid posting privileges to non-subscribers. Ideally, these two different semantics would be captured using new properties. However, for practical reasons, and to avoid privacy issues, we consider just the already existent sioc:has_subscriber property, and we populate it with the set of active members of a forum. Consequently, inactive members of the forum remain hidden, but this does not represent a problem due to the open world assumption.

Additionally, the Dublin Core (Dublin Core Metadata Element Set, Version 1.1, 2006) and Dublin Core Terms vocabularies are used to capture meta-data such as the message date (dcterms:created) and title (dc:title).

Given the distributed nature of RDF, it is expected that there will be different RDF datasets describing aspects of the same resources. The term *smushing* has been defined as the process of normalizing an RDF dataset in order to unify *a priori* different RDF resources which actually represent the same thing. The application which executes a *data smushing* process is called a *smusher*. The process comprises two stages:

First, redundant resources are identified; then, the dataset is updated to reflect the recently acquired knowledge. The latter is usually achieved by adding new triples to the model to relate the pairs of redundant resources. The OWL property owl:sameAs is often used for this purpose, although other properties without built-in logic interpretations can be used as well (e.g.: ex:hasSimilarName). Redundant resources can be spotted using a number of techniques. In this chapter, we explore two of them: (1) using logic inference and (2) comparing labels.

COLLECTING DATA INTO THE SOCIAL SEMANTIC WEB

Since SIOC is a recent specification, its adoption is still low, and only a few sites export SIOC data. There exist a number of techniques that can be used to bootstrap a network of semantic descriptions from current social web sites. We classify them in two main categories: intrusive and non-intrusive techniques.

On the one hand, methods which require direct access to the underlying database behind the social web site are **intrusive** techniques. The web application acts as the controller and publishes different views of the model in formats such as HTML and RSS. In terms of this pattern, publishing SIOC data is as simple as adding a new view. From a functional point of view, this is the most powerful scenario, because it allows a lossless publication due to the direct access to the back-end database. The SIOC community has contributed a number of plugins for some popular web community-building applications, such as Drupal, WordPress and PhpBB2. Mailing lists are also covered by SWAML, which is described in the next section. There is, however, a major blocker for this approach. All these software components need a deployment in the server side (where the database is). This is a burden for system administrators, who are often unwilling to make a move that would make it more difficult to maintain, keep secure and upgrade their systems.

This is particularly true when there is no obvious immediate benefit of exporting SIOC data.

On the other hand, methods which do not require direct access to the database and can operate on resources already published on the web are **non-intrusive**. One technique is the use of cooked HTML views of the information, the same ones that are rendered by web browsers for human consumption. An example could be RSS/Atom feeds, which have become very popular in the recent years. They can be easily translated into SIOC instances using XSLT stylesheets (for XML-based feeds) or SPARQL queries (for RSS 1.0, which is actually RDF). Unfortunately, these feeds often contain just partial descriptions. Another technique is the use of public APIs. The Web 2.0 trend has pushed some social web sites to export (part of) their functionality through APIs in order to enable their consumption by third-party mash-ups and applications. Where available, these APIs offer an excellent opportunity to create RDF views of the data. A shared aspect of these sources is their ubiquitous availability through web protocols and languages, such as HTTP and XML. Therefore, they can be consumed anywhere, and thus system administrators are freed of taking care of any additional deployment. In contrast, they cannot compete with the intrusive approaches in terms of information quality, as their access to the data is not primary.

SWAML PROJECT

SWAML (Fernández et al, 2008) is a Python tool that reads mailing list archives in raw format, typically stored in a "mailbox" (or "mbox"), as defined in RFC 4155 (Hall 2005). It parses mailboxes and outputs RDF descriptions of the messages, mailing lists and users as instances of the SIOC ontology. Internally, it re-constructs the structure of the conversations in a tree structure, and it exploits this structure to produce links between the posts. This script is highly configurable

Figure 1. SIOC post example in RDF/XML

```
<rdf:RDF
  xmlns:dcterms='http://purl.org/dc/terms/'
  xmlns:sioc='http://rdfs.org/sioc/ns#'
  xmlns:rdf='http://www.w3.org/1999/02/22-rdf-syntax-ns#'
  xmlns:dc='http://purl.org/dc/elements/1.1/'
  xml:base='http://example.org/swaml-devel/'>
  <sioc:Post rdf:about="2006-Sep/post-52">
    <dc:title>Re: [swaml-devel] Changing SWAML ontology</dc:title>
    <sioc:has_creator rdf:resource="subscriber/s10"/>
    <dcterms:created>Wed, 6 Sep 2006 20:14:44 +0200</dcterms:created>
    <sioc:content><!-- ommitted --></sioc:content>
    <sioc:has_reply rdf:resource="2006-Sep/post-69"/>
    <sioc:previous_by_date rdf:resource="2006-Sep/post-51"/>
    <sioc:next_by_date rdf:resource="2006-Sep/post-53"/>
  </sioc:Post>
</rdf:RDF>
```

and non-interactive, and has been designed to be invoked by the system task scheduler. This low-coupling with the software that runs the mailing list eases its portability and deployment.

SWAML could be classified as an intrusive technique because it requires access to the primary data source, even if in this case it is not a relational database but a text file (for instance, the approach followed by mle (Michael Hausenblas at al., 2007) is considered completely non-intrusive). Anyway, it is worth mentioning that some servers publish these text files (mailboxes) through HTTP. Therefore, sometimes it is possible to retrieve the mailbox and build a perfect replica of the primary database in another box. In such cases, SWAML can be used without the participation of the system administration of the original web server.

There are many ways in which a mailing list message might be related with other messages. However, we consider just two scenarios. The first one links a post with its replies (sioc:has_reply). Actually, due to sequential layout of the messages in the most widely used format to store mailing list archives (mailbox), it is easier to generate the inverse property (sioc:reply_of). Anyway, the has_reply property can be generated either by a description logics reasoner or by performing two passes over the sequence.

The second link among messages is established between a post and its immediate successor (or predecessor) in chronological order. It is worth to note that this link is not strictly necessary, because the following (or preceding) message can be obtained by sorting by date the sequence of posts. However, this is a rather expensive operation, because the whole set of posts is required in order to perform the sorting. The open world assumption makes this query even more challenging. Therefore, considering that browsing to the previous or next message is a common use case, and the complete set of posts can be very large or even unavailable, we introduced two new properties, next_by_date and prev_by_date. These properties where eventually accepted into the SIOC ontology. An RDF representation of a sample message is shown in Figure 1.

SWAML is essentially a mailbox parser and translator implemented in Python. Its output is a number of SIOC instances (Forum, Posts and Users) in a set of RDF files. SWAML can be invoked by the system task scheduler.

Parsing the mailbox and rebuilding the discussion threads may be sometimes tricky. Although each mail message has a supposedly unique identifier in its header, the Message-ID, defined by RFC 2822 (Resnick, 2001), in practice its unique-

Figure 2. Buxon is an end-user application that consumes sioc:Forum instances, which in turn can be generated from mailboxes using SWAML.

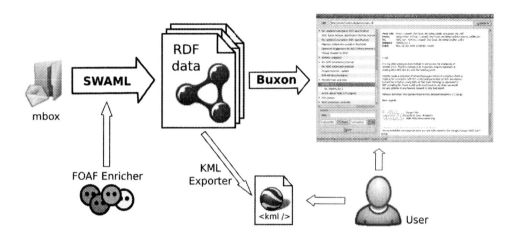

ness cannot be taken for granted. Actually, we have found some messages with repeated identifiers in some mailing lists, probably due to non-RFC compliant or ill-configured mail transport agents. Therefore, SWAML assumes that any reference to a message (such as those created by the In-Reply-To header) is in fact a reference to the most recent message with that ID in the mailbox (obviously, only previous messages are considered). Using this rule of thumb, SWAML builds an in-memory tree representation of the conversation threads, so sioc:Posts can be properly linked.

Actually, SWAML goes further than just a format-translation tool. A dedicated subroutine that runs as part of the batch execution but may be also separately invoked on any sioc:Forum, tries to find a FOAF description for each sioc:User.

One important requirement of the semantic web is to be an extension (and not a replacement) of the current document-based web. Ideally, each user agent must be able to retrieve the information in their format of choice. For instance, current web browsers prefer (X)HTML documents, because they can be rendered and presented to the end user. However, semantic web agents require information to be available in a serialized RDF format, such as RDF/XML or N3. Furthermore,

different representations of the same information resource should share a unique URI. Fortunately, the HTTP protocol supports this feature by using "content-negotiation". Clients of the protocol can declare their preferred formats in the headers of an HTTP request using the Accept header. Web servers will deliver the information in the most suited available format, using the Content-type header of the HTTP response to specify the actual format of the returned delivered content. MIME types such as text/html and application/rdf+xml are used as identifiers of the requested and available formats.

Setting up the content negotiation in the server-side usually requires some tuning of the web server configuration. It also depends on some choices made by the publisher of the information, such as the namespace scheme for the URIs or the fragmentation of the information. In (Miles et al, 2006) there is a list of some common scenarios, which are described to great detail, and configuration examples for the Apache web server are provided. The most suitable scenarios (or recipes, as they are called) to publish mailing list metadata are the fifth and sixth, i.e., multiple documents available both in HTML and RDF.

Figure 3. A sample htaccess configuration file for Apache generated by SWAML. These two rules redirect the request to the proper file based on the content negotiation field of the HTTP request. Some lines have been wrapped for readability.

```
RewriteEngine On
RewriteBase /demos/swaml-devel/
AddType application/rdf+xml .rdf
Options -MultiViews

RewriteCond %{HTTP_ACCEPT} text/html [OR]
RewriteCond %{HTTP_ACCEPT} application/xhtml\+xml [OR]
RewriteCond %{HTTP_USER_AGENT} ^Mozilla/.*
RewriteRule ^/([0-9]{4})-([A-Za-z]+)/post-([0-9]+)$
            $1-$2/post-$3.xhtml [R=303]

RewriteCond %{HTTP_ACCEPT} application/rdf\+xml
RewriteRule ^/([0-9]{4})-([A-Za-z]+)/post-([0-9]+)$
            $1-$2/post-$3.rdf [R=303]
```

The fifth scenario is extensively described in the referred source, and it has been implemented in SWAML. At the same time RDF and HTML files are written, SWAML also produces htaccess local configuration files for Apache. One of these configuration file is shown in Figure 3, while a sample request/response negotiation is depicted in Figure 4.

RDF metadata generated by SWAML can grow to a large size for lists with a high traffic and several years of operation, where there are tens of thousands of messages. The partition of the information might be an issue in such cases. On the one hand, information chunks are preferred to be small so any conceivable use case can be satisfied without retrieving a significant overload of unneeded information. However, scattering the metadata across a myriad of small files has some disadvantages. For instance, the number of resources that must be retrieved to fulfill a single query is greatly increased. Therefore, storing the RDF graph in a specialized database is an appealing alternative.

Fortunately, a common protocol to access semantic repositories using SPARQL as the query language is available (Clark 2006) and is gaining support by the RDF databases. This protocol exposes a simple API to execute and retrieve the results of SPARQL queries (at the present moment, SPARQL is a read-only query language, although

Figure 4. An HTTP dialog with content negotiation

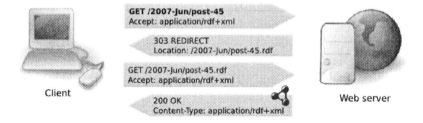

Figure 5. Sample Apache web server rewrite rule to translate HTTP request into SPARQL queries using a Sesame RDF repository. The last line has been wrapped for readability.

```
RewriteEngine On
RewriteBase /lists/archives

RewriteCond %{HTTP_ACCEPT} application/rdf\+xml
RewriteRule ^mylist/(.+)
        http://internal-server/sesame-server/repositories/mylist-rep/
        ?query=CONSTRUCT+{<http://example.org/lists/mylist/$1>+?y+?z}
        +WHERE+{<http://example.org/lists/mylist/$1>+?y+?z}
        &queryLn=sparql [R=303]
```

there are proposals to extend it with full CRUD capabilities such as those of SQL). This abstract query API may be realized by different means, such as SOAP bindings (described by a WSDL 2.0 interface) and HTTP bindings. The former enables interoperability with web service frameworks, while the latter can be exploited without the full-blown web service machinery.

Web service endpoints which implement the SPARQL protocol are sprouting on the web, some of them pouring huge amounts of data into the semantic web. We argue that metadata of large mailing lists can be conveniently exposed as SPARQL endpoints. That means to effectively translate the decision on data selection to the client (Pan 2006), and therefore minimizing the number of requests and the data overload. For instance, the client agent can retrieve all the headers of the messages in a given date range, but skip the body of the messages, saving a considerable amount of bandwidth.

However, non SPARQL-aware agents still need to access the information. This is the scenario of the sixth scenario (recipe) of the above cited document, but unfortunately this one is still being discussed. We propose a simple solution based on URL rewriting of the requests in order to translate conventional HTTP requests for resources into SPARQL queries that dynamically generate an RDF subgraph that contains the requested information about the resource. The rewriting mechanism, the SPARQL query and

even the presence of a data repository instead of static files is kept completely hidden to the client. At the same time, by avoiding the undesirable data replication, this technique helps to keep the information consistent. The most representative feature of our proposal is that it does not require any kind of server side script or application to translate the queries, because the data repository can serve the information directly in the format desired by the client.

We have implemented this technique using the Apache web server and Sesame 2.0 RDF repository (Broekstra et al, 2006). Figure 6 reproduces the hand-made htaccess file (as opposed to the ones that are automatically produced by SWAML). Unfortunately, Of course, the rewrite rule must be fired only when RDF data is requested, while requests for HTML must go through it.

We note, however, that our proposal presents some security-related issues. In particular, it is easily vulnerable to SPARQL-injection. Therefore, we strongly discourage the use of this technique in production environments. Nevertheless, some changes in the regular expressions are possible in order to prevent this kind of attack.

There is another different approach to publishing metadata: to embed it into the HTML content. W3C is pushing two complementary technologies, RDFa (Adida & Birbeck, 2007) and GRDDL (Connolly, 2007), which respectively encode into, and extract RDF data from XHTML documents. We have also explored this path. SWAML gener-

Figure 6. A single message rendered as XHTML code with RDFa and GRDDL markup by SWAML.

```
<html xmlns='http://www.w3.org/1999/xhtml'
      xmlns:dcterms='http://purl.org/dc/terms/'
      xmlns:sioc='http://rdfs.org/sioc/ns#'
      xmlns:dc='http://purl.org/dc/elements/1.1/'>
  <head profile='http://www.w3.org/2003/g/data-view'>
  <link href='http://www-sop.inria.fr/acacia/soft/RDFa2RDFXML.xsl'
        rel='transformation' />
  <title>[swaml-devel] CfP: FEWS2007</title>
  </head>
  <body>
    <div about='http://example.org/swaml/post/2007-May/5'
         typeof='sioc:Post'>
      <h1 property='dc:title'>[swaml-devel] CfP: FEWS2007</h1>
      <p>strong>From: </strong>
        <a href='http://example.org/swaml/subscriber/s2'
           rel='sioc:has_creator'>Diego Berrueta</a>
      </p>
      <p><strong>To: </strong>
        <a href='http://example.org/swaml/forum'
           rel='sioc:has_container'>SWAML Devel</a>
      </p>
      <p><strong>Date: </strong>
        <span property='dcterms:created'>
        Tue, 15 May 2007 19:24:49
        </span>
      </p>
      <pre property='sioc:content'><!-- omitted --></pre>
      <p>Previous by Date:
        <a href='http://example.org/swaml/post/2006-Sep/4'
           rel='sioc:previous_by_date'>previous</a>
      </p>
      <p>Next by Date:
        <a href='http://example.org/swaml/post/2007-Mar/6'
           rel='sioc:next_by_date'>next</a>
      </p>
    </div>
  </body>
</html>
```

ates simple XHTML pages for each message to illustrate the usage of both RDFa and GRDDL. We must remark that these pages are just a proof-of-concept of the semantic enrichment, and they lack many of the fancy features and complex templates of the already-existent applications which generate plain HTML.

CONSUMING MAILING LIST METADATA

Buxon

Buxon is a multi-platform desktop application written in PyGTK. It allows end users to browse the archives of mailing lists as if they were using their desktop mail application. Buxon takes the URI of a sioc:Forum instance (for example, a mailing list exported by SWAML, although any sioc:Forum instance is accepted) and fetches the data, retrieving additional files if necessary. Then, it rebuilds the conversation structure and displays the familiar message thread list (see Figure 7).

Buxon also gives users the ability to query the messages, searching for terms or filtering the messages in a date range. All these queries are internally translated to SPARQL (Prud'hommeaux & Seaborne, 2007) to be executed over the RDF graph. Newer versions of Buxon can send the sioc:Forum URI to PingTheSemanticWeb.com, a

Figure 7. Buxon browsing SIOC-Dev mailing list.

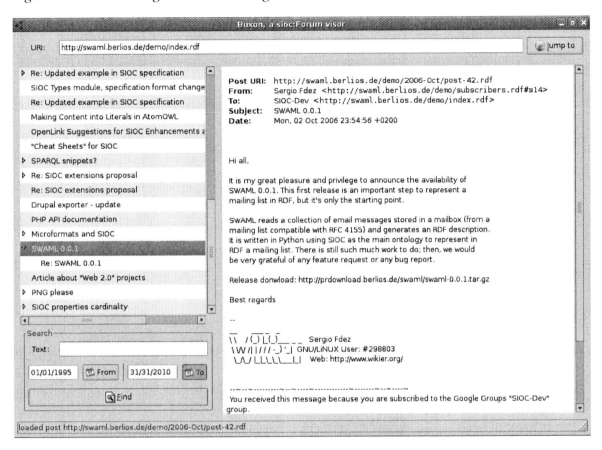

social web service that tracks semantic web documents. That way, Buxon contributes to establish an infrastructure that lets people easily create, find and publish RDF documents.

Other Browsers and Clients

The SIOC RDF data can be explored and queried using any generic RDF browser, such as Tabulator (Berners-Lee et al., 2006). The most interesting applications appear when instances of sioc:User are linked to FOAF descriptions of these users. For instance, it is trivial to write a query to obtain the geographical coordinates of members of a mailing list and to codify them into a KML file (Ricket 2006), provided they describe their location in their FOAF file using the basic geo vocabulary (Brickley 2006). The KML file can be plotted using a map web service such as Google Maps (Figure 8).

It is also possible execute visualize the messages in a time line view using the Timeline DHTML widget by the MIT SIMILE project using a query like the one we propose in Figure 9.

EXPERIMENTATION

A corpus of RDF data with many foaf:Person instances was assembled by crawling and scrapping five online communities. There is a shared topic in these communities, namely open source development; hence we expect them to have a significant number of people in common. We continue the work started in Berrueta et al (2007) to mine online discussion communities, and we

Figure 8. Plotting the geographical coordinates of the members of a mailing list using KML and Google Maps.

extend it to new information sources. More details are described in Berrueta et al We use the following sources:

- *GNOME Desktop mailings lists:* All the authors of messages in four mailing lists (evolution-hackers, gnome-accessibility-devel, gtk-devel and xml) within the date range July 1998 to June 2008 were exported to RDF using SWAML.
- *Debian mailing lists:* All the authors of messages in four mailing lists (debian-devel, debian-gtk-gnome, debian-java and debian-user) during years 2005 and 2006 were scrapped from the HTML versions of the archives with a set of XSLT style sheets to produce RDF triples.
- *Advogato:* This community exports its data as FOAF files. We used an RDF crawler starting at Miguel de Icaza's profile. Although Advogato claims to have +13,000 registered users, only +4,000 were found by the crawler.
- *Ohloh:* The RDFohloh (S. Fernández, 2008) project exposes the information

from this directory of open source projects and developers as Linked Data. Due to API usage restrictions, we could only get data about the +12,000 oldest user accounts.
- *Debian packages:* Descriptions of Debian packages maintainers were extracted from apt database of Debian packages in the main section of the unstable distribution.

Instances generated from these data sources were assigned a URI in a different namespace for each source. Some of these data sources do not directly produce instances of foaf:Person, but just instances of sioc:User. An assumption is made that there is a foaf:Person instance for each sioc:User, with the same e-mail address and name. These instances were automatically created when missing. This assumption obviously leads to redundant instances of foaf:Person which will be later detected by the smusher.

The ultimate goal of our experiments is to exercise the smushing processes described previously against a realistic dataset. Two million RDF triples were extracted from the sources described above, and put into OpenLink Virtuoso server

Figure 9. SPARQL query to extract the information required to visualize a time line of the messages posted to any sioc:Forum instance.

```
PREFIX sioc: <http://rdfs.org/sioc/ns#>
PREFIX rdf: <http://www.w3.org/1999/02/22-rdf-syntax-ns#>
PREFIX dcterms: <http://purl.org/dc/terms/>
PREFIX dc: <http://purl.org/dc/elements/1.1/>
SELECT ?start ?title ?description ?link
WHERE {
   ?post rdf:type sioc:Post .
   ?post dcterms:created ?start .
   ?post dc:title ?title .
   ?post sioc:link ?link .
   ?post sioc:content ?description
}
```

which provides not only an effective triple store, but also a SPARQL endpoint that was used to execute queries using scripts.

We evaluated two smushers: the first one smushed foaf:Person instances assuming that foaf:mbox_sha1sum is an IFP; the second one smushed the same instances comparing their foaf:name labels for string strict equality, without any normalization. Both smushers were implemented using SPARQL CONSTRUCT rules. The newly created owl:sameAs triples were put in different named graphs. These links were analyzed to find co-occurrences of people in different communities.

Some communities use the e-mail address as their primary key to identify its users. However, other communities use a different primary key, thus allowing users to repeat their e-mail addresses. For instance, a small number of users have registered more than one account in Advogato with the same e-mail (these accounts have been manually reviewed, and they seem to be accounts created for testing purposes).

Our data acquisition process introduces a key difference between how user accounts are interpreted in Debian mailing lists and GNOME mailing lists. The former considers e-mail address as globally unique, i.e., the same e-mail address posting in different Debian mailing lists is assumed to belong to the same user.

On the other hand, a more strict interpretation of how Mailman works is made with respect to the GNOME mailing lists, where identical e-mail address posting in different mailing lists are assumed to belong to a priori different users. In the second case, we rely on the smushing process to merge the identities of these users.

Although they must be handled with extreme care due to the issues afore-mentioned, the combined results of the two smushing processes are consistent with the expected ones. For instance, there is a very high overlap between the Debian developers (maintainers of Debian packages) and the Debian mailing lists. Obviously, Debian developers are a relatively small group at the core of the Debian community, thus they are very active in its mailing lists. Another example is the overlap between Advogato and GNOME mailing lists. Advogato is a reputation-based social web site that blossomed at the same time that the GNOME project was gaining momentum. Advogato was passionately embraced by the GNOME developers, who used Advogato to rate each others' development abilities.

We also studied whether there are some people that are present in many of the communities at the same time. We chose communities which are closely related to each other, consequently, we expected a high number of cross-community subscribers. There are several people who are present in many communities. We can conclude that almost all the most active open source developers in our dataset are core members of the Debian community. Another interesting fact is that only a few people among the top members of the communities consistently use a single e-mail address and just one variant of their names. This fact proves the difficulty of the smushing process, but also its usefulness.

CONCLUSION AND FUTURE WORK

There are a lot of ongoing efforts to translate data already reachable on the web into formats which are semantic web-friendly. Most of that work focuses on relational databases, micro-formats and web services. However, at the time of this writing and to the best of our knowledge, e-mail was almost excluded from the Semantic Web. Our project, in combination with the generic SIOC framework, fills this gap, conveniently providing an ontology and a parser to publish machine-readable versions of the archives of the countless mailing lists that exist on the Internet.

Furthermore, the SWAML project fulfills a much-needed requirement for the Semantic Web: to be able to refer to semantic versions of e-mail messages and their properties using resource URIs. By re-using the SIOC vocabulary for describing online discussions, SWAML allows any semantic web document (in particular, SIOC documents) to refer to e-mail messages from other discussions taking place on forums, blogs, etc., so that distributed conversations can occur across these discussion media. Also, by providing e-mail messages in RDF format, SWAML is providing a rich source of data, namely mailing lists, for use in SIOC applications.

The availability of these data leads to some benefits. In the first place, data can be fetched by user applications to provide handy browsing through the archives of the mailing lists, providing

features that exceed what is now offered by static HTML versions of the archives on the web.

Secondly, the crawlers of the web search engines can use the enhanced expressivity of the RDF data to refine search results. For instance, precise semantic descriptions of the messages permit to filter out repeated messages, advance in the fight against spam, or introduce additional filter criteria in the search forms.

Another consequence of no lesser importance is that each e-mail message is assigned a URI that can be resolved to a machine-readable description of the message. This actually makes possible to link a message like any other web resource, and therefore enriches the expressivity of the web.

Integration of the SWAML process with popular HTML-based mailing list archivers, such as Hypermail or Pipermail, would be a giant push to speed up the adoption of SWAML. It is well known that one of the most awkward problems of any new technology is to gain a critical mass of users. The semantic web is not an exception. A good recipe to tackle this problem is to integrate the new technology into old tools, making a smooth transition without requiring any extra effort from users. Merging the SWAML process into the batch flow of tools such as Hypermail would allow users to generate both RDF and production-quality, semantically enriched HTML versions of the archives.

So far, no semantic annotation relative to the meaning of the messages is considered. Obviously, such information can not be automatically derived from a RFC 4155-compliant mailbox. However, it is conceivable that it could be added by other means, such as social tagging using folksonomies, or parsing the metadata added by the authors of the messages using micro-formats or RDFa when posting in XHTML format. The inherent community-based nature of mailing lists can be exploited to build recommendation systems (Celma 2006).

We have also explored smushing techniques to spot redundant RDF instances in large datasets.

We have tested these techniques with more than 36,000 instances of foaf:Person in a dataset automatically extracted from different online open source communities. We have used only public data sources, consequently, these instances lack detailed personal information.

We are aware of the extreme simplicity of our experimentation using label comparison. In our opinion, however, it contributes to show the potential of this smushing technique. We note that it is possible to have more usages for it, for instance, smushing not just by people's names, but also by their publications, their organizations, etc. Surprisingly, the named-based smushing finds a high number of redundant resources even if the comparison strategy for labels (names) is very simplistic (in this case, case-sensitive string equality comparison). More intelligent comparison functions should lead to a higher recall. In this direction, we are evaluating some normalization functions for names. We have also evaluated classical information retrieval comparison functions that take into account the similarity of the strings (e.g., Levenshtein); nevertheless, their applicability to compare people's names is open to discussion.

We believe that the ratio of smushing can be further improved if the dataset is enriched with more detailed descriptions about people. Experiments are being carried out to retrieve additional RDF data from semantic web search engines as a previous step to smushing.

We have implemented a smusher application for persons, and we intend to use it to further investigate the potential for the optimization of the smushing process. The way in which these techniques are translated into actual algorithms is critical to achieve a promising performance of the smushing process, especially for very large datasets. In parallel, increasing the precision of smushing will require to study how to enable different smushing strategies to interrelate and reciprocally collaborate.

ACKNOWLEDGMENT

The authors would like to express their gratitude to Dr. John Breslin and Uldis Bojārs from DERI Galway, whose support and contributions have been a great help to this work. Also thanks to Ignacio Barrientos for his contribution packaging SWAML for Debian GNU/Linux.

REFERENCES

Adida, B., & Birbeck, M. (2008). *RDFa Primer*. Technical Report, W3C Working Draft.

Berners-Lee, T. (2006). *Linked Data Design Issues*. Available at http://www.w3.org/DesignIssues/LinkedData.html

Berners-Lee, T., et al. (2006). Tabulator: Exploring and Analyzing linked data on the Semantic Web. *Proceedings of the 3rd International Semantic Web User Interaction Workshop (SWUI06) workshop*, Athens, Georgia.

Berrueta, D. et al, (2008). *Best practice recipes for publishing RDF vocabularies*. Technical Report, W3C Note.

Berrueta, D., Fernández, S., & Shi, L. (2007). Bootstrapping the Semantic Web of Social Online Communities. *In Proceedings of workshop on Social Web Search and Mining (SWSM2008), co-located with WWW2008*, Beijing, China.

Bojārs, U., & Breslin, J. (2007). *SIOC Core Ontology Specification*. Available at http://rdfs.org/sioc/spec/.

Breslin, J., et al. (2005). Towards Semantically-Interlinked Online Communities. *Proceedings of the 2nd European Semantic Web Conference, ESWC 2005*, Heraklion, Crete, Greece.

Breslin, J. (2006). SIOC: an approach to connect web-based communities. *International Journal of Web Based Communities, 2*(2), 133–142.

Brickley, D. (2006). *Basic geo (WGS84 lat/long) vocabulary*. Technical report, W3C Informal Note.

Brickley, D., & Miller, L. (2005). *FOAF Vocabulary Specification*. Technical report.

Broekstra, J. (2006). Sesame: A generic architecture for storing and querying RDF and RDF Schema. In *Springer . Lecture Notes in Computer Science, 2342*, 54–68. doi:10.1007/3-540-48005-6_7

Celma, O. (2006). FOAFing the music: Bridging the semantic gap in music recommendation. *Proceedings of the 5th International Semantic Web Conference*, Athens, USA.

Clark, K. G. (2008). *SPARQL protocol for RDF*. Technical report, W3C Recommendation.

Connolly, D. (2007). *Gleaning Resource Descriptions from Dialects of Languages (GRDDL)*. Technical report, W3C Candidate Recommendation.

Fernández, S., Berrueta, D., & Labra, J. E. (2008). A Semantic Web Approach to Publish and Consume Mailing Lists. *IADIS International Journal on WWW/Internet, 6*, 90-102.

Fernándrez, S. (2008). *RDFohloh, a RDF Wrapper of Ohloh*. Proceedings of *1ˢᵗ workshop on Social Data on the Web (SDoW2008), collocated with 7ᵗʰ International Semantic Web Conference*, Karlsruhe, Germany.

Hall, E. (2005). *RFC 4155 - the application/mbox media type*. Technical report, The Internet Society.

Hausenblas, M., & Rehatschek, H. (2007). mle: Enhancing the Exploration of Mailing List Archives Through Making Semantics Explicit. *Semantic Web Challenge 07*, Busan, South Korea.

Klyne, G., & Carroll, J. J. (2004). *Resource Description Framework (RDF): Concepts and abstract syntax*. Technical report, W3C Recommendation.

Pan, Z., et al. (2006). *An investigation into the feasibility of the semantic web*. Technical Report LU-CSE-06-025, Dept. of Computer Science and Engineering, Lehigh University.

Patel-Schneider, P. F., Hayes, P., & Horrocks, I. (2004). *OWL Web Ontology Language: Semantics and Abstract Syntax*. Recommendation, W3C, February.

Prud'hommeaux, E., & Seaborne, A. (2008). *SPARQL Query Language for RDF*. Technical report, W3C recommendation.

Resnick, P. (2001). *RFC 2822 - internet message format*, Technical report, The Internet Society.

Ricket, D. (2006). Google Maps and Google Earth integration using KML. In *American Geophysical Union 2006 Fall Meeting*.

Shi, L., Berrueta, D., Fernández, S., Polo, L., & Fernández, S. (2008). Smushing RDF instances: Are Alice and Bob the same open source developer? *Proceedings of 3rd ExpertFinder workshop on Personal Identification and Collaborations: Knowledge Mediation and Extraction (PICKME 2008), collocated with 7ᵗʰ International Semantic Web Conference*, Karlsruhe, Germany.

This work was previously published in Social Web Evolution: Integrating Semantic Applications and Web 2.0 Technologies, edited by M. D. Lytras; P. Ordonez de Pablos, pp. 42-56, copyright 2009 by Information Science Reference (an imprint of IGI Global).

Chapter 4.13
Communicative Networking and Linguistic Mashups on Web 2.0

Mark Pegrum
University of Western Australia, Australia

ABSTRACT

This chapter discusses the application of a range of Web 2.0 technologies to language education. It argues that Web 2.0 is fundamentally about networking, community building, and identity negotiation. Given the textual nature of the Web, all of this is made possible primarily through the medium of language. Consequently, Web 2.0 is ideally suited to the teaching of language and literacy. To be most effective, this requires a broadly social constructivist pedagogical approach as well as a willingness to work with the messy reality of linguistic "mashups," the hybrid uses of languages, codes, and media which inform Web 2.0.

INTRODUCTION

There continues to be widespread confusion and apprehension about the effects of the Internet and new technologies on education. Recent discussions of the web in versions ranging from 1.0 to 3.0 have done little to alleviate this situation, with at least one spurious reference to Web 6.0 (Motteram & Ioannou-Georgiou, 2007) making the point that labels and numbers are not the important thing. However, a glance at Web 1.0 and Web 3.0 can be helpful in an understanding of Web 2.0, the term popularized by Tim O'Reilly through the first Web 2.0 Conference in 2004 (O'Reilly, 2005) and now commonly used to describe the current state of the web.

The retrospective term Web 1.0 refers to the initial *information-oriented web*, authored by a small number of people for a very large number of users. Consisting mainly of static webpages, it offered little room for interactivity. Educational uses largely fell into two categories: information retrieval (as in webquests) or rote training (drill exercises). While there were some clear benefits in terms of student autonomy, use of authentic materials and exposure to multiliteracies, and while problem-based learning and guided discovery approaches to Web 1.0 were not unknown, it was most often used in ways corresponding to traditional transmission or behaviourist models of pedagogy.

Web 3.0, a speculative term describing a possible future version of the web, refers most commonly to the *semantic web*, where software agents will collate and integrate information to give intelligent responses to human operators, and/or the *geospatial web*, where location will be used to index information. These are, however, long-term projections, whose educational implications are impossible to assess at present.

DOI: 10.4018/978-1-60566-190-2.ch002

In between is the presently dominant Web 2.0, also known as the *social web*, which comprises a loose grouping of newer generation social technologies whose users are actively involved in communicating and collaborating with each other as they build connections and communities across the world, negotiating their online identities in the process. What happened, as Davies puts it, was that "society got more technical while software got more social" (2003, p. 5). The 2007 Horizon Report describes Web 2.0's social networking sites as being "fundamentally about community" (New Media Consortium, 2007, p. 12), while Jimmy Wales (2007), founder of Wikipedia, has linked Web 2.0 to the new digital literacies concerned with "inclusion, collaboration and participation". In brief, Web 2.0 technologies, from blogs and wikis through social networking sites and folksonomies to podcasting and virtual worlds, are all about communicative networking. Such networking is likely to become increasingly important as a digital native ethos takes over from a digital immigrant one (Prensky, 2001), as more technologies become available to those with little specialist expertise in IT, and as today's technologies converge to form ever more versatile hybrids.

Web 2.0 has many applications in education, both current and potential, but its greatest impact may well be in subjects which foreground language and communication. After all, given the textual nature of the web, all the connections made online and all the communities established there are enabled primarily through the medium of language. As a result, for language and literacy educators, the advent of Web 2.0 presents great opportunities: to decentralize the role of the classroom (Coleman, 2007), escape the language lab, and engage with the younger generation of digital natives on their own territory. It is a territory whose geography is forged through language and whose key navigation tools are literacies. Teachers can help their students develop greater language competence and additional linguistic tools to navigate Web 2.0, as the students engage in the process of making

connections, building communities and shaping their own self-representations online. In this way, language and literacy educators can play a key role in the collaborative enterprise that is Web 2.0. It is important to acknowledge, however, that effective use of Web 2.0 requires a rethinking of approaches to literacy and pedagogy which may have traditionally seemed unproblematic, but which are less than ideally suited to the new online environment — or the wider world in which it is embedded.

This chapter begins by examining recent changes in conceptions of literacy and pedagogy which may enable educators to better frame their use of Web 2.0. It then goes on to discuss common Web 2.0 tools and their applications to language education, focusing firstly on collaborative technologies such as discussion boards, blogs and wikis; secondly on social networking technologies; thirdly on information linking technologies like folksonomies and RSS; and fourthly on cutting-edge technologies such as podcasting, m-learning and virtual worlds. Finally, the chapter explores some of the main limitations of Web 2.0 in education, in a discussion which ranges across pedagogical, social, sociopolitical and philosophical issues. Drawing these threads together, the conclusion offers recommendations for language and literacy educators who wish to use Web 2.0 more extensively in their teaching.

CHANGING LITERACIES AND PEDAGOGIES

It has been clear for some time that traditional print literacy alone is no longer sufficient to allow people to operate effectively in society. Web 2.0 greatly exacerbates the problematical aspects of this situation. As a result, there is an urgent need to pluralize the concept of literacy, as has been claimed in recent work on litera*cies* and *multi*literacies (Barton & Hamilton, 2000; Cope & Kalantzis, 2000; Kist, 2004; Street, 1994;

Unsworth, 2001). It is important to challenge the focus on "formalised, monolingual, monocultural, and rule-governed forms of language" inherent in print literacy pedagogy (New London Group, 2000, p. 9). In their place, multiliteracies should be promoted and developed to facilitate the navigation of "our culturally and linguistically diverse and increasingly globalised societies" as well as "the burgeoning variety of text forms associated with information and multimedia technologies" (ibid.). The multiliteracies paradigm can thus refer to multiple cultural and linguistic codes on the one hand, and to multiple media on the other. Both aspects, but particularly the latter, are reflected in the rapidly multiplying treatises on computer, electronic and hypertext literacies (Dudfield, 1999; Kern, 2006; Selber, 2004; Warschauer, 1999, 2003; Wray, 2004).

In short: in the Web 2.0 environment, there is a dynamic fusion of media and a rich blend of cultures, languages and, within languages, evolving codes and registers. While English may be the default lingua franca, it is less a single international English and more a loosely concatenated assemblage of World Englishes. And generational differences ensure that, even among speakers of single varieties of English, there is a bewildering mixture of modes of self-expression. Indeed, the multilingualism and multiliteracies which underpin Web 2.0 parallel the increasingly productive mixing of pre-existing video, graphics, music and text commonly referred to as *mashups* (a term derived from the hip hop practice of mixing songs to create new hybrids). "Linguistic mashups," then, would seem to be in the nature of international socialization and online networking: the emphasis is on communication, which involves sophisticated aggregations of multiple media drawing on increasingly porous cultural and linguistic codes. Web 2.0 is not about neat definitions or clear borders. Rather, its users must find ways to work with the global cacophony of voices which make up its textual fabric.

Fortunately, there is a range of appropriate pedagogical tools at hand. While Web 1.0 lent itself to transmission pedagogies and behaviourist drills, working effectively with Web 2.0 demands a more constructivist orientation. Social constructivist pedagogy, with its roots in the work of Vygotsky and carrying influences from Dewey and progressivism, views social interaction as the source of all learning. Acknowledging and valuing students' pre-existing knowledges and multiple perspectives, it helps students deconstruct and reconstruct these as they engage actively and collaboratively in building new understandings through scaffolded learning experiences (Dalgarno, 2001; Finger, Russell, Jamieson-Proctor & Russell, 2007, p. 119; Jonassen, 1992). As Hoppe, Joiner, Milrad and Sharples (2003) state, "there is an imperative to move from a view of e- and m-learning as solely delivery mechanisms for content"—the transmission approach typical of Web 1.0—and to embrace contemporary pedagogy with its "high valuation of *active, productive, creative and collaborative learning methods* [which go] much beyond the 'absorption' of codified information" (p. 255; italics in original). It might be argued that a constructivist approach is becoming ever more relevant in a world where, as Warschauer (2007) indicates, "[t]he ability to draw on rote answers is inadequate" because "yesterday's answers are outdated faster than ever" (p. 42). What is relevant in such a world is the ability to seek out information through networks of contacts, and to collaboratively build understanding with others engaged in similar pursuits. The social networking, dialogue building and collaborative knowledge construction tools of Web 2.0 are uniquely suited to preparing students for this world.

Another useful perspective is provided by the communities of practice paradigm, where learning is conceived of as "social participation," meaning that people engage in the "process of being active participants in the *practices* of social communities and constructing *identities* in relation to these communities" (Wenger, 1998, p. 4; italics in original). Communities of practice have, in fact, been defined as "networked learning systems" which connect "all participants and learning system components across multiple levels of practice and inquiry" (Quinton, 2006, p. 563). This is precisely the kind of educational networking that can be fostered by Web 2.0 applications. As students begin to use these tools, they are not only gaining important future skills but may well find themselves entering, as legitimate peripheral participants, the very communities of practice in which they will eventually become full participants. It is implicitly a community of practice orientation that Holmes, Tangney, FitzGibbon, Savage and Mehan (2001) ascribe to when they express the hope that, in a "communal constructivist" approach to new technologies, "students will not simply pass through a course like water through a sieve but instead leave their own imprint in the development of the course, their school or university, and ideally the discipline" (p. 1).

In language teaching itself, the last decade of the twentieth century witnessed a move away from the ideals of the communicative approach — which, having dealt with some of the key limitations of preceding approaches, came to create its own problems — and towards a conception of intercultural communicative competence. While continuing to recognize the importance of the communicative element, the intercultural communicative competence movement has rejected any insistence on the imitation of native speaker models along with the accompanying goal of integration into a target culture. Rather, the language learner is encouraged to move into a "third place" (Kramsch, 1993) between cultures; from here, he or she will be able to explore his/her own culture as well as other cultures, which are not seen as static entities into which full integration might be possible, but rather as multiple, contradictory and in flux (Byram, 1997; Corbett, 2003; Kramsch, 1998; Phipps & Gonzalez, 2004). Intercultural competence is thus very much about negotiat-

ing communication in "the messy real world of cultural flows and mixes" (Pegrum, forthcoming 2008a) — one whose messiness is exponentially increased by the technological affordances and communicative possibilities of Web 2.0.

In the new millennium, the notion of identity has also emerged as a major focus of research in language pedagogy, thanks in large part to the work of Norton (2000), who observes that "an investment in the target language is also an investment in a learner's own identity" (p. 11). Pavlenko and Blackledge (2004) foreground the questions of power and em*power*ment which underpin identity concerns:

individuals are agentive beings who are constantly in search of new social and linguistic resources which allow them to resist identities that position them in undesirable ways, produce new identities, and assign alternative meanings to the links between identities and linguistic varieties. (p. 27)

Ricento (2005) goes even further in describing:

the central role of language in the negotiation of a person's sense of self at different points in time and in different contexts, and in allowing a person access (or lack thereof) to powerful social networks that give learners the opportunity to speak. (p. 898)

Web 2.0 places an even greater premium on such issues for language teachers and learners: it elevates to the level of a constituting principle the notion that identity is constructed through language.

In sum, if the limitations of a "single-mode, single-language, single-culture literacy" (Pegrum, forthcoming 2008a) were always apparent to some, they are all the more obvious in our shrinking world, where members of the net generation are simultaneously bound together and yet differentiated from each other through their use of Web 2.0

tools. What Pennycook (2007) has recently written in regard to the rapidly globalizing culture of hip hop—original source of the mashup—applies equally to students' desire for linguistic and cultural self-realisation on Web 2.0:

If we believe that education needs to proceed by taking student knowledge, identity and desire into account, we need to engage with multiple ways of speaking, being and learning, with multilayered modes of identity at global, regional, national and local levels.

Unless we get in touch with this as educators, the flow will pass us by. ... Languages will flow and change around us, new combinations of languages and cultures will be put together, texts will be sampled and mixed in ever new juxtapositions. Students are in the flow; pedagogy needs to go with the flow. (p. 158)

Of course, it is not only about multiple Englishes, but multiple languages. It is not only about multiple texts, but multiple textualities. It is time, as Canagarajah (2003) has suggested, to begin teaching the "fluid literacies" (p. xi) essential for navigation and negotiation in this new hybrid world:

Rather than developing mastery in a 'target language,' we should strive for competence in a repertoire of codes and discourses. Rather than simply joining a speech community, we should teach students to shuttle between communities. Not satisfied with teaching students to be context-sensitive, we should teach them to be context-transforming. (p. xiii)

Few can doubt that students are part of this world already, on the web and beyond it. But that does not mean they are fully accomplished navigators, have all the language and literacy skills they need, or always exercise appropriate critical

judgement. Most students, Hubbard (2004) notes, can "profit from some formal, sustained training in how to take *operational* competence in a given computer application and transfer that into *learning* competence" (p. 51). More than this, students need to learn critical literacy skills to sort through, evaluate and prioritize the masses of data with which they are confronted, turning information into understanding (McFarlane, Roche & Triggs, 2007; Pesce, 2007). They also need a grasp of the powerful linguistic and media options at their disposal for shaping their identities and engaging with others online. It is a fallacy to think that educators in this new virtual world are no more than facilitators. As has been widely argued in the literature about online learning, and in line with social constructivist pedagogical models, teachers must be prepared to play a central organizing, guiding and mentoring role (Garrison & Anderson, 2003; Pegrum, 2007; Warschauer, 2007).

In doing so, they have a golden opportunity to engage with their students. They can support the latter's online self-presentations and endorse their community building by helping to enhance their language and literacy skills. At the same time, teachers should be open to learning from their students about their digital lifestyles — and in the process, teachers may well find their own language and literacy skills enhanced in unexpected ways. Collaboration which brings together teachers' pedagogical and critical expertise and students' technological and practical expertise is the only way to unlock the full educational potential of Web 2.0.

THINKING COLLABORATIVELY

Much of Web 2.0 is devoted to fostering communities of interest or practice which nurture collaborative thinking. As such, it effectively illustrates the potential, noted by Kaye in the early days of computer-mediated communication, for the "weaving together of ideas and information

Figure 1. Sample discussion thread replies from Third Space Trial 1, Feb. 2007

```
Re: Only Native Englishes can be taught meh??? by          - Wednesday, 7 February 2007, 11:53 PM
    Maybe ... by          - Sunday, 11 February 2007, 04:11 PM
Re: Only Native Englishes can be taught meh??? by          - Thursday, 8 February 2007, 12:25 PM
    Nurturing global listeners by          - Friday, 9 February 2007, 05:00 AM
        Re: Nurturing global listeners by          - Saturday, 10 February 2007, 06:24 AM
            Re: Nurturing global listeners by          - Wednesday, 14 February 2007, 12:32 PM
                Openness to World Englishes by          - Thursday, 15 February 2007, 08:52 AM
                Re: Nurturing global listeners by          - Friday, 16 February 2007, 04:47 AM
        Re: Only Native Englishes can be taught meh??? by          - Friday, 16 February 2007, 04:56 AM
    Passive awareness by          - Monday, 19 February 2007, 04:24 AM
        Re: Passive awareness by          - Monday, 19 February 2007, 10:19 PM
            Re: Passive awareness by          - Wednesday, 21 February 2007, 01:57 AM
                Re: Passive awareness by          - Wednesday, 21 February 2007, 03:40 AM
                    Re: Passive awareness by          - Wednesday, 21 February 2007, 04:52 AM
```

from many peoples' [sic] minds" (1989, p. 3). This principle underpins asynchronous discussion boards (DBs), in some ways a spiritual precursor of Web 2.0, along with the more multifaceted blogs, wikis and hybrid blikis (or blokis), all of which may contain in-built discussion or comments features.

Being text-based, asynchronous DBs are natural vehicles for the development of writing skills, while there is some limited evidence they may also support the development of oral skills (Burgmer, 2006, p. 96; Levy & Stockwell, 2006, p. 182). It has been widely observed that writing on the Internet, because of its conversational nature, often takes the form of a hybrid code, mixing together features of speech and writing with its own peculiar elements (Crystal, 2001a, 2001b; cf. Al-Sa'Di & Hamdan, 2005, on synchronous chat). It is worth bearing in mind, then, that DBs may not only help students learn about standard spoken and written language, but about hybridized language uses of the kind with which they need to be familiar in order to enter fully into many online environments.

If structured carefully, asynchronous DBs can promote the formation of learning communities where students, reacting to and building on each other's ideas in branching discussion threads, collaboratively construct their understandings of the subject matter at hand — all through the medium of written language, which is probably more conducive to reflective educational dis-

cussion than newer voice alternatives (whether synchronous VoIP or asynchronous voiceboards). See Figure 1 for an example of threaded postings in an international Master's forum for language teachers. Used in conjunction with face-to-face classes, DBs may help cater to differing learning styles and needs. For example, they allow more time to be spent on composition of contributions by less extroverted or non-native students; the time-independence of DBs may thus "mitigate the effects of certain inequalities" (Locke, 2007, p. 188). It has also been widely claimed that DB exchanges typically display a high level of cognitive sophistication (e.g., Garrison & Anderson, 2003, p.26; Heckman & Annabi, 2005; Hiltz & Goldman, 2005, p.6). This may be because "[t] he historical divide between speech and writing has been overcome with the interactional and reflective aspects of language merged in a single medium" (Warschauer, 1999, p.6). This particular aspect of online hybridity would certainly seem to have major advantages.

When they involve multilingual or multicultural cohorts of students, DBs may equally promote the development of intercultural competence. In the ongoing *Third Space in Online Discussion* research project, which involves language teachers enrolled in Master's courses at the University of Western Australia and Canterbury Christ Church University, UK, discussion forums (like that seen in Figure 1) are being analyzed as educational "third spaces" which exist in the interstices between students' cultural and educational experiences, and where there is ample space for the deconstruction and reconstruction of pedagogical, linguistic and cultural knowledge and understanding (Pegrum & Bax, 2007). It is apparent that, as Zieghahn (2001) realized some years ago, "the online environment offers a unique medium through which to reflect upon individual cultural position and on inter-cultural communication" (p. 144). While most educational DBs necessarily operate in a single lingua franca, multilingual forums are possible in some language learning situations. Linguistically as well as culturally, then, DBs can help educators respond to Canagarajah's aforementioned plea to teach students to shuttle between communities. In the process, their sense of their online — and perhaps offline — selves may be shaped through their interactions with peers.

While blogs — described by Doctorow (2002) as "outboard brain[s]" — can function as reflective diaries, they can also be conversational centre-pieces: readers may leave comments for a blog's author and each other, thereby forging connections and community around topics of mutual interest. Students can certainly join the conversations on others' blogs, but they can equally set up their own. Receiving feedback on blog entries from peers and teachers can facilitate knowledge con-struction as well as perspective shifts as they go about developing their online personas. Indeed, with fully public blogs, students can potentially receive feedback from anyone on the entire Internet and may, as a result, invest themselves more fully in writing and publishing tasks.

Because blogs can be multilingual (allowing some mixing of the mother tongue with the target language), multimodal (allowing pictures, video and audio to support written text), and carefully designed (drawing on technical knowledge and artistic flair), students at even the lowest levels of linguistic proficiency need not feel the work they are creating fails to capture or express important as-pects of their identities or beliefs. At higher levels, as students' linguistic competence develops, they

can present more nuanced versions of themselves. As Kazan indicates, "[w]ithin cyberspace, writers have flexibility in how they construct a self and the more strategies they acquire, the more flexibility they have" (2007, p. 264). The task for teachers is to help students make more "informed rhetori-cal decisions" (ibid.), which will allow them not only to shape their online identities as they wish, but also to "develop a public voice about issues they care about" and so come to understand "their literacies as citizenship skills as well as avenues to entertainment" (Rheingold, 2007).

Wikis are even more strongly oriented towards collaboration than blogs since they are effectively co-operatively authored websites. They turn the element of collective intelligence implicit in blogging communities into a structural principle. Students are able to engage in a form of process writing in which they draft and redraft work collaboratively, each contributor adding to and modifying the work of peers. With a private wiki, feedback can be received from the class teacher and peers, or, with a public wiki, from the entire Internet. As Mitchell (2005) notes, it has even been suggested that wikis are an example of "the tried and trusted system of peer review taken to a new level" (p.120).

One option is for students to contribute to pre-existing wikis such as Wikipedia or, for learners, Simple English Wikipedia, thereby entering into established communities of practice. Alternatively, dedicated class wikis can be set up on subjects of relevance or interest, and in time new communities of practice may form around these. Even a course constrained by a tight, exam-oriented syllabus can exploit wiki technology: under the guidance of the teacher, each individual's or group's research could feed into a network of student-constructed documents reviewing material to be covered in the exam. This might include vocabulary ac-companied by definitions and examples; gram-mar points accompanied by explanations and illustrations; or set literature accompanied by summaries and quotations. Once again, there is ample opportunity for multilingual, multimodal, technically sophisticated and artistically creative presentation. The more sophisticated the wiki, the greater the students' facility with multiliteracies will need to be — or become.

SOCIAL NETWORKING

Social networking technologies also promote collaborative thinking, many of them effectively harnessing the power of collective intelligence, but the accent is on the networking aspect. It has been suggested that Facebook, for example, "puts the social community first, with content—including, but not limited to, educational content—being the medium of exchange" (Downes, 2007). Some observers claim that virtual networks are replacing the gradually disappearing or increasingly inaccessible public spaces in which young people formerly gathered (boyd, 2006). These networks are intimately bound up with selfhood; the sense of empowerment that comes from the crafting of personal identity on social sites (Coghlan, 2007) goes hand in hand with negotiating membership of the groups of friends and acquaintances who congregate there. The potential effects on language education are an extension of the paradigm shift neatly captured at the start of the millennium by Kramsch, A'Ness & Lam (2000, p. 97) in their comments on language learning through participation in informal online interaction:

The kind of language experience ... in which rules are learned first and then put to use in conversation, has given way to a learning by doing, and learning to meet the demands of doing in specific contexts, to solve immediate problems together in the small culture of communities of practice (Holliday, 1999; Lave & Wenger, 1991; Uber Grosse & Leto, 1999; Wenger, 1999). Rather than an object of reverence or study in itself, language is viewed as a tool which brings people together and creates intimacy (Harmon, 1999). What is important is how you relate, emotionally, and physically, to that world.

Social networking sites, with MySpace and Facebook being by far the most popular, allow each user to set up an online identity, or profile, and to keep in touch with friends and acquaintances by constantly updating this profile while regularly viewing others' profiles; new contacts can be established through mutual acquaintances or shared interests. Since 2006, Facebook has used a news feed system to keep users updated on changes to the profiles of their contacts. Typically, social networking sites integrate a range of other communication channels, which may include email, instant messaging (IM) and even blogs, with facilities for sharing photos, videos and audio files. There is a fine line separating these sites from social sharing services, such as Flickr for photos or YouTube for videos. Facebook allows the integration of Flickr photos as well as del.icio.us tags (see below) into profiles, while it is now also possible for users to assemble friends and acquaintances from the virtual world Second Life alongside their other contacts.

Social networking sites are perhaps the most maligned feature of Web 2.0, mainly due to fears of Internet predation but also because of concerns over time spent online, as well as the possible degeneration of literacy skills as the digital natives communicate ever more rapidly in ever more truncated "netspeak." Yet the reality is that students are already using social networking sites and educators have the choice to work with or against them. The advantage of the former strategy is that it is possible to openly address concerns over Internet safety or time spent online, attempting to provide guidance in such areas. This might be extended to include a focus on what Barney (2007, p. 279) refers to as "critical technological literacy": asking questions about the presuppositions and blind spots, the benefits and drawbacks, in short, the "affordances and ... denials" of different technologies. Helping students adopt a critical distance to all technologies will do them a much greater service in the long run than simply closing down all discussion in the classroom, leaving them to conduct their explorations, unguided, in their own time.

At the same time, there are many educationally beneficial aspects of social sites which can be more fully exploited. According to recent US statistics, some 59% of 9-17 year olds say they talk about topics broadly related to education on social networking sites, while 50% claim to discuss schoolwork (National School Boards Association, 2007, p.1). Thus, whatever educators may think, students have already appropriated social networking as a constructivist learning tool. However, educators could certainly do more to encourage the use of this tool for groupwork outside the classroom. The potential for language learning partnerships is undoubtedly great. Lakshimi (2007), discussing her English language students' use of the social networking site Orkut, comments: "Students who have been incommunicado in the classroom are so interactive on Orkut that it leaves me wondering if Orkut would be a better teacher than I am in helping students learn to use English to be socially interactive" (n.p.). Interaction, of course, is precisely the motivation: the wish to communicate and participate, with language being an essential tool.

Social sharing sites offer the additional possibility of posting individual or collaborative work to the web, with students viewing each other's materials and, for example, commenting on their peers' photographed posters (Flickr), PowerPoint slides (Slideshare), presentations (YouTube) or short films posted to blogs (such as the *English Advertising Class*). As Coghlan (2007) observes with regard to student-created advertisements on the last of these sites, some examples may involve little traditional language use, but there is a lot of learning potential in the areas of "multiliteracy, digital literacy and e-literacy."

The communication on social networking and social sharing sites offers, finally, a unique opportunity to explore with students the nature and uses of netspeak, when and where it is appropriate, and how to codeswitch between netspeak and more standardised language forms. One of the main reasons for the widely criticized spread of netspeak into more traditional domains of literacy may well be students' ignorance of codeswitching or their inability to carry it out appropriately. Teachers' failure to explicitly address this area with students can only limit the latter's repertoire of literacies and constrain their ability to access and move between linguistic communities.

INFORMATION LINKING

Folksonomies are a step beyond social sharing. Relying very much on the principle of collective intelligence, they are a way of indexing distributed knowledge, which is then typically presented in the semi-organic form of a tag cloud, as seen in Figure 2. In essence, they allow information linking with a social element, because people (the "folk") have a central organizing role, which gives rise to rich "person-mediated serendipity" (Lambe, 2006, n.p.). After all, people who use the same tags are likely to have similar interests; and a folksonomy allows tags to be traced to users, and those users' other tags to be explored. The potential for "collaborative information discovery" (Alexander, 2006, p. 36) may be exploited by students working together to create class folksonomies dependent on criteria negotiated and evaluated by the students themselves. This could even involve the tagging of the students' own material posted on wikis or social sharing sites. Given the usefulness of well-constructed folksonomies, they might also be consulted by members of wider communities of practice on the Internet and could provide a means of entry into such communities; as Wenger (1998) reminds readers, learning communities should not be isolated but should "use the world around them as a learning resource and be a learning resource for the world" (p. 275). In all

Figure 2. Extract from E-language Tag Cloud (http://e-language.wikispaces.com/e-learning-tagcloud)

cases, tagging, like indexing of any kind, requires a high level of facility with the language being used for classification. With sufficient scaffolding, folksonomy building can function as a literacy enhancement exercise.

RSS (Really Simple Syndication) feeds provide automatic updates of syndicated content — ranging from blog entries to podcasts—from sites to which a user subscribes. Many homepage, blog and wiki services now make it very easy to include selected RSS feeds on webpages. Drawing in feeds from other sites in this way amounts to the incorporation of others' views and perspectives, leading to the co-construction of knowledge within a new frame. At the same time, as Anderson (2006) notes with respect to blog feeds, distribution of content by RSS allows "public review, argument and resolution of topic issues by students globally— in the process creating outstanding international learning opportunities" (p. 146).

Incoming feeds naturally entail a constant stream of information flowing into a desktop aggregator or webpage. The language could be that of native speakers; thus, learners could conceivably subscribe to media or blog feeds in languages they know or are learning, and would be exposed to extensive authentic input. There is also an argument, however, for subscribing to non-native language feeds. For example, TESOL students working in a World Englishes paradigm might find it beneficial to subscribe to feeds from Kachru's outer or expanding circles. Incorporating

both native and non-native feeds would lead to a rich patchwork of first and additional language usage, approximating in some ways the multi-dialectal reality of today's world. Awareness of multiliteracies can be enhanced through feeds which distribute audio or video content in addition to or in place of written text.

MASHUP FRONTIERS

Some of the greatest educational promise is to be found in the areas of podcasting, vodcasting, m-learning and virtual worlds, all of which offer considerable language learning opportunities, especially for those prepared to work with multiple literacies and language mashups.

M-learning refers to education involving mobile technology. The best-known example is podcasting, where syndicated audio files, potentially with accompanying text or image files, are downloaded from the web and transferred to a portable device such as an iPod or MP3 player, thus facilitating "time and place shifting to access the content" (Molina & 2006 EDUCAUSE Evolving Technologies Committee, 2006, p. 122). Listening to podcasts is widely perceived as advantageous for learning foreign languages or even brushing up on grammar, vocabulary or style in one's first language. Surveying a selection of national iTunes stores on the randomly selected date of 17 October, 2007, for instance, it was found that the majority of the 25 most popular educational podcasts in each country were related to foreign language learning or first language improvement: 24 in Spain, 22 in Germany and Switzerland, 21 in Australia, New Zealand and the UK, 20 in Canada and Ireland, 19 in France, Sweden and the US, and 17 in Italy.

M-learning can also involve regularly sending students digestible chunks of information via mobile phones, as has been done, for example, with Italian vocabulary accompanied by quizzes at Griffith University in Australia (Levy & Kennedy, 2005). However, there is the potential for greater levels of interactivity than this, as suggested in a recently proposed definition of m-learning as "the processes of coming to know through conversations across multiple contexts among people and personal interactive technologies" (Sharples, Taylor & Vavoula, 2007, p.225). For example, students can work individually or, better still, collaboratively to create podcasts or even vodcasts – as video podcasts are usually known – for publication to the web. Moblogging, or mobile blogging, allows students to use devices like mobile phones to post text, audio or video files to blogs. Peers and teachers can then respond to these postings in traditional text or mixed-media formats, addressing the communicative intent while possibly also critiquing features of language or composition. In many cases, spoken language will be foregrounded, thus helping to balance out the heavy emphasis on written text still typical of the web, including Web 2.0. Sometimes there may be room for multiple linguistic codes and registers if not multiple dialects or languages. More sophisticated versions of m-learning involve participants interacting with real-world environments and each other with the aid of GPS-enabled phones and other portable devices, which may provide instructions and information as well as a variety of communication channels; salient examples range from the MOBIlearn Uffizi Gallery trial in Florence, Italy (Sharples, Taylor & Vavoula, 2007, pp.236-242) to the *Handheld Augmented Reality Project,* or

HARP, conducted at Harvard University in the USA (Harvard University, n.d.).

Virtual worlds are perhaps the most striking realization of the possibilities of Web 2.0. The avatars which inhabit them are certainly Web 2.0's clearest example of the potential for identity creation, shaping and development. These worlds are very much about networking. Within them, avatars' understandings of their new environment are constructed largely through their engagement—their sharing and building of knowledge — with other avatars. Externally, virtual worlds are supported by and increasingly integrated with blogs, wikis, and social networking sites. Operating around and through these sites are distributed knowledge systems where, as in the gaming communities discussed by Williamson and Facer (2004), the key information is found "in the interconnections between the 'nodes' (the people, texts, tools and technologies) in the network, rather than with isolated individuals" (p. 266, with reference to Gee). In a comment which captures something of the richness of the virtual/non-virtual interface, the best-known of these worlds, Second Life (SL), has been described as "a playground [and] a crucible for ideas about how people can augment their interaction through constructive, and constructivist, play/work/whatever" (Stevens, 2007, n.p.).

Since the rollout of voice technology to SL in mid-2007, in-world avatar-to-avatar interactions can involve a mixture of spoken and written language not unlike that found in the real world. This creates valuable opportunities for students to try out new language, building up confidence and fluency before embarking on real world encounters. Language teachers have been quick to pick up on this potential, with the inaugural SLanguages Colloquium taking place on 23 June, 2007, and bringing together around 50 educators from across the globe; a snapshot of the opening talk by Gavin Dudeney is shown in Figure 3. Language teaching is already underway in SL, with English classes on offer, for example, through The English Village and Languagelab.com. SL also offers immersive

Figure 3. Inaugural SLanguages Colloquium on EduNation in Second Life, 23 June 2007. Reproduced by kind permission of Gavin Dudeney, EduNation.

linguistic experiences outside formal classes, a point emphasised at the inaugural in-world Festival of European Languages in 2007, which promoted the idea of learners seeking out target language areas of SL in which to practise their skills.

A certain degree of linguistic versatility is advantageous for anyone wishing to develop a fuller SL presence, since language is the glue which holds together any community which establishes itself there. Community, in fact, has been described as the killer app of SL (Yowell, cited in Panganiban, 2007). Different languages, and certainly different dialects and registers, are necessary for effective participation in a range of contexts and communities, with an increased linguistic repertoire being a concomitant of increased community involvement and wider social networking. This is not unlike the real world, except it is now possible to cross linguistic and cultural boundaries without leaving one's desk.

Anecdotal evidence suggests multilingual interactions in SL are becoming more common. A striking example of a four-person, five-language (Catalan, English, French, Portuguese and Spanish) conversation has been described by Gavin Dudeney, who writes of "the ease with which some of us switched between the languages we knew, and typed furiously to reformulate things we thought one of the others wouldn't understand into a language they would," resulting in "a very rich

evening" (personal communication, 11 Oct. 2007). Vance Stevens (2007) quotes a comment about SL which hints at intriguing language education possibilities: "Yesterday a cheerful Italian gave me a Babbler translator so we started teaching each other Italian and Hungarian using English as the common language, which was real fun, especially that we were figure ice-skating meanwhile" (n.p.). Participation in such conversations — and teaching scenarios — requires a willingness to engage with the unruliness of linguistic globalization as reflected through virtual world encounters. It demands a capacity to codeswitch and a facility with intercultural communicative competence skills: in short, the agility to shuttle between linguistic and cultural communities. This, in turn, reads like a set of lesson aims compiled from recent thinking on language pedagogy. While a single target language will necessarily remain the focus of most language lessons — and can be supported with SL immersion experiences — there is no reason why students should not occasionally be exposed to multilingual, multicultural interactions, especially as these are likely to become ever more central not only to the SL microcosm, but to the wider web, and indeed the world which lies beyond it.

LIMITATIONS OF WEB 2.0 IN EDUCATION

This chapter has discussed the potential of Web 2.0 for education generally and language education specifically. However, it will take time for current practices to become more widespread and for the potential of Web 2.0 to be fully realized. This requires further "normalization" of computing, so that the majority of educators eventually come to regard it with neither fear nor awe, but see it as simply providing a set of tools which may be used in the service of particular pedagogical goals (Bax, 2003; Chambers & Bax, 2006). Teacher training has a major role to play in demystifying computing. Specifically, this entails providing teachers with appropriate pedagogical frameworks for e-learning; an overview of the range of tools available; and adequate technological skills so that they do not feel intimidated by their students' know-how and, moreover, have the confidence to draw on the latter's technological expertise to complement their own pedagogical expertise. In addition, Web 2.0 provides very serviceable tools for building social constructivist professional development forums, and it is possible to imagine that in time "Web 2.0 may well become the biggest training institution in the world" (Consultants-E, 2007). This point will only be reached, however, if intensive preparatory work is carried out by today's teacher training institutions.

While learning about the advantages of Web 2.0, teachers must equally come to understand that e-learning is not, in and of itself, automatically constructivist or pedagogically progressive (Pegrum, forthcoming 2008b), and demands for speed, flexibility and cost saving can easily lead to impoverished content delivery systems. As suggested earlier, some creativity is needed to work within the constraints of rigid syllabi or assessments. As rewarding as it may be, well-designed online learning will normally require a heavy investment of time and energy by both staff and students. There is also a danger that, in their current state of "continuous partial attention" (Stone, 2006), technology users will lose the ability to focus clearly as well as the will to occasionally power down their multifarious communication channels and make time for reflection—a crucial part of education (Pegrum, 2005). And, even while acknowledging the benefits of constructivism, it might be asked whether it is possible or desirable to teach everything in a constructivist manner all of the time. It is important to maintain balance in all of the above areas.

If students are already spending a lot of time online, added educational demands should have a clear value. The identity issues permeating online presence are complex and delicate, and educators should beware of aggravating narcissistic tendencies which may be nourished by social networking (Ryan, 2007). Teachers must also face the fact they may not be welcome to approach students on some sites and through some channels; sensitivity is needed in negotiating educational uses with students.

Collaborative work raises questions of authorship and ownership, while non-participation is often not an option, as Conrad (2002) has noted with regard to virtual learning environments: "you cannot run *and* you cannot hide. Online life is a fishbowl existence" (p.208; italics in original). There is some cause for concern over privacy on social networking sites like Facebook (boyd, 2008). What is more, a lot of online material is preserved indefinitely so that, as Friedman (2006) warns in a more general context, "whatever you do, whatever mistakes you make, will be searchable one day" (p. 185).

Of course, the continued presence of a digital divide—or, more accurately perhaps, a digital spectrum (Haythornthwaite, 2007)—means that not everyone around the world, or within any given society, has equal access to the Internet. While the rapid spread of mobile technologies partially alleviates this situation, it is not the end of the issue: in recent years, the digital divide has come to be seen less in terms of access to technology and more in terms of skills and patterns of use (*ibid.*; Warschauer, 2003) or, in short, digital literacy. It should also be remembered that "global communication technologies are cultural artifacts that are produced by and productive of socio-historically located subjects" (Belz & Thorne 2006, p. xviii), and that they carry the Anglo-centric and, more broadly, Western values of their creators (Ess, 2007; Goodfellow, 2003; Reeder, Macfadyen, Chase & Roche, 2004). Students from varying linguistic, cultural, ethnic, religious, social and educational backgrounds may have their reasons for not wishing to participate in some or all online activities—reasons whose legitimacy is often eclipsed in Western secular education. Compromises must be sought with students who, for example, may struggle with the radically egalitarian nature of social networking technologies or who, as Sabre (2007) notes, might be uncomfortable with virtual worlds because of religious prohibitions on graphic representations of humans.

But perhaps the greatest single issue for would-be Web 2.0 educators may be an inability to step outside traditional philosophical and sociopolitical frames of reference. This could mean an inability to see outside the frame of Enlightenment rationalism and objectivism and to grasp the socially constructed nature of knowledge and learning, a fundamental flaw in Keen's timely if hyperbolic critique, *The Cult of the Amateur* (2007). It might mean an inability to value collaboration and community on their own terms outside of a capitalist paradigm of competition, as seen in Tapscott and Williams' otherwise informative *Wikinomics* (2006). It could mean an inability to perceive that, for the net generation, the notion of a prophylactic divide between "virtual" and "real" life makes little sense: like the radio or the telephone for older generations, the virtual is just another part of the real (cf. Davies, 2003; Thorne, 2006, p. 20). In fact, the connections between them are becoming ubiquitous, as seen in services such as

Vodafone's InsideOut, which allows calls between the physical world and Second Life.

For this reason, despite initial evidence which points to a lowering of cognitive performance and efficiency through multitasking (Baron, 2008; Wallis, 2006), it is possible that students who monitor multiple IM channels while writing assignments or who send text messages during lectures are engaging in what, for them, is "a natural way to interact and construct their own learning" (Reddekopp, 2006). Through practice, they may have adapted to such behaviour (Baron, 2008). What if, moreover, such a melding of learning, networking and identity building could give rise to lateral connections and a more holistic mode of education? In the absence of empirical evidence, these reflections are necessarily speculative. However, it is important not to close off new possibilities before they are fully apparent, thereby perhaps losing valuable educational opportunities—and losing students' allegiance along the way. While the digital natives have much to learn about language and literacy from an older generation of teachers, the teaching profession as a whole has much to learn from its digital native students, especially here at the technological and social frontier of Web 2.0.

CONCLUSION

The technologies covered in this chapter—discussion boards, blogs, wikis, social networking, social sharing, folksonomies, RSS, podcasting, vodcasting, m-learning and virtual worlds — comprise a representative Web 2.0 list, but one which is both incomplete and unstable. New technologies and applications are constantly appearing, while there is an overall tendency towards functional convergence. Yet, however this list might look a few years from now, it is likely to still be informed by the fundamental features this chapter has described as underpinning Web 2.0: communicative networking, community building and identity negotiation, performed through hybrid codes, multiple media and linguacultural mashups.

Writing of Web 2.0, McIntosh (2006) suggests that "[t]he reason these social technologies work is because they are social. But they are also changing the way that we socialise" (p. 72). As has been seen, socializing and networking on Web 2.0 are very much dependent on language. Web 2.0 is, after all, "a means whereby just about anyone can contribute to an ongoing 'conversation' in which knowledge is both discovered and constructed as it goes on" (Freedman, 2006, p.13), and there can be no conversation without language. It is little wonder, then, that Crystal (2001a, 2001b) has called the Internet a linguistic revolution; that Macfadyen & Doff (2005, following Cicognani) have claimed that cyberspace must be viewed in linguistic terms; or that some observers feel Web 2.0 comes close to realizing Tim Berners-Lee's original idea of the web as a "read-write medium" (Lee & Berry, 2006, p. 20).

It has been suggested in this chapter that language and literacy educators are in an ideal position to exploit the linguistic nature of Web 2.0. This requires a conception of literacy – indeed, of multiliteracies – which is appropriate to Web 2.0 and the increasingly interconnected world of which it is both a symbol and a product. It requires a suitable pedagogical base for e-learning, drawing on social constructivism, communities of practice, intercultural communicative competence and identity studies. It requires a familiarity with the advantages and drawbacks of each Web 2.0 tool, coupled with an ability to tailor such tools to particular cultural contexts. It requires some reflection on how to address pedagogical, social, sociopolitical and philosophical limitations on the use of Web 2.0 in education. In all of the above, teacher training has an important role to play.

Beyond this, if language and literacy educators are to fully exploit the potential of Web 2.0 as a platform to enhance language teaching and to help their students become more sophisticated users of language(s) within — and beyond — the digital environment, they need to adopt an open, exploratory and flexible attitude. They need to appreciate and work with the social orientation of Web 2.0. They need to become comfortable with linguistic and media mashups and actively foster the codeswitching and shuttling skills demanded by the untidy realities of globalization, on- and offline. And, while continuing to provide the same level of educational input and guidance as good teachers have always done, they need to trust the digital natives to help them map what, for education, is still largely uncharted territory.

REFERENCES

Al-Sa'Di, R. A., & Hamdan, J. M. (2005). Synchronous online chat English: Computer-mediated communication. *World Englishes, 24*(4), 409–424.

Alexander, B. (2006). Web 2.0: A new wave of innovation for teaching and learning? *EDUCAUSE Review, 41*(2), 32-44. Retrieved November 29, 2007, from http://www.educause.edu/ir/library/pdf/erm0621.pdf

Anderson, T. (2006). Interaction in learning and teaching on the educational Semantic Web. In C. Juwah (Ed.), *Interactions in online education: Implications for theory and practice* (pp.141-155). London: Routledge.

Barney, D. (2007). The question of education in technological society. In J. Lockard & M. Pegrum (Eds.), *Brave new classrooms: Democratic education and the Internet* (pp. 271-284). New York: Peter Lang.

Baron, N. (2008). Adjusting the volume: Technology and multitasking in discourse control. In J.E. Katz (Ed.), *Handbook of mobile communication studies* (pp.177-194). Cambridge, MA: MIT Press.

Barton, D., & Hamilton, M. (2000). Literacy practices. In D. Barton, M. Hamilton & R. Ivanič (Eds.), *Situated literacies: Reading and writing in context* (pp. 7-15). London: Routledge.

Bax, S. (2003). CALL – Past, present and future. *System, 31*, 13–28. doi:10.1016/S0346-251X(02)00071-4

Belz, J. A., & Thorne, S. L. (2006). Introduction: Internet-mediated intercultural foreign language education and the intercultural speaker. In J.A. Belz & S.L. Thorne (Eds.), *Internet-mediated intercultural foreign language education* (pp. viii-xxv). Boston: Heinle & Heinle. boyd, d. (2006). *Identity production in a networked culture: Why youth heart MySpace.* Paper presented to American Association for the Advancement of Science, 19 February. Retrieved November 29, 2007, from http://www.danah.org/papers/AAAS2006.html boyd, d. (2008). Facebook's privacy trainwreck: Exposure, invasion, and social convergence. *Convergence, 14*(1), 13-20.

Burgmer, C. (2006). *Computer-mediated communication (CMC): A beneficial tool for modern language learning?* Unpublished M. Phil. dissertation, University of Dundee, UK.

Byram, M. (1997). *Teaching and assessing intercultural communicative competence.* Clevedon: Multilingual Matters.

Canagarajah, S. (2003). Foreword. In G. Smitherman & V. Villanueva (Eds.), *Language diversity in the classroom: From intention to practice* (pp. ix-xiv). Carbondale, IL: Southern Illinois University Press.

Chambers, A., & Bax, S. (2006). Making CALL work: Towards normalisation. *System, 34*, 465–479. doi:10.1016/j.system.2006.08.001

Coghlan, M. (2007). *Language learning in a connected world.* Paper presented at New and Emerging Technologies in ELT, Loyola College, Chennai, India, 3-5 Aug.

Coleman, J. (2007). *Eeyore and the pixel dropout: What's wrong with technology-enhanced learning?* Paper presented at New and Emerging Technologies in ELT, Loyola College, Chennai, India, 3-5 Aug.

Conrad, D. (2002). Inhibition, integrity and etiquette among online learners: The art of niceness. *Distance Education, 23*(2), 197–212. doi:10.1080/0158791022000009204

Cope, B., & Kalantzis, M. (Eds.). (2000). *Multiliteracies: Literacy learning and the design of social futures.* London: Routledge.

Corbett, J. (2003). *An intercultural approach to English language teaching.* Clevedon: Multilingual Matters.

Crystal, D. (2001a). *Language and the Internet.* Cambridge: Cambridge University Press.

Crystal, D. (2001b). A linguistic revolution? *Education Communication and Information, 1*(2), 93–97.

Dalgarno, B. (2001). Interpretations of constructivism and consequences for computer assisted learning. *British Journal of Educational Technology, 32*(2), 183–194. doi:10.1111/1467-8535.00189

Davies, W. (2003). *You don't know me but… Social capital and social software.* London: The Work Foundation. Retrieved November 29, 2007, from http://www.theworkfoundation.com/Assets/PDFs/you_dontknowme.pdf

Doctorow, C. (2002). My blog, my outboard brain. *O'Reilly WebDev Center*, 31 May. Retrieved November 29, 2007, from http://www.oreillynet.com/lpt/a/javascript/2002/01/01/cory.html

Downes, S. (2007). Places to go: Facebook. *Innovate, 4*(1). Retrieved November 29, 2007, from http://www.innovateonline.info/index.php?view=article&id=517

Dudfield, A. (1999). Literacy and cyberculture. *Reading Online.* Retrieved November 29, 2007, from http://www.readingonline.org/articles/dudfield/main.html

Ess, C. (2007). Liberal arts and distance education: Can Socratic virtue and Confucius' exemplary person be taught online? In J. Lockard & M. Pegrum (Eds.), *Brave new classrooms: Democratic education and the Internet* (pp. 189-212). New York: Peter Lang.

Finger, G., Russell, G., Jamieson-Proctor, R., & Russell, N. (2007). *Transforming learning with ICT: Making it happen.* Frenchs Forest: Pearson.

Freedman, T. (2006). Introduction. In T. Freedman (Ed.), *Coming of age: An introduction to the new world wide web* (pp.13-14). Ilford: Terry Freedman. Retrieved November 29, 2007, from http://fullmeasure.co.uk/Coming_of_age_v1-2.pdf

Friedman, T. L. (2006). *The world is flat: The globalized world in the twenty-first century* (2nd ed.). London: Penguin.

Garrison, D. R., & Anderson, T. (2003). *E-learning in the 21st century: A framework for research and practice.* London: Routledge Falmer.

Goodfellow, R. (2003). *Literacies, technologies, and learning communities: Speaking and writing in the virtual classroom.* Paper presented at EuroCALL 03, Limerick, Ireland, 5 Sept. Retrieved November 29, 2007, from http://iet.open.ac.uk/pp/r.goodfellow/Euroc03/talk.htm

Harvard University. (n.d.). *Handheld augmented reality project (HARP).* Retrieved November 29, 2007, from http://isites.harvard.edu/icb/icb.do?keyword=harp

Haythornthwaite, C. (2007). Digital divide and e-learning. In R. Andrews & C. Haythornthwaite (Eds.), *The Sage handbook of e-learning research* (pp.97-118). Los Angeles: Sage.

Heckman, R., & Annabi, H. (2005). A content analytic comparison of learning processes in online and face-to-face case study discussions. *Journal of Computer-Mediated Communication, 10*(2). Retrieved November 29, 2007, from http://jcmc.indiana.edu/vol10/issue2/heckman.html

Hiltz, S. R., & Goldman, R. (2005). What are asynchronous learning networks? In S.R. Hiltz & R. Goldman (Eds.), *Learning together online: Research on asynchronous learning networks* (pp.3-18). Mahwah, NJ: Lawrence Erlbaum.

Holmes, B., Tangney, B., FitzGibbon, A., Savage, T., & Mehan, S. (2001). *Communal constructivism: Students constructing learning for as well as with others.* Dublin: University of Dublin Department of Computer Science. Retrieved November 29, 2007, from https://www.cs.tcd.ie/publications/tech-reports/reports.01/TCD-CS-2001-04.pdf

Hoppe, H. U., Joiner, R., Milrad, M., & Sharples, M. (2003). Guest editorial: Wireless and mobile technologies in education. *Journal of Computer Assisted Learning, 19*(3), 255–259. doi:10.1046/j.0266-4909.2003.00027.x

Hubbard, P. (2004). Learner training for effective use of CALL. In S. Fotos & C. Browne (Eds.), *New perspectives on CALL for second language classrooms* (pp. 45-68). Mahwah, NJ: Lawrence Erlbaum.

Jonassen, D. H. (1992). Evaluating constructivistic learning. In T. M. Duffy & D. H. Jonassen (Eds.), *Constructivism and the technology of instruction: A conversation* (pp. 137-148). Hillsdale, NJ: Lawrence Erlbaum.

Kaye, A. (1989). Computer-mediated communication and distance education. In R. Mason & A.R. Kaye (Eds.), *Mindweave: Communication, computers and distance education* (pp. 3-21). Oxford: Pergamon.

Kazan, T. S. (2007). Braving the body: Embodiment and (cyber-)texts. In J. Lockard & M. Pegrum (Eds.), *Brave new classrooms: Democratic education and the Internet* (pp. 251-269). New York: Peter Lang.

Keen, A. (2007). *The cult of the amateur: How today's Internet is killing our culture.* London: Nicholas Brealey.

Kern, R. (2006). Perspectives on technology in learning and teaching languages. *TESOL Quarterly, 40*(1), 183–210.

Kist, W. (2004). *New literacies in action: Teaching and learning in multiple media.* New York: Teachers' College Press.

Kramsch, C. (1993). *Context and culture in language teaching.* Oxford: Oxford University Press.

Kramsch, C. (1998). The privilege of the intercultural speaker. In M. Byram & M. Fleming (Eds.), *Language learning in intercultural perspective: Approaches through drama and ethnography* (pp. 16-31). Cambridge: Cambridge University Press.

Kramsch, C., A'Ness, F., & Lam, W. S. E. (2000). Authenticity and authorship in the computer-mediated acquisition of L2 literacy. *Language Learning & Technology, 4*(2). Retrieved 29 Nov., 2007 from http://llt.msu.edu/vol4num2/kramsch/default.html

Lakshimi, S. K. C. (2007). *The role of teachers and the modern tool of online community networks in facilitating social interaction.* Paper presented at New and Emerging Technologies in ELT, Loyola College, Chennai, India, 3-5 Aug.

Lambe, P. (2006). Folksonomies and rich serendipity. *Green Chameleon,* 20 Oct. Retrieved November 29, 2007, from http://www.greenchameleon.com/gc/blog_detail/folksonomies_and_rich_serendipity/

Lee, S., & Berry, M. (2006). Effective e-learning through collaboration. In T. Freedman (Ed.), *Coming of age: An introduction to the new world wide web* (pp. 19-28). Ilford: Terry Freedman. Retrieved November 29, 2007, from http://fullmeasure.co.uk/Coming_of_age_v1-2.pdf

Levy, M., & Kennedy, C. (2005). Learning Italian via mobile SMS. In A. Kukulska-Hulme & J. Traxler (Eds.), *Mobile learning: A handbook for educators and trainers* (pp. 76-83). London: Routledge.

Levy, M., & Stockwell, G. (2006). *CALL dimensions: Options and issues in computer assisted language learning.* Mahwah, NJ: Lawrence Erlbaum.

Locke, T. (2007). E-learning and the reshaping of rhetorical space. In R. Andrews & C. Haythornthwaite (Eds.), *The Sage handbook of e-learning research* (pp. 179-201). London: Sage.

Macfadyen, L. P., & Doff, S. (2005). The language of cyberspace: Text, discourse, cultural tool. In C. Ghaoui (Ed.), *Encyclopedia of human-computer interaction.* Hershey, PA: The Idea Group. Retrieved November 1, 2006, from http://homepage.mac.com/leahmac/LM/Docs/C65MacfadyenDoff.pdf

McFarlane, A., Roche, N., & Triggs, P. (2007). *Mobile learning: Research findings. Report to BECTA.* Coventry: BECTA. Retrieved January 14, 2008, from http://partners.becta.org.uk/upload-dir/downloads/page_documents/research/mobile_learning_july07.pdf

McIntosh, E. (2006). Podcasting and wikis. In T. Freedman (Ed.), *Coming of age: An introduction to the new World Wide Web* (pp.71-75). Ilford: Terry Freedman. Retrieved November 29, 2007, from http://fullmeasure.co.uk/Coming_of_age_v1-2.pdf

Mitchell, P. (2005). Wikis in education. In J. Klobas et al., *Wikis: Tools for information, work and collaboration* (pp. 119-147). Oxford: Chandos.

Molina, P. G. 2006 EDUCAUSE Evolving Technologies Committee. (2006). Pioneering new territory and technologies. *EDUCAUSE Review, 41*(5), 112-134. Retrieved January 14, 2008, from http://www.educause.edu/ir/library/pdf/erm0659.pdf

Motteram, G., & Ioannou-Georgiou, S. (2007). *Are teachers fit for Web 6.0?* Paper presented at New and Emerging Technologies in ELT, Loyola College, Chennai, India, 3-5 Aug.

National School Boards Association [USA]. (2007). *Creating and connecting: Research and guidelines on online social—and educational —networking.* Alexandria, VA: National School Boards Association. Retrieved November 29, 2007, from http://www.nsba.org/site/docs/41400/41340.pdf

Norton, B. (2000). *Identity and language learning: Gender, ethnicity and educational change.* Harlow: Longman.

O'Reilly, T. (2005). What is Web 2.0: Design patterns and business models for the next generation of software. *O'Reilly,* 30 Sept. Retrieved January 14, 2008, from http://www.oreillynet.com/pub/a/oreilly/tim/news/2005/09/30/what-is-web-20.html?page=1

Panganiban, R. (2007). SLCC Day 1: 'Second Life has the killer app, which is community'. *The Click Heard Round the World,* 25 Aug. Retrieved November 29, 2007, from http://www.rikomatic.com/blog/2007/08/slcc-day-1-seco.html

Pavlenko, A., & Blackledge, A. (2004). Introduction: New theoretical approaches to the study of negotiation of identities in multilingual contexts. In A. Pavlenko & A. Blackledge (Eds.), *Negotiation of identities in multilingual contexts* (pp. 1-33). Clevedon: Multilingual Matters.

Pegrum, M. (2005). Speed kills: Slowing down online language teacher training. In B. Beaven (Ed.), *IATEFL 2005: Cardiff Conference selections* (pp. 156-158). Canterbury: IATEFL.

Pegrum, M. (2007). Socrates and Plato meet neo-liberalism in the virtual agora: Online dialog and the development of oppositional pedagogies. In J. Lockard & M. Pegrum (Eds.), *Brave new classrooms: Democratic education and the Internet* (pp. 13-34). New York: Peter Lang.

Pegrum, M. (2008a). Film, culture and identity: Critical intercultural literacies for the language classroom. *Language and Intercultural Communication, 8*(2), 136–154. doi:10.1080/14708470802271073

Pegrum, M. (forthcoming, 2008b). From hype to hope: 10 myths of e-learning. In S. Ioannou-Georgiou & P. Pavlou (Eds.), *Learning technologies in the language classroom: Research and reflections.* Canterbury: IATEFL.

Pegrum, M., & Bax, S. (2007). *Catering to diversity through asynchronous online discussion: Linking teachers across continents.* Paper presented at Diversity: A Catalyst for Innovation — The 20th English Australia Conference, Sydney, Australia, 13-15 Sept.

Pennycook, A. (2007). *Global Englishes and transcultural flows.* London: Routledge.

Pesce, M. (2007). *Challenges and opportunities: Peer-produced knowledge and Australian education.* Education.au. Retrieved November 29, 2007, from http://blogs.educationau.edu.au/gputland/wp-content/uploads/2007/08/challenges-and-opportunities.doc

Phipps, A., & Gonzalez, M. (2004). *Modern languages: Learning and teaching in an intercultural field.* London: Sage.

Prensky, M. (2001). Digital natives, digital immigrants. *On the Horizon, 9*(5). Retrieved November 29, 2007, from http://www.marcprensky.com/writing/Prensky%20-%20Digital%20 Natives,%20Digital%20Immigrants%20-%20 Part1.pdf

Quinton, S. (2006). A brief critique on the future of learning: Assessing the potential for research. In D.L. Fisher & M.S. Khine (Eds.), *Contemporary approaches to research on learning environments: Worldviews* (pp. 543-578). Singapore: World Scientific Publishing.

Reddekopp, C. (2006). Multitasking and student learning: Possible explanations for a growing phenomenon. *Occasional Papers in Educational Technology.* Saskatoon: University of Saskatchewan. Retrieved November 29, 2007, from http://www.usask.ca/education/coursework/802papers/redekopp/index.htm

Reeder, K., Macfadyen, L. P., Chase, M., & Roche, J. (2004). Falling through the (cultural) gaps? Intercultural communication challenges in cyberspace. In F. Sudweeks & C. Ess (Eds.), *Fourth International Conference on Cultural Attitudes towards Technology and Communication* (pp.123-134). Perth: Murdoch University.

Rheingold, H. (2007). *Vision of the future.* Paper presented to Education.au, 2 October. Retrieved November 29, 2007, from http://www.educationau.edu.au/jahia/Jahia/pid/521

Ricento, T. (2005). Considerations of identity in L2 learning. In E. Hinkel (Ed.), *Handbook of research in second language teaching and learning* (pp. 895-910). Mahwah, NJ: Lawrence Erlbaum.

Ryan, Y. (2007). *Do you YouTube? Wanna come to MySpace? Musings on narcissism in the 21st century student.* Paper presented at First Year in Higher Education Conference, QUT, Brisbane, Australia. Retrieved November, 29, 2007, from http://www.fyhe.qut.edu.au/past_papers/papers07/final_papers/Do%20you%20YouTube%20_2_.pdf

Sabre, G. (2007). SL education vs personal beliefs. *The Metaverse Journal,* 10 Sept. Retrieved January 14, 2008, from http://www.metaversejournal.com/2007/09/10/sl-education-vs-personal-beliefs/

Selber, S. A. (2004). *Multiliteracies for a digital age.* Carbondale, IL: Southern Illinois University Press.

Sharples, M., Taylor, J., & Vavoula, G. (2007). A theory of learning for the mobile age. In R. Andrews & C. Haythornthwaite (Eds.), *The Sage handbook of E-Learning research* (pp. 221-247). London: Sage.

Stevens, V. (2007). *Second Life and online collaboration through peer-to-peer distributed learning networks.* Paper presented at METSMaC Conference, Abu Dhabi, UAE, 17-19 Mar. Retrieved November 29, 2007, from http://www.homestead.com/prosites-vstevens/files/efi/papers/metsmac/metsmac_secondlife.htm

Stone, L. (2006). *Attention: The real aphrodisiac.* Paper presented at ETech, San Diego, 6-9 Mar. Retrieved November 29, 2007, from http://radar.oreilly.com/archives/2006/03/etech_linda_stone_1.html

Street, B. V. (1994). Struggles over the meaning(s) of literacy. In M. Hamilton, D. Barton & R. Ivanič (Eds.), *Worlds of literacy* (pp.15-20). Clevedon: Multilingual Matters.

Tapscott, D., & Williams, A. D. (2006). *Wikinomics: How mass collaboration changes everything.* New York: Portfolio.

The Consultants-E. (2007, Nov.). A potted history of technology in teaching – present. *The Consultants-E Newsletter.* Retrieved January 14, 2008, from http://www.theconsultants-e.com/newsletter/The%20Consultants-E%20Newsletter%20-%20November%202007.pdf

The New London Group. (2000). A pedagogy of multiliteracies: Designing social futures. In B. Cope & M. Kalantzis (Eds.), *Multiliteracies: Literacy learning and the design of social futures* (pp. 9-37). London: Routledge.

The New Media Consortium/The EDUCAUSE Learning Initiative. (2007). *The horizon report: 2007 edition.* Austin, TX: The New Media Consortium. Retrieved November 29, 2007, from http://www.nmc.org/pdf/2007_Horizon_Report.pdf

Thorne, S. L. (2006). Pedagogical and praxiological lessons from Internet-mediated intercultural foreign language education research. In J.A. Belz & S.L. Thorne (Eds.), *Internet-mediated intercultural foreign language education* (pp.2-30). Boston: Heinle & Heinle.

Unsworth, L. (2001). *Teaching multiliteracies across the curriculum: Changing contexts of text and image in classroom practice.* Buckingham: Open University Press.

Wales, J. (2007). *Challenging how knowledge is created.* Education.au. Retrieved November 29, 2007, from http://www.educationau.edu.au/jahia/Jahia/home/challenging

Wallis, C. (2006). The multitasking generation. *Time, 10*(April), 46–53.

Warschauer, M. (1999). *Electronic literacies: Language, culture and power in online education.* Mahwah, NJ: Lawrence Erlbaum.

Warschauer, M. (2003). *Technology and social inclusion: Rethinking the digital divide.* Cambridge, MA: MIT Press.

Warschauer, M. (2007). The paradoxical future of digital learning. *Learning Inquiry, 1*(1), 41–49. doi:10.1007/s11519-007-0001-5

Wenger, E. (1998). *Communities of practice: Learning, meaning, and identity.* Cambridge: Cambridge University Press.

Williamson, B., & Facer, K. (2004). More than 'just a game': The implications for schools of children's computer games communities. *Education Communication and Information, 4*(2/3), 253–268.

Wray, D. (Ed.). (2004). *Literacy: Major themes in education.* Vol. 4: New literacies: The impact of technology. London: Routledge Falmer.

Zieghahn, L. (2001). 'Talk' about culture online: The potential for transformation. *Distance Education, 22*(1), 144–150. doi:10.1080/0158791010220109

KEY TERMS

Codeswitching: This term refers to the use of more than one language or language variety in a given context, for example to aid communication or to signal aspects of identity.

Continuous Partial Attention: According to Linda Stone, citizens of Western societies increasingly live in a state of *continuous partial attention*, as they continuously monitor multiple communication and information channels in an attempt not to miss anything. She argues that this is a post-multitasking behavior motivated less by the need to save time or be efficient than by the desire to always be connected to the network.

Folksonomy: An index produced in a bottom-up manner by adding user-generated tags to webpages of interest through a service such as del.icio.us. The resulting list of tags is known as a *folksonomy* and may be displayed in the form of a *tag cloud*, in which more prominent tags are shown in larger and darker type.

Mashup: This term, which stems from the hip hop practice of mixing music and/or lyrics from different songs to create new hybrids, can refer to web applications which combine data from different sources or, more commonly, to digital files which mix together pre-existing video, graphics, music, text, etc, in new combinations.

Social Constructivism: *Social constructivism* is a theory of learning which draws heavily on the work of the Soviet psychologist Lev Vygotsky (1896-1934). It suggests that learners add to and reshape their mental models of reality through social collaboration, building new understandings as they actively engage in learning experiences. Scaffolding, or guidance, is provided by teachers or more experienced peers in the learner's zone of proximal development, that is, the zone between what a learner can achieve independently and what s/he may achieve with support.

Third Place: This term is used by Claire Kramsch to refer to the space between cultures which language learners may reach as they develop intercultural (communicative) competence.

Web 1.0: A retrospective term which emerged after the advent of Web 2.0, *Web 1.0* refers to the original, information-oriented version of the World Wide Web. Created by Tim Berners-Lee in 1989/1990, it consisted of largely static web-pages developed by a small number of authors for consumption by a large audience.

This work was previously published in Handbook of Research on Web 2.0 and Second Language Learning, edited by M. Thomas, pp. 20-41, copyright 2009 by Information Science Reference (an imprint of IGI Global).

Chapter 4.14
Adoption of Web Services in Digital Libraries:
An Exploratory Study

Fatih Oguz
Valdosta State University, USA

ABSTRACT

This chapter describes a research study with an objective to explore and describe decision factors related to technology adoption. The study utilized theories of diffusion of innovations and communities of practice as frameworks and a case study of Web services (WS) technology in the digital library (DL) environment to develop an understanding of the decision-making process. A qualitative case study approach was used to investigate the research problems and data was collected through semistructured interviews, documentary evidence (e.g., meeting minutes), and a comprehensive member check. Face-to-face and phone interviews were conducted with respondents from five different DL programs in the U.S., selected based on distinctive characteristics (e.g., size of the DL program). Findings of the research suggest that the decision-making process is a complex procedure in which a number of factors are considered when making WS adoption decisions. These factors are categorized as organizational, individual, and technology-specific factors.

DOI: 10.4018/978-1-60566-042-4.ch014

INTRODUCTION

With the advent of the Internet and specifically the World Wide Web (WWW) application, means of accessing data and information have changed forever. The Internet brought great opportunities for libraries as well as dilemmas and problems, such as technology choice and readiness.

Digital libraries (DL) were envisioned as network-accessible repositories in the 1990s. Now, DLs extend the classical brick-and-mortar library concept, bring value to society, and transform information landscape by improving and changing the means of knowledge access, creation, use, and discovery across disciplines, regardless of temporal and geographical barriers (Larsen & Watctlar, 2003; Reddy & Wladawsky-Berger, 2001).

The speed of technological advances in information technologies (IT) in the last 10 years has enabled DLs to provide innovative resources and services to people. The information landscape is changing as a result of the revolutionary developments in IT, incompleteness of content on Internet, ever increasing digital content along with the evolution of networked technologies and applications, lack of standards, ineffective information retrieval mechanisms, and minimal cataloging. These factors present challenges to the future of DL development efforts (Borgman, 1999; Reddy & Wladawsky-Berger, 2001).

The concept of Web services (WS) has emerged as the next generation of Web-based technology for exchanging information. This effort began with the submission of the SOAP 1.1 to the World Wide Web Consortium (W3C) (Barefoot, 2002). WS are self-contained applications that can be described, published, invoked, and located over the Internet (or any network). Once a Web service is deployed, other applications can discover and invoke the service. WS provide a programmable interface for other applications without requiring custom programming and proprietary solutions regardless of the operating systems and programming languages to share information as opposed to providing users with a graphical user interface (Boss, 2004).

According to the W3C, a Web service is defined as a software system designed to support interoperable machine-to-machine interaction over a network by using XML for sending and receiving messages (Booth, Haas, McCabe, Newcomer, Champion, Ferris, et al., 2004). Simplicity and flexibility of XML made it a definitive standard for data transmission and storage. XML is an open standard and can be accessed and processed by any tool capable of reading and writing American standard code for information interchange (ASCII) text. By definition, the only requirement for a Web service is to use XML.

The basic WS platform is composed of XML and a transport protocol. HTTP is the commonly used transport protocol on the Internet (Hickey, 2003). XML, simple object access protocol (SOAP), and Web services description language (WSDL) are tools to create WS. A Web service provides the framework for creating the next generation of distributed systems by which organizations can encapsulate existing business processes, publish them as services, search for and subscribe to other services, and exchange information throughout and beyond the enterprise (Adams, Gisolfi, Snell, & Varadan, 2002). Besides recognizing heterogeneity of networked resources and applications as a fundamental ingredient, WS are independent of platform and the development environment can be packaged and published on the Internet. Also, WS enable just-in-time integration and interoperability with legacy applications (Oguz & Moen, 2006).

The development and widespread deployment of more intelligent knowledge environments that not only support scholarly inquiry and communication but also that are open, accessible to all, and transparent in their operation remains as a fundamental challenge for DL practitioners and researchers.

DL applications need to have some room to accommodate future technological innovations regardless how they are built, using off-the-shelf software vs. custom-built, and thus decision makers who include managers, coordinators, designers, and developers need to make important decisions at some point in time to adopt or reject an innovation, including a specific technology, application, framework or idea related with DLs. Decision makers who need information about an innovation may seek this information through both informal and formal communication channels while making such critical decisions.

In the context of DLs, roles and influence of informal communication channels on the decision-making process to adopt or reject WS technology has not been investigated before. The adoption of a new technology, WS, which is its early stages of adoption in the DL environment, may provide a significant opportunity to investigate decision factors. The goal of this study is to shed a light on the decision-making process to adopt or reject a new technology, WS, in the context of DLs.

As technologies rapidly change and the information landscape is transformed, DLs find themselves dealing with the issues of technology adoption decisions to exploit this dynamically changing technology environment to meet their users' needs and expectations. Therefore, understanding the decision-making process regarding adoption of WS technologies in the context of DLs is important.

BACKGROUND

This study used the diffusion of innovations (DOI) and communities of practice (CoPs) as theoretical frameworks and a case study of WS technologies in the DL environment to develop an understanding of the decision-making process.

Diffusion of Innovations and Communities of Practice as Theoretical Frameworks

The DOI research methodology provides required instruments, both quantitative and qualitative, to assess the rate and pattern of diffusion of an innovation and identifies various factors that facilitate or hinder its adoption and implementation (Fichman, 1992). These major factors include properties of the innovation, characteristics of adopters, and the means leading to adoption.

An innovation can be an idea, behavior, practice, or object perceived as new by the adopter (e.g., organization, individual). The concept of newness may be determined by the human reaction to it as well as the time passed since its discovery or first use. If the idea seems new to an individual or organization, it is considered an innovation (Daft, 1978; Rogers, 1995).

DOI researchers study the characteristics of the innovation to explain the rate of adoption of an innovation. Rogers (1995) classifies characteristics of innovations into five general categories: relative advantage, compatibility, triability, observability, and complexity. Innovations with greater relative advantage, compatibility, triability, observability, and less complexity are more likely to be adopted faster than others that lack these characteristics (Rogers, 1995). However, there are structural factors (e.g., formalization and centralization) as well as other innovation characteristics (e.g., cost, profitability, social approval) influencing adoption of an innovation, and therefore Rogers' DOI theory needs to be extended to accommodate such factors, specifically in organizational settings (Daft, 1978; Damanpour, 1991). In addition, Tornatzky and Klein (1982) found that relative advantage, compatibility, and complexity have the most consistent relationships with the adoption of innovations across a wide range of industries.

Rogers (1995, p. 23) defines a social system as "a set of interrelated units that are engaged in joint problem-solving to accomplish a common goal" and the members or units of a social system may be composed of individuals, organizations, and informal groups. Patterned social relationships (e.g., hierarchical positions) among the members of a social system define the social structure of a system which, in return, can facilitate or delay the diffusion of an innovation and lays out a framework for making predictions about the human behavior in a system since such structure provides regularity and stability to human behavior (Rogers, 1995).

Established behavior patterns called norms are the ruling principles of a social system, which may also influence diffusion (Rogers, 1995). In other words, norms serve as a guide or a standard for the members against which they can assess their own behavior. Norms may slow the diffusion process when an innovation does not comply with the norms of a social system even if the adoption of an innovation offers important benefits for the system (Raghavan & Chand, 1989).

The innovation-decision can be made by an individual member of a system as well as by the entire system. The decision can be made collectively by reaching a consensus among the members of a social system or by a relatively few individuals who possess status, power, or technical expertise (Rogers, 1995). A decision made by an individual to adopt or reject a new idea independently from other members of a system is called an optional-innovation decision (Rogers, 1995). An adoption decision may be influenced by the norms of the system and informal communication channels. In this case, the decision is made by an individual member of the system rather than the entire social system, and the individual member is fully responsible for the consequences of the decision. Collective-innovation decisions are made by members of a system through a consensus to adopt or reject a new idea. All the units within the social system are expected to comply with the decision. However, reaching a collective decision may be a time-consuming process because it is made by a consensus among the members. Authority-innovation decisions are made by a select set of members of a social system who have authority and higher status in the organizational chart; in this decision-making process an individual member has little or no influence on the decision. In organizational settings, collective and authority-innovation decisions are more common than the optional-innovation decisions, and authority-innovation decisions result in higher rate of adoption than others (Rogers, 1995).

Diffusion of an innovation is a social process that is influenced by various factors such as characteristics of the innovation (e.g., relative advantage) and the decision-making unit (e.g., individual characteristics), depending on the level of adoption (individual vs. organizational). The information about the innovation is communicated through formal (e.g., mass media) and informal in the course of the innovation-decision process. Rogers (1995) suggests that having some exposure to mass media and informal communication channels such as interpersonal networks increases a potential adopter's chance of knowing about an innovation earlier than others. This chapter specifically focuses on CoPs which serve as an informal communication channel.

CoPs are composed of people who share a concern, common problems, or a passion about the domain, and who want to gain more knowledge and expertise pertaining to the domain by inter-

acting regularly (Wenger, McDermott, & Snyder, 2002). CoPs provide a learning environment through social participation, where participation refers to being active participants in the practice and building a sense of identity associated with the CoP to which they belong.

CoPs embody individuals with diverse backgrounds and social structures (e.g., other CoPs, organizations), which in turn, reduce the learning curve and rework, and promote innovation by enabling them to share and disseminate both tacit and explicit knowledge (Lesser & Storck, 2001). Sharing tacit knowledge requires personal interaction and CoPs provide such an informal learning platform through conversation and apprenticeship, for example. Members of the community become aware of their peers' expertise, knowledge, and skills through creating a venue for them to interact with each other. Thus, they are able to compare, verify, and benchmark their professionally developed expertise in the field against their colleagues' knowledge. When these benefits of CoPs are considered, their contribution to DL development efforts is vital in making informed technology, specifically WS, adoption decisions. The literature (e.g., Borgman, 1999; Marchionini, 1998) and nature of DL development efforts (e.g., open source) suggest the existence of informal structures such as CoPs.

As the organizations, specifically commercial ones, expand in size, geographical coverage, and complexity, knowledge has become the key to improving organizational performance and the formation of informal social groups like CoPs become a natural part of organizational life (Lesser & Storck, 2001; Wenger et al., 2002). CoPs make knowledge an integral part of their ongoing activities and interactions. Interpersonal interactions play an important role, especially in sharing tacit knowledge; the learning tools utilized by CoPs such as storytelling, conversation, and apprenticeship increase the efficient use of knowledge. CoPs act as a "living repository" for collective knowledge through creating a value for both the members and the organizations supporting and sponsoring these social structures (Wenger et al., 2002).

The DL conferences, funding agencies, workshops, and professional societies (e.g., Association for Computing Machinery) play important roles both in building and cultivating the CoPs in the DL field, and such meetings serve as a breeding ground for future collaboration in DL development efforts (Borgman, 1999). In addition, the experts in the field reached a consensus that "efforts associated with development of digital libraries are primarily collaborative" in a Delphi study conducted by Kochtanek and Hein (1999, p. 253).

Web Services in Digital Libraries

In general, DLs enable far broader range of users than traditional physical and organizational arrangements (e.g., libraries) to access information. Gathering, organizing, sharing, and maintaining such information resources require a flexible, scalable, and interoperable infrastructure (Larsen & Watctlar, 2003). Interoperability is an important issue where various system architectures, operating systems, and programming languages are required to communicate with each other. In addition, DL development efforts are closely related with the progress in general purpose technologies such as high-speed networking, security, and interoperability (Marchionini, 1998). However, the size, heterogeneity, and complexity of the today's information resources become critical factors when building DL systems because such factors may create immense challenges for interoperability, or the ability to ensure seamless information exchange across multiple DLs and information resources (Akscyn & Witten, 1998; Gonçalves et al., 2002; Marchionini, 1998). Marchionini (1998) addresses interoperability in two levels. The first level is the efforts to create standards for data storage and transmission, for query representation, and for vocabulary control; DLs adopt such standards and modify their content and services

at the local level. However, standards development is a complex social process and requires consensus among stakeholders (Moen, 1997). The second level encourages individual DLs to create standards-based services that can be easily accessible and used by other DLs.

A vision set forth for the DLs by the President's Information Technology Advisory Committee (PITAC) Panel on Digital Libraries is that of providing the means of searching and accessing all human knowledge anytime and anywhere via Internet for all citizens (Reddy & Wladawsky-Berger, 2001). One of the key issues in accomplishing this vision is improving the ability to store and retrieve digital content across disparate and independent systems and collections by improving interoperability among diverse DL implementations (Reddy & Wladawsky-Berger, 2001). Thus, interoperability is an important factor to consider in the DL environment when making decisions to adopt WS technologies.

Important decisions have been made in the past as to adopt or reject a new technology for various reasons including the pursuit of this vision, delivering content in more efficient and advanced manner, and social status (e.g., being a pioneer in offering new DL services) (Pasquinelli, 2002). Some of the key technologies and standards related with interoperability that have been adopted in the past in DL environments such as the ANSI/NISO Z39.50 protocol, open archives initiative protocol for metadata harvesting (OAI-PMH), and open URL.

Hickey (2003) lists various ways of using WS technology in DLs from registering different types of objects and search services to navigating hierarchies and decomposing objects into simpler objects. The search/retrieve Web service (SRW) is a standardized Web service built on the 20 years of experience of the Z39.50 information retrieval protocol. SRW provides an easy way to implement the protocol with the power of older and more complex Z39.50 (Sanderson, 2004). Even some libraries are replacing Z39.50 with WS technologies as the protocol of choice between library portals and online electronic resources (Boss, 2004). WS facilitate access to electronic databases, and digital libraries providing access to such resources benefit from this technology (Boss, 2004).

The flexible and extensible digital object and repository architecture (Fedora) system, designed by the Cornell University Information Science and The University of Virginia Library's Digital Library Research and Development Group (DLR&D), is a promising open source digital library software initiative. Fedora was originally implemented based on CORBA architecture; however, the next release (Fedora 2.0) has adopted a service-oriented approach (SOA) based on WS ("Tutorial 1: Introduction," 2005). DSpace is another open source system, developed by Hewlett-Packard and MIT Libraries, to store the digital research and educational material produced by an organization or institution as a repository. Greenstone is yet another open source digital library software from New Zealand Digital Library Project at the University of Waikato that has a focus on publishing (Don, Buchanan, & Witten, 2005). The DELOS network pays close attention and contributes to the use of WS technologies in digital libraries. EBSCO publishing, a provider of a broad range of full-text and bibliographic databases, has introduced its WS interface to EBSCOhost, an electronic journal service for academic and corporate subscribers, forming a basis of real-time communications among library systems, portals, and all other systems in the future (Boss, 2004).

The major strength of WS is its reliance on XML. Given the characteristics of WS technologies and current use in DLs and e-commerce, WS are poised to play an important role as a technology providing interoperable standards-based access to DLs.

MAIN THRUST OF THE CHAPTER

This chapter attempts to explore and describe factors, activities, processes, and forces involved in the decision-making process related to adoption of WS technologies in DLs.

Research Problems and Methodology

The research strategy consisted of two components: a qualitative methodology and a case study. This strategy provided a framework of methods and data that would yield answers to the two research questions: (1) What are the key decision factors that lead decision makers to adopt or reject WS in the DL environment? and (2) What are the activities and entities that influence the decision regarding adoption of WS technologies in the DL environment?

The exploratory and descriptive nature of the study justified the use of a qualitative research approach that allows discovery and description of the social processes involved in decision making. Although quantitative methods have been predominant in information technology (IT) adoption research (Choudrie & Dwivedi, 2005), this chapter aims to develop a better understanding of decision factors influencing adoption of WS technologies in the context of DLs.

In-depth information about this complex social process involving decision makers was acquired through semistructured interviews and documentary evidence (e.g., meeting minutes and reports). The interview respondents and academic libraries that they are associated with were selected based on characteristics of DL programs identified by Greenstein and Thorin (2002). These characteristics included age of the program, staff size, and organization and orientation of the program. Seven respondents with different responsibilities (administrative vs. technical) were interviewed from five different DL programs in the US. These DL programs included big (i.e., staff size) programs such as California Digital Library and University of Texas at Austin and relatively smaller ones such as University of North Texas and University of Texas at Dallas.

Following Patton's (2002) guidelines, purposeful sampling, specifically maximum variation sampling, was employed when selecting the respondents who had the best knowledge, expertise, and overview about the topic of the research. The maximum variation sampling aimed at "capturing and describing the central themes that cut cross great deal of variation" (Patton, 2002, p. 234).

The respondents were from DL programs at the California Digital Library, University of North Texas, University of Texas at Dallas, University of Texas at Austin, and a university in the American Southeast. Some of the participating libraries are members of various influential professional societies and organizations in the DL field, including Digital Library Federation (DLF), Association of Research Libraries (ARL), and Coalition for Networked Information (CNI). Seven interviews were conducted with administrators and technical personnel who were involved in the decision-making process at these five academic libraries' DL programs.

Patton (2002) sets no rules for the sample size in qualitative inquiry by arguing that "the validity, meaningfulness, and the insights generated from qualitative inquiry have more to do with the information richness of the cases selected and the observational/analytical capabilities of the researcher than with sample size" (p. 245). The researcher stopped conducting interviews when data saturation was reached to meet the research goal, that is, to understand and describe decision factors related to WS adoption. Data saturation is defined as the point in a data collection process where new information becomes redundant (Bogdan & Biklen, 1992). Romney, Batchelder, and Weller (1986) conclude that samples as small as four participants could be enough to meet research objectives where purposeful sampling is

carefully carried out to include information-rich respondents.

Documentary evidence provided additional and clarifying information supplemental to the data collected through interviews. Further, a comprehensive member check was conducted which allowed to obtain additional information from respondents and to have study findings reviewed by them. This final verification process allowed respondents to evaluate the researcher's interpretation of findings and analysis of data from their perspectives (Lincoln & Guba, 1985; Patton, 2002).

Results and Findings

Data revealed a number of factors that influenced and informed the decision-making process in WS adoption. These factors are categorized at organizational, individual, and technical levels.

Characteristics of DL programs that appeared to influence the decision-making process and categorized as organizational level factors included: organizational culture, program's relationships with surrounding academic units and external partners, management style and work structure, focus and direction of a program, formalization (e.g., flexibility in hierarchal order), functional differentiation in a program, size and age of a program, administrative attitude toward change, financial resources, technology readiness (e.g., expertise, technology infrastructure), and program's expectations (e.g., user needs). These organizational level factors appeared to play a critical role, especially in influencing members' information-seeking and communication behaviors. Individual level factors included members' connectedness with their colleagues, skill-set (e.g., competence), participation in CoPs, perception of organizational culture and goals, and openness to new ideas. Technical level factors included: interoperability, modularity, scalability, flexibility, addressability, rapid deployment of services, subscription service, and open-standards base of WS.

Some of the organizational level factors include management style, focus and direction of the program, size and age of the program, and organizational culture. Organizational level factors were closely associated with the organization itself and indirectly impacted by a DL program's staff, for example. Administrative personnel had an influence on some of organizational level factors (e.g., management style). Other factors could be regarded as more individual characteristics of DL staff members in terms of their information-seeking and communication behavior. Impact of individual level factors on decision-making vary from one technology to another depending on role of the technology (i.e., mission critical vs. non-mission critical) in the DL program.

Respondents identified financial concerns as a critical factor in guiding technology adoption decisions, and these concerns included: initial cost, ongoing cost, payoff, budgetary restrictions, and funding requirements. However, the extent of influence of these factors on WS adoption decisions appeared to vary from one DL program to another depending on the DL program's expectations from the technology and needs, focus, and direction of the program. These expectations and needs were closely related with size and age of the program. Data suggested that as programs grew in size over time, so did their collections, responsibilities, and user expectations. For example, although respondents formed positive opinions regarding open source software, they were aware that the lack of necessary skills in the program would be an important factor when getting a project initiated and providing technical support if they chose to use open source software. In addition, acquiring necessary technology skills through hiring new staff members and additional training were also factors impacting cost. Lack of technical expertise as a decision factor appeared to reflect the importance of Davis' (1989) "ease of use," Tornatzky and Klein's (1982) "ease of operation," and Rogers' (1995) "complexity" as innovation characteristics since adopters' technical background and skills were closely associated with perception of these characteristics.

Technology readiness of the DL program was another organizational factor that appeared to have an influence in the decision-making process. Technology readiness had two aspects: a human aspect (e.g., expertise, staffing), and the technological compatibility of WS technologies with existing technical infrastructure (i.e., hardware, software, and standards). In addition, technology readiness was also closely associated with availability of financial resources in case a hardware or software upgrade was needed. Respondents noted that compatibility of WS technologies with their existing technological infrastructure was an important factor that informed the decision-making. Tornatzky and Klein (1982) found compatibility as one of the most addressed innovation attributes. Compatibility also refers to consistency of an innovation with existing values and norms of the DL program. Furthermore, technology readiness was also an important factor for triability purposes. Small scale experiments were generally conducted in DL programs prior to making an adoption decision.

Individual level adoption decisions could be made especially for the use of WS technologies in nonmission critical applications. A personal positive experience with WS, existing skill-set, potential benefits for the work (i.e., Davis' [1985] perceived usefulness), and having easy access to experienced-based knowledge through CoPs appeared to influence an individual's perception and lowered the individual's learning curve. Technology and specific factors such as interoperability, modularity, flexibility, and WS subscription service were also decision factors in this case. In DL programs where WS had already been adopted, adoption decisions were made collectively and WS technologies were used for major and mission-critical applications. Both organizational and technology-specific factors were taken into consideration.

Another important decision factor was technology-specific benefits offered by WS, including interoperability, modularity, and open standards. WS provides an interoperable platform and is built on open standards (e.g., XML) where programs written in different programming languages and running on different operating systems are able to communicate with each other based on open standards and protocols. Data suggested that interoperability was an important factor since WS would not require major changes in existing technical infrastructure. In addition to interoperability, respondents identified additional technology-specific factors. For example:

- **Modularity and flexibility:** Ability to act as building blocks to create distributed applications through reuse of existing applications that can be published and accessed over the internet or intranets.
- **Rapid deployment of Services:** Development time for new applications or services is greatly reduced through use of standard interfaces (e.g., WSDL) and open standards.
- Scalability: Ability to handle a growing amount of usage loads (e.g., Web caching, load balancing).
- **WS subscription service (UDDI):** A registry services for WS and allows other WS applications to automatically discover services and use them.

Small DL programs often looked to older and bigger DL programs when it came to adopting new technologies and standards. Their limited financial resources, staff size, and skill set were important barriers preventing them from taking initiatives that might be considered risky. These initiatives included technologies or standards that have not been tried or are in early stages of adoption in other DL programs. They often chose to rely on experiences of other DL programs so that they would be less likely to fail and run into unexpected problems. As for bigger programs, it

appeared that they sometimes wanted to be the first or early adopters of some technologies in the DL environment to set an example for other programs. Though setting an example for other DL programs or wanting to be an early adopter was not a key decision factor, it was one of the factors occasionally taken into consideration in the decision-making processes.

Data suggested that availability of financial resources, focus and direction, size and age, collection size, users' and programs' expectations, and technology readiness were important factors influencing decision makers. Especially when making an optional-innovation decision, a potential adopter's existing technical skill-set and connectedness with the adopter's colleagues were key factors. At the technical level, interoperability, modularity, scalability, flexibility, addressability, rapid deployment of services, subscription services, and the open standards base of WS were key decision factors leading decision makers to adopt or reject WS in the DL environment.

Figure 1 presents a conceptual framework for the study informed by the theoretical frameworks in light of results and findings discussed earlier. Organizational and technical (i.e., technology specific) level factors have an influence both on adopters' information seeking behaviors and on the adoption decision itself depending on the type of innovation decision (i.e., optional, collective, and authority) made. Individual level factors (i.e., individual characteristics) guide adopters' information seeking activities (e.g., participation in CoPs) and influence their perception of organizational values which in turn inform adopters' contribution to the decision-making process. As shown in Figure 1, potential adopters may acquire information about an innovation through formal (e.g., mass media) and informal (e.g., interpersonal) communication channels. The information acquired through these channels includes perceived characteristics of an innovation that may play a key role as decision factors in the decision-making process. Data suggested that use of information collected through

Figure 1. Conceptual framework

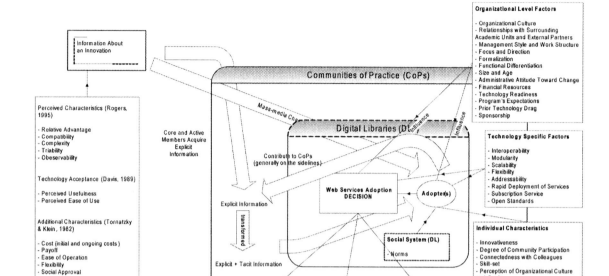

these channels in the decision-making process vary due to adopters' degree of participation in CoPs, characteristics of knowledge (explicit vs. tacit) acquired, and factors at organizational, technical, and individual levels.

On the other hand, there were number of activities that members of DL programs participated in, entities that provided them with guidance, processes that helped them develop an understanding of WS, motivations that encouraged or discouraged them towards WS technologies, and forces that informed and guided their information seeking and communication behaviors. These activities, entities, processes, and forces were in play when making a decision regarding adoption of WS technologies in the DL environment.

DL programs had good ties with surrounding academic departments and information services, including other library departments, IT department, library and information school, and faculty.

DL programs benefited from such connections not only by accessing their expertise but also by acquiring their content and collections.

DL staff members' interactions with others appeared to be maintained informally and the organizational structure of DL programs encouraged informal communication. Informality in communicating with others is one of the key characteristics of CoPs. Respondents interacted with their colleagues who were part of their own DL programs, as well as people from libraries, other university units, or external institutions and organizations to advance and share their knowledge and contribute to the field. Informal communication was also cited as an important part of the technology assessment process.

Some of the participating academic libraries were members of various professional associations and organizations which have an influence on DL-related issues, including use of DL technologies, digital preservation, standards, and DL development activities. Participation in these organizations (e.g., DLF, CNI, ARL) provided venues for DL programs to share their work and connect with other DL programs. The DLF promotes work on DL structures, standards, preservation, and use, CNI is interested in various areas critical to present and future of DLs, and ARL is one of the sponsor organizations of CNI and its member institutions are very active in the field. Further, these organizations engage in collaborative activities with each other in pursuit of their missions and goals. Collegial activities that were made possible through these relationships with these external entities appeared to play a central role in formation and continuation of informal communities that can be characterized as CoPs. Entities in the DL environment generally included CoPs, surrounding academic units and external partners, funding agencies, and the program itself.

In addition, attending national and international conferences were the most commonly used venues to obtain new information and served as a breeding ground for building personal contacts with colleagues. These collegial activities were regarded as communal activities. Preexisting personal contacts and the connections established in various venues with other institutions, organizations, and DL initiatives appeared to be very important for information access and sharing purposes.

CoPs attracted individuals with diverse backgrounds and skills from all around the world regardless of their geographical locations and provided an informal learning platform for their members. These CoPs were generally built and maintained in an online environment and occasionally supported with face-to-face interactions. In addition to distributed virtual CoPs, there were other CoPs, which may be subgroups of a broader CoP, that were locally networked and physically located. Participation of members in discussions in CoPs enabled online communities to cultivate and nurture knowledge acquired thorough experience, print, or other online resources and, in turn, these

discussions enhanced and improved members' understanding of the technology. In other words, this mediating process gave rise to cross-fertilization of ideas and appeared to improve credibility of the knowledge generated and housed in CoPs. CoPs provided a living repository for the knowledge generated within the community while they were also perceived as places where up-to-date and quality information could be acquired. CoPs were also used to verify information acquired from different sources.

The conceptual framework (see Figure 1) helped to structure the data-found analysis in a format which may help the reader see this very complex landscape and understand this complex social process. Further, this chapter provided evidence that Rogers' DOI model needs to be complemented with organizational level factors identified by other researchers such as Daft (1978), Davis (1989), and Tornatzky and Klein (1992) to understand and describe diffusion of innovations in organizational settings.

CONCLUSION

This research was an exploratory and descriptive study to shed a light on the decision-making process to adopt or reject a new technology, WS, in the context of DLs and the unit of analysis was the decision to adopt or reject a new technology. The information landscape is transformed as technologies rapidly change and DLs often find themselves in a critical position to make a decision whether to adopt or reject emerging technologies such as WS.

Since the study employed a qualitative case study approach that supported the exploratory and descriptive nature of the research, results and findings of the study are not intended to be statistically generalizable to other technology adoption cases. However, detailed description in the narrative may assist the reader of this case study research to determine applicability of these findings to other technology adoption decisions in the reader's own setting.

This chapter provides evidence that CoPs as informal communication channels practice play an important role in enabling staff members of a DL program to access up-to-date and experienced-based knowledge, providing a distributed problem-solving and learning platform, facilitating informal communication and collaborative activities among DL programs, and informing the decision-making process. Technical characteristics (e.g., interoperability, open standards), compatibility with existing technical infrastructure, applicability to existing DL projects, total cost of ownership (e.g., licensing, maintenance cost), technical expertise in the DL program (e.g., staffing, training, learning curve), and success of a pilot project are cited as key decision factors influencing adoption Web services technologies in the DL environment. This chapter provides an adequate foundation for further research on the impact of organizational, individual, and technology-specific factors on decision-making processes in the DL environment.

The complexity of the decision-making process and the variety of factors that informed and influenced this process are reflected. A review of the relevant literature suggests that this is a complex process, and the findings inform and provide details about the complexity, as presented in Figure 1. The theoretical frameworks selected for this chapter proved useful to achieve the goal of the study. The chapter attempts to provide a complete account of decision factors related with adoption of WS technologies in the DL environment. An outcome of this study suggests that an exploratory and descriptive study such as this is an important step towards understanding the decision-making process as technologies rapidly change in the DL environment.

ACKNOWLEDGMENT

The author thanks Corrie Marsh for her valuable feedback in writing of this chapter and to Dr. William Moen for his guidance and support for this research.

REFERENCES

Adams, H., Gisolfi, D., Snell, J., & Varadan, R. (2002). Best practices for Web services: Part 1 - formation of a semantic framework. *IBM developerWorks*. Retrieved March 5, 2004, from http://www-106.ibm.com/developerworks/Web-services/library/ws-best1/

Akscyn, R. M., & Witten, I. H. (1998). *Report of First Summit on international cooperation on digital libraries.* Retrieved May 3, 2005, from http://Web.archive.org/Web/20010529104724/ks.com/idla-wp-oct98/

Barefoot, D. (2002). *Web services primer*. Cape-Science.

Bogdan, R. C., & Biklen, S. R. (1992). *Qualitative research for education: An introduction to theory and methods* (2nd ed.). Boston: Allyn and Bacon.

Booth, D., Haas, H., McCabe, F., Newcomer, E., Champion, M., Ferris, C., et al. (2004, February). *Web services architecture* (W3C Working Group Note 11). The World Wide Web Consortium (W3C).

Borgman, C. L. (1999). What are digital libraries? Competing visions. *Information Processing & Management, 35*(3), 227–243. doi:10.1016/S0306-4573(98)00059-4

Boss, R. W. (2004). *Web services*. Retrieved November 1, 2005, from http://www.ala.org/ala/pla/plapubs/technotes/Webservices.htm

Choudrie, J., & Dwivedi, Y. K. (2005). Investigating the research approaches for examining technology adoption issues. *Journal of Research Practice, 1*(1).

Daft, R. L. (1978). A dual-core model of organizational innovation. *Academy of Management Journal, 21*(2), 193. doi:10.2307/255754

Damanpour, F. (1991). Organizational inertia and momentum: A dynamic model of strategic change. *Academy of Management Journal, 34*(3), 555–591. doi:10.2307/256406

Davis, F. D. (1989). Perceived usefulness, perceived ease of use, and user acceptance of information technology. *MIS Quarterly, 13*(3), 318. doi:10.2307/249008

Don, K., Buchanan, G., & Witten, I. H. (2005). *Greenstone 3: A modular digital library.* Retrieved November 1, 2005, from http://www.sadl.uleth.ca/greenstone3/manual.pdf

Fichman, R. G. (1992, December). *Information technology diffusion: A review of empirical research.* Paper presented at the Thirteenth International Conference on Information Systems (ICIS), Dallas.

Gonçalves, M. A., Fox, E. A., Watsom, L. T., & Kipp, N. A. (2002). Streams, structures, spaces, scenarios, societies (5s): A formal model for digital libraries. [TOIS]. *ACM Transactions on Information Systems, 22*(2), 270–312. doi:10.1145/984321.984325

Greenstein, D., & Thorin, S. E. (2002). *The digital library: A biography.* Digital Library Federation.

Hickey, T. B. (2003). *Web services for digital libraries.* Paper presented at the Cross Language Applications and The Web 27th Library Systems Seminar, Bern, Switzerland.

Kochtanek, T. R., & Hein, K. K. (1999). Delphi study of digital libraries. *Information Processing & Management, 35*(3), 245–254. doi:10.1016/S0306-4573(98)00060-0

Larsen, R. L., & Watctlar, H. D. (2003). *Knowledge lost in information.* Report of the NSF Workshop on Research Directions for Digital Libraries.

Lesser, E. L., & Storck, J. (2001). Communities of practice and organizational performance. *IBM Systems Journal, 40*(4), 831–931.

Lincoln, Y. S., & Guba, E. G. (1985). *Naturalistic inquiry.* Beverly Hills, CA: Sage Publications, Inc.

Marchionini, G. (1998). Research and development in digital libraries. In A. Kent (Ed.), *Encyclopedia of library and information science* (Vol. 63, pp. 259-279). New York: Marcel Dekker.

Moen, W. E. (1997). *The Development of ANSI/NISO Z39.50: A Case Study in Standards Evolution.* Unpublished Dissertation, Syracuse University.

Oguz, F., & Moen, W. E. (2006). *Texas library directory Web services application: The potential for Web services to enhance information access to legacy data.* Paper presented at the International Conference on Next Generation Web Services Practices (NWeSP'06), Korea.

Pasquinelli, A. (2002). *Digital library technology trends.* Retrieved December, 9, 2005, from http://www.sun.com/products-n-solutions/edu/whitepapers/pdf/digital_library_trends.pdf

Patton, M. Q. (2002). *Qualitative research and evaluation methods* (3rd ed.). Thousand Oaks, CA: Sage Publications, Inc.

Raghavan, S. A., & Chand, D. R. (1989). Diffusing Software-Engineering Methods. *IEEE Software, 6*(4), 81–90. doi:10.1109/52.31655

Reddy, R., & Wladawsky-Berger, I. (2001). *Digital libraries: Universal access to human knowledge: A report to the President.* President's Information Technology Advisory Committee (PITAC), Panel on Digital Libraries.

Rogers, E. M. (1995). *Diffusion of Innovations* (4th ed.). New York: The Free Press.

Romney, A., Batchelder, W., & Weller, S. (1986). Culture as consensus: A theory of culture and informant accuracy. *American Anthropologist, 88,* 313–338. doi:10.1525/aa.1986.88.2.02a00020

Sanderson, R. (2004). *SRW: Search/retrieve Web-service version 1.1.* Retrieved February 2, 2005, from http://srw.cheshire3.org/SRW-1.1.pdf

Tornatzky, L. G., & Klein, K. J. (1982). Innovation characteristics and innovation adoption-implementation: A meta-analysis of findings. *IEEE Transactions on Engineering Management, 29*(1), 28–45.

Tutorial 1: Introduction. (2005). Retrieved August 15, 2005, from http://www.fedora.info/download/2.0/userdocs/tutorials/tutorial1.pdf

Wenger, E., McDermott, R., & Snyder, W. M. (2002). *A guide to managing knowledge: Cultivating communities of practice.* Boston: Harvard Business School Press.

Chapter 4.15
A Context–Based Approach to Web 2.0 and Language Education

Gary Motteram
University of Manchester, UK

Susan Brown
University of Manchester, UK

ABSTRACT

Web 2.0 offers potentially powerful tools for the field of language education. As language teacher tutors exploring Web 2.0 with participants on an MA in Educational Technology and TESOL at the University of Manchester, UK, we see that the potential of Web 2.0 is intimately linked with teachers' perceptions of their teaching contexts. This chapter will describe a "context-based" approach to the exploration of Web 2.0 on a module focusing on the potential role of distributed courseware in language education. It will begin by giving an overall picture of where and how the exploration of Web 2.0 tools fits into the MA program. It will then describe the main aims and aspects of the module and discuss in some detail our context-based approach in relation to participants as well as Web 2.0 in existing literature. The chapter will conclude with two case studies concerning how teachers incorporate Web 2.0 technologies in courseware for their contexts.

DOI: 10.4018/978-1-60566-190-2.ch007

INTRODUCTION

This chapter explores the way that participants on a module run as part of an MA in Educational Technology and TESOL learn about, make use of and evaluate Web 2.0 technologies. This module is a new departure for the course and represents the ongoing need for the MA to refresh itself and to bring new and developing technologies into its domain.

Web 2.0 has its advocates and its detractors; however, it has become a *de facto* part of today's Internet landscape. The very nature of Web 2.0, its emphasis on such features as collaboration, interactivity and user-generated content, seems to make it an obvious choice for a focus of discussion when it comes to looking at current trends in the use of technology in language education. These trends, as shall be later discussed, reflect a focus on learner centered, collaborative tasks which, in Second Language Acquisition terms, allow channels for authentic language input and output (Chapelle, 1998).

However, it is important to realize that for many language teachers Web 2.0 may simply appear to be another technological innovation that will pass them by along with the many others that they have seen during their career, despite the slowly increasing range of references to the uses and benefits of key Web 2.0 technologies (e.g. blogs, podcasts and wikis) in language education.

As people and communities in various parts of the world increasingly embrace Web 2.0, some educational institutions are inevitably responding to those societal trends and trying to harness Web 2.0 in their learning programs. Others, although they are in societies where technology is more normalized (Bax, 2003a) have, for various reasons, not taken those technologies on board. Perhaps now, more than at any other time, language teachers may need to negotiate these changes as they impact, or not, on their institutions, and consider the implications of ever greater technology use for their language teaching. They may be inspired or effectively obliged to engage with the nature of Web 2.0 and analyze its affordances for language education. Other teachers, even if they are aware that it is being used in the wider world may currently see no application for it in language education.

Web 2.0 is described as relatively easy to use and therefore accessible to anybody with access to the Internet. This is in contrast to its Web 1.0 predecessor which is seen to require at least some familiarity with HTML as a minimum. Setting up and contributing to a blog for example may seem comparatively uncomplicated. However, once a blog has been set up the user may be confronted with concepts and technicalities that may be more difficult to get to grips with, RSS, by way of example. Teachers struggling to understand the concept behind RSS, and the different technologies that support it, are unlikely to be able to stand back and evaluate its uses in language learning terms.

Such issues notwithstanding Web 2.0 tools do appear to offer a lot of what language teachers would want in order to support learners language development: they can potentially distribute the learning and enable students to be in regular touch with a world-wide community of learners; they appear to enable an easier connection to be made between the classroom and the "real" world; they might enable learners to take some control over their learning making use of tools that excite them and which they are using in their everyday lives; they seem to offer engagement in active rather than passive learning, in process as well as product; learners can also potentially engage in discourses that take them beyond the classroom.

On the MA program in Educational Technology and TESOL at the School of Education, University of Manchester, it is important to explore Web 2.0 technologies in language education and help teachers understand generic functions of Web 2.0 in order to facilitate their evaluation of its potential uses. An evaluation of this potential should not, and cannot, be divorced from considerations pertaining to the "ecology" of the teaching environment in which teachers work, or have worked in the past and how that pertains to the wider changes in society. The use of the term "ecology" here signifies all of the rich, interacting elements that create the dynamic of teachers' teaching contexts including top down societal, curricula and institutional influences and the bottom up influences which may stem from teachers' knowledge of and enthusiasm for Web 2.0.

In this regard the MA tutors continue to observe that the way teachers "make sense" of Web 2.0 genres, i.e. understand how their various intrinsic operations — a process which is intimately bound up with teachers' "evaluation" of the potential affordances of such software for their contexts — is mediated by the teachers' perceptions of the context in which they work, or have worked in the past.

Considerations of context are bound up on the MA program with those of pedagogy, and the "fit" of Web 2.0 genres to pedagogical approaches. We have always worked as teacher-educators on the principle that the use of technology in language education should be firmly underpinned by considerations of pedagogy and appropriate methodology (Holliday, 1994). The functions of the technologies explored on the MA program are therefore considered according to how they can facilitate and possibly enhance pedagogical approaches that respond to the specificities of different contexts and the needs of learners in that context. In other words we adopt a context and pedagogic driven rather than a technology driven model. This central focus on pedagogy as it is relates to context and the role that technology can play in contexts has led us to evaluate the affordances of Web 2.0 as they might respond to contextual factors, what we have started to term a "niche" approach to evaluating Web 2.0

The main discussion in this chapter will centre on one of eight component modules that the MA program participants take, entitled "Courseware Development for Distributed and Blended Learning" (CDDBL) and the context-based approach to CDDBL introduced above. This module explores a range of Web 2.0 tools and how they may be exploited both for blending and distributing courseware. The chapter describes the module's explorations of Web 2.0 and tutors' evolving thinking about the way to best approach Web 2.0. The changing nature of participants on the module since its inception in 2005 is discussed and two case studies will illustrate ways in which participants have employed or how they envisage employing Web 2.0 in their own contexts.

In what follows the chapter gives the reader an overall view of the MA course and how Web 2.0 is included, describing our current approach to exploring Web 2.0 in CDDBL and discussing aspects of the literature informing the module. It then focuses on two case studies illustrating how former participants on the course evaluated Web 2.0 in relation to their own contexts. The chapter concludes by discussing possible future developments in our context approach to Web 2.0 on CDDBL.

THE MA PROGRAMME

Brief Overview of the Program

The participants on the Master's program in Educational Technology and TESOL come from different parts of the world including South America, Asia, the Middle East and Western and Eastern Europe and may be either non-native or native speakers of English. They all have at least three years teaching experience. This level of experience is a prerequisite for entry onto the degree as its whole focus is not on our (the tutors) forming and shaping of the participants' thinking about teaching, but on facilitating the reflective process that will allow the participants, drawing from their teaching experience, to shape their own thinking about their teaching. The participants' experiences of using technology vary and range from no use to a significant engagement. This obviously affects the extent to which they can reflect on their own practice using technology.

The MA was set up in the 1980s (in those days it was an MEd) to meet the needs of teachers who were becoming interested in using video and computers as part of their language teaching processes. The course has changed considerably over time, but still keeps as its main foundational aim a focus on the pedagogical implications of the uses of technology (see Wildner, 1999). The specific modules that are relevant to technology and language learning include: Language Learning and Technology, which explores the general uses made of technology in language classrooms to support language skills development; Multimedia in Language Education, which combines an exploration of second language acquisition processes with the design and development of language tasks using Web 1.0 technologies; Teaching and Learning Online, in which we ask the participants to explore and reflect on experiences of online learning. The fourth technology-focused module, Courseware Development for Distributed and Blended Learning (CDDBL), is the one that is described in detail in this chapter. Other modules that students do reflect a more general TESOL diet.

We have both onsite and offsite (distance) participants. The offsite participants study part time as they are generally practicing teachers and via an online virtual learning environment (VLE – currently WebCT). Onsite participants are studying for the most part full-time and are therefore removed from their teaching context, particularly if that context is not in the locality of Manchester or is overseas.

COURSEWARE FOR DISTRIBUTED AND BLENDED LEARNING

The nature of the program we offer means that there is a continual refreshment of the modules and CDDBL is the latest re-working, the first run of this new module taking place in 2005. The aim of the module is to assist in the development of skills that will enable teachers to review and create effective blended and distributed learning materials for their context, with all of the attendant considerations that this involves. While "Multimedia in Language Education" looks at materials design at task level, CDDBL considers the integration of activities at the level of a course or scheme of work.

Early on in the development of CDDBL we took the decision to focus primarily on Web 2.0 tools and their affordances in distributed courseware. We had originally intended to focus solely on Virtual Learning Environments (VLEs) but realized that in doing so we would be missing the opportunity to explore emerging technologies from the perspective of courseware development, technologies that potentially change the way we view that development, both in terms of the greater ease with which courseware might be created by tutors but also in the degree of control that the participants themselves have in the materials design process.

As we designed the first iteration of the module it occurred to us that unlike Web 1.0 technologies, where the extent of interactivity that a learner can engage in is more likely to be determined by the designer/tutor, with Web 2.0 technologies the development of courseware need not be the preserve of the tutor designer, but also of learners. Such differences between Web 1.0 and Web 2.0 technologies are explicitly discussed on CDDBL as are the ways that the two technology types can be effectively combined to suit the specificities of teaching contexts.

The current iteration of CDDBL therefore explores the following Web 2.0 tools: blogs; wikis; social bookmarking; e-portfolio software; and podcasting. It further focuses on two VLE platforms, WebCT and Moodle, an open source VLE which, in response to ongoing feedback from designers/tutors using the software, continues to have new tools incorporated into it, the majority of which are Web 2.0 tools such as blogs.

The assessment procedure for CDDBL requires participants to create sample courseware materials which combine Web 2.0 technologies and which address issues related to language learning in their context. They are currently asked to articulate the thinking behind their courseware through a 30-minute presentation and short executive summary and to discuss the courseware in relation to relevant educational literature.

PERSPECTIVES ON WEB 2.0 IN THE LITERATURE AND CDDBL

There are areas of difference and confluence between perspectives on Web 2.0 in the educational literature and our own perspective on important considerations relating to Web 2.0. in courseware development. We have said that the way participants on CDDBL evaluate the potential of Web 2.0 technologies is intertwined with their perceptions of the contexts in which they teach; this is having an increasing influence on the ongoing development of the module and on our approach to the exploration of Web 2.0 genres.

It is fair to say that the relationship between considerations of context in the educational literature and the nature and potential of Web 2.0 has not, as yet, been extensively explored. Much of the current literature on Web 2.0 in education discusses it from a general perspective, e.g. with regard to the uptake of Web 2.0 in society and particularly among the digital or net generation, and mainly with regard to tertiary education (see Oblinger, 2005; Bryant, 2006). Little of the discussion on Web 2.0 is, as yet, localized. This is not the case with discussion on Web 1.0 technologies, where a number of studies relate to the specificities of different local contexts (see, for example, Zhong & Shen, 2002). In CDDBL we explore with participants the general themes in the literature on Web 2.0; we provide a summary of some of these below.

Those in the field of education who write on Web 2.0 technologies see it as holding significant possibilities for the field. A lot of Web 2.0 discussion is subsumed under the epithet of "social software" which is perhaps both indicative of the cryptic nature of the term Web 2.0 and of the significance of the term "social" in the educational field where it is widely argued, partly based on the ideas of socio-cultural theorists such as Vygotsky (1978), that learning takes place through mediated social interactions. This potential is discussed in relation to the creation of new learning communities which may offer the "personalised collaborative learning experiences such as those that are already emerging in the world outside the school gates" (Owen et al., 2006, p. 11). Such communities can expand discussion beyond the classroom and provide new ways for students to collaborate within their class and across the world (Bryant, 2006). Wenger (1998) is regularly cited when discussions of the building of communities beyond classrooms is proposed.

As with the discussion in the educational field generally, the term Web 2.0 has not, as yet, been used extensively in the literature on language teaching. The tools associated with the term tend to be subsumed under the umbrella terms of Computer Mediated Communication (CMC) and social networking. Nevertheless the potential of those tools, as articulated in relation to social networking and CMC, is increasingly recognized. They may offer scope for exposure to, and production of, authentic language use in real life intracultural and intercultural Internet contexts (Kern, Ware & Warschauer, 2004). They also offer the learner the chance to use language as it is used on the Internet and be exposed to "emerging genres of language use" (Thorne & Payne, 2005, p. 372). Such opportunities for authentic language output and the concomitant opportunities for "noticing" and "negotiation of meaning" sit comfortably with notions of how SLA takes place (See Chapelle, 1998). Wikis for example, with their text editing features, may provide the learner opportunities to "correct their linguistic output" and "engage in target language interaction whose structure can be modified for negotiation of meaning" (Chapelle, 1998, pp. 23-24). With these opportunities for greater levels of authentic, autonomous language engagement more emphasis will need to be placed by teachers on the development of metacognitive skills among learners, i.e. the skills that learners need to order and develop their own learning. In some ways many Web 2.0 genres have inbuilt features, e.g. the wiki edit facility which can facilitate metacognitive thinking. Web 2.0 therefore, may offer the most genuine medium yet for breaking down the barriers between the classroom and the real world as not only can the learner use English in an authentic medium but that medium also provides the tools which allows learners to focus in an authentic way on how language is used. However, in the same way that Web 2.0 is an extension of Web 1.0 and can be seen to have some of its characteristics, it is not a good idea to view the uses of Web 2.0 technologies as somehow divorced from what has been occurring for many years in the world of Computer Assisted

Language Learning. This field has certainly advocated extensive use of a variety of technologies to promote language learning and has made use of a wide variety of tools to do this. It has also drawn heavily on popular theory from a range of contexts to support its practices. What is potentially different is the way that uses are more easily managed by the learners themselves and materials can be more easily learner generated.

In all the above examples the value of the learning that can potentially occur through Web 2.0 is seen in relation to the extent to which it is allied to, driven by and a part of the social, cultural and economic trends that are shaping the world. There is a prevailing discourse of urgency evident in some of the literature relating to technology in education, perhaps most pithily encapsulated in the phrase, "You can't not do it" (Collis & Moonen, 2001). This discourse sees the world changing at speed, where economies will be driven by a technologically savvy population, where academic institutions will need to gear themselves to offering flexible learning programs through various technologies and where the "digital/net generation" is not only at home with digital technologies but will be increasingly mystified as to why they are not an integral feature of their education (Oblinger, 2005). If the net generation's thinking and expectations are shaped by their experiences as net citizens and participants then they will bring those expectations into the educational context where Web 2.0 which is geared around interaction, will really count.

The literature identifies important caveats relating to the uptake of technology, not least the need for pedagogy to drive the way technology is used rather than the contrary. Salaberry, (2001) in his overview of the uses of technology and their impact on language learning during the twentieth century, makes the point that, "new technologies—revolutionary as they may be from a strictly technological point of view—are normally regarded as revolutionary from a pedagogical standpoint as well" (p. 39). Pedagogical approaches rooted

in socio-cultural theory which views humans as embedded in learning communities where social activity, collaboration and interaction are prime factors in the learning process, are seen as fortuitously consonant with what Web 2.0 appears to have on offer. However, there is perhaps a tendency in the literature to assume that there is a direct unmediated link between Web 2.0 and socio cultural pedagogical approaches and that the introduction of Web 2.0 automatically engenders greater learner participation and interaction. Web 2.0 tools may be predicated on the user as broadcaster rather than audience, as creator rather than recipient (Horizon Report, 2007) but when such tools are harnessed in educational contexts, the way that the teacher designs and scaffolds activities within these tools has a prime affect on the extent of and ways that students participate. Web 2.0 tools may offer the teacher a malleable medium for moulding learner development but it is the teacher's understanding of how best to work and craft that medium which may well determine how it works in a language teaching context. The importance of the tutor as designer is stressed to CDDBL participants.

The way that teachers choose to harness Web 2.0 will depend in large part on their teaching context and we are particularly careful on CD-DBL that in focusing on the way pedagogy can be enhanced by technology we do not neglect considerations of context. While in the literature on language education there has been some discussion on the need for a "context approach" i.e. "an approach that places context at the heart of the profession" (Bax, 2003b, p. 278) and on an "ecological perspective" which looks at the dynamic and negotiated relationship between the richness of a teaching context and methodology (Tudor, 2003), a "context approach" tends to be sidelined when it comes to thinking of the triadic relationship between pedagogy, technology and context. In arguing that there are snug and beneficial fits between a technology and a single pedagogical approach, e.g. social constructivism, there is a risk of propounding a one-fits-all pedagogy which is unresponsive to specificities of context. In fact what we would contend is that the inherent flexibility of Web 2.0 can allow for a blended pedagogical approach which can respond to local educational contexts. There is an expanding strand in the literature that argues that technology, as it is harnessed in careful instructional design, can be effectively used in this way (see, for example, Alonso et al., 2005).

THE PARTICIPANTS' CONTEXTS

The importance of a "context approach" on CD-DBL is underscored with every new cohort that participates on the module. CDDBL participants come from a multiplicity of teaching contexts around the globe, from South and South East Asia to the Middle East to South and North America to Eastern and Western Europe.

A preponderance of participants on CDDBL comes from low and mid-tech contexts. We describe low, mid and high-tech contexts here both from the perspective of the institution and of the learner (see Figure 1). The extent to which we consider an institution as low, mid or high tech depends on a number of factors; primary among these is the level of computer resources available to learners and teachers in the institution and the level of computer know-how among staff in the institution. From the learner perspective we describe context as low, mid or high-tech ostensibly according to the level of access they have to computer technology inside or outside of the teaching institution and their familiarity with that technology. While in a low or mid-tech context some teachers do use Web 1.0 technologies such as PowerPoint, it is more uncommon for Web 2.0 technologies to be used although a clutch of participants on the current run of the module are using Web 2.0 largely as resource areas for their learners. As yet we have not had any participants that we consider to be from high-tech contexts. By high-tech contexts we mean contexts where

the use of technology has become "normalized," in the institution, or as part of the learning process (Bax, 2003a) that is to say where the use of technology has become an integral, assumed and unnoticed aspect of the learning process and where learners consider it perfectly natural to engage in language learning, as facilitated by technology, in the institution as well as in their own time outside of the educational environment.

THE IMPACT OF CONTEXT ON EVALUATION OF WEB 2.0 TECHNOLOGIES

We have mentioned the complex and interacting factors that make up the teaching contexts of participants on CDDBL. These will be different for every participant on the module and therefore are best represented on an individual basis (See section entitled Two Case Scenarios). The low, mid and high-tech categories however, provide us with a general starting point for analyzing the way participants on the CDDBL evaluate Web 2.0 technologies. A top down and bottom up perspective on the use of technologies also provide a useful conceptual framework for analyzing this dynamic. By top down is meant societal, curricula and institutional factors that push for the further integration of technologies. Bottom up means influences that may derive from teachers who are enthusiastic technology users and may see its potential in language education.

Our observations to date have led us to conclude that such contextual factors and the way participants represent these as "context-in-mind," in other words their perceptions of context as they see it in their mind's eye, (Brown, in preparation), have some impact on the way they evaluate the potential of Web. 2.0. We have, over recent months variously described this representation; we have used a "smorgasbord" versus "empty table" metaphor where the smorgasbord represents a participant's perception of the major potential of Web 2.0 in relation to context and where the empty table is

Figure 1. High-tech and low-tech context

	High-tech context	
Full access to and integration of technology with extensive know-how as to when and how to use technology. Technology is normalized.	Learners have extensive access to technology, are used to working with technology and presume that technology will be used in the educational context.	
	Institution / Teacher / Learner	
Little or no access to computers/digital technologies/broad band. Little or no know-how among staff.	Little or no access to computer/digital technologies.	
	Low-tech context	

indicative of a context that a participant sees as entirely unconducive to the use of such technology. Generally, the empty table metaphor applies to the perceptions of participants working in low-tech contexts. There have been perhaps three or four participants on CDDBL out of the fifty or so participants since the inception of the module who have perceived Web 2.0 as a smorgasbord. These participants work in mid-tech contexts and have generally excellent IT skills. They are all to greater or lesser extents bottom up introducers of Web 2.0 in institutions that are generally receptive to their ideas.

We also characterize the way participants represent their context in terms of "considerations," "challenges," and "constraints." We find that a participant talks in terms of considerations when they can see ways of using Web 2.0 technologies in their context, but where there are issues they feel they need to take into account, e.g. the level of the language learner in order to effectively do that. The word "challenge" we relate to when a participant sees obstacles to the use of Web 2.0, obstacles that they see as surmountable and where they can envisage themselves playing a role in overcoming them. We use the term constraint to signify times when a participant sees their context

as hostile to the use of Web 2.0, and where they feel they have no power to alter that situation (once again such a perception of constraints generally, but not exclusively, relates to participants working in low-tech contexts).

In whichever way we choose to describe participant perceptions of Web 2.0 in relation to context, such perceptions do seem to be the primary factor in how participants relate to and evaluate Web 2.0. In CDDBL therefore, we are increasingly trying to steer our approach so that participants perceive strong connections between what they are doing on the module and what they will be able to do in context. While discussion of the literature relating to the use of such technology can give the participant a general sense of the possible value of Web 2.0, it does not seem to lead to those moments of recognition and connection when a participant "visualizes" themselves using the technology in a way that will beneficially address issues they have in their context or come to a keen understanding of why a particular Web 2.0 tool is not useful. A decision that a Web 2.0 tool cannot offer useful affordances for a specific context should be an informed decision coming from strong critical engagement with, and analysis of, the tool.

Figure 2. Private language school case scenario

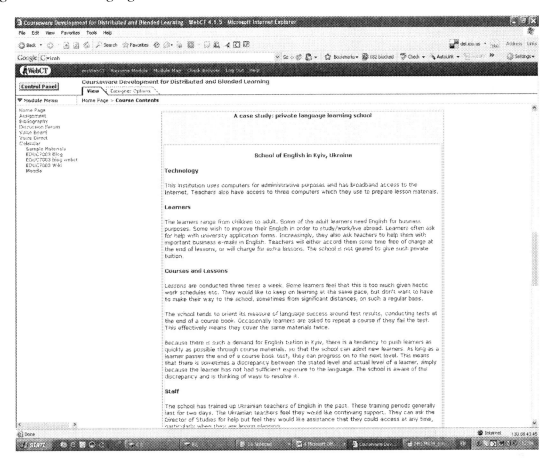

A CLOSER LOOK AT THE "CONTEXT APPROACH" ON CDDBL

We are using different strategies to facilitate the moments of recognition and connection which allow participants to visualize a role for Web 2.0 in their teaching. One of these is a "case study approach." One facet of this approach is the use of a semi-authentic case scenario centering on a private language school. In this scenario (illustrated in three descriptions: see Figure 2 for the first of these) a number of issues are flagged. CDDBL participants are asked to think about the role Web 2.0 genres may play in addressing these. The issues relate, for example, to the number of face-to-face sessions the learners at the school are required to attend, which, given their busy lives

and the location of the school can prove difficult, and to a pervasive testing system where learners who do not pass the test have to repeat exactly the same course book materials.

Along with the case scenario, we also draw on actual Web 2.0 courseware examples (see Figure 3 for the Web resource page containing these examples) which correspond to specific contexts. Where possible we try to obtain accounts from the courseware developers themselves about the way they have developed the courseware in response to considerations of context. Increasingly we are using courseware examples developed by previous participants on CDDBL and hope to create a bank of exemplars which address various aspects of context. Some previous participants on CDDBL have begun to use courseware conceived on the

Figure 3. Courseware examples

module in their local contexts and we hope that we will be able to tap into their experiences of this in order to see how their evaluation of the affordances of Web 2.0 works out in practice. We hope that this will lead to the formation of a "community of practice" (Wenger, 1998) centering on the use of Web 2.0 for language education.

Another approach we are currently exploring to facilitate "moments of recognition and connection" relates to our "niche" evaluation of Web 2.0. Earlier in this chapter we described Web 2.0 as a malleable medium that teachers can harness to suit the needs of their local contexts and it is this inherent flexibility which is at the root of the niche approach. The emphasis in this approach is not on Web 2.0 tools as killer applications that will change the face of language teaching. Instead, we look at the intrinsic functions of Web 2.0 genres to get a better sense of how they may address specific and perhaps seemingly minor issues within various

contexts e.g. a lack of time to develop process writing skills in face-to-face language lessons. Web 2.0 has a broad and expanding set of functions — that expansion of functions stemming from the loop development of Web 2.0 genres in response to the way users employ or wish to employ those genres. These functions resultantly offer a varied range of affordances for language education. We feel that the range of functions of Web 2.0 is well suited to a blended pedagogical approach.

An Exploration of Blogs

It is perhaps best to illustrate this emerging niche approach to Web 2.0 through a discussion of the functions and affordances of one Web 2.0 tool. We have chosen to focus on blogs to do this partly because the educational literature on blogs is currently more substantial than the literature on other Web 2.0 tools. This literature is beginning to analyze the increasingly varied nature of blog types and blog interactions and flesh out pedagogical approaches that relate to these. In doing so it usefully corresponds to our own emerging thinking around Web 2.0 and we can therefore discuss our approach in close relation to recent literature.

A growing number of articles on blogs in education discuss their role in fostering communicative and collaborative interactions (Belderrain, 2006; Cereijol & Myers, 2006; Efimova & Moor, 2005; Owen et al., 2006; Williams & Jacobs, 2004). Owen et al. (2006) define the interactional aspect of Weblogs as those properties that allow "readers to comment on postings, to post links to other blogs and through using pingback and trackback functions (which essentially constitute referencing systems between comments on different blog sites) to keep track of other blogs referencing their posts" (Owen et al., 2006, p. 41). Efimova and Moore discuss the "distributed" generally "spontaneous" conversational interactions which blogs can engender (2005, p. 1), conversations that are tightly associated with the functions of blogs, namely the "comment" feature, "trackback" function and RSS aggregator. Efimova and Moor's research into conversational blogging is particularly useful in its explorations of how specific functions of blogs may relate to the types of interactions that take place through it.

As blogging becomes increasingly popular new tailored blogging environments have been created that respond to and cater for changes in interactional types. Twitter (http://twitter.com/) and Jaiku (http://www.jaiku.com/) are both mobile blogging environments which support brief and frequent "What I'm doing now" type interactions. Such mobile software applications with their ability to provide for embedded/contextualized interactions may potentially offer "virtual and real-world support for social interactions and collaboration in a real-world context" (de Jong et al., 2008, p. 121). The thinking behind such interactive software

applications may be juxtaposed with the thinking behind the "slow blogging" movement. The slow blogging movement has its own manifesto rejecting "immediate" blogging and the "disintegration into the one-liners" (Slow blogging manifesto, online) "what I am doing now" type blogging. It expounds, in contrast, an unhurried, reflective "speaking like it matters" approach to blogging which has its roots in the conception of blogging as a diary space.

We can see from such discussion in the literature that blogging may be used in educational settings for a variety of purposes serving to promote interactions and conversations of various types and reflective thinking that is not predicated on interaction. While blogging may be consonant with pedagogical approaches rooted in socio-cultural theory and therefore predicated on social interactions, it might equally support approaches that are not necessarily intrinsically connected with such interaction, approaches, by way of example, rooted in cognitive theory. On CDDBL we discuss how the various uses that blog environments can be put to and the types of user behavior they can engender can relate to the specificities of CDDBL participants' teaching contexts. To this end we are increasingly using terms which reference the specific character and variety of blog spaces such as micro blogs, slow blogs, soap blogs etc.

We also focus on the setting panel in blogs, an aspect of blogs that has been little explored in the educational literature. The settings area of blogs (the areas that provides customization functions) allows the blog owner to disable blog comments and trackback functions which can effectively seal a blog off from interaction. Comments can be approved or rejected by a blog owner before they appear on the blog and the owner can also determine who views their blog and who has a role as an author.

Knowing about these blog properties is important for teachers as they allow for a nuanced methodology in relation to context. Group blogs may be set up by teachers to allow the full range of interactions that blogs can afford, including learner permission to edit the blog. Learners can set up their own blogs and have full control of the permissions on that blog. However a teacher can take a more prominent controlling role of a group blog space, in order to facilitate scaffolded interaction. Such setting functions may prove useful in some contexts.

The participants on CDDBL who work in South Asian and South East Asian locations talk about the "teacher-centered" contexts they work in where the teacher is expected to be the "sage on the stage," rather than the "ghost in the wings," a metaphor for a teacher who plays a hands-off facilitory role (see Mazzolini & Maddison, 2003). Such participants, while they see major potential for a more learner-centered approach — which they view particularly as a beneficial means of developing fluency skills in English — council a carefully scaffolded approach which slowly introduces learners to greater autonomous peer-peer interaction (see the case study on Andrew Prosser). The setting affordances of blog environments can support that transition.

TWO CASE STUDIES

This chapter has discussed the reasons why a context-based approach has been adopted, particularly as it regards CDDBL participant perceptions of their teaching context. It has explored the way the context-based approach aims to help teachers critically evaluate Web 2.0 for their contexts by focusing on the flexibility of Web 2.0 and the range of pedagogical approaches it may be associated with. In what follows, ways in which two CDDBL participants have perceived the potential of Web 2.0 for their context are presented and their approach to harnessing the affordances of Web 2.0 tools to address aspects of those contexts explored. The two participants work in two diverse contexts. One of the contexts may be characterized as verging on high-tech and one as mid-tech.

Both participants have called on the affordance of Web 2.0 tools in interesting ways to address issues within their context.

Vida Zorko: University of Ljubljana (Offsite Participant on the First Run of CDDBL, 2005)

Vida teaches English for Specific Purposes (ESP) and develops courseware for groups of sociology students studying at the Faculty of Social Sciences at the University of Ljubljana who receive ESP tuition as a part of their degree. Vida felt that a move from a "traditional" lecture-based approach to Problem Based Learning (PBL) (Savin-Baden, 2000) would better serve the students in their learning. She was instrumental in introducing that approach, an approach for the most part approved of in the Sociology Department. This inevitably required a change in ways of working, both on the part of teachers and students, and impacted on the ESP provision. Vida felt that the introduction of a wiki (in this case a pbwiki), which she considered well suited to the social constructivist learning that underpins PBL, could play an instrumental role in facilitating this change. She combined the use of a wiki, in which students working in small groups solved real-life sociology related problems, with a blog space, which she used to co-ordinate aspects of the blended online and face-to-face learning approach and to offer advice and help when students encountered problems. The students could also access Web 1.0 html pages, which were used for the delivery of language learning resources and activities.

Vida felt that the role of the wiki would prove valuable in:

- Promoting peer-to-peer, teacher-teacher and student-teacher interactions necessary (as Vida sees it) for the successful institution of a problem based teaching approach.

- Increasing motivation by publicly displaying group products.
- Facilitating the sharing of knowledge among students and teachers.
- Empowering students with the authority to construct their own knowledge.
- Enabling teachers to better assess students' progress by monitoring the history of the process.

Vida felt that these potential collaborative affordances link to the following features of the PBwiki:

- An interface which is easy to modify to make it more transparent for users.
- 1-click access to all areas, thus promoting greater sharing of knowledge, making student and tutor contributions easily accessible and allowing tutors to better monitor student progress and to collate reoccurring language problems and deal with them in a face-to-face environment.
- The "whose online" and "edit" function that allow tutors to see who is working in the wiki at a given time, and to respond almost immediately to student contributions. From this perspective Vida characterizes the wiki as "almost a synchronous space."
- A comment area that allows for easy dialogue between student and student, and student and tutor.

However, Vida was aware that such functions, in and of themselves, would not bring about the benefits she felt the use of a wiki would introduce. The student wiki pages all adhere to a certain format (though students can adjust that format themselves) that scaffolds the way the students work with each other, as in the example in Figure 4.

In Vida's case the "smorgasbord" metaphor referred to earlier in this chapter is entirely appropriate as she saw, as a participant on CDDBL,

an abundance of opportunities offered by Web 2.0 for her context. She looked on wikis as a tool that with careful scaffolding could facilitate the PBL approach that she had instituted and support a sea change in ways of learning in the Sociology Department. The PBL approach adopted by Vida and the Sociology Department is generally perceived, in the literature, as consonant with the nature of Web 2.0. The Sociology Department was, moreover, amenable to Vida's ideas. In these respects Vida's context arguably offered fertile ground for the introduction of Web 2.0 and may have made it easier for Vida to evaluate Web 2.0 and envisage for it a concrete role. Nevertheless, the introduction of Web 2.0 stemmed largely from Vida's bottom up initiatives and efforts to persuade tutors of the value of the wiki. She saw this process as an enjoyable "challenge," referring back to the three "c" considerations, challenges and constraints framework, rather than as a constraint that would impede the introduction of Web 2.0.

It is perhaps possible that the bottom up influence from Vida, and increasingly her fellow tutors, along with the top down department approval will conspire to normalize Web 2.0 in the faculty, making it the first context we have encountered where this is the case. Early indications through research Vida conducted for her MA dissertation show that the wiki has proved valuable in instigating greater collaborative learning and is fast becoming a "normalized" tool (Bax, 2003a).

Andrew Prosser, Private Language School, Seoul (Offsite Participant on Second Run of CDDBL, 2006)

We might contrast Vida's context with that of Andrew Prosser's. Andrew's is a mid-tech context and is in some ways amenable to Web 2.0 use in that his learners all have access to computers and have some familiarity with Web 2.0 as the majority of them enjoy blogging, a popular Web 2.0 tool in Korea.

Figure 4. Example page of Vida's wiki environment

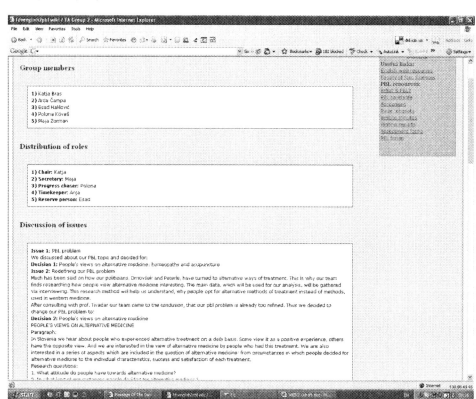

It would, however, be an exaggeration to say that Andrew saw Web 2.0 in terms of a smorgasbord of opportunity for his context, particularly where Web 2.0 is associated with highly learner-centered, autonomous learning. Andrew described his context as essentially teacher-centered, where the teacher is viewed as the "sage on the stage" (Mazzolini & Maddison, 2003), "transmitting" knowledge to be memorized by learners. He saw the value of a more learner-centered approach in encouraging greater learner autonomy and learner interactions which would, in turn, have dividends in terms of language development. However, he did not advocate a total shift to a learner-centered approach and argued that nudging learners towards greater autonomy would require a careful structuring of courseware. He had a cautiously optimistic approach to the value of Web 2.0 in such courseware but once again felt that its value would be highly contingent on careful scaffolding.

Andrew harnessed the popularity of blogging in his teaching context by creating courseware with blogs and in Moodle that would lead ultimately to the learners creating their own "tourist guide to Seoul" blogs. He drew, in the initial stages of his courseware, on those affordances of Moodle and blogs that he considered in keeping with an "associative" instructional design approach to courseware design, an instructional design approach which is mainly tutor determined and uses a linear navigational design structure which asks learners to go through a series of tasks in order to assist learners in mastering a specific language structure or skill. To this end he created controlled Web 1.0 practice exercises in Moodle (see Figure 5), and a blog that modeled the way learners may approach their tourist blog. Through this scaffolding process he gradually shifted from a teacher-centered approach, to the more learner-centered

Figure 5. Andrew's Moodle environment

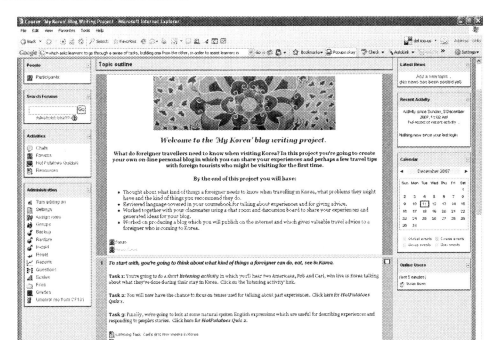

blog task that tapped into the learner-centered affordances of blogs.

Andrew's Web 1.0 and Web 2.0 meld and his perceptions of the potential of Web 2.0 for blending pedagogies in many ways constitute a "niche" approach to his own context.

CONCLUDING REMARKS: THE FUTURE OF CDDBL

In choosing to focus on Vida and Andrew we have illustrated two contexts in which both teachers have envisaged a key role for Web 2.0. and successfully incorporated it into courseware. There is not scope in this chapter to explore case scenarios where CDDBL participants have perceived the introduction of Web 2.0 in their contexts entirely in terms of "empty tables" or "constraints" militating against their incorporation. However, as we have discussed earlier a number of participants

on CDDBL perceive their contexts in these terms and we do not anticipate that this situation will change any time soon. This said, if Web 2.0 continues to be integrated into the fabric of societies at its current speed then it is likely in the longer term that institutions and the teachers within them will increasingly need to negotiate their use. The issue then will be less one of "empty tables" and "constraints" and more one of how Web 2.0 can best be used. This may well engender the type of bottom up thinking demonstrated by Vida Zorko and the "niche" thinking of Andrew. Teachers may increasingly also need to negotiate top-down decisions about the use of technology and the extent to which the use of technology should be Web 1.0 based and Web 2.0 based. We hope that CDDBL will help participants see clear ways to play a role in, and negotiate these influences.

In the latest 2007 offsite run of CDDBL a small proportion of the participants were already enthusiastically using Web 2.0 in their contexts before the module commenced and are indeed bottom up initiators of its use. They have a strong grasp of the functions of the technologies, even if they have not greatly explored their pedagogical possibilities. By the end of the module all of the participants are actively contemplating using Web 2.0 technologies in their teaching and learning situations. Assignment presentations that we have viewed include: the use of online video to encourage better presentation skills for trainee teachers in Japan; the introduction of blogs to encourage more accurate writing skills in Mexico; the use of Moodle as a delivery platform to supplement in class activity; the use of Ning as a tool to increase participation in e-learning; the use of RSS feeds to support the development of learner autonomy in Japan; the use of blogs as an e-portfolio in primary schools in Greece; the use of Moodle, wikis and instant messaging to introduce a greater language element into cultural visits in the UK.

There will continue to be participants who view Web 2.0 with skepticism largely because they see their context as militating against its use. However, interest in the module grows and assignment presentations show the inventiveness of the module participants, their increased ability to analyze their contexts, to bring theory to bear and to integrate a variety of Web 2.0 technologies into their teaching. We feel that the context-based, niche approach we are adopting, which we will continue to develop, will help to increase this interest and give our module participants opportunities to use Web 2.0 in ways they feel will enhance their learning context however minor or substantial these modifications may be.

There will continue to be debate and argument about whether Web 2.0 is somehow different and transformative in its very nature. We have argued here that, given its flexibility, which we see as conducive to a bended pedagogical approach, and the possibilities that it offers for breaking down the barriers between the real world and the classroom, it does have a different and possibly transformative potential. We have also argued that the potential for Web 2.0 goes hand-in-hand with the way it is harnessed by tutors/designers to suit local contexts.

It is clear that information/digital technologies are an increasing feature of net migrants' lives and that for the generations coming through the ability to stay socialized via technologies will be a significant part of their identities. Of course, this landscape will continue to change and the elements on the table will constantly refresh, however, we believe that our particular approach will enable both ourselves and the module participants to deal with these changes in an informed and pedagogically appropriate way.

ACKNOWLEDGMENTS

The authors would like to thank Vida Zorko and Andrew Prosser for their kind permission to write about their perceptions of Web 2.0 and their contexts and for their invaluable assistance in ensuring these were faithfully represented.

REFERENCES

Alonso, F., Lopez, G., Manrique, D., & Vines, J. (2005). An instructional model for Web-based E-Learning education with a blended learning process approach. *British Journal of Educational Technology, 36*(2), 217–235. doi:10.1111/j.1467-8535.2005.00454.x

Bax, S. (2003a). CALL — past, present and future. *System, 36*(1), 13–28. doi:10.1016/S0346-251X(02)00071-4

Bax, S. (2003b). The end of CLT: A context approach to language teaching. *English Language Teaching Journal, 57*(3), 278–287.

Beldarrain, Y. (2006). Distance education trends: integrating new technologies to foster student interaction and collaboration. *Distance Education, 27*(2), 139-153. Retrieved November 24, 2007, from http://www.informaworld.com/smpp/content~content=a749174134

Brown, S. (in preparation). *Context-in-mind: A cultural historical perspective on language teachers' perceptions of social software.*

Bryant, T. (2006). Social software in academia. *EDUCAUSE Quarterly, 2,* 61-64. Retrieved November 25, 2007, from http://www.educause.edu/ir/library/pdf/eqm0627.pdf

Cereijo, M., & Myers, C. (2006). Weblogs: New communication technology uses in resource limited environments. In Gonzales et al., (Eds), *Current Developments in Technology Assisted Education, 1 (*pp.720-726). Retrieved November 24, 2007, from http://www.formatex.org/micte2006/Downloadable-files/oral/Weblogs.pdf

Chapelle, C. (1998). Multimedia call: Lessons to be learned from research on instructed SLA. *Language Learning & Technology, 2*(1), 22–34.

Collis, B., & Moonen, J. (2001). *Flexible learning in a digital world.* London: Kogan Page.

De Jong, T., Sprecht, M., & Koper, R. (2008). A Reference model for mobile social software for learning. *Int. J. Cont. Engineering, Education and Lifelong Learning, 18*(1), 118-138. Retrieved November 25, 2007, from http://dspace.learningnetworks.org/bitstream/1820/996/6/08+De+JONG_16.pdf

Efimova, L., & Moor, A. (2005). An exploratory study of conversational blogging practices. *Proceedings of the 38th Hawaii International Conference on Systems Sciences.* Retrieved November 24, 2007, from http://ieeexplore.ieee.org/iel5/9518/30166/01385452.pdf?tp=&isnumber=&arnumber=1385452

Holliday, A. (1994). *Appropriate methodology and social context.* Cambridge: Cambridge University Press.

Kern, R., Ware, P., & Warschauer, M. (2004). Crossing frontiers: New directions in online pedagogy and research. *Annual Review of Applied Linguistics, 24*(1), 243–260.

Kumaravadivelu, B. (2001). Towards a post-method pedagogy. *TESOL Quarterly, 35*(4), 537–559. doi:10.2307/3588427

Mazzolini, M., & Maddison, S. (2003). Sage, guide or ghost? The effect of instructor intervention on student participation in online discussion forums. *Computers & Education, 40,* 237–253. doi:10.1016/S0360-1315(02)00129-X

Oblinger, D. (2005). *Educating the Net generation.* EDUCAUSE e-book, Boulder, Colorado. Retrieved November 25, 2007, from http://www.educause.edu/LibraryDetailPage/666?ID=PUB7101

Owen, M., Grant, L., Sayers, S., & Facer, K. (2006). *Social software and learning: An Opening Education report from Futurelab.* Retrieved November 30, 2007, from http://www.futurelab.org.uk/research/opening_education/social_software_01.htm

Report, H. (2007). *New Media Consortium.* Retrieved January 29, 2007, from http://www.nmc.org/pdf/2007_Horizon_Report.pdf

Salaberry, R. (2001). The use of technology for second language learning and teaching: A retrospective. *Modern Language Journal, 85*(1), 39–56. doi:10.1111/0026-7902.00096

Savin-Baden, M. (2000). *Problem-based learning in higher education: untold stories.* SRHE & Open University Press, Buckingham.

Thorne, S. L., & Payne, J. S. (2005). Evolutionary trajectories, Internet-mediated expression, and language education. *CALICO Journal, 22*(3), 371–397. Retrieved November 30, 2007, from http://language.la.psu.edu/~thorne/thorne_payne_calico2005.pdf

Tudor, I. (2003). Learning to live with complexity: towards an ecological perspective on language teaching. *System, 31*(1), 1–12. doi:10.1016/S0346-251X(02)00070-2

Vygotsky, L. S. (1978). *Mind in society*. Cambridge, MA: Harvard University Press.

Wenger, E. (1998). *Communities of practice: Learning, meaning, and identity*. New York: Cambridge University Press.

Wildner, S. (1999). Technology integration into preservice foreign language teacher education programs. *CALICO Journal, 17*(2), 223–250.

Williams, J. B., & Jacobs, J. (2004). Exploring the use of blogs as learning spaces in the higher education sector. *Australasian Journal of Educational Technology, 20*(2), 232–247.

Zhong, Y., & Shen, H. (2002). Where is the technology-induced pedagogy? Snap-shots from two multimedia EFL classrooms. *British Journal of Educational Technology, 33*(1), 39–52. doi:10.1111/1467-8535.00237

KEY TERMS

Context-Based Approach: An approach that encourages teachers to have the confidence to creatively reflect on their teaching practice as it responds to the particularities of their own teaching contexts. Kumaradivelu refers to this as a "teacher generated theory of practice" (2001, p. 541). This means that the potential of technologies cannot be evaluated in abstract terms but as it is interlinked with contextually appropriate practice.

Ecology (Teaching Environment): The teaching ecology refers to all the rich, interacting elements that create the dynamic of a teacher's context. These may include top down societal, curricula and institutional elements and bottom up elements such as learner requests to use more technology in the classroom.

High-Tech Contexts: One where the use of technology is integrated into everyday life, so you would expect there to be easy access to the internet, probably these days through wi-fi; for the bulk of the population to carry mobile phones and for technology to feature strongly in the education system.

Low-Tech Contexts: Whilst the middle classes may have access to mobile phones and access to the internet at home, schools may only have traditional computer rooms which may not well be networked. Access to the internet for the general population is via internet cafes in urban areas rather than through wi-fi.

Pbwiki: One of a burgeoning number of wiki environments. The following page provides a useful comparative analysis of different wiki environments: http://www.wikimatrix.org.

Trackback/Pingback: Links that allow blog users to reference content on each others' blogs. For example, say every learner in a class has their own blog and one learner embeds a video file in their blog about a trip they have been on, if other learners comment on the video in their own blogs and use the trackback function, this will automatically show in the blog of the learner who embedded the video. Note that blogger.com does not currently offer the trackback and pingback function

This work was previously published in Handbook of Research on Web 2.0 and Second Language Learning, edited by M. Thomas, pp. 119-136, copyright 2009 by Information Science Reference (an imprint of IGI Global).

Chapter 4.16
An Adaptive and Context-Aware Scenario Model Based on a Web Service Architecture for Pervasive Learning Systems

Cuong Pham-Nguyen
TELECOM, France

Serge Garlatti
TELECOM, France

B.-Y.-Simon Lau
Multimedia University, Malaysia

Benjamin Barbry
University of Sciences and Technologies of Lille, France

Thomas Vantroys
University of Sciences and Technologies of Lille, France

ABSTRACT

Pervasive learning will become increasingly important in technology-enhanced learning (TEL). In this context, development efforts focus on features such as context-awareness, adaptation, services retrieval and orchestration mechanisms. This paper proposes a process to assist the development of such systems, from conception through to execution. This paper focuses mainly on pervasive TEL systems in a learning situation at the workplace. We introduce a context-aware scenario model of corporate learning and working scenarios in e-retail environments such as shops and hypermarkets. This model enables us to integrate contextual information into scenarios and to select how to perform activities according to the current situation. Our pervasive learning system is based on a service oriented architecture that consists of an infrastructure for service management and execution that is flexible enough to reuse learning components and to deal with context changes that are not known in advance and discovered on the fly.. [Article copies are available for purchase from InfoSci-on-Demand.com]

INTRODUCTION

Nowadays, technology-enhanced learning (TEL) systems must have the capability to reuse learning resources and web services from large repositories, to take into account the context and to allow dynamic adaptation to different learners based on substantial advances in pedagogical theories and knowledge models (Balacheff, 2006). This is particularly true of mobile learning, where context is variable. The reuse of learning resources and web services requires interoperability at a semantic level. In other words, it is necessary to have a semantic web approach to design TEL systems. Moreover, knowledge models and pedagogical theories can be fully represented by means of a semantic web approach. In the mobile learning area, a number of terms are commonly used; mobile, pervasive and ubiquitous learning systems (Brodersen, Christensen, Gronboek, Dindler, & Sundararajah, 2005; Hundebol & Helms, 2006; Sharples, 2005; Thomas, 2007). In computer science, mobile computing is mainly about increasing our capability to physically move computing tools and services with us. The computer becomes an ever-present device that expands our capabilities by reducing the device size and/or by providing access to computing capacity over the network (Lyytinen & Yoo, 2002). In mobile computing, an important limitation is that the computing model does not change while we move. This is because the device cannot obtain information about the context in which the computing takes place and adjust it accordingly. In pervasive computing, the computer has the capability to inquire, detect and explore its environment to obtain information and to dynamically build environment models.

This process is reciprocal: the environment also does it and becomes "intelligent". In ubiquitous computing, the main goal is to integrate large-scale mobility with pervasive computing functionalities.

In this article, we consider that mobile, pervasive and ubiquitous learning systems have the properties of mobile, pervasive and ubiquitous computing systems respectively. We focus our attention on pervasive learning systems. Mobile learning is not just about learning at anytime, at any place and in any form using lightweight devices, but learning in context and across contexts. It is best viewed as providing mediating tools in the learning process (Sharples, 2006). Many definitions of pervasive learning are given in the literature (Bomsdorf, 2005; Hundebol & Helms, 2006; Jones & Jo, 2004; Thomas, 2007). One useful definition is that a "pervasive learning environment is a context (or state) for mediating learning in a physical environment enriched with additional site-specific and situation dependent elements – be it plain data, graphics, information -, knowledge -, and learning objects, or, ultimately, audio-visually enhanced virtual layers" (Hundebol & Helms, 2006). One could consider pervasive learning as an extension to mobile learning where the roles of the intelligent environment and of the context are emphasized (Laine & Joy, 2008). In pervasive learning, computers can obtain information about the context of learning from the learning environment where small devices, sensors, pads, badges, large LCD screens, people, and so on, are embedded and communicate mutually. The physical environment is directly related to learning goals and activities. The learning system is dynamically adapted to the learning context. Consequently, a pervasive learning system needs to have an appropriate software architecture to support these features.

In the workplace context, learning can occur in purposeful situations in which there is an explicit goal to learn as well as in incidental situations in which there is no explicit learning goal or interest. Working involves an activity or a related set of activities that require effort and are aimed at achieving one or more objectives. Learning emphasizes what a learner knows or is able to do, while, in contrast, working is related to performance improvement (Michael-Spector & Wang, 2002). In other words, when performing a work task, it often happens that learning also occurs. The performance and quality of work may also be enhanced following learning experiences. Working activities are mainly about solving problems, and in knowledge-intensive organizations this implies continuous learning. Carrying out the particular working task is the priority; learning is just a means (Farmer, Lindstaedt, Droschl, & Luttenberger, 2004). The distinction between learning and working activity is blurring, working being a way of learning, and vice versa. Simon (2007) asserts that traditional methodologies such as formal classroom teaching and even Internet based, content oriented courses and programs have their place at the worksite. Nevertheless, these approaches are generally inflexible to the demands of contextualised, learner centred, performance related challenges (Simon, 2007). Thus, learning processes need to be embedded in organizations, so that learning becomes pervasive and a natural part of work. A particular architecture is required to facilitate the redefinition of learning to mean a work activity and to provide an infrastructure for seamless work-learning integration (Simon, 2007). In such framework, situated learning can be used, where the location, time, environment and tasks, etc. are taken into account. It provides the right learning support at the right time according to the situation parameters and to the goals in the working context. Situated learning increases the quality of learning and is attractive for learning at the workplace and for work-learning integration (Oppermann & Specht, 2006).

In the p-LearNet project (p-LearNet, 2006), a pervasive learning system aims to integrate context-aware corporate learning and working activities within the e-retail framework (retail activities through shops and hypermarkets). In such a framework, we are interested in the following learning issues: the combination of formal learning (formal classroom at the workplace, etc.) and work-learning integration, integration of mobile devices in broader lifelong learning and working scenarios, learning in context, seamless learning across different contexts and context-as-construct (Balacheff, 2006; Sharples, 2006; Vavoula & Sharples, 2008). In such a framework, we focus on a scenario-based approach for TEL system design. Scenarios are used to describe the learning, working and tutoring activities to acquire some domain knowledge and know-how, solve a particular problem or support working activities. Scenario analysis reveals that learning and working situations can be modeled by an explicit hierarchical task model because working and learning activities are well structured and stable. In pervasive learning systems, activities, represented by tasks, can be achieved in different ways according to the current situation. Methods associated with tasks enable us to provide different ways to carrying out those tasks. Activities need to have access to supporting resources or web services. Thus, a context-aware and adaptive mechanism is necessary to select relevant methods associated with a task and their corresponding resources and web services. For a particular couple (Task, Method), resources and web services may also be selected according to the current situation.

In pervasive computing, the computing device has to seamlessly and flexibly obtain information about its environment in which the computing takes place and to adjust itself accordingly. From a software architecture viewpoint, a pervasive learning system has to be flexible enough to reuse learning components (learning resources or learning web services) which are not known in advance and discovered on the fly. A service oriented architecture (SOA) approach facilitates the deployment of an adaptive learning environment based on the aggregation and orchestration of the services needed by an organization. This approach can be effective for pervasive learning systems if one provides for continuous adaptation based on the available services and other contextual information.

The main contribution of this article is an adaptive and context-aware model of scenarios for a pervasive learning system supporting working and learning activities. The pervasive learning system architecture is based on a service oriented architecture to meet pervasive computing requirements. Web services are retrieved and orchestrated, and can be used for different working and learning activities. Thus, the scenario model can invoke web services to undertake activities. The scenario model and the web service retrieval and orchestration are based on a semantic web approach which enables us to represent the explicit common knowledge of the communities of practice involved in the p-LearNet project. The scenario model is based on a hierarchical task model having the task/method paradigm. An activity, represented by a task, may have several associated methods. A method represents a way of performing a task in a particular situation. The context-aware and adaptive mechanism can be viewed as the selection of the relevant content (methods or web services) for a given task according to the current working and/or learning situation. This mechanism is based on matching content description to the current situation for filtering, annotation and ranking. Content and situation need to have corresponding features for adaptation purposes. Methods are described by contextual features while web services are described by metadata. Situations are described according to a context model. For managing web services, we also define the service requirement specification for web service retrieval. Moreover, a pervasive learning system architecture is proposed to facilitate its design and execution in a workplace environment, based on Open Services Gateway initiatives (OSGi) and Universal Plug and Play (UPnP). SOA enables us to design an architecture that is able to inquire, detect and

explore its environment to obtain information and to dynamically build environment models. As web services are closely related to learning needs by means of the scenario model, we can provide the right learning support according to the current situation and deal with pervasive computing issues.

In the next section we begin by presenting the p-LearNet project and e-retail system goals. Secondly, we present our pervasive learning system architecture based on SOA that serves as a platform of service management in e-retail systems. Thirdly, our context management model (organization, features) is detailed and linked to a situation. Fourthly, we present our context-aware scenario model and its relationships with the context management model. Fifthly, the web service requirements and specifications are presented and also the semantic metadata schema describing the web services. Sixthly, the context management process, i.e. the detection and creation of new situations are explained. Seventhly, the adaptation process which links the context model, the scenario model, the metadata schema and the context management is presented. Finally, a conclusion highlights the main results of this study and some perspectives on the results.

P-LEARNET PROJECT AND E-RETAIL SYSTEMS

The 3-year p-LearNet project is an exploratory work on adaptive services and usages for human learning in the context of pervasive communication. One aim is concerned with providing learning to professionals during their work activities. This project therefore addresses concepts and methodologies to facilitate this type of learning. In such a framework, the main issues of the p-LearNet project are: work-integrated learning and customer learning support, continuous professional learning at the workplace, professional learning whatever the place, the time, the organisational and technological contexts of the individual or collective learning and working processes, context-as-construct and seamless learning. The design and engineering of pervasive learning systems must be considered as an interdisciplinary problem requiring the integration of different scientific approaches from computer science, education, commerce, social sciences, etc. Learning focuses mainly on how to support individual and group learning processes through pedagogical guidance and how to enhance the learner's knowledge and know-how. In this project, one of our corporate partners is an international retail companies having chains of shops and hypermarkets wishing to explore sales staff learning at the workplace. Corporate partners identify the problems and requirements about quality and efficiency of information and services to increase market share and the corresponding learning goals. Several innovative scenarios have been set up according to two main learning and/or working situations for both a seller and a customer as learners: i) Seller or customer, outside the shop counters: seller in the back office or storage areas, customer at home or elsewhere; ii) Seller in his department, alone or with a customer having resources from the Smart Spaces (large LCD screen, printers,

RFID, etc.) surrounding them (Derycke, Chevrin, & Vantroys, 2007).

In the e-retail framework, the context is continuously evolving during the selling process: a seller can communicate with customers while revising his/her knowledge, checking the inventory or contacting the supplier about products, etc. Sometimes learning and working are interwoven in a pervasive environment. A substantial part of learning does not happen during training but during working activities. Learning and professional activity support must therefore be integrated. A learning system must overcome three main obstacles: time pressure, inadequate learning support in the working context and cognitive and structural disconnection between work, knowledge, and learning (Farmer, Lindstaedt, Droschl, & Luttenberger, 2004). For example, a seller equipped with a portable device, for example a PDA or a UMPC, close to shelves (without a customer) can revise thier knowledge about products and selling techniques or can continue thier previous learning activities to improve their knowledge, or they can verify product labeling or access to product information. During the selling process or the selection / decision phase, the seller can use his/her mobile device as a coach to help them, etc.

Figure 1. Learning requirements and needs at the workplace

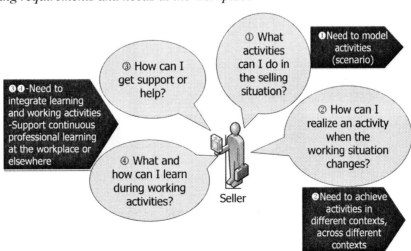

In such a framework, the following needs are required (cf. Figure 1).

One of the key problems is the requirement for continuously following the user into a wide variety of contexts, and our efforts address this issue inside the intermediation infrastructure, between the service universe and the communication universe, by adding "intelligence" to provide seamless services regardless of channel. The next section will present the pervasive learning system architecture we developed to deal with our requirements. We then explain in more detail the context and the context-aware scenario model.

PERVASIVE LEARNING SYSTEM ARCHITECTURE

We developed a generic and flexible software infrastructure (cf. Figure 2) to support learning and working activities at workplace. As described in the introduction, learning in context must support certain functionalities, as listed below.

Firstly, we have to recover information or data from the context, such as activities (current and available), location, and devices available in the environment. We identified two main sources for context recovery. One is the user's environment,

which is composed here of a set of devices offering services. These devices can communicate with each other and they can be reachable by anyone, within the constraints of access rules (e.g. sellers can access more services than customers, etc.). Thus, the selling space becomes a part of the process and can collect information (Derycke, Vantroys, Barbry, & Laporte, 2008). Our pervasive learning system can access services provided by devices, external services and semantic composition services. External services may be provided by the company information system. Semantic composition services are mainly composed of four modules (scenario, metadata, context and domain) corresponding to the models mentioned in the next sections. Each module is itself a set of services and managed by the Context Manager System component (cf. Figure 2). These services can be used by the devices and by anyone in the sales department (sellers, customers, etc.). Activities are another source for context.

Secondly, our architecture allows us to aggregate and to coordinate all available services, both from software (learning system, database access, information system, etc.) and from the environment (televisions, webcams, printers, etc.). It is what we call extensibility and modularity. Extensibility means that we can integrate

Figure 2. An overview of pervasive learning system architecture

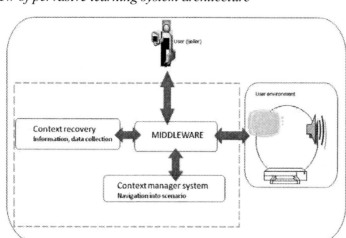

and use any new services (e-learning modules) or devices (printers, televisions, etc.) We have to support live detection of service abilities. For example when a device is turned on or off, the system knows if its services are available or not. Then, we need semantic discovery of all available services. Modularity means addition or removal of some interactive elements, for adaptation to the needs of a particular retail company. The services provided have to be modular too: the system can provide services with different implementations to match the location, time, users, devices, etc. And, finally, our system has to be compliant with existing services. Our system can use services which have already been developed by a particular company. For practical purposes, we do not want to re-develop services already used for e-learning activities.

Thirdly, in order to present all services to the user in a relevant way, we need adapt available services for user applications (see the section "Adaptation" below). Our system uses multi-channel and multimodal intermediations between a mobile personal user device and a collection of e-services (Chevrin, Sockeel, & Derycke, 2006).

To satisfy these requirements we have chosen the following technologies. The modular archi-

tecture is possible thanks to OSGi (OSGi, 2007). OSGi is a software layer over Java. It reuses the dynamic class loading capabilities of the Java language. It enables a development model where applications are (dynamically) composed of many different (reusable) components (bundles). It acts as a shell over the Java Virtual Machine: it manages the component life cycle, so we can dynamically add or remove components. Each component hides their implementation from other components while communicating through *services*, which are objects that are specifically shared between components. A similar implementation example is the Eclipse IDE, which is also built on an OSGi framework. Each Eclipse plug-in is an OSGi bundle, which is why we can easily add or remove plug-ins.

To communicate easily with external services, such as our context management system, we used web services access (using a SOAP-based implementation). To discover devices present in the selling space, we use the UPnP (UPnP, 2007) protocol. UPnP is a communication protocol allowing the creation of spontaneous networks of devices (TV sets, HVAC, light control etc.) and control points (PDA, Smartphone, touch panels, etc.). UPnP enables live detection of devices and

Figure 3. Middleware architecture

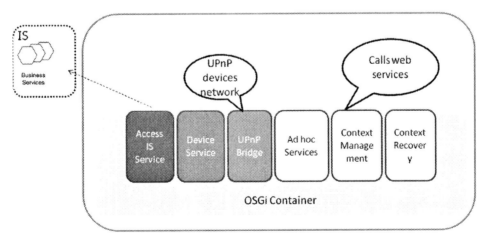

their use via the SOAP protocol, so the services provided by devices are also seen as web services.

As a consequence, we have to allow communication between different services from different protocols, each with their own formalism. Therefore we have implemented a dedicated communication middleware based on OSGi technology, as shown in Figure 3. Our system is built by assembling services in an OSGi container. Each service can communicate with external components using web services. For example, the context recovery service calls our context manager system as a web service. Moreover, thanks to different OSGi bridges, physical devices can be seen as UPnP devices. The gateway allows us to plug in any kind of device as long as a suitable OSGi driver is available. Each device company can provide such drivers, OSGi and UPnP being open protocols.

CONTEXT MODELING

In mobile learning, context may be viewed as "context-as-construct", i.e. "context should be reconceived as a construct that is continually created by the interaction of learners, teachers, physical settings, and social environments" (Sharples, 2006) and "learning not only occurs in the context, it also creates context through continual interaction" (Balacheff, 2006). Dourish (2004) outlines certain modeling characteristics of the context that need to be tailored for structuring contextual information: i) Contextuality is a relational property that holds between objects or activities; ii) The context is not defined in advance. On the contrary, the scope of contextual features is defined dynamically; iii) Context is an occasioned property, relevant to particular settings, particular instances of activities; iv) Context arises from the activities. Context cannot be separated from activities. It is actively produced, maintained and enacted during activities. We claim that activi-

ties embedded in a particular physical world (or environment) are key issues to give us intention and meaning according to different situations and finally to determine the relevant features describing the different situations. Many definitions of context are given in the literature, including: *"learning context is used to describe the current situation of a person related to a learning activity; in addition to attributes relying on the physical world model* (Derntl & Hummel, 2005); *"information and content in use to support a specific activity (being individual or collaborative) in a particular physical environment"* (Kurti, Milrad, Alserin, & Gustafsson, 2006).

In our framework, the context model has to deal with learning in context, seamless learning across different contexts and context-as-construct. In other words, we have to manage the context to provide the right learning support. According to these features, a context management model must have the following properties: dynamic and "context-as-construct". Therefore, context settings could be "unpredictable" because it is dynamically created and modified through continual interactions with users and the environment. Context and activities are central to determine learning goals and to choose how achieve them, more particularly in a working environment.

According to these requirements and issues, our context management model is composed of a context model, a context metadata schema, several context views and a set of situations. It is organized as follows (cf. Figure 4).

There is a context model, defining a set of relevant context dimensions and their features. The context dimensions are divided into two categories: abstract dimensions and atomic dimensions. An abstract dimension can be recursively broken down into sub-dimensions which are either abstract or atomic. An atomic dimension consists only of a set of features. Potentially, our context dimensions are the scenario (a hierarchal task model having a task/method paradigm), the user (an employee, a sales person, an expert,

Figure 4. Context Management Model

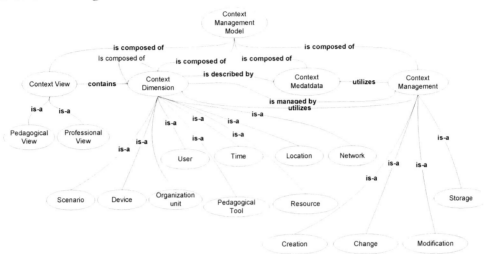

etc.) with sub-dimensions: the role, previous knowledge, know-how, preferences, loyalty card, purchase intentions, intention of use), the device, the location (office, shelf, stockroom, cash desk, etc.), the time, the learning tools, the network, the physical environment and the resources (e.g. learning object, services, media resource, system resource, etc.). The context metadata schema is described by a set of properties (some of these are shown in Table 1). Dimensions and features are described by context metadata to deal with "unpredictable" context settings. The main idea is to specify in advance for each type of context property how to manage it for creation, change, and adaptation. In Table 1, the four displayed features are used to manage adaptation. Thus, we apply a specific adaptation policy according to the values of these features.

There is also a set of views. A view consists of a subset of context features which are relevant to a given content category (methods, resources, or web services) and a given activity type (learning or working) for adaptation. An adaptation process does not manage the same features for different content categories. In the adaptation process, the current situation, filtered by a view and the corresponding content description are compared. Potentially, a view can also be created for a sub-category of content category or activity type (for example, a sub-category of web services or learning activities). The predicate contextViewFeatures described below in F-logic specifies all context features for a view identified by a content category (*AC*) and an activity type (*AT*). Context views are used to define different viewpoints for adaptation. Consequently, different adaptation categories are specified accordingly (see Box 1).

A set of situations is organized in historical dependencies. A situation is a partial instantiation of the context model consisting of the obtained

Table 1. A subset of context metadata properties

Some context metadata features	Description
State	{Mandatory, Transitory}.
ContentType	{methods, resources, web services}
ActivityType	{learning, professional, etc.}

features describing the current learning or working situation and its physical environment. It defines a complete context state associating all interactions between the user and the learning system at the workplace in a given time interval. A user activity can be influenced by his previous work and learning activities. As soon as a new situation occurs, the next stage can be chosen according to the historical dependencies, for instance, to ensure seamless learning. So far, we do not have enough details from our experiments to define relevant strategies to manage seamless learning across contexts. Future experiments will gives us more detail about this issue and also about the real set of features describing the context management model. At present, it is mainly a kind of generic context management model having an accurate structure and associated principles to manage learning in context and seamless learning across contexts in our pervasive learning system, in other words adaptation. Consequently, our context-aware scenario model is defined according to this context management model.

CONTEXT-AWARE SCENARIO MODEL

In our framework, the goal of scenarios is to describe the learning, working and tutoring activities to acquire some knowledge domain and know-how to solve a particular problem or to support working activities. The main role of a scenario model is to integrate mobile devices into broader learning and working scenarios, to combine formal (formal classroom at the workplace) and work-learning integration and to enable us to manage seamless

learning across contexts. As a scenario describes user activities, an author/designer can manage a global activity consistently. In this article, we focus on the work-learning integration context given in Figure 6 (described in detail later).

In pervasive learning systems, activities cannot be achieved in the same way in different situations. It is necessary to have a context-aware and adaptive mechanism to decide how to perform an activity according to a given situation. Derntl and Hummel address these needs by introducing a UML-based modeling extension for including relationships between context and learning activities in the learning design models (Derntl & Hummel, 2005). Several research studies in artificial intelligence focus on the hierarchical task model using the task/method paradigm (Trichet & Tchounikine, 1999; Wielinga, Velde, Schreiber, & Akkermans, 1992; Willamowski, Chevenet, & François, 1994). In a learning environment, hierarchical task models were also used for designing, for instance, authoring tools (Ikeda, Seta, & Mizoguchi, 1997) and learning systems (Betbeder & Tchounikine, 2003; Choquet, Danna, Tchounikine, & Trichet, 1998; Ullrich, 2005). The mechanism of hierarchical and recursive decomposition of a problem into sub-problems is one of the basic characteristics of the hierarchical task model (Trichet & Tchounikine, 1999; Wielinga et al., 1992; Willamowski et al., 1994). In the MODALES project, an adaptive and context-aware model of scenarios has been successfully proposed and implemented. It is based on an interdisciplinary approach (didactics, physics and its epistemology, computer science and education) (Tetchueng, Garlatti, & Laubé, 2008). This hierarchical task model has been reused and modified according to our new requirements.

Box 1.

```
FORALL AT, CC, ViewFeature  contextViewFeatures(AT, CC, ViewFeature)
    <- EXISTS cm cm:ContextMetadata AND cm[ActivityType->>AT; ContentType-
>>CC; ForContextFeature->>ViewFeature].
```

The Task/Method Concept

Within the framework of the Task/Method paradigm, tasks represent activities and sub-activities managed by a knowledge-based system (cf. Figure 5). A method describes how a particular task can be achieved. There are two types of tasks: abstract tasks and atomic tasks. An atomic task is not composed of sub-tasks. It can be achieved by a simple procedure defined inside a method. An abstract task represents a high level activity composed of sub-activities. A method defines how an abstract task is composed of sub-tasks which can be either abstract or atomic. A method associated with an abstract task defines a control structure that allows the recursive decomposition of tasks into sub-tasks and the sub-task order at runtime by means of operators. At present, three different operators are used: sequence, alternative and parallel. A method associated with an atomic task can have: i) a resource specification for resource retrieval; ii) a service specification for web service retrieval; iii) a procedure/function specification for a simple procedure or function. For a given task, several methods can be used to achieve it. Methods are described by contextual features for selection and adaptation.

Learning Scenario for Sellers at the Workplace

In our framework, all activities (working and learning) are integrated into a single scenario that is modeled by a hierarchical structure of tasks/methods (cf. Figure 6). The selection of the relevant method to achieve a given task according to the current situation, restricted to the relevant context view and the context descriptor, are compared.

Figure 6 shows a part of the e-retail scenario, which represents the decomposition of the task "S.3 – Sale assistance in situation" by a method "M13" in a sequence order of sub-tasks ("S.3_T.1" and "S.3_T.2"). The task "S.3_T.1" can be achieved in two different situations: one without a customer and one with a customer. Thus, the decomposition of the task "S.3_T.1" can be made by two different methods ("M131", "M132"). Each one is associated to a set of contextual features (context descriptor), which specifies the relevant situations for which the method could be selected. Because the task "S.3_T.1" is an abstract task, its methods decompose it into sub-tasks by means of operators determining the sub-task execution order. The method "M131" aims to provide to the seller

Figure 5. Context-aware task model description

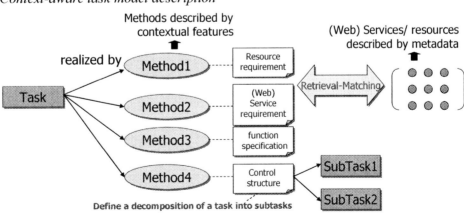

Figure 6. A small part of the e-retail scenario

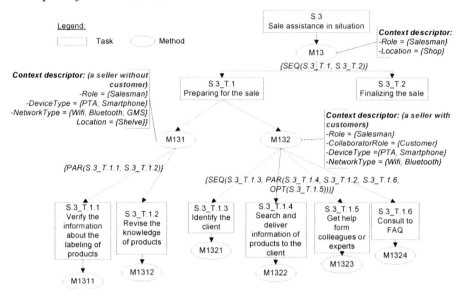

with both activities available ("S.3_T.1.1 - verify information about the labeling of products" and "S.3_T.1.2 - revise the product knowledge") when s/he approaches shelves without customers (Location = {Shelves}). The method "M132" achieves the task "S.3_T.1" for the seller with a customer (CollaboratorRole = {Customer}). It is divided into four sub-tasks that are carried out as follows: (SEQ (S.3_T.1.3, PAR (S.3_T.1.4, S.3_T.1.5, S.3_T.1.6))) means that we start with the sub-task "S.3_T.1.3" then follow with one of three sub-tasks ("S.3_T.1.4", "S.3_T.1.5" and "S.3_T.1.6") that will be executed in parallel.

We shall use this part of scenario as an example. A task can be achieved by using web services, so in the next section we will show how services are described and annotated for retrieval, orchestration and adaptation in the scope of the task requirements.

SERVICE SPECIFICATIONS AND REQUIREMENTS

In pervasive computing, service oriented architectures are increasingly used to design learning

systems. A review of current literature reveals numerous ongoing efforts aimed at exploiting semantic web technologies for web service retrieval and adaptation (Janssen, Lins, Schlegel, Kühner, & Wanner, 2004; Keidl & Kemper, 2004; Pathak, Koul, Caragea, & Honavar, 2005; Sheshagiri, Sadeh, & Gandon, 2004). Semantic modeling of web services is a pre-requisite for successful service retrieval. Service descriptions should specify what the service offers, how the service works and how to access the service (Yang, Lan & Chung, 2005). Work in this area utilises WSDL+DAML-OIL (Sivashanmugam, Verma, Sheth, & Miller, 2003), WSDL-S (Akkiraju et al., 2005) and OWL-S (Martin et al., 2004) among other technologies. Pathak et al. (2005) incorporate OWL-S descriptions to describe service requests and providers that can be processed by a matchmaking engine that is aware of the relevant domain ontologies. The framework supports selecting services based on the user's functional and non-functional requirements, which are then ranked based on user-specified criteria. Dolog et al. (2004) propose a service-based architecture for establishing personalized e-Learning provided by various web-services, including personalization services and support services. Their work encompasses annotation schema and ontologies for learning resources which may include web services, though these are not mentioned explicitly (Dolog, Henze, Nejdl, & Sintek, 2004).

In our learning and working scenarios, an activity may be realized by either a simple internal service or a set of external services. The problem to solve is to search for a service or a number of services that may be composed in a certain order to fulfill the requirements of the current task / method pair. Towards this goal, services have to be semantically annotated. In systems without context adaptation, web services are statically bound to a method at design time. In this regard, the problem is to bind, invoke and execute these web services in a "known" order. Take for instance Task "S.3_T.1.4" in Figure 6. Web service A can be bound to this task (through its method "M132") at design time for searching for product information and resources (images, sound messages, documents, etc.). At runtime, logic is built-in to web service A to search for relevant resources annotated with description metadata from repositories or from the database and deliver them to the client making the request.

The proposed solution is semi-dynamic service searching and matching. The relevant services in this regard can be a single matched service or a set of matched services. The latter is aimed at searching for all the relevant services provided by service providers according to the current situation and the service requirement identified in the selected method. This is done based on an adaptation process applied to services (Please refer to the Context Management, Service Requirement Specification and Adaptation Process sections). Taking Task "S.3_T.1.4" above for example, the realization solution consists of four phases. Each phase is considered as a single service or a set of matched services:

- Phase 1: a search of web services (in a service repository) which provide information about a selected product or a product type required by the Service Requirement Specification of the method "M132" is first carried out according to the current situation.

- Phase 2: All relevant web services of all the suppliers are organized, invoked and executed for searching for product information and resources.

- Phase 3: The found resources are assembled and adapted according to the current situation. They are filtered and sorted according to their degree of relevance.

- Phase 4: The relevant resources are delivered to the target devices. All services are managed and executed by our pervasive learning system architecture previously described.

SERVICE REQUIREMENT WSPECIFICATION

The characteristics and functionalities of a service required for a relevant task or activity have to be specified semantically to facilitate accurate and efficient discovery and matching of the relevant services. The primary goal of a service requirement is the description of how a service is to be "desired". It is a request issued by the system wishing to interact with a service provider in order that a task should be performed on behalf of the learner in the current situation. By our definition, a service satisfies a service requirement by providing a set of desired output parameters for a desired goal with a set of pre-existing input parameters and situational context features. Our proposed service requirement is summarized as follows:

- **Functional requirements:** describe the capabilities of web services desired by a user. It is characterized by input parameters, expected output parameters, pre-conditions and expected post-conditions;

- **Non functional requirements:** include the identity of a service (e.g. name, owner, type etc.) as well as performance related characteristics, such as Quality of Service (QoS), security etc;

• **Content requirements:** specify a list of domain concepts or a query identifying the content requirements of services (e.g. Mark, Price, ProductModel etc.).

Table 2 shows an example of a service requirement specification "SRS_M1322" for the method "M1322" which realizes the task "S.3_T.1.4 – Search and deliver information on products to clients". This specification consists of three main parts. In the functional requirement part, the input is composed of three parameters (ProductType ?pt, ProductInfoType ?pi and DeliveredResourceType ?rt) describing desired capabilities of the service for retrieving the desired resource (e.g. document, media, voice file, pages, database, etc.). The pre-condition is a predicate that verifies, for example a mandatory presence of a *ProductType*. The output describes a list of relevant resources to be delivered to the client. The non-functional requirements portion represents QoS related context features that can be used for ranking purposes. Finally, the content requirement presents a list of domain

concepts that covers a sub-domain (ontology of products) for query refinement. These concepts are used to "compare" with the DomainContent category of a service (see Table 3) through the domain ontology.

Service Description

Service requests and provision are modeled with a common service description metadata model to formally specify the functional and non-functional requirements of services. The fundamental consideration in describing a web service to support accurate and efficient service discovery and matching is to fulfill a three-part ontology (Milanovic & Malek, 2004): *function, behavior* and *interface. Interface* dictates how the service can be invoked and what resources are to be assembled to provide the desired functionalities of the service. It is syntactic in nature. We propose to follow the WSDL binding standard for message format and protocol details for interoperability. Hence, the problem of searching and matching the right service provision to a client service requirement in a web service architecture is basically reduced to a problem of matching the service

Table 2. An example illustrating the service requirement specification for the method "M132"

Service Request	SRS_M1322	
Functional Requirement	(	
	input	(ProductType ?pt)
		(ProductInfoType ?pi)
		(DeliveredResourceType ?rt)
	output	(ProductResource ?pr)
	pre-condition	(isNotNull ?pt)
	post-condition	
	)	(isNotNull ?rt)

function and *behavior* descriptions to the service requirement specification. In this article, we propose a service description ontology to describe web services with a service description feature set. Table 3 enlists features which are generally applicable to most web services.

These features can be extended to include features which describe more specific functionalities of web services such as pedagogy. The features on a feature list can either be mandatory or optional. They serve to index a service for searching, filtering and ranking purposes. As soon as a web service has been chosen according to the service specification and requirements, it is achieved and managed by our pervasive learning system architecture.

CONTEXT MANAGEMENT PROCESS

The context management process integrates all parts and models of the system in a permanent way to deal with complex and dynamic context changes and demands of situated learning at runtime. To this end, it detects the situation changes and then generates a new situation or updates the current situation for maintaining activity relevance, seamlessly. This process is divided into five main stages (see Figure 7):

- Stage 1: Context change detection and aggregation: this stage determines context changes and checks whether these changes lead to the creation of a new situation or an update of the current one. The changes can come from collaborators (colleagues, customers, tutors or learners), user interactions, location, network, device, time, scenario, etc.;
- Stage 2: Gathering of the initial context information to create the new situation, this is done by a partial or complete copy of the last situation and/or by querying the context ontology;
- Stage 3: Selection of the current task: the last task status can be restored in the new situation to ensure seamless learning and working based on the historical dependencies of

Table 3. Service global feature set

Sub categories	Feature set
General	{name, description, language, owner, type (name, taxonomy, value), entityType}
Meta-metadata	{metadataCreator, metadataValidator, creationDate, validationDate, language, format}
Life-cycle	{creator, dateCreated, version, status, contributor, publisher, dateUpdated, extentOfValidity}
Right	{IP, accessRight, signature, provenance, dateCreated, dateUpdated}
Technical	{URI, resource, resourceURI, resourceFormat, replacedBy, realisation, modeOfInteraction}
ServiceRequirement	{listInput(name, type, value, ontologyURI), listOutput(name, type, value, ontologyURI), expectedEffect}
DomainContent	{listDomainConcepts}
Context	{roleModels, location(coordinate, spatialLocation, locationRelativity), physical(deliveryChannel, deliverySystem, deviceModel, tool), informaticResource(hardware, software), temporal(temporalCoverage, frequencyRequirement)}

situations. When the last task is finished, the next one is selected according to the current scenario and the historical dependencies of situations. When the last task is not finished, it is necessary to continue it;

- Stage 4: Searching for the relevant couples (Task, Method): According to the current situation and the task, the adaptation process has to select the relevant methods. The main role of the adaptation process is to maintain consistency between the learning system, the physical environment and the current learning or working situation and also to ensure seamless learning and working;

- Stage 5: Discovery and execution of relevant web services to serve the current task: Realization of a task requires the discovery, orchestration, invocation and execution of relevant web services. Service requirement specification which specifies the required service functionalities and characteristics is defined in the selected method of the selected Task/Method pair in Stage 4. The adaptation process is hence aimed at searching for the relevant web services to realize the current task according to this specification and the current situation. The specification and management of web services is described in the next section.

ADAPTATION

The fundamental issue in a pervasive learning environment is how to provide learners with the right activities, the right learning content at the right time and in the right way. Thus, adaptation is mandatory to all types of learning activities in pervasive learning environments (Bomsdorf, 2005). At present, we focus on adaptation mechanisms dedicated to two content categories: method and web service adaptation. At the scenario level, adaptation is aimed at accomplishing an activity according to the current situation, or in other words, how to select the relevant methods for a given task. The learning system has to dynamically select the relevant way to perform the different tasks of a scenario. At the service level, adaptation has to refine the service retrieval process for perform an atomic task. Thus, web services are only available in atomic tasks. The learning system needs to select the relevant web services according to the current couple (task, method) and the current situation. As context is dynamic, it is not possible to know in advance how the next situation will be structured. In other words, it is not possible to anticipate the set of features composing the different situations. For managing adaptation, it is necessary to trigger rules using the contextual features of methods and the service

Figure 7. The context management process

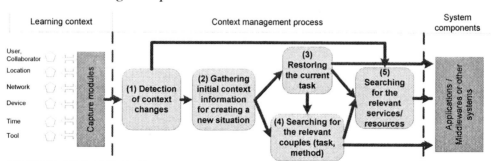

description of web services which are defined a priori and the set of situation features which can be unexpected – not known in advance. Consequently, it is not possible to define rules for each possible configuration of features in a situation.

Like the Mobilearn European project (Lonsdale & Beale, 2004), we associate specific metadata with situation properties and/or dimensions for managing adaptation. Situation features are divided into two categories: permanent and transitory. Features describing scenarios and users which are available in all situations are permanent features in a situation. Thus, it is possible to manage them as usual because they are known a priori. Other features are transitory. For them, it is necessary to analyse how each property contributes to content adaptation – methods and services selection - differently according to its role in the adaptation process. Some of them are used to filter the content while others are used to rank or annotate it where filtering, ranking and annotation are the adaptation techniques. For instance, learning and working methods can be filtered according to learning places or used devices while it is annotated according to the user's knowledge or preferences. As soon as features are used to filter content (methods or services), it is easy to manage them. In other words, content will or will not be filtered out by a present transitory feature. At present, all transitory features of content are used to filter. Nevertheless, we shall have to investigate this issue in depth according to more detailed scenarios in future.

Adaptation Process

The adaptation process is specified for a content type (methods and web services) and an adaptation category. The input content of the adaptation process can be achieved in different ways depending on the content type: input methods are specified directly by the current task while input services are selected by a search process based on a query which "compares" the service requirement of the selected couple (task, method) with the service description. The three stages of the adaptation process are presented as follows (cf. Figure 8):

- Evaluation/Classification: input content is classified according to the current situation in several equivalence classes: two classes *{"Good", "Bad"}* for each transitory feature and up to five equivalence classes *{"Very-Bad", "Bad", "ToConsider", "Good", "VeryGood"}* for all permanent situation features, together. The content belongs to an equivalent class if it satisfies its membership rules.
- Filtering: all content belonging to "Bad" classes are filtered out. In other words, these content are discarded. For example, with the network dimension, the class *"Good"* is considered as relevant while the class *"Bad"* is not. This means that the system hence will eliminate all content that belongs to the class *"Bad"*.

Figure 8. Adaptation principle

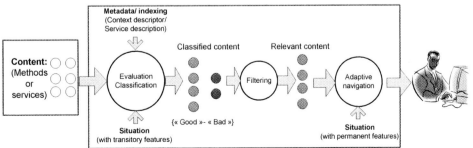

- Adaptive navigation: permanent situation features are used to evaluate and classify the remaining content. An adaptive technique can be chosen by the system or by the user according to an author decision. All content belonging to the same equivalence class are treated in the same way. Annotation and sorting are processed according to the total order of equivalence classes. For hiding, only contents belonging to the class "Good" and "VeryGood" are maintained.

Adaptation of Methods

Method adaptation is specified as follows: 1) All context dimensions for this adaptation category possess the same set of equivalent classes {"Good", "Bad"}; 2) All methods for which the current context and the user features match up to the corresponding method's contextual features (or "belong to" for multiple-valued features) belong to the class "Good" and others belong to the class "Bad"; 3) If the class "Good" is empty, it is considered as a problematic situation and required a designer action to remediate or to provide a new method and context adapted to the user and the task. Otherwise, all methods, belonging to the

class "Good", can be provided to the user. The user can choose one of the relevant methods to carry out the current task.

Table 4 shows an example of two membership rules described in a reduced form using F-Logic syntax. The first rule *EvaluateBadMethod* verifies if a method belongs to the class "Bad" according to a situation. It is done based on the mismatching between the method's context descriptor and contextual features of a situation. The mismatching of each contextual feature is verified by each sub rule. The second rule *EvaluateBadLocationForMethod* is a sub rule that verifies the mismatching of the current situation's location feature and the corresponding the supported location list of a method. The predicate *contextViewFeatures* verifies if the location feature is one context view feature for methods. For the filtering, all methods which do not belong to class "Bad" are considered as relevant methods (see the rule *MethodFiltering* in Table 4).

Adaptation of Services

Firstly, a service retrieval process is carried out to search relevant services in the repository based on the Service description to fulfill the Service

Table 4. Illustration of a membership rule of the equivalent class "Bad" for methods

```
RULE EvaluateBadMethod:
FORALL aMethod, aSituation belongingToBad (aMethod, aSituation)
<- EXISTS aCxtDescriptor (aMethod[has_Context_Descriptor->> aCxtDescriptor] AND (
IsMismatchedLocation(aSituation->>hasLocationPlace, aCxtDescriptor->>Location) OR
IsMismatchedNetwork(aSituation->>hasCurrentNetwork, aCxtDescriptor->>hasNextworkTypes) OR
IsMismatchedDevice(aSituation->>hasUsedDevice, aCxtDescriptor->>hasDeviceType) OR
IsMismatchedCollaborator(aSituation->>hasCollaborator, aCxtDescriptor->>hasCollaboratorRole) OR
IsMismatchedRole(aSituation->>hasCurrentUser->>hasRole, aCxtDescriptor->>hasRole) OR
IsMismatchedKnowHow(aSituation->>hasCurrentUser, aCxtDescriptor->>hasPrerequisiteKnowHow))).

RULE EvaluateBadLocationForMethod:
FORALL aLocation1, aListLocation2 IsMismatchedLocation (aLocation1, aListLocation2)
 <- NOT inList(aListLocation2, aLocation1)  OR NOT contextViewFeatures("Method", "Learning", getCorrespondingCon
textFeature(aLocation1)).

RULE MethodFiltering:
FORALL aMethod, aSituation isRelevant(aMethods, aSituation) <- aMethod:Methods AND NOT
belongingToBad(aMethod, aSituation).
```

request for a task. This is done by querying the Service descriptor metadata repository (matching particularly the ServiceRequirement and DomainContent of Services with the functional, non-functional and content requirements of a request). Secondly, the relevant Services serve as the input for the adaptation phase which is aimed at refining the relevant services according to the current situation and user's interest. Adaptation of services is specified as follows: 1) all transitory context features in the Context category are used to classify input services into two equivalent classes {"Good", "Bad"}; 2) all services belong to class "Bad" will be eliminated; 3) some context features from the Context, Quality, Financial, etc. categories are taken into account for the service ranking process. This process is based on user interest features. For example, users can choose *qualityRating* of services as with high priority while others may be more interested in *performance*. Moreover, ranking requirements also depend on the type of services. With services for voice communications, the performance is very important while with services for financial transactions, security is a high priority. Therefore, the user can build an "interested" feature priority list by annotating each feature with an "interest" level (from very low to very high). This information will be stored in the user's profile for later reuse and be part of the current situation information for this user. Based on the list of "interest" features, the system can rank all matched services.

CONCLUSION

We have proposed an adaptive and context-aware model of a scenario based on a hierarchical task model having the task/method paradigm - with methods defining how to achieve a task - for a pervasive learning system supporting working and learning situations. This model enables us to include contextual information in learning scenarios at the design stage and to choose how to achieve activities according to the current situation at runtime. In other words, the relevant methods are selected dynamically according to the current situation for performing activities. We have also integrated web services described at the semantic level for indexing services. From a scenario perspective, the system can dynamically select and adapt learning components (resources and services) that are not known in advance for achieving an atomic task. Our context model and adaptation process deal with dynamic "context-as-construct" by means of transitory and permanent situation features managed in different ways. A service oriented architecture approach is suitable for pervasive learning systems to deal with such dynamic learning content and environments. At present, because our scenarios are limited, issues of seamless learning and working across contexts are managed in a limited way. The integration of scenarios and learning resources is not actually taken into account. As an area for future work, we will enrich our scenarios and from that, we can study in greater depth the transitory and per-

Figure 9. Service retrieval and adaptation

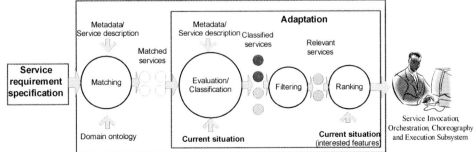

manent situation features and adaptation policies needed to manage different adaptation categories and seamless learning. Our model will lead to experiments in the scope of the p-LearNet project with our industrial partners to be evaluated in real situations.

ACKNOWLEDGMENT

This work is supported by the p-LearNet project funded by the ANR "Agence Nationale de la Recherche" in France. It receives the support of the PICOM "Pôle de Compétitivité des Industries du Commerce".

REFERENCES

Akkiraju, R., Farrel, J., Miller, J., Nagarajan, M., Marc-Thomas, Schmidt, et al. (2005). Web Service Semantics - WSDL-S. Retrieved 15 November, 2008, from http://www.w3.org/Submission/2005/SUBM-WSDL-S-20051107/

Balacheff, N. (2006). 10 issues to think about the future of research on TEL. *Les Cahiers Leibniz, Kaleidoscope Research Report* (147).

Betbeder, M.-L., & Tchounikine, P. (2003). *Structuring collective activities with tasks and plans*. Paper presented at the IEEE International Conference on Advanced Learning Technologies (ICALT'2003).

Bomsdorf, B. (2005). *Adaptation of Learning Spaces: Supporting Ubiquitous Learning in Higher Distance Education*. Paper presented at the Mobile Computing and Ambient Intelligence: The Challenge of Multimedia, Dagstuhl Seminar Proceedings.

Brodersen, C., Christensen, B. G., Gronboek, K., Dindler, C., & Sundararajah, B. (2005). *eBag: a ubiquitous Web infrastructure for nomadic learning*. Paper presented at the Proceedings of the 14th international conference on World Wide Web.

Chevrin, V., Sockeel, S., & Derycke, A. (2006, June 26-29). *An Intermediation Middleware for supporting Ubiquitous Interaction in Mobile Commerce*. Paper presented at the ICPS'06, IEEE International Conference on Pervasive Services, Lyon.

Choquet, C., Danna, F., Tchounikine, P., & F. Trichet. (1998). *Modelling Knowledge-Based Components of a Learning Environment within the Task/Method Paradigm*. Paper presented at the Intelligent tutoring Systems, ITS'98, San Antonio (USA).

Derntl, M., & Hummel, K. A. (2005). *Modeling Context-Aware E-learning Scenarios*. Paper presented at the Pervasive Computing and Communications Workshops. *3rd IEEE PerCom 2005 Workshops*.

Derycke, A., Chevrin, V., & Vantroys, T. (2007, 13th May). *P-Learning and e-retail: a case and a flexible Sotware Architecture*. Paper presented at the Pervasive Learning 2007. *An International Workshop on Pervasive Learning*, Toronto, Ontario, Canada.

Derycke, A., Vantroys, T., Barbry, B., & Laporte, P. (2008). *E-retail: Interaction of Intelligent Selling Space with Personal Selling Assistant*. Paper presented at the ICEIS 2008, an International Conference on Enterprise Information System, Barcelona, Spain.

Dolog, P., Henze, N., Nejdl, W., & Sintek, M. (2004). *Personalization in distributed e-learning environments*. Paper presented at the Proceedings of the 13th international World Wide Web conference on Alternate track papers & posters.

Dourish, P. (2004). What we talk about when we talk about context. *Personal Ubiquitous Comput., 8*(1), 19-30.

Farmer, J., Lindstaedt, S. N., Droschl, G., & Luttenberger, P. (2004, April 2-3). *AD-HOC - Work-*

integrated Technology-supported Teaching and Learning. Paper presented at the 5th conference on Organisational Knowledge, Learning and Capabilities, Innsbruck, Austria.

Hundebol, J., & Helms, N. H. (2006). Pervasive e-Learning - In Situ Leaning in Changing Contexts.

Ikeda, M., Seta, K., & Mizoguchi, R. (1997). *Task Ontology Makes It Easier To Use Authoring Tools.* Paper presented at the IJCAI.

Janssen, D., Lins, A., Schlegel, T., Kühner, M., & Wanner, G. (2004). *A Framework for Semantic Web Service Retrieval.* Fraunhofer Institute for Industrial Engineering and University of Applied Sciences, Schellingstr.

Jones, V., & Jo, J. H. (2004). *Ubiquitous Learning Environment: an Adaptive Teaching System using Ubiquitous Technology.* Paper presented at the ASCILITE, Perth, Australia.

Keidl, M., & Kemper, A. (2004). *Towards Context-Aware Adaptable Web Services.* Paper presented at the In Proceedings of the 13th International World Wide Web Conference (WWW'04).

Kurti, A., Milrad, M., Alserin, F., & Gustafsson, J. (2006, October 4-6). *Designing and implementing ubuquitous learning activities supported by mobile and positioning technologies.* Paper presented at the the Ninth IASTED International Conference computers and Advanced Technology in Education, Lima, Peru.

Laine, T. H., & Joy, M. (2008). *Survey on Context-aware Pervasive Learning Environments.* Paper presented at the Mlearn 2008, the bridge from text to Context, Wolverhampton.

Lonsdale, P., & Beale, R. (2004). Towards a dynamic process model of context. *Proceedings of Ubicomp 2004 workshop on Advanced Context Modeling, Reasoning and Manage.*

Lyytinen, K., & Yoo, Y. (2002). Issues and challenges in ubiquitous computing. *SPECIAL ISSUE:*

Issues and challenges in ubiquitous computing, 45(12).

Martin, D., Burstein, M., Hobbs, J., Lassila, O., McDermott, D., McIlraith, S., et al. (2004). *OWL-S: Semantic Markup for Web Services.* Retrieved 15 November, 2008, from http://www.w3.org/Submission/OWL-S

Michael-Spector, J., & Wang, X. (2002). Integrating Technology into Learning and Working: Promising Opportunities and Problematic Issues. *Educational Technology & Society, 5*(1).

Milanovic, N., & Malek, M. (2004). *Current Solutions for Web Service Composition.* Berlin.

Oppermann, R., & Specht, M. (2006). Situated Learning in the Process of Work. In S. Netherlands (Ed.), *Engaged Learning with Emerging Technologies* (pp. 69-89).

OSGi. (2007). *OSGi Alliance.* from http://www.osgi.org

p-LearNet. (2006). *p-LearNet project.* Retrieved from http://p-learnet.univ-lille1.fr/web/guest/home.

Pathak, J., Koul, N., Caragea, D., & Honavar, V. G. (2005). *A framework for semantic web services discovery.* Paper presented at the Workshop On Web Information And Data Management. *Proceedings of the 7th annual ACM international workshop on Web information and data management*, Bremen, Germany

Sharples, M. (2005). Learning As Conversation: Transforming Education in the Mobile Age. In *Proceedings of Conference on Seeing, Understanding, Learning in the Mobile Age* (pp. 147-152), Budapest, Hungary.

Sharples, M. (2006). *Big Issues in Mobile Learning: Report of a workshop by the Kaleidoscope Network of Excellence Mobile Learning Initiative.* LSRI, University of Nottingham.

Sheshagiri, M., Sadeh, N. M., & Gandon, F. (2004). *Using Semantic Web Services for Context-Aware Mobile Applications*. Paper presented at the MobiSys 2004 Workshop on Context Awareness.

Simon, A. (2007). Blurring the lines between learning and working. *Yellow Edge, The Performance Architect*. Retrieved One, from http://www.yellowedge.com.au/Downloads/Issue%201%20-%20Blurring%20the%20lines%20between%20learning%20and%20work.pdf

Thomas, S. (2007, May 13). *Pervasive Scale: A model of pervasive, ubiquitous, and ambient learning*. Paper presented at the An International Workshop on Pervasive Learning, in conjunction with Pervasive 2007, Toronto, Ontario, Canada.

Sivashanmugam, K., Verma, K., Sheth, A. P., & Miller, J. A. (2003). *Adding semantics to web services standards*. Paper presented at the Proceedings of the International Conference on Web Services, ICWS '03, CSREA Press.

Tetchueng, J. L., Garlatti, S., & Laubé, S. (2008). A Context-Aware Learning System based on generic scenarios and the theory in didactic anthropology of knowledge. *International Journal of Computer Science and Applications, 5*(Special Issue on New Trends on AI Techniques for Educational Technologies), 71-87.

Trichet, F., & Tchounikine, P. (1999). DSTM: a Framework to Operationalize and Refine a Problem-Solving Method modeled in terms of

Tasks and Methods. *International Journal of Expert Systems With Applications, Elsevier Science, 16*, 105-120.

Ullrich, C. (2005). Course generation based on HTN planning. In J. A. & B. B. (Eds.), *Proceedings of 13th annual Workshop of the SIG Adaptivity and User Modeling in Interactive Systems* (pp. 75-79).

UPnP. (2007). *UPnP, Official web site*. from http://www.upnp.org

Vavoula, G. N., & Sharples, M. (2008). *Challenges in Evaluating Mobile Learning*. Paper presented at the mLearn 2008, the international conference on mobile learning, University of Wolverhampton, School of Computing and IT, UK.

Wielinga, B., Velde, W. V. d., Schreiber, G., & Akkermans, H. (1992). The KADS Knowledge Modelling Approach. In R. Mizoguchi & H. Motoda (Eds.), *Proceedings of the 2nd Japanese Knowledge Acquisition for Knowledge-Based Systems Workshop* (pp. 23-42). Hitachi, Advanced Research Laboratory, Hatoyama, Saitama, Japan.

Willamowski, J., Chevenet, F., & François, J. M. (1994). A development shell for cooperative problem-solving environments. *Mathematics and computers in simulation, 36*(4-6), 361-379.

Yang, S, Lan, B., & Chung, J. (2005, 29 March-1 April 2005). *A new approach for context aware SOA*. Paper presented at the The 2005 IEEE International Conference on e-Technology, e-Commerce and e-Service, 2005. *EEE '05. Proceedings*.

This work was previously published in International Journal of Mobile and Blended Learning, Vol. 1, Issue 3, edited by D. Parsons, pp. 41-69 , copyright 2009 by IGI Publishing (an imprint of IGI Global).

Chapter 4.17
Exploring the Effects of Web–Enabled Self–Regulated Learning and Online Class Frequency on Students' Computing Skills in Blended Learning Courses

Pei-Di Shen
Ming Chuan University, Taiwan

Chia-Wen Tsai
Ming Chuan University, Taiwan

ABSTRACT

Web-based courses have shown to be successful in providing quality distance education. However, due to a national education policy, pure online courses are not permitted in Taiwan. In addition, there exists a lack of appropriate design and delivery of blended learning courses. In this study, the authors conducted a quasi-experiment to examine the effects in applying blended learning (BL) with web-enabled self-regulated learning (SRL) to enhance students' skills of deploying database management system (DBMS). Four class sections with a total of 172 second-year students were taken as four distinct groups. The results showed that students in the SRL and BL groups with 5 online classes had the highest grades for using DBMS among the four groups. Students who received the treatments of web-enabled SRL also outperformed a control group that did not have the benefit of instruction in SRL. The implications of this study are also discussed.

INTRODUCTION

The goals of vocational schools concentrate on developing a highly skilled workforce (Lee & Huang, 1996). Professionals with a vocational degree represent a major portion of the work force in Taiwan (Shen, Lee, Tsai, 2007a). However, vocational education in Taiwan is highly competitive in that it must attract sufficient student enrollments in the face of a continually decreasing birth rate and rapidly increasing number of schools. Schools, facing the high pressure of market competition, often emphasize the proportion of students awarded certificates before they graduate. That is, teaching in this sector usually focuses on helping vocational students to pass the certification examinations (Shen, Lee & Tsai, 2007). The grades on students' certificates and the numbers achieved are the main criteria to evaluate teachers' teaching and students' learning. In this regard, how to help students enhance their professional skills and pass the certificate examinations is a major concern to many teachers in vocational schools in Taiwan.

Web-assisted instruction has been advocated by contemporary educators and researchers (Liu & Tsai, 2008). Asynchronous, web-based educational programs have been shown to be quite successful in providing quality distance education (Overbaugh & Casiello, 2008). However, the policy of e-learning in Taiwan is relatively conservative in contrast with that in the U.S. For example, earning an academic degree entirely through online courses is still not allowed at present. That is, teachers in some nations with conservative institutions and implementations of e-learning, have to adopt a mode of blended learning (BL) rather than pure online learning when implementing e-learning. The effectiveness of BL has already been demonstrated (Liu, Chiang & Huang, 2007; Pereira, Pleguezuelos, Merí, Molina-Ros, Molina-Tomás & Masdeu, 2007; Shen, Lee & Tsai, 2007b), nevertheless, due to limited research on how BL can be conducted effectively using the Internet, it is essential to investigate and develop an appropriate design and arrangement of BL courses for schools and teachers. For example, what frequency of online classes in a BL course is more appropriate to the students, particularly for those with low self-regulatory skills? The authors conducted an experiment to explore the appropriate online class frequency that supports student learning.

Through the Internet, learners are free to access new information without restrictions (Li, Tsai & Tsai, 2008); however, this may also be one of its greatest dangers. There is a continuing debate about the effectiveness of online learning environment designs (Azevedo, 2005; Jacobson, 2005). Online learning differs from didactic presentation, where the student has few opportunities to deviate from the teacher's presentation of the material (Greene & Azevedo, 2007). Moreover, it is indicated that vocational students are more Internet-addicted than students in general (Yang & Tung, 2007). Many vocational students are addicted to shopping websites, online games, and online messengers, and prefer this rather than getting involved in courses, particularly online courses (Shen, Lee, Tsai & Ting, 2008). This addiction to the Internet and the lack of on-the-spot teacher monitoring in web-based instruction makes it even more difficult for students to concentrate on online learning (Shen, Lee & Tsai, 2008). To respond to this challenge, the authors adopt self-regulated learning (SRL) that can help students better regulate and improve their learning.

As more and more institutions of higher education provide online courses, the question arises whether they can be as effective as those offered in the traditional classroom format (Shelley, Swartz & Cole, 2007). However, few studies have discussed effective online instructional methods for vocational students (Shen, Lee, and Tsai, 2007a). Furthermore, we expect that innovative teaching methods and technologies could improve students learning in BL courses. Specifically, this study explores the potential effects of web-based SRL with variations in online class frequency on the development of vocational students' computing skills. Based on suggestions from earlier research, we have re-designed the course and conducted a series of quasi-experiments to examine the effects of web-enabled SRL, varying with frequency of online classes on vocational students' computing skills.

SELF-REGULATED LEARNING

Zimmerman and Schunk (1989) define SRL in terms of self-generated thoughts, feelings, and actions, which are systematically oriented toward attainment of the students' own goals. SRL is an active, constructive process whereby learners set goals for their learning and then attempt to monitor, regulate, and control their cognition, motivation, and behavior in the service of those goals (Winne, 2001; Winne & Hadwin, 1998; Zimmerman & Schunk, 2001). Characteristics attributed to self-regulated persons coincide with those attributed to high-performance, high-capacity students, as opposed to those with low performance, who show a deficit in metacognitive, motivational, and behavioral variables (Montalvo & Torres, 2004; Reyero & Tourón, 2003; Roces & González Torres, 1998; Zimmerman, 1998).

In an SRL environment, students take charge of their own learning by choosing and setting goals, using individual strategies in order to monitor, regulate and control the different aspects influencing the learning process and evaluating their actions. Eventually, they become less dependent on others and on the contextual features in a learning situation (Järvelä, Näykki, Laru & Luokkanen, 2007). Bielaczyc, Pirolli and Brown (1995) incorporated self-explanation and self-regulation strategies in the attainment of the cognitive skill of computer programming. They found that their treatment group, which incorporated self-regulation strategies, outperformed a control group that did not have the benefit of instruction in these strategies.

Moreover, Nota, Soresi and Zimmerman (2004) indicate that the cognitive self-regulation strategy of organizing and transforming proves to be a significant predictor of the students' course grades in mathematics and technical subjects in high school, their subsequent average course grades and examinations passed at university.

Previous studies have established that self-regulation skills can help foster learning from any instructional method (see Ertmer, Newby & MacDougall, 1996; Weinstein, 1989; Zimmerman, 1990). In addition, many educators and teachers recognize the importance of SRL in online learning environments. In Lynch and Dembo's (2004) study that investigates the relationship between self-regulation and online learning in a BL context, it is indicated that verbal ability and self-efficacy related significantly to performance, together explaining 12 percent of the variance in course grades. Moreover, it is indicated that successful students in an online course generally used SRL strategies and the effect of self-regulation on students' success was statistically significant (Yukselturk & Bulut, 2007). Therefore, in this study, SRL is applied in this BL course to enhance students' computing skills.

BLENDED LEARNING

Blended learning (BL) is a form of technology-mediated learning that improves learning outcomes through an alternation of face-to-face courses and Internet courses (Lai, Lee, Yeh & Ho, 2005). Marino (2000) discovered that some students experienced difficulty adjusting to the structure of online courses, managing their time in such environments, and maintaining self-motivation. Students may feel frustration in fully online courses, particularly those who are dependent learners, are less self-regulated, and need frequent direction and reinforcement from a visible instructor. These frustrations could be eased when the online course is combined with periodic opportunities for face-to-face interactions (Rovai & Jordan, 2004).

With regard to the effects of BL in previous research, Yushau (2006) shows the positive effect of blended e-learning on students' attitude toward computers and mathematics. It is found that performance, as measured by the final mark of the course under a hybrid teaching method that incorporated both traditional face-to-face lectures and electronic delivery and communication methods, is higher than that of using a traditional teaching method alone (Dowling, Godfrey & Gyles, 2003). In Castelijn and Janssen's (2006) study, their statistical results also indicated that BL students had higher exam scores in a financial management course.

As for the effects of BL on student success rates in learning to program, Boyle, Bradley, Chalk, Jones, and Pickard's (2003) research results indicate a generally positive evaluation of the main elements of the blend, and widespread use of the new online features. Moreover, students in the BL group attained significantly higher average scores than those in the traditional teaching group. Similarly, Pereira et al. (2007) concluded that BL was more effective than traditional teaching. Therefore, BL is applied in this study to help students learn and develop their skills in using application software.

METHODS

Subjects

The subjects in this study were 172 vocational students from two consecutive semesters taking a compulsory course entitled 'Database Management Systems'. Students at this university are expected to spend much more time and effort in mastering a variety of technological skills when compared to those in comprehensive universities in Taiwan. None of students in this study majors in information or computer technology, and the

pre-test confirmed that all participants had average or little knowledge of the course content. In addition, there was no student who had taken a web-based course before. We evenly and randomly divided the students into the four experimental groups.

Course Setting

The course is a semester-long, 2 credit-hour class, targeting second-year college students from different major fields of study. The major focus of this course is to develop students' skills in applying the functions of a database management system (DBMS), which is a powerful tool for creating and managing large amounts of data efficiently, robustly and safely, over long periods of time (Матросова, 2007). Students received a study task dealing with the subject of Microsoft Access, one of the popular DBMS applications. Further, according to the school's policy, the course targets helping students to earn a certificate in database applications. That is, students have to take a certification test in Access at the end of the semester.

Experimental Design and Procedure

The experimental design is a factorial pretest - post test design. Four classes were selected from two successive years for this quasi-experiment, with three classes chosen for BL classes and the last one used as a control group. In the first week, the lecturer declared in the three BL classes that the class section would be partially provided with innovative instructional methods mediated on the web as an intervention. Students had the freedom to drop this class section and take another teacher's class section, if preferred. After this declaration, 172 students continued in the three BL classes.

In the first week, students were pre-tested and the results showed that the differences of students' computing skills among the four groups were not statistically significant. That is, students in the four groups had similar levels of computing skills before they received the interventions. Then, participants were randomly assigned to one of the four experimental conditions. The 'SRL and BL with 10 online classes' group (C1, n=44), 'SRL and BL with 5 online classes' group (C2, n=41), 'non-SRL and BL with 5 online classes' group (C3, n=42) are experimental groups, while 'non-SRL and face-to-face' group (C4, n=45) is the control group. C2 and C3 were conducted in the first semester, while C1 and C4 were conducted in the second.

This experiment was implemented in the 'Database Management Systems' course. Students needed to pass the examination to earn the Microsoft Access certificate. The certificate examinations were held immediately after the completion of teaching the course (16th week of the semester). The detailed schedule of the experiment is depicted in Figure 1.

Intervention Concerning SRL

Students in C1 and C2 received instruction in an after-school class teaching SRL strategies. The students were gathered in a classroom and a two-hour lecture was delivered discussing how students could manage study time and regulate their learning. The content of this SRL course was composed of the four processes addressed by Zimmerman, Bonner & Kovach (1996), that is, self-evaluation and monitoring, goal-setting and strategy planning, strategy implementation and monitoring, and monitoring of the outcome of strategy. Students were taught how to implement these four processes to become more self-regulated learners.

In addition to the two-hour lecture, students in SRL groups were required to regularly preview and review the textbook, and practice the skills in using DBMS. The teacher assigned course work to students in the Assignments and Exercises section of the course website and students had to complete the assignments by the required deadline. They were also required to record their learning behavior on the course website every week. The button for submission became unavailable when the time was up. Activities and results of students' learning were captured and recorded on the course website instead of in their notebooks, to prevent falsification of records.

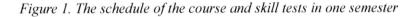

Figure 1. The schedule of the course and skill tests in one semester

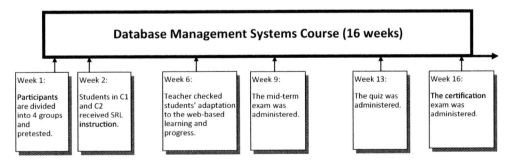

Intervention Concerning BL

Networked multimedia technologies and software were applied in the BL classes (C1, C2 and C3). A course website was provided for BL students. The teacher lectured about how to solve simulated computing problems through the Internet or in the classroom. The teacher recorded every lecture session whether in the classroom or via the Internet and later on translated lectures into HTML files with flash, video, and voice. These HTML files were then loaded onto the course website. Students could then preview and review the course sessions on this course website. They could also download the examples and upload their homework to the site.

From the third week, some course work to be delivered online, that is, five or ten non-contiguous weeks in total, was moved onto the website. At the beginning of the semester, the teacher urged students to adjust their learning gradually and smoothly. The remaining weeks' teaching was still conducted in the traditional classroom. In the set of face-to-face classes, the teacher gave lectures and students could ask questions. The mid-term examination, quiz, and certificate examination were all administered in the face-to-face classes.

Evaluation and Qualification

A detailed evaluation of the project was conducted. The authors explored the potential effects of web-based SRL with variations in online class frequency on students' skills in using Microsoft Access. To examine levels of change manipulated by variations in experimental conditions, we first measured students' Access skills as they entered the class. In the first week, students completed two database files in Access as a pretest. The pretest grades showed that the computer skills of almost all the students were low. This confirmed that all participants in the four classes had little knowledge or skill using this software package.

Differences in students' skills of using DBMS at the beginning stage among the four classes were not statistically significant. Thus, the researchers ruled out initial differences as a plausible alternative explanation for the differences detected after treatments (Gribbons & Herman, 1997).

The examinations for the certificate in Access were conducted immediately after the course concluded. There were two problems, each consisting of 5 to 7 sub-problems in the examinations. Before testing, students were assigned random seats. All students were tested at the same time. A student's grade came from their correctness and completeness in problem solving. A student could get professional certification using DBMS if his/her grade was higher than 70. Finally, we tested the differences between students' skills in using Access under different conditions.

Design of the Course Website

An open-source Learning Management System (LMS), Moodle, was adopted as the platform for the course website in this study. Teachers who use this LMS can access an array of powerful tools such as assignments, forums, journals, quizzes, surveys, chat rooms, and workshops (Cole, 2005). The course website mainly consisted of five sections: Course Information, Course Content, Course Discussion, Student System, and Assignments and Exercises. Course Information provides course description, syllabus, assignments, grading and course-related information. Course Content includes lectures delivered, conversations that happened in the classroom and the students' exercise files. Students can download the files and listen to audio recordings to review or complete exercises, repeatedly. Teachers may ask questions in the Course Discussion board in order to promote discussion and interaction. Students' personal information and their logs are recorded in the Student System. They could also write their learning journals as blogs in this section. Finally, teachers can assign course work to students in

Assignments and Exercises section and students have to complete and upload the assignments according to deadlines.

RESULTS

A 'one-way ANOVA' was used to compare students' computing skills in using DBMS under different conditions. As shown in Table 1, students from the control group (C4) received the lowest grades among the four groups, and differences in grades among them are significant. However, the difference among the three BL groups (C1, C2 and C3) in students' computing skills is not statistically significant. Further analysis is needed to explore whether the online class frequency influenced students' learning.

The independent samples t-test is used to compare the difference of students' computing skills between 'SRL and BL with 10 online classes'

group (C1) and 'SRL and BL with 5 online classes' group (C2). As shown in Table 2, students' average grade for DBMS in C2 (93.83) is significantly higher than that in C1 (84.85) group. This is, a blended course with 5 online classes contributed to better learning effects for vocational students than that with 10 online classes.

Results from Table 3 show that the students' average grade for DBMS in C2 (93.83) is higher than that in the C3 group (86.40). Thus, the effects of web-based SRL on students' skills in using DBMS are positive, and higher than those without SRL intervention.

DISCUSSION AND IMPLICATIONS

Many researchers and educators have highlighted the importance of using technologies to help students learning (Chen, Kinshuk, Wei, Chen &

Table 1. One-way ANOVA: Students' Grades for Using DBMS

Grades	(I) Groups	(J) Groups	Mean Difference (I-J)	Std. Error	Sig.	95% Confidence Interval	
						Lower Bound	Upper Bound
1	2		-8.981	3.816	.141	-19.76	1.79
	3		-1.556	3.792	.982	-12.27	9.15
	4		19.256(*)	3.727	.000	8.73	29.78
2	1		8.981	3.816	.141	-1.79	19.76
	3		7.425	3.859	.299	-3.47	18.32
	4		28.237(*)	3.795	.000	17.52	38.95
3	1		1.556	3.792	.982	-9.15	12.27
	2		-7.425	3.859	.299	-18.32	3.47
	4		20.812(*)	3.771	.000	10.16	31.46
4	1		-19.256(*)	3.727	.000	-29.78	-8.73
	2		-28.237(*)	3.795	.000	-38.95	-17.52
	3		-20.812(*)	3.771	.000	-31.46	-10.16

* The mean difference is significant at the .05 level

Table 2. Independent samples t-test: Scores of C1 and C2

Group	n	Mean	S. D.	F	t-value	df	p
C1	44	84.85	17.350	1.274	-2.493	83	.015**
C2	41	93.83	15.749				

*Note. **p < 0.05*

Table 3. Independent samples t-test: Scores of C2 and C3

Group	n	Mean	S. D.	F	t-value	df	p
C2	41	93.83	15.749	.857	2.507	81	.014**
C3	42	86.40	10.834				

*Note. **p < 0.05*

Wang, 2007; Connolly, MacArthur, Stansfield & McLellan, 2007; Liu & Tsai, 2008; Shen, Lee & Tsai, 2007b). There are several advantages in applying a BL approach (Boyle *et al.*, 2003). It is also found that many students studying in undergraduate and part-time graduate programs indicated their preferences for retaining some form of face-to-face teaching while at the same time taking advantage of e-learning (Lee and Chan, 2007). Meanwhile, the policy of e-learning in Taiwan is relatively conservative in contrast with that in the U.S. Teachers in this context have to adopt BL if they want to implement e-learning in their courses. Moreover, many vocational students are addicted to shopping websites, online games, and online messengers (Shen, Lee, Tsai & Ting, 2008). In this regard, it is necessary to develop an appropriate design and arrangement for BL courses.

To improve our understanding of this issue, the authors brought in and then tested rigorously a set of hypotheses among four conditions. According to the findings of this study, we believe that our research has made some contributions to e-learning theory in three different ways.

Firstly, our research contributed to the existing literature by demonstrating that lower online class frequency in a BL course is more helpful to students learning. Second, this study specifies how teachers help students to regulate their learning by applying web-enabled SRL in a BL course, and further contribute to their learning. Finally, this empirical study demonstrated that a BL course with SRL strategies was more effective in developing students' computing skills than a course in the traditional classroom.

Effects of Online Class Frequency

As the results showed in Table 1, the effects of BL on students' scores for computing skills is significantly higher than those who learned through traditional teaching. Students' computing skills in C1, C2 and C3 were significantly higher than those in C4. The result in this study is similar to Castelijn and Janssen's (2006), Shen, Lee, and Tsai's (2007b), and Yushau's (2006) studies that show the positive effect of blended e-learning on students' learning and attitude toward computers and mathematics.

Moreover, this study attempted to further understand and develop the appropriate design and arrangement of BL courses for schools and teachers. It is shown in Table 2 that a BL course with 5 online classes could result in significantly better learning effects than that with 10 online classes ($p = 0.015$). It is mentioned that students in the vocational system tend to have lower levels of academic achievement (Lee, 2003), have low confidence and motivation in learning (Su, 2005), have low interest and negative attitude toward their learning (Chen & Tien, 2005), do not adequately get involved in their schoolwork, and do not care so much about their grades (Shen, Lee & Tsai, 2007a). In this specific context, teachers could adopt technologies and teaching websites to help students achieve better learning performance. For example, the BL course and audio-recorded content provide the flexibility and opportunities for students to attend class, review the course content, and practice what they learn at their convenience, particularly before the certificate examinations. However, the online class frequency in a blended course is also one of the critical factors that influences students learning. In the online classes, the physical absence of the instructor and the increased responsibility demanded of learners to effectively engage in learning tasks may present difficulties for learners, particularly those with low self-regulatory skills (Dabbagh & Kitsantas, 2005). Students retreating to the isolation of their computers may avoid school activities and course involvement (Treuer & Belote, 1997). Too many online classes in a BL course may even damage low-achieving students' learning. In this regard, teachers should arrange the appropriate mix of blended classes for students. For example, one traditional class session accompanied the last online class for students to ask questions or for the teacher to check students' progress. With appropriate design, BL could really contribute to students learning.

The Effects of Web-Enabled SRL

With respect to the effects of web-enabled SRL, the results shown in Table 3 indicate that the difference of students' computing skills between C2 and C3 groups is statistically significant ($p = 0.014$). The success in online courses often depends on students' abilities to successfully direct their own learning efforts (Cennamo, Ross & Rogers, 2002). E-learning should be treated as self-directed learning because the learner attends lectures only to register time, place, subject, and to alter the order of attending lectures (Lee & Lee, 2008). Through the intervention of SRL, the teacher assigned course work to students in the course website and students had to complete and submit the assignments at the required time. The web-enabled SRL helped students regulate their learning behaviors, and further contributed to their learning effects. This result is similar to Chang's (2005), and Yukselturk and Bulut's (2007) studies indicating that self-regulation helped students become more responsible for their learning and contribute to further success.

Based on our findings, we provide suggestions for teachers who teach application software, particularly for those emphasize earning certification. Teachers who wish to stick to traditional methods of teaching, without applying networked multimedia, may no longer be employing a fruitful approach. Students from the control group (C4) received the lowest grades among four groups (see Table 1). In this traditional learning environment, students have neither chance nor channel to review or practice for the tests, and usually ignored the problems of their inadequate skills and knowledge. Therefore, it is suggested that teachers should redesign their courses, design appropriate arrangement of BL courses, and adopt new instructional methods and technologies to fully exploit the benefits of web-based learning environments.

In conclusion, this study explores that the effects of web-based SRL with variations in frequency of online classes on the development of vocational students' computing skills. This study highlights the necessity of applying innovative teaching methods and technologies, and appropriate arrangement of BL courses to help students learn and pass the certificate examinations. Furthermore, this research may provide reference about the intervention of web-enabled SRL and arrangement of online classes in BL courses for schools, scholars and teachers preparing for or presently engaged in implementing e-learning.

REFERENCES

Azevedo, R. (2005). Using hypermedia as a meta-cognitive tool for enhancing student learning? The role of self-regulated learning. *Educational Psychologist, 40*(4), 199-209.

Bielaczyc, K, Pirolli, P., & Brown, A. (1995). Training in self-explanation and self-regulation strategies: investigating the effects of knowledge acquisition activities on problem solving. *Cognition and Instruction, 13*(2), 221-252.

Boyle. T., Bradley, C., Chalk, P., Jones, R., & Pickard, P. (2003). Using blended learning to improve student success rates in learning to program. *Learning, Media and Technology, 28*(2 & 3), 165-178.

Castelijn, P., & Janssen, B. (2006). *Effectiveness of Blended Learning in a Distance Education Setting.* Retrieved July 15, 2008, from http://www.ou.nl/Docs/Faculteiten/MW/MW%20Working%20Papers/gr%2006%2006%20castelijn.pdf

Cennamo, K.S., Ross, J. D., & Rogers, C.S. (2002). Evolution of a web-enhanced course: Incorporating strategies for self-regulation. *Educause Quarterly, 25*(1), 28-33.

Chen, C.H., & Tien, C.J. (2005). *Market Segmentation Analysis for Taking Skill Test by Students in an Institute of Technology.* Retrieved July 15, 2008, from http://www.voced.edu.au/td/tnc_85.574

Chen, N.S., Kinshuk, Wei, C.W., Chen, Y.R., & Wang, Y.C. (2007). Classroom climate and learning effectiveness comparison for physical and cyber F2F interaction in holistic-blended learning environment. *Proceedings of the 7th IEEE International Conference on Advanced Learning Technologies* (pp. 313-317).

Chang, M.M. (2005). Applying self-regulated learning strategies in a web-based instruction - An investigation of motivation perception. *Computer Assisted Language Learning, 18*(3), 217-230.

Cole, J. (2005). *Using Moodle: Teaching with the Popular Open Source Course Management System.* O'Reilly Media, CA.

Connolly, T.M., MacArthur, E., Stansfield, M.H., & McLellan, E. (2007). A quasi-experimental study of three online learning courses in computing. *Computers & Education, 49*(2), 345-359.

Dabbagh, N., & Kitsantas, K. (2005). Using web-based pedagogical tools as scaffolds for self-regulated learning. *Instructional Science, 33*(5–6), 513-540.

Dowling, C., Godfrey, J.M., & Gyles, N. (2003). Do hybrid flexible delivery teaching methods improve accounting student learning outcomes? *Accounting Education: An International Journal, 12*(4), 373-391.

Ertmer, P.A., Newby, T.J., & MacDougall, M. (1996). Students' approaches to learning from case-based instruction: The role of reflective self-regulation. *American Educational Research Journal, 33*(3), 719-752.

Gribbons, B. & Herman, J. (1997). True and quasi-experimental designs. *Practical Assessment, Research & Evaluation, 5*(14). retrieved

July 15, 2008, from http://PAREonline.net/getvn.asp?v=5&n=14

Greene, J.A., & Azevedo, R. (2007). Adolescents' use of self-regulatory processes and their relation to qualitative mental model shifts while using hypermedia. *Journal of Educational Computing Research, 36*(2), 125-148.

Jacobson, M.J. (2005). From non-adaptive to adaptive educational hypermedia: Theory, research, and design issues. In S. Chen & G. Magalas (Eds.), *Advances in Web-based education: Personalized learning environments* (pp.302-330). Hershey, PA: Idea Group.

Järvelä, S., Näykki, P., Laru, J., & Luokkanen, T. (2007). Structuring and regulating collaborative learning in higher education with wireless networks and mobile tools. *Educational Technology & Society, 10*(4), 71-79.

Lai, S.Q., Lee, C.L., Yeh, Y.J., & Ho, C.T. (2005). A study of satisfaction in blended learning for small and medium enterprises. *International Journal of Innovation and Learning, 2*(3), 319-334.

Lee, P.W.R., & Chan, F.T. (2007). Blended learning: Experiences of adult learners in Hong Kong. In J. Fong & F. L. Wang, (Eds.), *Blended Learning* (pp. 79-87). Retrieved July 15, 2008, from http://www.cs.cityu.edu.hk/~wbl2007/WBL2007_Proceedings_HTML/WBL2007_PP079-087_Lee.pdf

Lee, J.K., & Lee, W.K. (2008). The relationship of e-Learner's self-regulatory efficacy and perception of e-Learning environmental quality. *Computers in Human Behavior, 24*(1), 32-47.

Lee, L.S., & Huang, J.J. (1996, May 27-29). *Technological and vocational teacher education in Taiwan, R. O. C.* Paper presented at the Taiwan-Australia Conference on Vocational Education and Training, Melbourne, Australia.

Lee, Y.M. (2003). *An Investigation of Taiwanese Graduate Students' Level of Civic Scientific Literacy.* Ph. D. dissertation. Austin, The University of Texas.

Li, K.C., Tsai, Y.T., & Tsai, C.K. (2008). Toward development of distance learning environment in the grid. *International Journal of Distance Education Technologies, 6*(3), 45-57.

Liu, C.C., & Tsai, C.C. (2008). An analysis of peer interaction patterns as discoursed by on-line small group problem-solving activity. *Computers and Education, 50*(3), 627-639.

Liu, C.H., Chiang, T.C., & Huang, Y.M. (2007). Assessment of effectiveness of web-based training on demand. *Interactive Learning Environments, 15*(3), 217-235.

Lynch, R., & Dembo, M. (2004). The relationship between self-regulation and online learning in a blended learning context. *International Review of Research in Open and Distance Learning, 5*(2). Retrieved July 15, 2008, from http://www.irrodl.org/index.php/irrodl/article/view/189/799

Marino, T.A. (2000). Learning Online: A view from both sides. *The National Teaching & Learning Forum, 9*(4), 4-6.

Матросова, C.T.A. (2007). *Computer World.* Retrieved July 15, 2008, from http://venec.ulstu.ru/lib/go.php?id=1566

Montalvo, F., & Torres, R. (2004). Self-regulated learning: Current and future directions. *Electronic Journal of Research in Educational Psychology, 2*(1), 1-34.

Nota, L., Soresi, S., & Zimmerman, B.J. (2004). Self-regulation and academic achievement and resilience: a longitudinal study. *International Journal of Educational Research, 41*(3), 198–251.

Overbaugh, R.C., & Casiello, A.R. (2008). Distributed collaborative problem-based graduate-level learning: Students' perspectives on communication tool selection and efficacy. *Computers in Human Behavior, 24*(2), 497-515.

Pereira, J.A., Pleguezuelos, E., Merí, A., Molina-Ros, A., Molina-Tomás, M.C., & Masdeu, C. (2007). Effectiveness of using blended learning strategies for teaching and learning human anatomy. *Medical Education, 41*(2), 189-195.

Reyero, M., & Tourón, J. (2003). The development of talent: acceleration as an educational strategy. A Coruña, Netbiblo.

Roces, C., & González Torres, M.C. (1998). Ability to self-regulate learning. In J.A. González Pienda, & J.C. Núñez (Eds.), *Dificultadesde aprendizaje escolar*. Madrid, Pirámide/Psicología.

Rovai, A.P., & Jordan, H.M. (2004). Blended learning and sense of community: A comparative analysis with traditional and fully online graduate courses. *International Review of Research in Open and Distance Learning, 5*(2). Retrieved July 15, 2008, from http://www.irrodl.org/index.php/irrodl/article/view/192/274

Shelley, D.J., Swartz, L.B., & Cole, M.T. (2007). A comparative analysis of online and traditional undergraduate business law classes. *International Journal of Information and Communication Technology Education, 3*(1), 10-21.

Shen, P.D., Lee, T.H., & Tsai, C.W. (2007a). Applying Web-Enabled Problem-Based Learning and Self-Regulated Learning to Enhance Computing Skills of Taiwan's Vocational Students: A Quasi-Experimental Study of a Short-Term Module. *Electronic Journal of e-Learning, 5*(2), 147-156.

Shen, P.D., Lee, T.H., & Tsai, C.W. (2007b, September 15-17). Facilitating Students to Pass Certificate Tests via Blended E-Learning with Self-Regulated Learning: A Quasi-experimental Approach. *WSEAS Proceedings on Multimedia, Internet & Video Technologies*. Beijing, China

Shen, P.D., Lee, T.H., & Tsai, C.W. (2008). Enhancing Skills of Application Software via Web-Enabled Problem-Based Learning and Self-Regulated Learning: An Exploratory Study.

Journal of Distance Education Technologies, 6(3), 69-84.

Shen, P.D., Lee, T.H., Tsai, C.W., & Ting, C.J. (2008). Exploring the Effects of Web-Enabled Problem-Based Learning and Self-Regulated Learning on Vocational Students' Involvement in Learning. *European Journal of Open, Distance and E-Learning,* 2008(1). Retrieved July 15, 2008, from http://www.eurodl.org/materials/contrib/2008/Shen_Lee_Tsai_Ting.htm

Su, M.H.M. (2005). A study of EFL technological and vocational college students' language learning strategies and their self-perceived English proficiency. *Electronic Journal of Foreign Language Teaching, 2*(1), 44-56.

Treuer, P., & Belote, L. (1997). Current and emerging applications of technology to promote student involvement and learning. *New Directions for Student Services, 78,* 17-30.

Weinstein, C. (1989). Teacher education students' preconceptions of teaching. *Journal of Teacher Education, 40*(2), 53-60.

Winne, P.H. (2001). Self-regulated learning viewed from models of information processing. In B. J. Zimmerman & D. Schunk (Eds.), *Self-regulated learning and academic achievement: Theoretical perspectives* (pp. 153-189). Mahwah, NJ: Erlbaum.

Winne, P.H., & Hadwin, A. (1998). Studying as self-regulated learning. In D. J. Hacker, J. Dunlosky, & A. Graesser (Eds.), *Metacognition in educational theory and practice* (pp. 277-304). Hillsdale, NJ: Erlbaum.

Yang, S.C., & Tung, C.J. (2007). Comparison of Internet Addicts and Non-addicts in Taiwanese High School. *Computers in Human Behavior, 23*(1), 79-96.

Yukselturk, E., & Bulut, S. (2007). Predictors for student success in an online course. *Educational Technology & Society, 10*(2), 71-83.

Yushau, B. (2006). The effects of blended e-learning on mathematics and computer attitudes in pre-calculus algebra. *The Montana Mathematics Enthusiast, 3*(2), 176-183.

Zimmerman, B.J. (1990). Self-regulated learning and academic achievement: An overview. *Educational Psychologist, 25*(1), 3-17.

Zimmerman, B.J. (1998). Developing self-regulation cycles of academic regulation: An analysis of exemplary instructional model. In D. H. Schunk & B. J. Zimmerman (Eds.), *Self-regulated learning: From teaching to self-reflective practice.* New York: Guilford.

Zimmerman, B.J., & Schunk, D.H. (1989). *Self-Regulated Learning and Academic Achievement: Theory, Research, and Practice.* New York: Springer-Verlag.

Zimmerman, B.J., & Schunk, D.H. (2001). *Self-Regulated Learning and Academic Achievement: Theoretical Perspectives.* Mahwah, NJ: Erlbaum.

Zimmerman, B.J., Bonner, S., & Kovach, R. (1996). *Developing self-regulated learners: Beyond achievement to self-efficacy.* Washington, DC: American Psychological Association.

This work was previously published in International Journal of Mobile and Blended Learning, Vol. 1, Issue 3, edited by D. Parsons, pp. 1-16, copyright 2009 by IGI Publishing (an imprint of IGI Global).

Section V
Organizational and
Social Implications

This section includes a wide range of research pertaining to the social and organizational impact of Web technologies around the world. Chapters included in this section analyze social marketing, e-government, Web vendors, and Web tourism. The inquiries and methods presented in this section offer insight into the implications of Web technologies at both a personal and organizational level, while also emphasizing potential areas of study within the discipline.

Chapter 5.1
Building Trust in E–Commerce through Web Interface

Muneesh Kumar
University of Delhi South Campus, India, & ESC-PAU, France

Mamta Sareen
University of Delhi, India

ABSTRACT

The emergence of Internet has revolutionalized the way businesses are conducted. The impact of e-commerce is pervasive, both on companies and society as a whole. It has the potential to impact the pace of economic development and in turn influence the process of human development at the global level. However, the growth in e-commerce is being impaired by the issue of trust in the buyer-seller relationship which is arising due to the virtual nature of e-commerce environment. The online trading environment is constrained by a number of factors including web interface that in turn influences user experience. This article identifies various dimensions of web interface that have the potential to influence trust in e-commerce. The empirical evidence presented in the article is based on a survey of the web interfaces of 65 Indian e-Marketplaces. [Article

copies are available for purchase from InfoSci-on-Demand.com]

INTRODUCTION

Convergence of Information Technology and telecommunication technology has resulted in emergence of a new economy wherein the buying and selling process is being executed through Internet and other computer networks. This is being termed as e-commerce. The proliferation of Internet technologies into business has fundamentally changed the relationship between suppliers and consumers. It has provided faster access and better knowledge of commodities and prices. The ability to exchange information in both directions between producer and consumer has created a relationship not previously possible. E-commerce is changing the way business is being conducted and eventually all companies will have to make the transition to remain competitive because soon all customers will expect this level of service and it will inevitably become the standard for customer satisfaction (Rust & Kannan, 2003)

The impact of e-commerce is pervasive, both on companies and society as a whole. It is the first mass application of information and communication technologies in the movement towards digital economy. It has broken all man-made boundaries and provided an opportunity for both buyers and sellers to interact among themselves regardless of difference in language, society, culture and tradition.

The rapid growth of e-commerce is now being related to economic development and is often been cited as a driver of economic growth. E-commerce is also been touted as a powerful medium through which less developed economies can exploit the potential of global markets. It, thus, has the potential to impact the pace of economic development and in turn influence the process of human development at the global level. However, the growth in e-commerce is being impaired by the issue of trust which is arising due to virtual nature of e-commerce environment. This virtual nature of e-commerce environment imposes certain constraints on buyer-seller relationship that did not exist in traditional face-to-face transactions. The on-line trading environment basically thrives on 'virtuality' *(Handy, 1995)* and 'user experience' (Marsh, 2000). Since, the transactions in this virtual environment *are conducted through the 'veil' of web interface, trust becomes an important issue. The web interface acts like the only 'contact point' among the buyers and sellers. Hence, there is a need for the web interface to induce trust in online environment. The focus of the present article is to identify various trust inducing web dimensions that may enhance the effectiveness of web interface and there by help in inducing trust among the e-commerce players.*

TRUST IN E-COMMERCE

Trust is defined as "the willingness of a party to be vulnerable to the actions of another party based on the expectations that the other party will perform a particular action important to the trustor, irrespective of the ability to monitor or control that other party" (Mayer, Davis and Schoorman 1995). In the context of e-commerce, trust may be regarded as a judgment made by the user, based on general experience learned from being a customer/seller and from the perception of a particular merchant. In other words, trust is also seen as a generalized expectancy that the word, promise, or written statement of another party can be relied on (Rotter, 1980).

To date, research on understanding online trust and e-commerce is limited (Grabner-Kräuter and Kaluscha 2003; Yoon 2002; Corritore et al. 2003; Kolsaker and Payne 2002). In their critical reviews of website and/or ecommerce trust, Corritore et al. (2003) and Grabner- Kräuter and Kaluscha (2003) argued that there is a lack a conceptual understanding of online trust and theoretical support for its role in online transactions and relationships. Without trust, businesses are unable to function (Reichheld et al. 2000). Jian, Bisantz, and Drury (2000) and Bailey et al. (2003) claim that trust not only plays a strong role in human-to-human interactions, but also plays a critical role in human-to-computer interactions.

LITERATURE REVIEW

A rich web interface may have a positive impact on trust in the faceless environment of e-commerce. Several studies like Fogg et al 2001; Lee and Kim & Moon, 2000; Neilsen, 1999, 2005 etc. reported evaluations of a list of design features that could potentially appear on the web interface to impact trust. Ang and Lee (2000) stated that if the web site does not lead the buyer to believe that the seller is trustworthy, no business can be conducted. In other words, one key consideration in fostering online trust in e-commerce is to build a trust inducing web interface. Lohse and Spiller (1998) identified four interface design features that affect the effectiveness of the web interface. Their results indicated that features like effective navigation, detailed product descriptions, links, etc. affect the trust in e-commerce activity. Xiling Zhou asserted that poor quality of web interface, lack of proper content in the web sites, unintuitive navigation, etc. can diminish the trust in the concerned company in e-commerce activities. Bailey et al stressed that visual aesthetics and navigation quality of a web site help to assess its trustworthiness in e-commerce activities. Jarvenpa et al, 1999 stated that a web site with trust inducing features functions as a skillful sales person for that company and therefore moderates the disadvantages of an impersonal web site. It is believed that online buyers in e-commerce look for the presence of positive cues about a site's general trustworthiness, as well as for the absence of negative cues. Hence, the e-commerce players by carefully designing their site to set and meet user expectations can influence the trustworthiness of other players.

Arion et al. (1994) asserted that user interface is the point where trust is generated. They stated that trust is a dynamic process, initially based on faith due to the lack of evidence that seeks to reach a certain level of confidence, i.e., where there is conclusive evidence in favor of trusting behavior. In their consideration of computer-supported cooperative work (CSCW) systems, Arion et al. (1994) argued that development of trust in the human-computer interaction need to be supported by the infrastructure/system.

A web interface provides total "user experience". Hence, an effective web interface can make this contact point between the trading partners more meaningful and help in building up trust. The effectiveness of the web interface may also be determined by factors such as the aesthetic appearance of the site, the content and the way the information is presented to the user. The web interface is not just how it looks; it is how easy it is to learn, how well it recedes into the sub consciousness of users, and how well it supports users' tasks. Different authors have suggested various features for making the web interface more effective (Egger, 2003; Neilson, 1999; Wang et al 2007 and others). These features can be classified into three broad categories i.e. ***appeal, content and usability.***

Appeal: It refers to 'attitude' component and the first impression a user gets when accessing a site for the first time Lindgaard (1999) stated that an immediate negative impression may well determine the subsequent perception of the site's quality and usability, whereas one may inherently judge a site by its first impression. Literature from psychology also stresses the important role of a party's first impression, as someone's confirmation bias would entail that all user actions will unconsciously seek to confirm the first impression rather than falsify it (Kahneman & Tversy, 1973; Good, 1988). Fogg et al. (2002) reported, in their large study about how people evaluate the credibility of websites that, almost 50% of all comments made by participants referred to graphic design. They therefore argue that, in the context of online credibility and trust, findings indicate that *looking* good is often interpreted as *being* good, credible and trustworthy. Hence, appeal has largely to do with the site's graphics design and layout. In addition, Demonstrating important clients or providing links towards company's various policies also instills trust among the users (Doney and Canon, 1997).

Usability: Usability is the measure of the quality of a user's experience when interacting with the web site Sweden Canada Link (2001) stated that usability is about making the visit to the website as effective as possible for the users. The focus of usability is on enabling users, whatever their interests and needs, by removing barriers and making the system as easy to use as possible. According to usability expert Jakob Nielsen, usability is a necessary condition for survival on the web. If a web site is difficult to use, people leave. If the homepage fails to clearly state what a company offers and what users can do on the site, people leave. Indeed, *visual design* is presented to the user passively, while the user actively needs to *navigate* the website in order to access relevant information. Usability is all the more important in the context of online shopping as it is known to be an important condition for the acceptance and adoption of new technologies. The Technology Acceptance Model (TAM), as defined by Davis (1989), holds that usefulness and ease of use are both strong predictors of trust. This model has also been explicitly used to relate trust and e-commerce by researchers like Gefen and Straub (2000), Pavlou (2001), amongst others.

Content: Websites contain information and serve as a medium that predominantly is used for the transfer of information (either technical or not). This plays an important role in the effectiveness of the site. Product information has historically been regarded as a critical element of the content of web interface. A number of researchers have investigated the relationship between web interface and information structure (e.g., Gay et al., 1991: Radha and Murphy, 1992; Mohageg, 1992; Utting and Yankelovich, 1989), concluding that information structure is an essential element of an effective web interface. However, a web site may also contain other information such as detailed and relevant information about the company, its complete offline address, seals of approvals from various trusted third parties, etc. Green (1998) stated that in the e-commerce environment, information plays an important role as business audiences seek more information about products/ services and the company. To be able to convey the information effectively, it is necessary to structure it properly. Correct and detailed descriptions of the products and services offered by the company helps the users to make informed decisions about their transactions. Features that reduce user costs, such as comparisons with competitive products,

may also be seen as a sign of honesty and competence (Egger, 2002). In addition, the provision of related content, if relevant, can also be interpreted as the company truly understanding its customers' needs. The credibility of the information has also been observed to be very important about a company's ethical standards.

Various dimensions of the web interface address the appeal, usability and content features of an effective web interface. Various authors have identified a number of such dimensions (Kim 1998; Egger 2003; Wang et al 2006; etc.). Some of these dimensions are categorized as trust inducing dimensions. Kim (1998) had identified four interface design features which contribute to trustworthiness of the web site. Wang et al. (2007) also stressed on certain web dimensions to enhance the richness of web interface. He proposed four broad dimensions of web interface namely, graphic design dimension, Structure design dimension, Content design dimension and Social-cue design dimension that may influence trust. However, the various studies do not include features that are commonly found in any modern e-commerce web site and the e-commerce players are interested in. These include reference to the kind of security policy, privacy policy being followed by the company for online transactions, the technology related policies and procedures followed by the company to address the security, privacy etc. issues, the statements from well known customers, media excerpts, etc. Thus, there is a need for a more comprehensive model relating trust and web interface.

WEB INTERFACE AND TRUST MODEL

In order to incorporate the various gaps in the earlier model relating trust with web interface, the present article proposes five trust inducing dimensions of an effective web interface. These dimensions are: a) User Interface Dimension; b)

Figure 1. Web interface and trust model

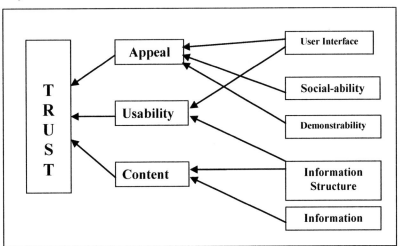

Information Structure Dimension; c) Information Content Dimension; d) Demonstrability Dimension; and e) Social-ability Dimension. The relationships between these dimensions and three features identified earlier are exhibited in the Figure 1.

- **User Interface Dimension:** User Interface indicates the appearance and the tools available for accessing the information contained in the web site/portal. Constaine (1995) pointed out that interface is important aspect as the more intuitive the user interface is, the easier it is to use and trust. The website must be recognizable as from the organization. That is, it must be obvious that the look of the site – colors, logos, layout, etc. is consistent with other collateral from the organization. The various features offered by the web site that normally giving the first impression about the company lays the initial foundation of trust building process. Kim and Moon, (1999) reported that the overall color layout and graphical interface influences the trustworthiness of the web site. This dimension aids in addressing the appeal aspect of an effective web interface. Various features that may be useful in enhancing

trust levels among the users include: a) Home Page; b) Graphics Interface; c) Links; d) Professionalism; and e) Loading Time.

- **Information Structure Dimension:** The structure dimension defines the overall organization and accessibility of displayed information on the web site. Ease of navigation has frequently been mentioned as a key to promote online trust (e.g., Cheskin/Sapient Report, 1999; Neilsen, 1998). In other words, users must be able to easily locate the information they seek on the web site. This ease-of- use reflects two characteristics of a trustworthy web site: simplicity and consistency. Buyers appreciate simplicity or a clear design of e-commerce web sites because it reduces the perceived risks of deception, frustration, and wasting time. When the structure and design of the web site are consistent, users feel more confident using the site because they can transfer their learning from one sub-site to the next rather than having to learn everything over again for each new page and trust is build (Neilsen, 1998,). For example, broken links, meaningless images, and similar "hygiene factors" may relate to users dissatisfaction with a web site (Zhang et al., 1999). Key features of structure dimension of a web site may include: a) Navigation; b) Accessibility; c) Functionality; d) Consistency; and e) Learnibility.

- **Information Content Dimension:** This dimension refers to the informational components that can be included on the web site, either textual or graphical. A logically structured web site providing comprehensive, correct, and current product information instills trust among the users (Egger, 2001; Neilsen, 1999). If the information regarding the products is precise, factual and contains links of details required, if necessary, then trust is build (Bhattacharya, 2001). Recent market surveys include that some of the companies are using their web sites as a part of integrated communication strategy to create trust and action (Sheehan and Doherty, 2001). In such cases the website interface plays an important role in e-business transactions. The contents should be displayed as being less complex and more users friendly that enriches the visitor's experience and motivates him/her to visit the site again (G.Chakraborty et al 2003). key features of structure dimension of a web site may include: a) Navigation; b) Accessibility; c) Functionality; d) Consistency; and e) Learn-ability.

- **Demonstrability Dimension:** Several researchers stress the importance of "demonstrability" in e-commerce, which is to promote the brand reputation of a company online. It is often seen that various features like offline address of the company, details about real people behind etc play the same role of offering certain clues about the credibility of the company as the physical clues in the brick and mortar business transactions. These clues help the potential trading partners to assess the credibility of the company. Especially displaying the seals of approval from various trusted third parties and the accreditations earned help in building trust levels.

- **Social-ability Dimension:** This dimension relates to embedding social cues, such as face-to-face interaction and social presence, into web site interfaces via different communication media, because a lack of the "human touch" or presence may constitute a barrier for at least some consumers to trust online merchants (e.g., Riegelsberger & Sasse, 2002). The effectiveness of a personalization system improves in the long run. Weiner and A. Mehrabian (1968) stated that the choice of language can help create a sense of psychological closeness and warmth. Where as Nass and Steuer (1993) stressed that the use of natural and informal language can impact perceived social presence. Yoon (2002) also showed that web site trust is influenced by consumer familiarity. Every time a customer interacts with the web site, the personalization mechanism collects new data about the user's preferences, so that a more and more satisfactory service can be offered.

METHODOLOGY AND RESULTS

A list of 100 B2B web e-marketplaces operating in India was prepared through the use of various search engines like Google, Yahoo, MSN etc. The criterion for the selection of these e-marketplaces was random. On visiting these web sites, it was found that some of the web portals were merely a directory of sellers and buyers and not actually carrying out e-commerce transactions. Such web portals were excluded from the sample. Hence, a total of 65 B2B web sites/e-marketplaces were selected for the purpose of the survey. Based on the number of elements present, the web site was to be rated on a 5 point Likert scale for each of the trust inducing dimension. Finally, an overall trust rating of the web portal was also to be obtained for each web interface of the select e-marketplace.

Initially, 25 participants were requested to rate six e-marketplaces. The participants were IT savvy in the age range of 30-45 years and came from a variety of background like public sector, business sector, private sector, banking sector and academic sector. The participants were asked to provide their own ratings of each dimension and also the overall rating of the web site based on a questionnaire consisting of 20 questions. Hence, a total of 120 responses were received from each of the 25 participants. Cronbach's Alpha Scale Reliability test was used to test the reliability of the questionnaire and it was found to be 0.8751, which is fairly good degree of reliability.

In order to study the significance of these trust inducing dimensions for the level of trust, linear regression model was used (the limitations of linear regression model in this context may be recognized). The model used the level of trust as dependent variable and each of the trust inducing dimensions as independent variable. The purpose was to find out any redundant dimension included in the dimension. The regression analysis was carried out on the data collected from these 25 participants for each of the six e-marketplaces. The adjusted R^2 ranged from 86% to 92%. This would imply that more than 85% of the variation in the trust ratings could be collectively explained by the five trust inducing dimensions of an effective web interface. The results of regression analysis for the ratings given for one of the e-marketplaces are presented in Table 1.

During the systematic elimination process, all the five trust inducing dimensions were found to be significant. The results showed Demonstrability and Information Content dimension as significant trust inducing dimensions of web interface. This further strengthens the reasons of the present article for the inclusion of demonstrability dimension as a trust inducing dimension for web interface to the model proposed by Wang *et al*. The information structure dimension and the User Interface dimension of web interface also were found to be

having significant contribution towards building trust in web interface. This could be because of the fact that in India, complete virtual B2B transactions do not occur very often and they are aided with various offline channels like phone, fax, etc. However, the result assures that all these dimensions of an effective web interface as proposed in the model have a potential to enhance trust among the users. Further, socio-ability dimension, though considered important in B2C e-commerce activities, was not found to be contributing much towards trust levels in e-marketplaces.

In order to identify any bias in the evaluation of the web interfaces of the six e-marketplaces, the author also independently evaluated all the select e-marketplaces. The results of the evaluations were compared with the trust equation obtained of these select e-marketplaces. It was observed that the difference between the two results was not significant. This would imply that the evaluations of the e-marketplaces done by 25 participants and the author held nominal bias. Therefore, evaluation of the remaining 59 e-marketplaces was carried out independently by the author, in the same manner as it was done by the 25 participants.

The regression model used earlier was used on the data so collected from the evaluations of web interfaces of the selected e-marketplaces. The results of the linear regression analysis are presented in the Table 2. As may be observed from Table 2, all the five trust inducing web dimensions were found to be contributing towards trust in the web site.

All the dimensions of effective web interface as identified in the model were found to be good predictors of level of trust. The results were fairly comparable with the results obtained from the linear regression analysis carried out on the data collected through 25 participants with respect to six select e-marketplaces. Thus, it may be concluded that the five trust inducing web dimensions namely Information Content dimension, Demonstrability dimension, Information

Table 1. Trust ratings of an e-marketplace and trust inducing dimensions. Partial results of regression

Model	Unstandardized Coefficients		Standardized Coefficients		
	B	Std. error	Beta	t	Sig
(Constant)	-0.312	0.460	-	-0.677	0.506
User Interface	0.243	0.115	0.242	2.912	0.003
Info. Structure	0.225	0.116	0.265	2.093	0.009
Info. Content	0.327	0.217	0.327	3.209	0.001
Demonstrability	0.338	0.165	0.264	3.049	0.002
Socio-ability	0. 033	0.097	0.003	1.634	0.020

Table 2. Trust ratings of an e-marketplace and trust inducing dimensions. Partial results of regression

Model	Unstandardized Coefficients		Standardized Coefficients		
	B	Std. Error	Beta	t	Sig
(Constant)	-.633	0.232	-	-2.732	0.008
User Interface	0.178	0.114	0.242	2.816	0.008
Info. Structure	0.269	0.102	0.211	2.334	0.011
Info. Content	0.421	0.094	0.382	3.486	0.001
Demonstrability	0.296	0.105	0.261	2.836	0.006
Socio-ability	0.067	0.114	0.060	0.590	0.055

Structure dimension, User Interface dimension and the Social-ability dimension (in that order) positively contribute towards trust building processes in e-commerce.

LIMITATIONS AND SCOPE FOR FUTURE RESEARCH

The main limitation of this article could be the coverage of only e-marketplaces in validating trust in e-commerce. Since, e-commerce involves various other activities, it would be better, if the sample data would contain web interfaces from other segments of e-commerce also. Further, the model proposed in this article has tried to include

as many trust inducing dimensions as possible. It may, however, be possible that the article might have overlooked certain issues that might influence the web interface of the e-commerce sites. However, user experience is a very complex issue related to human-computer interface and may vary from individual to individual. Ideally, different individuals must have rated all the e-marketplaces. However, it was not possible for the present scope.

CONCLUSION

E-commerce has the potential to provide a flip to the pace of economic development and provide a unique opportunity to organizations in less developed countries to operate in global markets. This could also have implications on the socio-economic conditions of the less developed countries. Trust has been a major hurdle impeding the growth of e-commerce and the need for enhancing trust cannot be over-emphasized. The article, through validation, identifies various trust inducing dimensions for enriching the web interface and there by inducing trust. Focus on these dimensions, which demonstrate 'correct and concise' information, 'relevant structure' of information and 'usability', would help in inducing trust in the faceless environment of e-commerce. This in turn would improve the user experience and the buyer-seller relationship in online trading environment. This supports the earlier findings of Arion et al. (1994) wherein trust in human-computer interactions was stated to be supported by the system. It may, however, be noted that the trust in buyer-seller relationship is also influenced by a number of factors and the enhancement of features of web interface would need to be viewed as an integral part of an overall trust building strategy of an organization. Thus, by effectively incorporating various features of the trust inducing dimensions on the web interface, the merchant is able to provide a trust worthy platform for the customer across global boundaries to transact among each other. This has helped in the development of a virtual society which is driven by trust in technology and enhances the growth of e-commerce. Professional bodies and business organizations need to play an important role in this regard. Development and adherence to globally accepted standards in this regard can go a long way in enriching the 'user experience' in e-commerce.

REFERENCES

ACM Special Interest group on Computer-Human Interaction Group (1992). *ACM SIGCHI*, Technical Report. New York: ACM.

Arion, M., Numan, J. H., & Pitariu, H. (1994). Placing Trust in Human-Computer Interactions. *Proceedings of 7th European Cognitive Ergonomics Conference* (pp. 352-365).

Ba, S., & Pavlou, P. A. (2002). Evidence of the Effect of Trust Building Technology in Electronic Markets: Price Premiums and Buyer Behavior. *MIS Quarterly, 26*(3)

Bailey, J. P., & Faraj, S. (2000).The Role of Intermediaries in the Development of Trust on the WWW: The Use and Prominence of Trusted Third Parties and Privacy Statements. *JCMC*, 5(3).

Bailey. A. (2005). Consumer Awareness and Use of Product Review Websites. *Journal of Interactive Advertising, 6*(1), 90-108.

Bhattacherjee, A. (2002). Individual Trust in Online Firms: Scale Development and Initial Test. *Journal of Management Information Systems, 19*(1), 211-241.

Chakraborty, G., Lala, V., & Warren, D. (2002). An Empirical Investigation of Antecedents of B2B Websites Effectiveness. *Journal of Interactive Marketing, 16*(4), 51-72 .

Cheskin/Sapient Research and Studio Archetype/ Sapient. (1999). E-Commerce Trust Study, Retrieved June 10, 2008 from http://www.sapient.com/cheskin.

Corritore,C. l., Marble, R. P., Wiedenbeck, S., Kracher, B., & Chandran, A.(2005) Measuring Online Trust of Websites: Credibility, Perceived Ease of Use, and Risk. *Proceedings of the Eleventh Americas Conference on Information Systems*, Omaha, USA.

Davis, J., Mayer, R., & Shoorman, F. (1995). *An integrated model of organizational trust, the academy of management review, 20*(3), 705-734.

Davis F. D. (1989). Perceived usefulness, perceived ease of use and user acceptance of information technology. *MIS Quaterly, 13*(3), 319-340.

Doney, P. M., & Cannon, J. P. (1997). An Examination of the Nature of Trust in Buyer-Seller Relationships. *Journal of Marketing, 61*, 35-51.

Egger F. N. (2003). *From interactions to transactions: Designing the Trust Experience for Business-to-Consumer Electronic Commerce.*

Egger F. N. (2001). Affective Design of E-Commerce User Interfaces: How to maximize perceived trustworthiness. *Proceedings of The International Conference on Affective Human Factors Design.* London: Asean Academic Press.

Egger, F. N. (June 27-29, 2001). *Affective Design of E-Commerce User Interfaces: How to maximize perceived trustworthiness.* Conference on Affective Human Factors Design. Singapore, (pp. 317-324).

Fogg B. J., & Nass C. (1997). Effects of computers that flatter. *International Journal of Human-Computer Studies, 46*, 551-561.

Grabner-Kräuter & Kaluscha. (2003). Empirical research in on-line trust: a review and critical assessment. *International Journal of Human-Computer Studies, 58*(6), 783–812.

Gefen, D., & Straub, D. W. (2000). The Relative Importance of Perceived Ease-of-Use in IS Adoption: A Study of E-Commerce Adoption. *Journal of the Association for Information Systems, 1*(8), 1-28.

Gray, S. H. (1990). Using Protocol Analyses and Drawings to Study Mental Model Construction during Hypertext Navigation. *International Journal of Human-Computer Interaction, 2*(4), 359-377

Green, M. C. (2002). Perceptions of trust in Internet relationships. *Computer-supported social interaction conference*, Oxford, OH

Handy, C. (1995). Trust and the Virtual Organization. *Harvard Business Review, 73*(3), 40-50.

Jarvenpaa, S. L., & Tractinsky, N. (1999). Consumer Trust in an Internet Store: A Cross-Cultural Validation. *Journal of Computer Mediated Communication, 5*(2).

Jian, J-Y., Bisantz, A. M., & Drury, C. G. (1998). Towards an empirically determined scale of trust in computerized systems: Distinguishing concepts and types of trust. *In Proceedings of the Human Factors & Ergonomics Society 42nd Annual Meeting,* (pp. 501-505).

Keen, P. G. W. (1997). Are you ready for 'Trust' Economy. *Computer World, 31*(16), 80.

Kolsaker, A., & Payne, C. (2002). Engendering trust in e-commerce: a study of gender based concerns. *Marketing Intelligence & Planning, 20*(4), 206-214.

Lohse, G. L., & Spiller, P. (1998). Electronic Shopping: Quantifying the Effect of Customer Interfaces on Traffic and Sales. *Communications of the ACM, 41*(7)

Lee, J., Kim J., & Moon J. Y. (April 2000). What Makes Internet Users Visit Cyber Stores Again? Key Design Factors for Customer Loyalty. *Proceedings of the Computer-Human Interaction Conference on Human Factors in Computing Systems*, The Hague, Netherlands, (pp. 305-312).

Lee, J., & Huang, Y. (2005). The Design Factors of the Initial Trust in the Internet environment. *Proceedings of World Conference on Educational Multimedia, Hypermedia and Telecommunications,* (pp. 993-997).

Lingaard G. (1999). *Does emotional appeal determine perceived usability of web sites?* Retrieved June 8, 2008 from http://www.cyberg.com

Marsh, T., & Wright, P. (2000). Maintaining the illusion of interacting within a 3D virtual space. *Presence 2000: 3rd International Workshop on Presence*, Delft, The Netherlands.

Mayer, R. C., Davis, J. H., & Schoorman, F. D. (1995). An integrative model of organizational trust. *Academy of Management Review, 20*(3), 709-734.

McMahon, K. (2005). *An exploration of the importance of website usability from a business perspective.* Retrieved July 1, 2008 from http://www.flowtheory.com/KTMDissertation.pdf

Moon, J.-W., & Kim, Y.-G. (2001). Extending the TAM for a World-Wide-Web Context. *Information & Management, 38*, 217-230.

Nass, C., Steuer, J., Tauber, E., & Reeder, H. (1993). Anthropomorphism, Agency, & Ethopoeia: Computers as Social Actors. *Conference of the ACM/SIGCHI & the IFIP* Amsterdam, the Netherlands (pp. 24-29).

Nielsen, J. (1999). *Trust or Bust: Communicating Trustworthiness in Web Design. Jacob*

Nielsen's Alertbox. Retrieved April 10, 2008 from http://www.useit.com/alertbox/990307.html.

Nielsen, J. (May 16, 1999). *Who Commits the 'Top Ten Mistakes' of Web Design?* Jacob Nielsen's Alertbox. Retrieved August 2, 2008 from http://www.useit.com/alertbox/990516.html.

Neilsen Normen group (2000). *Trust: Design guidelines for e-commerce user experience.* Retrieved September 6, 2008 from http://www.nngroup.com

Sheehan, K. B., & Doherty, C. (2001). Re-weaving the Web: Integrating Print and Online Communications. *Journal of Interactive Marketing, 15*(2), 47-59.

Radha, R., & Murphy, C. (1992). Searching Versus Browsing in Hypertext. *Hypermedia. 4*(1), 31.

Reichheld, F. F., & Sasser, W. E. (1990). Zero defections: Quality comes to services. *Harvard Business Review, 68*, 105-111.

Resnick, P., Zeckhauser, R., Friedman, E., & Kuwabara, K. (2000). Reputation Systems. *Communications of the ACM, 43*(12), 45-48.

Riegelsberger, J., Sasse, M. A., & McCarthy, J. D. (2003). Trust at First Sight? A Test of Users' Ability to Identify Trustworthy e-Commerce Sites. *Proceedings of HCI2003*, 8-12 243-260.

Rotter J. B. (1980). Impersonal trust, Trustworthiness and gullibility. *American Pschologist, 35*(1), 1-7.

Rust, R. T., & Kannan, P. K. (2003). E-Service: A new paradigm for business in the electronic environment. *Communications of the ACM, 46*(6), 36-43.

Utting, K., & N. Yankelovich (1989). Context and Orientation in Hypermedia Networks. *ACM Transactions on Information Systems, 7*(1) 58-84.

Wang, E., Barrett, S., Caldwell & Gavriel, S. (2003). Usability comparison: similarity and differences between e-commerce and world wide web. *Journal of the Chinese Institute of Industrial Engineers, 20*(3), 258-266.

Weiner, M., & Mehrabian, A. (1968). *Language within Language: Immediacy, a Channel in Verbal Communication.* New York: Appleton-Century-Crofts.

Xiaoni, Z. (2003). Factors Contributing to Purchase Intentions. *Internet Journal of Internet Commerce, 2*(1).

Yoon, S. J. (2002). The antecedents and consequences of trust in online purchase decisions. *Journal of Interactive Marketing, 16*(2), 47-63.

This work was previously published in International Journal of Information Communication Technologies and Human Development, Vol. 1, Issue 1, edited by S. Chhabra, pp. 64-74, copyright 2009 by IGI Publishing (an imprint of IGI Global).

Chapter 5.2
Swift Trust in Web Vendors:
The Role of Appearance and Functionality[1]

Xin Li
University of North Carolina at Pembroke, USA

Guang Rong
Clemson University, USA

Jason B. Thatcher
Clemson University, USA

ABSTRACT

With the growth of product search engines such as pricegrabber.com, Web vendors have many more casual visitors. This research examines how Web vendors may foster "swift trust" as a means to convert casual visitors to paying customers. We examine whether perceptions of Web sites' appearance features (normality, social presence and third-party links) and functionality features (security, privacy, effort expectancy and performance expectancy) positively relate to swift trust in a Web vendor. Using a quasi-experimental research design, we empirically test the proposed relationships. Based on an analysis of 224 respondents, we found appearance and functionality features explained 61% of the variance in swift trust. The article concludes with a discussion of findings and implications.

INTRODUCTION

Trust is a key enabler of e-commerce (Lee & Turban, 2001; Kracher, Corritore, & Wiedenbeck, 2005). Extensive research has found that trust leads to online end users reporting higher levels of purchasing intention, expressing greater loyalty to a Web vendor, and engaging in actual purchasing behavior (Gefen, McKnight, Choudhury, & Kacmar, 2002; Gefen, 2002b; Karahanna, &

Straub, 2003a). Given the extensive support in the literature for ties from online end users trust to their behavior, it is important to direct attention to identifying levers that foster trust and encourage online end users to complete transactions.

Fostering trust has proven problematic among fast-moving online end users. Although search engines direct over 85% of consumers to vendor Web sites, 57% of consumers abandon their shopping carts prior to checkout (DoubleClick, 2004). Perhaps due to the ease of identifying alternatives through engines such as pricegrabber.com, online consumers frequently visit Web sites and fail to complete transactions. Thus, Web vendors are under the pressure to quickly win trust, retain first time visitors and convert them to paying customers.

In this article, we examine how Web vendors may foster swift trust. Swift trust refers to trust formed quickly in a new relationship (Meyerson, Weick, & Kramer, 1996). Unlike other forms of trust which rest on experience or familiarity with a vendor, swift trust develops quickly during a consumer's first exposure to an unfamiliar Web vendor. Although first time visitors may lack experience or knowledge of a Web vendor, their perceptions of the "working conditions" of e-commerce, including appearance and functionality of a Web site (Zhang, von Dran, Small, & Barcellos, 1999), influence their understanding of a vendor's ability to complete transactions and its trustworthiness. For example, Gefen et al. (2003a) suggested that a fair and open Web site that clearly states due process, policies that handle the relationship, and provides clear explanations, engenders consumer trust. Hence, designers emphasize a Web site's appearance and functionality as means to promote swift trust.

Although substantial research has examined the implications of trust in Web vendors, research has left unexplored the influence of appearance and functionality on swift trust in a Web vendor. To gain deeper insight into online consumer be-

havior, this study examines the following research question:

How do the appearance and functionality of a Web site influence online consumers' swift trust in a Web vendor?

The article unfolds as follows. First, we develop a general model tying appearance and functionality to consumers' swift trust and purchasing intention. In terms of appearance, we examine normality, social presence, and links to third-party assurance providers. In terms of functionality, we examine the roles of security, privacy, effort expectancy and performance expectancy. Next, we present the results of a quasi-experimental study that tests the proposed model. Then, we discuss our findings. The article concludes with implications for research and practice.

LITERATURE REVIEW AND MODEL DEVELOPMENT

Trust is a complex and abstract concept. Although defined differently in many literatures, trust most commonly refers to one's willingness to depend on another based on the expectation that the other has the attributes to be trusted (Mayer, Davis, & Schoorman, 1995). Trust is driven by: 1) risk and uncertainty in relationships, 2) the trusting party's vulnerability, and 3) his/her expectations of the trusted party. When these drivers are present, an individual must extend trust to another in order for a relationship to exist.

E-commerce researchers extended the traditional trust definition and drivers to online shopping and found that they are important in studying online end user behavior (McKnight et al., 2002; Gefen et al., 2003a) (see Table 1). For example, high uncertainty characterizes complex and anonymous online transaction processes. While traditional customers can pay at the counter and take the products home immediately, online end users do not directly observe vendors nor

Table 1. Extending trust definition and drivers to the domain of e-commerce

	Traditional	E-Commerce
Trust Definition	The willingness of a party to be vulnerable to the actions of another party based on the expectation that the other will perform a particular action important to the trustor, irrespective of the ability to monitor or control that other party (Mayer et al.., 1995 p. 712).	
Prerequisites: Trustor and Trustee in a relationship	Two parties—a trusting party (trustor) and a party to be trusted (trustee)—in a social relationship (Wang & Emurian, 2005)	In the context of online shopping, the relationship is predicated on the exchange of money for goods or services. Online consumer is the trustor. Web vendor is the trustee (Wang & Emurian, 2005).
Drivers of Trust: Risk and Uncertainty	Trust is necessary in risky situations (Kee & Knox, 1970). When the trustor has no control or even no means to monitor the trustee's behaviors, the trustee would have chances to act opportunistically. The higher the risks and uncertainty exist, the more trust is needed to enable behaviors in the context (Ruyter, Moorman, & Lemmink, 2001).	Because of high complexity and anonymity, the e-commerce environment is more risky and uncertain than the traditional market (Wang & Emurian, 2005). Unobservability causes even more information asymmetries than those in traditional markets (Tan & Thoen, 2002).
Drivers of Trust: Vulnerability	Vulnerability refers to the extent to which a trustor would lose to the trustee's opportunistic behaviors. The more a trustor will lose, the more vulnerable s/he is in specific circumstances, and the higher level of trust is needed to justify the participation in such circumstances (Hosmer, 1995; Mishra, 1996).	E-commerce customers are exposed to both financial loss (e.g., credit card theft, defective or below-expectation product, delivery delay and damage, etc.) and privacy loss (e.g., identity theft, spam mails, etc.) (Friedman, Kahn, & Howe, 2000; Gefen, 2002a).
Drivers of Trust: Expectations	Reasonable expectation refers to trustor's belief that the trustee can be relied on. Usually a trustor will form a set of expectations about the trustee, including its competence, benevolence and integrity (Mayer et al., 1995). Based on the expectations, the trustor grants trust.	Online customers form expectations or beliefs of an e-vendor in terms of competence (ability of the vendor to do what the customer needs), benevolence (the vendor's caring and motivation to act in the customer's interests) and integrity (the vendor's honesty and promise keeping) (McKnight et al., 2002; Gefen et al., 2003a).
Outcomes of Trust Trusting Behavior and Relationship	Trust leads to risk-taking behavior. The form of the action depends on the situation (Mayer et al., 1995). Trust also leads to long-term relationships and anticipated future interaction (Mayer et al., 1995; Doney & Cannon, 1997).	Consumers' trust in an e-vendor leads to their risk-taking behaviors, such as following advice, providing information, and making purchases (McKnight et al., 2002). It also plays an important role in developing long-term relationships, like enhancing customer loyalty.

directly view the actual products they purchase. Given the salience of risk and uncertainty in online environments (Wang & Emurian, 2005), understanding how to foster trust becomes essential for understanding how to encourage end users to purchase goods online.

In light of risk and uncertainty, e-consumers accept some degree of vulnerability when they make online purchases. For example, when purchasing a good, a consumer accepts exposure to the chance that an unfamiliar vendor could misuse the credit card information. Consumers who accept cookies also open themselves up to having their activities tracked and information stolen. When consumers perceive higher levels of vulnerability (McKnight et al., 2002), they must extend trust to justify entering a business relationship with a Web vendor.

Consumers extend trust based on their expectations of a Web vendor. Expectations refer to perceptions of a vendor's trusting attributes (McKnight et al., 2002). Typically, online trust is conceived as a set of beliefs and expectations that about a vendor's: a) capability to operate a business and complete transactions (i.e., competence); b) desire to positively interact with consumers (i.e., benevolence); and c) honesty and adherence to widely accepted principles (i.e., integrity) (Mayer et al., 1995; McKnight et al., 2002; Gefen et al., 2003a). When dealing with a new Web vendor, consumers may not have enough direct knowledge or experience. They have to build such expectations based on other sources.

Swift Trust

To retain quick moving consumers, vendors must foster swift trust. Swift trust refers to trust formed quickly in new or transitory relationships (Meyerson et al., 1996). It forms without the benefit of familiarity, past experience, and fulfilled promises. Swift trust is similar to initial trust in that it develops early in a relationship, reflects limited interaction between a trustor and trustee, and rests on cues derived from the environment (Meyerson et al., 1996; McKnight, Cummings, & Chervany, 1998) (see Table 2 for a comparison of forms of trust). However, unlike initial trust, swift trust is developed under time constraints due to environmental pressures or consumers' short attention span (Galleta, 2006). Jarvenpaa and Leidner (1999) argue that swift trust is characterized by short time frames, which limit trustors' ability to develop expectations of trustee. Once individuals form swift trust, they are inclined to pursue future interactions with a trustor.

Swift trust is particularly germane to understanding online consumer behavior. Product search engines usually organize results based on price. Frequently, low-cost vendors use low prices to overcome a lack of name recognition. In this case, online consumers do not have past experiences or direct interactions with an unfamiliar trustee—the Web vendor—suggested by a search engine. Due to their numerous shopping choices, the online consumers may expend limited time and effort exploring an unfamiliar Web site. To "close the deal," Web vendors must foster swift trust, or lose the new customers to competitors.

Table 2. Developed trust, initial trust and swift trust

	Definition	**Temporal**	**Studies**	**Trust Foundation**
Developed trust	Trust built on shared experience and direct interactions between the two parties.	In an established relationship	(Ganesan, 1994; Gefen et al., 2003a)	Familiarity, Past Experiences, Direct Interactions
Initial trust	Trust in an unfamiliar trustee; a trust relationship in which the actors do not yet have credible, meaningful information about, or affective bonds with, each other.	In a new relationship	(McKnight et al., 2002; Koufaris & Hampton-Sosa, 2004)	Disposition to Trust*, Institutional-Based Trust including Situational Normality and Structural Assurances
Swift trust	Trust formed quickly in a new or temporary system, without traditional sources of trust such as familiarity, past experience, and fulfilled promises.	In a new relationship, with time constraints	(Meyerson et al., 1996; Jarvenpaa & Leidner, 1999)	Disposition to Trust*, Imported Trust and Category-Driven Trust based on quick cues

Because individuals lack sufficient time to form perceptions of new trustees from scratch, swift trust is usually "imported from other settings and imposed quickly in categorical forms" (Meyerson et al., 1996, p. 174). To engender swift trust in online shopping, vendors embed cues in the Web site design to facilitate the importing and categorization processes. Some cues provide links for consumers to import trust from other trusted sources (i.e., trust transference [Stewart, 2003]). For example, the presence of Visa and FedEx icons provides signal to consumers about safe payment and fast delivery. Other cues invoke categorization processes to speed up the trust formation. For instance, some vendors utilize page layout and menu sets similar with those known and trusted Web sites to encourage new consumers to categorize them as familiar. Industry certificates or awards are usually placed prominently on the homepage for consumers to label the vendors as professional. More Web sites present BBB and Trust-e seals, so consumers will classify them as reliable vendors. Thus, through embedding cues in Web design, new vendors can successfully foster swift trust among first time visitors.

A Model of Swift Trust in Web Vendor

Web design consists of two major dimensions: appearance and functionality (Zhang et al., 1999). Appearance features refer to the look and feel of a Web site. They give the first impression to the Web visitors. Functionality features are more task-related. They refer to a Web site's ability to supply information and conclude transactions. Here, we propose a model (see Figure 1) depicting how a set of appearance and functionality features induce swift trust and purchase intention. In both appearance and functionality dimensions, we examine features that have been previously studied and are often noted as salient to fostering positive beliefs about a Web vendor and its Web site. While they are not exhaustive, the set of features will provide us some initial insight into swift trust formation. In the following sections, we discuss these appearance and functionality features and their relationships with swift trust and purchase intention.

Swift Trust and Purchase Intention

Purchase intention refers to online consumers' willingness to purchase from a Web vendor

Figure 1. A model of swift trust in Web vendor

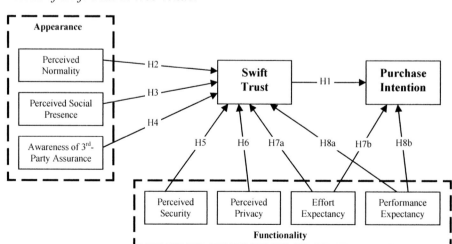

(Stewart, 2003). Prior research suggests that purchase intention is influenced by consumers' trust in a Web vendor (Stewart, 2003; van der Heijden, Verhagen, & Creemers, 2003; Gefen et al., 2003a). Although formed quickly at the early stage of a relationship, swift trust encourages further interactions and facilitates the development of purchase intention. If consumers grant swift trust towards a Web vendor, they tend to believe that this vendor will protect their privacy, sell high-quality products, and be capable of consummating online transactions. Thus, we hypothesize that as swift trust in a vendor grows, consumers will report higher purchase intentions.

H1: *Swift trust in a Web vendor positively affects purchase intention.*

Appearance Features

A Web site is an electronic storefront of a Web vendor. For a pure e-commerce company, the Web site is the only access point through which consumers may collect information on, and interact with, the goods and services. Because of the Web site's centrality in the consumer-Web vendor relationship, a Web site's appearance is an important source of signals about the vendor's trustworthiness. Prior trust literature has mentioned several appearance features that affect trust (McKnight et al., 2002; Gefen et al., 2003a; Gefen & Straub, 2004). Based on the literature, we believe online consumers will express swift trust when they perceive a Web site's appearance as normal and high on social presence, and they are aware of third-party assurances of trustworthiness. In the following paragraphs, we explain the logic behind these relationships.

Perceived Normality

Perceived normality refers to consumers' perception that a Web site performs in a normal or customary manner, which is consistent with their experience with similar Web vendors (Gefen et al., 2003a). Normality of a Web site signals to new consumers that the vendor will fulfill their expectations of a good shopping experience (i.e., product information can be easily acquired, transactions are completed smoothly and safely, and expected goods and services are received quickly) (Gefen et al., 2003a). If a Web site is perceived as normal, consumers will categorize it as trustworthy and extend swift trust. Alternatively, an unusual Web site design that is not well-known and requires learning new ways to access information may not be trusted.

When visiting a new Web site, consumers assess normality through their quick interaction with the Web site. Specifically, they evaluate their perceptions of: 1) the shopping process, 2) the information required to complete a purchase, and 3) the quality of their interaction with the Web site (Gefen et al., 2003a). For example, most consumers are familiar with one-click shopping. If, on a new Web site, consumers find that they must go through a complicated process and provide unusually detailed information to complete a transaction, or they have a complicated or unpleasant communication with online representatives, they will not trust the Web vendor and fail to complete a transaction. Thus, we anticipate that consumers who perceive normality of a Web site are more likely to form swift trust towards a Web vendor.

H2: *Perceived normality positively affects swift trust in Web vendor.*

Perceived Social Presence

Perceived social presence refers to consumers' perception that there is personal, sociable, and sensitive human contact and/or peer community on the Web site (Gefen & Straub, 2004). A Web site can project a social presence similar to what consumers experience in off-line stores. Gefen and Straub (2004) found that when a Web site is perceived as having a higher level of social presence, it enables more effective interaction and communication between a consumer and Web vendor, and thus, renders consumers more inclined to trust the Web vendor. By projecting social presence similar to off-line stores, a Web site may induce consumers to categorize the Web site as part of a trustworthy group of known, off-line vendors.

In practice, although Web vendors are not able to use salespersons or store assistants to physically interact with customers, they send cues or project social presence through images of high-quality products, happy customers, and live-chat customer service functions. For example, on Overstock.com, service representatives use interactive, pop-up windows to ask online consumers if they need more information, or offer to help complete a transaction. Many Web sites foster virtual communities, where customers can participate in peer discussions, provide product/store reviews, and receive peer assistance (e.g., newegg.com and target.com). If, during the first visit, consumers perceive a Web site as high on social presence, we anticipate they will extend swift trust to a Web vendor.

H3: *Perceived social presence positively affects swift trust in Web vendor.*

Awareness of Third-Party Assurance
Awareness of third-party assurance refers to consumers' knowledge and awareness of third-party institutional mechanisms that ensure a trustworthy environment for Web site operations and business transactions (McKnight et al., 2002). Several institutional mechanisms are widely used in e-commerce, including seal programs (e.g., Trust-e reliability and privacy seal programs, VeriSign security seal program), credit card protections (e.g., Visa card security and protection programs, MasterCard security and credit basics), and customer certified store ratings and feedback systems (e.g., BizRate.com) (Pavlou & Gefen, 2004). Prior research suggests that these mechanisms provide a safe and reliable environment for

online transactions. Through prominently placing seals and icons of these mechanisms, a Web site encourages consumers to extend trust based on their experiences with the established institutional structures. Based on the prior studies (McKnight et al., 2002; Stewart, 2003), consumers who are quickly aware of the third-party assurance on an unfamiliar Web site are more likely to extend swift trust towards the Web vendor.

H4: *Awareness of the third-party assurance positively affects swift trust in Web vendor.*

Functionality Features

Online customers' impression of a Web site's functionality, that is, its ability to successfully complete a transaction, influences their trust in the Web vendor. Although deep understanding of functionality requires extensive interaction with a Web site, cues in the Web site design may contribute to the formation of swift trust. Based on prior research, we direct our attention to four perceptions of functionality that may influence swift trust: security, privacy, effort expectancy and performance expectancy (Gefen et al., 2003a; Thatcher & George, 2004).

Perceived Security
Perceived security refers to consumers' perception that a Web site can safely complete transactions (Pavlou & Chellappa, 2001). When considering a transaction with an unknown party, consumers will evaluate the vendor's ability to protect their information, successfully complete a transaction, and offer help resolving a dispute. In the online environment, consumers usually perceive additional security threats than the traditional consumers, such as credit card theft, defective products/services, and delivery failure (Featherman & Pavlou, 2003). Consumers' security concerns are the major determinant of their online perceptions and behaviors (Salisbury, Pearson, Pearson, & Miller, 2001).

Consumers' assessment of the Web site's ability to safely complete transactions contributes to the formation of trust (Zhou, Dai, & Zhang, 2007). For example, Amazon.com provides notices when users sign in using the secure server. It gives customers easy access to the shipping and return policies on its homepage. By doing so, Amazon.com sends signals about its ability to facilitate safe, secure online shopping. Similarly, many Web vendors send signals about security through providing order status, real-time shipping tracking, and return assistance. When first time visitors feel fewer security concerns on a Web site, they will be more likely to report swift trust in the vendor.

H5: *Perceived security positively affects swift trust in Web vendor.*

Perceived Privacy

Perceived privacy refers to the consumers' belief that a Web vendor will protect consumers' personal and financial information (Pavlou & Chellappa, 2001). An online transaction requires consumers to provide more personal and financial information than traditional shopping channels. For example, online transactions require providing billing and shipping addresses, something that is not typically requested by brick-and-mortar stores. Also, e-commerce companies often use cookies to collect information and provide customized recommendations to consumers. Due to demands for consumer information, as well as a Web vendor's ability to collect information without consumers' notice, privacy concerns have become a defining issue for many Web consumers (Malhotra, Kim, & Agarwal, 2004).

When considering a transaction with an unfamiliar store, privacy may be a salient issue for a consumer (Liu, Marchewka, Lu, & Yu, 2005). A Web site may address privacy concerns through prominently featuring links to the privacy notice or policies, by briefly stating how they collect data on consumers, and by illustrating how such data may be used by the firm (Gefen et al., 2003a; Gefen, Rao, & Tractinsky, 2003b). When consumers quickly recognize that a Web vendor complies with the fair information practices and commits to protect its customers' privacy, they are more likely to express swift trust. Hence:

H6: *Perceived privacy positively affects swift trust in Web vendor.*

Effort Expectancy and Performance Expectancy

Within the domain of e-commerce, effort expectancy and performance expectancy have been tied to trust and purchase intentions (Pavlou, 2003; Gefen et al., 2003a). Effort expectancy (also referred to as ease of use [Venkatesh, Morris, Davis, & Davis, 2003]) refers to the degree to which the consumers believe that using a new Web site would be free of effort (Gefen et al., 2003a). Performance expectancy (also referred to as perceived usefulness [Venkatesh et al., 2003]) refers to the degree to which the consumers believe that using a new Web site would enhance their ability to safely, effectively purchase goods (Gefen et al., 2003a). Gefen et al. (2003a) found that customers' effort expectancy in using a Web site influences their trust. Their findings also indicate that trust, effort expectancy, and performance expectancy influence customers' usage intentions towards the Web site. Consistent with prior research, we hypothesize that when a new Web site is perceived as low on effort expectancy, consumers will be more likely to report swift trust as well as intentions to use a Web site. Hence:

H7a: *Effort expectancy negatively affects swift trust in Web vendor.*

H7b: *Effort expectancy negatively affects purchase intentions.*

In a departure from Gefen et al. (2003a), we argue that performance expectancy positively influences swift trust. Because first time visitors lack extensive experience with the tools provided by a Web vendor, expectations about performance reflect how they interpret cues embedded in a Web site. For example, a standard "useful" feature of a shopping site is the ability to search for products. Similarly, a comparison tool can help consumers compare similar products in terms of price, specifications and features in a more effective way. When consumers perceive that a Web site possesses tools that enable searching for and acquiring products, they will be more likely to express positive expectations of performance. Given that swift trust reflects limited interaction with a Web site, we anticipate that the presence of these "useful" tools positively influences swift trust and purchase intention. Hence:

H8a: *Performance expectancy positively affects swift trust in Web vendor.*

H8b: *Performance expectancy positively affects purchase intention.*

METHOD

A quasi-experimental survey design was used to test the research model. We used Overstock.com as our target Web site as it is a pure e-commerce company. Subjects would not confound trust in Overstock.com with their experiences at a real-world brick-and-mortar or click-and-mortar business.

We collected data at three public universities in the United States. Junior- and senior-level college students participated in the study. Although student samples have been criticized in many IS research contexts, evidence suggests that college students are active online shoppers, who do not differ from their working peers (Sen, King, & Shaw, 2006), and thus, represent a useful sample for testing our research model (Suh & Lee, 2005).

Study Procedure

The study consisted of a task and a survey. Participants were assigned a shopping task on Overstock. com. Specifically, subjects were asked to shop for a birthday gift for their significant others. They were given 10 minutes to view the Web pages and research a purchase. No actual purchase was required in the shopping task. Following completion of the task, subjects were asked to complete a survey about their experiences on Overstock. com. The survey collected data on all constructs in the research model and demographic information. Respondents were required to complete the task and survey in 25 minutes, thus engendering time pressure characteristic of situations involving swift trust.

Measurement Development

Where possible, we adapted measures from prior online trust research. Each item was measured using a seven-point Likert-type scale (anchored with 1=strongly disagree, 7=strongly agree). Purchase intention was measured using four items adapted from Pavlou's work (Pavlou, 2003; Pavlou & Gefen, 2004) (see Appendix I for the items).

Swift trust was operationalized as a second-order construct. It comprises three dimensions: competence, benevolence, and integrity. Each dimension was measured using three to four items adapted from McKnight et al. (2002).

Measures of most appearance features were adapted from prior studies. Perceived normality was measured by items adapted from Gefen et al. (2003a). Perceived social presence was measured by items adapted from Gefen and Straub (2004). To measure awareness of third-party assurance, we developed four items that directed attention to the presence of icons and links to trusted third parties such as VeriSign security seal program or credit card partners that appear on Overstock.com.

Functionality features measures were adapted from prior research. Effort expectancy and performance expectancy were adapted from Gefen et al. (2003a). Perceived security and perceived privacy were adapted from Salisbury et al. (2001), Yang and Jun (2002), and Smith et al. (1996).

Pilot Study and Data Collection

We conducted a pilot study to validate the measurement instruments and our quasi-experiment design. The instrument and task were well received by the pilot study participants. Minor changes were made in wording and the order of items. Also, we received feedback that our task was meaningful and induced a feeling of time pressure among our respondents.

Two-hundred eighty-one students participated in this study. We dropped 14 responses due to missing values. Also, we dropped 43 subjects because they reported prior experience with Overstock.com. This yielded a usable sample of 224 respondents that included 118 females and 106 males, with substantial Internet and online shopping experience. T-tests revealed that sample characteristics and responses across research sites were not significantly different. Table 3 presents sample characteristics.

RESULTS

We used partial least square (PLS), a structural equation modeling technique, to evaluate the hypotheses. Although a debate is emerging in the MIS literature on the merits of PLS, in the broader methods literature, PLS is considered a useful tool for theory building, specifically when one seeks to establish predictive validity in a structural model (Chwelos, Benbasat, & Dexter, 2001). As a result, we believe PLS is an appropriate tool for estimating our measurement and structural models. In the following sections, we present the results in two steps: measurement model and structural model.

Measurement Model

Two measurement models were evaluated. Following Agarwal and Karahanna's approach (2000), we first evaluated the measurement model for swift trust—a second order construct. Swift trust is formed by three reflective sub-dimensions: competence, benevolence and integrity. All items yielded high loadings (ranging from 0.855 to 0.948, $p < 0.000$) on the appropriate sub-dimension. Also, each sub-dimensions' internal consistency score (ranging from 0.908 to 0.941) and composite reli-

Table 3. Sample characteristics

Char.	Number	Percentage	Char.	Number	Percentage
Gender			Internet Experience – Years of Use		
Female	118	52.7%	0-3 years	5	2.2%
Male	106	47.3%	4-7 years	103	46.0%
Age			8 years or above	116	51.8%
Under 21	85	37.9%	Internet Experience - Often		
21 - 45	133	59.4%	Once a day or less	16	7.1%
Above 45	6	2.7%	Many times a day	208	92.9%
Internet Level			Online Shopping Experience – in past 2 years		
Beginner	2	0.9%	0-2 times	31	13.8%
Intermediate	34	15.2%	3-10 times	67	29.9%
Proficient	188	83.9%	11 time or above	126	56.3%

Table 4. Swift trust: Means, reliability and average variance extracted[1]

Dimension	Means	StDev	CR	Alpha	1	2	3
1. Competency	5.516	0.949	.952	.931	.832		
2. Benevolence	5.022	1.095	.943	.908	.707	.848	
3. Integrity	5.142	1.010	.958	.941	.698	.797	.852

[1]*Diagonal elements in the 'correlation of constructs' matrix are the square root of the average variance extracted. For adequate discriminant validity, diagonal elements should be greater than corresponding off-diagonal elements.*

Table 5. Overall measurement model: Means, reliability and average variance extracted[1]

	Means	StDev	CR	Alpha	1	2	3	4	5	6	7	8	9
1. Transaction Intention	5.008	1.348	.961	.944	.928								
2. Trust in Online Store	5.227	0.924	.933	.892	.533	.907							
3. Perceived Normality	5.961	1.028	.959	.935	.340	.538	.942						
4. Perceived Social Presence	4.231	1.351	.964	.953	.364	.396	.070	.918					
5. Awareness of 3rd-party	5.056	1.057	.927	.894	.414	.635	.400	.360	.872				
6. Effort Expectancy	6.221	0.921	.964	.949	.341	.520	.717	.119	.375	.933			
7. Performance Expectancy	5.498	1.144	.957	.940	.566	.530	.501	.338	.392	.583	.921		
8. Perceived Security	4.479	1.324	.960	.944	.413	.596	.316	.361	.545	.274	.349	.926	
9. Perceived Privacy	2.908	1.311	.947	.932	.064	.211	.185	.042	.184	.145	.087	.313	.864

[1]*Diagonal elements in the 'correlation of constructs' matrix are the square root of the average variance extracted. For adequate discriminant validity, diagonal elements should be greater than corresponding off-diagonal elements*

ability score (ranging from 0.943 to 0.958) were high. The detailed item loadings and reliability scores are reported in Appendix II (a) and Table 4, respectively. A confirmatory factor analysis was performed to assess the convergent and discriminant validity of the measures (see Appendix II (a) and Table 4). Briefly, all items load higher on the corresponding sub-dimensions than on other sub-dimensions, and each sub-dimension has a square root of the AVE (ranging from 0.832 to 0.852) greater than its correlations with other sub-dimensions. Hence, our analysis indicates adequate reliability, convergent, and discriminant validity of the swift trust measurement model.

Next, following Agarwal and Karahanna's approach (2000), we used the factor scores of the above three sub-dimensions as direct measures of swift trust to assess the full measurement model. Results are presented in Table 5 and Appendix II (b). All indicators load on the construct of interest, with loadings ranging from 0.829 to 0.965 (p < 0.000). Internal consistency scores range from 0.892 to 0.953. The composite reliability scores range from 0.927 to 0.964. All indicators loaded

higher on the construct of interest than other constructs. Every construct has square root of AVE (ranging from 0.864 – 0.942) greater than its correlations with any other constructs. Hence, our analysis indicates adequate convergent and discriminant validity for the overall measurement model.

Structural Model

Figure 2 presents the structural model results. Appearance and functionality features explain 61% of the variance in swift trust. Also, swift trust, effort expectancy, and performance expectancy explained 40% of the variance in purchase intention.

Swift Trust

In terms of appearance features, we found perceived normality (H2: .19, p<.01), perceived social presence (H3: .13, p<.01), and awareness of 3rd party assurance (H4: .28, p<.01) positively relating to swift trust. In terms of functionality features,

Figure 2. Research model with PLS results

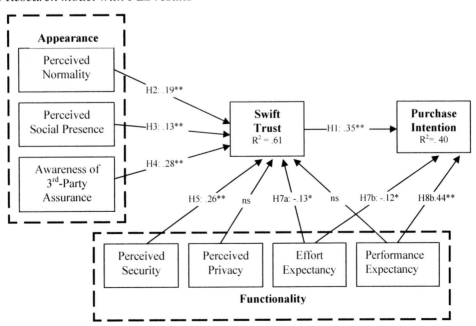

1217

perceived security (H5: .26, p<.01) positively related to swift trust while effort expectancy (H7a: -.13 p<.05) negatively related to swift trust. Perceived privacy (H6: n.s.) and performance expectancy (H8a: n.s.) were not significantly related to swift trust. Collectively, our results provide evidence that a Web site's appearance and functionality attributes influence swift trust.

Purchase Intention

The overall model explains 40% of the variance in purchase intention. Swift trust (H1: .36, p < 0.01) and performance expectancy (H8b: .44, p < 0.01) positively relates to purchase intention. Effort expectancy (H7b: -.12, p < 0.05) negatively relates to purchase intention.

DISCUSSION

This study examined sources and consequences of swift trust in Web vendors. In the following paragraphs, we discuss our findings and the implications.

Appearance Features and Swift Trust

All of the three appearance features that we examined positively relate to swift trust. The study findings show that perceived normality has a significant positive relationship with swift trust (H2: Supported). Similar to other groups of online consumers, our respondents had significant Internet and e-commerce experience. Among our study participants, similarity with familiar Web sites engendered their swift trust in an unfamiliar Web site. This finding suggests that Web designers should carefully consider how they visually and structurally differentiate their Web site from competitors. If a Web site employs an unusual or novel design, first time visitors may not extend trust to a Web vendor. For new Web vendors, in addition to relying on low price or novelty of prod-

uct lines/business models, our findings suggest patterning Web sites after successful e-commerce businesses in their market as a means to engender swift trust for first time visitors.

The study also shows that social presence positively related to swift trust in a Web vendor (H3: Supported). An unfamiliar Web site that projects social presence similar to real-world salespersons and customer service representatives engenders feelings of competence, benevolence, and integrity in online consumers (Gefen & Straub, 2004). Overstock.com uses images of satisfied customers and content employees to convey social presence. In addition, when customers check a product, a live assistance chat window frequently pops up and offers to provide more information or help completing a transaction. Further, below the item description, customers can read the product reviews posted by other customers or post their own reviews. All of these features give consumers the feeling like they were shopping at a physical store with helpful service representatives, and they were part of a community of shoppers (Thatcher & George, 2004). Thus, we suggest prominently projecting social presence as a useful means to foster consumers' swift trust.

First-time visitors reported higher levels of swift trust when they were aware of the third-party assurance (H4: Supported). Overstock.com places icons of third-party assurance providers on every Web page—including icons from credit card companies, payment options, VeriSign BBB Online, and BizRate.com. Our findings confirm that third-party icons signal that Overstock.com is operated in a safe and reliable environment, and the transactions in the environment are well protected (McKnight, Kacmar, & Choudhury, 2004). For practice, this finding directs Web designers to carefully consider the placement of third-party assurance icons and seals. If properly sized, placed at directly visible positions, repeated on different pages or different sections, the third-party assurance icons engender consumers' swift trust (McKnight et al., 2004).

Overall, appearance features are salient to understanding swift trust. This is probably because the appearance features are mostly visible to the first-time Web site visitors under time pressure. Our findings suggest that consumer perceptions of normality, social presence, and third-party assurances lead to swift trust in a Web vendor. For Web designers, these findings suggest that the look and feel of a Web site can be used to foster swift trust and convert first-time visitors to paying customers.

Functionality Features and Swift Trust

We found mixed results for functionality features' relationship with swift trust. Perceived security positively related to swift trust (H5: supported). Consumer perceptions of a Web site's capability to perform secure transactions influence their perceptions of the Web vendors' competence, benevolence, and integrity. Fully understanding the security features on a Web site may require time and extensive interaction. However, Web vendors can quickly signal their intention and ability to provide a safe shopping experience to the first time visitors through security cues. For example, Overstock.com provides prominent links to order tracking, shipping and return policies on its homepage. The transparent transaction processes may create a sense of security for online consumers. In addition, the "golden lock" signs on the login and check-out pages, as well as the timeouts and re-login requests, also provide quick signals of a Web site's security. If these security cues are prominently placed, first-time visitors can quickly perceive good protection and make quick inferences about the trustworthiness of a Web vendor. While most Web vendors expend significant efforts in developing security features that consumers may not directly see or understand, we suggest, to foster swift trust, Web vendors should give special attentions to how to signal the presence of the security features to online consumers.

Contrary to our expectations, perceived privacy was not significantly related to swift trust (H6: not supported). This finding may be a function of the task we used in our study. Participants searched for information and assessed features of a Web site; but they did not provide personal information required to complete a transaction. Perhaps due to the short and anonymous visit, our participants were not concerned with privacy issues associated with completing a purchase on Overstock.com. Because swift trust develops prior to making a purchase, we are comfortable with the strength of our research design. However, future research should examine ties between swift trust and an antecedent to privacy concerns. Hence, even though we did not find a relationship between privacy and swift trust, there remains room for future research on privacy and swift trust.

Effort expectancy negatively related to swift trust (H7a: Supported) and purchase intention (H7b: Supported). When using a Web site was perceived as relatively free of effort, consumers were more likely to perceive the Web vendor as competent, benevolent and high on integrity. While consistent with prior online consumer behavior research (Gefen et al., 2003a), our findings confirm the nomological net of relationships between effort expectancy, trust, and purchase intention. For practice, our findings underscore the importance of designing Web sites to be easy to navigate, easy to find product information, and easy to conclude transactions.

Performance expectancy was not related to swift trust (H8a: Not Supported) and it was related to purchase intention (H8b: Supported). Performance expectancy's influence on swift trust may have been washed out by perceived normality, perceived social presence, perceived security, and effort expectancy. While other perceptions refer to specific aspects of a Web site, performance expectancy requires consumers to make global assessments of a Web site. In light of this, it makes sense that perceptions of specific Web site attributes would exert greater influences on swift trust than a global assessment of a Web site. An alternative explanation for this finding may be that it requires consumers' substantial experience to form perceptions of performance expectancy. Because swift trust reflects only limited interaction with a Web site, online consumers may lack the experience to form beliefs about performance expectancy. Thus, it is not surprising that performance expectancy is not an antecedent to swift trust in a Web site. However, purchasing a product rests on general, well-developed perceptions of a Web site's functionality. Hence, performance expectancy, as expected, directly influences purchase intention (Gefen et al., 2003a).

Overall, online consumers report higher levels of swift trust when they report positive perceptions of a Web site's security and low levels of effort to use. The other functionality features may require more interactions to be realized and contribute to trust formation. Although perceptions of the features may evolve over time, Web vendors who embed noticeable signals that they are capable to complete secure, easy transactions are likely to engender consumers' swift trust and purchasing intention in their Web sites.

Swift Trust and Purchase Intention

Swift trust positively relates to purchase intention (H1: Supported). When online consumers quickly form trust, they are more likely to participate in further interaction with the Web site and eventually make actual purchases from the vendor. This finding is consistent with prior trust research (Gefen, 2002b; see Gefen et al., 2003a; 2003b; Pavlou & Gefen, 2004). Our finding also supports the idea that trust is relevant to purchasing intention even when consumers have limited time to familiarize themselves with a Web vendor. Hence, this finding underscores the importance of the previous findings on how appearance and functionality features influence the formation of swift trust in a Web vendor. For practice, although the casual visitors led by search engines may have many alternatives and move fast, Web vendors still can successfully foster swift trust and convert them to paying customers through the proper use of the appearance and functionality features.

CONCLUSION

This study examined swift trust in Web vendors. To induce conditions necessary for the formation of swift trust, we constrained study participants' time to visit a Web site. Also, we dropped responses from study participants with experience with our target Web site—Overstock.com. Based on our study, we found substantial support for appearance and functionality features positively relating to swift trust. Also, we found supports for swift trust, effort expectancy, and performance expectancy influencing purchase intention.

For research, this study provides initial evidence that swift trust has different antecedents than other forms of experience-based trust identified in the e-commerce literature—it was not affected by perceived privacy or performance expectancy. This suggests that future research should examine additional factors that shape the development of swift trust. For practice, our research underscores the importance of fostering swift trust as a means to increase purchase intention. Our findings direct attention to approaches under managerial control such as normality (i.e., using Web site designs similar to known vendors) and social presence (i.e., engendering a sense of community or having interactive help features) that positively influence the formation of swift trust.

In light of findings, it is important to note several limitations and opportunities for extending our research. An important limitation of this study is the use of a single Web site, Overstock.com. We used this approach to control for variance in how a Web site's features and respondents' experience influence swift trust. Overstock.com possesses many favorable features such as recommendation agents, icons, and product descriptions that may foster swift trust. In future research, it would be useful for researchers to examine how manipulating these features would influence consumers' swift trust in other unfamiliar Web vendors.

Also, future research should examine how to foster swift trust in diverse populations of online consumers. In this research, we drew on students who are active online consumers to examine swift trust. Although students are a valid sample for the current study, a pure student sample may include less variance in age, occupation, and Internet experience. For example, research suggests that age influences perceptions of technology among members of the workforce (Morris & Venkatesh, 2000). Hence, future research should examine differences in demographic factors such as age, income or occupation, which may relate to the formation of swift trust in e-commerce.

REFERENCES

Agarwal, R., & Karahanna, E. (2000). Time flies when you're having fun: Cognitive absorption and beliefs about information technology usage. *MIS Quarterly, 24*(4), 665-694.

Chwelos, P., Benbasat, I., & Dexter, A. (2001). Research report: Empirical test of an EDI adoption model. *Information Systems Research, 12*(3), 304-321.

Doney, P., & Cannon, J. (1997). An examination of the nature of trust in buyer-seller relationships. *Journal of Marketing, 61,* 35-51.

DoubleClick. (2004). *DoubleClick Q3 2004 ad serving trend report.* Doubleclick.com.

Featherman, M., & Pavlou, P. (2003). Predicting e-services adoption: A perceived risk facets perspective. *International Journal of Human-Computer Studies, 59*(4), 451-474.

Friedman, B., Kahn, P., & Howe, D. (2000). Trust online. *Communications of the ACM, 43*(12), 34-40.

Galleta, D., Henry, R., McCoy, S., & Polak, P. (2006). When the wait isn't so bad: The interacting effects of Web site speed, familiarity, and breadth. *Information Systems Research, 17*(1), 20-37.

Ganesan, S. (1994). Determinants of long-term orientation in buyer-seller relationships. *Journal of Marketing, 58*(2), 1-19.

Gefen, D. (2002a). Nurturing clients' trust to encourage engagement success during the customization of ERP systems. *Omega, 30,* 287-299.

Gefen, D. (2002b). Customer loyalty in e-commerce. *Journal of Association for Information Systems, 3,* 27-51.

Gefen, D., Karahanna, E., & Straub, D. (2003a). Trust and TAM in online shopping: An integrated model. *MIS Quarterly, 27*(1), 51-90.

Gefen, D., Rao, V., & Tractinsky, N. (2003b). The conceptualization of trust, risk and their relationship in electronic commerce: The need for clarifications. *Paper presented at the 36th Hawaii International Conference on System Sciences.* Big island, Hawaii.

Gefen, D., & Straub, D. (2004). Consumer trust in B2C e-commerce and the importance of social presence: Experiments in e-products and e-services. *Omega, 32,* 407-424.

Hosmer, L. (1995). Trust: The connecting link between organizational theory and philosophical ethics. *Academy of Management Review, 20*(2), 379-403.

Jarvenpaa, S., & Leidner, D. (1999). Communication and trust in global virtual teams. *Organization Science, 10*(6), 791-815.

Kee, H., & Knox, R. (1970). Conceptual and methodological considerations in the study of trust and suspicion. *Journal of Conflict Resolution, 14*(3), 357-366.

Koufaris, M., & Hampton-Sosa, W. (2004). The development of initial trust in an online company by new customers. *Information and Management, 41,* 377-397.

Kracher, B., Corritore, C., & Wiedenbeck, S. (2005). A foundation for understanding online trust in electronic commerce. *Information, Communications and Ethics in Society, 3*(3), 131-141.

Lee, M., & Turban, E. (2001). A trust model for consumer internet shopping. *International Journal of Electronic Commerce, 6*(1), 75-91.

Liu, C., Marchewka, J., Lu, J., & Yu, C. (2005). Beyond concern—a privacy-trust-behavioral intention model of electronic commerce. *Information and Management, 42,* 289-304.

Malhotra, N., Kim, S., & Agarwal, J. (2004). Internet users' information privacy concerns (IUIPC): The construct, the scale, and a causal model. *Information Systems Research, 15*(4), 336-355.

Mayer, R., Davis, J., & Schoorman, F. (1995). An integrative model of organizational trust. *Academy of Management Review, 20*(3), 709-734.

McKnight, D., Choudhury, V., & Kacmar, C. (2002). Developing and validating trust measures for e-commerce: An integrative typology. *Information Systems Research, 13*(3), 334-359.

McKnight, D., Cummings, L., & Chervany, N. (1998). Initial trust formation in new organizational relationships. *Academy of Management Review, 23*(3), 473-490.

McKnight, D., Kacmar, C., & Choudhury, V. (2004). Shifting factors and the ineffectiveness of third party assurance seals: A two-stage model of initial trust in a Web business. *Electronic Markets, 14*(3), 252-266.

Meyerson, D., Weick, K., & Kramer, R. (1996). Swift trust and temporary groups. In: R. Kramer & T. Tyler (Eds.), *Trust in organizations: Frontiers of theory and research,* (pp. 166-195). Thousand Oaks, CA: Sage Publications.

Mishra, A. (1996). Organizational responses to crisis: The centrality of trust. In: R. Kramer & T. Tyler (Eds.), *Trust in organizations,* (pp. 261-287). Newbury Park, CA: Sage Publications.

Morris, M., & Venkatesh, V. (2000). Age differences in technology adoption decisions: Implications for a changing workforce. *Personnel Psychology, 53*(2), 375-403.

Pavlou, P. (2003). Consumer acceptance of electronic commerce: Integrating trust and risk with the technology acceptance model. *International Journal of Electronic commerce, 7*(3), 101-134.

Pavlou, P., & Chellappa, R. (2001). The role of perceived privacy and perceived security in the development of trust in electronic commerce transaction. Unpublished work.

Pavlou, P., & Gefen, D. (2004). Building effective online marketplaces with institution-based trust. *Information Systems Research, 15*(1), 37-59.

Ruyter, K., Moorman, L., & Lemmink, J. (2001). Antecedents of commitment and trust in customer-supplier relationships in high technology markets. *Industrial Marketing Management, 30,* 271-286.

Salisbury, D., Pearson, R., Pearson, A., & Miller, D. (2001). Perceived security and World Wide Web purchase. *Industrial Management and Data Systems, 101*(3-4), 165-176.

Sen, R., King, R., & Shaw, M. (2006). Buyers' choice of online search strategy and its managerial implications. *Journal of Management Information systems, 23*(1), 211-238.

Smith, H., Milberg, S., & Burke, S. (1996). Information privacy: Measuring individuals' concerns about organizational practices. *MIS Quarterly, 20*(2), 167-196.

Stewart, K. (2003). Trust transfer on the World Wide Web. *Organizational Science, 14*(1), 5-17.

Suh, K., & Lee, Y. (2005). The effects of virtual reality on consumer learning: An empirical investigation. *MIS Quarterly, 29*(4), 673-697.

Tan, T., & Thoen, W. (2002). Formal aspects of a generic model of trust for electronic commerce. *Decision Support Systems, 33,* 233-246.

Thatcher, J., & George, J. (2004). Commitment, trust, and social involvement: An exploratory study of antecedents to Web shopper loyalty. *Journal of Organizational Computing and Electronic Commerce, 14*(4), 243-268.

van der Heijden, H., Verhagen, T., & Creemers, M. (2003). Understanding online purchase intentions: Contributions from technology and trust perspectives. *European Journal of Information Systems, 12,* 41-48.

Venkatesh, V., Morris, M., Davis, G., & Davis, F. (2003). User acceptance of information technology: Toward a unified view. *MIS Quarterly, 27*(3), 425-478.

Wang, T., & Emurian, H. (2005). An overview of online trust: Concepts, elements, and implications. *Computers in Human Behavior, 21,* 105-125.

Yang, Z., & Jun, M. (2002). Consumer perception of e-service quality: From Internet purchaser and non-purchaser perspectives. *Journal of Business Strategies, 19*(1), 19-41.

Zhang, P., von Dran, G., Small, R., & Barcellos, S. (1999). Web sites that satisfy users: A theoretical framework for Web user interface design and evaluation. *Paper presented at the 32nd Hawaii International Conference on System Sciences.* Maui, HI.

Zhou, L., Dai, L., & Zhang, D. (2007). Online shopping acceptance model—a critical survey of consumer factors in online shopping. *Journal of Electronic Commerce Research, 8*(1), 41-62.

ENDNOTE

[1] We specially thank the special issue editor for granting extra space to include the appendices.

APPENDIX I: SURVEYS AND MEASURES

Construct	Items
Appearance Features	
Perceived Normality	The steps required at this Web site to search for products and make orders are typical of other similar type Web sites.
	The information requested of me at this Web site is the type of information most similar type Web sites request.
	The nature of the interaction with this Web site is typical of other similar type Web sites.
Perceived Social Presence	There is a sense of human contact in this Web site.
	There is a sense of personalness in this Web site.
	There is a sense of sociability in this Web site.
	There is a sense of human warmth in this Web site.
	There is a sense of human sensitivity in this Web site.
Awareness of Third-Party Assurance	The display of the VeriSign icon on Overstock.com makes me feel that this Web site is trustworthy.
	The display of the BBBOnline icon on Overstock.com makes me feel that this Web site is trustworthy.
	The display of the Visa, MasterCard, American Express, and DiscoverCard icons on Overstock.com makes me feel that this Web site is trustworthy.
	The display of the BizRate.com icon on Overstock.com makes me feel that this Web site is trustworthy.
Functionality Features	
Effort Expectancy (Reverse Coded)	I find this Web site easy to use.
	It would be easy for me to become skillful at using this Web site.
	Learning to use this Web site would be easy to me.
	My interaction with this Web site is clear and understandable.
Performance Expectancy	I find this Web site useful.
	Using this Web site can improve my shopping performance.
	Using this Web site can enhance my shopping effectiveness.
	Using this Web site can increase my shopping productivity.
Perceived Security	I feel secure in providing sensitive information (e.g., credit card number) when transacting with Overstock.com.
	I would feel totally safe providing sensitive information about myself to Overstock.com.
	I would feel secure sending sensitive information to Overstock.com.
	Overall, Overstock.com is a safe place to send sensitive information.

Construct	Items
Perceived Privacy (Reverse Coded)	I am concerned that Overstock.com is collecting too much information about me.
	It bothers me when Overstock.com asks me for personal information.
	I am concerned about my privacy when browsing Overstock.com.
	I have doubts as to how well my privacy is protected on Overstock.com.
	My personal information could be misused when transacting with Overstock.com.
	My personal information could be accessed by unknown parties when transacting with Overstock.com.
Swift Trust in Online Store	
Competence	I believe this online store is effective in assisting and fulfilling my purchases.
	This online store performs its role of e-vendor very well.
	Overall, this online store is a capable and proficient e-vendor.
	In general, this online store is very knowledgeable about the business it operates.
Benevolence	I believe that this online store would act in my best interest.
	If I required help, this online store would do its best to help me.
	This online store is interested in my well-being, not just its own.
Integrity	This online store is truthful in its dealings with me.
	I would characterize this online store as honest.
	This online store would keep its commitments.
	This online store is sincere and genuine.
Purchase Intention	
	Given the need, I intend to transact with Overstock.com.
	Given the chance, I think that I would consider making purchases from Overstock.com.
	I would probably purchase from Overstock.com when I have a need.
	It is likely that I will actually buy products from Overstock.com in the near future.

APPENDIX II: CONFIRMATORY FACTOR ANALYSES: FACTOR LOADINGS & CONVERGENT VALIDITY

(a)   First-Order Constructs

	Com	Ben	Int
Com1	0.855	0.568	0.581
Com2	0.948	0.664	0.650
Com3	0.929	0.679	0.678
Com4	0.915	0.666	0.636
Ben1	0.693	0.935	0.755
Ben2	0.664	0.914	0.706
Ben3	0.597	0.914	0.741
Int1	0.639	0.743	0.917
Int2	0.689	0.746	0.947
Int3	0.633	0.706	0.895
Int4	0.616	0.748	0.933

(b)   Second-Order Constructs

	Intent	Trust	Normality	Social Presence	Aware-ness	Effort Expect.	Perf. Expect.	Security	Privacy
Intent1	0.936	0.489	0.336	0.309	0.370	0.298	0.475	0.382	0.080
Intent2	0.947	0.565	0.401	0.330	0.439	0.397	0.553	0.397	0.054
Intent3	0.958	0.498	0.344	0.353	0.395	0.350	0.556	0.395	0.084
Intent4	0.885	0.430	0.175	0.365	0.332	0.214	0.522	0.366	0.020
Com	0.479	0.886	0.561	0.267	0.567	0.532	0.480	0.494	0.206
Ben	0.499	0.925	0.449	0.405	0.562	0.445	0.505	0.566	0.214
Int	0.480	0.922	0.463	0.408	0.607	0.445	0.463	0.568	0.158
WN1	0.307	0.507	0.946	0.055	0.356	0.698	0.486	0.281	0.180
WN2	0.347	0.527	0.938	0.115	0.440	0.641	0.462	0.343	0.204
WN3	0.308	0.493	0.955	0.026	0.335	0.697	0.474	0.271	0.138
SP1	0.368	0.382	0.048	0.916	0.344	0.101	0.331	0.332	0.083
SP2	0.334	0.360	0.097	0.888	0.368	0.135	0.333	0.321	0.070
SP3	0.319	0.376	0.070	0.940	0.330	0.093	0.289	0.350	0.036
SP4	0.331	0.338	0.045	0.931	0.306	0.106	0.281	0.305	-0.044
SP5	0.326	0.368	0.064	0.937	0.311	0.115	0.324	0.354	0.041
AW1	0.348	0.612	0.410	0.289	0.893	0.397	0.354	0.500	0.214
AW2	0.307	0.544	0.289	0.274	0.886	0.317	0.364	0.444	0.164
AW3	0.374	0.537	0.393	0.322	0.848	0.328	0.311	0.445	0.119
AW4	0.426	0.524	0.301	0.384	0.875	0.261	0.342	0.519	0.138
PEOU1	0.334	0.520	0.688	0.128	0.368	0.950	0.583	0.273	0.186
PEOU2	0.302	0.474	0.706	0.080	0.361	0.921	0.531	0.233	0.123
PEOU3	0.306	0.444	0.619	0.103	0.280	0.923	0.512	0.217	0.136
PEOU4	0.333	0.505	0.672	0.133	0.391	0.953	0.554	0.300	0.098
PU1	0.482	0.480	0.478	0.271	0.340	0.589	0.836	0.330	0.159
PU2	0.548	0.496	0.463	0.299	0.386	0.512	0.965	0.315	0.041
PU3	0.538	0.500	0.450	0.337	0.373	0.541	0.958	0.317	0.026
PU4	0.526	0.485	0.466	0.343	0.350	0.519	0.936	0.332	0.102
Secu1	0.410	0.542	0.315	0.278	0.451	0.235	0.273	0.897	0.296
Secu2	0.364	0.511	0.251	0.378	0.493	0.217	0.338	0.939	0.300
Secu3	0.389	0.531	0.266	0.341	0.507	0.245	0.314	0.961	0.310
Secu4	0.375	0.620	0.335	0.347	0.567	0.312	0.367	0.924	0.263
Priv1	0.085	0.153	0.237	-0.057	0.174	0.230	0.098	0.218	0.829

(b) continued

Priv2	0.054	0.178	0.190	-0.001	0.179	0.174	0.095	0.273	0.839
Priv3	0.051	0.174	0.160	0.041	0.170	0.132	0.058	0.265	0.878
Priv4	0.061	0.219	0.174	0.019	0.167	0.133	0.095	0.321	0.929
Priv5	0.025	0.187	0.112	0.096	0.154	0.051	0.040	0.280	0.877
Priv6	0.062	0.182	0.104	0.107	0.117	0.057	0.068	0.259	0.855

This work was previously published in Journal of Organizational and End User Computing, Vol. 21, Issue 1, edited by M. Mahmood, pp. 88-108, copyright 2009 by IGI Publishing (an imprint of IGI Global).

Chapter 5.3

Understanding Brand Website Positioning in the New EU Member States:
The Case of the Czech Republic

Shintaro Okazaki
Universidad Autónoma de Madrid, Spain

Radoslav Škapa
Masaryk University Brno, Czech Republic

ABSTRACT

This study examines Websites created by American multinational corporations (MNCs) in the Czech Republic. Utilizing a content analysis technique, we scrutinized (1) the type of brand Website functions, and (2) the similarity ratings between the home (US) sites and Czech sites. Implications are discussed from the Website standardization versus localization perspective.

INTRODUCTION

Both academics and practitioners have long debated whether advertising messages should be standardized. The proponents of standardization argue that the use of uniform advertising would provide significant cost benefits, thus improving company performance in the short run, while creating a consistent brand image in multiple markets. In contrast, the proponents of localization contend

that ignoring the cultural, social, and economic characteristics of particular markets would cause psychological rejection by local consumers, thus decreasing profits in the long run. The debate has also produced a compromised or hybrid approach, which suggests that whether to standardize or localize advertising in a given market is a question of degree, and it is necessary to analyze many factors on a case-by-case basis (Mueller, 1991).

This debate is not limited to traditional media. As multinational corporations (MNCs) integrate their marketing communication with an emergent interactive medium, websites are becoming increasingly important for brand marketing and customer relationship management in multiple markets. This is because the Internet is, by definition, a *glocal* medium, which allows companies to create localized content with global access. In fact, many MNCs have established so-called "global gateway" sites with several language options. Consumers can first choose the language, then seek the information they desire. In this regard, the content of the local sites may need to be adapted to local consumers' tastes and preferences, in terms of design, layout, copy, message, and so forth. (Okazaki and Alonso, 2002).

Okazaki (2005) examined websites created by American MNCs' in four EU member states (i.e., the UK, France, Germany, and Spain), and found a high level of localization in website communication strategy. This research extends Okazaki's exploration into the new EU member states, by conducting a content analysis of the MNCs' websites created in the Czech Republic. Specifically, we address the following questions: (1) What types of brand website functions are used? (2) To what extent are the Czech sites standardized?

SIGNIFICANCE OF THE STUDY

This study will be an interesting addition to the literature of global information technology for two reasons. First, prior research provides little information on how the content created by the most globally diffused information technology, the Internet, has been standardized in foreign markets. Information managers in global markets should be aware of a question of transmitting culturally bound meanings into local sites. Secondly, this study addresses how design features and website functions can be used as a tool to create a universal imagery in global websites. Specifically, this study explores one of the most understudied countries in Europe: the Czech Republic. After joining the European Union, studies on information technology in this new member state is almost non-existent, thus, this research makes a unique contribution to the literature.

ENLARGEMENT OF THE EUROPEAN UNION

In 2004, the enlargement of the European Union increased its member states from 15 to 25, by adding 10 countries: Cyprus, the Czech Republic, Estonia, Hungary, Latvia, Lithuania, Malta, Poland, Slovakia, and Slovenia. In 2007, two more countries, Romania and Bulgaria became the member states, making the Union of 27 countries. This drastic expansion changed the way multinational corporations (MNCs) operate their businesses in Europe. Because of these countries' low labour costs and investment incentives (e.g., tax reduction, construction aid, etc.), many firms moved their production facilities from other regions to these new member states. For example, Sheram and Soubbotina (2000) report that "Countries seen as more advanced in market reforms—the Czech and Slovak Republics, Hungary, and Poland—attracted almost three-quarters of foreign investment" in transition economies. In fact, Poland received approximately $6.4 billion in foreign direct investment in 2003, an increase of $360 million over the previous year (MacKay 2004).

As these new EU Member States experience rapid economic expansion, global marketing influences consumers in them more and more. Their product experiences increasingly resemble those of their "Western" neighbours. In this light, it is reasonable to argue that the role of advertising in everyday consumption has also undergone a drastic transition, in both content and executions. For example, in the Czech Republic, advertising spending reached 563 million euros in 2004, while the average annual growth rate over the last 5 years has been 5%. Multinational corporations (MNCs) are the largest advertisers in these countries.

MEDIA USAGE IN EASTERN AND CENTRAL EUROPE

The Czech Republic

In the Czech Republic, television has traditionally been the primary vehicle for advertising, accounting for 46% of the MNCs' marketing budgets. Print media is the second medium with

34%, while outdoor advertising (i.e., billboard) is third, with 8% of total advertising expenditure (OMD Czech, 2005). However, the rapid growth of the Internet has significantly affected this media distribution. According to the Czech Publishers Association, the share of Internet advertising has been estimated at approximately 4%, or 25 million Euro (760 millions CZK), with a growth rate of almost 80% in 2004 (Unie vydavatelů, 2005). The telecommunications, financial, and automobile companies are the heaviest users of the Internet as an advertising medium (Unie vydavatelů, 2005).

In 2005, nearly 30% of Czech households had a personal computer (Czech Statistical Office, 2005). Internet penetration is increasing steadily in the Czech Republic. Nowadays, 35% of the adult population in the Czech Republic uses the Internet, almost twice the number of Internet users in 2000. The Czech Republic has thus clearly outmatched other Central European countries: for example, Bulgaria (16%), Hungary (22%), and Poland (31%). However, it has not yet achieved the levels of Internet penetration in Estonia (51%) or Slovenia (56%). The most dynamic increase is found in older people (GfK, 2006), even though the Internet use remains the domain of younger people. A quarter of Czech citizens have an Internet connection at home.

Searching for information is one of the most frequent activities on the Internet, according to a survey by the Czech Statistical Office (2005). In the most recent quarter to be surveyed, 62% of the Internet users used the Internet to find information about goods and services, 54% used it to find and download professional texts, 38% looked for services related to travel and accommodation, 36% to read and download on-line newspapers and magazines, and 28% to play or download games or music. However, the number of individuals with e-shopping experience increased rapidly between 2005 and 2006 (the survey was carried out in the first quarters of 2005 and 2006): it amounted to 14% in 2006, while a year before it had been only 6% (Czech Statistical Office, 2006). The

most popular items in the Internet shopping are electronics, books, journals, textbooks, tickets and travel services, and accommodation. Online shopping is typically used more by men than women, and by the younger generation groups, between 25 and 45 years.

Approximately 12,500 Czech enterprises purchased goods or services via the Internet in 2003, almost 30% of the total number. The value of Internet purchases reached 2.8% of total purchases, and the value of Internet sales reached nearly 2.1% of total sales in these enterprises.

Poland and Hungary

Along with the Czech Republic, Poland and Hungary make up the fastest-growing economic region within the new EU member states. For example, the rapid transformation of the Polish economy is reflected in the accelerated growth of its advertising market. Between 1996 and 1999, average annual growth in advertising expenditure was more than 40%, which can be attributed to the drastic structural changes, and the subsequent economic boom, in this period. With regard to media share, television was the most popular (48%), with print media second (35%). On-line advertising, including websites, remains far behind traditional media, representing approximately 1% of total media spending (Zenith Optimedia, 2004). The telecommunications, financial, and automobile industries are the heaviest users of the Internet for advertising, promotion, and transactions (Agora, 2005).

In 2005, 30% of households in Poland had the technical possibility of the Internet access. In term of quality of connections, the survey found that only 16% of Polish households used a broadband connection. The significant disparity in the Internet infrastructure is between urban areas and the countryside, where the penetration of broadband connections is four times lower than in urban areas (Eurostat, 2005).

The Internet usage by Polish enterprises is below the EU average: in 2005, 87% of enterprises used the Internet connection. The share of broadband the Internet connections was 43%. More than 67% of companies have their own website homepage (Eurostat, 2006). Online purchases have not yet become popular. Only 5% of Polish consumers ordered goods or services via the Internet in 2005 (Eurostat, 2006). According to the survey by GfK (2006), only 4% of the Internet users make a purchase on the Internet once a month or more. A further 6% buy online once every two to three months, while 18% go online sporadically with the intention of buying something. The most frequently purchased items include books, CDs, clothes, and shoes. Less frequently, people buy DVDs and air tickets (GfK, 2006).

In B2B the situation is similar. In 2005, only 9% of the enterprises surveyed ordered products or services via the Internet. Sales via the Internet were lower, with only 4% of enterprises selling via the Internet. In 2005, turnover from e-commerce via the Internet amounted to 1.6% of total turnover (Eurostat, 2005).

Similarly, the Hungarian market has shown a drastic growth in market size and advertising spending. According to the Budapest Business Journal (BBJ, 2004), advertising expenditure in television media reached 213 million euros by 2003. The print media also showed a drastic growth, to spending of 212 million euros. In 2003, the online advertising market expanded by approximately 30%, achieving a 2% share of the total media market. The principal reasons for this growth were an increased number of the Internet users in younger generations, and the rapid proliferation of broadband high-speed connection. The largest online advertisers include car dealers, telecommunication companies, beer makers, and cosmetics firms (BBJ, 2003).

Other EU Member States

In 2005, Slovenia had the highest rate of the Internet usage in the new member states, both for households (48%), and for enterprises (96%)

(Eurostat, 2006). The lowest rates of access were in Lithuania, for households (16%), and in Latvia, for enterprises (75%). The largest disparities in the Internet access between households and enterprises were recorded in the Czech Republic, Lithuania, and Slovakia. The number of individuals who have never used the Internet outweighs the number of regular users in the new member states. That differs from the situation in the old member states.

There is also disparity in the presence of companies' websites on the Internet. In January 2005, 62% of enterprises in the EU were equipped with a website, but only 49% in the new member states. The lowest percentages of companies with websites were found in Latvia, Hungary, and Lithuania. Most enterprises use the content of their web presentations mainly to market their products. Less than half use it to display catalogues of their products, services, and prices. One quarter use websites to offer after-sales service to their customers. Apart from the Czech Republic, enterprises in the new member states registered lower rates than the EU average for purchases, sales, and for total sales on the Internet, as a percentage of their overall turnover (Eurostat, 2006).

The e-readiness rankings of the Economist Intelligence Unit can be seen as a complex indicator of the level of ICT of a country's infrastructure. The index is a weighted collection of nearly 100 quantitative and qualitative criteria, which assesses the "state of play" of a country's information and communications technology (ICT) infrastructure, and the ability of its consumers, businesses, and governments to use ICT to their benefit. In the 2006 e-readiness rankings, Estonia achieved the best position of all the new EU member states (27th), whereas Latvia (39th) was lowest. By comparison, ten of the fifteen old EU members were in the top 20.

The Networked Readiness Index, published annually in the Global Information Technology Report, is a similar index. This index captures such aspects as available ICT infrastructure, and

Table 1. Descriptive statistics

	Population[1]	GDP per capita[2]	Advertising spending[3]	Advertising spending as % of GDP[4]	Internet penetration[5]	Internet household penetration[6]	No of local domains[7]	Online spending[8]	Internet Advertising spending[9]
Czech Rep.	10,288.9	73.6	769,186	0.65	50	29	1,502,537	7	22,734
Cyprus	776.0	88.9	89,073	0.54	33.6	37	75846	2	n.a.
Estonia	1,339.9	59.8	107,744	0.79	51.8	46	449,036	n.a.	3,607
Hungary	10,057.9	62.5	1,029,874	0.91	30.4	32	1,176,592	7	21,302
Latvia	3,385.7	48.6	129,961	0.81	45.2	42	132,204	1	7,277
Lithu-ania	2,280.5	52.1	150,07	0.50	35.9	35	240,592	2	3,086
Malta	407.7	71.7	n.a.	n.a.	33	53	20,673	n.a.	n.a.
Poland	3,8101.8	49.7	1,862,672	0.55	29.9	36	5,001,786	6	32,885
Slovakia	5,391.6	57.1	n.a.	n.a.	46.5	27	486,020	0	n.a.
Slovenia	2,010.3	81.9	242,656	0.64	55.5	54	64,284	9	5,484
EU 10	74,040.3	64.6			44	39	9,149,570		

Note: 1. Data in thousands for the 1st of January 2007. Source: Eurostat (2007)

2. GDP (in PPS per capita) in 2005. EU25=100%. Source: Eurostat (2007).

3. Global advertising expenditure 2006. In $US Thousands. Initiative Innovation (2007).

4. Initiative Innovation (2007) and The World Factbook, Central Intelligence Agency (2007)

5. Internet Usage in the European Union. Penetration (% Population) in 2007. Source: Internet World Stats (2007).

6. Percentage of households who have Internet access at home in 2006. Source: Eurostat (2007).

7. Number of local domains based on number of top-level domain in January 2007. Source: ISC Internet Domain Survey (2007).

8. The Internet turnover as percentage of the total turnover of enterprises with 10 or more employees in 2006. Source: Eurostat (2007).

9. Global advertising expenditure 2006. In thousands of $. Initiative Innovation (2007).

actual levels of ICT usage, and its purpose is to understand more thoroughly the impact of ICT on the competitiveness of nations. In this index, Estonia again scored best amongst the new members. Latvia and Poland had the lowest ratings.

STANDARDIZATION VS. LOCALIZATION

The issue of standardization arises from the desirability and feasibility of using a uniform marketing mix (4Ps) across national markets (Szymanski et al., 1993). Advertising has been examined more often than the other elements of this mix (Agrawal, 1995; Zandpour et al., 1994). A *standardized* approach is the use of uniform messages with no modification of headings,

illustrations, or copy, except for translation in international markets (Onkvisit and Shaw, 1987). The standardized school of thought argues that consumers anywhere in the world are likely to share the same wants and needs (Elinder, 1961; Levitt, 1983). On the other hand, the *localized* approach asserts that consumers differ across countries, and therefore advertising should be tailored according to culture, media availability, product life cycle stages, and industry structure (Synodinos et al., 1989; Wind, 1986). Combining these two extremes, the third school of thought states that the appropriateness of standardization depends on economic similarity, market position, the nature of the product, the environment, and organizational factors (Jain, 1989).

In the 1970s, empirical evidence showed a high degree of localization, due to both increasing nationalistic forces, and various well-publicized advertising blunders in the 1960s (Agrawal, 1995). This trend reversed, to favour standardization, in the 1980s, and went along with a drastic rise in the number of multinational advertising agencies (Yin, 1999). During this period, a series of content analysis studies attempted to identify cross-cultural differences between Japanese and U.S. advertising (Hong et al., 1987; Madden et al., 1986; Mueller, 1987).

In the 1990s, localization seemed to remain popular among MNCs operating in various regions of world markets. Harris (1994) found that 69% of 38 MNCs (19 American and 19 European) standardized their advertising campaigns to some extent throughout the EC markets, whilst the rest of the sample localized. Interestingly, only 8% of the sample used totally standardized advertising, providing "little evidence of any widespread practice of standardized pan-European advertising campaigns" (Harris, 1994). Kanso and Nelson (2002) found that 62% of 193 firms (both American and non-American subsidiaries) in Finland and Sweden use localization, and place a strong emphasis on local cultures. Similarly, Samiee et al. (2003) found that MNCs operating in Southeast Asia tend to localize advertising. They examined 113 firms in Hong Kong, PRC, Taiwan, and Singapore, and found that both environmental and economic factors were the primary drivers of this tendency.

WEBSITE POSITIONING AS GLOBAL INFORMATION MANAGEMENT

Although these issues have been debated for decades in traditional media, a new stream of research has emerged recently, on the standardization versus localization of global websites in multiple markets. With the rapid expansion of the Internet, and the resulting connections between local, regional, and international markets, an increasing number of MNCs are shifting from off-line to on-line marketing. This frequently entails creating a diverse range of websites in multiple markets (Donthu and Garcia, 1999). By 2001, more than 36 million domains for commercial websites had already been established: these "dot coms" are projected to attract an astonishing $6.8 trillion in business by 2004 (Forrester, 2002; Internet Software Consortium, 2001).

Such numbers incline observers to see the Internet as a door to the "global village wonderland", as advocated by Levitt (1983): that is, an entity that creates an environment for more standardized marketing communication in world markets. Product-based websites are replacing such shopping venues as mail-order catalogues and television-based home shopping, and also offer a new format for global advertising among culturally and linguistically diverse groups (Pastor, 2001). An increase in the quantity and quality of product/brand information on the Internet is generating extraordinary consumer interest, which extends beyond physical and political boundaries (Donthu and Garcia, 1999). Accordingly, Roberts and Ko (2001) asserted that websites, with their ability to uniformly blend textual and visual content, constitute the best communication medium in which to develop brand images.

One roadblock that MNCs face involves localized websites: primarily, the need to satisfy the linguistic requirements of a diverse population of potential customers (Warden et al., 2002). According to Quelch and Klein (1996), establishing localized relationships with international consumers is best achieved by creating regional Web content. However, creating regional commercial websites may not be cost-effective if, to elicit return visits, a company is obliged to update information continuously. Such intense website maintenance on a regional level can jeopardize consistent brand strategies, by eliminating the "advantage of centralized management of a firm's Websites" (Warden et al., 2002).

In a pioneering study, Okazaki and Alonso (2002) examined Japanese websites in Japan,

Table 2. Network and e-readiness statistics

	Networked Readiness Index [1]	Networked Readiness Index (Rank) [1]	e-readiness rankings [2]	e-readiness rankings, general index [2]	e-readiness rankings, Connectivity index [2]	e-readiness rankings, Business Environment index [2]	Enterprises selling via Internet 2005 in % [3]	Enterprises availability of the Internet 2005 in % [3]
Czech Republic	0.36	32	32	6.14	4.90	7.39	13	92
Cyprus	0.36	33	n.a.	n.a.	n.a.	n.a.	4	85
Estonia	0.96	23	27	6.71	6.60	7.81	8	90
Hungary	0.27	37	32	6.14	4.80	7.34	4	78
Latvia	-0.03	52	39	5.30	3.95	7.21	1	75
Lithuania	0.08	44	38	5.45	4.65	7.28	6	86
Malta	0.51	30	n.a.	n.a.	n.a.	n.a.	16	90
Poland	-0.09	53	32	5.76	4.30	7.28	5	87
Slovakia	0.19	41	36	5.65	4.05	7.35	7	92
Slovenia	0.34	35	28	6.34	5.90	7.45	12	96

Note: n.a. = not available.

1. Global Information Technology Report 2005-2006
2. Economist Intelligence Unit (2006).
3. Eurostat (2005).

Spain, and the U.S.A., and found that cultural dimensions (power distance, uncertainty avoidance, masculinity – femininity, individualism-collectivism, and long-term orientation) and communication style (high context versus low context) were the primary drivers of cross-cultural differences in MNCs' website communication strategies. Focusing on more operational aspects, Okazaki (2005) examined American brands' website standardization in France, Germany, Spain, and the UK. He argued that the progress of the EU enlargement and economic integration via the euro provided firms with an incentive to use a uniform website communication across the EU member states. However, the findings were mixed, in that the level of standardization of American brands' websites in the European countries was low, compared to their respective home-country (American) websites. On the other hand, differences within the EU were minimal: the websites created within the European markets were somewhat "regionalized", especially for durable and industrial goods. A summary of prior research on website content analysis is shown in Table 3.

COMMUNICATION IN THE GLOBAL WEBSITE ENVIRONMENT

What is the primary factor influencing MNCs that operate in European markets? They now face more and more pressure to generate more comprehensive marketing strategies on the web. Among the various forms of the online environment, websites have been one of the most popular platforms, allowing consumers to see, consult, and obtain product-related information at any time, anywhere. Such websites can be seen as a new form of global marketing communications, offering opportunities to strengthen effective relational marketing in international markets (Robert and Ko, 2002). The creation of a localized URL in Europe, therefore, may be a necessary strategic move, because cultural and linguistic barriers are

Table 3. Prior research on website content analysis

Year	Authors	Countries examined	Unit of analysis	Analyzed content	Sample size	Statistical design
1999	Ju-Pak	US, UK & S.Korea	Product-based websites	Information content, creative strategies, design	110 (EE.UU.) 100 (UK) 100(S.Korea)	Chi-square, ANOVA
1999	Oh, Cho & Leckenby	US & S.Korea	Target ads	Information content, creative strategies	50 for each country	Chi-square
1999	Yoon & Cropp	US & S.Korea	Brand websites	Information content, emotional appeals, cultural aspects	20 for each country	Chi-square
2000	Lee & Sego	US & S.Korea	*Banners*	Information content, emotional appeals, colours, etc.	252 in total	Chi-square
2000	Chung & Ahn	US & S.Korea	*Banners*	Information content, "call-to-action" messages, demographics, etc.	251 (EE.UU.) 221 (S.Korea)	Chi-square
2000	Yoon	US	Product-based websites	Information content, celebrity endorsement, etc.	200 in total	Chi-square, ANOVA
2002	Okazaki & Alonso	Japan, Spain & EE.UU.	Product-based websites	Information content, cultural values, creative strategies	20 for each country	Chi-square, ANOVA
2002	Dou, Nielsen & Tan	Canada, Denmark & Malaysia	Commercial websites	Communication systems, transactional functions, etc.	150 for each country	ANOVA
2002	Zahir, Dobing & Hunter	26 countries	National portals	Linguistic aspects, design, colours, Hofstede's cultural dimensions, etc.	26 portals	Descriptive stat
2003	Robbins & Stylianou	16 countries	Corporate websites	Design, presentation, links, security, information content, financial content, corporate information, etc.	90 in total	ANOVA
2005	Okazaki	US, UK, France, Germany & Spain	Brand websites	Brand website functions, similarity ratings	244	ANOVA, discriminant analysis, multiple regression

perhaps the most difficult obstacles to overcome in marketing communications across European nations (Kahle, Beatty, and Mager, 1994). Such localization, however, could cost a great deal. Hence, MNCs may intuitively favour standardization, given the benefits associated with offline marketing standardization, such as consistent brand image and corporate identity, cost savings, and organizational control. Furthermore, websites seem to be an effective medium for establishing a global brand image, by offering consistent textual and visual information to international consumers. Unfortunately, there seems to be a lack of empirical research regarding the standardization versus localization issue in the online environment, leaving important questions unanswered.

What are the determining factors in international marketing communications on the web? In a recent criticism of the slow progress of international advertising research, Taylor and Johnson (2001) argue that the standardization debate should "focus on what executions can be standardized and when they can be standardized". Following this suggestion, this study intends to fill this gap, by identifying to what extent MNCs have adopted a standardized approach for their websites created in European markets. In order to ensure cross-national data equivalency, we examined only the websites created by America's top brands for the UK, France, Germany, and Spain. These countries differ importantly in terms of cultural and linguistic characteristics, but are relatively homogeneous in socioeconomic conditions and technological infrastructure, and have online markets of a reasonable size.

Furthermore, 3.3%, 6.5%, and 8.1% of the world's online population consist of French, German, and Spanish speaking consumers, respectively, compared to 35.2% of English speakers (Global Reach, 2003). Therefore, these four countries represent an important segment of world online consumers. On the other hand, the languages spoken in the new EU member states, such as Polish or Czech, account for a very small portion of the online population. In fact, the impact of these countries, on both the world economy and the world online population, is negligible (Table 4). Thus, an important question arises: is it worthwhile for MNCs to consider local adaptation in such new markets? Or is it better to use a standardization approach in these markets, to take advantage of cost savings and efficient website maintenance? To address these questions, this study will examine websites created by MNCs for the Czech Republic.

CONCEPTUAL FRAMEWORK

Figure 1 shows the conceptual framework for this study. These concepts are essentially based on the matrix proposed by Quelch and Klein (1996), who suggested two primary models of website: the communication model and the transaction model. Originally, their matrix was not intended to be a theoretical model for formal testing, but since then it has been used as a conceptual base (e.g., see Dou, Nielsen, and Tan, 2002). In our modified matrix,

communication and transaction feature form two ends of one axis, which should be balanced with the other axis, consisting of fact and image. The resulting four quadrants need to be effectively combined to achieve the desired level of website standardization. The components in each quadrant can be considered the most relevant programmes for website brand communications.

The extent of website standardization should be determined on the basis of the two major roles of global online programmes: (1) to enhance worldwide transactions by establishing a localized relationship, and (2) to develop a standardized brand image, using the appropriate combination of content, graphics, backgrounds, and multimedia effects in all the MNC's websites in different languages (Roberts and Ko, 2003). In the following section, each principal feature of our proposed model is therefore analyzed in the light of these perspectives.

METHODOLOGY

This study adopts content analysis as a research methodology. This method has been widely used in cross-cultural research (Brislin, 1980), as well as in the Internet research (McMillan, 2000; Okazaki and Alonso, 2002).

Company selection. A website content analysis was performed, to examine the degree of website standardization of American brands' websites created for the Czech market. Methodological recommendations from prior research were adopted, to establish a high reliability (Dou et al., 2002; Okazaki and Alonso, 2002; Philport and Arbittier, 1997). To create a dataset, a ranking of "The 100 Top Global Brands" from *Business Week (2002)* was used. Only brands with America as country of origin (by the classification of *Business Week*) were chosen to match home versus host country website pairs. In total, 66 brands were found, of which 34 brands had websites in the Czech Republic. Here, it is important to note that these

Table 4. World online population and language use

Language type	Internet access [1]	% of world online pop.	Total pop. [1]	GDP[2]	% of world economy	GDP per capita [3]
English	238.5	35.2	508	n.a.	n.a.	n.a.
Non-English	439.8	64.8	5,822	n.a.	n.a.	n.a.
European Languages (non-English)	238.1	35.1	1,218	12,968	30.3	n.a.
Czech	4.0	n.a.	12	121	n.a.	10.0
Dutch	13.2	2.0	20	575	n.a.	28.5
Finnish	2.8	n.a.	6	142	n.a.	23.6
French	22.7	3.3	77	1517	4.2	19.7
German	44.4	6.5	100	2,679	5.8	26.8
Greek	2.0	n.a.	12	189	n.a.	15.8
Hungarian	1.6	n.a.	10	96	n.a.	9.6
Italian	24.1	3.6	62	1,251	3.6	20.1
Polish	6.9	n.a.	44	359	n.a.	8.1
Portuguese	19.3	2.8	176	1,487	3.6	8.4
Romanian	2.4	n.a.	26	108	n.a.	4.2
Russian	18.4	2.7	167	822	1.8	4.9
Scandinavian languages (total)	13.5	2.0	20	550	1.3	27.9
Serbo-Croatian	1.0	n.a.	20	n.a.	n.a.	n.a.
Slovak	1.0	n.a.	6	47	n.a.	8.7
Slovenian	0.7	n.a.	2	22.9	n.a.	10.9
Spanish	54.8	8.1	350	2500	8.9	7.1
Turkish	4.6	n.a.	67	431	n.a.	6.4
Ukrainian	0.9	n.a.	47	115	n.a.	2.3
TOTAL EUROPEAN LANGUAGES (non-English)	238.1	35.1	1,218	12,968	33.9	n.a.
TOTAL ASIAN LANGUAGES	201.7	29.7	n.a.	n.a.	n.a.	n.a.
TOTAL WORLD	648.7		6,330	41,400	n.a.	n.a.

Note: 1 US$ in million; 2 US$ in billion, 3 US$ in Thousand.
Source: Global Reach (2003)

firms are considered as representative of American firms doing business in the Czech Republic, because their Internet presence can be considered as the initial step of market entry mode.

Coding categories. Next, a detailed coding sheet was first developed, with detailed operational definitions. The variables include (1) brand website functions, and (2) similarity ratings (Table 5). With regard to the former, the coding categories were adopted from Okazaki (2005), who suggested 23 website communication functions. Similar categories have been suggested in the past (e.g., Ghose and Dou, 1998; Leogn, Huang, and Stanners, 1998). Each variable was measured on a categorical dichotomy as to the existence of each function on a website. Values of "1" and "0" were assigned for answers of "Yes" and "No", respectively. For example, websites that had appropriate information associated with "job/career development" were assigned "1" for this

Figure 1. Conceptualization of website program standardization

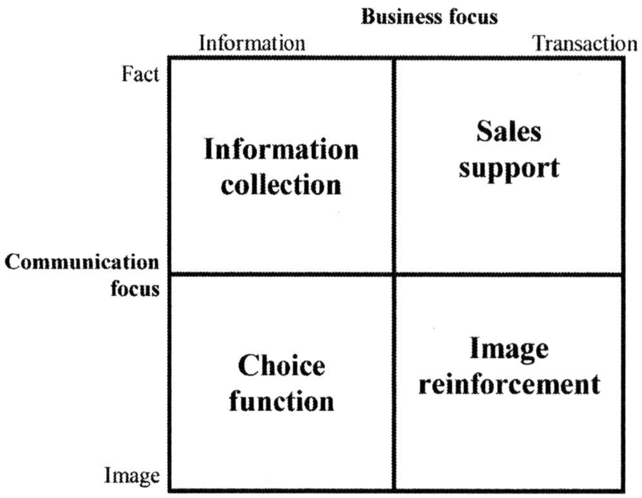

attribute. Those that did not were assigned "0". These values were considered dependent variables in the analysis. The similarity rating refers to the degree of similarity between home-country and host-country websites. This "similarity rating" measure was also adopted from Okazaki (2005), and was originally inspired by Mueller (1991). The textual and visual components of websites created for local markets were assessed for the extent to which they were similar or dissimilar to those created at home. The similarity rating was coded for each pair of websites (i.e., U.S.A.-Czech sites) on a five-point semantic scale, ranging from "very different" (coded as 1) to "very similar" (coded as 5), with an intermediate scale point "not determinable" (coded as 3). The components included copy, headlines, text, layout, colour, photographs associated with the product, with human models, and with background scenes, illustrations, charts, graphs, and interactive images.

Coding instrument. All coding instruments were originally prepared in English, and then translated into Czech, using the "back translation" technique. Each typology was supplemented with additional examples, to give a better illustration. The unit of analysis was determined as the homep-

age, which has been considered a central gate to Web-based communication. This is appropriate, given the primary objective of the study: to identify major differences in the main text, pictures, and graphics. We examined the first and second levels of websites, because it is practically impossible to scrutinize every detail of an entire site. The existence of online brand communications was primarily determined by the main menu or index provided on the homepage. For instance, if the menu included a link labelled "corporate information", the site was coded as having this variable. The only exception occurred when analyzing direct or indirect online transactions, because in some cases these functions may not be listed on the main index. In this case, the coders were asked to examine the submenu of the websites.

Coder training and reliability. Following the recommendations by Kolbe and Burnett (1991), two bilingual Czech judges, both of whom were unaware of the purpose of the study, were hired and first trained to grasp the operational definitions of all the variables. During the training period, the coders practised independently, by examining 20 randomly chosen websites from non-American firms. Then, the coded results were compared,

Table 5. Measurement schemes

Measure	Coding categories	Scale type
Brand website functions	Global/Local site options, Corporate information, Corporate news release, Product/Brand news release, General product information, Brand specific information, Investor relationships, Direct online transaction, Indirect online transaction, Office/Store locator, Country/Language option, Search engine, Jobs/Career development, Promotion/Prizes/Sweepstakes, Education/Training, Culture/Entertainment, Client registration/Log-in, Guest book/Customer feedback, E-mail alert, FAQs, Free download, Sitemap, Links	Nominal scale (Yes=1, No=0)
Similarity ratings	Company logo, Company logo placement, Major copy, Major copy placement, Major headline, Major headline placement, Major text, Layout in top half / right half, Layout in bottom half / left half, Colour in top half / right half, Colour in bottom half / left half, Major photograph 1 (product), Major photograph 2 (human model), Major photograph 3 (background scene), Major illustrations, Major chart or graph, Interactive image 1 (flash as opening), Interactive image 2 (pop-ups), Interactive image 3 (animated banners), Interactive image 4 (layers, pop-unders, etc.)	Interval scale (1=very different, 5=very similar)

and differences were reconciled through discussion. An inter-judge reliability was calculated using the reliability index suggested by Perreault and Leigh's reliability index (I_r) (1989). Various researchers consider this estimation method to be the best among available alternatives (e.g., Kolbe and Burnett, 1991).

As Table 6 shows, the majority of the resulting indexes far exceeded a widely accepted minimum .80???, and was thus deemed satisfactory. It was recognized that there would be a potential loss of information in similarity evaluation between American and Czech sites, because non-native English speakers had analyzed American websites. However, it was accepted that such potential bias was minimized by the coders' extensive preparation: the subjective interpretation of textual information was minimal, since the coders were responsible for examining only *major* copy, headlines, and text on the websites. Otherwise, they were instructed to objectively measure the similarity of non-textual information.

RESULTS

Table 7 summarizes the frequency distribution of brand website functions. For the sake of comparison, the information provided in Okazaki's (2005) previous exploration was used as a reference with regard to the U.S., UK, French, and German markets. This comparison should help our understanding of MNCs' website standardization in existing versus new EU member states.

The Chi-square analysis detected significant differences in 8 categories: global/local site options, general product information, investor relations, online purchase, email contact, promotion/prizes/sweepstakes, culture/entertainment, and guest book/customer feedback. It appears that American MNCs tend to apply a different website communication strategy in the Czech market because, in prior research, Okazaki (2005) found significant differences in only 3 of 23 variables, suggesting that the frequency of the usage of brand website functions in the UK, France, Germany, and Spain was relatively uniform. In observing the frequencies of brand website functions in the Czech sites, email contact was used more frequently, but the other tools were used much less than in the other markets.

Next, in order to capture the relationships between the brand website functions and country domain, we performed a multiple correspondence analysis via optimal scaling technique. This method is appropriate for nominal variables, from which a multidimensional map can be created. We used the existence of the brand website functions

Table 6. Intercoder reliability

Measure	Coding categories	Perreault & Leigh's *lr*
Brand website functions	Brand specific information	0.82
	Client registration/Log-in	0.91
	Corporate information	1.00
	Corporate news release	0.97
	Country/Language option	1.00
	Culture/Entertainment	0.97
	Direct online transaction	1.00
	Education/Training	0.94
	E-mail alert	1.00
	FAQs	1.00
	Free download	0.94
	General product information	0.97
	Global/Local site options	0.94
	Guest book/Customer feedback	1.00
	Indirect online transaction	1.00
	Investor relations	0.97
	Jobs/Career development	0.97
	Links	0.91
	Office/Store locator	1.00
	Product/Brand news release	1.00
	Promotion/Prizes/Sweepstakes	0.97
	Search engine	1.00
	Sitemap	1.00
Similarity ratings	Text	0.91
	Major photograph: product	0.75
	Major photograph: model	0.56
	Major photograph: background scene	0.92
	Major illustrations	0.82
	Major chart or graph	
	Layout in top half / right half	0.93
	Layout in bottom half / left half	0.98
	Headline placement	0.74
	Headline	0.69
	Copy placement	0.73
	Copy	0.91
	Company logo placement	0.95
	Company logo	0.96
	Colour in top half / right half	0.93
	Colour in bottom half / left half	0.91

Table 7. Results of brand website functions

1. Brand website features	US (n=66)	UK (n=57)	France (n=49)	Germany (n=57)	Czech (n=34)	p
Global/Local site options	37.9	84.2	65.3	75.4	**64.4**	.000
Corporate information	89.4	86.0	87.8	84.2	**86.1**	.956
Corporate news release	53.0	54.4	55.1	59.6	**55.6**	.983
Product/Brand news release	51.5	49.1	53.1	52.6	**55.6**	.990
General product information	80.3	84.2	83.7	78.9	**47.2**	.000
Brand specific information	75.8	68.4	73.5	68.4	**69.4**	.858
Investor relationships	45.5	26.3	16.3	22.8	**11.1**	.001
Online purchase	71.2	42.1	42.6	43.9	**25.0**	.000
Email contact	22.7	31.6	28.6	24.6	**77.8**	.000
Office/Store locator	33.3	33.3	32.7	26.3	**13.9**	.346
Country/Language option	62.1	57.9	71.4	61.4	**52.8**	.536
Search engine	68.2	57.9	55.1	50.9	**52.8**	.442
Jobs/Career development	62.1	47.4	46.9	54.4	**61.1**	.374
Promotion/Prizes/Sweepstakes	56.1	63.2	44.9	47.4	**11.1**	.000
Education/Training	39.4	33.3	26.5	24.6	**25.0**	.331
Culture/Entertainment	47.0	57.9	53.1	42.1	**13.9**	.001
Client registration/Log-in	51.5	36.8	38.8	36.8	**41.7**	.398
Guest book/Customer feedback	78.8	82.5	75.5	77.2	**22.2**	.000
E-mail alert	25.8	15.8	20.4	19.3	**25.0**	.483
FAQs	18.2	22.8	16.3	19.3	**8.3**	.647
Free download	19.7	26.3	26.5	28.1	**36.1**	.643
Sitemap	45.5	42.1	44.9	36.8	**38.9**	.905
Links	4.5	12.3	8.2	3.5	**19.4**	.053

Note: The data of the US, UK, France and Germany are based on Okazaki (2005)

(yes or no) as descriptive variables, and the type of country domain (U.S.A. or Czech Republic) as classification variables. Figure 2 shows the resulting biplot component loadings. As clearly seen, the majority of brand website functions are more closely associated with U.S. sites (represented by "1"), while only a limited number of brand website functions are associated with Czech sites (represented by "2"). Specifically, global/local site options, links, and indirect online transactions are concentrated in the lower left quadrant (which U.S. sites appear to dominate), but the rest of the brand website functions are concentrated in the upper right quadrant (where Czech sites appear to dominate).

Lastly, Table 8 summarizes the results of the similarity ratings. A higher similarity rating indicates a higher degree of standardization. As the results clearly show, the similarity between the American and Czech sites was notably higher, especially in logo, copy, and colour. In comparison with the other sites, headlines and major photographs also exhibit higher similarity. On this basis, it appears clear that the American MNCs tend to create highly standardized websites in the Czech Republic.

Figure 2. Multiple correspondence analysis

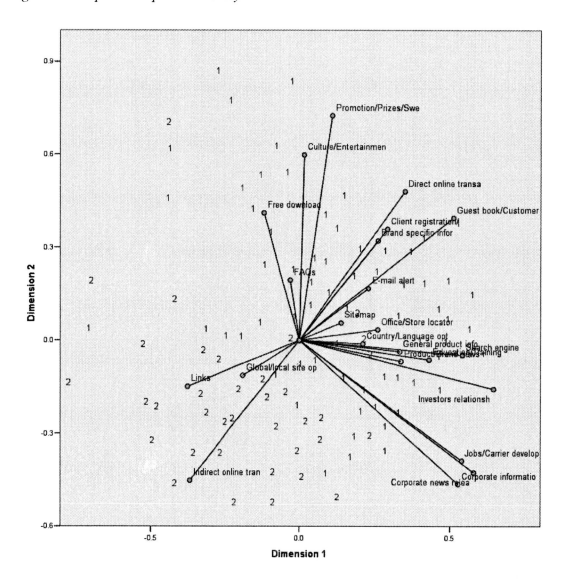

DISCUSSION

This study attempts to examine the website communication strategy used by American MNCs in a new EU member state, the Czech Republic. We performed a content analysis of 34 Czech sites created by America's top brands in terms of brand website functions, and similarity between the home and host sites. The findings indicate that American MNCs appear to standardize their Czech sites. Given that the Czech Republic is a growing market that attracts more and more foreign direct investment, this case could be considered indicative of the general tendency in the other new EU member states.

First, American MNCs tend to use general product information less frequently in the Czech market than in the other EU markets, which suggests two possible scenarios. First, they have not yet commercialized their products in this market, and therefore dispose of little information. In this case, the primary objective of their websites would

Table 8. Results of similarity ratings

Components	UK (n=57)	France (n=49)	Germany (n=57)	Czech (n=34)
Company logo	4.51	4.61	4.39	**4.58**
Major copy	1.43	1.36	1.14	**4.00**
Major headline	1.23	1.17	1.02	**3.47**
Major text	2.84	2.53	2.68	**2.32**
Layout	3.35	3.32	3.29	**3.88**

be to provide a preliminary information platform in a new market. Second, they might have needed to localize product information to a great extent, especially in the local language, with more adapted product usage. However, it appears that the most logical conclusion would be that the lack of online product information is because American firms are still in the very early mode of market entry in the Czech Republic.

The second scenario seems very unlikely when we address the following question: Why would large multinational firms devote resources to extensive adaptations of Czech websites? The country's population is only 10 million and, according to the most recent Eurostat (2006), only 19% of Czech homes had the Internet access in 2005, including 5% with broadband connections. As much as 63% of the population has never used the Internet. Only one in six people who used the Internet (5.5%) bought anything online in 2005, and these purchases were limited largely to electronic goods (2.1%), books (1.6%), and clothing (1.1%). Therefore, if the total market in a given product category is currently only 100,000 or so, and if adapting the website is only going to improve website effectiveness by 5% to 10%, is there any incentive to adapt and then to continue managing that adaptation? Consistent with this argument, our findings indicate that online purchase functions are rarely used in the Czech sites. This suggests that American MNCs may have neither distribution channels nor local investors in the Czech market. Similarly, the much less frequent use of guest book/

customer feedback indicates that American brands are less willing to offer personalized contact to the local Czech consumers, probably because of the unavailability of local outlets, representatives, or staff. In contrast, in the Czech Republic, they offer general email addresses more frequently than in the other countries, as an alternative contact mode for general inquiries.

Third, by the same token, culture/entertainment and promotion/prices/sweepstakes are used much less in the Czech market than in the others, because these elements need to be matched to local consumer tastes, and require more personalized content. It would make little sense to offer presents or incentives when the companies actually have no local sales activities.

Finally, a surprisingly high level of similarity ratings for both textual and visual components indicates a lack of any cultural adaptation of websites to the Czech market. This contrasts with Okazaki's (2005) findings regarding American MNCs' website strategy in the UK, France, Germany, and Spain, where clearly localized websites have been created in the existing EU member states. This finding is consistent with the frequency of brand website functions: the Czech sites use far fewer brand website functions with highly standardized textual and visual components.

It is clear that American MNCs consider the EU a single market, and one that is strategically dissimilar to their home market. If we observe only the websites created in the "older" member states, there seems to exist a "regionalization" strategy across Europe, in that the level of similarity ratings among the European samples was relatively uniform. This may be due to the close geographical proximity of the three countries, which would, logically, provide more opportunities for personal interaction and the accumulation of greater knowledge. However, in the case of the Czech Republic, website adaptation has not yet advanced, probably due to many unknown factors: in particular, specific information regarding local consumers' tastes and preferences.

To make our findings more objective, we should recognize a few limitations. First, the current study examined only one country that has recently joined the European Union. Future research should expand this study into other new EU member states, especially Poland and Hungary, because these two countries, along with the Czech Republic, are the most economically developed regions. Because of the extreme scarcity of research related to these countries, any such extension will contribute significantly to the literature. Second, while content analysis could provide useful information regarding the manifest content, the findings should be treated with caution. The findings by no means explain practitioners' "true" intentions in website communication strategy. In this regard, it will be interesting to extend this study in the future, by conducting a questionnaire survey of advertisers and marketers who are actually responsible for the new EU member states.

LIMITATIONS

While this study makes significant contributions to the global information management literature, some important limitations must also be recognized. First, content analysis is, by definition, an observational method that examines only manifest content. Our findings have little or nothing to do with marketers' "true" intentions on global website positioning. Second, our unit of analysis was limited to the menu and submenu of the homepages. However, it is possible that a more localized strategy might have been observed in further links. Finally, we examined only one of the new EU member states, thus, any generalization of our findings should be treated with caution.

FUTURE RESEARCH DIRECTIONS

First, future extensions should examine websites created for the other new EU member states, such as Poland, Hungary, Latvia, Lithuania, and Malta. Information technology management for website positioning in these countries is virtually unknown, and analyzing brands' websites positioning in these countries should help us to draw more generalisable implications. In particular, researchers are planning to examine Polish and Hungarian websites in the next stage because, in these countries, the total online as well as offline advertising spending is substantial, in comparison with the other new EU member sates.

Second, in furthering our explorations, content analysis methodology should be improved. Specifically, we need to examine the level of standardization or localization at deeper levels of websites. While this study scrutinized the first level of websites or homepages, some may claim that much information was lost by ignoring the second and third levels of websites. For example, the lack of direct online transactions need not necessarily mean that the website does not have a link to the online shopping sites of different companies. This was the case for consumer electronics, in that computer or office machine products are sold on "general" e-commerce (or even auction) sites. More specific coding instructions should be established, to enable the coders to improve their analysis with a higher level of inter-coder reliability.

Third, we also should conduct a survey that targets foreign subsidiaries' managers. It will be interesting to compare the findings of this paper with the managers' perceptions. In particular, several questions appear of special interest. For example, are their websites created or controlled locally or globally? What level of control do senior executives of foreign subsidiaries actually have of their electronic commerce planning and executions?

Finally, in an attempt to capture a clearer picture of global website positioning in multiple markets, more collaboration will be needed by researchers in information systems management and other disciplines: in particular, marketing management. Needless to say, a higher level of international cooperation is necessary to conduct more objective and reliable data collection in multiple markets.

REFERENCES

Agora (2005). Advertising market.

Agrawal, M. (1995). Review of a 40-year debate in international advertising. *International Marketing Review*, *12*(1), 26–48. doi:10.1108/02651339510080089

ARBOmedia. (2005a). Standardní reklamní rok přinese médiím 17,8 miliard.

ARBOmedia. (2005b). Standardní reklamní rok přinese médiím 17,8 miliard".

Brislin, R. W. (1980). Translation and Content Analysis of Oral and Written Material. In H. C. Triandis and Berry, J. W. (eds.), *Handbook of Cross-cultural Psychology* (Vol. 2, pp. 389-444), Boston: Allyn and Bacon.

Budapest business journal (2003). Web-based advertising making ground. September 16, 2003,

Budapest business journal (2004). Online advertising boom. August 18, 2004,

BusinessWeek (2002). The 100 Top Brands. August 5, 95-99.

Czech, O. M. D. (2005). Odhady reklamních výdajů.

Czech Publishers Association. (2006). Internetová reklama v roce 2005 přesáhla 1 miliardu Kč. Press release,

Czech Statistical Office (2006), *The survey on ICT usage in households and by individuals in the Czech Republic in 2006* (in Czech).

Donthu, N., & Garcia, A. (1999). The Internet Shopper. *Journal of Advertising Research*, *39*(5), 52–58.

Dou, W., Nielsen, U. O., & Tan, C. M. (2002). Using corporate websites for exporting marketing. *Journal of Advertising Research*, *42*(5), 105–115.

Economist Intelligence Unit (2006), *The 2006 e-readiness rankings*.

Elinder, E. (1961). How International Can Advertising Be?" in S. W. Dunn (ed.), *International Handbook of Advertising*, NY: McGraw-Hill, 59-71.

Eurostat (2005), *Europe in figures: Eurostat yearbook 2005*.

Eurostat (2006), *Community survey on ICT usage in households and by individuals*.

Factum, T. N. S. (2004). Firemní weby a marketing.

Factum, T. N. S. (2005). Češi a reklama v roce 2004.

Forrester (2002), *Forrester's Global eCommerce Predictions For 2004*.

GfK. (2006). Increasingly more kids use the Internet. One in three Polish Internet users willing to buy music on the Internet. Press release,

Ghose, S., & Dou, W. (1998). Interactive Functions and Their Impacts on the Appeal of Internet Presence Sites. *Journal of Advertising Research, 38*(2), 29–43.

Harris, G. (1994). International Advertising Standardization: What Do the Multinationals Actually Standardize? *Journal of International Marketing, 2*(4), 13–30.

Hong, J. W., Muderrisoglu, A., & Zinkhan, G. M. (1987). Cultural differences and advertising expression: a comparative content analysis of Japanese and U.S. magazine advertising. *Journal of Advertising, 16*(1), 55–62, 68.

Internet Software Consortium. (2001), *Distribution of Top-Level Domain Names by Host Count, Jul 2002.*

Jain, S. C. (1989). Standardization of International Marketing Strategy: Some Research Hypotheses. *Journal of Marketing, 53*(January), 70–79. doi:10.2307/1251525

Ju-Pak, K. H. (1999). Content dimensions of Web advertising: a cross-national comparison. *International Journal of Advertising, 18*(2), 207–231.

Kanso, A., & Nelson, R. A. (2002). Advertising Localization Overshadows Standardization. *Journal of Advertising Research, 42*(1), 79–89.

Kolbe, R. H., & Burnett, M. S. (1991). Content-Analysis Research: An Examination of Applications with Directives for Improving Research Reliability and Objectivity . *The Journal of Consumer Research, 18*(September), 243–250. doi:10.1086/209256

Koudelova, R., & Whitelock, J. (2001). A cross-cultural analysis of television advertising in the UK and the Czech Republic. *International Marketing Review, 18*(3), 286–300. doi:10.1108/02651330110695611

Leong, E. K. F., Huang, X., & Stanners, P. J. (1998). Comparing the Effectiveness of the Web site with Traditional Media. *Journal of Advertising Research, 38*(5), 44–51.

Levitt, T. (1983). The Globalization of Market. *Harvard Business Review, 61*(May/June), 92–102.

Mackay, S. (2004). Parliament Approves New Government. *Executive Perspectives: Poland, Price Waterhouse Coopers.*

Madden, C. S., Caballero, M. J., & Matsukubo, S. (1986). Analysis of information content in U.S. and Japanese magazine advertising. *Journal of Advertising, 15*(3), 38–45.

McMillan, S. J. (2000). The Microscope and The Moving Target: The Challenge of Applying Content Analysis to The World Wide Web. *Journalism & Mass Communication Quarterly, 77*(1), 80–98.

Mueller, B. (1991). An analysis of information content in standardized vs. specialized multinational advertisements. *Journal of International Business Studies*, First Quarter, 23-39.

OBP. (2001). Advertising in Poland.

Oh, K. W., Cho, C. H., & Leckenby, J. D. (1999). A Comparative Analysis of Korean and U.S. Web Advertising. *Proceedings of the 1999 Conference of the American Academy of Advertising*, Gainesville: University of Florida, 73-77.

Okazaki, S. (2005). Searching the Web for global brands: How American brands standardise their websites in Europe. *European Journal of Marketing, 39*(1/2), 87–109. doi:10.1108/03090560510572034

Okazaki, S., & Alonso, J. (2002). A content analysis of Web communication strategies: Cross-cultural research framework and pre-testing. *Internet Research: Electronic Networking . Applications and Policy, 12*(5), 380–390.

Onkvisit, S., & Shaw, J. J. (1987). Standardized International Advertising: A Review and Critical Evaluation of the Theoretical and Empirical Evidence. *The Columbia Journal of World Business, 22*(Fall), 43–55.

Optimedia, Z. (2004). Poland's advertising market in 2004.

Perreault, W. D., & Leigh, L. E. (1989). Reliability of nominal data based on qualitative judgments. *JMR, Journal of Marketing Research, 26*(May), 135–148. doi:10.2307/3172601

Philport, J. C., & Arbittier, J. (1997). Advertising: Brand communications styles in established media and the Internet. *Journal of Advertising Research, 37*(2), 68–76.

Quelch, J. A., & Klein, L. R. (1996). The Internet and International Marketing. *Sloan Management Review, 38*(Spring), 60–75.

Roberts, M. S., & Ko, H. (2001). Global Interactive Advertising: Defining What We Mean and Using What We Have Learned. *Journal of Interactive Advertising,* 1 (2),

Root, F. R. (1994), *Entry Strategies for International Markets.* Heath, Washington DC: Lexington.

Sheram, K., & Soubbotina, T. P. (2000), *Beyond Economic Growth: Meeting the Challenges of Global Development,* Washington D.C.: World Bank. Taylor, Charles R., P. Greg Bonner and Michael Dolezal (2002). Advertising in the Czech Republic: Czech perceptions of effective advertising and advertising clutter. In Charles R. Taylor (ed.), *New direction in International Advertising Research* (Vol 12, pp. 137-149), San Diego, CA: Elsevier.

Synodinos, N., Keown, C., & Jacobs, L. (1989). Transitional Advertising Practices: A Survey of Leading Brand Advertisers. *Journal of Advertising Research, 29*(2), 43–50.

Szymanski, D. M., Bharadwaj, S. G., & Varadarajan, P. R. (1993). Standardization versus Adaptation of International Marketing Strategy: An Empirical Investigation. *Journal of Marketing, 57*(October), 1–17.

Taylor, C. R., & Johnson, C. M. (2002). Standardized vs. specialized international advertising campaigns: What we have learned from academic research in the 1990s. *New Directions in International Advertising Research, 12,* 45–66. doi:10.1016/S1474-7979(02)12019-9

Unie vydavatelů (2005). Internetová reklama v roce 2004 dosáhla 760 milionů Kč.

van REPEN, Erica, Rik Pieters, Jana Fidrmucova and Peter Roosenboom. (2000). The Information Content of Magazine Advertising in Market and Transition Economies. *Journal of Consumer Policy, 23,* 257–283. doi:10.1023/A:1007138219753

West, D. C., & Paliwoda, S. J. (1996). Advertising adoption in a developing market economy: The case of Poland. *International Marketing Review, 13*(4), 82–101. doi:10.1108/02651339610127266

World Advertising Resource Center (WARC) (2004). *European Marketing Pocket Book.*

Zandpour, F., Campos, V., Catalano, J., Chang, C., Cho, Y. D., & Hoobyar, R. (1994). Global Reach and Local Touch: Achieving Cultural Fitness in TV Advertising. *Journal of Advertising Research, 34*(5), 35–63.

ADDITIONAL READING

Batra, R., Myers, J. G., & Aaker, D. A. (1996). *Advertising Management,* Prentice Hall, Englewood Cliffs, NJ.

De Mooij, M. (1998). *Global marketing and advertising: Understanding cultural paradox.* Sage Publications, Thousand Oaks, CA.

Duncan, T., & Ramaprasad, J. (1995). Standardized multinational advertising: The influencing factors. *Journal of Advertising, 24*(3), 55–67.

Ghose, S., & Dou, W. (1998). Interactive functions and their impacts on the appeal of Internet presence sites. *Journal of Advertising Research, 38*(3), 29–43.

Ha, L., & James, E. L. (1998). Interactivity reexamined: A baseline analysis of early business Web sites. *Journal of Broadcasting & Electronic Media, 42*(4), 457–469.

Hwang, J. S., McMillan, S. J., & Lee, G. (2003). Corporate Web sites as advertising: An analysis of function, audience, and message strategy. *Journal of Interactive Advertising, 3*(2).

Jain, S. (1989). Standardization of international marketing strategy: Some research hypotheses. *Journal of Marketing, 53*(1), 70–79. doi:10.2307/1251525

Krippendorff, K. (1980). *Content analysis: An introduction to its methodology.* Sage Publications, Newbury Park, CA.

Laroche, M., Kirpalani, V. H., Pens, F., & Zhou, L. (2001). A model of advertising standardization in multinational corporations. *Journal of International Business Studies, 32*(2), 250–265. doi:10.1057/palgrave.jibs.8490951

Lynch, P. D., Kent, R. J., & Srinivasan, S. S. (2001). The global Internet shopper: Evidence from shopping tasks in twelve countries. *Journal of Advertising Research, 41*(3), 15–22.

Okazaki, S. (2004). Do multinationals standardise or localise? The cross-cultural dimensionality of product-based Web sites. *Internet Research: Electronic Networking . Applications and Policy, 14*(1), 81–94.

Okazaki, S., & Alonso, J. (2003). Right messages at the right site: on-line creative strategies by Japanese multinational corporations. *Journal of Marketing Communications, 9*(4), 221–239. doi:10.1080/1352726032000129908

Okazaki, S., & Alonso, J. (2003). Beyond the Net: Cultural Values Reflected in Japanese Multinationals' Web Communication Strategies. *Journal of International Consumer Marketing, 16*(1), 47–70. doi:10.1300/J046v16n01_04

Tharp, M., & Jeong, J. (2001). Executive insights: The global network communications agency. *Journal of International Marketing, 9*(4), 111–131. doi:10.1509/jimk.9.4.111.19939

Warden, C. A., Lai, M., & Wu, W. Y. (2003). How world-wide is marketing communication on the World Wide Web? *Journal of Advertising Research, 43*(5), 72–84.

This work was previously published in Encyclopedia of Data Warehousing and Mining, edited by J. Wang, pp. 885-890, copyright 2005 by Information Science Reference (an imprint of IGI Global).

Chapter 5.4

WEB 2.0, Social Marketing Strategies and Distribution Channels for City Destinations:
Enhancing the Participatory Role of Travelers and Exploiting their Collective Intelligence

Marianna Sigala
University of the Aegean, Greece

ABSTRACT

During the last decades, the use of Web 2.0 applications for the generation, dissemination, and sharing of user-generated content (UGC) and the creation of new value added services are enormous. Web 2.0 tools have tremendously changed the way people search, find, read, gather, share, develop, and consume information, as well as on the way people communicate with each other and collaboratively create new knowledge. UGC and Web 2.0 are also having a tremendous impact not only on the behaviour and decision-making of Internet users, but also on the e-business model that organizations need to develop and/or adapt in order to conduct business on the Internet. Organizations responsible to market and promote cities on the Internet are not an exception from these developments. This chapter aims to inform city tourism organizations responsible for the development of city portals about (a) the use of the major Web 2.0 tools in tourism and their impact on the tourism demand and supply; and (b) the ways and practices for integrating the use of Web 2.0 into their e-business model and e-marketing practices.

INTRODUCTION

During the last years, the number and use of numerous Web 2.0 tools, whereby Internet users produce, read and share multimedia content (User Generated Content, UGC), is mushrooming (eMarketer, 2007a). It is estimated (eMarketer, 2007b) that 75.2 million USA Internet users currently use UGC, and this is expected to increase to 101 million by 2011. eMarketer (2007c) also found that over 25 million USA adults regularly share advice on products or services online.

DOI: 10.4018/978-1-60566-134-6.ch011

The Web 2.0 technologies and applications (e.g. tags, RSS, blogs, wikis, podcasts, etc.) are considered as the *tools of mass collaboration*, since they empower Internet users to collaboratively produce, consume and distribute information and knowledge. In other words, Web 2.0 tools do nothing more than realizing and exploiting the full potential of the genuine concept and role of the Internet (i.e. the network of the networks that is created and exists for its users). This has tremendously changed the way people search, find, read, gather, share, develop and consume information, as well as on the way people communicate with each other and collaboratively create new knowledge (Sigala, 2008). UGC and Web 2.0 technologies are also having a tremendous impact not only on the behavior and decision-making of Internet users, but also on the e-business model that organizations need to develop and/or adapt in order to conduct business on the Internet (Bughin, 2007).

The tourism industry is not an exception from such developments. On the contrary, as information is the lifeblood of tourism, the use and diffusion of Web 2.0 technologies have a substantial impact of both tourism demand and supply. Indeed, more than ¼ of Internet users have used a weblog to review information about a destination or travel supplier in the last 12 months (Harteveldt, Johnson, Epps & Tesch, 2006), many new Web 2.0 enabled tourism cyber-intermediaries have risen challenging the e-business model of existing online tourism suppliers and intermediaries who in turn need to transform their e-business model and e-marketing practices in order to survive (Adam, Cobos & Liu, 2007). As the Internet plays an important role for the e-marketing of city destinations (Sigala, 2003; Yuan, Gretzel, & Fesenmaier, 2006), Web 2.0 tools and applications also create both threats and opportunities for organizations developing and maintaining destination management systems and portals. In this vein, this chapter aims to inform city tourism organizations responsible for the development of city portals about: a) the use of the major Web 2.0 tools in tourism and their

impact on tourism demand and supply; and b) the ways and practices for integrating the use of Web 2.0 into their e-business model and e-marketing practices.

WEB 2.0 TOOLS IN TOURISM: USE, IMPACT AND APPLICATIONS IN CITY MARKETING

RSS (Really Simple Syndication)

Definition, Features and Use

RSS allow users to subscribe to a webpage for receiving new content, e.g. subscribe to receive online distributions of news, blogs, podcasts etc, and so, RSS allows the creation of links and interactive communication amongst other Web 2.0 applications and users. This is done either through a news aggregator (similar to an email inbox) or a news reader (a web-based environment) (Winer, 2005). By doing so, one does not have to visit each individual website that he/she is interesting to read any new information, but rather the RSS feeds all new updated information to the users' RSS reader. RSS readers enable Internet users to gather and read all new information that is customized to the user's profile within one consolidated message. Many free RSS exist on the Internet, e.g. FeedDemon, NewsGator, Rojo, software on the website of Google™, MyYahoo®, etc.

RSS allows new communication and interaction modes with information (Figure 1) (Farmer, 2004). In e-mail, the control of the communication channel is held entirely by the instigator of the communication. Consequently, e-mail communication is characterized at times by flame wars, antisocial behavior and feelings of intrusion by the participants, while the information artifact is transitory, unfixed and not archived except in individual instances. In discussion boards, information artifacts are fixed, frequently archived and can be interacted with through threading and comments,

Figure 1. Communication types

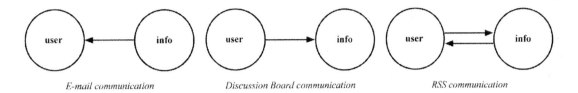

but for accessing information, the user must deliberately visit a dedicated online area. In contrast, in RSS, both the communicator and the reader of information have control of the communication process, i.e. the former sends information only to those that users have selected to aggregate the RSS feed, while the later select from where and how (e.g. summaries, titles, or full entries) to receive communication. Further, as most RSS aggregators are either integrated with or stand-alone desktop/web applications, readers need only to check the aggregator for new items.

Impact on Tourism Demand

RSS feeders have a tremendous impact on the way consumers search and read information nowadays. RSS has the following benefits for users:

- saves a lot of time spent on information searching;
- provides users with consolidated personalized information;
- is less obstructive and more personalized to users' interests than other Internet based communication, and so, RSS entice subscribers to visit the related websites, thus helping in building website traffic and visitation;
- RSS boosts viral marketing and online word-of-mouth as users tend to forward items in RSS feeds to their friends, family and co-workers, much like the 'forward this message' feature in eNewsletters.

Business Applications for City Marketing

As RSS is an information distribution technology that is characterized as a demand pull rather than a supply push model, many tourism destination organizations have adopted and incorporated RSS feeds in their websites in order to communicate with their potential and current travelers in a less disrupted and personal way. Some examples of RSS include:

- Keep a communication with their travelers such as sending them Newsletters and/or updates of the programme of cultural events organized in the city.
- RSS helps organizations to enhance their Search Engine Optimization by creating inbound links to a company's website and by informing search engines whenever new content is uploaded on a website, so that they can index it.
- RSS is used for syndicating content to other Websites expanding the original website's readership and reach.

For example, the destination marketing organization of Las Vegas has included an RSS on its website (visitlasvegas.com), whereby users can subscribe to feeds that automatically notify them of current travel specials. Almost all of the information (e.g. events' news, weather updates, special offers, etc.) on the official city website of Dublin created by the city tourism board (visitdublin.com) is available to any traveler and/or other website through RSS. RSS are offered for free for anyone for reading and/or enriching his/her own web site, provided that the latter follows the proper format, terms and conditions and attribution, e.g. attribution such as *"Content provided by Dublin Tourism"*. In such a way, visitdublin.com aims to enhance readership of its content, continuous personal communication with its customers, viral marketing, and search engine optimization through content syndication and incoming links.

Blogs (or Weblogs)

Definition, Features and Use

Weblogs began as personal writing spaces that store and update regularly multimedia content (in reverse chronological order) and links of interest to the author. Thus, blogs are used for recording its author's journey and sharing it with others by using links, RSS, trackbacks, comments, taglines, archives, permanent links, blogrolls, etc. (Blood, 2000). Weblogs are defined as a "… site consists of dated entries" (Blood, 2000), whereby entries are episodic or conversational in a diary or "story telling" format. Motivated by different reasons (Forrester Research, 2006), such as documenting one's life, providing commentary and opinions, expressing deeply felt emotions, articulating ideas through writing, and forming and maintaining community forum, weblogs (or blogs) are a *"new form of mainstream personal communication"* (Rosenbloom, 2004, p. 31) for millions of people to publish and exchange knowledge/information, and to establish networks or build relationships in the world of all blogs. Indeed, blogging tools enabling between-blog interactivity are building up the "blogosphere" whereby social networks among bloggers are created. Du and Wagner (2006) identified the following characteristics of blogs:

- **Personalized:** blogs are designed for individual use and their style is personal and informal. Blogger.com offers a "team

blog" collaborative feature enabling also multi-person weblog.
- **Web-based:** blogs are easy to access and frequently maintain by simply using a web browser.
- **Community-supported:** Weblogs can link to other weblogs and websites (e.g. photos, videos, web-texts), enabling the synthesis and linkage of ideas from different users, and so, stimulating meta-knowledge, i.e. the generation of new knowledge through sharing.
- **Automated:** Blogging tools are easy to create and maintain without the need of HTML programming skills and knowledge; so, bloggers can solely concentrate on the content.

Du & Wagner (2006) also identified 3 types of blogging tools and features: type I features of blogging (such as text, diary, hyperlinks, user friendly editor) provide easy-to-use and learn tools for editing, presentation, publishing and interlinking of content. Such blogs are heavily used by those that solely seek a channel of self-expression. Type II blogging tools (such as Indexed archive, search, "permalink": a permanent URL for each weblog entry enabling referencing of specific past entries like other web-source. "Trackback": a reverse hyperlink tracking the referrer weblogs "making these formally invisible connections visible", categorisation & syndication) are used by bloggers who wish to easily share rich media (e.g. videos, pictures etc), to have a sophisticated content management system and to enable between-blog commenting or hyper linking, e.g. through "permalink" or trackback (Blood, 2000). Nowadays, the emerging Type III of blogging tools provide improved content distribution and between-blog connectivity (e.g. "pingback", alert of other bloggers' comments or new posts), as well as integrated applications for further enhancing social networking and community building such as the following examples:

- Workflow or project management (e.g. Lycos Circles workflow for a party, from invitation to management of responses and to travel directions),
- Polls, Intrasite messaging (e.g. ModBlog allows users to track friends' newest entries, or to know who are the most "recent visitors"),
- Web invitation, picture/music sharing (e.g. MSN Space picture/music sharing, and remote posting of updates via email or mobile devices).

Impact on Tourism Demand

Numerous examples of general and-or (content or user) specific blogs have been created in the tourism industry, such as tripadvisor.com, hotelchatter. com, bugbitten.com, placeblogger.com, realtravel. com, travelpod.com, igougo.com, gazetters.com (a B2B blog for travel agents). Many travelers and tourists also develop and maintain their own blogs for sharing their travel experiences with others and distributing their feedback (reviews) of travel suppliers for achieving fun, social recognition, prestige and-or self-expression. Due to the unbiased information shared in blogs based on first-hand authentic travel experiences, many travelers tend to use and trust blogs' information for searching for travel information, tips and selecting travel suppliers and destinations. Blogs have the power of the impartial information and the electronic word-of-mouth that is diffusing online like a virus. Hence, blogs are becoming a very important information source for international travelers for getting travel advice and suggestions. Moreover, when reading others' travel experiences through weblogs, this also creates to the reader the willingness to travel and visit the same destination or suppliers. Indeed, research has shown that UGC at blogs has a similar AIDA effect to users as paid advertisements have. The latter is because blog's content can (Lin & Huang, 2006): 1) **A**ttract the attention, eyeballs of other

Internet users and increase traffic on a website, 2) create **I**nterest to users who can now seek more and additional information, 3) develop someone's **D**esire to also visit a destination and/or buy the product and 4) foster an **A**ction (e.g. book a hotel or organize a trip to a destination). Of course, it should be noted that the power of blogs can also be negative, i.e. spread a bad experience of a tourist to million of online Internet users. Therefore, it is very important that tourism companies authorize a public relations staff as the responsible representative of the company to first scan and read blogs' content and then respond to formally any positive and negative users' comments. Guidelines and corporate policies for responding to UGC should also be established. Nowadays, many blogs take the form and are presented in a video format (Vlog, video blog). The first travel website to implement vlogs exclusively is endlesseurope. com. Due to the multimedia features of video content and the intangible nature of the tourism product, it is argued that vlogs are going to have a much greater impact and influence on travelers' decision making and evaluation of alternative tourism products and suppliers.

Business Applications for City Marketing

Blogs generate and distribute a plethora of UGC related to travelers' experiences, suppliers' and destination reviews, travel tips and advices. City destination management organizations can exploit and use such content for:

- monitoring and influencing electronic word-of-mouth;
- conducting an easy, free, timely and reliable market research about travelers' preferences, feedback and profile;
- communicating with current and prospective travelers in a very personal and informal way;

- gathering travelers' feedback and responding to customers' complaints;
- enhancing search engine optimization: blogs are becoming very important tools affecting information search since their links, content and popularity can dictate the position of a company on a search engine search.

There are many search engines that one can use for identifying and locating weblogs. The most popular one is technorati.com, which also provides statistics about the online activity of weblogs, e.g. about the popularity of a blog and its potential influence on search engines results.

Apart from exploiting others' blogs, many tourism suppliers and destination management organizations have also adopted a pro-active strategy by creating and incorporating blogs on their own websites. For example, Marriott has created its own blog on its website (www.blogs.marriott.com), while Starwood has created a blog to communicate with its Preferred Guests and enhance their loyalty through the website www.thelobby.com. Company initiated and moderated blogs can offer the following benefits: solicit and gather feedback from customers; conduct free online market research; become recognized as an expert on a specific topic; communicate and update your customers with latest news; and use others' customers' suggestions for helping customers select and evaluate products such as what amazon.com is doing by allowing users to upload books' reviews on its website. For example, Eurostar has initiated a blog (www.voiceofacity.com) whereby it has commissioned local Parisians to post blogs for creating a travelers' guidebook with a truly ground-roots feel. The destination organization of the city of Los Angeles has created a blog supporting the sharing of bloggers' experiences and insights on their adventures of the diversity of Los Angeles' arts and culture (http://blog.experiencela.com/). The fully Web 2.0 enabled official portal of Holland features a blog capability (i.e.

the triplog) enabling Dutch travelers and locals to share and post the experiences they lived in Holland (http://us.holland.com/blog.php?sf=e.pagerank&so=DESC&sel=popular). In this vein, blogs are becoming a useful tool for enabling local communities to get more involved in destination marketing, communicate and blur with tourists. As a result, blogs and web 2.0 tools can support and foster community participation in city tourism development and marketing practices. Community participation can ensure a better blend between locals and tourists reducing any inter-cultural conflicts, creating social relations and respect and understanding amongst different cultures as well as enabling multi-stakeholder understanding and communication in tourism decision making and activities.

Social Networking– Collaborative Networking

Definition, Features and Use

Social networking websites enable users to create their profile and invite others with similar profile to take part in their online community. The most popular websites such as myspace.com and bebo.com reflect the willingness of Internet users to transform websites as a gathering place of people with similar profiles.

Impact on Tourism Demand

Many social networking websites have been created in the tourism industry allowing travelers and prospective travelers to network with one another based on shared interests or attributes, such as tripmates.com, gusto.com, triporama.com, triphub.com, traveltogether.com and wayn.com. Travelers log into websites and create a personal profile detailing their travel experience and interests, then network with others o share travel advice and stories, and even plan trips together. Hence, social networking websites have a tremendous impact on how tourists nowadays create, organize and consume tourism experiences. Many tourists nowadays prefer to have the reassurance of other users sharing similar profile with them that the trip, the travel company, destination and/or the itinerary that they have scheduled is a good one and it matches their preferences and tastes. Many tourists also wish to use the Internet for collaboratively organizing a group trip with their friends. Websites such as tripup.com, traveltogether.com and travelpost.com enable tourists to create an itinerary, e-mail and share it online with others, who in turn can edit, modify and enhance it, post it back to others for further comments and / or invite and read other travelers' comments and advices on the trip they organized in order to finally achieve a consensus and proceed to a group booking.

Business Applications for City Marketing

Since sharing travel experiences in a social website can significantly inspire travel and boosts one's willingness to visit a destination or supplier, several tourism websites are incorporating social networking tools in their e-business models. For example, existing cyberintermediaries, such as Yahoo!® Trip Planner has adopted a collaborative trip organizing and booking tools. The official website of the city of Philadelphia has also features a collaborative trip planning tool (www. planit.pcvb.org), that potential travelers can use for organizing their itinerary in Philadelphia with friends as well as soliciting feedback and comments from other travelers and locals.

Lufthansa created and operates its own social networking website, named as Jetfriends, for enabling its young flyers to share flight experiences and indoctrinate them into the Lufthansa brand and frequent flyers' club (http://www.jetfriends. com/jetfriends/kids/). Sheraton also re-organized and re-designed its website (which is nowadays titled as the Sheraton Belong Neighborhood), whereby Sheraton's guests can subscribe to the website, upload their experiences, stories, pictures, videos and comments for sharing them with other website visitors and users. The social networking of Sheraton's website enables potential travelers to organize and book their holiday and hotel experience at any Sheraton property that matches their profile and preferences by reading and reflecting on the comments and first-hand experiences written by previous Sheraton customers. The impact of social networking features for persuading potential travelers to select a particular hotel and/or destination is very powerful, because through social networking websites, travelers can search website content based on keywords and stories contributed by other travelers that may be more relevant and make more sense to them than keywords and experiences being created and pushed by the website developers themselves. For example, on Sheraton's website one can search an hotel experience based on the comments and tags contributed by a previous guests referring to *"nice walking in beaches nearby Sheraton hotels"* or *"relaxing family holidays in Sheraton properties"* rather than using the Sheraton's search engine to find hotel based on its location, facilities etc.

Nowadays, many city destination organizations have also incorporated social networking features into their e-business model and strategy in order to further enhance their communication with customers and take benefit of the electronic word-of-mouth that they can create. For example, the official website of Los Angeles invites any cultural and art organization-institution to become a partner with experiencela.com in order to share and distribute related content on their website. Experiencela.com has also created a cooperation e-business strategy with the social networking websites clickr.com and myspace.com. Specifically, the destination management organization of LA created a special webpage for LA on flickr.com (http://www.flickr.com/groups/21164279@N00/pool/) and myspace.com (http://www.myspace.com/experiencela) in order to enable the users of the formers that are also funs and travelers of LA to share personal photographs, comments and stories about LA. The city of LA has realized that such UGC can crucially drive traffic to their website, boost their search engine optimization strategy, instil travelers' desire to visit LA and use customer intelligence for providing reliable and timely advice and suggestions for trips to potential travelers to LA.

Tagging (Social Search and Tag clouds)

Definition, Features and Use

Tagging represents a new way for categorizing information. Users tag a piece of content (e.g. an audio, a picture, a word) with a meaning (a word or phrase) and then this information is categorized in categories based on this meaning. Community tagging is a bottom-up, grass-roots phenomenon, in which users classify resources with searchable keywords. The tags are free-form labels chosen by the user, not selected from a controlled vocabulary. Tagging is also known as consumer-generated taxonomy. Forrester (2006) defines tagging as 'the act of categorizing and retrieving Web content using open-ended labels called tags'. Tagging provides customer value, because it allows them to assign their own word or words to mark products and content online in order to categorize content that they find relevant, i.e. such as what bookmarking allows users to do. Words that users choose for categorizing website and content then become a navigation shortcut that a person can use to browse and search content throughout that site.

Tagging is used not only for saving and sorting a user's content but also for sharing content with others. Websites with tagging capabilities can also allow users to share their personal tags and navigation ways with other users. Moreover, some tag enabled websites enable users not only to share their tag navigations, but also their profile. In this way, users can see who has tagged something, and try to search and find information based on

the search behavior of users with similar profiles and mental maps with them (personalized social searching). In this vein, tagging has a great effect on how search engines identify and present information results in keyword searches to users.

Flickr.com represents the first wide-spread of tags, whereby users can add their own tags to any photo they wish to share, aggregate pictures into photosets, create public or private groups, search photos by tags and easily add flickr-stored photos to a blog. Nowadays, there are numerous websites enabling tagging and searching based on tags, e.g. del.icio.us, a bookmarking service, Technorati, a blog cataloging site, and digg, a gathering place for tech fans. These sites create clickable "tag clouds" for resources, groupings of tags arranged alphabetically, with the most used or popular keywords shown in a larger font. In this way, these websites present other websites that users think are important or relevant to them. Many such sites make use of RSS to notify interested users of changes and new developments, e.g. in flickr.com, RSS feeds can be attached to individual tags, or to photos and discussions. In addition to RSS, flickr.com and other social networking sites typically offer functions such as search (for users and tags), comments (and comment trails), and APIs (application program interfaces) for posting to or from the tools, that can be used in combination with blogs. An interesting use of RSS that is combined with tagging is the Flashcard exchange, where, one can view or subscribe to all flashcards posted for learning Spanish (or other languages).

Although the tagging process is by no means simply technical—a way of categorizing resources—it has a strong social dimension as users of the website find common interests and create on-line communities. It represents another example of the fuzziness separating consumers and creators on the Web. A contribution to a tagging site, seen by other users, may cause additional tags or comments to be added, automatically building and updating and thus ultimately defining a resource. Instead of one person making a judgment about a blog entry, photo, or other resource, a consensual classification is created. In effect, a text or object identifies itself over time. This creation of "folksonomies" (as the user defines how to sort information which in turn defines how others search and find information) can be seen as a democratic implementation of the Semantic Web. Thus, for some, tagging helps and boosts the creation of the semantic web (Web 3.0), whereby web content and search is directly related to its meaning for the users.

Impact on Tourism Demand

Several websites offer the capability for users to sort, share and categories travel related content based on tagging, e.g. flickr.com (for pictures sorting and sharing), travbuddy.com (for travel experiences sharing), travelistic.com (for tagging video content). However, although more and more users are using collaborative tools for identifying and sorting travel content, tagging is still an emerging technology: only 5% of USA online leisure travelers—slightly more than 5 million of the 114 million USA adults who travel for leisure and go online regularly—tag Web pages or other content on sites like del.icio.us or Flickr™ (Epps, 2007). Moreover, the social capabilities of tagging for community building and social collaboratively construction of concepts' meaning and of travel experiences could have numerous innovative applications in tourism as well. For examples, travelers may be enabled and offered the opportunity to build structural tags in a text using XML for creating word groups or simply finding appropriate keywords to describe a travel experience. This would offer additional options to Internet users to collaboratively develop travel itineraries and search of travel information with others sharing a similar profile with them.

Business Applications for City Marketing

Because of the power of the folsconomy to provide enhanced user-value and influence the results/page ranking of search engines' search, many tourism firms nowadays include and consider tagging when designing their websites and e-business strategy. For example, Thomson's website provides an affiliate link to deli.ci.ous.com (http://www.thomson.co.uk/), so that its users can tag and sort its website content through this technology.

However, tourism firms may adopt different strategies regarding the way they use and incorporate tagging into their websites (Epps et al., 2007). For example, Triporama.com has launched its tagging system, titled "Triporama Bookmarks", which allows its website users to download a free software in their PC for tagging content in their own words from anywhere on the Web to their Triporama group trip plan, which they can then share with their travel companions. Such a solution provides differentiation customer value for Triporama, because as travelers visit many different Websites while planning a trip, Triporama's bookmarking tool lets travelers collect, label, and share the content they have found on the Web with other members of their group. Users also have the option to make their tags publicly available, while Triporama also aims to edit and curate these public tags into features like "top 10" lists to give other users ideas for planning their own group trips. When redesigning its website, Sheraton introduced its "Vacation Ideas" feature whereby guests are invited to write stories about their hotel stay, users give Sheraton their consent for publishing their stories online and the entire story becomes a tag. A tag cloud is created, titled the "Buzz Barometer", whereby word occurring most frequently in stories appear in bigger fonts, while based on the number of stories shared containing different words a "Vacation Ideas page" is created (http://www.starwoodhotels.com/sheraton/index.html). For example, by clicking on the "Beach" guide brings up the five hotels whose stories mention "beach" most frequently (weighted by the number of stories relative to the size of the property). By making storytelling the method by which the tags are created, Sheraton has made tagging so friendly and easy for its guests that they do not even know that they are tagging content. Sheraton benefits from this tagging strategy because:

- It helps first time website users: Vacation Ideas gives travelers, not knowing where they want to go and/or not familiar with the Sheraton brand, a more creative, user friendly and understandable way to search and book hotels than the customary destination-based and company pushed search.
- It helps Sheraton to build long lasting relations with its guests by maintaining a close relationship with the travelers before, during and after the trip. This is because the website provides guests having stayed at a Sheraton's hotel to return to the Sheraton's website in order to contribute, solicit or read other travelers' stories.
- It improves organizational learning, since Sheraton gets insights into Sheraton's hotel properties and customers' experiences. Instead of conducting expensive and time consuming research, Sheraton uses tagging as a simple and reliable way for gathering customer feedback and intelligence about its products and services. Based on the customer knowledge that is gained, operation managers can improve organizational processes, while marketers get to know what and how customers think and talk about the brand, in order to better position the Sheraton brand in the market and enhance the guest experience at the hotels in ways that reinforce guests' perspective of the Sheraton brand.

Yahoo!® Travel introduced new tagging features into its Yahoo!® TripPlanner that enable users to tag their own or others' Trip Plans with suggested or custom tags, which are later analyzed and used by Yahoo! for identifying and feeding recommendations on the Yahoo! Travel home. Users can set their preferred level of privacy at the level of the Trip Plan (private, shared with invited friends, or visible to any user). Users are provided around 30 tags (e.g. ("budget," "luxury", "weekend", "honeymoon") to choose from for labeling trip plans from the style of the trip, however, Yahoo! monitors the tags used most frequently by its users for augmenting its list of proposed tags. By using taxonomy-directed tagging, Yahoo!® eliminates many of the inherent problems of folksonomies created when users label similar things differently using synonyms or different forms of the same word (e.g. lodging, accommodation, hotel etc.). Tagging has helped Yahoo!® to: a) make its content (750,000 Trips Maps, photos, users' comments etc.) more useful, accessible, searchable and understandable to its users; and b) to gather, analyze and use customers' intelligence (where they live, where they have traveled, and what content they have viewed) and further refines that knowledge through the lens of the tags they use to search in order to create targeted, personalized recommendations for destinations and deals sold through its vertical search website Yahoo!® FareChase. In other words, tagging helps to further refine the collaborative filtering process that Yahoo! uses in order to provide personalized recommendations and suggestions to its users. Personalized suggestions for cross and up sales can significantly drive and enhance booking and sales levels as well as provide additional functional and emotional value to website users that in turn enhances customer loyalty.

In the same vein, the official destination portal of Holland uses tagging technology in order to provide travelers an easy way to search the website content and its multimedia information (video, photos etc.) (http://us.holland.com/). Actually, tags are used as an user constructed and defined search engine rather than providing a search engine designed by the website developer that reflects a top down business defined search process. Tag clouds appear on the left with different font sizes to reflect words used more or less frequently, while "Top 10" suggestions for each tag (e.g. restaurant) are also constructed and updated continuously when new content and UGC is shared on the website. The portal also provides users the possibility to comment each others' contributions and comments as well as to tag the Holland's webpage content by using different social booking technology such as Digg and Furl.

Overall, it becomes evident that city tourism organizations should consider including tagging into their websites, as tagging can help them overcome the following issues (Epps, Harteverldt & McGowan, 2007):

- Very frequently websites do not speak the same language and they do not use the same terminology as their users. City destination organizations should consider using tagging in order to make their website content more accessible, understandable and appealing to its users. For example, the marketer of a city might promote as the major value of the destination its easy accessibility by air transportation, however, travelers may perceive as the most valuable feature of the destination the fact that it is "a safe city to walk around".

- Tagging can help and further enhance keyword search by supporting nuanced, adjective-based searches. Tagging also enables social search whereby users can see who has tagged something, how credible or relevant its suggestions are based on his/her profile and his/her evaluation by other users.

- Tagging helps organize and display user-generated content uploaded on websites. As more and more city tourism organizations invite their users to upload and share their UGC (e.g. reviews, itineraries, photos,

videos, and podcasts), they later struggle to make this UGC relevant and accessible to their users and tags can help in addressing the latter.

- City tourism organizations can gather reliable and timely customer intelligence and feedback regarding the image of their destination, the mental maps of their travelers and how they view and perceive their destination etc. Such customer knowledge can be later used for marketing campaigns as well as for improving the products and services of the city as a destination.

- Customer information gathered through social tagging can also be used for improving search engine optimization campaigns. For example, words used frequently as tags by travelers can be used as metatags-metadata for building the portal's website as well as for spending money on keyword sensitive search engines such as Google™ AdWords.

However, when deciding whether and how to use tagging, city tourism organizations responsible for the development of the city portal should also decide the process, the policy and the way for developing their tagging system regarding the following issues: a) does the company edit the tags incorporated by users? This is important specifically if tags are uploaded with spelling mistakes or they include anti-social and embarrassing words. In other words, editing and a clear policy may be required in order to protect the consistency, the ethos and the good image of the website; b) are the tags and taggers' profiles made publicly available for everyone? What consent and agreement are required to take from the users and how the privacy policy of the website should be amended to incorporate the former?; c) is a software going to be purchased to manage the tagging process or is this going to be done manually? Are the required and skilled labor sources available? and d) how tags are going to be created? Are the tags going to be provided by the users or are the tags restricted by the website owner? Forrester (2006) recommends that companies use *taxonomy-directed* tagging, as it makes the tagging process more efficient and easier to use and it promotes consistency among tags. This is because when users create a tag, they can choose from existing suggested tags, or they can add their own.

Wikis

Definition, Features and Use

Wiki is a piece of server software permitting users to freely create and edit (hyperlinked) content via any browser and without the need to have access to and know to use any programming language. A wiki is a collaborative website whose content can be edited by anyone who has access to it. Wiki features include easy editing, versioning capabilities, and article discussions. So, wiki technologies enable users to add, delete, and in general edit the content of a website. Wiki users-creators are notified about new content, and they review only new content. As a result, such websites are developed collaboratively through their users, and a wiki becomes a collaboratively expandable collection of interlinked webpages, a hypertext system for storing and modifying information—a database, where each page is easily edited by any user with a forms-capable Web browser client. Neus and Scherf (2005) defined wiki as web content management systems allowing collaborative creation, connection and edition of contents, while Pereira and Soares (2007) defined wiki as a shared information work space that facilitates access to information content, organizational communications, and group collaboration. In other words, wikis represent another way of content publishing and communication as well as for group collaboration. In this vein, wikis and blogs have some similarities but they differ regarding the notification of new content, editing format, and structure. In other words, *'a wiki can be a blog, but a blog does not have to be a wiki'*.

Impact on Tourism Demand

The most popular wiki is the famous online encyclopedia, titled wikipedia.com, that is created and continually updated by its users. In tourism, wikitravel.org represents a wiki based effort of Internet users to collaboratively create and continuously update an online global travel guide including world-wide destinations. The number of readers, creators and content at wikitravel.org are continuously mushrooming. At wikitravel.org, one can find guides for any destination irrespective of its size and/or geographic location, as well as create a guide for any destination that he/she wishes. Wikitravel.com is further enriched with other web 2.0 tools and technologies such as maps, tags, podcasts etc.

Business Applications for City Marketing

Many tourism organizations take the opportunity to promote and create links to their websites through wikitravel.com in order to create and drive traffic to their own websites (http://wikitravel.org/en/London). Many other destination management organizations exploit and incorporate the wiki technology in their website portals in order to enable its users (travelers and locals) to collaboratively create and share their perceptions and mental images and opinions about their destination. For example, the National Library of Australia has included a wiki on its portal (http://wiki.nla.gov.au) inviting users to share their understanding and knowledge of local Australian dances as well as negotiate their meaning and create metaknowledge by synthesizing different views and perspectives. The National Library of Australia has also developed a wiki and social network website (www.pictureaustralia.org) whereby users can share their pictures about Australia and tell their story. In this way, the Library aims to help democratize history and establish a collective memory of places and events around the country. Ancient Times website (http://ancient.arts.ubc.ca/community.html) includes several collaborative tools, such as a wiki, blog and an arts metaverse enabling any user and history student to collaboratively develop and negotiate the meaning and construction of old cities and destinations, such as Giza and Athens. These cultural guides can significantly enhance the appeal and the interpretation of the cultural artifacts of historical cities and destination by providing several edutainment services and benefits to their users/visitors (Sigala, 2005a). Other wiki applications can also be provided on the city portals in order to boost website loyalty, repeat traffic, and travelers' desire to visit the destination. For example, a destination organization can design and incorporate a wiki on its portal for enabling potential travelers and locals to exchange and collaboratively develop recipes of local dishes and food.

Podcasting and Online Video

Definition, Features and Use

Podcasting refers to the uploading of audio and video files by users on websites. The most popular website for sharing such content with others is youtobe.com. Podcasting represents repositories of audio (podcasts) and video (vodcasts) or "video podcasting" materials that can be "pushed" to subscribers, even without user intervention, through RSS aggregate feeds of audio and video content facilitating users to search the latest services. Podcasting-capable aggregators or "podcatchers" are used to download podcasts. These files can also be downloaded to portable media players that can be taken anywhere, providing the potential for "anytime, anywhere" learning experiences (mobile learning). Podcasting's essence is about creating content (audio or video) for an audience that wants to listen when they want, where they want, and how they want. Podcasting differs from webcasting. A podcast has a persistent site, capable of synchronizing with a portable multimedia device, e.g. an MP3 player or iPod, whereas webcasting is streamed from the internet and requires the user to be connected to the internet while playing or viewing the webcast files. Webcasting is closely related to real-time downloading and synchronous broadcasting. Podcasting adds spatial flexibility to the temporal flexibility that webcasting offers and affords itself for creating personally-customizable media environments. Podcasting offers customer value in terms of the flexibility possibilities to hear personalized content whenever and whatever device one wishes, e.g. one can download the "Economist"'s or "CNN"'s personalized news' and press releases to his/her iPod and listen to its favorite news while he/she driving at work. As podcasting does not rely on the visual senses, it allows users to carry out other tasks while listening.

Impact on Tourism Demand

Tourism experiences are intangible. One cannot experience, feel and try a travel experience before he/she buys and before he/she travels to a destination. As a result, the purchase risk of a travel—tourism experience is high and it is difficult to persuade a user for the qualities of a tourism service. Due to its multimedia features, podcasting helps users to better and easier evaluate travel alternatives by experiencing in someway a travel experience before they decide to buy and consume it and/or travel to a destination. This is because audio and video files of hotels, destinations, and other travel products created and uploaded for sharing by other users are considered as more unbiased information and not staged experiences produced by the supplier aiming to promote his/her own product as the best one. Podcasting has also been used as mobile guides for travelers, e.g. Virgin Atlantic provides through its website free podcasts-guides of cities whereby they fly to.

Impact on Tourism Supply

Many tourism suppliers are using Podcasting as a marketing, information and customer communication tool. For example, Jumeirah hotel uploads podcasts on its website for delivering and updating its potential guests about what is happening in its properties at every single day, and-or delivering to website users and potential buyers the experiences of VIPs that have stayed at their property. Tate Gallery enables their visitors that have experienced their paintings and exhibition to record themselves, upload their audio-video on the Tate Gallery website, and which others can later download and use them as a mobile interpretation guide while visiting the gallery. Orbitz.com provides podcasting of many destinations that travelers can download to their MP3 players and use them as guides while visiting the destination. In a similar way, MGM Grand Hotel Las Vegas has lauded online video on its website under the title "Maximum Vegas" in order to better illustrate to its potential guests the experience and services of its hotel and gaming resort. Similarly, city destination organizations should consider enhancing the content and marketing appeal of their website portals by enabling podcasting opportunities, i.e. either allow users to share content or push their own created podcasting content (e.g. http://www. visitlondon.com/maps/podcasts/, Podcasts at the official portal of London). For developing podcasts, city tourism organizations can outsource this function to companies such as soundwalk. com, podtrip.com and heartbeatguides.com that specialize in the development and dissemination of destination podcasts.

METAVERSES: MASSIVELY MULTIPLAYER ONLINE ROLE PLAYING GAME (MMORPG)

Definition, Features and Use

Metaverses are three dimensional virtual worlds whereby Internet users collaboratively play "online MMORPG games" with others. However, these platforms are wrongly perceived as "simple games" and "virtual" worlds, since they frequently represent an extension to our physical day-to-day world to which users add new socio-economic and political situations. MMORPG are games that are played by numerous players (e.g. millions of users) and they could be considered as an intermediate step from 'computer' to 'ambient' era. Some of these games (e.g. World of Warcraft) develop around a theme defining the goals of the game, while other games, such as SecondLife.com, there. com, cokemusic.com, habbohotel.com and http:// play.toontown.com/about.php, encourage a freestyle of playing, allowing the users to make what they want out of it. Metaverse environments are internet-based 3-D virtual world whereby their users, called residents, can interact with each other through motional avatars (an internet user's representation of him/herself) providing an advanced level of a social network service. Although it is difficult to measure the size and growth of such games, it is estimated that the market for massively multiplayer online games is now worth more than $1bn in the West world (Book, 2003). For example, one can simply consider the size of and growth of Second Life®® itself. Second Life® has more than 5 million users, while about half a billion US$ are being transacted every year on Second Life's® website (as reported on SecondLife.com on April 2007).

Impact on Tourism Demand

Tourists and travelers participate in such games either for fun and-or for ways of expression of oneself and for achieving satisfaction through task—accomplishment, self-actualization and creation—design of something new. For example, many people dream and try to become and excel on a profession that they could not achieve in their real life, others try to design a new product and service hoping that other players will adapt and pay for it and so they can gain money and/or head hunters would spot their talents and recruit them in their real or virtual companies.

Business Applications for City Marketing

Many tourism and travel related companies have already created their representative offices and headquarters in metaverse environments such as SecondLife.com. Embassies (e.g. that of Sweden), Tourism Authorities (e.g. that of Maldives) of many countries and many tourism companies (e.g. TUI, Burj Al Arab Hotel, Marriott, Costa Cruises) have created their offices and companies on islands of SecondLife.com for boosting their marketing practices such as enhancing customer communication and education about their products/services, building brand reputation and user communities, and achieving word of mouth (WOM) and advertising. Hyatt used residents of Second Life® and exploited their intelligence and knowledge for designing a new hotel concept, named as Aloft; architects and guests were involved in designing the hotel providing their feedback, preferences and specialist knowledge (read the related blog at http://www.virtualaloft.com/). As a result of the popularity of the new hotel, the first Aloft hotel will open and operate in real life in New York in January 2008. Apart from collaborative new product development, a firm can further exploit the social intelligence gathered and generated at SecondLife.com and other metaverse environments in order to conduct market research and to test new product ideas and new advertising campaigns, e.g. Toyota first tested the campaign

of its new brand Scion on SecondLife® and then, widely broadcasted the new campaign in real life. Other companies, use SecondLife® for recruiting and identifying new talents e.g. CNN does head hunting of new journalists online.

Many destinations are also moving into the futuristic world of virtual reality and metaverse, as many city and country destination organizations create their virtual destinations. Netherlands Tourism Board recently opened a national tourism board in SecondLife® (http://us.holland.com/secondlife.php), the city of Galveston launched a virtual replica of itself in SecondLife® (http://www.galveston.com/secondlife/), providing their visitors with the chance to become part of an interactive community (Figure 10 and 11). The aim is to provide digital travelers the chance to take guided virtual tours, learn about the history, culture and daily life of the destination, and interact with new virtual friends from around the world. Tourism Ireland has also launched the world's first tourism marketing campaign in SecondLife® (http://dublinsl.com/index.php) including the sponsorship of a range of events and activities, including concerts, fashion shows, and photographic exhibitions, in Second Life's® replica city of Dublin. Dublin's representation in SecondLife.com is the first place-location in Ireland that the Tourism Board created its representation in Second Life®. Similiar to the Dublin creation, Amsterdam in Second Life® comes complete with Dutch signs, canals, trams and a lot of attention to detail. Overall, when investigating the impact of SecondLife.com on its residents' behavior, it becomes evident that historical landmarks and buildings such as Tour Eiffel, London Bridge, Ajax Football stadium etc., have a great effect in building virtual communities of people spending a lot of time on dwelling them. Since it is apparent that real world modern-day cities and their landmark attraction are probably the most effective at driving and retaining visitor traffic, city tourism organizations should exploit this inherent advantage and exploit their cultural and heritage assets in metaverse environments for boosting their city brand name, recognition and promotion.

Mash-Ups

Definition, Features and Use

Mash-ups describe the seamlessly combination of two or more different sources of content and-or software for creating a new value added service to users. Many mash-ups enrich their services with some geographical content such as Google™ Maps; e.g. *The New York Times Travel Section's "36 Hours In..."* mash-up, which allows users to search the *"36 Hours in ..."* story archive from a Google™ Map. For example, when visiting the website traintimes.org.uk, one can see on real time where trains are located and when they will arrive at destinations, since the website combines information from Google™ maps, and information from the British rail website about train time tables, delays etc.

There are several mash-up applications in tourism such as new cyberintermediaries including mapping services (e.g. earthbooker.com, tripmojo. com, reservemy.com) and meta-search engines such as farecompare.com. Other examples include: www.43places.com that combines Flickr photos, RSS feeds and Google™ Maps with tagging and user-generated content, allowing users to share their favorite destinations; www.randomdayout. co.uk combines a number of data sources to create a mapped itinerary, using Virtual Earth (Microsoft's equivalent of Google™ Maps). An innovate example related to destination marketing management is the case of the city of Pennsylvania (http://www.visitpa.com): based on a project amongst Google™ Earth, Carnegie Mellon University, NASA, the Pennsylvania Tourism Office and the National Civil War Museum, virtual tourists would have the chance to view Pennsylvania's Civil War trails online. More sophisticated examples of mash-ups are the "Marco Polo" function on

triptie.com and the "Trip Planner" function on Yahoo!® Travel, which allow users to integrate content from other websites into the user's own itinerary planning toolkit on the host website.

Impact on Tourism Demand

Travel decisions are complex and involve the searching, comparison and combination of several information located in many different websites. For example, a decision to travel to a destination requires various and a plethora of information about weather conditions, exchange rates, travel and accommodation alternatives and prices, attractions etc. As a result, tourists increasingly demand and expect to combine and cross-check information from different sources, so that they can better and easier make a holistic decision. For example, tourists may not be able to clearly understand where a hotel may be located when the description of the hotel websites states that the hotel is located on the beach, near the beach etc. Tourists easily get confused from different descriptions found in different websites. On the contrary, mash-up websites empowered with maps (e.g. earthbooker.com) enable users to see where exactly a hotel or other attraction is located (sometimes even locate the exact orientation and view of a hotel room and then decide whether to book this room at this hotel).

Business Implications for City Marketing

Mash-up applications have empowered the rise of new cyber- and info- intermediaries offering new sophisticated information services (e.g. flightcompare.com search and compare all flight information from different websites in order to provide comparable flight information within one webpage to its users). Moreover, many tourism suppliers and organizations also enrich their website content with maps in order to make it more user friendly and useful to their visitors, e.g. the official website of London and Dublin use

Google™ Maps with geotags for enabling tourists to identify points of interest, hotels etc. Moreover, many companies leave their software as an Open Application Programme Interface (API), so that users can create limitless combinations of their services. For example, backstage.bbc.co.uk represents BCC's services and opportunities offered to its users, who are enabled to take content from the BBC, re-structure it and present it the way they prefer. Enabling user innovation is another way that companies aim to exploit on users' creativity and intelligence instead of investigating solely on company's R&D efforts.

FUTURE TRENDS

It has become evident from the above mentioned analysis that the two major impacts of web 2.0 and its UGC on consumer behavior and marketing practices are: 1) the electronic word-of-mouth that is created; and b) the opportunities to build and maintain customer communities for enhancing the practices of Customer relationship Management and social marketing. Exploiting web 2.0 for city marketing can have a tremendous effect on the marketing effectiveness, since, as the following analysis and discussion illustrates, both previous issues significantly affect consumer loyalty and purchasing behavior.

Web 2.0 and Electronic Word-of-Mouth (WOM)

Word-of-mouth (WOM) is very important in tourism and in services in general, since objective information about a service experience cannot be easily provided before one buys and consumes the services themselves. Services are intangible and so they are difficult to be tested, tried and evaluated before buying them. Consumers also tend to rely more on consumer reviews when purchasing high involvement products (Park, Lee & Han, 2007), such as several travel products e.g. a honeymoon

trip, an adventure travel etc. In this vein, tourism decisions are very complex and risky. Indeed, the literature about information search in the tourism field has recognized the important role of WOM in travel planning and decision making (Hwang, Gretzell, Xiang & Fesenmaier, 2006; Murphy, Moscardo & Benckendorff, 2007). WOM has been found to be one of the most influential information sources for travel (Morrison, 2002). Research has also shown that those with past experience with a specific travel destination and that engage in digital word-of-mouth communication are most likely to be the most preferred and the most influential source of information in the pre-trip stage of travel decision making (Crotts, 1999).

To make travel decisions easier, travelers need to reduce the inherent information complexity of travel decisions as well as the risk related to the service firm (i.e. is that a good and reliable company), the service risk (i.e. is that a service that fits my preferences and needs?) and the purchasing risk (i.e. is that a trustworthy booking and buying channel to use for buying a travel service?). To achieve that, consumers use recommendation-based heuristics and other users' feedback to reduce uncertainty, eliminate the related risks as well as filter and process the plethora of information that must be processed when making decisions (Olshavsky & Granbois, 1979). WOM-based information is heavily used and trusted by consumers for taking travel decisions, because it is seen as more vivid, easier to use, and more trustworthy as it is based on actual experience and typically provided without direct benefits (Smith, Menon & Sivakumar, 2005).

As demonstrated in the above mentioned analysis of UGC in Web 2.0 websites, electronic WOM can take different names and forms such as virtual opinion platforms, consumer portals, social networking, blogs' comments, tag words, podcasting, virtual communities and online feedback mechanisms (Armstrong & Hagel, 1997; Bellman, 2006; Sigala, 2008). Users of Web 2.0 websites and tools may post their own experiences, videos, share their opinion, give advice, or look for answers to their questions. Consumers also perceive electronic WOM to be a reliable source of information (Gruen, Osmonbekov & Czaplewski, 2006). Dellarocas (2003) identified three different characteristics of online WOM relative to traditional WOM: 1) electronic WOM is larger in scale (both in terms of quantity and people impact) due to the Internet's low-cost and networking features; 2) electronic WOM is a powerful and reliable market research tool giving organizations the ability to monitor on real time their operations; and 3) it is difficult to convey contextual cues (e.g. facial expression) through the Internet and peer review websites for example, and so not knowing or seeing who the information provider is makes, it is harder to interpret the subjective information in online interaction. To address this problem, websites often display demographic or other data about reviewers (for example, the length of membership, their location, etc.) in order to help build credibility and trust. Websites may even provide the possibility to users to upload and share their own feedback and evaluation (by incorporating each review into a rating of the reviewer) about the quality of the reviews written by other members. Moreover, because Web 2.0 enables users to identify and use personalized and contextual information (e.g. look at what others' with similar profiles are saying), electronic WOM is considered as both more relevant and unbiased than traditional WOM, whereby one cannot easily track and relate the content with the profile of its original messenger.

Smith, Menon and Sivakumar (2005) claim that consumers prefer such peer recommendations over other forms of input, while Amis (2007) advocated that social network sites have as much influence on consumers as television and more than newspapers. Statistics actually provide evidence of consumers' reliance on electronic word-of-mouth. More than 80% of web shoppers said they use other consumers' reviews when making purchasing decisions (Forrester, 2006).

eMarketer (2007d) reports that nearly 6/10 consumers prefer websites with peer-written reviews, and that websites with reviews experience greater conversion rates.

Overall, Dellarocas (2003) summarized organizations' benefits of electronic WOM in the following: brand building; customer relationship management; customer acquisition; addressing customer complaints; market research; product development; quality control and supply chain quality assurance activities.

Web 2.0, Customer Relationship Management (CRM) and Social Marketing

The major aim of CRM is to personalize business services and products as well as develop a 1:1 communications and long lasting relation with profitable customers (Sigala, 2005b). eCRM also requires the development of customers' communities for providing loyal customers with functional, emotional and social benefits and value (Sigala, 2006). The previous section provided practical examples illustrating the way in which web 2.0 applications and tools enable the formation and development of customer virtual communities. By identifying and reviewing the limited related studies that have been conducted so far, the following analysis further supports the capability of web 2.0 to build virtual communities of users and enhance the community benefits (functional and emotional/social) to its users.

Ying and Davis (2007) and, Lento, Welser, Gu and Smith (2006) illustrated how blogs create and maintain strong online communities through their social ties tools such as blogrolls, permalinks, comments and trackbacks. Indeed, many authors (e.g. Lin, Su & Chien, 2006; Ying & Davis, 2007) have started to apply social network analysis for measuring and illustrating the social bonds, networking and communication structures created within the blogsphere. Li and Stronberg (2007) summarized blogs' benefits for firms as follows: search engine optimization; e-word-of-mouth (eWOW); improved brand perception and visibility; instantaneous client feedback; market research and insight; increased sales efficiency; and reduced impact from negative user-generated content. Damianos et al. (2007) advocated that social bookmarking generates social influence and bonds as well as creates value by: enabling resource management, information sharing and discovery, expert finding, and social networking; providing teams with a place to share resources; forming and supporting social networks around interest areas; and feeding expertise finding and user profiling. Awad and Zhang (2007) discussed the marketing benefits of eWOW generated in online review communities and debated firms' efforts and strategies addressing it. By examining the communication tools and social cues of myspace.com, Dwyer (2007) demonstrated the impact of social networking sites on developing customer interrelations and communities. In their study of videos' tags on Del.ici.ous, Paolillo and Penumarthy (2007) found that social tagging can generate community benefits such as: easy retrieval (as users use words they can remember and have useful meaning to them); contribution and sharing; attract attention; opinion expression; play; and self-presentation. Thus, since tagging can be used for providing functional services, creating social ties, market research on users' opinions and interests, and WOW, social tagging's ability in creating user communities is evident. Forrester (2006) demonstrated web 2.0's ability to generate customer and business value in different processes: customer service (e.g. community self-service savings); sales (e.g. community loyalty and sales reduces commissions and price competitions); marketing (e.g. credibility of eWOW); production (e.g. co-design reduces waste); and R&D (e.g. community input raises success rate).

A significant amount of literature also highlights the business benefits from developing virtual communities particularly in the area of CRM and social marketing. Analytically, Wang and

Fesenmaier (2004) illustrated that virtual tourist communities are useful for managing customer relations by: attracting customers through in-depth, focused and member-generated content; engaging customers through social interactions; and retaining customers through relation building with other members. Online communities also build customer value (Wang & Fesenmaier, 2004) by generating users with all types of relational benefits namely functional, social, hedonic and psychological (Gwinner, Gremmler & Bitner, 1998). Kim, Lee and Hiemstra (2004) provided evidence of the impact of virtual communities on travelers' loyalty and product purchase decision making. Andersen (2005) explored the use of online brand communities for developing interactive communication channels and establishing social and structural bonds with devoted users. Jang, Ko and Koh (2007) showed that online brand communities posses and develop features - such as, quality and credibility of information, service quality, member interaction and leadership, brand reputation and (intrinsic and extrinsic) rewards for members' activities- that in turn, contribute to increased users' brand loyalty, commitment and sales. Erat, Desouza, Schafer-Juger and Kurzawa (2006) discussed how different types of communities of practice (e.g. B2C, C2C) can be used for acquiring and sharing customer knowledge in order to improve business processes and performance. Beyond collecting customer knowledge, online communities can also be used for co-operating with customers for New Product Development (NPD) and innovation (Rowley, Teahan & Leeming, 2007). A plethora of cases and research studies (e.g. in Lagrosen, 2005; Pitta & Fowler, 2006) reflects the possibility to use virtual communities for NPD as well.

Table 1. Web 2.0 extended CRM implementation

	Low market integration	High market integration
High customer integration	**Many-to-one** Target: clients' networks Active customers' involvement *e.g. Lonelyplanet.com, Sheraton.com*	**Many-to-many** Co-exploitation of customers' profiles with other network partners *e.g. mash-ups, earthbooker.com, flightcompare.com*
Low customer integration	**One-to-one** Target: individual customers	**One-to-many** Ecosystems of partners offering a seamless experience to individual clients (cross-selling, products' bundling) *e.g. travelocity.com*

Proposed Models for Exploiting Web 2.0 in Enhancing Marketing Communication and CRM

The previous analysis and industry examples illustrate that web 2.0 tools and applications have a twofold impact on the way CRM is implemented: 1) web 2.0's networking and connectivity capabilities provide enormous opportunities to communicate and co-operate with customers and industry partners in many different directions (e.g. many-to-one, many-to-many) (Table 1) the social intelligence and knowledge created collaboratively in web 2.0 platforms (i.e. the user-generated content) can be exploited in different ways for identifying, developing, enhancing and maintaining relations with profitable customers (Table 2).

Table 2. Exploiting social intelligence for managing and enhancing customer relationships through their lifecycle

Phase	Type of customer information/ intelligence	CRM implementation activities
Acquisition	Of the customer information: transaction and personal data	Create brand awareness and recognition amongst customers and virtual communities by building and supporting electronic word-of-mouth
		Develop brand reinforcement and trust by educating and informing customers about the brand, its services, functionalities etc
		Use customer intelligence in order to identify and target new customers, e.g. clone the profile of existing product-service users, use the connections and recommendations of existing customers etc.
		Use customer intelligence to understand how customers use the service, what functionalities they prefer or not
		Use customer intelligence for profiling customers
Retention	For the customer information: relationship and product data	Use customer intelligence for enhancing customer service and transactions
		Use customer intelligence for personalizing services and products
		Build and develop community of customers-users
		Use customer intelligence for innovation & NPD
Expansion	For the customer information: relationship and product data	Use customer intelligence for cross selling, e.g. suggest compatible products based on other users' purchases
		Use customer intelligence for up-selling
		Use customer intelligence for developing affiliation and loyalty programmes
Win back	By the customer information: feedback and monitoring data	Use customer intelligence (feedback, reviews etc) for identifying pitfalls and faults
		Use customer intelligence and communities for handling customers' complaints
		Use customer intelligence and communities for monitoring and managing the firm's reputation, status and prestige

In other words, CRM cannot anymore be considered as synonymous to one-to-one communication and personalized service at an individual basis. Web 2.0 augment CRM practices and implementation to include various forms of communications with clients and business partners. Following Gibbert, Leibold and Probst (2002), Table 3 reflects a two dimensional matrix, whereby the vertical axis represents how firms integrate customers into their value chains and the horizontal axis represents the integration of business partners into the firm's value chain. Companies can use web 2.0 technologies to communicate and enable dialogues and interactions not only between them and their customers, but also between customers themselves (C2C), between business partners, among all of them etc. When engaged in two directional communication both customers and partners, firms can involve the former in their value chain in order to create customer value and benefits. For example, as explained earlier, when customers communicate with other customers in virtual communities, customers provide social and emotional support to others as well as functional benefits (e.g. free consultancy in trip planning). Also, when co-operating and sharing content and applications with other businesses (e.g. in mash-up websites), firms can collaborate with and integrate other partners in their value chain in order to provide additional services to their clients, e.g. a holistic tourism product-services such as a dynamic packaging.

Moreover, in developing successful relationships with profitable clients, firms need to understand and manage all phases through which relations are evolved, as each phase is characterized by differences in behaviors and orientations and so, it requires different CRM approaches. Theory and practical evidence has shown that customer relations evolve over three major distinct phases related to the customer lifecycle (see Sigala, 2008): initiation, maintenance and retention or termination. Hence, all CRM implementation models reflect practices that collect and use three forms of customer information / intelligence in order to manage each relational phase. "Of-the-customer" information includes customers' personal and transaction data for understanding and measuring their profile, e.g. sales, profitability, purchasing patterns, preferences. "For-the-customer" information refers to product, service and firm information perceived as useful by clients for making more informed decisions. "By-the-customer" information reflects customer feedback (e.g. customer complaints, suggestions, reviews) used for new product development or business improvement. As illustrated previously, Web 2.0's user-generated content mushrooms these three types of customer information and provides firms with several opportunities not only to collect, but also to get access to such types of customer intelligence. In other words, Web 2.0 platforms can be exploited as a free and real time market research and intelligence tool. Table 2 summarizes how firms can exploit web 2.0 tools and platforms for collecting and analyzing this customer intelligence for augmenting and supporting their CRM practices.

Overall, it becomes evident that web 2.0 enabled CRM reflects a cultural shift from product *'designing for customers'* to *'designing with'* and *'design by'* customers. For firms to achieve such a cultural shift, crucial organizational changes should also take place. Importantly, the role of marketers should be changed from being sales people to becoming community builders and perceiving customers not as targets to identify and sell, but as partners to collaborate with. Firms should also realize that they should use customer intelligence not only for learning about their customers and identifying new target markets (opportunistic behavior), that they should also use customer intelligence for learning and improving processes and products with their customers as well as with different business partners (partnership relation). In other words, firms derive and realize maximum benefits when they exploit web 2.0 tools for establishing and maintaining cocreation and co-learning adaptable and flexible ecosystems with their customers and business partners (Table 3).

CONCLUSION

Internet users and travelers are nowadays empowered to create and synthesize in their own way the travel content that they also wish to distribute and share it with others through users' controlled distribution channels. In this vein, Web 2.0 technologies enable Internet users to become the co-producers, the co-designers, the co-marketers and the co-distributors of tourism experiences and services as well as the co-entrepreneurs of new tourism products and new e-business models. As the diffusion of Web 2.0 applications becomes wide and consumers incorporate them within their daily and professional life, travelers expect tourism firms and organizations to provide similar Web 2.0 enabled services. The previous analysis aimed at identifying and illustrating the business implications created for tourism and hospitality enterprises as well as strategies and tactics that they can adopt for eliminating threats while exploiting the arising opportunities. Therefore, as Web 2.0 is here to stay, it is evident that unless a city tourism organization adopts and incorporates Web 2.0 tools into its e-business model and strategies for marketing and managing its destination, the competitiveness of the latter is threaten. Nevertheless, in order to be successful, the adoption and use of any web 2.0 tools should be accompanied with appropriate organizational and cultural changes within the firm regarding the roles, job descriptions and tasks of its staff, users and business partners. Further research is required in order to understand and examine how firms are achieving and trying to implement such organizational changes when incorporating web 2.0 into their e-business model.

REFERENCES

Adam, J., Cobos, X., & Liu, S. (2007). *Travel 2.0: Trends in Industry Awareness and Adoption.* New York University and PhoCusWright Inc.

Amis, R. (2007, May). You can't ignore social media: How to measure Internet efforts to your organization's best advantage. *Tactics*, 10.

Andersen, P. H. (2005). RM and brand involvement of professionals through Web-enhanced brand communities: Coloplast case. *Industrial Marketing Management, 34*(3), 285–297. doi:10.1016/j.indmarman.2004.07.007

Armstrong, A., & Hagel, J. (1997). *Net gain: Expanding markets through virtual communities.* Boston, MA: Harvard Business School Press.

Awad, N. F., & Zhang, S. (2007, January). *Stay out of my forum! Evaluating firm involvement in online ratings communities.* Paper presented at the 40th HICSS, Waikoloa, Big Island, Hawaii.

Bellman, S., Johnson, E., Lohse, G., & Mandel, N. (2006). Designing marketplaces of the artificial with consumers in mind. *Journal of Interactive Marketing, 20*(1), 21–33. doi:10.1002/dir.20053

Bickart, B., & Schindler, R. M. (2001). Internet forums as influential sources of consumer information. *Journal of Interactive Marketing, 15*(3), 31–40. doi:10.1002/dir.1014

Blood, R. (2000). Weblogs: A history and perspective. Retrieved October 15, 2007, from http://www.rebeccablood.net/essays/weblog_history.html

Book, B. (2003, July). *Traveling through cyberspace: Tourism and photography in virtual worlds.* Paper presented at the conference Tourism & Photography: Still Visions - Changing Lives in Sheffield, UK.

Bughin, J. R. (2007, August). How companies can make the most of user-generated content. *The McKinsey Quarterly*, Research in Brief, Web Exclusive.

Crotts, J. (1999). Consumer decision making and prepurchase information search. In Y. Mansfield & A. Pizam (Eds.), *Consumer behavior in travel and tourism* (pp. 149-168). Binghamton, NY: Haworth Press.

Damianos, L., Cuomo, D., & Griffith, J. Hirst, D., & Smallwood, J. (2007, January). *Adoption, utility, and social influences of social bookmarking*. Paper presented at the 40th HICSS, Waikoloa, Big Island, Hawaii.

Dellarocas, C. (2003). The digitization of word-of-mouth: Promise and challenges of online feedback mechanisms. *Management Science, 49*(10), 1407–1424. doi:10.1287/mnsc.49.10.1407.17308

Du, H. S., & Wagner, C. (2006). Weblog success: Exploring the role of technology. *International Journal of Human-Computer Studies, 64*, 789–798. doi:10.1016/j.ijhcs.2006.04.002

Dwyer, C. (2007, January). *Digital relationships in the 'MySpace' generation: Results from a qualitative study*. Paper presented at the 40th HICSS, Waikoloa, Big Island, Hawaii. eMarketer (2007a). *Web 2.0 sites draw more visitors*. Retrieved May 2, 2007, from http://www.eMarketer.com.

eMarketer (2007b). *UGC users outnumber creators*. Retrieved July 2, 2007, from http://www.eMarketer.com.

eMarketer (2007c). *The rising roar of word-of-mouth*. Retrieved June 29, 2007, from http://www.eMarketer.com.

eMarketer (2007d). *Reviews boost e-commerce conversions*. Retrieved May 25, 2007, from http://www.eMarketer.com.

Epps, S. R. (2007). *Demystifying tagging for travel sellers*. Forrester Research Report.

Epps, S. R., Harteveldt, H. H., & McGowan, B. (2007). *Executive Q&A: Social tagging for ebusiness. Answers to E-Business professionals' common questions about social tagging*. Forrester Research.

Erat, P., Desouza, K., Schafer-Jugel, A., & Kurzawa, M. (2006). Business customer communities and knowledge sharing: studying the critical issues. *European Journal of IS, 15*, 511–524.

Farmer, J. (2004). Communication dynamics: Discussion boards, Weblogs and the development of communities of inquiry in online learning environments. In R. Atkinson, C. McBeath, D. Jonas-Dwyer, & R. Phillips (Eds.), *Beyond the comfort zone* (pp. 274-283). *Proceedings of the 21st ASCILITE Conference*.

Forrester Research. (2006). *Social computing*. Retrieved September 14, 2007, from http://www.forrester.com.

Gibbert, M., Leibold, M., & Probst, G. (2002). Five styles of CKM, and how smart companies use them to create value. *European Management Journal, 20*(5), 459–469. doi:10.1016/S0263-2373(02)00101-9

Gruen, T. W., Osmonbekov, T., & Czaplewski, A. J. (2006). eWOM: The impact of customer-to-customer online know-how exchange on customer value and loyalty. *Journal of Business Research, 59*, 449–456. doi:10.1016/j.jbusres.2005.10.004

Gwinner, K. P., Gremmler, D. D., & Bitner, M. J. (1998). Relational benefits in services: The customer's perspective. *Journal of the Academy of Marketing Science, 26*(2), 101–114. doi:10.1177/0092070398262002

Harteveldt, H., Johnson, C. A., Epps, S. R., & Tesch, B. (2006).*Travelers embrace social computing technologies. Guidelines for travel e-commerce and marketing executives and managers*. Cambridge, MA, USA: Forrester Research.

Haven, B. (2007). *Making podcasts work for your brand*. Cambridge, MA, USA: Forrester Research.

Hwang, Y., Gretzel, U., Xiang, Z., & Fesenmaier, D. (2006). Information search for travel decisions. In D. Fesenmaier, H. Werthner & K. Wöber (Eds.), *Destination recommendation systems: Behavioral foundations and applications* (pp. 3-16). Cambridge, MA: CAB International.

Jang, H. Y., Ko, I. S., & Koh, J. (2007, January). *The influence of online brand community characteristics on community commitment and brand loyalty*. Paper presented at the 40th HICSS, Waikoloa, Big Island, Hawaii.

Kim, W. G., Lee, C., & Hiemstra, S. J. (2004). Effects of an online virtual community on customer loyalty and travel product purchases. *Tourism Management, 25*(3), 343–355. doi:10.1016/S0261-5177(03)00142-0

Lagrosen, S. (2005). Customer involvement in NPD: A relationship marketing perspective. *European Journal of Innovation, 8*(4), 424–436. doi:10.1108/14601060510627803

Lento, T., Welser, H. T., Gu, L., & Smith, M. (2006). The ties that blog: Relationship between social ties and continued participation in blogs. *Workshop on Weblogging* Edinburgh.

Li, C., & Stromberg, C. (2007). *The ROI of blogging*. Cambridge, MA: Forrester Research.

Lin, Y., & Huang, J. (2006). Internet blogs as a tourism marketing medium: A case study. *Journal of Business Research, 59*, 1201–1205. doi:10.1016/j.jbusres.2005.11.005

Lin, Y., Su, H. Y., & Chien, S. (2006). Knowledge-enabled procedure for customer relationship management. *Industrial Marketing Management, 35*, 446–456. doi:10.1016/j.indmarman.2005.04.002

Morrison, A. (2002). *Hospitality and tourism marketing* (3rd ed.). Albany, NY: Delmar.

Murphy, L., Moscardo, G., & Benckendorff, P. (2007). Exploring word-of-mouth influences on travel decisions: friends and relatives vs. other travelers. *International Journal of Consumer Studies, 31*(5), 517–527. doi:10.1111/j.1470-6431.2007.00608.x

Neus, A., & Scherf, P. (2005). Opening minds: Cultural change with the introduction of open-source collaboration methods. *IBM Systems Journal, 44*(2), 215–225.

Olshavsky, R. W., & Granbois, D. H. (1979). Consumer decision making: Fact or Fiction? *The Journal of Consumer Research, 6*, 93–100. doi:10.1086/208753

Paolillo, J. C., & Penumarthy, S. (2007, January). *The social structure of tagging internet video on del.icio.us*. Paper presented at the 40th HICSS, Waikoloa, Big Island, Hawaii.

Park, D. H., Lee, J., & Han, J. (2007). The effect of online consumer reviews on consumer purchasing intention: The moderating role of involvement. *International Journal of Electronic Commerce, 11*(4), 125–148. doi:10.2753/JEC1086-4415110405

Pereira, C. S., & Soares, A. L. (2007). Improving the quality of collaboration requirements for IM through social networks analysis. *International Journal of Information Management, 27*, 86–103. doi:10.1016/j.ijinfomgt.2006.10.003

Pitta, D., & Fowler, D. (2005). Online consumer communities and their value to new product developers. *Journal of Product and Brand Management, 14*(5), 283–291. doi:10.1108/10610420510616313

Rosenbloom, A. (2004). The blogosphere. *Communications of the ACM, 47*(12), 31–33. doi:10.1145/1035134.1035161

Rowley, J., Teahan, B., & Leeming, E. (2007). Customer community and co-creation: A case study. *Marketing Intelligence & Planning, 25*(2), 136–146. doi:10.1108/02634500710737924

Sigala, M. (2003). Developing and benchmarking internet marketing strategies in the hotel sector in Greece. *Journal of Hospitality & Tourism Research (Washington, D.C. Print), 27*(4), 375–401. doi:10.1177/10963480030274001

Sigala, M. (2005a). In search of online postmodern authenticity: Assessing the quality of learning experiences at eternalegypt.org. In M. SIGALA & D. Leslie (Eds.), *International Cultural Tourism: Management, implications and cases* (pp. 123–136). Oxford, UK: Butterworth Heinemann, Elsevier.

Sigala, M. (2005b). Integrating customer relationship management in hotel operations: Managerial and operational implications. *International Journal of Hospitality Management, 24*(3), 391–413. doi:10.1016/j.ijhm.2004.08.008

Sigala, M. (2006). e-Customer relationship management in the hotel sector: Guests' perceptions of perceived e-service quality levels. *Tourism: An International Interdisciplinary Journal, 54*(4), 333–344.

Sigala, M. (2008, January). Developing and implementing an eCRM 2.0 strategy: Usage and readiness of Greek tourism firms. *ENTER 2008 conference*, Innsbruck, Austria.

Smith, D., Menon, S., & Sivakumar, K. (2005). Online peer and editorial recommendations, trust, and choice in virtual markets. *Journal of Interactive Marketing, 19*(3), 15–37. doi:10.1002/dir.20041

Wang, Y., & Fesenmaier, D. R. (2004). Modeling participation in an online travel community. *Journal of Travel Research, 42*(3), 261–270. doi:10.1177/0047287503258824

Winer, D. (2005). What is a. River of News. style aggregator? *Really Simple Syndication.* Retrieved June 22, 2005, from http://www.reallysimplesyndication.com/riverOfNews

Ying, Z., & Davis, J. (2007, January). *Web communities in blogspace.* Paper presented at the 40th HICSS, Waikoloa, Big Island, Hawaii.

Yuan, Y., Gretzel, U., & Fesenmaier, D. R. (2006). The role of information technology use in American convention and visitors bureaus. *Tourism Management, 27*(2), 326–341. doi:10.1016/j.tourman.2004.12.001

This work was previously published in Information Communication Technologies and City Marketing: Digital Opportunities for Cities Around the World, edited by M. Gasco-Hernandez; T. Torres-Coronas, pp. 221-245, copyright 2009 by Information Science Reference (an imprint of IGI Global).

Chapter 5.5

City Brands and their Communication through Web Sites:
Identification of Problems and Proposals for Improvement

José Fernández-Cavia
Universitat Pompeu Fabra, Spain

Assumpció Huertas-Roig
Universitat Rovira i Virgili, Spain

ABSTRACT

City marketing tries to position cities in the mind of the public, although the process of creating and communicating city brands is still at an early stage of its development. One of the main tools for the communication of these brands is now the World Wide Web. This chapter describes the results of two combined studies (qualitative and quantitative) that analyzes a sample of official city Web sites. The results show that official Web sites of cities give much attention to ease of navigation, but interactivity is much less implemented, especially between users. Furthermore, some lack of attention to the communication aspects of city brands can also be found. Finally, the chapter submits a number of improvement proposals.

INTRODUCTION

In the current world of cities, competition has increased and the centre of interest has moved to include much broader spheres. Already, cities do not try only to be just significant tourist nuclei, but they also compete in aspects such as quality of life, economic development and sustainability. Aside from tourist interest, cities try to position themselves as comfortable areas to live and important centers of economic development that attract all types of investment.

To achieve this, it is necessary to know the opinions and evaluations of the publics (Prebensen, 2007)[1], to find out what image they have of the city and determine the positioning that it would be desirable to achieve. Therefore, a vision of the city must be formulated and, consequently, a program of identity must be created that is transmitted through a brand and a visual logo and, later, an adequate and effective communication program must be

DOI: 10.4018/978-1-60566-134-6.ch002

run. With this objective, citymarketing tries to position cities in the minds of the public. In spite of this, the process of creating and disseminating city brands is still in a very early stage of its development.

This chapter tries to show, on one hand, that the concept and application of city brands are still very incipient and, on the other hand, that the official websites, in part due to city brands being underdeveloped, do not pay enough attention to the dissemination of the graphic, functional, and emotional aspects of the brand. With this, there is still a long way to go in the dissemination of cities through their brands on the Internet.

THE CONCEPT OF CITY BRAND

The concept of brand applied to destinations, places or cities is relatively new. It started to spread with the Travel and Tourism Research Association's Annual Conference in 1998 (Blain, Levy & Brent Ritchie, 2005). From that moment, the concept has been developed widely and has been studied from diverse perspectives, especially from the point of view of tourism. All in all, studies on city brands and destinations are still under developed and knowledge on the subject is limited. Some authors consider that it's not correct to talk about branding or place branding in relation to territories, cities or countries. They believe that it is incorrect to associate communicational and marketing terms to realities with their own identity like cities. Nevertheless, the majority or authors appreciate that the territories and the cities do not have the same characteristics as commercial products, but agree that they can apply the same marketing strategies to the territories (Olins, 2002).

The first difficulty we come up against in the study of city brands is the confusion of concepts. Therefore, it is fundamental to distinguish between city brand and brand image (Cai, 2002). Many studies confuse the analysis of the brand image

with the brand itself and the branding done by the destination.

The city brand is a new concept and is not very well defined. It is currently very much in fashion, and many people have theories, but few have dared to define it. It is a construct composed of a name, a logo, some symbols and some values that we try to associate with a city, representing its identity, with the objective of creating a position and a vision of the city in the minds of the public. Each city must have its own brand, and each city brand must be the result of a citymarketing plan and a competitive city strategy.

A very complete definition of destination brand, fully applicable to the city brand, which is based on the previous definitions of Aaker (1991) and Ritchie and Ritchie (1998) is that of Blain, Levy and Brent Ritchie (2005), which implies:

The creation of a name, symbol, logo, word mark or other graphic that both identify and differentiate a destination; that convey the promise of a memorable travel experience that is uniquely associated with the destination; and that serve to consolidate and reinforce the emotional connection between the visitor and the destination; that reduce consumer search costs and perceived risk; all with the intent purpose of creating a destination image that positively influences consumer destination choice. (p. 337)

However, the brand image is the result of the branding process, which is the perception created in the minds of individuals. It is *"networks of knowledge elements stored in long-term memory, and the core of such a network is the brand name which is linked to a number of other knowledge elements and/or associations"* (Riezebos, 2003).

As confirmed by Bill Baker:[2] *"A destination without a clear and attractive brand image is like a person without a personality. They blend into the crowd, are seen as uninteresting, and don't get the attention they deserve"*.

As consequence of this dichotomy between

city brand and brand image, there are two types of studies on the topic. On one hand, those that analyze the brand names themselves, their names, symbols, logos, their identification, purposes and meanings. Our research is included within this first type. And on the other, those that are based on the associations and relationships that the brand names create with the public, that is, the brand image that is created among consumers.

We also consider it is important to distinguish another conceptual aspect. Place branding is not the same as destination branding. Place branding is based on the construction of a global image of the territory that promotes the place in its globality: economical, touristic and as a place of residence. Even in some occasions, tourist branding can be contradictory with place branding. This is why we consider it necessary to give a definition of place branding. It is the sum of beliefs and impressions people hold about places. Images represent a simplification of a large number of associations and pieces of information connected with a place. They are a product of the mind trying to process and pick out essential information from huge amounts of data about a place (Kotler, Haider & Rein, 1993).

Having clarified these concepts, we will concentrate on the city brand, which is the purpose of our analysis. This, like all brands, has its raison d'être, which is based on two basic functions (Aaker, 1991). One of these is the identification of the brand with the town and the attribution of a symbology and some values to the destination. The cities must have new signs of identity, an image and a position. Therefore, the first function of the brand is to attribute functional and emotional values to a city that identify the different cities globally and by consensus.

The second function of the brand is based on differentiating the cities from each other. This has always been the principal mission of all brands. According to the American Marketing Association: "the brand is a name, term, design, symbol, or any other feature that identifies one

seller's good or service as distinct from those of other sellers".

Blain, Levy and Brent Ritchie (2005) add three concrete purposes of city brands to the two classics stated previously by Aaker (1991). On one hand, to give the visitors the security of a quality experience at the destination. On the other, to reduce the search costs on the part of the visitors and, finally, to offer a single purchase proposal. But we must be conscious of the difficulties of creating city brands, and the limitations that still exist with respect to their functions.

Moreover, Hankinson (2004) uses the concept of brand networks, in which the destination and city brands have four functions: brands as communicators that represent a differentiation between cities, brands as perceptual entities that appeal to the senses and emotions, brands as values, and brands as relationships.

Having reviewed the theoretical framework of destination and city brands, and defined the concept of city brand, from which the study starts, we will now make a simple classification. As we understand, city brands can be classified according to their degree of evolution and development in the following categories:

1. The graphic brand, which only implies the creation of a symbol and a logo. Logos are the basic element for the creation of a brand and the main vehicle for communicating an image.[3]

2. The functional conceptual brand. This type of brand adds the symbolization of some of the territory's characteristics to the logo, which are real and tangible, and which are to be promoted, being adopted as strong points of the city. These attributes may be: good climate, beaches, nightlife, quality of life and, level of innovation.

3. The emotional conceptual brand, created by a body, entity or public institution, also trying to transmit abstract, symbolic and personifiable values to the city, such as innovation,

multiculturality, modernization, passion, etc. With this combination of values, the aim is to position and distinguish the image of the city from the competition. Previous studies (Ekinci & Hosany, 2006; Hosany, Ekinci & Uysal, 2006)[4] have shown that the emotional and personifiable values of the destination brands have positive influences in the prior choices of purchase and recommendation of these destinations.

Various authors agree that the brand image of a destination has two basic dimensions (Lawson & Band-Bovy, 1977): cognitive and affective, which would correspond with the emotional and functional conceptual brand. The cognitive component would be made up of the beliefs and knowledge of the physical attributes of a city, the functional conceptual brand; meanwhile, the affective component would refer to the feelings about these attributes, the emotional conceptual brand (Baloglu & McCleary, 1999). From the perspective of understanding the brand image as a "cluster of attributes and associations that the consumers connect to a brand", Biel (1997) understands the existence of "hard" associations, which refer to the tangible and functional attributes, and "soft" associations, emotional attributes. Biel acknowledges that the personality of the brand belongs to the emotional aspect of the brand image. Along the same lines, authors such as Etchner and Brent Ritchie (1991), Kapferer (1997) or De Chernatory and Dall' Olmo Riley (1997) confirm that the brand and its image are composed of two attributes: the functional or tangible, and the symbolic or intangible[5].

However, the emotional conceptual brand must be agreed upon by consensus, created jointly by public and private institutions and citizens of the region, which involves both the internal and external public, and is not identified with or property of a single institution, but of the whole region.

The valid significance of a brand is that registered by its public. Certainly, a brand must be adopted by all the public, starting with the city's own residents, companies and institutions; and for this purpose it is fundamental that these are involved in its creation, that they adopt it as their own and thus help with its dissemination. A study by Blain, Levy and Brent Ritchie (2005), based on interviews with the heads of marketing of the destinations, showed that the opinion of the residents and the visitors must be fundamental in the process of creating city brands.

So, in light of the classification above, an existing city brand may be understood as more or less developed according to its degree of preparation. Some city brands are simply logos that do not represent any specific aspect of the destination, while others have elaborate brands agreed by consensus, which come from a prior marketing plan and represent functional and emotional values that can be identified with the city.

QUALITATIVE ANALYSIS OF CITY BRANDS

Having stated the definition, functions and classification of city brands, we performed an initial qualitative study on eight brands of important world cities on their official websites. The study showed the limitations of city brands in their current process of creation, implementation and dissemination.

The objective of the investigation centered on finding out the degree of evolution and development of a sample of city brands, and their dissemination through the websites of their official institutions. The analysis consisted of two stages. The first centered on the prior examination of the city brand itself and its degree of development. The method used in this part of the study was based on the classification of the degree of advance preparation and evolution. In other words, in the analysis of the graphics and logo, the functional and emotional values assigned and the knowledge of the moment of creation, motivation and agents involved in the process of creating the city brand.

The second phase of the investigation centered on the study of how the city brands were treated on the official websites of the destinations. The analytical method used was the BIWAM (Brand Identity Web Analysis Method). This is a technique for qualitative analysis of the establishment of brands on the web, created by Martín Barbero and Sandulli (2005), which includes eight dimensions of analysis, of which we applied six to our study of city brands:

1.	Analysis of the Appearance, which corresponds to the strong, real and objective points of the destination (the functional element of the brand) and how it is communicated on the web.
2.	Analysis of the Personality. This implies the assessment of the symbolic and emotional elements that are attributed to city brands and their treatment on the websites.
3.	Analysis of Humanity. This refers to the interactivity of the page.
4.	Analysis of the Style. This analyses the graphic part of the brand, specifically, the relationship of the logo with the colors and the typography of the website.
5.	Analysis of the Medium, and the communicative functionality of the websites.
6.	Analysis of the Credibility. This refers to errors, slow loading speed, internal coherence, etc.

We only applied six dimensions of analysis created by Martín Barbero and Sandulli (2005) because the other two could be applied to product brands, but no to city brands.

The sample consisted of eight city brands that correspond to international tourism capitals, which have created their city brands, but show different degrees of evolution according to the typology stated above. The city brands selected for the sample were: Barcelona, Madrid, Edin-burgh, Amsterdam, Cincinnati, Toronto, Dubai and Hong Kong.

RESULTS OF THE QUALITATIVE STUDY: EVOLUTION AND LIMITATIONS OF CITY BRANDS

The results of the study showed that city brands are a concept of recent creation and still incipient development. Actually, the majority of brands analyzed in the study were created in 2005. Many large world cities still have not created their city brands. And among those that have, the degree of evolution of their brands is still mostly in the initial stages. The vast majority are stuck in the stage of creating logos based on strong points or characteristics of the city that they wish to boost. However, very few cities try to identify themselves with an emotional conceptual brand, based on the appropriation of personifiable values and the creation of a city marketing strategy.

Our results coincide with those of a study by ESADE (2004) on the evolution of the positioning of Spanish tourist destinations and their tourism brands. This stated that the brands, as strategic realities of tourist destinations, are usually fairly general, based on functional values without dealing with emotional aspects. They do not segment their range much and are only transmitted externally, forgetting the internal public, and do not evolve with the passage of time.

Other studies in tourist marketing have shown that, in general, the application of marketing techniques in destinations is still scarcely developed (Gnoth, 1998; Pritchard & Morgan, 2002).

The causes of the lack of evolution of city brands are related to a series of limitations the brands experience in their implementation. The first consists of the complexity of combining a segmentation strategy with the creation of a single brand image. The cities are directed at diverse sectors of the public (citizens, investors, businesspersons, tourists) with whom they wish to communicate. As each sector of the public has certain interests and certain needs, the cities generally create different marketing strategies for each of them. For this reason, it may be complicated, or even contradictory, to create different strategies and integrate them into one single brand positioning.

Another difficulty is found in the existence of more than one brand per city. It often occurs that different institutions create city brands for their websites or for independent use. The result is dispersion, incoherence and the impossibility of creating a single image that is recognizable and adopted throughout the community. For example, the City Council of Madrid has a municipal website (munimadrid) with a brand and a logo that has nothing to do with the Madrid brand on the municipal tourism portal (esmadrid), or with the website of the region (turismomadrid). It is easy to understand that it is absolutely essential to make the effort to coordinate and negotiate when creating a single brand that is not property of one institution in particular, but of all the citizens, and applicable to all the websites related to a destination.

With respect to the second function of the brand, that of differentiating cities from each other, it is possible that different cities try to identify themselves with the same values. The research that we have performed shows that the emotional conceptual brand, that which attributes some personifiable values to a city with the purpose of differentiating it from other cities, is usually created in a very broad and ambiguous way, and this does not fulfill its differentiating function. The majority of cities do not identify with a single value, but with many, some of which are shared by different brands, which, in fact, encourages confusion.

Kotler (1993) already stated that all images of a destination must be simple and distinctive. The main function of a brand must be to differentiate it with respect to the competition. However, in the study it was demonstrated that the majority of cities prefer to be identified with diverse values

or characteristics at the same time, perhaps to be attractive to more sectors of the public, maybe because they are values that are currently very attractive in society and which they do not want to renounce although they have been adopted by other destinations. This is shown in the eight city brands analyzed, Amsterdam and Toronto identify themselves as creative; Barcelona and Dubai, adventurous; Barcelona and Edinburgh, friendly; Edinburgh and Toronto, imaginative; Barcelona, Amsterdam and Edinburgh, diverse; Hong Kong, Barcelona and Amsterdam, cosmopolitan; and finally, Barcelona, Amsterdam, Edinburgh and Toronto, innovative. In this sense, the city brand completely loses its distinctive or differentiating function and this limits the creation of a single image for every destination. Similarly, Morgan, Pritchard and Piggott (2002) also showed that the images created of destinations and cities are not different and do not usually contain a single idea or single purchase proposition.

Our research also revealed that the majority of city brands have been created according to a specific event. For example, Madrid's brand was created to promote the destination internationally when the city was selected as a possible candidate for the Olympic games of 2012. Barcelona, however, created its brand to promote the Forum 2004, and Cincinnati, after the results of an economic study, took notice of the need to connect the three States of Ohio, Kentucky and Indiana, and as a result, created its brand with this unifying objective. This fact may also be negative for city brands, which should never be associated with a specific political event, as they must represent a city and not a municipal government, a social or sporting event or any private interest.

The motive that generally moves public bodies to create city brands is mainly based on tourist or economic interests, and thus the brand created usually is identified with these interests. This is an error, a reductionist conception that limits the potential of the city brand. In addition, on occasions, after an election or change of party in the town halls, the city brands and their representation and meanings are changed, precisely with the intention of breaking away from the previous image and promoting a new improved image related to the political party that has formed the municipal government. These changes create dysfunction, as the brands need time to be implemented and require their evolution to be homogenous and coherent. The persistence and durability of a brand is key for its implementation and acceptance by all sectors of the public. Therefore, brand changes only create more confusion in the identities and images of the cities.

Finally, but importantly, difficulty in the creation of city brands lies in coordination, taking into account the umbrella brands of destinations greater than the cities. In tourism, the broader destinations (regions, nations, states or countries) include those within them in their brand for the promotion of tourism. So this presents us with a number of questions: Should the umbrella brands take into account and be coherent with the city brands that they include? Should they all be related? Should they be coherent with each other? Should they have common features? Should the attributes of the umbrella brands be shared by the brands of the respective cities that are represented?

TREATMENT OF CITY BRANDS ON THE WEB

The Internet and new information technologies play a key role in communicating the cities and their brands. They are an important source of information. Destination Management Systems are more than simple websites. In addition to the information, they offer advertising, marketing and sales applications, and have interactive resources that, in an entertaining way, provide services and attract the attention of the users.

Currently, through a city's tourism website, you can get information, make reservations, etc. However, in the promotion of the cities, not only as tourist destinations, but also as business centers and residential areas, portals or broader websites are starting to be created, which offer, in addition to tourist information, business and leisure information for the citizens.

In this sense, and from the field of communication, the brand websites have been marked as the future of marketing communication on the Internet, as they have the potential to provide high levels of information and, in addition, create virtual product experiences (Klein, 2003). Brand websites are capable of combining both of the basic objectives of commercial communication in this channel: to create a brand image and achieve a direct response (Hollis, 2005). As Cho and Cheon (2005) describe, the websites may serve for diverse communication purposes: public relations, sales promotion, advertising or direct marketing.

In the second part of the study, the results of our analysis of city brands on the web showed that the aspects that make up the corporate image, that is, the colors, the lines and the logo of the city brand, in general, are used very little to create graphic coherence and brand image throughout the website. There are some exceptions, such as the sites of Amsterdam or Madrid, that show effective graphic coherence for transmitting the brand, but habitually the typography and the colors of the logo are only used in auxiliary hyperlinked pages, but not the whole official site.

The study showed that what is best transmitted through the web is the functional conceptual brand of the cities, the strong points or the potential that they wish to promote; but in no way the emotional conceptual brand, which ascribes personifiable values to the destination. The exception is a hyperlink that some official websites have, such as Edinburgh or Amsterdam, which links to a page exclusively dedicated to explaining the emotional brand.

Starting with the results of the studies of Hosany, Ekinci and Uysal (2006), where it is demonstrated that the emotional and personifiable values have positive influences on the intention to visit, purchase and recommend destinations on the part of consumers, it is surprising that it is actually the emotional aspect and the personality of the brand that are the least developed aspects on the official websites of the cities analyzed. The heads of marketing of the cities should develop strategies and campaigns that promote the distinctive personality of the destinations, based on the emotional components of these cities, which create better positioning and a more favorable image among users.

Thus, in conclusion, the under use of websites to promote city brands has been verified. The websites centre on the functional conceptual aspects of the brand, that is, all the strong points that are notable in the city, but lack, in general, coherent graphic treatment and the expression of the emotional conceptual brand. The design of the websites tries to be useful and functional to provide the users with the information and services they wish to obtain, but they are not at all creative to disseminate the emotional values attributable to the city through its brand. McMillan (2004) coincides with our statements, arguing that advertising on the Internet and websites must be more creative, that is, better designed, with greater impact, more varied and more entertaining.

Once at this point, and in light of other studies and a bibliography centered on more technical questions of the websites, we decided to analyze other characteristic aspects of the websites that also influence the dissemination and perception of city brands. We considered that dealing with city brands should not be limited to an analysis of the websites' content only, but should take into account aspects such as the interactivity or usability of their pages.

Different research on websites shows that usability is a key aspect in the creation of a good brand image. The sites that seem to be or are easier to open, navigate or use, create a more favorable attitude and image among users (Chen & Wells, 1999; Chen, Gillenson & Sherrell, 2002; Heijden, 2003). Thus, small websites, with very

basic iconography and ease of use, such as that of Barcelona, would transmit a good city brand image. However, extensive and complicated sites that are slow to open and that have a confused internal structure, such as that of Toronto, cause less positive or even unfavorable attitudes to be created.

Along the same lines, Jared M. Spool (1996)[6] did a study comparing websites, which demonstrated that the usability of a website considerably and positively affects the brand and the branding process. His results showed that the users that navigate more easily through a website and find the information that they want quickly end up with a better impression of the brand, as it has satisfied their expectations to a greater degree. Contrarily, the obstacles that the users find when navigating negatively and directly affect their perception of the brand. Therefore, usability is essential for effective branding.

Regarding interactivity, Liu (2003) defends the idea that the concept of interactivity unites three correlated but different factors: the active control of information, bidirectional communication and the synchronicity or simultaneity of communication. In a previous article (Liu & Shrum, 2002), the same author classified the brand websites in the maximum range of the three factors stated. This study showed, by the way of bidirectional communication, that the Internet is the only medium that can be used for commercial transactions without the help of other tools, since necessary activities such as showing the product, placing orders, making payments or even, in categories such as music, software or transport titles, distributing the product can happen through the web.

Other authors (Cho & Cheon, 2005) prefer to divide the concept of interactivity into three fields of action or types: consumer-message interactivity, consumer-consumer interactivity and consumer-marketer interactivity. Consumer-message interactivity refers to the capability of the user to personalize his or her relationship with the contents of the page according to his or her interests and motives. Consumer-marketer interactivity centers on the communication between the user of a website and the organizers or those responsible for the content; this relationship may be bidirectional, from user to administrator (questions, suggestions, complaints) or from administrator to user (obtaining personal data, answering questions, etc.). Consumer-consumer interactivity is the relationship that may be created between the people that access a website (virtual communities, chats, forums, etc.).

More recent studies (Sicilia, Ruiz & Munuera, 2005; Ko, Cho & Roberts, 2005) show that interactivity enables the information to be processed better and generates more favorable attitudes towards the website and towards the product and the brand, and greater intention to purchase.

Based on these previous studies on the usability and interactivity of websites we decided to make a broader quantitative analysis about the treatment of city brands on the Internet. In addition to the items related to graphic, functional and emotional aspects of the brand, in the trial we analyzed usability and interactivity characteristics of the websites as elements that also influence the dissemination of a good brand image.

PURPOSE AND METHOD OF QUANTITATIVE STUDY. USABILITY, INTERACTIVITY AND THE CITY BRAND ON THE WEB

The first qualitative study was wider. It analyzed the city brands and their treatment in websites in depth. But later, we decided to carry out a quantitative study analyzing more webs and variables. We had to develop a different questionnaire of analysis that could be measured by quantitative methods.

The main objective of this quantitative study consisted in analyzing the degree of usability, interactivity and treatment of city brands on the official websites of tourist cities.

For this empirical study, we used a quantative method based on a WTO (World Tourism Organization, 1999) analysis model. This was extended with the contribution of recent studies (McMillan, 2003; Liu, 2003; Cho & Cheon, 2005) and adding newly created interactive resources, which appeared as new features on destination websites at the time the study was carried out. At the same time, the model was also extended with aspects to analyze about how city brands are dealt with on the web, the databases that the websites may obtain about their users, and other aspects of website information not considered in the initial model.

The analysis was applied to 40 official websites of important tourist cities of the five continents during 2006. This sample was selected by means of a ranking evaluating the main tourist cities of the world, taking into account the *World's Top Tourism Destinations* of the WTO (World Tourism Organization), the number of visitors and the importance of the city as a tourist destination.

We observed 135 indicators, of which 87 are representative of the three variables analyzed: usability, interactivity and the brand. Interactivity is analyzed in the three factors mentioned previously: consumer-message interactivity, consumer-marketer interactivity and consumer-consumer interactivity. Its analysis, through the SPSS program, was centered on descriptive statistics and the combination of variables, using Gamma as a correlation index.

RESULTS OF THE QUANTATIVE STUDY. USABILITY

The concept of usability is defined as "the extent to which a product can be used by specified users to achieve specified goals with effectiveness, efficiency and satisfaction in a specified context of use"[7]. This ease of use, nevertheless, is related to very diverse aspects, that go from the page design, to the content quality, the ease of locating information and the simplicity of navigation, all

Table 1. Items of usability (Source: Authors' compilation)

Indexes of usability	Frequency	Percentage
List of contents on all pages	36	90.0%
Link the home page	37	92.5%
External links related sites	38	95.0%
Up-to-date information	39	97.5%
Sitemap	23	57.5%
Indication of the navigation path	16	40.0%

Table 2. Ranking of websites with the most and least points with respect to usability (Source: Authors' compilation)

Web sites with high scores in structure, design and usability		Web sites with low scores in structure, design and usability	
Score	City Web sites	Score	City Web sites
11	London	5	Cairo
11	Hong Kong	5	Beijing
10	Bangkok	6	Lisbon
10	Budapest		
10	Sydney		
10	Amsterdam		
10	Tokyo		
10	Buenos Aires		
10	Mexico City		

of which are related, in addition, to the subjective perceptions of the user.

The indicators used in the study to measure the usability variable are those that provide the navigability for the website: the access menu for the sections always being visible, the indication of the navigation path, constant links to the home page, the existence of a sitemap and an internal search engine; the possibility of user help by telephone, e-mail, chat or web call; and external links to related sites.

The majority of sites analyzed in the study showed high levels of structure, which means that the websites are, in general, well designed. At a global level, high percentages were seen for the variables that make up the structure, usability and design of the websites.

As seen in Table 1, the majority of the sites analyzed have a list of the site contents that appears on all of the pages, along with a link to the home page from each page. These two resources give the user his or her location on the web, clarify the structure of the site and simplify its use. In addition, almost all the websites have external links with other related sites. Through these links they can provide complementary information and services. In some cases connection to the official sites of the town halls and institutions are provided, in others, the purchase of services, for example the link on Barcelona's website to ServiCaixa, through which you can purchase tickets for entertainment.

With respect to the help that the websites offer their users, 90% of the sites analyzed provided e-mail contact. In addition, 65% provided a telephone helpline. But, however, only one website offered help by chat and none used web calls (calls from marketing staff from the destinations where you request them to call you at a certain time) or human clicks (communication in real time of a visitor to a website with its administrators).

All in all, the results stated up to now show that the majority of websites are well structured and designed. Therefore, they have a high degree of usability.

Table 2 shows the rankings of the websites with best structure, design and usability, along with those that have the least points in these aspects. The structure variable ranges between 5 and 11, with sites with 5 having the worst structure and those with 11 the best.

The initial Hong Kong web page (Figure 1), one of the best in usability of our study, is simple, graphic and structured. It shows only a big image and the list of different languages the user can choose.

When you enter in the initial page of the selected

Figure 1. Hong Kong Web site

language you can observe that it has the content list in all the pages, visual and graphic links and shows a constant simplicity in the entire site.

Interactivity

The interactivity variable, as explained previously, was analyzed using three aspects: consumer-message interactivity, consumer-marketer interactivity and consumer-consumer interactivity. We measured the concept of interactivity using the three aforementioned typologies of Cho and Cheon (2005).

Consumer-message interactivity is measured with indicators such as: the existence of search engines, user help, the option to customize the display, displaying virtual reality, multimedia presentations, directional maps, virtual leaflets, the option of downloads to mobiles, and on-line games, among others. However, consumer-marketer interactivity is based on indicators of

relationships with the marketing organizers of the cities. They offer the possibility of questions and complaints from users, opinion surveys, chats with promotional or sales agents, bulletin boards for users, or the possibility of placing orders and making reservations on line. Finally, consumer-consumer interactivity is measured using indicators of the relationship between them, such as the existence of chats or an email service.

Consumer-Message Interactivity

The first result we can see is that, in general, the majority of websites analyzed use many more resources that belong to the consumer-message interaction, than to the consumer-marketer, and consumer-consumer interaction. Therefore, the sites offer the navigator a greater interactivity with the messages that they wish to transmit than with the people that are in charge of marketing the destinations and other consumers. And within the resources of the consumer-message interaction, the most used in all the websites, that is, those that show the highest percentages, are the interactive travel organizers.

So, this shows that the majority of websites analyzed offer services of interactive travel organizers. We refer to organizers without the possibility of purchase. They help users to plan their trips by providing fully personalized information adapted to the needs and interests of the users. The interactive travel organizers allow the users to plan their trips in a fully complete and personalized way, from their transport to the destination to their accommodation and other complementary tourist services.

However, there are other interactive consumer-message resources that are hardly used by the websites analyzed. Certainly, 62.5% have directional maps of the cities to orient the users and 82.5% have geographical markers on the maps with zoom, which offer the possibility of searching for and locating elements on the map in detail. But only three of the sites allow the user to customize the home page, four show virtual excursions or online games for children, five offer virtual flights of the city from the air or allow users to create their own virtual leaflets in folders, which they can save with the personalized information that interests them.

The informative services using optional downloads to mobiles, whether metro maps, information on monuments or audio downloads are also resources that are barely used by the websites analyzed.

All of these interactive resources, in addition to offering information, provide a certain entertainment and distraction to the users of the websites, making them more attractive and interesting.

Consumer-Marketer Interactivity

The resources of the consumer-marketer interaction are still less used by the websites analyzed that those of consumer-message interaction. The possibility of placing orders or online reservations is offered by 35% of the sites, and 32.5% allow the user to track the orders placed. For these two resources, the prior registration is usually required of the user, and with this the websites can obtain personal information about their consumers. In 22.5% of the sites, users can fill in surveys or opinion polls and 12.5% offer the option of complaints by consumers.

The rest of the consumer-marketer interactive resources are barely used by the websites analyzed. For example, only Rome's site offers the users the possibility of asking what they want about the city, the services offered or the entity that organizes the marketing of the destinations. Only the websites of Dublin and Istanbul have an electronic bulletin board available to the users. And finally, the sites of Madrid, Amsterdam and Montreal are the only ones that allow the consumers to sponsor the website. This means that any organization can pay some money to sponsor the website. All the conditions are very well explained on the site. In exchange, the sponsor can put its logo on the website.

Not one of the websites analyzed offered the users the possibility to propose new products or services, chats with the marketing agents, or "call me" buttons with time and language selection for those responsible for promoting the city to call the interested users to provide them with the information they want, personally by telephone.

Consumer-Consumer Interactivity

With respect to the consumer-consumer interaction, there are even fewer resources available. The resource of this type that is most used in the sites analyzed is the on-line postcards service, featuring in 40% of the websites, of which 37.5% do not require registration. This resource, which is offered more and more by the destination websites and is mostly used by young users, enables them to send on-line postcards, without the delay or costs of sending them.

Table 3. Resources used in the websites of interactive travel organizers (Source: Authors' compilation)

		Frequency	Percentage
Interactive travel organizers (without possibility of purchase)	How to get there	33	**82.5**
	What to do	39	**97.5**
	Attractions/events	38	**95.0**
	Leisure activities	38	**95.0**
	Cultural activities	37	**92.5**
	Where to stay	38	**95.0**
	Transport	39	**97.5**
	Excursions	33	**82.5**
	Rentals	**16**	40.0

Moreover, only Krakow's site has a chat for users, and the possibility for consumers to tell their stories, experiences and summaries of trips is only found on the sites of Hong Kong, Rome and Toronto. Finally, none of the websites analyzed offer the services of a cyber club of users with advantages or a cyber community with common interests. Cyber clubs which offer some advantages of information, discounts and special conditions to the loyal users. The cyber club of users would allow the marketing organizers of the destinations to create loyalty programs for clients using the offer of advantages and discounts. Moreover, the creation of a cyber community would enable the users of this group to build relationships with each other, broaden information in their interest, and create a strong position with respect to these common interests.

So, we can see that there is a great inequality in the use of interactive resources by official websites of destinations. The most used are those that belong to the consumer-message interaction, and especially, the interactive travel organizers. All in all, generally, the percentages of use of interactive resources are still underused, in particular those of the consumer-marketer and consumer-consumer interaction. These results coincide with those of the study by Anton (2004) about the Internet presence of the main tourist destinations of the

Spanish Mediterranean coast. In it, he highlights the absence of instruments that promote interactivity in the websites, such as on-line forms, pages of visitor comments, etc. (Table 3)

The degree of global interactivity of the websites analyzed, which may range between 4 and 28, can be seen in the ranking in Table 4. These numbers represent the number of interactive tools they use.

Visit Dublin's web page it's the most interactive out of all the analyzed sites. If we only observe the first part of the page we can find a searcher and in the graphic frontal there is the option to click and see a video about the city. The whole page is very interactive.

In the accommodation section the user can search information, but can also reserve and buy the products.

Even the maps of the city and the maps of public transport are interactive. They show the routes that the user requires in personalized way.

Treatment of City Brands on the Web

In the analysis of the communication and dissemination of city brands through websites, it is necessary to differentiate the concepts of city brand and brand image. As previously explained, the city brand is a construct composed of a name,

Table 4. Ranking of websites with the most and least points with respect to interactivity (Source: Authors' compilation)

Most interactive websites		Least interactive websites	
Score	City websites	Score	City websites
28	Dublin	4	Moscow
23	Hong Kong	4	Kiev
21	Valencia	7	Sydney
20	Madrid	8	Cairo
18	Berlin	8	Seville
18	Istanbul		
18	Rome		

Table 5. Ranking of the best and worst treatment of city brands in websites (Source: Authors' compilation)

Websites that deal with their city brands best		Websites that deal with city brands worst	
Score	City websites	Score	City websites
10	Amsterdam	3	Kuala Lumpur
8	Hong Kong	5	Madrid
8	Athens	5	Zagreb
8	Dublin	5	Cairo
8	Toronto	5	Sydney
		5	Moscow
		5	Lisbon
		5	Montreal
		5	Rome
		5	Mexico City
		5	Kiev

a logo, some symbols and values that we try to associate with a city representing its identity, with the objective of creating a positioning and a vision of the city in the minds of the public, which must be based on a citymarketing plan and projected through a communication program. On the other hand, the brand image is that which is created in the minds of the public as a consequence of the communication of the city brand, in conjunction with the perceptions and subjective values of individuals. (Table 5, Figure 2, Figure 3, Figure 4, Figure 5, Figure 6)

In the study, the degree of communication and dissemination of the city brands through the websites was measured using the presence of the brand and the logo, whether there is a description of the city brand, whether the graphic and photographic images represent the brand, whether the colors and the typography of the page are coordinated with the logo, and the functional and emotional brand is disseminated.

The results show that city brands are treated poorly on the websites analyzed. Their treatment is even less developed than that of interactivity.

All in all, the vast majority of websites (97.5%) have the logo on all of the pages, and this is usually situated in the upper left part. However, it must also be taken into account that three of the websites analyzed show more than one logo for the same city brand, which creates dysfunctionality and incoherence.

Of the websites, 92.5% offer a brief description of the destination, but only 5% (two of the sites analyzed) have a minimum explanation of the city brand, of its creation and symbolism. Similarly, only 35% of the websites state the marketing objectives of the tourist institutions of the cities.

The graphic images, in general, also are an underused resource in the dissemination of the city brands. All the websites transmit the functional brand through photographic images, but only half of them (50%) communicate the emotional brand through the photographs. On the other hand, the rest of the graphic images are not used to disseminate the brand at all.

Finally, the graphic and typographic coherence between the brand and the web has not been taken into account either in the majority of websites

Figure 2. Visit Dublin Web site

Figure 3. Visit Dublin accomodation section

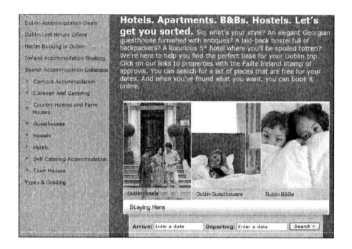

Figure 4. Visit Dublin maps section

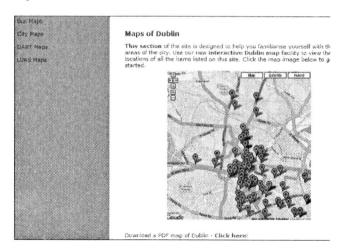

Figure 5. I Amsterdam Web site

analyzed. Only 27.5% of the sites have the predominant colors of the website coordinated with the logo, and 23.5% use the same typography on the page and the brand. On the other hand, only one of the sites analyzed includes elements of the advertising campaign transmitted through the conventional media.

The degree of global treatment of the city brands on the websites analyzed, which ranges between 3 and 10, can be seen in the ranking in Table 5.

The web of Amsterdam, which best disseminates the city brand, does not only deal with the functional and emotional brand on the web, but in addition it pays attention to many other graphic and visual aspects. For example, the emotional brand, which is disseminated through very few websites, in that of Amsterdam it is dealt with both by changing photographs on the page, which show people of the city, and by an introductory page that explains in depth what the brand symbolizes. In it, it explains what the brand "Iamsterdam" is, who

Figure 6. I Amsterdam manifesto page

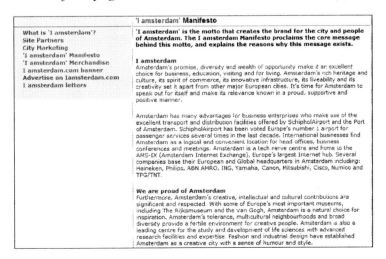

created it, when and why; and what it symbolizes and means. As can be seen in the home page, the logotype is present in the entire site. The brand is based on the idea that the value of Amsterdam is their people. It plays with 'I am sterdam' and 'I am Amsterdam'. The photographs of the site try to communicate these emotional values through different types of people of differing ages, race and profession instead of showing monuments or landscapes and scenery.

But the official site of Amsterdam also pays attention to other aspects related to the brand, such as the typography. It uses the same combination of colors and type of letters as the logo in the whole website, creating a graphical coherence that boosts and constantly reminds of the city brand.

Finally, this web page contains information on the city marketing, their objectives and strategies and also an explicit explanation of the brand (which you can read in the I Amsterdam manifesto), advertising of the city and the merchandising of products.

CONCLUSION

The study indicates that the majority of websites analyzed have high usability indexes. Therefore, the official websites of cities pay a lot of attention to ease of navigation, so that the user can easily navigate and find the information he or she wants.

Contrarily, interactivity is much less implemented in the websites analyzed. The interactive resources that are most used are those that correspond to the consumer-message or consumer-marketer relationship, despite being generally underused.

So, it can be confirmed that the websites analyzed in this study have a better structure, design and usability, than interactivity. The websites are more usable and structured than interactive. And, in addition, there is no correlation between these two variables. Therefore, the interactive capacity

of the websites may be higher than now without affecting the other variables at all.

As a consequence of the under use of interactive resources, the possibilities of user records, contained in the interactive resources, also decrease. This means that the information obtained on the part of the website users is minimum. As has been previously confirmed, the possibility of obtaining more information for more direct one-to-one marketing that would produce special offers according to the needs of the consumers is being wasted.

On the other hand, there is even less treatment of the brands on the websites analyzed. Only the graphic images, basically the logo, are disseminated and in part the functional brand. However, very few communicate the emotional brand. Similarly, few websites show graphic and typological coherence with the logo, or a relationship with the advertising or the marketing objectives of the destinations.

These results show that, in general, there is a certain lack of attention to the communicative aspects in the construction of the city websites. They seem to be made by information technologists, who pay great attention to usability, and also, to a lesser extent, interactivity, but do not take into account the communication of the brand. Therefore, you can sense the existence of a certain lack of co-ordination between the IT and communication and marketing departments of the entities promoting the cities.

To effectively create websites that disseminate city brands and promote the image of the destinations, it is fundamental to be conscious of what an important tool for image, communication and marketing these websites are for the destinations and cities.

As we go further into the Information Era, the role of websites is changing. They are evolving from being merely sources of information, that is, intermediaries between tourists and destinations, to being involved in tourist transactions. Therefore, tourism and Internet make an ideal combination. The Internet provides the users with a way of obtaining much more varied and detailed information on the destinations and the cities than that which existed before. However, in addition it enables them to, through the same web space, make consultations and reservations quickly and easily.

The websites are considered the future of communication on the Internet, as they offer a large quantity of information and, in addition, create virtual product experiences (Klein 2003). Websites, on one hand, create a brand image and, on the other, can provoke a direct response (Hollis, 2005). As Cho & Cheon (2005) confirm, websites offer different communication possibilities: public relations, sales promotion, advertising, direct marketing and brand image creation. As a consequence, this communicative potential must be promoted and made use of in the field of cities.

With respect to how little city brands are dealt with on the websites analyzed, it is due, firstly, to insufficient conceptualization, creation and development. As we have already stated, city brands are a recently created concept that is still at a very incipient stage. For this reason, the web deal poorly with them. Firstly, it is necessary to create elaborate city brands, based on a strategy of citymarketing, to be communicated later to the public and, if not, disseminated through the websites.

Despite the studies mentioned above (Spool, 1996; Chen & Wells, 1999; Chen & al., 2002; Heijden, 2003) that show the importance of usability in promoting a more positive brand image among users; and the effect of interactivity, which produces more favorable attitudes towards the web, the brand and greater intentions of purchase (Sicilia & al., 2005; Ko & al., 2005), we can confirm that high indexes of usability and moderate indexes of interactivity do little good in the websites analyzed in the promotion of city brands. First it is necessary to correctly create the city brand, to later disseminate it through the websites of the cities. And only after this first step, will usability and interactivity be complementary and effective aspects in the promotion of city brands.

Improvement Proposals

The creation of the city brand must not be an act restricted to the activity of citymarketing. Exactly the opposite, it must be coherent with the whole marketing plan and be derived from a competitive city strategy.

It must start with a prior diagnosis of the current situation of the city image and the competition, to later formulate the vision of the city and the positioning that is desirable to achieve in the world urban system.

Only after the two first stages should an identity program for the city be determined, which must take into account a historical analysis, and the perceptions of the internal and external public. Then the visual identity of the city, its logo, colors, typography should be determined; along with the functional and emotional values of the brand. In this whole process it is essential to identify the internal and external public (citizens, visitors, investors, mass media, public institutions, neighborhood associations), to address them directly and achieve that they take on the identity and the city brand to be promoted as their own and, if possible, this should be by consensus.

Finally, the city brand they must be disseminated by a communication plan to each sector of the public through all types of actions *above* and *below the line,* with the intention of continuity in time, for the values of the brand to catch on coherently in the perceptions of all their sectors of the public and be integrated in the rest of the citymarketing actions.

But city brands must not only comply with a creation process inserted into the citymarketing actions, they must also have certain characteristics:

1. The city brand must be made up of three basic elements: the graphic brand, the creation of a symbol and a logo; the functional brand, based on the real strong and attractive points of the city; and the emotional brand, the symbolic and personalizable values that are associated with the city. Without one of these three elements, the city brand is incomplete, losing its identificative and persuasive power.

2. A single city brand must be created, with a single strategy, that is applicable to the diverse sectors of the public, but that at the same time identifies the brand with unique values, which allow the cities to de identified and differentiated from each other. In addition, this brand must be adopted by all the organizations and entities, avoiding the proliferation of several brands that create dysfunctionality.

3. Finally, and independently of the municipal political changes, city brands must be created to last a long time. If they are agreed upon by consensus when created, and therefore, do not belong to the municipal governments, they will evolve independently of the political channels and have a greater possibility of being consolidated in the minds of the public.

Once the city brand is completely and adequately created, and starting with the importance of websites as tools for communication, promotion and marketing of the cities, attention must be paid to three key aspects in the promotion of city brands through the Internet:

1. The treatment of the city brand through the constant and unique presence of the logo, with an explanation of its symbology and objectives, with the representation of the functional and emotional values that are desirable to associate both textually and as graphically, and by means of the graphic

and typographic coherence throughout the website.

2. Maximum development of usability throughout the page, which facilitates user navigation and promotes a positive image increasing the possibilities of recommendation and marketing.

3. Maximum creative use of the interactive resources, as these improve the brand image and the users feel drawn to navigate.

REFERENCES

Aaker, D. (1991). *Managing brand equity*. New York, NY: Free Press.

Anton Claver, S. (2004). La presencia en Internet de los principales destinos turísticos del litoral mediterráneo español. *Actas del Congreso TURITEC 2004*. Universidad de Málaga, 2004. Retrieved June 1, 2008, from http://www.turismo.uma.es/turitec/turitec2004/index.htm

Baker, B. (2007). Places: The new brand frontier. *Total destination management*. Retrieved June 1, 2008, from www.DestinationBranding.com

Baloglu, S., & McCleary, K. (1999). A model of destination image formation. *Annals of Tourism Research, 26*, 868–897. doi:10.1016/S0160-7383(99)00030-4

Biel, A. (1997). Discovering brand magic: The hardness of the softer side of branding. *International Journal of Advertising, 16*, 199–210.

Blain, C., Levy, S. E., & Brent Ritchie, J. R. (2005). Destination branding: Insights and practices from destination management organizations. *Journal of Travel Research, 43*, 328–338. doi:10.1177/0047287505274646

Buhalis, D. (2002). *eTourism. Information technology for strategic tourism management*. UK: Prentice Hall.

Buhalis, D., & Costa, C. (2006). *Tourism, management dynamics. Trends, management and tools.* Oxford: Elsevier Butterworth Heinemann.

Cai, L. (2002). Cooperative branding for rural destination. *Annals of Tourism Research, 29,* 720–742. doi:10.1016/S0160-7383(01)00080-9

Chaves, N. (2004, April). *La marca destino turístico, cinco estrategias gráficas.* Paper presented at the XIII Simposi Internacional de Turisme i Lleure ESADE-Fira de Barcelona. Retrieved April 30, 2007, from www.esade.es/cedit2004/cat/est_estudios.php

Chen, L. D., Gillenson, M. L., & Sherrell, D. L. (2002). Exciting online consumers: an extended technology acceptance perspective. *Information & Management, 39,* 705–719. doi:10.1016/S0378-7206(01)00127-6

Chen, L. D., & Wells, W. D. (1999). Attitude toward the site. *Journal of Advertising Research, 39*(5), 27–38.

Cho, C.-H., & Cheon, H. J. (2005, Summer). Cross-cultural comparisons of interactivity on corporate Web sites. *Journal of Advertising, 43*(2), 99–115.

De Chernatony, L., & Dall'Olmo Riley, F. (1997). Modelling the components of the brand. *European Journal of Marketing, 32*(11/12), 1074–1090. doi:10.1108/03090569810243721

Ekinci, Y., & Hosany, S. (2006). Destination personality: An application of brand personality to tourism destinations. *Journal of Travel Research, 45,* 127–139. doi:10.1177/0047287506291603

ESADE, & BDDO Consulting (2004, April). *Evolución del posicionamiento de los destinos turísticos españoles: De lugares de vacación a marcas de turismo.* Paper presented at the XIII Simposi Internacional de Turisme i Lleure ESADE-Fira de Barcelona. Retrieved April 30, 2007, from www.esade.es/cedit2004/cat/est_estudios.php

Etchner, C. M., & Brent Ritchie, F. (1991). The meaning and measurement of destination image. *Journal of Tourism Studies, 2*(2), 2–12.

Gnoth, J. (1998). Conference reports: Branding tourism destinations. *Annals of Tourism Research, 25,* 750–760.

Hankinson, G. (2004). The brand images of tourism destinations: A study of the saliency of organic images. *Journal of Product and Brand Management, 13*(1), 6–14. doi:10.1108/10610420410523803

Hankinson, G. (2005). Destination brand images: A business tourism perspective. *Journal of Services Marketing, 19*(1), 24–32. doi:10.1108/08876040510579361

Heijden, H. (2003). Factors influencing the usage of web sites: The case of a generic portal in The Netherlands. *Information & Management, 40,* 541–549. doi:10.1016/S0378-7206(02)00079-4

Hollis, N. (2005, June). Ten years of learning on how online advertising builds brands. *Journal of Advertising Research,* 255–268. doi:10.1017/S0021849905050270

Hosany, S., Ekinci, Y., & Uysal, M. (2006). Destination image and destination personality: An application of branding theories to tourism places. *Journal of Business Research, 59,* 638–642. doi:10.1016/j.jbusres.2006.01.001

Kapferer, J. N. (1997). *Strategic brand management.* London: Kogan Page.

Keller, K. (1993). Conceptualizing, measuring, and managing customer-based brand equity. *Journal of Marketing, 57,* 1–22. doi:10.2307/1252054

Klein, L. R. (2003). Creating virtual product experiences: The role of telepresence. *Journal of Interactive Marketing, 17*(1), 41–55. doi:10.1002/dir.10046

Ko, H., Cho, C.-H., & Roberts, M. S. (2005). Internet uses and gratifications. A structural equation model of interactive advertising. *Journal of Advertising, 34*(2), 57–70.

Konecnik, M., & Gartner, W. C. (2006). Customer-based brand equity for a destination. *Annals of Tourism Research, 34*(2), 400–421. doi:10.1016/j.annals.2006.10.005

Kotler, P., Haider, D. H., & Rein, I. (1993). *Marketing places: Attracting investment, industry and tourism to cities, states and nations.* New York, NY: Free Press.

Lawson, F., & Band-Bovy, M. (1977). *Tourism and recreational development.* London: Architectural Press.

Liu, Y. (2003, June). Developing a scale to measure the interactivity of Web sites. *Journal of Advertising Research,* 207–216.

Liu, Y., & Shrum, L. J. (2002). What is interactivity and is it always such a good thing? Implications of definition, person and situation for the influence of interactivity on advertising effectiveness. *Journal of Advertising, 31*(4), 53–64.

López Lita, R., & Benlloch, M. T. (2005). La marca territorio. El marketing de ciudad, una herramienta al sevicio de las marcas territorio. *99% com, 2,* 8.

Lynch, P. J., & Horton, S. (2004). *Manual de estilo web. Principios de diseño básico para la creación de sitios Web.* Barcelona: Gustavo Gili, SA.

Martín Barbero, S., & Sandulli, F. (2005). *Marcating en la Web: BIWAM. Identidad desnuda.* Madrid: Dossat 2000.

McMillan, S. (2004). Internet advertising: One face or many? In D. Schumann and E. Thorson (Eds.), *Internet advertising: Theory and research (2nd edition).* New York, NY: Lawrence Erlbaum.

McMillan, S., Hwang, J.-S., & Lee, G. (2003, December). Effects of structural and perceptual factors on attitudes toward the website. *Journal of Advertising Research,* 400–409.

Morgan, N., Pritchard, A., & Piggott, R. (2002). New Zeland, 100% Pure: The creation of a powerful niche destination brand. *Journal of Brand Management, 9*(4/5), 335–354. doi:10.1057/palgrave.bm.2540082

Morgan, N., Pritchard, A., & Pride, R. (2004). *Destination branding. Creating the unique destination proposition.* Oxford: Elsevier.

Nielsen, J. (2002). *Usabilidad. Diseño de sitios web.* Madrid: Prentice Hall.

Padín Fabeiro, C. (2004, April). *La formación de la imagen de un nuevo destino.* Paper presented at the XIII Simposi Internacional de Turisme i Lleure ESADE-Fira de Barcelona. Paper presented at the XIII Simposi Internacional de Turisme i Lleure ESADE-Fira de Barcelona. Retrieved April 30, 2007, from www.esade.es/cedit2004/cat/est_estudios.php

Park, C. W., Jaworski, B. J., & MacInnis, D. J. (1986, October). Strategic brand concept management . *Journal of Marketing, 50,* 135–145. doi:10.2307/1251291

Prebensen, N. K. (2007). Exploring tourists' images of a distant destination. *Tourism Management, 28,* 747–756. doi:10.1016/j.tourman.2006.05.005

Riezebos, R. (2003). *Brand management. A theoretical and practical approach.* Harlow, UK: Prentice-Hall.

Ritchie, B., & Ritchie, R. (1998). *The branding of tourism destination: Past achievements and future trends.* Paper presented at the 48th Congress, AIEST, St-Gall.

Sicilia, M., Ruiz, S., & Munuera, J. L. (2005). Effects of interactivity in a Web site. *Journal of Advertising, 34*(3), 31–45.

Simon, S. J. (2001). The Impact of culture and gender on web sites: An empirical study . *The Data Base for Advances in Information Systems, 3*(1), 18–37.

Spool, J. M. (1996, January 1). Branding and usability. *User Interface Engineering*. Retrieved June 1, 2008, from www.uie.com/articles/branding_usability.

Tsikriktsis, N. (2002). Does culture influence web site quality expectations? An empirical study. *Journal of Service Research, 5*(2), 101–112. doi:10.1177/109467002237490

World Tourism Organisation. (1999). *Promoción de destinos turísticos en el Ciberespacio*. Madrid: WTO.

World Tourism Organisation. (2001). *Comercio electrónico y turismo*. Madrid: WTO.

ENDNOTES

[1] According to Nina K. Prebensen (2007), to build a good city brand, with the most suitable elements, that create a positive image, the opinion and knowledge of the visitors or future visitors is fundamental.

[2] Bill Baker is the founder and President of Total Destination Management. He is internationally recognised as an expert in building brand recognition for destinations and communities. TDM is a Portland, Oregon based team of destination branding, tourism planning and marketing specialists. www. DestinationBranding.com consulted in July 2007.

[3] Blain, Levy and Brent Ritchie (2005) confirm that the logos of city brands globally represent the experience that the visitors expect of a destination or city. Effectively, logos stimulate the communication of the attributes desired among the visitors and influence the tourists' decision to visit a place.

[4] Hosany, Ekinci and Uysal (2006) demonstrated that there is a relationship between the image of a destination and its personality. They also demonstrated that the image of a destination's brand is fundamental to position it effectively.

[5] Other authors, such as Keller (1993) and Park (1986) add a third category or element to the city brand: experiential attributes, which refer to the experiences, satisfaction and feelings of the destination's visitors.

[6] Spool compared two websites: one more usable and informative and the other very graphically meticulous. He showed that the more usable site created a better brand image, as it satisfied the expectations of the users to a greater degree. Therefore, the graphic aspects of a website, such as logos and photographs, have less effect on the branding than expected.

[7] International Organization for Standardization (ISO). In: http://www.iso.org/iso/home.htm

APPENDIX: LIST OF WEBSITES ANALYSED

America

Table 6. America

México D.F.	www.mexicocity.gob.mx
Los Ángeles	www.lacvb.com
Montreal	www.tourisme-montreal.org
New York	www.nycvisit.com/home/index.cfm
Toronto	www.torontotourism.com
Buenos Aires	www.buenosaires.gov.ar/areas/turismo/home
Río de Janeiro	www.riodejaneiro-turismo.com.br/en/home.php

Africa

Table 7. Africa

El Cairo	www.cairotourist.com
Marrakesh	www.ilove-marrakesh.com

Asia

Table 8. Asia

Bei-jing	english.bjta.gov.cn
Tokyo	www.tourism.metro.tokyo.jp/english/index.html
Hong Kong	www.discoverhongkong.com
Kuala Lumpur	www.kualalumpur.gov.my
Bangkok	www.bangkoktourist.com
Macau	www.macautourism.gov.mo
Bali	www.balitourismauthority.net/home.asp
Delhi	delhitourism.nic.in

Oceania

Table 9. Oceania

Sydney	www.cityofsydney.nsw.gov.au

Europe

Table 10. Europe

Amsterdam	www.iamsterdam.nl
Athens	www.cityofathens.gr
Dublin	www.visitdublin.com

Istanbul	english.istanbul.com
Florence	www.firenzeturismo.it/en_default.asp
Helsinki	www.hel2.fi/tourism
Lisbon	www.cm-lisboa.pt/turismo
London	www.visitlondon.com
Paris	www.parisinfo.com
Prague	www.visitprague.cz
Roma	www.romaturismo.com
Vienne	info.wien.at
Berlin	www.berlin-tourist-information.de
Kiev	www.kmv.gov.ua
Krakow	www.krakow.pl
Budapest	www.budapestinfo.hu
Moscow	www.moscowcity.com
Zagreb	www.zagreb-touristinfo.hr

Spain

Table 11. Spain

Barcelona	www.bcn.es/turisme/catala/turisme/welcome.htm
Madrid	www.esmadrid.com
Sevilla	www.turismo.sevilla.org
València	www.turisvalencia.es

Chapter 5.6
Assessing the Performance of Airline Web Sites:
The ARTFLY Case

Elad Harison
University of Groningen, The Netherlands

Albert Boonstra
University of Groningen, The Netherlands

EXECUTIVE SUMMARY

This case takes place in the increasingly competitive environment of the airline sector. Airline websites and Internet-based booking systems enable transformation of airline operations and become strategic weapons for the majority of airlines worldwide. Established airlines are attempting to stimulate customers to use the Internet, in response to entry of low cost carriers that capture shares of their market and in order to reduce their sales costs. Nonetheless, the development and maintenance of websites and e-commerce platforms requires substantial investments in capital and labor. Therefore, airlines need to assess the performance of their e-commerce channels in terms of profitability, customer appreciation and volume of sales on a continuous basis. However, the design of an assessment model that can serve the managers of ARTFLY, one of the established airlines in the industry that deals with the recent challenges of the intensifying competition, is open for a wide variety of interpretations and should be determined due to the firm's nature of operations and due to its aim to increase the volume of its online sales.

ORGANIZATIONAL BACKGROUND

ARTFLY, founded in 1919, is a major airline that operates on a worldwide basis. In 2004 ARTFLY merged with the Air Minoli group and became a division within the joint Air Minoli/ARTFLY group. Air Minoli/ARTFLY has a worldwide coverage, in terms of destinations, flight routes and marketing units. The group uses two main European airports as their main hubs and offers air transport to 128 destinations in 65 countries in 5 continents. To illustrate the volume of the group's activities in 2004-2005 the ARTFLY group transported more than 20 million passengers and more than 600,000 tons of cargo, generating profits of 255 million Euros ($300 million U.S.).

In 1995, ARTFLY was one of the first European airlines that introduced fully integrated e-business into its ticketing process, in response to radical changes in the air transport market (Rubin & Joy, 2005). In particular, the entry of low cost airlines and the price war that followed presented a tangible threat to ARTFLY's market. Low cost carriers succeeded in attracting increasing numbers of passengers who previously purchased their tickets through travel agents and airline branches and have shifted to booking their flights online via the Web sites of those carriers (see Figure 1). For example, the rise of EasyJet and Ryanair to dominance in the British market, flying 55 million passengers from and to the U.K., was achieved in part as a consequence of online ticket sales (ABTA, 2005). ARTFLY replaced its previous procedures with online bookings, electronic tickets, and electronic check-ins and boarding passes. Reducing its costs

by direct sales and using the Internet as a prominent marketing channel were immediate actions that were taken by ARTFLY's management and assisted in surviving the intense competition in the market and maintaining its major position in this rapidly changing business environment.

In March 1996, the company launched its first Web site, which was mainly an electronic brochure with information on flights. A year later, new functionality was added including real-time information on departure and arrival times, a reservations module and electronic ordering of tickets. From 2001, a complete electronic booking system was included in ARTFLY's homepage and, since then, the Web site is continuously maintained and often face-lifted due to changes in the market and new technological possibilities.

ARTFLY bases its marketing and sales activities on four main distribution channels that include its own Web site, online travel agencies (e.g., Expedia.com and Kayak.com), ARTFLY branches and "physical" travel agencies (see Table 1). The firm has defined its Web site, ARTFLY.

Figure 1. Channels of low cost flight bookings (Source: ABTA, 2005)

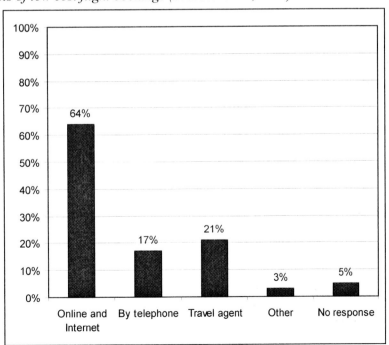

com, as the most important channel in its home market. The company is keen to increase the share of online bookings via the Web site (together with other online travel agencies) from 25% up to 40%. Outside its home market, ARTFLY branches are its main sell points. The branches are located at major airports and in the centers of large cities worldwide, hence enabling accessibility of customers to its booking services. In addition, ARTFLY operates through local travel agencies. However, the firm aims at replacing part of its offline sales by increasing the share of online bookings, as the physical distribution channels involve either higher operating expenses (e.g., personnel and location costs) or commissions paid to independent travel agencies.

The targets of ARTFLY can be compared to the industry's benchmarks. In 2006, the Airline IT Trends Survey (SITA, 2006) measured the relative share of bookings in each distribution channel in 98 major airlines worldwide. It concludes that, on average, the airlines' own Web sites (the direct online channel) captured 21.5% of the bookings, 8.2% of the tickets were purchased through online travel agencies (the indirect online channel), 17.7% of the bookings were made in the branches

Table 1. Four distribution channels of ARTFLY

	Direct	Indirect
Online channel Now (2005/06): 12% Target (2008/09): 40%	1 www.ARTFLY.com	2 Online travel agencies (e.g., Expedia.com)
Offline channel Now (2005/06): 88% Target (2008/09): 60%	3 ARTFLY branches	4 Travel agencies with branches (e.g., Thomas Cook, but mostly operate on local, regional or national scales)

Figure 2. Use of online channels for flight bookings (Source: SITA, 2006)

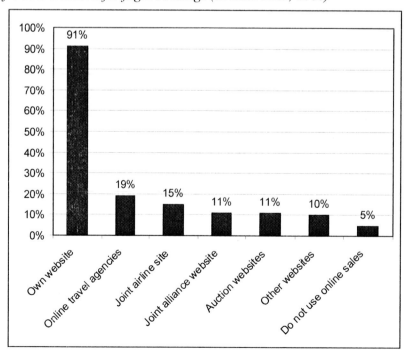

of flight companies (the direct offline channel), while the majority of bookings – 52.6% of the flight tickets sold in 2006 – were made through "physical" travel agencies (the indirect traditional channel). On the supply side, 91% of the firms in the survey offer their customers the possibility to book their flights via their own Web sites, and only a small proportion of the firms (5%) do not have any direct or indirect online channels (see Figure 2).

The firm's policy, that is, setting a 40% share of sales from online sources, stems from three main objectives, as follows:

- *Cost-reductions* that result from simplifying the booking and payment processes and reducing the scale of human interventions in the ticketing process by emailing e-tickets to customers.
- *Better services* are provided by a faster check-in procedure and by enabling online customers to select their seats while booking their flight. Doing so, customers do not have to wait for their boarding pass and can shorten their stay at the airport.
- *Increased market share* is achieved by gaining better performance on the Internet than its competitors. This aim involves both high degrees of Internet presence and use of intelligent strategies and customer relationship management (CRM) tools to identify the preferences and patterns of purchasing decisions among online customers.

Over time, ARTFLY's Web site has become increasingly important for the firm in terms of its growing volume of sales and as an attractor of potential customers. To illustrate the growth of its online channel of distribution, in 1997 ARTFLY's Web site received approximately 3,000 visitors per week, while during 2007 it attracted more than one million weekly visitors. In 2001, the site reached average monthly revenues of 0.5 million Euros, while the monthly online revenues in 2007

were approximately 156 million Euros (source: Reference Document ARTFLY/Air Minoli, 2006). However, the exponential increase in the use of ARTFLY's Web site led to larger volumes of online traffic and to demands from customers for new and advanced features, availability and reliability of the Web site.[1] Consequently, ARTFLY's online operations required a new assessment model that captures the multiple dimensions of its online operations and their effectiveness in terms of additional profits and growth of its customer base.

Currently, the evaluation of ARTFLY's online activities and performance is coordinated by the CEO through a series of monthly meetings that involve managers of different divisions and units. The managers report the changes in the indicators for which they are responsible and recommend on adapting existing online tools and campaigns or highlight the needs to develop new systems. Then, the feasibility of developing or modifying new tools, their expected contribution to the organization and their costs are discussed within this forum. However, this process suffers from two major shortcomings: First, the configuration of the current performance evaluation process requires significant coordination efforts due to the involvement of different divisions and organizational units and due to the broad distribution of responsibilities among them (see Figure 3). Second, the CEO can assess the performance of ARTFLY's Web sites only in a monthly resolution and cannot receive continuous measurements of performance to assess it within shorter periods (for example, on a daily or on a weekly timeline).

SETTING THE STAGE

Recent studies in marketing and in ICT emphasized the potential of Web sites and e-commerce tools as new distribution channels that can create new opportunities for cost savings and profits for new and existing companies (Buhalis, 2004; Xing & Grandt, 2006). In particular, early air transport studies identified how Internet technologies can be implemented by airlines to increase the volumes of their online ticket sales and to expand their marketing channels (Alamdari, 2002; Jarach, 2002; Lubbe, 2007; Shon, Chen & Chang, 2003; Yoon, Yoon & Yang, 2006). Recent studies focussed on assessing the impact of commercial Web sites on broader dimensions of activities and performance of firms (see, for example, Agarwal & Venkatesh, 2002; Gianforte, 2004; Huizingh, 2002; Otim & Grover, 2006; Park & Gretzel, 2007).

Those studies seem to be of a major importance particularly to airline companies, as their market is characterized on the one hand by strong competition and on the other hand by opportunities to sustain customer relations and loyalty (e.g., via frequent flyer programs, Gasson, 2003). In addition, the entry of low-cost airline companies in recent years intensified price competition and put higher pressure on the profit margins of many firms (Klein & Loebecke, 2003; Klein, Klein, Kohne & Oorni, 2004). In this respect, the Internet assists airlines in developing alternative marketing and distribution channels, reducing direct costs, reaching new customers and maintaining long-term relations with existing customers. However, the strong competition in the market and the openness of the Internet as a communications medium enabled firms to learn and to apply similar online business practices, Web site designs and e-commerce tools. In other cases, the rapid development of Internet technologies has made within a short period Web sites less user friendly or less attractive in comparison to Web sites of competitors, and sometimes even obsolete (Law & Leung, 2000). Consequently, marketing managers in airline firms, as well as in other sorts of organizations that base a large part of their activities on electronic commerce, are in need of an evaluation tool to assess the effectiveness and the reach of their online operations and to indicate what improvements in it should be made.

Internet marketing and e-commerce are largely based on site building, promoting it online (e.g.,

via search engine) and via traditional marketing campaigns and attracting potential customers that enter it to purchase goods and services (Chu, 2001). The accessibility to the Web site and the knowledge of consumers of its existence and the range of information and services that it provides are major factors in its success, as well as the choice of advertising channels with high potential to attract customers (Monsuwe, Dellaert & Ruyter, 2004). It is also important to enhance their presence and the volume of Web traffic to them by other means, such as association with related search terms and Web-based campaigns. Complementary off-line campaigns can also reinforce the exposure of Web sites to potential Web-surfers and customers. Drèze and Zufryden (2004) describe nine categories of traffic building strategies that should be taken into account while constructing Web-traffic plans: off-line advertising of a Web site, offline news reports, Internet advertising/banner ads, links from other Web sites, links from search sites, links from online directories, online news reports, reference in an e-mail and discussion/newsgroups. The exposure of Web sites increases not only but including it in search engines and search-word based advertising, but also by more "traditional" means, such as banners, TV campaigns and press releases. Attracting large numbers of visitors to the firm's Web site is an important step to the successful of Web-based exposure and merchandizing.

Although financial indicators of the operations of the firm (including its online marketing, distribution and sales)[2] are essential for evaluating the performance of Web sites, a different approach that is based on a broader framework of the firm's operations and competitive position is often needed (Toh & Raven, 2003). Financial measurements of the performance of Web sites and online tools mostly reflect short-term measurements, such as costs and revenues and overlook other performance measures of online activities and long-term effects on the firm.

Figure 3. ARTFLY's organizational structure (Divisions and units participating in the evaluation of the performance of ARTFLY's Web sites are marked in grey)

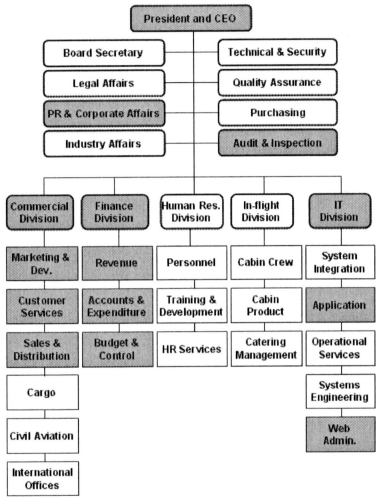

Analyses of Internet ventures, including those of *non-Internet* product and service providers, should be done at the industry level. When an individual tool fails to meet the industry's standards, the firm is advised not to engage in developing online marketing and distribution channels. For example, if an airline company invests an online booking system and the volume of bookings are inferior to other players in the market, it should either modify the system or abolish it and turn to its traditional distribution channels (e.g., agents and call centers, Smyth & Wagner, 2006).

CASE DESCRIPTION

By the end of 2006 the Finance Director, Mrs. Eva van Duinen, started a discussion during a weekly board meeting, in which she expressed her doubts about the performance of the Web site of ARTFLY. She felt that the usual growth of online sales were stagnating. The CEO, Mr. Jim Manzetti, agreed with her that it would be wise to give more attention to this theme. The first thing to do for a more thorough discussion in the management team would be to collect all relevant data on Web site performance. The members of

Table 2. Comparative measures of ARTFLY's Web site use in subsequent periods

Measures	2005 Q4	2006 Q4
1 Financial overview:		
Revenues from online bookings (in USD)	88,359	84,563
Number of tickets sold via Web site	209,523	206,251
Costs of Web site maintenance (in thousands of USD)	12,450	14,429
2 Customer appreciation of Web site according panel		
Ease of finding the Web site (on scale of 1 – 10)	7.3	7.3
Overall appreciation of Web site (on scale of 1 – 10)	6.9	6.5
3 Contact		
Number of visitors	5.133.935	4.988.238

the management team agreed that they would look for this information, especially the information that compares Web site performance between the 4th quarter of 2005 and 2006.

One week later, the Web site performance theme was again on the agenda. The Finance director reported that the revenues from online bookings had gone down with nearly 5%, compared with the last quarter of 2005. She also mentioned that the costs of Web site development and maintenance had gone up by 12%. John Simons, IT director, explained this rise of IT costs by growing costs of maintenance as a result of the increasing number of Web pages and the hiring of external experts. He said that more Web pages and more online traffic automatically lead to higher costs in terms of maintenance. External experts were needed in order to make Web sites more aesthetically pleasing. Developing such expertise in-house would be much more expensive.

Mr. Otto Caroll, director of the sales department delivered additional figures that showed that the number of tickets sold is also slightly decreasing. In addition to this, other indicators revealed that the volume of use of the Web sites by new and returning ("loyal") customers is lower than in the previous years and its popularity among them is decreasing. During the same meeting, the public relations manager, Mrs. Anna Jacobsson,

reported from a panel discussion with customers that the overall appreciation of the Web site by the panelists was also gone down a little bit. These panel discussions were held with a group of twenty customers on a quarterly basis and covered many issues related to customer services and customer satisfaction of ARTFLY.

The data on Web site performance were grouped by a staff member in Table 2. Based on these data, a discussion started among the various directors. Eva van Duinen, the Finance Director, felt strongly that a program of cost cutting would be necessary to align investments in online channels with the performance of those channels.

Director Otto Caroll from Sales argued that the figures reflect a growing and intense competition, especially with low-cost airlines, which directly compete with ARTFLY in its existing routes, and that a substantial share of ARTFLY's customers have preferred to book their flights online via their Web sites. He argued that ARTFLY should know what they are doing wrong with their Web sites, before cutting costs.

The IT director contributed to the discussion by saying that a strategy of promoting the online channel should be supported by high investments in quality and attractiveness of the Web sites. He thinks that cost saving programs will jeopardize such a policy.

All directors agreed that the available information as reflected in table 1 was not appropriate for making far reaching decisions on investment programs or savings on ARTFLY Web sites. The participants were missing comparisons with the performance of other airlines as well as figures about the performance of off-line channels. Others were asking what the determinants of customer satisfaction of airline Web sites are. Speed? Attractiveness? Completeness? It would not be wise to invest or to save costs without having a thorough knowledge on important relevant issues that determine the performance of online channels.

When the discussion continued, it became clear the directors did not completely agree on the most relevant issues that determine Web site performance. The financial director emphasized the financial justification of investments in Web sites. Others agreed that this is important, but the financial performance will be determined by actual sales. These are determined by issues like the easiness to find a Web site, the speed and loading time of a Web site, attractiveness and so on. The IT director, John Simons added to this by saying that ARTFLY also pays considerable amounts of money to search engines like Google and Yahoo. Costs of clicks from those sites varied from 0.20 – 0.30 cents. To his opinion, it would be important to assess whether these costs can be justified by increased online sales. Marketing manager, George Veldman emphasized that Web sites also realize important cross sales in terms of hotel bookings, car rentals and so on. He felt that the profits from cross selling should be captured in the whole decision making process.

The CEO concluded this discussion by saying that the company needed a Web site performance monitoring system that includes the issues raised by the various directors. Such a system should have to lead to frequent reports that show how the company's Web sites are performing. This would help to make rational decisions with regard to investments and cost saving programs much easier. He emphasized that the system should

also be related to the strategy of ARTFLY, which includes a careful move to online channels, while maintaining off-line channels and keeping customers satisfied who prefer off-line channels.

IN NEED OF AN ASSESSMENT MODEL: DEFINING KEY INDICATORS TO ASSESS THE PERFORMANCE OF ARTFLY'S WEB SITE

Recent studies in marketing and in ICT have addressed the potential of Web sites and e-commerce tools to provide new distribution channels that can increase the profitability of flight companies. Online bookings can significantly increase the volume of sales by reaching new customers via Internet presence and campaigns and can reduce the operation costs of firms by eliminating the need to pay commissions to travel agents (Xing & Grandt, 2006). Major airlines were aware of the need for an assessment model to evaluate the performance of their online activities (notably, their Web sites and online ticket sales) and have adopted various models for this purpose (Alamdari, 2002; Jarach, 2002; Lubbe, 2007; Shon et al., 2003; Yoon et al., 2006). However, most of these models address only limited aspects of the online activities and Web site operation, such as the number of entries per period or the user-friendliness of the booking system, and do not provide a coherent overview of the indicators that define in detail the role of the Web sites. For example, most of these assessment methods overlook the additional added value of the Web sites in terms of their impact on sales, contribution to the airlines' profitability, reputation and presence in the market. A second type of indicators that is often omitted from the assessment models that are described in the literature evaluates the Web sites in terms of the quality of their technical operation. For example, the proportion of down time and the number of malfunctions can be included in the model as indicators for technical performance. The assessment of the technical performance of Web sites is particularly important as the availability of their online booking systems strongly affects the volume of online sales and the level of customer satisfaction. On the other hand, the period in which a Web site cannot be accessed can be directly translated to loss of sales and potential bookings. Even when some of the customers decide to complete their order via another marketing channel, such as call centers or travel agencies, it would be less profitable for the firm in comparison to online bookings.

The impact of commercial Web sites on the performance of the firm can be assessed through a broad prism that includes both financial key performance indicators as well as via qualitative and quantitative measures. Those measures should reflect the satisfaction of clients from the airline's Web site and the accessibility to its contents and to the booking system.

The financial appraisal of the firm's operations is the direct and most important indicator to evaluate its e-commerce channel. Therefore, online operations, and particularly the construction and the maintenance of a Web site, can be assessed from the financial standpoint by means used to evaluate other IT investment decisions: Profitability is the most important objective and it reflects the proportion between profits and investments. In addition, the risks associated with the development and operation of a Web site and an online booking system should be taken into the account of the expected financial gains (Renkema & Berghout, 1997). However, the financial measurements present the costs and revenues and do not include other measures that can affect the performance of the firm, such as service quality, reputation and brand loyalty. Therefore, the financial measures should be complemented by qualitative and quantitative indicators.

In addition to those indicators, nonfinancial factors that affect the performance of airline Web sites can be assessed via the following categories:

- **Customer satisfaction:** the ability of customers to locate the Web site of the company, to access it with ease and to use its contents in ways that meet their needs. This indicator is measured through customer surveys and focus groups.
- **Accessibility:** the ease of finding a Web site and the exposure of potential customers to it. This criterion includes also the technical aspects of accessing the Web sites with different Web browsers, presenting the contents properly and downloading the Web site in a reasonable time when various Internet connections are used.
- **Traceability:** measures the traffic to the Web site, access to the different contents and Web pages within it, its presence in online portals and its position (rating) in search engines. The criterion is measured by online traffic measurement tools.
- **Contact:** a sales-based criterion that reflects the interest of customers in the online services of the firm. It measures the volume of online visitors that access the Web site in a given time and the distribution between new and returning visitors. The number of visitors is especially important as it is used also to assess the traceability of the Web site and the accessibility of consumers to it. Contact data are obtained from customers that visit Web sites after viewing advertisements in the media (newspapers, radio and TV), follow Internet advertisements (banners flash videos and pop-up windows) and *adsense* advertisements that link terms used in search engines to commercial Web sites[3]. Therefore, it is possible to provide a measure for the effectiveness of each advertising channel by tracking the volume of traffic that originates from it.
- **Sales:** indicators measure the revenues and the profits from online sales in a given period. The firm can compare between sales from "off-line" marketing channels, such as

travel agents and ARTFLY's offices, and the volume of orders that are completed via its Web site. Changes in the relative share of online bookings reflect changes in consumers' behavior and trust in purchasing services via ARTFLY's Web site and can signal the need for a proactive online marketing, such as Internet-based campaigns and additional Web advertising. Sales data by channel can be obtained from ARTFLY's financial and accounting systems.

- **After-sales:** records data on service quality, the volumes and costs of online transactions (in comparison to off-line sales) and the satisfaction of customers from their online bookings.
- **Customer support:** measures the total number of visitors that apply for support services, such as technical assistance and follow-up on online bookings, in a given period, as well as assessing the costs of customer support services regarding the operation of the Web site and its various features.

Table 3. Criteria and measures for assessing ARTFLY's online products and services

Criteria	Indicators
Financial overview	Costs Revenues Direct revenues from bookings
Customer satisfaction	Ease of finding the Web site Ease of booking a flight online Speed of downloading the Web site and contents Speed of operating the Web site Overall appreciation of Web site Appreciation of services
Traceability	Number of domain names in use
Accessibility	Loading time Number of languages supported by Web site

Contact	Total:
	  Number of visitors
	  Number of new visitors
	
	Per channel:
	  Number of visitors
	  Costs per visitor
	  Sales per visitor
	  Average bookings per visitor

Sales	Total revenues Total sales Sales per product Profits per product Total profits Volume of bookings Total conversion Conversion per product Ratio of online to offline revenues
After-sales	Costs per booking Number of bookings Use in relation to sales Customer appreciation
Customer support	Use of the product Use of the product per visitor Costs of use Customer appreciation

Since the beginning of 2007, the model, presented in Table 3, was applied in various ways to measure the short-term and long-term performance of ARTFLY's Web site. The various indicators have formed a baseline that can provide information on changes in consumers' behaviour (such as growing demand for particular lines or seasonal trends). Further, by following the indicators of the model over time ARTFLY can monitor its online operations and assess the effectiveness of new contents and features, Internet-based promotions, different advertising channels and online marketing campaigns. Table 4 demonstrates the measures of the assessment model after implementing it for two years. However, the application of ARTFLY's assessment model is only in its initial stages and the firm plans to expand its use (such as assessing the use of the booking system by regular passengers vs. members of the frequent flier program) and to broaden the set of measurement indicators.

The metrics collected for the assessment model provide useful insights that can assist in managing the firms' online strategy and activities. After the implementation of the assessment model, ART-FLY's managers can identify major changes and market trends with ease and to respond to them. The model is often used to assess current practices and strategies of the firm, such as its advertising strategy and the distribution of its advertising budget between online and traditional media.

CURRENT CHALLENGES/PROBLEMS FACING THE ORGANIZATION

As mentioned previously, the airline market is dynamic and it is dominated by intensifying competition, particularly from low-cost carriers. In this business environment, ARTFLY aims at increasing the share of the online bookings ac-

Table 4. Comparative measures of the assessment model in subsequent periods.

Measures	2006 Q4	2007 Q1
	105,489	108,549
1 Financial overview:	14,759	15,563
Revenues (in thousands of Euros)	89,467	91,263
Costs (in thousands of Euros)		
Direct revenues from online bookings		
2 Customer satisfaction	7.1	7.2
Ease of finding the Web site	6.6	7.1
Speed	6.3	6.7
Overall appreciation of Web site	365	389
Appreciation of services		
3 Traceability		
Number of domain names		
	6.123669	6.23657
4 Accessibility		
Loading time in seconds		
Languages supported by Web site		
	8.36	7.92
5 Contact	11	14
Number of visitors		
Visitors from Google		
Sales to visitors from Google (millions of Euros)	4.563.236	5.239.246
Costs per click from Google (Euros)	562.346	599.756
Visitors from Yahoo	6.235	6.539
Sales to visitors from Yahoo (millions of Euros)	0.21	0.23
Costs per click from Yahoo (Euros)	123.756	142.153
	953	843
	0.30	0.29

complished by its customers, as those sustain its market share. Further, online bookings accommodate a tangible potential to lower ARTFLY's operational costs.

ARTFLY's management assesses the performance of its Web sites and online tools particularly on the basis of financial indicators, that is, the additional revenues and profits gained from those distribution channels in comparison to the financial investments necessary to construct and to maintain those electronic commerce platforms and online campaigns. However, the impact of ARTFLY's presence over the Internet goes beyond the direct and immediate financial prospects and has significant positive effects in terms of customer satisfaction, reputation and the quality of the information and services that it provides. Further, ARTFLY's management concluded the way the performance assessment of the Web sites and online booking facilities is carried out could be considerably improved. Hence, ARTFLY's actual challenges and questions are as follows and are followed by elaboration of the relevant aspects:

• What are the possible dimensions through which the performance of Web sites can be determined and assessed?

The current assessment model can be seen as a starting point for the evaluation of the performance of Web sites. Firms should address the following questions: Which dimensions are used in the current model, which aspects are emphasized and which are ignored? What are the choices that are made and how do they reflect the strategy of the company?

• How can ARTFLY's assessment model can be extended and improved?

Since the model as reflected in Table 3 and 4 are an early version of the model management should think about further refinements of it, as well as about removing less relevant elements of the model.

• How frequent should a performance measurement system of Web sites be operated to report to firm managers?

Information should be provided to support decision making that promote the use, the improvement and the maintenance of Web sites. These decisions also support the outphasing or abandonment of Web sites when needed. Management teams should determine how often they have to consider these issues.

• How should the evaluation process of the performance of Web sites be organized?

To realize actual use, data have to be collected, data have to entered into the system, information has to produced by the system and the information has to be distributed to the relevant people. Management should specify these generic activities and the responsibilities of carrying them out on a continuous basis.

• Which organizational units should be responsible for the performance evaluation and take part in it?

This issue is related to the question of who is primary responsible for the use and for the success of Web sites. Depending on the organizational structure and the roles and responsibilities of workers, Web site responsibilities can be divided in different ways. Alternative options are: Web site managers, business process managers, business unit managers, financial managers, division managers or CEO's.

• How can a performance measurement system be related to the strategies and to the strategic priorities of firms?

Firms have various strategic priorities, for example, they can follow a low cost strategy, a differention strategy, a global strategy or a niche strategy that can be monitored by the measurement system. However, those different strategies may be evaluated and monitored by different criteria that assess online processes and functions, as well as the Web sites themselves.

REFERENCES

Agarwal, R., & Venkatesh, V. (2002). Assessing a firm's web presence: A heuristic evaluation procedure for the measurement of usability. *Information Systems Research, 13*(2), 169.

Alamdari, F. (2002). Regional development in airlines and travel agents relationship. *Journal of Air Transport Management, 8*(5), 339-348.

Association of British Travel Agents (2005). *Travel statistics and trends*. London: ABTA Press.

Buhalis, D. (2004). eAirlines: Strategic and tactical use of ICTs in the airline industry. *Information & Management, 41*(7), 805-825.

Chu, R. (2001). What online Hong Kong travelers look for on airline/travel websites? *International Journal of Hospitality Management, 20*(1), 95-100.

Drèze, X., & Zufryden, F. (2004). Measurement of online visibility and its impact on Internet traffic. *Journal of Interactive Marketing, 18*(1), 20-37.

Gasson, S. (2003). *The impact of e-commerce technology on the air travel industry*. Hershey, PA: Idea Group Inc.

Gianforte, G. (2004). The world at our fingertips— How online travel companies can turn clicks into bookings. *Journal of Vacation Marketing, 10*(1), 79-87.

Huizingh, K. R. E. (2002). Towards successful e-business strategies: A hierarchy of three management models. *Journal of Marketing Management, 18*(7-8), 721-747.

Klein, S., & Loebbecke, C. (2003). Emerging pricing strategies on the web: Lessons from the airline industry. *Electronic Markets, 13*(1), 46-58.

Klein, S., Kohne, F., & Oorni, A. (2004). Barriers to online booking of scheduled airline tickets. *Journal of Travel & Tourism Marketing, 17*(2/3), 27-39.

Jarach, D. (2002). The digitalisation of market relationships in the airline business: The impact and prospects of e-business. *Journal of Air Transport Management, 8*(2), 115-120.

Law, R., & Leung, R. (2000). A study of airlines' online reservation services on the internet. *Journal of Travel Research, 39*(2), 202-213.

Monsuwe, T. P., Dellaert, B. G. C., & Ruyter, K. (2004). What drives consumers to shop online? A literature review. *International Journal of Service Industry Management, 15*(1), 102-121.

Lubbe, B. (2007). The effect of Internet apprehension and website satisfaction on air travellers' adoption of an airline's website. *Journal of Air Transport Management, 13*(2), 75-80.

Otim, S., & Grover, V. (2006). An empirical study on Web-based services and customer loyalty. *European Journal of Information Systems, 15*, 527–541.

Park, Y. A., & Gretzel, U. (2007). Success factors for destination marketing web sites: A qualitative meta-analysis. *Journal of Travel Research, 46*(1), 46-63.

Renkema, T. J. W., & Berghout, E. W. (1997). Methodologies for information system investment evaluation at the proposal stage: A comparative view. *Information and Software Technology, 39*(1), 1-13.

Rubin, R. M., & Joy, J. N. (2005). Where are the airlines headed? Implications of airline industry structure and change for consumers. *Journal of Consumer Affairs, 39*(1), 215-228.

Shon, Z. Y., Chen, F. Y., & Chang, Y. H. (2003). Airline e-commerce: The revolution in ticketing channels. *Journal of Air Transport Management, 9*(5), 325-331.

SITA (2006). *Airline IT trends survey.* Geneva: SITA Press.

Smyth, A., & Wagner, C. M. (2006). Business-to-business electronic marketplaces in the airline industry: Tool for enhanced efficiency in a volatile business. Transportation Research Record. 1951, 60-68.

Toh, R. S., & Raven, P. (2003). Perishable asset revenue management: Integrated internet marketing strategies for the airlines. *Transportation Journal, 42*(4), 30-43.

Xing, Y., & Grandt, D. B. (2006). Developing a framework for measuring physical distribution service quality of multi-channel and "pure player" internet retailers. *International Journal of Retail and Distribution Management, 34*(4), 278-289.

Yoon, M. G., Yoon, D. Y., & Yang, T. W. (2003). Impact of e-business on air travel markets: Distribution of airline tickets in Korea. *Journal of Air Transport Management, 12*(5), 253-260.

ENDNOTES

[1] Since the beginning of 2005, the latest version of the Web site is available in all the 65 countries and supports 20 different languages. ARTFLY's management demanded that the Web site would be available online in 99.99% of the time.

[2] On average, airlines expect to save 13% of their administrative costs by moving to online bookings (SITA, 2006).

[3] Google bases its activities and business model on linking the search terms of users to textual *adsense* advertisements. When customers click on featured advertisements, they open the promoted Web site. Then Google charges the advertiser per click.

This work was previously published in Journal of Cases on Information Technology, Vol. 11, Issue 1, edited by M. Khosrow-Pour, pp. 47-64, copyright 2009 by IGI Publishing (an imprint of IGI Global).

Chapter 5.7
Aviation–Related Expertise and Usability:
Implications for the Design of an FAA E–Government Web Site

Ferne Friedman-Berg
FAA Human Factors Team - Atlantic City, USA

Kenneth Allendoerfer
FAA Human Factors Team - Atlantic City, USA

Shantanu Pai
Engility Corporation, USA

ABSTRACT

The Federal Aviation Administration (FAA) Human Factors Team – Atlantic City conducted a usability assessment of the www.fly.faa.gov Web site to examine user satisfaction and identify site usability issues. The FAA Air Traffic Control System Command Center uses this Web site to provide information about airport conditions, such as arrival and departure delays, to the public and the aviation industry. The most important aspect of this assessment was its use of quantitative metrics to evaluate how successfully users with different levels of aviation-related expertise could complete common tasks, such as determining the amount of delay at an airport. The researchers used the findings from this assessment to make design recommendations for future system enhancements that would benefit all users. They discuss why usability assessments are an important part of the process of evaluating e-government Web sites and why their usability evaluation process should be applied to the development of other e-government Web sites.

INTRODUCTION

On November 15, 2007, President Bush announced actions to address aviation delays during the Thanksgiving holidays. As part of this announcement, he directed people to visit the Web site fly.

faa.gov, which is a Federal Aviation Administration (FAA) e-government Web site that provides real time information about airport delays.

Fourth, the federal government is using the Internet to provide real-time updates on flight delays. People in America have got to know there's a Web site called Fly.FAA.Gov; that's where the FAA transmits information on airport backups directly to passengers and their families. If you're interested in making sure that your plans can -- aren't going to be disrupted, you can get on the Web site of Fly.FAA.Gov. As well, if you want to, you can sign up to receive delay notices on your mobile phones. In other words, part of making sure people are not inconvenienced is there to be -- get transmission of sound, real-time information. (Bush, 2007)

There has also been a concerted effort by the FAA to publicize its Web site by placing advertisements in airports across the United States. Many news outlets now provide airport delay information as part of their weather forecasts, and this delay information comes, most often, directly from the fly.faa.gov Web site.

Because this Web site is the public face of a large federal agency, it is important that it presents the agency in the best light possible. An agency Web site should be a positive public relations vehicle and should not, in itself, create any public relations problems. Although use of e-government Web sites is increasing annually, low user acceptance of e-government Web sites is a recognized problem (Hung, Chang, & Yu, 2006). Many factors affect whether or not someone will use or accept an e-government Web site, including past positive experience with e-government Web sites (Carter & Bélanger, 2005; Reddick, 2005); the ease of use of the Web site (Carter & Bélanger, 2005; Horst, Kuttschreutter, & Gutteling, 2007); the perceived trustworthiness of the information presented on the Web site (Carter & Bélanger; Horst, et al., 2007); the perceived usefulness of

the Web site (Hung et al., 2006); and personal factors such as education level, race, level of current internet use, and income level (Reddick, 2005). If a Web site has many functional barriers, such as having a poor layout or producing incomplete search results, customers of the site may not use it (Bertot & Jaeger, 2006).

Early work in e-government has consistently ignored studying the needs of end users, and there has been little research focusing on the demand side of e-government (Reddick, 2005). That is, *what are customers looking for when coming to an e-government Web site?* Although there have been many benchmarking surveys conducted on e-government Web sites, benchmarking surveys often do not describe the benefits provided by a Web site and only enumerate the number of services offered by that site (Foley, 2005; Yildiz, 2007). Benchmarks do not evaluate the user's perception of sites and do not measure real progress in the government's delivery of e-services. However, governments often chase these benchmarks to the exclusion of all other forms of evaluation (Bannister, 2007).

E-government academics emphasize the importance of usability testing and highlight the need to focus on Web site functionality, usability, and accessibility testing (Barnes & Vigden, 2006; Bertot & Jaeger, 2006). However, despite its importance, many organizations still are not performing usability testing on e-government Web sites. Current work often does not address the needs of different user communities, employ user-centered design, or use rigorous methods to test the services being delivered (Bertot & Jaeger; Heeks & Bailur, 2007).

Governments around the world are working to review best practices for e-government evaluation methods (Foley, 2005). Because of the social and economic benefits of providing information online, it is important that e-government Web site designs meet the needs of its targeted users. In addition, it is important to document the benefits provided by the Web site to increase public support

(Foley). Carter and Bélanger (2005) point out that e-government Web sites should be easy to navigate. They note that the organization of information on the site should be congruent with citizens' needs. When consumers visit an e-government Web site, they are most frequently looking for information (Thomas & Streib, 2003), which they need to be able to find quickly and easily. If users encounter problems while using a Web site, they may become frustrated and be less likely to adopt or utilize e-government services in the future. A positive experience with an e-government Web site will be communicated to others (Carter & Bélanger), and a usable Web site can play a significant role in engendering trust in the agency itself.

Most Web usability research focuses on e-commerce sites and privately run Web sites (Hung et al., 2006), and people expect e-government Web sites to be as good or as usable as private sector sites (Irani, Love, & Montazemi, 2007). People are more likely to use an e-government Web site if the transactions with that site are compatible with previously conducted transactions on similar, non-government Web sites (Carter & Bélanger, 2005).

However, there are clear differences between e-government and e-commerce Web sites. For instance, e-government sites must provide universal accessibility so that all citizens have access to information. Additionally, e-government Web sites are accountable to the public, whereas commercial Web sites are only accountable to people who have a financial stake in the Web site. It is not always clear, however, where the boundary between these two types of sites lies (Salem, 2003). Additionally, there are often challenges faced in producing e-government Web sites that are not faced by commercial sites (Gil-Garcia & Pardo, 2005). For example, when creating e-government Web sites, designers need to consider whether the project goals align with the goals or mission of the government agency (Yildiz, 2007). They also must make sure that all project stakeholders are involved, determine whether they are in compli-

ance with all relevant government regulations, and work within government budget cycles and changing government contractors.

The FAA and fly.faa.gov

The FAA Air Traffic Control System Command Center provides information about airport conditions, such as arrival and departure delays, to the public and the aviation community via their Web site, www.fly.faa.gov. This Web site allows users to view airport conditions for specific airports.

The Web site has many different functions that help the user to search for delay information (see Figure 1). Using the **Search by Region** function, users are able to look up airports in different geographic regions, such as the Northeastern states and the Southeastern states. When using the **Search by Airport** function, users are able to search for airport delay information by typing in the name of a city, airport, or a three-letter airport code. The **View by Major Airport** function allows users to search for delay information using a drop down list of 40 major airports.

The site is also a repository of information for use by airlines, pilots, passengers, government personnel, academics, individual aircraft operators, and other stakeholders in the aviation community. It provides access to real-time and historical advisory information, real-time airport arrival demand information, current reroutes, and reroute restrictions. It also provides access to information related to air traffic management tools, a glossary of aviation terms, a national routes database, pilot tools for making arrival and departure reservations, a collection of National Airspace System documents, and many other air traffic tools.

The focus of this assessment was on the evaluation of site elements that the general public would access the most, such as the airport delay information and the glossary of aviation terms. From the user's point of view, the Web site needs to provide accurate information quickly, with minimal effort,

Figure 1. The www.fly.faa.gov home page, illustrating the View by Region, Search by Airport, View by Major Airport, and Site Map search methods

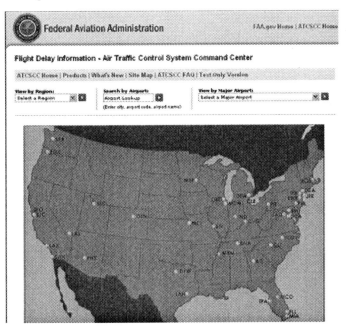

while minimizing potential mistakes. The site should be easy for users to learn and provide an appealing and satisfying experience.

We faced some unique issues and challenges when evaluating the fly.faa.gov Web site. First, the fly.faa.gov Web site presents real-time, up-to-the-minute data, whereas most e-government Web sites often present static information or information that changes infrequently. It was also clear that the expectations of site users were likely to be influenced by the information found on more commercial aviation sites. Because people have preconceived notions about the airlines and the reliability of information provided by airlines, it was possible that this perception could transfer to their perception of this Web site.

The Web site was also originally designed for use by people associated with the aviation industry, such as pilots and local airport authorities, who have at least a working knowledge of various aviation concepts. Because it is accessible on the internet and other travel sites have links to it, members of the traveling public (who may

have little, if any, understanding of aviation or its associated jargon) also frequently use the site. The Web site is also being touted (Bush, 2007) as the first place the public should visit on the Web when looking for travel-related delays in the aviation system. Therefore, it was important to evaluate whether this site is usable by people who do not have a background in aviation. In this usability assessment, we examined how effectively people with different levels of domain knowledge were able to use the site.

It was difficult to identify a single typology that described the Web site. Although the site often looks like a Government to Consumer (G2C) site (Hiller & Bélanger, 2001), its original purpose was to function as a Government to Business (G2B) site or a Government to Employee (G2E) site. The site allows people to perform basic transactions (Hiller & Bélanger, Stage 3), but it also attempts to be a full-service, one-stop site for many types of aviation related information (Hiller & Bélanger, Stage 4). For instance, although this evaluation did not focus on the G2B information, airlines often use the site to find delay information, and general aviation pilots use the site to make route reservations. Although the site tries to organize its content to meet the different needs of these different categories of users (Ho, 2002; Schelin, 2003), it is not clear how the organizational structure was determined or whether it is the most optimal organization for all types of users.

We conducted this formal usability assessment to determine how successfully the Web site meets these usability goals and the needs of its users, including both expert and novice users. The assessment employed techniques commonly used in usability evaluations (Ahlstrom & Longo, 2003; Nielsen, 2003). The participants completed a set of representative tasks using the Web site, while researchers observed and recorded their actions and comments. Users also answered a series of questions rating the usability of the site. The data collected through these activities helped us identify a number of problems. After identifying the final list of usability issues, we used a part of the heuristic evaluation technique (Nielsen) to determine the most critical issues. This article discusses the technique used in this evaluation, highlights some of the most critical issues, and provides suggestions to designers on how to fix them. We also discuss the benefits of applying this formal process to the development of other e-government Web sites.

METHODOLOGY

Participants

We recruited 32 adult volunteers from the FAA William J. Hughes Technical Center to serve as participants. Because the participants were FAA employees, many had greater aviation-related knowledge than the general public. However, many FAA employees, such as administrative assistants and facility support workers, do not have significant knowledge of aviation or air

traffic control. We included participants of both categories.

Equipment

The laptops used in the experiment contained fully interactive offline versions of the fly.faa.gov Web site. A User Script asked the participants to use the Web site to find information to answer 17 questions: 12 asked users to search for delay information, 3 asked users to find the definitions for aviation-related terms, and 2 asked users to identify the authority to be contacted when trying to obtain specific information. The script also asked users to use the **Search by Region**, **Search by Airport**, and **View by Major Airport** methods for specific questions. This allowed us to evaluate the usability of each function.

Procedure

Each session lasted 30 to 45 minutes. After signing an informed consent form, the participants completed a Background Questionnaire that collected information about the participants' knowledge of computers, Web sites, and aviation terminology.

After completing the Background Questionnaire, the participants next completed the User Script. We observed each participant during the experiment and recorded pertinent actions or comments. At the end of the experiment, the participants completed a Post-Session Questionnaire, where they rated their experience and identified usability issues.

Because using participants who all had a high level of aviation-related knowledge could have biased the results, we used the data to categorize the participants into three groups (novices, moderate knowledge users, and experts), based on their aviation-related knowledge. We analyzed the data by level of expertise to determine whether aviation-related knowledge had an impact on user performance. By analyzing the results in this way, we could make recommendations targeted toward making the site usable for the different user populations. When even individuals with a high level of aviation-related expertise had trouble using certain features, this provided strong evidence that those features needed to be redesigned. Even if novices were the only ones who had a problem with a feature, we rated that problem as severe if the impact for those users was severe.

RESULTS

Background Questionnaires

The Background Questionnaire asked the participants questions regarding their familiarity with aviation-related terms and acronyms. For example, participants were asked to list three-letter abbreviations for airports (e.g., Philadelphia International Airport = PHL), or were given the three-letter abbreviations and asked to list the airports associated with those abbreviations (e.g., MIA = Miami International Airport). Using the correct responses to these and other aviation-related questions, we categorized the participants as novices (n = 8), moderate knowledge users (n = 15), and experts (n = 9). The novices were slightly younger than both the experts and those with moderate-knowledge (M_{novice} = 41.6 years, $M_{moderate}$ = 49.9 years, M_{expert} = 49.1 years). More than 70% of novices and those with moderate knowledge reported never using the fly.faa.gov Web site. In contrast, 75% of the experts reported using the Web site a few times a year.

All the participants had extensive experience using computers and the Web. Because we found no discernable differences in reported Web and computer use among the participants, we were unable to stratify the participants based on these factors.

User Script Data: Overall Analysis

Of the 12 questions that asked users to find specific delay information, the participants answered 79.4% correctly. For the subset of five delay questions that allowed the participants to use their preferred search method, the participants answered 71.2% correctly. For the subset of four **Search by Airport** questions, 84.5% of the participants answered the questions correctly. For the **View by Major Airport** question, 90.6% of participants found the correct answer; for the **View by Region** question, 81.3% found the correct answer; and for the **Site Map** question, 87.5% found the correct answer.

Three questions asked the participants to use the site to provide the definition of three aviation related terms and abbreviations. Although 84.4 % of participants answered all three questions correctly, 6.3% answered one incorrectly, 3.1% answered two incorrectly, and 6.3% were not able to answer any of the questions. By comparing the percentage of participants who answered a question correctly, we determined that all three questions were equally difficult.

Two questions asked the participants to find whom to contact to obtain information about the status of an individual flight or why an airport was closed. For these questions, only 28.1% of the participants answered both questions correctly, 56.2% answered one incorrectly, and 15.6% answered both incorrectly.

User Script Data: Analysis by Level of Expertise

We analyzed the data by level of expertise to determine whether aviation-related knowledge had an impact on user performance. Analyzing all 17 questions, we found an effect of expertise on overall task performance, $F(2, 29) = 3.54, p =$

.04. Post hoc pairwise contrasts indicated expert participants were able to answer significantly more questions than novices (85.6% vs. 69.1%, *p* = .01), and there was a trend suggesting moderate-level users answered more questions than novices (79.6% vs. 69.1%, *p* = .07).

We performed ordinal (linear) chi-square tests on individual questions to determine whether the percentage correct increased or decreased across the user categories (Howell, 2007). Although only three of the questions were significant, 7 of the 12 delay questions showed the expected pattern of results (see Table 1). Therefore, we also tested the binomial probability that 7 of the 12 delay questions would show the expected ordering of expert > moderate > novice. We found that it was unlikely that this pattern would occur by chance 7 out of 12 times, *p* < .001. This suggests that experts were better able to find information on the fly.faa.gov Web site than moderate users,

Table 1. Percentage correct by level of aviation-related expertise

Questions	% Correct		
	Novices	**Moderate Users**	**Experts**
1. Los Angeles to Salt Lake City.**	75.0	100.0	100.0
2. Portland to Memphis.	25.0	53.3	33.3
3. Denver to Philadelphia. **Search by Airport.**	87.5	93.3	88.9
4. Houston to Chicago. **Search by Airport.****	62.5	73.3	100.0
5. Newark to Burlington.	50.0	73.3	88.9
6. Las Vegas to New York. **View by Major Airport.**	75.0	93.3	100
7. Phoenix to Dallas.*	12.5	73.3	77.8
8. Cincinnati/Northern Kentucky to Detroit. **View by Region.**	75.0	80.0	88.9
9. Pittsburgh to Washington DC. **Site Map.**	75.0	86.7	100.0
10. New York to San Jose. **Search by Airport.**	75.0	80.0	100.0
11. Orlando to St. Louis. **Search by Airport.**	87.5	86.7	77.8
12. Houston to Tulsa.	87.5	86.7	100.0
Using information available on the site, provide the definitions of the following aviation-related terms or abbreviations:			
13. CIGS	87.5	93.3	88.9
14. MULTI-TAXI	87.5	86.7	88.9
15. VOL	75.0	93.3	100.0
Using information available on the site, who should a visitor contact to obtain information about the following:			
16. Status of an individual flight	100.0	78.6	87.5
17. Why an individual airport was closed	50.0	26.7	44.4

* p < .10, two-tailed. ** p < .05, two-tailed.

who in turn were better than the novices. We did not find the same pattern for the aviation term or contact information questions.

We grouped the questions to analyze performance on the different subsets of questions. For the 12 questions that asked users to find specific delay information, novices, moderate-level users, and experts answered 65.6%, 81.7%, and 88% of the questions correctly, $F(2, 29) = 5.04, p = .01$. Post hoc pairwise contrasts indicated experts and moderate-level users were better able to find delay information than novices ($p = .005$ and $p = .021$, respectively).

We further divided the 12 delay questions into subcategories based on search method. For the subset of questions that allowed people to find information using their preferred search method, we found an effect of expertise on user performance, $F(2, 29) = 9.93, p = .001$. Experts and moderate users performed better than novices when searching for delay information using their preferred search method, answering an average of 80% and 77.3% of the questions correctly, while novices only answered an average of 50% correctly ($p < .001$ for both post hoc pairwise comparisons).

For the four delay questions that asked users to specifically use the **Search by Airport** method, novices, moderate users, and experts answered 78.1%, 83.3%, and 91.7% of them correctly. Although these results were not statistically significant, they demonstrated the same trend as the other sets.

Post-Session Questionnaire: Overall Analysis

The Post-Session Questionnaire asked the participants to rate their subjective experience with the fly.faa.gov Web site using 6-point scales. Except for the question asking about the level of detail, higher ratings indicated positive responses and lower ratings indicated negative responses. For the question that asked the users how detailed

the information on the site was, a rating of 1 indicated too little detail and a 6 indicated too much detail. For these summaries, we omitted responses from the participants who chose more than one number on the rating scale. The ratings indicated that the participants thought it was fairly easy to find information on the site ($M = 4.4, SD = .8$) and that they understood information once they found it ($M = 4.8, SD = 1.0$). The participants also found it fairly easy to navigate between pages on the site ($M = 4.9, SD = 1.2$) and found the design of the site to be consistent ($M = 4.9, SD = 1.0$). They indicated that there was somewhat too much detail ($M = 3.9, SD = 0.8$), but that information on the site was fairly readable ($M = 4.8, SD = 1.1$). Finally, they indicated that, overall, they were mostly satisfied with the site ($M = 4.7, SD = 0.8$). When we compared satisfaction ratings to actual performance, it was apparent that participants were not able to accurately estimate performance, given that they answered an average of 20.1% questions incorrectly. However, despite their performance, the participants still reported high satisfaction with the site. Given this dissociation between performance and satisfaction, it is important that usability experts evaluate not just user satisfaction, but actual user performance, when evaluating a Web site.

Post-Session Questionnaire: Analysis by Level of Expertise

We found no significant differences in the ratings between experts, moderate-level users, and novices. There were, however, some interesting trends in the data. The ratings on information comprehensibility indicated that experts found the information to be somewhat more comprehensible than moderate-level users, who, in turn, found the information to be more comprehensible than novices. In evaluating design and layout consistency, the experts were the least satisfied with the design consistency, with novices being the most satisfied, and moderate users falling somewhere in the middle. For the ratings on the level of detail, experts gave the highest ratings (i.e., slightly too much detail), with novices giving the lowest ratings (i.e., slightly too little detail), and moderate users falling in the middle (i.e., an appropriate level of detail).

Rating of Usability Issues

Using comments and questionnaire ratings made by the participants, along with our observations of the participants while they completed the User Script, we compiled a consolidated list of usability issues and rated the severity of each issue (for a comprehensive list, see Friedman-Berg, Allendoerfer, & Pai, 2007). When rating the severity of each problem, we considered the following factors (Nielsen, 2003).

1. **Frequency:** Is the problem very common or very rare?
2. **Impact:** How easy is it for the users to overcome the problem when navigating through the Web site?
3. **Persistence:** Can users overcome the problem once they know about it, or will the problem bother users repeatedly?

The researchers rated each issue as having high, medium, or low frequency, impact, and persistence, and then used these three ratings to determine a severity rating from 0 to 5. The severity rating scale was adapted from Nielsen (2003).

0 = I don't agree that this is a usability problem at all
1 = minor/ cosmetic problem only: not necessary to fix, should be given lowest priority
2 = usability problem: small benefit from fixing, should be given low priority
3 = moderate usability problem: moderate benefit from fixing, should be given medium priority

4 = major usability problem: important to fix, should be given high priority
5 = usability catastrophe: extremely important to fix, should be given highest priority

After each researcher independently assigned a severity rating for each issue, we averaged them to compute a consolidated severity rating (Nielsen, 2003). These consolidated severity ratings provide a good estimate of additional usability efforts needed when developers establish priorities for future enhancements. We rank ordered the usability issues from those having the highest severity rating to those having the lowest.

The following section discusses the eight usability issues that had the highest severity rating and provides suggestions and design recommendations regarding how these issues could be resolved. User interface design standards and best practices drive these suggestions (Ahlstrom & Longo, 2003). In some cases, we developed simple prototypes to demonstrate potential design concepts that designers could use to remediate some of these issues.

Issue 1: User Confusion Regarding Delay Types

The primary purpose of fly.faa.gov is to provide travelers with airport delay information. For example, a traveler going from Philadelphia to Miami might want to find out about departure delays at PHL and arrival delays at MIA. The traveler also might have some interest in the causes of delays, which can include factors like weather, airport construction, and traffic flow programs. However, the difference between delay types was not readily apparent to many participants. For example, one question asked users to find information about delays at their arrival destination. The arrival airport had no arrival delays, but did have general departure delays. Because the instructions indicated that they were arriving at that airport, the participants should have focused on the lack of an arrival delay, but only 40.6% of the participants answered this question correctly. Those who answered incorrectly seemed to be looking at the departure delay, which indicated that they did not understand which delays were relevant for them. This issue received a mean severity rating of 4.3, $SD = 0.5$.

It is important that the site provide users with the information they want without requiring them to understand difficult air traffic concepts. We also found that novices had greater difficulty in finding delay information than both moderate level users and experts. This was likely due to novice users not understanding more technical concepts. We recommend that the site not try to present difficult concepts to the lay public, but instead present information in a less technical manner. For instance, instead of referencing ground delay programs as the cause of a delay, the site could indicate that a delay was due to congestion. For users seeking more detailed information, the Web site could provide additional information about ground delay programs using links to additional pages.

Because the participants were not always able to identify relevant delays, we recommend that the site provide users with a capability that gives them easy access to pertinent delay information. For example, the site might provide an interactive tool that allows users to input departure and arrival airports or click on city pairs to generate a single report on relevant delays for air traffic traveling between a pair of airports.

Issue 2: Information Presentation: Clutter and Redundant Information

The participants' comments and researchers' observations suggested that there was too much information on the typical search results page (see Figure 2). This issue received a mean severity rating of 4.3, $SD = 0.5$. The site sometimes presented information for a single airport in multiple places on the same page. The information was dense, used too much text, and was not well organized. In many instances, the participants had difficulty finding the delays that were relevant for them. Displaying so much information can be especially problematic when users are in a hurry to find information. Users may scan too quickly and get lost. They may read the wrong line, overlook information they are looking for, or see a big block of text and give up.

We recommend simplifying and reorganizing these pages to make it easier for users to find and understand information on the page. The page could use a tabular layout arranged in columns and organized by arrivals and departures (see Figure 3). Much of the text information is not useful, creates clutter, and should therefore be removed. Because the distinction between general departure delays and destination-specific delays is not clear to users, it should be deemphasized or eliminated. Finally, all delay information related to an individual airport should be consolidated.

Presenting two sets of delay information for one airport, especially if the data are inconsistent, is confusing. The Web site should avoid going into too much technical detail regarding the causes of delays. It might instead use icons or graphics (e.g., clouds with snow, clouds with rain) to depict weather or other causes of delays. The Web site could offer links to additional information for advanced users.

Issue 3: Overuse of Aviation-Related Acronyms and Jargon

The site uses too many aviation-specific acronyms and jargon when providing specific information about the causes of delays. This issue received a mean severity rating of 4.0, $SD = 0.0$. Aviation-specific acronyms, abbreviations, and jargon are difficult for the general public to understand, and the glossary is difficult to find. The average user of the Web site may never be aware that it exists.

Figure 2. Crowded Airport Status Information page

AIRPORT STATUS INFORMATION
provided by the FAA's Air Traffic Control System Command Center

Waterloo Muni Airport (ALO) Real-time Status

The status information provided on this site indicates general airport conditions; it is not flight-specific. Check with your airline to determine if your flight is affected.

Delays by Destination:

- Due to WEATHER/WIND, departure traffic destined to **General Edward Lawrence Logan International Airport, Boston, MA (BOS)** is currently experiencing delays averaging **1 hour and 46 minutes.**
- Due to WEATHER/WIND, departure traffic destined to **Newark International Airport, Newark, NJ (EWR)** is currently experiencing delays averaging **2 hours and 17 minutes.**
- Due to WEATHER/LOW CIGS, departure traffic destined to **John F Kennedy International Airport, New York, NY (JFK)** is currently experiencing delays averaging **4 hours and 3 minutes.**
- Due to WEATHER/WIND, departure traffic destined to **La Guardia Airport, New York, NY (LGA)** is currently experiencing delays averaging **3 hours and 10 minutes.**
- Due to WEATHER/SNOW, departure traffic destined to **Chicago Midway Airport, Chicago, IL (MDW)** is currently experiencing delays averaging **1 hour and 9 minutes.**
- Due to WEATHER/SNOW, departure traffic destined to **Chicago OHare International Airport, Chicago, IL (ORD)** is currently experiencing delays averaging **1 hour and 10 minutes.**
- Due to WEATHER/WIND, departure traffic destined to **Philadelphia International Airport, Philadelphia, PA (PHL)** is currently experiencing delays averaging **3 hours and 38 minutes.**
- Due to WEATHER/WIND, departure traffic destined to **Teterboro Airport, Teterboro, NJ (TEB)** is currently experiencing delays averaging **1 hour and 3 minutes.**
- Due to WEATHER/TSTMS, departure traffic destined to **Newark International Airport, Newark, NJ (EWR)** will not be allowed to depart until at or after 4:15 pm CST.
- Due to WEATHER/TSTMS, departure traffic destined to **La Guardia Airport, New York, NY (LGA)** will not be allowed to depart until at or after 4:15 pm CST.
- Due to WEATHER/ENROUTE WX, departure traffic destined to **Philadelphia International Airport, Philadelphia, PA (PHL)** will not be allowed to depart until at or after 4:15 pm CST.

General Departure Delays: Traffic is experiencing gate hold and taxi delays lasting 15 minutes or less.

General Arrival Delays: Arrival traffic is experiencing airborne delays of 15 minutes or less.

Figure 3. Airport Status Information in a redesigned format

AIRPORT STATUS INFORMATION
provided by the FAA's Air Traffic Control System Command Center

Waterloo Muni Airport (ALO) Real-time Status

The status information provided on this site indicates general airport conditions; it is not flight-specific. Check with your airline to determine if your flight is affected.

Departure Delays			**Arrival Delays**
Are you flying to:			
Airport	**Delay**		Arrival traffic is experiencing airborne delays of 15 minutes or less.
Logan International Airport, Boston, MA (BOS)	1 hour 46 minutes	Snow	
Newark International Airport, Newark, NJ (EWR)	2 hours 17 minutes	Thunderstorms	
John F. Kennedy International Airport, New York, NY (JFK)	4 hours 3 minutes	Congestion	
LaGuardia Airport, New York, NY (LGA)	3 hours 10 minutes	Emergency	
Chicago Midway Airport, Chicago, IL (MDW)	1 hour 9 minutes	Equipment Outage	
Chicago O'Hare International Airport, Chicago, IL (ORD)	1 hour 10 minutes	Construction	
All other airports	Delays of 15 minutes or less		

When the participants had to find the definition of three aviation-related terms, 16% were unable to find the definition for at least one of them. Therefore, we recommend eliminating the use of these terms when they are not essential. This would eliminate unnecessary detail, simplify the site, and make it easier to use and understand.

Issue 4: User Confusion with Using the View by Region Maps

The fly.faa.gov Web site provides users with a **View by Region** search function that allows users to look up airports by searching in different geographic regions. These regions include the Northeast, North Central, Northwest, Southeast,

South Central, and Southwest regions, along with Alaska and Hawaii. When a user uses the **View by Region** function, they are taken to a map that contains only states that are part of a region. However, it is not easy for someone with little knowledge of geography to determine the region for a particular state. The participants got lost when looking for airports that were not on the main U.S. map because they were unable to determine the relationship of regional maps to the main U.S. map. This was especially difficult for states such as Ohio that lie at the edge of a region. These issues make the **View by Region** method difficult for the general public to use and the participants found the **View by Region** maps to be confusing. This issue received a mean severity rating of 4.0, *SD* = 0.0.

One question asked the participants to find delay information for an airport that was not available on the main map or on the **View by Major Airport** menu. Only 71.9% of the participants found the correct answer for this question, indicating that the participants had some difficulty finding information when they needed to drill down on the maps.

There are several recommendations that could alleviate some of the issues related to the use of the **View by Region** method. First, the site could place an outline around the different regions or use color coding to highlight the different regions on the U.S. map. This would help users identify which states belong in which region. The site could display split portions of the main U.S. map on the same page to better orient users to the different regions. To familiarize people with relevant geographic information, the site could label states, both on the main U.S. map and on the smaller regional maps. The site could also offer users a drop-down menu that listed the various airports by state.

Issue 5: Lack of User Knowledge Regarding Three-Letter Airport Identifiers

All commercial airports have three-letter identifiers, and using them is an efficient way to obtain delay information about an airport. The site provides a function that allows users to type a three-letter identifier directly into the **Search by Airport** text box, which will take the user to the details page for that airport. It also provides cues to site users by labeling airports on the main U.S. map with their three-letter identifiers (see Figure 1). However, many participants did not know the correct three-letter identifiers for airports and did not use the cues on the main map to determine the correct identifier. This issue received a mean severity rating of 3.3, *SD* = 0.6.

The site should emphasize that the **Search by Airport** text box accepts regular airport names and city names in addition to three-letter identifiers. Although the **Search by Airport** text box does have a label indicating that users can enter city, airport code, or airport name information in this field, we recommend that the Web site provide the user with specific examples to highlight and better explain the different search options.

Issue 6: The Search by Airport Function Returns Redundant and Irrelevant Results

City name searches using the **Search by Airport** function generate an intermediate results page that lists multiple airports. These listings often contain redundant and irrelevant results. This issue received a mean severity rating of 3.3, *SD* = 0.6. For example, a search for Chicago generates a search results page listing two airports: Midway and O'Hare International. The site lists each result twice, once under **City Name Matches** and once under **Airport Name Matches** (see Figure 4). This format is confusing and users may not

Figure 4. The www.fly.faa.gov results page for a Search by Airport search for Chicago

Airport Lookup Search Results - 'CHICAGO'

City Name Matches
* Chicago Midway Airport, Chicago, IL (MDW)
* Chicago OHare International Airport, Chicago, IL (ORD)

Airport Name Matches
* Chicago Midway Airport, Chicago, IL (MDW)
* Chicago OHare International Airport, Chicago, IL (ORD)

realize that both links take them to the same information. Some participants questioned why the site listed an airport twice. We recommend that the **Airport Lookup Search Results** page consolidate search results and list airports only once in any search results list.

Issue 7: User Spelling and Misspellings and Their Impact on the Search by Airport Function

User spellings and misspellings can have a serious impact on the **Search by Airport** function. In some instances, the correct spelling does not work, but a misspelling does. For example, typing *O'Hare* does not return any results, but *Ohare* does. Typing *LaGuardia* returns no results, but *La Guardia* does. In addition, common misspellings do not produce any results at all, even when the system could provide reasonable guesses about what the user intended. For example, *Newyork* does not produce any search results at all. This issue received a mean severity rating of 3.3, *SD* = 0.6. The participants quickly became frustrated and confused when the site did not return any search results for correct spellings or reasonable misspellings. The search function should always result in a hit when the correct spelling is used, should provide "best guess" search result even

when users make spelling mistakes, and should ignore spacing errors.

Issue 8: Inconsistent Use of Pop-up Windows

The fly.faa.gov Web site is inconsistent in its use of pop-up windows. When users access information using the **Search by Airport** method or when they click on the color-coded dots on the main site map, the Web site displays the search results in a pop-up window. However, when users access information using the **View by Major Airport** method, the site displays the same information in the current browser window rather than in a pop-up window. This issue received a mean severity rating of 3.0, *SD* = 0.0.

During the assessment, some participants accidentally closed the browser by clicking the **Close** button when search results appeared in the main browser window. These participants had become accustomed to results appearing in a pop-up window. When search results appeared in the main browser window, they still reacted as if they were in a pop-up window and accidentally closed down the site, along with the browser.

We recommend that the site be more consistent in how it returns search results and **Airport Status Information** pages. Users become confused when the site responds differently to similar actions. If the standard convention of the site is to bring up search results in pop-up windows, then the site should bring up all search results in pop-up windows.

DISCUSSION

The level of aviation-related expertise had an impact on many aspects of user performance. Experts were more likely than novices and moderate-level users to have had some prior interaction with the fly.faa.gov Web site. They were also better at finding delay information on the Web site. Experts appeared to have a better conceptual understanding of the different types of airport delays than both novices and moderate users. Finally, experts indicated that they found the information on the Web site to be slightly more comprehensible than both novices and moderate level users. Although we realize that there may be some performance decrement for people who have no affiliation with the FAA, we expect that their performance and their issues should be most similar to our novice users.

On the basis of performance differences, we recommend that the primary goal of site designers should be to make the site more usable for people who do not have an aviation background. If people in the general public visit this site without an aviation-related background, we would expect them to have substantial difficulty (a) understanding which delays were relevant for them, (b) understanding how airport delays differ from airline delays, and (c) interpreting much of the jargon used by aviation experts. Although both experts and novices use the site, simplifying the Web site should help all users, not just novices. Links to additional information can be provided for expert users.

Subjective reports indicated that the participants were generally satisfied with the fly.faa.gov Web site, and objective data revealed that they could successfully complete most tasks using the site. By evaluating user performance data in conjunction with user comments and researcher observations, we were able to identify a number of human factors issues with the Web site that we would not have identified by relying solely on subjective data.

After identifying issues, we rated each one in terms of its impact on site usability, discussed each issue in detail, identified supporting data when appropriate, and provided recommendations for improving the usability of the Web site. Many of the suggested improvements should be easy to implement and should further increase user satisfaction and site usability.

CONCLUSION

One of the primary lessons that we learned from this usability evaluation is that developers should not simply rely on subjective reports of usability when evaluating e-government Web sites. It is just as important to observe users interacting with a Web site and collect objective performance data to better identify usability issues. By having people use the Web site to find different types of information, we were better able to identify those areas of the site that caused problems for users. To encourage organizations to perform usability evaluations on e-government sites, we should ensure that they provide value by identifying important usability issues that can be remedied through redesign. As we saw in this evaluation, subjective reports often fail to identify these issues. If research on Web site usability fails to identify significant usability issues, it is likely that such evaluations will not be used.

We also found that having researchers rate the severity of usability issues improved our evaluation. Future e-government usability assessments could reap benefits by using this technique. Many times, when a usability assessment is performed, the output of the assessment is a laundry list of issues that usability experts present to site designers. If guidance is given on issue severity or criticality, it is usually ad hoc and is not derived using any formal methodology. By requiring evaluators to explicitly rate each item on frequency, impact, and severity, they are required to think about how and in what ways the problem will affect the user. This user-centric focus is the key element of this methodology. It allows site evaluators to provide designers with a roadmap of how they can best focus their effort to provide a more optimal user experience. Additionally, we recommend that usability assessments use more than one evaluator to make severity ratings. We found that different evaluators might have different priorities, but by using combined severity ratings from three or more evaluators, you can increase the reliability of the ratings (Nielsen, 2003).

By employing an evaluation processes like the one used in this study to evaluate e-government sites, whether they are G2B sites, G2C sites, or G2E sites, designers and system developers can better allocate limited resources during the design process. In general, it is important that e-government Web site designers take into consideration the demographics of those who will use their Web site or application. If an e-government Web site or application, initially targeted to users with a specific area of expertise, is going to be redesigned for use by the general public, the site must be evaluated for usability. Based on the results of such an evaluation, changes need to be made to ensure that the site is usable by the broadest possible audience.

REFERENCES

Ahlstrom, V., & Longo, K. (Eds.). (2003). *Human factors design standard for acquisition of commercial-off-the-shelf subsystems, non-developmental items, and developmental systems* (DOT/FAA/CT-03/05/HF-STD-001). Atlantic City International Airport, NJ: FAA William J. Hughes Technical Center.

Bannister, F. (2007). The curse of the benchmark: An assessment of the validity and value of e-government comparisons, *International Review of Administrative Services, 73*, 171-188.

Barne, S. J., & Vidgen, R. T. (2006). Data triangulation and Web quality metrics: A case study in e-government source. *Information and Management, 4*, 767-777.

Bertot, J. C., & Jaeger, P. T. (2006). User-centered e-government: Challenges and benefits for government Web sites. *Government Information Quarterly, 23*, 163-168.

Bush, G.W. (2007, November 15). President Bush discusses aviation congestion. *Office of the Press Secretary* [Press release]. Retrieved February 22, 2008, from http://www.whitehouse.gov/news/releases/2007/11/20071115-6.html

Carter, L., & Bélanger, F. (2005). The utilization of e-government services: Citizen trust, innovation and acceptance factors. *Information Systems Journal, 15*, 5-25.

Foley, P. (2005). The real benefits, beneficiaries and value of e-government. *Public Money & Management, 25*, 4-6.

Allendoerfer, K., Friedman-Berg, F., & Pai, S. (2007). *Usability assessment of the fly.faa.gov Web site* (DOT/FAA/TC-07/10). Atlantic City International Airport, NJ: Federal Aviation Administration William J. Hughes Technical Center.

Gil-García, J. R., & Pardo, T. A. (2005). E-government success factors: Mapping practical tools to theoretical foundations. *Government Information Quarterly, 22*, 187-216.

Heeks, R., & Bailur, S. (2007). Analysing eGovernment research. *Government Information Quarterly, 22*, 243-265.

Hiller, J., & Belanger, F. (2001). *Privacy strategies for electronic government*. E-Government series. Arlington, VA: Pricewaterhouse Coopers Endowment for the Business of Government.

Ho, A. (2002). Reinventing local government and the e-government initiative. *Public Administration Review, 62*, 434-444.

Horst, M., Kuttschreutter, M., & Gutteling, J. M. (2007). Perceived usefulness, personal experiences, risk perception, and trust as determinants of adoption of e-government services in the Netherlands. *Computers in Human Behavior, 23*, 1838-1852.

Howell, D. C. (2007). *Chi-square with ordinal data.* Retrieved January 22, 2007, from http://www.uvm.edu/~dhowell/StatPages/More_Stuff/OrdinalChisq/OrdinalChiSq.html

Hung, S. Y., Chang, C. M., & Yu, T. J. (2006). Determinants of user acceptance of the e-government services: The case of online tax filing and payment system, *Government Information Quarterly, 23*, 97-122.

Irani, Z., Love, P. E. D, & Montazemi, A. (2007). E-Government: Past, present, and future. *European Journal of Information Systems, 16*, 103-105.

Nielsen, J. (2003). *Severity ratings for usability problems.* Retrieved April 15, 2006, from http://www.useit.com/papers/heuristic/severityrating.html

Reddick, C.G. (2005). Citizen interaction with e-government: From the streets to servers? *Government Information Quarterly, 22*, 38-57.

Salem J. A. (2003). Public and private sector interests in e-government: A look at the DOE's PubSCIENCE. *Government Information Quarterly, 20*, 13-27.

Schelin, S. H. (2003). E-government: An overview. In G. D. Garson (Ed.), *Public information technology: Policy and management issues* (pp. 120-137).

Hershey, PA: Idea Group Publishing.

Thomas, J. C., & Streib, G. (2003). The new face of government: Citizen-initiated contacts in the era of e-government. *Journal of Public Administration Research and Theory, 13*, 83-102.

Yildiz, M. (2007). E-government research: Reviewing the literature, limitations, and ways forward. *Government Information Quarterly, 24*, 646-665.

This work was previously published in International Journal of Electronic Government Research, Vol. 5, Issue 1, edited by V. Weerakkody, pp. 64-79, copyright 2009 by IGI Publishing (an imprint of IGI Global).

Index

X

Y